W-X-Y-Z   Volume 21

The World Book Encyclopedia

World Book, Inc.

a Scott Fetzer company

Chicago   London   Sydney   Toronto

The World Book Encyclopedia

Copyright © 1990, U.S.A.
by
World Book, Inc.

Ww

W is the 23rd letter of our alphabet. The letter developed from a symbol used by the Semites, who once lived in Syria and Palestine. They named it *waw,* meaning *hook,* and adapted an Egyptian *hieroglyphic,* or picture symbol. The Romans, who took it from the Greeks, gave it a V shape. They first pronounced it as we pronounce *W,* but later pronounced it as *V.* During the 1000's, French scribes doubled the *V,* as *VV,* in order to write the Anglo-Saxon letter *wen,* for which they had no letter in their alphabet. The *VV* was also written in a rounded form as *UU.* It later came to be called "double *U"* in English. See **Alphabet.**

Uses. *W* or *w* is about the 19th most frequently used letter in books, newspapers, and other printed material in English. *W* is used to abbreviate *west.* In military titles, *W* often stands for *women* or *women's,* as in *WAC* for *Women's Army Corps.* In electricity, *w* is used for *watt.* In chemistry *W* is the symbol for the element tungsten.

Pronunciation. In English, *w* is pronounced by rounding the lips and raising the tongue toward the velum, or soft palate, in preparation for a vowel sound to follow. The velum is closed, and the vocal cords vibrate. *W* is silent in words such as *wrong* and *answer.* It rarely occurs in Scandinavian languages or in French and other Romance languages, except for a few words from other tongues. In German, it usually has the sound of *v.* See **Pronunciation.**   Marianne Cooley

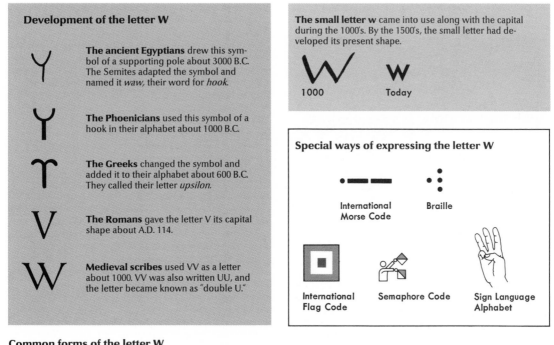

Development of the letter W

The ancient Egyptians drew this symbol of a supporting pole about 3000 B.C. The Semites adapted the symbol and named it *waw,* their word for *hook.*

The Phoenicians used this symbol of a hook in their alphabet about 1000 B.C.

The Greeks changed the symbol and added it to their alphabet about 600 B.C. They called their letter *upsilon.*

The Romans gave the letter V its capital shape about A.D. 114.

Medieval scribes used VV as a letter about 1000. VV was also written UU, and the letter became known as "double U."

The **small letter w** came into use along with the capital during the 1000's. By the 1500's, the small letter had developed its present shape.

1000   Today

Special ways of expressing the letter W

International Morse Code

Braille

International Flag Code

Semaphore Code

Sign Language Alphabet

Common forms of the letter W

Handwritten letters vary from person to person. *Manuscript* (printed) letters, *left,* have simple curves and straight lines. Cursive letters, *right,* have flowing lines.

Roman letters have small finishing strokes called *serifs* that extend from the main strokes. The type face shown above is Baskerville. The italic form appears at the right.

Sans-serif letters are also called *gothic letters.* They have no serifs. The type face shown above is called Futura. The italic form of Futura appears at the right.

Computer letters have special shapes. Computers can "read" these letters either optically or by means of the magnetic ink with which the letters may be printed.

Wabash River, *WAW bash,* is the best-known river in Indiana. It is 475 miles (764 kilometers) long. The Wabash rises in western Ohio and flows northwest into Indiana. It turns near Huntington, and flows west and southwest until it joins the Ohio River in the southwestern corner of Indiana. The Wabash forms part of the boundary between Indiana and Illinois (see **Indiana** [physical map]). The Wabash and its branches drain most of Indiana and a large area of Illinois. The river is mentioned in several songs, including Indiana's state song, "On the Banks of the Wabash, Far Away."

Indians used the Wabash as a transportation route as early as the 1300's. By the 1700's, the Wabash was an important transportation route for French traders and colonial settlers. In the 1850's, a new railroad system linked the major cities along the Wabash, and river transportation declined.   Michael E. Sullivan

WAC. See **Army, United States** (Women in the Army).

Waco, *WAY koh* (pop. 101,261; met. area pop. 170,755), is a manufacturing and distribution center in central Texas. The city lies on the Brazos River, about 100 miles (160 kilometers) south of Dallas. For location, see **Texas** (political map).

Industries in Waco manufacture candy, cottonseed products, glass, mobile homes, steel, and wood products. The city serves as a shipping center for the surrounding farm area, which produces cotton, dairy foods, fruit, hay, livestock, oats, poultry, vegetables, and wheat. Baylor University, the world's largest Baptist uni-

Baylor University

Baylor University's main campus is located in Waco. Pat Neff Hall houses the university's administrative offices.

versity, and Paul Quinn College are in Waco.

Waco was founded in 1849 on the site of a former Waco Indian village and was named for that tribe. That same year, the city's first permanent white settler, Captain Shapley P. Ross, established a ferry service across the Brazos River. The ferry made Waco an important gateway to the West. Construction of a bridge in 1870 enabled Waco to become a boom town. Waco is the county seat of McLennan County and has a council-manager form of government.   Robert C. Sadler

WAF. See **Air Force, United States** (Women in the Air Force).

Wager is a bet, or anything which is risked on the outcome of an event or the answer to a question. Money or other property may be wagered, or it may be agreed that the loser of the bet shall do a certain thing. Laws do not enforce the payment of wagers, except in certain countries and states where that kind of gambling is lawful. See also **Gambling; Lottery.**   Leonard Miller

Wages and hours. Wages are the price paid for work. They are usually figured by the hour or the week.

Wages are the main source of income for most people in the United States. Wages may be classified as *money wages* and *real wages.* Money wages are the actual amount of money a worker receives from an employer. Real wages represent the amount of goods and services workers can buy with their money wages. The prices of goods and services may change sharply over time. As a result, economists must compare real wages to determine how the ability of workers to buy changes. Such comparisons adjust for changing prices.

Real-wage comparisons are especially important over long periods. During such periods, money wages may increase sharply even though real wages may increase little or even decline. For example, from 1978 to 1987, money wages increased by 63 per cent while real wages actually declined by 5 per cent. Thus, workers could buy slightly more goods and services with their average weekly wages in 1978 than they could in 1987.

The growth of real wages over time is much more important than the growth of money wages because real-wage levels determine the purchasing power of workers. A main contributing factor in the growth of real wages over time is growth in productivity. When more goods and services are produced without an increase in the cost of production, prices stay low, and wages can buy more. The growth in productivity is measured by the workers' average *output per worker-hour.* Output per worker-hour measures the amount of goods and services an average worker produces in one hour. Output per worker-hour increases as workers become more skilled, and as machinery, tools, and factories become more efficient.

From 1909 to 1950, output per worker-hour in the United States rose an average of 2 per cent annually. From 1950 to 1969, it increased at an average annual rate of 2.8 per cent. However, from 1969 to 1987, the growth in average worker productivity per hour slowed to an average rate of 1.2 per cent yearly. In 1980 and 1982, worker productivity actually declined, contributing to the decline in real wages from 1978 to 1987.

Since the 1940's, employers have spent an increasing percentage of their labor costs on *fringe benefits,* rather than *take-home pay* for the worker. The most popular

Wages and hours in the United States
Average weekly wages

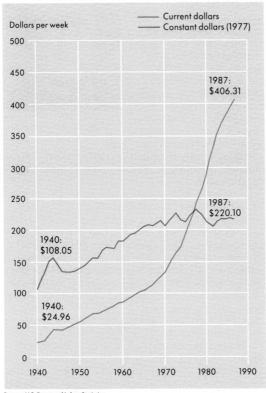

Average weekly hours

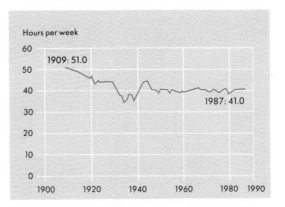

Average weekly wages

Year	Current dollars	Constant dollars (1977)
1940	$ 24.96	$ 108.05
1945	44.20	148.82
1950	58.32	146.80
1955	75.70	170.36
1960	89.72	183.48
1965	107.53	206.36
1970	133.33	208.00
1975	190.79	214.85
1980	288.62	212.06
1981	318.00	212.00
1982	330.26	207.71
1983	354.08	216.03
1984	374.03	220.67
1985	386.37	220.15
1986	396.01	222.23
1987	406.31	220.10

Source: U.S. Bureau of Labor Statistics

Average weekly gross wages (before social security and income tax deductions) have increased greatly since 1940, *above left.* Wages in constant dollars, which show current dollars adjusted for inflation, have risen more slowly. Average weekly working hours have fallen in the 1900's, *above right.* Both graphs report data only for production workers in manufacturing industries.

fringe benefits include pension plans, medical and dental insurance, paid holidays, and paid sick time. Employers usually consider fringe benefits as a substitute for wages, rather than as an additional contribution to the workers.

Hours. Before the Industrial Revolution, most people worked on farms where the workday ran from sunrise to sunset. Factory operators tried to enforce the same hours during the Industrial Revolution of the 1700's and early 1800's, despite the difference in working conditions and the type of work. Gradually, the 10-hour day and the 6-day week became the normal working period in U.S. and European factories.

Labor began its demands for an 8-hour day in the mid-1800's. But the 8-hour day did not become common in the United States until after World War I. During the 1930's, the 5-day, 40-hour workweek came into general practice in the United States. This practice has changed little through the years. By the early 1980's, the average workweek was 35 hours. Flexible work scheduling, called *flextime* or *flexitime,* began in West Germany in 1967 and spread to the United States during the 1970's. Flextime workers may choose their own daily work

hours, within certain limits, as long as they work the required number of hours per week. Most flextime systems require all employees to be present during a period called the *core hours.*   Paul L. Burgess

Related articles in *World Book* include:

Child labor	Minimum wage
Cost of living	Piecework
Labor, Department of	Profit sharing
Labor movement	Unemployment insurance

Wagner, *WAG nuhr,* **Honus,** *HOH nuhs* (1874-1955), is often considered baseball's greatest shortstop. Wagner played for the Pittsburgh Pirates from 1900 to 1917. He led the National League in batting a record eight years, including four seasons in a row. He batted .300 or higher in a league record 17 consecutive seasons. Wagner's lifetime batting average was .329. He led the league in stolen bases five times. Wagner holds the National League record for most triples with 252. He also ranks second in major league putouts by a shortstop.

Wagner was born in Mansfield (now Carnegie), Pa. His given and family name was John Peter Wagner. He was called *Honus,* a nickname for *Johannes,* the German form of John. Wagner began his major league career

Culver

Honus Wagner, a shortstop for the Pittsburgh Pirates, was one of the greatest hitters and fielders in baseball history.

Historical Pictures Service
Richard Wagner

thoven's ninth symphony in 1839. This renewed his faith in German music and inspired his first master-piece, *A Faust Overture* for orchestra (1840). Wagner no longer believed in *Rienzi.* But he completed it anyway, because a suc-cessful production in Paris would ensure his reputa-tion as an opera composer all over Europe. The opera was not produced, how-ever, and Wagner ran out of money. In 1841, during this period of misery in Paris, he wrote *The Flying Dutchman,* returning to the German romantic style.

His fortunes revived in 1842 with an offer to conduct at the Dresden opera house. In Dresden, Wagner com-posed *Tannhäuser* (1845) and *Lohengrin* (1848), two great treatments of the romantic view of medieval life.

Meanwhile, social revolution brewed in Germany. Wagner was convinced that musicians were being treated unjustly and that the organization and operation of the theaters were poor. His resentment led to his par-ticipation in an unsuccessful revolution in 1849. After-ward, a warrant was issued for his arrest and he fled to Switzerland. He was not allowed to return to Germany for 12 years.

Later career. During his first years in Switzerland, Wagner wrote no music. Instead, he examined his own philosophy of art and life and wrote on social and artis-tic problems. He also began the libretto for his greatest creation, *The Ring of the Nibelung.* He began work on the music for this cycle of four operas in 1853. He fin-ished *The Rhine Gold (Das Rheingold)* in 1854, *The Val-kyrie (Die Walküre)* in 1856, and the first two acts of *Siegfried* by 1857. Then he composed another work he had been planning, *Tristan and Isolde.* He did not com-pose the third act of *Siegfried* until 1869.

Tristan, completed by 1859, is a landmark in music because of the intensely *chromatic* style used to express the love interest in the story. This style increased the ex-pressive nature of a melody or chord. *Tristan* is a unique conception for the stage. It deals less with external events or actions than with the emotional lives of the characters, what Wagner called "soul states."

Getting *Tristan* produced was Wagner's chief concern after 1859. Debts piled up, and he was constantly threat-ened with financial ruin. In 1864, King Ludwig II of Ba-varia came to his rescue. Wagner became the king's ad-viser in Munich and *Tristan* was finally produced there in 1865. Meanwhile, Wagner had started work on his only mature comedy, *The Mastersingers of Nuremberg (Die Meistersinger von Nürnberg).* He finished this in Switzerland in 1867. In 1874 he concluded the entire *Ring* cycle with the completion of *The Twilight of the Gods (Die Götterdämmerung).* About 1864, Wagner fell in love with Cosima von Bülow, the married daughter of composer Franz Liszt. Cosima became his mistress and they were married in 1870.

With the king's aid, Wagner finally built a theater of his own in Bayreuth in which to perform the *Ring.* The

with the Louisville Colonels in 1897. He was elected to the National Baseball Hall of Fame in 1936.   Jack Lang

Wagner, *VAHG nuhr,* **Richard** (1813-1883), was a great German composer who fundamentally changed European musical, literary, and theatrical life. Wagner believed that the theater should be the center of a com-munity's culture rather than merely a place of entertain-ment. He finally built his own theater and founded Eu-rope's oldest summer music festival. He intended this festival and the ideal conditions it offered to performing artists to serve as a model for other theaters.

Wagner wrote his own opera *librettos* (words), bas-ing his mature works on episodes from history and from medieval myths and legends. In the music of his earlier works, he used elements of the German, French, and Italian operatic styles of his time. He reached a climax in *Lohengrin,* which brought these diverse elements into complete unity. After *Lohengrin,* Wagner developed a new "musical language." Composers like Mozart tended to explore a twofold set of melodies with properly matched keys, as in a symphonic movement. Wagner moved to a greater variety of melodies (called motives) and keys, using new ways to blend them into the unity of his musical dramas.

Early career. Wagner was born in Leipzig on May 22, 1813. He was educated at the best schools. Early in life, he showed a flair for the theater and might have be-come a great actor if he had not decided to become a musician. From 1833 to 1839, he worked as an opera conductor in several German cities. He wrote his first complete opera, *The Fairies* (1834), in the German ro-mantic style. He abandoned this style in his next opera, *The Ban on Love* (1835), based on Shakespeare's *Meas-ure for Measure.* In 1836, he married Minna Planer, an actress. It was a stormy marriage and the two lived apart in the last years before her death in 1866.

Wagner's next project was *Rienzi,* an opera in the im-posing style called French grand opera. He interrupted his work on *Rienzi* after hearing a performance of Bee-

first festival was held there in 1876. Wagner composed his last work, the opera *Parsifal* (1882), especially to be performed in this theater.

Wagner's philosophy. Wagner tried to find a new way of combining music and drama in the theater. He believed the basic error in opera was that music had become the sole end. Drama served merely as an excuse for the music. Wagner aimed at a work in which all the various elements in operatic composition were in perfect harmony and directed toward a single artistic end.

Wagner considered the orchestra the greatest artistic achievement of his time, and wanted to take greater advantage of its expressive possibilities. Wagner did not think the orchestra should accompany a vocal line with repeated chords like a "monstrous guitar." He believed it could be given a more elaborate musical texture in which the vocal line would be one independent strand. His use of recurrent motives permitted continuous music throughout an act, with no breaks until the end. Wagner disliked "operatic" acting, and insisted that singers use only movements required by the music.

Wagner waged one of the hardest battles ever fought in the cause of artistic freedom. His stormy and debt-ridden career forced many people to realize that creative artists deserve their support. Wagner's works were a dominant force in Western culture until World War I. He ranks with Bach, Mozart, and Beethoven as one of the world's greatest composers.   Robert Bailey

See also **Opera.**

Additional resources

Deathridge, John, and Dahlhaus, Carl. *The New Grove Wagner.* Norton, 1984.

Gregor-Dellin, Martin. *Richard Wagner: His Life, His Work, His Century.* Harcourt, 1983.
Osborne, Charles. *The World Theatre of Wagner: A Celebration of 150 Years of Wagner Productions.* Macmillan, 1982.

Wagner, *WAG nuhr,* **Robert Ferdinand** (1877-1953), an American statesman, served in the New York legislature and showed special interest in welfare questions. He was justice of the Supreme Court of New York from 1919 to 1926, and from then until 1949 was a U.S. Senator from New York. A Democrat, he introduced the National Labor Relations Act, or "Wagner Act," the National Industrial Recovery Act, the Social Security Act, and the U.S. Housing Act of 1937. He was born in Nastatten, near Wiesbaden, Germany.   Harvey Wish

Wagner Act. See National Labor Relations Act.

Wagon. The wheel and the wagon developed at the same time. This was at least 5,000 years ago, when people first found that they could pull sledges more easily if they fitted the sledges with wheels of solid wood. The Egyptians were among the earliest people to use wagons. The Scythians wandered the plains of southeastern Europe as early as 700 B.C., carrying their possessions on two-wheeled carts covered with reeds. The Greeks and the Romans developed chariots that were lighter and faster than Egyptian ones. The four-wheeled coach was developed in Germany during the Middle Ages.

English governors of American colonies introduced the first wagons in North America. Stagecoaches began to run over colonial roads about the time of George Washington. The *prairie schooner* (covered wagon), which was first built by the German farmers of Pennsylvania, was used in the development of the American West. Farm wagons carried crops to market until the

Detail of the Bayeux Tapestry (1000's-1100's); Bayeux Museum, Bayeux, France (Giraudon)

A wagon of the Middle Ages was used to carry weapons into battle.

Brown Brothers

The Conestoga wagon carried pioneers westward over the Allegheny Mountains from the early 1700's until about 1850. It was drawn by a team of four to six horses.

Brown Brothers

The New England buckboard wagon was a popular American carriage of the early 1900's. These open wagons were used for short business and pleasure trips.

Brown Brothers

A horse-drawn delivery wagon was a common sight during the early 1900's.

early 1900's. The present-day truck trailer is actually a kind of wagon.   Franklin M. Reck

See also **Chuck wagon; Conestoga wagon; Pioneer life in America** (The wagon train); **Stagecoach; Transportation** (pictures).

Wagon train. See **Pioneer life in America** (The wagon train); **Western frontier life** (Transportation).

Wahoo is a fish that lives in warm parts of the Atlantic, Indian, and Pacific oceans. In American waters, it is found from Florida to Venezuela in the Atlantic Ocean, and from Mexico to Ecuador and the Hawaiian Islands in the Pacific. The wahoo is known as *peto* in Latin America and as *ono* in Hawaii.

WORLD BOOK illustration by Colin Newman, Linden Artists Ltd.

The wahoo is an excellent game and food fish that lives in the warm waters of all oceans. It is an active swimmer.

The wahoo has a long body with a pointed snout and a long fin on the back. The back is dark blue and the sides are silver with wavy bars. Wahoos can grow to a length of more than 8 feet (2.4 meters) and can weigh more than 180 pounds (82 kilograms).

Scientific classification. The wahoo belongs to the mackerel family, Scombridae. It is *Acanthocybium solandri.*

Gary T. Sakagawa

Wailing Wall is a high wall in Jerusalem. It is also called the *Western Wall,* because during Biblical times it formed the western wall of the courtyard of the Jews' holy Temple. The wall is about 160 feet (49 meters) long and about 40 feet (12 meters) high. Archaeologists have discovered that 19 rows of stones extend about 20 feet (6 meters) underground.

Beginning in the 700's, the Arabs permitted Jews to assemble at the wall on the evenings before their Sabbath and before their feast days. In services at the wall, the Jews recalled their traditions and sufferings.

Jews continued to use the Wailing Wall after the British won control of Jerusalem during World War I. In 1948, Jordan captured the section of Jerusalem where the wall was located, and prohibited Jews from the new state of Israel from using it. But the Jews regained access to the wall when Israel captured the Jordanian section of Jerusalem in the Arab-Israeli war of June 1967. For location of the Wailing Wall, see **Jerusalem** (map).

Bruce M. Metzger

See also **Jerusalem** (Holy places; picture).

Wainwright, Jonathan Mayhew (1883-1953), was an American general whose courage made him a hero of World War II. After General Douglas MacArthur was ordered to leave the Philippines and go to Australia in March 1942, Wainwright remained in command of the American and Filipino forces on Bataan Peninsula and Corregidor. He was forced to surrender in May 1942, and was held a prisoner for three years by the Japanese. Wainwright was released in 1945, and participated in the surrender ceremony of the Japanese delegates aboard the U.S.S. *Missouri* in Tokyo Bay. On his return

to the United States, Wainwright became a full general and received the Congressional Medal of Honor.

Wainwright was born in Walla Walla, Wash., and was graduated from the United States Military Academy in 1906. He became a cavalry officer and served in the Philippines in 1909 and 1910. During World War I, he served on the general staff of the 82nd Division in France. After World War II, he commanded the Fourth Army. He retired in 1947.   Maurice Matloff

See also **Bataan Peninsula.**

Waite, *wayt,* **Morrison Remick** (1816-1888), served as chief justice of the United States from 1874 until his death. In the Granger Cases, his opinions upheld the power of state governments to regulate business (see **Granger Cases**). Later in Waite's term, this doctrine lost favor when the Supreme Court developed broad powers to enforce the 14th Amendment. However, the doctrine of broad power to regulate business was revived in the 1930's.

Waite was born in Lyme, Conn. He graduated from Yale University. In 1871, he was an American delegate to the Geneva Tribunal of Arbitration, which considered the *Alabama* claims (see **Alabama** [ship]). He helped found the Republican Party.   Jerre S. Williams

Wake is the custom of watching over a dead person before burial. Some form of the custom has been practiced in all parts of the world. But the practice is no longer used as widely in Western society as in earlier times.

In the traditional wake, family and friends gathered at the dead person's home. The custom probably began because of a concern over occasional errors made in the determination of death. It is also likely that some early people believed that the presence of the living would ward off the evil spirits that might possess a body prior to disposal.   Richard A. Kalish

Wake Island is a United States possession in the west-central Pacific Ocean (see **Pacific Islands** [map]). It is a triangular atoll made up of three small coral islets, Wake, Peale, and Wilkes. The islets cover a land area of about 3 square miles (8 square kilometers). They have about 300 people, all of whom are U.S. citizens. With a curving reef, they enclose a lagoon that is less than 4 square miles (10 square kilometers) in area. Wake has no fresh water, and its vegetation consists mainly of shrubs and bushes.

Spaniards probably sighted Wake when they explored the Pacific in the late 1500's. The British schooner *Prince William Henry* landed there in 1796. In 1841, Lieutenant Charles Wilkes of the United States Exploring Expedition surveyed Wake with the aid of the naturalist Titian Peale. They found no indication that the atoll had ever been inhabited. Wake Island became an unincorporated territory of the United States in 1898. The United States claimed Wake because it lay on the cable route from San Francisco to Manila. In 1935, Wake became a base for Pacific air traffic.

Wake Island was the site of an early World War II battle. For two weeks in December 1941, a force of 400 U.S. Marines and about 1,000 civilians fought off a Japanese invasion. But the Japanese captured Wake in late December 1941. The Japanese garrison on Wake surrendered at the end of the war, in 1945.

Today, Wake is used primarily for emergency stopovers for airplanes and ships. The U.S. National Weather Service and the U.S. National Oceanographic and Atmospheric Administration have research and monitoring units on the atoll.   Robert C. Kiste

Wake-robin. See Trillium.

Waksman, *WAKS muhn,* **Selman Abraham** (1888-1973), made outstanding contributions to soil microbiology and to the development of antibiotics. He taught and did research, especially on a group of microbes known as *actinomycetes.* He studied the effects of soil microbes on each other, on the fertility of the soil, and on the formation of humus.

During the early 1940's, Waksman and his co-workers tested about 10,000 soil microbes for antibiotic activity. This research led to the discovery of the antibiotic *streptomycin* in 1943 (see **Streptomycin**). Waksman gave his share of the royalties to establish an Institute of Microbiology at Rutgers University. He retired as the director of the institute in 1958. He won the 1952 Nobel Prize for physiology or medicine.

Waksman was born in Novaya Priluka, Russia. He moved to the United States in 1910.   Mordecai L. Gabriel

Walata, *wah LAH tah,* was a leading trading city in West Africa from the late 1000's to the 1500's. Copper, swords, and other goods were traded there for gold and sometimes for slaves. Today, Walata is a small town in Mauritania called *Oualata.*

During the 1000's, Muslim traders from the south settled in Walata. The city became part of the Mali Empire in the 1300's. The Tuareg of the south seized and occupied Walata in 1433. In the late 1400's, it became part of the Songhai Empire. After that empire fell, various peoples ruled Walata.   Leo Spitzer

Wald, George (1906-   ), an American biochemist, determined how chemical changes in the retina enable a person to see. He shared the 1967 Nobel Prize for physiology or medicine.

Wald analyzed the *pigment* (coloring matter) of *rods,* the cells in the retina that respond to dim light. He found that light causes certain changes in *retinene,* a chemical in the pigment. These changes trigger a nerve impulse that transmits to the brain an image of what is seen. Wald discovered that the body makes retinene from vitamin A. This discovery explained why a deficiency of vitamin A reduces vision at night.

Wald was born in New York City and earned a Ph.D. at Columbia University. He joined the faculty of Harvard University in 1934. He was an outspoken opponent of the Vietnam War (1957-1975).   Isaac Asimov

Wald, Lillian D. (1867-1940), founded the first visiting nurse program in the United States that was not affiliated with a religious group. Her contacts with the poor in New York City in the depression of 1892-1893 inspired her to found the Nurses' Settlement, later known as the Henry Street Settlement. It became a model for public-school nursing programs in the United States. She

Henry Street Settlement Archives
Lillian D. Wald

also worked with the founder of the first "ungraded" class for mentally retarded children.

Wald and social reformer Florence Kelley were the first to suggest to President Theodore Roosevelt the idea of a national children's bureau to study the needs of children. Congress set up the Children's Bureau as an agency of the U.S. government in 1912. In addition, Wald was active in the American Union Against Militarism, and her views were highly respected by President Woodrow Wilson and others who worked for peace. Lillian Wald was born in Cincinnati.   Elizabeth Fee

Waldenses, *wahl DEHN seez,* are members of a Christian religious group. The group was founded by Peter Waldo, a wealthy merchant of Lyon, France. In 1173, Waldo left his wife, gave his fortune to the church and charity, and began preaching in the streets of Lyon. His message of poverty and religious devotion attracted many followers. The followers were called the *poor men of Lyon.* At first, they were approved by Pope Alexander III and the Archbishop of Lyon. But the succeeding pope and archbishop forbade the Waldenses to preach because they were not priests and their teachings differed from those of the church. For example, they denied the pope's authority and the existence of purgatory. The Waldenses were excommunicated in 1184 by Pope Lucius III.

Many Waldeneses adopted the doctrines of the Reformation, which took place during the 1500's. There are now about 50,000 Waldenses in Europe and North and South America. Their headquarters are in Rome.   Eugene TeSelle

Waldheim, *VALT hym,* **Kurt,** *koort* (1918-   ), is an Austrian diplomat who served as secretary-general of the United Nations (UN) from 1972 to 1982. He replaced U Thant of Burma, who retired after holding the office for more than 10 years. Waldheim was the UN's fourth secretary-general.

As secretary general, Waldheim carried out difficult peacekeeping missions in the Middle East, Asia, and other areas. Although he failed to stop a war between China and Vietnam in 1979, the fighting ended that same year. In 1980, Waldheim sought, without success, the release of American hostages held in Iran. The Americans were freed in 1981. He also tried but failed to end the Iran-Iraq war that began in 1980.

In 1986, Waldheim was elected president of Austria, a largely ceremonial position. His campaign was marked by controversy when records surfaced concerning his possible involvement in Nazi atrocities during World War II. The documents showed that Waldheim was a German army officer in units that killed thousands of Yugoslav patriots and deported thousands of Greek Jews to concentration camps during the 1940's. Waldheim denied involvement in these actions.

Waldheim was born near Vienna. He attended the Vienna Consular Academy and earned a law degree at the University of Vienna. Waldheim entered the Austrian foreign service in 1945. He became permanent Austrian observer at the UN in 1955 and headed Austria's first delegation to the UN that same year. From 1964 to 1968, and again from 1970 to 1971, he served as Austria's representative at the UN. He was Austria's foreign minister from 1968 to 1970.   Raymond E. Lindgren

See also **United Nations** (The Secretariat [picture]).

Peter Baker Photography

Many cottages in northern Wales, such as the one above near Mount Snowdon, are small and built low to the ground.

G. R. Roberts from Carl Östman

A love for music is a famous characteristic of the Welsh people. The Welsh children shown above are playing recorders.

Wales

Wales is one of the four countries that make up the United Kingdom of Great Britain and Northern Ireland, often shortened to Great Britain or the United Kingdom. The other countries are England, Northern Ireland, and Scotland. Cardiff is the capital and largest city of Wales.

Wales occupies a wide peninsula on the west coast of the island of Great Britain. It takes up about a tenth of the island. Much of Wales is a land of low, broad mountains and deep, green valleys.

Most of the Welsh people live in coal-mining regions and industrial cities and towns in southern Wales. The Welsh have great pride in their country. Although Wales has been united with England for more than 400 years, the Welsh have kept alive their own language, literature, and traditions. The Welsh name for Wales is *Cymru* (pronounced *KUHM ree*).

This article tells about the people, geography, and economy of Wales. It also traces the country's history up to 1536, when Wales was united with England. For a discussion of Great Britain as a whole, of the relation of Wales to the other British countries, and of Britain's history, see the *World Book* article on **Great Britain.**

Government

Wales is part of Great Britain, a constitutional monarchy. Queen Elizabeth II is Britain's head of state, but a Cabinet of government officials called *ministers* actually

rules the nation. The prime minister is the chief governing official. Britain's laws are made by Parliament, which includes the House of Commons and the House of Lords. Wales elects 38 of the 650 members of the House of Commons. A majority of the members of the House of Lords are nobles who inherit their seats. For more information on the British government, see **Great Britain** (Government).

The chief administrative official of Wales is the *secretary of state for Wales,* who is appointed by the British prime minister and is a member of the Cabinet. The secretary of state heads the *Welsh Office* in Cardiff. The

Facts in brief

Capital: Cardiff.
Official languages: Welsh and English.
Area: 8,019 sq. mi. (20,768 km²). *Greatest distances*— north-south, 137 mi. (220 km); east-west, 116 mi. (187 km). *Coastline*— 614 mi. (988 km).
Elevation: *Highest*—Snowdon, 3,561 ft. (1,085 m) above sea level. *Lowest*—sea level, along the coast.
Population: *Estimated 1990 population*—2,861,000; density, 357 persons per sq. mi. (138 per km²); distribution, 76 per cent urban, 24 per cent rural. *1981 census*—2,791,581. *Estimated 1995 population*—2,901,000.
Chief products: *Agriculture*—barley, cattle, hay, oats, potatoes, rutabagas, sheep, turnips. *Manufacturing*—aluminum, chemicals, electrical and electronic equipment, iron, motor vehicle parts, petroleum products, plastics, steel, synthetic fibers, tin plate. *Mining*—coal, limestone, slate.
Money: *Basic unit*—pound. For its price in U.S. dollars, see **Money** (table: Exchange rates [Great Britain]). See also **Pound.**

D. Q. Bowen, the contributor of this article, is Professor of Geography at the University of London.

Welsh Office carries out the day-to-day administration of Wales. It is responsible for housing, local government, national parks, public health, roads, town planning, water and sewerage systems, and welfare programs.

Wales is divided into two types of units for purposes of local government. The main units are called *administrative counties.* These units are divided into *administrative districts.* Wales has 8 administrative counties and 37 administrative districts. Each administrative county and administrative district in Wales has its own elected council. Council members serve four-year terms.

Some Welsh people are satisfied with their system of government, but others object to being governed by Great Britain. *Plaid Cymru* is a Welsh nationalist party that seeks independence for Wales from Britain. Other Welsh people think that Wales should at least have its own legislative assembly to deal with legislation that directly affects the country. In the 1970's, the British government worked out a plan under which Wales would

The flag of Wales features a red dragon on a white and green background. The dragon has been a Welsh symbol for nearly 2,000 years.

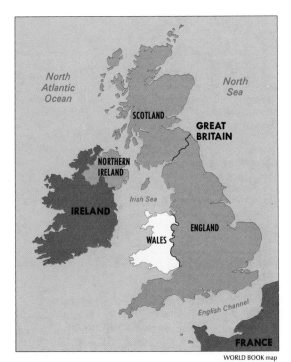

WORLD BOOK map

Wales occupies about a tenth of the island of Great Britain. England and Scotland are also on the island.

be given this *home rule* power. In 1979, the Welsh people voted to reject the plan.

People

Ancestry and population. Most of the Welsh are descended from peoples from the European mainland who began colonizing the western seaboards several thousand years ago. These people built prehistoric monuments called *megaliths* (see **Megalithic monuments**). Later, Celts, Romans, Anglo-Saxons, Vikings, Normans, and the English invaded Wales. But they were never able to conquer the country completely because of its difficult terrain. Struggles against these invaders, and efforts to earn a living from the rugged land, helped shape the strong, independent character of the people.

Wales has nearly 3 million people. A majority of them live in the southeast. Major population growth occurred here during the Industrial Revolution in the 1700's, when many people came to Wales from England. Cardiff, Swansea, and Newport, all on the southern coast, are the largest cities in Wales. Cardiff, the capital and largest city, has a population of about 270,000.

Language. Wales has two official languages, Welsh and English. Most Welsh-speaking people live in the western and northwestern parts of Wales. In some of these areas, almost three-fourths of the people speak Welsh. But nationwide, the number of people who speak Welsh declined from about one-half of the population in 1901 to about one-fifth today. Either English or Welsh may be used in the courts and for government business. Some newspapers are printed partly or entirely in Welsh, and radio and television programs are broadcast in both languages.

Welsh is a form of the ancient Celtic language and has been influenced by each group of invaders (see **Celts**). The letters *k, q, v,* and *z* are not used in Welsh, and the letters *w* and *y* are sometimes used as vowels. Many Welsh words have a double *l* or a double *d*. The *ll* is pronounced like the *thl* in *athletics.* The *dd* is pronounced like the *th* in *this.*

Way of life in industrial Welsh cities and towns is similar to that in industrial areas of England, Canada, and the United States. After work, the people take part in a variety of leisure activities. Many people watch television in the evenings. Wales has two television networks—the British Broadcasting Corporation (BBC) and the Independent Broadcasting Authority (IBA). As elsewhere in Great Britain, the *pub* (public house) is an important part of the social lives of many Welsh people. Pubs in Wales often serve local Welsh beer.

In the steep-sided coal mining valleys of southern Wales, many people live in *row houses*—houses of the same design that are attached in a row. The areas around the mining towns include much scenic beauty.

Although family ties and religious values have traditionally been important in Welsh life, they have become less important since World War II (1939-1945). They remain strongest in certain rural areas. The Welsh have long loved to sing. The choral tradition continues today, especially with outstanding male choirs.

A popular Welsh tradition is the *eisteddfod* (ay STEHTH vahd), a festival featuring poets, musicians, and singers. Eisteddfods began in the Middle Ages but died out. In the 1790's, some of the Welsh began to re-create

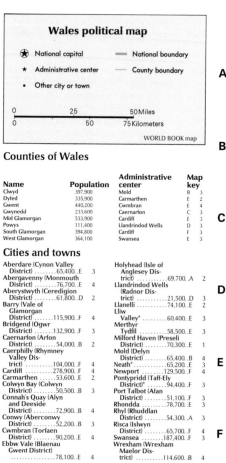

Wales political map

⊛ National capital   === National boundary

★ Administrative center   — County boundary

• Other city or town

0 ———— 25 ———— 50 Miles
0 ———— 50 ———— 75 Kilometers

WORLD BOOK map

Counties of Wales

Name	Population	Administrative center	Map key	
Clwyd	397,900	Mold	B	3
Dyfed	335,900	Carmarthen	E	2
Gwent	440,200	Cwmbran	E	4
Gwynedd	233,600	Caernarfon	C	3
Mid Glamorgan	533,900	Cardiff	E	3
Powys	111,400	Llandrindod Wells	D	3
South Glamorgan	394,800	Cardiff	F	3
West Glamorgan	364,100	Swansea	E	3

Cities and towns

Aberdare (Cynon Valley District) ....65,400..E 3
Abergavenny (Monmouth District) ....76,700..E 4
Aberystwyth (Ceredigion District) ....61,800..D 2
Barry (Vale of Glamorgan District) ....115,900..F 4
Bridgend (Ogwr District) ....132,900..F 3
Caernarfon (Arfon District) ....54,000..B 2
Caerphilly (Rhymney Valley District) ....104,000..F 4
Cardiff ....278,900..F 4
Carmarthen ......53,600..E 2
Colwyn Bay (Colwyn District) ....50,500..B 3
Connah's Quay (Alyn and Deeside District) ....72,900..B 4
Conwy (Aberconwy District) ....52,200..B 3
Cwmbran (Torfaen District) ....90,200..E 4
Ebbw Vale (Blaenau Gwent District) ....78,100..E 4

Holyhead (Isle of Anglesey District) ....69,700..A 2
Llandrindod Wells (Radnor District) ....21,500..D 3
Llanelli ....74,100..E 2
Lliw Valley* ....60,400..E 3
Merthyr Tydfil ....58,500..E 3
Milford Haven (Preseli District) ....70,300..E 1
Mold (Delyn District) ....65,400..B 4
Neath* ....65,200..E 3
Newport ....129,500..F 4
Pontypridd (Taff-Ely District)* ....94,400..F 3
Port Talbot (Afan District) ....51,100..E 3
Rhondda ....78,700..E 3
Rhyl (Rhuddlan District) ....54,300..A 3
Risca (Islwyn District) ....65,700..F 4
Swansea ....187,400..F 3
Wrexham (Wrexham Maelor District) ....114,600..B 4

*Does not appear on map; key shows general location.
Populations are for districts, which may include rural areas as well as the city or town. The British government does not report populations for individual cities and towns.
Source: 1985 official estimates.

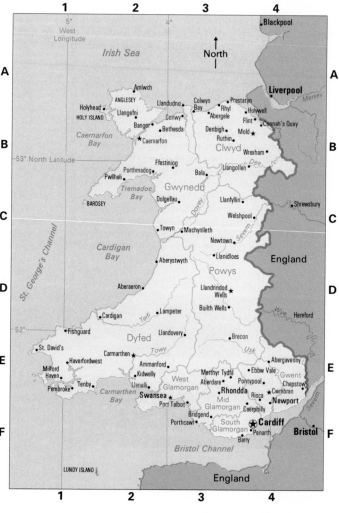

older cultural traditions. The modern eisteddfod arose from this movement. Each year, the people hold two world-famous eisteddfods. The Royal National Eisteddfod takes place in August. It is held in various cities and towns, alternately in northern and southern Wales. Only the Welsh language is used during this event. The International Music Eisteddfod is held in July at Llangollen in northern Wales. Both festivals attract visitors from throughout the world. The Welsh League of Youth holds an annual eisteddfod for children.

Food. Most Welsh cooking is simple. The people enjoy roast Welsh lamb, with mint sauce, and roast beef. The most famous dishes of Wales are *cawl,* which is a clear broth with vegetables; and *Welsh rarebit,* which consists of melted cheese and butter served on toast. Other specialties include *laver bread* (a dish made from seaweed and oatmeal); salmon and trout from Welsh rivers; and Welsh cakes.

Recreation. Rugby football is the national sport of Wales. The Welsh national Rugby team plays teams from countries throughout the world. In southern Wales, each village and town has its own team, and this feature is spreading in the north. See **Rugby football.**

Another popular sport is *football,* or soccer. The Foot-

ball Association of Wales supervises amateur teams. More than 90 professional teams belong to the Football League of England and Wales. Cricket is also played throughout Wales. See **Cricket; Soccer.**

In rural areas, many people fish and some hunt foxes. The rugged Welsh mountains, especially those in Snowdonia National Park in northwestern Wales, are excellent for climbing and other mountain sports.

Education. Wales and England have the same school system. It is supervised by the Department of Education and Science, a department of the British government, and by local education authorities.

All Welsh children between the ages of 5 and 16 must attend school. Until the age of 11, children attend *primary schools.* Then they enter *comprehensive schools.* Most students leave the comprehensive schools at age 16. Some go on to technical colleges or other forms of further education. Those who remain in school until age 18 or 19 may proceed to a university or other institute of higher education anywhere in Britain.

Wales has one federal university, the University of Wales. The first of the university's colleges was founded in Aberystwyth in 1872. Later, colleges were opened at Bangor—near Caernarfon—Cardiff, and Swansea. The university also includes St. David's College in Lampeter, near Carmarthen; and the Welsh School of Medicine and the Institute of Science and Technology, both in Cardiff. Its total enrollment is more than 20,000.

Religion. Nearly all the Welsh people are Protestants. The Methodist Church is the largest Protestant church in Wales. Others include the Anglican, Baptist, Presbyterian, and United Reformed churches. About 5 per cent of the people are Roman Catholics.

The Church of England became the official Welsh church in 1536. But by 1811, so many Welsh people had joined the Methodist Church that Wales formally separated from the Church of England. The Welsh Church Act of 1914 declared that the Church of England was no longer the official church of Wales.

The arts. Wales is a country of poets and singers. The traditions of Welsh literature and music date back more than 1,000 years to the *bards* (poet-singers) of the Middle Ages (see **Bard**).

The most notable of early Welsh poets were Taliesin and Aneirin. Aneirin wrote a poem called the *Gododdin* about the year 600. The poem describes the adventures of a band of noble warriors in the late 500's. The *Mabinogion,* a collection of 11 Welsh stories, is an important work of medieval European literature. These stories were probably written down around the year 1100. During the 1100's, Geoffrey of Monmouth wrote poems that helped spread the legends of King Arthur. Dayfydd ap Gwilym, one of the greatest Welsh poets of the Middle Ages, wrote on nature and love during the 1300's. Dylan Thomas ranks as the most famous Welsh poet of the 1900's. See **Mythology** (Celtic mythology).

The choral tradition of Wales continues today. Welsh songs are often hymn tunes, and many date from the 1700's, when a religious revival took place. The Welsh National Opera Company has become famous throughout the world. In addition, there are a number of modern theaters throughout Wales today.

The land

Wales occupies a broad peninsula on the west coast of Great Britain. It covers 8,019 square miles (20,768 square kilometers). England lies east of Wales. The Irish Sea on the north and St. George's Channel on the west separate Wales from Ireland. The Bristol Channel lies to the south. Wales has many areas of scenic beauty, including the irregular coastline, the peninsula of Gower in the south, and the national parks of Snowdonia in the north and the Brecon Beacons and the Pembrokeshire Coast in the south. For more information about the geography and climate of Wales, see *The land* and *Climate* sections of **Great Britain.**

Surface features. The Cambrian Mountains cover about two-thirds of Wales. In northern Wales, the mountains are steep and rugged. The highest peak in the country, 3,561-foot (1,085-meter) Snowdon (called *Eryri* in Welsh), rises in northwestern Wales. In central and southern Wales, the Cambrian range becomes flatter and forms large plateaus cut deeply by valleys. On the plateaus are pastures, grassy plains, and *bogs* (swamplands). In many areas, gorges mark the steep slopes leading from the plateaus to the valleys. Many small lakes and waterfalls dot the mountain region.

Coastal plains and river valleys cover about a third of

Wales. Low, narrow plains stretch along the south and west coasts. The broadest lowlands are along the Dee, Severn, and Wye rivers, near the English border.

A large island, the Isle of Anglesey (*Môn* in Welsh), lies off the northwest coast. The Menai Strait separates the island from the mainland.

Rivers and coastline. The longest rivers in Wales are the Severn and the Wye. Both begin near Aberystwyth, flow eastward into England, and then turn south and empty into the Bristol Channel. The Severn has a total length of 220 miles (354 kilometers), and the Wye 130 miles (209 kilometers). The River Dee, which flows northeastward from Bala Lake into the Irish Sea, forms part of the boundary between Wales and England. See **Severn, River.**

Much of the country's coastline is irregular and lined with cliffs. The coastline is 614 miles (988 kilometers) long. Many natural bays and harbors lie along the coast. Milford Haven, one of the natural harbors that have been developed as ports, is used by large ships that carry oil to Great Britain.

Economy

Coal mining and metal processing became the chief industries of Wales during the Industrial Revolution, which began in the 1700's. Today, however, the economy of Wales depends less on mining, and manufacturing and service industries have gained importance. Most mining and manufacturing activities are concentrated in southern Wales. Service industries include wholesale and retail trade, finance, and activities of the growing tourist industry.

Wales physical map

Most of Wales, except the coastal plains and river valleys, is covered by the Cambrian Mountains. A region of low plains, called the Welsh Marches, extends along the English border. The Welsh coast is irregular and has many bays and harbors.

WORLD BOOK map

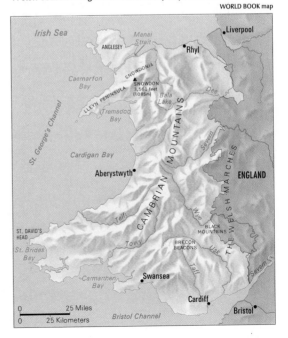

Natural resources. Coal is the most important natural resource of Wales. The most extensive deposits are in the South Wales Coalfield between the Tywi and Usk rivers. These deposits have been mined for nearly 200 years. A smaller coal field lies in northeast Wales. Limestone is also quarried in southern Wales.

Northwestern Wales is famous for its large slate quarries. The rocks of northern and central Wales also contain lead, zinc, and gold. Gold was mined by the Romans during Wales's early history.

The country has plentiful water resources, and large reservoirs have been formed by damming and flooding deep valleys. Some hydroelectric power is generated from this water. But most of the water is piped to large cities in England, notably Liverpool and Birmingham.

Manufacturing. Major steel works operate at Llanwern, near Newport, and at Port Talbot. Tin plate manufacturing is also important. However, metal manufacturing in Wales has declined in importance since the 1950's. It has been replaced by light industry, especially the manufacture of electronic equipment. A deep water oil tanker terminal at Milford Haven is a center of oil refining. Other products manufactured in Wales include chemicals, electrical equipment, motor vehicle parts, plastics, and synthetic fibers.

Agriculture. Most Welsh farms are in the coastal lowlands and in the major valleys of the interior mountains. Farmers raise beef and dairy cattle in the lowlands. Sheep are raised in the more mountainous areas. But the once famous and widespread Welsh woolen industry is now confined to a few mills.

Wales is not self-sufficient in food production and must depend on imports from other countries. The country's major crops are barley, oats, and potatoes. Hay, rutabagas, and turnips are grown to feed livestock.

Mining. Coal mining was once the most important industry in Wales, but it has declined steadily because of falling demand. Between 1947 and 1966, 115 coal mines closed in southern Wales. By the mid-1980's, only 15 mines employing about 12,000 miners remained.

History

Scholars believe that prehistoric people lived in caves in northern Wales some 200,000 years ago. People from the European mainland began settling in Wales thousands of years ago.

About 2000 B.C., people called the Beaker folk settled the Wales region. Their name comes from small clay containers called *beakers,* which they buried with their dead. The Beaker folk raised crops and made bronze tools. About 500 B.C., the Celts began arriving in the country. The largest group of Celtic immigrants into Wales arrived about 300 B.C. The Celts introduced the use of iron in Wales.

The Romans, who had invaded England in A.D. 43, conquered Wales between A.D. 60 and 75. They controlled the country for nearly 400 years and built roads, walls, cities, and castles throughout Wales.

Struggles against the Anglo-Saxons. The Romans left Wales and England in the early 400's. Soon afterward, Angles, Jutes, and Saxons from northeastern Europe invaded eastern, southern, and central England. They conquered all the Celtic tribes except the Britons, who fled to Wales. For hundreds of years, the Britons succeeded in keeping Wales independent.

During their long struggle against the Anglo-Saxons, the Welsh frequently sent raiders into England. To stop the raids, Offa II, ruler of Mercia, built a boundary between Mercia and Wales in the late 700's. The boundary, called *Offa's Dike,* still stands. It consists of a ditch and earthen wall from the River Wye to the River Dee.

Revolts against England. William the Conqueror and his Norman armies won control of England in 1066. In 1071, William declared himself lord of Wales. To keep the Welsh under control, he gave lands along the border between England and Wales to Norman barons. These borderlands were called the *Marches,* and the barons were known as *marcher lords.* The marcher lords built castles on their lands and gradually ex-

Important dates in Wales

A.D. 60-75 Roman armies conquered Wales.
1071 William the Conqueror declared himself lord of Wales.
1282 English troops killed Llewelyn ap Griffith, Prince of Wales, in battle, crushing a Welsh revolt.
1301 Edward I gave the title Prince of Wales to his son.
1402-1410 Owen Glendower revolted against English rule.
1485 Henry Tudor, a Welsh prince, became King Henry VII of England.
1536 Henry VIII united Wales and England.
(For later dates, see **England** [History]; **Great Britain** [History]).

Welsh mining villages have long rows of attached houses. The villages are known for being dreary, but they are surrounded by beautiful green countryside.

panded their estates. They soon controlled most of central and southern Wales. The Welsh people were divided into various tribes headed by chieftains. Some of the chieftains accepted the barons so that they could stay on their land. But many others fought for their independence, and the Welsh regained much of their land from the barons during the 1100's.

During the 1200's, Llewelyn ap Griffith, a Welsh prince, won control of most of Wales. King Henry III of England recognized Llewelyn as Prince of Wales in 1267. In return, Llewelyn had to recognize Henry as his superior. But after Henry died in 1272, Llewelyn refused to accept his son, Edward I, as a superior. The dispute led the Welsh to revolt in 1282. Llewelyn was killed in battle, and the revolt collapsed.

In 1284, Edward I issued the Statute of Rhuddlan. This order placed northern Wales directly under English control and established royal courts at Caernarfon. It also divided central and southern Wales into counties under the control of English sheriffs. In 1301, Edward I gave the title Prince of Wales to his son, Edward, who was born at Caernarfon Castle. Since then, all English monarchs except Edward II have given the title to their oldest son. During the 1300's, the Welsh revolted many times against English rule. In 1402, one rebel leader, Owen Glendower, drove the English out of much of Wales. But by 1410, the English regained control.

Union with England. In 1485, Henry Tudor, a Welsh prince, became King Henry VII of England. The Welsh people then gradually began to accept the idea of uniting with England. In 1536, Henry VII's son, Henry VIII, joined the two countries under a single government by the first Act of Union. Minor adjustments, such as changes in boundaries, were made over the next several years. The union was finalized in 1543, when the English government passed a second Act of Union. After Wales and England were united, the history of Wales became part of the history of England and, later, of Great Britain. For the story of England and Britain, see **England** (History); **Great Britain** (History).   D. Q. Bowen

Related articles in *World Book* include:

Biographies

Bradley, Francis H.
Geoffrey of Monmouth
Lawrence, T. E.
Lloyd George, David
Owen (Robert)
Thomas, Dylan
Williams, Emlyn

Cities and towns

Cardiff
Llanfairpwllgwyngyll
Swansea

Physical features

Bristol Channel
Severn, River

Other related articles

Bard
Celts
Clothing (picture: Traditional costumes)
David, Saint
Great Britain (picture: Mountain climbing)
Mythology (Celtic)
Prince of Wales

Outline

I. **Government**
II. **People**
  A. Ancestry and population
  B. Language
  C. Way of life
  D. Food
  E. Recreation
  F. Education
  G. Religion
  H. The arts
III. **The land**
  A. Surface features
  B. Rivers and coastline
IV. **Economy**
  A. Natural resources
  B. Manufacturing
  C. Agriculture
  D. Mining
V. **History**

Questions

What is an *eisteddfod*?
Who were the *marcher lords*?
How are *ll* and *dd* pronounced in Welsh?
What is *Plaid Cymru*?
Who has been the most famous Welsh poet of the 1900's?
What title do English monarchs give to their oldest son?
What two economic activities have gained importance in Wales today?
What are the most famous Welsh dishes?
What are the two official languages of Wales?
In what part of Wales do most Welsh people live?

Additional resources

Barber, W. T. *Exploring Wales.* David & Charles, 1982.
Morgan, Kenneth O. *Rebirth of a Nation: Wales, 1880-1980.* Oxford, 1981.
Morris, Jan. *The Matter of Wales: Epic Views of a Small Country.* Oxford, 1985.

Walesa, *vah WEHN sah,* **Lech,** *lehk* (1943-   ), became the leader of Poland's labor movement in 1980. Walesa's negotiations with Poland's government that year led to the government's recognition of Solidarity— an organization composed of about 50 Polish trade unions. This action marked the first time a Communist country recognized a labor organization that was independent of the country's Communist Party.

In 1980, Walesa was chosen as provisional head of Solidarity, and in October 1981, he was elected chairman. Solidarity faced

© B. Bisson, Sygma
Lech Walesa

growing hostility from Poland's Communist Party and the Soviet Union. In December 1981, Poland's government established martial law and suspended Solidarity's activities. Walesa and hundreds of other union leaders were imprisoned. In October 1982, the government officially outlawed Solidarity. Walesa was released in November 1982. The remaining prisoners were released over the next several years. The government ended its ban on Solidarity in 1989. Also in 1989, it allowed elections for a new Parliament. The elections were the freest ones in Poland since the country became a Communist state in 1945. Almost every candidate who was endorsed by Walesa and Solidarity won a seat in Parliament (see **Poland** [Recent developments]).

Walesa was born in Popow, north of Warsaw. In 1967, he became an electrician at the shipyards in Gdańsk. There, Walesa began taking part in the workers' rights movement. Walesa won the 1983 Nobel Peace Prize for his efforts to prevent violence while trying to gain workers' rights.   Janusz Bugajski

Walker, David (1785-1830), was a black American abolitionist who wrote a famous antislavery pamphlet. This pamphlet, called *An Appeal to the Colored Citizens of the World* (1829), urged American slaves to fight for their freedom. Its publication marked the beginning of the radical antislavery movement in the United States. The *Appeal* was the strongest attack on slavery made up to that time by a black writer.

Walker was born a free man in Wilmington, N.C. His father had been a slave, and his mother a free woman. Walker educated himself. In 1827, he settled in Boston and established a second-hand clothing business. He became a leader in Boston's Colored Association, which worked against slavery. He also wrote for and helped distribute *Freedom's Journal,* the first black newspaper in the United States.

After the publication of the *Appeal,* rumors circulated of large rewards being offered for Walker, dead or alive. Walker died under mysterious circumstances, reportedly of poisoning. Many abolitionists believed he had been murdered.   Otey M. Scruggs

Walker, James John (1881-1946), served as Democratic mayor of New York City from 1926 to 1932. Handsome and fun-loving, he came to symbolize the *Roaring Twenties.* In 1932, Governor Franklin D. Roosevelt asked Walker to explain corruption in the city's affairs. Investigation showed that Walker had been more careless than crooked, but his reputation was injured, and he resigned. Walker, who was known as Jimmy, was born in New York City.   John A. Garraty

Walker, Leroy Pope (1817-1884), served in 1861 as the first Confederate secretary of war. He was appointed because he was a leading Alabama secessionist. As war secretary, he worked hard to raise troops and obtain war materials for the Confederacy. The success of the Confederate armies during the first year of the Civil War owed much to his efforts. Walker later became a Confederate brigadier general. He was born in Huntsville, Ala.   Richard N. Current

Walker, Mary Edwards (1832-1919), was the only woman to receive the Medal of Honor, the highest military award given by the United States government. She was a pioneer woman physician and a supporter of the women's rights movement of the late 1800's.

Walker served as a surgeon with the Union Army during the Civil War. In 1864, she was captured and held for four months in a Confederate prison. She was released in exchange for a Confederate officer. In 1865, she was awarded the Medal of Honor for her medical treatment of Union soldiers.

Walker helped lead a movement aimed at ending the social restrictions on the way women dressed. She believed that women should be allowed to wear whatever they pleased and became known for wearing trousers. Walker also campaigned to give women the right to vote. She wrote several books on the role of women in society, including *Hit* (1871) and *Unmasked, or the Science of Immorality* (1878).

Walker was born in Oswego, N.Y., and graduated from Syracuse Medical College. In 1917, a federal review board revoked Walker's Medal of Honor. The review board claimed that Walker had never actually served in the Union Army. The Army restored Walker's award in 1977.   Miriam Schneir

Walker, William (1824-1860), was an American *filibuster* (military adventurer). He tried to make himself ruler of two Central American republics. In 1853, he gathered a company of soldiers and tried to conquer Lower California and the state of Sonora, both in Mexico. He failed, and United States officials arrested him for violating neutrality laws. He was freed, and in 1855 led a successful revolution in Nicaragua. He was president from 1856 to 1857, but then was forced to leave.

Walker tried to gain control of Honduras in 1860, but the Honduran government captured and executed him. He was born in Nashville, Tenn.   Wayne Gard

Walkie-talkie is a hand-held two-way radio that provides quick communication. Police officers, soldiers, amateur radio operators, sports enthusiasts, and workers use walkie-talkies.

Many walkie-talkies transmit with a power of less than one-tenth watt. They can send and receive messages over distances up to 1 mile (1.6 kilometers). Others have from 1 to 4 watts of power, and can send and receive messages over distances of 2 to 4 miles (3 to 6 kilometers). Under certain conditions, walkie-talkie signals can travel hundreds of miles or kilometers from the source. This happens when the signal *skips* (is reflected off the ionosphere). Electrical devices operating nearby, and such obstacles as buildings, may cut down a walkie-talkie's effective range.

Walkie-talkies of less than one-tenth watt that have been manufactured since Jan. 1, 1977, operate on frequencies between 49.82 and 49.90 megahertz. The more powerful types of walkie-talkies operate between 26.965 and 27.405 megahertz.

In the United States, a license is required to operate a walkie-talkie of more than one-tenth watt. Any citizen 18 years old or older may obtain a license from the Federal Communications Commission.   Stanley R. Alten

See also **Citizens band radio; Radio** (Two-way communication; picture).

Walking, as a competitive sport, is a race between two or more persons, or against time. Walking races are also called *race-walking.* Most races are held at distances ranging from 20 to 50 kilometers (12 to 31 miles). In one event, the winner is decided by which competitor covers the greatest distance in two hours.

Competitive walkers developed a method of walking called the "heel-and-toe." A long stride lands the foot on the heel and swings the walker forward to put weight quickly on the toe. The toe acts as a springboard for the next stride. At least part of one foot must always be on the ground and the leg must be completely straight, or *locked,* momentarily during each step. A nonracer walks 1 mile (1.6 kilometers) in 15 to 20 minutes. A heel-and-toe expert can do it in $6\frac{1}{2}$ minutes, only $2\frac{1}{2}$ minutes slower than a champion mile runner.

The walking contest was popular in England for centuries before it was introduced in the United States in the 1870's. At one time, U.S. contestants competed in six-day marathons on indoor tracks.   Bert Nelson

Walking leaf. See Leaf insect.

Walking stick is an insect that looks like a twig. The strange appearance of this insect hides it from its enemies. There are several kinds of these insects in the United States. The common walking stick of the Eastern states has long legs and a slender body that is 2 to 3

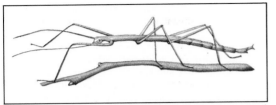

WORLD BOOK illustration by Oxford Illustrators Limited

The common walking stick resembles a twig.

Edward S. Ross

A long, slender walking stick, shown here hanging from a twig, is well hidden from its enemies. Walking sticks eat leaves and sometimes damage trees.

inches (5 to 8 centimeters) long. Unlike most insects, it has no wings. It may be brown or green. It eats leaves, and sometimes harms trees. The female usually drops her eggs on the ground. The young are neglected, and few survive. See also **Leaf insect.**

Scientific classification. Walking sticks make up the walking stick family, Phasmidae. The common walking stick is *Diapheromera femorata.*   Url Lanham

Wall of China. See Great Wall of China.
Wall painting. See Mural.
Wall Street is a short, narrow street in New York City. Along with Broad and New Streets, it forms a triangle where the New York Stock Exchange and many great commercial houses and banks are located. For location, see **New York City** (map). The district is the heart of U.S. banking and business and an international symbol of finance. See also **New York City** (Settlement); **Treaty** (picture).   Robert Sobel
Wallaby. See Kangaroo; Animal (picture).
Wallace, Alfred Russel (1823-1913), was a British naturalist and explorer. He became famous by reaching independently the same explanation for evolution as Charles Darwin did. He also laid the basis for the study of animal geography. He proposed an imaginary line in the southwestern Pacific, which became known as Wallace's Line, that divides the animal life of the Australian region from that of the Asian, or Oriental, region. Wallace spent five years in the Amazon Valley and nine in the East Indies collecting data on animals. He wrote *The Malay Archipelago* (1869), and *Geographical Distribution of Animals* (1876). Wallace was born in Usk, England.   Lorus J. and Margery Milne
See also **Darwin, Charles R.**

Wallace, George Corley (1919-   ), an American political leader, ran unsuccessfully for President three times and was elected governor of Alabama four times. He was a presidential candidate in 1968, 1972, and 1976. Wallace won the governorship in 1962, 1970, 1974, and 1982. He gained national attention in the early 1960's for his strong support of states' rights and his opposition to school integration.

Wallace was born in Clio, Ala., and graduated from the University of Alabama Law School in 1942. He was captain of the university boxing team and won academic honors in college. After serving three years in the Army Air Forces, he entered politics. A Democrat, he served in the Alabama legislature from 1947 to 1953 and as state judge from 1953 to 1958. He ran for governor in 1958, and lost. Four years later, he won.

Wallace opposed federal involvement in what he considered state problems, especially school integration. At his inauguration as governor in 1963, he pledged: "Segregation now, segregation tomorrow, and segregation forever." He denounced federal court orders to end school segregation. His "stand in the doorway" at the University of Alabama in 1963, opposing the enrollment of two black students, made him a hero to opponents of integration. Actually, many Alabama schools became integrated during Wallace's first term.

Wallace's wife, Lurleen, ran for governor in 1966 because at that time Alabama law prohibited Wallace from serving two terms in a row. But, most people understood that he would continue to act as governor. Mrs. Wallace won the election, but she died in office in 1968.

In 1968, Wallace was the presidential candidate of the American Independent Party (now called the American Party). He lost the election to Republican Richard M. Nixon and ran third behind Hubert H. Humphrey, the Democratic nominee. Wallace failed to achieve his goal of a deadlock in the Electoral College, which would have given him bargaining power to decide who became President. But he received almost 10 million votes. He carried five states and received 46 electoral votes. Wallace's running mate was retired Air Force General Curtis E. LeMay. See **American Party.**

In 1971, Wallace married Cornelia Ellis Snively, a niece of former Alabama Governor James E. Folsom. The couple were divorced in 1978. In 1981, Wallace married Lisa Taylor, a country music singer. The marriage ended in divorce in 1987.

Wallace was the victim of an attempted assassination in May 1972, during his campaign for the 1972 Democratic presidential nomination. He was shot and seriously wounded in Laurel, Md. Arthur H. Bremer, a 21-year-old man from Milwaukee, was convicted of the shooting and sentenced to 53 years in prison. The shooting left Wallace's legs paralyzed. He did not win the Democratic nomination. He also failed to win the Democratic nomination in 1976.

During the 1982 race for

The Wallace Campaign

George C. Wallace

governor, Wallace stressed his intention to help all needy Alabamians. He received strong support from black voters. Wallace retired from politics in 1987.

David S. Broder

Additional resources

Frady, Marshall. *Wallace.* Rev. ed. New American Library, 1976. A critical biography.
Greenhaw, Wayne. *Watch Out for George Wallace.* Prentice-Hall, 1976. A political campaign biography.

Wallace, Henry Agard (1888-1965), served as Vice President of the United States from 1941 to 1945 under President Franklin D. Roosevelt. He was also secretary of agriculture from 1933 to 1940 and secretary of commerce in 1945 and 1946. In 1948, he was the presidential nominee of the Progressive Party, a third political party. He was also an expert on plant culture, and developed a successful hybrid seed corn.

Wallace was one of the most controversial figures of the New Deal and Fair Deal periods (see **New Deal**). He urged adoption of the Agricultural Adjustment Act, the first of many New Deal plans to regulate the farm problem by government planning. In 1946, President Truman asked him to resign as secretary of commerce because of his outspoken criticism of the U.S. "get-tough" policy toward the Soviet Union.

Brown Bros.
Henry A. Wallace

Wallace became the first Vice President to take an active post in an administrative agency when Roosevelt appointed him chairman of the Board of Economic Warfare in 1941. The board was abolished in 1943 after a feud developed between Wallace and the Reconstruction Finance Corporation. Wallace was an important foreign policy adviser. He participated in decisions leading to the development of the atomic bomb, and headed the Supply Priorities and Allocations Board. He was not renominated in 1944 because Democrats did not like his social idealism and internationalism.

Wallace was born in Adair County, Iowa. He graduated from Iowa State College (now Iowa State University). When his father, Henry Cantwell Wallace, became U.S. secretary of agriculture in 1921, young Wallace took his place as editor of the family magazine, *Wallace's Farmer.* In 1950, he resigned from the Progressive Party because it had condemned U.S. intervention in Korea.

Irving G. Williams

Additional resources

Schapsmeier, Edward L. and F. H. *Henry A. Wallace of Iowa: The Agrarian Years, 1910-1940.* Iowa State Univ. Press, 1968. *Prophet in Politics: Henry A. Wallace and the War Years, 1940-1965.* 1970.
Walton, Richard J. *Henry Wallace, Harry Truman, and the Cold War.* Viking, 1976.

Wallace, Lew (1827-1905), was an American author, diplomat, lawyer, and military leader. He is best known for his historical novel *Ben-Hur* (1880), which tells of the rise of Christianity in the Roman Empire.

Lewis Wallace was born in Brookville, Ind. He was an officer in the Mexican War (1846-1848). He later practiced law and was elected to the Indiana Senate in 1856. Wallace rose to the rank of major general in the Union army during the Civil War (1861-1865). In 1862, his troops captured Fort Donelson, Tenn., weakening Confederate defenses. His bravery in delaying General Jubal A. Early's troops at Monocacy River helped prevent the capture of Washington, D.C., in 1864.

Wallace was a member of the court in 1865 that tried those involved in the assassination of President Abraham Lincoln. From 1878 to 1881, Wallace was governor of the territory of New Mexico. He served as U.S. minister to Turkey from 1881 to 1885.   Ronald T. Curran

Wallace, Sir William (1272?-1305), was a Scottish patriot who led a revolt against King Edward I of England. The story of his life has stirred the national pride of Scots for more than 600 years.

In 1296, King Edward drove out the king of Scotland and stationed English soldiers in the country. Wallace, known for his strength and courage, became the leader of bands of Scottish patriots who carried on a bitter war against the invaders. The English raised an army and advanced against Wallace. He defeated them in the battle of Stirling Bridge. At that point, King Edward hurried home from France and led a great army against the rebels. His heavily armored soldiers defeated the rebels at Falkirk. Wallace escaped and carried on the fight in the mountains. Seven years later, he was captured and executed for treason.   Paul M. Kendall

Wallboard is a kind of board made of fibers of wood, cane, and other fibrous materials. It is used to cover walls and ceilings. Wallboard gives protection against fire and weather, and insulation against heat and cold. It absorbs sound and also serves as a decoration. Wallboard is made in sheets $\frac{1}{10}$ inch to 3 inches (2.5 to 76 millimeters) thick. It is made in sections up to 8 feet (2.4 meters) wide and 20 feet (6 meters) long. A wall that is covered with wallboard is called a *dry wall.*

Fiberboard is made from cane or wood fiber pressed into sheets (see **Fiberboard**). The fibers may be loosely compressed, leaving air spaces for good heat insulation and sound absorption. The surface is usually fibrous, but some is veneered with paper-thin sheets of mahogany and other woods. Fiberboard is used for interior surfaces and also for outside wall sheathing that is to be covered with wood siding or brick veneer.

Hardboard is a kind of wallboard often used in making furniture. It is made by heating specially treated masses of wood fibers and placing them under pressure to form a dense, hard board. *Tempered board* is made by further treatment of hardboard with liquids and heat. *Plasterboard* has a core of gypsum sandwiched between layers of heavy paper.   George W. Washa

Wallenberg, Raoul (1912-   ?   ), a Swedish businessman and diplomat, helped save about 100,000 Hungarian Jews from being killed by the Nazis in 1944, during World War II. He often risked his life, and later won worldwide admiration for his heroic efforts.

Wallenberg was born in Kapptsta, near Stockholm. He was a member of a prominent family of bankers and industrialists. He visited Hungary on business in the early 1940's, during World War II. Wallenberg became increasingly disturbed by the campaign of Nazi leader

Adolf Hitler to kill all the Jews of Europe. In 1944, Wallenberg came to the attention of the World Jewish Congress and the American War Refugee Board. He accepted their invitation to head a program in Hungary to save remaining Jews there.

The Swedish government appointed Wallenberg to serve as a diplomat in Budapest, Hungary's capital. He issued Swedish passports to about 20,000 Jews, allowing them to claim the protection of the neutral Swedish government. He also sheltered Jews in houses he bought or rented with his own money or money from the groups that had sent him. Wallenberg, a Lutheran, was assisted by Roman Catholic and other non-Jewish leaders.

Adolf Eichmann, a Nazi official who directed the sending of Jews to concentration camps, ordered Wallenberg to stop interfering with German plans for the Jews. Wallenberg refused. Eichmann tried to have Wallenberg assassinated, but the attempt failed. In the final days before the liberation of Budapest by Soviet soldiers, Wallenberg persuaded the Nazis to cancel a plan to kill 70,000 Jews who were forced to live in a *ghetto* (segregated area) of the city.

In January 1945, Soviet forces took Wallenberg into custody. They apparently believed he was an American spy. In 1957, the Soviet government reported that Wallenberg had died of a heart attack in prison in 1947. But several people reported seeing him alive in Soviet prisons and hospitals after 1947. In 1981, the United States Congress made Wallenberg an honorary U.S. citizen.

Abraham Cooper

Wallendas, The. See Circus (Famous circus performers).

Wallenstein, *WAHL uhn STYN* or *VAHL uhn SHTYN,* **Albrecht Wenzel Eusebius von,** *AHL brehkt VEHN tsuhl oy ZAY bee us fuhn* (1583-1634), a Bohemian general, played an important role in the Thirty Years' War (1618-1648). He was the inspiration for *Wallenstein* (1798-1799), a tragedy by the German playwright Friedrich Schiller.

Wallenstein was born in Bohemia. His father was a Protestant nobleman. Wallenstein became a Roman Catholic and fought for Holy Roman Emperor Rudolf II, a Catholic, against the Turks.

Bohemian Protestants began the Thirty Years' War by rebelling against the Catholic Habsburg family, which ruled Bohemia as part of the Holy Roman Empire. Wallenstein remained loyal to the Holy Roman Empire and raised a small army for Emperor Ferdinand II. Ferdinand rewarded him with the title Duke of Friedland. Wallenstein, who had been made a general, recruited troops and led them in battles in Germany and Bohemia.

Wallenstein believed he was destined to play a great political role. His goal was a huge European empire that would dominate the Turks and western Europe. The Catholic princes resented his great ambition and power, and the emperor was alarmed by his intrigues with Swedish and German Protestant leaders. The emperor ordered his arrest, or death, and officers loyal to the emperor murdered him.   Charles W. Ingrao

See also **Thirty Years' War.**

Waller, Fats (1904-1943), was an American jazz pianist, songwriter, and entertainer. He became one of the most accomplished pianists in the history of jazz, though in his day he was known primarily as an entertainer.

RCA

Fats Waller was a popular American jazz pianist.

Many of Waller's songs have lively, witty lyrics. His first songs were published in 1924. In 1923, he started working with Andy Razaf, an American lyricist who wrote the words for some of Waller's most popular songs. Their compositions include "Ain't Misbehavin' " (1929), "Blue Turning Grey Over You" (1930), "Honeysuckle Rose" (1929), and "Jitterbug Waltz" (1942).

Waller made several hundred recordings, many of them with a small band that he led from 1934 until his death. He sang on many of these records. Waller weighed almost 300 pounds (140 kilograms). Thomas Wright Waller was born in New York City.   John Norris

See also **Jazz** (The golden age).

Walleye. See Fish (picture: Fish of temperate fresh waters); **Perch; Pike.**

Wallflower is a fragrant plant that originated in southern Europe. It blooms in the spring, and bears clusters

© Kent and Donna Dannen, Photo Researchers

Wallflowers have clusters of colorful blossoms.

of single or double golden, maroon, or purple flowers. The plant is called *wallflower* because its stems often grow on walls and cliffs for support. Wallflowers seem to thrive on the lime in cliffs. They grow well in England's cool climate and in warm southern areas of the United States. They are also called *gillyflowers.*

Scientific classification. Wallflowers are in the mustard family, Cruciferae. They are *Cheiranthus cheiri.*

Robert W. Schery

Walloons are a group of people who live in southern Belgium. The region they inhabit is called Wallonia. It consists of the provinces of Hainaut, Liège, Luxembourg, Namur, and the southern half of Brabant (see **Belgium** [political map]). The Walloons make up about 30 per cent of the Belgian population.

The Walloons are descended from a Celtic tribe known as the Belgae, who once lived in Flanders, the northern region of Belgium. The Belgae were forced to move south in the A.D. 400's when the Franks, a Germanic people, invaded Flanders. The descendants of the Franks, called the Flemings, now inhabit Flanders.

During the 1700's, Wallonia became one of Europe's most wealthy industrial regions. The Walloon cities of Liège and Charleroi became centers for coal mining and steelmaking. During the 1800's, the Belgians built extensive networks of canals and railroads in Wallonia. They also developed an advanced banking system.

Language and cultural differences have created friction between the Walloons and the Flemings. The Walloons speak French. The Flemings speak Dutch.

When Belgium became independent in 1830, the Walloons largely controlled the government. They made French the only official language of the country. The Flemings then began a movement to gain recognition of their own language and culture. Dutch became an official language of Belgium during the late 1800's.

Conflicts between the Walloons and the Flemings continued during the 1900's. In 1980, the Belgian government granted limited self-rule to Flanders and Wallonia.

Janet L. Polasky

See also **Belgium** (People); **Flemings.**

Wallpaper is decorative paper used to cover inside walls. Many wall coverings made of other materials—for example, burlap, linen, manufactured fibers, plastics, and thin sheets of wood—are also considered wallpaper. A special paste, which is brushed onto the undecorated side of wallpaper, makes it stick to a wall. Manufacturers sell most wallpaper in rolls of sheets that measure about 30 feet (9.1 meters) long and $2\frac{1}{4}$ feet (69 centimeters) wide.

Most people use wallpaper to make a room more attractive. Wallpaper also provides practical advantages. For example, it hides cracks, stains, and other flaws on walls. Paper made of plaster reinforced with plant fibers can be used to cover brick, concrete blocks, or rough plaster. Wallpaper made of a plastic material called *vinyl* can be scrubbed with a mild detergent and water. Many apartment dwellers and people who frequently redecorate use a special kind of wall covering called *strippable wallpaper.* It can be peeled off easily without damaging the wall.

Scholars believe the first wallpaper was made in England, France, or the Netherlands during the 1500's. Artists designed patterned wallpaper as a cheaper substi-

tute for the *tapestries* (woven wall hangings) that had decorated European palaces for centuries. Craftworkers painted designs on the paper by hand or printed them from carved blocks of wood. The Chinese began to make wallpaper in the early 1600's. They painted birds, flowers, and landscapes on rectangular sheets of rice paper. In the 1700's, the French decorated wallpaper with Chinese objects and patterns. This popular style became known as *chinoiserie.*

Wallpaper was first produced in the United States in Philadelphia in 1739. In 1947, vinyl-covered wallpaper was introduced. Prepasted paper, which sticks to a wall when the paper is moistened with water, was developed in the 1950's.   Howard A. Rickspoone

See also **Interior decoration.**

Walnut is the name of a type of tree valued for its nuts and wood. Several species of walnut trees grow in the United States. Two of these are native to the East—the *black walnut* and the *butternut,* also called the *white walnut.* Another species, the *English walnut* or *Persian walnut,* was brought to the United States from southern Europe. It is grown commercially in California and Oregon. Black and English walnut trees provide high-quality wood for furniture.

English walnut trees produce walnuts that have the greatest commercial value. They are large, spreading trees that grow up to 100 feet (30 meters) tall. They have gray bark, large leaflets, and soft wood. These trees

Oxford Scientific films from Earth Scenes

English walnut flowers, *above,* lack petals. They grow in clusters called *catkins.*

Debbie Dean

The nuts of the English walnut tree, *above,* have thin shells and a mild flavor.

Grant Heilman

The English walnut tree may grow up to 100 feet (30 meters) tall. The nuts of the English walnut tree have greater commercial value than those of any other variety.

have been grown commercially in Europe since ancient times.

The English walnut tree bears clusters of small flowers called *catkins*. The flowers may be cross-pollinated or self-pollinated. After flowering, the tree produces walnuts. The nuts have thin shells and taste mild and sweet. They contain mostly fats and some proteins.

Growers typically plant English walnut trees at least 60 feet (18 meters) apart in commercial orchards. However, growers have developed several varieties of these trees that may be planted closer together. English walnut trees thrive in deep, well-drained soil. After the nuts ripen, they are shaken from the trees, hulled, and dried. The nuts are taken to packing houses where they are sorted and sized. They may be packaged either in the shell or shelled. The poorer grades of nuts are used to make walnut oil.

Growers once left walnut shells that fell to the ground as waste. Today, the shells are collected and used in glues and plastics. They are also used to make solutions for cleaning and polishing metal surfaces.

The United States leads the world in the production of walnuts. Other major walnut-growing countries include China, Greece, the Soviet Union, and Turkey. In the United States, the walnut industry is centered in the area around Stockton, Calif. In addition, several hardy varieties of English walnut trees are grown in the Midwest and the East. However, growers usually do not plant large orchards of these varieties. English walnut trees do not grow well in the South.

Black walnut trees grow in forests from Massachusetts to Florida and east to Texas. They are hardy trees that are grown mainly for their lumber. The nuts also are harvested and sold. They have a distinctive and rich flavor, but their shell is hard and thick. They are usually shelled before they are sold. Growers have also developed a few thin-shelled varieties of these nuts.

Black walnut wood is dark purplish-brown, with a fine grain and luster. It is valuable for interior finishing, furniture, and gunstocks. This wood is becoming rare.

Scientific classification. Walnuts belong to the walnut family, Juglandaceae. The English walnut is *Juglans regia*. The black walnut is *J. nigra,* and the butternut is *J. cinerea.*

Richard A. Jaynes

See also **Butternut; Tree** (Familiar broadleaf and needleaf trees [picture]).

Walnut Canyon National Monument is in central Arizona. It contains 800-year-old cliff-dwelling ruins in shallow caves. The monument was established in 1915. For its area, see **National Park System** (table: National monuments).

Walpole is the family name of two famous Englishmen of the 1700's, father and son. They bore the title Earl of Orford. The father was a famous political leader, the son a noted writer.

Sir Robert Walpole (1676-1745) was the most influential politician in England during the first half of the 1700's. He became England's first prime minister, though the title was not official at the time. He sponsored no memorable legislation, and did nothing to raise the standard of conduct in government. But during the 21 years he governed Great Britain, he became famous for his ability to transact government business.

Walpole was born at Houghton, Norfolk, and was ed-

Bettmann Archive

Sir Robert Walpole, *seated center,* governed Great Britain from 1721 to 1742 as the country's first prime minister, though the title was not official at the time. He became famous for his ability to conduct government business.

ucated at Eton College and Cambridge University. He entered Parliament in 1701 and by 1710 was secretary at war and treasurer of the navy. Walpole showed ability, but he lost his offices when the Tories replaced the Whigs in 1710-1711. He then became the leader of the opposition in the House of Commons. The new government convicted Walpole of graft and sent him to prison in 1712. However, Walpole returned to Parliament in 1713.

After George I became king in 1714, Walpole's political stature increased. He became first lord of the treasury in 1715, but resigned in 1717. During the next few years, he attacked the government and built up his influence in the House of Commons. His greatest triumph in this period came in 1718 when he defeated the Peerage Bill, which sought to limit the House of Lords to 216 members. He also profited politically from the collapse of the speculative South Sea Company in 1720, which disgraced the men in office.

In 1721, Walpole again became first lord of the treasury and chancellor of the exchequer. For the next 20 years, he was the most powerful person in Great Britain. His primary purpose was to govern Britain with as little excitement as possible. He left the direction of foreign affairs to others, and worked to control the House of Commons and build his personal interests. For years,

Walpole defeated opposition by his debating skill, his power and influence, and his constant attendance in the House of Commons.

Eventually Walpole lost his vigor. In domestic affairs, his readiness to compromise and his preference for doing nothing brought criticism from William Pitt. Walpole was a man of peace who knew that in war even the victors lose. As the demand for war with Spain rose, his hold on the House of Commons declined. His loss of influence and failing health prompted him to resign in 1742. However, Walpole was almost immediately created Earl of Orford, and he influenced policies in the House of Lords until his death.   Charles F. Mullett

Horace Walpole (1717-1797), the youngest son of the prime minister, was a letter writer, author, and art lover. Even at a time when personal letters were considered a minor art form, Walpole's huge correspondence is remarkable. His witty letters provide an entertaining documentary of life in English high society. They report social and political gossip, and express Walpole's opinions on literature and the arts.

As a scholar fascinated by medieval life, Walpole greatly influenced the Gothic revival of the late 1700's. He transformed Strawberry Hill, his house in Twickenham, into a miniature Gothic castle. He built a printing press nearby, and published many of his own writings. His most influential literary work is *The Castle of Otranto* (1764). This tale of terror and the supernatural was the first of what became known as Gothic novels.

Walpole was born in London. He served in Parliament from 1741 to 1768. In 1791, he succeeded to the family title as the fourth Earl of Orford.   Martin C. Battestin

Additional resources

Dickinson, Harry T. *Walpole and the Whig Supremacy.* English Universities Press (London), 1973.
Fothergill, Brian. *The Strawberry Hill Set: Horace Walpole and His Circle.* Faber & Faber, 1984.
Lewis, Wilmarth S. *Horace Walpole.* Pantheon, 1961.
Plumb, John H. *Sir Robert Walpole.* Houghton, 1973. First published as 2 vols. 1956, 1961.

Walpole, Sir Hugh Seymour (1884-1941), was one of the most popular British novelists in the early 1900's. His finest novels are probably the *Herries Chronicles* (1930-1933), a series of four historical novels set in England in the 1700's. The series includes *Rogue Herries, Judith Paris, The Fortress,* and *Vanessa.* Walpole wrote over 30 other novels on a variety of subjects. In *The Dark Forest* (1916) and *The Secret City* (1919), he described his World War I experiences with the Red Cross in Russia. *The Cathedral* (1922) is based on his experiences as a clergyman's son. *Portrait of a Man with Red Hair* (1925) is a horror story about a brutal murderer.

Walpole was born in Auckland, New Zealand, and was sent to school in England at the age of five. He was knighted in 1937.   Sharon Basset

Walpurgis Night, *vahl PUR gihs,* is the eve of May Day, when German people celebrate the feast of St. Walpurgis. According to legend, witches gather on this night and celebrate their Sabbath on mist-covered Brocken, the highest peak in the Harz Mountains.

Walrus is a sea animal that lives in parts of the Arctic, North Atlantic, and North Pacific oceans. It has two ivory tusks, and its four feet are flattened into flippers. The flippers make the walrus a good swimmer.

Leonard Lee Rue III, Tom Stack & Assoc.

The walrus has long tusks that it uses mainly for defense. Its thick hide helps it survive in its cold environment.

During the winter and spring, walruses drift along on large floating fields of ice. In summer, some may rest on shore. A walrus spends much time in the water searching for clams, its favorite food. The animal uses its tongue to form a vacuum to suck clams into its mouth and to suck the flesh from the shell. A walrus has bristles on its upper lip. These bristles are sensitive to touch and probably help the walrus find food.

Scientists classify the walrus as a kind of large seal. An adult male grows about 12 feet (3.7 meters) long and weighs up to 3,000 pounds (1,400 kilograms).

The walrus is the only seal with tusks. The tusks, which are its upper canine teeth, point downward and may grow as long as 39 inches (99 centimeters). A walrus defends itself from polar bears with its tusks. It also uses them as hooks when climbing onto ice. Walruses do not attack people. However, an angry, wounded walrus can injure a hunter or damage a boat with its tusks. A walrus makes a loud bellow that can be heard for $\frac{1}{2}$ mile (0.8 kilometer). This bellowing helps hunters locate the animals.

Walruses are mammals. A female walrus usually has one calf every other year and cares for her young for about two years. Twins are very rare. Baby walruses are grayish-brown, and adults are rusty-brown. Some walruses live as long as 40 years.

Most walruses live in herds, but some live alone. Some Eskimos hunt walruses. They eat the meat, use the hides to make shelters or boats, and burn the blubber oil for heat and light. Some Eskimos carve walrus tusks into figures of animals and hunting scenes.

Scientific classification. The walrus is in the order Pinnipedia. It forms the walrus family, Odobenidae. It is *Odobenus rosmarus.*   Michael A. Bigg

See also **Animal** (picture: Animals of the polar regions); **Seal.**

Walt Disney World. See Florida (Places to visit).

Walter, *VAHL tuhr,* **Bruno,** *BROO noh* (1876-1962), was one of the leading symphony orchestra and opera conductors of the 1900's. He became noted for the warmth and insight of his musical interpretations. He was also known for his support of the music of his friend Gustav Mahler (see **Mahler, Gustav**).

Walter was born in Berlin, where he received his musical education. His real name was Bruno Walter Schlesinger. At the age of 18, he became an assistant to Mahler, who was director of the Hamburg Opera. Their association continued until Mahler died in 1911.

While still a young man, Walter became one of the most celebrated conductors in central Europe and held several important positions. He moved to the United States in 1939. Walter frequently conducted the New York Philharmonic Orchestra from 1941 to 1957 and at the Metropolitan Opera from 1941 to 1959.

Robert C. Marsh

Walter, Thomas Ustick, *YOO stihk* (1804-1887), an American architect, became noted for his buildings in the Greek Revival style. He is known chiefly as the architect of the United States Capitol from 1851 to 1865. He added the Senate and House wings, and the large cast-iron dome, painted to resemble stone. Walter was born in Philadelphia. With Richard Upjohn, he founded the American Institute of Architects.

Leland M. Roth

Walter Reed Army Medical Center, in Washington, D.C., provides care for active-duty and retired military personnel and their families. It also conducts scientific research and trains doctors in advanced methods. It covers 113 acres (46 hectares) in Washington and also includes 118 acres (48 hectares) in Forest Glen and 22 acres (9 hectares) in Glenhaven, both in Maryland. Major activities of the center are the treatment facility, the Walter Reed Army Institute of Research, the Institute of Dental Research, and the Armed Forces Institute of Pathology. The center was named for Walter Reed, an Army surgeon who helped conquer typhoid fever and yellow fever (see **Reed, Walter**).

Critically reviewed by the United States Army

Walther von der Vogelweide, *VAHL tuhr fawn duhr FOH guhl vy duh* (1170?-1230?), was perhaps the greatest of the medieval *minnesingers* (love poets). Walther was born in Austria, and he lived during the period when the elegance and grace of aristocratic culture flourished. He was a poet in the court of Vienna but apparently had to leave when his patron died. He then moved from court to court until, late in life, he received a grant of land from German Emperor Frederick II.

Walther's love poetry differed from the conventions of courtly *minnesang,* which celebrated a hopeless love for some high-born lady. Walther praised the love for a village girl. He also raised poems of political commentary to a high art. His large and varied poetic production shows originality. His technique ranges from simple to highly complex forms.

James F. Poag

Walton, Ernest Thomas Sinton (1903-   ), an Irish physicist, shared the 1951 Nobel Prize in physics with Sir John Cockcroft. They discovered jointly the transmutations of atomic nuclei by artificially accelerated particles in 1932. They constructed the first of the controlled particle accelerators, producing 500,000 volts. Their experiments confirmed Albert Einstein's theory that mass and energy are equivalent. Walton was born in Dungarvan.

Robert H. March

See also **Cockcroft, Sir John Douglas.**

Walton, George (1741-1804), a Georgia signer of the Declaration of Independence, was governor and chief justice of Georgia several times. In 1775, Walton became secretary of the provincial congress and president of the council of safety. He served in the Continental Congress from 1776 to 1781. Walton fought in the defense of Savannah in 1778, and was captured by the British. He was a United States senator in 1795 and 1796. Walton was born near Farmville, Va.

Richard B. Morris

Walton, Izaak (1593-1683), was an English author best known for his book on fishing, *The Compleat Angler.* The work is a classic example of a *pastoral* (about rural life) book in English literature. *The Compleat Angler* was first published in 1653 and went through four revisions during the author's lifetime. The book is written as a dialogue, primarily between Piscator, a fisherman, and Venator, a hunter. The work combines practical information about fish and fishing with songs, poems, and descriptions of country life and the English countryside. Walton also gained fame for his biographies, notably of the poets John Donne (1640, revised edition 1658) and George Herbert (1670) and the clergyman Richard Hooker (1665).

Walton was born in Stafford and became a wealthy London hardware merchant. He did not graduate from a university but read widely and became a friend of a number of famous men, including Donne and playwright Ben Jonson.

Steven N. Zwicker

See also **Biography** (The 1600's).

Walton, Sir William (1902-1983), was an English composer whose works are noted for their strong sense of melody and form. Walton was a slow and deliberate composer who produced a relatively small body of works. Most of his compositions are instrumental and many follow the symphonic form.

Walton's first major composition was *Façade* (1923), a chamber work set to poems by his friend Edith Sitwell. Walton's other important works include two symphonies and concertos for viola, violin, and cello. He also wrote *Sinfonia Concertante* (1927, revised 1943) for piano and orchestra. Among his other orchestral compositions are *Partita* (1958), *Variations on a Theme by Hindemith* (1963), and *Improvisations on an Impromptu of Benjamin Britten* (1970). Walton also composed marches, chamber music, and music for radio, television, and films. *Belshazzar's Feast* (1931), an oratorio, is his most famous vocal composition. Other vocal works include two operas and compositions for chorus and solo voice.

William Turner Walton was born in Oldham. He received his first musical training from his father, a music teacher. Walton later studied at Oxford University. He was knighted in 1951.

Mary Vinquist

Waltz is a ballroom dance in $\frac{3}{4}$ time characterized by its swift gliding turns. The term *waltz* is also used for the music that accompanies this dance. The waltz has been danced in two distinct styles, the *three-step* and the *two-step*. In Europe, especially in Vienna, the dancers waltzed much faster than in North America.

The waltz probably developed from an Austrian folk dance called the *Ländler.* Waltzes became popular in Germany in the late 1700's. Their popularity among young people led some authorities to outlaw waltzes because they thought it was immoral for couples to dance so closely. During the late 1700's and the 1800's, many composers wrote waltzes intended for listening rather than for dancing. Leading composers of *concert waltzes* included members of the Strauss family (see **Strauss, Johann, Jr.**). Waltz music and dancing also appear in many operas, operettas, and ballets.

Dianne L. Woodruff

See also **Dancing** (The rise of romanticism; picture).

Walvis Bay is a district of South Africa. It is separated from the rest of the country by the southern part of Namibia (South West Africa). The district lies along the Atlantic Ocean (see **Namibia** [map]). Walvis Bay covers 434 square miles (1,124 square kilometers) and has a population of 20,740. Its largest city, also called Walvis Bay, is the chief port for Namibia's trade. Industries of the district include meat processing, canning, and fishing.

Portuguese sailors were the first white people to see the Walvis Bay area. They landed there in 1487, but black Africans had settled in the area long before. Walvis Bay became part of South Africa when that country was established in 1910. In 1920, the League of Nations gave South Africa control of Namibia. Since then, South Africa has administered Walvis Bay as part of Namibia.

During the 1970's, representatives of South Africa and the United Nations began discussing plans to grant independence to Namibia. Walvis Bay became a center of controversy. Namibian leaders want Walvis Bay to become part of Namibia upon independence. But leaders of the South African government say the district should remain part of their country.   L. H. Gann

Wampanoag Indians. See Massasoit; Philip, King; Indian, American (Table of tribes); Rhode Island (King Philip's War).

Wampum is an American Indian word for purple or white beads made from shells. The beads were made mainly by North American Indians living near the Atlantic coast. The Indians decorated their clothing and other possessions with wampum. They also used it to keep records.

The Indians carved white beads from the shells of sea snails called *whelks* and purple beads from the shells of hard-shell clams. Manufacturing the beads required patience and skill because the shells were brittle and the beads were tiny. The beads were about $\frac{1}{8}$ inch (3 millimeters) in diameter and about $\frac{1}{4}$ inch (6 millimeters) long. The Indians drilled a fine hole in each bead. They then used the holes to string the beads or to sew them onto fabrics or animal skins.

The Indians often wove thousands of beads into wampum belts. They exchanged the belts as pledges to keep treaties and to assure friendships. The Indians recorded events on their belts by arranging beads in designs. In many cases, the colors of the beads had meanings. White often represented health, peace, and riches. Purple often meant grief or sympathy.

The Algonquian Indians made the first wampum about 1600. European fur traders exchanged wampum obtained from coastal tribes for the furs of inland Indians. Dutch and English colonists, who had few metal coins, adopted wampum as money. But wampum began to lose its value during the mid-1600's, when new metal coins appeared. In the 1700's, colonists manufactured wampum themselves for use in the fur trade with Great Plains and Northwest Coast Indians.   Lynn Ceci

Wandering Jew is a legendary figure who is condemned to wander throughout the world until the *Second Coming* of Jesus Christ. The most popular version of the legend of the Wandering Jew developed during the early 1600's in Germany. It tells of a Jewish shoemaker named Ahasuerus who cursed Jesus while Jesus was carrying His cross to the Crucifixion. As punishment, Jesus ordered Ahasuerus to wander until Jesus would return to earth. Ahasuerus thus became the Wandering Jew and the living witness of Jesus' Crucifixion.

According to legend, the Wandering Jew appears at various times and places and describes events that have happened since the time of Jesus. Since the 1600's, many writers have used the legend as the framework for political and social commentary, especially because the character had observed so much of world history. The legend of the Wandering Jew has also been used to promote prejudice against Jews.   Richard R. Ring

Wandering Jew is the common name for certain kinds of plants belonging to the spiderwort family. They grow in the southern United States, Mexico, and South America. The name refers to the old legend of the Jew who was doomed to wander over the earth forever because he mocked Jesus as He carried the cross. These plants seem to wander all over and live indefinitely. They are grown as house plants for the beauty of their leaves, which have a silvery sheen. In the strong sunlight these leaves show white or cream stripes above, and reddish-purple beneath. The wandering Jew plant requires much water and sunlight. The plant bears white or rose-red flowers.

Scientific classification. The plants belong to the spiderwort family, Commelinaceae. They are genus *Tradescantia,* species *T. fluminensis,* with white flowers, and *Zebrina pendula* with rose-red flowers.   Donald Wyman

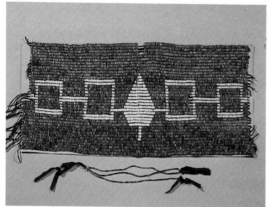

New York State Museum (WORLD BOOK photo)

Indian wampum, consisting of beads, was woven into belts to record important events. The belt in the upper part of this picture marked the union of five tribes. The Indians also strung wampum on cords, such as those shown under the belt.

Wang Wei (699-759) was a Chinese painter and poet known especially for his skill as a landscape artist. He painted beautiful *monochromatic* landscapes, which use shades, tones, and tints of a single color. Records tell of Wang Wei's many paintings on the walls of temples and palaces. He also painted on silk and probably on paper. None of his wallpaintings has survived, and only a few other existing paintings are said to be his. However, much of Wang Wei's poetry has been saved.

Wang Wei lived during the Tang dynasty (618-907), which is generally regarded as the golden age of Chinese civilization. He lived in the capital, Chang-an (now Xian), where he earned a high office in government. Wang Wei also produced beautiful Chinese *calligraphy* (handwriting) and was a skilled musician. He has come

The wandering Jew's striped leaves and graceful flowers make it a favorite ornamental plant for indoor cultivation.

Townsend P. Dickinson, Photo Researchers

to be recognized as a genius who brought painting, poetry, and calligraphy together into a unified art.

Robert A. Rorex

Wankel engine. See Rotary engine.
Want ad. See Advertising (Newspapers); **Careers** (Finding job opportunities).
Wapiti. See Elk; **Deer** (Kinds).
War. Since the dawn of history, people have fought against other people. Any struggle in which two large groups try to destroy or conquer each other is a war. There have been many kinds of wars. Families have fought against families, tribes against tribes, followers of one religion against followers of another. In modern times, wars have been fought between nations or groups of nations. Armies and navies once were almost the only factors in deciding the outcome of wars. Today, civilians must join in the war effort if it is to succeed.

Wars have always caused great suffering and hardship. Most people hate war, yet for hundreds of years war has been going on somewhere in the world nearly all the time. Earthquakes and floods *happen* to people, but people *make* war themselves. To understand why wars continue to go on when nearly everyone wants to

have peace, we must look into the nature of war.

Causes of war. In modern times, no nation or group chooses war if it can get what it wants peacefully. The fighting starts when a nation wants something so badly that it is willing to go to war to get it. Sometimes war results from a disagreement between two nations, and sometimes from a desire for conquest. Some of the basic causes of war may be a desire for more land, a desire for more wealth, a desire for more power, or a desire for security.

War for land to live on. In ancient times, people often fought so that they could get enough to eat. When the pasture lands in Central Asia dried up, hungry tribes would make war on their neighbors in order to get new lands. The neighbors sometimes fought back. More often they gave up their lands and tried to seize those of a still weaker tribe.

Much of the fighting that went on between early American pioneers and American Indians was this kind of war. The Indians wanted to roam freely over the land, hunting, trapping, or fishing. The pioneers wanted to clear the land and plant it in crops. Indian fighting was dangerous, and no one who already had a good farm was likely to go out and fight the Indians for another. But landless people from abroad preferred the dangers of war to the horrors of poverty.

This type of war has not entirely disappeared, but it is no longer common or important. The early war for land to live on usually had these two important characteristics: those who did the fighting made the decision to fight, and the fighters wanted something for themselves.

War for wealth. The peoples of ancient empires fought many wars for wealth. The decision to fight was made by the ruler of the empire and his or her advisers. The fighting was often done by hired armies. A ruler who sought to conquer new lands did not intend to drive the people out of the lands. Generally, he or she just wanted to collect taxes from the people in the territory invaded.

When Alexander the Great led his armies against the Persian Empire, the common people of the invaded lands paid little attention, except to hope that their own property would not be destroyed. It usually made little difference to these people which ruler collected taxes.

Detail of *Clearing After Snowfall Along the River* (1500's), an ink painting on paper; Honolulu Academy of Arts, Gift of Robert Lehman, 1960

A landscape in the style of Wang Wei shows this early Chinese artist's mastery of *monochromatic* painting. This technique uses shades, tones, and tints of a single color.

Wars were fought solely by rulers and their armies.

In the Middle Ages, there were many wars for wealth. Often one noble would try to seize the property of another. He would use his own soldiers and perhaps hire other leaders and their soldiers to help him. Sometimes the conqueror of a city would take a large money payment in return for leaving the city in peace.

War for power. The great European nations fought wars throughout the world to gain or increase their power. These wars united the people and strengthened the governments. Wars of conquest based on the ideas of a super-race or of a superior economic system are often wars to extend the power of a government.

War for security. Most countries fear the possibility of attack, and maintain armed forces to defend themselves. Sometimes this fear may be directed toward a particular country. In that case a nation may decide to choose its own time and strike the first blow. Or it may decide to conquer some weaker neighbor, and thus increase its own resources as a defense against attack.

Differences between causes and reasons. When a nation makes war, its government always states the *reasons* for the war. This is necessary if the people are to be united in the war effort. But the reasons given for a war need not be the same as its *causes.* For example, the government of the United States pointed to the British interference with American shipping and the impressment of American seamen as reasons for the War of 1812. A cause which was not stated was the desire on the part of some Americans to extend the United States into lands held by the British and their Spanish allies in North America. This was one of the important *causes* of the war, but it was not stated as a *reason.* The causes of war may be selfish, base, or even wicked, but the reasons stated are usually lofty and noble. Both sides in a war may show reasons which they consider to be valid.

War means absence of law. War is not the only kind of struggle in which there may be some right on both sides. Almost every case that comes to trial before a court has this same quality. In a suit over property, both sides can usually show a claim of some sort. The court has to decide which is the *better* claim. If there were no court, both persons claiming the property might feel justified in fighting for it.

In frontier days many Westerners carried guns and settled their disputes by fighting. Until courts and police forces were established, they had no other way to settle quarrels in which both sides were partly right. People often joined forces against horse thieves and other outlaws, but they could not handle quarrels between honest people who disagreed about their rights.

Today a similar problem exists among nations. The people in any country are likely to see their own interests more clearly than those of people in another country. People's own desires seem so reasonable and so important that the desires of people in another country are likely to look selfish and unreasonable. Laws and courts can settle such disputes *within* a country, but there has as yet been no effective law *between* countries. That is why the use of force to settle a dispute is a *crime* within a country and a *war* between countries. War can exist only where there is no effective law.

Most wars have several "causes." In modern times, a nation usually does not make war for a single simple reason. There may be dozens or hundreds of causes for war. In every country there are groups of people with different aims and different hopes. When nearly all these groups are willing, each for its own reasons, to run the risk of war, war will almost certainly result.

For example, some groups in the United States wanted to enter World War I because they were angry at the Germans for invading Belgium. Some groups wanted to make sure that Great Britain and France would win the war, because of America's close economic and cultural ties with these countries. Some people feared that the German submarine campaign might halt trade relations between the United States and the Allied countries, and cause a depression. Some were indignant at the sinking of the *Lusitania.* Others simply believed that the Germans were wrong and the Allies were right, and wanted to help the right side. A few persons saw that it would not be safe for the United States to allow Germany to dominate Europe.

Depression and war. Some economists and historians think there is a close connection between war and economic depression. They argue that in a worldwide depression every country tries to protect itself at the expense of other countries. Each nation wants to cut down unemployment at home, and tries to make sure that little is bought from abroad which could be made by its own workers at home. This can easily be done by raising tariffs. It is sometimes called a way of "exporting unemployment" to other countries.

The chief concern of any government during a depression is to get people back to work. One way to do this is by building armaments. If anger can be stirred up against another country, or if people can be made to feel that they are in danger of attack, funds for military preparation are readily voted. Besides, the armed forces themselves give employment to many.

A modern democracy, such as the United States, would never risk war in order to end a depression or put people to work. But war may provide more employment and give many people a larger share of food, clothing, and other good things than they can have in depression. For this reason, a long depression makes war seem less dreadful to those who have lost all hope, and may drive them to follow such leaders as Adolf Hitler.

War aims and peace aims. War seldom accomplishes the complete results any side has hoped for. Many people with different purposes may unite to make war, but they often start quarreling among themselves when the war is over. In order to hold a warring people or group of countries together, peace aims are usually stated in vague, general terms, so that everyone concerned can see in them a promise of what he wants. When the victory is won, general terms become specific, and usually do not satisfy all the winners.

Methods of warfare. Changes in the ways of waging war have had a great effect on the way people live. Some historians think that the idea of human equality came to be widely accepted because guns took the place of spears, swords, and arrows as the chief weapons of war. They point out that an armored knight in feudal days was more than a match for dozens of men who had no armor. But, these historians point out, the minutemen of Lexington and Concord, with guns in their hands, were equal or nearly equal to the same number of British soldiers. Following their theory, the historians go on to point out that when one soldier became the equal of another, some people decided that voting was an easy way to tell how a fight over an issue would come out. The idea of human equality gained strength when people accepted each individual's right to cast a vote that was just as important as any other individual's vote.

Modern warfare has moved away from the days when soldiers with rifles were the most important part of an army. War has been mechanized until it is in large part a contest in producing machinery. In Thomas Jefferson's day, it made sense to protect "the right to keep and bear arms," so that people could overthrow a tyrannical government. Today, the private citizen cannot keep the kinds of weapons that would serve this purpose.

The atomic bomb, used by the United States against Japan in 1945, has brought another great change into warfare. After the invention of the bomb, it seemed probable that future wars would be short and terribly destructive. Great cities could be destroyed and millions of people killed within a few hours. The only question was whether the nations of the world could change their habits fast enough to keep war from breaking out. See **Nuclear weapon.**

Total war is one in which a nation uses all its people, resources, and weapons. In such wars, civilians as well as military people take part in the war effort. For example, World Wars I and II were total wars in which entire populations took part. Civilians worked on such activities as civil defense and weapons manufacture, and many civilians were killed by bombs.

Limited war is one in which the warring nations limit the weapons they use, the targets they attack, or the areas involved. Since the invention of the atomic bomb, *limited war* has come to mean a war in which neither side uses atomic weapons. The Korean War (1950-1953) was a limited war in this sense. Only North and South Korea fought a total war. Neither the Soviet Union nor the United States used their nuclear weapons.

After World War II, several international disputes grew into wars. But fear of nuclear destruction prevented any of the wars from becoming total. These limited wars included the Vietnam War (1957-1975) and the Middle East wars of 1948, 1956, 1967, and 1973.

Is war "normal"? Democratic countries take it for granted that peace is normal, and that war means some-

thing has gone wrong. But it is hard to say just where peace ends and war begins. Nations may be on unfriendly terms for years, building up their armies and navies, seeking allies, and trying to win control of each other's markets, without any actual clash of armed forces. These countries might be considered to be merely observing a rest period between wars. Many historians consider the years between World Wars I and II as a breathing spell in a single great war.   Payson S. Wild

Related articles in *World Book* include:

Wars

Boer War	Punic Wars
Chinese-Japanese wars	Revolutionary War in America
Civil War	Russo-Japanese War
Cold War	Russo-Turkish wars
Crimean War	Seven Weeks' War
Crusades	Seven Years' War
Franco-Prussian War	Spanish-American War
French and Indian wars	Succession wars
Hundred Years' War	Thirty Years' War
Indian wars	Vietnam War
Korean War	War of 1812
Mexican War	Wars of the Roses
Peasants' War	World War I
Peloponnesian War	World War II

Other related articles

Air force	Embargo	Neutrality
Amphibious warfare	Espionage	Peace
Army	Geneva Conventions	Prisoner of war
Blockade	Guerrilla warfare	Propaganda
Censorship	Hostage	Psychological war-
Chemical-biological-	International law	fare
radiological war-	Jingoism	Truce
fare	Marine	Underground
Contraband	Military science	Weapon
Draft, Military	Navy	

Additional resources

Dyer, Gwynne. *War.* Crown, 1985.
Glossop, Ronald J. *Confronting War: An Examination of Humanity's Most Pressing Problem.* 2nd ed. McFarland, 1987.
Holmes, Richard. *Acts of War: The Behavior of Men in Battle.* Free Press, 1985.
Walzer, Michael L. *Just and Unjust Wars: A Moral Argument with Historical Illustrations.* Basic Books, 1977.

War aces are airplane pilots who shoot down at least five enemy aircraft during a war. The aircraft must either crash or be forced to land in the opponent's territory. The *downing* of an aircraft must be confirmed by an eyewitness or recorded on film to count as a *victory* or *kill.* Gunners and other crew members may also receive credit for a victory.

The term *ace* originated in France during World War I (1914-1918). At first, the term was an unofficial title given to the best pilots. Later, shooting down five aircraft became widely used as the standard for being an ace. The downing of any aircraft—including an airship or observation balloon—counted as a victory.

During World War I, the leading aces became national heroes. Many people thought of them as daring knights of the sky. Baron Manfred von Richthofen of Germany, called the *Red Baron* or *Red Knight,* became the top ace of the war. He shot down 80 enemy aircraft. Aces from other countries included Captain René Fonck of France with 75 victories, Major Edward Mannock of Great Britain with 72, and Major Billy Bishop of Canada with 72. Captain Eddie Rickenbacker, the top Ameri-

Wars involving the United States

Wars		U.S. military deaths	U.S. war costs
Revolutionary War	(1775-1783)	25,324*	$101,100,000
War of 1812	(1812-1815)	2,260	$90,000,000
Mexican War	(1846-1848)	13,283	$71,400,000
Civil War	(1861-1865)		
Union forces		360,222	$3,183,000,000
Confederate forces		260,000*	$2,000,000,000
Spanish-American War	(1898)	2,446	$283,200,000
World War I	(1914-1918)	116,516	$18,676,000,000
World War II	(1939-1945)	405,399	$263,259,000,000
Korean War	(1950-1953)	54,246	$67,386,000,000
Vietnam War	(1957-1975)	58,000*	$150,000,000,000*

*Estimate.

can ace, shot down 22 planes (3 shared) and 4 balloons in only six months.

During World War II (1939-1945), Germany produced the leading aces. Captain Erich Hartmann of Germany had 352 kills, a record. Aces from other countries included Warrant Officer Hiroyoshi Nishizawa of Japan with 87 kills and Major Richard I. Bong of the United States with 40. Lieutenant Colonel Heinz Bär of Germany became the first jet ace. He shot down 16 planes in a jet fighter toward the end of the war.

After World War II, most air combat involved jet fighter planes. Captain Joseph McConnell, Jr., of the United States became the top ace of the Korean War (1950-1953). He had 16 kills. During the Vietnam War (1957-1975), two American pilots—Captain Richard S. Ritchie and Lieutenant Randall H. Cunningham— became aces. Each of these pilots had five victories.

Edward H. Sims

See also **Air Force, United States** (History); **Bishop, Billy; Rickenbacker, Eddie.**

War and Peace. See Tolstoy, Leo (His masterpieces).

War Between the States. See Civil War.

War correspondent is one of the most dramatic news reporting jobs. A reporter on a war front runs the risk of being killed or wounded. War correspondents have covered fighting in all parts of the world.

Perhaps the first efforts to give readers quick and accurate news of a war were made by George W. Kendall, founder of the *New Orleans Picayune.* Kendall set up a system of messengers to speed the news of the Mexican War (1846-1848) back to the United States. Walt Whitman sent stories of the Civil War (1861-1865) to New York City papers.

The first roving war correspondent to become well known was Richard Harding Davis. Beginning in 1897 with the Cuban revolution against Spanish rule, he covered six major conflicts. Stephen Crane, an American novelist, reported the Spanish-American War in 1898.

Before World War I (1914-1918), reporters had remained behind the lines, getting their information from commanders. Beginning with World War I, they moved with the troops and wrote firsthand accounts. Ernie Pyle's descriptions of World War II (1939-1945) endeared him to readers in the United States. Pyle was killed by enemy fire in the Pacific.   Maurine H. Beasley

See also **Crane, Stephen; Davis, Richard Harding; Pyle, Ernie.**

War crime is a military violation of the rules of warfare. Since World War II (1939-1945), the term has referred to any crime, atrocity, or persecution committed during the course of a war.

For thousands of years, a wide variety of rules and customs have governed the conduct of warfare. These rules developed partly from the customs of chivalry and diplomacy and partly from the desire to limit the horror and destruction of war. Throughout history, many people have been tried for war crimes.

Since the late 1800's, most nations have signed international treaties establishing rules of warfare. These rules deal with fair treatment of war prisoners, outlawing of gas and germ warfare, and humane treatment of civilians in areas that are occupied by military forces.

World War I. After World War I (1914-1918), the Treaty of Versailles required Germany to turn over about 900 persons for trial by the Allies as war criminals. But the Germans held their own trials instead. Only 13 of the 900 were tried, and the few who were convicted received light sentences.

World War II. In 1943, during World War II, the Allies set up the United Nations (UN) War Crimes Commission in London. The commission collected evidence and compiled lists of war criminals. After the war, the main war crimes trials took place in Nuremberg, Germany; and Tokyo, Japan. The defendants were charged with starting wars of conquest and violating the rules of war. See **Nuremberg Trials.**

From 1945 to 1950, the Allies held many other war crimes trials in Europe and the Far East. Some countries that had been occupied by German or Japanese troops held their own trials of officers and occupation officials. West Germany also tried a number of Germans charged with war crimes committed during World War II. Some of these trials continued into the 1980's.

For years after World War II, Israeli agents sought Adolf Eichmann, a former German officer believed chiefly responsible for deporting Jews to Nazi extermination camps. In 1960, the agents found Eichmann in Argentina. They kidnaped him and took him to Israel, where a court found him guilty of war crimes and crimes against humanity. Eichmann was sentenced to death and hanged.

The Korean War. During the Korean War (1950-1953), the United States accused the Chinese and North Korean forces of war crimes against UN troops and South Korean civilians. In 1953, the UN General Assembly expressed "grave concern" over these reports. However, the war ended without any war crimes trials.

The Vietnam War. Beginning in 1965, the United States sent troops to Vietnam to aid South Vietnam against the Communist Viet Cong forces and the North Vietnamese. As the fighting grew heavier, each side accused the other of violating the rules of war. The United States and South Vietnam charged North Vietnam with violating the Geneva Conventions, which provide for humane treatment of war prisoners, wounded soldiers, and civilians (see **Geneva Conventions**).

In 1969, it was disclosed that in March 1968, United States troops had massacred hundreds of civilians in and around the hamlet of My Lai. As a result, United States courts-martial tried several officers and enlisted men for war crimes. One man, Lieutenant William L. Calley, Jr., was found guilty of murder and sentenced to prison.

The United Nations and war crimes. The war crimes trials after World War II drew criticism from some scholars and political leaders. They felt that international law provided no basis for the trials. In 1947, the UN established the International Law Commission to develop a code of international laws, including those governing war crimes. The commission prepared a code called the *Draft Code on Offences Against the Peace and Security of Mankind.* The UN has not yet adopted the code.

Many people believe that an international body, such as the UN, should conduct war crimes trials. They feel such a procedure would draw less criticism than trials held by individual nations.   Robert J. Pranger

See also **Genocide; Wiesenthal, Simon.**

War debt was one of the most difficult problems left by World War I. Huge war costs had forced some countries to borrow from others. The borrowed sums came to be known as *inter-Allied debts.*

The United States was the chief lender during the war. It loaned more than $10 billion. In 1922, Congress organized the World War Foreign Debts Commission. By 1930, the commission had made agreements with all the debtor countries except the Soviet Union and Nicaragua. Cuba and Liberia had paid their small debts in full. The United States tried to make all settlements in accordance with each nation's ability to pay.

German reparations. The Treaty of Versailles held Germany responsible for the losses that the Allied nations suffered during World War I. In 1921, a commission of Allied experts ordered Germany to make *reparations* (damage payments) of about $33 billion. It was to make some payments in money, and some in goods. Germany paid a few installments on the reparations. However, it claimed that the payments were wrecking its economic system.

In 1924, an international committee headed by Charles G. Dawes worked out a payment and loan plan to ease the financial strain on Germany (see **Dawes Plan**). But Germany insisted on a reduction in its payments. In 1929, an international commission of financial experts met in Paris to discuss German reparations. The outcome of the discussions was the Young Plan. This plan reduced the German debt to about $16 billion, and made payments easier. The members of the commission also established a Bank for International Settlements to handle payments. Meanwhile, general inflation and uncontrolled spending had led to a world-wide financial panic and depression. The panic threatened Germany with complete financial collapse.

The Hoover Moratorium. On June 30, 1931, President Herbert Hoover proposed that all intergovernmental debts be held up for one year. The purpose of this action, known as the *Hoover Moratorium,* was to provide a "breathing spell" for European countries. Germany took the opportunity to ask for a complete adjustment of all war debts.

The Lausanne Conference. In June 1932, an international conference met in Lausanne, Switzerland. The conference agreed to cancel all German reparations until better conditions returned to Germany.

The worldwide depression greatly hindered the government debt problem. On June 15, 1933, debt payments to the United States amounted to about 8 per cent of the total due. Only Finland made full payment. In 1934, the war-debt agreements totally collapsed.

During World War II, the United States was again the great financial power. The Lend-Lease Act of 1941 replaced the huge lending system of World War I. According to this act, the United States loaned goods and materials to nations fighting Germany and Japan. After the war, no repayment terms were decided upon. The United States canceled some war debts outright. During the Korean War, the U.S. loaned its allies about $11 billion in military goods.   Norman D. Palmer

See also **Bank for International Settlements; Lend-Lease.**

War Department was an executive department of the United States government from 1789 to 1947. It was set up to supervise all military activities and all phases of national defense. In 1798, Congress separated the naval forces from the land forces, creating a new Department of the Navy. The War Department retained control over the Army. The secretaries of both departments reported to the President, were members of the President's Cabinet, and cooperated through joint committees and conferences.

After World War II, government authorities decided that a unification of all three military services—the land, sea, and air forces—would result in greater national defense at lower cost. Congress passed the National Security Act in 1947, setting up the National Military Establishment (NME). The secretary of war became the secretary of the army, and lost his place in the President's Cabinet. A secretary of defense supervised the NME, which included the new Department of the Army and two other military departments. In 1949, the NME became the Department of Defense (see **Defense, Department of**).

The War Department was one of the first three departments established by the federal government. The secretary was chosen as an administrator, and not as a military expert. He relied on military officers for advice. The secretary was assisted by the *War Council,* which included his undersecretary and the chief of staff of the army. The *War Department General Staff,* which was established in 1903 under the chief of staff, provided professional military advice to the secretary of war and the President.

The War Department's principal job was to manage the Army. It had to recruit men, provide them with weapons and supplies, transport them, and protect their health. It also had to build fortifications, direct the education of officers, and supervise the National Guard (see **National Guard**).

In its early years, the War Department also had important nonmilitary functions. It conducted a large construction program in improving rivers and harbors, building dams and reservoirs, and developing other public works. Other government agencies took over much of this public works program during the 1930's. The War Department also managed the affairs of the island possessions of the United States through its Department of Insular Affairs. This agency was abolished in 1939, and its duties were transferred to the Department of the Interior.

One of the War Department's biggest tasks in the years before World War II was the administration of the Civilian Conservation Corps (CCC), an organization of about 300,000 young men who worked on government conservation projects. For a limited time, the War Department also had the responsibility of transporting all air mail.

Many famous men held the office of secretary of war. Some of the best known included James Monroe, Jefferson Davis, Edwin M. Stanton, Elihu Root, William Howard Taft, Newton D. Baker, and Henry L. Stimson. Baker was secretary during World War I, and Stimson during World War II.   John C. Bollens

See also **Army, Department of the; Air Force, Department of the.**

War Hawks. See War of 1812 (The War Hawks).

War Labor Board, National. See Arbitration.

Detail of *Perry's Victory on Lake Erie*, (about 1813), an engraving by A. Lawson, after a painting by Thomas Birch, New-York Historical Society, New York City, Olds Collection

The Battle of Lake Erie in 1813 was won by U.S. naval forces under Master-Commandant Oliver H. Perry. During the battle, Perry was rowed from his sinking ship to another vessel, *above*.

War of 1812

War of 1812. The War of 1812 was in many ways the strangest war in United States history. It could well be named the War of Faulty Communication. Two days before war was declared, the British government stated that it would repeal the laws which were the chief reason for fighting. If there had been telegraphic communication with Europe, the war might well have been avoided. Speedy communication would also have prevented the greatest battle of the war, which was fought at New Orleans 15 days after a treaty of peace had been signed.

The chief United States complaint against the British was interference with shipping. But New England, the great shipping section of the United States, bitterly opposed the idea of going to war. The demand for war came chiefly from the West and South.

It is strange also that the war, fought for freedom of the seas, began with the invasion of Canada. In addition, the treaty of peace that ended the war settled none of the issues over which it had supposedly been fought.

Another oddity was that the young United States was willing to risk war against powerful Great Britain. Finally, add that both sides claimed victory in the War of 1812, and it becomes clear that the whole struggle was a confused mass of contradictions.

Causes of the war

Napoleon Bonaparte, head of the French government after 1799 and emperor after 1804, had made himself the master of continental Europe. Except for one short breathing spell (1801-1803), Great Britain had been fighting France since 1793. Napoleon had long hoped to invade and conquer Britain, but in 1805 his navy was destroyed at the battle of Trafalgar. This forced Napoleon to give up the idea of taking an army across the English Channel. So he set out instead to ruin Great Britain by destroying British trade. Napoleon's Berlin and Milan decrees (1806-1807) were an attempt to shut off Great Britain from all trade with Europe. Great Britain, in turn, issued a series of Orders in Council which declared a blockade of French ports and of ports in Europe and elsewhere that were under French control. See **Continental System; Milan Decree; Order in Council.**

The British and French blockades had disastrous effects on United States shipping. Before 1806, the United States was getting rich on the European war. United States ships took goods to both Great Britain and France, and the value of trade carried increased fourfold from 1791 to 1805. Now the picture had suddenly changed. A United States ship bound for French ports had to stop first at a British port for inspection and payment of fees. Otherwise the British were likely to seize the ship. But Napoleon ordered neutral ships not to stop at British ports for inspection, and he also announced that he would order his forces to seize any United States ships which they found had obeyed the British Orders in Council.

The British navy controlled the seas. So the easiest thing for United States vessels was to trade only with other neutrals, with Great Britain, or under British license. A few adventurous spirits ran the British blockade for the sake of huge profits they could make, and continued the risky trade with continental Europe. The United States complained of both French and British policies as illegal "paper blockades," because neither side could really enforce such an extensive blockade. See **Blockade** (Paper blockade).

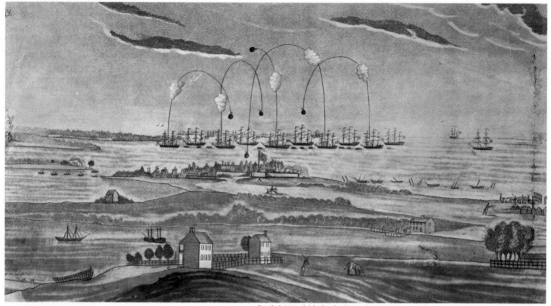

Detail of *A View of the Bombardment of Fort McHenry . . .* (about 1817), an aquatint engraving by J. Bower, The Peale Museum, Baltimore, Maryland, The Hambleton Collection

Bombs burst in the air over Fort McHenry in 1814 during a British attack on the Baltimore area. Francis Scott Key wrote "The Star-Spangled Banner" after watching this battle.

Impressment of seamen. The British navy was always in need of seamen. One reason for this need was that hundreds of deserters from the British navy had found work on United States ships. The British government claimed the right to stop neutral ships on the high seas, remove sailors of British birth, and *impress,* or force, them back into British naval service. The United States objected strongly to this practice, partly because many native-born Americans were impressed "by mistake" along with men who had actually been British seamen. See **Jefferson, Thomas** (The struggle for neutrality).

In June 1807, Captain James Barron of the frigate *Chesapeake* refused to let the British search his ship for deserters. The British frigate *Leopard* fired on the *Chesapeake,* removed four men whom the British called deserters, and hanged one of them. Anti-British feeling in the United States rose sharply. President Thomas Jefferson ordered all British naval vessels out of American harbors. Four years later, the British apologized for the incident and paid for the damage done, but the bitterness remained.

American reaction. The United States tried several times to get the British to change their policy toward neutral shipping and toward impressment. In April 1806, the United States Congress passed a Non-Importation Act, which barred British goods from American markets. The act was not put into continuous operation until December 1807. By that time, the *Chesapeake* incident had taken place and sterner measures were believed to be necessary. Also in December 1807, Congress passed the Embargo Act. This act prohibited exports from the United States and forbade American ships from sailing into foreign ports.

The embargo did not produce anything like the results Congress desired. Overseas trade nearly stopped,

Detail of *Washington,* an engraving by an unknown artist, from *The Stationer's Almanack,* London, 1815 (Library of Congress)

The British captured Washington, D.C., in 1814, *above.* They burned the Capitol, the White House, and other buildings.

WORLD BOOK map

The War of 1812 was fought mainly in the northern United States and southern Canada. This map shows where the major land and water battles took place.

almost ruining New England shipowners and putting many sailors out of work. Shipyards closed, and goods piled up in warehouses. The embargo also hurt Southern planters, who normally sold tobacco, rice, and cotton to Great Britain. Opponents of the embargo described its effects on the United States by spelling the word backward. They called the embargo the "O-Grab-Me" act. Even with the hardships the embargo caused for the United States, it failed as a policy. The British and the French were intent on winning the European war at all costs, and so both refused to yield to American pressure.

After 14 months, Congress gave up the embargo and tried a new device for hurting British and French commerce. It passed the Non-Intercourse Act in March 1809, permitting American ships to trade with any countries but Great Britain and France. The act also opened American ports to all but British and French ships. But this plan also failed.

In 1810, Congress passed Macon's Bill No. 2, which removed all restrictions on trade. The law went on to say that if either Great Britain or France would give up its orders or decrees, the United States would restore nonintercourse rules against the other nation, unless it also agreed to change its policy.

Macon's Bill really helped Napoleon, who was eager to get the United States into the war against Great Britain. He pretended to repeal his Berlin and Milan decrees so far as they applied to United States ships. President James Madison shut off all trade with Great Britain. In the summer of 1811, further attempts were made to reach an agreement with the British. But these attempts failed, and in November, Madison advised Congress to get ready for war.

The War Hawks. A group of young men known as "War Hawks" dominated Congress during this period.

Henry Clay of Kentucky and John C. Calhoun of South Carolina were the outstanding leaders of the group. Clay was then Speaker of the House of Representatives. Like Clay and Calhoun, most of the War Hawks came from Western and Southern states, where many of the people were in favor of going to war with Great Britain.

The people of New England generally opposed going to war because they feared that war with Great Britain would wipe out entirely the New England shipping trade which had already been heavily damaged. Another reason New England opposed war was because many New Englanders sympathized with Great Britain in its struggle against Napoleon.

Some historians have argued that a leading motive of the War Hawks was a desire for expansion. The people of the Northwest were meeting armed resistance in their attempt to take more land from the Indians, and they believed that the Indians had considerable British support. Friction between Westerners and Indians climaxed in November 1811 at the Battle of Tippecanoe near what is now Lafayette, Ind. Indians attacked an American army, and British guns were found on the battlefield. A desire to eliminate British aid to the Indians may have inspired some Westerners to seek an invasion of Canada, Britain's main possession in North America. But most Westerners favored such an invasion chiefly because of a deep resentment over long-lasting British insults at sea.

The main concerns of Congress were maritime rights, national honor, and the country's obligation to respond to foreign threats. The Federalists in Congress strongly opposed going to war. But the Democratic-Republicans believed that war was the only solution to America's dilemmas. They hoped a successful invasion of Canada would force Britain to change its policies. See **Democratic-Republican Party.**

Progress of the war

Declaration of war. On June 1, 1812, President Madison asked Congress to declare war against Great Britain. He gave as his reasons the impressment of United States seamen and the interference with United States trade. He charged also that the British had stirred up Indian warfare in the Northwest. Congress declared war

Important dates in the War of 1812

1812 (June 18) The United States declared war on Great Britain.

1812 (Oct. 13) British forces won the Battle of Queenston Heights in Canada.

1813 (April 27) The Americans captured York (now Toronto), the capital of Upper Canada. They later burned some public buildings.

1813 (Sept. 10) American forces under Master-Commandant Oliver Hazard Perry won the Battle of Lake Erie.

1813 (Oct. 5) The Americans won the Battle of the Thames River in Moraviantown, an Indian village in Canada.

1814 (Aug. 24) British troops invaded Washington, D.C., and burned the Capitol and the White House.

1814 (Sept. 11) American forces won the Battle of Lake Champlain.

1814 (Dec. 24) The Americans and the British signed a peace treaty in Ghent, Belgium.

1815 (Jan. 8) American forces won the Battle of New Orleans. News of the peace treaty did not reach the United States until after this battle.

on June 18, 1812. Two days earlier, the British foreign minister had announced that the Orders in Council would be repealed, but word of this announcement did not reach America until after the war had begun. Because President Madison asked for the declaration of war, many Federalists blamed him for the conflict, calling it "Mr. Madison's war."

Attitude of the nation. Congress had known for seven months that war was likely to come, but no real preparations had been made. There was little money in the U.S. treasury. The regular Army had less than 10,000 troops, and very few trained officers. The Navy had fewer than 20 seagoing ships.

To make matters worse, a large minority, both in Congress and in the country, was opposed to war. The declaration of war had passed by a vote of only 79 to 49 in the House, and 19 to 13 in the Senate. New England, the richest section in the country, bitterly opposed the war, and interfered with its progress by withholding both money and troops.

The war at sea. At sea, the United States depended primarily on *privateers*—that is, armed ships owned by private people and hired by the government to fight. This was because the tiny regular American navy was dwarfed by the massive British fleet. Several single-ship U.S. victories against British ships improved American morale but had no permanent effect on the naval struggle.

A British blockade was clamped on the United States coast, and United States trade almost disappeared. Because duties on imports were the chief source of federal revenue, the U.S. treasury drifted further and further into debt.

The only American naval victories that directly affected the course of the war were those won by Oliver Hazard Perry on Lake Erie, on Sept. 10, 1813, and by Thomas Macdonough on Lake Champlain, on Sept. 11, 1814. But United States naval vessels and privateers did considerable damage to British commerce, taking about 1,500 prize ships in all.

Land campaign of 1812. The American plan of attack called for a three-way invasion of Canada. Invasion forces were to start from Detroit, from the Niagara River, and from the foot of Lake Champlain.

At Detroit, General William Hull led about 2,000 troops across the Detroit River into Canada. The British commander, General Sir Isaac Brock, drove Hull's forces back into Detroit, surrounded them, and captured both the city and Hull's entire army. The British and Indians also captured Michilimackinac and Fort Dearborn (Chicago).

On the Niagara River, a United States force occupied Queenston Heights on the Canadian side. This force was defeated and captured when New York militia units refused to come to its support.

At Lake Champlain, the third United States army advanced from Plattsburgh, N.Y., to the Canadian frontier. Here, too, the militia refused to leave United States territory, and the army marched back again to Plattsburgh. Thus the first attempt to invade Canada failed completely.

Campaigns of 1813. In January 1813, an American army advancing toward Detroit was defeated and captured at Frenchtown on the Raisin River. In April, York

(now Toronto), the capital of Upper Canada, was captured by United States troops and held for a short time. Some of the public buildings were burned.

Perry's destruction of the British fleet on Lake Erie forced the British to pull out of Detroit, and much of the Michigan Territory came under United States control. General William Henry Harrison was able to take his army across the lake and defeat the retreating British at the Battle of the Thames.

In the autumn, General James Wilkinson and General Wade Hampton undertook a campaign against Montreal. This attempt failed, and the United States armies retreated into northern New York. In December, the British crossed the Niagara River, captured Fort Niagara, and burned Buffalo and neighboring villages.

Campaigns of 1814. By 1814, Napoleon had been defeated in Europe. Great Britain was then able to send over 15,000 troops to Canada, thus ending all American hopes of conquest. But the United States had at last built up a well-trained and disciplined army on the New York frontier. Under the able leadership of Major General Jacob Brown and Brigadier General Winfield Scott, this army crossed the Niagara River from Buffalo in July and defeated the British at the Battle of Chippewa. But soon after that, the Americans were turned back at the Battle of Lundy's Lane. After holding Fort Erie in Canada for several months, United States troops finally withdrew to the American side. This was the last attempt to invade Canada. Meanwhile, nearly 11,000 British troops had moved into New York by way of Lake Champlain. The troops retreated hastily when the destruction of the British fleet on the lake threatened their supply lines back to Canada.

Another British army, under General Robert Ross, was escorted by a fleet to Chesapeake Bay, scattered the United States troops at the Battle of Bladensburg, occupied Washington, D.C., and set fire to the Capitol, the White House, and other public buildings. Both the British army and the British fleet were driven back at Baltimore. This engagement inspired Francis Scott Key to write "The Star-Spangled Banner" (see **Star-Spangled Banner**).

"The needless battle." The Battle of New Orleans was the last engagement of the war. It was fought on Jan. 8, 1815. Like the declaration of war, this battle might have been prevented if there had been speedy communication. A treaty of peace had been signed at Ghent, Belgium, 15 days before the battle took place, but the treaty was not ratified by the United States until a month later.

The British had sent an army of more than 8,000 men to capture New Orleans. There were several possible routes to the city, but the British army chose to march straight toward the entrenchments that had been prepared by General Andrew Jackson. American artillery and sharpshooting riflemen killed or wounded about 1,500 British soldiers, including the commanding officer, General Sir Edward Pakenham. The Americans lost few men in the battle.

Treaty of Ghent. The British public was tired of war and especially of war taxes, and an increasing number of Americans feared disaster if the war continued. Commissioners of the two countries met at Ghent, Belgium, in August 1814.

The Battle of New Orleans was fought 15 days after the United States and Great Britain had signed a peace settlement. Word of the treaty had not reached New Orleans in time to prevent the fighting. Although the American victory had no effect on the outcome of the war, it gave the United States increased political standing in Europe.

Chicago Historical Society

The British at first insisted that the United States should give up certain territory on the northern frontier, and set up a large permanent Indian reservation in the Northwest. But American victories in the summer and fall of 1814 led the British to drop these demands. A treaty was finally signed on Dec. 24, 1814, in Ghent. By the terms of this treaty, all land that had been captured by either party was to be given up. Everything was to be exactly as it was before the war, and commissions from both of the countries were to settle any disputed points about boundaries. Nothing whatever was said in the treaty about impressments, blockades, or the British Orders in Council, although they supposedly had caused the war.

Results of the war

The United States had faced near disaster in 1814. But the victory at New Orleans and what seemed to be a successful fight against Britain increased national patriotism and helped to unite the United States into one nation.

The war settled none of the issues over which the United States had fought. But most of these issues faded out during the following years. In the long period of peace after 1815, the British had no occasion to make use of impressments or blockades. Indian troubles in the Northwest were practically ended by the death of the chief Tecumseh and by the rapid settlement of the region. The United States occupied part of Florida during the war, and was soon able to buy the rest of it from Spain.

One indirect result of the War of 1812 was the later election to the presidency of Andrew Jackson and of William Henry Harrison. Both of these men won military fame which had much to do with their elections. Another indirect result was the decline of Federalist power. New England leaders, most of them Federalists, met secretly in Hartford, Conn., to study amendments to the Constitution. Their opponents charged that they had

plotted treason, and the Federalists never recovered (see **Hartford Convention**).

Chief battles of the war

The War of 1812 was not an all-out struggle on either side. The United States was ill-prepared for the war militarily. Britain, which could devote only part of its resources to the conflict, viewed the war as just an annoying part of its struggle with Napoleon.

The chief battles of the war are described below.

Lake Champlain (Sept. 11, 1814). The British had four ships and about a dozen rowing galleys on Lake Champlain to protect the flank of General Sir George Prevost's army. Prevost was advancing against Plattsburgh on the west shore of the lake. Master-Commandant Thomas Macdonough commanded the American fleet of 4 ships and 10 rowing galleys. Macdonough anchored his ships across the mouth of Plattsburgh Bay, so the British had to approach him head on. He also arranged the anchors and cables of his flagship, the *Saratoga,* so he could turn the ship about to bring a fresh broadside to bear on the enemy at a critical point in the fighting. As a result of his careful planning, the entire British fleet surrendered.

Lake Erie (Sept. 10, 1813). At Erie, Pa., Master-Commandant Oliver Hazard Perry had built two fine brigs, each carrying 20 guns. In addition, he had under his command a smaller brig captured from the British, and six small schooners, each armed with one or two heavy guns. With these nine ships, Perry blockaded the British fleet of six ships at the western end of the lake. The British came out to fight, and at first had the advantage. When Perry's flagship, the *Lawrence,* was disabled, he transferred in a small boat to the *Niagara,* which had suffered little damage in the battle. He went on to defeat the British fleet and capture it. Perry reported his victory to General Harrison in the famous words, "We have met the enemy and they are ours."

Lundy's Lane (July 25, 1814). This battle took place on Canadian soil, about 1 mile (1.6 kilometers) from Niagara

Falls. The battle began when General Winfield Scott was advancing toward Queenston with about 1,000 men and came upon about 2,800 British troops. The American General Jacob Brown had some 2,700 men in Chippewa, about 3 miles (4.8 kilometers) away. The fighting began at about 5 o'clock in the afternoon. Before darkness fell General Brown had arrived on the field with reinforcements. The battle raged until midnight, and the losses were heavy.

Each side claimed victory in the battle. The Americans drove the British from their position and captured the chief British battery, but the British later retook the field and recaptured the guns. The battle of Lundy's Lane is remembered for brave fighting on both sides.

New Orleans (Jan. 8, 1815). This battle has already been described under the heading *"The needless battle."* It had no effect on the outcome of the war, but it helped to bring about a surging American nationalism. It also brought fame to General Andrew Jackson.

Queenston Heights (Oct. 13, 1812). This battle ended the second American attempt to invade Canada. General Sir Isaac Brock, the British commander, had about 1,500 men scattered along 36 miles (58 kilometers) of the Niagara River. The Americans, under Generals Stephen Van Rensselaer and Alexander Smyth, numbered more than 6,000. The Americans tried to cross the Niagara River from a point opposite Queenston Heights, 7 miles (11 kilometers) below Niagara Falls. About 400 Americans got across the river, and were attacked by a force under Brock. Brock was fatally wounded in the battle.

Later in the day, after both sides had received reinforcements, the British drove the invaders down to the river bank. Here the U.S. troops stopped, because they could not get back across the stream. The entire American force of about 900 surrendered. The British victory was clouded by the death of General Brock, who was one of the finest officers in either army. A monument to his memory stands on the battlefield.

Raisin River Massacre (Jan. 22, 1813) took place in Frenchtown (now Monroe, Mich.) on the Raisin River. A detachment of Kentucky troops, sent to drive the British from Frenchtown, was defeated and captured by the British and Indians. After the battle the British departed with the able-bodied American prisoners, leaving the wounded Americans behind with the Indians. The Indians massacred wounded prisoners.

Thames River (Oct. 5, 1813), also known as the Battle of Moraviantown, was the direct result of Perry's naval victory on Lake Erie. The British had to abandon Detroit. British troops withdrew from Detroit and crossed into Canada. The British were accompanied by 600 Indians under their chief, Tecumseh. After the British had entered Canada, about 3,000 United States troops under General Harrison pursued them for several days.

The British finally halted near Moraviantown, on the Thames River in Kent County, Ontario, and offered battle. British General Proctor and many of his men fled soon after the first volley, but Tecumseh died on the battlefield. The death of Tecumseh, the leading Indian chief, broke the league of Indian tribes which had been allied to the British and practically ended the cooperation of the British and Indians on the northwestern frontier. A court-martial later publicly reprimanded General Proctor and suspended him.   Reginald Horsman

Related articles in *World Book* include:

Biographies

Brock, Sir Isaac	Key, Francis Scott
Decatur, Stephen	Lawrence, James
Forten, James	Macdonough, Thomas
Harrison, William Henry	Madison, James (Events leading to war)
Hull, Isaac	Perry (Oliver H.)
Hull, William	Scott, Winfield
Jackson, Andrew (Jackson the soldier)	Secord, Laura I.

Other related articles

Constitution (ship)	Hartford Convention
Ghent, Treaty of	Star-Spangled Banner

Outline

I. **Causes of the war**
　A. Impressment of seamen
　B. American reaction
　C. The War Hawks
II. **Progress of the war**
　A. Declaration of war
　B. Attitude of the nation
　C. The war at sea
　D. Land campaign of 1812
　E. Campaigns of 1813
　F. Campaigns of 1814
　G. "The needless battle"
　H. Treaty of Ghent
III. **Results of the war**
IV. **Chief battles of the war**

Questions

Why might the War of 1812 be called the War of Faulty Communication?
What was *impressment*? Why did Americans object to it?
Who were the War Hawks?
What two American naval victories affected the course of the war?
When and by whom were these historic words written: "We have met the enemy and they are ours"?
When was the Capitol burned by the British?
What famous American patriotic song was written during the battle of Baltimore?
What battle is known as "The needless battle"? Why?

Additional resources

Berton, Pierre F. D. *The Invasion of Canada: 1812-1813.* McClelland (Toronto), 1980; Little, Brown, 1980. *Flames Across the Border: The Canadian-American Tragedy, 1813-1814.* 1981.
Caffrey, Kate. *The Twilight's Last Gleaming: Britain vs. America 1812-1815.* Stein & Day, 1977.
Marrin, Albert. *1812: The War Nobody Won.* Atheneum, 1985. For younger readers.
Stagg, John C. A. *Mr. Madison's War: Politics, Diplomacy, and Warfare in the Early American Republic, 1783-1830.* Princeton, 1983.

War of Secession. See Civil War.

War of the American Revolution. See Revolutionary War in America.

War on Poverty. See Johnson, Lyndon Baines (The national scene).

War Powers Resolution is a United States law designed to balance military powers of the President and Congress. The law, passed in 1973, is popularly known as the War Powers Act. According to Section 4(a)(1) of the resolution, the President must inform Congress within 48 hours if U.S. forces are sent into a hostile area without a declaration of war. In addition, the forces may remain no longer than 90 days unless Congress approves the President's action or declares war.

The resolution was created as a result of actions taken by Presidents Lyndon B. Johnson and Richard M. Nixon during the Vietnam War (1957-1975). Johnson and Nixon sent troops into battle even though Congress did not specifically approve such an action or declare war.

The resolution's 90-day limit has never been applied because no President who has ordered troops into combat areas since 1973 has referred to Section 4(a)(1) of the resolution. Instead, the Presidents have referred to their constitutional authority as commander in chief.

Congress took its first major action under the resolution in 1983 after U.S. Marines in Lebanon were attacked. President Ronald Reagan reported the situation. But he disagreed with Congress that the 90-day limit of the War Powers Resolution had been triggered because he did not mention Section 4(a)(1) in his report. Congress later passed a law allowing the troops to remain in Lebanon for 18 months.   Louis Fisher

War prisoner. See Prisoner of war.

Warbeck, Perkin (1474?-1499), became one of the most famous "pretenders" in European history. He appeared in Ireland during the shaky reign of Henry VII of England. He claimed to be Richard, the younger son of the Yorkist king, Edward IV. Richard and his brother, Edward V, had been imprisoned in the Tower of London by their uncle, Richard III, in 1483 and were never heard of again. Perkin's claim was supported by many followers of the House of York in England, and by several European princes who were King Henry's enemies.

Perkin tried to invade England in 1497, but he was captured and imprisoned. When he attempted to escape, Henry VII had him hanged. There is convincing evidence that Perkin was a Flemish youth of humble parentage.   Paul M. Kendall

Warble fly is a large, hairy fly that resembles a bumble bee. The *larvae,* or young, of the warble fly live under the skin of animals. The *cattle warble,* or *heel fly,* lays its eggs on the hairs of the feet or legs of cattle. The larvae, called *cattle grubs,* work their way through the skin of the animal. Under the skin of the back, the larvae cause painful swellings, called *warbles.*

Scientific classification. Warble flies are in the order Diptera. They make up the family Hypodermatidae. The two cattle warbles found in North America are *Hypoderma lineatum* and *H. bovis.*
          E. W. Cupp

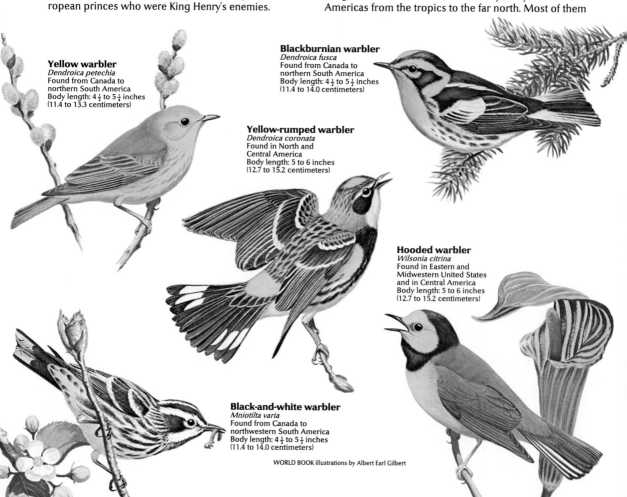

WORLD BOOK illustration by Oxford Illustrators Limited

Adult warble fly

See also Bot fly.

Warbler is the popular name of the small migratory songbirds of the wood warbler family. They live in the Americas from the tropics to the far north. Most of them

Yellow warbler
Dendroica petechia
Found from Canada to northern South America
Body length: $4\frac{1}{2}$ to $5\frac{1}{4}$ inches (11.4 to 13.3 centimeters)

Blackburnian warbler
Dendroica fusca
Found from Canada to northern South America
Body length: $4\frac{1}{2}$ to $5\frac{1}{2}$ inches (11.4 to 14.0 centimeters)

Yellow-rumped warbler
Dendroica coronata
Found in North and Central America
Body length: 5 to 6 inches (12.7 to 15.2 centimeters)

Hooded warbler
Wilsonia citrina
Found in Eastern and Midwestern United States and in Central America
Body length: 5 to 6 inches (12.7 to 15.2 centimeters)

Black-and-white warbler
Mniotilta varia
Found from Canada to northwestern South America
Body length: $4\frac{1}{2}$ to $5\frac{1}{2}$ inches (11.4 to 14.0 centimeters)

WORLD BOOK illustrations by Albert Earl Gilbert

are about $5\frac{1}{2}$ inches (14 centimeters) long. Warblers are hard to see because they are small and they keep close to the foliage of trees and bushes. Their feathers are of many beautiful colors. People enjoy the quick movements and abrupt, high-pitched songs of the warblers.

Many warblers winter in South and Central America, and migrate through the United States late in the spring. In May, they begin to appear in woods, in city parks, and in trees near buildings. Many species go on farther north for their nesting. Some warblers go as far north as the Hudson Bay and the Yukon Territory in Canada, but others nest in the Southern States.

Warblers build their nests in trees and bushes or on the ground. The nests are usually cup-shaped, and loosely built of twigs and grasses woven together, but some are compact structures of plant down. The female warbler lays from three to six eggs, which are whitish with brownish markings at the larger end.

Many kinds of warblers have fine singing voices. Others sing only weak, lisping notes. There are more than 150 species and subspecies of warblers. Some of the better-known ones are the *yellow warbler,* the *black-and-white warbler,* and the *yellow-rumped warbler.* Yellow warblers are quite common in city parks. The black-and-white warbler likes to creep along the branches of trees. The yellow-rumped warbler has four yellow patches on its head, rump, and breast.

Another well-known warbler is the *American redstart.* It is colored a striking black with salmon markings, and looks somewhat like a small oriole. The redstart is one of the most active and graceful of American warblers. The *Blackburnian warbler* has a bright orange throat. Two other warblers are named for their colors. They are the *black-throated green warbler* and the *black-throated blue warbler.* The *ovenbird* has a yellowish-brown stripe on its head, a white breast marked with black, and an olive-green back. It is named for its ovenlike nest.

Warblers help farmers by killing insects that destroy fruits and strip trees of their leaves. Warblers search in tiny cracks in the bark and in fruit buds for insects that might escape larger birds.

Scientific classification. Wood warblers make up the wood warbler family, Parulidae. The black-and-white warbler is *Mniotilta varia.* The American redstart is *Setophaga ruticilla.* The ovenbird is *Seiurus aurocapillus.* The yellow warbler is *Dendroica petechia,* and the yellow-rumped is *D. coronata.* The Blackburnian warbler is *D. fusca,* the black-throated green is *D. virens,* and the black-throated blue is *D. caerulescens.*

Albert Wolfson

See also **Bird** (pictures: Birds of forests and woodlands; Birds' eggs); **Chat; Ovenbird; Redstart; Yellowthroat.**

Ward is a word that once had much the same meaning as the word *guard.* The relationship between the two words may be seen in two of the present meanings of *ward* that are described below.

In law, a ward is a person who needs to be guarded or protected, and so the court has appointed a guardian for the ward. Most wards are *minors* (people under legal age). Spendthrifts or people who are mentally unsound, however, may be legally considered wards. A guardian's duty is to protect the ward's interests and act in the place of a parent (*in loco parentis*).

In politics, a ward is a political division of a city. The early use of this name started when cities were divided into wards so that they might be guarded more easily. But today cities are divided into wards chiefly to simplify city government and city elections. For purposes of government, each ward elects one or two *aldermen.* The aldermen help govern the city and look after the ward.

Carlfred B. Broderick

See also **Guardian.**

Ward, Aaron Montgomery (1844-1913), an American businessman, pioneered in the mail-order business in the United States. As a traveling salesman in the Middle West, he conceived the idea of buying merchandise in large quantities from manufacturers for cash and selling it directly to farmers for cash.

In 1872, Ward and his partner, George R. Thorne, began in the mail-order business in a livery-stable loft with $2,400 capital and a single-sheet catalog listing a few dry goods items. When he died, annual sales had risen to $40 million. Ward was born in Chatham, N.J., on Feb. 17, 1844. Kenneth Wiggins Porter

Ward, Artemus, *AHR tuh muhs* (1834-1867), was the pen name of Charles Farrar Browne, one of the most important American humorists of the 1800's. Ward's subjects varied from current events to general human weaknesses, all of which he treated in a light manner. He was largely responsible for the widespread use among humorists of intentionally misspelled words for comic effect. Ward also popularized comic lecturing.

Ward was born in Waterford, Me. His most famous works are the Artemus Ward letters, which describe the fictional adventures of a traveling showman. These letters first appeared in the Cleveland *Plain Dealer* in 1858. In 1866, Ward moved to London, where he enjoyed great popularity. He died there of tuberculosis at the age of 33. David B. Kesterson

Ward, Barbara (1914-1981), was a British economist and journalist. She became known for her books about the problems of economic development in developing nations. Ward argued for a more even distribution of the world's economic resources between the industrial and the developing countries. To achieve these goals, she favored international cooperation and programs to control population growth.

Barbara Mary Ward was born in York, England. She attended schools in Paris and in Germany before entering Oxford University in England in 1932. She graduated in 1935.

Ward joined the staff of *The Economist,* an influential weekly British newspaper, in 1939. In 1950, she married Sir Robert G. A. Jackson, an Australian economist and United Nations official. She received the title Dame Commander of the British Empire in 1974. In 1976, she was made a life *peeress* (member of the nobility) with the title Baroness Jackson of Lodsworth.

Ward wrote numerous books and essays. Her major works include *The Rich Nations and the Poor Nations* (1962), *Nationalism and Ideology* (1967), *The Lopsided World* (1968), *The Home of Man* (1976), and *Progress For a Small Planet* (1979). Daniel R. Fusfeld

Ward, Joseph (1838-1889), was a noted clergyman and educator, and a leader in South Dakota's drive for statehood. In 1879, he helped form a group that worked for South Dakota's statehood.

Ward became a Congregational minister in 1869, and

became a missionary in Yankton, then capital of the Dakota Territory. Because of his missionary work, some people call him the *Father of Congregationalism in Dakota*. In 1881, he helped establish Yankton College, a private school associated with the Congregational church. He served as president and professor of philosophy at Yankton until his death.

Ward was born in Perry Centre, N.Y. A statue of him represents South Dakota in the United States Capitol in Washington, D.C.   Richard A. Bartlett

Ward, Lynd Kendall (1905-1985), was an American artist. His reputation as a wood engraver was established with the publication of *God's Man* (1929) and five other novels in woodcut. They were the first such novels without text to be published in the United States. His works also appear in water color, oil, and lithography. He wrote and illustrated *The Biggest Bear* (1952), a children's book which received the Caldecott Medal in 1953. Ward and his wife, May McNeer, received the 1975 Regina Medal. Ward was born in Chicago. He graduated from Columbia University.   Marilyn Fain Apseloff

Ward, Montgomery. See Ward, Aaron Montgomery.

Warden. See Prison.

Warfare. See War; Guerrilla warfare.

Warhead. See Bomb; Guided missile (The warhead); Torpedo.

Warhol, *WAWR hawl,* **Andy** (1930?-1987), was an American artist known for pictures that consist of images of familiar objects or people. Warhol isolated and simplified these images, sometimes by enlarging them

Acrylic and silk-screen enamel painting on canvas (1962); Leo
Castelli Gallery, New York City

An Andy Warhol painting shows repeated images of movie star Marilyn Monroe. Many of Warhol's works deal with familiar subjects in a style that looks mass-produced and impersonal.

in a series of pictures in variant colors. He also repeated the same image many times in a single picture. His pictures became controversial because they seemed so different from traditional painting.

Warhol created most of his pictures with a mechanical stencil process called *silk-screen printing.* His pictures of commercial products, such as soup cans and soft-drink bottles, are among his best-known works. He also used silk-screen printing to reproduce pictures from newspaper photographs that showed death and destruction. In addition, he made portraits of movie star Marilyn Monroe and other celebrities. The silk-screen process gives his work a mass-produced and impersonal appearance. Warhol's style and choice of subject matter made him a leading figure in the pop art movement of the 1960's. See **Pop art.**

Warhol deliberately concealed information about his age and youth. He was born in Pennsylvania, probably in 1930. Warhol attended the art school at the Carnegie Institute of Technology in Pittsburgh. After graduating in 1949, he moved to New York City, where he became a successful commercial artist. Warhol's work as a painter became widely known in 1962.   George Ehrlich

Warlock. See Witchcraft.

Warm-blooded animal is an animal that almost always has about the same body temperature, regardless of the temperature of its surroundings. Birds and mammals, including human beings, are warm-blooded animals. Nearly all other kinds of animals are cold-blooded. Scientists refer to warm-blooded animals as *endothermic* or *homeothermic.*

The body of a warm-blooded animal produces heat by burning food. Shivering and physical activity also generate body heat. Young warm-blooded animals and some adult small mammals have heat-producing organs, called *brown fat,* on their neck, chest, and back.

A layer of fat beneath the skin, plus a covering of hair, fur, or feathers, helps keep a warm-blooded animal warm. The animal's body can also conserve heat by reducing the flow of blood to the limbs and to uncovered skin. The body becomes cooler by such means as panting and sweating.   James Edward Heath

See also **Bird** (The respiratory system); **Mammal; Cold-blooded animal; Temperature, Body.**

Warner, Pop (1871-1954), was one of the most influential coaches in the history of American college football. His many contributions to the game include the single-wing and double-wing formations, the screen pass, and the practice of numbering plays.

Warner was born in Springville, N.Y. His real name was Glenn Scobey Warner. He attended Cornell University, where he was captain of the 1894 football team. He acquired the nickname "Pop" while a freshman at Cornell because he was older than the average student. After briefly practicing law, Warner began coaching at Georgia in 1895. He later coached at Cornell, the Carlisle (Pa.) Indian Industrial School, Pittsburgh, Stanford, and Temple. He retired in 1938.   Joe Marcin

Warner, Seth (1743-1784), was an American soldier in the Revolutionary War. He is chiefly remembered for his role in forming and leading the famed regiment of Green Mountain Boys. His most important contribution to winning the war was his timely arrival to help reinforce the colonial troops at the Battle of Bennington on

Aug. 16, 1777. His support of John Stark clinched a decisive victory for the American forces. In recognition of his services, Warner was appointed a brigadier general in 1778. He was born in Roxbury, Conn. See also **Green Mountain Boys.**   Clinton Rossiter

Warrant, *WAHR uhnt,* is a document authorizing a person to do something. A *search warrant* authorizes a law officer to search a house or other premises for goods held illegally. A *bench warrant* authorizes a law officer to arrest and bring before the court a person charged with a crime, misdemeanor, or contempt of court. Other warrants certify or guarantee the quality and validity of things.   George T. Felkenes

See also **Arrest; Search warrant; Wiretapping.**

Warranty. See **Consumerism** (The right to quality); **Deed; Guaranty.**

Warren, Earl (1891-1974), became chief justice of the United States in 1953. He submitted his resignation in June 1968, but did not leave office. He remained on the court because a Senate filibuster prevented a vote on the nomination of associate justice Abe Fortas to succeed him as chief justice. Warren later agreed to remain in office until the end of the Supreme Court's term in the summer of 1969.

Warren had won recognition as a liberal and influential presiding officer. In 1954, he wrote the opinion for the unanimous ruling by the Supreme Court outlawing racial segregation in the public schools. He wrote the 1964 decision that states must apportion both houses of their legislatures on the basis of equal population. Also in 1964, he was chairman of a presidential committee that investigated the assassination of President John F. Kennedy (see **Warren Report**).

Wide World
Earl Warren

Warren was born in Los Angeles, and received his law degree from the University of California. He served as attorney general of California from 1939 to 1943, and as governor of California from 1943 to 1953. In 1946, he became the first candidate for governor to win both the Republican and Democratic nominations. Warren was the Republican nominee for Vice President in 1948.

Merlo J. Pusey

Warren, Joseph (1741-1775), was a leading Massachusetts statesman in the period before the Revolutionary War. He was among the first to die for the patriot cause when he was killed at the Battle of Bunker Hill. He spoke and wrote frequently for the colonial cause after 1765, and he helped draft some key Massachusetts protests against the British enactments. Warren's selection in 1775 as president of the Provincial Assembly and his election as major general in the Massachusetts forces reflected the respect he won. Warren was born in Roxbury, Mass. He studied at Harvard College.

Clarence L. Ver Steeg

Warren, Mercy Otis (1728-1814), was a colonial American writer. Her most important work was the three-volume *History of the Rise, Progress, and Termination of the American Revolution* (1805). She had helped encourage prerevolutionary feelings by ridiculing the British colonial government in such plays as *The Adulateur* (1773), *The Defeat* (1773), and *The Group* (1775).

Warren had extensive knowledge of political affairs and was a close friend of many leaders of the revolution, who included her brother, James Otis, and her husband, James Warren. Mercy Otis Warren expressed her political convictions even when they were unpopular. For example, she opposed ratification of the United States Constitution because she felt it gave too much power to the federal government. She favored increased safeguards for individual liberties and equal opportunities for women in education and public affairs. Warren was born in Barnstable, Mass.   Dean Doner

Warren, Robert Penn (1905-1989), was an American novelist, poet, and literary critic. Warren won the 1947 Pulitzer Prize for fiction for *All the King's Men* (1946). This novel describes the rise and fall of a ruthless Southern politician. Warren won the 1958 Pulitzer Prize for poetry for his collection *Promises: Poems 1954-1956,* which was published in 1957. He also won the 1979 poetry prize for his collection *Now and Then: Poems 1976-1978,* which was published in 1978. Warren served as the first poet laureate of the United States in 1986 and 1987.

In addition to *All the King's Men,* Warren's major novels include *World Enough and Time* (1950), *The Cave* (1959), and *Meet Me in the Green Glen* (1971). These books reflect the author's Southern heritage. They also emphasize the interaction of past and present, and what Warren believed is each person's struggle to determine his or her identity. Warren's poetry explores the themes of time, the individual, and the nature of evil. His long poem *Brother to Dragons* (1953) is typical of his verse. Warren also co-edited, with the critic Cleanth Brooks, two influential textbooks—*Understanding Poetry* (1938) and *Understanding Fiction* (1943). Warren was born in Guthrie, Ky.   John B. Vickery

Warren Report is a summary of events related to the assassination of President John F. Kennedy in Dallas, Tex., on Nov. 22, 1963. Issued by the Warren Commission in September 1964, it concluded that Lee Harvey Oswald, acting alone, shot Kennedy from a window on the sixth floor of the Texas School Book Depository building. The report also said that Jack Ruby acted alone in killing Oswald on Nov. 24, 1963, in a Dallas jail. The report found no evidence of a conspiracy involving Oswald and Ruby. It criticized the Secret Service and Federal Bureau of Investigation (FBI), and asked for better measures in the future to protect the President.

President Lyndon B. Johnson named Chief Justice Earl Warren to head the commission. The other members were Senator Richard B. Russell, Democrat of Georgia; Senator John S. Cooper, Republican of Kentucky; Representative T. Hale Boggs, Democrat of Louisiana; Representative Gerald R. Ford, Republican of Michigan; Allen W. Dulles, former director of the Central Intelligence Agency (CIA); and John J. McCloy, former adviser to President Kennedy.

The commission was appointed on Nov. 29, 1963. During 10 months, it took testimony from 552 witnesses. But critics accused the commission of not probing deeply enough into the possibility of a conspiracy.

During the late 1970's, a special committee of the U.S. House of Representatives reexamined the evidence. It concluded that Kennedy "was probably assassinated as a result of a conspiracy." See **Kennedy, John F.** (Assassination controversy).   Carol L. Thompson

Additional resources

Belin, David W. *November 22, 1963: You Are the Jury.* Quadrangle, 1973.
Goode, Stephen. *Assassination! Kennedy, King, Kennedy.* Watts, 1979. Suitable for younger readers.
Hurt, Henry. *Reasonable Doubt: An Investigation into the Assassination of John F. Kennedy.* Holt, 1986.
Kurtz, Michael L. *Crime of the Century: The Kennedy Assassination from a Historian's Perspective.* Univ. of Tennessee Press, 1982.

Wars of Succession. See Succession wars.

Wars of the Roses brought civil strife to England in the late 1400's. Two branches of the royal house fought for the English throne. The symbols adopted by each side gave the struggle its name. The House of York had long used a white rose as its emblem. The House of Lancaster became identified with a red rose, but historians are not certain when this took place. Some believe the red rose symbol did not appear until the final battle. The wars began in 1455 with the Battle of Saint Albans, and ended in 1485 with the Battle of Bosworth Field.

King Henry VI of the House of Lancaster held the throne when the Wars of the Roses began. His grandfather, Henry IV, had seized power in 1399. Richard, Duke of York, claimed that Henry VI had no right to be king. Richard was killed at the Battle of Wakefield in 1460. But his son Edward led the York forces that crushed the Lancastrians at the Battle of Towton in 1461. Edward then became king as Edward IV.

In 1470, the forces of Lancaster drove Edward from England and brought back Henry VI. Edward returned seven months later, defeated the Lancaster forces at the battles of Barnet and Tewkesbury, and regained the throne. The House of York ruled until Richard III lost his throne to the Lancaster descendant Henry Tudor, who became King Henry VII in 1485. Henry VII married Elizabeth, daughter of Edward IV, uniting the houses of Lancaster and York, and founding the Tudor dynasty.

Paul M. Kendall

See also **England** (The Wars of the Roses); **Lancaster; Tudor, House of; York.**

Warsaw, *WAWR saw* (pop. 1,659,400), is the capital and largest city of Poland. Its name in Polish is *Warszawa.* The city is a center of culture, science, and industry. It lies in east-central Poland, on both banks of the Vistula River. For location, see **Poland** (political map).

Warsaw has been the capital of an independent country throughout much of its history. But Prussia, Russia, and Germany have each controlled the city at various times. During World War II (1939-1945), German troops occupied Warsaw. The war left the city in ruins, its population reduced by about 85 per cent. Warsaw today is largely a city rebuilt from the ruins.

The city. Warsaw covers 174 square miles (450 square kilometers). The Vistula River divides the city. The left bank section lies west of the river, and the right bank section lies east of it. The center of Warsaw and most of the residential areas are on the left bank.

The Poles reconstructed many of Warsaw's historic buildings that had been damaged in the war. Churches and palaces built during the Middle Ages stand near modern hospitals, schools, and government buildings. Warsaw has spacious parks, and fine libraries, museums, and theaters. Statues of famous Poles stand throughout the city.

Famous landmarks, rebuilt since the war, include the Cathedral of St. John and the ancient city walls, both dating from the 1300's. Warsaw's opera house, also reconstructed since the war, is one of the largest in the world. The city's many monuments include the Column of King Sigismund, built in 1644. This monument honors the king who moved the Polish capital from Kraków to Warsaw.

Warsaw has modern housing developments and office buildings. New stores line Marszałkowska Street, the heart of the city's main shopping district. The huge Palace of Culture and Science, a gift from the Soviet Union in 1954, stands in a modern part of Warsaw. The city's many educational and research institutions include the University of Warsaw and the headquarters of the Polish Academy of Science.

Numerous cultural events take place in the capital. Each fall, the Festival of Contemporary Music attracts musicians from all Europe. Every five years, pianists from many parts of the world play in Warsaw's Frédéric Chopin International Piano Competition.

The people. World War II severely reduced Warsaw's population. But after the war, the population grew so rapidly that serious housing shortages developed. The government built many housing projects and restricted the flow of new residents into Warsaw.

Almost all the people of Warsaw are Poles. They share the same cultural, national, and racial backgrounds. The great majority of the people of Warsaw are Roman Catholics, and religion plays an important role in their lives. Religious festivals, such as the Corpus Christi procession in May or June, rank as major events.

Economy. Warsaw is an important center of Polish industry. Major industries in the city include food processing and the manufacture of automobiles, electronic equipment, machines, metals, and textiles. Warsaw has long been a trading city, and it is one of the chief railroad centers of eastern Europe. Thousands of Warsaw's citizens work in various agencies of the Polish government.

History. As early as the A.D. 900's, a small Slavic settlement existed in the area that is now Warsaw. During the late Middle Ages, from the 1200's to the 1500's, Warsaw was the home of the dukes of Mazovia. Mazovia entered the Polish kingdom in the 1500's, and King Sigismund III moved the capital from Kraków to Warsaw in 1596. Swedish forces invaded Poland in the mid-1600's and destroyed much of Warsaw in 1656. But Warsaw remained the capital of Poland until 1795. That year, Austria, Prussia, and Russia divided Poland among themselves, and Prussia took over Warsaw.

From 1807 to 1813, the city was the capital of the Duchy of Warsaw, a state created by the French emperor Napoleon. After Napoleon's defeat in eastern Europe, Russia gained control of Warsaw. The Poles rebelled against the Russians in 1830 and 1863, but these uprisings failed. During the late 1800's, the Russians tightened their control over Warsaw. World War I (1914-

Downtown Warsaw has wide streets lined with modern stores and office buildings. One of Poland's cultural centers, the city has numerous libraries, museums, theaters, and historic landmarks.

Horst Cerni, Shostal

1918) brought an end to the Russian rule. Germany controlled Warsaw from 1915 to 1918, when Poland again became independent.

World War II (1939-1945) brought the almost total destruction of Warsaw. In 1939, the Germans held the city in a three-week siege that caused great damage. Warsaw surrendered to the Germans, but the city became the heart of the Polish underground resistance movement.

The people of Warsaw suffered under the ruthless terror of the German troops. The Nazis staged mass arrests and public executions, and they forced many of Warsaw's people to leave the city. They confined about 500,000 Jews to a section of the city called the *ghetto*. Many of the Jews died of hunger and disease. The Germans executed thousands of others. In April 1943, about 60,000 Jews who still remained in the ghetto revolted. The Germans killed almost all of them.

By the summer of 1944, Soviet armies had pushed the Germans out of the Soviet Union and had reached the outskirts of Warsaw. On Aug. 1, 1944, the people of Warsaw rose against the Germans. At first, the Poles seized large parts of the city. But the nearby Soviet troops did not come to their aid, and the Poles soon weakened. In spite of massive German counterattacks, the Poles held on to isolated areas on the left bank of the Vistula River. They finally surrendered on October 3. The Germans evacuated the entire population of the left bank. They burned and dynamited the buildings and destroyed what remained of Warsaw. On Jan. 17, 1945, Soviet forces entered Warsaw. They set up a Polish Communist government in February, and Warsaw became the capital of the Polish People's Republic. Leslie Dienes

See also **Poland** (picture).

Warsaw grouper, a name for black Jewfish. See **Jewfish.**

Warsaw Pact is a treaty that holds most Communist nations of Europe in a military command under Soviet control. Albania, Bulgaria, Czechoslovakia, East Germany, Hungary, Poland, Romania, and the Soviet Union signed the treaty in Warsaw in May 1955. They claimed they signed the treaty as a response to the creation of the North Atlantic Treaty Organization (NATO), a defense alliance formed by the United States and its European allies. NATO, based on a treaty signed in 1949, had begun operations in 1950. Albania withdrew from the Warsaw Pact in 1968. A Soviet army general serves as supreme commander of Warsaw Pact forces, whose military headquarters are in Moscow. Stuart D. Goldman

Warship is a naval combat ship. Some kinds of warships attack enemy aircraft, surface ships, and submarines. They are heavily armed with such weapons as guns, missiles, rockets, and torpedoes. Others serve as bases for planes or helicopters. Still others transport troops, weapons, and equipment to battle areas.

Warships range in size from small vessels with only a few crew members to large aircraft carriers that carry more than 6,000 persons. Most warships have radar and sonar to detect and locate enemy planes, surface ships, and submarines. Radar detects aircraft and surface ships, and sonar locates submarines. Electronic intercept equipment can detect radio and radar transmissions from enemy ships and aircraft.

In ancient times and until the 1600's, warships and cargo ships were almost identical. However, warships gradually became highly specialized vessels used only for military purposes.

Kinds of warships

Large modern navies have many kinds of warships that are designed for certain combat operations. The United States Navy uses six principal types: (1) aircraft carriers, (2) amphibious warfare ships, (3) cruisers, (4) destroyers, (5) frigates, and (6) submarines. Many fleets also include small warships called *small combatants.*

Aircraft carriers are the largest and most powerful warships. They serve as bases for bomber and fighter planes. They also carry antisubmarine aircraft, helicopters, and small numbers of other kinds of planes. Aircraft carriers have few defensive weapons, and so they depend on other warships for protection.

A carrier has a large, flat flight deck with equipment that enables planes to take off and land without a long runway. The aircraft are launched by four catapults, each of which can put a plane into the air every 30 seconds. The landing area of the flight deck has steel wires stretched across it. A hook attached to the bottom of each plane catches onto a wire, bringing the aircraft to a quick stop.

The powerful radars of an aircraft carrier not only detect enemy planes but also guide the carrier's own aircraft. Short-range radars are used to detect enemy missiles. They also help the crew keep track of nearby ships at night and navigate the carrier near shore.

A warship in action. The frigate U.S.S. *Lockwood,* shown above, tests a missile for use against enemy surface ships and submarines. This ship is also armed with a 5-inch (127-millimeter) gun and antisubmarine torpedoes. It carries a helicopter for locating and attacking submarines.

Aircraft carriers are about 1,100 feet (335 meters) long and can carry from 85 to 95 planes. Carriers travel at speeds of over 30 knots (nautical miles per hour).

Amphibious warfare ships land troops, weapons, and vehicles on beaches held by the enemy. Some of these ships remain far from shore and use small landing craft, amphibious tractors, or helicopters to land the troops and cargo. Such ships have closed-off areas at sea level called *docking wells.* The docking wells are flooded and opened into the sea so that landing craft and amphibious tractors can float out through them.

Some amphibious warfare ships serve chiefly as helicopter carriers. They resemble small aircraft carriers but do not have the launching and landing equipment needed for conventional planes. These ships carry from 20 to 30 helicopters, as well as troops and small vehicles. The ships also can serve as bases for *V/STOL aircraft.* V/STOL's can take off and land vertically or on a very short runway. Other amphibious warfare ships have command and communications facilities to coordinate air, shore, and surface operations.

Amphibious warfare ships measure up to 800 feet (250 meters) long and travel at speeds of about 20 knots. They carry few defensive weapons.

Cruisers escort aircraft carriers and defend them against air and submarine attacks. Modern cruisers are called *guided missile cruisers.* They carry supersonic missiles that can be fired at aircraft that are from 15 to 85 miles (24 to 137 kilometers) from the ship. Cruisers also have antisubmarine rockets and torpedoes for use against enemy submarines. Some cruisers carry one or

two helicopters. After an enemy submarine has been detected by sonar, the helicopters pinpoint its location and attack it with torpedoes or depth bombs. Some cruisers also carry 5-inch (127-millimeter) guns. Modern cruisers are about 600 feet (180 meters) long and travel at speeds of more than 30 knots.

Destroyers are used chiefly to defend aircraft carriers, amphibious ships, and merchant ships. They also perform various independent missions, such as bombarding enemy shores and conducting search and rescue operations at sea.

Modern destroyers have 5-inch (127-millimeter) guns, short-range antiaircraft missiles, and antisubmarine weapons. They also carry one or two helicopters to attack submarines. Destroyers range in length from about 375 to 560 feet ($112\frac{1}{2}$ to 171 meters). They can reach speeds of 30 to 33 knots.

Frigates are used primarily to defend amphibious ships and merchant ships against enemy submarines. Frigates carry torpedoes, nuclear depth charges, and other antisubmarine weapons. They also have a helicopter for locating and attacking submarines. In addition, most of these warships carry missiles and one or two guns for defense against air and surface attacks. Modern frigates measure up to 445 feet (136 meters) long. They travel at speeds of 27 to 30 knots.

Some navies have small frigates called *corvettes* to patrol coastal waters. Corvettes measure about 150 feet (46 meters) long. The U.S. Navy does not use corvettes.

Submarines search out and attack enemy submarines and surface ships. Some can also fire missiles at enemy cities and military bases. Modern submarines have nuclear power systems that enable them to remain underwater for months at a time. The U.S. Navy has two principal kinds of submarines, *attack submarines* and *ballistic missile submarines.*

Attack submarines have large sonars for detecting submarines and surface ships from long distances. They carry torpedoes that are fired from tubes inside the hull. Antisubmarine missiles can also be fired from the torpedo tubes. In addition, these tubes carry mines that are laid off an enemy coast. Attack submarines range in length from 250 to 360 feet (76 to 110 meters). Some can travel underwater at speeds of more than 30 knots.

Ballistic missile submarines carry long-range missiles that can hit targets up to 4,000 miles (6,400 kilometers) away. These submarines are designed chiefly to attack enemy cities. They also carry torpedoes for defense against enemy surface ships and submarines. Ballistic missile submarines measure from about 380 to 550 feet (115 to 168 meters) long. They reach speeds of more than 20 knots underwater.

Small combatants include such ships as minesweepers, missile boats, and patrol boats. Minesweepers locate and remove underwater explosives. Missile boats carry guided missiles that can attack enemy surface ships from 10 to 60 miles (16 to 97 kilometers) away. Patrol boats guard rivers and coastal waters.

Small combatants are generally operated near coasts. The U.S. Navy has few of these ships because it conducts chiefly long-range ocean operations.

History

Ships have been used in combat for at least 3,000 years. Until the 1600's, however, there were few differences between warships and cargo ships. Any ship that fought in combat might also transport goods or carry explorers on long voyages.

Early warships. The ancient Greek and Roman navies used long, narrow wooden ships called *galleys.* These vessels were powered by oarsmen, who sat in one or more rows on each side. Galleys also had a rectangular sail called a *square sail,* which was used in a favorable wind. The bow ended in a long, sharp point that was rammed into the hull of an enemy ship.

During the A.D. 700's, the Vikings of northern Europe developed the *long ship.* It was powered by rowers and a square sail but weighed only about half as much as a galley. Long ships were strong and seaworthy, and they helped the Vikings control the seas until the 1000's.

Southern Europeans continued to use galleys in battle but gradually stopped attacking by ramming enemy ships. Instead, the rowers maneuvered their galley close to an enemy ship and then boarded it.

By the 1500's, most warships carried guns, and so battles no longer were fought aboard ship. Navies began to use warships as floating gun platforms and replaced galleys with larger, more heavily armed ships.

The age of sailing ships. During the 1500's, Europeans began to build large, heavy sailing ships designed for long ocean voyages by explorers. Such ships included *galleons,* which were also used as warships.

The Spanish Navy built large galleons that sailed high on the water. English galleons were smaller, lower, and easier to maneuver. In 1588, the Spanish Navy tried to invade England. The Spaniards called their fleet the "Invincible Armada" because they were sure it could not be defeated. But the English won the battle, partly because their galleons were more maneuverable warships than those of the Spaniards.

After Spain's defeat, navies began to build specialized fighting ships. These vessels included *capital ships,* an important type of warship during the 1600's and 1700's. Capital ships were fairly easy to maneuver and large enough to carry more than 100 guns. They became known as *ships of the line* because they could serve in the line of battle.

Warships of the 1800's. In 1814, Robert Fulton, an American artist and inventor, built the first steam-powered warship. Navies then began to use warships driven by steam, but the vessels were also powered by sails until the mid-1800's.

Naval guns that fired explosive shells, rather than solid cannon balls, were developed in the 1820's. The shells could easily tear huge holes in the sides of wooden ships. Therefore, navies began to build iron vessels and also *ironclad* ships. The hulls of these vessels were made of wood or iron, and were covered with thick plates of iron. Ironclads could withstand attack far better than wooden ships could. The first battle between these new types of warships occurred in 1862, during the American Civil War. The North's iron *Monitor* fought the South's ironclad *Merrimack* (then called the *Virginia*) at Hampton Roads, Va. Neither ship won, but the battle marked the beginning of the age of steel ships. It was also one of the first battles between ships powered only by steam.

Rotating gun turrets were invented in the mid-1800's, and the *Monitor* was the first ship in the U.S. Navy to use them. They enabled guns to be turned in various directions and ended the need for extensive maneuvers by warships. Heavy rifles became standard armament on combat vessels and greatly improved the range and accuracy of naval gunfire.

The birth of the modern battleship. In 1906, the British Navy introduced the *Dreadnought,* the first modern battleship. It was the forerunner of the massive battleships that ruled the seas for more than 35 years. The *Dreadnought* was faster, larger, and more heavily armed than any earlier warship.

During the early and mid-1900's, navies improved the basic design of the *Dreadnought* to make battleships larger and faster. Better communications methods developed within the ships increased the efficiency of their command. The battleship became the chief combat warship, and nations measured their power in the world by the number of battleships in their navies.

Warships in the two world wars. Battleships were the most powerful warships during World War I (1914-1918). However, the German Navy proved that submarines were also highly effective warships. German submarines, called *U-boats,* sank thousands of Allied merchant ships. These deadly attacks soon led to the development of sonar equipment and various antisubmarine ships.

Radar was perfected shortly before World War II began in 1939. It enabled warships to locate enemy aircraft and ships at night, through clouds, and at great distances. Improved *gun directors* were developed at

The development of warships

Ships have been used in battle since ancient times. But warships and cargo ships were almost identical until the 1600's, when navies began to build vessels designed only for combat. Today, large navies have many kinds of warships. Each type performs specific functions in battle. These illustrations show the development of some major warships from the 200's B.C. to modern times.

WORLD BOOK illustrations by George Suyeoka

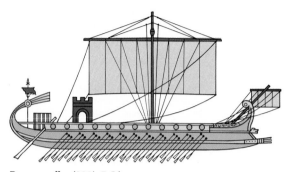

Roman galley (200's B.C.)
About 180 feet (55 meters) long

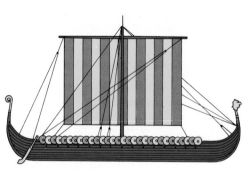

Viking long ship (about A.D. 1000)
About 80 feet (24 meters) long

Galleon (1500's)
About 140 feet (43 meters) long

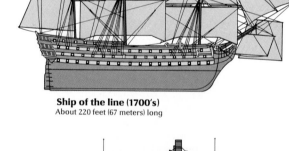

Ship of the line (1700's)
About 220 feet (67 meters) long

U.S. Civil War iron ship (1860's)
About 170 feet (52 meters) long

U.S. Civil War ironclad ship (1860's)
About 270 feet (182 meters) long

about the same time. They quickly tracked moving aircraft and directed gunfire at them. Gun directors were used with *proximity fuzes,* which exploded a shell as it neared its target and eliminated the need for a direct hit.

Aircraft became the most effective military weapons of World War II. The importance of battleships declined, and navies began to concentrate on building aircraft carriers. They also built large numbers of cruisers and destroyers to protect the carriers and installed antiaircraft weapons on all warships.

The U.S. Navy built thousands of amphibious warfare ships during World War II. One type, the *landing ship—tank (LST),* carried tanks and landed them on enemy beaches. Other amphibious warfare ships carried

troops, landing craft, and military supplies. Still others used guns, mortars, and rockets to bombard enemy beaches before invasions.

Warships in the nuclear age. After World War II ended in 1945, the U.S. Navy began to develop nuclear-powered warships. It launched the first nuclear-powered submarine, the *Nautilus,* in 1954. The *Nautilus* could travel much faster than the diesel-powered submarines then in use. Its nuclear power system also enabled the submarine to travel hundreds of thousands of miles underwater without refueling. Shortly after the *Nautilus* went to sea, the Soviet Union completed its first nuclear submarine. The navies of Great Britain, France, and China have also built nuclear submarines.

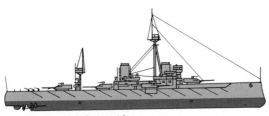

Dreadnought (early 1900's)
About 500 feet (150 meters) long

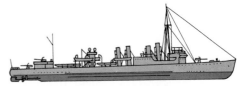

World War I destroyer (early 1900's)
About 300 feet (91 meters) long

World War II battleship (mid-1900's)
About 900 feet (274 meters) long

World War II submarine (mid-1900's)
About 300 feet (91 meters) long

Modern landing ship—tank (LST)
About 500 feet (150 meters) long

Minesweeper (1950's)
About 150 feet (46 meters) long

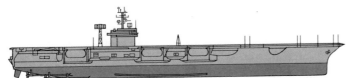

Modern nuclear-powered aircraft carrier
About 1,000 feet (300 meters) long

Modern missile boat
About 130 feet (40 meters) long

Modern nuclear-powered guided-missile cruiser
About 600 feet (180 meters) long

Modern nuclear-powered ballistic missile submarine
About 500 feet (150 meters) long

The development of powerful, long-range guided missiles also increased the capabilities of warships. These missiles can be launched from almost every kind of warship. In the early 1960's, the U.S. Navy developed the first ballistic missile submarine.

During the 1960's, the U.S. Navy also built nuclear-powered surface ships. In the 1970's, U.S. warships began to use gas turbine engines. These engines operated almost as effectively in surface ships as did nuclear power systems, and they cost much less. In the early 1980's, the U.S. Navy began to modernize and reactivate several World War II battleships.   Norman Polmar

Related articles in *World Book* include:

Kinds of ships

Aircraft carrier	Frigate	Missile boat
Amphibious ship	Galleon	Privateer
Battleship	Galley	PT boat
Cruiser	Minesweeper	Submarine
Destroyer		

Famous warships

Alabama	Constitution	Monitor
Bismarck	Graf Spee	and Merrimack
Constellation	Maine	

Other related articles

Depth charge	Navy	Sonar
Guided missile	Navy, United States	Torpedo
Mine warfare	Radar	V/STOL

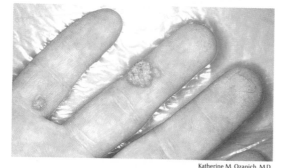

Katherine M. Ozanich, M.D.

Warts are hard, rough growths on the skin. They may appear on the hands, feet, face, or other parts of the body.

Wart is a hard, rough growth on the surface of the skin. Warts may appear in a wide range of shapes, sizes, and numbers anywhere on the skin. They can even appear on the lips or tongue. On moist parts of the body, warts may grow into masses like tiny cauliflowers. Warts that grow on the sole of the foot look like corns and make walking painful. Warts on the face may form little beard-like projections.

Warts result from infection by certain viruses. The viruses live in cells of the surface layer of the skin and do not infect the underlying tissue. The thickened surface layer forms folds into which little blood vessels grow. If a wart is scratched open, the virus may spread by contact to another part of the body or to another person. Contrary to superstition, touching the skin of a toad will not cause warts.

Some warts go away without treatment, perhaps because immunity to the virus develops. A vaccine cures wart infections in cattle, but it is not a practical treatment for people. Physicians often remove warts by burning or freezing the wart tissue, which causes little harm to the deep skin layers. Treatment for any wart should be done by a doctor.   Orville J. Stone

Wart hog is an African pig with large curved tusks protruding from its huge flattened head. These tusks may be as much as 2 feet (61 centimeters) long. Between the tusks and the eyes are three pairs of large "warts" from which the hog gets its name. The coarsely grained pale gray hide of the wart hog is thinly sprinkled with stiff, brownish-gray hairs. A thin mane of long bristly hair hangs over its back and head. A large boar may

Leonard Lee Rue III, Tom Stack & Assoc.

The wart hog is named for the "warts" on its head.

weigh over 200 pounds (91 kilograms) and measure about 30 inches (76 centimeters) high at the shoulder.

The Boer farmers call the wart hog *vlakte-vark* (pig of the plains). It lives in dry, sandy country from southern Africa to Ethiopia and prefers open forest with plenty of thickets for protection. The wart hog travels in small family groups. Old boars, however, usually prefer to live by themselves. The sow may produce as many as six to eight young at a time. Ordinarily, only half that number are born at one time. Wart hogs often enlarge and use burrows that have been made by other animals. They eat almost everything—roots, plants, birds' eggs, and even small mammals.

Scientific classification. The wart hog belongs to the Old World pig family, Suidae. Its scientific name is *Phacochoerus aethiopicus.*   Duane A. Schlitter

Warwick, *WAWR ihk* or *WAWR wihk* (pop. 87,123), is Rhode Island's second largest city and a commercial center of the state. Only Providence has more people. Warwick lies on Greenwich Bay, in east-central Rhode Island (see **Rhode Island** [political map]). Warwick helps form a metropolitan area with 618,514 people.

Warwick is the home of the Warwick Musical Theater. The city's industries produce textiles and metal products. Warwick is the headquarters for a division of an insurance company. The Theodore Francis Green State Airport, Rhode Island's largest airport, is in Warwick. Narragansett Bay, a sailing and fishing resort, is nearby. Warwick received its city charter in 1931. It has a mayor-council form of government.   Theodore Holmberg

Warwick, *WAWR ihk,* **Earl of** (1428-1471), was a famous English soldier and statesman. He is also known as the *Kingmaker* and as the *Last of the Barons.*

Warwick was one of the most powerful men in England during the Wars of the Roses. He commanded an army with great skill at the Battle of Saint Albans in 1455. In 1460, war broke out again. Warwick again took the field and won the Battle of Northampton, capturing King Henry VI. But later in the year the Yorkists were defeated at Wakefield. The Duke of York was captured and killed. Warwick became head of the Yorkists as guardian of his cousin, Prince Edward.

Another battle was fought at Saint Albans in 1461, and Warwick was defeated. But he boldly proclaimed Edward, the Duke of York, king of England, and had him crowned. Edward and Warwick soon quarreled. In 1470, an army led by Warwick invaded England from France and forced King Edward to flee. Warwick then restored Queen Margaret and Henry VI to the throne. But in 1471 Warwick met Edward in battle again, at Barnet, and was killed. Warwick's given and family name was Richard Neville.   André Maurois

Warwick, Guy of. See Guy of Warwick.

Wasatch Range, *WAW sach,* is a mountain range that extends for about 140 miles (225 kilometers) from southern Idaho into northern Utah. Its abrupt western face forms the western front of the Rocky Mountains and the eastern rim of the Great Basin. Salt Lake City lies at the foot of the range. The range's average elevation is 10,000 feet (3,000 meters). Mount Timpanogos (11,750 feet, or 3,581 meters) is the highest peak. Steep narrow valleys cut the range's western side. The eastern slope is less steep (see Utah [physical map]).   John H. Garland

See also **Salt Lake City** (picture); **Utah** (picture).

Washakie, *WAHSH uh kee* (1804?-1900), was a chief of the eastern Shoshone Indians in Utah and Wyoming. He became noted for his friendship toward white people and for his relentless warfare against his Indian enemies.

Washakie furnished aid to many immigrants moving west over the Oregon Trail, and also sent some Indians to General George Crook in the 1870's to serve as scouts against the Sioux.

He spent his later years in splendor as the ruler, guide, and counselor of his people. Washakie renounced many of the old Indian customs and joined the Protestant Episcopal Church.   *William H. Gilbert*

Washburn, Sherwood Larned (1911-   ), is an American anthropologist. He became noted for his studies of ape behavior and of human and ape anatomy. Washburn was one of the first scientists to study the behavior of apes in their natural surroundings. He taught at Columbia University and the University of Chicago, and he has taught at the University of California at Berkeley since 1959. He edited the *American Journal of Physical Anthropology* from 1955 to 1957. Washburn was born in Cambridge, Mass.   *Mordecai L. Gabriel*

Washing machine is a machine that quickly washes clothes, linens, and other items. Before the invention of the washing machine, people spent hours doing their laundry by hand. Some people soaked their clothes in streams and then beat them with rocks to get out the dirt. Later, people scrubbed their laundry on washboards. People in some parts of the world still use such methods today.

Most washing machines work automatically. The operator simply puts in laundry, pours in detergent, and sets the controls. One set of controls determines whether the machine uses hot, warm, or cold water. The water enters the machine through hoses connected to hot and cold water pipes. The operator also sets controls to select the length of washing and rinsing time and the amount of water that enters the machine. The machine, which is powered by an electric motor, then operates automatically. Many automatic washing machines have special features, such as filters that remove lint, and automatic dispensers for bleach and fabric softener.

Most automatic washers have an inner tub that is surrounded by an outer tub. The washing takes place in the inner tub, called the *washbasket.* After the laundry has been washed and rinsed, the washbasket spins rapidly. The spinning removes most of the water from the various items and throws it into the outer tub. The water is then pumped out of the machine through a drain hose. Finally, the operator dries the laundry in a clothes dryer or hangs it on a clothesline or elsewhere to dry.

There are two types of automatic washers, *agitator machines* and *tumbler machines.* Most automatic washers are agitator machines.

The operator of an agitator machine puts in laundry by lifting the lid of the washer. Inside the machine, a cone-shaped device called an *agitator* is mounted in the center of the washbasket. Most agitators have several projections called *fins.* As the agitator rotates, it continually reverses direction. This action moves the laundry through the water and forces water through the laundry items.

A tumbler machine is loaded through a door on the front of the machine. The washbasket revolves, and the laundry tumbles through the water.

Some washing machines are not automatic. A *semiautomatic machine* has controls like those of an automatic machine, but the operator must set them more than once. A *spinner machine* has two tubs that are set apart from each other. The operator transfers laundry from the washtub to the second tub, which spins rapidly and throws the water into a surrounding chamber. A *wringer machine* has two rollers that squeeze water out of the laundry. The operator removes the items from the tub before passing them through the rollers.

One of the first mechanical washers was patented about 1860 by Hamilton E. Smith of Philadelphia. A crank on this machine turned paddles inside, pushing the laundry through the water. An electric-powered washer was invented in 1910, and an automatic washing machine was introduced in 1937.   *Evan Powell*

Washing soda. See Soda.

How an agitator washing machine works

Hot- and cold-water inlet hoses ⎯
Controls
Agitator
Inner tub
Outer tub
Drain hose
Drain pump
Drain outlet hose to sewer
Drive mechanism

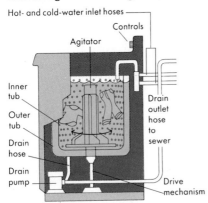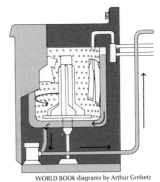

WORLD BOOK diagrams by Arthur Grebetz

Washing begins after water fills the tubs. The action of the agitator moves the laundry and forces water through it.

Rinsing occurs after the wash water is pumped out of the tubs. After the rinsing process, the rinse water is pumped out.

Spin drying. As the inner tub spins, excess water from the laundry goes into the outer tub. The water is then pumped out.

Seattle, the largest city in Washington, is an important manufacturing and trade center of the Pacific Northwest. Mount Rainier, Washington's highest peak, rises southeast of the city.

Washington *The Evergreen State*

Washington is the only state of the United States named for one of the nation's Presidents. It was named in honor of George Washington. The state lies on the Pacific Coast in the northwestern part of the country. Its location makes it a gateway for land, sea, and air travel to Alaska and to Asian countries across the Pacific Ocean.

Washington is famous for scenery of breathtaking beauty and sharp contrasts. High mountains rise above evergreen forests and sparkling coastal waters. The junglelike forests of the Olympic Peninsula in the west are among the rainiest places in the world. But the flat semidesert land that lies east of the Cascade Mountains stretches for long distances without a single tree.

Snow-covered peaks tower above the foothills and lowlands around them. Mount Rainier, the highest mountain in the state, appears to "float" on the horizon

The contributors of this article are Ronald Reed Boyce, Dean of the School of Social and Behavioral Sciences at Seattle Pacific University; and Robert C. Carriker, Professor of History at Gonzaga University.

southeast of Seattle and Tacoma. On a clear day, persons in the Seattle area can also see Mount Baker to the north, the Olympic Mountains to the west, and the Cascades to the east. Lodges and chair lifts in the mountains attract thousands of tourists and skiers.

Washington's coastline has several bays and inlets that make excellent harbors. Ships from all parts of the world dock at Bellingham, Seattle, Tacoma, and other ports on Puget Sound. Washington also has important shipping centers on the Pacific Ocean and the Columbia River. Washington fishing fleets catch salmon, halibut, and other fishes in the chilly waters off the northern Pacific Coast. The state is famous for seafoods, especially chinook and sockeye salmon.

Washington's nickname, the *Evergreen State*, comes from its many firs, hemlocks, pines, and other evergreen trees. Washington has large areas of thick forests, especially on the western slopes of the Cascades. The state produces large amounts of lumber, pulp and paper, and other wood products. The state's nickname also suggests the lush green lowlands found in western Washington. A mild, moist climate makes this region excellent

A. D. Lodwick, Black Star

Rain forests in Olympic National Park, with moss-covered trees and thick undergrowth, look like tropical jungles.

Interesting facts about Washington

One of the world's foremost aircraft and spacecraft manufacturers, the Boeing Company, was founded in Seattle in 1916. Boeing produced the booster rocket for the Apollo/Saturn 5 moon landing of 1969; the Lunar Rover, which transported astronauts and equipment on the moon; and the Mariner 10 spacecraft, which flew by Mercury and Venus in 1974.

Boeing aircraft and spacecraft

The first municipal monorail service in the United States began operating in Seattle in 1962. It was built to connect the World's Fair with downtown Seattle.

The city of George, Washington, has streets named after varieties of cherries, such as Bing and Maraschino avenues.

First monorail

Father's Day, first celebrated on June 19, 1910, was originated by Sonora Louise Smart Dodd of Spokane.

The greatest snowfall in North America in one season occurred at Rainier Paradise Ranger Station. A total of 1,122 inches (2,850 centimeters) fell from July 1971 through June 1972.

for dairy farming and for growing flower bulbs.

East of the Cascades, farmers raise livestock and wheat on large ranches. They grow fruits and vegetables in fertile, irrigated river valleys such as the Okanogan, Wenatchee, and Yakima. Delicious apples produced in these areas are a Washington specialty. Washington leads the states in apple production.

Giant dams on the Columbia River and its tributaries capture water for irrigation and power. The largest dam, Grand Coulee, is one of the engineering wonders of the world. Irrigation water is transforming the Columbia Basin, where farmers raise large crops of vegetables on land that once was dry and bare.

Washington contributes to the nuclear age with the U.S. Department of Energy's Hanford Site, a nuclear energy center near Richland. Washington also has a part in the space age. The Boeing Company, a leading producer of commercial airliners and spacecraft, has headquarters in Seattle and plants in Auburn, Kent, Renton, and near Everett.

Olympia is the capital of Washington. Seattle is the state's largest city.

Antje Gunnar, Bruce Coleman Inc.

The San Juan Islands, which lie near Canada's Vancouver Island, are noted for their scenic beauty. Vacation resorts on the islands attract many visitors.

Washington in brief

Symbols of Washington

The state flag, first adopted in 1923, bears the state seal. The flag's green field stands for Washington's forests. The seal, first adopted in 1889, has a likeness of George Washington, for whom the state was named. The first seal used a postage stamp for the likeness of Washington. Both the flag and seal were readopted in 1967 when a portrait for the seal by Gilbert Stuart, an American artist, was approved by the state legislature.

State flag

State seal

Washington (brown) ranks 20th in size among all the states and is the smallest of the Pacific Coast States (yellow).

The state capitol, called the Legislative Building, is in Olympia. Olympia has been the state capital since Washington became a state in 1889.

General information

Statehood: Nov. 11, 1889, the 42nd state.
State abbreviations: Wash. (traditional), WA (postal).
State motto: *Alki* (An Indian word for *Bye and Bye*).
State song: "Washington, My Home." Words and music by Helen Davis.

Land and climate

Area: 68,139 sq. mi. (176,479 km²), including 1,627 sq. mi. (4,215 km²) of inland water but excluding 2,397 sq. mi. (6,208 km²) of Pacific coastal water, Puget Sound, and the Straits of Georgia and Juan de Fuca.
Elevation: *Highest*—Mount Rainier, 14,410 ft. (4,392 m) above sea level. *Lowest*—sea level along the coast.
Coastline: 157 mi. (253 km).
Record high temperature: 118° F. (48° C) in Grant County on July 24, 1928, and at Ice Harbor Dam on Aug. 5, 1961.
Record low temperature: −48° F. (−44° C) at Mazama and at Winthrop on Dec. 30, 1968.
Average July temperature: 66° F. (19° C).
Average January temperature: 30° F. (−1° C).
Average yearly precipitation: 38 in. (97 cm).

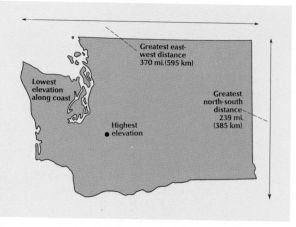

Greatest east-west distance 370 mi.(595 km)

Lowest elevation along coast

Greatest north-south distance 239 mi. (385 km)

Highest elevation

Important dates

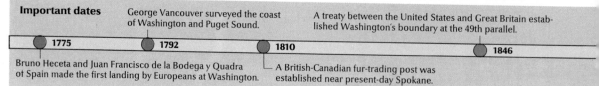

George Vancouver surveyed the coast of Washington and Puget Sound.

A treaty between the United States and Great Britain established Washington's boundary at the 49th parallel.

| 1775 | 1792 | 1810 | 1846 |

Bruno Heceta and Juan Francisco de la Bodega y Quadra of Spain made the first landing by Europeans at Washington.

A British-Canadian fur-trading post was established near present-day Spokane.

State bird
Willow goldfinch

State flower
Coast rhododendron

State tree
Western hemlock

People

Population: 4,132,204 (1980 census)
Rank among the states: 20th
Density: 61 persons per sq. mi. (24 per km²), U.S. average 67 per sq. mi. (26 per km²)
Distribution: 74 per cent urban, 26 per cent rural

Largest cities in Washington

Seattle	493,846
Spokane	171,300
Tacoma	158,501
Bellevue	73,903
Lakes District*	54,533
Everett	54,413

*Unincorporated place.
Source: U.S. Bureau of the Census.

Population trend

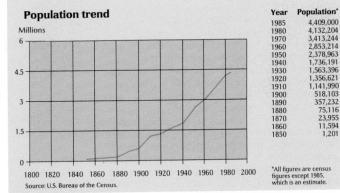

Millions

Source: U.S. Bureau of the Census.

Year	Population*
1985	4,409,000
1980	4,132,204
1970	3,413,244
1960	2,853,214
1950	2,378,963
1940	1,736,191
1930	1,563,396
1920	1,356,621
1910	1,141,990
1900	518,103
1890	357,232
1880	75,116
1870	23,955
1860	11,594
1850	1,201

*All figures are census figures except 1985, which is an estimate.

Economy

Chief products

Agriculture: timber, milk, beef cattle, apples, wheat.
Manufacturing: transportation equipment, food products, paper products, wood products, chemicals.

Gross state product

Value of goods and services produced in 1986, $77,683,000,000. *Services* include community, business, and personal services; finance; government; trade; and transportation, communication, and utilities. *Industry* includes construction, manufacturing, and mining. *Agriculture* includes agriculture, fishing, and forestry.

Source: U.S. Bureau of Economic Analysis.

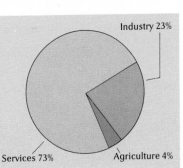

Industry 23%

Services 73%

Agriculture 4%

Government

State government

Governor: 4-year term
State senators: 49; 4-year terms
State representatives: 98; 2-year terms
Counties: 39

Federal government

United States senators: 2
United States representatives: 8
Electoral votes: 10

Sources of information

Tourism: Department of Trade and Economic Development, Tourism Development Division, 101 General Administration Building, Olympia, WA 98504
Economy: Department of Trade and Economic Development, Development Services Division, 101 General Administration Building, Olympia, WA 98504
Government: Superintendent of Public Instruction, Old Capitol Building, FG-11, Olympia, WA 98504-3211
History: Superintendent of Public Instruction, Old Capitol Building, FG-11, Olympia, WA 98504-3211

The Northern Pacific Railroad linked Washington and the East.

Grand Coulee Dam was completed.

| 1883 | 1889 | 1942 | 1980 |

Washington became the 42nd state on November 11.

Mount St. Helens volcano erupted, causing 57 deaths and enormous damage in southwestern Washington.

People

Population.

Population. The 1980 United States census reported that Washington had 4,132,204 people. The state's population had increased 21 per cent over the 1970 census figure, 3,413,244. The U.S. Bureau of the Census estimated that by 1985 the state's population had reached about 4,409,000.

About two-fifths of the people of Washington live in the Seattle metropolitan area in the western part of the state. Washington has nine metropolitan areas (see **Metropolitan area**). For the names and populations of the state's metropolitan areas, see the *Index* to the political map of Washington.

Most of the larger Washington cities are in the western part of the state along Puget Sound. Seattle, the state's largest city, is in this region. It serves as an important shipping and manufacturing center. Cities in the eastern part of the Seattle metropolitan area are experiencing rapid growth. Tacoma, an industrial and port city, is about 28 miles (45 kilometers) south of Seattle. Both Seattle and Tacoma began chiefly as ports for shipping lumber. Later, the two cities became shipping centers for trade with Alaska and Asia.

Most of the cities in eastern Washington developed as centers for farm trade, lumbering, or mining. Spokane, the largest eastern city, is an important railroad, manufacturing, grain, and financial center. The "Tri-Cities" of Richland, Pasco, and Kennewick in south-central Washington grew in size and importance after World War II. At that time, the Hanford nuclear energy center was established nearby. See the separate articles on the cities of Washington listed in the *Related articles* at the end of this article.

About 94 per cent of Washington's people, including

Population density

Most of the larger cities in Washington are located in the western part of the state along Puget Sound. About 40 per cent of the people live in the Seattle metropolitan area.

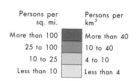

Persons per sq. mi.	Persons per km²
More than 100	More than 40
25 to 100	10 to 40
10 to 25	4 to 10
Less than 10	Less than 4

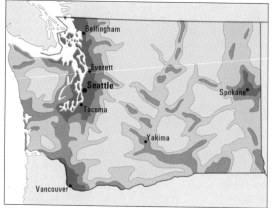

WORLD BOOK map; based on U.S. Bureau of the Census data.

many of Canadian and Oriental ancestry, were born in the United States. Canadians make up the largest group of people born in another country. Other foreign-born groups include people from Germany, Mexico, and Sweden. Washington has more than 65,000 American Indians. About a fourth of them live on the state's 25 reservations.

Joel W. Rogers, Earth Images

An Indian worker shovels herring into a loading net in Bellingham. More than 65,000 American Indians live in Washington. About one-fourth of them live on the state's 25 reservations.

Pacific Science Center

The Pacific Science Center, in Seattle, features exhibits of modern science. The children above are experimenting with one of the center's many scientific demonstrations.

Schools. The first school in Washington opened at Old Fort Vancouver in 1832. It was established for the children of employees of the Hudson's Bay Company, a British trading firm. In the 1830's, missionaries began teaching Indians in eastern Washington near present-day Spokane and Walla Walla. These early teachers included Marcus Whitman and his wife Narcissa, and Cushing Eells, Henry Spalding, and Elkanah Walker. In 1859, Whitman College, Washington's first institution of higher learning, was founded in Walla Walla. A state-wide public school system began in 1895. A law passed that year provided state financial support for schools.

An elected state superintendent of public instruction and a state board of education supervise Washington's public school system. Children between the ages of 8 and 15 must attend school. For the number of students and teachers in Washington, see **Education** (table).

Libraries. Washington's first library, the State Library in Olympia, began in 1853 as the Territorial Library. Today, about 70 public libraries and library systems serve the state. The Seattle Public Library has more than a million books, including collections on the Pacific

Northwest and on aeronautics. Many Washington colleges and universities also include outstanding libraries. The Henry Suzzallo Library at the University of Washington has several famous collections, including historical material on the Pacific Northwest, oceanography, and the fisheries industry.

Museums. The Thomas Burke Memorial Washington State Museum on the campus of the University of Washington features exhibits on natural history. Museums with relics of Washington history include the Museum of Native American Culture and the Cheney Cowles Memorial Museum in Spokane, the Washington State Historical Society in Tacoma, the Museum of History and Industry in Seattle, and the State Capital Museum in Olympia. The Seattle Art Museum has a fine collection of Oriental art. The museum also features works by artists of the Pacific Northwest. The Charles and Emma Frye Art Museum in Seattle displays paintings by European and American artists. The Maryhill Museum of Art in Goldendale has an excellent collection of items of European royalty. The Pacific Science Center in Seattle has exhibits of modern science.

David R. Frazier

Universities and colleges

Washington has 21 universities and colleges that offer bachelor's or advanced degrees and are accredited by the Northwest Association of Schools and Colleges. Locations shown below refer to the schools' mailing addresses. For further information, see **Universities and colleges** (table).

Name	Location
Central Washington University	Ellensburg
City University	Bellevue
Cornish College of the Arts	Seattle
Eastern Washington University	Cheney
Evergreen State College	Olympia
Gonzaga University	Spokane
Griffin College	Seattle
Heritage College	Toppenish
Lutheran Bible Institute of Seattle	Issaquah
Northwest College of the Assemblies of God	Kirkland
Pacific Lutheran University	Tacoma
Puget Sound, University of	Tacoma
St. Martin's College	Lacey
Seattle Pacific University	Seattle
Seattle University	Seattle
Walla Walla College	College Place
Washington, University of	Seattle
Washington State University	Pullman
Western Washington University	Bellingham
Whitman College	Walla Walla
Whitworth College	Spokane

Washington State University is located in Pullman. Bryan Hall, *left,* houses the university's philosophy department and is the center of a program for international students.

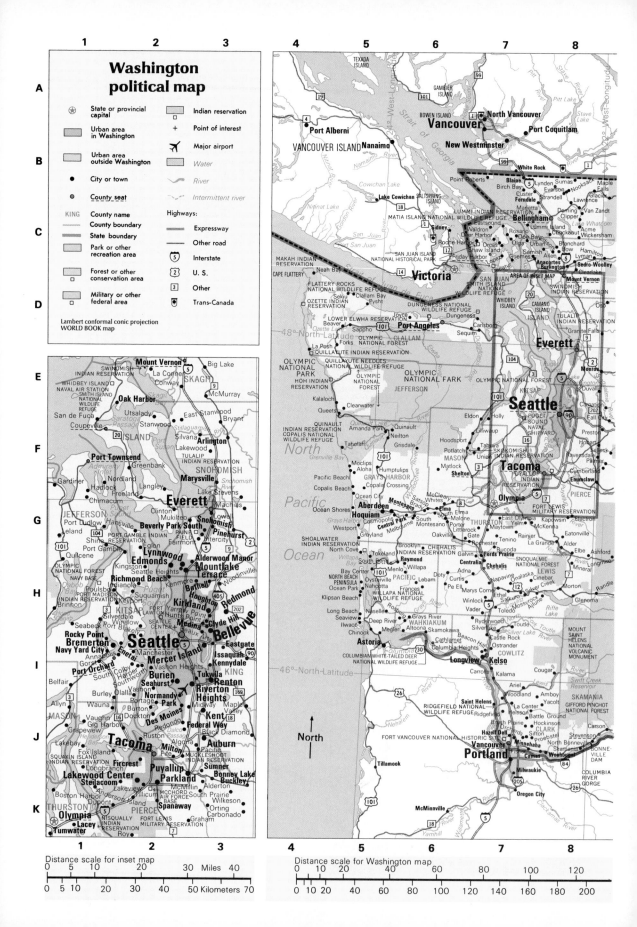

Washington political map

Legend:

- ⊛ State or provincial capital
- ▨ Urban area in Washington
- ▨ Urban area outside Washington
- ● City or town
- ◉ County seat
- KING County name
- ⸺ County boundary
- ⸺ State boundary
- ▨ Park or other recreation area
- ▨ Forest or other conservation area
- ▨ Military or other federal area
- ▨ Indian reservation
- + Point of interest
- ✈ Major airport
- ▨ Water
- ∿ River
- ⌇ Intermittent river

Highways:

- ⸺ Expressway
- ⸺ Other road
- ⑤ Interstate
- ② U.S.
- ③ Other
- ▣ Trans-Canada

Lambert conformal conic projection
WORLD BOOK map

Distance scale for inset map
0 5 10 20 30 40 50 Kilometers 70
0 5 10 20 30 Miles 40

Distance scale for Washington map
0 10 20 40 60 80 100 120 (Miles)
0 10 20 40 60 80 100 120 140 160 180 200 (Kilometers)

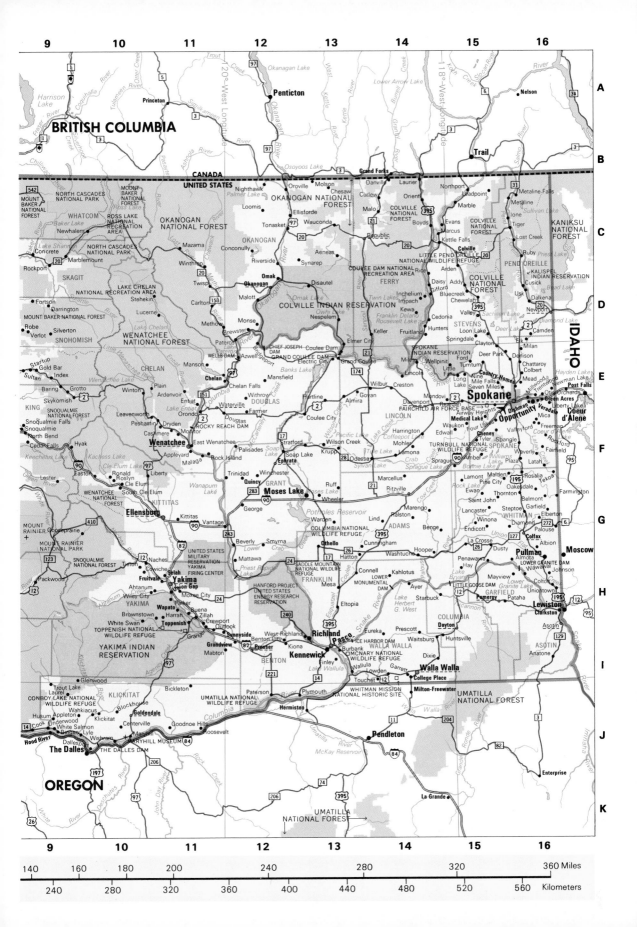

Washington map index

Metropolitan areas

- Bellingham 106,701
- Bremerton 147,152
- Olympia 124,264
- Richland-Kennewick-Pasco 144,469
- Seattle 1,607,469
- Spokane 341,835
- Tacoma 485,667
- Vancouver 192,227
- Yakima 172,508

Counties

- Adams 13,267 G 14
- Asotin 16,823 I 16
- Benton 109,444 I 12
- Chelan 45,061 D 10
- Clallam 51,648 D 6
- Clark 192,227 J 8
- Columbia 4,057 H 15
- Cowlitz 79,548 I 7
- Douglas 22,144 E 12
- Ferry 5,811 D 14
- Franklin 35,025 H 13
- Garfield 2,468 H 15
- Grant 48,522 F 12
- Grays Harbor 66,314 F 5
- Island 44,048 D 7
- Jefferson 15,965 E 6
- King 1,269,749 E 9
- Kitsap 147,152 E 7
- Kittitas 24,877 G 11
- Klickitat 15,822 I 10
- Lewis 56,025 H 8
- Lincoln 9,604 F 14
- Mason 31,184 F 6
- Okanogan 30,663 C 12
- Pacific 17,237 H 6
- Pend Oreille 8,580 C 16
- Pierce 485,667 G 8
- San Juan 7,838 D 7
- Skagit 64,138 D 9
- Skamania 7,919 I 8
- Snohomish 337,016 D 9
- Spokane 341,835 F 15
- Stevens 28,979 D 15
- Thurston 124,264 G 7
- Wahkiakum 3,832 H 6
- Walla Walla 47,435 I 14
- Whatcom 106,701 C 9
- Whitman 40,103 G 16
- Yakima 172,508 H 10

Cities and towns

- Aberdeen 18,739 G 5
- Acme C 8
- Addy D 15
- Adna H 7
- Ahtanum H 10
- Airway Heights 1,730 E 15
- Albion 631 G 16
- Alderwood, see Marietta[-Alderwood]
- Alderwood Manor 16,524 H 3
- Algona 1,467 J 3
- Allen C 8
- Allyn J 1
- Almira 330 E 13
- Altoona I 6
- Amanda Park F 5
- Amboy I 8
- Anacortes 9,013 C 7
- Anatone I 16
- Anderson Island K 1
- Appleyard F 11
- Arden C 15
- Ardenvoir E 11
- Ariel I 7
- Arlington 3,282 F 3
- Ashford G 8
- Asotin 943 °H 16
- Auburn 26,417 J 3
- Ault Field* 2,553 D 7
- Ayer H 14
- Baring E 9
- Battle Ground 2,774 J 7
- Bay Center H 5
- Beacon Hill 1,496 I 7
- Beaux Arts 328 I 3
- Beaver D 5
- Belfair I 1
- Bellevue 73,903 I 3
- Bellingham 45,794 °C 8
- Belmont G 16
- Benge G 14
- Benton City 1,980 I 12
- Beverly G 12
- Bickleton I 11
- Big Lake E 3
- Bingen 644 J 9
- Birch Bay B 7
- Black Diamond 1,170 J 3
- Blaine 2,363 B 7
- Blanchard C 8
- Bluecreek D 15
- Bonney Lake 5,328 K 3
- Boston Harbor K 1
- Bothell 7,943 H 3
- Boulevard Park* 8,382 E 9
- Bow C 8
- Boyds C 14
- Brady G 6
- Bremerton 36,208 I 1
- Brewster 1,337 D 12
- Bridgeport 1,174 E 12
- Brier* 2,915 E 8
- Brinnon H 1
- Brownstown H 10
- Brush Prairie J 7
- Bryant F 3
- Bryn Mawr* 11,754 E 9
- Buckley 3,143 K 3
- Bucoda 519 G 7
- Buena H 11
- Burbank I 13
- Burien 23,189 I 2
- Burley I 1
- Burlington 3,894 C 8
- Burton J 2
- Camas 5,681 J 8
- Carbonado 456 K 3
- Carlsborg D 7
- Carlton D 11
- Carnation 913 E 8
- Carrolls I 7
- Carson J 9
- Cascade* 16,939 E 9
- Cashmere 2,240 F 11
- Castle Rock 2,162 I 7
- Cathlamet 635 °I 6
- Centerville J 10
- Central Park 2,709 G 6
- Centralia 11,555 H 7
- Chattaroy E 16
- Chehalis 6,100 °H 7
- Chelan 2,802 E 11
- Chelan Falls E 12
- Cheney 7,630 F 15
- Chesaw B 13
- Chewelah 1,888 D 15
- Chimacum G 1
- Chinook H 5
- Clallam Bay D 5
- Clarkston 6,903 H 16
- Clayton E 15
- Cle Elum 1,773 F 10
- Clearlake C 8
- Clearwater E 5
- Clinton G 2
- Clipper C 8
- Clyde Hill 3,229 H 3
- Colfax 2,780 °G 16
- College Place 5,771 I 14
- Colton 307 H 16
- Columbia Heights 2,515 I 7
- Colville 4,510 °C 15
- Conconully 157 C 12
- Concrete 592 C 9
- Connell 1,981 H 13
- Conway E 2
- Cook J 9
- Copalis Beach G 5
- Copalis Crossing G 5
- Cosmopolis 1,575 G 5
- Cottage Lake* 4,435 E 9
- Coulee City 510 F 13
- Coulee Dam 1,412 E 13
- Country Homes E 16
- Coupeville 1,006 °F 1
- Cowiche H 10
- Creston 309 E 14
- Crewport H 11
- Cumberland F 8
- Curlew B 14
- Cusick 246 D 16
- Custer B 7
- Dalkena D 16
- Dallesport J 10
- Danville B 14
- Darrington 1,064 D 9
- Davenport 1,559 °E 14
- Dayton 2,565 °H 15
- Decatur C 7
- Deer Harbor C 7
- Deer Park 2,140 E 15
- Deming C 8
- Des Moines 7,378 J 2
- Diamond G 15
- Disautel D 13
- Dishman 10,169 E 16
- Dixie I 14
- Dockton J 2
- Doe Bay C 7
- Doty H 6
- Dryden F 11
- Dumas Bay* 14,535 E 9
- Dungeness D 7
- Dupont 559 K 1
- Duvall 729 E 8
- East Farms, see Otis Orchards [-East Farms]
- East Olympia G 7
- East Port Orchard* 4,631 F 7
- East Renton Highlands* 12,033 E 9
- East Wenatchee 1,640 F 11
- East Wenatchee Bench* 11,410 F 11
- Eastgate 8,341 I 3
- Easton F 10
- Eastsound C 7
- Eatonville 998 G 8
- Edison C 8
- Edmonds 27,679 H 2
- Edwall F 15
- Eglon G 2
- Elbe G 8
- Elberton G 16
- Electric City 927 E 13
- Elk D 16
- Ellensburg 11,752 °G 11
- Ellisforde C 12
- Elma 2,720 G 6
- Elmer City 312 E 13
- Eltopia H 13
- Endicott 290 G 15
- Enetai 2,638 I 2
- Entiat 445 E 11
- Enumclaw 5,427 F 8
- Ephrata 5,359 °F 12
- Erlands Point* 1,254 E 7
- Esperance* 11,120 D 9
- Ethel H 7
- Evans C 15
- Everett 54,413 °E 8
- Everson 898 B 8
- Ewan G 15
- Fairchild* 5,353 E 15
- Fairfield 582 F 16
- Fairmont [-Intercity] 6,997 G 3
- Fairview* 2,788 H 11
- Fairwood* 5,337 F 15
- Fall City 1,528 F 8
- Farmington 176 G 16
- Federal Way J 2
- Ferndale 3,855 C 7
- Fife 1,823 J 2
- Fircrest 5,477 J 2
- Fisher J 7
- Ford E 15
- Fords Prairie 2,582 G 7
- Forks 3,060 E 5
- Fort Lewis* 23,761 G 7
- Four Lakes F 15
- Fox Island J 1
- Frances H 6
- Freeland G 2
- Freeman F 16
- Friday Harbor 1,200 °C 7
- Fruitvale 3,967 H 11
- Galvin G 7
- Gardiner F 1
- Garfield 599 G 16
- Garrett 1,134 I 14
- Geneva* 1,423 C 8
- George 261 G 12
- Gifford D 14
- Gig Harbor 2,429 J 2
- Glacier B 8
- Glenoma H 8
- Gold Bar 794 E 9
- Goldendale 3,575 °J 10
- Gorst I 1
- Graham K 3
- Grand Coulee 1,180 E 13
- Grandview 5,615 I 12
- Granger 1,812 H 11
- Granite Falls 911 D 8
- Grapeview J 1
- Grayland G 5
- Grays River H 6
- Green Acres E 16
- Greenbank F 2
- Grisdale F 6
- Grotto E 9
- Guemes C 7
- Hadlock [-Irondale] 1,752 G 1
- Hamilton 268 C 8
- Hansville G 2
- Harper I 2
- Harrah 343 H 11
- Harrington 507 F 14
- Hartline 165 E 13
- Hatton 81 G 13
- Hay H 15
- Hazel Dell 15,386 J 7
- Heisson J 7
- Highland, see West Clarkston[-Highland]
- Hobart F 8
- Hockinson J 7
- Holly F 7
- Hoodsport F 6
- Hoquiam 9,719 G 5
- Humptulips F 5
- Hunters D 14
- Hunts Point 480 H 3
- Husum J 9
- Hyak F 9
- Ilwaco 604 H 5
- Inchelium D 14
- Index 147 E 9
- Indianola H 2
- Inglewood* 12,467 E 9
- Intercity, see Fairmount [-Intercity]
- Ione 594 C 15
- Irondale, see Hadlock [-Irondale]
- Issaquah 5,536 I 3
- Johnson H 16
- Joyce D 6
- Juanita* 17,232 E 9
- Kahlotus 203 H 14
- Kalama 1,216 I 7
- Kapowsin G 8
- Keller D 14
- Kelso 11,129 °I 7
- Kenmore 7,281 H 3
- Kennewick 34,397 I 13
- Kennydale I 3
- Kent 22,967 J 3
- Kettle Falls 1,087 C 15
- Keyport H 1
- Kingsgate* 12,652 E 9
- Kingston H 2
- Kiona I 12
- Kirkland 18,779 H 3
- Kitsap Lake* 1,260 E 7
- Kittitas 782 G 11
- Klickitat J 10
- Klipsan Beach H 5
- Krupp 83 F 13
- La Center 439 J 7
- Lacey 13,940 K 1
- La Conner 633 E 2
- La Crosse 373 G 15
- Lake Forest North* 7,995 E 9
- Lake Forest Park* 2,485 E 8
- Lake Stevens 1,660 G 3
- Lake Stickney* 6,135 D 9
- Lakebay J 1
- Lakeland North* 11,648 E 9
- Lakeland South* 5,225 E 9
- Lakes District* 54,533 F 8
- Lakeview K 2
- Lakewood F 3
- Lakewood Center K 2
- Lamont 101 F 15
- Langley 650 G 2
- La Push E 4
- Latah 155 F 16
- Lawrence C 8
- Leavenworth 1,522 F 10
- Lebam H 6
- Leland G 1
- Lester F 9
- Lexington* 1,907 I 7
- Liberty F 10
- Liberty Lake 1,599 E 16
- Lilliwaup F 7
- Lincoln E 14
- Lind 567 G 14
- Little Falls E 15
- Littlerock G 7
- Lone Oak* 1,121 I 7
- Long Beach 1,199 H 5
- Long Lake E 15
- Longbranch J 1
- Longmire G 9
- Longview 31,052 I 7
- Loomis C 12
- Loon Lake D 15
- Lopez C 7
- Lowden I 14
- Lummi Island C 7
- Lyle J 9
- Lyman 285 C 8
- Lynden 4,022 B 8
- Lynnwood 22,641 H 2
- Mabton 1,248 I 11
- Machias G 3
- Malaga F 11
- Malden 200 F 15
- Malone G 6
- Malott D 12
- Manchester I 2
- Mansfield 315 E 12
- Manson E 11
- Maple Falls B 8
- Maple Valley J 3
- Marblemount C 9
- Marcellus F 14
- Marcus 174 C 14
- Marietta [-Alderwood] 2,324 C 7
- Martha Lake* 7,022 D 9
- Marysville 5,080 F 3
- Matlock F 6
- Mattawa 299 H 12
- Mazama C 11
- McChord* 5,746 G 8
- McCleary 1,419 G 6
- McKenna G 7
- McMillin K 3
- McMurray E 3
- Mead E 16
- Medical Lake 3,600 F 15
- Medina 3,220 I 3
- Melbourne G 6
- Menlo H 6
- Mercer Island 21,522 I 3
- Mesa 278 H 13
- Metaline 190 C 16
- Metaline Falls 296 B 16
- Methow D 11
- Mica F 16
- Milan E 16
- Millwood 1,717 E 16
- Milton 3,162 J 2
- Mineral H 8
- Minnehaha J 7
- Moclips F 5
- Mohler F 14
- Molson B 13
- Monitor F 11
- Monroe 2,869 E 8
- Montesano 3,247 °G 6
- Morton 1,264 H 8
- Moses Lake 10,629 G 13
- Moses Lake North* 3,348 G 13
- Mossyrock 463 H 7
- Mount Vernon 13,009 °D 8
- Mountlake Terrace 16,534 H 2
- Moxee City 687 H 11
- Mukilteo 1,426 G 2
- Naches 644 H 10
- Nahcotta H 5
- Napavine 611 H 7
- Naselle H 5
- Navy Yard City 2,594 I 1
- Neah Bay D 4
- Neilton F 5
- Nespelem 284 D 13
- Newhalem C 10
- Newman Lake E 16
- Newport 1,665 °D 16
- Newport Hills* 12,245 E 9
- Nine Mile Falls E 15
- Nooksack 429 B 8
- Nordland F 1
- Normandy Park 4,268 I 2
- North Bend 1,701 F 9
- North Bonneville 394 J 8
- North City* 13,551 E 9
- North Cove G 5
- North Hill* 10,170 E 9
- North Marysville* 15,159 D 8
- North Selah* 1,901 H 11
- Northport 368 B 15
- Oak Harbor 12,271 E 1
- Oakesdale 444 G 16
- Oakville 537 G 6
- Ocean Beach* 2,108 I 7
- Ocean Park H 5
- Ocean Shores 1,692 G 5
- Odessa 1,009 F 14
- Okanogan 2,326 °D 12
- Olalla I 2
- Olga C 7
- Olympia 27,447 °G 7
- Omak 4,007 D 12
- Onalaska H 7
- Opportunity 21,241 E 16
- Orcas C 7
- Orchards 8,828 J 7
- Orient C 14
- Orondo E 11
- Oroville 1,483 B 12
- Orting 1,787 K 3
- Oso D 8
- Ostrander I 7
- Othello 4,454 G 13
- Otis Orchards [-East Farms] 4,597 E 16
- Outlook H 11
- Oysterville H 5
- Pacific 2,261 J 3
- Pacific Beach F 5
- Packwood H 9
- Palouse 1,005 G 16
- Parker H 11
- Parkland 23,355 K 2
- Parkwood* 4,599 E 7
- Pasco 18,425 °I 13
- Pateros 555 D 12
- Paterson I 12
- Pe Ell 617 H 6
- Peshastin F 11
- Pine City F 15
- Plaza F 16
- Plymouth I 13
- Point Roberts B 7
- Pomeroy 1,716 °H 15
- Port Angeles 17,311 °D 6
- Port Angeles East* 2,786 D 6
- Port Blakely I 2
- Port Gamble G 2
- Port Ludlow G 1
- Port Orchard 4,787 °I 1
- Port Townsend 6,067 °F 1
- Portage J 2
- Porter G 6
- Potlatch F 6
- Poulsbo 3,453 H 1
- Poverty Bay* 8,353 E 9
- Prescott 341 I 14
- Preston F 8
- Proebstel J 7
- Prosser 3,896 °I 12
- Pullman 23,579 G 16
- Puyallup 18,251 K 2
- Queets E 5
- Quilcene H 1
- Quinault F 5
- Quincy 3,525 F 12
- Rainier 891 G 7
- Ralston G 14
- Randle H 8
- Ravensdale F 8
- Raymond 2,991 H 5
- Reardan 498 E 15
- Redmond 23,318 H 3
- Redondo J 2
- Renton 30,612 I 3

Republic ....1,018.°C 13
Retsil* ....1,524..F 7
Rice ....D 14
Richland ....33,578..I 13
Richmond
　Beach ....6,700..H 2
Richmond
　Highlands* .....24,463..E 8
Ridgefield ....1,062..J 7
Ritzville ....1,800.°G 14
Riverside ....243..C 12
Riverton* ......14,182..E 8
Riverton Heights ....I 3
Robe ....D 9
Roche Harbor ....C 7
Rochester ....G 7
Rock Island .....491..F 11
Rockford ....442..F 16
Rockport ....C 9
Rocky Point ....1,495..I 1
Ronald ....F 10
Roosevelt ....J 11
Rosalia ....572..F 16
Rosario ....C 7
Rosburg ....H 6
Rose Hill* ......7,616..E 8
Roslyn ....938..F 10
Roy ....417..K 2
Royal City* .....676..G 12
Ruby ....C 16
Ruff ....G 13
Ruston ....612..J 2
Ryderwood ....H 7
St. John ....529..G 15
Salkum ....H 7
Saltwater. see
　Zenith[-Saltwater]
Samish ....C 8
San de Fuca ....F 1
Sappho ....D 5
Satsop ....G 6
Seabeck ....H 1
Seahurst ....I 2

Seattle ......493,846.°E 8
Seattle Heights ....H 2
Seaview ....H 5
Sedro-Woolley ...6,110..C 8
Sekiu ....D 5
Selah ....4,500..H 11
Selleck ....F 9
Sequim ....3,013..D 7
Shaw Island ....C 7
Shelton ....7,629.°F 7
Sheridan
　Beach* ....6,873..E 8
Shine ....G 1
Shorewood. see
　White Center
　[-Shorewood]
Sifton ....J 7
Silvana ....F 3
Silver Creek ....H 7
Silverdale ....H 1
Silverlake .....10,299..H 7
Silverton ....D 9
Skamania ....I 8
Skamokawa ....I 6
Skykomish ....209..E 9
Snohomish .....5,294..G 3
Snoqualmie ....1,370..F 9
Snoqualmie Falls ....F 9
Soap Lake .....1,196..F 12
South Bend ....1,686..H 5
South
　Broadway* ....3,500..H 11
South Cle Elum ...449..G 10
South Colby ....I 2
South Prairie ....202..K 3
South
　Wenatchee* ...1,376..F 11
Southworth ....I 2
Spanaway ......8,868..K 2
Spangle ....276..F 16
Spokane ....171,300.°E 16
Sprague ....473..F 15
Springdale ......281..D 15

Stanwood ....1,646..F 2
Starbuck ....198..H 14
Startup ....E 9
Stehekin ....D 10
Steilacoom ....4,886..K 2
Steptoe ....G 16
Stevenson .....1,172.°J 8
Stratford ....F 13
Sultan ....1,578..E 9
Sumas ....712..B 8
Sumner ....4,936..J 3
Sunnyside .....9,225..I 11
Sunnyslope* ...1,485..F 11
Suquamish .....1,498..H 2
Tacoma .....158,501.°F 8
Taholah ....F 5
Tahuya ....F 6
Tanglewilde, see
　Thompson
　Place[-Tanglewilde]
Tekoa ....854..F 16
Tenino ....1,280..G 7
Terrace
　Heights* .....3,199..H 11
Thompson Place
　[-Tanglewilde]* ..5,910..G 7
Thornton ....G 16
Tieton ....528..H 10
Tiger ....C 16
Tillicum ....K 2
Tokeland ....G 5
Toledo ....637..H 7
Tonasket ....985..C 12
Toppenish .....6,517..H 11
Touchet ....I 14
Toutle ....H 7
Town and
　Country* .....5,578..E 16
Tracyton* .....2,304..E 7
Trentwood ....E 16
Trinidad ....F 12
Trout Lake ....I 9

Tukwila ....3,578..I 3
Tumtum ....E 15
Tumwater ......6,705..K 1
Twisp ....911..D 11
Tyler ....F 15
Underwood ....J 9
Union ....F 7
Union Gap .....3,184..H 11
Union Mills* ..4,623..G 7
Uniontown ....286..H 16
University
　Place* ....20,381..F 2
Urban ....C 7
Usk ....D 16
Utsalady ....F 2
Vader ....406..H 7
Valley ....D 15
Valley
　Ridge* ......17,961..E 8
Valleyford ....F 16
Vancouver ....42,834.°J 7
Vantage ....G 11
Van Zandt ....C 8
Vashon ....I 2
Vashon Heights ......I 2
Vaughn ....J 1
Veradale ......7,256..E 16
Verlot ....D 9
Wahkiacus ....J 10
Waitsburg .....1,035..I 14
Waldron ....C 7
Walla Walla ..25,618.°I 14
Walla Walla
　East* ....3,285..I 14
Wallula ....I 13
Wapato ....3,307..H 11
Warden ....1,479..G 13
Washougal .....3,834..J 8
Washtucna ....266..G 14
Waterville ......908.°E 11
Wauconda ....C 13
Waukon ....F 15

Wauna ....J 1
Waverly ....99..F 16
Wellpinit ....E 15
Wenatchee ....17,257.°F 11
West Clarkston-
　[Highland]* ...3,683..H 16
West Federal
　Way* ....16,872..E 8
West Pasco* ...5,729..I 13
West Richland .2,938..I 13
West
　Wenatchee* ...2,187..F 11
Westport ......1,954..G 5
Wheeler ....G 13
White Center
　[-Shorewood]* .19,362..E 8
White Salmon ..1,853..J 9
White Swan ....H 10
Whites ....G 6
Wickersham ....C 8
Wilbur ....1,122..E 14
Wilkeson ....321..K 3
Willapa ....H 6
Wilson Creek ....222..F 13
Winchester ....F 12
Winlock ....1,052..H 7
Winona ....G 15
Winslow ....2,196..H 2
Winthrop ....413..C 11
Winton ....J 10
Wishram ....J 10
Withrow ....E 12
Woodinville ....H 3
Woodland ......2,341..J 7
Woodway* ....832..E 8
Yacolt ....544..J 8
Yakima ....49,826.°H 11
Yarrow Point ..1,064..H 3
Yelm ....1,294..G 7
Zenith
　[-Saltwater]* .8,982..E 8
Zillah ....1,599..H 11

*Does not appear on map; key shows general location.
°County seat.
Source: 1980 census. Places without population figures are unincorporated areas.

James P. Rowan

Tacoma, Washington's third largest city, rises behind shipyards on Puget Sound. Washington ranks as a leading shipbuilding center. Seattle and Bremerton also have major shipyards.

Washington is a paradise for people who enjoy the outdoors. It offers some of the best hunting and fishing in the nation. People who fish for sport catch more than a million salmon each year off the state's Pacific coast. Every winter and spring, skiers flock to the slopes of Mount Spokane and areas in the Cascade Range such as Crystal Mountain, Mission Ridge, Mount Baker, Mount Rainier, Snoqualmie Pass, Stevens Pass, and White Pass.

In summer, rugged mountains and wilderness areas attract hikers and mountain climbers.

Washington's many annual events include Indian festivals, flower exhibitions, sports competitions, and regional fairs. Perhaps the outstanding annual event is Seafair, held in Seattle from mid-July through early August. This show features parades, water carnivals, and boat races on Lake Washington.

Owen Blauman, Seattle Seafair

Boat race at the Seattle Seafair

Places to visit

Following are brief descriptions of some of Washington's many interesting places to visit:

Grand Coulee Dam, 92 miles (148 kilometers) west of Spokane, is the largest concrete dam in the United States (see **Grand Coulee Dam**).

Lewis and Clark Interpretive Center, near Ilwaco, features maps and paintings illustrating the Lewis and Clark expedition between Missouri and the Pacific Coast.

Maryhill Castle, in Maryhill, is an art museum in an elaborate mansion built in 1926 by multimillionaire Samuel Hill. The gray stone structure stands on a high bluff overlooking the scenic Columbia River Gorge.

Point Defiance Park, in Tacoma, has a zoo, an Oriental garden, and replicas of an old fort and a logging camp.

Rocky Reach Dam, near Wenatchee, has a museum and an underground room where visitors can watch salmon swim upstream to lay their eggs.

Seattle Center includes the Pacific Science Center from Century 21, a world's fair held in 1962. The Space Needle, a tower 607 feet (185 meters) high, is in the area. It has an observation deck. A monorail links the center and downtown Seattle.

National parks and forests. Washington has three national parks—Mount Rainier, North Cascades, and Olympic. These parks include some of the country's most scenic areas. Part of Klondike Gold Rush National Historical Park is in Washington. The other part is in Alaska. Washington has nine national forests. Seven of them lie entirely within the state. They are Oka-

nogan, Gifford Pinchot, Mount Baker, Snoqualmie, Wenatchee, Olympic, and Colville. Kaniksu National Forest is shared by Washington, Idaho, and Montana. Umatilla National Forest, in the Blue Mountains, lies in both Washington and Oregon. Several areas in Washington's national forests are set aside as national wilderness areas, to be preserved in their natural condition. For the area and chief features of each national park, see **National Park System.** See also the separate articles on the national parks.

National historic sites. Whitman Mission National Historic Site marks the spot of the Indian mission founded by Marcus Whitman and his wife in 1836. It was also the scene of the Indian massacre of 1847 in which the Whitmans and others lost their lives. The place became a national monument in 1936, and a historic site in 1963. See **Whitman Mission National Historic Site.** Fort Vancouver National Historic Site was the western headquarters of the Hudson's Bay Company from 1825 to 1849. Established in 1948 as a national monument, the area became a national historic site in 1961. Mount St. Helens National Volcanic Monument, site of a volcano that erupted in 1980, became a national monument in 1982. Ebey's Landing National Historical Reserve, on Whidbey Island, has forts built in the 1890's and 1940's.

State parks. Washington has over a hundred developed parks and historic and geologic sites under the administration of the state parks and recreation commission. The park system includes several undeveloped tracts. For information on state parks, write to Director, Washington State Parks and Recreation Commission, 7150 Cleanwater Lane, Olympia, WA 98504.

Annual events

January-May

International Boat Show in Seattle (January); Northwest Bach Festival in Spokane (January); Tacoma Dome Boat Show in Tacoma (February); Annual Gray Whale Migration in Westport and Ocean Shores (March); Daffodil Festival in Tacoma (March); Apple Blossom Festival in Wenatchee (late April and early May); Lilac Festival in Spokane (May); Rhododendron Festival in Port Townsend (late May).

June-August

Lummi Stommish Water Carnival near Bellingham (June); Outboard Hydroplane Races in Electric City (June); Toppenish Indian Pow Wow in Toppenish (July 3-4); Pacific Northwest Arts and Crafts Fair in Bellevue (July); King County Fair in Enumclaw (July); Omak Stampede and Suicide Race (August); Logger's Jubilee and Mountain Air Art Fair in Morton (August).

September-December

Ellensburg Rodeo (early September); Lake Chelan Sailing Regatta (September); Western Washington State Fair in Puyallup (September); Autumn Leaf Festival in Leavenworth (late September and early October); Yule Log Festival in Poulsbo (December).

Cindy McIntyre, West Stock

Japanese Garden at Point Defiance Park in Tacoma

Crystal Mountain ski area

Don Mason, West Stock

© Steve Solum, Bruce Coleman Inc.

Ruby Beach at Olympic National Park

Land and climate

Land regions. Washington has six main land regions: (1) the Olympic Mountains, (2) the Coast Range, (3) the Puget Sound Lowland, (4) the Cascade Mountains, (5) the Columbia Plateau, and (6) the Rocky Mountains.

The Olympic Mountains region lies in the northwest corner of the state. It is bordered by the Strait of Juan de Fuca on the north and the Pacific Ocean on the west. Most of the region lies within Olympic National Park. The rugged snow-capped Olympic Mountains are one of the wildest parts of the United States. Some areas of these mountains have never been explored. The chief industry in the region is logging in the foothills of the mountains.

The Coast Range region covers the southwestern corner of Washington and extends southward into Oregon. The Willapa Hills, which overlook Willapa Bay, are the chief land feature of this region in Washington. Logging and lumber milling are the region's most important economic activities. Many people also work in fishing and dairying.

The Puget Sound Lowland region is wedged between the Olympic Mountains on the west and the Cascade Mountains on the east. It extends northward into British Columbia and southward into Oregon. The valley of the Chehalis River is also part of the region. The valley extends westward to the Pacific Ocean between the Willapa Hills on the south and the Olympic Mountains on the north.

Puget Sound, a huge bay almost completely enclosed by land, covers the north-central part of the lowland region. The Strait of Juan de Fuca connects Puget Sound with the Pacific Ocean. Narrow, twisting branches of the sound extend far inland. These branches reach south to the cities of Tacoma and Olympia.

About three-fourths of Washington's people live on the lowland plain. The plain has about three-fifths of the state's cities, and most of its factories and sawmills.

The Cascade Mountains region, east of the Puget Sound Lowland, separates the western section of the state from the eastern section. The Cascade Mountains of Washington are part of a long mountain range that stretches southward from British Columbia into northern California. The peaks of several volcanoes rise above the main chain of mountains. Most of these volcanoes

are inactive. However, Mount St. Helens in southwestern Washington erupted in 1980. Its elevation is 8,364 feet (2,549 meters).

Mount Rainier, the highest point in the state and one of the highest mountains in the United States, is a long-quiet volcano. It rises 14,410 feet (4,392 meters). Other high peaks include Mount Adams (12,307 feet, or 3,751 meters); Mount Baker (10,778 feet, or 3,285 meters); and Glacier Peak (10,541 feet, or 3,213 meters). All these mountains have glaciers and permanent snowfields on their upper slopes. Farther down the slopes, and on the lower mountains, are magnificent forests. Tall Douglas fir trees grow on the rainy western slopes. Most of the forested area lies within national forests.

The Columbia Plateau covers most of central and southeastern Washington. This great basin lies from 500 to 2,000 feet (150 to 610 meters) or more above sea level, and is surrounded by a rim of higher lands. It makes up part of the largest lava plateau in the world. The basin was formed by lava which flowed out of cracks in the earth's crust thousands of years ago.

Interesting features of the Columbia Plateau are its *coulees* and *scablands,* especially in the Big Bend region. This area lies south and east of a great bend in the Columbia River. Coulees are trenchlike dry canyons with steep walls. They were formed thousands of years ago, when glaciers blocked the Columbia River. Rushing streams of river water and melting ice cut new channels across the lava plateau. After the glacial period ended,

Land regions of Washington

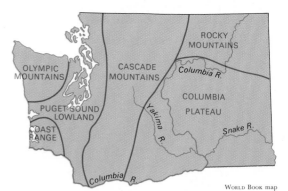

WORLD BOOK map

Map index

Badger Mountain	B	6	Frenchman Hills	C	6	Lincoln Plateau	C	5	Olympic Nat'l. Park		
Bald Butte	C	9	Glacier Peak	A	5	Lincoln Rock	B	6	Ocean Strip	B	2
Banks Lake	B	7	Gorge High Dam	A	5	Little Spokane R.	B	9	Omak Lake	A	7
Bauer Coulee	B	8	Grand Coulee Dam	B	8	Lost Horse Plateau	C		Ozette Lake	A	2
Blue Mts.	C	9	Grays Harbor	C	2	Mayfield Res.	C	4	Palouse R.	C	8
Bonneville Dam	D	5	Green Lookout			McNary Dam	D	7	Pend Oreille R.	A	9
Boundary Bay	A	4	Mountain	D	4	Methow R.	A	6	Pt. Brown	C	2
Cape			Green R.	B	4	Michigan Prairie	C	8	Potholes Res.	B	7
Disappointment	C	2	Hoh R.	B	2	Moses Coulee	B	6	Priest Rapids Res.	C	7
Cape Elizabeth	B	2	Hood Canal	B	3	Moses Lake	B	7	Puget Sound	B	4
Cape Flattery	A	2	Horse Heaven Hills	C	6	Mt. Adams	C	5	Puyallup R.	B	4
Cape Shoalwater	C	2	Howard Hanson Res.	B	5	Mt. Baker	A	5	Quinault R.	B	2
Cascade Range	C	4	Huckleberry Mts.	A	8	Mt. Logan	A	6	Rattlesnake Flat	C	8
Cascade Tunnel	B	5	Ice Harbor Dam	C	8	Mt. Olympus	B	3	Rattlesnake Hills	C	6
Cedar R.	B	4	Indian Nation	C	6	Mt. Rainier (highest			Rimrock Lake	C	5
Cedar Valley	C	5	Jack Mountain	A	6	point in			Rock Island Dam	B	6
Chehalis R.	C	3	Kamiak Butte	C	9	Washington)	C	5	Rock Creek	B	9
Chelan Mts.	A	6	Kettle R.	A	8	Mt. Rainier Nat'l			Rocky Coulee	B	7
Chief Joseph Dam	B	7	Kettle River Range	A	8	Park	C	5	Rocky Reach Dam	B	6
Clearwater R.	C	10	Kittitas Valley	B	6	Mt. St. Helens	C	4	Ross Dam	A	5
Columbia Basin	B	7	Klickitat R.	C	5	Mt. Spokane	B	9	Rufus Woods Lake	A	7
Columbia R.	D	6	Lake Chelan	A	6	Mud Mountain Lake	B	5	Saddle Mts.	C	6
Colville R.	A	9	Lake Creek	B	8	Naches R.	B	5	Sanpoil R.	A	8
Cowlitz R.	C	4	Lake Cushman	B	3	Nisqually R.	B	4	Sauk R.	A	5
Crab Creek	B	8	Lake Entiat	A	6	North Cascades Nat'l.			Sawtooth Ridge	A	6
Diablo Dam	A	5	Lake Quinault	B	3	Park	A	5	Simcoe Mts.	C	6
Elwha R.	B	3	Lake Shannon	A	5	Okanogan Range	A	7	Skagit R.	A	5
Entiat Mts.	A	6	Lake Whatcom	A	4	Okanogan R.	A	7	Skykomish R.	B	5
Esquatzel Coulee	C	7	Leadbetter Pt.	C	2	Olympic Mts.	B	2	Snake R.	C	8
Franklin D. Roosevelt			Lenore Lake	B	7	Olympic Nat'l. Park	B	3	Snoqualmie Pass	B	5
Lake	A	8	Lewis R.	D	4				Snow Peak	A	8

Soleduck R.	B	2
South Fork Res.	B	5
Spokane R.	B	8
Sprague Lake	B	8
Stillaguamish R.	A	4
Swift Res.	C	4
Tekoa Mountain	B	9
Tieton R.	C	5
Tiffany Mountain	A	7
Toppenish Ridge	C	6
Touchet R.	C	8
Toutle R.	C	4
Tucannon Canyon	C	9
Union Flat Creek	C	9
Upper Baker Dam	A	5
Walla Walla R.	C	8
Walville Peak	C	3
Wanapum Res.	B	7
Wenatchee Mts.	B	5
Wenatchee R.	B	6
West Fork Methow R.	A	6
White Pass	C	5
White R.	B	5
White Salmon R.	C	5
Willapa Bay	C	2
Willapa Hills	C	3
Windy Peak	A	7
Wynoochee R.	B	3
Yakima Ridge	C	6
Yakima R.	C	6
Yakima Valley	C	6

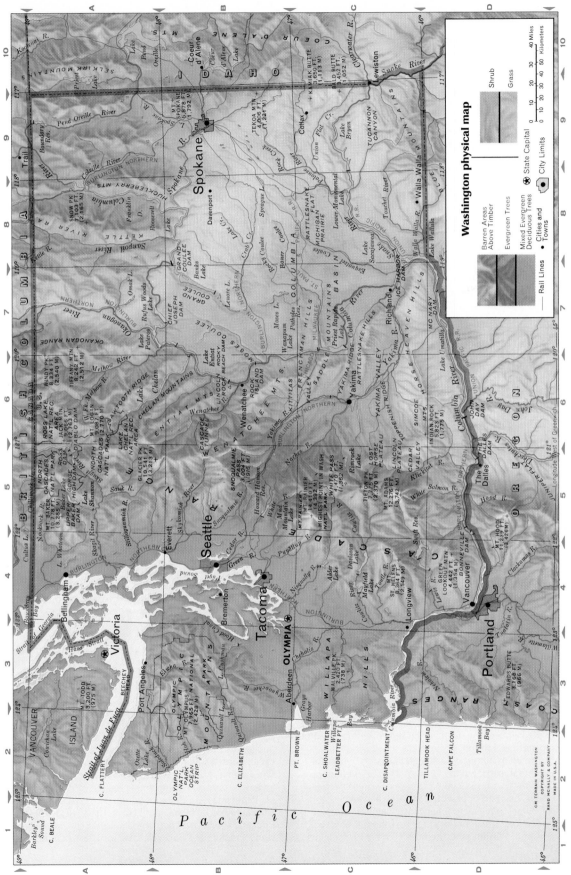

Washington physical map

State Capital

⊛ City Limits

● Cities and Towns

— Rail Lines

Barren Areas Above Timber

Evergreen Trees

Mixed Evergreen Deciduous Trees

Shrub

Grass

0   10   20   30   40 Miles
0 10 20 30 40 50 Kilometers

Specially created for *The World Book Encyclopedia* by Rand McNally and World Book editors

Doug Wilson, Black Star

Washington apples are famous throughout the United States. The state is the nation's leading producer of apples. Most are grown in the irrigated valleys of central Washington.

the Columbia settled into its present course. The other streams dried up, leaving empty canyons. Grand Coulee and Moses Coulee are the chief dry canyons. Scablands are areas where patches of hard lava rock lie on the surface of the plateau.

The Wenatchee, Yakima, Snake, Walla Walla, and other irrigated river valleys in the Columbia Plateau region contain fertile cropland. Much of the desert-like Columbia Basin is good for growing crops when the land is irrigated. The Yakima Valley in south-central Washington is one of the most productive farm areas in the nation. Farmers there raise beef and dairy cattle, and grow large crops of hops, potatoes, and orchard fruits.

Another important part of the Columbia Plateau is the Palouse country in the southeast. Much of Washington's valuable wheat crop is grown on the gently rolling hills of the Palouse. The deep, fertile soils of this region hold moisture and permit dry farming.

The Blue Mountains in the southeastern corner of Washington extend into Oregon. They are neither as high nor as rugged as the Cascades. Farmers grow grains, hay, and other crops in the larger valleys, and the slopes serve as summer pastures for livestock.

The Rocky Mountains cut across the northeastern corner of Washington. The branch of the Rockies in

Washington is also called the Columbia Mountains. These mountains consist of several ridges with valleys in between. The Columbia River and its branch, the Okanogan, are the main rivers in the region. Minerals found in this area include clay, copper, gold, lead, limestone, magnesite, silver, and zinc.

Coastline. Washington's general coastline measures 157 miles (253 kilometers). Its *tidal shoreline* measures 3,026 miles (4,870 kilometers). This measurement includes the shoreline along the Strait of Juan de Fuca, along Puget Sound, and around the islands in Puget Sound. These islands include Bainbridge, Camano, Fidalgo, Vashon, Whidbey, and the more than 170 islands of the San Juan group. Puget Sound has many good protected harbors, but other parts of Washington's coast have few natural ports. The lack of other ports makes Puget Sound's harbors highly valuable.

Rivers, waterfalls, and lakes. The mighty Columbia River, one of the longest rivers in the United States, flows through Washington for more than 700 miles (1,100 kilometers). It enters the state at the eastern end of the border with British Columbia. Then it makes a giant southward curve through central Washington. At the Washington-Oregon border it makes a sharp turn to the west and flows to the Pacific Ocean. The river forms most of the boundary between the two states. The Columbia drains more than half of Washington. Many dams on the Columbia and its tributaries control floods and provide water for irrigation and power. The Snake River, which flows into the Columbia in south-central Washington, is the second longest river in the state. Other tributaries of the Columbia River in eastern and central Washington include the Colville, Methow, Okanogan, Pend Oreille, Sanpoil, Spokane, Wenatchee, and Yakima rivers.

Many rivers of western Washington, including the Skagit, Skykomish, and Puyallup, flow from the mountains into Puget Sound. These rivers furnish water for many cities, and provide power for industry. Some of them teem with salmon and other kinds of fishes that travel upstream to lay their eggs. Logging companies use the rivers to float logs to sawmills. Other important rivers include the Chehalis, which flows into the Pacific Ocean at Grays Harbor, and the Cowlitz, which flows into the Columbia River near Longview. Parts of many rivers in western Washington are named for Indian tribes that dominated those areas during the years of white settlement.

Many of the state's rivers break into falls and rapids in mountainous areas. The chief waterfalls include Cascade, Fairy, Horseshoe, Klickitat, Ladder Creek, Metaline, Nooksack, Palouse, Rainbow, Snoqualmie, Spokane, and White River.

A number of lakes were formed around Puget Sound when glaciers scooped out the land and water filled the hollow places. Some were formed when soil and rock pushed by the glaciers dammed river valleys. The largest and best known of these glacial lakes are Washington, Sammamish, and Whatcom. Other fresh-water lakes include Ozette, Crescent, and Quinault, all on the Olympic Peninsula west of Puget Sound. The Cascade Mountains area has many beautiful lakes. The largest is Lake Chelan, 51 miles (82 kilometers) long, on the eastern slope. Franklin D. Roosevelt Lake, formed by Grand Coulee Dam, covers 130 square miles (337 square kilometers) and is the state's largest lake.

Plant and animal life. Forests cover more than half of Washington. In the western part of the state, important softwood trees include the Douglas-fir, Sitka spruce, western hemlock, and western redcedar. In the eastern section, softwoods include the Douglas-fir, lodgepole pine, ponderosa (western yellow) pine, and western larch. Common hardwoods include alder, aspen, cottonwood, and maple. Many kinds of plants grow in Washington because of the great variety of climates and elevations. Rare wild flowers bloom in mountain meadows. Colorful lupine, brown-eyed Susan, and goldenrod grow in fields and along roads. Flowering plants such as the western rhododendron and the western dogwood brighten the forests and hillsides.

Game animals found in Washington include bears and four kinds of deer—elks, Columbian black-tailed deer, mule deer, and western white-tailed deer. Washington also has many small fur-bearing animals, such as beavers, martens, minks, muskrats, and western bobcats. The state's game birds include pheasants, quail, ruffed grouse, sage grouse, wild ducks, and wild geese.

Fishes in Washington's many freshwater rivers and lakes include grayling, cutthroat trout, rainbow trout, steelhead trout, and whitefish. Huge sturgeon have been caught in the Columbia and Snake rivers. Saltwater fishes include cod, flounder, halibut, and salmon. Crabs, oysters, and several kinds of clams live in the coastal waters.

Climate. Western Washington has a milder climate than any other region in the United States that is as far north. Westerly winds from the Pacific Ocean help keep the summers pleasantly cool and the winters relatively warm. Seattle's temperature averages about 66° F. (19° C) in July and 41° F. (5° C) in January.

Eastern Washington has warmer summers and colder winters than western Washington. Spokane, near the Idaho border, has an average temperature of 70° F. (21° C) in July and 25° F. (−4° C) in January.

The state's highest temperature, 118° F. (48° C), occurred in Grant County on July 24, 1928, and at Ice Harbor Dam in southeastern Washington on Aug. 5, 1961. The lowest, −48° F. (−44° C), occurred at Mazama and at Winthrop in the northeast on Dec. 30, 1968.

Moist winds from the Pacific Ocean bring much rain to western Washington. By the time the winds reach eastern Washington, they have lost much moisture. As a result, the east has a much drier climate than the west. *Precipitation* (rain, melted snow, and other forms of moisture) averages over 135 inches (343 centimeters) a year in parts of the Olympic Peninsula. But Washington's central plateau receives only 6 inches (15 centimeters). Much of this area is semidesert.

Snowfall in Washington averages about 5 inches (13 centimeters) a year along the coast. Mount Rainier receives 50 to 75 inches (130 to 191 centimeters) on its lower slopes and over 500 inches (1,300 centimeters) on its higher slopes. In 1970-1971, Paradise Ranger Station on Mount Rainier recorded the nation's heaviest snowfall for one winter—1,027 inches (2,609 centimeters).

Average monthly weather

	Seattle						Spokane				
	Temperatures				Days of rain or snow		Temperatures				Days of rain or snow
	F°		C°				F°		C°		
	High	Low	High	Low			High	Low	High	Low	
Jan.	43	31	6	−1	19	Jan.	30	20	−1	−7	17
Feb.	48	34	9	1	16	Feb.	36	23	2	−5	12
Mar.	52	37	11	3	17	Mar.	46	30	8	−1	13
Apr.	58	40	14	4	13	Apr.	56	37	13	3	7
May	65	45	18	7	10	May	66	44	19	7	9
June	70	50	21	10	11	June	72	51	22	11	8
July	75	53	24	12	6	July	82	57	28	14	4
Aug.	74	53	23	12	6	Aug.	81	55	27	13	4
Sept.	68	49	20	9	8	Sept.	71	48	22	9	5
Oct.	59	44	15	7	16	Oct.	58	39	14	4	10
Nov.	50	38	10	3	18	Nov.	42	30	6	−1	12
Dec.	45	34	7	1	20	Dec.	34	24	1	−4	16

Average January temperatures

Winds from the Pacific Ocean keep western Washington's winters relatively warm. Eastern Washington is the coldest.

Average July temperatures

The eastern part of the state has the warmest summers. Ocean winds keep the coast pleasantly mild in summertime.

Average yearly precipitation

Washington has wide variations in precipitation. The west has a rainy climate. The central area is the driest.

WORLD BOOK maps

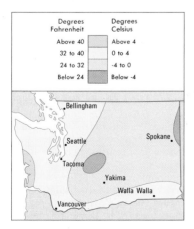

Degrees Fahrenheit	Degrees Celsius
Above 40	Above 4
32 to 40	0 to 4
24 to 32	-4 to 0
Below 24	Below -4

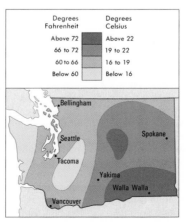

Degrees Fahrenheit	Degrees Celsius
Above 72	Above 22
66 to 72	19 to 22
60 to 66	16 to 19
Below 60	Below 16

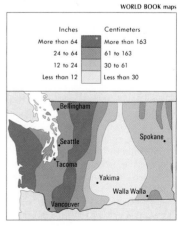

Inches	Centimeters
More than 64	More than 163
24 to 64	61 to 163
12 to 24	30 to 61
Less than 12	Less than 30

Service industries, taken together, make up almost three-fourths of Washington's *gross state product*—the total value of all goods and services produced in a state in a year. Wholesale and retail trade is the leading economic activity in Washington. The state is closer to Asian ports than most other parts of the country, so foreign trade is especially important. The manufacture of aircraft and the processing of farm and forest products are also major parts of the state's economy.

Natural resources. Washington's many natural resources include a plentiful water supply, large timber reserves, and fertile soils.

Water is one of the state's most important resources. Melted snow from the mountains feeds the rivers of western Washington and provides water for industry, electric power, irrigation, and home use. The Columbia River and its tributaries are valuable sources of water in central and eastern Washington. Inlets and bays in the Puget Sound region and along the coast encourage shipping, commercial fishing, and pleasure boating.

Forests cover about 23 million acres (9.3 million hectares) in Washington. About 18 million acres (7.3 million hectares) are of commercial value. In the west, where the rainfall is heaviest, the western hemlock is the leading timber tree. Douglas-fir, Sitka spruce, and western redcedar are also common. The Douglas-fir is the chief timber tree in the drier eastern section. Ponderosa pine, western larch, and lodgepole pine also grow there. The eastern forests lie chiefly along the slopes of the Cascades, in the northeastern highlands, and in the Blue Mountains. The most common Washington hardwoods include alder, aspen, cottonwood, and maple.

The state government, the U.S. government, and many private companies work to conserve Washington's valuable timber resources. They use harvesting methods that leave enough trees for natural reseeding. They also grow seedlings in tree nurseries for use in reforestation projects. Tree seeds are scattered from helicopters in areas that are difficult to reach by land. Helicopters and small airplanes are also used to spray insecticides on forests.

Soils. Washington's best soils for agriculture are the silts and sands of the river valleys and of the irrigated dry lands east of the Cascades. The soils of the Palouse region in southeastern Washington, especially in Whitman County, were built up from fine materials carried by winds from the west. The Puget Sound area and most of the high mountain areas have rocky soils.

Minerals. Washington has the only large coal deposits on the Pacific Coast. The largest coal fields lie in western Washington, especially in Lewis County. Magnesite deposits occur near Chewelah. Gold deposits are found on the eastern slopes of the Cascades and in the Okanogan Mountains. Lead and zinc occur mainly in northeastern Washington. Clay, limestone, and sand and gravel occur in many areas. The state also has deposits of barite, copper, diatomite, gypsum, olivine, peat, pumice, silver, soapstone, talc, and tungsten.

Service industries account for 73 per cent of the gross state product of Washington. Most of these industries are concentrated in the state's nine metropolitan areas.

Wholesale and retail trade is Washington's leading economic activity in terms of the gross state product.

Production and workers by economic activities

Economic activities	Per cent of GSP* produced	Employed workers	
		Number of persons	Per cent of total
Wholesale & retail trade	19	436,500	24
Manufacturing	17	305,000	17
Finance, insurance, & real estate	16	104,900	6
Community, social, & personal services	15	391,000	21
Government	15	348,900	19
Transportation, communication, & utilities	8	96,200	5
Construction	6	84,500	5
Agriculture	4	64,100	3
Mining	†	2,900	†
Total	100	1,834,000	100

*GSP = gross state product, the total value of goods and services produced in a year.
†Less than one-half of 1 per cent.
Figures are for 1986.
Sources: *World Book* estimates based on data from U.S. Bureau of Economic Analysis, U.S. Bureau of Labor Statistics, and U.S. Department of Agriculture.

This industry also is the state's leading employer. The wholesale trade of automobiles, chemicals, groceries, and forest products is especially important. Much of the wholesale trade involves goods shipped through ports along Puget Sound. Univar, one of the world's major chemical wholesalers, is headquartered in Seattle. Major types of retail establishments include food stores, discount stores, and restaurants. Seattle is also the home of Nordstrom, a large retail clothing company.

Finance, insurance, and real estate form the state's second most important service industry in terms of the gross state product. Seattle is the state's top financial center. The city is the home of a major banking company, Washington Mutual Savings, and a major insurance firm, Safeco. Real estate is an important part of the economy because of the large sums of money involved in the buying and selling of homes and other property.

Next in importance among the state's service industries are (1) community, social, and personal services, and (2) government. Community, social, and personal services consist of a variety of businesses, including doctors' offices and private hospitals, computer programming and engineering companies, law firms, and repair shops. The Seattle-Tacoma area has many companies that specialize in programming computer software. Private health care is one of the fastest-growing businesses.

Government services include public schools and hospitals, and military bases. Fort Lewis, the largest U.S. Army post on the Pacific Coast, is located between Olympia and Tacoma. The U.S. Air Force operates a missile base near Spokane, and the U.S. Department of Energy runs the Hanford Site, a nuclear energy center near Richland. Washington's public school system employs many people. State government offices are based in Olympia, the state capital.

Transportation, communication, and utilities rank last among the state's service industries. Two major U.S. transportation companies, Alaska Air Group and Airborne Freight, are headquartered in Seattle. Telephone companies are the most important part of the communications sector. More information about transportation and communication appears later in this section.

Manufacturing in Washington accounts for 17 per cent of the gross state product. Products manufactured in the state have a *value added by manufacture* of about $16 billion a year. Value added by manufacture represents the increase in value of raw materials after they become finished products.

Transportation equipment is Washington's leading product in terms of value added by manufacture. Washington is a leading center of the aircraft and space industry. The Boeing Company, with headquarters in Seattle and plants in Auburn, Kent, Renton, Spokane, and near Everett, leads the nation in producing commercial airliners. It employs about 100,000 workers in Washington—more than any other manufacturer in the state.

Washington is also a leading shipbuilding center. It has major shipyards at Bremerton, Seattle, and Tacoma. The Puget Sound Naval Shipyard at Bremerton is one of the largest naval shipyards on the Pacific Coast.

Food products rank second in value among Washington manufacturers. Food-processing activities include milling flour; potato processing; packing fish and meats; canning, freezing, and preserving fruits, vegetables, and berries; and producing butter, cheese, milk, wine, breakfast foods, and bakery goods.

Next in importance among Washington's manufactured goods are paper products and wood products. Weyerhaeuser, a company that ranks among the leading makers of paper and wood products, is headquartered in Tacoma. Several other large forest products companies have operations in Washington, and many areas in the western part of the state have factories that make paper and wood products.

Other products manufactured in Washington, in order of value, include chemicals, machinery, printed materials, and primary metals. Major kinds of machinery are computers and construction equipment. Washington leads the states in aluminum production.

Agriculture accounts for 4 per cent of Washington's gross state product. Washington has about 38,000 farms. They average about 420 acres (170 hectares) in size.

Farmers produce good crops both by dry farming methods and by irrigation. The chief irrigated regions are in the Columbia Basin and in the valleys of the Okanogan, Snake, Spokane, Walla Walla, Wenatchee, and Yakima rivers. The state has about 13,000 irrigated farms.

Timber is the most valuable agricultural product in Washington. The annual timber harvest in Washington is larger than that of any other state except Oregon. Douglas-fir and western hemlock are the state's most valuable timber trees.

Wheat is Washington's most valuable crop. Farmers in eastern Washington raise spring and winter wheat. Washington leads the nation in the production of hops, used in making beer. The state ranks high in the production of potatoes, grown mainly in Grant, Yakima, and other counties of south-central Washington. Washington also ranks among the leading producers of asparagus, carrots, and green peas, and of barley and other grains. It also produces dry beans, dry peas, onions, sweet corn, and hay.

Washington grows more apples than any other state. People throughout the country enjoy such famous kinds of Washington apples as the Red Delicious and Golden Delicious. Washington is a top cherry-producing state. The state also ranks high in the production of apricots, berries, grapes, pears, and plums and prunes. Most fruit is grown in central Washington's irrigated valleys.

Flower bulbs are also an important Washington crop. The state is one of the world's chief producers of iris, tulip, and daffodil bulbs. Washington growers also produce alfalfa seed, grass seed, and mint.

Livestock and livestock products account for about a third of Washington's income from farm products. Milk and beef cattle are by far the most important livestock products in Washington. Most of the dairy farms are in the western part of the state. Beef cattle are raised chiefly on ranches in eastern Washington. The state's

Farm, mineral, and forest products

This map shows where the state's leading farm, mineral, and forest products are produced. The major urban areas (shown on the map in red) are the state's important manufacturing centers.

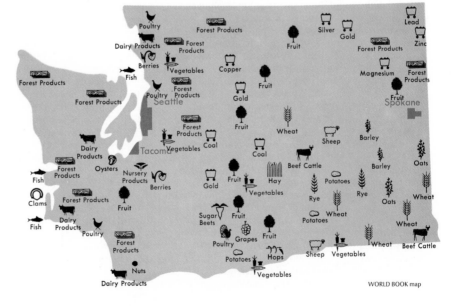

WORLD BOOK map

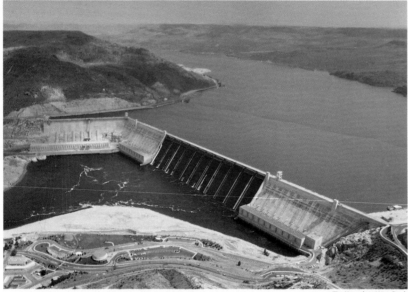

Grand Coulee Dam, the largest concrete dam in the United States, lies on the Columbia River in northeastern Washington. The dam has three power plants and is one of the world's greatest sources of water power.

© Tim Heneghan, West Stock

other livestock products include eggs and *broilers* (chickens between 5 and 12 weeks old).

Mining contributes less than 1 per cent of Washington's gross state product. The state's leading mineral products are coal, gold, magnesium, and sand and gravel. Coal mines lie south of Olympia. Chelan and Ferry counties have gold mines. Magnesium is produced in Stevens County. Sand and gravel are produced near the largest cities. Washington's other mineral products include clays, crushed stone, gypsum, and silver.

Fishing. Washington has an annual fish catch valued at about $130 million. The state has won fame for its seafoods, especially chinook and sockeye salmon. The Washington fish catch also includes chum, coho, and pink salmon; clams; cod; crabs; flounder; halibut; herring; oysters; rockfish; shrimp; steelhead trout; and tuna. Seattle ranks as the chief U.S. market for halibut and salmon caught in Alaskan and Canadian waters.

Electric power. Washington has more potential water power than any other state. It has developed only about half of its potential water power. But it leads the states in hydroelectric power production.

Grand Coulee Dam, the largest concrete dam in the world, is also one of the world's greatest sources of water power. Other large dams on the Columbia River include Bonneville, Chief Joseph, John Day, McNary, Priest Rapids, Rock Island, Rocky Reach, The Dalles, and Wanapum. There are also many dams on the Snake River. Power-producing dams on smaller rivers include Diablo and Ross, both on the Upper Skagit; Alder, on the Nisqually; and Mossyrock, on the Cowlitz. Washington receives about 85 per cent of its power from hydroelectric plants. The rest of the power comes from nuclear plants and plants that burn coal.

Transportation facilities in Washington help link the United States with Asia and Western Canada. They also provide a means for shipping the state's goods to major markets in other states, which lie far away.

The Seattle-Tacoma International Airport is one of the

world's busiest airports. Spokane has the state's second busiest airport.

About 15 rail lines provide freight service in Washington. Passenger trains serve 13 Washington cities. In 1883, the Northern Pacific line reached Washington, and in 1887 it was extended across the Cascade Mountains to Tacoma. The Cascade Tunnel, 7.79 miles (12.54 kilometers) long, was completed in 1929. It is the longest railroad tunnel in the Western Hemisphere.

Roads and highways extend for about 86,000 miles (138,000 kilometers) throughout Washington. About three-fourths are surfaced. Two floating concrete pontoon bridges cross Seattle's Lake Washington. The longest one has a floating portion that is 7,518 feet (2,291 meters) long. The structure is the longest concrete pontoon bridge in the United States. The Tacoma Narrows Bridge, one of the world's longest suspension bridges, crosses a part of Puget Sound.

Anacortes, Seattle, Tacoma, and several other Puget Sound cities are important seaports. Oceangoing ships enter Puget Sound through the Strait of Juan de Fuca. They bring products from Asia, South America, and other parts of the world. Longview and Vancouver on the Columbia River and Grays Harbor on the Pacific Ocean are also major ports. The Port of Seattle and the Port of Tacoma are growing rapidly as *container ports.* These ports service *container ships*—ships that carry goods in metal containers the size of railroad cars.

An artificial waterway, the Lake Washington Ship Canal, cuts across Seattle. It connects Lake Washington and Lake Union with Puget Sound. The Seattle fishing fleet, many pleasure boats, and some ocean vessels travel up the canal to landlocked harbors. An extensive, state-owned ferry system links the San Juan Islands and the mainland. Privately owned ferries link Seattle to cities in British Columbia.

Communication. Washington's first newspaper, the *Columbian,* began in Olympia in 1852. Today, Washington has about 145 newspapers, including about 25 dailies. Washington newspapers with the largest circulations are the *Seattle Post-Intelligencer,* the *Seattle Times,* the *Spokane Daily Chronicle, The* (Spokane) *SpokesmanReview,* and the *Tacoma News-Tribune.* Washington publishers also issue about 130 periodicals.

Washington's first commercial radio broadcast was made from Everett in 1920 by station KFBL (now KRKO). KING-TV, the state's first television station, began operating in Seattle in 1948. Today, the state has about 170 radio stations and about 20 TV stations.

Government

Constitution. Washington is governed under its original Constitution, adopted in 1889. The Constitution has been amended more than 75 times. Amendments to the Constitution may be proposed by the state Legislature, or by a constitutional convention called by a majority of the legislators with the approval of a majority of the voters. All amendments must be approved by two-thirds of the legislators in both houses, and then by a majority of the voters in a statewide election.

Executive. The governor of Washington serves a four-year term and may be reelected an unlimited number of times. The governor has the power to appoint more than 350 lesser state officials. The governor may also fill vacancies that occur in elective executive offices and among the superior and Supreme Court judges. The governor may veto bills that have been passed by the Legislature. Washington's governor also has the power to veto individual items in any bill without killing the whole bill.

Other top state officials are the lieutenant governor, secretary of state, treasurer, auditor, attorney general, superintendent of public instruction, commissioner of public lands, and insurance commissioner. They serve four-year terms, and may be reelected an unlimited number of times. The superintendent of public instruction is elected by *nonpartisan* (no-party) ballot.

Legislature consists of a 49-member Senate and a 98-member House of Representatives. By law, the House of Representatives cannot have less than 63 members or more than 99. The number of senators cannot be more than one-half or less than one-third of the number of representatives. The state has 49 legislative districts. Voters in each district elect one senator and two representatives. Senators serve four-year terms, and representatives serve two-year terms. Regular legislative sessions begin on the second Monday in January each year. The law limits these sessions to 60 days in even-numbered years and 105 days in odd-numbered years. The governor may call special sessions.

In June 1964, the Supreme Court of the United States ruled that representation in both houses of a state's Legislature must be apportioned on the basis of equal population in all voting districts. In July, a federal court ordered the Legislature to reapportion itself. It did so in 1965. In early 1972, state legislators failed to agree on a reapportionment plan for the 1970's. Later that year, a federal court redrew the districts. The districts were reapportioned by the Legislature again in 1981.

Courts. The highest court in Washington is the state Supreme Court. It has nine judges elected to six-year terms. The voters elect three Supreme Court judges in each general election, every two years. The judge with the shortest remaining term serves as chief justice. If two or more judges have equal terms remaining, the other judges decide which one will be chief justice. The next highest court is the state court of appeals. It has 12 justices elected to six-year terms. Other Washington courts include district superior courts, headed by one or more judges elected for four years, and justice-of-the-peace courts, with justices elected for four years.

Local government. A 1948 amendment to the Washington Constitution gave counties the right to choose their own form of county government. In most of Washington's 39 counties, a three-member board of commissioners has both executive and lawmaking powers. The commissioners are elected to four-year terms. Other county officials include the prosecuting attorney, superintendent of schools, sheriff, clerk, and treasurer. A county may also have an auditor, assessor, coroner, health officer, relief administrator, and other officials.

Washington has 266 incorporated cities and towns. The state Constitution provides that any city with 20,000 or more residents may have *home rule.* That is, it may choose its own form of local government. Ten Washington cities have home rule. Some have a council-manager form of government, some a commission form, and some a mayor-council form. Most smaller cities are run by a mayor and a city council.

Revenue. The state government receives about 70 per cent of its *general revenue* (income) from state taxes. Almost all the rest comes from federal grants and other U.S. government programs. Washington's main source of tax revenue is a general retail sales tax. Retail sales taxes total about 42 per cent of state taxes. The state also receives much of its revenue from excise taxes, such as those on alcoholic beverages, motor fuels, and tobacco. Washington also has taxes on public utilities and

The governors of Washington

	Party	Term
Elisha P. Ferry	Republican	1889-1893
John Harte McGraw	Republican	1893-1897
John Rankin Rogers	Democratic-Populist	1897-1901
Henry McBride	Republican	1901-1905
Albert Edward Mead	Republican	1905-1909
Samuel G. Cosgrove	Republican	1909
Marion E. Hay	Republican	1909-1913
Ernest Lister	Democratic	1913-1919
Louis Folwell Hart	Republican	1919-1925
Roland H. Hartley	Republican	1925-1933
Clarence D. Martin	Democratic	1933-1941
Arthur B. Langlie	Republican	1941-1945
Monrad C. Wallgren	Democratic	1945-1949
Arthur B. Langlie	Republican	1949-1957
Albert D. Rossellini	Democratic	1957-1965
Daniel J. Evans	Republican	1965-1977
Dixy Lee Ray	Democratic	1977-1981
John D. Spellman	Republican	1981-1985
Booth Gardner	Democratic	1985-

insurance, and a license tax on motor vehicles.

Politics. In the 1912 presidential election, Washington supported the Progressive Party. In the other elections, the state has supported Republicans about 60 per cent of the time, and Democrats about 40 per cent. For the state's voting record in presidential elections since 1892, see **Electoral College** (table).

Voters of farm areas and suburbs have generally favored Republicans. People in the cities of western Washington have usually supported the Democrats.

History

Indian days. Many Indians lived in the Washington region before white people came. Tribes of the plateau Indian group lived on the plains and in river valleys east of the Cascades. These included the Cayuse, Colville, Nez Percé, Okanogan, Spokane, and Yakima. The coastal Indians lived west of the Cascade Mountains. These tribes included the Chinook, Clallam, Clatsop, Nisqually, Nooksack, and Puyallup. They lived mainly on salmon and other fish and clams. They also gathered wild fruits and vegetables once a year. They carved masks and other items from wood.

Discovery and exploration. The first white people to see the Pacific Northwest were probably Spanish and English explorers who sailed northward along the coast from California during the 1500's. The Europeans did not land in what is now Washington until the late 1700's. After the mid-1700's, Russian fur traders settled in what is now Alaska. The Spaniards feared that the Russians would move to occupy the region farther south. To prevent this expansion, Spain sent several expeditions to establish Spanish rights to the area.

In 1775, Bruno Heceta and Juan Francisco de la Bodega y Quadra were the first Europeans to land on Washington soil, near present-day Point Grenville. They claimed the region for Spain.

The first English explorer to reach the area was Captain James Cook, in 1778. He did not touch the coast or, because of stormy weather, see much of it. Captain George Vancouver, another English explorer, made a survey of Puget Sound and Georgia Gulf between 1792 and 1794. One of his officers, Peter Puget, reached Puget Sound in 1792. England based its claim to the region on the explorations of Cook and Vancouver.

Captain Robert Gray, an American, headed a fur-trading expedition sent by a Boston company. Gray sailed into the harbor that now bears his name. In 1792, he reached the mouth of the Columbia River. Gray's arrival at the Columbia became a basis for American claims to the region. In 1805, the explorers Meriwether Lewis and William Clark crossed the Rocky Mountains. They reached the Columbia River and followed it to the Pacific Ocean. Their voyage gave the United States a second claim to the Northwest. Between 1807 and 1811, the British strengthened their claim when David Thompson, a Canadian explorer and geographer, traveled down the Columbia to the Pacific.

Settlement. During the early 1800's, British and American fur traders both operated in the region. In 1810, the Canadian North West Company established Spokane House near present-day Spokane for the purpose of trading with the Indians. In 1811, a company sent by the American trader John Jacob Astor set up a fur-trading post at Astoria, in present-day Oregon. Astor's group also founded Fort Okanogan, the first permanent American settlement established on land that now lies within the state of Washington.

During the War of 1812 between the United States and Great Britain, Astor's company gave up its trading posts. After the war, the two countries could not agree on a boundary line to separate their territories west of the Rocky Mountains. They signed a treaty in 1818 permitting citizens of both countries to trade and settle in the region, which was called the Oregon Country. John McLoughlin of the Hudson's Bay Company, a British trading firm, completed Fort Vancouver (now Vancouver) on the Columbia River in 1825.

During the 1840's, many Americans settled in the Oregon Country. The boundary dispute between the United States and Great Britain reached a climax during the presidential campaign of 1844. James K. Polk partially based his campaign on the claim that all the region south of latitude 54° 40' belonged to the United States (see **Fifty-Four Forty or Fight**). In 1846, President Polk signed a treaty with Great Britain which set the boundary line at the 49th parallel, Washington's present northern border. Great Britain kept Vancouver Island, part of which lies south of the 49th parallel.

Territorial days. A bill creating the Oregon Territory, of which Washington was a part, passed Congress in 1848. General Joseph Lane was appointed governor. In 1853, President Millard Fillmore signed a bill creating the Washington Territory. This region included the present state of Washington, northern Idaho, and western Montana. The capital was established at Olympia. The President appointed Isaac Ingalls Stevens as the first governor of the new territory. Stevens sought treaties with the Indians, in order to put them on reservations and free more territory for white settlers. The coastal Indians signed the treaties. But Stevens' efforts in 1855 to sign treaties with the plateau Indians led to war. Kamiakin, a Yakima Indian chief, led the warring tribes. The fighting ended in 1858, soon after the Indians lost a battle near Four Lakes. Treaties were ratified in 1859.

In 1859, the Washington Territory was expanded to include the southern parts of what are now the states of Idaho and Wyoming. Washington received its present boundaries in 1863, when the Idaho Territory was established. Increasing numbers of settlers streamed into Washington after 1860, partly because of the discovery of gold in Idaho, Oregon, and British Columbia. But there were no major gold strikes in Washington. Many who had hoped to find gold in Washington stayed to become farmers or loggers.

Statehood. The completion of a railroad connection with the East in 1883 brought more settlers. President Benjamin Harrison proclaimed the territory as the 42nd state on Nov. 11, 1889. Elisha P. Ferry, former governor of the territory, was elected Washington's first state governor. Olympia remained the capital.

Between 1890 and 1900, parts of the desertlike lands

Historic Washington

Captain George Vancouver, an English explorer, surveyed the coast of Washington and Puget Sound between 1792 and 1794.

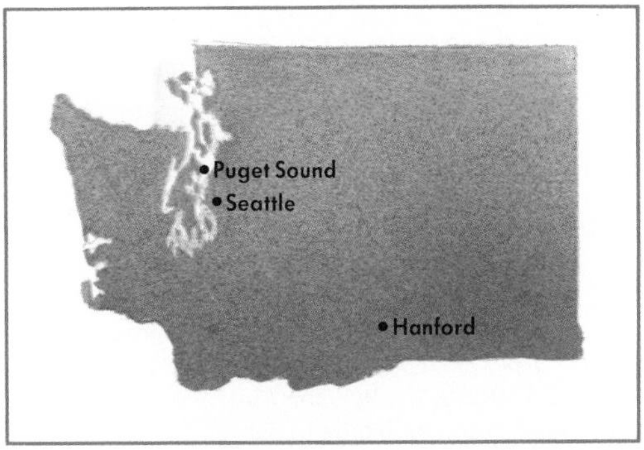

"Fifty-Four Forty or Fight" was the cry during the presidential campaign of 1844. But the boundary between Washington and Canada was fixed at latitude 49° by the 1846 Treaty of Oregon.

A nuclear energy center was built by the federal government at Hanford in 1943. The center helped make the first atomic bombs. In the 1960's, the facility began producing electricity.

The Space Needle was built for Century 21, a world's fair held in Seattle in 1962. The observation tower rises 607 feet (185 meters).

Lewis and Clark reached the Pacific in the autumn of 1805 after crossing the Rockies and descending the Snake and Columbia rivers. Thomas Jefferson had commissioned them to explore the upper Louisiana Territory.

WORLD BOOK illustrations by Kevin Chadwick

Important dates in Washington

1775 Bruno Heceta and Juan Francisco de la Bodega y Quadra of Spain became the first Europeans to land on Washington soil.

1792 Robert Gray sailed into Grays Harbor and the Columbia River. George Vancouver surveyed the coast of Washington and Puget Sound.

1805 Lewis and Clark reached Washington and the Pacific Ocean.

1810 A British-Canadian fur-trading post was established near present-day Spokane.

1818 Great Britain and the United States agreed to a joint occupation of the Oregon region, including Washington.

1846 A treaty between the United States and Great Britain established Washington's boundary at the 49th parallel.

1853 Congress created the Washington Territory.

1855-1858 Indian wars raged in the Washington Territory.

1883 The Northern Pacific Railroad linked Washington and the East.

1889 Washington became the 42nd state on November 11.

1909 The Alaska-Yukon-Pacific Exposition was held in Seattle.

1917 The Lake Washington Ship Canal opened.

1942 Grand Coulee Dam was completed.

1954 A $40,000,000 oil refinery opened at Ferndale.

1962 Century 21, a world's fair, was held in Seattle.

1964 The Columbia River Treaty of 1961 and related agreements received final approval from the U.S. and Canadian governments.

1974 Expo '74, a world's fair, was held in Spokane.

1980 Mount St. Helens volcano erupted causing 57 deaths and enormous damage in southwestern Washington.

of eastern Washington were reclaimed by irrigation. Large numbers of wheat ranchers and fruit growers came to the state. By 1900, much of the open cattle range had been replaced by wheat fields and fruit orchards. Lumbering, fishing, and mining also increased rapidly, and shipping to the Far East and Alaska became a leading activity. The shipping industry added to the wealth of the ports and railway centers. The state also profited greatly by the Klondike and Alaska gold rush of 1897-1898 (see **Alaska** [The gold rush]). Seattle profited most as the chief supply center for the prospectors, but all of western Washington increased in population and prosperity. Farmers in eastern Washington also profited.

The early 1900's. In 1909, the Alaska-Yukon-Pacific Exposition was held in Seattle to celebrate the growth of the port of Seattle. After the United States entered World War I in 1917, Washington's economy boomed as it provided needed forest products, agricultural commodities, and ships for the war effort.

The end of the war brought sharp cutbacks in production. Much unemployment resulted. Organized labor protested with general strikes, including the "Seattle Revolution of 1919," in which about 60,000 workers walked off their jobs. The Great Depression during the 1930's brought even greater reductions in many industries. Food processing remained Washington's only stable industry. Other industries that kept producing on a small scale included metalworking and aircraft construction. These activities, along with construction work on the Bonneville and Grand Coulee dams, helped the state regain some prosperity in the late 1930's.

The mid-1900's. During World War II (1939-1945), Washington industries produced aircraft and ships. Expansion occurred in truck and railroad car construction, the wood products industry, and agriculture. In 1943, the government built a nuclear energy center, the Hanford Works, in southeastern Washington. The center helped make the first atomic bombs. In the 1960's, it began to produce electricity. It later became known as the Hanford Site of the U.S. Department of Energy.

Many Washington cities grew as a result of the construction and expansion of military bases. Thousands of people who came to the state to work in defense plants stayed after the war to build new careers in the aluminum and aircraft industries. The importance of forest products and agriculture declined in Washington after World War II. However, farms in the central part of the state benefited from Columbia River irrigation projects. These projects resulted from the construction of a number of federal dams on the river. Development of the Columbia River also led to the growth of inland ports and an increase in river shipping. In 1964, the United States and Canada approved a cooperative plan for hydroelectric and river-control projects on the Columbia and connecting streams.

In 1962, Century 21, a world's fair held in Seattle, helped promote tourism, an important industry in the state. The fairgrounds and buildings and the 607-foot (185-meter) Space Needle observation tower remain as a year-round civic and tourist center. Seattle and its suburbs spent $130 million in a nine-year project to clean up polluted Lake Washington and Elliott Bay, two major recreation areas. In 1968, Seattle-area voters approved a $333-million improvement program called "Forward

Thrust." Plans included a $118-million expansion of park and recreational facilities.

In the late 1960's, industry and population increased rapidly in Seattle and the Puget Sound area. An important reason for the expansion was the growth of the Boeing Company. Boeing Company, a major military airplane builder in wartime, expanded into both the commercial jet and aerospace industries. At one time, nearly 10 per cent of the work force in Washington was employed in jet aircraft and related businesses. From 1969 to 1971, the aerospace industry slumped. Much of the industry's work force was laid off, and Washington's economy suffered.

Recent developments. During the early 1970's, state officials attempted to attract other industries. Interest in Washington's highly skilled labor force drew several electronics companies. The aerospace industry began its recovery in the mid-1970's, when the production of jet-powered commercial aircraft increased.

Douglas Miller, West Stock

The eruptions of Mount St. Helens in southwestern Washington in 1980 spread volcanic ash over a wide area. The volcanic eruptions caused billions of dollars of damage.

Washington's commercial salmon fishing industry was deeply hurt in 1974. That year, U.S. District Judge George Boldt ruled that existing treaties allow Indians the right to half the harvest of salmon returning to off-reservation waters in Washington. The Supreme Court of the United States upheld this decision in 1979.

Also in the 1970's, the Washington Public Power Supply System (WPPSS) began to build five nuclear power plants to meet increasing needs for electric power. But the project became burdened with cost overruns. In 1983, WPPSS defaulted on $2¼ billion in municipal bonds and, having completed only two plants, ceased construction. WPPSS was the most expensive civil works project in history. Its default also was the largest of its kind.

On May 18, 1980, volcanic eruptions of Mount St. Helens in southwestern Washington resulted in 57 deaths and billions of dollars in damage. The eruptions caused floods and forest fires and spread a thick layer of ash over a wide area.

Washington today faces several challenges. State officials want to help the state grow economically without destroying its natural resources. They are especially trying to attract new kinds of industry and depend less on federal aerospace and defense contracts. State leaders are also working to solve the problems of a weak timber industry and declining agricultural prices. In addition, they are concerned about the U.S. government's interest in storing nuclear waste at the Hanford Site.

Ronald Reed Boyce and Robert C. Carriker

Study aids

Related articles in *World Book* include:

Biographies

Foley, Thomas Stephen	Ray, Dixy Lee
Jackson, Henry M.	Vancouver, George
Joseph, Chief	Wainwright, Jonathan M.
Joseph, Mother	Whitman, Marcus
Landes, Bertha Knight	Whitman, Narcissa
Puget, Peter	

Cities

Olympia	Seattle	Tacoma
Richland	Spokane	Vancouver

History

Chinook Indians	Oregon (Exploration)
Lewis and Clark expedition	Oregon Territory
Nootka Indians	Western frontier life

National parks and historic sites

Mount Rainier National Park	Whitman Mission National
North Cascades National Park	Historic Site
Olympic National Park	

Physical features

Bonneville Dam	Mount Saint Helens
Cascade Range	Mud Mountain Dam
Cascade Tunnel	Olympic Mountains
Coast Range	Puget Sound
Columbia River	Ross Dam
Grand Coulee Dam	Snake River
Mount Rainier	

Other related articles

Pacific Northwest	Puget Sound Naval Shipyard

Outline

I. People
 A. Population
 B. Schools
 C. Libraries
 D. Museums

II. Visitor's guide
 A. Places to visit
 B. Annual events

III. Land and climate
 A. Land regions
 B. Coastline
 C. Rivers, waterfalls, and lakes
 D. Plant and animal life
 E. Climate

IV. Economy
 A. Natural resources
 B. Service industries
 C. Manufacturing
 D. Agriculture
 E. Mining
 F. Fishing
 G. Electric power
 H. Transportation
 I. Communication

V. Government
 A. Constitution
 B. Executive
 C. Legislature
 D. Courts
 E. Local government
 F. Revenue
 G. Politics

VI. History

Questions

On what grounds did both England and the United States claim the region that is now Washington?

Where is the longest railroad tunnel in the United States?

Why does western Washington have a mild climate?

What is Washington's most valuable crop?

In what ways does Washington benefit from the dams in the Columbia River system?

How does the state protect its forest resources?

What is the Space Needle?

In what region do most of Washington's people live?

What is the largest concrete dam in the world?

What are *coulees*? What are *scablands*?

Additional resources

Level I

Carpenter, Allan. *Washington*. Rev. ed. Childrens Press, 1979.

Fradin, Dennis B. *Washington in Words and Pictures*. Childrens Press, 1980.

Thompson, Kathleen. *Washington*. Raintree, 1987.

Level II

Avery, Mary W. *Washington: A History of the Evergreen State*. Univ. of Washington Press, 1965.

Clark, Norman H. *Washington: A Bicentennial History*. Norton, 1976.

Ficken, Robert E. *Lumber and Politics: The Career of Mark E. Reed*. Univ. of Washington Press, 1980. A look at industry and government in the state through the story of a lumberman and politician.

Johansen, Dorothy O., and Gates, C. M. *Empire of the Columbia: A History of the Pacific Northwest*. 2nd ed. Harper, 1967.

Kirk, Ruth, and Daugherty, R. D. *Exploring Washington Archaeology*. Univ. of Washington Press, 1979.

Manning, Harvey. *Washington Wilderness: The Unfinished Work*. Mountaineers, 1985. A look at land use policies in the state.

Nelson, Gerald B. *Seattle: The Life and Times of an American City*. Knopf, 1977.

Richards, Kent D. *Isaac I. Stevens: Young Man in a Hurry*. Brigham Young Univ. Press, 1979. A biography of the first governor of the Washington Territory.

Scott, James W., and De Lorme, R. L. *Historical Atlas of Washington*. Univ. of Oklahoma Press, 1988.

Washington State: A Literary Chronicle. Ed. by William Storrs Lee. Crowell, 1969.

Robert H. Glaze, Artstreet

The United States Capitol, in Washington, D.C., is the place where Congress makes the nation's laws. Tourists flock to this magnificent building to enjoy its beauty and to see Congress in action.

Washington, D.C.

Washington, D.C., is the capital of the United States. It is also one of the country's most beautiful and historic cities and the site of many of its most popular tourist attractions.

Washington serves as the headquarters of the federal government. The President of the United States, the members of Congress, the Supreme Court justices, and about 374,000 other federal government employees work in the Washington area. Decisions made by government leaders in the city affect the lives of people throughout the United States and, sometimes, in other parts of the world. For example, the President suggests laws to Congress and directs U.S. relations with other countries. The members of Congress pass laws that every American citizen must obey. The Supreme Court justices decide whether the government's laws and practices are constitutional.

Washington is important to the American people in

The contributors of this article are Eunice S. Grier, a consultant in the Washington, D.C., area on public policy; and Atlee E. Shidler, president of the Greater Washington Research Center.

another way. The city is a symbol of their country's unity, history, and democratic tradition.

Every year, millions of people from all parts of the United States and from other countries visit Washington. They go there to see such important government buildings as the United States Capitol, where Congress meets, and the White House, where the President lives and works. They visit the Washington Monument, Lincoln Memorial, and other famous structures dedicated to American heroes of the past. They also tour the city's many museums, which together house the world's largest collection of items from America's past.

Most of Washington's main government buildings,

Facts in brief

Population: *City*—638,432. *Metropolitan area*—3,250,822.
Area: *City*—69 sq. mi. (179 km²). *Metropolitan area*—3,957 sq. mi. (10,249 km²).
Altitude: 25 feet (7.6 meters) above sea level.
Climate: *Average temperatures*—January, 37° F. (3° C); July, 78° F. (26° C). *Average annual precipitation* (rainfall, melted snow, and other forms of moisture)—50 in. (127 cm). For the monthly weather in Washington, D.C., see **Maryland** (Climate).
Government: Federal District under the authority of Congress. Mayor and city council, elected to four-year terms, help run the government.
Founded: Site chosen, 1791. Became capital, 1800.

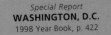

Special Report
WASHINGTON, D.C.
1998 Year Book, p. 422

monuments, and museums stand in the west-central part of the city. This area ranks among the nation's most beautiful places. Many of its buildings and monuments are magnificent white marble structures. Scenic parks and gardens, and—in springtime—gorgeous blossoms of Japanese cherry trees, add natural beauty to the man-made splendor of the area.

Outside the west-central area, Washington is much like other big cities. It has large residential areas, including wealthy, middle-class, and poor sections. Suburbs spread out from the city in all directions. Washington faces problems common to all cities, including crime, poverty, traffic jams, and a shortage of good moderate-cost housing. Unlike most cities, Washington has no large industrial areas. This is so because government, rather than manufacturing or trade, has always been the city's main business.

About 70 per cent of Washington's people are blacks. No other major city in the United States has so large a percentage of black people. But in Washington's suburbs, whites account for about 78 per cent of the population.

Washington lies in the southeastern United States, between Maryland and Virginia. It is the only American city or town that is not part of a state. Washington covers the entire area of the District of Columbia, a section of land that is under the jurisdiction of the federal government.

Washington is one of the few cities in the world that was designed before it was built. President George Washington chose the city's site in 1791. He hired Pierre Charles L'Enfant, a French engineer, to draw up plans for the city. Washington replaced Philadelphia as the nation's capital in 1800. L'Enfant and other members of a commission appointed to plan the city named it in honor of George Washington. The *D.C.* in the city's name stands for *District of Columbia.*

WORLD BOOK map

Washington, D.C., the capital of the United States, lies between Maryland and Virginia on the Potomac River.

Most of Washington's government buildings, famous monuments and museums, and other tourist attractions are located in the west-central part of the city. This area extends from Capitol Hill, which rises near the center of the city, westward to the Potomac River. This section describes the main features of the area. The two-page map provides an overview of it. The last part of the section deals with interesting sights in other parts of Washington and its suburbs. Many of Washington's points of interest also have separate articles in *World Book.* See the list of *Related articles* at the end of this article.

This section also tells—in general terms—about the activities of the federal government. But for much greater detail, see the article **United States, Government of the,** and its list of *Related articles.*

Capitol Hill

Capitol Hill rises 88 feet (26.8 meters) near the center of Washington. Several huge government buildings stand on the hill. They include the United States Capitol, congressional office buildings, the Library of Congress, the Supreme Court Building, and the conservatory of the United States Botanic Garden. The Folger Shakespeare Library, a private institution, is also located on Capitol Hill.

United States Capitol is the place where the members of Congress meet to discuss and vote on proposed legislation. The Capitol ranks among Washington's most magnificent buildings. Many tall Corinthian columns and an enormous dome beautify its white marble exterior. A bronze Statue of Freedom $19\frac{1}{2}$ feet (5.94 meters) high stands on top of the dome. The Capitol, including the statue, rises almost 300 feet (91 meters) above the ground.

The Capitol has 540 rooms. Many of them contain beautiful paintings, sculptures, and wall carvings that portray events and people important in American history. Such works of art, along with gorgeous furnishings, give the interior of the Capitol the splendor of a fine museum or a palace.

Many people visit the Capitol just to enjoy its beauty and its reminders of the country's past. But visitors may also attend sessions of Congress. To do so, however, they must first get a pass from one of the people who represents them in Congress.

Congressional office buildings. Six buildings provide office space for the members of Congress. They are the Dirksen, Hart, and Russell Senate office buildings, all north of the Capitol; and the Cannon, Longworth, and Rayburn House of Representatives office buildings, south of the Capitol. The members of Congress welcome visits to their offices by people they represent.

Library of Congress is probably the world's largest library. Its huge collection of about 84 million items includes books, manuscripts, films, and recordings. The Library of Congress has three huge buildings, all east of the Capitol. The main building is a gray sandstone structure. The Library of Congress Thomas Jefferson Building (formerly called the Annex) is of white marble. The third building, of granite and marble, is called the Library of Congress James Madison Memorial Building. It is the newest of the library buildings.

Milt & Joan Mann

The Capitol's Great Rotunda, or room under its dome, has many works of art related to American history. These works include paintings of important events and statues of famous people.

Milt & Joan Mann

The Supreme Court Building resembles a Greek temple. In a courtroom inside, the Supreme Court justices make legal decisions that may affect the lives of every American.

The library serves the reference needs of Congress. The public may also use its materials and tour the buildings. The library's many items of special interest to tourists include most of Mathew Brady's Civil War photographs, a Gutenberg Bible printed in the 1450's, and one of the original copies of Abraham Lincoln's Gettysburg Address.

Supreme Court Building also stands east of the Capitol. In this building, the nine justices of the Supreme Court of the United States decide on the constitutionality of laws, government practices, and decisions of lower courts.

The white marble exterior of the Supreme Court Building resembles a Greek temple. The room where the justices hear cases is decorated with long, red drapes, copper gates, and marble columns. Visitors may attend sessions of the court. But seating is limited and is available on a first-come, first-served basis.

United States Botanic Garden is located on the southwest side of Capitol Hill. It exhibits more than 10,000 kinds of plants, including many rare species.

Folger Shakespeare Library, east of the main Library of Congress building, houses the world's most important collection of works by and about William Shakespeare. Only scholars may use its materials. But the library displays rare books and manuscripts for public viewing.

The National Mall

A long, narrow parklike area stretches westward from Capitol Hill. Called the *National Mall,* or simply the *Mall,* it provides open space amid west-central Washington's many huge buildings. It is also the location of some of the city's leading tourist attractions.

Several outstanding museums that are part of the Smithsonian Institution stand along the Mall a little west of Capitol Hill. The National Gallery of Art, which houses a world-famous collection of paintings and sculptures by Americans and Europeans, is also located there. Farther west are the Washington Monument and Lincoln Memorial. A long, narrow body of water called the *Reflecting Pool* lies between these two magnificent structures. Mirrorlike reflections of the monument and memorial can be seen in the pool's water. The Vietnam Veterans Memorial is located northeast of the Lincoln Memorial. Dedicated to those who served in the Vietnam War, it includes two black granite walls that meet at an angle. The names of all Americans who died in the war, or who remained classified as missing in action when the walls were built, are inscribed on the walls. The memorial also includes a large bronze sculpture of three servicemen.

The Jefferson Memorial lies south of the Washington Monument. It overlooks a lagoon called the *Tidal Basin.* Hundreds of Japanese cherry trees encircle the basin. In springtime, gorgeous pink and white cherry blossoms bloom on the trees. They create a sight of magnificent beauty that attracts huge crowds of visitors. The period when the trees are likely to be in bloom is set aside for a festival called the *Cherry Blossom Festival.*

Smithsonian museums. The Smithsonian Institution is a government corporation that operates cultural, educational, and scientific facilities throughout Washington. The facilities include several museums on the Mall that house a total of more than 130 million items. Among the items are many of the world's greatest paintings, objects of importance to American history, and countless objects from the everyday life of America's past. The original building of the Smithsonian Institution, popularly called "the castle," is one of the Mall's most impressive structures. Formerly a museum, it now houses the institution's offices. But the building remains a tourist attraction because it resembles a medieval castle and it contains maps and plans of Washington. The names of the Smithsonian museums and some highlights of their collections follow.

Hellmuth, Obata & Kassabaum, Architects

Visitors to the Air and Space Museum view historic aircraft and space vehicles. The museum, a part of the Smithsonian Institution, exhibits the Wright brothers' first airplane, *above.*

National Air and Space Museum has exhibits that trace the history of flight. Its attractions include the airplane Orville Wright used in making the first successful flight, and the one in which Charles Lindbergh made the first solo flight across the Atlantic Ocean. The exhibits also include spacecraft that carried American astronauts into outer space and rocks that astronauts brought back from the moon.

National Museum of American History displays the flag that inspired Francis Scott Key to write the national anthem. It has large collections of historical automobiles, railroad trains, and industrial machinery. It also houses an enormous collection of everyday objects from the past, including clothing, kitchen utensils, and home furnishings.

National Museum of Natural History exhibits stuffed animals from many parts of the world and skeletons of prehistoric animals. It has lifelike exhibits that show how American Indians and Eskimos lived long ago. The museum also features an outstanding gem collection, which includes the famous Hope Diamond.

Wally McNamee, Woodfin Camp, Inc.

Sylvia Johnson, Woodfin Camp, Inc.

Vietnam Veterans Memorial includes two adjoining black granite walls, *far left.* The walls are inscribed with the names of all Americans who died in the Vietnam War, or who remained classified as missing in action when the walls were built. The memorial also includes a bronze sculpture of three servicemen, *near left.*

Dean Brown from Nancy Palmer

Robert H. Glaze, Artstreet

Milt & Joan Mann

Monuments to three American Presidents are located on the National Mall. The Jefferson Memorial, *left,* stands in a beautiful setting among Japanese cherry trees at the edge of the Tidal Basin. The towering Washington Monument, *center,* ranks as the city's tallest structure. The majestic Lincoln Memorial, *right,* has a famous statue of Lincoln inside.

Smithsonian Arts and Industries Building houses a collection of items from the 1800's. These include locomotives, military weapons, and industrial machinery.

Art museums. Four of the Smithsonian museums on the Mall are art galleries. The *Hirshhorn Museum and Sculpture Garden* has an outstanding collection of modern American works of art. The *Freer Gallery of Art* and the *Arthur M. Sackler Gallery* feature collections of Asian art. The *National Museum of African Art* exhibits works by black Africans. Both the Sackler and the African museums are housed in a complex called the Quadrangle. The *National Gallery of Art,* also on the Mall, is affiliated with the Smithsonian museums.

The Smithsonian Institution also operates art museums in other parts of Washington. Its Fine Arts and Portrait Galleries Building, at 7th and F streets a few blocks north of the Mall, houses two outstanding museums. They are the *National Museum of American Art,* which surveys American art from colonial days to the present; and the *National Portrait Gallery,* which includes paintings of persons important in American history. The *Renwick Gallery,* at 17th Street and Pennsylvania Avenue also north of the Mall, features exhibits of American crafts, design, and decorative art.

Washington Monument is a towering, slender, white marble *obelisk* (pillar) dedicated to the memory of George Washington. The tallest structure in Washington, D.C., it rises 555 feet 5 $\frac{1}{8}$ inches (169.29 meters). An elevator inside carries visitors to the top. From there, a person can see much of the Washington area.

Lincoln Memorial is a templelike white marble monument that honors Abraham Lincoln. On the outside, 36

Doric columns—one for each state that existed when Lincoln died—support the roof. Inside is a majestic marble statue of Lincoln seated in a chair. Paintings that symbolize Lincoln's accomplishments, and quotations from Lincoln's writings, appear on the interior walls.

Jefferson Memorial honors Thomas Jefferson. It is a circular white marble structure ringed by 26 Ionic columns and topped by a beautiful dome. A bronze statue of Jefferson stands inside. Quotations from Jefferson's writings appear on the interior walls.

North of the Mall

Many huge government buildings crowd the area north of the Mall. Most of them stand along or near Pennsylvania Avenue. This broad, tree-lined street runs northwestward from Capitol Hill. It connects the Capitol and the White House, and serves as Washington's main parade route.

The White House ranks as the most important government building in the area. Most of the other buildings house offices of the executive branch of the government. The executive branch, headed by the President, is responsible for carrying out government policies. It includes the Executive Office of the President, 14 executive departments, and many other agencies of the federal government.

Several nongovernment organizations—including the American Red Cross, the Daughters of the American Revolution (DAR), the National Academy of Sciences, and the World Bank—have their headquarters near the government buildings. Also nearby is a major tourist attraction—Ford's Theatre.

White House, at 1600 Pennsylvania Avenue, has served as the home and the office of every United States President except George Washington. Some of the world's most historic decisions have been made in this famous building.

The White House is constructed of white sandstone and has 132 rooms. Five of the rooms are open to the public. They are the Blue Room, East Room, Green Room, Red Room, and State Dining Room. These rooms are famous for their magnificent works of art and furnishings. Visitors are not allowed in the rooms where the President lives and works. But occasionally, the President or a member of the President's family stops by to greet tourists in the public rooms.

The White House stands on a beautifully landscaped plot that covers 18 acres (7.3 hectares). Lafayette Square lies north of the White House grounds, and the Ellipse lies to the south. These parklike areas, together with the White House grounds, are sometimes called the *President's Square,* or *Park.* Blair House, a mansion on the west side of Lafayette Square, serves as a guesthouse for high-ranking foreign officials who come to visit the President. President Harry S. Truman lived in Blair House from 1948 to 1952, while the White House was being repaired.

Executive branch buildings. The main Executive Office Building stands directly west of the White House. An additional Executive Office Building is located north of the main building, across Pennsylvania Avenue. Many of the President's closest advisers work in these buildings. The headquarters of the Department of the Treasury, one of the government's executive departments, are just east of the White House.

Several huge executive branch buildings stand close together on the south side of Pennsylvania Avenue between the White House and the Capitol. This group of buildings is called the *Federal Triangle* because it forms the shape of a triangle. The Federal Triangle includes

the headquarters of the executive departments of Commerce and Justice. It also contains the following federal government agencies: the Federal Trade Commission, Internal Revenue Service, Interstate Commerce Commission, National Archives, and United States Customs Service.

The Department of Labor—an executive department —and the headquarters of the Federal Bureau of Investigation (FBI) lie north of Pennsylvania Avenue between the White House and the Capitol. The FBI headquarters is called the J. Edgar Hoover Building. Two other executive departments—the Department of State and the Department of the Interior—lie several blocks southwest of the White House.

Almost all the executive departments and agencies offer tours of their buildings. Especially popular are the tours of the National Archives and the headquarters of the FBI. The National Archives stores government documents. It displays three of the most important documents for public viewing. These are the original copies of the United States Constitution, the Bill of Rights, and the Declaration of Independence. At FBI headquarters, bureau agents conduct tours that feature highlights of the agency's history and show how the FBI works today. The tours end with a demonstration of agents taking target practice.

Ford's Theatre, the playhouse where Abraham Lincoln was shot, stands about $1\frac{1}{2}$ blocks north of Pennsylvania Avenue, between the White House and Capitol. The theater houses a collection of items related to Lincoln's life and death. *Petersen House,* the house where Lincoln died, is across the street from the theater.

South of the Mall

Originally, almost all the executive branch buildings were located near the White House. But the executive branch has grown tremendously and has spread out to other parts of Washington. Several government build-

The White House has served as the home and office of every United States President with the exception of George Washington. The picture at the left shows the south side of the White House.

Washington, D.C.

This map illustrates west-central Washington, the site of most of the city's main points of interest. Dozens of important buildings and monuments are shown in blue on the map and keyed with a number to the map index, *below.*

1. American Art Portrait Gallery Building B 4
2. Arthur M. Sackler Gallery C 5
3. Blair House C 1
4. Bureau of Engraving and Printing D 4
5. Bureau of Indian Affairs D 2
6. Cannon House Office Building B 8
7. Corcoran Gallery of Art D 2
8. Department of Agriculture D 5
9. Department of Commerce C 3
10. Department of Education C 7
11. Department of Energy C 5
12. Department of Health and Human Services C 7
13. Department of Housing and Urban Development C 6
14. Department of Justice C 4
15. Department of Labor B 6
16. Department of State D 1
17. Department of the Interior D 2
18. Department of the Treasury C 2
19. Department of Transportation C 7
20. Dirksen and Hart Senate Office Buildings A 7
21. Executive Office Buildings C 1
22. Federal Aviation Administration C 6
23. Federal Bureau of Investigation C 4
24. Federal Reserve System D 1
25. Federal Trade Commission B 5
26. Folger Shakespeare Library A 8
27. Ford's Theatre B 4
28. Freer Gallery of Art C 5

29. General Services Administration D 1
30. Government Printing Office A 5
31. Hirshhorn Museum and Sculpture Garden C 5
— House Office Buildings (see 6, 39, and 51)
32. Internal Revenue Service C 4
33. Interstate Commerce Commission C 4
34. Jefferson Memorial E 5
35. Library of Congress B 8
36. Library of Congress Thomas Jefferson Building B 8
37. Library of Congress James Madison Memorial Building B 8
38. Lincoln Memorial E 1
39. Longworth House Office Building B 8
40. Martin Luther King Memorial Library B 3
41. National Aeronautics and Space Administration C 6
42. National Air and Space Museum C 6
43. National Archives C 5
44. National Gallery of Art B 6
45. National Museum of African Art C 5
— National Museum of American Art (housed in number 1)
46. National Museum of American History C 4
47. National Museum of Natural History C 4
48. National Museum of the Building Arts (Pension Building) B 5
— National Portrait Gallery (housed in number 1)
49. Office of Personnel Management D 1
50. Old Post Office Building C 4

51. Rayburn House Office Building B 7
52. Renwick Gallery C 1
53. Russell Senate Office Building A 7
— Senate Office Buildings (see 20 and 53)
54. Smithsonian Arts and Industries Building C 5
55. Smithsonian Institution Building (administrative offices) C 5
— Smithsonian Museums (see 1, 28, 31, 42, 44, 45, 46, 47, 52, and 54)
56. Supreme Court Building A 8
57. Union Station A 6
58. United States Botanic Garden B 7
59. United States Capitol B 7
60. United States Customs Service C 4
61. United States Postal Service D 6
62. Vietnam Veterans Memorial E 1
63. Washington Monument D 3
64. White House C 2

This map was drawn by George Suyeoka.
Reference material was provided by Sanborn Map Co. and Air Photographics, Inc.
The map was critically reviewed by the National Capital Planning Commission.

Jack Rottier, National Parks Service

Ford's Theatre was the scene of the assassination of Abraham Lincoln. The President was sitting in a box seat behind the flags when he was shot. The box overlooks the stage.

ings now stand south of the Mall. They include the buildings of six executive departments. These departments are Agriculture, Education, Energy, Health and Human Services, Housing and Urban Development, and Transportation. In addition, the United States Postal Service, a government agency, is there.

The Bureau of Engraving and Printing ranks as the major tourist attraction south of the Mall. There, government workers engrave and print the country's paper money. Large crowds of visitors flock to the bureau to see these fascinating processes.

Other points of interest

The Washington area has dozens of interesting sights in addition to those already described and shown on the two-page map. Some of the most famous ones appear below. Others are included under *The city* section later in this article.

John F. Kennedy Center for the Performing Arts borders the Potomac River northwest of the Lincoln Memorial. Dramatic groups, ballet and opera companies, and orchestras from all parts of the world perform in this modern building. The Kennedy Center also serves as the permanent residence of the American Film Institute, the American National Theater, the Washington Opera, and the National Symphony Orchestra. Performances at the Kennedy Center attract large crowds. Thousands of people also visit the center every year to honor the memory of President John F. Kennedy, to whom it is dedicated.

Watergate is a group of luxurious, modern apartment and office buildings just north of the Kennedy Center. The Watergate Complex became internationally famous in 1972 when campaign workers for President Richard M. Nixon, a Republican, were caught breaking into Democratic political headquarters there. The break-

Milt and Joan Mann

The Bureau of Engraving and Printing makes the nation's paper money. The employee shown above is inspecting large sheets of newly printed $1 bills.

Dennis Brack, Black Star

John F. Kennedy Center for the Performing Arts features concerts, *above,* as well as ballets, films, operas, and plays. Its activities help make Washington a leading cultural center.

in marked the start of a major American political scandal, which led to Nixon's resignation.

National Zoological Park is a zoo about 2 miles (3 kilometers) north of the White House. The zoo contains about 2,800 animals. The animals include two pandas that the Chinese government gave to the United States in 1972.

Pentagon Building, the headquarters of the Department of Defense, ranks as the world's largest office building. It covers 29 acres (11.7 hectares) in Arlington, Va., across the Potomac from Washington.

Arlington National Cemetery, northwest of the Pentagon in Arlington, contains the graves of thousands of persons who served in the United States armed forces. It includes the Tomb of the Unknowns, where four unidentified servicemen who died in action are buried. Arlington National Cemetery also includes the gravesites of President John F. Kennedy and Senator Robert F. Kennedy.

Marine Corps War Memorial, north of Arlington Cemetery, ranks among Washington's most famous monuments. Often called the *Iwo Jima Statue,* this dramatic bronze sculpture shows five marines and a Navy medical corpsman raising the American flag on the island of Iwo Jima during World War II.

Mount Vernon was the private estate of George Washington. It is located in Fairfax County, Virginia, about 15 miles (24 kilometers) south of the city. The first President's home, many of his belongings, and his grave are there.

Other museums. Washington has many outstanding museums in addition to the Smithsonian museums. Two of the most famous ones are the Corcoran Gallery of Art and the Phillips Collection. The Corcoran Gallery, about 2 blocks southwest of the White House, displays masterpieces by American painters. The Phillips Collection, at 21st and Q streets about 10 blocks northwest of the White House, houses works by artists from El Greco to the present.

Architectural styles. Many visitors to Washington enjoy the rich and varied architecture of the city's buildings and monuments. Many structures, including the Capitol, Supreme Court Building, and Lincoln Memorial are built in the classical architectural style of ancient Greece and Rome. Washington Cathedral, an Episcopal church at Massachusetts and Wisconsin avenues in northwestern Washington, features the Gothic style of medieval Europe. The National Shrine of the Immaculate Conception, near 4th Street and Michigan Avenue in northeastern Washington, has elements of two other medieval styles—Byzantine and Romanesque. The *mosque* (Moslem house of worship) of the Islamic Center is a fine example of the Islamic style of architecture. It stands along Massachusetts Avenue near Rock Creek Park in the northwestern part of the city.

Many buildings in Georgetown, a neighborhood northwest of the White House, provide examples of colonial American residential architecture. Some of the city's newest office and apartment buildings reflect modern American architecture. But a law limits the height of buildings in the city. As a result, Washington—unlike most other large cities—has no skyscrapers.

Paul S. Conklin
Arlington National Cemetery, in Arlington, Va., includes the gravesite of President John F. Kennedy, *foreground.* Thousands of people who served in the armed forces are buried there.

James H. Pickerell
The Marine Corps War Memorial shows servicemen raising the American flag on Iwo Jima during World War II. It stands in Arlington, Va., across the Potomac River from Washington.

Washington, D.C., lies along the northeast bank of the Potomac River. The city covers 69 square miles (179 square kilometers) and has a population of 638,432. The state of Maryland borders Washington on the north, east, and south. Virginia lies across the Potomac River to the west and south.

Suburban communities of Maryland and Virginia surround Washington. The city and its suburbs form a metropolitan area that covers 3,957 square miles (10,249 square kilometers) and has a population of 3,250,822.

The United States Capitol stands near the center of Washington. Broad streets extend out from the Capitol in all directions like the spokes of a wheel. They include North Capitol Street, which runs north from the Capitol; East Capitol Street, which runs east; and South Capitol Street, which runs south. These streets, together with the Mall that extends west from the Capitol, divide Washington into four sections. The sections are *Northwest, Northeast, Southeast,* and *Southwest.* Each section is named for its direction from the Capitol. Each address in Washington is followed by one of four abbreviations that tells what section the address is in. The abbreviations and their meanings are: *NW* (Northwest), *NE* (Northeast), *SE* (Southeast), and *SW* (Southwest).

Paul S. Conklin

Row houses line the streets of many Washington neighborhoods. Large numbers of Washington's black residents live in neighborhoods similar to the one above.

Northwest section includes the part of Washington between North Capitol Street and the south side of the Mall. Washington's largest section, it covers about half the city's area and has almost half of its people. The Northwest section is also Washington's main center of cultural, economic, and government activity.

The southern part of Northwest Washington includes the White House and the many government buildings near it, the Smithsonian museums, and the Washington Monument and Lincoln Memorial. For detailed information on this part of the city, see the *Visitor's guide* section in this article.

Washington's main shopping districts lie in the Northwest section. One district is just to the north of Pennsylvania Avenue between the White House and the Capitol, and the other district is in the vicinity of Connecticut Avenue and K Street. In these districts, department stores and small specialty shops serve the shopping needs of residents and tourists alike.

West of the shopping district, Rock Creek Park winds through Northwest Washington in a north-south direction. The official residence of the Vice President of the United States is on the grounds of the Naval Observatory on Massachusetts Avenue near the park. Embassies of countries that have diplomatic relations with the United States are also along Massachusetts Avenue.

Large residential areas lie west and east of the park. Georgetown, an area to the west, ranks among the nation's wealthiest places. It is famous for its beautiful old houses—some dating from the 1700's—and for its shops that sell antiques and other luxury items. Other residential areas in the Northwest section include high-income, middle-income, and low-income neighborhoods.

Five of the city's largest universities have their campuses in Northwest Washington. They are: American, George Washington, Georgetown, and Howard universities; and the University of the District of Columbia.

Northeast section lies between North Capitol and East Capitol streets. It covers about a fourth of the city

Milt & Joan Mann

Georgetown, a wealthy neighborhood in Northwest Washington, has fine examples of early American architecture. Many of its buildings are 100 to 200 years old, but in excellent condition.

and has about a fourth of its people. Northeast is chiefly a residential area, and has both middle-class and low-income neighborhoods.

The Bethune Museum Archives and other institutions dedicated to promoting black culture are located in the Northeast section. The campus of Catholic University of America—the national university of the Roman Catholic Church—lies about 3 miles (5 kilometers) north of the Capitol in this section.

The Anacostia River cuts through Northeast Washington east of the Capitol. The National Arboretum and the Kenilworth Aquatic Gardens lie along the river. The arboretum contains trees and shrubs from many parts of the world. The Kenilworth Gardens includes numerous ponds filled with colorful water plants.

Southeast section is the area between East Capitol and South Capitol streets. It covers about a fourth of the city and has about a fourth of its people. A wealthy residential neighborhood of luxury apartments and restored

old houses lies close to the Capitol in the Southeast section. It also extends into the Northeast. Nearby is an old-fashioned market called the *Eastern Market.* Farmers from the area around Washington come to the market to sell such products as fresh fruits and vegetables, cider, eggs, and flowers. Merchants offer bakery products, meat cut to order, and other goods.

The Anacostia River winds through this section farther south. The area south of the river, called *Anacostia,* includes many crowded and run-down sections.

Southwest section extends from South Capitol Street to the south side of the Mall. Washington's smallest section, it covers about an eighth of the city's land and has only about 4 per cent of its people. Almost all of Southwest Washington has been rebuilt since the 1950's as part of a major urban renewal program. As a result, the section has many relatively new houses and apartment and office buildings. The government's five newest executive departments—Education, Energy, Health and

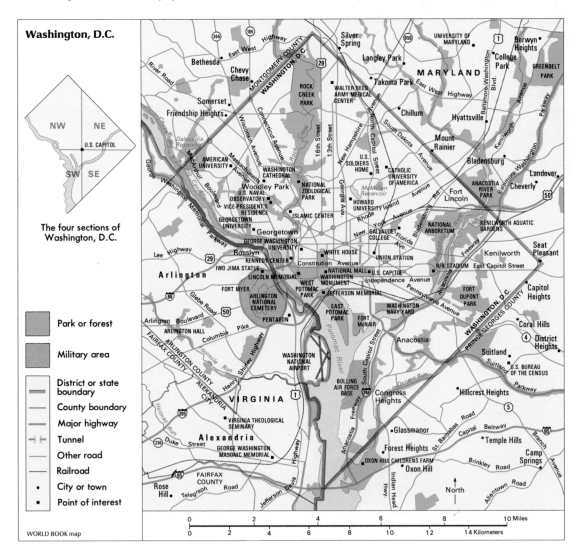

Washington, D.C.

The four sections of Washington, D.C.

Park or forest

Military area

District or state boundary
County boundary
Major highway
Tunnel
Other road
Railroad
• City or town
▪ Point of interest

WORLD BOOK map

Human Services, Housing and Urban Development, and Transportation—are there. The Department of Agriculture is also there.

Metropolitan area. The Washington metropolitan area, as defined by the federal government, includes the city; Calvert, Charles, Frederick, Montgomery, and Prince Georges counties in Maryland; Arlington, Fairfax, Loudoun, Prince William, and Stafford counties in Virginia; and five Virginia cities that are not part of a county—Alexandria, Fairfax, Falls Church, Manassas, and Manassas Park.

The counties of Washington's metropolitan area include both suburban cities and towns and large open areas of hills, woods, and farms. Most of the suburban cities and towns are under the jurisdiction of the counties in which they are located.

In the Washington area, as in other metropolitan areas, thousands of people who live in the suburbs work in the city. But during the 1900's, many government agencies have moved from the city to the suburbs. Also, many private businesses have been established there. As a result, large numbers of people—from both the city and the suburbs—work in the suburbs. For example, more than 23,000 people work for the Department of Defense in the Pentagon in Arlington, Va. Other government agencies that are located in the suburbs include the National Institutes of Health and the Naval Hospital in Bethesda, Md.; the Central Intelligence Agency in McLean, Va.; and the Bureau of the Census in Suitland, Md.

James H. Pickerell

Single-family houses line a curving street in the Washington suburb of Bethesda, Md. Thousands of people in the Washington area live in suburbs and commute to jobs in the city.

Two of the most famous *new towns* in the United States—Columbia, Md., and Reston, Va.—are located near Washington. Begun during the early 1960's, these two communities were carefully planned before they were built (see **City planning** [Building new communities]).

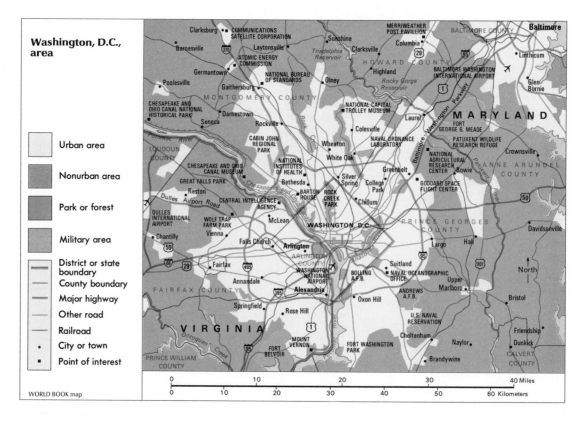

WORLD BOOK map

About 70 per cent of Washington's people are blacks. No other major American city has so large a percentage of black people. Whites make up about 27 per cent of the city's population. The other 3 per cent includes small groups of American Indians and Asians—especially Chinese, Filipinos, and Japanese.

The racial makeup of Washington's suburbs contrasts sharply with that of the city. In the suburbs, about 78 per cent of the people are whites, and about 17 per cent are blacks. American Indians, Asians, and members of other races account for the other 5 per cent.

About 41,000 people who live in Washington are citizens of countries other than the United States. Many of these people work for foreign embassies or for international organizations in the city. The foreign population includes people from almost every country, and gives the city a *cosmopolitan* (international) flavor.

Ethnic groups. Black people make up Washington's largest ethnic group. About 449,000 blacks live in the city. Black people make up a majority of the population in each of Washington's four sections. They account for about 89 per cent of the population in Northeast Washington, 90 per cent in Southeast, 60 per cent in Southwest, and 51 per cent in Northwest.

Thousands of Washington's blacks live in neighborhoods made up almost entirely of people of their own

Robert H. Glaze, Artstreet

Black Washingtonians visit an art exhibit at Howard University, *above.* Washington has a higher percentage of black people than any other major American city, about 70 per cent.

race. The neighborhoods range from poor, to middle-income, to upper-income ones. Many black Washingtonians also live in middle- and upper-income racially integrated areas, both in the city and the suburbs.

About 172,000 white people live in Washington. In many cities, large numbers of whites of the same ethnic group—such as people of Irish, Italian, or Polish ancestry—live in the same neighborhoods. But most of Washington's predominantly white neighborhoods are made up of people of many ethnic backgrounds.

Since the mid-1900's, many refugees from countries torn by war and political turmoil have settled in Washington and its suburbs. They include many people of Southeast Asian and Hispanic origins. Many of these people of the same ethnic group live close together. They have opened restaurants, shops, and other businesses in their neighborhoods.

Housing. About half of Washington's people live in one- or two-family houses, and about half live in apartment buildings. Only about 36 per cent of Washington's families own their homes. The others rent them. The national average for the percentage of families in cities who own their homes is about 48 per cent.

Washington has some of the nation's most luxurious housing, including the Watergate apartments and the mansions and town houses of Georgetown. It also has much good middle-class housing. However, the city faces a shortage of good housing for low-income, as well as moderate-income, families. This housing shortage exists in both the city and the suburbs, and ranks among the Washington area's biggest problems.

Several factors make the housing problem difficult to solve. Each year, some housing units become so run-down that people abandon them, thus reducing the number of usable low-income units. In other cases, low-income units are remodeled and then rented or sold to higher-income households. In addition, since the 1960's, the cost of housing has risen faster in Washington than

Paul S. Conklin

Embassy officials from many nations mix at a party at the Argentine Embassy, *above.* Washington's many embassies give the city a *cosmopolitan* (international) flavor.

in most parts of the country. Rising costs further reduce the amount of housing available to people with low and moderate incomes.

Education. The Washington public school system includes about 185 schools with more than 87,000 students. An additional 25,000 students attend about 80 private schools in the city.

The District of Columbia Board of Education governs the public school system. The board consists of 11 members elected by the people to four-year terms. The members appoint a superintendent to administer the system. About 88 per cent of the money needed to run Washington's public schools comes from local taxes, and about 12 per cent from the federal government.

Washington has 17 accredited universities and colleges. The University of the District of Columbia, established in 1976, has three campuses in the city. Howard University is one of the country's largest predominantly black universities. Catholic University of America is the national university of the Roman Catholic Church in the United States.

Social problems. Washington faces a variety of social problems. Among them are poverty and crime.

Overall, the people of Washington have a high standard of living. But thousands of people in both the city and suburbs do not share in the wealth. About 15 per cent of all the families in the city and about 4 per cent of the families in the suburbs have incomes that classify them as poor by federal government standards. In Washington as elsewhere, poverty affects blacks more than whites. About 14 per cent of all the black families in the metropolitan area are poor, compared to about 3 per cent of all the white families.

Paul S. Conklin

A soccer game on the Ellipse provides recreation for a group of Washington young people, *above*. The Washington Monument rises above the trees in the background.

Universities and colleges

Washington, D.C., has 17 universities and colleges that grant bachelor's or advanced degrees and are accredited by the Middle States Association of Colleges and Schools. For enrollments and further information, see **Universities and colleges** (table).

Name	Founded
American University	1893
Catholic University of America	1887
Corcoran School of Art	1890
Defense Intelligence College	1962
De Sales School of Theology	1949
District of Columbia, University of the	1976
Dominican House of Studies	1902
Gallaudet University	1864
George Washington University	1821
Georgetown University	1789
Howard University	1867
Mount Vernon College	1875
Oblate College	1916
Southeastern University	1879
Strayer College	1904
Trinity College	1897
Wesley Theological Seminary	1882

Much of the crime in the Washington area takes place in the city, especially in poor neighborhoods. But in recent years, crime rates have been rising more rapidly in the suburbs than in the city. Washington's crime problem receives more nationwide publicity than that of any other city with the possible exception of New York City. Whenever a government official is the victim of a crime, the news is reported throughout the country. As a result, many people believe Washington has one of the nation's highest crime rates. But more than 60 metropolitan areas have a higher crime rate. Over a dozen metropolitan areas lead Washington in the rate of violent crimes, such as assault and murder.

Cultural life and recreation. The museums, government buildings, monuments, libraries, parks, and theaters described under *Visitor's guide* help make Washington a leading cultural and recreational center. Residents as well as tourists enjoy these facilities.

Washington also has many cultural and recreational facilities used chiefly by its residents. These include a public library system with about 1,400,000 volumes. The system includes a main library and about 25 branch libraries. The main library is the Martin Luther King Memorial Library at 9th and G streets NW. Washington has many neighborhood museums, including some that specialize in exhibits of black culture. The city's main playhouses—in addition to the Kennedy Center—include the National Theatre at 13th and E streets NW, the Arena Stage at 6th and M streets SW, Ford's Theatre, and the Shakespeare Theatre at the Folger.

Washington has about 150 parks. Many Washingtonians enjoy boating on the Potomac River. Three professional sports teams play in the Washington area. The Washington Redskins of the National Football League play in the Robert F. Kennedy, or RFK, Stadium, about 2 miles (3 kilometers) east of the Capitol. The Washington Bullets of the National Basketball Association and the Washington Capitals of the National Hockey League play in the Capital Centre, in Largo, Md.

Washington's economy is based on the activities of the federal government. The government employs more of the Washington area's workers than does any kind of private business. It also generates much of Washington's private economic activity.

The federal government provides jobs for about 400,000 people in Washington and its suburbs. The best-known and most important government employees include the President and the President's close advisers, the members of Congress, and the Supreme Court justices. But these key policy-making officials account for only a tiny portion of Washington's government workers. Hundreds of lower-ranking officials help carry out the day-to-day operations of the government. Thousands of office workers—including lawyers, accountants, clerks, and secretaries—assist them.

Private business. The government's attractions make Washington one of the world's leading centers of tourism. Every year, millions of tourists visit the city to see the government in action and to enjoy its many interesting and historic sights. The money the tourists spend helps support—and provides jobs in—many hotels, motels, restaurants, and other businesses.

Many other economically important businesses and private organizations are located in Washington chiefly because the government is there. They include law and accounting firms, public affairs research organizations, and communications companies. They also include numerous trade associations and labor unions that have their headquarters in the city so they can try to influence government policies in the best interests of their members. The people who work to influence the government are called *lobbyists.* Finance, insurance, real estate, and wholesale and retail trade also provide many jobs.

Manufacturing is far less important in Washington than it is in most large cities. Only a small portion of the area's labor force works in manufacturing industries. Printing and publishing firms employ many of these workers.

Transportation. Automobiles provide the main means of transportation within Washington and between the city and its suburbs. About 70 per cent of the people who work in the Washington area use cars to get to and from their jobs. The government has built several superhighways to handle the heavy automobile traffic. Even so, huge traffic jams often occur in and around the city during rush hours.

The Washington Area Metropolitan Transit Authority, a public corporation, provides public transportation in the Washington area. Called *Metro,* the transit authority operates a bus service throughout the city and its suburbs. In 1969, Congress passed legislation providing for a subway system to be operated by Metro. Parts of the system, which extends throughout the city and well into the suburbs, first began operating in 1976. The entire subway system is scheduled for completion in the 1990's.

Three major airports handle Washington's commercial air traffic. Washington National Airport lies just across the Potomac River in Virginia. Dulles International Airport, also in Virginia, lies about 25 miles (40 kilometers) west of the city. Baltimore-Washington Interna-

Cameramann International, Ltd.

Government workers jam Pennsylvania Avenue, *above,* on their way to and from work. The federal government is the largest employer in the Washington area.

tional Airport (formerly Friendship International) is in Maryland, about 30 miles (48 kilometers) northeast of Washington.

Union Station lies north of the Capitol. The station serves passenger trains that run between Washington and other parts of the country.

Communication. Washington ranks as a leading communication center. Many of the world's major newspapers, magazines, and radio and television networks have permanent correspondents in the city. These reporters provide their readers, listeners, and viewers with firsthand news of the activities of the government.

The government makes Washington one of the nation's chief publishing centers. Its departments and agencies produce pamphlets and books on thousands of subjects. The subjects range from census information to how to solve farm problems and where to go for medical help.

A number of national magazines are published in Washington. They include *National Geographic Magazine, U.S. News & World Report, The New Republic,* and the *National Journal.*

Washington has two general daily newspapers, the *Washington Post* and the *Washington Times. USA Today,* a national daily paper, is published in the Washington area. Fourteen television stations and more than 40 radio stations serve the Washington area.

Washington has an unusual local government. As in many cities, the people elect a mayor and a city council to make laws and carry out government functions. But the federal government has final authority in all matters relating to Washington's government.

The mayor serves a four-year term and is responsible for the administration of the government. The mayor appoints the heads of the city's local government departments, such as the police and sanitation departments. The mayor also prepares the city's budget and proposes local laws.

Washington's city council has 13 members. Five of the council's members—including its chairman—are elected in citywide elections. In addition, one council member is elected from each of Washington's eight election districts. All members serve four-year terms.

The city council passes local laws. But Congress also has the power to make laws for the city, including ones that overrule council decisions. The council approves the mayor's budget. But Congress and the Office of Management and Budget in the Executive Office of the President must approve the budget.

The mayor can *veto* (reject) legislation passed by the city council. The council can *override* (set aside) a veto with a two-thirds majority vote of those voting on the question.

Washington's flag was adopted in 1938. Its design is based on George Washington's coat of arms.

The city seal, adopted in 1871, shows Justice placing a wreath on a statue of George Washington.

Washington's city government gets about two-thirds of its revenue from taxes, including property, sales, and local income taxes. The federal government provides most of the rest of the revenue.

Washington's present system of local government was established by an act of Congress in 1973 and approved by the people in 1974. For 100 years before that time, the people of Washington had almost no voice in their government. The President, rather than the people, chose the three commissioners who made up the government. See the *History* section of this article for details on Washington's former system of local government.

History

The first people known to have lived in the Washington area were Piscataway Indians. Whites moved into the area during the late 1600's and established farms and plantations. In 1749, settlers founded Alexandria, the area's first town, in what was then the colony of Virginia.

Washington becomes the capital. Several different cities served as the national capital during the early years of the United States (see **United States capitals**). In 1783, Congress decided that the country should have a permanent center of government. But the states could not agree on a location for it. People assumed that the new capital would become an important commercial and industrial city. As a result, each state wanted it to be located within its borders. Also, both Northerners and Southerners believed the capital should be in their part of the country.

In 1790, Secretary of the Treasury Alexander Hamilton worked out a solution. He proposed that the capital be built on land that belonged to the federal government, rather than to a state. He and others persuaded Northern political leaders to agree to locate the capital in the South. In return, Southern leaders supported certain government policies favored by the North.

Once the disagreements were settled, Congress decided to locate the capital along the Potomac River. It asked President George Washington, who had been raised in the Potomac area, to choose the exact site.

The President's choice, made in 1791, included not only the land now occupied by Washington, but also about 30 square miles (78 square kilometers) of land west of the Potomac. The city's present territory had belonged to Maryland, and the land southwest of the river

was part of Virginia. The two states turned over the territory to the federal government.

Early days. George Washington hired Pierre Charles L'Enfant, a French engineer, to create a plan for the physical layout of the city. L'Enfant's plan dealt only with the area between the Anacostia River and Georgetown.

Detail from an engraving by Andrew Ellicott (1792);
Library of Congress, Geography and Map Division

Pierre L'Enfant's plan for Washington showed the location of the Capitol, White House, and Mall. President George Washington hired L'Enfant, a French engineer, to plan the city.

View of the Capitol at Washington, D.C., a hand-tinted engraving by C. J. Bentley after a painting by W. H. Bartlett; from *American Scenery,* published in 1840 by George Virtue

Pennsylvania Avenue in 1827 was a quiet dirt road. The Capitol, *background,* had a different dome and was smaller than it is today. The present Capitol design dates from the 1850's.

But it established the pattern for the entire city. It made the Capitol the center of Washington. The American surveyors Andrew Ellicott and Benjamin Banneker helped work out the plan for the new city.

The federal government moved to Washington from its temporary capital in Philadelphia in 1800. At that time, the entire Washington area had only about 8,000 people. In 1814, during the War of 1812, British soldiers captured Washington. They burned the Capitol, the White House, and other government buildings. Reconstruction of the buildings was completed in 1819.

The Constitution of the United States gave Congress the power to govern Washington. But in 1802, Congress established a local government, including a mayor and a city council, to help run the city. The people of Washington were given the right to elect council members in 1802 and the mayor in 1820, but they were not allowed to vote for members of Congress or the President.

The predictions that Washington would become an important commercial and industrial center did not come true. The city could not compete economically with such long-established cities as Boston, New York, Philadelphia, Baltimore, and Charleston. Lacking economic growth, Washington remained a small city. By the 1840's, it had only about 50,000 people, and only a small part of its present area was built up. As a result, in 1846, Congress returned to Virginia the land that the state had earlier given to the federal government.

Growth and development. Washington's main periods of growth have been times of crisis, such as wars and depressions. During such times, the role of the federal government has been greatly expanded to help meet the crises. Large numbers of people moved to the city to handle the new jobs that resulted.

The Civil War (1861-1865) was the first crisis that caused Washington to grow. During the war, the city's population soared from about 60,000 to 120,000. The Union stationed thousands of troops in Washington to protect the city from Confederate attacks. Large num-

bers of people flocked to the city to help direct the Union's war effort and to establish businesses. In addition, thousands of slaves who had been freed during the war moved to the city. The enormous population growth led to a severe housing shortage. In addition, the city's streets, sewer and water systems, and other public facilities could not handle the increased population.

Congress began a major rebuilding and expansion program in Washington after the war. The program solved the city's physical problems. But it indirectly led to an end of the people's right to choose their government leaders. Congress believed that a reorganization of Washington's local government was necessary for a successful rebuilding program. At first, in 1871, it established a territorial government that included a governor appointed by the President, and an elected assembly. Then, in 1874, Congress established a local government made up of three commissioners appointed by the President. Washington became the only American city in which the people did not elect its local officials.

Washington grew gradually for many years after the Civil War. But in 1917, when the United States entered World War I, another period of enormous growth began. Again, the government needed new workers to help direct a war effort, and businesses and services were needed to support them. The city's population increased from about 350,000 when the United States entered the war to more than 450,000 in 1918, when the war ended. Shortages developed in housing, office space, schools, and public facilities. The automobile had replaced the horse as the main means of transportation in the city. To accommodate the cars, the Mall was turned into a parking lot. Many new houses, office buildings, and schools went up during the 1920's.

During the Great Depression of the 1930's, jobs became scarce in all parts of the United States except Washington. The federal government became deeply involved in projects designed to end the depression, and thousands of new government jobs became available in the capital. The city's population grew from about 485,000 to 665,000 between 1930 and 1940.

Recent developments. Several factors have caused the federal government to grow with few interruptions since the depression. These factors include the country's participation in World War II from 1941 to 1945, its leadership of the Western world after the war, and the federal government's increased responsibilities in the field of social welfare. The government's growth has brought about steady growth of the Washington area. The city's population reached a peak of more than 800,000 by 1950. Since then, it has decreased by about 160,000. However, the population of the suburbs has soared. Between 1950 and 1980, Washington's metropolitan area population grew faster than that of any other large city. It increased from about 1½ million to more than 3 million.

Blacks made up a majority of the population for the first time in the 1950's. Until the late 1960's, almost all the people who moved to the suburbs of Washington were whites. Blacks then began moving to the suburbs in large numbers.

After World War II, many Washingtonians began demanding the right to participate in government. Congress and the states passed a constitutional amendment that allowed the people to vote in presidential elections for the first time in 1964. In 1970, Congress passed legislation that permitted Washington to have a delegate in the United States House of Representatives for the first time since 1875. The delegate was elected by the voters in 1971. The delegate may vote in House committees, but not in House votes. In 1973, Congress gave the people of Washington the right to elect local officials for the first time in 100 years. Walter E. Washington, appointed as the city's chief administrative officer in 1967, won election as mayor in 1974. In 1978, Marion S. Barry, Jr., was elected mayor.

In 1978, Congress approved a constitutional amendment that would allow Washington residents to elect voting delegates to the United States House of Representatives and Senate. The amendment never took effect because it was not *ratified* (approved) by at least three-fourths of the states within the required time limit of seven years.

In the 1970's, many Washingtonians began to support a movement to make the District of Columbia a state. In a 1980 election, a majority of Washington's voters supported statehood. In January 1982, a constitutional convention met and drew up a state Constitution. This Constitution was approved by the city's voters in November 1982. Washington's voters also approved the name *New Columbia* for the proposed state. The Constitution was sent to the U.S. Congress for final approval in September 1983, but no congressional vote had been taken by mid-1989.

In 1989, as a result of severe drug problems in Washington, the federal government mounted a $70-million to $80-million program to combat drug abuse. The program aims at increasing efforts to identify drug dealers, establishing more detainment facilities for drug criminals, and providing more effective rehabilitation of drug abusers.   Eunice S. Grier and Atlee E. Shidler

Related articles in *World Book* include:

Interesting places to visit

Arlington National Cemetery
Capitol, United States
Corcoran Gallery of Art
Folger Shakespeare Library
Freer Gallery of Art
Hirshhorn Museum and Sculpture Garden
Jefferson Memorial
Kennedy Center for the Performing Arts
Library of Congress
Lincoln Memorial
Mount Vernon
National Air and Space Museum
National Archives

National Gallery of Art
National Museum of American History
National Museum of Natural History
National Zoological Park
Pentagon Building
Smithsonian Institution
Statuary Hall
Supreme Court of the United States
United States Botanic Garden
Unknown Soldier
Washington Cathedral
Washington Monument
White House

Other related articles

Latrobe, Benjamin H.   L'Enfant, Pierre C.

Outline

I. **Visitor's guide**
  A. Capitol Hill
  B. The National Mall
  C. North of the Mall
  D. South of the Mall
  E. Other points of interest
II. **The city**
  A. Northwest section
  B. Northeast section
  C. Southeast section
  D. Southwest section
  E. Metropolitan area
III. **People**
  A. Ethnic groups
  B. Housing
  C. Education
  D. Social problems
  E. Cultural life and recreation
IV. **Economy**
  A. The federal government
  B. Private business
  C. Transportation
  D. Communication
V. **Local government**
VI. **History**

Questions

How does the federal government influence Washington's economy?
Who planned the physical layout of Washington?
What are some of Washington's tourist attractions?
How are the four sections of Washington named?
Why is Washington's local government unusual?
What have been the chief causes of the city's growth?
Why does Washington have no skyscrapers?
What are Washington's chief social problems?
Why does Washington face a low-income housing shortage?
Why did Congress have a difficult time deciding where to locate the capital?

Additional resources

Green, Constance W. *Washington.* 2 vols. Princeton, 1976. First published in 1962-1963.
Lewis, David L. *District of Columbia: A Bicentennial History.* Norton, 1976.

Washington, Booker T. (1856-1915), was the most influential black leader and educator of his time in the United States. He became prominent largely because of his role as founder and head of Tuskegee Institute, a vocational school for blacks in Tuskegee, Ala.

Washington advised two Presidents—Theodore Roosevelt and William Howard Taft—on racial problems and policies. He also influenced the appointment of several blacks to federal office, especially during Roosevelt's

Administration. Washington described his rise from slavery to national prominence as an educator in his best-selling autobiography, *Up from Slavery* (1901).

Early life. Booker Taliaferro Washington was born a slave in Hales Ford, Va., near Roanoke. After the U.S. government freed all slaves in 1865, Washington's family moved to Malden, W. Va. There, Washington worked in coal mines and salt furnaces. From 1872 to 1875, he attended the Hampton Institute, an industrial school for blacks in Hampton, Va. He became a teacher at the institute in 1879. Washington based many of his later educational theories on his training at Hampton.

Educator. In 1881, Washington founded and became principal of Tuskegee Normal and Industrial Institute. He started this school in an old abandoned church and a shanty. The school's name was later changed to Tuskegee Institute (now Tuskegee University). The school taught specific trades, such as carpentry, farming, and mechanics, and trained teachers. As it expanded, Washington spent much of his time raising funds. Under Washington's leadership, the institute became famous as a model of industrial education. The Tuskegee Institute National Historic Site, established in 1974, includes Washington's home, student-made college buildings, and the George Washington Carver Museum.

Washington believed that blacks could benefit more from a practical, vocational education rather than a college education. Most blacks lived in poverty in the rural South, and Washington felt they should learn skills, work hard, and acquire property. He believed that the development of work skills would lead to economic prosperity. Washington predicted that blacks would be granted civil and political rights after gaining a strong economic foundation. He explained his theories in *Up from Slavery* and in other publications.

Racial leader. In the late 1800's, more and more blacks became victims of lynchings and *Jim Crow* laws that segregated blacks (see **Jim Crow**). To reduce racial conflicts, Washington advised blacks to stop demanding equal rights and to simply get along with whites. He urged whites to give blacks better jobs.

In a speech given in Atlanta, Ga., in 1895, Washington declared: "In all things that are purely social we can be as separate as the fingers, yet one as the hand in all things essential to mutual progress." This speech was often called the *Atlanta Compromise* because Washington accepted inequality and segregation for blacks in exchange for economic advancement. The speech was widely quoted in newspapers and helped make him a prominent national figure and black spokesman.

Washington became a shrewd political leader and advised not only Presidents, but also members of Congress and governors, on political appointments for blacks and sympathetic whites. He urged wealthy people to contribute to various black organizations. He also owned or financially supported many black newspapers. In 1900, Washington founded the National Negro Business League to help black business firms.

Throughout his life, Washington tried to please whites in both the North and the South through his public actions and his speeches. He never publicly supported black political causes that were unpopular with Southern whites. However, Washington secretly financed lawsuits opposing segregation and upholding

the right of blacks to vote and to serve on juries.

Opposition to Washington came chiefly from W. E. B. Du Bois, a historian and sociologist. Du Bois criticized Washington's educational and political philosophy and practices. Du Bois supported higher education for talented blacks who could serve as leaders. He feared that the success of Washington's industrial school would limit the development of true higher education for blacks. Du Bois accepted the need for industrial training. However, he believed that blacks should also have the opportunity to obtain a college education.

Du Bois attacked Washington's compromising views on political and civil rights. Du Bois felt that blacks must openly strive for their rights. He criticized what he regarded as Washington's surrender of rights and human dignity for economic gain. Du Bois also attacked some ways that Washington used his power. By controlling many black newspapers, for example, Washington made it difficult for differing views to be published. And because he was acclaimed as the foremost black leader, Washington helped determine what racial policies and practices were "acceptable." Du Bois outlined his criticisms in his book *The Souls of Black Folk* (1903).

By 1910, Washington's influence had started to decline as Du Bois and others began new movements. These movements led to the creation of such organizations as the National Association for the Advancement of Colored People (NAACP) and the National Urban League.

Raymond W. Smock

See also **Du Bois, W. E. B.; Black Americans** (The rise of new black leaders); **Niagara Movement; Tuskegee University.**

Additional resources

Bontemps, Arna. *Young Booker: Booker T. Washington's Early Days.* Dodd, 1972.
Harlan, Louis R. *Booker T. Washington: The Making of a Black Leader, 1856-1901.* Oxford, 1972. *Booker T. Washington: The Wizard of Tuskegee, 1901-1915.* 1983.
Washington, Booker T. *Up from Slavery: An Autobiography.* Corner House, 1971. First published in 1901.

Booker T. Washington National Monument

Booker T. Washington, a black leader and educator, founded Tuskegee Institute and headed the school from 1881 to 1915.

**1st President of
the United States 1789-1797**

Washington
1st President
1789-1797
No political
party

J. Adams
2nd President
1797-1801
Federalist

John Adams
Vice President
1789-1797

Oil painting on canvas (1796) by Gilbert Stuart; Jointly owned by the National Portrait Gallery, Smithsonian Institution, and the Museum of Fine Arts, Boston

Washington, George (1732-1799), won a lasting place in American history as the "Father of our Country." For nearly 20 years, he guided his country much as a father cares for a growing child.

In three important ways, Washington helped shape the beginning of the United States. First, he commanded the Continental Army that won American independence from Great Britain in the Revolutionary War. Second, Washington served as president of the convention that wrote the United States Constitution. Third, he was elected the first President of the United States.

The people of his day loved Washington. His army officers would have made him king if he had let them. From the Revolutionary War on, his birthday was celebrated each year throughout the country.

Washington lived an exciting life in exciting times. As a boy, he explored the wilderness. When he grew older, he helped the British fight the French and Indians. Many times he was nearly killed. As a general, he suffered hardships with his troops in the cold winters at Valley Forge, Pa., and Morristown, N.J. He lost many battles, but led the American army to final victory at Yorktown, Va. After he became President, he successfully solved many problems in turning the plans of the Constitution into a working government.

Washington went to school only until he was about 14 or 15. But he learned to make the most of all his abilities and opportunities. Washington's remarkable patience and his understanding of others helped him win people to his side in times of hardship and discouragement.

There are great differences between the United States of Washington's day and that of today. The new nation was small and weak. It stretched west only to the Mississippi River and had fewer than 4,000,000 people. Most people made their living by farming. Few children went to school. Few men or women could read or write. Transportation and communication were slow. It took Washington 3 days to travel about 90 miles (140 kilometers) from New York City to Philadelphia, longer than it now takes to fly around the world. There were only 11 states in the Union when Washington became President and 16 when he left office.

Many stories have been told about Washington. Most are probably not true. So far as we know, he did not chop down his father's cherry tree, then confess by saying: "Father, I cannot tell a lie." He probably never threw a stone across the broad Rappahannock River. But such stories show that people were willing to believe almost anything about his honesty and his great strength. One of Washington's officers, Henry "Light Horse Harry" Lee, summed up the way Americans felt and still feel about Washington:

"First in war, first in peace, and first in the hearts of his countrymen."

Washington the man

Washington's appearance caused admiration and respect. He was tall, strong, and broad-shouldered. As he grew older, cares lined his face and gave him a somewhat stern appearance. Perhaps the best description of Washington was written by a friend, George Mercer, in 1760:

"He may be described as being straight as an Indian, measuring 6 feet 2 inches in his stockings, and weighing 175 pounds . . . A large and straight rather than a prominent nose; blue-gray penetrating eyes . . . He has a clear though rather colorless pale skin which burns with the

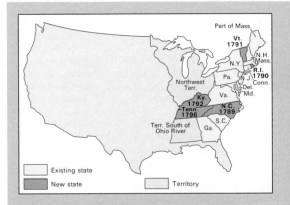

Part of Mass.

Vt.
1791

N.H.
N.Y. Mass.

Pa. R.I.
J. 1790 Conn.

Northwest
Terr. Del.
Md.
Ky. Va.
1792
Tenn. N.C.
1796 1789
S.C.
Terr. South of Ga.
Ohio River

Existing state

New state   Territory

Only 11 states made up the United States when Washington became the new nation's first President in 1789. Five states joined the Union during Washington's presidency.

The U.S. flag adopted in 1794 recognized the addition of Vermont and Kentucky to the Union. It served as the nation's flag until 1818.

The world of President Washington

The French Revolution began in 1789. In one of the first major acts of rebellion, French citizens captured the Bastille, a royal fortress and hated symbol of oppression.

The first U.S. census was begun in August 1790, and took 18 months to complete. It counted 3,929,214 people.

The Industrial Revolution in the United States made a big advance in 1790, when Samuel Slater established the nation's first water-powered cotton mill in Pawtucket, R. I.

Plans for a permanent national capital moved forward when President Washington selected a site on the Potomac River in 1791. Construction of the White House began the next year.

The Bill of Rights became law in 1791. These first 10 amendments to the U.S. Constitution guaranteed basic liberties.

The New York Stock Exchange was established in 1792.

Eli Whitney's cotton gin, patented in 1793, revolutionized the economy of the South. The device led to mass production of cotton and increased the demand for slave labor.

General Anthony Wayne defeated the Indians in 1794 in the Battle of Fallen Timbers. A treaty signed the following year opened a huge tract of land in Ohio to white settlers.

The first hard-surfaced road in the United States was completed in 1795 between Philadelphia and Lancaster, Pa. Other toll roads built in the 1790's encouraged development in New England and the Middle Atlantic region.

The first smallpox vaccination was given by English physician Edward Jenner in 1796. It represented a major advance in the battle against this dread disease.

WORLD BOOK map

sun . . . dark brown hair which he wears in a queue . . . His mouth is large and generally firmly closed, but which from time to time discloses some defective teeth . . . His movements and gestures are graceful, his walk majestic, and he is a splendid horseman."

Washington set his own strict rules of conduct, but he also enjoyed having a good time. He laughed at jokes, though he seldom told any.

One of the best descriptions of Washington's charac-

Important dates in Washington's life

1732 (Feb. 22) Born in Westmoreland County, Virginia.
1749 Became official surveyor for Culpeper County, Virginia.
1751 Went to Barbados Island, British West Indies.
1753 Carried British ultimatum to French in Ohio River Valley, as a major.
1754 Surrendered Fort Necessity in the French and Indian War, as a colonel.
1755 (July 9) With General Edward Braddock when ambushed by French and Indians.
1755-1758 Commanded Virginia's frontier troops, as a colonel.
1759 (Jan. 6) Married Mrs. Martha Dandridge Custis.
1774 Elected delegate to First Continental Congress.
1775 Elected delegate to Second Continental Congress.
1775 (June 15) Elected commander in chief of Continental Army.
1781 (Oct. 19) Victory at Yorktown.
1787 (May 25) Elected president of the Constitutional Convention.
1789 Elected first President of the United States.
1792 Reelected President of the United States.
1796 (Sept. 19) Published *Farewell Address,* refusing a third term.
1798 (July 4) Commissioned lieutenant general and commander in chief of new United States Army.
1799 (Dec. 14) Died at Mount Vernon at age 67.

ter was written after his death by his good friend Thomas Jefferson:

"His mind was great and powerful . . . as far as he saw, no judgment was ever sounder. It was slow in operation, being little aided by invention or imagination, but sure in conclusion. . . .

"Perhaps the strongest feature in his character was prudence, never acting until every circumstance, every consideration, was maturely weighed; refraining when he saw a doubt, but, when once decided, going through with his purpose whatever obstacles opposed.

"His integrity was most pure, his justice the most inflexible I have ever known . . .

"He was indeed, in every sense of the words, a wise, a good and a great man. . . . On the whole, his character

David R. White, Stockfile

A memorial mansion stands on the site of George Washington's birthplace on Pope's Creek in Westmoreland County, Virginia. The original house burned down in 1780.

was, in its mass, perfect . . . it may truly be said, that never did nature and fortune combine more perfectly to make a man great . . ."

Early life (1732-1746)

Family background. George Washington inherited much more than a good mind and a strong body. Washington belonged to an old colonial family that believed in hard work, in public service, and in worshiping God. The Washington family has been traced back to 1260 in England. The name at that time was de Wessington. It was later spelled Washington. Sulgrave Manor in England is regarded as the home of George Washington's ancestors (see **Sulgrave Manor**).

George's great-grandfather, John Washington (1632-1677), came to live in America by accident. He was mate on a small English ship that went aground in the Potomac River in 1656 or 1657. By the time the ship was repaired, he had decided to marry and settle in Virginia. He started with little money. Within 20 years he owned more than 5,000 acres (2,000 hectares), including the land that later became Mount Vernon. Lawrence Washington (1659-1698), the eldest son of John, was the grandfather of George.

Washington's parents. George's father, Augustine Washington (1694-1743), was Lawrence's youngest son. After iron ore was discovered on some of his land, he spent most of his time developing an ironworks. He had four children by his first wife, Jane Butler. She died in 1729. In March 1731, he married Mary Ball (1709?-1789), who became George's mother.

Mary Ball did not have a very happy childhood. Her father and mother both died before she was 13. Although she had a large fortune, she spent all her life worrying about money. After her son George became a man, she wrote him many letters asking for money even though she did not need it.

Augustine and Mary Ball Washington had six children. Besides George, there were: Betty (1733-1797), Samuel (1734-1781), John Augustine (1736-1787), Charles (1738-1799), and Mildred (1739-1740).

Boyhood. George Washington was born on Pope's Creek Farm in Westmoreland County, Virginia, on February 22, 1732 (February 11, on the Old Style Calendar then in use; see **Calendar**). When George was almost 3, his family moved to the large, undeveloped plantation that was later called Mount Vernon. It lay about 50 miles (80 kilometers) up the Potomac River in Virginia and was then called Little Hunting Creek Farm. Here George's only playmates were his younger sister and brothers. No neighbors lived close by. But George had fun exploring the nearby woods and helping out in farm work as well as a small boy could. He saw little of his father, who made many trips to his ironworks, about 30 miles (48 kilometers) away.

In 1738, when George was nearly 7, his father decided to move closer to the ironworks. He bought the 260-acre (105-hectare) Ferry Farm which lay on the Rappahannock River across from Fredericksburg, Va.

Education. George probably began going to school in Fredericksburg soon after the family moved to Ferry Farm. No accurate records have been found that tell who his teachers were. Altogether, he had no more than seven or eight years of school. His favorite subject was arithmetic. He wrote his lessons in ink on heavy paper. His mother then sewed the paper into notebooks.

George studied enough history and geography to know something of the outside world. But he never learned as much about literature, foreign languages, and history as did Thomas Jefferson or James Madison. They had the advantage of much more formal education.

By the time he ended his schoolwork at the age of 14 or 15, George could keep business accounts, write clear letters, and do simple figuring. During the rest of his life he kept diaries and careful accounts of his expenses.

George's father had probably planned to send him to school in England because there were few schools in Virginia. But Augustine Washington died when George was only 11, and the plans came to nothing. After his father's death, George's mother did not like to have him away from home for long. George was to inherit Ferry Farm when he reached 21. Meanwhile, he, his younger sister and brothers, and the farm were left in the care of his mother.

Plantation life. Growing up at Ferry Farm, young George helped manage a plantation worked by 20 black slaves. He was observant and hard-working. He learned how to plant and produce tobacco, fruit, grains, and vegetables. He saw how many things a plantation needed to keep operating, such as cloth and iron tools. He also developed his lifelong love for horses.

At the same time, Washington enjoyed the life of a young Virginia country gentleman. He had boyhood romances and wrote love poems. He became an expert dancer. And he enjoyed hunting, fishing, and boating on the river.

Development of character. As a youth, Washington was sober, quiet, attentive, and dignified. His respect for religion and his dependability made him admired. He experienced the hardships of colonial life on the edge of the wilderness. He learned that life was difficult. This helped make him become strong and patient.

As a schoolboy, Washington copied rules of behavior in an exercise book, perhaps at the suggestion of his mother. Following are some of these rules in his own spelling, capitalization, and punctuation:

> Turn not your Back to others especially in Speaking, Jog not the Table or Desk on which Another reads or writes, lean not upon any one.
> Use no Reproachfull Language against any one neither Curse nor Revile.
> Play not the Peacock, looking every where about you, to See if you be well Deck't, if your Shoes fit well, if your Stockings Sit neatly, and Cloths handsomely.
> While you are talking, Point not with your Finger at him of Whom you Discourse nor Approach too near him to whom you talk especially to his face.
> Be not Curious to Know the Affairs of Others neither approach those that Speak in Private.
> It's unbecoming to Stoop much to ones Meat. Keep your Fingers clean & when foul wipe them on a Corner of your Table Napkin.

George Washington's admiration for his half-brother Lawrence (1718-1752) also influenced his development. Lawrence had been educated in England. He had the polish of a young English gentleman. From 1740 to 1742, Lawrence had gone to Central America as a Virginia militia captain in a brief war between Great Britain and Spain. The militia took no part in the actual fighting. But Lawrence returned to Virginia with many war stories.

Washington became a surveyor when he was a teen-ager. He began as an assistant and soon earned enough to support himself. He made several survey trips to the Virginia wilderness.

These tales excited George's imagination. George became a frequent visitor to the fashionable new house that Lawrence had built at Mount Vernon.

Lawrence decided that 14-year-old George should join the British Royal Navy. George wanted to go, but he needed his mother's permission. No matter how much he argued, she would not let him go. She asked advice of her brother, Joseph Ball. He suggested somewhat jokingly that rather than let George become a sailor, it would be better to apprentice him to a *tinker,* a mender of pots and pans.

Washington the surveyor (1747-1752)

After teen-aged George Washington gave up hopes of becoming a sailor, he became interested in exploring the frontier. Becoming a surveyor and marking out new farms in the wilderness would give him a chance to leave home to seek adventure. He enjoyed mathematics, and he easily picked up an understanding of fractions and geometry. Then he took his father's old set of surveying instruments out of storage. At 15, he began to earn money as an assistant to local surveyors.

On one of his frequent visits to Mount Vernon, George met Lord Fairfax, the largest property owner in Virginia. Fairfax was a cousin of Lawrence Washington's wife. He owned more than 5 million acres (2 million hectares) of land in northern Virginia. These lands extended to the Allegheny Mountains and included most of the Shenandoah Valley.

First expedition. Lord Fairfax began planning an expedition to survey his western lands. James Genn, an expert surveyor, was put in charge of the expedition. Sixteen-year-old George Washington was invited to go along. The boy persuaded his mother to let him make his first long trip away from home.

The month-long expedition set out on horseback in March 1748. Washington learned to sleep in the open and hunt for food. By the time he returned to Mount Vernon, he felt he had grown into a man. He also was now shaving.

Professional surveyor. In the summer of 1749, Washington helped lay out the newly established town of Alexandria, Va. Later that year he was appointed official surveyor for Culpeper County. In November, Lord Fairfax hired him to make a short surveying trip into the Shenandoah Valley.

Washington lived at Mount Vernon most of that winter. He now supported himself. His surveying work paid him well. It was one of the few occupations in which a person could expect to be paid in cash. Most other business in Virginia was carried on with payments in tobacco. Washington kept track in his account book of small loans he made to his relatives and friends. He also wrote down winnings and losses at playing cards and billiards.

During 1750, Washington made more and more surveys as settlers moved into the Shenandoah Valley. He carefully saved his money. When he saw a particularly good piece of land, he bought it. By the end of the year he owned nearly 1,500 acres (607 hectares).

Only foreign trip. In 1751, George Washington made his only trip away from the shores of America. Lawrence Washington had become seriously ill. He decided to sail to the warm climate of Barbados Island in the British West Indies for his health. He asked George to go along.

The brothers arrived at the island in November. George's diary shows he was interested in comparing farming methods on the island with those of Virginia. Two weeks after arriving, George became ill with smallpox. He carried a few pox scars on his face the rest of his life. A week after recovering, George decided to return to Virginia while Lawrence remained in the tropics.

George was now 20. He fell in love with 16-year-old Betsy Fauntleroy, the daughter of a Richmond County planter and shipowner. George proposed to her at least twice. Each time he was refused. He sadly wrote that she had given him a "cruel sentence."

In June 1752, Lawrence Washington suddenly returned home. He died of tuberculosis six weeks later. Lawrence left Mount Vernon to his wife for as long as she lived, then to his daughter. He provided that the estate should go to George if his daughter died with no children of her own. He also left George an equal share of his land with his other three brothers.

Early military career (1753-1758)

At the age of 20, George Washington had no experience or training as a soldier. But Lawrence's war stories had interested him in military affairs. He applied to the governor for a commission in the militia. In February 1753, he was commissioned as a major and put in charge of training militia in southern Virginia. Washington immediately began reading books on tactics and military affairs.

Messenger to the French. In October 1753, Washington learned that Robert Dinwiddie, the acting governor of Virginia, planned to send a message to the French military commander in the Ohio River Valley. Dinwiddie intended to warn the French that they must withdraw their troops from the region. The French wanted the Ohio River Valley for fur trading, but the British wanted it for farming. Washington volunteered to carry the message. Dinwiddie gave him the task.

In mid-November, Washington set out into the dangerous wilderness. With him went Christopher Gist, a frontier guide; an interpreter; and four frontiersmen. Washington's party traveled north into western Pennsylvania. Sometimes the men covered as much as 20 miles (32 kilometers) in a day. They stopped at an Indian village at the site of present-day Pittsburgh, Pa. There, three Indian chiefs agreed to accompany the party to visit the French. The Indians gave George the name *Caunotaucarius,* which meant Towntaker.

Early in December, Washington reached French headquarters at Fort Le Boeuf, just south of present-day Erie, Pa. The French commander rejected Dinwiddie's warning. He said that his orders were to take and hold the Ohio River Valley. He gave Washington a letter to carry back to the British.

Washington experienced many hardships and dangers on the return trip to Virginia. It was late December and bitterly cold. Snow lay deep on the ground. Once an Indian tried to kill Washington. Another time Washington nearly drowned trying to cross the Allegheny River on a raft.

On Jan. 16, 1754, Washington reached Williamsburg and delivered the French reply to Dinwiddie. Washington urged Dinwiddie to build a fort where the Ohio and Allegheny rivers joined (the site of present-day Pittsburgh). He also drew detailed maps of the region. Within five days, Dinwiddie sent a force of frontiersmen to build the fort. The governor had unknowingly taken the first step toward a war that was to spread to many other countries—known in America as the French and Indian War, and in Europe as the Seven Years' War.

First military action. The 22-year-old Washington was promoted to lieutenant colonel. He received orders to enlist troops to man the new fort. He found Americans resentful because the British refused to pay them as much as regular British soldiers. Washington himself angrily threatened to resign because his pay was lower than that of a lieutenant colonel in the regular British army. Perhaps for the first time he realized that the British treated American colonists unfairly. It also may have been the first time he thought of himself as an American rather than as an Englishman.

Washington set out with about 160 poorly trained soldiers in April 1754. He was still 200 miles (320 kilometers) from the fort when he learned the French had captured it. Washington decided to move on toward the fort, which the French had named Fort Duquesne.

On May 28, 1754, Washington captured the first French prisoners of the war. He surprised a group of French troops, killed 10, wounded 1, and took 21 prisoners. Only one of Washington's men was killed. Washington described his feelings in the short fight: "I heard the bullets whistle, and believe me there is something charming in the sound."

Surrender of Fort Necessity. Washington's men built a fort about 60 miles (97 kilometers) south of Fort Duquesne. They completed it in June and named it Fort Necessity. Meanwhile, Washington had been promoted to the rank of colonel.

Early in June, about 180 Virginia militia arrived to reinforce Fort Necessity. Some friendly Indians also joined Washington's forces. But no food arrived. On June 14, just as the last food was being eaten, a company of about 100 British regular army troops arrived. They brought with them some vitally needed supplies.

On July 3, the French attacked Fort Necessity. Washington had only 400 men. A third of the troops were sick, and the rest hungry. The French fired from behind trees and rocks. About 30 of Fort Necessity's defenders were killed and 70 wounded. A rainstorm turned the battlefield into a sea of mud. As night fell, the young colonel had few men, little food, and no dry gunpowder. His position was hopeless. About midnight, Washington agreed to surrender Fort Necessity. The French let him march out of the fort and return to Virginia with his men and guns.

A discouraged Washington returned to Williamsburg two weeks later. The colonists did not blame the young colonel for losing the fort. They praised Washington and his men for their bravery.

In October, Washington again visited Williamsburg. He was shocked when Dinwiddie told him he had orders from London to lower the rank of all colonial officers. Washington wanted a military career, but he angrily resigned, rather than be lowered from the rank of colonel to captain.

Washington had inherited Ferry Farm from his father, but he did not wish to go there to live with his mother. Instead, he decided to rent Mount Vernon from the widow of his brother Lawrence. He agreed to pay a rent of 15,000 pounds (6,800 kilograms) of tobacco a year.

Braddock's defeat. In March 1755, Washington received a message from Major General Edward Braddock. The British general invited Washington to help him in a new campaign against the French at Fort Duquesne. Washington agreed to serve without pay as one of Braddock's aides. He believed this was an excellent opportunity to learn military affairs from an experienced general.

Braddock assembled his forces at Fort Cumberland, Md., about 90 miles (140 kilometers) southeast of Fort Duquesne. On June 7, the troops started across the rough country. Washington was upset by the slow march. He wrote in a letter: "They were halting to level every mole hill and to erect bridges over every brook; by which means we were four days getting 12 miles."

During the second week of the march, Washington became seriously ill with a high fever. He was forced to remain behind in camp for nearly three weeks. He warned Braddock to be careful of "the mode of attack which, more than probably, he would experience from the Canadian French and their Indians."

On July 9, the British had nearly reached Fort Duquesne. Braddock ordered his long column to march forward. Wearing bright red uniforms, the British soldiers looked as though they were parading before the king. Washington was not yet well, but he had rejoined the army and rode his horse with pillows tied to the saddle. Braddock was confident that the French would wait at their fort for his attack. What happened next was later described by Washington:

"We were attacked (very unexpectedly I must own) by about 300 French and Indians. Our numbers consisted of about 1,300 well armed men, chiefly regulars, who

During the French and Indian War, Washington served as an aide to British General Edward Braddock. Braddock was killed in July 1755, after leading his troops to defeat at Fort Duquesne. Washington is shown above reading the burial service over Braddock's body.

were immediately struck with such a deadly panic that nothing but confusion and disobedience of orders prevailed amongst them.

". . . the English soldiers . . . broke and ran as sheep before the hounds . . . The general (Braddock) was wounded behind in the shoulder and into the breast, of which he died three days after . . .

"I luckily escaped without a wound, though I had four bullets through my coat and two horses shot under me . . ."

With Braddock's defeat and death, Washington was released from service. He rode home to Mount Vernon. Shortly after, in a letter to one of his brothers, he summed up his military career thus far:

"I was employed to go a journey in the winter (when I believe few or none would have undertaken it) and what did I get by it? My expenses borne! I then was appointed with trifling pay to conduct a handful of men to the Ohio. What did I get by this? Why, after putting myself to a considerable expense by equipping and providing necessaries for the campaign, I went out, was soundly beaten, lost them all—came in, and had my commission taken from me, or in other words, my command reduced, under pretense of an order from home . . . I have been on the losing order ever since I entered the service . . ."

Frontier commander. The French encouraged the Indians to attack English settlers. In August 1755, Dinwiddie persuaded Washington to accept a new commis-

sion as colonel. Washington would take command of Virginia's colonial troops to defend the colony's 350-mile (563-kilometer) western frontier.

Many of the Virginians recruited by Washington and his officers were homeless men. A British officer described them as "an extremely bad collection of broken inn-keepers, horse jockeys, and Indian traders."

Washington constantly urged that a new attack be made on Fort Duquesne. The British finally decided in 1758 to attack Fort Duquesne again. An advance British force of 800 men again was ambushed by the French and Indians. More than 300 British soldiers were killed. When the main army, including Washington, finally reached the fort in late November, the French had burned it and retreated toward Canada.

Washington returned to Virginia to hang up his sword. He was now the most famous American-born soldier. Perhaps the most important thing he had learned was that the British army could be beaten.

The peaceful years (1759-1773)

At the age of 26, Washington turned to seek happiness as a country gentleman and to build a fortune. During the next 16 years, he became known as a skilled farmer, an intelligent businessman, a popular legislator, a conscientious warden of the Church of England, and a wise county court judge.

Marriage. On Jan. 6, 1759, Washington married Mrs. Martha Dandridge Custis (see **Washington, Martha Cus-**

Washington married Mrs. Martha Dandridge Custis, a wealthy Virginia widow, in 1759. He became a loving stepfather to Martha's two children, "Patsy" and "Jackie."

tis). She was a widow, eight months older than George. The marriage probably took place in New Kent County, Virginia, at the bride's plantation home, which was called the *White House.* Her first husband had left a fortune of about 17,000 acres (6,880 hectares) of land and $360,000. This was divided equally among the widow and her two children, John "Jackie" Parke Custis (1754-1781) and Martha "Patsy" Parke Custis (1756-1773). Washington became a loving stepfather to the children and gave them many gifts. He and Martha had no children of their own.

Legislator. After a six-week honeymoon at the White House, Washington took his new family to Williamsburg. There he served for the first time in the colonial legislature. He had been elected to the House of Burgesses in 1758, while still on the frontier. Although he had not personally campaigned, he had paid bills for his friends to entertain voters during the campaign.

During the next 15 years, Washington was reelected time after time to the legislature. He seldom made speeches and did not put any important bills before the legislature. More important, he learned the process of representative government. He saw the difficulties in getting a law passed. The experience gave him patience in later years when he had to deal with Congress during the Revolutionary War and as President. He also became acquainted with Thomas Jefferson, Patrick Henry, and other Virginia leaders.

Farmer and landowner. Washington brought his wife and children to Mount Vernon in April 1759. He found it badly run down by the neglect of his overseers.

In 1761, Washington inherited Mount Vernon because his half-brother Lawrence's widow and daughter had both died. He began to buy farms that lay around the estate. He also bought western lands for future development. In 1770, Washington made a trip west as far as the present town of Gallipolis, Ohio, searching for good land to buy. By 1773, he owned about 40,000 acres (16,000 hectares). He also controlled the large Custis es-

tate of his wife and her children. He rented much of his land to tenant farmers.

Washington was a careful businessman. He did his own bookkeeping and recorded every penny of expense or profit. His ledgers tell us when he bought gifts for his family, and what prices he received for his crops.

As a large landowner, Washington had to supervise many different activities. He wanted to learn more about farming, so he bought the latest books on the subject. When he discovered he could not grow the best grade of tobacco at Mount Vernon, he switched to raising wheat. He saw the profit in making flour, so he built his own flour mills. Large schools of fish swam in the Potomac River, and Mount Vernon became known for the barrels of salted fish it produced. Washington experimented with tree grafting to improve his fruit orchards. His weavers made cloth for the black slaves. He hired out his carpenters, bricklayers, and blacksmiths to other plantation owners.

Social life at Mount Vernon and nearby plantations was merry and light-hearted. The men shot ducks, fished, and hunted wild game. The greatest social events were the fox hunts. On weekends when hunts were planned, Mount Vernon housed many guests and their servants. Barbecues, dinners, dancing, and games made the hours pass quickly and pleasantly.

The coming revolution (1774-1775)

The American colonists in the late 1760's and early 1770's grew angrier and angrier at the taxes placed on them by Great Britain. As a legislator and as a leading landowner, Washington was deeply concerned as relations with Great Britain became worse. During this time his knowledge of colonial affairs increased under the guidance of his neighbor, George Mason, a leading statesman of the time (see **Mason, George**).

Lord Botetourt, the British governor, dismissed the Virginia legislature in 1769 because the representatives had protested the taxation imposed by the British Townshend Acts. Washington met with other legislators in a Williamsburg tavern. He presented a plan prepared by Mason for an association to boycott imports of British goods. The plan was quickly adopted.

Washington became one of the first American leaders to consider using force to "maintain the liberty." He wrote Mason in April 1769: ". . . That no man should scruple, or hesitate a moment to use arms in defense of so valuable a blessing, on which all the good and evil of life depends, is clearly my opinion; yet Arms, I would beg leave to add, should be the last . . . resort."

In 1774, the British closed the port of Boston as punishment for the Boston Tea Party. Virginia legislators who protested were dismissed by Governor Lord Dunmore. Again the representatives met as private citizens. They elected seven delegates, including Washington, to attend the First Continental Congress in Philadelphia. Washington wrote: ". . . shall we supinely sit and see one province after another fall a prey to despotism?"

First Continental Congress. The Continental Congress met in September 1774. There, Washington had his first chance to meet and talk with leaders of other colonies. The members were impressed with his judgment and military knowledge. Washington made no speeches and he was not appointed to any committees. But he worked to have trade with Great Britain stopped by all the colonies. The trade boycott was approved by the Congress. Then Congress adjourned.

In March 1775, representatives from each Virginia county met in a church in Richmond, Va. Washington and the others thrilled to Patrick Henry's famous speech in which he cried: "Give me liberty or give me death!"

The representatives again elected Washington to attend the Second Continental Congress in Philadelphia. See **Continental Congress.**

Elected commander in chief. By the time Washington left Mount Vernon to attend the Second Continental Congress, the Battles of Lexington and Concord already had been fought in Massachusetts. The Congress opened on May 10, 1775. For six weeks the delegates to the Congress debated and studied the problems facing the colonies. The majority, including Washington, wanted to avoid war. At the same time, they feared they could not avoid it.

To express his desire for action, Washington began wearing his red and blue uniform of the French and Indian War. He was appointed to one military committee after another. He was asked to prepare a defense of New York City, to study ways to obtain gunpowder, to make plans for an army, and to write army regulations.

Then, on June 14, Congress called on Pennsylvania, Maryland, and Virginia to send troops to aid Boston, which had been placed under British military rule. John Adams, who in later years would be Washington's Vice President and successor as President, rose to discuss the need of electing a commander in chief. Adams praised Washington highly and said his popularity would help unite the colonies. Many New England delegates believed a northerner should be made commander in chief. But the following day Washington was elected unanimously.

Washington had not sought the position. He particularly wanted to make everyone understand he did not want the $500 monthly pay that had been voted. He said

A View of Mount Vernon, oil painting on canvas (about 1790) by an unknown artist of the American School; National Gallery of Art, Washington, D.C., gift of Edgar William and Bernice Chrysler Garbisch

Washington's estate at Mount Vernon included an impressive mansion overlooking the Potomac River, and about 8,000 acres (3,200 hectares) of farmland and forests. Washington brought his family to Mount Vernon in 1759. He died there in 1799, two years after leaving the presidency.

John Adams Proposing Washington for Commander-in-Chief (Second Continental Congress, Philadelphia, June 15, 1775), oil painting on canvas (1913) by John Ward Dunsmore; Fraunces Tavern Museum, Sons of the Revolution in the State of New York, New York City

Washington was chosen to be commander in chief of the colonial army at the Second Continental Congress in 1775. John Adams, *center,* proposed Washington, *standing left,* for the position. The delegates elected him unanimously. He accepted reluctantly and refused pay for his services.

he would keep track of his expenses, and would accept nothing else for his services. His acceptance speech, on June 16, was presented with modesty.

"I beg it may be remembered by every gentleman in the room," Washington said, "that I this day declare with the utmost sincerity, I do not think myself equal to the command I am honored with."

"First in war" (1775-1783)

"These are the times that try men's souls," Thomas Paine wrote during the Revolutionary War. "The summer soldier and the sunshine patriot will in this crisis shrink from the service of his country . . ."

During the eight years of war, Washington's soul was tried many times both by "summer soldiers," who did not care to fight in winter, and by "sunshine patriots," who were friendly to the American cause only when things went well. Only his strong will to win made it possible for Washington to overcome his many discouragements.

The following sections describe the most important problems that Washington overcame to win the Revolutionary War. For an account of the main battles, see the article **Revolutionary War in America.**

Symbol of independence. To most Americans of his time, Washington became the chief symbol of what they were fighting for. The colonists had been brought up to respect the British king. They did not easily accept the

idea of independence. The Congress that approved the Declaration of Independence on July 4, 1776, was not elected by the people, but by the legislatures of the states. And the legislatures were elected only by property owners. As a result, some people who did not own property and had no vote viewed independence with suspicion. Thousands of *Loyalists,* as British sympathizers were called, refused to help the fight for independence in any way.

Although many people did not especially wish for independence and did not trust Congress, they came to believe in Washington. They sympathized with him for the misery he shared with his soldiers. They cheered his courage in carrying on the fight.

"Washington retreats like a general and acts like a hero," the *Pennsylvania Journal* said in 1777. "Had he lived in the days of idolatry, he had been worshiped as a god." That same year, the Marquis de Lafayette wrote to Washington: ". . . if you were lost for America, there is nobody who could keep the Army and Revolution for six months."

Discouragement. Praise did not keep Washington from feeling discouraged. Often he believed he could not hold out long enough to win. Following are several comments he wrote throughout the war.

1776—"Such is my situation that if I were to wish the bitterest curse to an enemy on this side of the grave, I should put him in my stead with my feelings . . ."

1779—". . . there is every appearance that the Army will infallibly disband in a fortnight."

1781—". . . it is vain to think that an Army can be kept together much longer, under such a variety of sufferings as ours has experienced."

The army. Throughout the war, Washington seldom commanded more than 10,000 troops at any one time. He described his soldiers as "raw militia, badly officered, and with no government." There were two kinds of troops: (1) soldiers of the Continental Army, organized by Congress, and (2) militia, organized by the states.

Washington had trouble keeping soldiers in the Continental Army. At the beginning of the war, Congress let soldiers enlist for only a few months. Toward the end of the war, Washington convinced Congress that enlistments had to be longer. When their enlistments were up, the soldiers of the Continental Army went home. Sometimes a thousand men marched off at once.

Washington often had to plan battles for certain dates, because if he waited longer the soldiers' enlistments would be up. For example, Washington attacked the Hessian (German) troops at Trenton, N.J., on the day after Christmas in 1776 for this reason. His army had shrunk to only about 5,000 men and the enlistments of most of his soldiers would be up at the end of December. The victory at Trenton inspired many of his soldiers to reenlist.

From time to time, Washington asked the states to call out their militia to help in a particular battle. The militia included storekeepers, farmers, and other private citizens. They were poorly trained and did not like being called from their homes to fight. The Continental Army complained so much that troops of the Continental Army called them "long faces." Washington's army was defeated many times because the militia turned and ran when they saw redcoated British soldiers.

Desertion by his soldiers was another one of Washington's major problems. Many soldiers enlisted only to collect bonuses offered by Congress. At some times, as many men deserted each day as were enlisted. Washington authorized harsh punishment for deserters. He had some hanged. Dangerous mutinies also occurred.

"We are, during the winter, dreaming of independence and peace, without using the means to become so," Washington wrote in 1780. "In the spring, when our recruits are with the Army in training, we have just discovered the necessity of calling for them, and by the fall, after a distressed and inglorious campaign for want of them, we begin to get a few men, which come in just in time enough to eat our provisions . . ."

From the time Washington took command to the end of the war, he had few capable generals. Congress appointed the generals without asking Washington's advice. The states appointed officers in the militia. Most officers were chosen for political reasons. Some generals, such as Charles Lee and Horatio Gates, believed they should have been chosen commander in chief. They sometimes failed to obey Washington's orders in an effort to make him look like a poor general. One foreign-born general, Thomas Conway, organized a conspiracy known as the *Conway cabal* to make Major General Horatio Gates commander in chief (see **Cabal**). Washington sometimes hesitated to give orders to generals older than himself. In planning a battle or campaign, he usually called for a council of his generals and accepted the opinion of the majority.

Shortage of supplies. Washington's troops lacked food, clothing, ammunition, and other supplies through-

The Battle of Trenton in December 1776, ended in a resounding victory for the patriots. Washington led his troops across the icy Delaware River and launched a successful surprise attack against the Hessians.

Granger Collection

Winter at Valley Forge was a period of great suffering for the Continental Army. Washington and the French General Marquis de Lafayette led their discouraged troops through several months of hardships, including bitter cold, inadequate shelter, and shortages of food and clothing.

out the war. If the British had attacked the Americans around Boston in 1775, Washington could have issued only enough gunpowder for nine shots to each soldier. He had to give up Philadelphia to the British in 1777 because he could not risk losing the few supplies he had. The army repeatedly ran out of meat and bread. Sometimes hundreds of troops had to march barefoot in the snow because they had no shoes.

"The want of clothing, added to the misery of the season," Washington wrote in the winter of 1777-1778 at Valley Forge, Pa., "has occasioned (the soldiers) to suffer such hardships as will not be credited but by those who have been spectators."

In the winter of 1779-1780 at Morristown, N.J., Major General Nathanael Greene described Washington's army: "Poor fellows! They exhibit a picture truly distressing—more than half naked and two thirds starved. A country overflowing with plenty are now suffering an Army, employed for the defense of everything that is dear and valuable, to perish for want of food."

Winning the war. From the beginning of the war, Washington knew the powerful British navy gave the enemy a great advantage. The ships of the British could carry their army anywhere along the American coast. Washington's tiny, ragged army could not possibly defend every American port.

On the other hand, Washington knew from his experience in the French and Indian War that the British army moved slowly on land. He also knew it could be beaten. He proved that he could stay one jump ahead of the British by quick retreats. Meanwhile, Washington waited and prayed for the French to send a large fleet of

warships to America. He hoped then to trap the British while the French navy prevented them from escaping.

Washington's prayers came true at Yorktown, Va. There, on Sept. 28, 1781, he surrounded Lord Cornwallis' army. The French fleet prevented the British from escaping by ship. Washington began attacking on October 6. On October 19, Cornwallis and 8,000 men surrendered.

Turning down a crown. After Cornwallis surrendered, the British lost interest in continuing the war. Peace talks dragged on in Paris for many months.

In May 1782, Colonel Lewis Nicola sent a document to Washington on behalf of his officers. It complained of injustices the army had suffered from Congress. It suggested that the army set up a monarchy with Washington as king. Washington replied that he read the idea "with abhorrence." He ordered Nicola to "banish these thoughts from your mind."

In November 1783, word finally arrived that the Treaty of Paris had been signed two months earlier. The last British soldiers went aboard ships at New York City on November 25. That same day Washington led his troops into the city. About a week later, on December 4, he said good-by to his officers at Fraunces Tavern.

On his way home to Virginia, he stopped at Annapolis, Md., where Congress was meeting. He returned his commission as commander in chief, saying ". . . I resign with satisfaction the appointment I accepted with diffidence."

"First in peace" (1784-1789)

Washington, now 51 years old, reached Mount Vernon in time to spend Christmas, 1783, with Martha. The war had aged him. He now wore glasses. As he had told his officers: "I have grown gray in your service and now find myself growing blind."

For the next five years, Washington lived the life of a Virginia planter. Many guests and visitors dropped in at Mount Vernon. His entertainment expenses were large. In 1787, he wrote: "My estate for the last eleven years has not been able to make both ends meet."

Washington believed strongly in the future development of the West. This made him search for more land to buy. In 1784, he made a 680-mile (1,090-kilometer) trip on horseback through the wilderness to visit his land holdings southwest of Pittsburgh. He helped promote two companies interested in building canals along the Potomac and James rivers. He took part in plans to drain the Dismal Swamp in southern Virginia.

Washington also widened his interest in farming. In many ways his farm methods were ahead of the times. He began breeding mules. He introduced rotation of crops to his farms. He began using waste materials from his fishing industry as fertilizer. He also took steps to prevent soil erosion.

Constitutional Convention. In 1786, Washington wrote: "We are fast verging to anarchy and confusion." In Massachusetts, open revolt broke out (see **Shays' Rebellion**). Finally, the states agreed to call a meeting in 1787 to consider revising the weak Articles of Confederation

(See **Articles of Confederation**). Washington was elected unanimously to head the Virginia delegates. A huge welcome greeted him when he arrived in Philadelphia in May. All the bells in the city were rung. The Constitutional Convention opened on May 25. The delegates elected Washington president of the convention.

Debate on the proposed constitution went on throughout the hot summer. Washington wrote: "I see no end to my staying here. To please all is impossible . . ." As president, Washington took little part in the debates, but helped hold the convention together. The convention finally reached agreement in September. See **Constitution of the United States.**

Elected President. By the summer of 1788, enough states had approved the Constitution so the government could be organized. Throughout the country, people linked Washington's name directly to the new Constitution. They took it for granted that he would be chosen as the first President. But Washington had many doubts as to whether he should accept the position. He wrote: ". . . If I should receive the appointment, and if I should be prevailed upon to accept it, the acceptance would be attended with more diffidence and reluctance than I ever experienced before in my life."

In February 1789, members of the first Electoral College met in their own states and voted (see **Electoral College**). At that time, each elector voted for two

Detail of *George Washington Addressing the Constitutional Convention,* oil painting on canvas (1856) by Junius Brutus Stearns; Virginia Museum of Fine Arts, Richmond

Washington presided over the Constitutional Convention that was held in Philadelphia in 1787 to write a constitution for the United States. Although he participated little in the discussions, he helped keep the convention together for months of debate before agreement was reached.

Library of Congress

The future President learned of his election from Charles Thomson, secretary of Congress, at Mount Vernon.

candidates. The candidate with the most votes became President, and the runner-up became Vice President. Washington was elected President with 69 votes—the largest number possible—from the 69 electors. John Adams was elected Vice President with 34 votes.

First Administration (1789-1793)

Washington's journey from Mount Vernon to New York City was the parade of a national hero. Every town and city along the way held a celebration.

Inauguration Day was April 30, 1789. The 57-year-old Washington rode in a cream-colored coach to Federal Hall at Broad and Wall streets. Washington walked upstairs to the Senate Chamber, then out onto a balcony. Thousands watched as Washington raised his right hand and placed his left hand on an open Bible. Solemnly he repeated the presidential oath of office

Vice President and Cabinet

Vice President	* John Adams
Secretary of state	* Thomas Jefferson
	* Edmund Randolph (1794)
	* Timothy Pickering (1795)
Secretary of the treasury	* Alexander Hamilton
	* Oliver Wolcott, Jr. (1795)
Secretary of war	* Henry Knox
	* Timothy Pickering (1795)
	* James McHenry (1796)
Attorney general	* Edmund Randolph
	William Bradford (1794)
	Charles Lee (1795)

*Has a separate biography in *World Book.*

given by Robert R. Livingston of New York. Washington added the words, "So help me God!" and kissed the Bible. Cannons fired a 13-gun salute. Then President Washington walked back to the Senate Chamber and delivered his inaugural address.

Life in the Executive Mansion. The house of Samuel Osgood on Cherry Street in New York City was the first Executive Mansion. In February 1790, Washington moved to a larger house on Broadway. When Congress later made Philadelphia the capital, the Washingtons moved into the home there of financier Robert Morris. It was the finest house in the city.

The Washingtons entertained a great deal. They had a large staff of servants and slaves. The President held two afternoon receptions each week so he could meet the hundreds of people who wanted to see him. Every Friday night, Mrs. Washington held a formal reception. These affairs ended at 9 p.m. because, she said, the President "always retires at 9 in the evening." Each year on his birthday Washington gave a ball at which dancing lasted until well after midnight.

Martha Washington's two young grandchildren, Eleanor Parke Custis and George Washington Parke Custis, came to live with the Washingtons in the early 1780's. Their father, John Custis, had died during the Revolutionary War and their mother had remarried.

Evacuation Day, lithograph (1879) by E. P. and L. Restein; Library of Congress

President-elect Washington arrived in New York City for his inauguration in April 1789. Jubilant citizens had greeted him in every city and town on the road from Mount Vernon to New York.

Washington took the oath of office as first President of the United States on the balcony of Federal Hall in New York City. His second inauguration took place in Philadelphia.

Washington gave an inaugural address in the Senate Chamber of Federal Hall after taking the oath of office. He thus established a tradition that every other President has followed.

Martha Washington was described in a letter by Abigail Adams, wife of the Vice President: "She is plain in her dress, but that plainness is the best of every article . . . Her hair is white, her teeth beautiful, her person rather short . . . Her manners are modest and unassuming, dignified and feminine . . ."

The Washingtons made many trips home to Mount Vernon during the next eight years. The President sometimes stayed there as long as three months when Congress was not in session.

New precedents of government. "I walk on untrodden ground," Washington said as he began the new responsibilities of his office. "There is scarcely any part of my conduct that may not hereafter be drawn into precedent."

Washington believed strongly in the constitutional provision that the executive, legislative, and judicial branches of the government should be kept as separate as possible. He thought the President should not try to influence the kinds of laws Congress passed. But he be-

Washington's Cabinet consisted of four men that he knew and trusted. This picture shows Washington with, *left to right,* Secretary of War Henry Knox, Secretary of the Treasury Alexander Hamilton, Secretary of State Thomas Jefferson, and Attorney General Edmund Randolph.

lieved that if he disapproved of a bill, he should let Congress know by vetoing it. He regarded the duties of his office largely as administering the laws of Congress and supervising relations with other countries.

The Union included only 11 states when Washington became President. In November 1789, North Carolina accepted the Constitution, and in 1790 Rhode Island joined the Union. Vermont was admitted in 1791, and Kentucky in 1792.

On July 4, 1789, Washington received the first important bill passed by the new Congress. It provided income to run the government by setting taxes on imports. He signed it with no comment.

By September, Congress had established three executive departments to help run the government: the Department of Foreign Affairs (now Department of State), and the Departments of War and the Treasury. Congress provided for an Attorney General and a continuation of the Post Office. Congress also adopted the Bill of Rights amendments to the Constitution, and established a system of federal courts.

Cabinet. In September, Washington began making important appointments. He chose men whom he knew and could trust:

Chief justice of the United States—John Jay, who had been Secretary of Foreign Affairs under the Articles of Confederation.

Secretary of state—Thomas Jefferson, who had served

Unfinished portrait of Martha Washington (1796) by Gilbert Stuart; Jointly owned by the National Portrait Gallery, Smithsonian Institution, and the Museum of Fine Arts, Boston

Martha Washington handled her duties as first lady with grace and dignity, though she said she felt like a "state prisoner" in the role. She was 65 years old when this portrait was painted.

The Republican Court by Daniel Huntington; The Brooklyn Museum, Gift of the Crescent-Hamilton Athletic Club

The Washingtons entertained a great deal in the executive mansions they occupied in New York and Philadelphia. Martha Washington held a formal reception each Friday evening, *above*. These gatherings ended at 9 p.m., when, according to the first lady, the President always retired.

Quotations from Washington

The following quotations come from some of George Washington's speeches and writings. His famous Farewell Address was prepared with the assistance of Alexander Hamilton, among others.

Discipline is the soul of an army. It makes small numbers formidable; procures success to the weak, and esteem to all.
Letter of instructions to the captains of the Virginia Regiments, July 29, 1759

I am embarked on a wide ocean, boundless in its prospects, and in which, perhaps, no safe harbor is to be found.
Written in 1775, a few days before going to Boston as commander in chief of the Revolutionary forces

The time is now near at hand which must probably determine whether Americans are to be freemen or slaves . . . The fate of unborn millions will now depend, under God, on the courage and conduct of this army. Our cruel and unrelenting enemy leaves us only the choice of brave resistance, or the most abject submission. We have, therefore, to resolve to conquer or die.
Address to the Continental Army, Aug. 27, 1776

It is too probable that no plan we propose will be adopted. Perhaps another dreadful conflict is to be sustained. If to please the people, we offer what we ourselves disapprove, how can we afterwards defend our work? Let us raise a standard to which the wise and honest can repair.
Speech at the Constitutional Convention, 1787

Liberty, when it begins to take root, is a plant of rapid growth.
Letter to James Madison, March 2, 1789

The preservation of the sacred fire of liberty, and the destiny of the republican model of government, are justly considered as deeply, perhaps as finally staked, on the experiment entrusted to the hands of the American people.
First Inaugural Address, April 30, 1789

To be prepared for war is one of the most effectual means of preserving peace.
First Annual Address, presented to both houses of Congress, Jan. 8, 1790

If the laws are to be so trampled upon with impunity, and

a minority . . . is to dictate to the majority, there is an end put, at one stroke, to republican government.
Response to the Whiskey Rebellion, 1794

. . . The basis of our political system is the right of the people to make and to alter their constitutions of government. But the Constitution which at any time exists, 'till changed by an explicit and authentic act of the whole People, is sacredly obligatory upon all . . .

. . . Let me now warn you in the most solemn manner against the baneful effects of the spirit of party . . . It agitates the Community with ill founded jealousies and false alarms, kindles the animosity of one part against another, foments occasionally riot and insurrection.

. . . Of all the dispositions and habits which lead to political prosperity, religion and morality are indispensable supports.

. . . Promote . . . institutions for the general diffusion of knowledge . . . it is essential that public opinion should be enlightened.

. . . Observe good faith and justice toward all Nations. Cultivate peace and harmony with all . . . nothing is more essential than that permanent, inveterate antipathies against particular Nations and passionate attachments for others should be excluded . . . The nation which indulges toward another an habitual hatred or an habitual fondness is in some degree a slave. It is a slave to its animosity or to its affection, either of which is sufficient to lead it astray from its duty and its interest.

. . . 'Tis our true policy to steer clear of permanent Alliances, with any portion of the foreign world . . . Taking care always to keep ourselves, by suitable establishments, on a respectable defensive posture, we may safely trust to temporary alliances for extraordinary emergencies . . . There can be no greater error than to expect or calculate upon real favors from nation to nation.
Farewell Address, published in the American Daily Advertiser, a Philadelphia newspaper, Sept. 19, 1796

---

with Washington for five years in Virginia's legislature.

Secretary of war—Henry Knox, Washington's chief of artillery during the Revolutionary War.

Secretary of the treasury—Alexander Hamilton, who had been one of Washington's military aides.

Attorney general—Edmund Randolph, former governor of Virginia and a member of the Constitutional Convention. He had been Washington's friend for years.

During his first Administration, Washington relied heavily on the advice of Hamilton and James Madison, a congressman from Virginia. At first, Washington did not call his department heads together as a group. Instead, he asked them to give him written opinions or to talk with him individually. Washington allowed his department heads to act independently. He did not try to prevent Hamilton, Jefferson, or the others from influencing Congress. Toward the end of his first Administration, he began calling the group together for meetings. In 1793, Madison first used the term *cabinet* to refer to the group (see **Cabinet**).

Finances. Washington's new government had millions of dollars in debts which the Congress of the Articles of Confederation had been unable to pay. Hamilton drew up a plan to straighten out the finances. There was much argument, but finally the plan passed in July 1790. The law provided that the national government would

assume the wartime debts of the states. It also called for borrowing $12 million from other countries and for paying interest on the public debts.

New national capital. Congress approved a bill in July to transfer the government to Philadelphia until 1800. After that, the capital would be moved to a federal district to be located on the Potomac River. The President took up residence in Philadelphia in November 1790. During the next several years, Washington devoted much time to the plans for the new national capital, which came to bear his name.

Constitutional debate. Hamilton obtained passage in 1791 of a bill setting up the First Bank of the United States (see **Bank of the United States**). Washington had to decide whether the government had powers under the Constitution to charter such a corporation. Jefferson and Randolph believed that the bill was unconstitutional. They said such powers were not mentioned in the Constitution. Hamilton argued that the government could use all powers except those denied by the Constitution. Washington, who believed in a strong national government, took Hamilton's side and signed the law.

First veto by Washington of congressional legislation was made in April 1792. The first census of the United States had shown that the population was 3,929,214, including 697,000 slaves. Congress then passed a bill in March to raise the number of U.S. representatives from 67 to 120. Washington believed the bill was unconstitutional because some states would have greater representation in proportion to population than other states. Many persons thought the bill favored Northern states over Southern states. Congress failed to override Washington's veto, and then revised the bill to provide for a House of 103 members.

Rise of political parties. Washington was disturbed as he saw that Jefferson and Hamilton were disagreeing more and more with each other. Men and newspapers who supported Hamilton's views of a stronger and stronger national government called themselves *Federalists* (see **Federalist Party**). The Federalists became the party of the Northern states and of banking and manufacturing interests. Those who favored Jefferson's ideas of a strict interpretation of the Constitution in defending states' rights became known as *Anti-Federalists,* or *Democratic-Republicans* (see **Democratic-Republican Party**). The Democratic-Republicans mainly represented the Southern states and the farmers.

Washington attempted to favor neither party. He tried to bring Hamilton and Jefferson into agreement and tried to discourage the growth of political parties.

Reelection. In 1792, Washington began to make plans for retirement. In May he asked Madison to help him prepare a farewell address. Madison did so, but urged Washington to accept reelection. Hamilton, Knox, Jefferson, and Randolph each asked Washington to continue as President. Perhaps one of the strongest arguments came from Jefferson, who wrote: "Your being at the helm will be more than an answer to every argument which can be used to alarm and lead the people in any quarter into violence or secession. North and South will hang together if they have you to hang on."

Members of the Electoral College cast their votes in December 1792. Their ballots were counted on Feb. 13, 1793, and Washington again was elected President with the largest number of votes possible—132. Adams received 77 votes and was again the runner-up and Vice President.

Second Administration (1793-1797)

Washington's second inauguration took place in Congress Hall in Philadelphia on March 4, 1793. The 61-year-old Washington faced greater problems during his second Administration than during his first.

Neutrality proclamation. Word came in April 1793 that a general war had begun in Europe. England, Spain, Austria, and Prussia were all fighting against the new French republic. Although the United States had signed an alliance with the French king in 1778, Washington wanted to "maintain a strict neutrality." Jefferson, who favored the recent French Revolution, did not want to issue a neutrality statement. Hamilton believed neutrality was necessary. Washington ordered Attorney General Randolph to write up a statement. On April 22, the President signed the Neutrality Proclamation which called for "conduct friendly and impartial" to all the warring nations. It also forbade American ships from carrying war supplies to the fighting countries.

Relations with France. The United States decision to stay out of the European war pleased the English, but it angered the French. Leaders of the French Revolution believed the United States should stand by its alliance of 1778 with King Louis XVI. But the revolutionaries had beheaded the king who made the alliance. This posed a delicate point in international law, and Washington had no precedents to guide him. He finally decided to be cool and formal in receiving Edmond Genêt, the new minister appointed by the French republic.

Genêt seemed determined to draw Americans into the war on the side of France. He tried secretly to win Democratic-Republicans to the French cause during the spring and summer of 1793. This upset Washington. The President's patience gave out when Genêt tried to outfit warships in American ports and send them to sea against the British. After a stormy Cabinet meeting in July 1793, Washington asked France to recall Genêt because he endangered American neutrality. Genêt was stripped of his power, but was allowed to stay in the United States. The neutrality crisis of 1793 passed, and the United States remained at peace.

Whiskey Rebellion. In 1794, Washington proved that the government could enforce federal laws in the states. Farmers in four counties in western Pennsylvania had refused to pay federal taxes on manufacturing whiskey. They armed themselves and attacked federal officials. Washington raised 15,000 troops and sent them to western Pennsylvania. By November 1794, the rebellion had been crushed and the ringleaders arrested.

Relations with Britain. Washington worried as relations with Great Britain grew worse. British warships stopped American ships carrying food supplies to France and seized their cargoes. They sometimes took seamen off the American ships and forced them into the British navy. British troops refused to give up western frontier forts they were supposed to have surrendered under terms of the treaty of 1783. The British also were stirring up Indian fighting on the western frontier. In an effort to settle problems with Britain, Washington sent Chief Justice John Jay to London in 1794.

In March 1795, Washington received a copy of a treaty Jay had signed on Nov. 19, 1794. Earlier copies had been lost in the mail. Most of the treaty had to do with regulation of trade between America and Britain. It also called for British troops to give up the frontier forts in 1796. But it contained no agreement that British ships would stop waylaying American ships and taking seamen. See **Jay Treaty**.

Washington called a special session of the Senate in June to study the treaty. Federalists supported the Jay Treaty because it insured continuing trade with Britain. The Democratic-Republicans violently opposed the treaty because they believed it would harm France. The Federalists controlled the Senate, so the treaty was ratified by a vote of 20 to 10, except for one section. This section opened trade with the British West Indies to United States ships, but it also severely restricted this trade. Washington could not make up his mind whether or not to sign the treaty. He went home to Mount Vernon to think about it.

At Mount Vernon, the President received word of riots in many cities protesting the Jay Treaty. A mob in New York City stoned Hamilton. A Philadelphia mob broke windows at the British embassy.

Cabinet scandal. Washington returned to Philadelphia on Aug. 11, 1795. He learned that the British had captured a French diplomatic message which seemed to indicate that Edmund Randolph, who was now secretary of state, was a traitor. Washington read a translation of the French message. He believed that Randolph might have sold secrets to the French.

Without saying anything to Randolph about his suspicions, Washington called a Cabinet meeting to discuss the Jay Treaty. At the meeting, Randolph argued against signing the treaty as long as Britain continued to seize American ships. Washington became convinced Randolph was in the pay of France, and so he signed the treaty.

As soon as the Jay Treaty had been delivered to the British embassy, Washington called in Randolph and showed him the French message. Randolph denied his guilt, but resigned. He swore he would prove his innocence. Randolph later published a book in which he declared that he had never betrayed his country.

Washington now suffered the bitterest criticism of his career. He was accused by Democratic-Republican newspapers of falling victim to a Federalist plot in signing the Jay Treaty. It was even suggested that he should be impeached because he had overdrawn his $25,000 salary. Washington's feelings were badly hurt.

Public opinion of Washington began to improve when he was able to announce a few months later that a treaty had been negotiated with Spain opening up the Mississippi River to trade. Agreement also had been reached with the pirates of the Barbary States to release American prisoners and to let American ships alone for a payment of $800,000 ransom, plus $24,000 tribute each year. Peace treaties also had been signed with Indian tribes on the frontier.

Farewell Address. Washington, who believed the office of President should be above political attack, had become tired of public office. The new House of Representatives had a large Democratic-Republican majority and was unfriendly to Washington. He also felt himself growing old.

In May 1796, Washington dusted off the draft of his *Farewell Address* that he and James Madison had worked on four years earlier. He sent it to Jay and to Hamilton for their suggestions. Finally, in September, the much edited address, all in Washington's handwriting, was ready. He gave it to the editor of the *American Daily Advertiser,* a Philadelphia newspaper, which published it on September 19.

In the election campaign that followed, Washington favored John Adams, the Federalist candidate for President. But Washington did not take an active part in the campaigning. The Democratic-Republican candidate was Thomas Jefferson. When the Electoral College met, it gave 71 votes to Adams and 68 to Jefferson. Under the existing constitutional provision, Adams became President and Jefferson Vice President.

At the inauguration in March 1797, Adams sensed Washington's relief at retirement. Adams wrote to his wife: "He seemed to me to enjoy a triumph over me. Methought I heard him say, 'Ay! I am fairly out and you fairly in! See which of us will be the happiest!' "

"First in the hearts of his countrymen" (1797-1799)

Washington was 65. He happily went home to Mount Vernon. Friends said he looked even older. But he did not lose touch with public affairs. Almost every day visitors dropped in to see him. On July 31, 1797, he wrote: "Unless someone pops in unexpectedly—Mrs. Washington and myself will do what has not been done within the last twenty years by us—that is to set down to dinner by ourselves."

He described his daily routine in a letter:

"I begin . . . with the sun . . . if my hirelings are not in their places at that time I send them messages expressive of my sorrow for their indisposition . . . breakfast—a little after seven o'clock . . . This over, I mount my horse and ride round the farms . . . The usual time of sitting at table, a walk, and tea, brings me within the dawn of candlelight . . . I resolve that . . . I will retire to my writing table and acknowledge the letters I have received; but when the lights are brought, I feel tired, and disinclined to engage in this work."

Managing the several farms which made up the more than 8,000 acres (3,200 hectares) of Mount Vernon took much of his time. He made frequent trips to watch construction in the new city of Washington, D.C., which then was called the Federal City.

Recall to duty. While Washington enjoyed his retirement, relations between the United States and France grew worse. The government decided to raise an army for defense. President Adams asked Washington's help. On July 4, 1798, Washington was commissioned as "Lieutenant General and Commander in Chief of the armies raised or to be raised."

He went to Philadelphia for a few weeks in November to help plan the new army. He had dinner one night in debtors' prison with financier Robert Morris, in whose Philadelphia home he had lived while President. Morris had been sent to prison because he could not pay his debts.

During his last year of life, Washington wrote many letters to the various men he chose as generals for the new army. Federalist leaders asked if he would consider running for a third term. He said no. Washington also was saddened by the deaths of friends and relatives. Patrick Henry died on June 6, 1799, and Washington's last living brother, Charles Washington, died on Sept. 20, 1799.

Death. On December 12, Washington wrote his last letter. It was to Alexander Hamilton. In it he discussed the importance of establishing a national military academy. After finishing the letter, Washington went for his daily horseback ride around Mount Vernon. The day was cold, with snow turning into rain and sleet. Washington returned after about five hours and sat down to dinner without changing his damp clothes. The next day he awoke with a sore throat. He went for a walk. Then he made his last entry in his diary, noting down the weather: "Morning Snowing and abt. 3 inches deep . . . Mer. 28 at Night." These were his last written words.

Between 2 and 3 a.m. on Dec. 14, 1799, Washington awakened Martha. He had difficulty speaking and was quite ill. But he would not let her send for a doctor until dawn. James Craik, who had been his friend and doctor since he was a young man, hurried to Mount Vernon. By the time he arrived, Washington already had called in an overseer and had about a cup of blood drained from his veins. Craik examined Washington and said the illness was "inflammatory quinsy." Craik bled Washington

The Washington Family, oil painting on canvas (1796) by Edward Savage; National Gallery of Art, Washington, D.C., Andrew W. Mellon Collection

The Washingtons had no children of their own, but they raised Martha's children from her first marriage. Then they cared for two of her grandchildren, whose father died during the Revolutionary War. This painting shows the Washingtons with the grandchildren, George and Eleanor.

again. Present-day doctors believe the illness was a streptococcal infection of the throat.

Two more doctors arrived in the afternoon. Again Washington was bled. Late in the afternoon he could hardly speak, but told the doctors: "You had better not take any more trouble about me, but let me go off quietly. I cannot last long."

About 10 p.m. on December 14, Washington whispered: "I am just going. Have me decently buried, and do not let my body be put in the vault in less than two days after I am dead. Do you understand me?" His secretary answered: "Yes, sir." Washington said: "'Tis well." He felt for his own pulse. Then he died.

On December 18, Washington was given a military funeral. His body was laid to rest in the family tomb at Mount Vernon. Throughout the world people were saddened by his death. In the United States, thousands of people wore mourning clothes for months.

No other American has been honored more than Washington. The nation's capital, Washington, D.C., was named for him. There, the giant Washington Monument stands. The state of Washington is the only state named after a President. Many counties, cities, towns, streets, bridges, lakes, parks, and schools bear his name. Washington's portrait appears on postage stamps, on the $1 bill, and on the quarter.

After the siege of Boston in 1776, the Massachusetts legislature in a resolution had said: ". . . may future gen-

erations, in the peaceful enjoyment of that freedom, the exercise of which your sword shall have established, raise the richest and most lasting monuments to the name of Washington." The legislators foresaw the place he would hold forever in the hearts of Americans.

At the time of his death, Washington held the title of lieutenant general, then the highest military rank in the United States. But through the years, he was outranked by many U.S. Army officers. In 1976, Congress granted Washington the nation's highest military title, General of the Armies of the United States. This action confirmed him as the senior general officer on the Army rolls.

Critically reviewed by Mary Wells Ashworth and John Alexander Carroll

Related articles in *World Book* include:

Adams, John
Braddock, Edward
Cabinet
Constitution of the U.S.
Custis, George W. P.
French and Indian wars
Genêt, Edmond
George Washington Birthplace National Monument
Hamilton, Alexander
Jefferson, Thomas
Knox, Henry
Lafayette, Marquis de
Masonry (picture)
Mount Rushmore National Memorial

Mount Vernon
President of the U.S.
Randolph (family)
Revolutionary War
Sculpture (American; picture)
Stamp collecting (picture)
Stuart, Gilbert Charles
Sulgrave Manor
Valley Forge
Virginia (picture)
Washington, D.C.
Washington, Martha Custis
Washington Monument
Washington's Birthday
Whiskey Rebellion

Outline

I. Washington the man
II. Early life (1732-1746)
  A. Family background
  B. Washington's parents
  C. Boyhood
  D. Education
  E. Plantation life
  F. Development of
    character
III. Washington the surveyor (1747-1752)
IV. Early military career (1753-1758)
  A. Messenger to the French
  B. First military action
  C. Surrender of Fort Necessity
  D. Braddock's defeat
  E. Frontier commander
V. The peaceful years (1759-1773)
  A. Marriage
  B. Legislator
  C. Farmer and landowner
  D. Social life
VI. The coming revolution (1774-1775)
  A. First Continental Congress
  B. Elected commander in chief
VII. "First in war" (1775-1783)
  A. Symbol of independence
  B. Discouragement
  C. The army
  D. Shortage of supplies
  E. Winning the war
  F. Turning down a crown
VIII. "First in peace" (1784-1789)
  A. Constitutional Convention
  B. Elected President
IX. First Administration (1789-1793)
  A. Inauguration day
  B. Life in the Executive
    Mansion
  C. New precedents of gov-
    ernment
  D. Cabinet
  E. Finances
  F. New national capital
  G. Constitutional debate
  H. First veto
  I. Rise of political parties
  J. Reelection
X. Second Administration (1793-1797)
  A. Neutrality proclamation
  B. Relations with France
  C. Whiskey Rebellion
  D. Relations with Britain
  E. Cabinet scandal
  F. Farewell address
XI. "First in the hearts of his countrymen" (1797-1799)
  A. Recall to duty
  B. Death

Questions

Why is Washington called the "Father of His Country"?
When did Washington first notice that the British treated Americans as second-class citizens?
How did Washington react to his first sound of bullets in war?
What was Washington referring to when he said: "I went out, was soundly beaten, lost them all . . ."?
How did Washington acquire Mount Vernon?
When and why did Washington make his only trip outside of America?
Why did Washington's presidential receptions usually end at 9 p.m.?
As a farmer, how was Washington ahead of his time?
How did Washington show the Second Continental Congress that he was ready to defy Great Britain?
Who praised Washington as "First in war, first in peace, and first in the hearts of his countrymen"?

Reading and Study Guide

See *Washington, George,* in the Research Guide/Index, Volume 22, for a *Reading and Study Guide.*

Additional resources

Cunliffe, Marcus F. *George Washington: Man and Monument.* Rev. ed. New American Library, 1982.
Flexner, James T. *Washington: The Indispensable Man.* Little, Brown, 1974.
Freeman, Douglas S. *George Washington: A Biography.* 7 vols. Augustus Kelley, 1975-1981. First published 1948-1957.
Meltzer, Milton. *George Washington and the Birth of Our Nation.* Watts, 1986. For younger readers.

Washington, Harold (1922-1987), won election as the first black mayor of Chicago in 1983. Washington, a Democrat, defeated Republican Bernard E. Epton, a former state representative. Washington received about 52 per cent of the total vote. He won support from about 99 per cent of Chicago's black voters and 18 per cent of its white voters, including Hispanics. Blacks make up about 40 per cent of the city's population. Washington was reelected in April 1987. He had a fatal heart attack in November 1987.

Antonio Dickey
Harold Washington

Washington was the first black mayoral nominee of Chicago's Democratic Party. He became the nominee by defeating Mayor Jane M. Byrne and Cook County State's Attorney Richard M. Daley in a primary election.

Washington was born in Chicago. His father was a lawyer and a Methodist minister. Washington graduated from Roosevelt University in 1949 and from the Northwestern University School of Law in 1952. He became a lawyer in 1953. He served in the Illinois House of Representatives from 1965 to 1976 and in the Illinois Senate from 1976 to 1980. Washington represented Illinois's First Congressional District in the U.S. House of Representatives from 1981 to 1983.   Basil B. Talbott, Jr.

Washington, Lawrence. See **Washington, George** (Development of character; Only foreign trip).

Washington, Martha Custis (1731-1802), was the wife of George Washington. When he took office as the first President in 1789, she became America's first first lady.

Martha Washington was born on June 2, 1731, near Williamsburg, Va. Her father, Colonel John Dandridge, was a wealthy landowner. Martha had no formal schooling. Until she married Washington, she had never traveled beyond Virginia. At the age of 17, she married Daniel Parke Custis, a wealthy Virginia planter who was 13 years older than she. They had four children, two of whom died in childhood. The other two children died before Washington became President. The death of Custis in 1757 made Martha one of the richest women in Virginia.

No one knows when Martha Custis first met George Washington. They may have met at a neighbor's home in Williamsburg early in 1758. Washington was then a colonel in the militia. She was eight months older than he. They were married on Jan. 6, 1759.

Washington called his wife by her childhood nickname, "Patsy." During the Revolutionary War, she traveled long distances to share his hardships. Mrs. Washington joined him at his camp at Valley Forge, Pa., during the winter of 1777-1778. She also spent the harsh winters of 1778-1779 and 1779-1780 with him in camp at Morristown, N.J. She organized a women's sewing circle and mended clothes for the troops.

As first lady, Mrs. Washington managed the President's home with dignity and grace. But she did not enjoy being first lady. She said she felt like a "state prisoner." Many people called her "Lady Washington." But Mrs. Washington dressed so plainly that people often mistook her for the family maid.

After Washington's death in 1799, she continued to live at Mount Vernon, their estate. Shortly before she died on May 22, 1802, she burned the letters Washington had written her. Mrs. Washington was buried at Mount Vernon. *Critically reviewed by Mary Wells Ashworth*

See also **Washington, George.**

Washington, Mount. See Mount Washington.

Washington, Treaty of, was a treaty signed in 1871 by the United States and Great Britain in Washington, D.C. The treaty settled a number of disputes between the two countries. It provided that the *Alabama* Claims be referred to a special court for arbitration (see **Alabama** [ship]). The court met at Geneva, Switzerland. The settlement of the claims came to be known as the Geneva Arbitration. U.S. Secretary of State Hamilton Fish negotiated the treaty. The treaty also ended quarrels about fishing rights in Canadian waters.

The treaty set down three rules for the court to follow in settling the *Alabama* Claims. (1) It provided that a neutral country should guard against the arming of any vessels within its jurisdiction which might be intended for the use of a country at war. (2) It provided that a neutral country should close its ports to any belligerent which tried to use them as bases for naval operations. (3) It placed on a neutral country the responsibility of guarding against any violations of the first two provisions.

The Washington Treaty granted the U.S. fishing industry the continued use of the waters off the coasts of Quebec, Nova Scotia, New Brunswick, and Prince Edward Island. The British also gained similar fishing rights along the U.S. coast north of the 39th parallel.

The treaty also referred the United States claim to the San Juan, or Haro, Islands, off Puget Sound, to the German emperor for arbitration. His decision upheld the United States claim. *John Donald Hicks*

Washington, University of, is a coeducational state-supported institution in Seattle. It has colleges of architecture and urban planning, arts and sciences, education, engineering, forest resources, ocean and fishery sciences, and pharmacy. It also has a graduate school and schools of business administration, dentistry, law, librarianship, medicine, nursing, public affairs, public health and community medicine, and social work. The university grants bachelor's, master's, and doctor's degrees.

The University of Washington was founded in 1861 in what is now downtown Seattle. The school moved to its present location along Lake Washington in 1895. For enrollment, see **Universities and colleges** (table).

Critically reviewed by the University of Washington

Washington Cathedral, also called the National Cathedral, is an Episcopal church in Washington, D.C. Its official name is the Cathedral Church of Saint Peter and Saint Paul.

The building is laid out in the form of a cross, 525 feet (160 meters) long and 275 feet (84 meters) wide at its widest point. It is Gothic in style, with pointed arches and vaulted ceilings. The cathedral is noted for its rich carvings and beautiful stained-glass windows. Stones from historic buildings and shrines in all parts of the world were used in building it. The *Gloria* tower of the

cathedral contains a large carillon with 53 bells and a 10-bell English peal.

Work on the cathedral began in 1907, and services have been held in some of its chapels since 1912. President Woodrow Wilson and Admiral George Dewey are among the well-known people buried in the cathedral. *Alan Gowans*

Washington Conference was a meeting held in Washington, D.C., to discuss naval disarmament and certain problems involving east Asia. It took place from November 1921 to February 1922. Nations represented were Belgium, China, France, Great Britain, Italy, Japan, the Netherlands, Portugal, and the United States. It led to one of the few successful disarmament agreements in modern times.

Three major treaties resulted from the conference. The Five-Power Naval Limitation Treaty, adopted by Britain, France, Italy, Japan, and the United States, ended a growing build-up of major warships among these nations. It resulted in destruction of *capital ships* (battleships) and a 10-year prohibition on construction of more battleships. The Four-Power Treaty, signed by Britain, France, Japan, and the United States, recognized each nation's possession of certain islands in the Pacific Ocean. The Nine-Power Treaty was signed by all the countries at the conference. Its chief purpose was to guarantee the independence of China. The treaty was observed until 1931, when Japan invaded Manchuria, a region in northeastern China. *Thomas H. Buckley*

Washington Monument is a great obelisk built in honor of George Washington. It stands in Washington, D.C., near the Potomac River, about halfway between the Capitol and the Lincoln Memorial.

The monument has the shape of the obelisks of ancient Egypt, but it is several times larger than they were. It is 555 feet $5\frac{1}{8}$ inches (169.29 meters) high, and measures 55 feet $1\frac{1}{8}$ inches (16.79 meters) along each of its four sides at the bottom. The sides slant gradually inward as they rise to the base of the *pyramidion* (small pyramid) which tops the pillar. At this point, each side of the pillar is 34 feet $5\frac{1}{2}$ inches (10.50 meters) long. The pyramidion rises 55 feet (16.8 meters). The walls of the monument are 15 feet (4.6 meters) thick at the bottom and 18 inches (46 centimeters) thick at the top. They are covered with white marble from Maryland. The stones covering the pyramidion are 7 inches (18 centimeters) thick. A cap of cast aluminum protects the tip.

Inside, the monument is hollow. The inner walls are set with 189 carved memorial stones, many of historic interest. The stones were presented by individuals, societies, cities, states, and other countries. Visitors must take an elevator to the top of the monument. To descend, they can either take the elevator or walk down the 898 steps leading from the top. The view of Washington, D.C., is impressive. More than a million people visit the Washington Monument each year.

Some people planned a memorial to Washington while he was still alive, but he objected to the expense. In 1833, the Washington National Monument Society began raising funds for a monument. A design by Robert Mills had already been accepted in part. The government approved the project, and the cornerstone was laid on July 4, 1848, with the same trowel that Washington had used to lay the cornerstone of the Capitol in

1793. But engineers found the ground too soft, so they moved the site to the north.

Many people donated stones for the monument. Pope Pius IX sent a marble block from the Temple of Concord in Rome. One night in 1854, a group believed to be Know-Nothings, or members of the American Party, stole this block (see **Know-Nothings**). This act shocked the public, and contributions almost stopped. In 1855, Congress agreed to give some financial aid to the project. But Know-Nothings broke into the society's offices and claimed possession of the monument. In 1876, Congress voted to finish the project at government expense. Work began on Aug. 17, 1880. It was completed on Dec. 6, 1884. The monument was dedicated on Feb. 21, 1885, and opened to the public on Oct. 9, 1888. Its total cost was $1,187,710.31. The monument is maintained as a national memorial by the National Park Service.

James J. Cullinane

See also **Washington, D.C.** (picture).

Washington State University is a coeducational, state-controlled land-grant institution in Pullman, Wash. It has colleges of agriculture and home economics, business and economics, education, engineering and architecture, nursing, pharmacy, sciences and arts, and veterinary medicine. It also offers master's degrees in 62 fields and doctor's degrees in 44 areas. It was founded in 1890. For enrollment, see **Universities and colleges** (table). Critically reviewed by Washington State University

Washington's Birthday is celebrated as a federal holiday on the third Monday in February. It honors the first President of the United States. George Washington was born on Feb. 22, 1732, according to the calendar we now use. But according to the Old Style Calendar then in use, his birth date was February 11. People first celebrated the anniversary in the late 1700's, some on the 11th and some on the 22nd. Today, some states also honor President Abraham Lincoln and other Presidents on the third Monday in February, and call the holiday *Presidents' Day.*

Washita River. See **Ouachita River.**

Wasp is any of a large number of insects closely related to bees and ants. There are more than 17,000 species of true wasps. They are characterized by a narrowing of the abdomen into a thin "wasp waist," and by the presence of a stinger in the female.

Wasps are most common in regions with tropical or warm climates. Only a few species live in cold regions. About 3,800 species are found in the United States and Canada. Most wasps have wings and fly. However, the females of a few species, called *velvet ants,* lack wings. The majority of wasps are yellow, reddish, bluish-black, or black in color. Some are black and white, black and yellow, or black and red. Others have stripes of black and a bright color across the body.

Scientists divide wasps into two groups: (1) solitary and (2) social. Each group has different nesting habits. Among solitary wasps, the female does all the work of nesting by herself. Common solitary wasps include mud daubers, cuckoo wasps, and digger wasps. Social wasps have a social system in which members of the community help build and maintain the nest. Hornets and yellow jackets are two common kinds of social wasps.

Body. A wasp's body, like that of any insect, has three parts: (1) a head, (2) a thorax, and (3) an abdomen. On each side of its head, a wasp has two *compound* eyes made up of many tiny lenses. Two antennae between the eyes serve primarily as organs of smell and touch. A wasp's mouthparts are designed both for chewing food and for sucking up liquids.

The thorax is the middle part of a wasp's body. The insect's wings and legs are connected to the thorax. Wasps have four wings and six legs.

A wasp's abdomen contains organs of digestion and reproduction. Female wasps have a stinger hidden near the end of the abdomen. Solitary wasps use their stinger to paralyze prey. Social wasps also use their stinger to defend their nest against intruders. Attached to a wasp's stinger are glands that produce poison. The poison of social wasps contains chemical compounds that are irritating to higher animals. People who are especially sensitive to these poisonous compounds can die from being stung.

Life cycle. Wasps develop in four stages: (1) egg, (2) larva, (3) pupa, and (4) adult. The tiny egg of a wasp hatches into a wormlike larva, also called a *grub.* The larva reaches its full size in 7 to 20 days, depending on the species and the weather. It then spins a covering known as a *cocoon.* Most solitary wasps that live in cool climates spend the winter in the cocoon. Most social wasps stay in the cocoon about two weeks. While in the

Some kinds of wasps There are more than 17,000 species of true wasps. The drawings below show three species that live in North America. The scientific name of each species appears in italics.

WORLD BOOK illustrations by John Eggert and Oxford Illustrators Limited

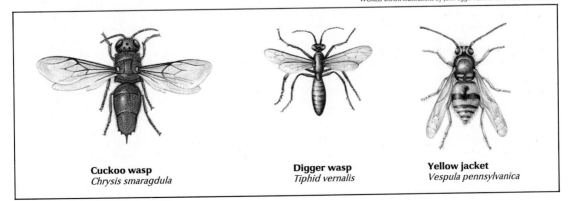

Cuckoo wasp
Chrysis smaragdula

Digger wasp
Tiphid vernalis

Yellow jacket
Vespula pennsylvanica

Wasp nests vary in form and in the building materials used. Polistes wasps build open paper nests, such as the one shown above. Mud daubers construct nests of mud. A cross section of a mud dauber nest, *right,* shows the tube-shaped cells where the off-spring hatch and grow.

cocoon, the larva becomes a pupa, a stage during which the insect changes dramatically into an adult. At the end of the pupal stage, the adult breaks out of the cocoon.

Male and female social wasps most commonly mate in the fall. Most males die a few weeks later. The female stores *sperm* (male sex cells) in a sac near the end of her abdomen. She hibernates during winter in a protected place and emerges in the spring to start a nest. When she lays an egg, she may fertilize it with sperm. Fertilized eggs become female wasps. Unfertilized eggs become males. Female solitary wasps hibernate as larvae and mate in the spring, after they have become adults. Mated female social wasps may live up to a year. Male wasps and unmated females live two months or less.

Food. Adult wasps feed mainly on the nectar of flowers. They prey on other insects and on spiders chiefly to provide food for developing offspring. Most species of wasps hunt a particular kind of prey. For example, one species of sphecid wasp preys on cockroaches, and another preys on bumble bees.

In most species of solitary wasps, the female captures and paralyzes a prey by stinging it. She then lays an egg on the animal's body. The larva that hatches from the egg feeds on the prey. A few solitary wasps and most social wasps capture a prey and immediately eat it. Later, they *regurgitate* (spit up) the food to their larvae.

Nests. Wasps are talented nest-builders. Most solitary wasps dig nesting burrows in the ground. Some nest above the ground in hollow twigs or abandoned beetle burrows. They separate the chambers for each offspring with bits of grass, stone, or mud. Other solitary wasps build nests completely of mud.

Most social wasps make their nests of paper. The female produces the paper by chewing up plant fibers or old wood. She spreads the paper in thin layers to make cells in which she lays her eggs. Some species of wasps, including a group called *Polistes,* build open nests with a single comb of cells. Other species, such as hornets and yellow jackets, construct nests of many cells enclosed by a paper covering with a single entrance. The nests may be suspended from trees, or they may be built underground in abandoned rodent burrows.

Group life. Solitary wasps do not live in groups. In most species, the male and female get together only to mate. The female maintains the nest and provides food for her offspring. Soon after emerging from the cocoon, each of the offspring leaves the nest and seeks a mate.

Social wasps live in organized communities that consist largely of members of the same family. In the spring, the mated female, called the *queen,* builds the first cells of the nest and lays eggs. Her first offspring are small females, most of which cannot reproduce. These females, called *workers,* enlarge the nest, care for new larvae, and defend the nest from intruders. The queen continues to lay eggs until late summer. Her last offspring include both males and larger females that can reproduce. Among some species, the queen may be joined by other queens, usually her sisters. If the founding queen dies, one of the other queens will take over her position.

Some social wasps that live in tropical climates establish new communities by *swarming.* Swarming occurs when a nest becomes overcrowded. One or more of the young queens leave the nest with several workers. Huddled together, the wasps fly to another location and build a new nest.

Scientific classification. Wasps belong to the order Hymenoptera. True wasps make up the division Aculeata in the suborder Apocrita.   H. Jane Brockmann

See also **Hornet; Insect** (pictures: The compound eyes of a wasp; A fierce battle); **Yellow jacket.**

Wassermann, *WAH suhr muhn* or *VAHS uhr MAHN,* **August von,** *OW goost fuhn* (1866-1925), was a German bacteriologist and immunologist. He became well known for the development of an important blood test used to diagnose syphilis called the *Wassermann test.* The test, announced in 1906, became a model for later research on blood tests to determine the presence of antibodies to viruses and other disease agents. Today, the Wassermann test has been largely replaced by other tests for syphilis.

Wassermann was born in Bamberg, Germany. He began work under the great German physician Robert Koch in 1883. During the 1890's, Wassermann became noted for his research on cholera and diphtheria immunity. He discovered that people possess varying amounts of resistance to diseases. After 1900, Wassermann helped develop diagnostic tests for tuberculosis. In 1913, he became director of his own institute of experimental therapy.   John Scarborough

Waste disposal is the process of getting rid of human waste products. People produce *gaseous waste,* such as carbon monoxide from cars; *liquid waste,* such as sewage; and *solid waste.* The almost countless kinds of solid waste include paper and plastic products, glass bottles, aluminum and steel cans, garbage, and junked automobiles. Solid waste is also called *refuse.* If not disposed of properly, it looks ugly, smells foul, and attracts insects, rats, and other animals that spread disease. This article deals with the disposal of solid waste. For information on gaseous waste, see the *World Book* article on **Environmental pollution.** See also **Sewage.**

People produce millions of tons of solid wastes each year, and the production is increasing rapidly. They also produce more and more wastes that are difficult to handle. For example, tin and steel cans that rust and become part of the soil are being replaced by aluminum cans that stay in their original state for years. Paper packaging that decays and burns easily is being replaced by plastic packaging that decays slowly and gives off gases when burned.

Solid waste from homes, office buildings, and restaurants is called *municipal solid waste*. This article discusses how to dispose of such waste.

Solid waste also comes from industries and farms. For information on these two sources of waste, see the *World Book* article on **Environmental pollution.**

Methods of waste disposal. Solid waste disposal regulations in the United States were established by the Resource Conservation and Recovery Act of 1976 and similar laws. Most U.S. cities and towns have a waste-collecting department or a private firm that gathers refuse from homes and other buildings. Workers haul the refuse away in trucks. Communities use two chief methods to dispose of municipal solid waste: (1) land disposal and (2) incineration.

Land disposal involves hauling the refuse to an area owned by a community or by a private firm. In the United States, such areas range from unsanitary *open dumps* to properly operated *sanitary landfills.*

Open dumps are a poor method of waste disposal because they cause environmental problems. For example, they can ruin the appearance of an area and provide a home for rats and other animals that spread disease. If garbage is exposed, it rots and smells foul. Most dumps allow some burning, which causes smoke and foul-smelling air. In addition, rain water can drain through refuse and carry harmful substances to streams.

Properly operated sanitary landfills cause little damage to the environment. The wastes are packed firmly together by tractors and covered with earth each day. The cover of earth prevents insects and rodents from getting into the refuse. Operators of these sites forbid burning. In time, sanitary landfill sites become filled up. Many communities then cover the site for a final time and use the area for recreational purposes.

Many communities do not operate their sanitary landfills properly. For example, a community may allow burning at the site, or it may cover the site with earth only occasionally. Concern for the environment has caused many communities and states to establish strict laws to control land disposal sites.

Incineration burns waste products. Many large cities use incinerators because they do not have enough vacant areas for land disposal sites nearby. Large numbers of municipal incinerators lack adequate air pollution control devices. Burning in many of these plants releases gases and solid particles that may harm human health, damage property, and kill plants.

Some homes have small household incinerators or backyard burners that burn trash and garbage produced by the occupants. Many communities prohibit open backyard burning at residences.

Uses of solid waste. Many substances in refuse have value. They include glass, wood fiber from paper products, and metal. Scientists have developed ways of recycling many wastes so they can be used again. Extensive recycling would greatly reduce the amount of waste that must be burned or buried. See **Recycling.**

The heat from the burning of wastes can also be used. In some communities, the heat from municipal incinerators is used to produce steam. The steam drives engines that produce electric power.   Mary Lynne Bowman

See also **Energy supply** (Solid wastes); **Garbage disposer; Hazardous wastes; Nuclear energy** (Wastes).

Additional resources

Epstein, Samuel S., and others. *Hazardous Waste in America.* Sierra Club, 1982.
Miller, Christina G., and Berry, L. A. *Wastes.* Watts, 1986. For younger readers.
Zipko, Stephen J. *Toxic Threat: How Hazardous Substances Poison Our Lives.* Messner, 1986.

Wat Tyler's Rebellion, also called the Peasants' Revolt, was an uprising by English farm laborers in 1381. The peasants objected to the harsh conditions under which they lived, such as forced labor and heavy taxation. An unfair new tax touched off the uprising. During eight days, blacksmith Wat Tyler dominated the movement. It was supported by many small landholders, tradespeople, and skilled workers.

Riots broke out in many parts of England. Mobs destroyed private property and killed many wealthy persons. On June 12, 1381, Tyler and Jack Straw gathered together more than 100,000 angry peasants from Kent and Essex and led them in a march on London. Once the mob reached London, the leaders demanded to see King Richard II. The king was only 14 years old. Richard faced the angry mob alone, because his royal advisers had deserted him. But Richard could not quiet the rioters, and he finally agreed to listen to their demands at Mile-End on June 14.

The rebels demanded an end to serfdom, and a low rental payment on freed lands. They also called for a repeal of oppressive labor laws. The young king agreed to their terms, and most of the mob disbanded. However, Tyler remained with about 30,000 supporters to gain further advantages for his people. He grew bold and demanding. His attitude led to his being killed by the mayor of London. Meanwhile, troops came to support the king, and drove the rebels away. The promises of the king were put aside and the oppression of the peasants continued. However, Wat Tyler's Rebellion inspired other popular movements for freedom and equality in England.   Robert S. Hoyt

Watauga Association was a group of early American settlers. In 1772, they drew up one of the first written constitutions in North America. In 1769, a party of settlers established a colony on the banks of the Watauga River in what is now the state of Tennessee. They thought their settlement fell within the boundaries of the colony of Virginia. But in 1771, the Watauga settlers discovered that their territory lay within the limits of the colony of North Carolina. North Carolina refused to give legal protection to the settlers. The Watauga pioneers decided to keep order in their colony by organizing their own government. The leaders of the movement were John Sevier and James Robertson. Robertson was one of the founders of Nashville, Tenn.

In 1772, the Watauga group became the first American-born settlers to form a free and independent community. They drew up a document which they called the *Articles of the Watauga Association.* The Articles provided for an executive council, a legislature, a sheriff, and an attorney. In 1776, the Watauga community, known as the Washington District, sent representatives to the assembly of North Carolina. Later, it became part of the state of Tennessee.   John R. Alden

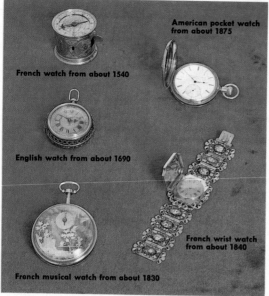

American pocket watch
from about 1875

French watch from about 1540

English watch from about 1690

French wrist watch
from about 1840

French musical watch from about 1830

Time Museum, Rockford, Ill. (WORLD BOOK photo)

Some early watches are shown above. The French watch from about 1540 has only an hour hand. The English watch has a hairspring. The French musical watch tells time by playing a melody. The French wrist watch has a gold and enamel bracelet. The American pocket watch is enclosed in a hinged gold case.

Watch is a small, portable clock. People use watches to tell time and also wear or carry them as personal accessories. More than 60 million watches are sold in the United States annually.

Portable clocks were first used during the 1500's by town watchmen in Europe. As the watchmen made their rounds, they carried the portable clocks on straps around their necks. As other people began carrying timepieces, the name was shortened to watch.

Kinds of watches

Most modern watches are worn on the wrist. Before the 1920's, they were almost always carried in the pocket or purse. In the past, women sometimes used watches as decorative accessories, wearing them as necklaces, rings, or pins. Today's watches range from plain models costing less than $10 to ones decorated with precious stones that cost more than $50,000. Watches have traditionally displayed the time by means of hands pointing to numerals or markers on a dial. This method is known as *analog display.* Today, lighted numerals are also used to display time by a method called *digital display.*

Many watches give information in addition to the passing of hours and minutes. Most also show the passage of seconds. Many show the day of the week, the day of the month, and the year. Some watches sound an alarm at any desired time. Some novelty and special function watches show the wearer's pulse or body temperature. Some include electronic games or tiny calculators for solving mathematical problems.

How watches work

Every watch has two main parts, the *case* and the *movement,* or *works,* inside the case. The movement

shows the time, provides power to run the watch, and regulates the speed of the watch. Watches differ according to how their movements perform these functions. This article divides watches into two groups—(1) mechanical watches and (2) electronic watches—based on how they are powered.

Mechanical watches are powered by a coiled spring called a *mainspring.* In many watches, the mainspring is wound by turning a knob, or *crown,* that is connected to a shaft inside the case. Other watches, called *self-winding watches,* contain a weight mechanism that winds the mainspring automatically when the watch is moved about. As the watch runs, the mainspring unwinds. The power supplied by the unwinding mainspring turns several tiny gear wheels that are connected in a series called the *train.* A watch's hands are attached to individual gear wheels that turn at specific speeds. The speed of the wheels is partially determined by a mechanism called the *escapement.*

The escapement includes an *escape wheel,* a *balance wheel,* a *balance spring,* and a *pallet lever.* The escape wheel is connected to the train and turns when the watch runs. It also transmits energy to the balance wheel, which is the time base, or timekeeping device, of the watch. The balance spring, also called the *hairspring,* makes the balance wheel *oscillate* (swing back and forth) at a specific frequency. Most balance wheels oscillate 5 or 6 times a second. The pallet lever has two *pallets* (hooks)—one at either end—that catch on the escape wheel. Each oscillation of the balance wheel causes the pallet lever to swing, thus enabling the escape wheel briefly to escape the grip of the pallets. The escape wheel then turns slightly before the pallets again catch on it. This catching action stops the movement of the escape wheel and also produces the characteristic ticking sound of a mechanical watch. Each slight movement of the escape wheel is transmitted through the other wheels in the train to the hands of the watch. Because the oscillations of the balance wheel regulate the speed of the escape wheel, they are responsible for the accuracy of the timepiece.

Many mechanical watches have more than 100 parts. In the most expensive watches, some parts are finished by hand to assure accuracy and durability. In addition, the pallets and various other parts of such watches are made from tiny, hard jewels, such as natural or synthetic rubies, to reduce wear. Such timepieces contain 15 or more jewels.

One type of mechanical watch sold in the United States is called a *pin-lever watch.* In pin-lever watches, the parts are not finished by hand, and the pallets on the pallet lever are metal pins instead of jewels. These watches are inexpensive, but they wear out sooner than do finer watches. If a pin-lever watch is adjusted very carefully by a jeweler, it can be just as accurate as a more expensive jeweled watch.

Electronic watches contain tiny quartz crystals. Some are accurate to within 60 seconds a year. The time base for this type of watch is its vibrating quartz crystal. Most crystals vibrate 32,768 times a second. Quartz-based watches contain a battery-powered electronic integrated circuit on a tiny piece of silicon called a *chip* (see **Electronics** [picture: Devices used in microelectronics]). This chip keeps the crystal vibrating, and it

A mechanical watch has hands that show the time on a dial. The movement of a mechanical watch, *far right,* includes a *mainspring,* which powers the watch. A *balance wheel* regulates the watch's speed. It moves the *pallet lever,* which allows the *escape wheel* to move slightly. This action moves a train of gears that turn the hands on the watch face.

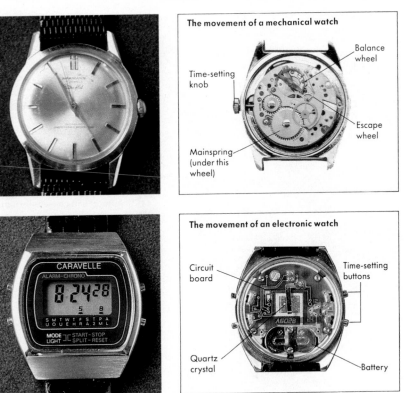

The movement of a mechanical watch

Balance wheel

Time-setting knob

Escape wheel

Mainspring (under this wheel)

A digital electronic watch displays the time in digits that form when electric current passes through patterns of liquid crystal. The movement of an electronic watch, *far right,* includes a *battery,* which makes a *quartz crystal* vibrate. An integrated circuit on a *circuit board* translates the vibrations into information for display on the face of the watch.

The movement of an electronic watch

Circuit board

Time-setting buttons

Quartz crystal

Battery

WORLD BOOK photos

translates the vibrations into electric impulses. In electronic analog watches, these impulses activate a tiny motor that moves the watch hands at the correct speeds.

Another electronic watch, the *solid-state watch,* also uses quartz as its time base. However, it has no moving parts. Instead, the circuits of a solid-state watch translate the time information directly into a *liquid crystal display* (LCD) on the watch face. Most LCD's show the time in the form of digits. In a digital LCD, a thin layer of liquid crystal is sandwiched between two layers of glass. Digital patterns are printed onto the glass with transparent conductive coatings. Normally, these patterns are invisible. However, when an electric charge is applied to the coatings, the liquid crystal becomes visible as a dark numeral. In analog LCD watches, the liquid crystal forms the pattern of watch hands, instead of digits, to indicate the time. A liquid crystal display requires little power from the battery and therefore appears continuously. But the display cannot be seen clearly in dim light. Some LCD watches have a light that can be turned on to illuminate the face.

History

Peter Henlein, a German locksmith, traditionally has been credited with making the first watch. In the early 1500's, Henlein invented a mainspring to power clocks. Until then, clocks had been driven by falling weights and had to remain stationary and stand upright for the weights to operate. Mainsprings enabled clockmakers to produce small, portable clocks. Watchmaking soon spread to England, France, and Switzerland.

The earliest watches were heavy and inaccurate. They weighed so much that they had to be suspended from a cord or chain and worn around the neck or hanging from a belt. Early watches had only an hour hand, and their cases were spherical or drum-shaped. Unusual shapes, including skulls and crosses, became popular during the mid-1600's.

Many watches had a minute hand by the late 1600's, but a hand for the seconds did not become common until the 1900's. The balance spring and escape lever mechanisms had been developed by the late 1700's.

During the late 1600's, watches became small and light enough to fit into a pocket of a jacket or vest. These *pocket watches* were the most popular style of watch for more than 200 years. Wrist watches became common in the late 1800's, but they were designed for women only. During World War I (1914-1918), soldiers realized that wrist watches were more convenient than pocket watches. As a result, wrist watches soon became accepted as accessories for men as well.

Electric analog watches, which were powered by a tiny battery, were introduced in the 1950's. Originally, these watches used a balance wheel as a time base. But later models contained a vibrating tuning fork that acted as a time base in much the same way as quartz crystals do in electronic watches. Quartz-based watches appeared in the early 1970's and, because of their accuracy, soon made earlier electric watches obsolete.

Milton C. Stevens

See also **Clock; Switzerland** (picture: Switzerland's watchmaking industry).

Watch Tower Bible and Tract Society. See Jehovah's Witnesses.

Cameramann International, Ltd. from Marilyn Gartman

Waterfalls flow over rocky cliffs.

Frederick Figall from Artstreet

A flood can cause enormous destruction of property.

© Robert Frerck, Woodfin Camp, Inc.

Waterways are used to transport bulky goods.

Water

Water is the most common substance on earth. It covers more than 70 per cent of the earth's surface. It fills the oceans, rivers, and lakes, and is in the ground and in the air we breathe. Water is everywhere.

Without water, there can be no life. Every living thing—plants, animals, and people—must have water to live. In fact, every living thing consists mostly of water. Your body is about two-thirds water. A chicken is about three-fourths water, and a pineapple is about four-fifths water. Most scientists believe that life itself began in water—in the salty water of the sea.

Ever since the world began, water has been shaping the earth. Rain hammers at the land and washes soil into rivers. The oceans pound against the shores, chiseling cliffs and carrying away land. Rivers knife through rock, carve canyons, and build up land where they empty into the sea. Glaciers plow valleys and cut down mountains.

Water helps keep the earth's climate from getting too hot or too cold. Land absorbs and releases heat from the sun quickly. But the oceans absorb and release the sun's heat slowly. So breezes from the oceans bring warmth to the land in winter and coolness in summer.

Throughout history, water has been people's slave—

Thomas M. Keinath, the contributor of this article, is head of the Department of Environmental Systems Engineering at Clemson University.

and their master. Great civilizations have risen where water supplies were plentiful. They have fallen when these supplies failed. People have killed one another for a muddy water hole. They have worshiped rain gods and prayed for rain. Often, when rains have failed to come, crops have withered and starvation has spread across a land. Sometimes the rains have fallen too heavily and too suddenly. Then rivers have overflowed their banks, drowning everything and everyone in their paths.

Today, more than ever, water is both slave and master to people. We use water in our homes for cleaning, cooking, bathing, and carrying away wastes. We use water to irrigate dry farmlands so we can grow more food. Our factories use more water than any other material. We use the water in rushing rivers and thundering waterfalls to produce electricity.

Our demand for water is constantly increasing. Every year, there are more people in the world. Factories turn out more and more products, and need more and more water. We live in a world of water. But almost all of it—about 97 per cent—is in the oceans. This water is too salty to be used for drinking, farming, and manufacturing. Only about 3 per cent of the world's water is *fresh* (unsalty). Most of this water is not easily available to people because it is locked in glaciers and icecaps. By the year 2000, the world demand for fresh water may be double what it was in the 1980's. But there will still be enough to meet people's needs.

There is as much water on earth today as there ever was—or ever will be. Almost every drop of water we use

© E. Schulthess, Black Star

Ice is the solid form of water.

© Alexander Lowrey, Photo Researchers

Many people enjoy the recreational uses of water.

Bureau of Reclamation

Falling water from a dam produces energy.

finds its way to the oceans. There, it is evaporated by the sun. It then falls back to the earth as rain. Water is used and reused over and over again. It is never used up.

Although the world as a whole has plenty of fresh water, some regions have a water shortage. Rain does not fall evenly over the earth. Some regions are always too dry, and others too wet. A region that usually gets enough rain may suddenly have a serious dry spell, and another region may be flooded with too much rain.

Some regions have a water shortage because the people have managed their supply poorly. People settle where water is plentiful—near lakes and rivers. Cities grow, and factories spring up. The cities and factories dump their wastes into the lakes and rivers, polluting them. Then the people look for new sources of water. Shortages also occur because some cities do not make full use of their supply. They have plenty of water, but they do not have enough storage tanks and distribution pipes to meet the people's needs.

As our demand for water grows and grows, we will have to make better and better use of our supply. The more we learn about water, the better we will be able to meet this challenge.

This article tells broadly about water. It discusses water's importance to civilization and to life itself. It describes the nature of water. For a discussion of our water problems and how we use and abuse our water supply, see **Water pollution.** Separate articles, including **Climate, Conservation, Lake, Ocean, Rain,** and **River,** provide details about the broad subject of water.

Interesting facts about water

How much water is on the earth? There are about 326 million cubic miles (1.4 billion cubic kilometers) of water. There are over a million million (1,000,000,000,000) gallons of water per cubic mile (0.9 million million liters per cubic kilometer).

How much of the earth's water is fresh? Only about 3 per cent of the earth's water is fresh. About three-fourths of the fresh water is frozen in glaciers and icecaps. Glaciers and icecaps contain as much water as flows in all the earth's rivers in about 1,000 years.

How much water do living things contain? All living things consist mostly of water. For example, the body of a human being is about 65 per cent water. An elephant is about 70 per cent water. A potato is about 80 per cent water. A tomato is about 95 per cent water.

How much water does a person take in over a lifetime? On the average, a person takes in about 16,000 gallons (60,600 liters) of water during his or her life.

What are the different forms of water? Water is the only substance on earth that is naturally present in three different forms—as a liquid, a solid (ice), and a gas (water vapor).

How much water does a person use every day? On the average, each person in the United States uses about 70 gallons (260 liters) of water a day in the home.

What is the largest single use of water? The largest single use of water is by industry. It takes about 150 gallons (568 liters) of water to make the paper for one Sunday newspaper, and about 160 gallons of water per pound (1,340 liters per kilogram) of aluminum.

Can water ever be used up? Water is used and reused over and over again—it is never used up. Every glass of water you drink contains molecules of water that have been used countless times before.

Every plant, animal, and human being needs water to stay alive. This is because all the life processes—from taking in food to getting rid of wastes—require water. But people depend on water for more than just to stay alive. We also need it for our way of life. We need water in our homes—to brush our teeth, cook food, and wash dishes. We need water in our factories—to manufacture almost everything from automobiles to zippers. We need water for irrigation—to raise crops in regions that do not get enough rain.

Water in living things. Every *organism* (living thing) consists mostly of water. Your body is about 65 per cent water. So is that of a mouse. An elephant and an ear of corn are about 70 per cent water. A potato and an earthworm are about 80 per cent water. A tomato is about 95 per cent water.

All living things need a lot of water to carry out their life processes. Plants, animals, and human beings must take in *nutrients* (food substances). Watery solutions help dissolve these nutrients and carry them to all parts of an organism. Through chemical reactions, the organism turns the nutrients into energy, or into the materials it needs to grow or to repair itself. These important chemical reactions can take place only in a watery solution. Finally, the organism needs water to carry away waste products.

Every living thing must keep its water supply near normal, or it will die. A person can live without food for more than two months, but can live without water for only about a week. If the body loses more than 20 per cent of its normal water content, a person will die painfully. Human beings must take in about $2\frac{1}{2}$ quarts (2.4 liters) of water a day. This intake can be in the form of the water or beverages we drink, or the water in the food we eat.

Water in our homes. In our homes, we use far more water than the amount we need simply to stay alive. We require water for cleaning, cooking, bathing, and carrying away wastes. For many people, such water is a luxury. Millions of homes in Asia, Africa, and South America have no running water. The people must haul water up by hand from the village well, or carry it in jars from pools and rivers far from their homes.

The United States has more homes with kitchen faucets and flush toilets than any other country. Every American uses an average of about 70 gallons (260 liters) of water a day in the home. It takes about 3 gallons (11 liters) of water to flush a toilet. It takes 30 to 40 gallons (115 to 150 liters) to take a bath, and each minute under a shower takes at least 5 gallons (19 liters). It takes up to 10 gallons (38 liters) of water to wash the dishes, and up to 30 gallons (115 liters) to run an automatic washing machine.

Water for irrigation. Most of the plants that people raise need great quantities of water. For example, it takes 115 gallons (435 liters) of water to grow enough wheat to bake a loaf of bread. People raise most of their crops in areas that have plenty of rain. But to raise enough food for their needs, people must also irrigate dry areas. The rainfall that crops use to grow is not considered a water use, because the water does not come from a country's supply. Irrigation, on the other hand, is a water use because the water is drawn from a nation's rivers, lakes, or wells.

The water a nation uses for irrigation is important to its water supply because none of the water remains for reuse. Plants take in water through their roots. They then pass it out through their leaves into the air as a gas called *water vapor*. Winds carry away the vapor, and the liquid water is gone. On the other hand, nearly all the water used in our homes is returned to the water supply. The water is carried by sewer pipes back to rivers, and can be used again.

The United States uses about 110 billion gallons (416 billion liters) of water a day for irrigation. This is enough water to fill a lake 5 miles (8 kilometers) long, 1 mile (1.6 kilometers) wide, and 100 feet (30 meters) deep. About 41 per cent of all the water used in the United States is for irrigation. For a discussion of irrigation systems, see the article **Irrigation.**

Water for industry. The largest single use of water is by industry. It takes about 270 tons of water to make a ton of steel and about 250 tons of water to make a ton of paper. Manufacturers use about 10 gallons (38 liters) of water to refine 1 gallon (3.8 liters) of gasoline or to brew 1 gallon of beer. Factories in the United States draw about 140 billion gallons (530 billion liters) of water every day from wells, rivers, or lakes. This total accounts for about 52 per cent of all the water used in the country. In addition, many factories buy water from city water systems.

Industry uses water in many ways. It uses water for cleaning fruits and vegetables before canning and freezing them. It uses water as a raw material in soft drinks, canned foods, and many other products. It uses water to air-condition and clean factories. But most of the water used by industry is for cooling. For example, water cools the steam used in producing electric power from fuel. It cools the hot gases produced in refining oil, and the hot steel made by steel mills.

Although industry uses a lot of water, only about 2 per cent of it is consumed. Most of the water used for cooling is piped back to the rivers or lakes from which it is taken. The water consumed by industry is the water added to soft drinks and other products, and the small amount of water that turns to vapor in the cooling processes.

Water for power. People also use water to produce electric power to light homes and to run factories. Electric power stations burn coal or other fuel to turn water into steam. The steam supplies the energy to run machines that produce electricity. Hydroelectric power stations use the energy of falling water from waterfalls and dams to produce electricity. See **Water power; Electric power.**

Water for transportation and recreation. After people learned to build crude small boats, they began using rivers and lakes to carry themselves and their goods. Later, they built larger boats and sailed the ocean in search of new lands and new trade routes. Today, people still depend on water transportation to carry such heavy and bulky products as machinery, coal, grain, and oil. See **Transportation.**

People build most of their recreation areas along lakes, rivers, and seas. They enjoy water sports, such as swimming, fishing, and sailing. Many people also enjoy the beauty of a quiet lake, a thundering waterfall, or a roaring surf.

U.S. water budget

On the average, 4,200,000,000,000 gallons (15,900,000,000,000 liters) of precipitation fall on the United States every day. About 70 per cent of this moisture returns directly to the air by evaporation, or is used by plants where it falls. People use about 6 per cent of the precipitation.

WORLD BOOK diagram by Murrie-White & Associates, Inc.

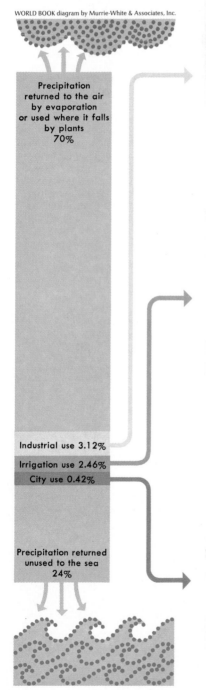

Precipitation returned to the air by evaporation or used where it falls by plants
70%

Industrial use 3.12%

Irrigation use 2.46%

City use 0.42%

Precipitation returned unused to the sea
24%

Canfield Beverage Co. (WORLD BOOK photo)
Soft drink manufacturing

Jones & Laughlin Steel Corporation
Cooling hot steel

© Robert P. Carr, Bruce Coleman Inc.
Irrigation for raising crops in dry areas

WORLD BOOK photo
Drinking

© George Hall, Woodfin Camp, Inc.
Fire fighting

The waters of the earth move continuously from the oceans, to the air, to the land, and back to the oceans again. The sun's heat evaporates water from the oceans. The water rises as invisible vapor, and falls back to the earth as rain, snow, or some other form of moisture. This moisture is called *precipitation*. Most precipitation drops back directly into the oceans. The remainder falls on the rest of the earth. In time, this water also returns to the sea, and the cycle starts again. This unending circulation of the earth's waters is called the *water cycle* or *hydrologic cycle*.

Because of nature's water cycle, there is as much water on earth today as there ever was—or ever will be. Water changes only from one form to another, and moves from one place to another. The water you bathed in last night might have flowed in the Soviet Union's Volga River last month. Or perhaps Alexander the Great drank it more than 2,000 years ago.

The waters of the earth. The earth has a tremendous amount of water, but almost all of it is in the oceans. The oceans cover about 70 per cent of the earth's surface. They contain about 97 per cent of all the water on earth, and are the source of most precipitation that falls to earth. Ocean water is too salty to be used for drinking, agriculture, or industry. But the salt is left behind during evaporation, and the precipitation that falls to earth is fresh water.

Only about 3 per cent of the water on earth is fresh water—and most of it is not easily available to people. It includes water locked in glaciers and icecaps, more than 2 per cent of the earth's water. About half of 1 per cent of the earth's water is beneath the earth's surface. Rivers and lakes contain only about one-fiftieth of 1 per cent of the earth's water.

Water in the air. At one time or another, all the water on earth enters the air, or atmosphere, as water vapor. This vapor becomes the life-giving rain that falls to the earth. Yet, the atmosphere contains only one-thousandth of 1 per cent of the earth's water.

Moisture in the air comes mostly from evaporation. The sun's heat evaporates water from land, lakes, rivers, and, especially, the oceans. About 85 per cent of the vapor in the air comes from the oceans. Plants also add moisture. After plants have drawn water from the ground through their roots, they pass it out through their leaves as vapor in a process called *transpiration*. For example, a birch tree gives off about 70 gallons (260 liters) of water a day. Corn gives off about 4,000 gallons per acre (37,000 liters per hectare) daily. See **Evaporation; Leaf** (Transpiration).

Precipitation. Vapor is carried by the air moving over the earth. The moisture-filled air cools wherever it is forced up by colder air or by mountains or hills. As the air cools, the vapor *condenses* into droplets of liq-

The water cycle

This diagram traces the never-ending circulation of the earth's water as it makes its long journey from the oceans, to the air, to the land, and back to the oceans again.

WORLD BOOK diagram by George Suyeoka

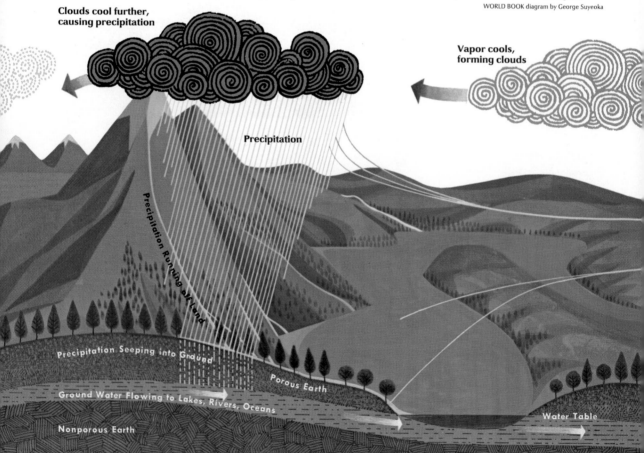

Clouds cool further, causing precipitation

Vapor cools, forming clouds

Precipitation

Precipitation Running off Land

Precipitation Seeping into Ground

Porous Earth

Ground Water Flowing to Lakes, Rivers, Oceans

Water Table

Nonporous Earth

uid water, forming clouds. The droplets fall to the earth as rain. If the vapor is chilled enough, it condenses into ice crystals, and falls as snow.

About 75 per cent of the precipitation falls back directly on the oceans. Some of the rest evaporates immediately—from the surface of the ground, from rooftops, from puddles in the streets. Some of it runs off the land to rivers. From the rivers, it flows back to the sea. The rest of the precipitation soaks into the earth and becomes part of the *ground water* supply. Ground water moves slowly through the ground to the rivers and returns to the sea. This movement of ground water to rivers keeps the rivers flowing during periods without rain. See **Rain; Snow; Weather; Ground water.**

How water shapes the earth. Water changes the face of the earth as it moves through the great water cycle. Water wears down mountains, carves valleys, and cuts deep canyons. It also builds deltas and straightens coastlines.

During precipitation, some water falls on highlands and mountains. The force of gravity pulls the water downhill. As the water flows to lower levels, it *erodes* (wears away) the soil and rocks. In this way, after many thousands of years, mountains are worn down. The water that runs off the land during precipitation cuts small channels. The small channels drain into larger channels. The larger channels drain into still larger

ones, until finally the water empties into the main stream that runs to the sea. The water carries to the sea the materials it has eroded from the land. See **River.**

Some of the precipitation that falls is captured in mountain glaciers. As the glaciers slide down mountainsides, they cut the mountains into sharp and jagged peaks. See **Glacier.**

The ocean also changes the face of the land. As waves pound against the shore, they cut away land and leave steep cliffs. Much of the material the waves wear away from the land is carried far out to sea. Some piles up near shore in sand bars. For more information on how water shapes the earth, see the *World Book* articles **Earth** (How the earth changes); **Erosion; Ocean** (The changing shoreline).

How water began. The question of how water began on earth is part of the question of how the earth itself began. Many scientists believe the earth was formed from materials that came from the hot sun. These materials included the elements that make up water. As the earth cooled and grew solid, water was trapped in rocks in the earth's crust. The water was gradually released, and the ocean basins filled with water. Other scientists have other ideas about how the earth and water began. For a discussion of these ideas, see the articles **Earth** (How the earth began) and **Ocean** (How the oceans began).

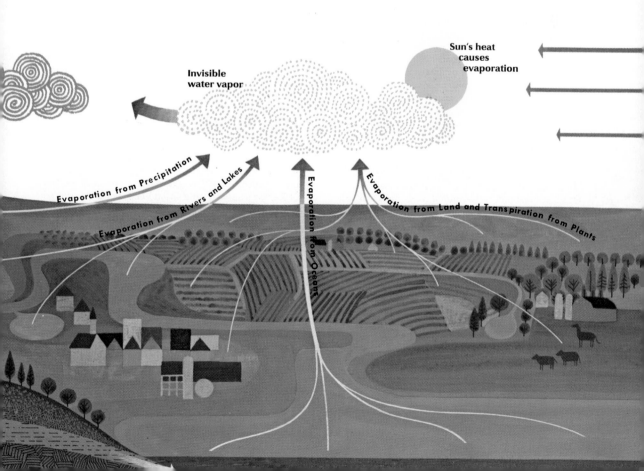

Shortages of fresh water have troubled people throughout history. Today, they trouble people more than ever because the demand for water is growing rapidly. Many people fear that the world does not have enough water to meet all our needs. Yet the world has—and always will have—the same amount of water it has always had. All the water we use passes through the great water cycle and can be used again and again.

The total amount of water on earth is enough for all our needs. However, the earth's water is distributed unevenly. Some regions suffer a constant *drought* (lack of rain). Other regions generally have plenty of water, but they may be struck by drought at times. In addition, people have created many water problems by mismanaging the supply.

World distribution of water. The earth has an enormous amount of water—about 326 million cubic miles (1.4 billion cubic kilometers) of it. In a cubic mile, there are more than a million million—1,000,000,000,000—gallons, or 3.8 million million liters. But 97 per cent of this water is in the salty oceans, and more than 2 per cent is in glaciers and icecaps. The rest totals less than 1 per cent. Most of this water is underground, and the remainder includes the water in lakes, rivers, springs, pools, and ponds. It also includes rain and snow, and the vapor in the air.

A country's water supply is determined by its precipitation. In regions with plenty of precipitation year after year, there is plenty of water in lakes, rivers, and underground reservoirs.

The earth as a whole receives plentiful rain. If this rain fell evenly, all the land would receive about 26 inches (66 centimeters) a year. But the rain is distributed unevenly. For example, over 400 inches (1,000 centimeters) drenches northeastern India every year. But northern Chile may not get rain for years.

Generally, the world's most heavily populated areas receive enough rain for their needs. These areas include most of Europe, Southeast Asia, the Eastern United States, India, much of China, and the northwestern region of the Soviet Union. But about half the earth's land does not get enough rain. These dry areas include most of Asia, central Australia, most of northern Africa, and the Middle East.

The United States has plenty of water. It averages about 30 inches (76 centimeters) of rain annually. This total is large, but it is distributed unevenly. Over 135 inches (343 centimeters) soaks parts of western Washington each year, but Nevada averages only about 7 inches (18 centimeters). Most states east of the Mississippi get 30 to 50 inches (76 to 130 centimeters) of precipitation a year—more than enough to grow crops. But large regions in the West get less than 10 inches (25 centimeters). There, only a little grass and shrubs can grow without irrigation.

Canada's annual precipitation is also distributed unevenly. In the southeast, it ranges from 30 inches (76 centimeters) in central Ontario to 55 inches (140 centimeters) in eastern Nova Scotia. From 14 to 20 inches (36 to 51 centimeters) of precipitation falls in most of the Prairie Provinces. Parts of the west coast get over 100 inches (250 centimeters).

Water shortages. Many regions of the world have a constant water shortage because they never get enough rain. But even a region that normally has enough rain may suddenly have a dry year or several dry years. The climates in regions that receive only light rainfall are especially changeable. Such regions can have a series of destructive dry years.

In the 1930's, one of the worst droughts in United States history struck the Southwest, an already dry region. Winds whipped the dry soil into gigantic dust storms, and most of the region became known as the *Dust Bowl.* Hundreds of farm families had to leave their homes. See **Dust Bowl.**

Periods of low rainfall alternate with periods of high rainfall from year to year and from place to place. During the 1960's, for example, drought struck the Northeastern United States, and parts of China, Brazil, Nicaragua, Portugal, and other countries. Meanwhile, floodwaters spilled over the land in the Midwestern and Western United States, and in parts of Italy, Mexico, Honduras, and other countries.

Many regions have water shortages because the people have not prepared for a period of less than normal rainfall. These water shortages could have been prevented if the people had built artificial lakes, storage tanks, and other facilities to carry them through a drought.

The United States is especially rich in water. But every year, a number of U.S. communities must ration their water. As a result, many people fear that the country is running out of water. The United States as a whole has as much water today as the land had when Christopher Columbus sailed to the New World. But rainfall patterns change. In addition, the demand for water is increasing faster in the United States than in any other country. More and more Americans want air conditioners, garbage disposers, automatic washers, and an extra bathroom. Industry also demands more water as production rises. When drought strikes a water-hungry U.S. community, the effects can be severe—especially if the people are not prepared.

During the 1960's, rainfall in the Northeastern United States fell below normal for several years. Many cities had to restrict the use of water. New York City suffered especially, because it is so heavily populated. To save water, people turned off their air conditioners and let their lawns wither. Restaurants tried not to serve water to customers. The city was declared a disaster area. New York City's troubles came about because the city did not have enough storage tanks, distribution lines, and other facilities to supply the city with water during a long period of light rainfall.

Water management and conservation. Throughout history, people have attempted to increase their water supply by trying to "make rain." They have prayed to rain gods and performed rain dances (see **Rain dance**). They have sprayed the clouds with chemicals to make them release their moisture (see **Rainmaking**). People also have always looked to the sea as a source of water (see the section *Fresh water from the sea*). But often, people do not need more water. They only need to manage the supply better.

Many water problems in the United States have arisen because the country has had a plentiful and easily available water supply. Water has been cheap, and people have been careless and wasteful. They have dumped untreated sewage and other wastes into rivers and lakes, spoiling the water (see **Water pollution**). In most U.S. cities, people pay about 45 cents per 1,000 gallons (3,800 liters) of water. In contrast, New York City, which has had severe water shortages, supplies free water to many people. Many landlords pay a fixed fee, and the tenants can let the water run as long as they like, wasting much of it. Neither the tenant nor the landlord pays a penny extra.

The supply of cheap, easily available water is shrinking in the United States. The development of new supplies will become more and more costly. It will then be cheaper to reuse water from old supplies. For example, steel companies use great quantities of water for cooling. As costs rise, the companies may use a small amount of water over and over in a circulating cooling system.

Sewage can be treated and turned into usable water. Such water is used today and will be used more in the future. Many Texas communities water their lawns with treated sewage water. In Santee, Calif., people swim and fish in lakes of purified sewage water.

The unequal distribution of precipitation

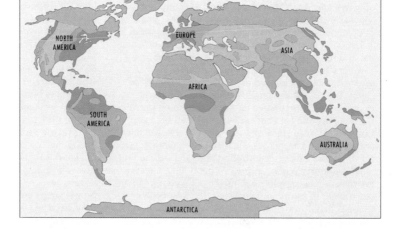

Always Enough Rain

Usually Enough Rain

Usually Not Enough Rain

Never Enough Rain

WORLD BOOK map

Artstreet

A tropical rain forest receives plentiful rainfall and remains green throughout the year.

Photri from Marilyn Gartman

A desert receives little rainfall, resulting in a dry landscape that can support little vegetation or animal life.

Artstreet

A drought occurs when a region receives less than normal rainfall over a long time, often leaving soil parched and cracked.

AP/Wide World

A mudslide can occur when a sudden downpour drenches an area that seldom receives large amounts of rain.

City water systems

When you turn on a faucet, you expect clean, pure water to flow out. You also expect your city to have plenty of water for its industries, for fighting fires, and for cleaning streets. The job of supplying a modern city with water is tremendous. First of all, there must be sources of plentiful water to meet the demands of a growing city. Then, the water must be purified. Next, it must be piped into every house, office building, factory, and hotel in the city. Finally, the used water must be piped away. Public water supply systems in the United States serve about 185 million people, or about 80 per cent of the population.

Sources of supply. Cities can draw fresh water from only two sources: (1) rivers and lakes, or (2) the ground. Most U.S. cities, especially those with fewer than 5,000 people, get water from underground supplies. Most larger cities get theirs from rivers or lakes. Nationwide, most Americans get water from rivers and lakes.

Rivers and lakes. Most cities that depend on rivers for their water are located on small rivers—simply because most rivers are small. The amount of water in a river can vary from time to time, depending on rainfall. During a dry spell, a river's water level may fall sharply, especially if it is a small river. Then, a city may not have enough water. For this reason, many cities that depend on small rivers store water during rainy periods so they will always have a good supply. Some build a dam on the river and store water behind it in a reservoir. Others store water in a pond or small lake. See **Reservoir.**

A city that draws its water from a lake has a natural storage reservoir in the lake itself. Lakes are fed by rivers and by waters moving through the ground. During wet spells, lakes store some of the extra water they receive. This extra water helps keep lake levels from dropping below normal during dry periods.

Ground water. Many cities are not near rivers or lakes large enough for their needs. They use water that is stored underground. This water comes from rain that soaks into the ground. As it trickles downward, it fills the spaces between grains of sand and cracks and pores in rocks. In time, the water reaches a layer of rock or other material that is watertight. The water collects above the watertight layer, and the ground becomes *saturated* (soaked). This saturated zone is called an *aquifer.* The upper limit of the zone is called the *water table.* Cities obtain underground water by drilling wells that reach below the water table and pumping up the water. See **Ground water; Well** (Water wells).

Uses of city water supplies. Public waterworks supply U.S. cities with a total of about 25 billion gallons (95 billion liters) of water a day. They provide each person with an average of 70 gallons (260 liters) a day that is used in the home. Factories and such businesses as hotels and restaurants also use about 70 gallons of water a day for each person in a city. In addition, city water systems provide water for fighting fires, cleaning streets, and sprinkling park lawns. On the average, these uses total about 10 gallons (38 liters) a day for each city dweller.

Another "use" of a city's water is waste. In many cities, homeowners pay a flat fee, no matter how much water they use. They do not have meters that measure the water they use. If their faucets leak, the water is wasted. Water is also wasted through leaks in a city's under-

How Chicago treats its water   This diagram traces the eight-hour course of water as it flows through the Central Water Filtration Plant. The water enters intake cribs (1) about 2½ miles (4 kilometers) out in Lake Michigan, and flows through tunnels (2) under the lake into the plant's intake basin (3). Water can also enter the plant directly through a shore intake (4). Screens (5) keep out fish, plants, and trash. Pumps (6) lift the water about 20 feet (6 meters) above the lake level, so that it flows by gravity through the filtration processes. Alum, chlorine, lime, fluoride, and other chemicals are added (7), and then thor-

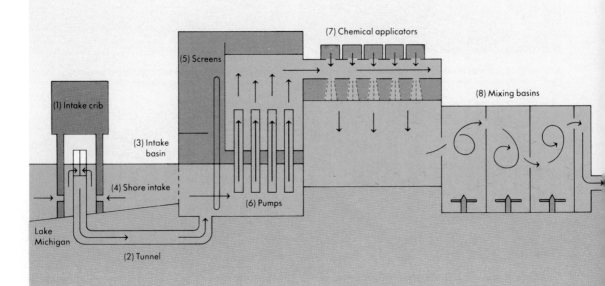

Artstreet

Chicago's main water purification plant is the largest water treatment plant in the world. It serves about $4\frac{1}{2}$ million people in Chicago and nearby suburbs, and can produce nearly $1\frac{3}{4}$ billion gallons (6.6 billion liters) of water a day. The plant is on a 61-acre (25-hectare) artificially created peninsula that extends into Lake Michigan.

oughly mixed with the water in mixing basins (8). Bacteria, silt, and other impurities stick to the alum, which sinks to the bottom of settling basins (9). The water then trickles through sand and gravel filters (10), which screen out any remaining impurities. The filtered water collects in clear wells (11), and then flows to reservoirs (12), where it receives a final treatment with chlorine and other chemicals. The purified water passes through tunnels (13) to pumping stations (14). The stations send the water through underground mains to homes, factories, and other buildings.

WORLD BOOK diagram by Zorica Dabich

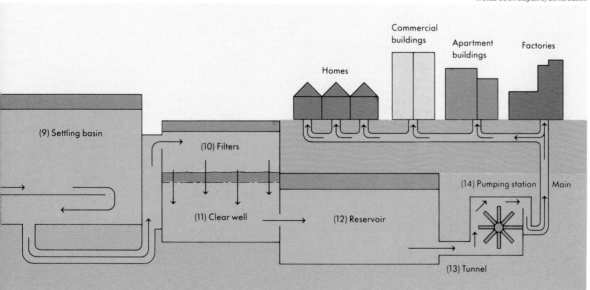

ground pipes. Generally, water lost through leakage is at least 20 per cent of a city's water use. Chicago loses about 150 million gallons (568 million liters) of water daily through leakage—about five times as much as all the city's downtown buildings use.

Purifying and treating water. People want drinking water that is free of bacteria, sparkling clear, and without an objectionable taste or odor. Water in its natural state seldom has these qualities. So after water is drawn from a source, it is piped into a treatment plant. The plant may put the water through one or several processes, depending on the quality of the untreated water, and on a city's standards. Many cities use three basic processes: (1) coagulation and settling, (2) filtration, and (3) disinfection.

Coagulation and settling. The *raw* (untreated) water flows into the treatment plant and is mixed with chemicals. Some of these chemicals are *coagulants.* The most widely used coagulant is a fine powder called *aluminum sulfate* or *alum.* In the water, the alum forms tiny, sticky globs called *flocs.* Bacteria, mud, and other impurities stick to the flocs. The water then passes into a *settling basin,* where the flocs settle to the bottom. Coagulation and settling remove most impurities.

Filtration. The water is then passed through a filter. The filter consists of a bed of sand usually about $2\frac{1}{2}$ feet (76 centimeters) deep on top of a bed of gravel about 1 foot (30 centimeters) deep. As the water trickles down through the filter, any remaining particles are screened out. The water then flows to huge reservoirs for a final treatment that kills bacteria.

Disinfection kills disease-carrying bacteria. Most plants disinfect water by adding a substance called *chlorine.* Chlorine is usually added before coagulation and settling, and after filtration. Most cities chlorinate their water, even if they do not treat it in any other way. See **Chlorine.**

Sally Wayland

A water tower is a part of the water system in many towns and cities. It provides storage and helps maintain water pressure.

Other processes are also used to remove unpleasant tastes or smells, or to give water special qualities. *Aeration* improves taste and odor. In this process, water is usually sprayed or trickled through the air. The oxygen in the air takes away the bad taste and odor. Many communities have water containing minerals that make it *hard.* Hard water requires lots of soap to make a lather. It also forms deposits on pipes and other equipment. Several processes can be used to *soften* the water (see **Water softening**). Some cities add *lime* to their water to help prevent pipes from rusting. *Activated carbon* helps get rid of fishy odors and remove toxic chemicals. Many

A small town water system

WORLD BOOK diagram by Zorica Dabich

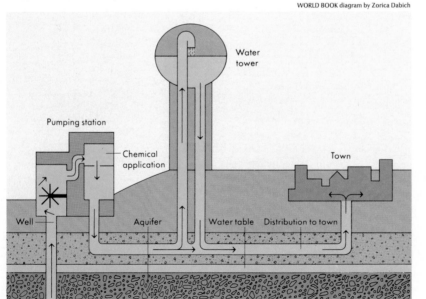

Water tower

Pumping station

Chemical application

Town

Well

Aquifer

Water table

Distribution to town

Most small U.S. towns get water by drilling wells and pumping up underground water. The water is chemically treated and then pumped to consumers. Most towns also pump water into tall water towers. When water is released from these towers, the force of gravity distributes it through the piping system.

communities add a substance called *fluoride* to their water to help reduce tooth decay (see **Fluoridation**).

Distributing water. The treated water flows to a pumping station, where it is pumped into large cast iron pipes called *water mains*. Water mains run beneath the streets. They carry water to every fire hydrant, and connect with smaller pipes that lead to every home, office building, and restaurant. The pumping station sends the water into the mains under enough pressure to carry it to every faucet. This pressure is usually so high that you cannot hold back the water by putting your finger under a fully opened faucet.

Sometimes the demand for water may be too great for the pressure a pumping station can supply. Then, water may only trickle from the faucets. This can happen on a hot summer day when many people in the neighborhood are watering their lawns, filling backyard pools, or taking showers. The water pressure may also fall when fire fighters use a large amount of water to fight a large fire.

Most cities pump water into storage tanks to help keep their water pressure high at all times. The tanks are built on hills, or they are tall water towers. When water is released from these tanks, gravity pulls the water downward, giving it the pressure to rush through the water mains.

Disposing of used water. Most of the water in our homes is used to carry away wastes. This water, and the wastes it carries, is called *sewage*. Factories also use water to wash away such industrial wastes as acids and greases. In most U.S. cities, a piping system under the streets carries away the sewage from homes, factories, hotels, and other buildings. This system is called a *sewerage system*.

Sewage has a bad odor. But more important, it contains disease-producing bacteria. Most cities have treatment plants that clean sewage water and kill the bacteria in it. The treated water can then be dumped into a river, stream, or lake. To learn how sewage is treated, see the **Sewage** article.

Almost all of the sewage in the United States undergoes some type of sewage treatment. Only a little of the sewage is dumped untreated into rivers. The dumping of untreated sewage causes serious problems for the cities downstream that take their water from the same rivers.

Fresh water from the sea

About 97 per cent of the water on earth is in the salty oceans. In their thirst for water, people have looked longingly throughout history at this endless supply. Today, more than ever, many people believe that desalting ocean water holds the answer to the ever-increasing demand for fresh water.

The salt in seawater is mostly common table salt. A person can safely drink water that contains less than $\frac{1}{2}$ pound of salt to 100 pounds of water, or 0.5 kilogram to every 100 kilograms. But seawater has about 7 times this amount of salt. A person who drinks only seawater will die of thirst because the kidneys cannot get rid of all the salt. The person's body will *dehydrate* (dry out) as it tries to wash out the excess salt. Nor can people use seawater in agriculture or industry. It kills most crops, and quickly rusts most machinery.

People have found many ways to *desalinate* (remove the salt from) seawater. Desalination offers hope of relieving water shortages near seacoasts. However, desalination does not hold the answer to all the water problems. Even if the oceans contained fresh water, people would still have such problems as pollution and flood control.

There are three main desalination processes: (1) distillation, (2) electrodialysis, and (3) freezing. Distillation and freezing remove the water from the salt. Electrodialysis takes the salt from the water.

Distillation is the oldest and most common method of turning seawater into fresh water. Most ocean ships use it to obtain drinking water. Seawater can be distilled simply by boiling it in a teapot, and piping the steam into a cool bottle. The steam rises, leaving the salt behind. As the steam cools in the bottle, it condenses into fresh water.

Every day, the sun evaporates millions of tons of water from the ocean's surface. The water vapor then condenses and falls back to earth as fresh water. For centuries, people have copied nature and used the sun's heat to distill seawater. Two thousand years ago, Julius Caesar used solar distillation in Egypt to obtain drinking water for his soldiers. Today, the people of Guam, the Galapagos Islands, and other places still use the sun's heat to distill seawater.

Solar distillation can be done simply by filling a shallow basin with seawater and covering it with a transparent plastic dome, or a sloping sheet of glass. The salt water turns to vapor under the sun's heat. The vapor rises until it hits the underside of the dome or glass, where it condenses. The fresh water runs down into collecting troughs. This type of distillation produces little water. In one day, such a basin in a sunny climate can produce only about 6,500 gallons of water per acre (60,800 liters per hectare) of the basin's area.

Most modern desalting plants use a process called *multistage flash distillation*. This is a type of the age-old method of boiling and condensation. In flash distillation, hot seawater flows into a large chamber in which the pressure is low. The low pressure causes some of the water to *flash* (turn quickly) into steam. The steam is condensed into salt-free water. The seawater passes through several distillation chambers. Often, the final water is so pure that it is tasteless, and some salt must be tossed back in to give it flavor. The desalting plants at the United States naval base at Guantánamo Bay, Cuba, and at Key West, Fla., use this process. They each produce over 2 million gallons (8 million liters) of fresh water a day.

Another distilling process called *forced-circulation vapor-compression* is used by the United States government's Roswell, N.Mex., desalting plant. This plant can produce 1 million gallons (4 million liters) of fresh water a day.

Electrodialysis is used chiefly to desalt *brackish* (slightly salty) ground water. Electrodialysis is based on the fact that when salt is dissolved in water, it breaks up into *ions* (electrically charged particles) of sodium and chloride. Sodium ions carry a positive charge, and chloride ions carry a negative charge.

The process uses a large chamber divided into many compartments by thin plastic sheets called *membranes.* Two types of membranes are used, and they are placed alternately. One type allows only positive ions to pass through it. The other lets only negative ions through. One of the end compartments contains a positive *electrode* (electrical pole). The other end compartment contains a negative electrode.

When an electric current is sent through the water, the negative ions are drawn through the membranes permeable to negative ions toward the positive electrode. The positive ions are drawn through the membranes permeable to positive ions toward the negative electrode. Thus, the salt in every other compartment is drawn off, leaving fresh water.

The U.S. government's plant in Webster, S.Dak., uses the electrodialysis process. This plant produces about 250,000 gallons (946,000 liters) of water daily from the region's brackish ground water.

Freezing. Ice is pure water. When seawater freezes, the ice crystals produced are pure water in solid form. The salt is separated and trapped between the ice crystals. There are several freezing processes. The main problem lies in separating the ice crystals from the salt. This is usually done by washing off the salt with fresh water. The ice is then melted and becomes fresh liquid water.

The United States government's plant in Wrightsville Beach, N.C., uses a freezing process. It can produce about 200,000 gallons (760,000 liters) of fresh water a day.

Other desalting processes are also being studied. One of the most promising is *reverse osmosis.* In normal osmosis, a less concentrated liquid flows through a membrane into a more concentrated liquid. Thus, if salt water and fresh water are separated in a chamber by a

semipermeable membrane, the fresh water will flow through the membrane into the salt water. However, if enough pressure is placed on the salt water, this normal flow can be reversed. Fresh water will then be squeezed from the salt water as it passes through the membrane, leaving the salt behind. The reverse osmosis desalting process works in this way.

The future of desalting. All methods of desalination require large amounts of energy. Producing energy is expensive, whether it comes from hydroelectric, fuel-burning, or nuclear power plants. In the United States, it costs about $1 to produce 1,000 gallons (3,800 liters) of fresh water from seawater. In comparison, U.S. cities pay an average of only about 45 cents for 1,000 gallons taken and distributed from fresh sources.

Desalination can relieve water shortages chiefly in dry regions along seacoasts. But it offers little hope of ending shortages in cities far from a seacoast or in mountains. The cost of bringing the water to such cities could be greater than the cost of desalting.

In places where only seawater is available, the high cost of desalination is less important. For this reason, more than 200 desalting plants have been built throughout the world—from Australia to California, and from Greenland to South America. Most of these plants are small. Many of them serve military posts in isolated regions, oil-drilling crews in deserts, island resorts, or industrial plants.

The world's desalting plants produce a total of more than 980 million gallons (3.8 billion liters) of fresh water each day. This production meets only a small fraction of the world's daily demand for fresh water. A large desalting facility, such as the one at Ash Shuwaykh in Kuwait, can alone produce about 75 million gallons (284 million liters) of fresh water daily.

Much government and private research is centered on building large nuclear-powered dual purpose desalination plants to lower the cost of desalting. These plants would be able to produce electricity as well as desalted water.

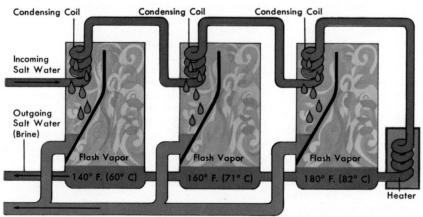

Flash distillation is the most widely used desalting process. Incoming seawater is heated and then released into a low-pressure chamber. This causes part of the water to flash into steam, even though its temperature is below 212° F. (100° C). The steam condenses into fresh water on a condensing coil, which is cooled by incoming seawater. The remaining seawater passes through similar chambers, each at a successively lower pressure.

Electrodialysis is based on the fact that when salt dissolves in water, it breaks up into negatively and positively charged ions. This diagram, showing three compartments of an electrodialysis unit, illustrates how the ions are drawn from the middle one.

Freezing. In the process shown, seawater enters a vacuum freezing chamber. Part of the water flashes into vapor, and part turns into an icy slush. The salt is washed off the ice in a separation unit. The ice melts and the vapor condenses in a melter.

WORLD BOOK diagrams by Murrie-White & Associates, Inc.

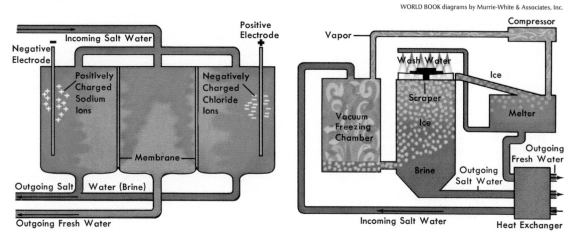

What water is and how it behaves

Water is not only the most common substance on earth, it is also one of the most unusual. No other substance can do all the things that water can do. Water is an exception to many of nature's rules because of its unusual *properties* (qualities).

The chemistry of water. Water consists of tiny particles called *molecules*. A drop of water contains many millions of molecules. Each molecule, in turn, consists of even smaller particles called *atoms*. Water molecules consist of atoms of hydrogen and oxygen. Hydrogen and oxygen by themselves are gases. But when two atoms of hydrogen combine with one atom of oxygen, they form the chemical compound H_2O—water.

Even the purest water contains substances besides ordinary hydrogen and oxygen. For example, water contains very tiny portions of *deuterium,* a hydrogen atom that weighs more than the ordinary hydrogen atom. Water formed by a combination of deuterium and oxygen is called *heavy water* (see **Heavy water; Deuterium**). Water is a combination of several different substances, but these substances make up only a small fraction of it.

The properties of water. Water can be a solid, a liquid, or a gas. No other substance appears in these three forms within the earth's normal range of temperature. The molecules that make up water are always moving, and the form water takes depends on how fast they move. The molecules in solid water (ice) are far apart and almost motionless. The molecules in liquid water are close together and move about freely. The molecules in water vapor, a gas, move about violently and bump into one another.

Ice. Most substances contract as they grow colder. But when water is cooled, it contracts only until its temperature reaches 39° F. (4° C). Water expands when it becomes colder than 39° F. For this reason, when ice forms at 32° F. (0° C), it floats on liquid water. If water contracted upon freezing, any volume of ice would be heavier than an equal volume of liquid water. Ice would then

sink. If ice sank, the earth would become a lifeless arctic desert. Each winter, more and more ice would pile up on the bottom of lakes, rivers, and oceans. In summer, the sun's heat could not reach deep enough to melt the ice. Water life would die. The hydrologic cycle would slow down. In time, all of the water would turn to solid ice, except perhaps for a thin layer of water over the ice during the summer.

The water molecule

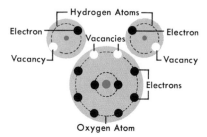

A water molecule is made up of two hydrogen atoms and one oxygen atom. Each hydrogen atom has room for another electron around its nucleus. The oxygen atom has room for two more electrons around its nucleus.

Water Molecule

The two hydrogen atoms and one oxygen atom fill their empty spaces by sharing electrons. The resulting water molecule is an extremely tight structure because its atoms share electrons.

Liquid. Water is a liquid at temperatures found in most places on the earth. No other common substance is liquid at ordinary temperatures. In fact, the temperatures at which water is a liquid are unusual. Water is a liquid between 32° F. (0° C), its freezing point, and 212° F. (100° C), its boiling point. But substances with a structure like that of water are not liquid in this temperature range. These substances include gases with the formulas H_2Te, H_2Se, and H_2S. As their formulas show, they are closely related to water (H_2O). Each has two atoms of hydrogen, plus an atom of the elements tellurium, selenium, or sulfur. If water behaved like these close relatives, it would be a liquid between about −148° F. (−100° C) and −130° F. (−90° C). In that case, there would be no liquid water on earth because the earth's temperatures are far higher than −130° F.

Water weighs about 62.4 pounds per cubic foot (1 kilogram per liter). Scientists compare the weight of other substances with the weight of water in order to find the *specific gravity* of the substance (see **Density**).

Vapor. If an uncovered glass of water stands for a few days, the water will gradually disappear because the water molecules are moving constantly. Those at the surface break free of those below and enter the air as vapor. The higher the temperature of the water, the faster it evaporates, because the water molecules move faster.

Water can also be turned into vapor by boiling it, and creating *steam.* It takes an enormous amount of heat to produce steam. Water boils at 212° F. (100° C). But when water reaches the boiling point, it does not immediately turn into steam. First there is a pause, during which the water absorbs additional heat without any rise in the temperature. This heat is called *latent heat.* More than five times as much heat is required to turn boiling water into steam as to bring freezing water to a boil. Thus, steam holds a great amount of latent heat energy. People use this energy to run machinery.

Water vapor in the air also holds a tremendous amount of latent heat energy. This energy is released when the vapor cools and condenses, and falls as rain. The high latent heat of water is related to water's remarkable heat capacity.

Heat capacity is the ability of a substance to absorb heat without becoming much warmer itself. Water has a greater heat capacity than any other substance except ammonia. To illustrate water's unusual heat capacity, imagine a pound of water, a pound of gold, and a pound of iron—all at −459.67° F. (−273.15° C). This is *absolute zero,* the temperature at which a substance supposedly contains no heat at all. If all three substances were heated and each absorbed the same amount of energy, the gold would melt at 2016° F. (1102° C). But the ice would still be at −300° F. (−184° C). When the iron began to melt at 2370° F. (1299° C), the ice would finally have reached 32° F. (0° C).

Surface tension is the ability of a substance to stick to itself and pull itself together. Water's surface tension is extremely high. A dripping faucet shows how water sticks to itself. As the water drips, each drop clings to the faucet, stretches, lets go, and then snaps into a tiny ball. Water molecules cling together so tightly that water can support objects heavier than itself. For example, a needle or a razor blade can float on water. Insects

A *World Book* science project
How detergents reduce the surface tension of water

The purpose of this project is to determine how various detergents reduce surface tension and how this ability is related to their cost. The ability to reduce surface tension is an important part of a detergent's cleaning action.

Surface tension makes the surface of water act like a film. This "film" can support a small, flat object, such as a button, that is actually too heavy to float. Surface tension also makes it hard for water to clean soiled materials, and so a detergent must reduce surface tension in order to work effectively. You can approximately measure a detergent's ability to reduce surface tension by resting a button on the surface of some water and counting the drops of detergent needed to weaken the "film" so that the button sinks.

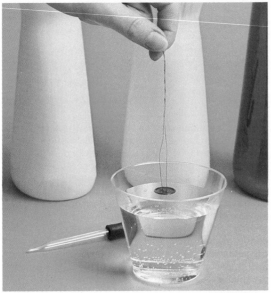

WORLD BOOK photo

Materials

- Glass or plastic container
- Stirring rod
- Several plastic buttons
- Short piece of thread
- Eyedropper
- Assorted brands of liquid dishwashing detergent
- Several quarts or liters of tap water at room temperature

can walk on water. Water can also stick to other substances, such as cloth, glass, and soil. By sticking to these substances, water wets them. See **Surface tension.**

Capillarity is the ability of a liquid to climb up a surface against the pull of gravity. You can see water's climbing ability in a glass of water. The water is higher around the edges, where it touches the glass. The capillarity of water helps it circulate through soil, and up through the roots and stems of plants. It also helps circulate blood, which is mostly water, throughout our bodies. See **Capillarity.**

Dissolving ability. Water can dissolve almost any substance. It dissolves the hardest rocks as it runs over the land and seeps through the ground. In time, it carries the dissolved materials to the oceans. Water also dis-

Procedure

1. Fill the container with 8 ounces (237 milliliters) of the water to be used in the tests.
2. Loop the thread through the holes of the button. Holding the thread, gently lower the button onto the surface of the water. If the button sinks, try other buttons until you find one that rests on the surface.
3. Remove the button and dry it thoroughly.
4. Using the eyedropper, place one drop of the first detergent to be tested in the container of water. Stir the solution thoroughly with the stirring rod.
5. Carefully lower the button and rest it on the water's surface. Remove the button and dry it thoroughly.
6. Repeat steps 4 and 5, adding a drop of detergent each time, until the button sinks when lowered onto the water. Keep track of the number of drops you add to the water.
7. After the button sinks, record the number of drops of detergent you added. Remove the button and rinse and dry it. Pour the water into the sink and rinse and dry the container thoroughly. Repeat all the steps for each of the detergents to be tested.

Organizing your information

1. For each detergent tested, divide the cost of the detergent in cents by the number of ounces or milliliters in an unopened bottle to find the *cost per unit quantity.*
2. Make a table that shows the following information for each detergent: the number of drops used in the test, the cost per unit quantity, and the *economic rating.* Calculate the economic rating by using this formula:

number of drops × cost per unit quantity = economic rating

The economic rating provides a way of comparing the costs of using the detergents tested. The detergent with the smallest economic rating reduces surface tension most economically.

3. Prepare a series of graphs, such as the ones shown below, to illustrate the information in your table. Which detergent is most economical to use?

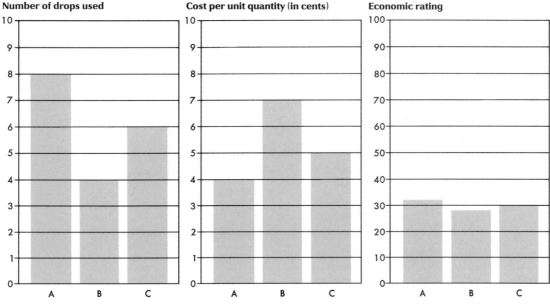

solves the nutrients that all living things need. Water dissolves and carries the nutrients in the soil to plants and to the cells within plants. Water also dissolves the food that people and animals eat, and then carries this food to the cells.

How water is held together. Water's unusual properties depend on the forces that hold it together. These forces are (1) chemical bonds and (2) hydrogen bonds.

Chemical bonds are the forces that hold the two hydrogen atoms and the one oxygen atom together in a water molecule. Each hydrogen atom has one electron whirling in orbit around its nucleus. But each of these atoms has room for two electrons. The oxygen atom has six electrons in its outer orbit, but it has room for eight. The hydrogen and oxygen atoms each fill their empty spaces by sharing their electrons. The two electrons

from the two hydrogen atoms enter the orbit of the oxygen atom. At the same time, two electrons from the oxygen atom fill the empty spaces in the two hydrogen atoms. The resulting water molecule is an extremely tight structure.

Hydrogen bonds are the forces that link water molecules together. Water molecules have a lopsided shape because the two hydrogen atoms bulge from one end of the oxygen atom. The hydrogen end of the water molecule has a positive electric charge. At the opposite end, the molecule has a negative charge. Water molecules link together because the positive and negative charges attract. The positive ends of water molecules attach to the negative ends of other water molecules, whose positive ends attach to the negative ends of still other water molecules.

Water and civilization. Water has been vital to the development and survival of civilization. The first great civilizations arose in the valleys of great rivers—in the Nile Valley of Egypt, the Tigris-Euphrates Valley of Mesopotamia, the Indus Valley of Pakistan, and the Huang He Valley of China. All these civilizations built large irrigation systems, made the land productive, and prospered.

Civilizations crumbled when water supplies failed or were poorly managed. Many historians believe the Sumerian civilization of Mesopotamia fell because of poor irrigation practices. Salt in irrigation water is left behind during evaporation, and tends to build up in the soil. This can be avoided by washing the salt away with extra water. But if the land is not well drained, it becomes water-logged. The Sumerians failed to achieve a balance between salt accumulation and drainage. The salt and excess water harmed their crops. Farm production gradually declined, and food shortages developed. With the collapse of agriculture, the Sumerian civilization fell.

The ancient Romans built aqueducts, canals, and reservoirs throughout their empire. They turned regions along the coast of northern Africa into prosperous civilizations. After the Romans left, their water projects were abandoned. Today, these places are desert.

The challenge of today, as in ancient times, is for people to make the best use of water. But the challenge is greater than ever before because more and more water is needed as industry and population grow. The earth has enough water to meet the growing demand, but the water is distributed unevenly. Also, people waste and pollute water and manage it poorly in other ways.

People are beginning to realize how precious water is, and how necessary it is to understand water problems in order to solve them. During the late 1960's and the 1970's, the United States government and individual state governments established various antipollution programs. In addition, the federal government and private companies worked to improve processes for desalting seawater.

Nations have begun to cooperate with one another in trying to solve water problems. In 1965, the First International Symposium on Water Desalination was held in Washington, D.C. At this conference, representatives from more than 60 countries shared their knowledge of desalting techniques.

Since 1965, about 70 nations have taken part in the International Hydrological Decade, a program directed by the United Nations to promote scientific research on water resources. A United Nations Water Conference was held in 1977 to help plan more efficient ways of using and conserving the world's water supply.

Thomas M. Keinath

Study aids

Related articles in *World Book* include:

Forms of water

Artesian well	Hail	Sleet
Cloud	Heavy water	Snow
Dew	Humidity	Spring
Fog	Ice	Steam
Frost	Iceberg	Waterfall
Geyser	Liquid	Waterspout
Glacier	Mineral water	Well
Ground water	Rain	Whirlpool

Purification and distribution of water

Aqueduct	Fluoridation	Sanitation
Chlorine	Plumbing	Sewage
Dam	Pump	Water meter
Filter	Reservoir	Water softening

Other related articles

Boiling point	Flood	Ocean
Canal	Hydraulics	Osmosis
Capillarity	Hydrography	Rainmaking
Climate	Hydrology	River
Conservation (Water	Hydrolysis	Salt
conservation)	Hydroponics	Surface tension
Deuterium	Hydrosphere	Transportation
Electric power	Irrigation	Water pollution
Erosion	Lake	Water power
Eutrophication	Life (The chemical	Water wheel
Evaporation	basis of life)	Weather

Outline

I. Water in our daily lives
  A. Water in living things   E. Water for power
  B. Water in our homes   F. Water for transportation
  C. Water for irrigation   and recreation
  D. Water for industry
II. Nature's water cycle
  A. The waters of the earth B. Water in the air
  C. Precipitation
  D. How water shapes the
    earth
  E. How water began
III. The water supply problem
  A. World distribution of water
  B. Water shortages
  C. Water management and conservation
IV. City water systems
  A. Sources of supply
  B. Uses of city water supplies
  C. Purifying and treating water
  D. Distributing water
  E. Disposing of used water
V. Fresh water from the sea
  A. Distillation   D. Other desalting processes
  B. Electrodialysis   E. The future of desalting
  C. Freezing
VI. What water is and how it behaves
  A. The chemistry of water
  B. The properties of water
  C. How water is held together
VII. Water and the course of history

Questions

What are some of the ways in which people use water?

Why do all living things need water to live?

What are some reasons for water shortages? What can be done to conserve water?

Why would people die if they drank only seawater?

What are some ways in which water shapes the earth?

How much of the earth is covered with water?

Why would the earth become a lifeless arctic desert if ice did not float?

What is the *water,* or *hydrologic, cycle?*

Reading and Study Guide

See *Water* in the Research Guide/Index, Volume 22, for a *Reading and Study Guide.*

Additional resources

Level I

Ardley, Neil. *Working with Water.* Watts, 1983. A collection of experiments.

Branley, Franklyn M. *Water for the World.* T. Y. Crowell, 1982.

Gardner, Robert. *Water: The Life Sustaining Resource.* Messner, 1982.

Gunston, Bill. *Water.* Silver Burdett, 1982.

Level II

Angel, Heather, and Wolseley, Pat. *The Water Naturalist.* Facts on File, 1982. Includes simple projects.

Goldin, Augusta R. *Water: Too Much, Too Little, Too Polluted?* Harcourt, 1983.

Powledge, Fred. *Water: The Nature, Uses, and Future of Our Most Precious and Abused Resource.* Farrar, 1982.

Pringle, Laurence P. *Water: The Next Great Resource Battle.* Macmillan, 1982.

Sheaffer, John R., and Stevens, L. A. *Future Water: An Exciting Solution to America's Most Serious Resource Crisis.* Morrow, 1983.

Water beech. See Ironwood.

Water beetle
is the name given to many separate families of beetles that live in the water. Typical water beetles are the *whirligigs,* the *predaceous diving beetles,* and the *giant water scavenger beetles.* Some of these insects live in the water all their lives. Others live in or near the water only in the *larval* (young) stage.

Whirligigs whirl on the top of the water. They have short *antennae* (feelers), long-clawed front legs, and paddle-shaped hind legs. Their eyes are divided into a lower pair and an upper pair. Whirligigs produce an applelike scent when handled. Predaceous diving beetles have long, threadlike antennae. Their hind legs are flat and fringed. Giant water scavenger beetles have short, stubby antennae. Predaceous diving and giant water scavenger beetles are fierce predators and eat small fish and insect larvae.

WORLD BOOK illustration by Shirley Hooper, Oxford Illustrators Limited

Giant water scavenger

Scientific classification. Water beetles are in the order Coleoptera. Whirligig beetles belong to the family Gyrinidae, predaceous diving beetles to the family Dytiscidae, and giant water scavenger beetles to the family Hydrophilidae.

David J. Shetlar

See also **Beetle** (pictures).

Water bird. For examples, see Bird (pictures: Birds of inland waters and marshes; Birds of the seacoasts) and also the lists of Swimming and diving birds and Wading birds in the *Related articles* section.

Water boa. See Anaconda.

Water boatman. See Water bug; Insect (Beneficial insects).

Water buffalo. Several kinds of wild oxen may be called water buffaloes. Some have been domesticated, and are among the most useful of all farm animals. The water buffalo of India is one of the largest of wild cattle. The *bulls* (males) are often 5 to 6½ feet (1.5 to 2 meters) tall, and their horns may spread 12 feet (3.7 meters) from

L. R. Dawson, Bruce Coleman Ltd.

The water buffalo has large curved horns. The Indian water buffalo, *above,* is a farm animal used in Asian rice fields.

tip to tip, measured along the curve. The horns sweep out and back to form almost a circle, and are three-sided. The Indian buffalo's hide is bluish black, and is easy to see through its thin hair. Wild Indian buffaloes graze in herds of about 50 animals. Both wild and domesticated buffaloes have a keen sense of smell.

They like to wallow in the mud and water a large part of the day. They are fierce when wild, and a water buffalo is said to be a match for a large lion or tiger. The Indian buffalo has long been used in the rice fields of Asia, and makes rice farming possible on a large scale. This powerful animal can plow knee deep in mud. The Indian buffalo has also been taken to many other parts of the world—Egypt, Spain, Italy, Hungary, southern Soviet regions, southern Asia, the East Indies, and the Philippines.

Buffalo hide is tough and thick, and makes good leather. The milk of the cow is nourishing, with more fat than the milk of domestic cows. It is used in India for making a liquid butter.

The *carabao* is a smaller water buffalo of the Philippines. It is also important in farming. A native wild buffalo on Mindoro Island is called the *tamarau.* Africa is the home of two types of wild buffalo that are not actually water buffaloes. These are the big Cape buffalo, which has flattened horns, and the smaller Congo buffalo of central Africa.

Scientific classification. Water buffaloes are in the subfamily Bovinae of the bovid family, Bovidae. The Indian water buffalo is *Bubalus bubalis.*　C. Richard Taylor

See also **Buffalo; Carabao.**

Water bug is the common name for insects that spend most of their lives in the water. Most kinds of water bugs inhabit freshwater ponds, slow-moving streams, or pools of standing water. A few kinds live in salt water.

Water bugs may be divided into five groups—*water boatmen, back swimmers, water scorpions, giant water bugs,* and *water striders.* Most water bugs measure ⅛ to 1¾ inches (0.3 to 4.4 centimeters) long. Giant water bugs grow to 2⅓ inches (6 centimeters) long.

Water boatmen have weakly developed mouthparts. They use their short forelegs to collect algae and other submerged food particles. All other water bugs have biting, piercing, or sucking mouthparts that enable them to feed on other insects, tadpoles, small fish, and salamanders. All water bugs except water boatmen can cause painful bites.

Water boatmen and back swimmers have long, flat, hair-fringed back legs that they use like oars when they swim. Back swimmers swim on their backs. They are able to swim up beneath their prey, and they can stay underwater for several hours at a time. Water scorpions generally live on the bottom of ponds. A water scorpion has oval disks on

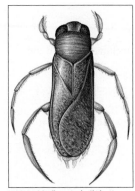

WORLD BOOK illustration by Shirley Hooper, Oxford Illustrators Limited

Water boatman

its abdomen. The disks probably help the insect adjust to changes in water pressure and depth. Water striders have long, stiltlike back legs that enable them to dart across the water's surface. They do not actually swim.

Scientific classification. Water bugs belong to the order Heteroptera in the class Insecta. Water boatmen are included in the family Corixidae; back swimmers, in the family Notonectidae; water scorpions, in the family Nepidae; giant water bugs, in the family Belostomatidae; and water striders, in the family Gerridae.   P. A. McLaughlin

Water chestnut is the common name for two very different kinds of aquatic plants. The *Chinese water chestnut* is a grasslike plant grown for its edible *corms* (underground stems). The other kind of water chestnut is a leafy, floating aquatic plant. It is also called the *water caltrop.*

The Chinese water chestnut has tube-shaped, leafless green stems that grow to about 5 feet (1.5 meters) high. It is cultivated in flooded fields similar to rice paddies. The small, rounded corms have a crispy white flesh and can be eaten raw, slightly boiled, broiled, pickled, or canned. They are a popular ingredient in Chinese foods. The Chinese water chestnut is native to China and is

widely cultivated in southern China and parts of the Philippines. The plant was introduced into the United States in 1934 and grows well along much of the Atlantic Coast.

Water caltrops bear nutlike fruits that are a delicacy throughout Asia. These plants grow chiefly in tropical and subtropical regions of Asia and Africa. They also can be found in some streams and lakes in the Eastern and Southern United States.

Scientific classification. The Chinese water chestnut belongs to the sedge family, Cyperaceae. It is *Eleocharis dulcis.* Water caltrops belong to the genus *Trapa* in the water chestnut family, Trapaceae.   Chien Yi Wang

Water clock, also called *clepsydra* (*KLEHP suh druh*), was an instrument that recorded time by measuring water escaping from a vessel. Its invention is generally accredited to Plato about 400 B.C. People used it long before modern clocks were invented.

The water clock consisted of a glass jar, with a scale of markings on its side. These were so arranged that, as the water ran out, the water left in the jar marked the time. Various improvements were made in the device, such as having a floating figure point to the hour. Another design caused the dripping water to turn a small wheel that was connected to the hands on the face of a dial. The water clock was used in Rome as early as 159 B.C. It was used in Athens to regulate the length of speeches in the law courts.   James Jespersen

Water color. See Painting (Water color painting).

Water conservation. See Conservation (Water conservation); **Water** (Water management).

Water cress. See Cress.

Water cycle. See Water (picture: The water cycle).

Water dog. See Mudpuppy.

Water flea is the common name of a group of tiny animals that live primarily in freshwater ponds and lakes. A few species of water fleas live in the ocean. Water fleas are a major source of food for many fish. Water fleas measure about $\frac{1}{125}$ to $\frac{3}{4}$ inch (0.2 to 18 millimeters) long. They received their name because their jerky swimming motions resemble the jumping of a flea. They swim by making a rowing movement with their *antennae* (feelers), which extend from the front of the head.

A water flea's body is covered by a transparent *carapace* (shell). The action of the heart and other organs can be seen through the carapace. As a result, water fleas

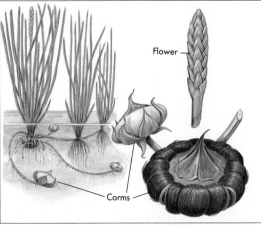

WORLD BOOK illustration by John F. Eggert

Chinese water chestnut, *above,* is a grasslike plant that is cultivated in flooded fields. Its edible underground stems, called *corms,* are a popular ingredient in Chinese foods.

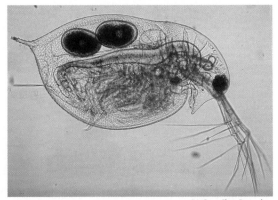

Eric Grave, Photo Researchers

A water flea is a tiny shellfish with a transparent body covering. It uses its feelers as oars to skim and jump through water.

are often used in scientific experiments to observe the effects of drugs on body organs. The water flea's head is not covered by the carapace. Water fleas use their four to six pairs of legs, called *appendages,* for filtering food particles from the water.

Scientific classification. Water fleas belong to the orders Cnomopoda and Ctenopoda in the class Branchiopoda.

P. A. McLaughlin

Water glass, also known as *soluble glass* (chemical formula Na_2SiO_3), is a jellylike compound of sodium, silicon, and oxygen. Its chemical name is sodium silicate. Pure water glass is colorless, and readily dissolves in water. It is insoluble in alcohol and acids.

Water glass is used in detergents and soaps, in preserving wood, and in fireproofing wood, cloth, and paper. The solution will also waterproof walls. Industry uses it as an adhesive in manufacturing fiberboard shipping cases, greaseproof boxes, and similar containers. It is also used in cement manufacture, and for hardening concrete. Water glass is used in the purification of fats and oils, in refining petroleum, and in the manufacture of silica gel and *catalysts* (substances that speed up chemical reactions). Geoffrey E. Dolbear

Water hen. See Gallinule.

Water hyacinth is a plant that grows chiefly in the tropical regions of the world. It floats on lakes, rivers, and swamps and grows to a height of about 2 feet (61 centimeters) above the water. It has as many as 38 purple flowers grouped around the top of the stem.

Diseases and insects control the growth of water hyacinths in South America, where the plants first grew. But in the Southern United States and other regions where people have introduced the plant, there are no natural controls on its growth. In those regions, water hyacinths are a serious environmental problem because they grow so fast. The plants may double in number every 10 days. They form floating mats that can cover entire water surfaces and destroy the plant and animal life below. Plants need sunlight to live, and fish must have oxygen. The thick growth of water hyacinths blocks the sunlight, and the roots of the plants use up the oxygen in the water. In addition, boats cannot travel on waterways that are choked with water hyacinths.

Many scientists are exploring possible uses of water

Agricultural Research Service, USDA
Water hyacinths are an environmental problem in the Southern United States. The plants have blocked this canal in Florida.

hyacinths. In the early 1970's, researchers began the experimental use of the plants to clean up polluted streams. Water hyacinths can absorb many chemicals—including sewage and industrial wastes—from the water in which the plants grow. Thus, polluted water might be purified by passing it through tanks that contain water hyacinths. Other people are studying the possibility of making cattle feed from dried water hyacinths.

Scientific classification. The water hyacinth belongs to the pickerelweed family, Pontederiaceae. It is *Eichhornia crassipes.* James D. Mauseth

Water lily, also called *pond lily,* is the popular name for various beautiful water plants that grow in both temperate and hot climates. Water lilies send their long, stout leaf and flower stalks up from the mud bottom of clear, shallow water. Their narrow to round green leaves usually are seen floating on the surface of the water but may also be submerged. The flowers are usually raised above the water on long flower stalks. The white-flowered water lily is the most common. The flowers may be as large as 1 foot (30 centimeters) across. Some of the water lilies bloom during the day and others during the night. The water lily is the flower for the

John L. Tveten
Water lilies grow in clear, shallow water in temperate and hot climates. The plants' beautiful flowers grow on long stalks that rise from the mud bottom.

month of July. See also **Flower** (picture: Flowers of woodlands and forests).

Scientific classification. Water lilies belong to the water lily family, Nymphaeaceae. The most common white water lily of the Eastern United States is *Nymphia ordorata.* Thomas B. Croat

Water meter is a device that measures the volume of water that flows through a pipe or a large channel. The most widely known type of water meter turns numbers on a register that operates like an *odometer* (mileage recorder) of an automobile. This type is used by water companies to measure the water used in homes, factories, and business establishments.

In mild climates, such a home water meter is installed in a small box outside a house on the *service line* (pipe) leading to the street. In cold climates, the meter is installed inside a house—usually in the basement—to pro-

Badger Meter, Inc.

A water meter measures the volume of water that flows through a pipe. The meters above measure water in gallons, *left*, and in cubic feet, *right*. Water companies use such meters to measure water consumed in homes, factories, and businesses.

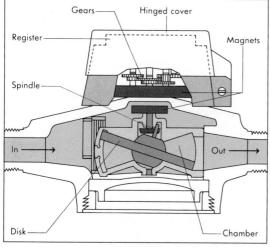

WORLD BOOK diagram by William Graham adapted from information furnished by Badger Meter, Inc.

How a water meter works. Water flows through a chamber and causes a disk to wobble. This motion rotates a spindle and a drive magnet. The rotation passes to a second magnet, which turns the meter register, indicating the amount of water used.

tect it from freeze-ups during winter. The meter is often connected to a register mounted outside the house so that the meter reader does not have to go inside.

The measuring chamber of a residential-type water meter usually contains a disk. Incoming water causes the disk to wobble. The amount of water that flows through the chamber determines how much the disk moves. The motion of the disk turns the numbers on the register. Many water meters use a magnetic coupling to transfer the disk's motion to the register. The register records the flow of water in cubic feet, gallons, or liters.

Other types of meters continuously register the flow of water on a chart-recording instrument. These meters are used in filtration plants, pumping stations, and industries.

The *venturi meter* and the *orifice meter* restrict the passage through which the water moves. They are used to measure the difference in water pressure to determine the amount of the flow.

The *magnetic flow meter* uses two electrodes mounted flush in the walls of a pipe, outside of which

have been mounted powerful magnets. *Ions* (electrically charged atoms or groups of atoms) carried in the water pass through the magnetic field and generate voltage used by the meter to measure the water flow.

Electronic meters measure water flow by measuring changes in the wavelength of the sounds made by moving water. A variety of other devices are used to measure the flow of water in open channels, such as sewers and rivers.   Evan Powell

Water moccasin is a poisonous snake that lives in the southeastern United States. It is also called *moccasin snake* and *cottonmouth.* Water moccasins live in the area south of a line running from Cape Charles, Va., to the middle of the Alabama-Georgia boundary, then to southern Illinois, and from there to the point where the Pecos River and the Rio Grande meet in Texas. Water moccasins rarely appear above this line.

The water moccasin is a pit viper, like the rattlesnake. It has a hollow, or pit, in the side of its head, between and slightly below the eye and nostril. Several harmless water snakes have a broad head like the moccasin, but they all lack the pit.

Adult water moccasins are about $3\frac{1}{2}$ feet (107 centimeters) long, though some grow to more than 5 feet (1.5 meters) long. They usually have broad dark bands across their bodies. Water moccasins feed on a wide variety of animals, including frogs, fish, small mammals, and birds. The young are born alive in the summer.

Water moccasins are most often seen in watery

WORLD BOOK illustration by John F. Eggert

The water moccasin is one of several poisonous snakes in North America. It lives in southern swamps and bayous.

places, in the swampy backwaters of rivers and streams, and on marshy lake shores. Knowing this makes it easier for people to avoid the water moccasin. The bite of the water moccasin is highly dangerous, and may be fatal. This snake is also called a cottonmouth because when threatened it throws back its head and flashes its white-lined mouth as a warning signal.

Scientific classification. The water moccasin belongs to the family Viperidae. It is *Agkistrodon piscivorus.*   D. Bruce Means

See also **Snake** (picture: Anatomy); **Viper.**

Water ouzel. See Dipper.

Water pipit. See Pipit.

Water plant, also called *aquatic plant* or *hydrophyte,* is a name used for any plant that is specially adapted to live in water. Many botanists also consider the term *water plant* to include those plants that grow in water-saturated soils.

Water plants may be rooted in the mud and have their leaves and blossoms above or at the surface of the water. Some kinds grow completely underwater. Submerged water plants often have air bladders or large air pores in their stems and leaves that help the plants stand upright or stay afloat. Some of the best-known water plants are water lilies, sedges, and cattails. These plants often grow in lakes and ponds. Some biologists consider certain types of algae to be water plants. However, most scientists do not include algae in the plant kingdom. They classify algae in the kingdoms Protista and Monera.   David A. Francko

Related articles in *World Book* include:

Bladderwort	Duckweed	Rush
Bulrush	Lotus	Seaweed
Cattail	Papyrus	Water hyacinth
Cress	Pondweed	Water lily

Water pollution is one of our most serious environmental problems. It occurs when water is contaminated by such substances as human and other animal wastes, toxic chemicals, metals, and oils. Pollution can affect rain, rivers, lakes, oceans, and the water beneath the surface of the earth, called *ground water*.

Polluted water may look clean or dirty, but it all contains germs, chemicals, or other materials that can cause inconvenience, illness, or death. Impurities must be removed before such water can be used safely for drinking, cooking, washing, or laundering. Even some industries must clean the water before it can be used in their manufacturing processes.

Water pollution has become a serious problem in most countries, including Canada, China, India, Japan, the Soviet Union, and the United States. Governments have passed laws limiting the amount and kinds of waste that can be dumped into water. Governments, industries, cities, and towns have spent billions of dollars on research and water treatment plants to reduce pollution. But there are still serious problems. In the United States, several large cities, including Boston and New York City, release a huge volume of untreated sewage into their harbors or coastal waters. Also, pollution that does not come from a direct point, such as a sewage outlet or factory drain, is largely uncontrolled. These *nonpoint sources* of pollution include water that runs off construction sites and farmland and carries *sediment* (soil particles) and nutrients into streams and lakes.

Sources

There are three chief sources of water pollution: (1) industrial wastes, (2) sewage, and (3) agricultural chemicals and wastes.

How eutrophication affects a lake

Eutrophication, the process by which wastes add nutrients to water, changes the balance of life there. The diagram at the left shows a lake with few waste nutrients added. Algae grow, using nutrients already in the lake, and provide food for fish. As the fish and algae die, their remains become organic wastes. Bacteria, using oxygen from the water, convert these wastes into nutrients and the cycle repeats. Nutrients and organic wastes added by people unbalance the cycle, as shown at the right. Nutrients increase the growth of algae. As the algae die, they add to the wastes. Bacteria use so much oxygen converting wastes into nutrients that few fish survive.

Balanced cycle

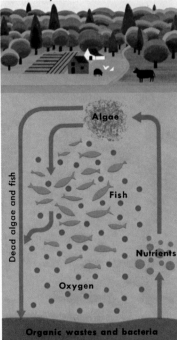

Unbalanced cycle

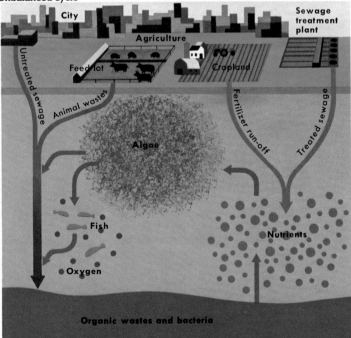

Industrial wastes. U.S. industries discharge three to four times as many pollutants into wastewater as do all the country's sewerage systems. These wastewaters contain many toxic chemicals. Much of this chemical waste is discharged directly into water systems. Also, the burning of coal, oil, and other fuels by power plants, factories, and automobiles produces sulfur and nitrogen oxides. These pollutants cause *acid rain,* which falls to the earth and enters streams and lakes. See **Acid rain.**

Some industries may pollute water in another way. They use large quantities of water to cool equipment. Heat from the equipment makes the water hot. When discharged into a river or a lake, it may cause *thermal pollution* that can harm plant and animal life.

Sewage consists of human wastes, garbage, and water that has been used for laundering or bathing. By the year 2020, the United States will probably produce three times as much sewage as it did in 1970. Most of the sewage in the United States goes through treatment plants that remove solids and such dissolved substances as nitrogen and phosphorus. About 10 per cent passes through *septic tanks* before filtering through *leaching fields* into the land (see **Sewage** [Rural sewerage systems]). The remaining 10 per cent of the sewage in the United States goes untreated directly into waterways or the ocean.

Agricultural chemicals and wastes. Water from rain or melted snow flows from farmland into streams and carries chemical fertilizers and pesticides that farmers have used on the land. Animal wastes also may cause water pollution, particularly from feed lots with large numbers of animals. Cattle, hogs, sheep, and poultry that are raised on feed lots do not distribute their wastes over widespread pastureland. Instead, much of their wastes runs off into nearby streams. Water used for irrigation also may be polluted by salt, agricultural pesticides, and toxic chemicals on the soil surface before it flows back into the ground.

Effects

Water polluted with human and animal wastes can spread typhoid fever, cholera, dysentery, and other diseases. About 75 per cent of U.S. community water supplies are disinfected with chlorine to kill disease-causing germs. However, disinfection does not remove chemicals and metals, such as polychlorinated biphenyls (PCB's), chloroform, arsenic, lead, and mercury. The careless release of these toxic wastes, primarily in waste dumps, is seriously threatening ground water supplies. PCB's, chloroform, and pesticides have been found in some municipal drinking water supplies. Scientists are concerned that drinking even small quantities of these substances over many years may have harmful effects.

Pollution prevents people from using and enjoying water for recreation. For example, odors and floating debris make boating and swimming unpleasant, and the risk of disease makes polluted water unsafe. Oil spilled from ships or from offshore oil wells may float to shore. The oil can cause serious pollution and kill water birds, shellfish, and other wildlife. In addition, water pollution affects fishing, both commercial and sport. Fish have been killed by oil or by a lack of oxygen in the water. Industrial wastes, particularly PCB's, also harm fish. See **Polychlorinated biphenyl (PCB).**

Water pollution also upsets various processes that occur naturally in water. These processes, which use the oxygen dissolved in water, help to make wastes harmless. In a process called *mineralization, aerobic bacteria* break down organic wastes into simpler substances. Some of these substances, such as phosphates and nitrates, serve as *nutrients* (food) for plants.

Aerobic bacteria use oxygen in the water when breaking down organic wastes. Scientists can find out how much organic matter the water contains by measuring how much oxygen the bacteria use in breaking it down. This measurement is called the *biochemical oxygen demand* (BOD) of the water. If the water contains too much organic waste, the bacteria will use up most or all of the oxygen in it. Some species of game fish—such as salmon, sturgeon, trout, and whitefish—will then be unable to live in the water. Fish that need less oxygen, such as carp and catfish, will replace them. If all the oxygen is used up, most aquatic life will be unable to survive.

Too many nutrients in water may lead to a process called *eutrophication.* Many nutrients result from the natural disintegration of rocks and from mineralization of organic matter. But additional nutrients come from fertilizers draining off farmland, or from detergents or other parts of sewage. All the nutrients fertilize microscopic *algae* (simple plantlike organisms), as well as such plants as pondweeds and duckweeds (see **Algae**). More algae and plants grow as a result of the additional nutrients. As more grow, more also die. Algae and plants *respire*—that is, they break down food to release oxygen. They also decay. Both of these processes consume oxygen. In extreme cases, the river or lake may become so eutrophic that all the oxygen dissolved in water is consumed during portions of the day.

Thermal pollution can also reduce the amount of oxygen that dissolves in water. In addition, the high temperature of the water can kill some kinds of plants and fish.

Control

Sewage treatment. The most efficient sewage treatment plants use three separate processes—*primary treatment, secondary treatment,* and *tertiary treatment.* But few sewage treatment plants use all three processes. As a result, most treated sewage still contains nutrients, which may cause eutrophication, and chemicals. See **Sewage** (Urban sewerage systems).

Pretreatment of wastes. Industries can reduce pollution by treating wastes to remove harmful chemicals before dumping the wastes into water. Industrial wastes can also be reduced by using manufacturing processes that recover and reuse polluting chemicals.

Drinking water standards. In 1974, the U.S. Congress passed the Safe Drinking Water Act to help protect the nation's public water supply against pollution. This act authorized the Environmental Protection Agency (EPA) to establish uniform quality standards for about 240,000 public water systems throughout the United States. The standards were designed to reduce the amount of harmful bacteria, chemicals, and metals in drinking water. The EPA, together with the state governments, began enforcing its standards in 1977.

In 1979, the EPA issued rules to limit the amount of chloroform and other related organic chemicals called *trihalomethanes* (THM) in the drinking water of large cities. These chemicals are formed at treatment plants when chlorine is added to drinking water to kill disease-causing bacteria. Extended exposure to high levels of THM's, especially chloroform, is thought to increase the risk of cancer.   Gene E. Likens

Related articles in *World Book* include:

Acid rain	Ocean
Atlantic Ocean (People and the Atlantic)	Phosphate
	Polychlorinated biphenyl (PCB)
Environmental pollution	Sanitation
Environmental Protection Agency	Sewage
Eutrophication	Thermal pollution
Great Lakes (Pollution)	

See also *Environmental pollution* in the Research Guide/Index, Volume 22, for a *Reading and Study Guide.*

Additional resources

The Enduring Great Lakes. Ed. by John Rousmaniere. Norton, 1979.
Knight, Allen W., and Simmons, M. A. *Water Pollution: A Guide to Information Sources.* Gale Research, 1980.

Water polo is a sport similar to hockey or soccer. Two teams in a pool try to score by throwing or pushing a hollow rubber ball into the opponent's goal. One point is scored for each goal. Water polo is one of the roughest sports because the players kick and wrestle or sometimes hold an opponent's head under the water, though such actions are against the rules.

Men's water polo is played in an area that measures from 66 to 98 feet (20 to 30 meters) long and 26 to 66 feet (8 to 20 meters) wide. Women's matches are played in an area no larger than 82 by 56 feet (25 by 17 meters). The goals are 10 feet (3 meters) wide and usually 3 feet (.9 meter) above the water.

A team consists of a goalie and six field players. The goalie can handle the ball with both hands, but the field players may use only one hand at a time. Players move the ball by passing it or swimming with it. Each time a team gets the ball, it has 35 seconds to try to score. If it does not shoot the ball at the goal within that time, the other team gets the ball.

If a player commits a minor foul, the other team is given three seconds to pass the ball without opposition. When a major foul is committed, the player must leave the game—without a substitute—for 45 seconds or until a goal is scored. An even more serious foul results in a

penalty throw, in which an opposing player shoots at the goal with only the goalie defending it.

Men's games are 28 minutes long and are divided into 7-minute quarters. Women's matches last 24 minutes and are divided into 6-minute quarters. Water polo originated in England in the 1870's.

Critically reviewed by United States Water Polo

Water power is a valuable source of energy. When such fuels as coal, oil, and even nuclear fuels are burned up as a source of energy, they cannot be reused. But water used as a source of energy is not used up. The earth's constant flow of water can be harnessed to produce useful mechanical and electric power.

Wheels mounted on a frame over a river were the first devices used to harness water power. Blades around the outside of the wheels dipped into the river, and the flowing water striking the blades caused the wheels to turn. The ancient Romans connected water wheels to grinding stones and used the power to mill grain.

During the Industrial Revolution, large water wheels were used to run machinery in factories. The power was not completely reliable, however. Floodwaters created more power than was needed, and droughts left the factories without power. By the end of the 1800's, the steam engine had replaced water power in most factories.

The first water-powered plant for generating electricity was built in Appleton, Wis., in 1882. This *hydroelectric plant* established water power as an important source of electricity. Hydroelectric power is now used all over the world. Today, almost all water power is used to generate electricity. Many hydroelectric plants are combined with *thermal power plants* (those using fuel). With this combination, the thermal plant can supply power if the hydroelectric plant is affected by drought. Hydroelectric plants are especially useful for producing electricity during periods when it is in great demand, because they can be turned on and off rapidly.

The mechanics of water power. Water cannot create power unless it is flowing from a higher place to a lower place as in a river, a waterfall, or a dam. People use the effects of *gravity* (the attraction the earth exerts on an object) pulling the water downward when they harness water for power. For example, in the customary system of measurement, a cubic foot of water weighs

© Jerry Cooke, *Sports Illustrated,* Time Inc.

Water polo is a rough sport played in a pool. Two teams try to score by throwing or pushing a hollow rubber ball into their opponent's goal. This picture shows the team in black caps trying to catch the ball after the opposing team in white caps has thrown it toward their goal. The goalie, *right foreground,* wears a red cap.

62.4 pounds. The pull of gravity then creates a pressure of 6,240 pounds per square foot at the base of a body of water 100 feet tall. If this water were released from a nozzle at the bottom of its source, the stream of water would travel at a speed of about 80 feet per second. The force of this stream striking the blades of a water wheel would cause the wheel to turn, producing useful mechanical energy.

World water power production. The potential water power of the world is about $2\frac{1}{4}$ billion kilowatts of electric power. This is a very general estimate, because the flow of many large rivers has not been measured. Of this potential, about 500 million kilowatts is developed.

The United States has about a sixth of the world's developed power. Canada and Europe have most of the rest of the developed power. The potential of Asia, Africa, and Latin America is just beginning to be developed.

The world's largest hydroelectric power plants in operation include the Grand Coulee on the Columbia River in the United States and the Sayano-Shushensk on the Yenisey River in the Soviet Union. Each of these plants has a capacity to produce about $6\frac{1}{2}$ million kilowatts. The Itaipu power plant of Brazil and Paraguay on the Paraná River will have a capacity of about $12\frac{1}{2}$ million kilowatts when it is completed in the early 1990's.

Vijay P. Singh

Related articles. See the section on *Electric power* in state articles, such as **Arizona** (Electric power). See also:

Conservation	Irrigation
Dam	Reservoir
Electric power	Turbine

Water purification. See Water (City water systems); Kuwait (Land).

Water safety. See Boating; Safety; Swimming.

Water-skiing is a popular sport in which a person wearing special skis is pulled over the water by a speeding motorboat. The skier holds on to a line attached to the boat. Millions of people throughout the world water-ski for recreation, and many compete in tournaments.

Water skis are wider than skis used on snow. They are made of fiberglass or various kinds of wood and are available in many lengths. The skier's feet fit into flexible rubber *bindings,* which come off easily if the person falls, thus helping to prevent injury. A water-skier should always wear a life jacket for maximum safety.

The skier grasps a handle at one end of the towline, which measures about 75 feet (23 meters) long. The other end of the line is connected to the stern of the boat. A boat with a V-shaped hull is best for waterskiing because it pulls the skier on a straighter course than a flat-bottomed boat. The minimum speed for water-skiing is about 20 miles (32 kilometers) per hour. Experts are pulled at speeds of up to 100 miles (160 kilometers) per hour.

A water-skier starts from a dock or in the water. When the skier begins to move, the front end of the skis should be above the water. The person's back should be straight, the arms held straight ahead, and the knees slightly bent. Water-skiing is easy to learn and requires only a good sense of balance.

In the United States, water-skiing tournaments are held by the American Water Ski Association and by

© Pierre Kopp, West Light

Water-skiing requires a good sense of balance but is easy to learn. Water-skiers wear life jackets for maximum safety.

water-skiing clubs. These tournaments include competition in *jumping,* and *slalom,* and *trick skiing.* In jumping, the skiers soar off a ramp in the water. The longest jump wins. The slalom involves skiing as fast as possible around a series of buoys. In trick skiing, water-skiers are judged on how well they perform jumps, turns, and other difficult maneuvers.   William D. Clifford

Water softening is a method of removing from water the minerals that make it hard. Hard water does not dissolve soap readily. It forms scale in pipes, boilers, and other equipment in which it is used. The principal methods of softening water are the lime soda process and the ion exchange process.

In the *lime soda process,* soda ash and lime are added to the water in amounts determined by chemical tests. These chemicals combine with the calcium and magnesium in the water to make insoluble compounds that settle to the bottom of the water tank.

In the *ion exchange process,* the water filters through minerals called *zeolites.* As the water passes through the filter, the sodium ions in the zeolite are exchanged for the calcium and magnesium ions in the water, and the water is softened. After household softeners become exhausted, a strong solution of *sodium chloride* (salt) is passed through the filter to replace the sodium that has been lost. The use of two exchange materials makes it possible to remove both metal and acid ions from water. Some cities and towns, however, prohibit or restrict the use of ion exchange equipment on drinking water, pending the results of studies on how people are affected by the consumption of the added sodium in softened water.   Evan Powell

Water sports. See Boating; Diving; Fishing; Rafting; Skin diving; Surfing; Swimming; Water-skiing.

Water supply. See Water.

Water table. See Drainage; Ground water; Irrigation (Bringing irrigation water to farms).

Water turbine. See Turbine (Water turbines).

Water vapor. See Humidity.

Water wheel changes the energy of falling water into mechanical energy which can be used for running machinery. The best source of water power in nature is found in waterfalls and rapids in rivers. The water is directed into the wheel through a chute. The wheel is mounted on an axle, which is connected by belts or gearing with the machinery it is to operate.

There are two main types of water wheels, vertical and horizontal. The vertical wheels include the overshot and the undershot.

The overshot water wheel has many scooplike buckets around its edge. Water is delivered to the top of the wheel. The weight of the water falling into the buckets causes the wheel to turn. An overshot water wheel may have an efficiency of up to 80 per cent. That is, it may turn as much as 80 per cent of the energy of the water fed to it into mechanical energy.

The undershot water wheel is built so the water strikes against blades at the bottom of the wheel. The power of the wheel depends on the speed of the water as it strikes the blades. The undershot wheel has such a low efficiency that it is rarely used.

Most modern water wheels are horizontal. A horizontal wheel rotates on a vertical shaft. It is driven by the force of the water striking the blades on one side of the wheel. Horizontal wheels are highly efficient if properly designed for the conditions of their use.

Historians believe the water wheel was developed in the 100's B.C. It was used mainly to grind grain. Later it was used for many kinds of mechanical operations. It was a major source of power until the development of the steam engine in the 1700's.　　Ray K. Linsley

See also **Water power; Turbine** (Water turbines).

E. R. Degginger

This overshot water wheel in Virginia has been used to power a mill for grinding grain since the early 1800's.

Water witch. See Grebe.

Waterbuck. See Antelope (Kinds).

Waterbury (pop. 103,266; met. area 204,968) is one of the largest cities in Connecticut. It lies on the Naugatuck River (see **Connecticut** [political map]). Products made in Waterbury include buttons for clothing, watches and clocks, and foundry and machine-shop products. The city also has industries that provide health, financial, and insurance services. It is the home of Post College and Mattatuck Community College.

In 1802, Waterbury began manufacturing products made of brass. It later became first among the cities of the United States in production of brass products. It came to be called the *Brass Center of the World.* It manufactured such brass products as sheeting, screws and rivets, and ammunition casings. After World War II ended in 1945, Waterbury's production of brass goods began to decline dramatically. Brass products are now manufactured there only on a limited scale.

People in nearby Farmington bought the Waterbury area from Indians in 1674. They established a frontier outpost called Mattatuck in the area. The name became Waterbury when the town was incorporated in 1686. Waterbury received its city charter in 1853. The government of the city is headed by a mayor and a board of aldermen.　　Robert D. Veillette

Waterfall is any sudden descent of a stream from a higher to a lower level. In wearing down its channel, a river uncovers certain layers of rock that are softer than others. If the hard rock is farther upstream than the soft, the channel below is worn more rapidly, and a waterfall results. Sometimes the hard ledge forms the edge of a vertical cliff, over which the water plunges.

If the volume of water is small, the fall may be called a *cascade.* If the volume of water is large, a fall of this sort is called a *cataract.* Niagara Falls is such a cataract. Other noted cataracts are Victoria Falls on the Zambezi River in Africa and Churchill Falls of the Churchill River in Labrador. Usually, however, the term *cataract* is applied to a series of rapids or falls caused by the flow of the stream over a rapidly sloping rocky bed. Examples of these are the cataracts of the Nile and the Orinoco rivers. Cataracts which have small, gradual falls are termed *rapids.* Some of the most noted rapids in North America are those at Sault Sainte Marie, at the outlet of Lake Superior, and the rapids in the Saint Lawrence River.

Small waterfalls or cascades are often of great height. Such are the Upper Yosemite Falls in California, 1,430 feet (436 meters) high; and Sutherland Falls in New Zealand, 1,904 feet (580 meters). Some lower waterfalls are noted for their beauty. These include Montmorency Falls, near Quebec; Multnomah Falls, near the Columbia River, Oregon; and the Upper and Lower falls in Yellowstone National Park.

Falls usually occur in mountainous countries. But sometimes they are caused by the descent of streams to a flood plain. The line along which several rivers flowing into the same body of water descend to this lower level is called the *fall line.* The fall line of those rivers south of Chesapeake Bay which flow into the Atlantic Ocean is marked by the location of manufacturing cities whose sites were chosen because they were near water power, which later became even more valuable as hydroelectric power. Examples of these industrial centers are Rich-

Famous waterfalls

Photographs of some of the world's most striking waterfalls appear below and on the opposite page. The charts below compare the heights of these falls. If the falls charted are the highest in a series of falls, the total height of the drop is also given.

Niagara Falls, New York

© James Blank, West Stock

Gene Ahrens, Shostal

Multnomah Falls

© Charles Moore, Black Star

Yosemite Falls

© James Blank, West Stock

Yellowstone Lower Falls

Ribbon Falls

C. G. Maxwell, FPG

Ribbon Falls

2,000 feet
(610 meters)

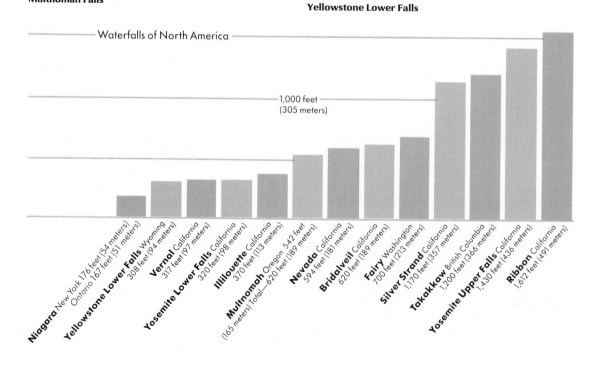

Waterfalls of North America

1,000 feet
(305 meters)

Niagara New York 176 feet (54 meters)
Ontario 167 feet (51 meters)

Yellowstone Lower Falls Wyoming 308 feet (94 meters)

Vernal California 317 feet (97 meters)

Yosemite Lower Falls California 320 feet (98 meters)

Illilouette California 370 feet (113 meters)

Multnomah Oregon 542 feet (165 meters) Total—620 feet (189 meters)

Nevada California 594 feet (181 meters)

Bridalveil California 620 feet (189 meters)

Fairy Washington 700 feet (213 meters)

Silver Strand California 1,170 feet (357 meters)

Takakkaw British Columbia 1,200 feet (366 meters)

Yosemite Upper Falls California 1,430 feet (436 meters)

Ribbon California 1,612 feet (491 meters)

© Mark Boulton, Bruce Coleman Inc.

Victoria Falls on the Zambia-Zimbabwe border

Kim Hart, Black Star

Vettisfoss Falls

George de Steinheil, Shostal

Angel Falls

© John Elk III, Wheeler Pictures

Gavarnie Falls

© Ray Manley, Shostal

Sutherland Falls

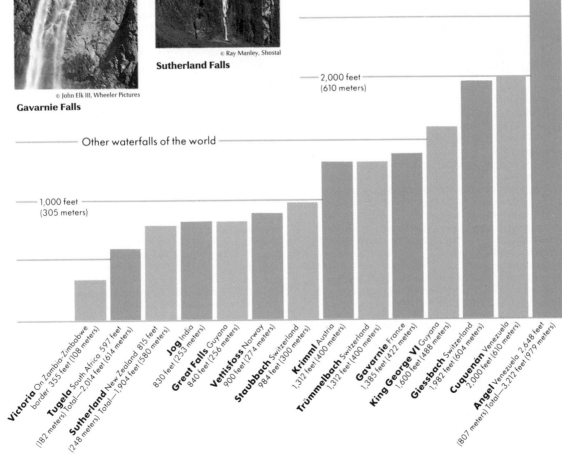

3,000 feet
(914 meters)

2,000 feet
(610 meters)

Other waterfalls of the world

1,000 feet
(305 meters)

Victoria On Zambia-Zimbabwe
border 355 feet (108 meters)

Tugela South Africa 597 feet
(182 meters) Total—2,014 feet (614 meters)

Sutherland New Zealand 815 feet
(248 meters) Total—1,904 feet (580 meters)

Jog India
830 feet (253 meters)

Great Falls Guyana
840 feet (256 meters)

Vettisfoss Norway
900 feet (274 meters)

Staubbach Switzerland
984 feet (300 meters)

Krimml Austria
1,312 feet (400 meters)

Trümmelbach Switzerland
1,312 feet (400 meters)

Gavarnie France
1,385 feet (422 meters)

King George VI Guyana
1,600 feet (488 meters)

Giessbach Switzerland
1,982 feet (604 meters)

Cuquenán Venezuela
2,000 feet (610 meters)

Angel Venezuela 2,648 feet
(807 meters) Total—3,212 feet (979 meters)

mond, Va., Raleigh, N.C., Augusta and Columbus, Ga., and Columbia, S.C.   Samuel N. Dicken

Related articles in *World Book* include:

Angel Falls	King George VI	Ribbon Falls
Argentina (picture)	Falls	Sutherland Falls
Brazil (picture)	Minnehaha Falls	Takakkaw Falls
Bridalveil Fall	Nevada Falls	Victoria Falls
Cuquenán Falls	Niagara Falls	Wyoming (picture)
Ethiopia (picture)	Reversing Falls	Yosemite Falls
Fall line	of Saint John	

Waterford (pop 39,516) is a city in southeastern Ireland. It lies on the River Suir, about 10 miles (16 kilometers) from the point at which the river enters Waterford Harbour. For location, see **Ireland** (map). Waterford is an industrial center and an important port for container ships. It is also a service and shopping area for southeastern Ireland.

The city's best-known industry is the manufacture of Waterford crystal glass. Waterford glassware was first manufactured in 1783, and it soon became known worldwide. Its production was ended in 1851, and was resumed in 1952. See **Glass** (picture: Waterford crystal jar). The city's other products include chemicals, electrical equipment, furniture, metal products, optical goods, and processed foods. Many of Waterford's modern factories are in an industrial area built in the 1960's.

Waterford was established by Viking raiders, who arrived there in the A.D. 800's. Norman invaders from England captured Waterford in 1170. During the late 1700's and early 1800's, the town prospered based on its export of agricultural products and its glassware industry.

Desmond A. Gillmor

Watergate was the name of the biggest political scandal in United States history. It included various illegal activities designed to help President Richard M. Nixon win reelection in 1972. Watergate resulted in Nixon's resignation from the presidency in 1974.

Watergate differed from most previous political scandals because personal greed apparently did not play an important role. Instead, Watergate represented an attack on one of the chief features of a democracy—free and open elections.

The Watergate activities included burglary, wiretapping, violations of campaign financing laws, and sabotage and the attempted use of government agencies to harm political opponents. The scandal also involved a cover-up of many of those actions. About 40 people were charged with crimes in the scandal and with related crimes. Most of these people were convicted by juries or pleaded guilty.

Watergate involved more high-level government officials than any previous political scandal. It led to the conviction on criminal charges in 1975 of former Attorney General John N. Mitchell and two of Nixon's top aides, John D. Ehrlichman and H. R. Haldeman. Also in 1975, former Secretary of Commerce Maurice H. Stans, a leader of Nixon's reelection campaign, pleaded guilty to Watergate criminal charges and was fined $5,000. Watergate also had resulted in the resignation of Attorney General Richard G. Kleindienst in 1973.

The break-in and cover-up. The scandal took its name from the Watergate complex of apartment and office buildings in Washington, D.C. On June 17, 1972, police arrested five men for breaking into the Democratic Party's national headquarters there. One of the burglars

was James W. McCord, Jr., the security coordinator of the Committee for the Re-election of the President (CRP). The five men—along with G. Gordon Liddy, another CRP aide; and E. Howard Hunt, Jr., a White House consultant—were indicted for a number of crimes, including burglary and wiretapping. In January 1973, five of the seven, including Hunt, pleaded guilty. The other two—Liddy and McCord—were found guilty by a jury.

Nixon's press secretary had said repeatedly that the scandal involved no member of the White House staff. But the press found evidence that White House aides had helped finance sabotage and spying operations against candidates for the 1972 Democratic presidential nomination. Reporters Carl Bernstein and Bob Woodward of *The Washington Post* led the investigation.

Early in 1973, evidence was uncovered that tied several top White House aides to plans for the Watergate break-in or to concealment of evidence that implicated members of the Nixon Administration. The evidence indicated that White House officials had tried to involve the Central Intelligence Agency and the Federal Bureau of Investigation in the cover-up. These officials falsely claimed that national security was involved.

On April 30, 1973, Nixon stated that he had no part in either planning the Watergate break-in or covering it up. He promised that the Department of Justice would appoint a special prosecutor to handle the case. In May, Archibald Cox, a Harvard Law School professor, was named to that position. Also in May, the Senate Select Committee on Presidential Campaign Activities began hearings on Watergate. Senator Sam J. Ervin, Jr., of North Carolina headed the committee. Former Presidential Counsel John W. Dean III became the chief witness against Nixon in the hearings. Dean admitted that he had played a major role in a White House cover-up and charged that Nixon knew of his activities. Dean also revealed Administration plans to use the Internal Revenue Service and other government agencies to punish opponents whom the White House had placed on so-called enemies lists. Dean was later sentenced to a prison term of 1 to 4 years. After serving four months, his sentence was reduced to that time and he was released.

The tape controversy. In July, the Senate committee learned that Nixon had secretly made tape recordings of conversations in his White House offices since 1971. The committee and Cox believed the tapes could answer key questions raised in their investigations. They asked Nixon to supply them with certain tapes, but he refused to do so. Nixon argued that, as President, he had a constitutional right to keep the tapes confidential. In August, Cox and the committee sued Nixon to obtain the tapes. U.S. District Court Judge John J. Sirica decided to review the tapes himself and ordered Nixon to give them to him. Nixon appealed the order, but a U.S. court of appeals supported Sirica.

In October, Nixon offered to provide summaries of the tapes. But Cox declared that summaries would be unacceptable as evidence in court and rejected the offer. Nixon ordered Attorney General Elliot L. Richardson to fire Cox, but Richardson refused to do so and resigned. Deputy Attorney General William D. Ruckelshaus also resigned after being ordered to dismiss Cox. Nixon then named Solicitor General Robert H. Bork acting attorney general, and Bork fired Cox. Leon Jaworski, a noted Texas attorney, later succeeded Cox.

The President's actions angered many Americans. In October, a number of members of the House of Representatives began steps to impeach him. Later in 1973, Nixon agreed to supply the tapes to Sirica. Then it was discovered that three key conversations were missing. The White House said that the tape-recording system failed to work properly during two of the talks and that the third had been accidentally erased.

In April 1974, Jaworski served Nixon with a *subpoena* (legal order) to furnish tape recordings and documents relating to 64 White House conversations. Jaworski said the materials contained evidence in the cover-up case. At the end of April, Nixon released 1,254 pages of edited transcripts of White House conversations. He said they told the full Watergate story.

Jaworski, however, insisted on receiving the original tapes and documents that he had requested. Nixon again claimed he had a constitutional right to protect confidential documents. Jaworski then sued the President in federal court. In July, the Supreme Court of the United States ordered Nixon to give Jaworski the materials. The Supreme Court ruled unanimously that a President cannot withhold evidence in a criminal case.

The cover-up trial. In March 1974, seven former officials of Nixon's Administration or his 1972 reelection committee were indicted on charges of conspiracy in covering up the Watergate break-in. Among them were Domestic Council Chief Ehrlichman, White House Chief of Staff Haldeman, and Attorney General Mitchell.

The trial lasted from October 1974 to January 1975. Ehrlichman, Haldeman, and Mitchell were each convicted of conspiracy, obstruction of justice, and perjury, and sentenced to a prison term of from $2\frac{1}{2}$ to 8 years. The sentences were later reduced to 1 to 4 years.

The resignation of Nixon. The President suffered another major setback in July 1974, when the House Judiciary Committee recommended that he be impeached. The committee adopted three articles of impeachment for consideration by the full House of Representatives. The first article accused Nixon of obstructing justice in the scandal. The other two articles accused him of abusing presidential powers and illegally withholding evidence from the judiciary committee.

Nixon's chief defenders continued to argue that the President had committed no impeachable offense. But on August 5, Nixon released additional transcripts of taped White House conversations. The transcripts convinced most Americans that Nixon had authorized the Watergate cover-up at least as early as June 23, 1972—six days after the break-in. Nixon immediately lost almost all his remaining support in Congress. He resigned on August 9, and Vice President Gerald R. Ford took office as President that day. On September 8, Ford pardoned Nixon for all federal crimes that Nixon might have committed while serving as President.

Other effects of Watergate. In 1974, Congress approved reforms in the financing of federal election campaigns. Some reforms limit the amount of money contributors may give to candidates for President, Vice President, and Congress. Other financial reforms require detailed reporting of both contributions and expenses. Many state legislatures limited contributions and spending in state election campaigns and adopted codes of ethics for all government employees.

Critically reviewed by J. Anthony Lukas

Additional resources

Bernstein, Carl, and Woodward, Bob. *All the President's Men.* Simon & Schuster, 1974.
Cook, Fred J. *The Crimes of Watergate.* Watts, 1981.
Kurland, Philip B. *Watergate and the Constitution.* Univ. of Chicago Press, 1978.
Lang, Gladys E. and Kurt. *The Battle for Public Opinion: The President, the Press, and the Polls During Watergate.* Columbia Univ. Press, 1983.
Lukas, J. Anthony. *Nightmare: The Underside of the Nixon Years.* Viking, 1976.

Waterloo, Battle of, fought on June 18, 1815, was the final battle of the French military genius, Napoleon Bonaparte. It put an end to his political ambitions to rule Europe. His defeat was so crushing that, when a person suffers a disastrous reverse, we say the person has "met his (or her) Waterloo."

Napoleon returns to France. After abdicating in 1814, Napoleon was exiled to the island of Elba, off the coast of Italy. He spent less than a year there before he decided to return to rule France. He saw that the allies at the Congress of Vienna seemed unable to settle their differences, and he hoped to take advantage of this split to regain power.

But the allies joined forces against Napoleon as soon as they heard of his return to France. Napoleon marched north into Belgium to meet this threat. The Duke of Wellington commanded the allied forces of Belgium, Great Britain, Hanover, and the Netherlands. Neither commander had good intelligence services. Napoleon was not in good health at the time, and failed to display his earlier energy and military grasp.

The battle took place at Waterloo, a small town near Brussels. The two armies were about equal in size. Napoleon had about 74,000 troops, and superior cavalry and artillery. Wellington had about 67,000 troops. He placed them in a strong defensive position. The French started a fierce attack against the allied lines on June 18. Wellington's troops resisted the French assaults.

Napoleon might have won at Waterloo if he had attacked earlier in the day. But he waited until noon because of a heavy rain the night before. This delay permitted Marshal Gebhard von Blücher to arrive with his Prussian troops to reinforce Wellington. The battle was a draw until the arrival of Blücher's forces. These forces helped turn the battle against the French.

Napoleon made one last effort to win the battle. He flung his best troops, the famous "Old Guard," against the enemy's lines. Three battalions of the Guard fought bravely. However, they were overwhelmed. The French troops then retreated from a fierce bayonet counterattack.

Both sides lost many killed and wounded in the battle. The French suffered about 40,000 casualties, and the allies about 23,000. After this defeat, Napoleon failed to gather a new army. He had no choice left but to abdicate a second time.   Robert B. Holtman

See also **Blücher, Gebhard L. von; Napoleon I; Wellington, Duke of.**

Watermark is an identifying mark pressed into paper as it is formed by a papermaking machine. Usually, it is the mark left by wires bent into the watermark pattern and attached to the *dandy roll* of a Fourdrinier machine (see **Paper** [diagram: How paper is made]). As the wire pattern comes into contact with the layer of wet pulp, a translucent impression is made, which can be seen when the finished paper is held in front of a light. A mark that looks like a watermark can also be produced chemically on finished paper. Watermarked paper is often used for important documents to help prevent counterfeiting.   Larry L. Graham

Watermelon is a large, sweet fruit. Watermelons consist of about 93 per cent water. They have a smooth *rind* (hard outer skin) and juicy, edible flesh. Most watermelons also have many seeds. The rind is striped or solid and ranges in color from gray-green to dark green. The flesh of ripe watermelons is white, greenish-white, yellow, orange, pink, or red. Most watermelons weigh from 5 to 40 pounds (2.3 to 18.1 kilograms), but some weigh as much as 100 pounds (45.4 kilograms). Their shape varies from round to oblong.

Watermelons provide a good source of potassium and vitamins A and C. They are eaten fresh, often in salads or as a dessert. The rind is sometimes pickled and used to make relish.

Watermelons grow on vines. For this reason—and because they must be replanted annually—watermelons are considered by horticulturists to be vegetables. The plants require a long, warm growing season, and they thrive in slightly acid, sandy soil. Growers plant the seeds about 4 feet (1.2 meters) apart in rows spaced about 10 feet (3 meters) from one another. In colder climates, where the growing season is short, the seeds are often planted in a greenhouse first. They are transplanted into fields after the danger of frost has passed.

The vines grow long, trailing stems called *runners.* Some runners grow up to 40 feet (12.2 meters) long. They produce slender, coiling *tendrils* and yellow blossoms. The tendrils attach themselves to objects in the field and prevent the watermelons from rolling in high winds and thus becoming scarred. Fruit develops from pollinated flowers. It matures four to six weeks after pol-

lination. As a watermelon ripens, the rind color becomes dull and the top of the fruit flattens slightly. A ripe watermelon makes a hollow thud when thumped.

A fungal disease called *wilt* is one of the most common threats to watermelon plants. The wilt fungus remains in the soil and may infect new watermelon plants for several years. Growers control wilt by rotating the watermelon crop to a different field each year.

The watermelon plant probably originated in Africa. Watermelons are known to have been grown in New England as early as 1629. Today, Turkey and China are the world's leading producers of watermelons. Major watermelon-producing states in the United States include Florida, Texas, and Georgia. Varieties of watermelon grown in the Western United States include Klondike and Peacock. Those grown in the East include Charleston Gray, Crimson Sweet, and Jubilee. Triple Sweet and Tri X 313 are two seedless varieties.

Scientific classification. The watermelon plant belongs to the gourd family, Cucurbitaceae. It is classified as *Citrullus lanatus.*   Gary W. Elmstrom

Waterproofing is a way of treating cloth, leather, wood, or other materials so that they will shed water. Many different chemical solutions are used in waterproofing. Nearly all of them work by forming a protective coating over the material to be waterproofed.

Materials which have pores are often soaked in solutions of rubber, linseed oil, paraffin, or some other substance which is itself waterproof. The waterproof solution fills the pores. Silicone is widely used to waterproof clothing and building materials (see **Silicone**).

The textile industry uses the most advanced methods of waterproofing. The fibers of cloth may be coated either before or after they are woven. Water-repellent solutions in spray containers are sold for home use.

In 1823, Charles Macintosh of England invented a waterproof fabric made of cloth and rubber. A raincoat made of his protective material came to be commonly known as a *mackintosh.*   Elizabeth Chesley Baity

Waters, Ethel (1900-1977), was a popular black American singer and actress. She gained recognition as a singer of both blues and popular songs. Waters starred in several Broadway musicals, including *Africana* (1927), *As Thousands Cheer* (1933), *At Home Abroad* (1935), and *Cabin in the Sky* (1940). She introduced a number of well-known songs during her stage career, including "I'm Coming Virginia," "Heat Wave," and "Taking a Chance on Love." She also appeared in dramatic roles. Waters won particular acclaim for her performances in the motion picture *Pinky* (1949) and the play *The Member of the Wedding* (1950).

Waters was born in Chester, Pa. She began singing in nightclubs and in vaudeville when she was 17 years old. Waters wrote a highly praised autobiography, *His Eye Is on the Sparrow* (1951).

Gerald Bordman

Watershed. See Forestry (Water).

WORLD BOOK illustration by Kate Lloyd-Jones, Linden Artists

Watermelons are popular fruits that have sweet, juicy flesh. The fruits develop from the yellow flowers of the watermelon plant after the blossoms are pollinated.

Alfredo Valente

Ethel Waters

Waterspout is a whirling cloud mass over a lake or ocean. It is a rotating column that consists of air and watery mist. Lake water or seawater may be drawn up at its base. Some waterspouts cause strong winds and may damage ships, but others are harmless.

Most waterspouts occur in tropical regions. The severe type forms under unstable weather conditions. A center of low pressure develops, and winds begin to

© Chesher, Photo Researchers

A waterspout's whirling column is a spectacular sight and may be dangerous. This waterspout occurred off Key West, Fla.

whirl around it. Many harmful waterspouts develop from clouds that bring thunderstorms. They begin to form in the clouds and develop downward. A harmless waterspout forms when the wind is weak and weather conditions are fairly stable. It receives its energy from the surface of the water.   Wayne M. Wendland

Waterton-Glacier International Peace Park is on the United States-Canadian boundary line between Montana and Alberta. It covers over 1 million acres (400,000 hectares) on the United States side, and over 130,000 acres (52,600 hectares) in Canada. The park unites Glacier National Park in Montana with Waterton Lakes National Park in Alberta. See also **Glacier National Park.**   Critically reviewed by Glacier National Park

Watie, Stand (1806-1871), became the only Indian brigadier general in the Confederate Army. Born near Rome, Ga., he moved to Oklahoma with the Cherokee Indians in 1838 and became a tribal leader. Watie entered the army after forming an alliance between the Cherokee and the Confederacy in 1861. He led a regiment of Cherokee volunteers called the Cherokee Mounted Rifles. In 1864, he was made a brigadier general. Watie was one of the last Confederate officers to surrender.   Michael D. Green

Watson, Homer (1856-1936), was a Canadian landscape painter. His works show the beauty and majesty of Canadian woods, fields, and streams. Watson was the first president of the Canadian Art Club, and was president of the Royal Canadian Academy from 1918 to 1922. He was born in Doon, Ont.   William R. Willoughby

Watson, James Dewey (1928-   ), is an American biologist. He shared the 1962 Nobel Prize for physiology

or medicine with biologist Francis H. C. Crick and biophysicist Maurice H. F. Wilkins, both of Great Britain. In 1953, Watson and Crick, relying mainly on experimental data provided by Wilkins, devised a model of the molecular structure of *deoxyribonucleic acid* (DNA). DNA is the substance that makes up *genes,* the material in cells that determines the characteristics of an organism.

The *Watson-Crick model* shows that a DNA molecule forms a *double helix*—that is, it resembles a twisted ladder. Each "rung" consists of one of two pairs of chemicals. If the ladder is divided at the middle of each rung, the legs form two new ladders, each identical to the original ladder. The model thus suggested how genetic information is passed from one generation to the next. See **Heredity** (The chemical basis of heredity).

Watson was born in Chicago. He studied at the University of Chicago and Indiana University. In 1955, Watson joined the biology faculty at Harvard University. In 1968, he became director of the Cold Spring Harbor Laboratory on Long Island, New York. That same year, he published *The Double Helix,* an account of the discovery of the DNA structure. In 1988, Watson was named an associate director of the National Institutes of Health in Bethesda, Md., and director of the agency's Office for Human Genome Research. In that position, he became responsible for coordinating a project to locate and analyze the sequences of chemical pairs in the *human genome* (all the genes in a human cell).

Daniel J. Kevles

See also **Cell** (The 1900's; picture: A model of a DNA molecule); **Science** (picture).

Watson, John Broadus (1878-1958), was an American psychologist. In the early 1900's, he became the leader of a revolutionary movement in psychology called *behaviorism.* At that time, Watson claimed that psychology was not a true science because it was based on the examination of thought processes and feelings. He believed that psychology would become a true science only if it came to be based on directly observed behavior.

Watson thought that almost all behavior is a direct result of certain stimuli in a person's environment. His belief that the environment shapes an individual's behavior was so extreme that he claimed he could teach any healthy child any talent or skill. Although Watson generally opposed the notion of innate abilities, he did allow for three inborn emotions—fear, anger, and love.

Watson was attracted to the Russian physiologist Ivan P. Pavlov's description of behavior as a *conditioned reflex* (see **Pavlov, Ivan P.**). Watson used this idea as the chief model of behavior in his *Psychology from the Standpoint of a Behaviorist* (1919).

Watson's extreme views are not widely held today. But his work helped lead to the development of scientific psychology, particularly in the United States. Watson's behaviorism greatly influenced the American psychologist B. F. Skinner (see **Skinner, B. F.**). Watson was born in Greenville, S.C.   Phillip L. Rice

See also **Psychology** (Behaviorism).

Watson, Thomas Augustus. See Bell, Alexander Graham; Telephone (History).

Watson, Thomas Edward (1856-1922), was an American political leader. Elected to the United States House of Representatives as a Democrat in 1890, he joined the new Populist Party, which represented the farmers (see **Populism**). The Populists nominated Watson for Vice President of the United States in 1896 and for President in 1904. As a newspaper editor and author in Atlanta and New York City, he agitated for radical reforms. He later became a Democrat again, and was elected to the Senate in 1920. Watson was born near Thomson, Ga.   Nelson M. Blake

Watson, Thomas John (1874-1956), was a famous American industrialist. He worked for the National Cash Register Company (now NCR Corporation) for 15 years. Then in 1914, he was made president of a company which became International Business Machines Corporation (IBM) in 1924. Under his leadership from 1914 to 1956, it became an international organization. He was born in Campbell, N.Y.   W. H. Baughn

Watson-Watt, Sir Robert Alexander (1892-1973), a Scottish electronics engineer and inventor, helped develop radar. He patented in 1935 a radar device that could detect and follow a flying airplane. He invented a crude form of radio direction finder in 1919 while associated with the British weather bureau. He described the finder as "useful for meteorological purposes such as the location of atmospheric discharges." He received his patent while doing radio research with the Department of Scientific and Industrial Research and with the National Physical Laboratory.

Watson-Watt was born in Brechin, Scotland, and graduated from University College at St. Andrew's University. He was knighted in 1942. He received many other honors, including the Hughes Medal of the Royal Society, the United States Medal of Merit, and many honorary degrees.   G. Gamow

See also **Radar** (The first uses of radar).

Watt is a unit of *power* in the metric system. Power is the rate of producing or using energy. The symbol for the watt is W. The watt is commonly used to measure electric power, even in countries that have not adopted the metric system. An electric device uses 1 watt when 1 volt of electric potential drives 1 ampere of current through it. The number on a light bulb shows its power requirement in watts. For example, a light bulb operating at 100 volts and using 2 amperes consumes 200 watts (100 volts $\times$ 2 amperes). Often, power is measured in *kilowatts*. One kilowatt equals 1,000 watts.

The watt also is used to measure mechanical power. A machine requires a power of 1 watt if it uses 1 joule of energy in 1 second. The watt was named for the Scottish engineer and inventor James Watt.   Gregory Benford

See also **Ampere; Joule; Kilowatt; Watt, James.**

Watt, James (1736-1819), was a Scottish engineer whose improved engine design first made steam power practicable. Crude steam engines were used before Watt's time, but they burned large amounts of coal and produced little power. Their *lateral* (back-and-forth) motion restricted their use to operating pumps. Watt's invention of the "separate condenser" made steam engines more efficient, and his later improvements made possible their wide application.

Watt, the son of a shopkeeper and carpenter, was born in Greenock, Scotland. When Watt was 18, he went to Glasgow and then to London to learn the trade of a mathematical instrument maker. In 1757, Watt became instrument maker at the University of Glasgow.

Illustration of 1788 engine; Granger Collection

James Watt's steam engine, developed during the late 1700's, led to the widespread use of steam power by industry.

In 1763, Watt received a model of a Newcomen steam engine to repair. Although he made it work, Watt was not satisfied with how it operated and set about to improve it. He obtained advice from students and professors, and discovered the principle of the separate condenser. Watt patented his discovery in 1769.

In the old engines, steam filled the cylinder space under the piston. The steam was then condensed, leaving a vacuum into which the piston was pushed by atmospheric pressure. This meant alternately heating and chilling the cylinder. Watt reasoned that because steam was an elastic vapor, it would fill any container into which it was admitted. If the steam-filled cylinder opened into a separate, chilled container, steam would move into the container and condense, producing the vacuum in the cylinder without having to chill it.

Watt spent several years trying to develop an operating engine of the new design. He also worked as a surveyor and construction engineer during this period. In 1774, he obtained the support of Matthew Boulton, an energetic Birmingham manufacturer. Boulton persuaded Parliament to renew Watt's patent for 25 years. The two then organized a company to rent the design of the new engine and to supervise its construction and operation. The firm succeeded.

Watt developed crank movements so the engine could turn wheels. He also invented an "expansive, double-acting" engine, a throttle valve, a governor for regulating engine speed, and many other devices. He did scientific research in chemistry and metallurgy, and was one of the first persons to suggest that water is a compound, not an element. He retired as a wealthy man in 1800. The power unit, the watt, is named in his honor (see **Watt**).   Robert E. Schofield

See also **Steam engine** (History); **Invention** (picture: James Watt's steam engine).

Additional resources

Dickinson, Henry W. *James Watt: Craftsman and Engineer.* Macmillan, 1936. A classic biography.
Dickinson, Henry W., and Jenkins, Rhys. *James Watt and the Steam Engine.* Oxford, 1927. A standard work.
Robinson, Eric, and Musson, A. E. *James Watt and the Steam Revolution.* Kelley, 1969.

Watt-hour meter. See Electric meter.

Watteau, *wah TOH,* **Antoine,** *an TWAHN* (1684-1721), a French painter, developed a style and subject matter that began the rococo movement. Watteau's specialty was the small, intimate painting called the *fête galante* (elegant party) or *fête champêtre* (country party). In these works, elegant young men and women wear shimmering satins and silks. They play music, dance, talk, flirt, and fall in love in rich, leafy garden settings. Watteau also painted portraits of familiar characters from the French theater.

Watteau's popularity was part of a reaction against the large, cold academic paintings of serious subjects that dominated French art about 1700. When Watteau applied for admission to the Royal Academy of Painting and Sculpture, he was given the unprecedented honor of choosing his own subject matter for his admission picture. Watteau painted *The Embarkation for Cythera* (1717), based upon a play of the day. The painting shows lovers who have traveled to Cythera, the island of Aphrodite, the Greek goddess of love. At the end of their visit, they prepare to board boats to return to the everyday world. The scene reflects a mood of melancholy as the lovers leave their paradise with regretful backward glances. The painting appears in **Painting** (Rococo).

Jean Antoine Watteau was born in Valenciennes. He moved to Paris in 1702. There he studied decorative painting and theatrical scene design. As a youth, he worked for a patron, the collector Pierre Crozat. Later, Watteau became one of the first major painters to operate outside the patronage system and live by selling his works through a dealer.   Ann Friedman

See also **Rococo.**

Watterson, Henry (1840-1921), an American newspaper editor, won the 1918 Pulitzer Prize for editorial writing. He was associated in 1868 in the consolidation of Louisville's newspapers into the *Courier-Journal,* and was its outspoken editor for 50 years. He hated slavery and thought secession wrong, but out of loyalty to the South served in the Confederate Army during the Civil War. Watterson left the *Courier-Journal* in 1919 because it supported the League of Nations. He was born in Washington, D.C.   Alvin E. Austin

Wattle. See Australia (Native plants).

Wattmeter is an instrument used to measure electric power. The most commonly used type of wattmeter is called an *electrodynamic wattmeter.* The electrodynamic wattmeter has two coils of wire. A *fixed* coil is arranged to receive the current of the circuit to be measured. A *movable* coil, supported by jeweled pivots that permit it to turn, is arranged to receive a current proportional to the voltage of the circuit to be measured. When the circuit is energized, the magnetic fields produced by the currents make the movable coil try to turn so that its axis is parallel to the axis of the fixed coil. Springs stop it in a position that de-

Simpson Electric Company

Wattmeter

pends on the power in the circuit. A pointer shows the power in watts on a scale.   Gregory Benford

Watts, Isaac (1674-1748), an English clergyman, wrote more than 700 hymns and psalms. He also wrote theological treatises, volumes of sermons, and books on ethics, psychology, and teaching. He was considered one of the greatest preachers of his time.

Watts's best hymns are notable for simplicity of poetic structure, apt use of figures of speech, and emotional vitality. A number of them still appear in most English hymnals. He wrote "Joy to the World," "O God, Our Help in Ages Past," "When I Survey the Wondrous Cross," and "There Is a Land of Pure Delight." He adapted many Old Testament psalms to a Christian point of view.

Watts was born in Southampton, England. He became pastor of London's Mark Lane Independent Chapel in 1702.   Leonard W. Van Camp

Watusi, another name for Tutsi. See **Burundi** (People; History); **Rwanda** (People; History).

Waugh, *waw,* **Evelyn,** *EEV lihn* (1903-1966), was an English author best known for his satirical novels about wealthy London society. Waugh also wrote novels that combined comic satire with spiritual and religious themes.

In his novels, Waugh explored the pretentious and absurd qualities he saw in ambitious, upper middle-class English people. Waugh's characters were often only thinly disguised portraits of actual people who were well known in England during the mid-1900's. Waugh strongly believed that the upper classes should have special rights and privileges. But his novels reflect his belief that the behavior of the upper classes was sometimes heartless and superficial. Waugh's first satirical novel was *Decline and Fall* (1928). His other important satires include *Vile Bodies* (1930), *Black Mischief* (1932), and *A Handful of Dust* (1934).

Waugh converted to Roman Catholicism in 1930. The novels written after his conversion show an increasing concern with religious questions. Although Waugh continued to write such humorous satires as *Scoop* (1938) and *The Loved One* (1948), he also wrote more serious, searching novels. The most famous of these later novels is *Brideshead Revisited* (1945), a study of an aristocratic Catholic family. Waugh's other later novels include the autobiographical *The Ordeal of Gilbert Pinfold* (1957) and three related novels about World War II. These books are *Men at Arms* (1952), *Officers and Gentlemen* (1955), and *Unconditional Surrender* (American title *The End of the Battle,* 1961).

Waugh also wrote much nonfiction, including travel books, biographies, and essays. A selection of Waugh's nonfiction was published after his death as *The Essays, Articles and Reviews of Evelyn Waugh* (1984). In his autobiography, *A Little Learning* (1964), he described his childhood and youth. Waugh's *Diaries* (1976) and *Letters* (1980), published after his death, are filled with gossip and personal opinion that is often malicious, snobbish, or prejudiced. Evelyn Arthur St. John Waugh was born in London.   James Douglas Merritt

Wave theory. See Light (Early ideas about light).

Waveband. See Frequency band.

Wavelength. See Electromagnetic waves; Light (The nature of light); Waves.

Waverley novels. See Scott, Sir Walter.

Waves are motions that carry energy, but not matter, from one place to another. A simple experiment will show how waves carry energy but not matter. First have two boys hold the ends of a rope. When one boy moves his end of the rope up and down sharply, energy passes from one section to the next as a wave. Each part of the rope is set into motion as the wave passes, but the rope itself does not move forward with the wave. The boy holding the other end will feel the energy carried by the wave move his hand.

Next, have one boy throw a baseball to the other. The catcher feels some of the energy used in throwing the ball. But unlike the wave, the matter—that is, the ball—moves forward. As the ball moves, it carries the energy with it.

Waves on a rope or water are familiar examples of waves, but many other waves move around us all the time. For example, the sound of people speaking travels to our ears as waves. Radio and television programs travel to our homes as waves.

Many kinds of waves travel on or in a material. Scientists call the substance through which the waves travel the wave *medium.* For waves on a rope, the rope is the medium. Ocean waves travel on the surface of the water

and *seismic* (earthquake) waves travel through the earth. Some waves do not need to travel through a material medium. For example, the electromagnetic waves that carry light, radio, and television signals can travel through a vacuum. The medium for these waves is an electric and magnetic *field* (area containing lines of force).

Characteristics of waves

Waves are caused when something disturbs a medium. A rock dropped into a still pond sets water waves in motion. The rock is called the *source* of the waves. When you move the free end of a rope, you become the source of the waves on the rope. If you move the rope high and low, you will make large waves. Scientists call the top part of any wave the *crest* and the bottom part the *trough.* The height of a crest above the level of the rope when no waves are moving on it is called the *amplitude* of the wave. Amplitude can also be measured from the bottom of the trough to the still rope.

By moving the free end of the rope up and down faster, you make more waves on the rope. You have increased the *frequency* of the waves because more waves pass any point in one second. But no matter how

The shape of a wave

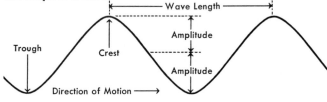

Many waves resemble hills and valleys. Scientists have various terms to describe waves, *left.* They call the hills *crests* and the valleys *troughs.* The *amplitude* is a measure of how much the medium carrying the wave rises or falls from its usual position. *Wave length* is the distance between comparable points on two waves next to each other.

Transverse wave

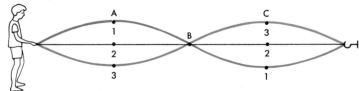

Transverse waves cause individual particles of the medium to move up and down while the wave moves forward. As a single wave moves down the rope away from the boy, *left,* the crest passes from point A to point B and then to point C. But the three points themselves do not move along the rope.

Standing wave

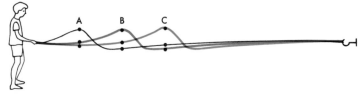

Standing waves do not move along the medium. Instead, they vibrate in a certain whole number of loops. To make two loops, the boy makes a wave with a wave length equal to the length of the rope. Then he holds his end still. Points A and C on the loops move, but point B—between them—does not move.

Longitudinal wave

Longitudinal waves, also called *compressional waves,* cause individual particles of the medium to move back and forth. Unlike transverse waves, the particles move in the same direction the wave moves, not across the direction of wave motion. If one end of a stretched spring receives a sharp push, a longitudinal wave travels along the spring. The wave moves the spring's coils closer together when it passes along them. After it passes, the coils move farther apart again.

A *World Book* science project

The purpose of this project is to learn about the behavior of waves by studying water waves in a ripple tank. Wave behavior such as reflection, diffraction, and interference is shown in the photos taken of a homemade ripple tank. Experiment with various objects in the tank to see how they affect the motion of the waves.

To make a ripple tank, cut a strip of wire screen to fit the inside edge of a baking dish. Then tape a layer of gauze inside the screen as shown. Fill the tank about one-third full of water and place the round stick near one end. Drop water from a medicine dropper or slightly lift one end of the tank and drop it to make waves. Two hat pins in a block of wax will make waves that come from two points. Attach the wax to a yardstick with rubber bands. Then set the yardstick over the tank so that the pins just touch the water when the stick vibrates up and down.

Materials needed

Baking dish   Round stick   Gauze bandage

Paraffin wax   Medicine dropper   Wire screen

Rubber bands   Hat pins   Adhesive tape

Wave patterns in a ripple tank

Reflected waves form curved arches near the barrier that reflected them. The original waves form nearly complete circles near the top of the picture.

Curved diffracted waves in the top half of the picture, *below,* resulted when parts of parallel waves passed through the small slit in the barrier.

Interfering waves cancel each other along the faint gray lines coming from the center. They strengthen themselves where the bright dashed lines occur.

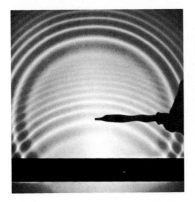

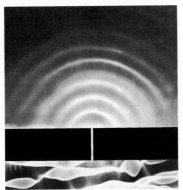

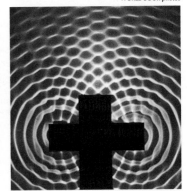

fast or how high you make the rope move, you cannot make the waves travel faster. The speed of a wave does not depend on either its amplitude or its frequency. The speed of the wave depends only on the stiffness and *density* (mass of a unit of volume) of the medium (see **Density**). For example, a tightly stretched rope will have a higher wave speed than a slack rope. Waves will also travel faster on a light, less dense rope that is stretched the same amount as a heavy rope.

When you increase the frequency of the waves, you also shorten the distance between the crests or troughs. Scientists call this distance the *wave length.* You can find the wave length by dividing the frequency into the wave speed.

The frequency of sound waves is also called the *pitch.* The pitch of a note produced by a stringed instrument can be raised by tightening or shortening the string. Strings designed to produce lower frequencies generally are heavier, longer, and less tightly stretched.

Wave motion

When a wave moves along a medium, there are really two motions to watch. One is the motion of the wave and the other is the motion of the medium itself.

Transverse waves cause the medium to move up and down while the wave travels along it. Waves that move this way are called transverse waves, because the motion of the medium is perpendicular to the motion of the waves. Rope waves are transverse. Other examples of transverse waves include electromagnetic waves such as light, and water waves. If the rope moves vertically or horizontally, the waves have a vertical or horizontal *polarization.* That is, the medium vibrates in only one direction. Only transverse waves can have polarization.

Longitudinal waves, also called *compressional waves,* travel in the same direction that the medium moves. For example, these waves are made in a stretched spring by compressing a few coils at one end and then releasing them. Sound waves and some earthquake waves are longitudinal waves.

Traveling and standing waves. In the previous examples with waves on a rope, the waves have traveled from one end of the rope to the other. These waves are *traveling waves.* However, under certain conditions, waves may be trapped in a medium. For example, if a string is held at both ends and plucked, the energy in the waves cannot leave the string at either end. This creates patterns called *standing waves.* The size of the space in which the waves are confined determines the wave length the waves can have. Standing waves can exist on a surface such as a drumhead, or within an enclosed space, such as a room. The possible wave lengths are still determined by the size of the medium.

How waves behave

So far, only individual waves in a single medium have been discussed. But waves behave differently when they move from one medium to another, when some part of the waves are stopped, or when other waves are also present in the medium.

Reflection and refraction. When waves leave one medium and enter another, some of the energy in the waves is reflected and some is *refracted* (transmitted) into the new medium. The amount of energy that is reflected and refracted depends on the angle at which the *incident* (incoming) waves strike the new medium. The larger the angle between the path of the waves and an imaginary line perpendicular to the surface of the new medium, the more the waves will be reflected.

The amount of reflection and refraction also depends on certain properties of the two mediums. For example, reflection and refraction of sound waves depends on the density of the two mediums and the speed of sound in them. If the two properties are nearly the same, most of the sound will be refracted into the new medium. If they are different, most of the sound will be reflected. Air is much less dense than the ground and carries sound much more slowly. Consequently, most of the energy in sound waves is reflected from the ground.

Diffraction. An expanding ring of waves moves away from a stone dropped into a still pond. As the ring becomes larger, any short part of the *wave front* (the outside edge of the ring) becomes a nearly straight line. But if the wave front passes through a small slit in a barrier, the wave coming out on the other side will not form a straight line. Instead, it will spread out from the slit in a curved line.

The changing of the straight wave front into a curved wave is called *diffraction.* Diffraction occurs because each point on the wave front is a source of a tiny curved wave called a *wavelet.* The wavelets along the front combine to make the straight wave. But the slit lets only a few wavelets pass through. The wavelets on either side are cut off and the front is no longer straight.

Interference. Where the crests of two waves with the same frequency pass a given point at the same time, the waves are in *phase.* But, if the crest of one wave passes the point at the same time as the trough of the other, one wave is half a wave length ahead of the other. Scientists measure the difference in phase between two waves in degrees. They multiply the number of degrees in a circle (360) by the fraction of the wave length between the two waves. In this case, the waves are 180° out of phase.

Waves of the same frequency make each other stronger where they are in phase and cancel each other where they are 180° out of phase. Scientists say the two sources *interfere* with each other. The waves will travel away stronger in some directions and weaker in others.

Wave theory. The ideas that apply to light, sound, and other waves also apply to the tiny parts of atoms. Scientists have discovered that electrons, neutrons, and protons, which are usually thought of as particles, sometimes behave like waves. Their waves are called *matter waves.* The wave theory of atomic particles has given scientists a greater understanding of the structure of atoms and their nuclei. See **Physics** (Einstein and relativity); **Quantum mechanics.**   L. Wallace Dean

Related articles in *World Book* include:

Electromagnetic waves	Pulsar
Heat (How heat travels)	Radio (How radio works)
Interference	Reflection
Laser	Refraction
Light (The nature of	Seismology
light)	Sound
Maser	Television (How television
Ocean (Ocean waves)	works)
Polarized light	Tidal wave

WAVES. See Navy, United States (Women in the Navy).

Wax is a fatty substance that is widely used as a protective coating for various surfaces. It resists air, water, and chemical change. Most wax is solid at room temperature. It softens when heated. The word *wax* comes from the Anglo-Saxon word *weax,* meaning *beeswax.*

Manufacturers produce three chief kinds of wax: (1) mineral, (2) animal, and (3) vegetable. Most manufacturers blend two or more types of wax to give their product the desired qualities.

Mineral wax. Most wax comes from petroleum. Manufacturers chill and filter oil and then use various chemical processes to separate the wax from it. There are three major kinds of petroleum wax: (1) *paraffin wax,* (2) *microcrystalline wax,* and (3) *petrolatum.* These waxes differ in color, hardness, and melting point.

Petroleum wax resists moisture and chemicals and has no odor or taste. It serves as a waterproof coating for such paper products as milk cartons and waxed paper. Petroleum wax also is used in making polishes for automobiles, floors, and furniture. It does not conduct electricity, and so it can serve as an electric insulator. Manufacturers use wax molds in casting jewelry and machinery parts. Most candles are made from paraffin wax. Microcrystalline wax is used mostly in making paper for packaging. Petrolatum, also called *petroleum jelly,* is used in making cosmetics and medicines.

Other mineral waxes include *montan wax,* obtained from coal; *ozokerite,* made from shale; and *peat wax,* made from peat. *Synthetic* (artificially made) wax comes from *glycol,* a chemical obtained from petroleum. These waxes are usually blended with petroleum wax.

Animal wax is used alone or is blended with petroleum wax in making candles, polishes, and other products. Bees produce *beeswax* in building honeycombs. *Wool wax* comes from a greasy coating on unprocessed wool. *Lanolin,* a form of wool wax, is used in making cosmetics. *Spermaceti,* obtained from the oil of the sperm whale, is used in making creams and salves.

Vegetable wax. Many plants have a natural wax coating that protects them from heat and moisture. *Carnauba wax,* the hardest and most widely used vegetable wax, coats the leaves of the carnauba palm tree. It remains solid in hot weather and is an important ingredient in automobile wax and other polishes. Other vegetable waxes include *bayberry wax, candelilla wax, Japan wax,* and *sugar cane wax.*   Richard F. Blewitt

Related articles in *World Book* include:

Beeswax	Painting (Encaustic	Polish
Candle	painting)	Sealing wax
Carnauba wax	Paraffin	Spermaceti
Microcrystalline wax	Petrolatum	

Wax myrtle is a large, fragrant evergreen shrub or small tree found along the eastern coast of the United States. It grows from southern New Jersey to southern Florida and as far west as Texas. It also is found in the West Indies. The wax myrtle grows up to 35 feet (11 meters) tall and has small, greenish flowers. The 2- to 4-inch (5- to 10-centimeter) leaves are covered with tiny amber to brown dots. The wax myrtle is grown as an ornamental shrub and does best in damp soil.

Scientific classification. The wax myrtle belongs to the bayberry or wax myrtle family, Myricaceae. It is *Myrica cerifera.*
Walter S. Judd

Waxwing is a silky-feathered, grayish-brown bird that is larger than a sparrow, with a conspicuous crest or topknot. The waxwing has a band of yellow across the end of its tail. It has red, waxlike drops on its wing feathers.

The *cedar waxwing* is the best known of these birds. It lives in most parts of North America, as far north as central Canada and Labrador. These birds eat berries and fruits, and insects. They build bulky nests, usually in a fruit or shade tree. Many cedar waxwings are found on the islands of Lake Superior and around the lakes of Ontario and northern Minnesota in the summer. The birds cannot sing, but they produce a soft, high-pitched whistle. The female lays three to five eggs which are a pale bluish or purplish gray, speckled with black, brown, or purple. See **Bird** (picture: Birds of forests and woodlands).

The *Bohemian waxwing* is a slightly larger bird. It has yellow marks on its wings and reddish-brown undertail feathers. This bird lives in the northern latitudes of the world. In winter, the Bohemian waxwing appears in the

Ken Carmichael, Animals Animals
Cedar waxwings live in most parts of North America. They build bulky nests and eat berries, fruits, and insects.

Jack Wilburn, Animals Animals
The Bohemian waxwing lives in forests near the Arctic but flies south to temperate regions in the winter.

northwestern and central northern United States and northern Europe. The *Siberian waxwing* lives in southeastern Siberia and Japan.

Scientific classification. Waxwings belong to the waxwing family, Bombycillidae. The cedar waxwing is *Bombycilla cedrorum;* the Bohemian, *B. garrulus,* and the Siberian, *B. japonica.*   Fred J. Alsop, III

See also **Bird** (picture: How birds feed).

Waybill. See Bill of lading.

Wayland Baptist University. See Universities and colleges (table).

Wayne, Anthony (1745-1796), was an American officer in the Revolutionary War. He became known as "Mad Anthony" Wayne because of his reckless courage. He was the hero of the recapture of Stony Point, N.Y., a British post on the Hudson River, in 1779. Wayne commanded the attack, which was considered one of the most daring of the war.

He was born on Jan. 1, 1745, in Chester County, Pennsylvania. He studied at an academy in Philadelphia where he qualified as a surveyor. A Philadelphia land company sent him to Nova Scotia in 1765 to supervise the surveying and settlement of land. He returned to Pennsylvania and served in the colonial assembly. When the war began in 1775, he raised a regiment for the Canadian campaign, and later served in the garrison at Ticonderoga.

In 1777, Wayne became a brigadier general and joined Washington's army to command the Pennsylvania line. He led a division at Brandywine, commanded the right wing at Germantown, and spent the winter with Washington at Valley Forge. Wayne led the advance attack at Monmouth the next year. In 1781, Wayne served with the Marquis de Lafayette against General Cornwallis, and took part in the siege of Yorktown. Cornwallis' surrender at Yorktown helped bring the Revolutionary War to an end.

In 1783, Wayne became a brevet major general, but he retired the same year. He represented Georgia in Congress in 1791, but the seat was declared vacant because of election irregularities. He returned to the army in 1791 as a major general and commander in chief. He fought against the Indians in Ohio in 1794, defeating them at the Battle of Fallen Timbers. Wayne made a treaty with the Indians in 1795 which secured a great tract of land for the United States. He died at Presque Isle (now Erie, Pa.) the next year.   John R. Alden

See also **Indian wars** (picture: "Mad Anthony").

Wayne, John (1907-1979), an American motion-picture actor, became famous for his he-man roles. He starred in such western films as *Red River* (1948) and in other action movies, including *Sands of Iwo Jima* (1950) and *The Quiet Man* (1952). He won an Academy Award for *True Grit* (1969). Wayne made more than 175 movies.

Warner Bros. Inc.

John Wayne

Wayne, whose real name was Marion Michael Morrison, was born in Winterset, Iowa. He made his film debut in 1928 after working as a prop boy. He failed in a leading role in *The Big Trail* (1930) and then worked mostly in low-budget westerns until the late 1930's under the name of Duke Morrison. He became a star after director John Ford cast him in the classic Western movie *Stagecoach* (1939). Wayne's other notable films include *The Long Voyage Home* (1940), *The Spoilers* (1942), *She Wore a Yellow Ribbon* (1949), *The Searchers* (1956), *Rio Bravo* (1959), *The Comancheros* (1961), and *The Green Berets* (1969).   Rachel Gallagher

Wayne State University. See Universities and colleges (table).

WCTU. See Woman's Christian Temperance Union.

Weakfish, also called *squeteague,* pronounced *skwee TEEG,* is a saltwater food fish of the croaker family. Its name comes from the fact that its mouth is tender and easily torn. The fish reaches a length of 1 to 2 feet (30 to 61 centimeters) or more. Although *sea trout* is one of its common names, it is not even closely related to the trout. The squeteague lives along the eastern and Gulf coasts of the United States from Massachusetts to Texas. The four kinds are the *common squeteague,* the *spotted squeteague,* the *silver squeteague,* and the *sand sque-*

Detail of oil painting on paper (1794?), probably by F. Kemmelmeyer (Henry Francis du Pont Winterthur Museum)

Pastel on paper (about 1796) by James Sharples, Sr.; Independence National Historical Park Collection, Philadelphia

"Mad Anthony" Wayne, *above,* led American troops against a confederation of Indian tribes in Ohio at the Battle of Fallen Timbers, *left,* in 1794.

teague. Most weakfish weigh less than 15 pounds (7 kilograms), but some weigh up to 30 pounds (14 kilograms).

Scientific classification. Squeteagues, or sea trout, belong to the drum family, Sciaenidae. The common squeteague is *Cynoscion regalis;* the silver is *C. nothus;* and the spotted is *C. nebulosus.*   Carl L. Hubbs

Weapon. Weapons have played an important part in the history of humanity. They have helped people conquer vast areas of wilderness and defend their homes and families from enemies. Nations use weapons to carry on wars. They continue to develop new weapons that kill more and more people. Many people believe nuclear weapons are the greatest threat to humanity because of their destructive power.   Frances M. Lussier

Related articles in *World Book.* See **Firearm** and its list of *Related articles.* See also the following:

Explosives

Bomb	Detonator	Gunpowder	RDX
Bullet	Fragmentation	Nitroglycerin	Shrapnel
Cartridge	Fuse	Nuclear	TNT
Cordite	Grenade	weapon	Torpedo
Depth charge	Guncotton	PETN	

Other weapons

Ax	Catapult	Guided missile	Sling
Bayonet	Crossbow	Knife	Spear
Blowgun	Dagger	Mace	Sword
Boomerang	Flail	Machete	Tomahawk
Bowie knife	Flame thrower	Rocket	

Other related articles

Ammunition	Greek fire
Archery	Magazine
Arrowhead	Mine warfare
Ballistics	Ordnance
Chemical-biological-radiological warfare	Powder horn
	Prehistoric people (Weapons)
Disarmament	Shot tower

Weasel is a small furry animal that has a long, slender body and short legs. Weasels have alert black or dark brown eyes and small, rounded ears. They are found on every continent except Africa, Australia, and Antarctica. The *long-tailed weasel* grows from 12 to 18 inches (30 to 46 centimeters) long, and weighs up to 9 ounces (255 grams). The females are smaller and weigh 3 to 4 ounces (85 to 115 grams). The *ermine* is a type of small weasel. Male ermines grow from 9 to 13 inches (22 to 34 centimeters) long. The *least weasel* is the smallest flesh-eating animal in the world. It grows up to 10 inches (25 centimeters) long and weighs about 2 ounces (55 grams).

Most weasels have brownish, reddish-brown, or yellowish-brown fur on the back and sides, and white, yellowish, or tan fur on the underparts. In winter, the fur of weasels that live in cold climates changes to white, except for a black-tipped tail. The white fur provides camouflage in the snow. The black-tipped tail may catch the eye of an attacking predator, such as a hawk or owl, and cause the attacker to miss the weasel. Weasels found in Florida and the Southwestern United States sometimes have distinctive whitish or buff markings on the face.

Weasels have keen smell and vision. They are amazingly strong for their size and prey on mice and squirrels. They usually bite their victims on the neck or at the base of the skull. Weasels also eat earthworms, insects,

Bob and Clara Calhoun, Bruce Coleman Ltd.

A weasel is a small furry animal with a slender body and short legs. The *long-tailed* weasel is a common species in North America. During the winter, the long-tailed weasel has a coat of white fur, *above.* During the rest of the year, the animal's coat is brown, with light-colored fur on its underside, *below.*

frogs, lizards, rabbits, shrews, snakes, and birds. The weasel's slender body enables it to easily invade mouse burrows, rock crevices, and squirrel burrows. Weasels often raid chicken yards and kill more chickens than they need for food. As a result, many farmers dislike weasels even though they destroy farmyard pests. The weasel's chief enemies are great horned owls and people. Weasels, like skunks, discharge a foul-smelling liquid called *musk* when they are threatened or attacked.

Weasels live in a variety of environments. They make dens in rock piles, under tree stumps, and in abandoned rodent burrows. They sometimes catch food in their dens and make nests using the fur and feathers of their victims. Weasels are most active at night. Most females have four to eight young born at a time.

Scientific classification. Weasels belong to the weasel family, Mustelidae. The long-tailed weasel is *Mustela frenata.* The ermine is *M. erminea,* and the least weasel is *M. nivalis*
          Charles A. Long

Related articles in *World Book* include:

Badger	Mink	Sable
Ermine	Otter	Skunk
Ferret	Polecat	Tayra
Grison	Ratel	Wolverine
Marten		

Milt and Joan Mann

A television weather report gives the day's weather conditions locally and across the nation. It also predicts the local weather for the next several days. Millions of people rely on TV forecasts to find out what kind of weather they can expect in the coming days.

Weather

Weather is the condition of the air that surrounds the earth. The weather may be hot or cold, cloudy or clear, windy or calm. It may bring rain, snow, sleet, or hail.

The weather affects our lives in numerous ways. For example, the type of clothing we wear depends largely on the weather. We put on heavy clothes when it is cold and dress lightly when it is hot. We also heat our homes in cold weather and cool them in hot weather. In many cases, we decide whether to spend our leisure time outdoors or inside according to the weather. The weather even affects our moods. People often feel more cheerful on a sunny day than on a gloomy one.

The weather has an enormous impact on agriculture. Farmers need clear weather to plant and harvest their crops. The plants require the right amount of sunlight and rain to grow and ripen. A storm or a sudden frost can damage or kill much of a crop. In such cases, the food produced from the plants that survive costs more.

Industry, transportation, and communication also suffer during bad weather. The construction of buildings, bridges, and roads may be delayed by rain, snow, or extreme cold. Snow may make trains late. Fog often prevents airplanes from taking off. Icy highways slow traffic. Storms may break power lines and telephone wires. Thunderstorms may disrupt radio and television broadcasts. Even more serious is the loss of lives that sometimes results from severe storms.

Weather is not the same as climate. Weather is the condition of the air during a brief period. Climate is the average weather of an area over a long time. Scientists often describe climate in terms of the average temperature of a region and the amount of rain and snow the area receives. A region's weather may change greatly from day to day. But the average temperature and the amount of rain and snow remain about the same from year to year. See **Climate**.

People have tried to predict the weather for thousands of years. Today, scientists use complex instruments, such as radar, satellites, and computers, to forecast the weather. The forecasts are broadcast on radio and television stations and published in newspapers. Modern scientific instruments have made weather forecasting today more accurate than ever before. But predicting the weather remains a difficult, inexact science.

Yoshi Kazu Sasaki, the contributor of this article, is George L. Cross Research Professor of Meteorology at the University of Oklahoma.

All weather develops in the *atmosphere,* the air that surrounds the earth. The atmosphere consists chiefly of the gases nitrogen and oxygen. It also has small amounts of other gases. Water vapor and particles of dust are mixed in the atmosphere. The atmosphere extends far above the earth's surface. Above a height of about 100 miles (160 kilometers), there is almost no air. This region is called *space.*

Nearly all weather occurs in the lowest layer of the atmosphere. This layer, called the *troposphere,* begins at the surface of the earth and extends from 6 to 10 miles (10 to 16 kilometers) away from the surface. Weather conditions in the troposphere—and on the earth—depend on four elements: (1) temperature, (2) air pressure, (3) wind, and (4) moisture.

Temperature is the degree of heat in the atmosphere. This heat comes from the sun. But only about one two-billionth of the heat given off by the sun enters the atmosphere. The rest is lost in space. About 34 per cent of the sunlight that enters the atmosphere is reflected back into space, chiefly by clouds. About 19 per cent is absorbed by the atmosphere and warms the air. However, the atmosphere gets most of its heat in another way. About 47 per cent of the sunlight that enters the atmosphere reaches the earth's surface and warms the ground and the seas. Heat from the ground and the seas then warms the atmosphere. The atmosphere absorbs the heat and prevents it from easily passing back into space. This result is called the *greenhouse effect* because the process resembles the way a greenhouse works. A greenhouse is a glass or clear plastic building in which plants can be grown throughout the year. A greenhouse lets sunlight in to heat the plants, but it prevents much of the heat from escaping.

Air pressure is the force of the atmosphere pushing on the earth. Temperature has a great effect on air pressure. Warm air weighs less than cool air. As a result, warm air puts less pressure on the earth than does cool air. The warm air forms a *low-pressure area,* also called a *low.* Cool air forms a *high-pressure area,* or a *high.* The force of air pressure tends to push air from high-pressure areas to low-pressure areas.

Weather terms

Air mass is an enormous body of air that forms over a region in which the temperature is fairly constant. The air mass takes on the temperature of the region and has a great influence on the weather.

Front is a zone that develops when the edge of a cold air mass and the edge of a warm air mass meet. Most changes in the weather occur along fronts.

High-pressure area is an area in which the force of the atmosphere on the earth is relatively high. High-pressure areas usually have clear skies.

Humidity is the measure of the amount of water vapor in the air.

Low-pressure area is an area in which the force of the atmosphere on the earth is relatively low. Low-pressure areas usually have cloudy skies.

Precipitation is moisture that falls from clouds in the form of rain, snow, sleet, or hail.

Temperature is the degree of heat in the atmosphere.

Wind is the movement of air. Air tends to move from a high-pressure area to a low-pressure area. Winds are named for the direction from which they blow. For example, a north wind blows from the north.

Wind chill is an estimate of how cold the wind makes a person feel. For example, when the temperature is 20° F. (−6.7° C) and the wind is blowing at 10 miles (16 kilometers) per hour, the wind chill temperature is 3° F. (−16.1° C). Thus, a person feels as cold as when the temperature is 3° F. (−16.1° C) and the wind is calm. See **Wind chill.**

Wind is the movement of air from a high-pressure area to a low-pressure area. The greater the difference in pressure between the two areas, the stronger the wind will be. Winds are named for the direction from which they blow. For example, a north wind blows from the north.

As air moves into a low-pressure area, it forces some of the air that was already there to move upward. The rising air expands and cools. Cool air cannot hold as much water vapor as warm air can. As a result, the water vapor in the air *condenses*—that is, it changes into tiny drops of water. The drops are held aloft by the rising air. When billions of these drops of water cluster together, they form a cloud. Thus, low-pressure areas are usually cloudy.

Weather extremes around the world

Highest temperature recorded was 136° F. (58.0° C) at Al Aziziyah, Libya, on Sept. 13, 1922. The highest temperature recorded in North America was 134° F. (57° C) in Death Valley, Calif., on July 10, 1913.

Lowest temperature observed on the earth's surface was −128.6° F. (−89.2° C) at Vostok Station in Antarctica, on July 21, 1983. The record low in the United States was −80° F. (−62° C) at Prospect Creek, Alaska, on Jan. 23, 1971.

Highest air pressure at sea level was recorded at Agata, in the Soviet Union, on Dec. 31, 1968, when the barometric pressure reached 32.01 inches (81.31 centimeters or 108.4 kilopascals).

Lowest air pressure at sea level was estimated at 25.69 inches (65.25 centimeters or 87.00 kilopascals), during a typhoon in the Philippine Sea on Oct. 12, 1979.

Strongest winds measured on the earth's surface were recorded at Mount Washington, N.H., on April 12, 1934. For five minutes the wind blew at 188 mph (303 kph). One gust reached 231 mph (372 kph).

Driest place on earth is Arica, Chile. In one 59-year period, the average annual rainfall was $\frac{3}{100}$ inch (0.76 millimeter). No rain fell in Arica for a 14-year period.

Heaviest rainfall recorded in 24 hours was 73.62 inches (186.99 centimeters) on March 15-16, 1952, at Cilaos, on the island of Reunion in the Indian Ocean. The most rain in one year was at Cherrapunji, India. From August 1860 to July 1861, 1,041.78 inches (2,646.12 centimeters) fell. The wettest place is Mount Waialeale, on the island of Kauai in Hawaii, with an average annual rainfall of 460 inches (1,168 centimeters).

Heaviest snowfall recorded in North America in 24 hours—76 inches (193 centimeters)—fell at Silver Lake, Colo., on April 14-15, 1921. The most snow recorded in North America in one winter—1,122 inches (2,850 centimeters)—fell at Rainier Paradise Ranger Station in Washington in 1971-1972.

Largest hailstone in the United States fell in Coffeyville, Kans., on Sept. 3, 1970. The hailstone measured $17\frac{1}{2}$ inches (44.5 centimeters) in circumference, and it weighed $1\frac{2}{3}$ pounds (0.76 kilogram).

Source: National Oceanic and Atmospheric Administration.

Elements of weather   All weather develops in the atmosphere. Weather conditions in the atmosphere—and on the earth—depend on four elements: (1) temperature, (2) air pressure, (3) wind, and (4) moisture.

WORLD BOOK diagrams by Zorica Dabich

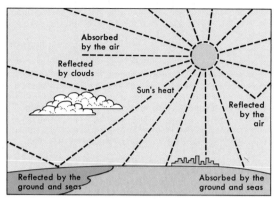

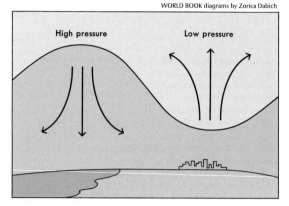

Temperature is the degree of heat in the atmosphere. The ground, seas, and air absorb about two-thirds of the sun's heat that enters the atmosphere. The rest is reflected into space.

Air pressure is the force of the atmosphere on the earth. Warm air weighs less than cool air. Warm air thus forms an area of low pressure and cool air forms an area of high pressure.

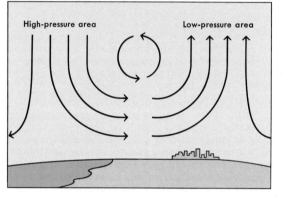

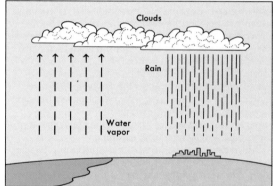

Wind is the movement of air. Air moves from a high-pressure area to a low-pressure area. As air moves into a low-pressure area, it forces the air that was already there to move upward.

Moisture enters the air as water vapor, which comes from the oceans. As the vapor rises, it may change into drops of water and form clouds. If the drops get big enough, they fall to earth.

As air near the ground flows out of a high-pressure area, the air above sinks and replaces it. The sinking air is compressed and becomes warmer. Because the warmer air can hold more water vapor, it can evaporate any clouds in the area. As a result, high-pressure areas are usually clear.

Moisture enters the atmosphere in the form of water vapor. Nearly all the vapor comes from water that evaporates from the oceans. The amount of water vapor in the air is called *humidity.* The more moisture there is in the air, the higher the humidity. Air that holds as much moisture as it can is *saturated.* The temperature at which the air becomes saturated is called the *dew point.* If the temperature falls below the dew point, the moisture in the air condenses.

On calm, clear nights, the air just above the ground cools rapidly. If the temperature of this air falls below the dew point, drops of water settle on grass, leaves, and windows and other surfaces. These drops of water are called *dew.* If the dew point is at or below freezing,

frost forms. Sometimes, warm, moist air near the ground is cooled to its dew point. In such cases, low clouds called *fog* may develop. Fog can form at night or during the day.

A cooling of the air may also cause moisture to fall to the earth as *precipitation.* Precipitation may occur in the form of *rain, snow, sleet,* or *hail.* Rain falls when the drops of water that form clouds combine and become so heavy that the air can no longer hold them up. If the temperature of the clouds is below freezing, ice crystals form. The ice crystals can turn to snow if the temperature of the air near the ground is as high as about 37° F. (2.78° C). If the temperature is between about 37° and 39° F. (2.78° and 3.89° C), the crystals change to sleet. At higher temperatures, the ice crystals melt as they fall and reach the earth as rain. Hail forms when strong air currents carry ice crystals up and down between the top and bottom layers of a thundercloud. The crystals become larger and larger until they fall to the earth as hailstones.

General circulation of the atmosphere depends largely on the way the sun's rays strike different parts of the earth. The sun's rays beat almost straight down at the equator. As a result, the equator is always hot and is an area of low pressure. The sun's rays strike the rest of the earth at various angles. The angle is sharpest at the North and South poles. The poles thus receive less heat and are always cold. They are areas of high pressure.

If the earth did not rotate, wind would move directly from the high-pressure areas of the poles to the low-pressure area of the equator. The cold air from the poles would flow under the warm air of the equator and push it upward. The air from the equator would then flow toward the poles. The movement of air between the poles and the equator would go on continuously.

The rotation of the earth prevents winds from the poles and the equator from moving directly north or south. The earth rotates from west to east. As a result, winds that blow toward the equator seem to curve toward the west. Winds that move away from the equator seem to curve toward the east. This effect is known as the *Coriolis force* (see **Coriolis force**). Because of the Coriolis force, the general circulation of the atmosphere consists of winds that circle the earth in wide bands. There are six belts of these *prevailing winds*—three in the Northern Hemisphere and three in the Southern Hemisphere. They are known as the *trade winds,* the *prevailing westerlies,* and the *polar easterlies.*

The trade winds blow toward the equator. Because the area of the equator is so hot, the air above it is always rising. As the air rises, the trade winds move in

from the north and south to take its place. The Coriolis force makes the trade winds seem to blow from the east. As a result of the earth's rotation, weather in the area of the trade winds moves from east to west. The trade winds from the north and south meet near the equator in an area called the *doldrums.* The doldrums is usually calm, but it is quite rainy and may have periods of gusty winds.

The prevailing westerlies occur north of the trade winds in the Northern Hemisphere and south of the trade winds in the Southern Hemisphere. The prevailing westerlies move away from the equator. They seem to blow from the west because of the Coriolis force. Weather in the area of the prevailing westerlies moves from west to east. Prevailing westerlies blow across most of the United States and Canada.

An area called the *horse latitudes* divides the prevailing westerlies from the trade winds. Because the prevailing westerlies and the trade winds move away from one another, air in the horse latitudes moves downward to fill the space. The winds in the horse latitudes are very light. The area may have been named by Spanish sailors of the 1600's who were bringing horses to America. Many of their sailing ships became stalled in the light winds of the area. The ships were there so long that water for the horses ran out and the animals had to be thrown overboard.

The polar easterlies blow from the North and South poles. Air above the poles sinks downward because it is so cold. When the air reaches the ground, it spreads out and moves toward the equator, forming the polar east-

General circulation of the atmosphere

The sun's rays beat almost straight down at the equator and at a sharp angle at the poles. The equator thus is hot and an area of low pressure. The poles are cold and areas of high pressure. These conditions create six belts of *prevailing winds,* which always move in the same pattern.

WORLD BOOK diagrams by Zorica Dabich

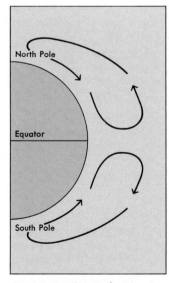

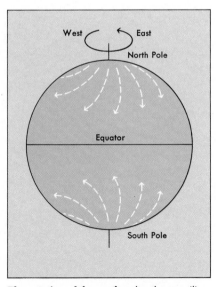

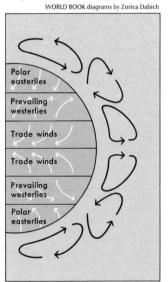

On a nonrotating earth, rising air over the equator would flow directly to the poles. Sinking air over the poles would flow to the equator.

The rotation of the earth makes the prevailing winds seem to curve. For example, winds that flow toward the equator seem to flow from the east. This effect is called the *Coriolis force.*

Prevailing winds circle the earth. The *trade winds* and *polar easterlies* flow toward the equator. The *prevailing westerlies* flow toward the poles.

erlies. The Coriolis force makes these winds seem to blow from the east. Weather in the area of the polar easterlies moves from east to west.

The polar easterlies and the prevailing westerlies meet at the *polar front,* a cloudy, rainy area. Above the polar front is a band of west winds called a *jet stream.* It occurs about 6 to 9 miles (10 to 15 kilometers) above the ground. Its winds may exceed 200 miles (320 kilometers) per hour. See **Jet stream.**

Pressure systems are highs or lows that cover an extremely large area. The area may be as big as 1 million square miles (2.5 million square kilometers), though most pressure systems are smaller. In the United States and Canada, most pressure systems develop along the polar front. There, the cold winds of the polar easterlies and the warmer winds of the prevailing westerlies blow past one another and create swirling winds called *eddies.* The prevailing westerlies carry these eddies eastward across the United States and Canada. There are two types of eddies—*cyclones* and *anticyclones.*

Cyclones formed by eddies are not the same as the storms known as cyclones. The winds of the eddies that create cyclones swirl inward toward a center of low pressure. The cyclone and its low-pressure area form a *low-pressure system.* Because of the rotation of the earth, cyclones that develop north of the equator move in a counterclockwise direction. Cyclones that form south of the equator move in a clockwise direction. In North America, cyclones generally approach on brisk winds, bringing cloudy skies and, usually, rain or snow.

Anticyclones swirl outward around a center of high pressure, forming a *high-pressure system.* North of the equator, anticyclones move in a clockwise direction. South of the equator, they swirl in a counterclockwise direction. Anticyclones follow cyclones, bringing dry, gradually clearing weather, and light winds.

Air masses are enormous bodies of air that form over areas in which the temperature is fairly constant. The air masses take on the temperature of these areas. Air masses may cover 5 million square miles (13 million square kilometers).

The general circulation of the atmosphere continually blows air masses from one area to another. Air masses take on the temperature of the area over which they move, but they do so very slowly because of their great size. Before an area can significantly change an air mass, the air mass influences the area's weather.

There are four major types of air masses: (1) continental polar, (2) continental tropical, (3) maritime polar, and (4) maritime tropical. Continental polar air masses are cold and dry. They develop over such regions as Greenland, northern Canada, and the extreme northern parts of Asia and Europe. Continental tropical air masses are hot and dry. They form over such areas as northern Africa and northern Australia. Maritime polar air masses are cool and moist. They develop over the northern and southern parts of the Atlantic and Pacific oceans. Maritime tropical air masses are warm and moist. They form over the middle of the Atlantic and Pacific oceans and over the Indian Ocean.

How air masses affect North America's weather

The weather in North America is greatly influenced by the movements of *air masses.* These enormous bodies of air form over areas in which the temperature is fairly constant. The air masses take on the temperature of these areas. As the air masses move across great distances, they influence the weather below. The *polar* and *maritime tropical* air masses affect the weather the year around. However, the polar air masses are strongest in winter, and the tropical air masses are strongest in summer. The *Arctic* air mass affects the continent only in winter. The *continental tropical* air mass forms during the warm months and disappears in winter.

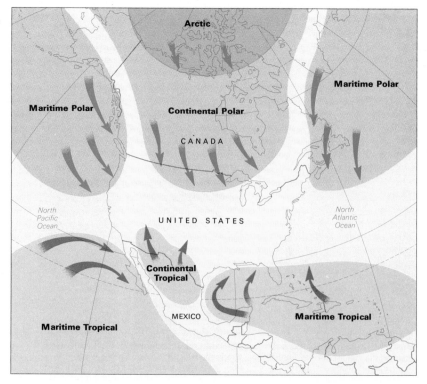

In North America, the continental polar air mass over northern Canada blows cold, dry air into southern Canada and the United States. Maritime polar air masses off the northeast and northwest coasts of North America bring cool, damp weather to the continent. Maritime tropical air masses from the southeast and southwest coasts bring warm, muggy weather. The polar air masses are strongest in the winter, and the tropical air masses are strongest in the summer. During winter, a cold *Arctic* air mass from the North Pole also influences the weather of North America. A continental tropical air mass forms over the southwestern United States during the warm months. It disappears in winter.

Fronts. When a cold air mass and a warm air mass meet, they form a zone called a *front.* There are two main types of fronts—*cold fronts* and *warm fronts.* In a cold front, the edge of an advancing mass of cold air moves under a mass of warm air. The warm air is forced upward, and the cold air replaces it at ground level. In a warm front, the edge of an advancing mass of warm air moves over a retreating mass of cold air. Warm air replaces the retreating cold air at ground level.

Most changes in the weather occur along fronts. The movement of fronts depends on the formation of pressure systems. Cyclones push fronts along at speeds of 20 to 30 miles (32 to 48 kilometers) per hour. Anticy-clones blow into an area after a front has passed.

Cold fronts cause sudden changes in the weather. The kinds of changes depend largely on the amount of moisture in the air that is being replaced. If the air is dry, the front may bring partly cloudy weather but no precipitation. If the air is humid, large clouds may form, bringing rain or snow. The precipitation caused by most cold fronts is heavy but does not last long. Cold fronts also may bring strong winds. The passing of most cold fronts brings a sharp drop in temperature, rapidly clearing skies, and a decrease in humidity.

Warm fronts produce more gradual changes in the weather than do cold fronts. The changes depend chiefly on the humidity of the advancing warm air mass. If the air is dry, wispy clouds may form, and there will be little or no precipitation. If the air is humid, the sky becomes gray. Light, steady rain or snow may fall for several days. In some cases, heavy fog forms. Warm fronts usually have light winds. The passing of a warm front brings a sharp rise in temperature, clearing skies, and an increase in humidity.

Cold fronts travel about twice as fast as warm fronts. As a result, cold fronts often catch up to warm fronts. When a cold front reaches a warm front, an *occluded front* develops. There are two types of occluded fronts—*cold-front occlusions* and *warm-front occlusions.* In a

The formation of fronts   A *front* forms when a cold air mass and a warm air mass meet. The main types of fronts are *cold fronts* and *warm fronts.* Cold fronts travel faster than warm fronts. When a cold front catches up to a warm front, an *occluded front* develops—either a *cold-front occlusion* or a *warm-front occlusion.*

WORLD BOOK diagrams by Zorica Dabich

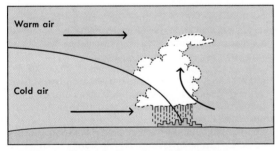

In a cold front, the edge of a mass of cold air moves under a mass of warm air. A cold front often brings periods of heavy precipitation. The passing of the front brings colder weather.

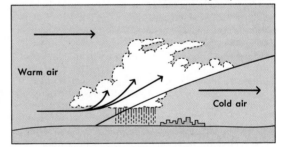

In a warm front, the edge of a mass of warm air moves over a mass of cold air. Warm fronts often produce light, steady precipitation. The passing of a warm front brings warmer weather.

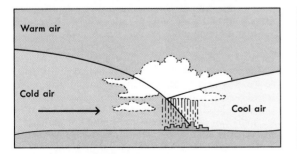

In a cold-front occlusion, the air behind the cold front is colder than the air ahead of the warm front. Such occlusions produce weather like that of a cold front, but not as extreme.

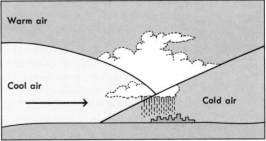

In a warm-front occlusion, the air behind the cold front is warmer than the air ahead of the warm front. Such occlusions result in weather like that of a warm front, though less extreme.

How geographical features affect the weather

When an ocean wind blows against a mountain, the air is lifted and cooled. The water vapor in the air condenses, and large clouds form. The peaks of some mountains are covered by clouds at all times. Because of the rising air currents, the windward side of a mountain usually gets more rain or snow than the other side. In some mountain ranges, the windward side also has more plant life. As air flows over a mountain and down the other side, the air becomes warmer and the clouds evaporate.

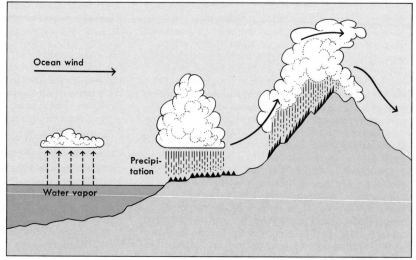

Ocean wind

Precipitation

Water vapor

WORLD BOOK diagram by Zorica Dabich

cold-front occlusion, the air behind the cold front is colder than the air ahead of the warm front. The weather of a cold-front occlusion resembles that of a cold front. In a warm-front occlusion, the air behind the cold front is warmer than the air ahead of the warm front. The weather of a warm-front occlusion resembles that of a warm front. But occluded fronts produce less extreme weather than do cold fronts and warm fronts.

Another type of front occurs when a cold air mass and a warm air mass meet but then move very little. Such a front is called a *stationary front*. It may remain over an area for several days. The weather of a stationary front is usually moderate.

Geographical features of the earth influence the weather in a number of ways. Features that have the greatest effect include mountains and such bodies of water as oceans and huge lakes. But even the geographical difference between a city and the surrounding countryside can affect the weather.

When wind blows against mountains, the air rises and is cooled. The water vapor in the cool air condenses, and clouds form. The peaks of some mountains are covered by clouds at all times. Because of the rising air currents, the windward side of a mountain usually gets more rain and snow than the other side.

As air flows over a mountain and down the other side, the air becomes warmer and takes up moisture by evaporation. In the Rocky Mountains, a warm, dry wind called a *chinook* sometimes flows down the eastern slopes. A chinook may raise the temperature at the foot of the mountains as much as 40° F. (22° C) in three hours. It can melt snow on the ground at the rate of about 1 inch (2.5 centimeters) an hour. Such winds also blow in the Alps and other European mountain systems, where they are known as *foehns*.

Oceans contribute to changes in temperature in coastal areas. Land absorbs heat from the sun faster than the oceans do. But the oceans absorb more heat, and they hold it longer. During the day, the land along coastlines becomes warmer than the seas. As a result, the air

above the land rises, and cool sea breezes blow in to take its place. In tropical climates, a sea breeze may cause a drop in temperature of from 15° to 20° F. (8° to 11° C) within half an hour. Large lakes, such as the Great Lakes, have a similar effect on the weather. In summer, for example, lakes never become as warm as the surrounding land. During the day, lake breezes keep the shoreline cooler than inland areas.

Cities usually have higher temperatures than the surrounding countryside. Automobiles, factories, and the heating systems of buildings create much of the added heat in cities. In addition, such surfaces as pavements and the walls of buildings absorb much heat from the sun and thus warm the air.

The automobiles, factories, and heating plants in cities also release pollutants into the air, including various particles of solid or liquid matter. Water vapor condenses on these particles, forming raindrops. Thus, most cities are rainier than the surrounding area. In addition, sunlight may act on certain pollutants and form a gas called *ozone*. In large amounts, ozone can kill plants and irritate a person's eyes, nose, and throat. A weather condition called a *thermal inversion* enables pollutants to build up over a city. A thermal inversion occurs when a layer of warm air settles over a layer of cool air that lies near the ground. This condition prevents pollutants from rising and scattering.

Storms are periods of violent weather. The main types of storms include (1) thunderstorms, (2) winter storms, (3) tornadoes, and (4) hurricanes.

Thunderstorms are the most common type of storm. As many as 50,000 thunderstorms occur throughout the world each day. In North America, most thunderstorms take place in spring and summer. They develop from tall, puffy *cumulonimbus clouds*. During hot, humid weather, the top of these clouds may reach a height of 80,000 feet (24,000 meters), where the temperature is well below freezing. Inside the cloud, air currents move up and down as fast as 5,000 feet (1,500 meters) per minute. The water vapor in this air condenses rapidly, re-

Some kinds of storms

Storms are periods of violent weather. They can kill people and destroy property. The main types of storms include (1) thunderstorms, (2) winter storms, (3) tornadoes, and (4) hurricanes.

Robert H. Glaze, Artstreet

A thunderstorm brings lightning, thunder, and rain.

Robert H. Glaze, Artstreet

A winter storm can be a cold, blinding snowstorm.

E. R. Degginger, Earth Scenes

A tornado is a deadly, spinning funnel cloud.

E. R. Degginger, Earth Scenes

A hurricane's swirling winds form over tropic seas.

sulting in heavy rain. The motion of the air also causes electrical charges to build up inside the cloud. These charges produce lightning. When lightning flashes, it heats the air around it. The air expands violently and creates the sound waves known as thunder.

Winter storms include *ice storms* and *blizzards*. Most ice storms occur when the temperature is just below freezing. In an ice storm, precipitation falls as rain but freezes as it hits the ground. As a result, a coating of ice forms on the ground and on streets and other surfaces. Ice storms make streets and sidewalks slick and often cause traffic accidents. The weight of the ice can also break power lines, telephone wires, and the branches of trees.

Blizzards are snowstorms with high winds and low temperatures. During a blizzard, the wind blows at 35 miles (56 kilometers) per hour or more, and the temperature may be 10° F. (−12° C) or less. Blowing snow makes it impossible to see more than a short distance. The wind may also pile the snow into huge drifts. See **Blizzard.**

Tornadoes are the most violent of all storms. They consist of winds that swirl in the shape of a funnel at speeds of up to 200 miles (320 kilometers) per hour. The storms destroy almost everything in their path. Most tornadoes measure less than one-half mile (0.8 kilometer) in diameter. A tornado is actually a small, violent cyclone, and tornadoes are sometimes called cyclones. Tornadoes form during thunderstorms and are common in the Midwestern and Southern regions of the United States. See **Tornado.**

Hurricanes are large, whirling storms that form near the equator over the oceans. They may have a diameter of 200 to 300 miles (320 to 480 kilometers). Winds swirl around the *eye* (center) of the storm at speeds of 75 miles (121 kilometers) per hour or more. Hurricanes hit land with tremendous force, bringing huge waves and heavy rain. Thunderstorms often form within hurricanes and produce tornadoes. Many hurricanes cause severe flooding. However, a hurricane weakens rapidly after it strikes land. Most hurricanes in the United States hit areas near the Atlantic Ocean and the Gulf of Mexico. In the western Pacific Ocean, hurricanes are known as *typhoons.* See **Hurricane; Typhoon.**

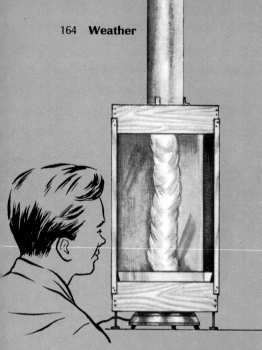

The hurricane generator. A real hurricane begins when the sun heats the ocean, producing a rising cloud of warm, moist air. In the hurricane generator, a cloud of water vapor is formed by heating water in a pan. Cool air enters at the sides of the generator, forcing the cloud to twist upward like a real hurricane.

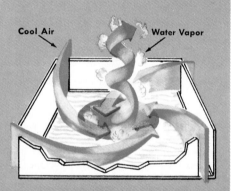

Cool Air   Water Vapor

The direction of spin is controlled by sliding the glass panels to the left or right. A Northern Hemisphere hurricane, *above,* twists counterclockwise. A Southern Hemisphere hurricane, *below,* twists upward in a clockwise way.

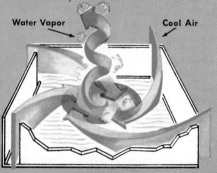

Water Vapor   Cool Air

A *World Book* science project

A homemade hurricane

The purpose of this project is to show how hurricanes form and to demonstrate how the winds of a hurricane spin in different directions in the Northern and Southern Hemispheres.

Caution: This project involves working with electricity, which can cause burns, shock, or fire. If you are not familiar with the precautions for working with electricity, you must have a knowledgeable person help you.

Materials and assembly

You can buy all the materials you need for this project at a hardware store. To build the hurricane generator, first assemble the wooden boxes that serve as the top and bottom. Then attach the corner metal angles to the bottom box, insert three glass walls and a Masonite wall, and attach the upper box and stovepipe. Paint the inside of the top box white to reflect light and heat. Paint the rest of the hurricane generator black.

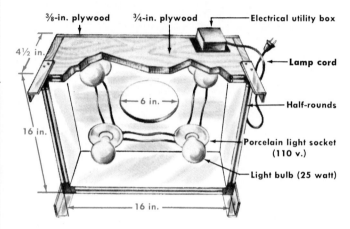

⅜-in. plywood   ¾-in. plywood   Electrical utility box
4½ in.
6 in.   Lamp cord
16 in.   Half-rounds
Porcelain light socket (110 v.)
Light bulb (25 watt)
16 in.

The upper box is built of ¾-inch plywood side pieces and a ⅜-inch plywood top piece. Cut a 6-inch hole in the top for the stovepipe. Cut a 1-inch hole in one side and screw the electrical box over the hole. Fasten half-rounds on the inside and outside edges of the bottom of the box. The half-rounds serve as guides for sliding the pieces of glass and the Masonite.

The lower box is also built of ¾-inch and ⅜-inch plywood. Cut an $8\frac{1}{2}$-inch hole in the top so that a standard 9-inch pie pan fits snugly just below its rim. A close fit is necessary to prevent air from entering around the pan. Drill seven ¼-inch ventilating holes near the top of any two facing sides. Fasten seven half-rounds to the edges of the top of the box. One side should have only an inside half-round so that the Masonite wall can be pulled out easily. You can make legs by nailing strap iron pieces across each corner. Drill a ⅜-inch hole in each piece and use ⅜-inch bolts as legs.

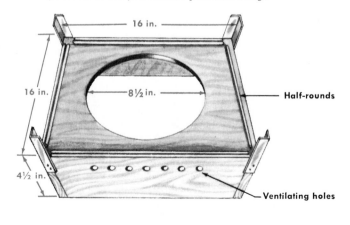

16 in.
16 in.   8½ in.   Half-rounds
4½ in.
Ventilating holes

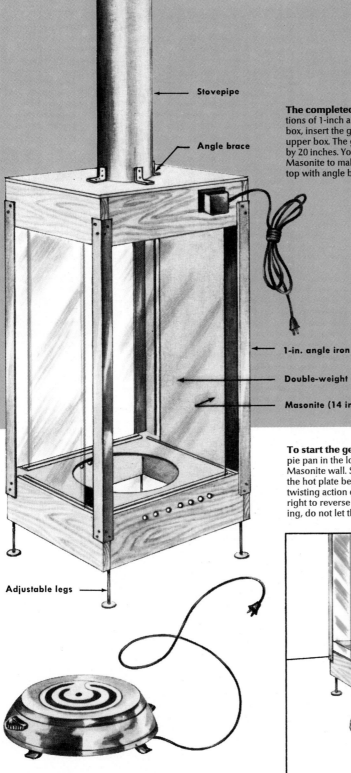

Stovepipe

Angle brace

1-in. angle iron

Double-weight glass (14 in. X 20 in.)

Masonite (14 in. X 20 in.)

Adjustable legs

Electric hot plate (600 to 1100 watt)

The completed generator is assembled using four 2-foot sections of 1-inch angle iron. Attach the angle irons to the bottom box, insert the glass and Masonite side pieces, and attach the upper box. The glass and Masonite should measure 14 inches by 20 inches. You can attach two drawer pulls to the piece of Masonite to make it easier to handle. Attach the stovepipe to the top with angle braces.

To start the generator, remove the Masonite wall and place a pie pan in the lower box. Fill the pan with water and replace the Masonite wall. Slide the glass and Masonite walls to the left. Put the hot plate beneath the generator and turn it on. Note the twisting action of the cloud of vapor. Then move the walls to the right to reverse the direction of the twisting. To avoid overheating, do not let the generator run without water in the pan.

Illustrated by Betty Davis for WORLD BOOK

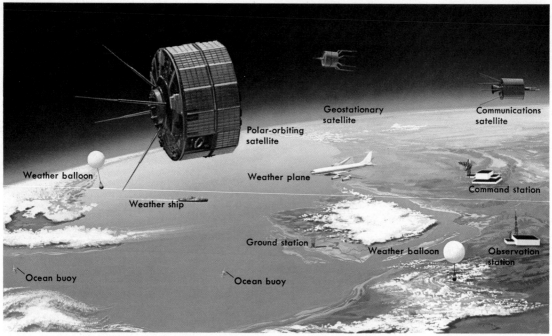

Weather observations around the world are made by a number of facilities, as shown in the artist's representation above. Observation stations measure conditions on land. Balloons send data to ground stations or satellites. Planes and ships also take weather measurements. Buoys transmit data on conditions at sea to satellites. Polar-orbiting and geostationary satellites beam pictures of the earth to command stations. Communications satellites also relay some weather information.

Weather forecasting enables us to make plans based on probable changes in the weather. Every day, millions of people check the weather reports broadcast on radio and television stations and published in newspapers. For most of us, it is usually just a convenience to know in advance what the weather may be. Forecasts help us decide what clothes to wear and whether to plan outdoor activities. But weather forecasts also have much greater importance. For example, reports on the direction and speed of the wind enable airplane pilots to determine how much fuel they need for a flight. Before builders pour concrete, they need to know if it will rain and ruin the concrete before it hardens. If farmers receive warning of a frost, they can take steps to protect their crops. Predictions of tornadoes, hurricanes, and floods can save many lives and reduce the damage to property.

In the United States, an agency of the federal government called the National Weather Service prepares and issues weather forecasts. An agency of the Canadian government, the Atmospheric Environment Service, provides weather forecasts in Canada. Both agencies also issue warnings of severe storms, keep weather records, and study ways to improve weather forecasting.

The scientists who forecast the weather are called *meteorologists.* They collect data on the condition of the atmosphere throughout the world. They use this information to prepare maps that show the temperature, air pressure, wind, and moisture in various areas. The me-

teorologists then analyze the maps and prepare their forecasts.

Observing the weather

Accurate weather forecasts depend on frequent observations of weather conditions throughout the world. Nations probably have shown greater cooperation in exchanging weather data than in any other activity. The World Meteorological Organization (WMO), an agency of the United Nations, sponsors the *World Weather Watch* program. Through this program, weather information is collected by the more than 140 nations that belong to the WMO. The information is then distributed among the member nations by means of a worldwide communications network. The meteorological agencies of the member nations provide the facilities for the program. The facilities for observing the weather include (1) observation stations, (2) weather balloons, and (3) satellites.

Observation stations record weather conditions on land. There are more than 3,500 stations around the world. They take hourly measurements of temperature, air pressure, wind direction and speed, humidity, rainfall, and other conditions. The stations transmit the information to centers where weather forecasts are prepared.

Observation stations use various instruments to record weather conditions. *Thermometers* measure the temperature of the air. *Barometers* show the air pressure. *Weather vanes* indicate the direction of the wind. *Anemometers* measure wind speed. *Hygrometers* measure the amount of moisture in the air. *Rain gauges* measure the amount of rainfall or snowfall. For more information, see the separate articles on these instruments in *World Book.*

Some observation stations also use radar to detect distant areas where rain is falling. A radar system sends out radio waves, which are reflected by raindrops and ice particles in clouds. The returning waves can be detected up to about 250 miles (400 kilometers) away. The location of the rainy area appears on a screen that resembles a television screen. By using radar, meteorologists can determine the direction in which a storm is moving and its speed. In many cases, the strength of the reflected waves reveals what type of storm is approaching. For example, the waves returned by hailstones in a thunderstorm are quite strong. Radar enables meteorologists to predict when a storm will pass over a certain area.

Weather balloons measure conditions in the upper atmosphere. Every day, about 800 observation stations around the world launch two balloons each. The balloons are filled with helium or hydrogen and carry an instrument called a *radiosonde.* Radiosondes take *soundings* (measurements) of the atmosphere and send the information to stations on the ground by means of a radio transmitter. The instruments measure the temperature, air pressure, and humidity of the air at various altitudes. The direction and speed of the wind are determined by tracking the movement of the balloons with direction-finding equipment on the ground. As the balloons rise, the gas inside expands. When the balloons reach a height of about 90,000 feet (27,000 meters), they burst. A parachute attached to the radiosonde then opens and carries the device back to the ground.

Emil Schulthess, Black Star

Weather balloons carry instruments that measure the conditions of the atmosphere at high altitudes and transmit the data to earth. This balloon is being released from a station in Antarctica.

Another type of weather balloon, called a *constant-level balloon,* floats at a certain altitude. The gas inside these balloons remains at a fairly constant pressure. The size of the balloon determines the altitude at which it floats. Constant-level balloons can remain aloft for many months. They provide long-term measurements of weather conditions at a certain altitude. The balloons transmit the data to satellites, which relay the information to stations on the ground.

Satellites carry television cameras that take pictures of the earth. The pictures show the pattern of clouds above the earth and large areas of snow and ice on the ground. The satellites beam picture signals to stations on the ground, where photographs are prepared from the signals. By studying these photographs, meteorologists can spot hurricanes and other dangerous storms developing over the oceans. The weather service can then issue warnings before the storms hit land. Satellites also take measurements of temperature and humidity. In addition, meteorologists can determine wind direction and speed by observing the movement of clouds in a series of satellite photographs.

There are two main kinds of weather satellites—*polar-orbiting* and *geostationary.* Polar-orbiting weather satellites circle the earth at an altitude of between about 500 and 900 miles (800 and 1,400 kilometers). The satel-

Milt and Joan Mann

Weather radar helps meteorologists detect areas where rain is falling. Radio waves sent out by a radar system are reflected by raindrops, and the rainy areas appear on a screen, *above.*

National Oceanic and Atmospheric Administration

A satellite photograph of North America shows the pattern of clouds over the continent. The swirling pattern off the northeast coast of the United States is a hurricane.

lite's orbit carries it over the North and South poles. Because the earth rotates, the satellite passes over different areas of the earth each orbit. The pictures taken by a polar-orbiting satellite may cover up to 4 million square miles (10 million square kilometers), or about 2 per cent of the earth's surface. Some polar-orbiting satellites can photograph the entire earth twice a day.

Geostationary satellites, also called *geosynchronous satellites,* orbit the equator at an altitude of about 22,300

miles (35,890 kilometers). At this altitude, the satellite's motion is *synchronized* with the earth's rotation—that is, the satellite moves in unison with the earth. The satellite completes one orbit during the time that the earth makes one rotation. Thus, it stays in one position over the earth. Because geostationary satellites orbit at such a high altitude, they can take pictures that cover a much wider area than those of polar-orbiting satellites. The pictures from four properly placed geostationary satellites can cover the entire earth at once.

Other observation facilities include airplanes and ships. Some commercial airplanes have special equipment that records the direction and speed of the wind and the temperature at flight level. A number of the planes can transmit the information to geostationary satellites. Special weather planes also take measurements of atmospheric conditions. In addition, the planes release a type of radiosonde called a *dropsonde,* which records weather conditions as it floats to the ground by parachute.

Merchant ships and weather ships relay information on weather conditions to ground stations by means of radio transmitters. Weather ships also launch balloons that record conditions in the upper atmosphere. In addition, the ships release special ocean *buoys,* devices that float on water. The buoys record weather conditions at sea level and transmit the information to polar-orbiting satellites. Some buoys are anchored in the water, and others drift with the current.

Analyzing weather information

Making a weather map. The information collected by observation stations, balloons, satellites, and other facilities is used to make weather maps. In the United States, computers of the National Weather Service

---

A weather map

Maps like the one below appear in many U.S. daily newspapers and are based on National Weather Service reports. The map shows the weather conditions expected across the nation at a certain time of the day. It also predicts the high and low temperature for the day in various cities.

Weather map symbols

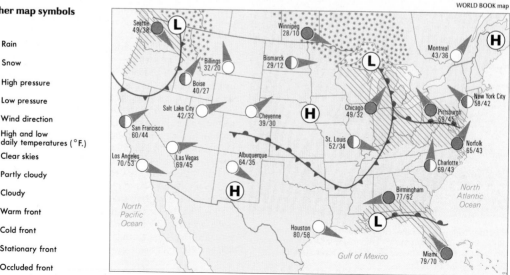

WORLD BOOK map

prepare maps of the nation, the continent, and the world. Simplified versions of the maps of the United States appear in newspapers and on television weather reports.

Meteorologists at the National Weather Service use several types of maps and charts in making their forecasts. A *surface weather map* shows the weather conditions that were measured at the earth's surface at a certain time of day. The maps have lines called *isotherms,* which connect places that recorded the same temperature. Lines called *isobars* connect places that had the same air pressure. Winds tend to blow almost parallel to isobars. If the isobars are close together, the winds are strong. If they are far apart, the winds are light. Surface weather maps also indicate the positions of fronts. Shaded areas on the maps represent precipitation.

A *500-millibar chart* shows the temperature, wind direction and speed, and humidity that were measured at an average altitude of about 18,400 feet (5,608 meters). At this altitude, air pressure equals about *500 millibars,* or about half the average air pressure at sea level. A *temperature chart* indicates the highest and lowest surface temperatures in various places over a 24-hour period. A *precipitation chart* tells where precipitation occurred during a 24-hour period. *Forecast maps* predict the temperature, air pressure, wind direction and speed, humidity, and precipitation at a certain time on a particular day. Computers prepare these maps by solving complex mathematical formulas, using the weather observations as a starting point.

Predicting the weather involves analyzing the various types of maps and charts. The National Weather Service prepares two main kinds of forecasts—*short-range forecasts* and *extended forecasts.* Short-range forecasts predict the weather over the next 18 to 36 hours. These forecasts are updated several times a day as meteorologists receive new weather data. There are several types of extended forecasts. One kind predicts the weather over the next 5 days. Meteorologists update 5-day forecasts daily. Another type of forecast covers the next 6 to 10 days. These forecasts are updated three times a week. Meteorologists also prepare 30-day forecasts. These forecasts are updated twice a month. The longer the period a forecast covers, the fewer details it includes and the less likely it is to be accurate.

Meteorologists cannot rely on forecast maps alone to make accurate predictions. For a number of reasons, the computer forecast maps are often wrong. One reason is that the formulas used by the computers are only approximate descriptions of the behavior of the atmosphere. In addition, exact predictions are often inaccurate because there are so many possible weather conditions and the conditions change so quickly. Forecast maps are more accurate in predicting general conditions of the atmosphere than in predicting the weather at a certain place and a certain time.

In addition to forecast maps, meteorologists analyze other maps and charts to predict the weather in a particular city. One reason some of their predictions are inaccurate is that not enough weather observations are made throughout the world. Most land areas have some observation stations. But not enough weather planes, ships, and ocean buoys are available to observe all of the oceans, which cover more than two-thirds of the earth's surface. The condition of the atmosphere over large areas of the ocean is rarely observed except by satellite. Satellites alone do not provide enough information on these areas. Thus, meteorologists cannot always tell what type of weather will be moving to a certain part of the world.

Milt and Joan Mann

Computers of the U.S. National Weather Service constantly receive weather data from such sources as observation stations, balloons, and satellites. The computers analyze and use the information to prepare the latest weather maps and forecasts.

People have tried to predict the weather for thousands of years. More than 4,000 years ago, people made forecasts based on the position of the stars. Some ancient peoples believed such weather conditions as rain, thunder, and wind were controlled by various gods.

The earliest weather instrument, the rain gauge, was probably invented before the 300's B.C. The weather vane was developed by about 50 B.C. But weather forecasting did not become reliable until the invention of a number of other scientific instruments.

Beginnings of modern weather forecasting. In A.D. 1593, the Italian scientist Galileo developed a type of thermometer. In 1643, Evangelista Torricelli of Italy, a pupil of Galileo's, invented a simple barometer. Scientists soon realized that differences in air pressure accounted for certain changes in the weather. The English astronomer Edmond Halley made the first weather map in 1686. The map charted the flow of the trade winds. In 1783, Horace Bénédict de Saussure of Switzerland first described the principle of the hair hygrometer, which uses hair to measure humidity.

Weather maps of the early 1800's showed that weather systems move with the prevailing winds. But at the time, this knowledge could not be used to warn people of approaching storms. Reports of weather observations were sent by mail, and the storms arrived before the mail.

In 1844, the American inventor Samuel F. B. Morse perfected the telegraph. The telegraph enabled meteorologists to quickly send weather observations from one city to another. In 1849, Joseph Henry, the secretary of the Smithsonian Institution in Washington, D.C., received the first weather report sent by telegraph in the United States. In 1856, France became the first nation to establish a weather service that relied on telegraphed reports. Great Britain began a similar service in 1860. Canada established its weather service in 1871.

The first national weather forecasting agency in the United States was formed in 1870 as part of the Army Signal Service. In 1890, Congress organized an agency called the Weather Bureau. Its name was changed to the National Weather Service in 1970.

Scientific advances in the 1900's. Until the early 1900's, weather forecasting consisted largely of predicting the movement of high- and low-pressure areas. Then, a Norwegian physicist named Vilhelm Bjerknes developed a new explanation for changes in the weather. Bjerknes believed that the movement of enormous masses of air greatly influenced weather conditions. He suggested that when a warm air mass and a cold air mass meet, a zone of rapidly changing weather develops. Bjerknes called these weather zones *fronts.* This theory greatly improved the accuracy of weather forecasting.

Lewis Fry Richardson, a British mathematician, believed that, because the behavior of the atmosphere follows the laws of physics, mathematics could be used to predict the weather. In the 1920's, Richardson developed calculations that applied the laws of physics to the varying conditions of the atmosphere. Using these calculations, scientists could forecast changes in the condition of the atmosphere. However, Richardson's calculations took so much time to perform that weather conditions passed before a forecast could be prepared.

In the 1940's, the first practical electronic digital computers were developed. A group of American meteorologists and mathematicians led by John von Neumann began formulating equations that would enable computers to predict the weather. The first successful weather forecast prepared by computer was announced in 1950. Since then, scientists have worked to perfect the equations for computer forecasting.

During the 1900's, great advances have been made in the development of equipment for observing the weather. In the 1930's, radiosondes came into common use. Radar was first used for weather observation in the 1940's. In 1959, the United States launched the first satellite to send weather information back to earth. *Tiros I,* the first weather satellite equipped with a television camera, was put into orbit in 1960. The first full-time weather satellite in geostationary orbit was launched in 1974.

Attempts to control the weather. Throughout history, people have tried to control the weather. Today, scientists are experimenting with methods to control such weather conditions as rain, fog, hail, hurricanes, and lightning. They have achieved the greatest success in producing rain by a method called *cloud seeding.* In this method, various chemicals are either sprayed or dropped into clouds by airplanes, or they are released from the ground and carried upward by the wind. The chemicals cause the drops of water in the clouds to fall. See **Rainmaking.**

Cloud seeding has most often been used to increase rainfall in dry regions. However, the method does not work unless clouds are almost ready to produce rain. Cloud seeding also has been used to prevent heavy rainfall that could damage crops in certain areas. Seeding causes most of the rain to fall before the clouds reach such areas.   Yoshi Kazu Sasaki

Study aids

Related articles in *World Book* include:

Elements of weather

Blizzard	Dew	Fog	Lightning
Calms, Regions of	Doldrums	Frost	Monsoon
Chinook	Drought	Hail	Norther
Cloud	Dust devil	Harmattan	Prevailing westerly
Cloudburst	Dust storm	Horse latitudes	Rain
Cyclone	Foehn	Humidity	Rainbow
		Hurricane	Sandstorm
		Ice	Sirocco
		Jet stream	Sleet

Snow	Thunder	Typhoon
Squall	Tornado	Waterspout
Storm	Trade wind	Wind
Temperature		

Weather instruments

Anemometer	Radiosonde
Balloon (Scientific uses)	Rain gauge
Barometer	Space travel (Weather
Hygrometer	satellites)
Kite	Thermocouple
Radar (In weather observation	Thermometer
and forecasting)	Weather vane

Other related articles

Air	Meteorology
Airport (Watching the	Rainmaking
weather)	Season
Autumn	Spring
Boating (picture: Warning	Summer
signals)	Sunspot
Climate	Troposphere
Dust	Weather Service,
Evaporation	National
Flag (picture: Flags that talk)	Wind chill
Indian summer	Winter
Isobar	World Meteorological
Isotherm	Organization
Langmuir, Irving	

Outline

I. What makes up weather
  A. Temperature   C. Wind
  B. Air pressure   D. Moisture
II. How weather develops and changes
  A. General circulation of   D. Fronts
     the atmosphere   E. Geographical features
  B. Pressure systems   F. Storms
  C. Air masses
III. Weather forecasting
  A. Observing the weather
  B. Analyzing weather information
IV. Development of weather forecasting

Questions

What is the *Coriolis force?*
Why are some weather predictions inaccurate?
What is the difference between a region's weather and its climate?
What is a *front?* How do cold fronts and warm fronts affect the weather?
What is the *dew point?*
In what direction does weather move in the area of the prevailing westerlies?
What is a *radiosonde?*
What kinds of weather information do satellites provide?
What is *cloud seeding?*
In what way does the atmosphere get most of its heat?

Additional resources

Level I
Adler, David. *World of Weather.* Troll, 1983.
Lambert, David. *Weather.* Watts, 1983.
Sattler, Helen R. *Nature's Weather Forecasters.* Nelson, 1978.
Weiss, Malcolm E. *What's Happening to Our Climate?* Simon & Messner, 1978.

Level II
Battan, Louis J. *Weather in Your Life.* Freeman, 1983.
Dunlop, S., and Wilson, F. *The Larousse Guide to Weather Forecasting.* Larousse, 1982.
Hardy, Ralph, and others. *The Weather Book.* Little, Brown, 1982.
Holford, Ingrid. *The Guinness Book of Weather: Facts & Feats.* 2nd ed. Guinness Superlatives, 1984.
Lydolph, Paul E. *Weather and Climate.* Rowman and Allanheld, 1985.

The Weather Almanac. Ed. by James A. Ruffner and F. E. Bair. 5th ed. Gale Research, 1987.

Weather balloon. See Balloon; Weather (Weather balloons; pictures).

Weather bureau. See Weather Service, National.

Weather forecasting. See Weather (Weather forecasting; Development of weather forecasting).

Weather satellite. See Weather (Satellites; Scientific advances in the 1900's; pictures).

Weather Service, National, provides forecasts, warnings, statements, observations, and records of the weather and certain water resources in the United States and its territories. It is a part of the National Oceanic and Atmospheric Administration (NOAA) of the U.S. Department of Commerce. The National Weather Service issues warnings of hurricanes, tornadoes, severe thunderstorms, flash floods, and other dangerous storms. It measures rainfall and river levels to forecast navigation, flood, and water-supply conditions, and issues special weather information for farmers, airplane pilots, mariners, and fire fighters. The National Weather Service records the climate of the United States and other countries, and studies ways to improve weather forecasting.

The agency has administrative headquarters in Washington, D.C., and regional offices on Long Island, N.Y., and in Kansas City, Mo.; Fort Worth, Texas; Salt Lake City, Utah; Honolulu, Hawaii; and Anchorage, Alaska. About 300 weather stations in the United States and its possessions have full-time staffs. These stations generally take observations every hour. They observe weather conditions and issue local information. The National Weather Service also has over 12,000 substations that gather climate information.

Weather reports pour into the National Meteorological Center, the Weather Service's central computer complex located near Washington, D.C. There, the Analysis and Forecast, Computation, and Extended Forecast branches analyze the reports. They make generalized forecasts with the aid of high-speed computers and distribute this material to local offices. The Weather Service also exchanges reports with other nations.

The National Severe Storm Forecast Center at Kansas City, Mo., watches the entire nation for conditions that may produce tornadoes or other severe local storms. The National Hurricane Center in Miami, Fla., provides forecasts and warnings of tropical storms threatening the East and Gulf coasts of the United States. Hurricane centers in San Francisco and Honolulu provide such information for Pacific areas.

Several federal agencies work with the Weather Service. For example, the Coast Guard gathers information about the weather from merchant ships. The Federal Aviation Administration helps gather weather information at airport stations, and it supplies weather reports to pilots.

Weather advice, forecasts, reports, and warnings are given to the public by means of newspapers, radio, television, and telephone. The Weather Service also broadcasts reports through its own radio program, NOAA Weather Radio (NWR). The public tunes into a local NWR station by using a special high-frequency receiver.

The U.S. public weather service began in 1870 as part of the Army Signal Service. In 1890, Congress organized the Weather Bureau under the Department of Agriculture. The President transferred the bureau to the Department of Commerce in 1940. In 1965, Congress made it part of the Environmental Science Services Administration, a branch of the Department of Commerce. The bureau was renamed the National Weather Service in 1970, when it became part of the National Oceanic and Atmospheric Administration.

Critically reviewed by the National Weather Service

See also **Weather** (Weather forecasting; Development of weather forecasting).

Weather vane is a device that turns freely on an upright rod and points in the direction from which wind comes. It is also called a *wind vane* or *weathercock.* The weather vane is one of the oldest weather instruments and is often ornamental in shape.

The part of the vane which turns into the wind is usu-

Shostal

A weather vane shows the direction from which wind blows. The weather vane is one of the oldest weather instruments.

ally shaped like an arrow. The other end is wide, so it will catch the smallest breeze. The breeze turns the arrow until it catches both sides of the wide end equally. Thus, the arrow always points into the wind. Below the arrow is a round plate on which the directions are marked. Some vanes, such as those used at weather stations, have electrical connections that record and display wind direction in a room that is far from the vane itself.   David D. Houghton

Weathering. See Earth (How the earth changes); **Soil** (How soil is formed).

Weaver, Robert Clifton (1907-   ), served as secretary of the Department of Housing and Urban Development under President Lyndon B. Johnson from 1966 through 1968. As head of the new department, Weaver became the first black Cabinet member in United States history.

Weaver was born in Washington, D.C. He received B.S., M.A., and Ph.D. degrees from Harvard University. He began his government career in 1933 as adviser on black affairs in the Department of the Interior. Weaver was named New York Deputy State Housing Commissioner in 1954. Appointed State Rent Administrator in 1955, he became the first black to attain New York state cabinet rank. From 1961 to 1966 he served as administrator of the federal Housing and Home Finance Agency.

Weaver also served as chairman of the National Association for the Advancement of Colored People (NAACP). He received the Spingarn Medal in 1962. Weaver was president of Bernard M. Baruch College in New York City from 1969 to 1970.   Carl T. Rowan

Weaverbird is a type of small bird that usually weaves a hanging nest. There are about 290 kinds of weaverbirds. They live in most parts of the world. The familiar *house sparrow* found in the United States is a weaverbird. Weaverbirds eat seeds and grain. They chatter continually. Most females and young weaverbirds are plainly colored. But the males are generally brightly colored during the mating season.

The *sociable weaver* of South Africa builds an umbrella-shaped community roof of sticks and grass in a tree. The roof may be up to 25 feet (7.6 meters) long and 15 feet (4.6 meters) wide. The underside of the roof is divided into compartments, each occupied by a pair of birds. As many as 95 individual nests have been counted under one roof. The female lays three or four speckled, purple-gray eggs.

The *village weaver* of Africa tears palm leaves with its beak and then uses the shredded leaves to weave its nest. The *baya weaver* of India and Sri Lanka builds a flask-shaped nest with a long tunnel entrance.

Scientific classification. Weaverbirds belong to the families Passeridae and Ploceidae. The house sparrow is *Passer domesticus,* and the sociable weaver is *Philetairus socius.* The village weaver is *Ploceus cucullatus,* and the baya is *Ploceus philippinus.*   Fred J. Alsop III

See also **Bird** (picture: Birds of Africa).

Arthur Gloor, Animals Animals

A weaverbird builds a hanging nest by weaving grass and twigs together. Some nests have tunnel entrances.

The craft of weaving has been practiced throughout the world for thousands of years. These Tunisian girls are handweaving a colorful wool rug with traditional patterns on a large floor loom in their home.

Marge Kathan

Weaving is the process of making cloth by crossing two sets of threads over and under each other. Many fabrics and most blankets, clothing, and rugs are woven. Weavers may use thread spun from such natural fibers as cotton, silk, and wool. Strong artificially made fibers, including nylon and Orlon, are also popular.

Narrow strips of almost any flexible material can also be woven. People learned to weave thousands of years ago with grasses, leafstalks, palm leaves, and thin strips of wood. Today, craftworkers throughout the world still use such fibers to weave baskets, hats, and other articles. Weaving also plays an important part in the manufacture of such products as screens, metal fences, and rubber tire cord.

Weaving ranks as a major industry in Japan, the Soviet Union, the United States, and many other countries. In the United States, the value of factory-woven goods totals more than $3\frac{1}{2}$ billion yearly. Weaving is also a popular craft. Artists exhibit and sell decorative woven items at art fairs, galleries, and museums. Many people design and weave colorful fabrics as a hobby.

Types of weaves

Weavers use three basic kinds of weaves: (1) the *plain weave,* or *tabby weave;* (2) the *twill weave;* and (3) the *satin weave.* More complex types of weaves are known as *fancy weaves.* All weaves consist of two sets of threads. One set, called the *warp,* stretches lengthwise on a loom or frame. To make cloth, the weaver repeatedly draws a set of crosswise threads called the *weft* over and under the warp. The weft is sometimes called the *woof* or the *filling.*

The plain weave, or *tabby weave,* is the simplest and most common type of weave. In the odd-numbered rows of this weave, a weft thread passes under the first warp thread, over the second, and so on. In the even-numbered rows, the weft passes over the first warp, under the second, and so on. This close weave produces a strong, flat-textured cloth that wears well. Plain-woven fabrics include gingham, muslin, and percale.

The *basket weave,* a variation of the plain weave, has a bulkier texture that resembles the weaves of a basket. The weft is drawn under two or more warp threads, then over the same number of threads, and so on. This method adds fullness to the weave.

The twill weave produces sturdy cloth that has raised diagonal lines. Each weft thread crosses two, three, or four warp threads at a time, creating extra width. This added width makes a decorative fabric that holds its shape despite repeated wear. Each row of weft threads follows the same pattern. But each row's pattern begins slightly to the right or left of the pattern in the

Some kinds of weaves

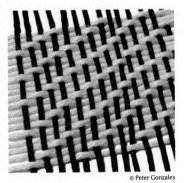

© Peter Gonzales

The plain, or tabby, weave is the simplest type of weave. A *weft* (crosswise thread) passes under one *warp* (lengthwise thread), over the next, and so on.

The twill weave forms diagonal lines in fabric. The weft crosses several warps at once. Each row's pattern begins slightly left or right of that of the previous row.

The satin weave produces such luxurious fabrics as rayon, satin, and silk. Each weft spans up to 12 warps in creating a smooth, glossy finish.

previous row. This technique puts a series of diagonal lines in the fabric. The weaver may create unusual patterns by changing the direction of the weave and adding various colored threads.

Common twill fabrics include denim, flannel, gabardine, and serge. The twill weave produces strong, tightly-woven cloth used to make coats, work clothes, and men's suits.

The satin weave makes soft, luxurious fabrics, such as damask, sateen, and satin. The wefts of a satin weave can cover as many as 12 warps. The threads may interlace at such wide intervals that the diagonal line of the weave cannot be seen without a magnifying glass. Satinweave cloth may snag easily. It is used to make such products as draperies and formal clothes.

Fancy weaves produce a variety of designs and textures in fabric. A *pile weave* has cut or looped weft yarns that extend above the fabric surface and provide a furry texture. Pile weaves include corduroy, terrycloth, velvet, and most carpet fabrics. A *double weave* binds two layers of cloth together for added strength and warmth. Blankets, coats, drapes, and upholstery fabrics may be double woven. A *gauze weave* is a loose, open weave that makes a sheer, lightweight fabric. The warp threads are arranged in pairs and twisted around the weft threads. Gauze-woven cotton, rayon, and silk make attractive curtains and lightweight clothing.

Weaving on a loom

How a loom works. Almost all looms have the same basic features and weave fabric in much the same way. On most looms, cloth is woven on a metal or wooden frame located at the front of the loom and parallel to the floor.

The weaver must thread the loom before weaving. A set of warp threads is wound onto a cylinder called the *warp beam* at the back of the loom. Each warp thread is then passed through one of two or more vertical frames called *harnesses*. The number of harnesses depends on the complexity of the weave. In the harnesses, each

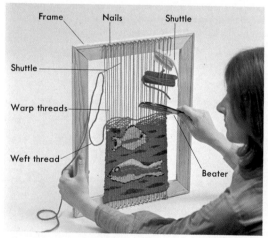

Frame   Nails   Shuttle

Shuttle

Warp threads

Weft thread

Beater

WORLD BOOK photo

A simple hand loom can be made from a picture frame. Nails hammered into the top and bottom of the frame hold the warp in place. This photograph shows a weaver using a comb as the beater. A needle and two pieces of cardboard serve as shuttles.

warp is threaded through a narrow opening in one of many strings or wires called *heddles.* The heddles hold the individual threads in place and prevent them from tangling. The warp threads then stretch over the weaving frame.

Next, the weaver winds the weft thread around a spool called the *bobbin.* The bobbin is held in an oblong metal or wood container called the *shuttle.* The shuttle serves as a needle that draws the weft thread over and under the warp. The weaving process begins when the weaver lifts the harness that holds the odd-numbered threads. This action creates a space called the *shed* through which the shuttle and weft then pass. Finally, the weaver lowers the first harness and pushes the newly woven row into place with a device called the *beater,* or *reed.* The beater is in a frame located in front of, and parallel to, the harnesses. It has comblike "teeth" made of steel wires that push each weft row compactly into place to tighten the weave.

To weave the next row, the weaver raises the second harness and passes the shuttle through the shed. The weaving of each row involves the same process. The finished cloth is wound around a bar called the *apron beam,* or *cloth beam,* at the front of the loom.

Kinds of looms. There are two basic types of looms, hand looms and power looms. A hand loom is any loom that is not power driven, such as a *table loom* or a *floor loom.*

A table loom is a compact, portable device that stands on a table or some other flat surface. Table looms of various sizes can weave cloth that measures from 8 to 36 inches (20 to 91 centimeters) wide. Table looms generally have from 2 to 8 harnesses, which the weaver controls by raising and lowering levers by hand. A table loom threads easily and costs less than most other kinds of looms. But weaving on a hand loom can be tiring because the weaver must put down the shuttle and operate the harnesses manually after every row.

Floor looms are large and stationary and measure from 20 inches (51 centimeters) to 5 feet (1.5 meters) wide. The weaver raises and lowers the harnesses of a floor loom by pressing foot pedals called *treadles.* This action frees the weaver's hands to pass the shuttle rhythmically through the sheds. Such rhythm adds speed and enjoyment to the weaving process.

Power looms produce millions of yards of textiles on factory assembly lines yearly. Looms run by steam, electricity, or water power have shuttles that refill automatically and can move as fast as 60 miles (97 kilometers) an hour. The beaters and harnesses on power looms move faster than the eye can follow.

Weaving without a loom

Artists and hobbyists have developed many ways to weave without a mechanical loom. In *paper weaving,* for example, strips of colored construction paper serve as the warps and wefts. The weaver interlaces the strips by hand to make place mats, wallhangings, and other decorative objects.

In *finger weaving,* or *Indian braiding,* several pieces of cord tied together at one end serve as the warp. A longer cord, also attached to the warp, is threaded over and under the lengthwise pieces to make belts and sashes. Some artists weave reeds, yarn, and other mate-

Burlington Industries, Inc.

Large commercial looms can weave about 19 yards (17 meters) of plain, heavyweight fabric per hour.

rials through flexible wire screens. The weaver can then bend the decorated wire into sculptural forms.

A loom made from a piece of cardboard can be used to weave yarn place mats, potholders, and purses. Evenly spaced notches cut at the top and bottom of the cardboard hold the warps in place. The weaver slips a stick under alternate warp threads to create a shed and passes a threaded needle through the shed.

History

Thousands of years ago, people discovered how to weave baskets from grasses. Historians do not know when the process of weaving cloth developed. But civilizations in central Europe, the Middle East, and Pakistan probably had learned to weave textiles by 2500 B.C. Ancient wall-paintings illustrate weaving techniques mastered by the Egyptians as early as 5000 B.C.

The Chinese learned to weave sometime between 2500 and 1200 B.C. They became famous for spinning silk thread that was woven into exquisite brocade and damask fabrics in Persia (now Iran) and Syria.

The Pueblo and other Indian tribes of what is now the Southwestern United States began to weave cotton textiles during the A.D. 700's. The two-bar loom mounted in a frame was used in Europe by the 1200's. By the 1400's, the art of weaving had become highly developed in Europe. For example, skilled weavers in the city of Arras, in what is now France, produced beautiful tapestries that decorated castles and cathedrals.

The greatest improvements in machinery for weaving came during the Industrial Revolution, a period of rapid industrial growth in Europe during the 1700's and early 1800's. In 1785, an English inventor named Edmund Cartwright developed the first power loom (see **Cartwright, Edmund**). The French inventor Joseph M. Jacquard developed the Jacquard loom in 1801. It uses punched cards and other attachments that guide the threads in weaving complex patterns.

Today, many textile firms use high-speed looms that have many tiny shuttles called *darts* instead of a single large shuttle. The darts pick up weft yarns that lie beside the loom and pass them through the shed faster than other kinds of shuttles.   Dona Z. Meilach

Related articles in *World Book* include:

Basket making	Ireland (picture)
Beadwork	Jacquard, Joseph M.
Colonial life in America (picture:	Northern Ireland (picture)
Spinning and weaving)	Rugs and carpets
Handicraft (picture)	Spinning jenny
Indian, American (pictures)	Tapestry
Industrial Revolution (The textile	Textile
industry)	

Additional resources

Black, Mary E. *The Key to Weaving: A Textbook of Hand Weaving for the Beginning Weaver.* Rev. ed. Macmillan, 1980.
Held, Shirley E. *Weaving: A Handbook of the Fiber Arts.* 2nd ed. Holt, 1978.
Morrison, Phylis. *Spiders' Games: A Book for Beginning Weavers.* Univ. of Washington Press, 1979. Explains weaving without a loom.

Web. See Spider.

Webb, Sidney and Beatrice, were British social reformers. The Webbs, husband and wife, were also noted historians of the labor movement in Great Britain. Their activities led to reforms that aided the poor, strengthened the labor movement, and improved public education.

Sidney James Webb (1859-1947) was born in London. His father was a bookkeeper. In 1885, Sidney joined the Fabian Society, an organization of British socialists. He remained one of its leaders for the rest of his life and helped make social research the society's chief interest.

Beatrice Webb (1858-1943) was born into a wealthy and socially prominent family on an estate near Gloucester. Her maiden name was Martha Beatrice Potter. Her interest in social research brought her into contact with Sidney Webb, and they were married in 1892.

Sidney entered politics as a member of the London County Council in 1892. In the council, he helped reshape education programs in London. The Webbs took the lead in founding the London School of Economics and Political Science in 1895. Beatrice's wealth enabled the couple to devote themselves to the study of the British labor movement. They wrote a number of pioneering books, notably *The History of Trade Unionism* (1894) and *Industrial Democracy* (1897).

From 1906 to 1909, Beatrice served on the Royal Commission on the Poor Law, which investigated poverty in Britain. She and Sidney wrote a minority report for the commission that called for passage of legislation that would guarantee a minimum standard of living for all citizens. In 1913, the Webbs established the *New Statesman,* a weekly periodical, to promote their socialist views.

Sidney became active in the Labour Party during World War I (1914-1918) and was elected to its executive committee. He prepared the statement in 1918 that first committed the party to socialism. In 1922, Sidney was elected to Parliament. He held Cabinet posts in Labour governments in 1924 and from 1929 to 1931.

During the 1920's and 1930's, Beatrice revised and edited the detailed diary she had kept since 1872. The resulting books, *My Apprenticeship* (1926) and *Our Partnership* (1948), form an eloquent record of the Webbs' productive careers.   Willard Wolfe

Webelos. See Boy Scouts (Cub Scouting).

Weber, *VAY buhr* or *WEE buhr,* is a unit used to measure magnetic flux in a magnetic field. The concentration of flux determines the strength of a magnetic field. A strong magnetic field may have a strength of two or more webers per square meter. The weber was named for the German physicist Wilhelm Weber. It equals 100 million units called *maxwells.*   Samuel Seely

Weber, *VAY buhr,* **Carl Maria von** (1786-1826), was the first important composer of German romantic opera. This kind of opera is based on conflict between a mortal and a supernatural being.

Weber's most popular romantic opera is *Der Freischütz (The Free-Shooter,* 1821). This opera tells about a pact that a hunter makes with the devil to get magic bullets that will strike anything he chooses. An important romantic feature of *Der Freischütz* is its atmospheric settings. A major scene takes place in a frightening wild rocky place called the "Wolf's Glen." The rest of the story is set in a friendlier region inhabited by hunters and farmers. Weber's other operas include *Euryanthe* (1823) and *Oberon* (1826). His other works include the piano piece *Invitation to the Dance* (1819). Weber was born in Eutin, near Lübeck.

Robert Bailey

Weber, *VAY buhr,* **Max** (1864-1920), was a German sociologist and economist. His theories and writings helped establish the foundations of modern sociology. Weber considered *bureaucracy* to be the most important feature of modern society. Bureaucracy is a method of organization based on specialization of duties, action according to rules, and a stable order of authority. Weber also developed an *ideal type* method for studying society. This method studies the basic elements of social institutions and how these elements relate to one another.

In "The Protestant Ethic and the Spirit of Capitalism" (1904-1905), Weber developed a theory that certain Protestant religious beliefs promoted capitalism. He argued that the Calvinist belief in working hard and avoiding luxury promoted the expansion of business enterprise. According to Weber, the Calvinist doctrine of business success as a sign of spiritual salvation justified the desire for profits. Weber also wrote on other religions and their relationship to the social system.

Weber was born in Erfurt, Germany. He studied at the universities of Berlin, Göttingen, and Heidelberg. Other important works by Weber that have been translated into English include *From Max Weber: Essays in Sociology* and *The Theory of Social and Economic Organization.*   Daniel R. Fusfeld

See also **Bureaucracy; Protestant ethic.**

Weber, *WEHB ur,* **Max** (1881-1961), was a pioneer modern painter in America. He is best known for the abstract works he painted between 1912 and 1919, and for his later paintings of figures with expressive gestures and the appearance of motion. Several of his pictures deal with Jewish themes, reflecting his background.

Weber was born in Western Russia and moved with his family to New York City when he was ten. He came under the influence of modern artists while painting and studying in Paris from 1905 to 1908. Until the late 1920's, many critics considered his work too extreme. Then Weber's paintings began to receive favorable criticism.

In 1930, the Museum of Modern Art in New York City presented a one-man show of Weber's works. It marked the first time the museum devoted a show to one living American artist.   George Ehrlich

Webern, *VAY buhrn,* **Anton** (1883-1945), was an Austrian composer. Webern, Alban Berg, and their teacher, Arnold Schoenberg, were the most important members of the modern Viennese school. This group of composers produced their most influential work from 1910 to the mid-1930's.

Webern's earliest compositions show the impact of Schoenberg's style (see **Schoenberg, Arnold**). These works include *Passacaglia* (1908) and *Five Movements for String Quartet* (1909). *String Trio* (1927), *Symphony* (1928), and other Webern compositions of the 1920's influenced composers of the period following the end of World War II in 1945. More than half of Webern's music consists of choral works and songs for individual voices. His major choral works include *Das Augenlicht* (1935), *First Cantata* (1939), and *Second Cantata* (1943). Webern's cantatas are his longest and most lyrical works. Most of his music lasts less than 10 minutes.

Webern was born in Vienna. The Nazis banned his work in 1938 after taking over Austria.   Miloš Velimirović

Webster, Daniel (1782-1852), was the best-known American orator, and one of the ablest lawyers and statesmen of his time. He gained his greatest fame as the champion of a strong national government. For years after his death, students memorized thrilling lines from his speeches. Such words as "Liberty *and* Union, now and forever, one and inseparable!" inspired many Northern soldiers during the Civil War.

Early career. Webster was born on Jan. 18, 1782, in Salisbury (now Franklin), N.H., and was graduated from Dartmouth College. He studied law in Boston, and then became a successful lawyer in Portsmouth, N.H. At the beginning of his career, Webster did not favor a strong

Detail of an oil painting on canvas (about 1850) by
G. P. A. Healy; Faneuil Hall, Boston (City of Boston Art Commission)

Daniel Webster, *right,* opposed Senator Robert Y. Hayne in a famous Senate debate in 1830 over states' rights. Webster rejected Hayne's view that a state could nullify federal laws.

national government. Instead, he stood for the rights of the states.

Portsmouth was a thriving seaport until President Thomas Jefferson's embargo and the War of 1812 destroyed most of its overseas trade. Siding with the local shipowners, Webster opposed trade restrictions and war. As a Federalist in the United States House of Representatives from 1813 to 1817, he objected to war taxes, and helped defeat a bill for drafting soldiers. He said that state governments should "interpose" to protect their citizens from the national government.

Webster moved to Boston in 1816. New spinning and weaving mills were springing up along New England streams where there was water power. In much of the Northeast, manufacturing came to be more important than shipping. The manufacturers desired a strong national government that could aid business.

As a friend and attorney of northeastern businessmen, Webster changed his views on national power and states' rights. In the Dartmouth College case, he argued against New Hampshire's claim to control the college and won the verdict of the Supreme Court of the United States (see **Dartmouth College case**). In another famous case, he held that it was constitutional for the federal government to charter a national bank. Representing Massachusetts in the United States House of Representatives from 1823 to 1827, he insisted that a protective tariff was unconstitutional. But after his election to the United States Senate in 1827, he became the country's most eloquent tariff advocate.

The U.S. senator. The so-called "tariff of abominations," passed in 1828, led John C. Calhoun of South Carolina to develop the theory that a state could "nullify" federal laws, and refuse to obey them (see **Nullification**). Senator Robert Y. Hayne of South Carolina brilliantly defended nullification in 1830, and Webster answered him with a famous speech declaring that the Constitution had created a single, unified nation (see **Hayne, Robert Young**). In 1832, when South Carolina tried to put nullification into effect, Webster gave strong support to President Andrew Jackson in resisting the attempt.

But Webster disagreed with Jackson on other issues, especially on the question of the Bank of the United States. When Jackson vetoed a bill for rechartering the bank, Webster did his best to save the institution, but failed (see **Bank of the United States**).

During his last years in the Senate, Webster opposed adding Texas to the Union, and also opposed the war with Mexico. He feared that the country might break up because of a quarrel over territories in the West. Most Northerners wished to keep slavery from spreading into the new territories, but Southerners were ready to leave the Union if the spread of slavery was prevented. In a "Union-saving" speech, Webster favored the Compromise of 1850, and helped get it passed (see **Compromise of 1850**). Some Northerners denounced him because he was willing to give Southerners part of what they wanted.

Secretary of state. Webster served as secretary of state under Presidents William Henry Harrison and John Tyler, and then under President Millard Fillmore. Under Tyler, he negotiated the Webster-Ashburton Treaty which settled the Maine boundary dispute and avoided a war with Great Britain (see **Webster-Ashburton**

Treaty). Under Fillmore, he befriended the Hungarian patriot Lajos Kossuth and spoke for Hungarian independence (see **Kossuth, Lajos**).

The man. Webster was a handsome, imposing man with deep-set, penetrating eyes, craggy brows, dark complexion, and a rich voice. After the founding of the Whig Party in the 1830's, Webster became one of its top leaders, along with his great rival, Henry Clay. His Whig friends thought he deserved to be President, and he ran as one of the party's three candidates in 1836. His later failures to become President made him bitter at the end of his life. A statue of him represents New Hampshire in Statuary Hall in the U.S. Capitol.   Richard N. Current

Additional resources

Bartlett, Irving H. *Daniel Webster.* Norton, 1981. First published in 1978.
Baxter, Maurice G. *One and Inseparable: Daniel Webster and the Union.* Harvard, 1984.
Current, Richard N. *Daniel Webster and the Rise of National Conservatism.* Little, Brown, 1962. First published in 1955.

Webster, John (1580?-1625?), an English playwright, is noted for two tragedies, *The White Devil* (completed about 1612) and *The Duchess of Malfi* (completed about 1613). Essentially, both plays deal with the common Elizabethan subject of revenge. But their power lies in the complexity of the characters' motives for acting as they do, the physical horror of the situations, and poetic dialogue which is second only to that of William Shakespeare. The plays show the world as corrupt and immoral. However, Webster used dramatic action to express the concern of all great tragic writers in the restoration of moral order.

Webster was born in London, but little is known of his life. He wrote or collaborated in writing more than a dozen plays and entertainments and his works were apparently popular with audiences.   Albert Wertheim

Webster, Noah (1758-1843), was an American educator and journalist who won fame for compiling *Webster's Dictionary.* This work was the finest English dictionary of its time. Its most recently revised form is *Webster's Third New International Dictionary.*

Webster was born in the village of West Hartford, Conn., on Oct. 16, 1758. He was descended from John Webster, governor of Connecticut in 1656, and from William Bradford, who governed Plymouth Colony for more than 30 years. Webster graduated from Yale College. He then studied law and was admitted to the bar at Hartford. But Webster practiced law only briefly.

While teaching school at Goshen, N.Y., in the 1780's, he compiled an elementary spelling book. He then compiled a grammar, and, finally, a reader for schoolchildren. Millions of copies of the speller were sold well into the 1900's, and they helped to standardize spelling and pronunciation in the United States.

Webster campaigned for the first American copyright laws. He became an active member of the Federalist party, and wrote

Brown Bros.

Noah Webster

many political pamphlets. In 1793, he became the editor of two Federalist newspapers. After 1803, he devoted most of his time to dictionary work.

In 1806, Webster published his first dictionary. He thought of it as a preliminary effort. His great dictionary, *An American Dictionary of the English Language,* appeared in two volumes in 1828. This work, which was enlarged for an edition in 1840, included 12,000 words and 40,000 definitions that had never before appeared in a dictionary. After his death, Webster's heirs sold the dictionary rights to the G. and C. Merriam Co. of Springfield, Mass. Bert Hitchcock

See also **Dictionary** (History).

Webster-Ashburton Treaty was an agreement signed by representatives of the United States and Great Britain. It settled a number of annoying disputes between the two countries.

Secretary of State Daniel Webster signed it for the United States and Lord Ashburton for Great Britain at Washington, D.C., in August, 1842.

The most important dispute settled was the fixing of the boundary line between Canada and the state of Maine. The United States received more than half of the disputed area of 12,000 square miles (31,100 square kilometers). The treaty settled other disputes of a minor nature, and a clause of the treaty provided for the mutual extradition of criminals.

The negotiations also provided opportunity for the peaceful discussion of problems arising from British efforts to suppress the African slave trade. The Webster-Ashburton Treaty was one of the many instances in which the United States and Great Britain settled disputes without going to war. John Donald Hicks

Webster College. See **Universities and colleges** (table).

Wedding. See **Marriage.**

Wedding anniversary. It is customary for married couples to celebrate their wedding anniversaries. The 10th, 25th, and 50th anniversaries generally receive special attention. A certain type of gift is appropriate for many anniversaries. For example, silver is given to a couple married for 25 years and gold, for 50 years.

Invitations to an anniversary celebration may be simple, handwritten notes or formal, printed or engraved cards, depending on the number of guests expected. In early years of marriage, the couple usually hosts a party for close friends to celebrate the anniversary. In later years, their children and grandchildren may honor them with a party or send them on a cruise or a trip. Examples of traditional gifts are listed below. Letitia Baldrige

Wedekind, *VAY duh kihnt,* **Frank** (1864-1918), was a German playwright who savagely attacked the smugness, hypocrisy, and corruption he saw in middle-class morality. His characters are overdrawn and sometimes grotesque symbols of the individual's sexual freedom and physical vitality. They scorn the conformity of the middle class. The plays *Earth Spirit* (1894), *Pandora's Box* (1894), and *The Marquis von Keith* (1900) are variations on Wedekind's view of society. An earlier play, *Spring's Awakening* (1890-1891), established Wedekind's reputation as a controversial playwright. In this play, Wedekind says the torments of youth are caused by the cruelty and narrow-mindedness of the adult world.

Wedekind was born in Hanover and grew up in Switzerland. In 1912, he formed a theater company that toured Germany performing his plays. Peter Gontrum

Wedge is a device that has two or more sloping surfaces that taper either to a sharp edge or to a point. Wedges are used to split or pierce materials, and to adjust the positions of heavy objects. Knives, chisels, axes, pins, needles, and nails are wedges.

A wedge must overcome the resistance of friction as well as the resistance of the material it is being used on. The total resistance may be high enough to require heavy blows from a hammer to drive the wedge forward. The greater the angle between the surfaces of a wedge, the greater the force needed to advance it. If the wedge angle is too great, it is impossible to drive the wedge into the material. The limiting angle varies from 90° to 180°, depending on the amount of friction acting on the wedge surfaces.

See also **Machine** (picture: Six simple machines).

Wedgwood, Josiah, *joh SY uh* (1730-1795), was the outstanding leader in the pottery industry during the greatest period of British pottery making. He became a master potter at 29, and was successful in his own business. Three years later, in partnership with Thomas Bentley, a London merchant, he started the Etruria factory at Hanley. There he perfected the clays, glazes, and processes that made Wedgwood ware famous (see **Wedgwood ware**). Wedgwood improved the known processes of his time, and invented and perfected new ones. Wedgwood was born in Burslem, Staffordshire, a district rich in pottery clays. Eugene F. Bunker, Jr.

Wedgwood ware is a type of pottery first made by the English potter Josiah Wedgwood about 1759. The term *Wedgwood ware* generally refers to Wedgwood's fine *creamware,* a cream-colored earthenware. In 1765, Queen Charlotte, wife of King George III, ordered a set of creamware tableware. She was so pleased with it that

Wedding anniversary gifts

First	Paper, plastics, furniture	Thirteenth	Lace
Second	Cotton, china	Fourteenth	Ivory, agate
Third	Leather, any leatherlike article	Fifteenth	Crystal, glass
Fourth	Linen, silk, synthetic silks	Twentieth	China or occasional furniture
Fifth	Wood and decorative accessories for the home	Twenty-fifth	Silver
Sixth	Iron	Thirtieth	Pearls or personal gifts
Seventh	Wool, copper, brass	Thirty-fifth	Coral, jade
Eighth	Bronze, electrical appliances	Fortieth	Rubies, garnets
Ninth	Pottery, china, glass, crystal	Forty-fifth	Sapphires, tourmalines
Tenth	Tin, aluminum	Fiftieth	Gold
Eleventh	Steel	Fifty-fifth	Emeralds, turquoise
Twelfth	Linen, silk, nylon	Sixtieth, Seventy-fifth	Diamonds, diamondlike stones, gold

Dwight M. Beeson, the Wedgwood Society of New York

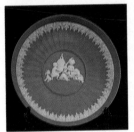

Leonard S. Rakow, M.D., the Wedgwood Society of New York

Wedgwood ware is a popular type of English pottery. The term generally refers to a cream-colored earthenware known as *creamware* or *Queens ware, above.* A type of stoneware called *jasper, left,* often features white raised designs on a blue background. Both plates were created during the late 1700's.

she allowed Wedgwood to name the pottery *Queens ware.* It is still known and sold by that name.

In addition to Queens ware, Wedgwood produced other kinds of pottery. They included *Egyptian black* or *black basalt,* a black stoneware; *rosso antico,* a red stoneware; and a stoneware called *jasper* that came in blue, green, lavender, pink, and yellow. Many of the jasper pieces had delicate raised designs, usually in white.

Wedgwood's pottery reflected the English taste for ancient Greek and Roman designs. He made copies of antique vases and sculptured ornaments as well as chess sets, buttons, cameos for jewelry, and plaques to decorate furniture. Wedgwood also manufactured statuettes, flowerpots, and other practical or decorative objects. Wedgwood ware is still made today in Barlaston, near Stoke-on-Trent.   William C. Gates, Jr.

Wednesday, *WEHNZ dee,* or *WEHNZ day,* is the English name for the fourth day of the week. This day gets its name from Woden, or Odin, the chief god in Teutonic mythology, to whom it was sacred. At the beginning of the Christian Era, the Germans called the day Woden's-day. Its name later changed to *Wednesday.* The first to name the days of the week after gods in mythology were the ancient Romans. They called the fourth day of the week after the god Mercury. From this name, the French called Wednesday *mercredi.* See also **Ash Wednesday; Odin; Week.**   Grace Humphrey

Weed is any plant that grows where people do not want it to grow. A plant may be considered a weed in one place but not in another. For example, a morning-glory in an alfalfa field is a weed pest, but a morning-glory in a garden is a lovely flower. Some plants, such as poison ivy and poison oak, are called weeds wherever they grow because they have no known use.

Many weeds are destructive. These species reduce both the quality and quantity of crops by competing with them for sunlight, water, and nourishing substances in the soil. Some types of weeds also shelter insects and diseases that damage nearby crops. Farmers in the United States spend more than $6 billion annually to control weeds. Nevertheless, the yearly loss due to weeds in crops totals about $7\frac{1}{2}$ billion. Weeds are usually considered unsightly in gardens, parks, and playgrounds. They interfere with transportation if allowed to grow unchecked along highways, railroad tracks, and waterways.

Some kinds of weeds, such as jimson weed and locoweed, are poisonous to human beings and other animals. Certain weeds, including nettles and poison ivy, produce severe skin reactions in most people. Ragweed pollen causes hay fever in many individuals.

Weeds can be beneficial in some cases. For example, they reduce soil erosion on land where cultivated plants do not grow. They also provide shelter and food for birds and other wildlife. A weed such as quack grass may serve as food for livestock if other food is not available. People in some countries eat parts of dandelions, lamb's-quarters, and other weeds. Fireweed, one of many weeds used in making certain medicines, helps relieve pain. Other weeds, such as goldenrod and wild carrot, are attractive in gardens.

How weeds grow. Weeds are classified as *annuals, biennials,* and *perennials,* depending on how long they live. Annual weeds grow from seeds and live one year or less. There are two kinds of annual weeds, *summer annuals* and *winter annuals.* Summer annuals start to grow in spring and produce seeds before dying in fall. Winter annuals begin to grow in fall and produce roots and a group of leaves, called a *rosette,* before winter. The plant then remains inactive until spring, when it grows to maturity. Common annual weeds include crabgrass, dodder, and ragweed.

Biennial weeds grow from seeds and live about two years. They produce roots and a rosette during the first year and then remain inactive until spring. Biennials produce stems, flowers, and seeds during the second year. Examples of biennial weeds include burdock, poison hemlock, and wild parsnip.

Perennial weeds, which live longer than two years, grow from seeds or from other parts of a plant. New growth may start from the roots, bulbs, or stems if the upper part of a plant dies or is cut down. Most perennials are difficult to control because they have extremely deep root systems. Canada thistle, dandelion, and quack grass are common perennial weeds.

Weeds may spread from one area to another in a variety of ways. Many weed seeds have special structures that enable them to travel great distances on wind currents. For example, the dandelion has a fluffy seed structure that can be blown for miles. Birds and other animals also scatter seeds of weeds. People spread weeds by means of seeds caught on farm and lawn equipment. In addition, weed seeds may be moved from one place to another in animal feed and among crop seeds.

Weed control. There are four general methods of weed control—*cultural, mechanical, biological,* and *chemical.* Cultural control is the use of efficient crop production to prevent weeds from growing. One such technique involves planting crop seeds that are free of weed seeds. Crop rotation helps keep weeds from adapting to a certain area. In small areas, a covering called a *mulch* is placed on the ground around plants to prevent weed growth. Common types of mulches include grass clippings, wood chips, and plastic sheets. See **Mulch.**

Mechanical control is the destruction of weeds manually or by machine. Farmers use a machine called a *cultivator* to dig up large weeds and cover smaller ones with soil. Tall weeds in pastures and on roadsides are controlled by mowing. Hoeing weeds or pulling them out of the ground by hand can be effective in small gardens, flower beds, and lawns.

Biological control involves the use of natural enemies of weeds growing in a specific area. For example, insects and other small animals that eat certain weeds may be put into a field where those weeds are growing. Bacteria and other organisms are used to spread diseases among specific species of weeds.

Chemical control is the use of chemical compounds called *herbicides.* Most herbicides are *selective*—that is, they kill weeds but do not harm crops. Herbicides must be used carefully to avoid harm to crops, human beings, and wildlife.   Harold D. Coble

Related articles in *World Book* include:

Amaranth	Grass	Nettle	Sow thistle
Beggarweed	Hemlock	Parsnip	Spurge
Bindweed	Herbicide	Pigweed	family
Brome grass	Horsetail	Plantain	Stickseed
Burdock	Indian mallow	Poison ivy	Teasel
Canada thistle	Jimson weed	Poison oak	Thistle
Cinquefoil	Knotgrass	Pokeweed	Toadflax
Cocklebur	Lamb's-	Purslane	Tumbleweed
Compass plant	quarters	Ragweed	Viper's
Dandelion	Lawn	Saint-John's-	bugloss
Dock	Locoweed	wort	Water
Dodder	Lupine	Smartweed	hyacinth
Glasswort	Milkweed	Solanum	Wild barley
Goldenrod	Mullein	Sorrel	Wild carrot

Weed, Thurlow (1797-1882), was an American journalist and political leader. He became a leader of the Whig and Republican parties, and was largely responsible for the election of two Whig presidents, William Henry Harrison and Zachary Taylor. His support of William H. Seward, U.S. secretary of state, led to Weed's appointment as a commissioner to England and France at the outset of the Civil War. Weed was born at Cairo, N.Y. In 1830 he established the Albany (N.Y.) *Evening Journal.*

John Eldridge Drewry

Weedkiller. See Weed.

Week is a division of time which includes seven days. We do not know exactly how this division of time began, but the ancient Hebrews were among the first to use it. The book of Genesis in the Bible says that the world was created in six days and the seventh day, or Sabbath, was a day of rest and worship.

The ancient Egyptians named each day of the week for one of the planets. They considered the seventh day merely as a day of rest and play. Among the later Romans, the seven days of the week were named after the sun, moon, and five planets which were then known. Each day was considered sacred to the Roman god who was associated with that planet. The days were known as Sun's-day, Moon's-day, Mars'-day, and so on. This system was used about the beginning of the Christian Era.

The English names for the days *Tuesday, Wednesday, Thursday,* and *Friday* were derived from the names of Norse gods.   Paul Sollenberger

See also separate articles in *World Book* on each day of the week.

Weems, Mason Locke (1759-1825), was an American clergyman who became famous as a writer and traveling bookseller. An Episcopal priest, he was often called "Parson" Weems. He wrote the first popular biography of George Washington, *The Life and Memorable Actions of George Washington* (about 1800). It includes many tales which Weems apparently invented, notably the one about the young Washington chopping down a cherry tree. Weems also wrote biographies of other leading Americans, as well as several moral tracts. Weems was born in Anne Arundel County, Maryland.

Marcus Klein

Weevil, *WEE vuhl,* is the name of many kinds of beetles with a long snout. They are among the worst insect pests that attack farm crops. The cotton boll weevil, commonly called the *boll weevil,* is one of the most destructive insects in the United States. The name weevil is also given to the *grubs* (larvae) of these beetles. Both grubs and adult weevils cause damage.

Adult weevils are sometimes so small that they are hard to see. They have long snouts that may be longer than the rest of the body. These insects lay their eggs in the stalk, seed, or fruit of the plant. The grub then feeds on these plant parts, causing great damage.

Besides the boll weevil, there are other kinds that attack grain, fruit, clover, and alfalfa. The *granary weevil* is harmful to wheat and other seeds. It lays its eggs on the seed after it is stored, and the grubs burrow into the grain. The *rice weevil* destroys rice and other cereals in the same way. The *alfalfa weevil* first appeared in Salt Lake City about 1904. It has spread rapidly and causes great loss in alfalfa-growing regions every year. This insect is less than $\frac{1}{4}$ inch (6 millimeters) long and is grayish-brown to almost black. It came to the United States from southern Europe. In its native home it has many insect enemies that attack the weevil and its eggs, and keep it in check. The U. S. Department of Agriculture has imported large numbers of weevil enemies. It has spread them among the weevils to keep down the damage to alfalfa.

There are also many kinds of fruit weevils. The *plum*

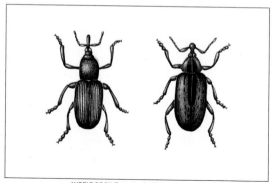

WORLD BOOK illustration by Shirley Hooper, Oxford Illustrators Limited
Weevils are insect pests that damage crops. These small insects include the rice weevil, *left,* and the alfalfa weevil, *right.*

curculio is the most important of the group that attacks apples, cherries, and plums. The larvae of these insects feed on the fruit, which falls off or becomes wormy.

Scientific classification. Weevils belong to the weevil or snout-beetle family, Curculionidae.   Ellis W. Huddleston

See also **Boll weevil; Grain weevil.**

Wegener, Alfred. See Continental drift (Evidence for the theory).

Weighing scale. See Scale, Weighing.

Weight is the gravitational force put forth on an object by the planet on which the object is located. The weight of an object depends on (1) the distance from the object to the center of the planet, (2) the *mass* (amount of matter) of the object, and (3) the mass of the planet.

An object's weight is largest if the object is on the surface of the planet. The weight becomes smaller if the object is moved away from the planet. The object has no weight in space, where the gravitational force acting on it is too weak to be measured. If the object were to penetrate inside the planet, its weight would also be smaller.

The mass of the planet also affects the weight of objects on its surface. If the planet has a mass smaller than Earth's, its gravitational force is also smaller. For example, a man who weighs 200 pounds (91 kilograms) on Earth would weigh only 76 pounds (34 kilograms) on Mars. He would weigh 180 pounds (82 kilograms) on Venus and 516 pounds (234 kilograms) on Jupiter.

Common units used to measure weight are the *ounce* and the *pound.* The *gram* and *kilogram* are units of mass that are also used to measure weight in the metric system.   Lucille B. Garmon

See also **Gravitation; Weights and measures; Scale, Weighing.**

Weight, Atomic. See Atom (Atomic weight).

Weight, Tables of. For boys and girls, see **Growth.**

Weight control is the process of losing or avoiding excessive body fat. It is based on the relationship between the amount of food you eat and the amount of exercise you get. The less you eat and the more you exercise, the less fat you will have. Weight control has medical importance because being *obese* (too fat) can lead to health problems. Emotional and social problems may result from obesity. Overweight people may not be obese, though the word *overweight* is often used for *obese.* Being overweight simply means weighing more than the average for a certain height.

Some people weigh less than average for their height because they have small bones and muscles. Others are underweight because they have less fat. In either case, being underweight is not unhealthy. But people may be underweight as the result of a disease—cancer, diabetes, or tuberculosis, for example. In some children, underweight may be the first sign of growth failure. An underweight person should consult a doctor. If no illness is found, there is no reason to worry.

An overweight person who is not too fat does not need to lose weight for health reasons. The person would do better simply to stay physically fit with such exercise as walking or taking part in sports.

Dangers of obesity

Obese people are more likely than thin people to get certain diseases. The treatment of these diseases among the obese is also less likely to succeed. Such diseases include appendicitis, cirrhosis, diabetes, and diseases of the heart and blood vessels, especially coronary heart disease. A fat patient with one of these diseases has a better chance of recovery if he or she reduces.

Obese people have more falls and other accidents than thin people because they are slower and clumsier. Their recovery from injury is often difficult because surgery performed on them is dangerous. Obesity cuts down freedom of movement, especially in the elderly, and thus can lower general health because of lack of exercise. The decreased freedom of movement in obese patients with arthritis also makes treatment difficult.

In many parts of the world, obese people may be rejected in various ways. Fat people are often treated unkindly by others, including their classmates in school. They generally have less social success than other people, and may find it harder to get jobs.

Causes of obesity

Overeating. You will gain or lose weight as a result of eating more or fewer calories than you need. A calorie is a unit used to measure the heat energy that the body gets from a certain amount of food. If you eat more calories than you use, they will turn into body fat. If you eat fewer than you use, your body will convert its own fat into energy. During any period of days or weeks, if you eat 3,500 more calories than you use, you will gain 1 pound (0.5 kilogram). You will lose a pound if you eat 3,500 fewer calories than you use. Some countries that use the metric system measure the heat energy obtained from food in *joules* instead of calories. About 4,182 joules equal one calorie.

A surplus of calories is necessary for growth in children and pregnant women. But they will gain body fat if they eat too many calories. See **Calorie.**

The amount of food you eat plays a much more important role in weight control than the kinds of food. People who are overweight, of normal weight, or underweight may all eat the same kinds of food. Their weight difference results from the amount of food they eat in relation to the amount of energy they use.

Certain centers in the brain control appetite, hunger, and *satiety,* the group of sensations that cause you to stop eating when your appetite and hunger have been satisfied. These brain centers normally make people eat an amount of food that provides enough energy for their needs. The *feeding centers* cause people to want to eat. The *satiety centers* act as a brake on the feeding centers and make people want to stop eating.

The feeding and satiety centers are extremely complicated mechanisms. They may be disturbed by such causes as emotional pressures and physical characteristics. For example, emotional pressures such as great disappointment cause some people to stop all physical activity. At such times, these people eat more than they usually do —and gain weight. Other people move around more and eat much less—and lose weight.

Some scientists believe that overfeeding infants causes them to develop too many fat cells. They claim that these cells store fat so readily that such people are likely to be obese for the rest of their lives.

Physical inactivity can lead to obesity among all age groups. It does so especially among children and teenagers, who are the most active groups. Most obese young people do not eat more than those of normal weight. In fact, most of them eat less. But they are so inactive that, even with a moderate appetite, they eat more than they need—and accumulate excess fat.

Exercise uses up many calories, and the more vigorous the activity, the more calories are used. A 150-pound (68-kilogram) person walking at an average speed of $3\frac{1}{2}$ miles (5.6 kilometers) per hour will use up 502 calories—the number of calories in a malted milk shake—in 97 minutes. That person will use up the same number of calories in 61 minutes by riding a bicycle, or in 26 minutes by running.

The number of calories used is proportional to a person's weight. If you weigh 75 pounds, for example, you will use up half as many calories as a 150-pound person by doing the same exercise for the same length of time.

The appetite of active people will increase if they become very active. If they become inactive, their appetite will not necessarily decrease. Appetite does not go below a minimum level even if activity drops.

Heredity. Scientists have learned much about the relationship between heredity and obesity in animals, especially mice. This relationship is based on *genes,* the basic units in cells that determine inherited characteristics. Scientists have discovered that some mice have a gene that causes the satiety center not to operate. Other genes in some mice cause their bodies to overproduce certain chemical substances called *hormones.* As a result of these hormones, the mice make body fat too easily or use it up with difficulty. Still other genes cause some mice to become obese more quickly than others when physically inactive or when given a diet high in fat. See **Gene; Hormone.**

In human beings, the action of genes is not so well known as in animals. But there is evidence that some people are more likely to become obese than others because of their genes. For example, studies of high school students show that only about 8 per cent of the children of thin parents were obese. Among families where one parent was obese, 70 per cent of the children were fat. Among families with both parents obese, 80 per cent of the children were fat. Adopted children do not show this relationship to their adoptive parents.

The role of genes in obesity is also indicated by the fact that certain inherited body types are more likely to become fat than others. People with broad hands and short, stubby fingers are more likely to be obese than people with narrow hands and long fingers. A child with obese parents is not doomed to obesity. The child still would have to eat more calories than are needed.

Diseases and other causes. Obesity may result from a number of diseases. Some ailments of the endocrine glands cause these glands to release too much of a hormone into the blood stream. The excess hormone disturbs the feeding and satiety centers of the brain. Obesity also can result from damage to these brain centers caused by infection, injury, or a tumor.

How to control obesity

You should consult a physician and have a medical checkup before starting an extensive weight reduction program. The advice of a dietitian is also useful. An obese person may need psychological help as well, especially if the person is young and has been teased and made to feel guilty, hopeless, or worthless. The first step in psychological treatment is to remove these feelings and to treat the obesity as a medical problem.

Energy equivalents of food calories

This table shows the calories in some foods, and the minutes it would take a 150-pound (68-kilogram) person to use them up in various ways. A person half as heavy would need twice as long.

Food	Calories	Minutes of lying down	Minutes of walking ($2\frac{1}{2}$ mph)	Minutes of walking (4 mph)	Minutes of bicycle riding (9 mph)	Minutes of swimming	Minutes of running (7 mph)
Apple, large	125	83	34	23	20	14	14
Beans, green, canned, 1 cup	25	17	7	5	4	3	3
Bread and butter	100	67	27	18	16	11	11
Cake, yellow, with chocolate frosting, 1 piece	235	157	64	43	38	26	26
Carrot, grated, raw, 1 cup	45	30	12	8	7	5	5
Chicken, potpie, 1 pie	545	363	149	99	87	60	60
Egg, fried	95	63	26	17	15	10	10
Ham, 2 slices	140	93	38	25	22	15	15
Hamburger sandwich	245	163	67	45	39	27	27
Ice cream, vanilla, $\frac{1}{2}$ cup	135	90	37	25	22	15	15
Malted milk shake, 10 ounces	335	223	91	61	54	37	37
Milk, whole (3.3% fat), 1 cup	150	100	41	27	24	16	16
Milk, lowfat (2% fat), 1 cup	120	80	33	22	19	13	13
Pancake with syrup	121	81	33	22	19	13	13
Peas, green, canned, $\frac{1}{2}$ cup	57	38	16	10	9	6	6
Pie, apple, $\frac{1}{8}$ of pie	405	270	110	74	65	44	44
Pizza, cheese, 15-inch diameter, $\frac{1}{8}$ of pizza	290	193	79	53	46	32	32
Pork chop, pan fried,	335	223	91	61	54	37	37
Shrimp, french-fried, 7 medium	200	133	55	36	32	22	22
Spaghetti with tomato sauce and cheese	190	127	52	35	30	21	21
Steak, sirloin, 3 ounces	240	160	65	44	38	26	26
Strawberry shortcake	417	278	114	76	67	45	45

Energy equivalent values based on figures compiled by Robert E. Johnson, Professor Emeritus, University of Illinois.
Calorie content of food based on *Nutritive Value of Foods,* U.S. Dept. of Agriculture, 1985.

Diet. Any reducing diet must provide fewer calories. If a man needs 3,000 calories a day to maintain his weight with his habits of life, he should eat only 2,000 calories a day to lose 2 pounds (0.9 kilogram) a week. It is generally dangerous to lose weight any faster.

The foods in a reducing diet must be well-balanced. That is, they must provide enough of all the nutrients needed for good health. There is no evidence that extreme diets—for example, "low carbohydrate" or "low protein" diets, or diets based on single foods—have any advantage over a well-balanced diet. (For information on well-balanced diets and their importance to good health, see **Nutrition.**) A reducing diet should also be good tasting and easy to buy and to cook.

A weight reducer should study charts that give the number of calories in various foods. Many people believe that such foods as baked potatoes and bread have many more calories than they do. They also underestimate the calories in such foods as steak.

The distribution of calories among meals and snacks is up to the individual. Some people do not get too hungry if they divide their calories among four or five light meals or snacks a day. Others are able to follow a diet better if they eat three meals a day and have no snacks.

Exercise. A person going on a reducing diet should get more exercise. But an obese person—even one who is otherwise healthy—should not suddenly start a program of prolonged, heavy exercise. The strain on the heart would be dangerous. An exercise program should be developed gradually. One good way to start is to take daily walks, increasing their duration. More demanding exercises can be added as the person becomes thinner and fitter.

Surgery. Extremely fat people whose obesity is life-threatening and who fail at dieting may have to undergo a surgical operation to reduce the size of the stomach. In one such operation, called *gastroplasty* or *gastric stapling procedure,* the surgeon uses a giant stapling device to close off most of the patient's stomach. After the surgery, the patient can eat only a small amount of food before becoming full.   Jean Mayer

See also **Diet; Nutrition.**

Additional resources

Brody, Jane E. *Jane Brody's Nutrition Book: A Lifetime Guide to Good Eating for Better Health and Weight Control.* Norton, 1981.
Goulart, Frances S. *Beyond Baby Fat: Weight-Loss Plans for Children and Teenagers.* McGraw, 1985.
Mayer, Jean. *A Diet for Living.* McKay, 1975.
Schwartz, Hillel. *Never Satisfied: A Cultural History of Diets, Fantasies, and Fat.* Free Press, 1986.
Silberstein, Warren P., and Galton, Lawrence. *Helping Your Child Grow Slim: Safe Dieting for Overweight Children and Adolescents.* Simon & Schuster, 1982.

Weight lifting involves the lifting of weights attached to a barbell. It serves as the basis of competitive sports called *weightlifting* (written as one word) and *powerlifting.* In these sports, athletes compete against one another to determine who can lift the most weight. Such competitions match lifters with similar body weights. Athletes who participate in other sports sometimes lift weights to increase their strength and flexibility. Lifting weights is also a popular hobby for improving muscle tone and general health. Professional body builders lift weights to improve their muscular development. They

© Douglas Kirkland, Sygma

A powerful weight lifter raises a heavy metal barbell over his head during competition in the Olympic Games.

exhibit their physiques in organized competitions. Judges determine which body builder has the best body.

In the sport of weightlifting, there are two types of lifts—the *snatch* and the *clean and jerk.* In the snatch, lifters bend down and grasp the barbell. They then lift the bar in a quick motion, raising it above their head while squatting under it. In the clean and jerk, the lifter brings the bar to a resting position at the shoulders, then jerks the barbell over the head by thrusting out the arms and legs.

Participants may attempt each lift up to three times. Weights are added to the barbell after each successful attempt. A panel of three referees determines whether each lift was properly executed. The lifter in each class who lifts the highest total weight wins. Weightlifting is an event in the Summer Olympic Games.

In the sport of powerlifting, the three chief types of lifts are the *squat,* the *bench press,* and the *dead lift.* In the squat, lifters stand upright with the barbell resting at shoulder height. They then lower themselves to a squatting position, pause, and again rise to an upright position. In the bench press, lifters raise and lower the weight above their chest while lying on their back on a bench. In the dead lift, the barbell rests on the floor in front of the lifter. The competitor bends to grasp it, then lifts it in one motion and straightens to a standing position, keeping the weight hanging at arm's length.

Critically reviewed by the United States Weightlifting Federation

See also **Olympic Games** (table); **Body building.**

Additional resources

Berger, Richard A. *Introduction to Weight Training.* Prentice-Hall, 1984.
Hatfield, Frederick C. *Powerlifting: A Scientific Approach.* Contemporary Books, 1981.
Lear, John. *The Powerlifters' Manual.* Sterling, 1983.
Schwarzenegger, Arnold, and Dobbins, Bill. *Encyclopedia of Modern Bodybuilding.* Simon & Schuster, 1985.

Weightlessness. See **Space travel** (Living in space); **Astronaut** (Training the astronauts).

Weights and measures are the standards used to find the size of things. People in the United States and a few other countries use standards that belong to the *customary,* or *English, system of measurement.* This system was developed in England from older measurement standards, beginning about the 1200's. People in nearly all other countries—including England—now use a system of measurement called the *metric system.* The metric system was created in France in the 1790's. In 1975, the United States Congress passed the Metric Conversion Act, which called for a voluntary changeover to the metric system. For a complete discussion of metric measurement, see the article on the **Metric system.**

Weights and measures form one of the most important parts of our life today. Many weights and measures

Metric conversion table

This table can help you change measurements into or out of metric units. To use it, look up the unit you know in the left-hand column and multiply it by the number given. Your answer will be approximately the number of units in the right-hand column.

When you know:	Multiply by:	To find:
Length and distance		
inches (in.)	25	millimeters
feet (ft.)	30	centimeters
yards (yd.)	0.9	meters
miles (mi.)	1.6	kilometers
millimeters (mm)	0.04	inches
centimeters (cm)	0.4	inches
meters (m)	1.1	yards
kilometers (km)	0.6	miles
Surface or area		
square inches (sq. in.)	6.5	square centimeters
square feet (sq. ft.)	0.09	square meters
square yards (sq. yd.)	0.8	square meters
square miles (sq. mi.)	2.6	square kilometers
acres	0.4	hectares
square centimeters (cm²)	0.16	square inches
square meters (m²)	1.2	square yards
square kilometers (km²)	0.4	square miles
hectares (ha)	2.5	acres
Volume and capacity (liquid)		
fluid ounces (fl. oz.)	30	milliliters
pints (pt.), U.S.	0.47	liters
pints (pt.), imperial	0.568	liters
quarts (qt.), U.S.	0.95	liters
quarts (qt.), imperial	1.137	liters
gallons (gal.), U.S.	3.8	liters
gallons (gal.), imperial	4.546	liters
milliliters (ml)	0.034	fluid ounces
liters (l)	2.1	pints, U.S.
liters (l)	1.76	pints, imperial
liters (l)	1.06	quarts, U.S.
liters (l)	0.88	quarts, imperial
liters (l)	0.26	gallons, U.S.
liters (l)	0.22	gallons, imperial
Weight and mass		
ounces (oz.)	28	grams
pounds (lb.)	0.45	kilograms
short tons	0.9	metric tons
grams (g)	0.035	ounces
kilograms (kg)	2.2	pounds
metric tons (t)	1.1	short tons
Temperature		
degrees Fahrenheit (° F.)	$\frac{5}{9}$ (after subtracting 32)	degrees Celsius
degrees Celsius (° C)	$\frac{9}{5}$ (then add 32)	degrees Fahrenheit

Miscellaneous weights and measures

Angstrom is a unit once used with the metric system to measure small distances. It equals 0.0000001 of a millimeter (0.0000000039 inch).

Assay ton, used for testing ore, equals 29.167 grams (1.029 ounces).

Bolt, used in measuring cloth, equals 120 feet (36.6 meters).

Butt, formerly used for liquids, equals 126 gallons (477 liters).

Carat, used to weigh precious stones and pearls, equals 200 milligrams (0.007 ounce).

Catty, used to measure tea and other materials, weighs about 1 $\frac{1}{3}$ pounds (0.6 kilogram).

Chaldron, a capacity measure, equals 36 imperial bushels (1.31 cubic meters).

Cubit, in the customary system, is 18 inches (46 centimeters). It is based on the length of the forearm.

Ell, used in measuring cloth, equals 45 inches (114 centimeters).

Firkin, used to measure lard or butter, equals either about 9 imperial gallons (40.9 liters) or about 56 pounds (25 kilograms).

Fortnight is a period of 14 days.

Hand, used to measure the height of horses, from the ground to the withers, equals 4 inches (10 centimeters).

Hogshead, used to measure liquids, equals 63 gallons (238 liters).

Kilderkin, used to measure liquids, equals 18 imperial gallons (82 liters).

Knot is a speed of 1 nautical mile (1.1508 statute miles or 1.852 kilometers) per hour.

Light-year, the distance light travels in a year. It is about 5.88 trillion miles (9.46 trillion kilometers).

Line, used to measure buttons, is $\frac{1}{40}$ inch (0.6 millimeter).

Load, of earth or gravel, equals 1 cubic yard (0.76 cubic meter).

Mole is a metric base unit for the amount of a substance. It equals 602,257,000,000,000,000,000,000 atoms, molecules, or whatever other elemental particles are being measured.

Nail, used in measuring cloth, equals 2.25 inches (5.72 centimeters).

Palm equals 3 or 4 inches (8 or 10 centimeters).

Perch, used for masonry, equals 24.75 cubic feet (0.7 cubic meter).

Perch, a measure of length in the customary system, equals 1 rod (5.03 meters).

Pin, used to measure liquids, equals 4 $\frac{1}{2}$ gallons (17 liters).

Pipe, used to measure liquids, equals 126 gallons (477 liters).

Pole, a measure of length in the customary system, equals 1 rod (5.03 meters).

Puncheon, used to measure liquids, equals 84 gallons (318 liters).

Quarter, used to measure grain, equals 25 pounds (11 kilograms).

Rood, used to measure land, equals $\frac{1}{4}$ acre (0.1 hectare).

Score is a group of 20.

Skein, used to measure yarn, equals 360 feet (110 meters).

Square, used to measure floor or roofing material, is an area of 100 square feet (9.3 square meters).

Tierce, used to measure liquids, equals 42 gallons (159 liters).

Tun, used to measure liquids, equals 252 gallons (954 liters).

Vara, used to measure land, equals 33 $\frac{1}{3}$ inches (84.6 centimeters) in Texas; 33 inches (84 centimeters) in California; and from 32 to 43 inches (81 to 109 centimeters) in Spain, Portugal, and Latin-American countries.

Daniel V. De Simone, the contributor of this article, is Executive Director of the American Association of Engineering Societies and former Deputy Director of the Office of Technology Assessment, an agency of the United States Congress. He directed the U.S. Metric Study conducted by the government from 1968 to 1971.

have had a fascinating history. For a complete discussion of the history of measurement, see **Measurement**.

The tables in this article show how to convert from customary to metric units and from metric to customary units. Suppose you want to change customary units to metric units. Multiply the number of customary units—inches, feet, pounds, and so on—by the number of metric units in *one* of the customary unit. For example, to change 22 miles to kilometers, multiply 22, the number of miles, by 1.6093, the number of kilometers that make

up 1 mile: 22 × 1.6093 = 35.4046. So 22 customary-unit miles equal 35.4046 metric-unit kilometers.

Daniel V. De Simone

Related articles. See **Measurement** and its list of *Related articles.* See also the following articles:

Apothecaries' weight
Avoirdupois
International Bureau of Weights and Measures
Metric system
National Institute of Standards and Technology
Time
Troy weight
Weight

Length and distance

Lengths and distances are measured from one point to another, usually along a straight line. Length usually refers to the measurement of an object. Distance usually refers to the measurement of the space between two places. The customary and metric units for length and distance are listed in the tables below. The tables also show the nautical units used to measure distances at sea, and the chain units used to survey land.

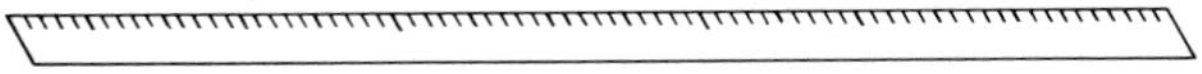

Customary			Metric		Metric			Customary	
1 inch (in.)		=	2.54	cm	1 nano-				
1 foot (ft.)	= 12 in.	=	30.48	cm	meter (nm)		=	0.00000003937	in.
1 yard (yd.)	= 3 ft.	=	0.9144	m	1 micron (μ)	= 1,000 nm	=	0.00003937	in.
1 rod (rd.)	= 5½ yd.	=	5.0292	m	1 milli-				
1 furlong (fur.)	= 40 rd., or ⅛ mi.	=	201.168	m	meter (mm)	= 1,000 μ	=	0.03937	in.
1 statute, or land,					1 centi-				
mile (mi.)	= 5,280 ft., or 0.86897624 nautical mi.	=	1.6093	km	meter (cm)	= 10 mm	=	0.3937	in.
					1 deci-				
					meter (dm)	= 10 cm	=	3.937	in.
1 statute					1 meter (m)	= 10 dm	=	39.37	in.
league	= 15,840 ft., or 3 statute mi., or 2.6069287 nautical mi.	=	4.8280	km	1 deka- meter (dam)	= 10 m	= 393.7		in.
					1 hecto- meter (hm)	= 10 dam	= 328.0833		ft.
					1 kilometer (km)	= 10 hm	=	0.62137	mi.

Nautical

					Customary		Metric	
1 span			=	9	in.	=	22.8	cm
1 fathom (fm.)	= 8 spans	=	6	ft.	=	1.83	m
1 cable's length	= 120 fathoms	=	720	ft.	=	219.46	m
1 nautical mile, or 1 International Nautical Mile (INM)		=	6,076.11549 ft., or 1.150779 statute mi.		=	1.852	km
1 nautical league	= 3 nautical mi.	=	18,228.346 ft., or 3.452338 statute mi.		=	5.556	km

Surveyor's, or Gunter's, Chain

				Customary		Metric	
1 link (li.)		=	7.92 in.	=	20.12	cm
1 chain (ch.)	= 100 li.	=	66 ft.	=	20.12	m
1 furlong (fur.)	= 10 ch.	=	660 ft.	=	201.168	m
1 statute mile (mi.)	= 8 fur.	=	5,280 ft.	=	1.6093	km

Engineer's Chain

				Customary		Metric	
1 link (li.)		=	1 ft.	=	30.48	cm
1 chain (ch.)	= 100 li.	=	100 ft.	=	30.48	m
1 mile (mi.)	= 52.8 ch.	=	5,280 ft.	=	1.6093	km

Surface or area

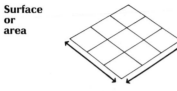

An area of land or the surface of an object is measured in square units. These units result from multiplying the length of the area or object by its width. The square units of both the customary and metric systems are based on units of length and distance. A small 2, placed to the right and above the symbol for a metric unit, indicates a square unit.

Customary				Metric	Metric			Customary	
1 square inch (sq. in.)			=	6.4516 cm²	1 square millimeter (mm²)		=	0.002	sq. in.
1 square foot (sq. ft.)	= 144	sq. in.	=	0.0929 m²	1 square centimeter (cm²)	= 100 mm² =		0.155	sq. in.
1 square yard (sq. yd.)	= 9	sq. ft.	=	0.8361 m²	1 square decimeter (dm²)	= 100 cm² =		15.5	sq. in.
1 square rod (sq. rd.)	= 30¼	sq. yd.	=	25.293 m²	1 square meter (m²)	= 100 dm² =		1,550	sq. in.
1 acre	= 160	sq. rd.	=	0.4047 ha	1 square dekameter (dam²)	= 100 m² =		119.6	sq. yd.
1 square mile (sq. mi.)	= 640	acres	=	258.9988 ha,	1 square hectometer (hm²)	= 100 dam² =		2.4711	acres
				or 2.590 km²	1 square kilometer (km²)	= 100 hm²	=	247.105	acres,
							or	0.3861	sq. mi.

Metric Land Measurement

Metric			Customary	
1 centiare (ca)		=	1,550	sq. in.
1 are (a)	= 100 ca	=	119.6	sq. yd.
1 hectare (ha)	= 100 a	=	2.4711	acres
1 square kilometer (km²)	= 100 ha	=	247.105	acres,
		or	0.3861	sq. mi.

Surveyor's Land Measurement

			Customary		Metric
1 square link (sq. li.)		=	62.73 sq. in.	=	404.686 cm²
1 square pole (sq. p.)	= 625 sq. li.	=	30.25 sq. yd.	=	25.293 m²
1 square chain (sq. ch.)	= 16 sq. p.	=	484 sq. yd.	=	404.686 m²
1 acre	= 10 sq. ch.	=	4,840 sq. yd.	=	4,046.856 m²
1 section (sec.)	= 640 acres	=	1 sq. mi.	=	2.590 km²
1 township (tp.)	= 36 sec.	=	36 sq. mi.	=	93.240 km²

Volume and capacity

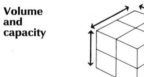

Volume refers to the amount of space occupied by an object. Capacity is the amount of a substance that a container can hold. Volume and capacity are both measured in cubic units. Cubic units combine length, width, and depth. But the names of many common cubic units, such as liter and quart, do not include the word *cubic*. A small 3, placed to the right and above the symbol for a metric unit, indicates a cubed unit.

Volume Measurement

Customary			Metric
1 cubic inch (cu. in.)		=	16.387 cm³
1 cubic foot (cu. ft.)	= 1,728 cu. in.	=	0.0283 m³
1 cubic yard (cu. yd.)	= 27 cu. ft.	=	0.7646 m³

Metric		Customary	
1 cubic millimeter (mm³)		= 0.00006	cu. in.
1 cubic centimeter (cm³)	= 1,000 mm³	= 0.0610	cu. in.
1 cubic decimeter (dm³)	= 1,000 cm³	= 0.0353	cu. ft.
1 cubic meter (m³)	= 1,000 dm³	= 1.308	cu. yd.
1 cubic dekameter (dam³)	= 1,000 m³	= 1,308	cu. yd.
1 cubic hectometer (hm³)	= 1,000 dam³	= 1,308,000	cu. yd.

Metric Capacity Measure

Metric			Customary	
1 milliliter (ml)		=	0.0610	cu. in.
1 centiliter (cl)	= 10 ml	=	0.6103	cu. in.
1 deciliter (dl)	= 10 cl	=	6.1025	cu. in.
1 liter (l)	= 10 dl	=	61.025	cu. in.,
		or	1.057	liquid qt.,
		or	0.908	dry qt.
1 dekaliter (dal)	= 10 l	=	610.25	cu. in.
1 hectoliter (hl)	= 10 dal	=	6,102.55	cu. in.
1 kiloliter (kl)	= 10 hl	=	35.316	cu. ft.,
		or	264.179	gal.,
		or	28.38	bu.

Household Capacity Measurement

Customary					Metric	
1 teaspoon			=	⅙ fl. oz. =	4.9	ml
1 tablespoon	=	3 teaspoons	=	½ fl. oz. =	14.8	ml
1 cup	=	16 tablespoons	=	8 fl. oz. =	236.6	ml
1 pint	=	2 cups	=	16 fl. oz. =	473.2	ml
1 quart	=	2 pints	=	32 fl. oz. =	946.3	ml
1 gallon	=	4 quarts	=	128 fl. oz. =	3.785 l	

Customary Liquid Capacity Measurement

	Customary				Metric
1 gill (gi.)			=	7.219 cu. in. =	0.1183 l
1 pint (pt.)	= 4	gi.	=	28.875 cu. in. =	0.4732 l
1 quart (qt.)	= 2	pt.	=	57.75 cu. in. =	0.9463 l
1 gallon (gal.)	= 4	qt.	=	231 cu. in. =	3.7854 l
1 barrel (bbl.), liquids	= 31.5	gal.	=	4.21 cu. ft. =	119.24 l
1 barrel (bbl.), petroleum	= 42	gal.	=	5.61 cu. ft. =	158.98 l

	Imperial		Customary		Metric
1 imperial pint	= 1.201 U.S. pt.	=	34.6775 cu. in.	=	0.568 l
1 imperial quart	= 1.201 U.S. qt.	=	69.354 cu. in.	=	1.13652 l
1 imperial gallon	= 1.201 U.S. gal.	=	277.42 cu. in.	=	4.54609 l

Customary Dry Capacity Measurement

	Customary		Metric	
1 pint (pt.)	=	33.600 cu. in. =	550.61	cm³
1 quart (qt.)	= 2 pt. =	67.20 cu. in. =	1,101.22	cm³
1 peck (pk.)	= 8 qt. =	537.61 cu. in. =	8,809.77	cm³
1 bushel (bu.)	= 4 pk. =	2,150.42 cu. in. =	0.035239	m³
1 barrel (bbl.)	=	4.08 cu. ft. =	0.115627	m³

	Imperial		Customary		Metric	
1 imperial pint	= 1.032 U.S. pt. =	34.6775 cu. in. =	568.26092	cm³
1 imperial quart	= 1.032 U.S. qt. =	69.354 cu. in. =	1,136.52	cm³
1 imperial bushel	= 1.032 U.S. bu. =	2,219.36 cu. in. =	0.03637	m³

Apothecaries' Fluid Measurement

			Customary		Metric
1 minim or drop (min. or ℔)		=	0.002083 fl. oz.	=	0.0616 ml
1 fluid dram (fl. dr. or ʒ)	= 60 min.	=	0.125 fl. oz.	=	3.6966 ml
1 fluid ounce (fl. oz. or ℥)	= 8 fl. dr.	=	1 fl. oz.	=	0.0296 l
1 pint (O.)	= 16 fl. oz.	=	16 fl. oz.	=	0.4732 l
1 gallon (C.)	= 8 O.	=	128 fl. oz.	=	3.7853 l

Shipping Capacity Measurement

		Customary		Metric
1 barrel bulk		=	5 cu. ft.	=	0.1416 m³
1 shipping ton, or 1 measurement ton, or 1 freight ton,	= 8 barrels bulk	=	40 cu. ft.	=	1.1327 m³
1 displacement ton		=	35 cu. ft.	=	0.9911 m³
1 register ton		=	100 cu. ft.	=	2.8317 m³

Weight and mass

The customary system measures the weight of various materials. Avoirdupois weight measures ordinary materials. Apothecaries' weight once measured drugs and medicines. Troy weight measures precious metals and gems. The metric system measures *mass* (amount of material something contains). An object's mass does not change, but its weight decreases with altitude. Mass and weight are equal at sea level, and the comparisons in this table are based on that location.

Avoirdupois Weight

				Metric
1 grain (gr.)	=			0.0648 g
1 dram (dr.)	=	27.34375	gr. =	1.7718 g
1 ounce (oz.)	=	16	dr. =	28.3495 g
1 pound (lb.)	=	16	oz. =	453.5924 g, or 0.4536 kg
1 hundred-weight (cwt.)	=	100	lb. =	45.3592 kg
1 short ton	=	2,000	lb. =	907.18 kg, or 0.9072 t

Special British Units	Customary			Metric	
1 stone (st.)	=	14	lb. =	6.35	kg
1 hundred-weight (cwt.)	=	112	lb. =	50.80	kg
1 long ton	=	2,240	lb. =	1,016.05	kg, or 1.0160 t

Metric Weight

					Avoirdupois
1 milligram (mg)				=	0.0154 gr.
1 centigram (cg)	=	10 mg	=		0.1543 gr.
1 decigram (dg)	=	10 cg	=		1.5432 gr.
1 gram (g)	=	10 dg	=		15.4324 gr.
1 dekagram (dag)	=	10 g	=		0.3527 oz.
1 hectogram (hg)	=	10 dag	=		3.5274 oz.
1 kilogram (kg)	=	10 hg	=		2.2046 lb.
1 metric ton (t)	=	1,000 kg	=		2,204.62 lb.

Apothecaries' Weight

				Avoirdupois			Metric	
1 grain (gr.)			=	0.002286	oz.	=	0.0648	g
1 scruple (s. ap. or ℈)	= 20	gr.	=	0.04571	oz.	=	1.296	g
1 dram (dr. ap. or ℨ)	= 3	s. ap.	=	0.1371	oz.	=	3.888	g
1 ounce (oz. ap. or ℥)	= 8	dr. ap.	=	1.0971	oz.	=	31.1035	g
1 pound (lb. ap. or ℔)	= 12	oz. ap.	=	13.1657	oz.	=	373.24	g, or 0.3732 kg

Troy Weight

				Avoirdupois			Metric	
1 grain (gr.)			=	0.002286	oz.	=	0.0648	g
1 pennyweight (dwt.)	= 24	gr.	=	0.054857	oz.	=	1.56	g
1 ounce (oz. t.)	= 20	dwt.	=	1.0971	oz.	=	31.1035	g
1 pound (lb. t.)	= 12	oz. t.	=	13.1657	oz.	=	373.24	g, or 0.3732 kg

Time

Both the customary and metric systems use the same units to measure time. The shortest unit of time in the customary system is the second. But the metric system has four units of time shorter than the second.

1 picosecond (ps)			=	0.000000000001 s
1 nanosecond (ns)			=	0.000000001 s
1 microsecond (μs)	=	1,000 ns	=	0.000001 s
1 millisecond (ms)	=	1,000 μs	=	0.001 s
1 second (s)	=	1,000 ms	=	$\frac{1}{3,600}$ h.
1 minute (min.)	=	60 s	=	$\frac{1}{60}$ h.
1 hour (h.)	=	60 min.		
1 day (d.)	=	24 h.		
1 week (wk.)	=	7 d.		
1 common lunar year (yr.)	=	354 d.		
1 common solar year	=	365 d.		
1 leap year	=	366 d.		
1 decade	=	10 yr.		
1 century	=	100 yr.		
1 millennium	=	1,000 yr.		

Temperature

The customary system measures temperature in Fahrenheit degrees. The metric system measures temperatures in Celsius degrees. The two temperature scales are shown below, with the freezing and boiling points of water indicated on both.

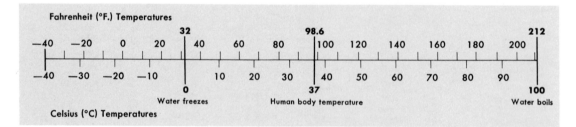

Fahrenheit (°F.) Temperatures

−40 −20 0 20 **32** 40 60 80 **98.6** 100 120 140 160 180 200 **212**

−40 −30 −20 −10 **0** 10 20 30 **37** 40 50 60 70 80 90 **100**

Water freezes   Human body temperature   Water boils

Celsius (°C) Temperatures

Other measures

The tables below and on the next page show other common measurement units. All these measurements are based on the customary system except for the metric wood measurement and the circular and angular measurement in radians.

Wood Measurement

		Customary		Metric	
1 board foot (bd. ft.)	=	144 cu. in. (1 ft. x 1 ft. x 1 in.)	=	.00236	m³
1 cord foot (cd. ft.)	=	16 cu. ft. (4 ft. x 4 ft. x 1 ft.)	=	0.4531	m³
1 cord (cd.)	=	8 cd. ft. (4 ft. x 4 ft. x 8 ft.)	=	3.625	m³

Circular and Angular Measurement

Degrees				Radians		
1 second ('')		=	$^1/_{1,296,000}$ circle	0.017454 radians (rad.) =		1°
1 minute (')	= 60 seconds	=	$^1/_{21,600}$ circle	1 radian	=	57.2958°
1 degree (°)	= 60 minutes	=	$^1/_{360}$ circle	2π radians	=	360°
1 quadrant,						
or 1 right angle	= 90 degrees	=	¼ circle	**Mils**		
1 circumference	= 4 quadrants	=	1 circle	1 mil =		0.056250°
				17.778 mils =		1°
				6,400 mils =		360°

Counting Measure						
	1 dozen (doz.)			=	12 units	
	1 gross (gr.)	=	12 doz.	=	144 units	
	1 great gross	=	12 gr.	=	1,728 units	

Paper Measure			
	1 quire (qr.)	=	24 or 25 sheets
	1 ream (rm.)	=	20 quires
	1 perfect ream	=	516 sheets
	1 bundle (bdl.)	=	2 reams
	1 bale	=	5 bundles

Printing Measure		Customary	Metric
	1 point	= approx. $^1/_{72}$ or 0.013837 in.	= 0.3514598 mm
	1 pica	= 12 points	= approx. ⅙ or 0.166044 in.
			= 4.2175176 mm

Weill, *vyl* or *wyl,* **Kurt** (1900-1950), was a German composer famous for his music for the theater. Weill is especially noted for music he composed for the plays of the German playwright Bertolt Brecht. The best-known work by Brecht and Weill is *The Threepenny Opera* (1928), which includes the popular song "Mack the Knife." They also wrote *Happy End* (1929), *The Rise and Fall of the City of Mahagonny* (1930), and *The Seven Deadly Sins* (1933).

Weill was born in Dessau and studied with the noted composers Engelbert Humperdinck and Ferruccio Busoni. He composed instrumental music and several works for the stage before starting his collaboration with Brecht. Weill left Germany in 1933 after the Nazis came to power. He settled in the United States in 1935.

Weill's first two works in America were the experimental musical plays *Johnny Johnson* (1936) and *The Eternal Road* (1937). His first traditional musical comedy, *Knickerbocker Holiday* (1938), features the famous ballad "September Song." Weill's other musicals include *One Touch of Venus* (1943), *Street Scene* (1947), *Down in the Valley* (1948), *Love Life* (1948), and *Lost in the Stars* (1949).

Thomas A. Erhard

Weimar Republic. See Germany (The Weimar Republic).

Weimaraner, *VY muh* RAH *nuhr* or *WY muh* RAH *nuhr,* is a hunting dog that originated in Weimar, Germany, in the 1800's. It was first bred to hunt big-game animals, such as deer and bears. Later, the dog became chiefly used to hunt game birds. The Weimaraner's gray coat, gray nose, and amber eyes give the dog a striking appearance. The dog has short fur and a tail cropped to be about 6 inches (15 centimeters) long when the dog is full grown. The Weimaraner weighs 60 to 80 pounds (27 to 36 kilograms) and is 24 to 28 inches (61 to 71 centimeters) high. It is intelligent, friendly, and obedient and has been used for many purposes, including obedience trials and field trials. It also makes an excellent pet. The dog is sometimes called the *gray ghost* because of its color and its silent movements when hunting.

Critically reviewed by the Weimaraner Club of America

See also **Dog** (picture: Sporting dogs).

Weinberger, Caspar Willard (1917-   ), was a Republican government official who held two Cabinet posts. He served as secretary of defense under President Ronald Reagan from 1981 to 1987 and helped direct a major increase in U.S. military forces. Weinberger was secretary of health, education, and welfare under President Richard M. Nixon from 1973 to 1975.

Weinberger was born in San Francisco and graduated from Harvard University in 1938. He earned a law degree from the Harvard Law School in 1941. In 1952, he won election to the California Assembly. In 1968, he became California state finance director. Nixon named Weinberger chairman of the Federal Trade Commission in 1970. In 1972, Nixon appointed him director of the Office of Management and Budget. Weinberger served in that post until his appointment to head the Department of Health, Education, and Welfare. In 1989, he became publisher of *Forbes* magazine.   Charles Bartlett

Weisgard, Leonard (1916-   ), is an American artist and illustrator of children's books. He won the Caldecott Medal in 1946 for his illustrations for *The Little Island* by Margaret Wise Brown, writing under the name Golden MacDonald. Weisgard illustrated over 20 other books by Brown and many picture books by other American authors. They include *Rain Drop Splash* (1946) by Alvin Tresselt and *The Courage of Sarah Noble* (1954) by Alice Dalgliesh. Weisgard has also written and illustrated over 20 books, including *My First Picture Book* (1953) and *The Plymouth Thanksgiving* (1967). He was born in New Haven, Conn.   Jill P. May

Weismann, *VYS mahn,* **August,** *OW gust* (1834-1914), a German biologist, is known chiefly for his theories of heredity and evolution. He stressed the independence from the rest of the body of the *germ plasm,* his name for the factors of inheritance in the sex cells. He denied that acquired characteristics can be inherited. He located the germ plasm in the chromosomes, a prediction that was proved correct early in the 1900's. Weismann upheld the theory of natural selection and was one of the first German scientists to support the British scientist Charles Darwin.

In Weismann's later years, he devoted himself chiefly to theoretical studies, and wrote extensively on heredity and evolution. His major work, *The Germ Plasm,* appeared in 1892. Weismann was born in Frankfurt, now part of West Germany. Mordecai L. Gabriel

Weissmuller, Johnny. See Olympic Games (The modern games).

Weizmann, *VYTS mahn* or *WYTS muhn,* **Chaim,** *KY ihm* (1874-1952), served as the first president of Israel from 1949 until his death. From 1920 to 1931 and from 1935 to 1948, Weizmann headed the World Zionist Organization, which worked to establish a national homeland for Jews in Palestine. He headed the Jewish delegation to the Paris Peace Conference in 1919, and worked there to have the League of Nations assign administration of Palestine to Great Britain. In 1917, Britain had issued the Balfour Declaration, which supported the idea of a Jewish national homeland in Palestine (see **Balfour Declaration**).

Wide World Photos
Chaim Weizmann

Weizmann was born in Motol, Russia, and he was educated in Germany and Switzerland. He taught chemistry at Manchester University in England from 1904 to 1914. During World War I, Weizmann discovered an improved method of making acetone and butyl alcohol for explosives. This discovery aided Britain's war effort.

Ellis Rivkin

Welding is a method of permanently joining two pieces of metal, usually by means of heat. Manufacturers use welding in making many products, including automobiles, home appliances, and furniture. Construction firms use it in erecting bridges, buildings, and other structures. The production of electronic equipment involves sophisticated microwelding processes.

There are more than 60 welding processes. Each process falls into one of three groups: (1) fusion welding, (2) solid-state bonding, and (3) brazing and soldering. However, some metallurgists do not consider brazing and soldering technically to be forms of welding.

Fusion welding uses heat to partially melt the metal surfaces that are to be joined. When the seam of melted metal cools and hardens, the two pieces are connected by a welded joint that may be as strong as any other part of the metal. Most fusion welding processes also use a *filler metal,* which is added to the weld in the form of a *welding rod* or a *consumable electrode.* The heat of the welding process melts the rod or electrode, which mixes with the melted base metal. The filler metal thus fills in the joint and strengthens it. The seam of hardened filler and base metal is called the *fusion zone.*

In most fusion welding processes, the heated metals must be shielded from hydrogen, nitrogen, and oxygen in the atmosphere. If the metals absorbed these gases, the weld could be weak or brittle. Shielding may be provided by spraying the metals during welding with an inactive gas, such as argon, carbon dioxide, or helium. Another method involves applying a nonmetallic *flux* to the metals before welding. The heat of welding melts the flux, which covers and protects the metals. A third way of shielding the metals is to weld in a vacuum.

There are a number of methods of fusion welding. They include the following.

Arc welding joins metals by using heat from an electric arc (see **Electric arc**). The welder uses an electrode holder, an electrode or welding rod, and a generator that produces an electric current. One type of arc welding, *shielded metal arc welding,* forms an electric arc between the metals and a flux-covered electrode. Heat from the electric arc melts the metal, the electrode, and the flux. In *submerged arc welding,* the electric arc is covered by powdered flux from a container attached to the welding tool. The arc forms between the metals and a consumable wire electrode that adds filler metal to the weld. The wire electrode is fed continuously through the welding tool from a coil.

Another type of arc welding is *gas tungsten arc welding.* In this process, an electric arc is directed between the metals and a bare wire electrode made from tungsten, which does not melt in the arc's heat. Argon or helium gas shields the metals. The welder must use a separate welding rod if filler metal is required. In *plasma arc welding,* argon or a similar gas is electrically heated until it forms an ionized gas called a *plasma.* An arc of plasma is directed on the metals to weld them, and a filler metal is supplied separately. The plasma arc also shields the metals. A plasma arc produces extremely high temperatures and can be used to weld metals that are difficult to join by other methods.

Resistance welding joins metals by means of the heat produced by resistance to the flow of an electric current. This process does not use filler metal or flux. The metals are clamped together, and electrodes apply pressure on opposite sides. An electric current passing through the electrodes meets resistance when it flows from one metal to the other. The resulting heat melts the metals and welds them together. In *resistance spot*

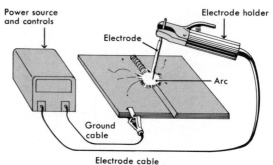
WORLD BOOK diagram
Arc welding joins metals by means of the heat produced by an electric arc. In shielded metal-arc welding, the arc forms between a flux-covered electrode and the metals to be welded.

Power source and controls
Electrode holder
Electrode
Arc
Ground cable
Electrode cable

A **welder** wears a mask with a special lens that protects the worker's eyes from the intense light of the welding process.

Phil Degginger

welding, rod-shaped electrodes form spot welds along the metals. In *resistance-seam welding,* electrodes in the form of rollers create a continuous seam.

Gas welding uses heat from a gas torch to join two metals. The most common welding gas is acetylene mixed with oxygen (see **Acetylene**). If the job requires a filler metal, the welder dips a welding rod into the liquid metal between the pieces being joined. A flux may be applied to the metal before welding.

Other fusion welding processes include those that use electron beams and lasers to produce the energy necessary to join metals. These methods require complex, specialized equipment. See **Laser.**

Solid-state bonding uses pressure as well as heat to bond metal and other materials. Common methods of solid-state bonding include the following.

Deformation bonding joins metals partly by means of pressure great enough to deform the pieces. The pressure forces the surfaces so close together that a strong joint forms by atomic attraction. Methods of exerting pressure include *roll bonding, friction* or *inertia welding, explosive bonding,* and *ultrasonic bonding.* In most cases, deformation bonding also involves heating metals to temperatures just below their melting points, so that atoms will move to the joint and fill in any gaps.

Diffusion bonding resembles deformation bonding but uses pressure insufficient to noticeably deform pieces. Diffusion bonding is especially suitable for joining unusual or reactive materials.

Brazing and soldering use a melted filler metal to join unusually close-fitting parts. The filler metal and a special flux are applied to the parts, which are then heated in an oven or with a gas torch. The temperature is too low to melt the parts. But the filler metal melts into the joint and welds the parts together. Brazing uses such fillers as brass, bronze, or a silver alloy. Soldering uses lead-tin alloys or other metals with comparatively lower melting points. See **Solder.**   Donald R. Askeland

Welfare generally refers to government programs that provide money, medical care, food, housing, and other necessities for needy people. People who receive welfare include children, the aged, the blind, the disabled, and others who cannot adequately provide for themselves and their families. Government welfare programs

are also called *public assistance.* Private charitable organizations, such as the Salvation Army, also give welfare assistance. All nations have some type of welfare.

Most public assistance in the United States comes from agencies of the federal and state governments. Public assistance benefits help many people who live below the *poverty line,* an income level established by the federal government. In the late 1980's, it was set at an annual income of about $12,000 for a family of four people. It is adjusted each year to account for inflation.

Public assistance differs from another type of government financial aid called *social insurance,* or *social security.* Social insurance programs are funded mainly by special payroll taxes on workers and their employers. Such programs in the United States include old-age, survivors, disability, and health insurance; unemployment insurance; and workers' compensation. Unlike welfare, social insurance programs provide benefits to people whether or not they are poor.

Welfare in the United States

Federal and state governments in the United States serve the needy through about 60 public assistance programs. Most people receive assistance chiefly through four major programs. These are (1) Medicaid, (2) Aid to Families with Dependent Children, (3) Supplemental Security Income for the Aged, Blind, and Disabled, and (4) the Food Stamp Program.

Medicaid provides free medical care to needy people. Eligibility criteria vary from state to state. In some states, people who can pay for their daily needs but cannot afford large medical bills may also qualify for Medicaid. Some services paid for include doctor visits, hospital treatment, and nursing home care. Medicaid also covers the cost of drugs, eyeglasses, hearing aids, and other medical items. Nearly half of all Medicaid expenses are for the aged and primarily cover the cost of nursing home care. Most Medicaid funding comes from the federal government. The rest comes from the state. Each state administers its own Medicaid program.

Aid to Families with Dependent Children (AFDC) provides cash benefits to dependent children and the parents or other adults caring for them. Most families that qualify for AFDC have just one parent in the home. About 80 per cent of these families are headed by a woman. AFDC also pays benefits to two-parent families if both parents are unemployed. Most AFDC funding comes from the federal government. The states provide the rest of the money and administer the program. The size of payments varies from state to state.

Supplemental Security Income for the Aged, Blind, and Disabled (SSI) provides financial aid to needy people who are at least 65 years old, or are blind or disabled. The federal government finances and administers SSI programs in most states, though some states supplement the federal payment and administer their own programs.

The Food Stamp Program helps low-income households buy more and better food than they could otherwise afford. Each participating household receives a certain number of coupons called *food stamps.* The stamps are issued by the federal government. The number of stamps a household receives varies with the family's size, income, and expenses. Cooperating grocery stores

Special Report
WELFARE
1995 Year Book, p. 438

accept the stamps like money for food purchases only.

Other welfare programs include public housing and energy assistance. Public housing provides low-cost rental apartments in government-owned buildings. Other federal housing programs give cash allowances to help low-income families rent privately owned housing. Energy assistance, which is federally financed but administered by the states, helps people pay fuel bills.

The federal government also finances and administers nutrition programs for low-income families. These programs furnish free food supplements for pregnant mothers and young children, and free or low-cost school lunches. Another federally funded program provides financial aid to college students from needy families. The federal government also offers financial aid, medical care, and other services to military veterans and their dependents.

The Earned Income Tax Credit (EITC) is a federal program financed and administered by the Internal Revenue Service. It provides a reduction in income tax to families that earn less than about $19,000 per year and have dependent children. Unlike other programs, the EITC aids families who live above the poverty line.

Finally, state and local governments fund and administer their own general assistance programs. These programs provide financial aid for needy people who do not qualify for other welfare. People waiting to receive assistance from other programs also may get temporary emergency aid from general assistance.

Criticism of the welfare system ranges over a number of economic and social issues. Some people criticize welfare programs for not providing high enough benefits to eliminate poverty. Spending on welfare would have to increase greatly to eliminate poverty, and many people believe the cost is already too high.

Many critics of the welfare system charge that providing a steady income to needy people encourages idleness. Actually, most welfare benefits go to elderly, blind, and disabled people and mothers with young children. But welfare does discourage some recipients from seeking employment, especially if they cannot get much more money from a job than they can get from benefits. Welfare discourages other recipients from working harder by reducing benefits if their income increases.

Many people also criticize the welfare system for being too complex and costly to administer. Each program has its own eligibility requirements and ways of calculating benefits, and these rules vary from state to state. Public officials collect detailed information about applicants to determine their eligibility for benefits. This process is time-consuming and costly.

Some people cheat the system by not reporting all the income they earn. But suppliers of services to welfare recipients account for most of the fraud in welfare. Some physicians, pharmacists, and others have been overpaid because they have made up false bills.

Welfare programs also may affect family stability. Unhappy marriages may break up partly because AFDC benefits are available. In addition, some people believe that welfare causes higher birth rates, with AFDC mothers deliberately having many children to increase their monthly benefits. But statistics show that there is no relationship between birth rates and AFDC programs. The availability of AFDC may enable needy parents to raise

their children themselves rather than give them up for adoption or foster care.

Welfare programs are also criticized for making recipients feel bad about themselves. Many people feel ashamed if poverty forces them to apply for welfare. In addition, some social workers look down on welfare recipients and treat them harshly.

Welfare in other nations

Welfare in Canada. The Canada Assistance Plan provides most of the public assistance in Canada. The plan is designed to provide financial aid to all of Canada's needy people. The provincial and national governments each pay half the cost of the program. The provincial governments administer the plan.

Welfare in Europe. Most European nations provide for their needy mainly through national programs that benefit all their citizens. In many countries, the government provides free medical and hospital care, family allowances, and retirement pensions. The programs in numerous Western European nations, such as Great Britain, Norway, and Sweden, are so complete that those countries are said to be *welfare states*. For more information, see the *Social welfare* section of the articles on **Great Britain, Norway,** and **Sweden.**

History

In early times, governments seldom took responsibility for relieving poverty. Charity to needy people generally came from relatives and neighbors. Religious groups also provided shelter, medical care, and financial assistance to the poor.

Early government welfare laws in England treated the poor harshly. For example, the Statute of Laborers, passed in 1349, prohibited charity because it might encourage idleness. In 1601, Parliament passed the Act for the Relief of the Poor, also known as the Elizabethan Poor Law. This law made local government units called *parishes* responsible for their own poor. The relief funds came from taxes collected in each parish.

Early welfare laws recognized two forms of assistance—*outdoor relief* and *indoor relief.* Outdoor relief was given to the needy in their own homes. To get indoor relief, however, the poor had to live in institutions known as *poorhouses, workhouses,* or *almshouses.* The terrible conditions in most such institutions discouraged all but the most desperate from seeking relief.

Early welfare in the United States resembled the English system. Local governments were responsible for aiding the poor. But the colonies, and later the states, sometimes helped the local government provide aid. The first federal welfare programs, begun after the Revolutionary War (1775-1783), provided pensions to war veterans. During the Civil War (1861-1865), these pensions were expanded to cover soldiers' widows and orphans. In the early 1900's, primary responsibility for providing welfare benefits shifted from local to state governments. During these years, states enacted programs to aid dependent children and the aged.

The Great Depression of the 1930's, an economic slump that brought joblessness and poverty to millions, led to a dramatic shift from state to federal responsibility. The Social Security Act of 1935 established federal assistance programs for dependent children, the blind, and the elderly, as well as old-age and unemployment insurance programs. The Social Security Act still provides the foundation for welfare in the United States.

Recent developments in welfare programs. Welfare benefits in the United States increased substantially during the 1950's and 1960's. A number of new programs were created, including the Food Stamp Program in 1964 and Medicaid in 1965, and existing programs received more funding. The SSI and EITC programs began in the mid-1970's. But during the 1970's, welfare benefits did not increase as fast as inflation. Also, Congress reduced benefits somewhat in the early 1980's.

Congress has also gradually changed the nature of AFDC. When the program began in 1935, most poor single mothers were widows, and AFDC was designed to enable them to stay home with their children. But by the 1980's, most poor single mothers were divorced or separated, or had never married. During the 1960's, Congress passed laws that provided incentives for AFDC mothers to find jobs. In the 1970's, the emphasis of legislation began to shift from work incentives to work requirements. Laws since the late 1960's have also increased the power of the federal government to require fathers of children receiving AFDC to provide some financial support.

The Family Support Act of 1988 contains strict work and child support requirements. The act provides that AFDC mothers must work if they have no children under 3 years of age. It also allows states to require mothers to work if they have no children under the age of 1. The act provides funding for child care and job training. It also requires the states to determine how much child support must be paid by a parent who does not have custody of a child and, in most cases, to withhold support payments from the parent's wages.   Irwin Garfinkel

Related articles in *World Book* include:

Aid to Families with   New Deal
 Dependent Children   Poverty
Food Stamp Program   School lunch
Housing (Public housing)   Social Security
Medicaid

Additional resources

Katz, Michael B. *In the Shadow of the Poorhouse: A Social History of Welfare in America.* Basic Books, 1986.
Law, Sylvia A. *The Rights of the Poor.* Avon, 1974.
The Welfare State. 3rd ed. Ed. by David L. Bender. Greenhaven, 1982. Suitable for younger readers.

Welfare state is a term sometimes applied to a country in which the government assumes major responsibility for the social welfare of its people. See also **Welfare** (Welfare in Europe).

Well is a hole in the earth from which a fluid is withdrawn. Water wells are the most common type. Oil and natural gas wells are also common. Mining companies also use wells to remove salt and sulfur from deep in the ground. They pump down steam or hot water to remove these materials.

Water wells. The underground water that flows into wells is called *ground water* (see **Ground water**). This water comes from rain that soaks into the ground and slowly moves down to the *ground water reservoir,* an area of soil and rock saturated with water. The top of this zone is the *water table,* the level at which water stands in a well that is not being pumped.

In damp places, the water table may lie just below the surface. It is easily reached by digging. A dug well is usually lined with bricks, stone, or porous concrete to keep the sides from caving in. In drier places, the water table may be hundreds of feet or meters down. It may then be necessary to drill the well and sink pipes. Power-driven pumps usually are used to draw the water out of deep wells.

In some areas, underground water moving down from the slopes of hills and mountains becomes trapped under watertight layers of clay or shale. Wells drilled through these layers in valleys and plains run into water under pressure. In such wells, called *flowing artesian wells,* the pressure may be strong enough to make water flow without pumping. See **Artesian well.**

Many people still depend on wells for their water

Kinds of water wells

Wells are used to draw water from the ground. They may be dug, driven, bored, or drilled into the earth. Dug wells can be constructed with hand tools or power tools. They measure up to 50 feet (15 meters) deep and have the greatest diameter of any water well. Driven wells consist of a series of pipes with a point at one end. The point is driven into the ground to a depth of up to 50 feet (15 meters). Bored wells, which are constructed with tools called *augers,* may be up to 100 feet (30 meters) deep. Drilled wells are constructed with special well-drilling equipment. They measure up to 1,000 feet (300 meters) deep.

WORLD BOOK diagrams by Arthur Grebetz

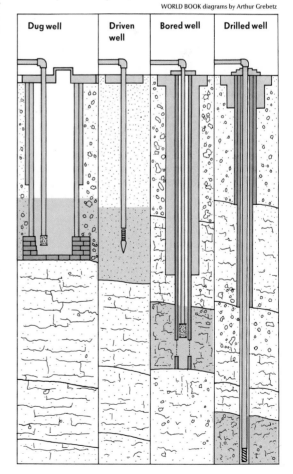

| Dug well | Driven well | Bored well | Drilled well |

supply, especially in rural areas. Many cities also get their water from wells. Underground water is usually pure, because the soil makes a good filter. It generally contains dissolved minerals. A well that taps water with a high mineral content is called a *mineral well.*

Water wells should be located so that they do not collect poisons or disease germs. A well should be at least 100 feet (30 meters) from a cesspool, and should never be located so that sewage drains toward it. Water from a well sunk through limestone may be dangerous because water runs through crevices and caves in limestone without being filtered. It is also important that surface water does not drain into a well.

Oil and natural gas wells. Oil and natural gas are lighter than water. Because of this, they would normally float upward and escape from the ground. But oil and gas become trapped beneath thick beds of rock in areas called *pools.* Wells penetrate deep into the earth to reach these pools and bring the oil and gas to the surface. *Wildcat wells* are drilled in search of new pools. A *production well* is drilled into a proven field.

Drilling oil and gas wells is a highly developed science. Workers who drill deep wells must have many years of training and experience. A deep oil well may cost several hundred thousand dollars. See **Gas** (From well to user; picture); **Petroleum** (Drilling an oil well).

Locating wells also requires a high degree of training. Geologists and engineers must be able to find where large amounts of oil or water lie, and determine at what rate they can take these materials out of the ground, and how much they can remove without damaging the natural resources.

Today, scientists and engineers use modern equipment such as seismographs to locate underground deposits (see **Seismograph**). But at one time, and sometimes even today, people have used a kind of magic in an attempt to locate water. For example, some people used a forked branch to do so. If such a branch, called a *divining rod,* is gripped firmly on the two forks and bent outward, the main stem will move up or down, unless the holder exerts effort to prevent this. A slight relaxation permits the main stem to point down. Some people believe that when this happens, the stem is pointing to a water source. People using this device sometimes succeed, but only because they have a common-sense idea of where water is usually found.   Ray K. Linsley

Welland Ship Canal is one of Canada's greatest engineering projects. It forms an important part of the St. Lawrence Seaway. The canal provides a navigable waterway 27 miles (44 kilometers) long between Lake Ontario and Lake Erie. The only natural connection between these two lakes is the Niagara River. But falls and rapids make much of the river useless as a commercial waterway.

The Welland Canal extends from Port Weller on Lake Ontario to Port Colborne on Lake Erie. Lake Erie is about 325 feet (99 meters) higher than Lake Ontario, so ships must be raised and lowered by locks. This is done by a series of eight locks.

The project to connect Lake Ontario and Lake Erie was completed in 1829. The original canal was built by a private company, with help from government loans, and cost about $7,700,000. It extended from Port Dalhousie, just west of Port Weller, on Lake Ontario to Port Robin-

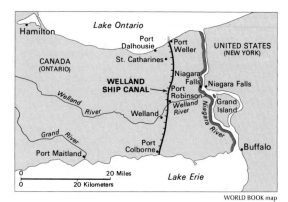

Location of the Welland Ship Canal

son on the Welland River. From Port Robinson, southbound ships sailed east along the Welland River to the Niagara River, and then went south along the Niagara to Lake Erie. But in 1833, workers completed an extension of the canal that stretched from Port Robinson south to Port Colborne (then called Gravelly Bay).

In a short time, the shipping industry wanted a larger waterway. In 1839, the project was taken over by the government of Upper Canada, which is now Ontario. The canal was greatly enlarged by 1845, and enlarged further by 1887. In 1912, the Canadian government began improvements that eventually resulted in the Welland Ship Canal of today. The canal officially opened on Aug. 6, 1932. It cost $130 million.

A reforestation project has been developed along the canal route to protect vessels from crosswinds. Loading docks service cities and factories along this route. The canal carries about 65 million short tons (60 million metric tons) of freight a year. It can be used by the largest bulk carriers on the Great Lakes. Ships can sail through the new canal in 8 hours or less, compared to the 16 hours required over the old waterway.

In 1973, workers completed a $110-million project to straighten and widen about 8 miles (13 kilometers) of the canal. The project also included the construction of several tunnels and bridges.   Carman Miller

See also **Saint Lawrence Seaway** (History; picture).

Weller, Thomas Huckle (1915-   ), a research biologist, shared the 1954 Nobel Prize for physiology or medicine with John F. Enders and Frederick C. Robbins (see **Enders, John F.; Robbins, F.C.**).

The men grew poliomyelitis viruses on tissues of human embryos outside the body (see **Poliomyelitis**). Weller also isolated and grew chicken pox, mumps, and shingles viruses. He was born in Ann Arbor, Mich. He became head of Harvard University's public health department in 1954.   Henry H. Fertig

Welles, *wehlz,* **Gideon** (1802-1878), was secretary of the Navy in the Cabinet of President Abraham Lincoln. Originally a Democrat, he joined the Republican Party when it was organized. Lincoln appointed him secretary of the Navy at the beginning of the Civil War. Under his management, the Union Navy set up a blockade along the Confederate coast, and formed a fleet of gunboats and ironclad vessels on the Mississippi River. Welles remained in the Cabinet of President Andrew Johnson, and vigorously upheld the President's Reconstruction policy.

Welles was born in Glastonbury, Conn. From 1826 to 1836, he edited the *Hartford* (Conn.) *Times.* He later served as chief of the Bureau of Provisions and Clothing of the U.S. Navy Department.   W. B. Hesseltine

Welles, Orson (1915-1985), was an actor and motion-picture director. While only in his early 20's, Welles was regarded as an important director of stage plays and radio series, in which he also performed. In 1938, his famous Halloween radio production of H. G. Wells's novel *The War of the Worlds* frightened many listeners by convincing them that Martians had actually invaded New Jersey. On the strength of this sensation, RKO studios hired Welles to write, direct, and act in his own films in Hollywood.

United Press Int.
Orson Welles

Welles's first film, *Citizen Kane* (1941), told the story of a powerful newspaperman, based on the life of publisher William Randolph Hearst. Polls of international film critics rank the film as one of the most important films in motion-picture history. It is regarded, especially for its camera and sound techniques, as perhaps the most influential film ever made in the United States.

Welles's next film, *The Magnificent Ambersons* (1942), is only partly his work. While he was abroad, RKO studios reedited the film and added a different ending. Thereafter, he wrote and directed only a few films in Hollywood, including *The Lady from Shanghai* (1948) and *Touch of Evil* (1958). Welles acted in more than 60 motion pictures, often to finance his independent film-making projects in Europe. Among these films are *The Trial* (1962) and *Falstaff* (1966). Although Welles was criticized for his flamboyance, his artistic independence inspired many young filmmakers. George Orson Welles was born in Kenosha, Wis.   Robert Sklar

See also **Motion picture** (Orson Welles).

Wellesley College is a privately controlled liberal arts school for women in Wellesley, Mass. It grants bachelor's degrees. Wellesley is noted for its art and library collections and its science laboratories. Henry Fowle Durant founded Wellesley College in 1870. It opened in 1875. For enrollment, see **Universities and colleges** (table).   Critically reviewed by Wellesley College

Wellington (pop. 325,697) is the capital and second largest city of New Zealand. It ranks as one of the country's chief seaports and manufacturing centers. Wellington lies along the harbor of Port Nicholson, on the southern coast of the North Island. For location, see **New Zealand** (map). Wellington and the surrounding area make up one of the most highly populated regions of New Zealand.

The port of Wellington handles foreign trade and also shipping and transportation between the North Island and the South Island, the largest islands of New Zealand. Factories in the Wellington area assemble automobiles and manufacture chemicals, clothing, electrical

machinery, processed foods, and other products.

Wellington is the home of Victoria University of Wellington. Other places of interest include the parliament buildings, two cathedrals, the Dominion Museum and National Art Gallery and the Sir Michael Fowler Centre.

British settlers founded Wellington in 1840. The capital was moved there from Auckland in 1865 because of Wellington's central location.   Brian Kitching

See also **New Zealand** (picture: The parliament).

Wellington, Duke of (1769-1852), was a British soldier and statesman who was known as *The Iron Duke.* He became famous as the general who overcame the armies of Napoleon in Spain and Portugal, and defeated Napoleon at the Battle of Waterloo. Later, Wellington became a leader of the Tory Party and served as prime minister.

Young soldier. Wellington was born Arthur Wellesley in Dublin, Ireland. He was the fourth son of Garrett Wellesley, Earl of Mornington. He was educated at Eton College and at a military college in France. At 18, he entered the army. Wellington rose rapidly and by 1796 had reached the rank of colonel. He first saw combat in 1794 in Flanders. In 1796, his regiment was sent to India, where his brother was governor general. Wellington became a major general before he was 35, and in 1803 he was given command of the British forces in the Mahratta War. He soon defeated the Mahratta chiefs and firmly established British power in India.

Peninsular War. In 1805, Wellington returned to England, and was elected the next year to Parliament. Two years later he was appointed chief secretary of Ireland. While there, he worked for new laws that would establish fair rents for tenants. He also laid the foundation for organization of the Irish police.

In 1808, Spain revolted against Napoleon, and the British sent troops there to help the Spanish. Wellington was promoted to lieutenant general and took command of one of the British divisions fighting in the peninsula of Spain and Portugal. Three weeks after he landed in Portugal, he defeated the French in the Battle of Vimeiro and forced them to leave Portugal.

Victory in Spain. In 1809, Wellington became commander of all British forces in the Peninsular War. He fought many battles with the help of Spanish forces and a Portuguese army that was organized by Great Britain. His small army won victory after victory. Slowly, he drove the French forces from the peninsula. In April 1814, Wellington won the Battle of Toulouse in France. Napoleon abdicated his throne, and the Peninsular War ended. Wellington returned to England in triumph, and he was given the title of Duke of Wellington.

Victory at Waterloo. In July 1814, Wellington was appointed ambassador to France. The following year, he represented Great Britain at the Congress of Vienna, although the Congress had completed most

Ewing Galloway
Duke of Wellington

of its work before he arrived (see **Vienna, Congress of**). He was at Vienna when the Congress heard of Napoleon's escape from Elba and return to France. Wellington signed the declaration that named Napoleon "the enemy and disturber of the peace of the world," and took command of the allied forces in the Netherlands. At the Battle of Waterloo, Wellington fought Napoleon himself for the first time. In this battle, Wellington rode at the head of his troops and, with Prince Gebhard Blücher's Prussian army, completely crushed Napoleon's power (see **Blücher, Gebhard L. von**). After that, Wellington commanded the army that occupied France for a short time. See **Waterloo, Battle of.**

Political career. In 1818 Wellington returned to England and held various government and diplomatic posts. He became commander in chief of the army in 1827, but resigned in 1828 to become prime minister of Great Britain.

Wellington belonged to the Tory Party, but he angered many in his party by pushing through a Catholic emancipation act that gave the vote to Roman Catholics and removed political liabilities from them. The British demanded parliamentary reform, and Wellington's opposition to a reform bill made his government unpopular. In 1830, he was forced to resign.

The Tory Party returned to power in 1834, but Wellington refused to become prime minister again. Seven years later, he became a member of Sir Robert Peel's cabinet and again served as commander in chief of the army. He retired in 1846. Although his opposition to reform made him unpopular at times, Wellington was respected as a national hero and was buried in Saint Paul's Cathedral.   Charles F. Mullett

Wells, H. G. (1866-1946), was a famous English novelist, historian, science writer, and author of science-fiction stories. Wells's novel *Tono-Bungay* (1909) best reveals his varied talents. The novel, a story of the dishonest promotion of a patent medicine, contains social criticism tinged with satire. In it, Wells described trips in airplanes and submarines at a time when such journeys seemed like science fiction.

Herbert George Wells was born in Bromley, Kent. He drew on his lower-middle-class background in some of his finest novels, including *Kipps* (1905) and *The History of Mr. Polly* (1909). His training as a scientist is reflected in his imaginative science-fiction stories. *The Time Machine* (1895) describes the adventures of a man who can transport himself into the future. Wells wrote about an invasion from Mars in *The War of the Worlds* (1898) and described a fictional utopia in *The Shape of Things to Come* (1933).

Wells supported social reform in the novel *The New Machiavelli* (1911), in the nonfiction study *The Work, Wealth and Happiness of Mankind* (1932), and in other books. He wrote *The Outline of History* (1920), a story of the development of the human race. The book shows Wells's knowledge of biol-

Culver
H. G. Wells

ogy and his liberal attitude in politics. With his son Geoffrey and Sir Julian Huxley, Wells wrote *The Science of Life* (1929-1930), a four-volume discussion of the principles of biology. Wells told his life story in *Experiment in Autobiography* (1934).   Sharon Bassett

Wells, Henry. See Wells, Fargo & Company.

Wells, Horace. See Dentistry (History of Dentistry).

Wells-Barnett, Ida Bell (1862-1931), was an American journalist and reformer. She was known chiefly for her campaign against the lynching of blacks during the late 1800's and early 1900's (see **Lynching**). Many blacks were lynched without even a trial after being accused of a crime, and others were lynched for no apparent reason at all. Wells-Barnett worked to expose such killings and to establish laws against lynching.

Ida Wells was born a slave in Holly Springs, Miss. She moved to Memphis in 1884. In 1889, she became part-owner and a reporter for *Free Speech,* a Memphis newspaper. In 1892, after three of her friends were hanged in Memphis, she began to investigate lynchings and other violence against blacks. Her work led to the establishment of many antilynching organizations.

She moved to Chicago in 1894 and the next year married Ferdinand L. Barnett, a lawyer and journalist. In 1909, Wells-Barnett helped found the National Association for the Advancement of Colored People (NAACP). She also took part in the campaign to give women the right to vote.   Otey M. Scruggs

Wells, Fargo & Company was an early American express and banking organization. Henry Wells and William G. Fargo founded the company in 1852. They planned an express service from San Francisco to New York City, with the American Express Company serving as eastern representative. In 1866, Benjamin Holladay sold his overland mail and stagecoach business to Wells, Fargo & Company, which soon became the most powerful firm in the Far West.

Wells, Fargo & Company carried passengers, freight, and mail. It specialized in shipping gold and silver from western mines. The Wells Fargo Nevada National Bank was formed in 1905. In 1918, Wells, Fargo & Company merged its express operations with two other major express companies to form the American Railway Express Company. The Wells Fargo Nevada National Bank continued its operations and later became the Wells Fargo Bank. Today, Wells, Fargo & Company and its subsidiaries provide a large network of banking and financial services.   W. Turrentine Jackson

See also **Fargo, William George.**

Welsbach, *WEHLZ bak* or *VEHLS bahk,* **Baron von** (1858-1929), was an Austrian chemist and pioneer in artificial lighting. He is noted chiefly as the inventor of a gaslight called the *Welsbach mantle.* He also invented the osmium filament for electric lamps and isolated the elements neodymium and praseodymium.

Welsbach was born Carl Auer in Vienna, and studied chemistry at the University of Heidelberg. Later, he attended the University of Vienna.   K. L. Kaufman

See also **Neodymium; Praseodymium.**

Welsh. See Wales (People).

Welsh corgi. See Cardigan Welsh corgi; Pembroke Welsh corgi.

Welsh pony. See Horse (table: Some types and breeds of horses; Ponies; picture).

Welsh springer spaniel looks like its relative, the English springer. It is a little smaller, and its coat is always red and white. As a sporting dog, the Welsh springer has a keen sense of smell, and will work well even in bad weather and rough brush. It can retrieve

WORLD BOOK photo by E. F. Hoppe

The Welsh springer spaniel has a keen sense of smell.

game on land or in the water. But unless the Welsh springer spaniel is trained well while it is young, it may be headstrong and independent.   Maxwell Riddle

Welsh terrier is one of the oldest English breeds of dogs. It has been known in Wales for several hundred years. It is closely related to the original black and tan terrier of England. The Welsh looks like a small-sized Airedale, with its wiry coat of deep red and jet-black markings. It has a long head and powerful jaws. This hearty hunting terrier weighs about 20 pounds (9 kilograms). The Welsh originally was bred for use in foxhunting. See also **Dog** (picture: Terriers).

Critically reviewed by the Welsh Terrier Club of America

Welty, Eudora, *yoo DOHR uh* (1909-   ), is an American short-story writer and novelist known for her searching studies of small-town life in the South. She has lived in Mississippi most of her life, and her affection for the South can be seen in her work.

Welty's style combines delicacy with shrewd, robust humor. The mixture of realism and fantasy in some of her stories gives them an almost mythical quality. Her major themes extend beyond the South—loneliness, the pain of growing up, and the need for people to understand themselves and their neighbors.

Welty's short stories appear in several collections, including *A Curtain of Green* (1941), *The Wide Net* (1943), and *The Bride of the Innisfallen* (1955). *The Collected Stories of Eudora Welty* was published in 1980. Her longer fiction consists of the novelettes *The Robber Bridegroom* (1942) and *The Ponder Heart* (1954) and the novels *Delta Wedding* (1946), *Losing Battles* (1970), and *The Optimist's Daughter* (1972). She received the 1973 Pulitzer Prize for *The Optimist's Daughter.* Her essays and reviews appear in *The Eye of the Story* (1978). She described the influence of her family and surroundings on her writing in *One Writer's Beginnings* (1984). Welty was born in Jackson, Miss.   John B. Vickery

Welwitschia, *wehl WIHCH ee uh,* also called *tumboa,* is a peculiar plant that grows in the sandy deserts of southwestern Africa. The Welwitschia resembles a giant, flattened mushroom. Its short, woody trunk rises from a large taproot and spreads like a table-top to a width of 5 to 6 feet (1.5 to 1.8 meters). The plant bears a single pair of leathery, green leaves that spread over the ground. The leaves are 2 to 3 feet (61 to 91 centimeters) wide and often twice as long. They grow in length for the life of the plant. Older plants appear to have many leaves because hot winds, blowing sand, and age split the two leaves into long, ribbonlike shreds.

Each year, stiff, jointed stemlike growths from 6 to 12 inches (15 to 30 centimeters) long develop at the point where the leaves join the trunk. These growths bear

Michael Fogden, Bruce Coleman Inc.

The Welwitschia resembles a giant, flattened mushroom. It bears two leaves that split into long, ribbonlike shreds.

small, erect flower spikes called *cone clusters.* Welwitschia plants are either male or female. Male plants produce small cones. Female plants bear larger cones that are bright scarlet. The cones are pollinated by insects. Welwitschia plants grow slowly and often live 1,000 to 2,000 years. The plant was named for Friedrich Welwitsch, an Austrian botanist of the 1800's.

Scientific classification. Welwitschia belongs to the division Gnetophyta. It is *Welwitschia mirabilis.*

Michael G. Barbour

Wen is a *cyst* (growth) in the skin. The skin contains *sebaceous glands* that secrete oil to lubricate the skin. A wen forms when these secretions collect inside a sebaceous gland. Wens may appear on any part of the skin except the soles of the feet or the palms of the hands. Wens usually appear on the scalp, face, or shoulder. They grow slowly, forming round or oval lumps, from the size of a pea to that of a walnut. Wens are soft and painless. They hold a yellowish-white matter, which may have a rancid odor. Wens may become infected, causing inflammation and pain. Any lump or growth in the skin should be seen promptly by a doctor.   Orville J. Stone

Wentworth, Thomas. See **Strafford, Earl of.**

Werewolf, according to superstition, is a person who changes into a wolf. The word comes from the Old English term *werwulf,* meaning *man-wolf.* Werewolves ap-

pear in many old stories. In some tales, they turn themselves into wolves by putting on a wolf skin, by drinking
water from a wolf's footprint, or by rubbing a magic
ointment on their bodies. In other stories, they are transformed by someone else's magic power.

The werewolves in most stories try to eat people. The
people in the stories who are threatened by werewolves
use various methods to bring them back to human form.
These methods include saying the werewolf's real name,
hitting the werewolf three times on the forehead, and
making the sign of the cross. According to the stories,
one way to find out a werewolf's identity is to wound it
and later look for a human with similar wounds.

Stories about werewolves have been most common
in Europe. Tales from other parts of the world tell of
people who turn into various other kinds of animals.

The technical word for werewolf is *lycanthrope*. This
word comes from *Lycaon,* the name of a king in Greek
mythology who was turned into a wolf by the god Zeus.
Lycanthropy is a form of mental illness in which a person imagines he or she is a wolf.   Alan Dundes

Wergeland, *VAIR guh lahn,* **Henrik Arnold** (1808-
1845), was a Norwegian patriot and author. He helped
arouse Norwegian national feeling by urging his fellow
citizens to seek independence from Sweden and to develop their own intellectual and cultural life. Many Nor-
wegians consider him a national hero.

Wergeland wrote poetry, drama, and prose, but his
poems are his greatest works. They include *Creation,
Man, and Messiah* (1830); *Jan van Huysum's Flower Piece*
(1840); *The Jew* (1842); *The Jewess* (1844), and *The English Pilot* (1844). Wergeland was born in Kristiansand,
Norway, the son of a clergyman.   Einar Haugen

Werner, *VEHR nur,* **Abraham Gottlob,** *AH brah
hahm GOHT lohp* (1749?-1817), a German geologist, for-
mulated a theory on the origin of the earth that was
widely accepted in his time. Werner believed all rocks
of the earth were formed from a giant ocean. Scientists
accepted this incorrect theory for many years because
Werner was the leading geologist of his day. He also introduced a system of identifying and classifying rocks
and created new methods of describing minerals.

Werner taught at the Freiberg School of Mines in
Freiberg from 1775 until his death. Students came from
throughout Europe to hear him explain complex ideas in
a simple way. His lectures helped geology gain respect
as an important area of study.   R. H. Dott, Jr.

See also **Geology** (The rock dispute).

Weser River, *VAY zuhr,* is an important German waterway. Its main headwater, the Werra, rises on the
southwestern slopes of the Thüringian Forest in central
Germany. The Weser winds 430 miles (700 kilometers) to
its mouth at the North Sea near Bremerhaven. For location, see **Germany** (physical map). In 1894, its channel
was deepened from the mouth to Bremen, about 45
miles (72 kilometers) to the south, so that large ships
could sail to Bremen.   Hugh D. Clout

Wesley, Charles (1707-1788), a clergyman of the
Church of England, was a founder of Methodism and
shared its leadership with his brother John. Charles is
best known as the author of more than 7,000 hymns,
many of which are still sung in Christian worship. They
include "Hark, the Herald Angels Sing," "Christ the Lord
Is Risen Today," and "Jesu, Lover of My Soul."

Wesley was born in Epworth, Lincolnshire. Like his
brother, he was educated at Christ Church College at
Oxford University in the 1720's. There he met with small
groups of other students for methodical study, spiritual
devotion, and practical good works. These activities
earned them the nickname "Methodist." For the next 20
years, Charles helped his brother shape the Methodist
movement. He was a vigorous evangelical preacher and
wrote about 480 of the 525 hymns in the Methodist *Collection of Hymns* (1780), widely regarded as a spiritual
classic. After his marriage in 1749, Charles settled into
parish ministry, though he continued to be a close adviser of his brother.   David Lowes Watson

See also **Methodists; Wesley, John.**

Wesley, John (1703-1791), a clergyman of the Church
of England, was a founder of Methodism. He was the
foremost leader in England of the Evangelical Revival, a
movement in Protestant Christianity during the 1700's
that emphasized personal faith and practical good
works. In carrying out his evangelical mission, Wesley
traveled about 250,000 miles (400,000 kilometers) and
preached over 40,000 sermons, often as many as 4 in a
day. His concern for the poor led him to provide loan
funds, establish homes for widows and orphans, extend
ministries to prisons and the armed forces, and open
free medical dispensaries.

Early years. Wesley was born in Epworth in Lincolnshire. He was the 15th of 19 children born to Susanna
Wesley and her husband, Samuel, an Anglican clergyman. Both parents were firmly committed to the Church
of England, yet came from Nonconformist families who
had separated from the Church of England. This background gave the young Wesley a deep sense of two traditions in English religious thought. One was the importance of the organized church, with its rules and
teachings. The other was the vitality of Puritan inward
religion, with its focus on a direct relationship with God.

Wesley was admitted to Christ Church College at Oxford University in 1720 and was ordained a priest in the
Church of England in 1728. He returned to Oxford in
1729 as a fellow of Lincoln College. There he became
spiritual adviser to some students, including his brother
Charles, who gathered in small groups to help each
other with study, devotions, and practical good works.
They were ridiculed by other students as "The Holy
Club" and "Bible Moths," but the nickname that prevailed
was "Methodists." Their practice of accountability in
small groups for the spiri-
tual life of all their members became the basic
structure of the later Methodist movement.

While Wesley was a mis-
sionary to Georgia from
1735 to 1737, he was influenced by the Moravians, a
German church that
stressed personal faith and
disciplined Christian living.
Its influence on Wesley led
to a spiritual crisis that was
not resolved until he re-
turned to England. In London on May 24, 1738, he

Detail of painting (1766) by
Nathaniel Hone; National
Portrait Gallery, London

John Wesley

attended a small religious meeting. There, according to his *Journal,* his heart was "strangely warmed" as he experienced the inward assurance of faith that so impressed him about the Moravians.

Leadership of the Methodist societies. Wesley increasingly assumed a leadership role in the Evangelical Revival. In 1739, at the invitation of George Whitefield, another prominent evangelist, he began to preach in the open air. For a number of years, he was joined in this activity by his brother Charles. Their "field preaching" became characteristic of Methodism, drawing large crowds. Those who responded to their message were incorporated into societies patterned on the religious societies of the Church of England dating back to the late 1600's.

Wesley's genius lay in organizing the Methodist societies into a movement. In 1743, he drew up a set of General Rules, which required members to attend weekly "class meetings." At the meetings, each member was asked to give an account of his or her discipleship according to well-defined guidelines. Wesley gave considerable responsibility to the leaders of these classes, who became a crucial link in the authority he exercised over the movement. Wesley also adopted *lay* (unordained) preachers as his assistants and helpers, and in 1744 he started an annual conference to consult on matters of doctrine and practice. The minutes of these conferences, along with his *Letters* and detailed *Journal,* are perhaps the fullest record of any religious movement. They have been published as part of a 34-volume edition of *The Works of John Wesley* (1976-   ).

Wesley's evangelical message created some controversy. It was opposed by many Anglican clergy as religiously fanatical and politically disruptive. The Calvinist wing of the Evangelical Revival criticized it as being too universal and putting too much emphasis on good works.

Formation of the Methodist Church. Wesley wanted Methodism to remain a reforming movement within the Church of England, and resisted separation from the church throughout his life. The issue was forced, however, by the need to provide for those who belonged to Methodist societies in the newly founded United States. In 1784, Wesley ordained Methodist preachers for North America, a step that led to the formation of the Methodist Episcopal Church, and then of the Methodist Church worldwide.   David Lowes Watson

See also **Methodists; Wesley, Charles; Whitefield, George.**

Additional resources

Ayling, Stanley E. *John Wesley.* Abingdon, 1983. First published in 1979.
Pudney, John. *John Wesley and His World.* Scribner, 1978.

Wesleyan Church is a religious denomination that was founded in 1968. It was formed by the merger of the Wesleyan Methodist Church and the Pilgrim Holiness Church. The Wesleyan Methodist Church had been established in 1843, and the Pilgrim Holiness Church in 1897. Many beliefs of the Wesleyan Church are based on doctrines set forth by the Dutch theologian Jacobus Arminius and the English minister John Wesley. The church conducts missionary work in Africa, Asia, Australia, Latin America, the Pacific Islands, and the Carib-

bean region. In the United States, it operates five colleges, two academies, and a children's home. Its headquarters are in Marion, Ind. See also **Arminius, Jacobus; Wesley, Charles; Wesley, John.**
Critically reviewed by the Wesleyan Church

Wessex. See **England** (The Anglo-Saxon period).
West, in international relations. See **Cold War.**
West, Benjamin (1738-1820), was an American painter who became famous for his large pictures of historical subjects. Many critics today agree with the painter Gilbert Stuart, who scorned West's "ten-acre pictures." But West influenced painters of his day, and taught many of the finest early American painters. His studio in London became a "school" for many American artists, including Ralph Earl, Samuel F. B. Morse, Charles Willson Peale, Rembrandt Peale, Gilbert Stuart, and John Trumbull.

West was born in Springfield, Pa. After some study with a local painter, West went to Italy when he was 21, and studied and copied the Roman sculptures and Renaissance and baroque paintings there for three years. West settled permanently in London in 1763. In the early 1770's, he gained fame for his paintings *The Death of General Wolfe* and *Penn's Treaty with the Indians.* In 1772, King George III of England made West his official painter of history. In 1792, West was elected the second president of the Royal Academy of Arts, which he had helped establish in 1768.   Elizabeth Garrity Ellis

See also **Wolfe, James** (picture); **United States, History of the** (picture: Early colonists); **Monroe, James** (picture: Elizabeth Kortright Monroe).

West, Jerry (1938-   ), became one of the greatest all-around players in the history of basketball. West, who played as a guard for the Los Angeles Lakers of the National Basketball Association (NBA), won fame for his scoring ability and ball-handling and defensive skills. West was head coach of the Lakers from 1976 to 1979 and became the team's general manager in 1982.

West played in the NBA from 1960 to 1974. When he retired as an active player, West ranked third in the NBA in regular-season scoring, with 25,192 points. West also became the first NBA player to score more than 4,000 points in play-off competition.

Jerome Allen West was born in Cabin Creek, W. Va., near Charleston. He won all-America honors at the University of West Virginia.   Bill Gleason

West, Jessamyn (1907-1984), was an American author. Her first and most famous book is *The Friendly Persuasion* (1945). In a series of sketches, it describes the rural life of a Quaker family in the mid-1800's.

West was a Quaker, and Quaker ideals of brotherhood can be found throughout her work. She wrote on various subjects. Her second novel, *The Witch Diggers* (1951), is a symbolic story set on a poor farm in southern Indiana. *Cress Delahanty* (1953) describes a girl midway between childhood and maturity. *Except for Thee and Me* (1969) is another novel about characters who appeared in *The Friendly Persuasion. Collected Stories of Jessamyn West* was published in 1986, after her death.

West was born in Indiana. Besides novels, stories, and essays, she wrote screenplays, including one for the film *Friendly Persuasion* (1956).   John Crossett

West, Mae (1892-1980), was an American actress who became famous for the humorous, bawdy sexuality of her stage and motion-picture performances. The success of her films *She Done Him Wrong* and *I'm No Angel* (both 1933) resulted in the Motion Picture Production Code to regulate the content of movies. To avoid having her material banned by the film censors, West spoke in double meanings, often cleverly parodying attitudes on sex. She became famous for such suggestive lines as "Come up and see me some time."

West was born in Brooklyn, N.Y. She worked in vaudeville and in stage revues from the age of 5. Her hit stage appearances in the 1920's brought her to Hollywood. In the first of her 12 films, *Night After Night* (1932), she displayed the wit and skill with racy wisecracks that made her an international celebrity. By 1936, West was the highest-paid woman in the United States. Her other films include *Belle of the Nineties* (1934) and *My Little Chickadee* (1940).   Rachel Gallagher

See also **Fields, W. C.** (picture).

West, Nathanael (1903?-1940), was an American novelist noted for a brilliant but bitter view of modern American life. He published only four short novels before he was killed in an automobile accident. All of West's fiction should be considered "experimental." *Miss Lonelyhearts* (1933) is a grim satire about a newspaperman who is assigned to write a column advising people on their problems. *The Day of the Locust* (1939) is a fantastic and sometimes nightmarish satire of life in Hollywood, where West wrote screenplays.

West was born in New York City. His real name was Nathan Wallenstein Weinstein. He wrote his first novel, *The Dream Life of Balso Snell,* in the mid-1920's. It was published in 1931. West also wrote *A Cool Million* (1934), a parody of a "rags to riches" story. West's reputation developed only after his death.   Victor A. Kramer

West, Dame Rebecca (1892-1983), was a British novelist, literary critic, and one of the greatest journalists of the 1900's. West analyzed the political and psychological reasons why people betray their countries in *The Meaning of Treason* (1947, revised as *The New Meaning of Treason,* 1964) and *A Train of Powder* (1955). In *Black Lamb and Grey Falcon* (1941), she wrote a penetrating study of the political history of Yugoslavia and other Balkan lands.

West's first book of literary criticism, *Henry James* (1916), describes the importance of James in shaping the modern novel. Her antiwar novel *The Return of the Soldier* (1918) shows James's influence in its emphasis on the psychological motives behind the characters' actions. The powerful novel *The Judge* (1922) is set in Edinburgh, Scotland, during the struggle for women's right to vote. West's autobiographical novel *The Fountain Overflows* (1956) was followed by two sequels published after her death, *This Real Night* (1984) and the unfinished *Cousin Rosamund* (1985). Another novel published after her death, *Sunflower* (1986), exploits her relationships with author H. G. Wells and newspaper tycoon Lord Beaverbrook. Her other novels include *The Thinking Reed* (1936) and *The Birds Fall Down* (1966).

West was born in London. Her given and family name was Cicely Isabel Fairfield. She became interested in women's rights and took the pen name Rebecca West from the strong-willed heroine of Henrik Ibsen's drama *Rosmersholm.* West was made Dame Commander in the Order of the British Empire in 1959.   Jane Marcus

West, The. In American history, the *frontier* (unsettled area) usually lay to the west of settled regions. For this reason, the terms *west* and *frontier* came to have the same meaning. To the first colonists, the frontier lay beyond the Appalachian Mountains. Later, pioneers who lived in the Midwest considered the plains and mountains farther west to be the frontier. See also **Pioneer life in America; Western frontier life; Westward movement.**   Walker D. Wyman

West, The, in international relations. See **Cold War.**

West Bank is a region that lies west of the River Jordan and the Dead Sea. It has an area of about 2,300 square miles (6,000 square kilometers) and a population of about 1 million. The West Bank was part of the area called Palestine from ancient times until 1950, when Jordan annexed it.

Since 1967, Israeli troops have held the West Bank. In 1974, Jordan gave up its claim to the region and called for the foundation of a Palestinian state there, should Israel withdraw. But Jordan continued to play key roles in the administration and financial support of the West Bank. Violence erupted in the region in 1982 and 1987 as Palestinians protested Israel's occupation. Israeli troops killed a number of demonstrators. The protests and violence continued into 1989. In 1988, Jordan ended its roles in the West Bank. For more details about the region, see **Jordan.**   Malcolm C. Peck

West Berlin. See **Berlin.**

West Germany. See **Germany.**

West Highland white terrier is the only all-white breed of Scottish terriers. The breed was developed

WORLD BOOK photo by E. F. Hoppe

West Highland white terriers are faithful pets.

from the white puppies in litters of cairn, Scottish, and Skye terriers. It has bright eyes and carries its tail high and its ears straight up. It has a wiry coat about 2 inches (5 centimeters) long. The dog weighs from 13 to 19 pounds (6 to 9 kilograms).   Josephine Z. Rine

West Indies are an island chain dividing the Caribbean Sea from the rest of the Atlantic Ocean. The islands stretch about 2,000 miles (3,200 kilometers) from near southern Florida to Venezuela's northern coast.

Three main island groups make up the West Indies. They are (1) the Bahamas in the north, (2) the Greater An-

The West Indies is an area of great natural beauty. Sandy beaches and tall palm trees line the coasts of many islands. The picture at the left shows a secluded beach on the island of Barbados. The West Indies extend from near southern Florida to the northern coast of Venezuela.

Andy Levin, Black Star

tilles near the center, and (3) the Lesser Antilles in the southeast. The Bahamas consist of about 3,000 small islands and reefs. The Greater Antilles include the large islands of Cuba, Jamaica, Hispaniola, and Puerto Rico. Politically, Hispaniola is divided into the Dominican Republic and Haiti. The Lesser Antilles are smaller islands southeast of Puerto Rico. All the islands except the Bahamas are sometimes called the Antilles.

Most of the islands of the West Indies were formed by volcanic eruptions. Others are coral and limestone formations. The warm climate, beautiful beaches, and tropical scenery attract large numbers of tourists. Most West Indians have black African, European, or mixed African and European ancestry. A majority of the people live in rural villages and farm for a living.

The first inhabitants of the West Indies were American Indians. In 1492, Christopher Columbus became the first European to reach the islands, when he landed on San Salvador in the Bahamas. He called them the Indies because he believed they were the East Indies islands of Asia. The islands were later given the name West Indies to distinguish them from the Asian islands. After Columbus visited the region, various European countries gained control of West Indies islands. Today, most of the islands make up, or form part of, independent nations. The rest are associated with France, Great Britain, the Netherlands, or the United States. For lists of the independent nations and the other political units of the West Indies, see the *tables* in this article.

People

Population and ancestry. The West Indies have a population of about 31 million. About a third of the people live on Cuba, the largest of the West Indies islands. Some West Indies islands are among the world's most densely populated places. About 55 per cent of the people live in rural areas, and about 45 per cent live in urban areas.

A majority of the people of the West Indies are descendants of black Africans who were brought to the islands as slaves to work on sugar and tobacco plantations. Most of the rest have British, Dutch, French, Portuguese, or Spanish ancestry; or mixed black African and European ancestry. Some people are descended from Chinese or East Indian farmworkers who arrived in the 1800's, after slavery was abolished. The area's origi-

nal Indian population has died out, except for small groups of Carib Indians who live in remote mountain regions of Dominica.

Languages. The many languages and dialects spoken in the West Indies reflect the cultural heritage of the European groups that colonized the area. For example, most of the people of Cuba, the Dominican Republic, and Puerto Rico speak Spanish. Dutch is the chief language of Aruba and the Netherlands Antilles. French is the official language of Haiti, Guadeloupe, and Martinique. English is the main language of the rest of the West Indies. Many West Indians use a dialect called *pat-*

People of the West Indies

Most people of the West Indies are descended from black Africans or Europeans. Some have Asian ancestry. The pictures below give an idea of the varied ancestry of the area's people.

Fred Ward, Black Star

Spanish descent

Nicholas Devore III, Bruce Coleman Inc.

Black African descent

Trinidad & Tobago Tourist Board

East Indian descent

Porterfield-Chickering, Photo Researchers

Dutch descent

Independent countries of the West Indies

Map key	Name	Area		Population	Capital	Official language	Date of independence
		In sq. mi.	In km²				
C7	Antigua and Barbuda	171	442	86,000	St. John's	English	1981
A3	Bahamas	5,385	13,878	251,000	Nassau	English	1973
D7	Barbados	166	431	260,000	Bridgetown	English	1966
B2	Cuba	42,804	110,861	10,297,000	Havana	Spanish	1898
D7	Dominica	290	751	98,000	Roseau	English	1978
C4	Dominican Republic	18,816	48,734	7,172,000	Santo Domingo	Spanish	1844
E7	Grenada	133	344	96,000	Saint George's	English	1974
C4	Haiti	10,714	27,750	5,777,000	Port-au-Prince	French	1804
C2	Jamaica	4,244	10,991	2,520,000	Kingston	English	1962
C6	St. Christopher and Nevis	101	261	48,000	Basseterre	English	1983
D7	St. Lucia	238	616	143,000	Castries	English	1979
D6	St. Vincent and the Grenadines	150	388	117,000	Kingstown	English	1979
E7	Trinidad and Tobago	1,980	5,128	1,283,000	Port-of-Spain	English	1962

Dependencies in the West Indies

Map key	Name	Area		Population	Status
		In sq. mi.	In km²		
C6	Anguilla	35	91	7,000	British dependency; some self-government
E4	Aruba	75	193	63,000	Self-governing part of the Netherlands
C2	Cayman Islands	100	259	19,000	British dependency
C7	Guadeloupe	658	1,704	328,000	Overseas department of France
D7	Martinique	425	1,102	329,000	Overseas department of France
C6	Montserrat	38	98	13,000	British dependency
E5;C6	Netherlands Antilles	310	800	185,000	Self-governing part of the Netherlands
C5	Puerto Rico	3,515	9,103	3,282,000	United States commonwealth
B4	Turks and Caicos Islands	166	430	9,000	British dependency
C6	Virgin Islands (U.S.)	132	342	111,000	U.S. organized unincorporated territory
C6	Virgin Islands, British	59	153	11,000	British dependency; some self-government

Each country and dependency in the West Indies has a separate article in *World Book.*

Populations are 1990 estimates for independent countries and 1990 and earlier estimates for dependencies based on figures from official government and United Nations sources.

ois (pronounced *PAT wah*), which is a mixture of African words and mainly English or French. A dialect called *Papiamento,* which is a combination of chiefly Dutch, English, Portuguese, and Spanish, is widely used in Aruba and the Netherlands Antilles.

Way of life. Nearly half the people of the West Indies make their living as farmers. Many work on large sugar or coffee plantations owned by wealthy people. Some own or rent small plots of land on which they raise crops and livestock. Many farm families must struggle to produce enough food for their own use. Most rural people live in one-room or two-room huts with thatched roofs. Wealthy landowners live in spacious wood or concrete homes with tile or metal roofs.

Most cities and towns of the West Indies lie in coastal areas. Many urban people work in hotels or other businesses connected with the tourist industry. Others have jobs in factories, shops, or government offices. Many poor urban families live in wooden shacks in crowded slum areas. Middle-income people live in modern apartments or small suburban houses. Many of the rich have beautiful homes on hillsides overlooking the sea.

Clothing in the West Indies is similar to that worn in the United States and Canada during warm weather.

Spence McConnell, Bruce Coleman Inc.

A crowded street market in Port-au-Prince, Haiti, features food, clothing, and household goods. Outdoor markets are common in many cities and towns in the West Indies.

M. Timothy O'Keefe, Bruce Coleman Inc.

Many rural houses in the West Indies are one- or two-room wooden structures. The scene above is in Jamaica. Most rural West Indians make their living as farmers.

West Indies

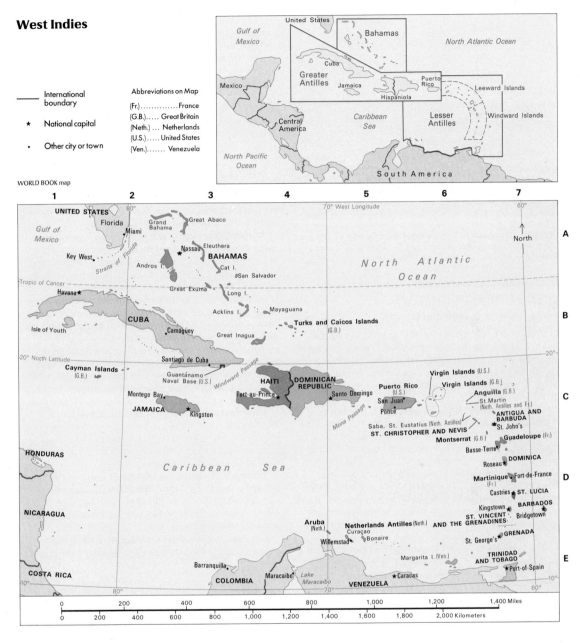

International
boundary

★ National capital

• Other city or town

Abbreviations on Map

(Fr.)..............France
(G.B.).....Great Britain
(Neth.) ... Netherlands
(U.S.).....United States
(Ven.).......Venezuela

WORLD BOOK map

Many farmers wear straw hats for protection from the sun. The diet of most West Indians includes beans, crabs, fish, rice, sweet potatoes, and such tropical fruits as bananas, mangoes, and oranges.

Religion. Most West Indians are Christians. Roman Catholicism is the main religion on the Spanish- and French-speaking islands. The English- and Dutch-speaking islands have a mixture of Catholics and Protestants. Small groups of Hindus, Jews, and Muslims also live in the West Indies. On several of the islands, many people practice traditional African religions. Voodoo, one of the best known of these, is widespread on Haiti. Ras Tafari, a religious group that worships former Emperor Haile Selassie I of Ethiopia as God, has numerous followers

on Jamaica and several other islands. See **Voodoo; Jamaica** (People).

Education. Government-sponsored elementary and secondary education is available throughout the West Indies. But schools in rural areas often face shortages of teachers and equipment, and many students drop out and get jobs to help support their families. The West Indies have a number of colleges and universities. Many islands have technical schools that prepare people for careers in agriculture, engineering, and other fields.

Recreation. Popular sports in the West Indies include baseball, basketball, cricket, soccer, and track and field. Cockfights are popular on most of the islands. Music is a favorite form of recreation. Most people

Nicholas Devore III, Bruce Coleman Inc.

Rugged mountains rise on many West Indian islands. Most of the urban communities—such as Port Elizabeth in St. Vincent and the Grenadines, *above*—lie in coastal areas.

enjoy performances of traditional songs and dances, and many play musical instruments.

Land and climate

The West Indies cover a land area of 90,699 square miles (234,909 square kilometers). The islands are part of an underwater mountain chain that linked North and South America in prehistoric times. Many of the islands were formed by volcanoes. Others were formed after wind and rain wore down the mountain peaks. These islands are mostly flat strips of coral and limestone.

Natural features. Volcanic mountains rise on a number of islands in the West Indies. Several of the volcanoes, including Mont Pelée on Martinique and Mount Soufrière on Saint Vincent, are still active. The highest point in the West Indies, Duarte Peak on Hispaniola, towers 10,417 feet (3,175 meters) above sea level. Strips of fertile lowland and white sand beaches line the coasts of many islands. Some of the coral islands rise only a few hundred feet or meters above sea level. They have large grassland areas and few trees.

The West Indies have a number of fine harbors, and many islands have numerous bays and inlets along their coasts. Swift-flowing rivers run on many islands, but most are too rough for boats other than canoes. The Puerto Rico Trench, which lies off the northern coast of Puerto Rico, includes one of the deepest spots in all the world's oceans. This place, called the Milwaukee Deep, is 28,374 feet (8,648 meters) below the ocean's surface.

Plant and animal life. Lush, tropical vegetation covers many of the islands of the West Indies. Bamboo, cedar, mahogany, and pine trees grow in the thick forests. Citrus and palm trees flourish along the coasts. The many varieties of flowering plants include bougainvillea, hibiscus, orchid, and poinsettia.

Iguanas, opossums, snakes, and many species of birds live on the islands. Large wild animals are not found in the West Indies. Tropical fish and such game fish as barracuda, marlin, and sailfish thrive in the blue-green waters surrounding the islands.

Climate. The islands of the West Indies have a warm, tropical climate. Steady ocean winds keep temperatures mild the year around. Temperatures average 81° F.

(27° C) in the summer and 75° F. (24° C) in the winter.

Rainfall in the West Indies averages 60 inches (150 centimeters) per year, with some mountainous areas receiving up to 200 inches (500 centimeters). Hurricanes frequently strike the islands, chiefly during the late summer and early fall. The heavy rains and violent winds of these storms sometimes cause many deaths and severe damage to houses and crops. Weather forecasters try to predict the storms hours, or even days, in advance to allow people to move to places of safety.

Economy

Agriculture is the chief economic activity of the West Indies. It employs over 50 per cent of the work force. About 30 per cent of the employed people work in government, tourism, or other service jobs. Most of the rest work in manufacturing, mining, or fishing.

Agriculture. Sugar cane is the area's leading crop. It is grown chiefly for export on large plantations. Other important export crops include bananas, citrus fruits, coffee, cotton, tobacco, and spices. Farmers produce cabbage, carrots, sweet potatoes, tomatoes, and other food crops throughout the West Indies. They also raise cattle, pigs, and other livestock. However, many islands cannot produce enough food to feed all the people and must import large quantities of food.

Tourism ranks second to agriculture among the most important economic activities of the West Indies. More than 8 million people visit the islands each year to enjoy the sunny climate, beaches, and tropical scenery. Many people take tours to the islands on cruise ships.

Manufacturing and processing activities in the West Indies include the production of cement, clothing, electrical parts, pharmaceuticals, rum, and salt. Oil refineries on Aruba and Curaçao process crude oil from Venezuela and other countries.

Mining is a relatively unimportant economic activity in most of the West Indies. There are some important oil and natural gas wells on Trinidad. Jamaica is one of the world's leading producers of bauxite. Cuba has large deposits of iron ore and nickel.

Fishing. Bonitos, sharks, tuna, and such shellfish as clams, crabs, and lobsters live in the waters surrounding

Fred Ward, Black Star

A Cuban farm worker gathers sugar cane by hand, *above*. Sugar cane is the most important crop of the West Indies. It is grown chiefly on large plantations.

the West Indies. Almost all the fish that are caught are sold in local markets.

Trade. Bananas, petroleum products, rum, and sugar are the main exports of the West Indies. Imports include automobiles, food, machinery, and raw materials. Canada, Great Britain, and the United States are the area's main trading partners. Cuba carries on much trade with the Soviet Union. A number of West Indian countries belong to the Caribbean Community and Common Market (CARICOM), an economic union that encourages trade among its members.

Transportation and communication. Most major West Indian cities have an international airport. Regional airlines serve smaller islands. Cargo and passenger ships from around the world visit West Indian ports. Paved roads link major cities with rural areas on many islands. Satellites beam radio and television programs from Europe and the United States to the West Indies. Most of the islands have at least one daily newspaper.

History

Early days. Ciboney Indians were the first inhabitants of the West Indies. They began living there during prehistoric times. Arawak Indians from South America began moving to the West Indies about A.D. 1000. They eventually settled in the Greater Antilles. They were soon followed by Carib Indians, who populated most of the Lesser Antilles. The Arawaks were a peaceful people who raised crops near their villages. The more warlike Caribs hunted and fished for a living.

The colonial period. Christopher Columbus landed on the island of San Salvador in the Bahamas in 1492. During the next 10 years, he reached, and claimed for Spain, almost all the West Indies islands. The Spanish set up the first permanent European settlement in the West Indies in 1496 at Santo Domingo on Hispaniola.

The search for gold and other riches drew thousands of Europeans to the West Indies. In the early 1500's, Spaniards founded colonies on Cuba, Jamaica, and Puerto Rico. They enslaved the Indians and forced them to work in gold mines. Disease and overwork and other harsh treatment killed almost all the Indians.

Other Europeans learned of the wealth of the West Indies. Pirates from England, France, and the Netherlands attacked Spanish ships and ports and stole valuable cargo. In the 1600's, the Danes, Dutch, English, and French established colonies on the smaller islands. In 1655, the English conquered Jamaica. The French took control of part of Hispaniola in 1697.

From the late 1600's through the 1700's, the colonial powers gained great wealth from sugar grown in the West Indies. The Europeans brought millions of black African slaves to the islands to work on plantations.

Independence movements. During the 1800's, revolutions weakened colonial control on several islands. In 1804, Haiti became the first independent nation in the West Indies after slaves on Hispaniola, led by Toussaint L'Ouverture, rebelled against their French rulers. The Dominican Republic broke off from Haiti and declared its independence in 1844. Slavery was abolished in all of the West Indies by the late 1800's. The plantation system then became much less profitable because plantation owners lost most of their cheap labor. As a result, European interest in the West Indies declined.

The United States began playing an active role in the West Indies in 1898. In that year, a revolution in Cuba drew the United States into the Spanish-American War against Spain. After the United States won the war, Cuba became independent and Puerto Rico became a U.S. colony. In 1917, the United States purchased what are now the U.S. Virgin Islands from Denmark.

Dictators controlled Cuba, the Dominican Republic, and Haiti during much of the first half of the 1900's. In 1959, Fidel Castro led a revolution in Cuba that overthrew the nation's government. He established a Communist state and became allied with the Soviet Union.

Many islands of the West Indies have become independent or have gained more control over their own affairs since 1945. Both the Netherlands Antilles and Puerto Rico gained almost complete self-government in the early 1950's. Ten British colonies formed the West Indies Federation in 1958. They were (1) Antigua, (2) Barbados, (3) Dominica, (4) Grenada, (5) Jamaica, (6) Montserrat, (7) St. Christopher (St. Kitts)-Nevis-Anguilla, (8) St. Lucia, (9) St. Vincent, and (10) Trinidad and Tobago. The federation was dissolved in 1962 after Jamaica and Trinidad and Tobago became independent.

In the late 1960's, Antigua, Dominica, Grenada, St. Christopher-Nevis-Anguilla, St. Lucia, and St. Vincent became states associated with Great Britain. Together, the six states were called the West Indies Associated States. By the early 1980's, all of the West Indies Associated States except for St. Christopher-Nevis-Anguilla had become independent nations. In 1980, Anguilla officially withdrew from St. Christopher-Nevis-Anguilla and became a separate British dependency. The rest of the state, called St. Christopher-Nevis, remained associated with Great Britain. In 1983, St. Christopher-Nevis became an independent nation. Its name was changed to St. Christopher and Nevis after independence.

For the year of independence of all the countries of the West Indies, see the *table* in this article.

The West Indies today face a number of economic and social problems, including overcrowding, poverty, and limited resources. Large numbers of West Indians cannot find jobs or must work for low wages. Many West Indian governments are trying to develop new industries to lessen dependence on agriculture and tourism. Such regional economic organizations as the Caribbean Development Bank and CARICOM are also working to stimulate industrial growth.   Thomas G. Mathews

Related articles in *World Book.* See the separate articles on countries and other political units in the West Indies listed in the *table* in this article. See also:

British West Indies   Grenadines   Windward Islands
French West Indies   Leeward Islands

West Indies Associated States. See West Indies (History).

West Indies Federation. See West Indies (History).

West Point, N.Y., a United States military reservation, has served as the site of the U.S. Military Academy since 1802. For location, see **New York** (political map). The reservation stands on a plateau above the west bank of the Hudson River. It also includes Constitution Island, in the river, site of several Revolutionary War forts. See also **United States Military Academy.**

West Roman Empire. See Rome, Ancient (Decline and fall; map: Division of the Roman Empire).

Bryan Allen, Shostal

The Allegheny Mountains cut through eastern West Virginia. Scenic mountains, steep hills, and narrow valleys cover almost all of the state, which has some of the nation's most rugged terrain.

West Virginia *The Mountain State*

West Virginia, in the Appalachian Highlands, has some of the most rugged land in the United States. The state has few large areas of level ground, except for strips of valley land that lie along the larger rivers. Mountain chains cover the eastern and central sections of West Virginia. Steep and rolling hills and narrow valleys make up the region west of the mountains. The extreme ruggedness of the land gives West Virginia its nickname, the *Mountain State.*

The beautiful mountain scenery of this rugged state attracts many visitors. Forests of valuable hardwood trees grow on the mountain slopes, and vast mineral deposits lie under the ground. West Virginia ranks third behind Kentucky and Wyoming in U.S. coal production. Coal deposits lie under about half the land. West Virginia industries are based on coal and other important mineral resources found in the state. These resources

The contributors of this article are Richard Stark Little, Associate Professor of Geography at West Virginia University; and George Parkinson, Curator and Associate Professor of History at West Virginia University.

include clay, limestone, natural gas, petroleum, salt, and sand. However, West Virginia's economic base is shifting. Today, service industries are growing rapidly and form the most important part of the economy.

Industrial cities line the banks of the broad Ohio River, which forms West Virginia's western border. Wheeling, Weirton, and other northern river cities produce iron and steel. Chemical plants operate in the Ohio and Kanawha river valleys. West Virginia's capital, Charleston, is in the Kanawha Valley. The Charleston area is a manufacturing center for chemicals and metal products. Huntington, Parkersburg, and many other cities have large plants that manufacture glassware and pottery.

West Virginia was part of the state of Virginia until the Civil War. Virginia joined the Confederate States in 1861. But the people of the northwestern counties remained loyal to the Union. They formed a new government, patterned after Virginia's, and broke away from the rest of the state. West Virginia became a separate state in 1863. The hardy independence of West Virginians is reflected in the state's motto, *Mountaineers Are Always Free.*

Interesting facts about West Virginia

WORLD BOOK illustrations by Kevin Chadwick

Weirton, in the Northern Panhandle of West Virginia, is the only city in the United States that borders two other states while touching its own state on more than one side. Weirton extends to Ohio on the west and Pennsylvania on the east. West Virginia surrounds it on the north and south.

The glass marble manufacturing center of the United States is located in West Virginia. A few factories in the Parkersburg area make most of the nation's glass marbles.

Glass marbles

A huge chandelier hangs in the golden dome of the state capitol in Charleston. The chandelier has 10,080 hand-cut Czechoslovakian crystals. It is 8 feet (2.4 meters) in diameter, weighs 2 short tons (1.8 metric tons), has 96 lights, and hangs from a 54-foot (16.5-meter) gold-plated chain.

West Virginia was the first state to levy a sales tax. The tax, enacted in 1921, was based on the gross receipts of the firms doing business in the state.

The town of Romney changed hands between Union and Confederate forces 56 times during the Civil War. West Virginia was the site of many battles during the war.

Romney

Rural Free Delivery originated in West Virginia. Postmaster General William L. Wilson introduced the idea to his home state. On Oct. 1, 1896, rural carriers began working out of post offices in Charles Town, Halltown, and Uvilla.

Lee Balterman from Marilyn Gartman

Coal mining is West Virginia's most important mining activity. Soft coal deposits lie under about half the state.

Bill Barley, Shostal

Downtown Charleston lies along the banks of the Kanawha River. Charleston is the capital and largest city of West Virginia. It ranks as the state's leading center of industry and trade.

West Virginia in brief

Symbols of West Virginia

The state flag, adopted in 1929, bears the front of the state seal. The seal was adopted in 1863. The design on the front includes a miner and a farmer. The rock between them shows the date of West Virginia's statehood. In the foreground, rifles symbolize the willingness to fight for freedom. The landscape on the back of the seal includes an oil derrick, a log cabin, sheep and cattle, a factory, a railroad, and wooded mountains.

State flag

State seal

West Virginia (brown) ranks 41st in size among all the states and 12th in size among the Southern States (yellow).

General information

Statehood: June 20, 1863, the 35th state.
State abbreviations: W. Va. (traditional); WV (postal).
State motto: *Montani Semper Liberi* (Mountaineers Are Always Free).
State song: "The West Virginia Hills." Words by Ellen King; music by H. E. Engle (one of three state songs).

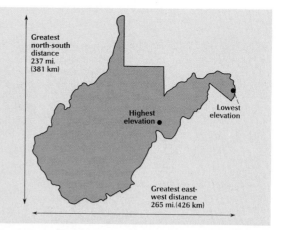

The State Capitol is in Charleston, West Virginia's capital since 1885. Earlier capitals were Wheeling (1863-1870), Charleston (1870-1875), and Wheeling (1875-1885).

Land and climate

Area: 24,231 sq. mi. (62,759 km²), including 112 sq. mi. (291 km²) of inland water.
Elevation: *Highest*—Spruce Knob, 4,863 ft. (1,482 m) above sea level. *Lowest*—240 ft. (73 m) above sea level along the Potomac River in Jefferson County.
Record high temperature: 112° F. (44° C) at Martinsburg on July 10, 1936, and at Moorefield on Aug. 4, 1930.
Record low temperature: −37° F. (−38° C) at Lewisburg on Dec. 30, 1917.
Average July temperature: 72° F. (22° C).
Average January temperature: 32° F. (0° C).
Average yearly precipitation: 44 in. (112 cm).

Greatest north-south distance 237 mi. (381 km)

Highest elevation

Lowest elevation

Greatest east-west distance 265 mi. (426 km)

Important dates

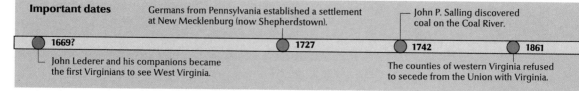

Germans from Pennsylvania established a settlement at New Mecklenburg (now Shepherdstown).

John P. Salling discovered coal on the Coal River.

1669?

1727

1742

1861

John Lederer and his companions became the first Virginians to see West Virginia.

The counties of western Virginia refused to secede from the Union with Virginia.

State bird
Cardinal

State flower
Rhododendron

State tree
Sugar maple

People

Population: 1,950,258 (1980 census)
Rank among the states: 34th
Density: 80 persons per sq. mi. (31 per km²), U.S. average 67 per sq. mi. (26 per km²)
Distribution: 64 per cent rural, 36 per cent urban
Largest cities in West Virginia

Charleston	63,968
Huntington	63,684
Wheeling	43,070
Parkersburg	39,946
Morgantown	27,605
Weirton	25,371

Source: U.S. Bureau of the Census.

Population trend

Millions

*All figures are census figures except 1985, which is an estimate.

Year	Population*
1985	1,936,000
1980	1,950,258
1970	1,744,237
1960	1,860,421
1950	2,005,552
1940	1,901,974
1930	1,729,205
1920	1,463,701
1910	1,221,119
1900	958,800
1890	762,794
1880	618,457
1870	442,014
1860	376,688
1850	302,313
1840	224,537
1830	176,924
1820	136,808
1810	105,469
1800	78,592
1790	55,873

Source: U.S. Bureau of the Census.

Economy

Chief products

Agriculture: beef cattle, milk, hay, chickens.
Manufacturing: chemicals; primary metals; stone, clay, and glass products.
Mining: coal, natural gas.

Gross state product

Value of goods and services produced in 1986, $24,096,000,000. *Services* include community, business, and personal services; finance; government; trade; and transportation, communication, and utilities. *Industry* includes construction, manufacturing, and mining. *Agriculture* includes agriculture, fishing, and forestry.

Source: U.S. Bureau of Economic Analysis.

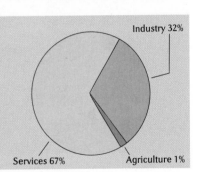

Industry 32%
Services 67%
Agriculture 1%

Government

State government

Governor: 4-year term
State senators: 34; 4-year terms
State delegates: 100; 2-year terms
Counties: 55

Federal government

United States senators: 2
United States representatives: 4
Electoral votes: 6

Sources of information

Tourism: West Virginia Department of Commerce, Division of Marketing Tourism, 2101 Washington Street East, Charleston, WV 25305
Economy: Community and Industrial Development, Building 6, Room B-504, Capitol Complex, Charleston, WV 25305
Government: Secretary of State's Office, Capitol Building, Charleston, WV 25305
History: West Virginia Department of Commerce, Division of Marketing Tourism, 2101 Washington Street East, Charleston, WV 25305

West Virginia became the 35th state on June 20.

The National Radio Astronomy Observatory began operating at Green Bank.

1863   **1920-1921**   **1959**   **1985**

Miners fought with mine guards, police, and federal troops in a dispute over organizing unions.

West Virginia established a state lottery.

Population. The 1980 United States census reported that West Virginia had 1,950,258 people. The population had increased 12 per cent over the 1970 figure, 1,744,-237. The U.S. Bureau of the Census estimated that by 1985 the state's population had reached about 1,936,000. Thousands of jobs created by a growth in the service industries and in coal production caused many people to move to West Virginia during the 1970's.

Almost two-thirds of the people of West Virginia live in rural areas. The state has about 210 cities, towns, and villages with populations of less than 2,500. Many were once coal-mining towns and trading centers for farm areas. West Virginia's large cities lie in river valleys, where the land is least hilly. They are centers for the chemical, iron, and steel industries. Charleston, Huntington, and Wheeling are the largest cities. See the sep-

arate articles on West Virginia cities listed in the *Related articles* at the end of this article.

The areas around Charleston, Huntington, Parkersburg, Weirton, and Wheeling are Metropolitan Statistical Areas (see **Metropolitan area**). The Cumberland, Md., metropolitan area also extends into West Virginia. For the populations of these areas, see the *Index* to the political map of West Virginia.

Almost all the people of West Virginia were born in the United States. Many of their ancestors came from Germany, Great Britain, Ireland, and Italy. Many immigrants came to West Virginia during the late 1800's and early 1900's to work in the state's coal mines.

Schools. Pioneer children in the West Virginia region attended classes in log cabins that served as both schools and churches. Parents paid the teachers in cash,

Gary T. Truman

An art and craft fair in Ripley features modern artwork and traditional West Virginia crafts. The blacksmith shown above is demonstrating the use of a hammer and tongs.

Population density

The most densely populated areas of West Virginia are the northern and southwestern parts of the state. Much of the mountainous southeastern part of the state is thinly populated.

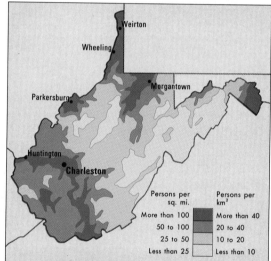

Persons per sq. mi.	Persons per km²
More than 100	More than 40
50 to 100	20 to 40
25 to 50	10 to 20
Less than 25	Less than 10

WORLD BOOK map; based on U.S. Bureau of the Census data.

Jodi Webb, Woodfin Camp, Inc.

A banjo player relaxes on his porch in a rural area of West Virginia. Thinly populated regions include most of the mountainous east and a large section in the central part of the state.

in farm products, and with "bed and board." In 1796, the Virginia legislature passed a law providing for free district schools in counties that wished to establish them. But few schools were set up, because most county officials believed parents should pay only to educate their own children. In 1810, the legislature created a literary fund for the education of poor children.

West Virginia established a free school system in 1863, after joining the Union. The state constitution of 1872 provided tax funds to support the schools. Until 1875, children in rural schools were not divided into different grades. Alexander L. Wade, a school superintendent in Monongalia County, developed a system of teaching subjects of various grade levels to children of different ages.

Today, a nine-member board of education determines educational policies and makes rules relating to those policies. The governor appoints the board members to nine-year terms. The board appoints a state superintendent of schools, who supervises the public school system. Children from age 7 through 15 must attend school. For the number of students and teachers in West Virginia, see **Education** (table).

Libraries. A subscription library was operating in Wheeling as early as 1808. Members of this library contributed money to buy books, which they could use without charge. Public libraries were not common until after 1900. A state library commission was established in 1929 to help regulate and expand library services.

Today, about 170 public library systems serve the people. Bookmobiles provide service for areas that lack libraries. The West Virginia University Library has the largest collection in the state. It includes the West Virginia Regional History Collection of manuscripts and books. Large public libraries include those at Charleston, Huntington, and Wheeling.

Museums. West Virginia's state museum is in the Cultural Center at the Capitol Complex in Charleston. The Sunrise Foundation in Charleston has an art gallery, children's museum, and planetarium. Art museums include the Huntington Galleries in Huntington, Parkersburg Art Center in Parkersburg, and the Oglebay Institute-Mansion Museum in Wheeling. Other museums include the Hawks Nest Museum at Hawks Nest State Park in Fayette County and the Marshall University Geology Museum in Huntington.

West Virginia University

West Virginia University is located in Morgantown. Woodburn Hall, *above,* is the oldest building on the campus.

Marshall University

The Marshall University campus is located in Huntington. The school, established in 1837, is one of the state's two oldest universities.

Universities and colleges

West Virginia has 19 universities and colleges that offer bachelor's or advanced degrees and are accredited by the North Central Association of Colleges and Schools. Locations shown below refer to the schools' mailing addresses. For enrollments and further information, see Universities and colleges (table).

Name	Location	Name	Location
Alderson-Broaddus College	Philippi	Shepherd College	Shepherdstown
Bethany College	Bethany	West Liberty State College	West Liberty
Bluefield State College	Bluefield	West Virginia College	
Charleston, University of	Charleston	of Graduate Studies	Institute
Concord College	Athens	West Virginia Institute of	
Davis and Elkins College	Elkins	Technology	Montgomery
Fairmont State College	Fairmont	West Virginia State College	Institute
Glenville State College	Glenville	West Virginia University	Morgantown
Marshall University	Huntington	West Virginia Wesleyan College	Buckhannon
Ohio Valley College	Parkersburg	Wheeling Jesuit College	Wheeling
Salem College	Salem		

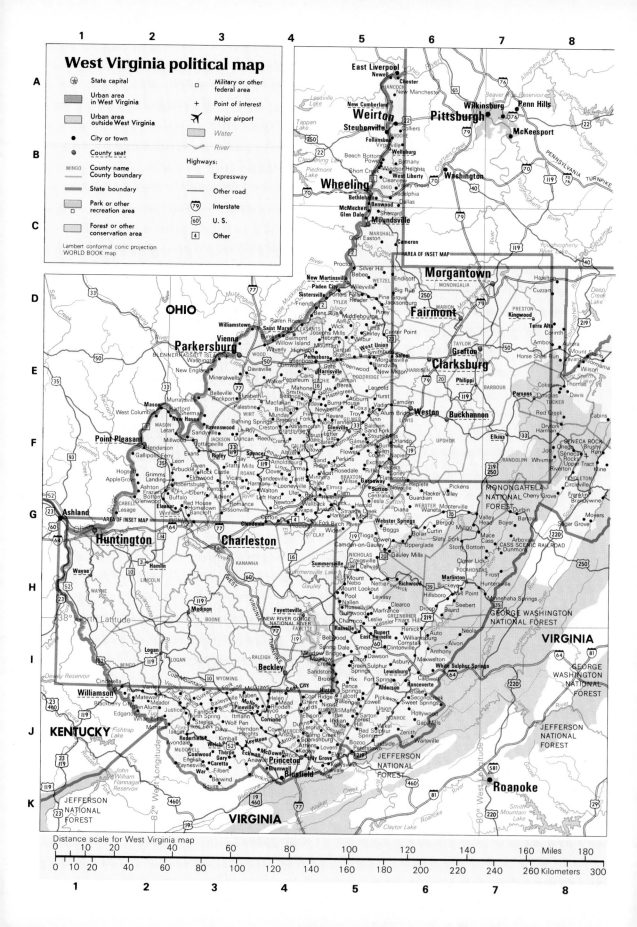

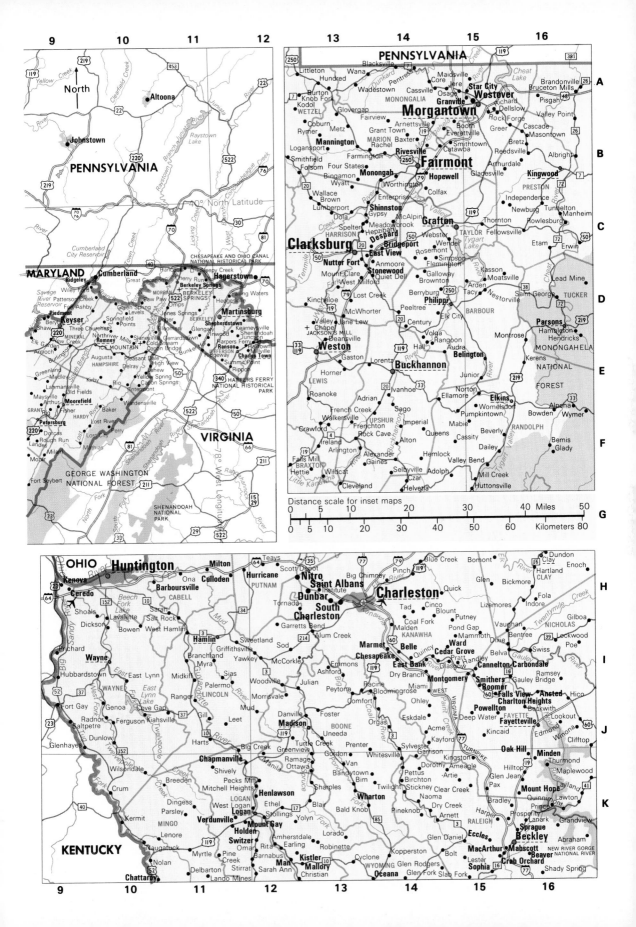

West Virginia map index

Metropolitan areas

Charleston ... 269,595
Cumberland (Md.) ... 107,782
(80,548 in Md.;
27,234 in W. Va.)
Huntington-
Ashland (Ky.) ... 336,410
(152,856 in W. Va.;
63,849 in O.;
119,705 in Ky.)
Parkersburg-
Marietta (O.) ... 157,914
(93,648 in W. Va.;
64,266 in O.)
Weirton-
Steubenville
(O.) ... 163,099
(91,564 in O.;
71,535 in W. Va.)
Wheeling ... 185,566
(102,997 in W. Va.;
82,569 in O.)

Counties

Barbour ... 16,639. .E 7
Berkeley ... 46,775. .D 11
Boone ... 30,447. .H 3
Braxton ... 13,894. .F 5
Brooke ... 31,117. .B 5
Cabell ... 106,835. .G 2
Calhoun ... 8,250. .F 4
Clay ... 11,265. .G 4
Doddridge ... 7,433. .E 5
Fayette ... 57,863. .I 4
Gilmer ... 8,334. .F 5
Grant ... 10,210. .E 9
Greenbrier ... 37,665. .H 5
Hampshire ... 14,867. .E 10
Hancock ... 41,053. .A 5
Hardy ... 10,030. .F 9
Harrison ... 77,710. .E 6
Jackson ... 25,794. .F 3
Jefferson ... 30,302. .E 11
Kanawha ... 231,414. .H 3
Lewis ... 18,813. .F 6
Lincoln ... 23,675. .H 2
Logan ... 50,679. .I 2
Marion ... 65,789. .D 6
Marshall ... 41,608. .C 5
Mason ... 27,045. .F 2
McDowell ... 49,899. .J 2
Mercer ... 73,942. .J 4
Mineral ... 27,234. .D 9
Mingo ... 37,336. .I 2
Monongalia ... 75,024. .D 6
Monroe ... 12,873. .J 5
Morgan ... 10,711. .D 10
Nicholas ... 28,126. .H 5
Ohio ... 61,389. .B 5
Pendleton ... 7,910. .F 8
Pleasants ... 8,236. .D 4
Pocahontas ... 9,919. .H 6
Preston ... 30,460. .D 7
Putnam ... 38,181. .G 2
Raleigh ... 86,821. .I 4
Randolph ... 28,734. .F 7
Ritchie ... 11,442. .E 4
Roane ... 15,952. .F 3
Summers ... 15,875. .J 4
Taylor ... 16,584. .E 6
Tucker ... 8,675. .E 8
Tyler ... 11,320. .D 5
Upshur ... 23,427. .F 6
Wayne ... 46,021. .H 1
Webster ... 12,245. .G 6
Wetzel ... 21,874. .D 5
Wirt ... 4,922. .F 3
Wood ... 93,627. .E 4
Wyoming ... 35,993. .I 3

Cities, towns, and villages

Abraham ... K 16
Acme ... J 14
Adolph ... F 15
Adrian ... E 14
Advent ... G 3
Albright ... 357. .B 16
Alderson ... 1,375. .I 5
Alexander ... F 14
Alma ... D 5
Alpena ... E 16
Altizer ... F 4
Alton ... F 14
Alum Creek ... I 13
Alvon ... I 6
Amboy ... E 8
Ameagle ... K 15
Amherstdale
[-Robinette]
... 1,075. .K 13
Anawalt ... 652. .J 3
Anmoore ... 865. .D 14
Annamoriah ... F 4
Ansted ... 1,952. .I 16
Anthony ... I 6
Antioch ... E 9
Apple Grove ... G 2
Arbovale ... G 7
Arbuckle ... F 2
Arden ... D 15
Arista ... J 4
Arlington ... F 13
Arnett ... K 14
Arnoldsburg ... F 4
Arthur ... E 9
Arthurdale ... 1,063. .B 16
Asbury ... I 5
Ashford ... I 13
Ashton ... G 2
Athens ... 1,147. .J 4
Auburn ... 116. .E 5
Audra ... E 15
Augusta ... E 10
Aurora ... E 8
Auto ... I 6
Avondale ... J 3
Baileysville ... J 3
Baker ... E 10
Bald Knob ... K 13
Baldwin ... F 5
Ballengee ... J 5
Bancroft ... 528. .G 3
Bandytown ... K 13
Barboursville ... 2,871. .H 10
Barnabus ... K 12
Barrackville* ... 1,815. .D 6
Bartow ... G 7
Baxter ... B 14
Bayard ... 540. .E 8
Beard ... H 6
Beatrice ... E 4
Beaver ... 1,122. .K 16
Bebee ... D 5
Beckley ... 20,492.°I 4
Beckwith ... J 16
Beech Bottom ... 507. .B 5
Belington ... 2,038. .E 15
Belle ... 1,621. .I 14
Belleville ... E 3
Bellwood ... I 5
Belmont ... 887. .D 4
Belva ... I 15
Bemis ... F 16
Bens Run ... D 4
Bentree ... I 15
Benwood ... 1,994. .C 5
Berea ... E 5
Bergoo ... G 6
Berkeley
Springs ... 789.°D 11
Berryburg ... D 15
Berwind ... K 3
Beryl ... D 9
Bethany ... 1,336. .B 6
Bethlehem ... 3,045. .C 5
Beverly ... 475. .F 15
Bickmore ... H 16
Big Chimney ... H 14
Big Creek ... J 12
Big Otter ... G 4
Big Run ... D 5
Bigbend ... F 4
Bim ... K 13
Bingamon ... B 13
Birch River ... G 5
Birchton ... K 14
Blackberry City ... J 2
Blacksville ... 248. .A 14
Blair ... K 13
Blandville ... E 5
Blennerhassett*
... 3,537. .E 3
Bloomery ... D 10
Bloomingrose ... I 13
Blount ... H 14
Blue Creek ... H 14
Bluefield ... 16,060. .K 4
Bluewell* ... 2,752. .J 4
Boggs ... G 5
Bolair ... G 6
Bolivar* ... 672. .E 12
Bolt ... K 14
Bomont ... H 15
Boomer ... 1,051. .I 15
Booth ... B 15
Bowden ... F 16
Bowen ... I 10
Boyer ... G 7
Bozoo ... J 5
Bradley ... 1,704. .K 15
Bradshaw* ... 1,002. .J 3
Bramwell ... 989. .J 4
Branchland ... I 11
Brandonville ... 92. .A 16
Brandywine ... G 8
Breeden ... K 11
Brenton ... 1,041. .J 3
Bretz ... B 16
Bridgeport ... 6,604. .C 14
Brohard ... F 4
Brookhaven* ... 1,661. .D 7
Brooks ... I 5
Brown ... C 13
Brownton ... D 14
Bruceton Mills ... 296. .A 16
Brushy Run ... F 8
Buckeye ... H 6
Buckhannon ... 6,820.°F 6
Buffalo ... 1,034. .G 2
Bunker Hill ... E 11
Burlington ... E 9
Burning Springs ... F 4
Burnsville ... 531. .F 5
Burnt House ... E 5
Burton ... A 13
Cabins ... F 9
Cairo ... 428. .E 4
Caldwell ... I 6
Camden ... E 5
Camden-on-
Gauley ... 236. .G 5
Cameron ... 1,474. .C 6
Camp Creek ... J 4
Cannelton-
Carbondale ... I 15
Canvas ... H 5
Capon Bridge ... 191. .E 10
Capon Springs ... E 10
Caretta ... J 3
Cascade ... B 16
Cass ... 148. .G 7
Cassity ... F 15
Cassville ... A 14
Catawba ... B 15
Cedar Grove ... 1,479. .I 14
Cedarville ... F 5
Center Point ... D 5
Central Station ... E 5
Centralia ... G 5
Century ... D 14
Ceredo ... 2,255. .H 9
Chapmanville ... 1,164. .J 12
Charles Town ... 2,857.°E 12
Charleston ... 63,968.°G 3
Charmco ... H 5
Chattaroy ... 1,383. .K 10
Cherry Grove ... G 8
Cherry Run ... D 11
Chesapeake ... 2,364. .I 14
Chester ... 3,297. .A 6
Chloe ... G 4
Christian ... K 12
Cinco ... H 14
Cinderella ... I 2
Circleville ... G 8
Clarksburg ... 22,371.°E 6
Clay ... 940.°H 16
Clear Creek ... K 15
Clear Fork ... J 3
Clearco ... H 5
Clearview ... 740. .B 5
Clem ... G 5
Clendenin ... 1,373. .G 4
Cleveland ... G 13
Clifftop ... J 16
Clintonville ... I 5
Clio ... G 4
Clover ... F 4
Clover Lick ... H 7
Coal City ... 2,324. .I 4
Coal Fork ... 2,775. .H 14
Coal Mountain ... I 3
Coalwood ... J 3
Coburn ... B 13
Coketon ... E 8
Cold Stream ... E 10
Colfax ... B 14
Colliers ... B 6
Comfort ... J 14
Cool Ridge ... I 4
Copen ... F 5
Core ... A 14
Corinth ... D 8
Corley ... F 5
Cornstalk ... I 6
Cornwallis ... E 4
Corrinne ... J 4
Corton ... G 4
Cottageville ... F 3
Cove Gap ... J 11
Covel ... J 4
Cowen ... 723. .G 5
Coxs Mills ... E 5
Crab Orchard ... 3,337. .K 15
Craigsville ... 1,562. .H 5
Crawford ... F 13
Cremo ... F 4
Creston ... F 4
Crum ... K 10
Culloden ... 2.931. .H 11
Curtin ... G 6
Cuzzart ... D 8
Cyclone ... K 13
Czar ... G 14
Dailey ... F 15
Dallas ... C 6
Daniels* ... 1,959. .I 4
Danville ... 727. .J 13
Davis ... 979. .E 8
Davisville ... E 3
Davy ... 882. .J 3
Dawson ... I 5
Deansville ... E 13
Deep Water ... J 15
Delbarton ... 981. .K 11
Dellslow ... A 15
Delray ... E 10
Despard ... 1,434. .C 14
Diana ... G 6
Dickson ... H 10
Dingess ... K 11
Dixie ... I 15
Dola ... C 13
Dorcas ... F 9
Dorothy ... K 14
Douglas ... E 8
Droop ... H 6
Dry Branch ... I 14
Dry Creek ... K 14
Dryfork ... F 8
Duck ... G 5
Dunbar ... 9,285. .H 13
Duncan ... F 3
Dundon ... H 16
Dunlow ... J 10
Dunmore ... G 7
Dunns ... J 4
Durbin ... 379. .G 7
Earling ... K 12
East Bank ... 1,155. .I 14
East Lynn ... I 10
East View ... 1,222. .C 13
Eccles ... 1,162. .K 15
Eckman ... J 3
Edgarton ... J 2
Edmond ... J 16
Eleanor ... 1,282. .G 2
Elgood ... J 5
Elizabeth ... 856.°E 4
Elk City ... D 14
Elk Garden ... 291. .D 9
Elkins ... 8,536.°F 7
Elkview* ... 1,161. .G 3
Ellamore ... E 14
Ellenboro ... 357. .E 4
Ellison ... J 4
Elmira ... G 5
Elmwood ... F 3
Elton ... I 5
Emmons ... I 13
Endicott ... D 5
English ... J 3
Enoch ... H 16
Enterprise ... 1,110. .C 14
Erwin ... C 16
Eskdale ... J 14
Etam ... C 16
Ethel ... K 12
Eureka ... D 4
Evans ... F 3
Everettville ... B 15
Exchange ... F 5
Fairlea* ... 1,888. .I 6
Fairmont ... 23,863.°D 6
Fairview ... 759. .A 14
Falling Spring ... 240. .I 6
Falling
Waters ... D 12
Falls View-Charlton
Heights ... I 15
Falls Mill ... F 12
Fanrock ... J 3
Farmington ... 583. .B 14
Fayetteville ... 2,366.°H 4
Fellowsville ... C 16
Fenwick ... H 5
Ferguson ... J 10
Filbert ... J 3
Fisher ... E 9
Five Forks ... F 4
Flatwoods ... 405. .F 5
Flemington ... 452. .C 14
Floe ... G 4
Flower ... F 5
Fola ... H 16
Follansbee ... 3,994. .B 5
Folsom ... B 13
Forest Hill ... J 5
Fort Ashby ... 1,205. .D 10
Fort Gay ... 886. .J 9
Fort Seybert ... G 9
Fort Spring ... I 6
Foster ... J 13
Four States ... B 13
Franklin ... 780.°G 8
Fraziers Bottom ... G 2
French Creek ... F 14
Frenchton ... F 13
Friars Hill ... H 6
Friendly ... 242. .D 4
Frost ... H 7
Gaines ... F 13
Gallipolis Ferry ... F 2
Galloway ... D 14
Gandeeville ... F 4
Gap Mills ... J 6
Garretts Bend ... I 12
Garrison ... J 14
Gary ... 2,233. .J 3
Gassaway ... 1,225. .G 5
Gaston ... E 13
Gauley
Bridge ... 1,177. .I 16
Gauley Mills ... G 5
Gay ... F 3
Gem ... F 5
Genoa ... I 10
Gerrardstown ... D 11
Ghent ... J 4
Gilbert ... 757. .J 2
Gilboa ... H 16
Gill ... J 11
Gilmer ... F 5
Given ... F 3
Glace ... I 6
Gladesville ... B 15
Glady ... F 16
Glasgow ... 1,031. .I 14
Glen ... H 15
Glen Alum ... J 2
Glen Dale ... 1,875. .C 5
Glen Daniel ... K 15
Glen Easton ... C 5
Glen Jean ... K 16
Glen Rodgers ... K 14
Glenfork ... K 14
Glengary ... D 11
Glenhayes ... J 9
Glenville ... 2,155.°F 5
Glenwood ... G 2
Glovergap ... A 13
Goffs ... E 4
Gordon ... J 13
Gormania ... E 8
Grafton ... 6,845.°E 7
Graham Heights* ... D 6
Grandview ... K 16
Grant Town ... 987. .B 14
Grantsville ... 788.°F 4
Granville ... 992. .A 15
Great Cacapon ... D 11
Green Spring ... D 10
Green Sulphur
Springs ... I 5
Greenland ... E 9
Greenview ... J 13
Greenwood ... E 5
Greer ... B 16
Griffithsville ... I 12
Grimms Landing ... G 2
Guardian ... G 6
Guyan ... J 3
Gypsy ... C 13
Hacker Valley ... G 6
Hall ... E 14
Hallburg ... G 4
Halltown ... E 12
Hambleton ... 403. .D 16
Hamlin ... 1,219.°H 2
Hancock ... D 11
Handley ... 633. .I 15
Harman ... 181. .F 8
Harmony ... G 3
Harper ... K 15
Harpers Ferry ... 361. .E 12
Harrison ... G 5
Harrisville ... 1,673.°E 4
Hartford ... 556. .F 2
Hartland ... H 16
Harts ... J 11
Hazelgreen ... E 5
Hazelton ... D 8
Heaters ... F 5
Hebron ... E 4
Hedgesville ... 217. .D 11
Helen ... J 4
Helvetia ... G 14
Hemlock ... F 14
Henderson ... 604. .F 2
Hendricks ... 390. .E 16
Henlawson ... K 12
Hepzibah ... C 13
Herndon Heights ... J 4
Herold ... G 5
Hettie ... F 13
Hico ... J 16
High View ... E 10
Highland ... E 4
Hillsboro ... 276. .H 6
Hilltop ... K 16
Hinton ... 4,622.°I 5
Hix ... I 5
Hogsett ... F 2
Holden ... 2,036. .K 11
Hollywood ... J 6
Hometown ... G 3
Hooverson
Heights* ... 3,111. .B 6
Hopewell ... B 14
Horner ... E 13
Horse Shoe Run ... E 8
Hubbardstown ... I 9
Hundred ... 485. .A 13
Huntersville ... H 7
Huntington ... 63,684.°G 1
Hurricane ... 3,751. .H 12
Hurst ... E 5
Huttonsville ... 242. .G 15
Iaeger ... 833. .J 3
Ikes Fork ... J 3
Imperial ... F 14
Independence ... C 15
Indian Mills ... J 5
Indore ... H 16
Ingleside ... J 4
Intermont ... E 10
Inwood ... 1,159. .D 11
Ireland ... F 13
Itmann ... J 4
Ivanhoe ... E 14
Ivydale ... G 4
Jacksonburg ... D 5
Jane Lew ... 406. .D 13
Jenkinjones ... K 4
Jere ... A 15
Jesse ... I 3
Job ... F 8
Jones Springs ... D 11
Josephs Mills ... D 5
Julian ... I 12
Junior ... 591. .E 15
Justice ... J 3
Kasson ... D 15
Kayford ... J 14
Kearneysville ... D 12
Kegley ... J 4
Kellysville ... J 5
Kenna ... G 3
Kenova ... 4,454. .H 9
Kentuck ... G 3
Kerens ... E 16
Kermit ... 705. .K 10
Kessler ... H 5
Keyser ... 6,569.°D 9
Keystone ... 902. .J 3

Kiahsville ...J 10
Kimball ...871 .J 3
Kincaid ...J 13
Kincheloe ...D 13
Kingston ...J 15
Kingwood ...2,877.°D 7
Kirby ...J 10
Kistler ...K 12
Kline ...F 9
Knob Fork ...A 13
Kodol ...A 12
Kopperston ...K 14
Lahmansville ...E 9
Lanark ...K 16
Landes ...F 9
Lando Mines ...K 11
Lavalette ...H 10
Lawton ...K 16
Layland ...K 16
Lead Mine ...D 10
Leet ...J 11
Left Hand ...G 4
Lehew ...E 10
Leivasy ...K 16
Lenore ...K 10
Leon ...228..F 4
Leopold ...E 5
Lerona ...J 4
Le Roy ...F 3
Lesage ...G 2
Leslie ...H 5
Lester ...626 .K 15
Letart ...F 2
Letherbark ...F 4
Letter Gap ...F 5
Levels ...F 10
Lewisburg ...3,065.°I 6
Liberty ...G 3
Lilly Grove ...J 4
Lima ...D 5
Linden ...F 4
Lindside ...J 5
Linn ...F 5
Littleton ...335..A 13
Lizemores ...H 16
Lockwood ...I 16
Logan ...3,029.°I 1
Logansport ...B 13
Lookout ...I 16
Looneyville ...G 4
Lorado ...K 13
Lorentz ...E 14
Lost City ...F 9
Lost Creek ...604..D 13
Lost River ...J 9
Lovern ...J 5
Lowell ...J 5
Lubeck* ...1,356..E 3
Lumberport ...939..C 13
Maben ...J 4
Mabie ...F 15
Mabscott ...1,668..K 15
MacArthur ...2,152..K 15
Mace ...D 7
Macfarlan ...E 4
Madison ...3,228.°H 4
Mahone ...E 4
Maidsville ...A 15
Malden ...H 4
Mallory ...1,330..K 12
Mammoth ...H 15
Man ...1,333..K 12
Manheim ...C 16
Manila ...J 12
Mannington ...3,036..B 13
Maplewood ...K 16
Marfrance ...H 5
Marie ...J 5
Marlinton ...1,352.°H 7
Marmet ...2,196..I 14
Martinsburg ...13,063.°D 11
Maryland
  Junction* ...1,042..D 9
Mason ...1,432..E 2
Masontown ...1,052..B 16
Matewan ...822..J 1
Mathias ...F 9
Matoaka ...613..J 4
Maxwelton ...I 6
Maysville ...E 9
McAlpin ...C 14
McCorkle ...I 12
McDowell ...K 4
McGraws ...K 15
McMechen ...2,402..C 5
McWhorter ...D 13
Mead ...J 4
Meador ...J 2
Meadow Bridge ...530..I 5
Meadow Creek ...I 5
Meadowbrook ...C 13
Medley ...B 13
Metz ...B 13
Miami ...I 14

Middlebourne ...941.°D 5
Midkiff ...J 11
Milam ...F 9
Mill Creek ...801..F 15
Mill Point ...H 6
Millville ...E 12
Millwood ...F 3
Milton ...2,178..H 11
Minden ...J 16
Mineralwells ...E 3
Mingo ...G 7
Minnehaha Springs ...H 7
Minnora ...F 4
Mitchell Heights ...342..K 12
Moatsville ...D 15
Mohawk ...J 2
Monongah ...1,132..B 14
Montcalm* ...1,544..K 4
Monterville ...G 7
Montgomery ...3,104..I 15
Montrose ...129..E 16
Moorefield ...2,257.°E 9
Morgansville ...E 5
Morgantown ...27,605.°D 7
Morris ...G 5
Morrisvale ...I 12
Moundsville ...12,419.°C 5
Mount Clare ...D 13
Mount Gay
  [-Shamrock] ...4,366..K 12
Mount Hope ...1,849..K 16
Mount Lookout ...H 5
Mount Nebo ...H 5
Mount Storm ...E 8
Mount Zion ...F 4
Mountain ...H 5
Moyers ...G 8
Mozer ...F 9
Mud ...J 12
Mullens ...2,919..J 4
Munday ...J 4
Murraysville ...E 3
Myra ...I- 11
Myrtle ...K 11
Nallen ...H 5
Naoma ...K 14
Napier ...F 5
Naugatuck ...K 10
Neola ...I 5
Nestorville ...D 15
Nettie ...H 5
New Creek ...E 9
New
  Cumberland ...1,752.°A 5
New England ...J 5
New Haven ...1,723..F 2
New Manchester ...A 5
New
  Martinsville ...7,109.°D 5
New Milton ...E 5
Newberne ...E 5
Newburg ...418..C 16
Newell ...2,032..A 5
Newton ...J 4
Newville ...G 5
Nicut ...J 4
Nimitz ...J 5
Nitro ...8,074..H 12
Nobe ...F 4
Nolan ...K 10
Normantown ...F 5
North Hills ...940..E 3
North Spring ...J 3
Northfork* ...660..J 3
Northriver Mills ...E 10
Norton ...E 15
Nutter Fort ...2,078..C 13
Oak Hill ...7,120..J 16
Oakvale ...208..J 5
Oceana ...2,143..K 14
Odd ...J 4
Ohley ...I 14
Old Fields ...E 9
Omar ...K 12
Omps ...D 11
Ona ...H 11
Onego ...F 8
Orgas ...J 14
Orlando ...E 14
Orma ...F 4
Osage ...285..A 15
Ottawa ...K 13
Ovapa- ...G 4
Paden City ...3,671..D 5
Palermo ...J 11
Palestine ...E 4
Parkersburg ...39,946.°E 3
Parsley ...K 11
Parsons ...1,937.°E 16
Patterson
  Creek ...D 10
Paw Paw ...644..D 10
Pax ...274..K 15
Paynesville ...J 2
Pecks Mill ...K 12

Peeltree ...D 14
Pence Springs ...I 5
Pennsboro ...1,652..E 5
Pentress ...A 14
Perkins ...I 5
Perry ...F 10
Petersburg ...2,084.°F 9
Peterstown ...648..J 5
Petroleum ...E 4
Pettus ...K 14
Peytona ...I 13
Philippi ...3,194.°E 7
Pickaway ...J 6
Pickens ...G 6
Pie ...J 2
Piedmont ...1,491..D 9
Pinch ...H 14
Pine Creek ...H 11
Pine Grove ...767..D 5
Pineknob ...K 14
Pineville ...1,140.°J 4
Piney ...J 16
Piney View* ...1,193..I 5
Pipestem ...J 5
Pisgah ...A 16
Pleasant Dale ...E 10
Pliny ...G 2
Poca ...1,142..G 3
Pocatalico* ...2,420..G 3
Poe ...J 16
Point
  Pleasant ...5,682.°F 2
Points ...D 10
Pond Gap ...I 15
Pool ...H 5
Porters Falls ...D 5
Powellton ...1,339..I 15
Power ...I 15
Pratt ...821..I 15
Prenter ...I 13
Prichard ...J 10
Prince ...K 16
Princeton ...7,493.°J 4
Procious ...G 4
Proctor ...C 5
Prosperity ...1,298..K 15
Pullman ...196..E 5
Pumpkintown ...F 15
Putney ...I 16
Queens ...F 14
Quick ...H 14
Quiet Dell ...D 14
Quincy ...I 14
Quinnimont ...K 16
Quinwood ...460..H 5
Rachel ...B 14
Racine ...I 13
Radnor ...J 10
Rainelle ...1,983..I 5
Ramage ...J 13
Ramsey ...J 16
Ranger ...J 11
Rangoon ...E 14
Ranson ...2,471..E 12
Raven Rock ...D 4
Ravenswood ...4,126..F 3
Reader ...D 5
Red Creek ...F 8
Red House ...G 3
Red Sulphur
  Springs ...J 5
Reedsville ...564..B 16
Reedy ...338..F 4
Renick ...I 6
Replete ...G 6
Revere ...E 15
Rhodell ...472..J 4
Richard ...A 15
Richwood ...3,568..H 6
Ridgeley ...994..D 9
Ridgeway ...E 11
Riffle ...D 14
Rig ...J 16
Rio ...E 10
Ripley ...3,464.°F 3
Rippon ...E 12
Rita ...K 15
Riverton ...F 8
Rivesville ...1,327..B 14
Roanoke ...E 13
Robertsburg ...G 2
Robinette, see
  Amherstdale
  [-Robinette]
Rock ...J 4
Rock Castle ...F 3
Rock Cave ...E 13
Rock Forge ...A 15
Rockport ...F 3
Roderfield ...K 3
Romance ...G 3
Romney ...2,094.°E 10
Ronceverte ...2,312..I 6
Rosedale ...F 5
Rosemont ...C 14

Rough Run ...F 9
Rowlesburg ...966..C 16
Rupert ...1,276..I 5
Russellville ...H 5
Ryan ...G 3
Rymer ...B 13
Sago ...E 14
St. Albans ...12,402..H 13
St. George ...D 16
St. Marys ...2,219.°D 4
Salem ...2,706..E 5
Salt Rock ...H 11
Saltpetre ...J 9
Sand Fork ...280..F 5
Sand Ridge ...F 4
Sandstone ...I 5
Sandyville ...F 3
Sarah ...H 11
Sarah Ann ...K 12
Sarton ...J 2
Scott Depot ...H 12
Secondcreek ...I 6
Seebert ...H 6
Selbyville ...F 14
Seneca Rocks ...F 8
Seth* ...I 13
Shady Spring ...1,786..K 16
Shamrock, see
  Mount Gay
  [-Shamrock]
Shanks* ...E 10
Sharples ...K 13
Shaw ...D 9
Shenandoah
  Junction ...D 12
Shepherds-
  town ...1,791..D 12
Sherman ...F 3
Sherrard ...D 5
Shinnston ...3,059..C 14
Shirley ...D 5
Shively ...I 11
Shoals ...H 10
Shock ...F 5
Short Creek ...B 5
Sias ...I 11
Silver Hill ...D 5
Simon ...J 3
Simpson ...C 14
Sissonville ...G 3
Sistersville ...2,367..D 5
Slab Fork ...K 15
Slanesville ...D 10
Slaty Fork ...G 6
Sleepy Creek ...D 11
Smithburg ...D 5
Smithers ...1,482..I 15
Smithfield ...278..B 12
Smithtown ...B 15
Smithville ...E 4
Smoot ...I 5
Sod ...H 12
Sophia ...1,216..K 15
South
  Charleston ...15,968..H 13
Spanishburg ...J 4
Spelter ...C 13
Spencer ...2,799.°F 4
Sprague ...K 16
Spring Dale ...I 5
Springfield ...D 10
Squire ...K 3
Stanaford* ...2,016..I 5
Star City ...1,464..A 15
Staten ...F 4
Statts Mills ...F 3
Steeles ...I 5
Stickney ...K 16
Stirrat ...K 12
Stollings ...K 12
Stonewood ...2,058..D 13
Stony Bottom ...G 7
Stouts Mills ...F 5
Strange Creek ...F 4
Stumptown ...F 4
Sugar Grove ...G 8
Summersville ...2,972.°H 5
Summit Point ...E 11
Sutton ...1,192.°G 5
Sweet
  Springs ...J 6
Sweetland ...I 11
Swiss ...I 16
Switzer ...1,034..K 12
Sylvester ...256..J 14
Tacy ...K 15
Tad ...H 14
Talcott ...I 5
Tams ...K 15
Tanner ...F 5
Tariff ...I 5
Teays ...H 12
Terra Alta ...1,946..D 8
Tesla ...G 5

Thomas ...747..E 8
Thornton ...C 15
Thorpe ...J 3
Three Churches ...D 10
Thurmond ...67..J 16
Thursday ...G 4
Tioga ...G 5
Toll Gate ...E 5
Tornado ...J 12
Triadelphia ...1,461..C 5
Troy ...F 5
True ...J 5
Tunnelton ...510..C 16
Turtle Creek ...J 12
Twilight ...K 14
Uler ...G 4
Uneeda ...J 13
Unger ...D 11
Union ...743.°J 6
Upper Tract ...F 8
Upperglade ...G 6
Vadis ...E 5
Valley Bend ...F 15
Valley Chapel ...D 13
Valley Grove ...597..B 5
Valley Head ...G 7
Valley Point ...A 16
Valleyfork ...G 4
Van ...J 13
Varney ...J 2
Vaughan ...I 16
Verdunville ...K 12
Verner ...J 2
Vicars ...I 15
Vienna ...11,618..E 3
Virginville ...B 6
Volga ...D 14
Wadestown ...A 13
Waiteville ...J 6
Walker ...E 4
Walkersville ...F 13
Wallace ...C 13
Wallback ...G 4
Walton ...G 4
Wana ...A 13
Waneta ...G 6
War ...2,158..K 3
Ward ...I 15
Wardensville ...241..E 9
Washington ...E 3
Waverly ...F 4
Wayne ...1,495.°H 1
Webster ...C 15
Webster
  Springs ...939.°G 6
Weirton ...25,371..B 5
Welch ...3,885.°J 3
Wellsburg ...3,963.°B 5
Wendel ...C 14
West
  Columbia ...F 2
West Hamlin ...643..J 11
West Liberty ...744..B 5
West Logan ...630..K 12
West Milford ...510..D 13
West Union ...1,090.°E 5
Weston ...6,250.°F 6
Westover ...4,884..A 15
Wharncliffe ...J 2
Wharton ...J 13
Wheeling ...43,070.°B 5
White Sulphur
  Springs ...3,371..I 6
Whitesville ...689..J 14
Whitman* ...1,651..J 2
Whitmer ...F 8
Wick ...D 5
Widen ...G 5
Wikel ...J 5
Wilbur ...F 5
Wildcat ...J 3
Wiley Ford ...1,224..D 10
Wileyville ...D 5
Williamsburg ...I 6
Williamson ...5,219.°I 1
Williamstown ...3,095..D 3
Willow Island ...E 4
Wilsie ...G 5
Wilson ...E 11
Wilsondale ...K 10
Windsor Heights ...B 5
Winfield ...329.°G 2
Winona ...I 16
Wolf Pen ...J 3
Womelsdorf ...306..E 15
Woodville ...J 12
Worthington ...329..B 14
Wyatt ...B 13
Wymer ...F 16
Yawkey ...J 12
Yellow
  Spring ...E 10
Yolyn ...K 12
Zenith ...J 6

'County seat.

*Does not appear on map; key shows general location.
Source: 1980 census. Places without population figures are unincorporated areas.

Beautiful scenery, mineral springs, and a variety of wildlife attract tourists, campers, hunters, and fishing enthusiasts to the mountains of West Virginia. The state's Allegheny and Cumberland mountain ranges offer alpine and nordic skiing. Kayakers, canoeists, and white water rafters enjoy such rivers as the New, the Gauley, the Bluestone, and the Shenandoah. West Virginia's state parks and forests attract hikers and back-packers. Tours of orchards, glass factories, and an exhi- bition coal mine offer glimpses into industries important to the state.

The Mountain State Forest Festival, held early in Oc- tober at Elkins, is among the most colorful annual events in West Virginia. Most of the festival takes place on the campus of Davis and Elkins College. Highlights of the festival include jousting tournaments, wood-chopping and sawing contests, and archery and shooting exhibi- tions.

Sternwheel Regatta in Charleston

Jack Zehrt, FPG

Places to visit

Following are brief descriptions of some of West Virginia's many interesting places to visit:

Berkeley Springs, a health resort city in Morgan County, was long called *Bath* after the famous resort city in Great Britain. George Washington noticed the health-giving qualities of the springs when he surveyed the land for Lord Fairfax. In 1776, Fairfax granted the site of the town to the Virginia Colony.

Blennerhassett Island, in the Ohio River near Parkersburg, was the site of a mansion built by Harman Blennerhassett about 1800. Blennerhassett, with Aaron Burr and others, was suspected of planning an independent government in the southwestern region of the United States. A reconstruction of the mansion has been built over the original foundation.

Cass, in Pocahontas County, has a state-owned scenic railroad powered by steam locomotives. Trains run through beautiful mountain country on the tracks of a former logging railroad.

Charles Town, the county seat of Jefferson County, was founded in 1786 by Charles Washington, younger brother of George Washington. A jury at the Jefferson County Court-house found John Brown guilty of murder and treason after his 1859 raid on Harpers Ferry. A stone marker designates the site of the John Brown Gallows. Several historic homes stand in the area around Charles Town. Harewood was built about 1770 for George Washington's brother Samuel. Dolley Payne Todd and James Madison were married in this house in 1794. Charles Washington built Mordington, or "Happy Retreat," about 1780. Bushrod Washington, grandnephew of the Presi-dent, built Claymont Court in 1820.

Jackson's Mill, near Weston, was the family farm where the Confederate General Stonewall Jackson spent his boyhood. In 1921 this area became the first state 4-H Club camp to be es-tablished in the United States.

National Radio Astronomy Observatory, in Green Bank, is a center for the study of radio waves from space. During the summer, visitors may inspect radio telescopes that measure the waves, and view a film about the observatory's work.

Seneca Rocks, in Pendleton County, tower 900 feet (275 me-ters) above the valley below. This landmark has many colorful layers of rock.

National forests and historical parks. Monongahela National Forest lies entirely within the boundaries of West Virginia. It is located in the eastern part of the state. Parts of George Washington and Jefferson national forests extend into West Virginia from Virginia.

The town of Harpers Ferry is famous in Civil War history. Har-pers Ferry National Historical Park lies on the boundary be-tween West Virginia and Maryland, as does the nearby Chesa-peake and Ohio Canal National Historical Park.

State parks and forests. West Virginia has 33 state parks and nine state forests. Among the best known state parks is Black-water Falls, near Davis. There, sparkling water tumbles 63 feet (19 meters) over a rocky ledge. For information on the parks and forests of West Virginia, write to Chief, Division of State Parks and Recreation, Department of Commerce, State Capitol Complex, 1900 Washington Street, East, Charleston, WV 25305.

Ron Snow, West Virginia Department of Commerce

Mountain State Forest Festival in Elkins

Annual events

January-May
Alpine Festival in Davis (March); House and Garden Tour in Martinsburg (April); Wildflower Pilgrimage at Blackwater Falls State Park (May); Strawberry Festival in Buckhannon (May); Allegheny Mountain Wool Fair in Mingo (May); Baseball Card and Sports Collectors' Show in Moundsville (May).

June-August
Folk Festival in Glenville (June); Mountain State Art and Craft Fair in Ripley (July); *Honey in the Rock* and *Hatfields and McCoys,* two plays about West Virginia history, at Grandview State Park (June through Sunday before Labor Day); New Martinsville Inboard Regatta in New Martinsville (July); Cherry River Festival in Richwood (August); West Virginia State Fair in Lewisburg (August); Appalachian Arts and Crafts Festival in Beckley (late August); West Virginia Italian Heritage Festival in Clarksburg (late August and early September); Sternwheel Regatta in Charleston (late August and early September).

September-December
Hardy County Heritage Weekend in Moorefield (September); Preston County Buckwheat Festival in Kingwood (September); West Virginia Oil and Gas Festival in Sistersville (September); Black Walnut Festival in Spencer (October); Festival of Lights in Wheeling (late November-January); 18th Century Christmas Market in Fairmont (December).

Harpers Ferry National Historical Park

Jeff Gnass, West Stock

Jodi Cobb, Woodfin Camp, Inc.

White water rafting on the New River

Land and climate

Land regions. In most places, West Virginia's boundaries follow the courses of rivers or the peaks of mountain chains. For this reason, the state has crooked boundaries. A narrow strip of West Virginia called the *Northern Panhandle* extends northward between Ohio and Pennsylvania. Another extension of West Virginia runs northward and eastward between Maryland and Virginia. It is called the *Eastern Panhandle.*

West Virginia has few large areas of level ground. Low mountains cover the eastern third of the state. Spruce Knob, the highest point in West Virginia, rises 4,863 feet (1,482 meters) above sea level near the eastern border. The widest valleys lie near the Ohio River in the west, and in parts of the Eastern Panhandle between the Allegheny and Blue Ridge mountains.

West Virginia has three main land regions: (1) the Appalachian Ridge and Valley Region, (2) the Appalachian Plateau, and (3) the Blue Ridge.

The Appalachian Ridge and Valley Region covers a wide strip of West Virginia along the state's eastern border. The Allegheny Mountains of this region belong to the Appalachian Mountain system. They form part of a series of long ridges and valleys that run from northeast to southwest across several eastern states. These mountains are made of folded layers of *sedimentary rock* (rock formed from deposits laid down by ancient rivers and seas). Erosion has worn down the softer layers, forming long parallel ridges of harder rock with valleys in between. Most streams and rivers run along the valleys between the ridges. A few streams cross the ridges in *water gaps* (breaks in the ridges). Water gaps occur where weak rock was worn away, or where streams cut

through hard rock as nature lifted and folded it. Caves and underground streams are common throughout the region. Forests cover the mountainsides.

The western border of the region lies along the *Allegheny Front.* The Allegheny Front occurs where the sharply folded rock layers of the Appalachian Ridge and Valley Region meet the more gently folded layers of the Appalachian Plateau. The front appears in some places as a high, rugged *escarpment* (slope). In southern West Virginia, it becomes lost in the roughness of the southern Allegheny Mountains.

The Appalachian Plateau covers the entire state west of the Appalachian Ridge and Valley Region. The plateau has a rugged surface. Streams have carved narrow valleys, leaving flat-topped uplands and rounded hills. The slopes are steep, especially in the west. Many peaks in the northeastern part of the region rise more than 4,000 feet (1,200 meters) above sea level.

Most of West Virginia's coal, salt, petroleum, and natural gas deposits are found in the Appalachian Plateau. Nearly all the state's larger cities lie in the wider river valleys of this region.

The Blue Ridge, a mountain range that forms part of the Appalachian system, touches the easternmost tip of West Virginia's Eastern Panhandle. The Blue Ridge Mountains are made of *igneous rock* (rock formed by the cooling of hot, melted material) and *metamorphic rock* (rock changed by heat and pressure). Apple and peach orchards grow on the slopes and in the fertile river valleys of this region.

Rivers and lakes. The Ohio River flows along the western boundary of West Virginia for over 275 miles

Stephen J. Shaluta, Jr., West Virginia Department of Commerce

Blackwater Falls tumbles 63 feet (19 meters) over a rocky ledge in Blackwater Falls State Park, near Davis. West Virginia has preserved its wilderness in many state parks and forests.

Land regions of West Virginia

WORLD BOOK map

Map index

Allegheny Mountains	C	5	
Allegheny Plateau	C	3	
Appalachian Mountains	D	4	
Bald Knob (Mtn.)	C	5	
Bickett Knob (Mtn.)	D	4	
Bickle Knob (Mtn.)	C	5	
Big Sandy R.	C	2	
Big Spruce Knob (Mtn.)	C	4	
Birch R.	C	4	
Bluestone Lake	D	4	
Bluestone R.	D	3	
Cacapon Mountain	B	6	
Cheat Lake	B	5	
Cheat Mountain	C	5	
Cheat R.	B	5	
Cottle Knob (Mtn.)	C	4	
Elk R.	C	3	
Fishing Creek	B	4	
Gauley R.	C	4	
Greenbrier R.	D	4	
Guyandotte R.	D	2	
Harpers Ferry Nat'l. Hist. Park	B	7	
High Knob (Mtn.)	B	6	
High Knob (Mtn.)	C	5	
Kanawha R.	C	3	
Keeney Mountain	D	4	
Knobly Mountain	B	5	
Laurel Mountain	B	5	
Little Kanawha R.	B	3	
Lost R.	B	6	
Meadow R.	C	4	
Middle Island Creek	C	3	
Mill Creek	C	3	
Mud R.	C	2	
New R.	C	3	
Ohio R.	C	2	
Opequon Creek	B	6	
Paddy Knob (Mtn.)	C	5	
Patterson Creek	B	5	
Peters Mountain	D	4	
Pine Swamp Knob (Mtn.)	B	5	
Pocatalico R.	C	3	
Potomac R.	B	6	
South Branch	C	6	
Reynolds Knob (Mtn.)	C	5	
Rich Mountain	C	4	
Shavers Fork	C	5	
Shavers Mountain	C	5	
Shenandoah R.	B	6	
Sideling Hill	B	6	
South Branch Mountain	B	6	
Spruce Knob (Mtn.) Highest Point in West Virginia	C	5	
Summersville Lake	C	4	
Sutton Lake	C	4	
Tug Fork	D	2	
Tygart Lake	B	4	
Tygart Valley R.	B	4	
West Fork R.	B	4	
Whitman Knob (Mtn.)	C	4	
Yew Mountain	C	4	

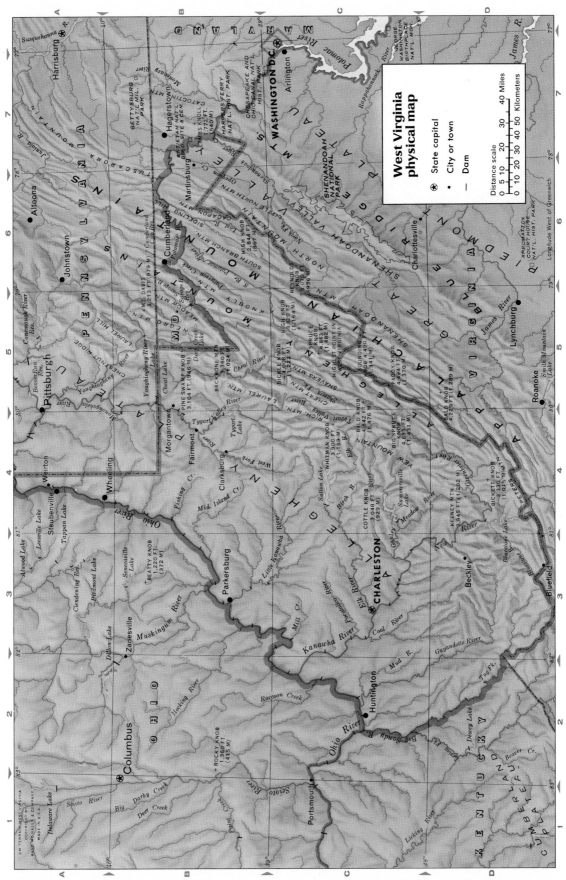

West Virginia physical map

* ⊛ State capital
* • City or town
* — Dam

Distance scale

0 5 10   20   30   40 Miles
0 10 20 30   40 50 Kilometers

Specially created for *The World Book Encyclopedia* by Rand McNally and World Book editors

The Kanawha River Valley, near Pliny, cuts through West Virginia's Appalachian Plateau region. The state's widest valleys lie in the western part of this region.

© Gary T. Truman

(442 kilometers). It provides a route to the Mississippi River and the Gulf of Mexico. The major rivers of the Appalachian Plateau flow northwestward into the Ohio. The Kanawha River is the Ohio's largest tributary in West Virginia. The Kanawha and New rivers and their branches drain a large portion of the state. The Big Sandy, Guyandotte, and Little Kanawha rivers also flow into the Ohio River.

The Monongahela River begins near the northern border of West Virginia. It flows northward through Pennsylvania and helps form the Ohio River at Pittsburgh. The Monongahela and its branches, including the Cheat, Tygart, and West Fork rivers, form the main drainage system of north-central West Virginia. A separate system drains the Eastern Panhandle. The Shenandoah and other rivers in that region flow northward and eastward into the Potomac River.

West Virginia has no large natural lakes. Dams and reservoirs have been built to hold back water during flood seasons and to release it during periods of low flow. The reservoirs serve as lakes for fishing and recreation.

Plant and animal life. Forests cover about four-fifths of West Virginia. The most important trees are such hardwoods as cherry, oak, and tulip trees. Evergreen trees, including hemlock, red spruce, and white pine, grow on mountain ridges and plateaus, and in river gorges.

The river valleys of West Virginia bloom with wild flowers from early spring to late fall. Bloodroot and hepaticas blossom beneath dogwood, redbud, white-blossomed hawthorn, and wild crab-apple trees. Azaleas and rhododendrons bloom in late spring and early summer. In autumn, the fields glow with asters, black-eyed Susans, and goldenrod.

White-tailed deer and black bears live in the mountains. Small woodland animals include gray and red foxes, minks, opossums, and raccoons. Many kinds of fish, including bass, trout, and walleyed pike, are found in the rivers and streams.

Climate. West Virginia has warm summers and moderately cold winters. The valleys are usually warmer than

the mountains. Maximum summer temperatures average over 85° F. (29° C), but in the mountains, they are from 5 to 10 degrees Fahrenheit (3 to 6 degrees Celsius) cooler. Minimum winter temperatures average about 25° F. (−4° C) in the central and northeastern mountains, and nearly 30° F. (−1° C) in the south and southwest. The state's highest recorded temperature, 112° F. (44° C), occurred at Moorefield on Aug. 4, 1930, and at Martinsburg on July 10, 1936. West Virginia's lowest recorded temperature, −37° F. (−38° C), was set at Lewisburg on Dec. 30, 1917.

Rainfall is plentiful in all parts of the state. It is heaviest in the southern mountains, and lightest in the upper Potomac River valley in the east. The ample rainfall benefits West Virginia's agriculture and industry, but it also creates problems. Summer thunderstorms sometimes cause flash floods that damage property in valley settlements. Heavy winter and spring floods occur in the lower river valleys of West Virginia. Thick fogs often cover the valleys.

The southwest has the lightest snowfall—less than 20 inches (51 centimeters) a year. The mountains sometimes get as much as 100 inches (250 centimeters) of snowfall annually.

Average monthly weather

	Charleston						Elkins				
	Temperatures				Days of		**Temperatures**				Days of
	F°		C°		rain or		F°		C°		rain or
	High	Low	High	Low	snow		High	Low	High	Low	snow
Jan.	46	27	8	−3	18	Jan.	43	22	6	−6	18
Feb.	49	28	9	−2	14	Feb.	44	21	7	−6	16
Mar.	57	33	14	1	16	Mar.	52	27	11	−3	17
Apr.	68	42	20	6	15	Apr.	63	36	17	2	15
May	77	50	25	10	14	May	72	45	22	7	14
June	85	60	29	16	11	June	79	54	26	12	15
July	87	64	31	18	12	July	83	57	28	14	14
Aug.	86	62	30	17	10	Aug.	81	56	27	13	12
Sept.	81	56	27	13	9	Sept.	76	50	24	10	10
Oct.	71	44	22	7	9	Oct.	65	38	18	3	11
Nov.	57	35	14	2	11	Nov.	52	29	11	−2	13
Dec.	48	29	9	−2	13	Dec.	43	22	6	−6	16

Average January temperatures
West Virginia has moderately cold winters. The southwestern section usually averages above freezing.

Average July temperatures
The state has warm summers, with the west and east being the hottest. The central mountains are milder.

Average yearly precipitation
Rain is plentiful throughout the state. It is the heaviest in the mountains and lighter on the east and west borders.

WORLD BOOK maps

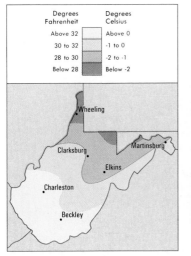

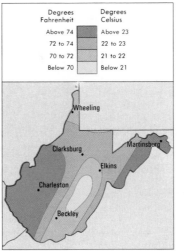

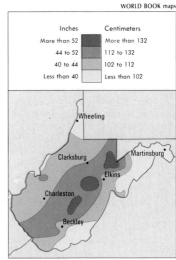

Economy

Service industries, taken together, provide about two-thirds of West Virginia's *gross state product*—the total value of goods and services produced in a year. Service industries include such activities as education, health care, real estate, and retail trade.

Chemical manufacturing and coal mining play major roles in the West Virginia economy. The Ohio and Kanawha river valleys are major centers of the nation's chemical industry. West Virginia is also a leading coal producer. But the increasing use of machines in the coal industry has reduced jobs. Jobs have also been lost due to the decline of West Virginia's steel and glass industries. As a result, the state has one of the nation's highest unemployment rates and lowest average incomes.

Natural resources. Few areas of similar size have so great a variety of resources as West Virginia. These resources include mineral deposits, scenic recreational areas, and abundant rainfall.

Minerals are West Virginia's most valuable natural resources. Deposits of *bituminous* (soft) coal lie under about half the state. Most of the coal deposits are in a broad belt that covers all the central counties. Fields of natural gas and petroleum-bearing sands are found in the western half of the state. Brine and rock salt come from the Ohio and Kanawha river valleys. Limestone is found in the mountains along the eastern border. Sand used in glassmaking comes from several north-central counties and from the Eastern Panhandle. Other minerals include clay, dolomite, sandstone, and shale.

Soils. The most fertile soils are in the river valleys. Some of the sandy soils that cover the rest of the state contain natural lime that makes the land especially good for grain crops and fruit trees.

Service industries account for 67 per cent of the gross state product of West Virginia. Most of the service

Production and workers by economic activities

Economic activities	Per cent of GSP* produced	Employed workers	
		Number of persons	Per cent of total
Finance, insurance, & real estate	15	23,700	4
Wholesale & retail trade	14	136,700	22
Manufacturing	14	86,800	14
Transportation, communication, & utilities	14	36,900	6
Community, social, & personal services	13	121,300	20
Mining	13	40,500	6
Government	11	128,900	21
Construction	5	22,800	4
Agriculture	1	19,300	3
Total	**100**	**616,800**	**100**

*GSP = gross state product, the total value of goods and services produced in a year.
Figures are for 1986.
Sources: *World Book* estimates based on data from U.S. Bureau of Economic Analysis, U.S. Bureau of Labor Statistics, and U.S. Department of Agriculture.

industries are concentrated in the state's six metropolitan areas. Several service industries benefit from the many tourists who visit the state's recreation areas, historic sites, and other attractions.

Finance, insurance, and real estate provide a larger share of the gross state product than any other economic activity in West Virginia. Real estate is the largest part of this industry because of the large sums of money that are involved in the selling and leasing of property. Charleston and Huntington are the state's chief financial centers.

Next in importance among service industries in West

Virginia are (1) wholesale and retail trade and (2) transportation, communication, and utilities. The wholesale trade of coal, chemicals, and groceries is important in the state. Leading types of retail businesses include department stores, food stores, and service stations. Heck's, a large department store chain, is headquartered in Nitro. Wholesale and retail trade is the leading employer in West Virginia.

Transportation, communication, and utilities provide a larger share of the gross state product in West Virginia than in any other state. Rail and water transportation are of major importance to the economy because they transport coal, chemicals, and other goods from production sites to markets. They also bring such goods as automobiles and groceries to West Virginia from other states. Trucking companies are also an important part of the transportation sector. Telephone companies are the major part of the communications sector. AT&T has a large branch office in West Virginia. Utility companies supply electric, gas, and water service. More information about transportation and communication appears later in this section.

Community, social, and personal service rank next in importance among the state's service industries. This industry consists of a variety of businesses, including doctors' offices and private hospitals, law firms, hotels, and repair shops.

Government ranks last among service industries in West Virginia. Government services include public

Eric Carle, Shostal

Coal barges move through the Greenup Locks on the Ohio River. West Virginia ranks among the nation's leading coal-mining states. Minerals are its most valuable natural resources.

Farm, mineral, and forest products

This map shows the areas where the state's leading farm, mineral, and forest products are produced. The major urban areas (shown in red) are the state's important manufacturing centers.

WORLD BOOK map

schools and hospitals. State government offices are based in Charleston, the state capital.

Manufacturing in West Virginia accounts for 14 per cent of the gross state product. Products manufactured in the state have a *value added by manufacture* of about $6 billion a year. Value added by manufacture represents the increase in value of raw materials after they have become finished products.

Chemicals are West Virginia's leading manufactured product by far. The chemical industry operates chiefly in the Kanawha and Ohio river valleys. It uses coal, natural gas, oil, and salt found in the region. Factories in Charleston, New Martinsville, Parkersburg, and South Charleston make dyes, detergents, paints, plastics, synthetic rubber, and salt cake.

Primary metals rank second in terms of value added by manufacture. This industry centers in the Northern Panhandle. Steel mills line the banks of the Ohio River near Wheeling and Weirton. Almost all the iron ore comes from mines in Minnesota and Michigan. Freighters bring the ore to ports along Lake Erie. From there, trains carry it to West Virginia. Weirton manufactures tin plate and sheet steel, and Wheeling produces structural steel. A huge chromeplating plant also operates in Weirton. Huntington has a large nickel plant.

Stone, clay, and glass products rank third in value. The state is famous for its glassware and pottery. Leading glass-producing communities in West Virginia include Huntington and Parkersburg. The Parkersburg area produces millions of glass marbles every year. Table glassware comes from Huntington, Milton, Morgantown, Moundsville, Salem, Weston, and Williamstown. Other glass products include blown glass, bottles, crystalware, plate glass, stained glass, and structural glass, such as glass bricks.

Most of the pottery plants are in Hancock County, although a few operate elsewhere along the Ohio River. They produce such products as chinaware, firebrick, paving brick, porcelain, and tile.

Other products manufactured in West Virginia, in order of value, include fabricated metal products, food products, printed materials, and machinery. Leading types of fabricated metal products made in the state are pipes, stampings, structural metal, and tools. Baked goods and soft drinks are the main food products made in West Virginia. Newspapers are the chief kind of printed material. Mining machinery is the leading type of machinery manufactured in the state.

Mining contributes 13 per cent of West Virginia's gross state product. Coal is the state's major mineral product. Only Kentucky and Wyoming mine more coal than West Virginia.

Coal accounts for 85 per cent of West Virginia's mining income. Bituminous coal is the only type of coal mined in the state. About three-fourths of it comes from underground mines. The rest comes from surface mines. About half of the state's land has coal beneath it. The southern part of West Virginia has the state's largest coal reserves.

West Virginia counties with the highest coal output are Boone, Logan, Mingo, and Monongalia. Boone and Logan counties each have about 80 coal mines.

Certain kinds of coal from the southern part of the state are popular because they cause relatively little air pollution when they burn. These coals have excellent heating and steam-producing qualities, and are rich in such by-products as coal tar and creosote.

Coal companies have made increasing use of advanced mining machinery and other technology to increase efficiency. This has resulted in a need for fewer workers. Unemployment in the coal-mining regions of West Virginia is at a higher rate than almost any other area in the United States.

Coal-mining companies are required by law to repair land where mining operations have been completed. But some of the companies have ignored this law and left the land badly scarred.

Among West Virginia's other mineral products, natural gas is the most important. Natural gas fields lie under most of the western part of the state. Much of the natural gas is piped to cities, where it is used to heat buildings. Some of the gas is converted to liquid form and

Ron Snow, West Virginia Chamber of Commerce

A glassmaker demonstrates his craft to a tour group in a factory in Williamstown. West Virginia is famous for its glassware and pottery.

transported by train or truck. Empty natural gas wells serve as storage places for gas from Louisiana, Oklahoma, or Texas. Pipelines carry the gas to West Virginia, where it is stored in the empty wells for use locally and in the northeastern states.

West Virginia also mines petroleum, crushed stone, salt, and sand and gravel. The northwestern part of the state produces the most petroleum. The petroleum is piped to refineries near St. Marys and Point Pleasant for processing.

Limestone is the main source of crushed stone. The eastern part of the state has most of the limestone quarries. Crushed stone is used mainly to make roadbeds.

Miners produce large quantities of salt from deep underground mines in Marshall County. The salt is removed from the mines by forcing water into the salt beds to dissolve the salt and pumping out the brine.

Most of West Virginia's sand and gravel is obtained by dredging operations in the Ohio River. Sand and gravel is used mainly to make concrete. A mountain near Berkeley Springs contains sand that is excellent for making glass.

Agriculture provides 1 per cent of the gross state product. Farmland covers about a fourth of the state. West Virginia's approximately 21,000 farms have an average size of 175 acres (71 hectares).

Livestock and livestock products provide most of the farm income in West Virginia. Beef cattle and milk are the most valuable farm products in the state. Most cattle and dairy farms lie in the river valleys of the Appalachian Plateau. Other important livestock products in West Virginia include *broilers* (chickens between 5 and 12 weeks old) and turkeys.

Hay is the most valuable field crop in West Virginia. Almost all the hay is fed to cattle. Corn and tobacco rank next in value. Much of the corn comes from the Ohio and Potomac river valleys. The lower Ohio Valley provides large amounts of tobacco.

West Virginia fruit growers raise large crops of apples and peaches. The easternmost part of West Virginia lies in the Shenandoah Valley, one of the best apple-growing regions in the United States. Farmers in West Virginia were the first to grow the Grimes Golden and Golden Delicious varieties of apples.

Electric power. Almost all of West Virginia's electric power comes from steam plants that burn coal. The state's many rivers and streams could furnish a vast amount of water power. But only a few hydroelectric projects have been built.

Transportation. Much of the transportation in West Virginia runs along the divides and valleys of the state's major streams. Herds of buffaloes opened trails along the waterways while migrating westward. Later, Indian war parties followed the same paths. Early settlers followed these trails and improved them for wagons. Many settlers traveled along the Ohio River. Most communities developed along railroad lines built in the late 1800's. Paved highways were developed in the 1920's.

West Virginia has about 35,000 miles (56,000 kilometers) of roads and highways. About three-fourths are surfaced. The West Virginia Turnpike runs 88 miles (142 kilometers) between Charleston and Princeton. The state has had difficulty developing a comprehensive road system because of rugged terrain.

Thirteen rail lines provide freight service in West Virginia. Passenger trains serve about 10 cities. The first railroad to reach the state, the Baltimore & Ohio, entered Harpers Ferry in 1836.

West Virginia has about 500 miles (800 kilometers) of navigable waterways. Ships and barges on West Virginia rivers carry chemicals, coal, lumber, oil, sand, steel, and other bulky products. During the 1930's, the federal government built a series of locks and dams on the Ohio River and its branches. These locks and dams improved the rivers of West Virginia for barge traffic. The United States Army Corps of Engineers has continued to develop the state's waterways.

Charleston has West Virginia's busiest airport. The state's other major airport lies near Huntington.

Communication. The state's first newspaper, the *Potomak Guardian and Berkeley Advertiser,* appeared in Shepherdstown in 1790. The state now has about 85 newspapers, approximately 25 of which are dailies. The *Intelligencer,* founded in 1852 in Wheeling, is still being published. Other dailies published in West Virginia include the *Bluefield Daily Telegraph,* the *Charleston Gazette,* the *Charleston Daily Mail,* the *Huntington Herald-Dispatch,* the *Parkersburg News,* and the *Wheeling News-Register.*

The state's first radio station, WSAZ, began broadcasting from Huntington in 1923. WSAZ-TV, the first television station, started operations in Huntington in 1949. Today, West Virginia has about 130 radio stations and 13 television stations.

Government

Constitution. West Virginia adopted its first constitution in 1863, when it became the 35th state in the Union. The state is now governed by its second constitution, adopted in 1872. The constitution has been amended more than 50 times. Constitutional amendments may be proposed in either house of the state legislature. They must be approved by a two-thirds majority of both houses, and then by a majority of the voters. The constitution may also be revised by a constitutional convention. Before a convention can be called, it must be approved by a majority of the legislators and the voters.

Executive. The governor of West Virginia is elected to a four-year term and may serve any number of terms, but not more than two terms in succession. The heads of many state administrative departments are appointed by the governor. Other top state officials include the secretary of state, auditor, treasurer, attorney general, and commissioner of agriculture. Each of these officials is elected to a four-year term.

Legislature of West Virginia consists of a senate and a house of delegates. The voters of each of the state's 17 senatorial districts elect two senators to four-year terms. The house of delegates has 100 members. They serve two-year terms. Each of the state's 40 delegate districts elects from 1 to 12 delegates, depending on population.

The legislature meets every year. Regular sessions

begin on the second Wednesday of January, except in the year after an election for governor is held. Then, the regular session starts on the second Wednesday of February. Regular sessions last 60 days. The governor may call special sessions.

Courts. The highest court in West Virginia is the Supreme Court of Appeals. It has five judges elected to 12-year terms. Every year, the court chooses a chief justice from among its members. The state is divided into 31 judicial circuits. Each circuit has a circuit court with one or more judges elected to eight-year terms. The circuit courts have jurisdiction in civil cases and cases involving felonies and misdemeanors. Each West Virginia county has one or more magistrate courts. The magistrate courts hear civil cases that involve amounts of money of $3,000 or less, and misdemeanor cases that are not handled by the circuit courts. Their judges, called magistrates, are elected to four-year terms.

Local government. Each of West Virginia's 55 counties elects a circuit clerk and a county clerk. All counties elect three county commissioners except for Jefferson County, which elects five, and Preston County, which elects eight. All of these officials serve six-year terms. Other elected county officials include a surveyor, prosecuting attorney, sheriff, and assessor. They serve four-year terms.

A 1936 amendment to the state constitution gives West Virginia cities with populations of over 2,000 the right to adopt or change their own charters. This right is called *home rule.* Only 10 West Virginia cities have taken advantage of the home-rule law. Most of these cities have a council-manager form of government. Most

Gerald S. Ratliff, West Virginia Chamber of Commerce

The West Virginia House of Delegates meets in the state capitol in Charleston. Its 100 members serve two-year terms.

of the state's other cities have a mayor-council government. West Virginia's home-rule cities are not so independent as home-rule cities of other states. This is because West Virginia courts still uphold the right of the state legislature to control many city affairs.

Revenue. Taxation provides about 60 per cent of the state government's *general revenue* (income). Most of the rest comes from federal grants and other U.S. government programs. West Virginia's most important sources of tax revenue are a general sales tax and a personal income tax. Other sources of tax revenue include taxes on insurance premiums, motor fuels, tobacco products, motor vehicle licenses and titles, and corporate profits.

Politics. Since 1864, West Virginia has divided its vote about equally between Republicans and Democrats in state and national elections. From 1896 to 1928, the Republicans won every state election except one. The Democrats won control of the state in 1932 and held it until 1956. Since then, about the same number of Democratic and Republican candidates have won the governorship. Democrats have usually won control of the state legislature. Since the early 1930's, West Virginia voters have greatly favored Democratic presidential candidates over Republican presidential candidates. For West Virginia's voting record in presidential elections, see **Electoral College** (table).

The governors of West Virginia

	Party	Term
Arthur I. Boreman	Republican	1863-1869
Daniel D. T. Farnsworth	Republican	1869
William E. Stevenson	Republican	1869-1871
John J. Jacob	Democratic	1871-1877
Henry M. Mathews	Democratic	1877-1881
Jacob B. Jackson	Democratic	1881-1885
Emanuel W. Wilson	Democratic	1885-1890
Aretas B. Fleming	Democratic	1890-1893
William A. MacCorkle	Democratic	1893-1897
George W. Atkinson	Republican	1897-1901
Albert B. White	Republican	1901-1905
William M. O. Dawson	Republican	1905-1909
William E. Glasscock	Republican	1909-1913
Henry D. Hatfield	Republican	1913-1917
John J. Cornwell	Democratic	1917-1921
Ephraim F. Morgan	Republican	1921-1925
Howard M. Gore	Republican	1925-1929
William G. Conley	Republican	1929-1933
Herman G. Kump	Democratic	1933-1937
Homer A. Holt	Democratic	1937-1941
Matthew M. Neely	Democratic	1941-1945
Clarence W. Meadows	Democratic	1945-1949
Okey L. Patteson	Democratic	1949-1953
William C. Marland	Democratic	1953-1957
Cecil H. Underwood	Republican	1957-1961
William Wallace Barron	Democratic	1961-1965
Hulett C. Smith	Democratic	1965-1969
Arch A. Moore, Jr.	Republican	1969-1977
John D. Rockefeller IV	Democratic	1977-1985
Arch A. Moore, Jr.	Republican	1985-1989
Gaston Caperton	Democratic	1989-

Indian days. The earliest Indians of the region were mound builders (see **Mound builders**). Hundreds of their burial mounds may still be seen in the Ohio and Kanawha river valleys. Later, the Woodlands Indians, including the Cherokee, Iroquois, and Shawnee tribes, moved into the region. Their villages were concentrated along major rivers. The Indians hunted game and gathered salt from pools of brine during the summer. They moved back to their homes in the east and north as winter approached. They often fought wars for control of the hunting grounds and brine pools. Many of these Indians were killed during the 1600's in tribal wars. Many others died as a result of epidemics of smallpox. When European and American settlers arrived, the area had a far smaller Indian population than did other areas. See **Indian, American** (Table of tribes).

Exploration. The area that became West Virginia formed part of the Virginia Colony. King James I granted the colony to the Virginia Company of London (see **London Company**), a group of British merchants and investors, in 1606. The boundaries reached from present-day South Carolina north to Pennsylvania, and extended westward and northwestward indefinitely. The German explorer John Lederer and his companions were probably the first Virginians to see the region that became West Virginia. Lederer's expedition reached the crest of the Blue Ridge, probably in 1669. In 1671, Thomas Batts and Robert Fallam led another expedition into the region in search of fur-hunting areas and transportation routes. Other exploring parties visited the region during the next few years.

Early settlement. One of the first settlers in the region was Morgan Morgan of Delaware, who built a cabin at Bunker Hill, probably in 1731. Germans seeking greater religious freedom came from Pennsylvania in 1727. They established a settlement called New Mecklenburg (now Shepherdstown). Other settlements were soon founded, many of them by other Germans and by Scotch-Irish from Northern Ireland. Most of these pioneer farmers settled in the Eastern Panhandle, in the Ohio Valley, and along the Greenbrier and New rivers.

The Indians often attacked the settlers, who were taking over their hunting grounds. The pioneers built a number of forts and blockhouses, many of which formed the beginnings of towns and cities. They included Fort Henry (now Wheeling), Fort Lee (Charleston), and Fort Randolph (Point Pleasant).

The explorer John P. Salling (also spelled Salley) discovered coal on the Coal River near Racine in 1742. But the deposits were not developed until railroads began expanding in the mid-1800's. The lumber industry began after 1755, when people started to use water-powered sawmills to produce lumber.

In 1763, King George III refused to let the colonists in America take any land west of the Alleghenies until treaties could be made with the Indians for peaceful settlement. The Scotch-Irish ignored the order. The Germans and the Dutch paid no attention to the order because they could not even read it.

Settlers pushed over the mountains into the forbidden green valleys in greater and greater numbers. They notched trees with their axes to mark their land claims. By treaties signed in 1768, the Cherokee and Iroquois gave up all claim to the lands they had used as hunting grounds between the Allegheny Mountains and the Ohio River. By 1775, about 30,000 settlers lived there.

Demands for separation. The Allegheny Mountains separated Virginia's western settlers from the seat of government at Williamsburg in the east. People in the west developed a social and economic life quite different from that of the eastern settlements. The soil was much more rugged in the western part than in the east, and plantation life could not be duplicated there. The western area also had less representation in Virginia's government than the east had, and received less support from the Virginia government.

Settlers in the west began to demand their own government as early as 1776, when they sent petitions to the Continental Congress. The Revolutionary War halted this attempt. The western settlers contributed their full share of men and supplies to the war. Indian armies led by British officers invaded the region three times between 1777 and 1782, but were driven out.

Industries began to develop during the Revolutionary War. In 1794, Peter Tarr built the first iron furnace west of the Alleghenies in the Northern Panhandle. In 1808, the Kanawha Valley began producing large quantities of salt.

Sectional strife. During the early 1800's, the differences between eastern and western Virginia became even greater. Much of the trade in the east moved to the Atlantic Ocean, while commerce in the west used waterways that flowed toward the Mississippi River. The land-owning, slaveholding aristocracy of eastern Virginia represented the larger part of the population. The easterners controlled state affairs. They opposed public improvements that the western farmers and industrialists wanted. Bitter disputes developed over slavery, taxation, use of public funds, education, and other issues.

Further discoveries of mineral resources continued economic development in the west. Natural gas had been discovered in 1775 near Charleston. In 1841, William Tompkins, a saltmaker in the Kanawha Valley, first used natural gas as a fuel for manufacturing. An oil well drilled at Burning Springs in 1860 began a stampede for oil. Burning Springs became a thriving village.

Civil War and statehood. Disputes over slavery reached a climax in 1859 when John Brown and his followers seized the federal arsenal at Harpers Ferry (see **Brown, John**). Virginia had to choose sides when Confederate troops in South Carolina fired on Fort Sumter on April 12, 1861. On April 17, a state convention voted for secession. But most of the western counties in Virginia supported the Union. These counties declared their independence and formed a government called the Restored Government of Virginia.

In August 1861, the western counties approved the formation of a new state called *Kanawha*. This Indian word is believed to mean *place of the white stone,* referring to the salt deposits in the region. The westerners prepared a state constitution in November 1861. In it, they changed the name of the proposed state to West Virginia. The people adopted the constitution in April 1862. Congress admitted West Virginia to the Union on June 20, 1863, as the 35th state. At that time, West Virginia had a population of about 380,000, including about 15,000 slaves. Arthur I. Boreman became the first governor. Wheeling became the state capital.

Historic West Virginia

Mound builders were the earliest Indians to inhabit what is now West Virginia. They built hundreds of burial mounds in the Ohio and Kanawha river valleys.

The Battle of Point Pleasant in 1774 is called "the first battle of the Revolutionary War" by some historians. Settlers defeated an Indian uprising in the Northwest Territory.

Several western counties that sided with the Union separated from Virginia at the beginning of the Civil War and formed their own government. They later became West Virginia.

John Brown, a famous abolitionist, captured the U.S. arsenal at Harpers Ferry in 1859 as part of an unsuccessful plan to start a rebellion of slaves.

Green Bank, the home of the National Radio Astronomy Observatory's main facility, opened in 1959.

Important dates in West Virginia

WORLD BOOK illustrations by Kevin Chadwick

1669? John Lederer and his companions became the first Virginians to see the West Virginia region.

1727 Germans from Pennsylvania established a settlement at New Mecklenburg (now Shepherdstown).

1742 John P. Salling discovered coal on the Coal River.

1754-1755 The French and Indians defeated troops led by George Washington and General Edward Braddock.

1775 Gas was discovered near Charleston.

1776 People in western Virginia sent petitions to the Continental Congress asking for a separate government.

1836 The first railroad reached the state at Harpers Ferry.

1859 John Brown and his followers raided the federal arsenal at Harpers Ferry.

1861 The counties of western Virginia refused to secede with Virginia. These counties organized a separate government that supported the Union.

1863 West Virginia became the 35th state on June 20.

1872 The people ratified the present state constitution.

1915 The Supreme Court of the United States ruled that West Virginia owed Virginia $12,393,929.50 as part of the state debt at the time of separation.

1920-1921 West Virginia miners fought with mine guards, police, and federal troops in a dispute over organizing unions.

1939 West Virginia made the final payment of its debt to Virginia.

1946 Major chemical industries began operating in the Ohio River Valley.

1959 The National Radio Astronomy Observatory began operating at Green Bank.

1968 Explosions and fire in a West Virginia coal mine took 78 lives. The disaster led to new mine safety laws.

1972 One of the worst floods in West Virginia history killed more than 100 persons near Man.

1985 The West Virginia legislature established a state lottery to help raise money for the state.

The new state furnished about 30,000 men to the Union armies. More than 8,000 men joined the Confederate armies. Battles raged in many parts of West Virginia during the first year of the war. After a series of defeats in 1861, Confederate forces stopped trying to capture land west of the Alleghenies. But they often raided the state for food, grain, and especially salt, which was scarce in the South. Small Confederate detachments also invaded West Virginia in an unsuccessful attempt to destroy the Baltimore and Ohio Railroad. This line connected the West and Washington, D.C.

Virginia asked West Virginia to reunite with it after the war ended in 1865, but West Virginia refused to do so. Virginia then insisted that West Virginia pay part of the state debt at the time of separation. Legal battles continued over this issue until 1915, when the Supreme Court of the United States ruled that West Virginia owed Virginia $12,393,929.50. West Virginia made its final payment on the debt in 1939.

A West Virginia law denied voting rights to about 15,000 men who had fought for the Confederacy or helped it in other ways. But the legislature repealed this law in 1871. A new constitution was adopted in 1872. Many Virginia aristocrats living in the southern part of the state controlled the government. They moved the state capital to Charleston in 1870. Wheeling became the capital in 1875, but the influential southerners in the state had the capital moved back to Charleston in 1885.

The development of railroads speeded industrial expansion after the Civil War. Railroads built during the late 1800's opened up mineral and timber resources in the state's interior. Coal production increased greatly to meet the needs of the railroads and new industries.

Experiments conducted in Pennsylvania in 1874 showed that natural gas could be used to produce industrial power on a large scale. Many industries came to West Virginia in the late 1800's to take advantage of this fuel. The lumber industry grew rapidly after 1881, when steam power replaced water power for sawmills.

Labor troubles. Between 1860 and 1920, West Virginia mining companies hired great numbers of immigrants. Wages were low and working conditions were poor. Coal miners tried to organize unions so they could make strong demands for better working conditions. The mining companies defeated most of these attempts. A few unions were organized during the 1870's, but working conditions improved only slightly. A single mine explosion in 1907 killed 361 miners.

Tent colonies such as Red Jacket, shown above in 1920, housed striking coal miners who were locked out of their company-owned homes. During the late 1800's and early 1900's, miners engaged in a bitter struggle to win higher wages and better working conditions.

The United Mine Workers of America began to organize workers in West Virginia in 1890. Miners at Paint Creek and at Cabin Creek went on strike in April 1912. Mineowners refused to talk with the workers. Twelve miners and four mine guards were killed in battles. Peace was restored only after Governor William E. Glasscock sent state militia to the area. In 1913, Governor Henry D. Hatfield proposed that the owners guarantee the miners a nine-hour workday and the right to organize. The miners and owners agreed to this plan, and the strike ended on April 28, 1913.

Labor disputes quieted down after the United States entered World War I in 1917. West Virginia provided raw materials and manufactured products for the war effort. Labor trouble flared up again after the war. In 1919, hundreds of union miners gathered near Charleston to march on Logan County to organize the miners there. Governor John J. Cornwell stopped the march by promising to investigate the union miners' complaints.

In May 1920, mineowners at Matewan, in Mingo County, locked union miners out of their jobs. The firms hired detectives to put the miners out of their company-owned homes. Fighting broke out, and the miners and city police routed the company detectives. Miners and mine guards in Mingo County fought again in August. Governor Cornwell requested the aid of federal troops, and President Woodrow Wilson sent 500 soldiers. The union then threatened a statewide strike unless the soldiers were withdrawn. Cornwell gave in, but fresh riots brought the troops back and the governor declared martial law.

The riots quieted during the winter, but broke out again early in 1921. Union miners marched on the city of Logan to organize the miners there. Mine guards met the miners with armed airplanes and machine guns. A four-day battle followed near Blair. The arrival of federal troops and a squadron of bombers forced the miners to retreat. Later, the state indicted 543 miners for taking part in the march. Twenty-two of them were tried for treason against West Virginia. A jury found them innocent. Many men left the union because of the miners' defeat. Almost 45,000 men were in the union in 1920; by 1932 only about 100 members remained.

After the National Recovery Administration (NRA) was established in 1933, many mine workers rejoined the union. Under the terms of the NRA, the mining companies raised wages, shortened work hours, and generally improved working conditions.

The mid-1900's. World War II (1939-1945) speeded industrial growth in West Virginia. Mines and factories produced coal, steel, chemicals, and other war supplies. The discovery of huge salt deposits in 1943 attracted major chemical industries to the Ohio River Valley in 1946. Employment reached record levels.

During the 1950's, West Virginia entered a period of economic adjustment. Defense industries no longer needed so many of the state's products. The demand for coal dropped as railroads shifted from coal-burning to diesel engines. More and more families began to use oil and gas as heating fuels. To meet this competition, the coal industry began to use more machines to do the work of coal miners. The machines lowered the price of coal, but many jobless workers left the state to seek other employment. West Virginia lost 7 per cent of its

population between 1950 and 1960 and 6 per cent between 1960 and 1970. Most of the people who left were young. Many older people who stayed behind received public welfare aid and government surplus food. However, the chemical and textile industries in the Ohio and Kanawha river valleys continued to grow, and glass and metal production also increased.

The 1960 presidential campaign brought Senator John F. Kennedy to West Virginia and focused national attention on the state's economic problems. Under Presidents Kennedy and Lyndon B. Johnson, federal aid was increased for West Virginia and other sections of the 11 Appalachian Mountain states. In 1965, Congress approved an aid-to-Appalachia program. This program provided funds for building roads, developing water resources and pasturelands, restoring forests, and retraining workers. In 1967, the state legislature passed laws to reduce water and air pollution and to control strip mining.

In 1968, coal mine explosions and a fire at Farmington trapped and killed 78 miners. After the tragedy, Congress passed stronger laws regulating mine safety and working conditions. These laws included provisions for benefits to miners disabled by *pneumoconiosis,* a coal dust disease known as "black lung."

Labor troubles continued in the 1960's. In 1969, retired coal miners marched on the West Virginia Capitol in a successful demand for increased benefits. Also in 1969, a public employee strike resulted in the mass firing of 2,600 state highway workers.

In 1972, the collapse of a dam on Buffalo Creek near Man caused one of the worst floods in West Virginia history. The flood killed more than 100 persons.

Recent developments. A nationwide energy shortage that developed in the 1970's at first strengthened West Virginia's coal-mining industry. New mines were opened and improved methods to process the increased amounts of coal were developed. The state's future as a supplier of cheap energy seemed secure.

New jobs created by the growth of manufacturing, coal production, and tourism helped West Virginia reverse its population decline. The state's population increased by 12 per cent between 1970 and 1980. But in the early 1980's, the availability of oil increased. The price of coal then dropped sharply, and many coal workers were laid off. In the mid-1980's, about a sixth of West Virginia's labor force was unemployed—the highest unemployment rate in the nation. These economic problems caused the population to decline again.

State officials have recognized the need to make West Virginia less dependent on the large coal and steel industries. To broaden the state's economy, officials have placed more emphasis on developing other manufacturing activities, service industries, and tourism. The state legislature, for example, has offered tax benefits to attract new industries. During the first half of the 1980's, many small factories replaced larger ones. Service industries also added many jobs. In addition, new interstate and state highways opened new areas of the state to industry and tourism. All these developments offer hope of raising economic levels in West Virginia. To help pay for road construction and other public works, the state legislature established a state lottery in 1985.

Richard Stark Little and George Parkinson

Related articles in *World Book* include:

Biographies

Boyd, Belle
Brown, John
Buck, Pearl S.
Byrd, Robert Carlyle
Cornstalk
Davis, Henry G.
Davis, John W.
Jackson, Stonewall

Kenna, John E.
Pierpont, Francis H.
Reuther, Walter P.
Rowan, Andrew S.
Vance, Cyrus R.
Washington, George
Yeager, Charles E.

Cities and towns

Charleston
Harpers Ferry
Huntington

Wheeling
White Sulphur Springs

Physical features

Allegheny Mountains
Kanawha River
Monongahela River

Ohio River
Potomac River

Other related articles

Civil War

Virginia (History)

Outline

I. **People**
  A. Population
  B. Schools
  C. Libraries
  D. Museums
II. **Visitor's guide**
  A. Places to visit   B. Annual events
III. **Land and climate**
  A. Land regions
  B. Rivers and lakes
  C. Plant and animal life
  D. Climate
IV. **Economy**
  A. Natural resources
  B. Service industries
  C. Manufacturing
  D. Mining
  E. Agriculture
  F. Electric power
  G. Transportation
  H. Communication
V. **Government**
  A. Constitution
  B. Executive
  C. Legislature
  D. Courts
  E. Local government
  F. Revenue
  G. Politics
VI. **History**

Questions

What were three reasons that led West Virginia to separate from Virginia?

Where do West Virginia's iron and steel industries get their iron ore supplies?

What two well-known varieties of apples were first grown in West Virginia?

How did the development of railroads affect West Virginia's economy?

Why did Governor John J. Cornwell call for federal troops in 1920?

What developments offer hope for improving the state's economy?

How does West Virginia rank among the states in coal production?

How has the nature of West Virginia's land influenced the state's economy?

How have changes in economic conditions in West Virginia af-

fected the state's population during the 1900's?

What is the most important field crop produced in West Virginia?

Additional resources

Level I

Carpenter, Allan. *West Virginia.* Rev. ed. Childrens Press, 1979.

Coffey, William E., and others. *West Virginia Government.* Education Foundation, 1984.

Fradin, Dennis B. *West Virginia in Words and Pictures.* Childrens Press, 1980.

Rice, Otis K. *West Virginia: The State and Its People.* McClain, 1979. First published in 1972.

Level II

Ash, Jerry W., and Douthat, S. L. *West Virginia USA.* Seawell Multimedia Corp., 1976.

Morgan, John G. *West Virginia Governors, 1863-1980.* 2nd ed. Charleston Newspapers, 1980.

Mountain Heritage. Ed. by Beryl B. Maurer. 5th ed. McClain, 1984.

Rice, Otis K. *The Allegheny Frontier: West Virginia Beginnings, 1730-1830.* Univ. Press of Kentucky, 1970. *West Virginia: A History.* 1985.

Stutler, Boyd B. *West Virginia in the Civil War.* 2nd ed. Education Foundation, 1966.

Tams, W. P. *The Smokeless Coal Fields of West Virginia: A Brief History.* West Virginia Univ. Press, 1983. First published in 1963.

West Virginia: A Guide to the Mountain State. Somerset, 1974. First published in 1941 as part of the American Guide Series.

Williams, John A. *West Virginia: A Bicentennial History.* Norton, 1976. *West Virginia and the Captains of Industry.* West Virginia Univ. Press, 1976.

West Virginia University is a state-controlled coeducational institution in Morgantown, W.Va. It has colleges of agriculture and forestry, arts and sciences, business and economics, creative arts, engineering, human resources and education, law, and mineral and energy resources. There are also schools of dentistry, journalism, medicine, nursing, pharmacy, physical education, and social work, and a center for extension and continuing education. Courses lead to bachelor's, master's, and doctor's degrees.

West Virginia University was founded in 1867. For information on the school's enrollment, see **Universities and colleges** (table).

Critically reviewed by West Virginia University

Westcott, Edward Noyes (1846-1898), wrote the novel *David Harum,* published shortly after his death. The story deals with a shrewd and humorous small-town banker in upstate New York. The novel and dramatic adaptation were extremely popular. Will Rogers starred in a film version of the novel.

Westcott was born in Syracuse, N.Y., where he became a successful banker. Westcott wrote *David Harum* while dying of tuberculosis.   Bert Hitchcock

Westergaard, Harald Malcolm (1888-1950), a distinguished American civil engineer and mathematician, became noted for his applications of mathematical analysis in the solution of engineering problems. He developed methods for the design of dams and of pavements for roads, bridges, and airports. Westergaard was born in Copenhagen, Denmark, and came to the United States in 1914.   Robert W. Abbett

Westerly wind. See Prevailing westerly.

Westermarck, Edward Alexander (1862-1939), was a Finnish anthropologist. Before reaching the age of 30, he wrote and published his major work, *The History*

of Human Marriage (1891). He was a professor at the University of London from 1907 to 1930. During this time, he wrote several works on marriage, the history and development of morals, and customs in Morocco. Westermarck was born in Helsinki.   David B. Stout

Western Australia is the largest state in the Commonwealth of Australia. This vast region covers the western third of the continent. Perth is its capital.

Location, size, and surface features. The state covers 975,100 square miles (2,525,500 square kilometers) in the western part of Australia (see **Australia** [political map]). Mountain ranges include the Hamersley Range in the northwest, the Darling Range along the western coast, the Stirling Range farther south, and extensive ranges in the Kimberly area of the northeast. The Ashburton, Fortescue, Gascoyne, and Murchison rivers flow across the western part of the state, but only during the wet season from November to March. The mountainous Kimberly area includes such rivers as the Fitzroy and the Ord. The Great Sandy Desert lies in the north, and the Great Victoria Desert covers part of the southeast. The Gibson Desert lies between them. Most of the land in these dry areas is not suited to agriculture, but the areas are rich in minerals.

Natural resources. Iron ore is the most important mineral in Western Australia. Other minerals include, in order of importance, bauxite, nickel, gold, mineral sands, and coal. There are oil and gas fields in the north and northwest parts of the state. The state's most fertile regions are in the southwest.

Climate. Temperatures in central Western Australia range from 80° to 90° F. (27° to 32° C) in January and average about 60° F. (16° C) in July. January temperatures north of the central area also average 80° to 90° F., and July temperatures range around 70° F. (21° C). Temperatures in the south vary from 70° to 80° F. (21° to 27° C) in January to 60° F. (16° C) in July. Less than 10 inches (25 centimeters) of rain falls annually in the central area. From 10 to 20 inches (25 to 51 centimeters) falls north and south of this region. Most coastal areas get 20 to 40 inches (51 to 100 centimeters).

The people and their work. Western Australia has a population of 1,406,929. About 37,000 of the people are *Aborigines* (descendants of the first inhabitants of Australia). About 70 per cent of the people live and work in the Perth area. Many of the state's people work in heavy industries, such as steel manufacturing and metal refin-ing. Others work in gold fields, iron ore mines, or farmlands. The chief crops include wheat, barley, oats, and potatoes. Other occupations include dairying, fishing, and stock raising. Perth is the only large city in Western Australia, and Kalgoorlie is the chief mining town.

Transportation. Rail and air lines link the state with the rest of the country. The state owns over 3,650 miles (5,874 kilometers) of railroads. One of the world's longest stretches of track without branches or rail connections extends about 1,000 miles (1,600 kilometers) from Kalgoorlie to Port Augusta, South Australia. There are about 72,000 miles (116,000 kilometers) of roads.

Education. All children must attend school from ages 6 to 15. The University of Western Australia and Murdoch University are in Perth.

Government. The British Crown appoints a governor for the state. A premier heads the government, assisted by a Cabinet of Ministers. The members of the Legislative Assembly, elected by popular vote, serve three years. Each member represents one electoral district. The members of the Legislative Council, elected by homeowners or occupants, serve six-year terms.

History. In 1616, the Dutch explorer Dirck Hartog became the first European to sight the coast of Western Australia. A military settlement was made at King George Sound in 1826. But full colonization did not begin until 1829. That year, Captain James Stirling founded the Swan River settlement and the towns of Perth and Fremantle. In 1901, Western Australia became one of the six original states of the Australian Commonwealth.   Mary Albertus Bain

See also **Perth.**

Western Bloc. See **Cold War** (introduction).

Western Church was a name given to the Roman Catholic Church after the Great Schism of the 800's to distinguish it from the Eastern Orthodox Church. See also **Roman Catholic Church.**

Western European Union (WEU) is a defense alliance that includes most of the Western European members of the North Atlantic Treaty Organization (NATO). NATO is the main military alliance of Western countries and includes the United States (see **North Atlantic Treaty Organization**). The WEU was formed in 1955 by Great Britain, France, Italy, Belgium, the Netherlands, Luxembourg, and West Germany. In 1988, Spain and Portugal joined. The organization works to strengthen the European part of NATO.   Stuart D. Goldman

© James L. Stanfield, National Geographic Society

Western Australia has vast areas of dry land through which transportation is difficult. Trucks pulling trailers carry cattle and other freight great distances through the areas. Such vehicles are called *road trains.*

New World Book Article
WESTERN FRONTIER LIFE
2006 Year Book, p. 472

Western frontier life

Western frontier life marks one of the most exciting chapters in American history. The settlement of the West represented the dreams of gold-hungry prospectors, and of homesteaders whose back-breaking labor transformed barren plains into fields of grain. It is the story of cowboys and the open range. It is the drama of Indians and outlaws, of the trains and stagecoaches they attacked, and of the citizens who brought order to the frontier. It is a living tradition that symbolizes to men and women everywhere the American achievement of taming a wild and beautiful land.

The far western frontier appeared about 1850, and vanished about 1890. Adventurous settlers had crossed the Appalachian Mountains during the 1700's and pushed through the Cumberland Gap in the 1770's. They built homes along the Mississippi River a few years later. Traders and scouts reached the Pacific Coast in the early 1800's. But the area west of the Mississippi—"the last frontier"—did not attract many settlers until after 1850. The final period of western settlement lasted from 1850 to 1890. For the complete story of western expansion in the United States, see **Westward movement.**

The western frontier produced many colorful figures. Some, such as Jesse James and Billy the Kid, symbolize outlaws who "died with their boots on." Others, such as Pat Garrett, gained fame as fearless defenders of law and order. "Buffalo Bill" Cody—scout, Indian fighter, and showman—probably did more than anyone else to create interest in the old West. Other figures, though less well-known, did more to develop the area itself. Charles Goodnight, a fiery rancher and cattle breeder, helped settle the Texas range. Granville Stuart of Montana, who had been an illiterate prospector, became United States minister to Paraguay and Uruguay. Adolph

Early settlers in the Far West crossed the plains to Oregon or California. Their high Conestoga wagons had already become museum pieces by the time of the last frontier.

Tom Hollyman, courtesy *Holiday*, © 1955 Curtis Publishing Co.

Sutro, a German immigrant, built a vast tunnel through Nevada's Comstock Lode, and later served as mayor of San Francisco.

The West promised to satisfy the needs and dreams of immigrants fresh from Europe as well as those of thousands of Americans unhappy with their life in the East. Some went west to find adventure, others to find happiness in the green valleys or among the tall mountains. Many sought wealth, but only a few were lucky. The West was a place where American Indians fought to keep their land, where accidents were common, and where hard work was the rule for all. Life on the western frontier seems colorful when we look back on it today. But the people who settled there found it difficult and dangerous—and even dull at times.

Building the frontier

For many years, the land on the western side of the Mississippi River formed the frontier of American settle-

Courtesy J. B. Lippincott Company from *Frederic Remington* by Harold McCracken

A stagecoach roars across the desert with Indian attackers in close pursuit. In *Downing the Nigh Leader,* the American artist Frederic Remington caught the drama and excitement that symbolize "the Wild West" to people throughout the world.

ment. Only a few thousand settlers had moved to Texas and California in the early 1800's. Land was still plentiful in the East, and treaties with the Indians forbade white settlements in many areas of the West. But, after 1850, many causes led to westward expansion. During the Civil War (1861-1865), the Union government encouraged mining, because the valuable ores helped pay for the war. The Homestead Act of 1862 provided cheap farm land for new settlers, as did gifts of huge tracts of land to the railroads. At the same time, thousands of Europeans wanted to come to America. Revolutionary movements had failed in many countries. Poor harvests caused famines in Ireland. The Scandinavian nations had become overpopulated. Government agents increased their persecution of the Jews in Russia, Poland, and other areas of central Europe.

The land between the Missouri River and the Pacific

Coast forms two great belts, running roughly north and south. The grasslands of the Great Plains stretch west from the Missouri River to the Rocky Mountains. Beyond the plains, from the Rockies to the Pacific Coast, lies a belt of land with many mountain ranges and several valleys. Because the Far West had many land regions and climates, it developed on several frontiers.

The rush to the west affected both belts of land, but it touched the Far West first. Settlers began moving to the Oregon region in large numbers in the early 1840's. In 1848, the Oregon Territory was established. California boomed with the discovery of gold at Sutter's mill in 1848, and it became a state in 1850. Washington also was settled before the Civil War. Congress created the Washington Territory in 1853.

The search for gold and silver attracted thousands of miners to the western mountains following the rush to California in 1849. At first, they mined in the Sierra Nevada mountains east of Sacramento. However, gold in this area became difficult to mine by the middle 1850's. So the prospectors moved eastward looking for *strikes,* or discoveries.

Several areas became important mining centers during the period from 1856 to 1875. The first was southern Arizona, where silver was found south of Tucson. Other silver discoveries were made there in the following years, including the giant strike in 1877 at Tombstone.

The next strike came in the Rocky Mountains west of Denver. It drew a great rush of fortune seekers, who vowed to reach "Pikes Peak or Bust." Central City and Leadville grew up almost overnight in Colorado. A third area centered on Virginia City in western Nevada, and encouraged further discoveries in the desert valleys and mountains. Both these areas began as gold fields. But black sand in Colorado and blue clay in Nevada clogged the machines the early miners used. The mines did not become profitable until mining companies found that the sands and clays had rich silver deposits.

Another mining region, in Idaho, Montana, and Washington, led to the settlement of such towns as Lewiston, Ida.; Helena, Mont.; and Walla Walla, Wash. The last great gold rush in the United States took place in the Black Hills of South Dakota in 1874 and 1875. Deadwood, founded in 1876, gained fame as one of the last frontier mining camps.

East meets West. The swarm of miners into the West showed the need for better transportation. Thousands of new settlers ran short of supplies. Prospectors could mine gold with pick, shovel, and pan, but silver-mining companies needed heavy machinery to dig the ore, and some means of shipping it to smelters. Such needs encouraged companies to build transcontinental railroad networks. Two companies began the first of these railroad systems in the early 1860's. Starting from the east was the Union Pacific, with Irish laborers who established such towns as Cheyenne and Laramie, Wyo.

The Central Pacific line, coming from the west, had thousands of Chinese in its road gangs. The two sets of tracks met at Promontory, near Ogden, Utah, in 1869. Other lines soon followed, including the Southern Pacific and the Atchison, Topeka, and Santa Fe. See **Railroad** (History; picture: The meeting of two railroads).

With the railroads to supply them, settlers had little fear of waterless deserts or hostile Indians. The growth of railroads almost led to the extermination of the bison, or American buffalo. Millions of these animals had roamed throughout the West, but hunters soon killed most of them. The hunters killed for buffalo hides, but seldom for meat.

The cattle boom. With the railroads came the period of "the cattle kingdom" on the Great Plains. Ranching started in southern Texas, where farmers raised long-horn cattle from Mexico. The ranchers branded the cattle to show ownership, and guarded them on horseback as they roamed the range. By the end of the Civil War, the number of cattle had increased, and people in the North had money to buy beef.

The era of the long drive, or trail drive, began when the ranchers saw that they could sell cattle in the East if they could get the animals to the railroads. A favorite route led along the Chisholm Trail, which ran from southern Texas to Abilene, Kan. Farther west, the Western Trail led to Dodge City, Kan. Millions of cattle plodded along these trails, sometimes as many as 4,000 in a single herd.

The open range did not last long. By 1885, overstocking had ruined many ranchers. They had more cattle than the land could support. Fierce blizzards in the winter of 1886-1887 spelled the end for many more. In a series of *range wars,* ranchers tried to keep out *nesters,* or permanent settlers. But the open range had disappeared, and the cattle boom came to an end.

Homesteading on the Great Plains had attracted few settlers before the Civil War. This was the land that novelist Hamlin Garland brought to life in his books and

Railroads helped tame the West. The train below ran out of Virginia City, Nev., on the Virginia & Truckee line.

The Western Pacific Railroad Company

In the gold fields, some miners spent Sunday reading the Bible or washing their clothes. Others wrestled or took part in horse racing.

Sunday Morning in the Mines by Charles Nahl. Permanent Collection E. B. Crocker Art Gallery, Sacramento, California

short stories. It is often called "the land of the straddle-bug." In the 1840's and 1850's, *locators,* or land sales agents, picked the best farms on the grassy plains. They marked their claims with *straddlebugs,* three boards fastened together like tepeepoles.

However, when *homesteaders,* or farmers, arrived later with their families, they often found themselves in trouble. They had little protection against the Plains Indians. When they rode horses, they could not use the long rifles they had carried in the woods back East. Also, water and trees were scarce in this region. When spring and late summer rains were scanty, crops withered and died. Farmers had difficulty finding wood for shelter, fuel, and fences.

New developments in the 1870's made it possible for eager settlers to farm the grasslands. Barbed wire, patented in 1873, provided the first cheap substitute for wood fences. Windmills solved the problem of bringing up water that lay far underground. Agricultural experts worked out methods of farming that would work in the dry climate (see **Dry farming**). With improved machinery, farmers could cultivate large areas. The railroads offered cheap land to homesteaders. Thousands of settlers moved into Kansas, Nebraska, and the Dakotas. The government opened a large section of Indian Territory in 1889, and the Oklahoma Territory was born (See **Indian Territory**). So much of the Far West had filled up by 1890 that the Bureau of the Census declared in a report that a definite frontier no longer existed.

Life on the frontier

The people of the western frontier formed a varied mixture. Americans streamed west from the East Coast, the Middle West, and the South. Some who had committed crimes went west because they wanted to get as far away from the law as possible. Others found life boring in the East, and wanted to try something new and different. Professional people and merchants cared for the needs of growing communities. Land speculators

hoped to make quick fortunes. But most settlers were farmers, laborers, unskilled mechanics, miners, and former soldiers. Many of these pioneers saw the West as a place of opportunity for themselves and their children. They were willing to risk their lives to be part of the development of this region.

Large numbers of blacks moved to the frontier to escape the prejudice they had experienced in the East and South. Thousands of black homesteaders settled in California, Kansas, Nebraska, and Texas during the second half of the 1800's. Some of the best-known cowboys of that period were blacks. A ranch hand named Nat Love gained fame for horsemanship and other skills on cattle drives. Bose Ikard, a former slave, was foreman of one of the largest ranches in Texas. Black soldiers in the U.S. Army fought Indians on the frontier.

Many other groups also lived in the Far West. Mexicans had settled in the Southwest and California since the 1700's. Indians furnished cheap labor. Basques from France and Spain herded sheep (see **Basques**). Scandinavians and other Europeans bought farms on the Great Plains. Miners came from England and Wales to join the search for precious metals. Chinese came to build the railroads, then drifted to mining camps where they ran laundries, restaurants, and small shops.

Most frontier people fell into two classes, *solid folk* and *boomers.* The solid folk settled down if they liked the life, or went home if they did not. Boomers were always heading for a new boom town. They seldom stayed long enough to make much money, and squandered their earnings in high living. Even among the steady people, few came to stay, as settlers had stayed on the land east of the Missouri River. Most of them wanted to get rich and go home.

The frontier was a man's world, and favored the jack-of-all-trades. Wyatt Earp was a law officer, buffalo hunter, stagecoach driver, and gambler. Hank Monk, a famous stagecoach driver, also mined, and rode the pony express. George Jackson, credited with discovering gold in the Rockies, had been a sheepherder, prospector, farm hand, miner, and roustabout, and later became a businessman.

Food on the frontier was usually simple. Flour served as the basic food, because it was nourishing and did not spoil. The people used it in sourdough biscuits and bread, and in *flapjacks,* or pancakes. Other important foods included dried beans; game, such as bison, deer, elk, antelope, and wild fowl; and preserved meats such as bacon, salt pork, and *jerky,* or dried meat. Ranchers could always eat beef, and sheep raisers had mutton. Frontier people rarely ate fresh fruit and vegetables or dairy products. Even cowboys did not milk cows.

People on the frontier had no need for fancy cooking—the men were too busy, and women were scarce. Meat with biscuits or flapjacks provided a feast. Old Len Martin of Carson City, Nev., declared while stewing a chicken that there was no sense "picking a chicken too darned close—anybody that don't like the feathers can skim 'em off."

Clothing had to be practical, and most people wore the same plain garments day after day. Men wore cowhide boots; woolen trousers or overalls; a wool shirt; a jacket or vest; and a felt hat. Some had socks. A man often wore a red bandanna handkerchief around his neck to protect himself from the dust and cold. Women wore sunbonnets and simple calico and gingham dresses. Cowboys wore leather *chaps* to protect their legs from brush. Cowboy hats, called *sombreros,* had a wide brim to shield the eyes, and a deep crown so that the hat would not blow off. Some men bought deerskin clothes from the Indians. Wealthy men and women bought clothes from New York City, London, or Paris.

Many frontiersmen, particularly outlaws and law-enforcement officers, carried weapons. Especially popular were Winchester rifles; Colt revolvers, including the famous six-shooter; and Bowie knives (see **Handgun** [picture]; **Bowie knife**).

Amusements on the frontier varied with the area and the type of settler. Homesteading families on the plains met for square dances, holiday celebrations, and house-raising or corn-husking bees. Miners and cowboys enjoyed spending their leisure time drinking and gambling in the saloons that sprang up in every town. Dance halls called *hurdy-gurdies* attracted many people, although men often had to dance with each other, because women were scarce. Informal rodeos featured expert horsemanship and other cowboy skills (see **Rodeo**). Throughout the West, people enjoyed horse races, shooting contests, and wrestling and boxing matches. In larger towns, settlers welcomed traveling dramatic groups and vaudeville shows. They applauded such famous performers as Edwin Booth, Laura Keene, and Helena Modjeska.

Religion came to the western frontier even before most white settlers arrived. In the early 1800's, Catholic and Protestant missionaries such as Father Pierre De Smet and Marcus Whitman had pushed into the Far West to convert the Indians (see **De Smet, Pierre Jean; Whitman, Marcus**). But new settlements often grew up far from the missions, and people had to rely on traveling preachers called *circuit riders* to perform religious services. These men rode about constantly. When they arrived in a town, they preached sermons and con-

Library of Congress

Virginia City bustled with activity in the 1860's. The town perched 6,500 feet (1,980 meters) high in the Sierra Nevada, close to Mt. Davidson, site of the fabulous Comstock Lode.

ducted marriages, baptisms, and other services for people who had sometimes waited many weeks. Among farm families on the plains, circuit riders set up Sunday schools and held summer camp meetings.

Frontier towns sprang up almost overnight. An early arrival in Bovard, Nev., told how he passed through the town in the morning and noticed four or five tents. When he returned in the afternoon, Main Street was 1 mile (1.6 kilometers) long and business was booming in a string of tent saloons. Some towns, such as Butte, Mont., started as shipping points for ore. Others, including Wichita, Kan., boomed as cattle transport centers. Many, such as Tombstone, Ariz., grew up around mines. Transportation centers usually grew and prospered. But most mining camps became ghost towns of rubble and sagebrush after the ores had been worked out or metal prices fell.

Most frontier towns provided few comforts. Miners often slept outdoors in summer, and built a dugout or crude shack in the winter. They might have a tent or make a shelter out of rocks, empty bottles, or packing cases. Two early settlers in Treasure City, Nev., collected all the rocks they could find for shelter against the winter. The next spring, they discovered that the walls were high-grade silver ore worth $75,000!

House furnishings were simple and often homemade. Miners needed blasting powder more than fine dishes. They papered their shacks with newspapers to make them warmer. Today, visitors can sometimes still read about events in a ghost town on the walls of its crumbling buildings. A few wealthy people shipped in furniture, tableware, and wallpaper at great expense. If a town became fairly permanent, the people built board sidewalks on each side of the dirt streets, lined with poles and stakes for hitching posts. Square false fronts made small buildings look impressive.

Life in frontier towns was difficult. People often lacked conveniences, and even necessities. Usually the only water available in mining camps was warm and dirty. Sometimes people hauled water a great distance and sold it for several dollars a barrel. In many areas on the plains, no trees grew.

Because of such shortages, western towns often grew

A teamster who "struck it rich" built this mansion near Virginia City. The teamster, whose name was Sandy Bowers, later went "ter Yoorup" to spend his fortune.

in groups, such as the one built around Virginia City, Nev. The rich silver and gold mines of the Comstock Lode centered around Virginia City, but the town had no wood or water. Other towns grew up nearby to supply these needs. Empire became a smelter town on the Carson River; Washoe, near the Sierra Nevadas, supplied fuel; and Reno grew up where the local railroad joined the main line of the Central Pacific.

During the 20-year period between 1860 and 1880, the Comstock Lode yielded more than $300 million worth of ore. Because of this great wealth, all the comforts of the day soon appeared in Virginia City. At first, supplies came in by muleback, a few at a time. When a road was built, slow freight wagons brought supplies. Finally, a railroad served the town with several trains a day. By 1876, Virginia City had 23,000 people, 20 laundries, 54 dry-good stores, 6 churches, and 150 saloons. The vice president of the express company built a four-story French-style mansion. An opera house and several theaters presented Italian light operas, vaudeville, lectures, and even Shakespeare's plays. The miners' union had a library. A local newspaper, the *Territorial Enterprise,* employed a young reporter who wrote under the name of Mark Twain. At any time, a person might find silver ore in the basement and be worth $1 million the next day. People had to be careful that they and their children did not fall into a neighbor's new mine.

Life in the country resembled that in the towns, except that settlers found it harder to obtain supplies. Prospectors roamed about with supplies loaded on a burro or two, but they had to return to a mining camp when they ran short. Country life on the frontier usually meant living on a ranch or a farm.

Ranches usually lay in mountain valleys watered by melting snow, or in broad uplands that had some moisture. Most ranches consisted only of a few simple buildings and some *corrals* (cattle pens) surrounded by high, strong fences made of stakes and poles. The grassland of the open range provided pastures. The *Texas house,* two log cabins joined by a roofed space, developed into the ranch-style house of today. The rancher used one cabin for cooking and eating, and the other for sleeping. As the ranch grew, the rancher might build a house for

the family, a cookshack, and a bunkhouse for the *hands* (cowboys).

Cattle ranchers let their herds graze on the open range, so they needed few buildings and no fences. But they did need cowboys to turn the cattle out to graze in spring, and move them to rich mountain pastures. Cowboys constantly guarded the herds against mountain lions and bands of rustlers. In the spring and fall, all the ranchers in an area held a *roundup* to gather in the cattle. Cowboys had already marked the grown cattle by branding them or cropping their ears. People from each ranch sorted out these cattle by their markings. New calves followed their mothers. Then cowboys cropped the calves' ears or branded them with the owner's mark.

Cowboys also drove herds to *cattle towns,* or *cow towns,* to be shipped east on the railroads. On the long drive, cattle moved in long lines, with riders ahead, behind, and on both sides. A *chuck wagon* carried food for the cowboys, and a *wrangler* took care of extra horses. When all went well, the cattle moved slowly but steadily. But they sometimes *stampeded* when they were afraid to swim a river, or were frightened by Indians or rustlers. After a few months, the drive plodded into a cattle town such as Abilene or Dodge City, where cowboys loaded the cattle into freight cars. For a description of cowboys and their work, see **Cowboy; Ranching.**

Farms, unlike ranches, depended on the soil, not the grass. Farmers plowed the grass under and raised grain, mainly wheat. Grasshoppers, hot winds, and prairie fires often made life hard for settlers on the plains. So did the ranchers, who resented the barbed-wire fences that destroyed the open range. Bloody fights developed in the range wars, or barbed-wire wars, that followed. Farmers fenced in watering places or blocked trails, then ranchers cut the wires. Barbed wire finally won, and farms spread farther and farther out over the rich grasslands of the Great Plains.

Life on the plains resembled that of pioneers east of the Missouri River. But there was a basic difference. While the farmer in Ohio might have too many trees, the

Texas Longhorns, an oil painting on canvas by Tom Lea; Dallas Museum of Art, gift of *LIFE* Magazine

Texas longhorn cattle, hardy and fierce, were descended from wild cattle brought to America by the Spanish. Ranch owners branded them or notched their ears to identify them.

farmer on the plains usually had no wood at all. The western farmer's land has often been called *the sod-house frontier,* because so many settlers built houses of dirt and sod. Farmers plowed furrows of sod and cut them crosswise into blocks about 1 foot (30 centimeters) square. They piled rows of sod blocks on top of each other to make walls, and covered them with a thatch roof. Sometimes they brought wood with them and built a frame to support the roof, or found a little wood nearby. A sod house remained warm in winter and cool in summer, but it had many disadvantages. Dirt sifted down on the food, crumbled from the walls, and rose from the clay floor. Rats and mice lived in the thatch, and snakes and gophers often dug tunnels through the walls or floor. For fuel, the farmer used twigs, grass, corncobs, peat, and buffalo *chips,* or manure. Later, settlers often improved their *soddies* by whitewashing the walls and hauling in lumber for doors and ceilings.

Transportation and communication

Transportation varied with the area and the means at hand. Until the railroads appeared, travel was always slow and uncomfortable, and often dangerous. Roads were few and bad, and schedules were irregular.

Most people traveled by stagecoach. A group of passengers could defend themselves more easily against Indians or bandits than a person alone. One famous line, the Butterfield Overland Mail, ran four coaches weekly between St. Louis and San Francisco. The coaches bumped along day and night, covering about 100 miles (160 kilometers) in 24 hours. The passengers, grimy with dust in summer and shivering with cold in winter, tried to sleep on the hard seats. Crude wood or adobe "stations" every 10 miles (16 kilometers) or so provided food for both passengers and horses. Travelers faced the constant danger of Indian attack and bad weather. Traveling alone was even more dangerous, but people in a hurry rode horseback. Settlers moving with their families traveled in wagons.

Wagon trains served as the best means of hauling freight before railroads were built. They usually included about 25 heavy, high-wheeled wagons, each pulled by a team of 6 to 20 oxen or mules. People called *bullwhackers* or *mule skinners* drove the wagons and guarded the freight. The wagons lumbered along at 1 or 2 miles (1.6 or 3.2 kilometers) per hour, or about 100 miles (160 kilometers) in a seven-day week, because "there was no Sunday west of Omaha." The wagons hauled ore from mines and brought in mining machinery and blasting powder. They carried the food and water that made life possible in desert camps. If blizzards stopped them, the price of flour might soar to $100 a sack. Famous freight lines included Ben Holladay's Central Overland California and Pikes Peak Express Company, and the Wells, Fargo line (see **Wells, Fargo & Company**). Frontier people also used burros to carry goods. Some even used camels, imported from Asia because they could live on the desert (see **Camel**).

Communication. News traveled slowly, most of it by stagecoach. A letter took months to go from California to the Middle West, and snows in the mountains cut off almost all communication in winter.

The pony express carried the mail between St. Joseph, Mo., and Sacramento, Calif., a distance of almost 2,000 miles (3,200 kilometers). The service had about 80 riders. Pony-express riders generally made two runs a week over their part of the route in each direction. At first, it cost $5 to send $\frac{1}{2}$ ounce (14 grams) of mail by pony express, so that this volume of *The World Book Encyclopedia,* for example, would have cost more than $400 to send. Pony-express riders changed horses every 10 to 15 miles (16 to 24 kilometers), and new riders took over every 75 miles (121 kilometers). The pony express covered more than 200 miles (320 kilometers) a day, so that mail usually traveled from St. Joseph to Sacramento in about 10 days. The trip often took up to 15 days during winter. This remarkable system began in April 1860, but lasted only about 19 months. It was discontinued after the telegraph reached California in October 1861. See **Pony express.**

Law and order

Farm families on the frontier lived quietly, but crime troubled the mining camps and cattle towns. These isolated settlements sometimes had great wealth in precious metals and attracted people who came to cheat and steal. Others meant well but wanted to have a good time. A mixture of gambling, drinking, and firearms sometimes led to violence. But the West was far from the "wild" place pictured in legend and story.

Crime often resulted from the temptations of gold and silver. Miners who had *struck it rich* usually celebrated by getting drunk. Then they might be stabbed and robbed, or cheated in a poker game by a *cardsharp* who used a marked deck of cards. Gold and silver also tempted bandits, who followed shipments on their way to California or to the East. They picked a deserted spot in which to attack a wagon or stagecoach. Criminals also included *claim jumpers,* who illegally took over mine claims that belonged to someone else. *Confidence men* (swindlers) often sold worthless stocks. Many dealt in "salted" mines, selling worthless holes after putting in small amounts of good ore.

Horses, cattle, and sheep also provided a temptation for lawbreakers. The animals roamed great areas, and could be moved under their own power. Rustlers stole cattle, drove them to a *shebang* (hideout), and altered their brands. One valley in the Pahranagat Range of southeastern Nevada became a refuge for rustlers who roamed through Utah, Arizona, Nevada, and Idaho. A rider passing through the valley could count as many as 350 different brands on cattle stolen from as many ranches. One story tells of a sheriff who returned from such a robbers' roost looking triumphant. "Get your man?" somebody asked. "No," the sheriff replied, "but I rode plumb through the place without getting shot."

Disturbances also arose from the constant feuding between cattle ranchers and the sheep owners and farmers. The Lincoln County War inflamed New Mexico in 1878 as cattlemen and other groups fought for control of the county. Army troops and Governor Lew Wallace finally quieted the rival cattle ranchers. See **New Mexico** (Territorial days). In 1892, cattle ranchers in Johnson County, Wyoming, imported a trainload of gunmen to terrorize farmers. The army finally ended this Johnson County Cattle War after several killings on both sides. See **Wyoming** (The Johnson County War).

The *desperadoes* (outlaws) usually worked together

Jesse James, according to an old ballad, "killed many a man, and robbed the Glendale train." He and his gang terrorized Missouri for several years. This scene, by Thomas Hart Benton, is a section of a mural in the state Capitol at Jefferson City.

Greg Leech, Missouri Department of Natural Resources

in gangs, such as those led by Henry Plummer, the Younger brothers, "the Dalton boys," and Frank and Jesse James. They robbed banks, trains, and stagecoaches throughout large areas. Sam Bass once stole $60,000 in gold from a single Union Pacific train traveling through Nebraska. Billy the Kid was said to have killed 21 men. Some of the most famous desperadoes were honest and kindly until drink or anger aroused them. Then they became killers. But even among lawbreakers, the code of the West demanded that people give each other a chance to defend themselves. A gunman who shot from behind or attacked an unarmed person was considered a coward. Outlaws who obeyed this code had many friends and admirers in spite of their crimes. They came to symbolize the independence and vitality of the West, and many legends grew up around them. Sooner or later most were shot or hanged.

Law enforcement. When Americans settled unorganized territory in the Far West, they brought with them federal, state, and local laws from their former homes. But these laws did not always help new communities. Often they did not take into account new and different situations, such as cattle rustling. Even when laws suited a community, enforcement proved difficult because of the great distances between settlements. For example, the sheriff at Pioche, Nev., was responsible for law and order as far away as the mining camp of El Dorado, 300 miles (480 kilometers) distant. If the sheriff did capture a murderer, there was often no jail to keep the prisoner in. And the outlaw's friends might kill innocent citizens to free the prisoner. Everyone had to be ready to "shoot it out." Judge Roy Bean, "the law west of the Pecos," held court in his saloon in Langtry, Tex., with the aid of a single law book and a six-shooter.

But law-abiding people lived in all parts of the frontier, and sooner or later they established order. The West often found law officers as fearless as the outlaws themselves. Many served as federal marshals. Tom Smith, the marshal of Abilene, Kan., did not drink or swear, but he shocked a tough cattle town into behaving by knocking out armed men with his bare fists. The Texas Rangers also helped maintain law and order (see **Texas Rangers**).

The citizens themselves provided another answer to the problem of law enforcement. They banded together in groups of *vigilantes* to capture and punish criminals. Sometimes these groups killed innocent people in their haste, but most victims deserved the punishment they received. See **Vigilante**.

Indian fighting disturbed the frontier for many years. The federal government had reserved large areas of western land for Indian use, but land-hungry white settlers constantly moved into these areas. Agents of the Indian Bureau tried to protect the Indians and to enforce laws for both Indians and whites. But most frontier troops, stationed in about 100 posts throughout the West, agreed with the claim many Westerners made that "the only good Indians are dead Indians." In 1864, an army force killed nearly 300 peaceful Indians near Sand Creek, Colo. Such events, and the revenge they inspired, aroused the whole frontier. For the story of Indian wars in the West, see **Indian wars.**

An American tradition

The frontier is gone now. Most of its mining camps have become empty ghost towns. Other settlements of the wild West have grown into peaceful communities. Denver, Cheyenne, Boise, and Salt Lake City now stand where settlers once pitched their tents. But western frontier life left behind a great American tradition because of its dramatic appeal. Even before "Buffalo Bill" Cody organized his "Wild West Show" in 1883, the western frontier had captured the interest of people in all parts of the world. Books, stories, paintings, songs, plays, and motion pictures about the old West still pour forth in a seemingly endless stream. Almost 450 works have appeared about Billy the Kid alone—including poems, novels, plays, ballets, and motion pictures. The West has also produced its own folklore heroes. Febold Feboldson performed amazing feats on the sod-house frontier of the Great Plains. Pecos Bill taught the cowboys all they knew, and even showed broncos how to buck. See **Febold Feboldson; Pecos Bill.**

Many works of poor quality have strayed far from the truth, presenting only the most sensational parts of frontier life. But other works have artistic merit, and give a true picture of those who settled the West.

Literature. Most of the early writing about the West came from men who had taken part in its development. Mark Twain's *Roughing It* became a frontier classic. Bret Harte's short stories and Joaquin Miller's poems found admirers in Europe as well as the United States. Owen Wister's novel about the West, *The Virginian,* stimulated much interest in the subject. Andy Adams, a cowboy, gave a truer picture of range life in *The Log of a Cowboy.* One of Emerson Hough's many novels, *The Covered Wagon,* became a popular motion picture. Hamlin Garland, with *A Son of the Middle Border,* and O. E. Rölvaag, with *Giants in the Earth,* immortalized the sod-house frontier. Zane Grey wrote over 50 colorful western novels. Later books include Walter Van Tilburg Clark's *The Oxbow Incident,* Conrad Richter's *The Sea of Grass,* and A. B. Guthrie's *The Big Sky.*

Music of the West, like literature, has been mainly popular, rather than serious. Famous songs include "The Chisholm Trail," "The Lone Prairie," and "Streets of Laredo." Many of these ballads grew out of English or Spanish folk songs that the cowboys sang to quiet the cattle, or to help fill the long, lonely, empty hours.

Serious music with western themes includes Giacomo Puccini's opera *The Girl of the Golden West,* Aaron Copland's ballets *Billy the Kid* and *Rodeo,* Ferde Grofé's *Grand Canyon Suite,* and Hershey Kay's ballet *Western Symphony.* One of the most popular of all American musical plays, *Oklahoma!,* by Richard Rodgers and Oscar Hammerstein II, tells how the cowboys clashed with the "hoe hands," or farmers.

Art. The color of the western landscape and the vigor of running horses, stampeding cattle, and rugged men have appealed to many artists. Frederic Remington, probably the most famous, painted and drew over 2,700 pictures of the West. Remington learned life on the frontier at first hand, and preserved it in realistic paintings, sketches, and statues. Others who have painted the West include Charles Marion Russell and N. C. Wyeth. Many artists, including Thomas Hart Benton and Georgia O'Keeffe, have used western backgrounds. Will James, Tom Lea, Ross Santee, and others have illustrated their own books on the West.

Entertainment. Motion pictures and television have made western frontier life familiar to people everywhere. With cowboys and soldiers fighting outlaws and Indians, the "western" offers endless opportunities for battles and thrilling chases through mountains and deserts. *The Squaw Man* of 1914, one of the first full-length films made in Hollywood, began a trend that continues today. William S. Hart, a typical two-gun cowboy, became a national hero. Other motion-picture cowboy idols have included Buck Jones, Tom Mix, Roy Rogers, John Wayne, and William Boyd, who made the first "Hopalong Cassidy" film in 1934. Many "westerns" provide poor entertainment, but some have been fine motion pictures. Among these, such films as *Stagecoach* and *High Noon* achieved a high level. On the stage, Will Rogers gained fame as "the cowboy philosopher." Radio and television present hundreds of western dramas every year. Rodeos, especially in the Western States, feature daring cowboys who ride bucking broncos and wild cattle. Thousands of people spend vacations on dude ranches, dressing like cowboys in settings that try to recapture a bygone era.   Odie B. Faulk

Related articles in *World Book.* See the articles on the various Western States, such as **Montana.** See also:

Famous westerners

Bass, Sam	Earp, Wyatt B. S.	Love, Nat
Bean, Judge Roy	Fargo, William G.	Masterson, Bat
Billy the Kid	Garrett, Patrick F.	Oakley, Annie
Buffalo Bill	Hickok, Wild Bill	Starr, Belle
Calamity Jane	James, Jesse	

Other related articles

Boom town	L'Amour, Louis	Turner,
Circuit rider	Pioneer life in Amer-	Frederick J.
Comstock Lode	ica	Vigilante
Cowboy	Pony express	Wells, Fargo &
Ghost town	Ranching	Company
Guthrie, A. B., Jr.	Rodeo	Westward move-
Homestead Act	Texas Rangers	ment
Indian wars		

Outline

I. Building the frontier
  A. The search for gold and silver
  B. East meets West
  C. The cattle boom
  D. Homesteading on the Great Plains

II. Life on the frontier
  A. The people   E. Religion
  B. Food   F. Frontier towns
  C. Clothing   G. Life in the country
  D. Amusements

III. Transportation and communication
  A. Transportation   B. Communication

IV. Law and order
  A. Crime   C. Indian fighting
  B. Law enforcement

V. An American tradition
  A. Literature   C. Art
  B. Music   D. Entertainment

Questions

Why was there so much crime on the western frontier? How did settlers enforce the law?

Why were traveling preachers called *circuit riders*?

What ended the period of the open range?

How did the first transcontinental railroad system affect the development of the western frontier?

Why was the western farmer's land often called "the sod-house frontier"?

What caused flour to become worth $100 a sack?

Why did some people import camels?

Why did some western towns grow up in groups?

Why was the pony express discontinued?

Additional resources

Level I

Freedman, Russell. *Children of the Wild West.* Clarion, 1983.
Laycock, George and Ellen. *How the Settlers Lived.* McKay, 1980.
The Old West. Time-Life Books, 1973-1979. Titles in this 26-volume series include *The Townsmen* (1975), *The Gamblers* (1978), and *The Women* (1978).
Tunis, Edwin. *Frontier Living.* Harper, 1976. First published in 1961.

Level II

At Home on the Range: Essays on the History of Western Social and Domestic Life. Ed. by John R. Wunder. Greenwood, 1985.
Mondy, Robert W. *Pioneers and Preachers: Stories of the Old Frontier.* Nelson-Hall, 1980.
The Western Frontier Library. Univ. of Oklahoma Press. Titles in this series of over 50 volumes include *When Buffalo Ran,* by G. B. Grinnell (1966) and *My Life on the Plains,* by G. A. Custer (1976).
The Women's West. Ed. by Susan Armitage and Elizabeth Jameson. Univ. of Oklahoma Press, 1987.

Western Hemisphere. See Hemisphere.

Western Isles. See Hebrides.

Western Reserve. In 1662, King Charles II of England granted the colony of Connecticut a charter. This charter gave Connecticut title to lands which stretched westward from the Atlantic Ocean to the Pacific. In 1786, Connecticut gave to the new United States government the great stretch of western land which it held under its original charter. But Connecticut kept a strip of land bordering Lake Erie in Ohio. This strip was called the *Western Reserve.* It extended westward about 120 miles (193 kilometers) from the northwestern boundary of Pennsylvania, and covered 3,667,000 acres (1,483,982 hectares).

In 1795, the Connecticut Land Company bought most of the Western Reserve for $1,200,000. In 1800, Connecticut and the U.S. government agreed to attach the land to the Ohio territory.   Richard Hofstadter

See also **Cleveland.**

Western Sahara, formerly *Spanish Sahara,* is an area on the northwest coast of Africa. It lies between Morocco, Algeria, Mauritania, and the Atlantic Ocean. For the location of Western Sahara, see **Africa** (political map). The area belonged to Spain in the early 1500's and again from 1860 to 1976. Today, it is claimed by Morocco. But Algeria and some of the people who live in Western Sahara oppose the claim.

About 180,000 people live in the area. Most are Arabs or Berbers. The majority are nomads who move about constantly, seeking water and grass for their herds of camels, goats, and sheep. Some people fish for a living along the coast of the Atlantic Ocean.

Western Sahara covers 102,700 square miles (266,000 square kilometers). Most of the land is barren, rocky desert which receives little rainfall. Vegetation is scanty except for patches of coarse grass and low bushes near the coast. But the land yields large quantities of valuable chemicals called *phosphates,* which are used as fertilizers and in the manufacture of some detergents.

Spain claimed the area in 1509. Morocco ruled it from 1524 until Spain regained control in 1860. Spain made the area one of its provinces—called the Province of Spanish Sahara—in 1958.

In 1976, Spain gave up its control of Spanish Sahara and ceded it to Morocco and Mauritania. The area came to be called Western Sahara. Morocco claimed the northern part of the former Spanish province, and Mau-

ritania claimed the southern part. Algeria and an organization of people of Western Sahara called the Polisario Front opposed these claims and demanded independence for the area. Fighting broke out between Polisario Front troops and troops from Morocco and Mauritania. Algeria and, later, Libya gave military aid to the Polisario Front. In 1979, Mauritania gave up its claim to Western Sahara and withdrew from the fighting. Morocco then claimed the part of Western Sahara that Mauritania had claimed. Fighting continued between the Polisario Front and Morocco. In 1984, Libya and Morocco signed a treaty of unity, and Libya stopped supplying military aid to the Polisario Front. In 1986, however, the treaty was dissolved. Fighting continued into the late 1980's.

James W. Fernandez

See also **Organization of African Unity.**

Western Samoa is an independent island country in the Pacific Ocean. It lies about 1,700 miles (2,740 kilometers) northeast of New Zealand. American Samoa, a United States territory, lies east of Western Samoa (see **American Samoa**). Western Samoa, one of the smallest countries in the world, consists of two main islands, Upolu and Savai'i, and several smaller islands.

Samoans are tall, brown-skinned Polynesians. Most live by raising their own food on small plots of land and have little income. By some standards, Western Samoa is a poor, or developing, country. But the people are healthy and have all the food and clothing they need.

Polynesians have lived in Western Samoa for at least 2,000 years. The first Europeans landed there in the 1700's, and Germany took control in 1900. During World War I, New Zealand occupied the islands. It ruled them until Western Samoa gained independence in 1962. The noted writer Robert Louis Stevenson lived in Western Samoa several years. He died there and was buried near

Western Samoa

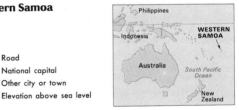

‐‐‐‐	Road
✪	National capital
•	Other city or town
+	Elevation above sea level

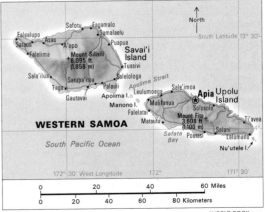

WORLD BOOK map

Nicholas Devore, Bruce Coleman Ltd.

Most Western Samoan houses have thatched roofs and open sides because of the country's warm, pleasant climate.

Hutchison Library

Polynesians make up about 90 per cent of the population of Western Samoa. Samoan life centers around family activities.

Apia in 1894. Stevenson's house, called Vailima, is now the residence of the head of state.

Western Samoa's official name in Samoan is *Samoa i Sisifo.* Apia, a city with about 33,000 people, is the capital and only city (see **Apia**).

Government. Western Samoa's head of state, Malietoa Tanumafili II, holds office for life. When he dies, the Legislative Assembly will elect a head of state for a five-year term.

The 47 members of the Legislative Assembly serve three-year terms. Forty-five members are elected by *matai* (heads of Samoan family groups) and two are elected by people—chiefly Europeans—who do not belong to matai. The assembly members elect the prime minister. The prime minister selects a cabinet from among these assembly members.

The prime minister and cabinet actually run the government. Laws passed by the assembly do not go into

Facts in brief

Capital: Apia.
Official languages: Samoan and English.
Area: 1,093 sq. mi. (2,831 km²). *Greatest distances*—east-west, on each of the two main islands, 47 mi. (76 km); north-south, 15 mi. (24 km) on Upolu, 27 mi. (43 km) on Savai'i. *Coastline* (total for both islands)—about 230 mi. (370 km).
Elevation: *Highest*—Mount Silisili (on Savai'i), 6,095 ft. (1,858 m). *Lowest*—sea level.
Population: *Estimated 1990 population*—170,000; density, 156 persons per sq. mi. (60 persons per km²); distribution, 77 per cent rural, 23 per cent urban. *1981 census*—158,349. *Estimated 1995 population*—178,000.
Chief products: *Agriculture*—bananas, cacao, coconuts.
Flag: The flag has a red field with a blue canton in the upper left-hand corner. Five white stars on the canton symbolize the Southern Cross constellation. Adopted in 1962. See **Flag** (picture: Flags of Asia and the Pacific).
Money: *Basic unit*—Tala.

effect until the head of state approves them. A *pulenu'u* (head chief) is appointed to represent the government in each village. There are two political parties, the Christian Democratic Party and the Human Rights Protection Party.

People. Most Samoans are of full Polynesian descent. About 10 per cent of the people are of mixed Samoan and European descent. A few Europeans, Chinese, and persons from other Pacific islands live in Western Samoa. The people speak *Samoan,* a Polynesian dialect. The better-educated people also speak English.

Samoans live simply, much as their ancestors did. Samoan life centers around the family. The people live with their relatives in extended family groups called *aiga.* The aiga elects a matai who serves as head of the family. Some of the young people resent the matai power, but the system is still strong.

The people live in open-sided *fale* (houses) that have a thatched roof supported by poles. They let down palm leaf blinds when it rains. Most Samoan men wear only a *lava-lava,* a piece of cloth wrapped around the waist like a skirt. Some wear a blouse or shirt with their lava-lava. Most of the women wear a long lava-lava and an upper garment called a *puletasi.*

Samoans greatly enjoy dancing. They also love to play their own version of cricket, a game they learned from the English missionaries. They play cricket with teams that may have from 10 to 300 players, compared to 11 players in a normal cricket game.

Almost all Samoans are Christians. The most important religious groups in the country are the Congregational, Methodist, and Roman Catholic.

Western Samoa provides good medical care and the people are generally healthy. Most districts have government hospitals that provide free care.

Most Samoans can read and write Samoan. About half can read and write English. Education is free, but not compulsory. The government operates elementary schools in most villages, and also has a few high schools. Some lessons are given by radio in all government schools. Many children attend mission schools. Western Samoa also has two colleges and a national university. Some Samoan students go overseas for further schooling.

Land. The islands of Western Samoa were formed by erupting volcanoes. A volcano on Savai'i is still active. It last erupted from 1905 to 1911, covering part of the island with lava rock that is still bare. The islands are fringed with coral reefs.

The island shores are lined with tall, graceful coconut palm trees. The rocky, reddish-brown soil near the coasts is fertile enough to produce bananas; *taro,* a plant with an edible underground stem; and *cacao,* a tree whose seeds are used to make chocolate and cocoa. Further inland, heavy rains have *leached* the soil (dissolved the minerals and washed them away). Few food crops can grow there. Tropical rain forests cover the high volcanic peaks at the center of the islands.

The climate is tropical and humid, but the southeast trade winds make it mild. Temperatures seldom rise above 85° F. (29° C) or fall below 75° F. (24° C). Rainfall ranges from about 70 inches (180 centimeters) a year on the northwest coast to over 150 inches (381 centimeters) in the southeast. The most pleasant months are from May to September, when the temperatures and rainfall are lowest.

Economy is based on agriculture, and about 70 per cent of the people are farmers. The chief food crops are bananas, coconuts, tropical fruit called *breadfruit,* and taro. The people also raise pigs and chickens and catch fish for food. They export some bananas, cacao, and *copra* (dried coconut meat).

The annual average income in Samoa is very low by world standards, but most Samoans have little need for money. They raise most of their own food, build their own houses, and make most of their own clothing.

Some of the people work for the government, for traders in Apia, or for the missions. People of mixed Samoan and European descent run many of the businesses. Western Samoa has few industries. It imports some manufactured goods, processed foods, and petroleum products from New Zealand, Australia, Great Britain, Japan, the United States, and West Germany.

Most villages are linked by roads. Small boats travel regularly between the islands. Samoa's airline, called Polynesian Airlines, flies to American Samoa, Tonga, and Fiji. Ocean-going ships dock at Apia, the only port.

History. People have lived in Samoa for at least 2,000 years, probably coming there from what are now Fiji and Vanuatu. The Samoans drove out invaders from the Tonga Islands and began forming their own nation about 1,000 years ago. Many chiefs ruled the people until a woman, Salamasina, united them in the 1500's.

Jacob Roggeveen, a Dutch explorer, was the first European to reach Samoa. He discovered the islands in 1722. But few Europeans visited Samoa until the first mission was established in Savai'i in 1830. Once the Samoans accepted the missionaries, whaling and trading ships began making regular stops in the islands.

Two royal families ruled different parts of Samoa during the mid-1800's, and they fought among themselves over who would be king. Germany, Great Britain, and the United States supported rival groups. In 1899, the three countries agreed that Germany and the United States would divide the islands, and Germany took control of Western Samoa in 1900. Germany improved farm production and also expanded the economy.

In 1914, a military force from New Zealand occupied German Samoa. After World War I, the League of Nations gave New Zealand a *mandate* (order) to govern Western Samoa.

New Zealand's rule began disastrously. An influenza epidemic struck Western Samoa in 1918 and about one-fifth of the people died. The New Zealand government became more and more unpopular in the 1920's. Some Samoans joined an organization called the Mau (testimony) movement, which favored Samoan traditions and opposed rule by New Zealand. The Mau movement urged nonviolent resistance. Samoans began to refuse to obey laws or to cooperate with the government. They continued their civil disobedience activities until 1936, when New Zealand officials met some of their demands.

After World War II, the United Nations made Western Samoa a trust territory and asked New Zealand to begin preparing the islands for independence. In 1957, members of the Legislative Assembly were elected for the first time and Samoan members controlled the assembly. A Cabinet headed by a Samoan prime minister gained executive powers in 1959. In 1961, the people voted to accept a new constitution. Western Samoa became independent on Jan. 1, 1962. It joined the Commonwealth of Nations in 1970 and the United Nations in 1976.   John Carter

Western Union owns and operates a commercial telegraph system and many other communication services in the United States. It also provides communications systems and services that are specially designed to meet the needs of individual business and government users. *Western Union* is short for *Western Union Telegraph Company.*

In 1851, a group of men in Rochester, N.Y., organized the New York and Mississippi Valley Printing Telegraph Company. The name of the firm was changed to Western Union Telegraph Company in 1856. The firm grew rapidly during the late 1800's and built a national telegraph system. In 1861, the company completed the first transcontinental telegraph line in the United States. This line made it possible for coast-to-coast messages to be received almost instantly. It also helped end the pony express (see **Pony express**). By 1900, Western Union operated two transatlantic cables and more than 1 million miles (1.6 million kilometers) of telegraph wire.

Through the years, Western Union has modernized its equipment and introduced new communication services. In 1945, for example, it started to send messages via radio beams relayed by a network of transmitting towers. Prior to this development, messages were sent by means of electrical impulses transmitted through telegraph wires. In 1970, the company introduced the Mailgram message service, which combines the facilities of Western Union and the U.S. Postal Service to deliver messages. Also in 1970, the Western Union Telegraph Company became the chief subsidiary of the Western Union Corporation.

In 1974, the telegraph company began operating the

first domestic satellite communications system in the United States. This system, called *Westar,* consists of three orbiting satellites and six transmitting stations on the earth. It handles telephone calls and TV programs in addition to telegraph transmissions.

In 1982, the telegraph company began operating a worldwide Telex service (see **Telegraph** [Special services]). That same year, the company introduced an electronic mail service called EasyLink. This service enables computer users anywhere in the world to communicate with each other by using their computers. Western Union's headquarters are at 1 Lake Street, Upper Saddle River, NJ 07458.

Critically reviewed by the Western Union Corporation

See also **Telegraph.**

Western Wall. See Wailing Wall.

Westinghouse, George (1846-1914), an American inventor and manufacturer, invented the air brake for railroad trains. He introduced alternating current for electric power transmission. He invented a system of pipes to conduct natural gas into homes safely. He also invented the gas meter.

Westinghouse was born on Oct. 6, 1846, in Central Bridge, N.Y. As a boy, he worked in his father's machine shop. At 15 he invented a rotary engine. He served in the Union army and navy during the Civil War.

By 1866, he had already perfected two inventions, a device for replacing derailed railroad cars and a railroad frog, which made it possible for a train to pass from one track to another. Westinghouse perfected the air brake in 1868. The brake was immediately successful, and he organized a company to produce it. He patented hundreds of inventions and organized over 50 companies. He was president of 30 corporations, including the Westinghouse Electric Company.   W. H. Baughn

See also **Brake.**

Westinghouse Electric Corporation is one of the world's largest suppliers of equipment and services relating to the control, distribution, generation, and use of electric power. The company produces a wide variety of products, ranging from office furniture and electric motors to nuclear reactors, radar systems for the armed services, and automated electrical systems for factories. The corporation also owns a finance company and is involved in various land development projects.

Westinghouse has designed and built nuclear reactors and related equipment for nuclear-powered generating stations throughout the United States and overseas. Nuclear reactors produced by Westinghouse provide power for most of the United States Navy's nuclear-powered submarines and surface ships.

The company has substantial holdings in the communications field. It owns 13 radio stations and 5 commercial television stations.

Westinghouse was founded in 1886 by George Westinghouse, an American inventor and manufacturer. Its headquarters are in Pittsburgh, Pa. For the sales, assets, and number of employees of Westinghouse, see **Manufacturing** (table: 50 leading U.S. manufacturers).

Critically reviewed by the Westinghouse Electric Corporation

Westminster, the government district of London. See London (Greater London; picture).

Westminster, Statute of. See Canada, Government of (International relations).

Westminster Abbey is a great national church that stands near the Houses of Parliament in London. This church is world-famous and is one of the most beautiful in England. Its official name is the Collegiate Church of Saint Peter. Its name of Abbey comes from the fact that it once served as the church of an ancient monastery.

Westminster Abbey marked the scene of many great events in English history. All the English rulers from the

Michael Freeman, Bruce Coleman Ltd.

The Coronation Chair in Westminster Abbey was built to hold the *Stone of Scone,* which Edward I took from Scotland in 1296.

Geoff Dore, Bruce Coleman Ltd.

Westminster Abbey in London is a national church of Great Britain. It was built in the French Gothic style of the 1200's.

time of William the Conqueror, except Edward V and Edward VIII, were crowned there. In the chapel of Edward the Confessor stands the old Coronation Chair that dates from 1300. See **Coronation.**

Burial in Westminster Abbey is one of the greatest honors England can give. Many kings and queens are buried in the chapel of Henry VII. Political leaders and other important people of England are buried in other parts of the Abbey. The bodies of many of England's greatest poets lie in the Poets' Corner.

Westminster Abbey became the seat of a bishop in 1539. This act made the Abbey a cathedral. However, only this one bishop has ever served there. A dean has headed the Abbey from the time of Queen Elizabeth I to the present day.

Edward the Confessor built a church on the site of the Abbey between about 1042 and 1065. But the main part of the Abbey was begun in 1245 by Henry III. He made the Abbey one of the best examples of French Gothic architecture in England (see **Gothic art**). In the 1500's, Henry VII added the chapel that bears his name. The towers were completed in 1740.

The floor plan of Westminster Abbey is in the shape of a Latin cross. The church is 513 feet (156 meters) long. The *transepts* (crossarms) extend 203 feet (62 meters). The *nave* (main hall) is 38 feet (12 meters) wide and 102 feet (31 meters) high. The twin towers on the west are 225 feet (69 meters) high. The square central tower barely rises above the roof.

Cloisters surrounding the Abbey date from the 1200's and 1300's. The chapter house was built in the 1200's. West of the main cloisters is the famous Jerusalem Chamber, dating from the 1300's. Air raids in World War II damaged parts of the Abbey. A program designed to completely restore Westminster Abbey and maintain it began in 1953.   Alan Gowans

Westminster Choir is one of the most famous choral organizations in the United States. It was founded in 1921 by John Finley Williamson in Dayton, Ohio. The choir is now a part of Westminster Choir College in Princeton, N.J.

Westminster Hall is a building connected with the House of Parliament in London. Originally, it was the great hall of the Palace of Westminster, where the rulers of England held court for almost 500 years. Many great events in English history took place in the hall. Sir Thomas More, Lady Jane Grey, the Earl of Strafford, and Warren Hastings stood trial there. Charles I was condemned to death there. William II built the hall from 1097 to 1099. Westminster Hall is 240 feet (73 meters) long, 68 feet (21 meters) wide, and 89½ feet (27 meters) high.   Talbot Hamlin

Westminster Kennel Club Show. See Dog (Dog shows).

Westminster School is one of the oldest public schools of England. Elizabeth I founded it about 1560 as part of Westminster Abbey. It is also called Saint Peter's College.

Westmoreland, William Childs (1914-   ), an American general, commanded United States forces in the Vietnam War from 1964 to 1968. He relied on ground operations that stressed the number of enemy dead over territory gained, a policy that became known as "search and destroy." In 1967, Westmoreland made sev-

eral optimistic reports on United States progress in the war. But in early 1968, enemy attacks against the major cities of South Vietnam raised doubts about the war's outcome. Later that year, Westmoreland returned to the United States to serve as Army chief of staff. He retired in 1972.

In 1982, a CBS-TV documentary, "The Uncounted Enemy: A Vietnam Deception," charged that Westmoreland underestimated enemy strength in 1967 and 1968 to make it appear that U.S. forces were winning the war. Westmoreland sued CBS, claiming that its charges about the underestimated troop figures were false and had damaged his reputation. During the trial, some former high-ranking military officials supported the CBS charges. Soon afterward, Westmoreland and CBS officials reached an agreement to drop the suit. They issued statements pledging mutual respect for each other, but CBS also stood by its broadcast.

Westmoreland was born in Spartanburg County, S.C. He graduated from the U.S. Military Academy in 1936. During World War II (1939-1945), he commanded artillery forces in North Africa, Sicily, and northern Europe. He led a paratroop regiment and became a brigadier general during the Korean War (1950-1953). He became a lieutenant general in 1963.   Allan R. Millett

Weston, Edward (1850-1936), an inventor and manufacturer, was noted for pioneering in the development of electric meters. He began manufacturing meters in 1882, and founded the Weston Electric Instrument Company in 1888.

Born near Wolverhampton, England, Weston moved to the United States in 1870. He entered the electroplating business, and developed an electroplating generator, an arc-lighting system, and an incandescent lighting system.   Robert P. Multhauf

Weston, Edward (1886-1958), was an American photographer. He produced dramatic pictures of people, landscapes, and such simple objects as seashells, seaweed, and rocks. Many of Weston's photographs emphasize the forms and textures of objects and scenes from nature.

Weston was born in Highland Park, Ill. Early in his career, he won many awards for his photographs in the hazy, out-of-focus style that had become popular in the late 1800's. In the 1920's, however, Weston adopted the technique of *straight photography,* a style featuring focused, detailed photographs that portray subjects simply and directly. In 1932, he helped form a group of progressive photographers who promoted straight photography.

In 1937, Weston became the first photographer to win a Guggenheim Fellowship. The award is a grant given to scholars, scientists, and artists to advance their work.
Charles Hagen

Westphalia, *wehst FAYL yuh,* is a former Prussian province of western Germany. *Westphalia,* or *Westfalen* in German, means *western plain.* It lies just east of the Netherlands. For location, see **Germany** (political map). Westphalia once belonged to the Duchy of Saxony. In the late 1100's, the name *Westphalia* was given to a region ruled by the Archbishop of Cologne. Prussia gained control of the area at the Congress of Vienna (1814-1815). In 1946, Westphalia became part of the state of North Rhine-Westphalia.   John W. Boyer

Oil painting on wood panel (1821) by Thomas Birch; Wadsworth Atheneum, Hartford, Conn. Bequest of Mrs. Clara Hinton Gould

Covered wagons carried thousands of pioneers westward across the United States. The sturdy Conestoga wagon, *shown above,* was first built by German immigrants in the early 1700's.

Westward movement

Westward movement carried settlers across America, from the Atlantic Ocean to the Pacific Ocean. The westward movement began in the early 1600's with European settlements along the Atlantic Coast of North America. It continued until the late 1800's. By that time, the western frontiers of the United States had been conquered.

An abundance of land and other natural resources lured America's pioneers westward. Fur traders, cattle ranchers, farmers, and miners led the push to the west. Merchants and other business people followed. These hard-working men and women faced great dangers, endured severe hardships, and suffered loneliness and boredom in the hope of making a better life for themselves and their children. Some of them looked to the west for wealth or adventure. Others sought to improve their social position or increase their political power.

The pioneers struggled westward across hills, mountains, and prairies on foot and on horseback. Some floated through the Erie Canal on barges or traveled down rivers on flatboats and steamboats. Others crossed the rugged wilderness in covered wagons. For many pioneers, the Cumberland Gap, the Oregon Trail, and other roads west became paths to opportunity.

Jerome O. Steffen, the contributor of this article, is Associate Professor of History at the University of Oklahoma.

The American frontier shifted westward in stages. The first American frontier ran along the Atlantic Coast. Settlers began to cross the Appalachian Mountains after territory west of the mountains came under British control in 1763. During the early 1800's, the next push westward took settlers into the Great Lakes region, the Mississippi River Valley, and the plains along the Gulf of Mexico. By the mid-1840's, adventurous pioneers had reached what are now California and Oregon in the Far West. The last frontier settled by the westward movement was the Great Plains between the Missouri River and the Rocky Mountains. The settlement of that region began in the 1860's.

In 1890, the U.S. Bureau of the Census reported that no frontiers remained in the United States. The pioneers had conquered the West.

For descriptions of the life of the people during this period, see the articles **Colonial life in America; Pioneer life in America;** and **Western frontier life.**

The first frontiers

The earliest settlements. Colonists from England, the Netherlands, and other European countries began to settle along the Atlantic Coast of North America in the early 1600's. Jamestown, the first permanent English settlement in North America, was founded in Virginia in 1607. Other early settlements included St. Marys City in Maryland; Plymouth and Boston in what is now Massachusetts; and New Amsterdam, which was the beginning of New York City.

The promise of owning land attracted many Europeans to the American Colonies. Some settlers were offered free land to develop. Others came as *indentured servants*. An indentured servant received free passage to America and food, housing, and clothing. In return, the servant agreed to work without wages for a specified period of time, usually four years. At the end of that period, indentured servants received their freedom. Beginning in 1619, black Africans also were brought to the colonies as indentured servants. Gradually, their periods of service were extended, and they began to be treated as slaves with no chance of freedom.

Some settlers came to America in search of religious freedom. Puritans, Quakers, and members of other groups sought to establish communities in which they could live according to their religious beliefs. Probably the best-known Puritans were the Pilgrims, who founded Plymouth Colony.

From the earliest settlements in Virginia and Maryland, colonists soon advanced inland along the valleys of the James, York, Rappahannock, and Potomac rivers. To the north, rich farmland drew settlers into the Connecticut, Merrimack, and Hudson river valleys. By the late 1600's, settlers had pushed as far west as the eastern edge of the Piedmont, the hilly uplands at the base of the Appalachian Mountains.

The Old West. Pioneers next moved into a region often called the Old West. It consisted of the Piedmont, the valleys of the Appalachians, and the back country of New England. In the Old West, fur traders offered Indians weapons and tools in exchange for deer hides, beaver pelts, and other skins and furs. Cattle owners in the Southern Colonies found ample grazing lands in the

Important dates in the westward movement

1775 Daniel Boone opened the Wilderness Road, which aided the settlement of Kentucky.

1785 The Ordinance of 1785 provided an orderly system for surveying and selling government lands.

1787 The Northwest Ordinance provided government for the Northwest Territory.

1794 Victory over the Indians and a treaty with Great Britain brought peace to the Northwest Territory.

1795 The Pinckney Treaty with Spain opened the Mississippi River to American traders.

1803 The Louisiana Purchase opened a vast area beyond the Mississippi River to American settlers.

1804-1806 Lewis and Clark explored the northern part of the Louisiana Territory.

1825 The Erie Canal opened, providing improved transportation westward.

1845 The United States annexed Texas.

1846 Britain gave the United States the southern part of the Oregon region.

1846-1848 War with Mexico resulted in the acquisition of California and the Southwest.

1848 The discovery of gold in California inspired the gold rush.

1862 The Homestead Act promised free land to settlers in the West.

1869 The nation's first transcontinental rail system was completed.

1890 Settlement of the main areas of the Western United States brought an end to the frontier.

Piedmont for their expanding herds, and cowboys led roundups and cattle drives. Farmers followed the fur traders and cattle ranchers into the Old West, settling in the Shenandoah Valley in Virginia and in the fertile hills and valleys of North and South Carolina.

Many kinds of people came to the Old West. Some owned small farms in the coastal lowlands but sought better land to the west. Others were the landless younger sons and daughters of established families in the East. These colonists were joined by new arrivals from Europe. For example, many German and Scotch-Irish immigrants fled hard times and religious persecution in Europe and settled in Pennsylvania during the early 1700's.

Settlers from different lands brought their own customs and way of life to the frontier. In the process, they helped create American culture. For example, Swedish settlers brought the log cabin to America. Other settlers copied the log cabin throughout the Old West. German gunsmiths in Pennsylvania adapted a European rifle to pioneer needs. The result—the Kentucky rifle—proved essential on the frontier for shooting game and for defense against wild animals.

Regional conflict. As each frontier became settled, tensions developed between western settlers and colonial governments in the east. The westerners resented paying taxes to distant governments that provided them with few benefits. The easterners, on the other hand, viewed the west as a backwoods inhabited by people incapable of governing themselves. At times, disputes between the two groups turned violent. In 1764, Pennsylvania frontiersmen known as "the Paxton Boys" marched on Philadelphia, the colony's capital. But the Pennsylvania statesman Benjamin Franklin persuaded them to turn back. In the Carolinas, a group of westerners known as the "Regulators" assembled to protest high taxes, insufficient representation in colonial government, and other

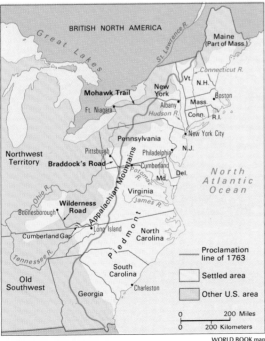

By 1790, the East Coast had been largely settled, and Americans had pushed beyond the Appalachians. Two new frontiers—the Northwest Territory and the Old Southwest—had opened.

WORLD BOOK map

injustices. A battle was narrowly avoided at the Saluda River in South Carolina in 1769. The Regulators fought and lost the Battle of Alamance in North Carolina in 1771.

The French and Indian War (1754-1763). The next frontier lay beyond the Appalachian Mountains. Both France and Great Britain claimed the territory between the Allegheny Mountains—a part of the Appalachians— and the Mississippi River. Their rivalry led to the French and Indian War between the French and the British, along with their Indian allies. The British defeated the French and gained nearly all of France's territory in North America.

The Proclamation of 1763. A vast territory west of the Appalachians lay open for settlement after the French and Indian War. However, Indians were pre-pared to defend their hunting grounds on that land. The British hoped to prevent costly Indian wars by keeping white settlers east of the Appalachians. For that reason, Britain issued the Proclamation of 1763. The proclama-tion drew a line through the mountains and forbade white settlements west of the line. It also ordered set-tlers already there to move back east and required trad-ers in the region to have licenses. Investors in land, farmers, and traders—all eager to take advantage of the new territory—resented the restrictions.

Crossing the Appalachians. The Proclamation of 1763 halted westward expansion for only a short time. Investors and colonists clamored for more land as the population in the East increased and the amount of available farmland decreased. Treaties negotiated with the Indians in 1768 shifted the proclamation line west-ward and opened the way for the settlement of what are now West Virginia and southwestern Pennsylvania. Pio-neers settled at Fort Pitt (now Pittsburgh) and in river val-leys nearby.

Some pioneers marched farther west into what are now eastern Kentucky and Tennessee. Daniel Boone was one of the most famous of those adventuresome pi-oneers. In 1775, he led a group of woodsmen from Ten-nessee through the Cumberland Gap into Kentucky. The trail they carved out became known as the Wilderness Road (see **Wilderness Road**). In Kentucky, Boone founded a settlement called Boonesborough. Other pio-neers, such as James Robertson and John Sevier, estab-lished frontier communities along the Holston, Wa-tauga, and Clinch rivers in eastern Tennessee. By the time the Revolutionary War began in April 1775, this frontier region swarmed with land speculators and the settlers they had attracted.

The Revolutionary War (1775-1783). During the Revolutionary War, the British encouraged Indians to at-tack American settlements along the western frontier. Many western settlers fled back east. In 1778 and 1779, Virginia sent troops under Lieutenant Colonel George Rogers Clark to strike at the British. Clark captured sev-eral settlements under British control in what are now Il-linois and Indiana. As a result of Clark's victories, the United States claimed the area between the Ohio River and the Great Lakes.

After the United States won its independence from Great Britain in 1783, it acquired British lands extending west to the Mississippi; north to Canada; and south to Florida, which was then a Spanish territory. Settled

areas west of the Appalachians soon became part of the United States. Kentucky joined the Union in 1792, and Tennessee followed in 1796.

Reaching the Mississippi River

After the Revolutionary War ended in 1783, the west-ward movement carried settlers onto two new frontiers. They were the Old Northwest and the Old Southwest. The Old Northwest extended from the Ohio River north to the Great Lakes and from Pennsylvania west to the Mississippi River. The Old Southwest at first consisted of Kentucky and Tennessee. It gradually expanded south to the Gulf of Mexico.

The Ordinance of 1785. Congress, eager for revenue from the sale of land in the Old Northwest, adopted the Ordinance of 1785. That law required the government to survey the Old Northwest before selling the land to the public. The territory was divided into townships of 6 miles (9.7 kilometers) square. These townships were fur-ther divided into 36 sections, each 1 mile (1.6 kilometers) square, an area that equals 640 acres (259 hectares). The 640-acre units were then auctioned off to the public for a price of at least $1 an acre.

Few farmers could afford to buy as much as 640 acres. Land speculators, such as the Ohio Company and the Scioto Company, grabbed up most of the land. These companies then divided the land into smaller sections and sold them at a profit.

Townships and sections

The Ordinance of 1785 provided a framework for orderly settle-ment of the Northwest Territory. Its system of townships and sections prevented boundary disputes, and was used in survey-ing all the territories later acquired by the United States.

WORLD BOOK illustration by Sarah Woodward

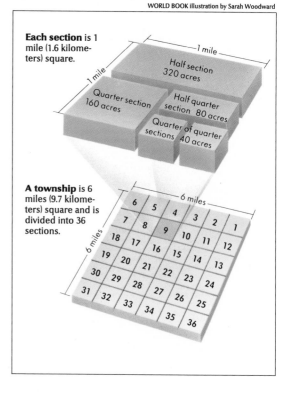

Each section is 1 mile (1.6 kilome-ters) square.

1 mile

Half section 320 acres

1 mile

Quarter section 160 acres

Half quarter section 80 acres

Quarter of quarter sections 40 acres

A township is 6 miles (9.7 kilome-ters) square and is divided into 36 sections.

6 miles

6 miles

Oil painting on canvas (1945) by Howard Chandler Christy (Ohio Historical Society)

Indians signed the Treaty of Greenville in 1795, opening up parts of Ohio and Indiana to pioneer settlement. The Indians were forced to sign many treaties, each time giving up more land.

The Northwest Ordinance of 1787 established a government for the Old Northwest, which then became known as the Northwest Territory. The ordinance also provided for the eventual division of the region into three to five states. Congress appointed the first officials of the territory—a governor, a secretary, and three judges. When the territory reached a population of 5,000 adult males, it could elect an assembly and send a nonvoting delegate to Congress. When any division of the territory reached a population of 60,000, it could apply for statehood.

The ordinances of 1785 and 1787 paved the way for full-scale migration to the west. The laws also established guidelines for the administration of all U.S. territories. Treaties with Great Britain and Spain further encouraged westward migration. Under the terms of the Jay Treaty, signed with Britain in 1794, the British agreed to abandon the military posts they still occupied in the Northwest Territory. In 1795, the United States signed the Pinckney Treaty with Spain, which then controlled Florida and the mouth of the Mississippi River. The treaty settled a dispute over the northern border of Florida, and it opened the Mississippi River to American traders.

Indian conflicts. America's rapid westward expansion led to warfare between white settlers and Indians. During the early 1790's, British traders in the Northwest Territory encouraged Indians to attack frontier settlements. The Indians in the Northwest twice fought off U.S. Army expeditions. But they were defeated by Major General Anthony Wayne at the Battle of Fallen Timbers near what is now Toledo, Ohio, in 1794. In the Treaty of Greenville, signed in 1795, the Indians gave up their claim to the southern two-thirds of what is now Ohio and the southeastern part of what is now Indiana. Pio-

neers rushed into the area. By 1800, the Ohio region had 45,000 settlers. In 1803, Ohio became the first section of the Northwest Territory to achieve statehood.

White settlers soon disregarded the line drawn by the Treaty of Greenville to separate their land from Indian land. As land-hungry pioneers advanced westward, the Indians were forced to sign many additional treaties, each time giving up more land. In the early 1800's, the Shawnee chief Tecumseh—aided by his brother, known as the Shawnee Prophet—tried to halt the invasion of white settlers. They worked to organize an alliance of Indian tribes from the Great Lakes to the Gulf of Mexico. But Tecumseh's plans for an alliance were largely destroyed when his forces were defeated at the Battle of Tippecanoe in the Indiana Territory in 1811.

The War of 1812 briefly interrupted America's westward expansion. During the war, many tribes in Tecumseh's alliance sided with the British against the United States. The Indians hoped that a U.S. defeat would allow them to keep their lands. However, two American victories hastened the downfall of Indian civilization east of the Mississippi River. In 1813, a combined British and Indian force suffered defeat at the Battle of the Thames in southern Canada. In 1814, Major General Andrew Jackson led soldiers to victory over the Creek Indians in the Battle of Horseshoe Bend in what is now Alabama.

By the mid-1800's, the U.S. government had moved almost all of the eastern Indians to the Indian Territory, an area set aside for the Indians west of the Mississippi River. That territory later became almost identical in area with present-day Oklahoma. Thousands of Indians died of starvation and disease on the march to the Indian Territory.

The Old Northwest. After the War of 1812, westward migration resumed at a brisk pace. By 1820, about

By 1840, pioneers had settled most of the land east of the Mississippi. Westward expansion had already carried many settlers across the river into Missouri, Arkansas, and Louisiana.

792,000 settlers had made their homes in the Old Northwest.

Pioneers headed to the Old Northwest over rough wagon roads and down the Ohio River. The Erie Canal, completed in 1825, provided another route westward, from the Hudson River to the Great Lakes. It also spurred the economic development of the Old Northwest. The canal allowed westerners to ship farm products efficiently and cheaply to the cities in the East. At the same time, Eastern cities could ship manufactured goods to the rapidly growing farm communities of the Northwest.

Steamboats and railroads encouraged further development of the Old Northwest during the next few decades. Pittsburgh, Louisville, Cincinnati, and other cities along the Ohio River became bustling centers of trade. Chicago and Detroit prospered along the Great Lakes.

The Old Southwest. The Adams-Onís Treaty, signed with Spain in 1819, gave the United States Florida and the southern strip of Alabama and Mississippi. Thousands of settlers poured into Florida. Pioneers also streamed onto the plains bordering the Gulf of Mexico that formed part of the Old Southwest.

Most of the settlers of the Old Southwest were cotton farmers. Farmers rushed first into western Georgia and then into Alabama and Mississippi after the federal government took over Indian lands in those states. Steamboats and an expanding network of roads sped the journey westward. Such cities as Natchez, Miss., New Orleans, and St. Louis prospered along the Mississippi River.

The best lands in the Old Southwest were held largely by plantation owners, unlike in the Old Northwest where small farms dotted the land. Plantation own-

ers dominated social and political life in most of the Old Southwest. As a result, the region developed an economy that depended almost entirely on cotton, and it experienced little industrial growth.

Exploring and settling the Far West

Settlers had begun to cross the Mississippi River by the 1820's. Yet American leaders misjudged the speed at which the nation was moving west. In 1801, President Thomas Jefferson foresaw a far distant time when the continent would be settled from coast to coast. However, pioneers reached California and other regions of the Far West during the 1840's.

The Louisiana Purchase. American settlement of the Far West began after President Thomas Jefferson purchased the Louisiana Territory from France in 1803. For about $15 million, the United States gained 827,987 square miles (2,144,476 square kilometers) of land. The purchase extended U.S. borders from the Mississippi River to the Rocky Mountains.

Before 1801, Spain had controlled the Louisiana Territory. The Spanish posed little threat to U.S. trade and westward expansion. But France, a more powerful and aggressive country, gained control of the territory in 1801. Jefferson feared French interference with U.S. trade along the Mississippi River and through the port of New Orleans. The Louisiana Purchase removed a possibly dangerous enemy from the western border of the United States.

Exploration. In 1803, Jefferson chose Meriwether Lewis, an Army captain, and William Clark, a former Army officer, to lead an expedition to explore the new territory. Jefferson wanted Lewis and Clark to trace the source of the Missouri River. He hoped that the explorers would find a water route from the Missouri to the Pacific Ocean. Jefferson also wanted the expedition to report on the natural resources and to establish friendly relations with Indians in the region.

In 1804, Lewis and Clark moved up the Missouri and across the Rockies. They reached the Snake River in the Oregon region in 1805 and followed the Columbia River to the Pacific. The expedition did not find a practical water route to the Pacific. But Lewis and Clark reported that the region was rich in furs, attracting fur traders and trappers to the area.

More government-sponsored expeditions followed the Lewis and Clark expedition. In 1806, Zebulon M. Pike, an Army officer, set out to explore the southern part of the Louisiana Purchase and gather information about neighboring Spanish territory. But he was captured by Spanish troops near the Rio Grande. After his release, Pike supplied the government with valuable information that later helped establish trade relations with Mexican settlements in the area. In 1820, Major Stephen H. Long led a small expedition up the Platte River to the Rocky Mountains. His report found the Great Plains unfit for settlement because it lacked trees and water. Long labeled the region the *Great American Desert*.

John C. Frémont, an Army surveyor, explored much of the Far West. Beginning in 1842, he led a series of expeditions that surveyed the Oregon Trail and mapped much of the Great Basin region between the Rockies and the Sierra Nevada. Frémont published a report on California, which drew many settlers to the region.

Fur traders and trappers also contributed greatly to the exploration of the Far West. Such well-known "mountain men" as Jim Bridger, Kit Carson, Thomas Fitzpatrick, and Jedediah Smith mapped many areas of the Rockies as they searched for beaver. Carson and Fitzpatrick served as guides on Frémont's expeditions. Bridger established a trading post that helped supply travelers along the Oregon Trail in what is now Wyoming. Jedediah Smith traveled more of the Far West than anyone of his time. In 1824, he used South Pass to cross the Rockies. It then became the route of many travelers. In 1826, Smith made the first overland trip to California.

The Santa Fe Trail. During the 1820's, traders also developed a trade network in the Southwest. In 1821, the trader William Becknell blazed the Santa Fe Trail, which extended from Independence, Mo., to Santa Fe in what is now New Mexico. New Mexico was then a province of Mexico. Another branch of the trail, opened in 1822, cut across the Cimarron Desert. It became the more popular route. Caravans of covered wagons journeyed to Santa Fe loaded with manufactured goods to exchange for Mexican silver, furs, and mules. The Santa Fe trade boosted Missouri's economy. It also made traders and explorers aware that Mexico had only a weak hold on New Mexico and its other northern provinces.

Texas. In the early 1820's, the Mexican government gave Stephen F. Austin, a pioneer from Missouri, permission to establish a colony in Texas. Texas belonged to Mexico as a result of the Adams-Onís Treaty of 1819, which defined the western border of the United States. The treaty drew a boundary line that zigzagged northwest from the Gulf of Mexico to the Pacific Ocean.

By 1835, American settlers outnumbered Mexicans in Texas, which made it difficult for Mexico to govern the territory. That year, the Texans rebelled. Texas gained its independence after its army, led by Samuel Houston, defeated the Mexicans at the Battle of San Jacinto in April 1836. Texas was an independent republic until December 1845, when the United States annexed Texas and made it a state.

The Oregon Trail. As Texans fought for their independence, other Americans looked to the Oregon region with great anticipation. Fur traders and missionaries were the first white settlers to reach the Pacific Northwest. Their glowing reports of fertile valleys attracted thousands of people to the region after 1835. Settlers followed the Oregon Trail. It began at Independence, Mo., and wound westward for about 2,000 miles (3,200 kilometers) across the Great Plains and the Rocky Mountains to the rich valleys of the Oregon region. Pioneer farmers, cattle ranchers, and sheep ranchers journeyed westward along the trail. The first large group of settlers, about 1,000, made the trip in 1843.

Travel on the Oregon Trail required strength and endurance. But the trek was not so lonely or dangerous as described in Western legend. The trail was crowded with wagon trains, army units, missionaries, hunting parties, traders, and even sightseeing tours. Some travelers complained that they sometimes had to stop early in the day to find a good campsite ahead of the crowd. Others spoke of the need to wear masks for protection against the dust kicked up by the heavy traffic. Stories about great numbers of pioneers killed by hostile Indians were also exaggerated. Of the 10,000 deaths that oc-

curred on the trail from 1835 to 1855, only 4 per cent resulted from Indian attacks. Such diseases as cholera and smallpox and firearms accidents were the chief causes of death on the trail.

The flood of immigrants to Oregon helped America achieve its territorial ambitions. Since the late 1700's, Great Britain and the United States had had overlapping claims in the Oregon region. The two countries signed a treaty in 1818, agreeing that citizens of both nations could occupy the disputed area. But by 1846, the growing number of American settlers in the Oregon region caused the British to abandon their hopes of keeping the area. In the Oregon Treaty of 1846, Great Britain gave up its claim to all of the Oregon territory south of the 49th parallel, except for Vancouver Island. That line later became the boundary between the United States and Canada.

The Southwest. In the Southwest, a border dispute led to war between the United States and Mexico in 1846. The Treaty of Guadalupe Hidalgo, signed in 1848, ended the Mexican War. The treaty gave the United States more than 525,000 square miles (1,360,000 square kilometers) of land. That huge territory covered all of present-day California, Nevada, and Utah; most of Arizona; and parts of Colorado, New Mexico, and Wyoming. In 1853, in the Gadsden Purchase, the United States bought from Mexico a strip of land that makes up southern Arizona and New Mexico. That purchase was made in part to provide a good southern route for a transcontinental railroad.

By the 1840's, many Americans believed that it was the destiny of the United States to rule all North America. Those Americans felt they had a mission to spread democracy to the West. The belief in the nation's inevitable expansion became known as the *doctrine of manifest destiny.* It encouraged America's bold and confident expansion westward.

Utah. Utah became the home of the Mormons, who came there in search of religious freedom. The Mormons had met hostility from non-Mormons in communities from New York to Illinois. In 1846, Brigham Young began leading Mormon settlers west from Illinois. In 1847, a small advance party established a settlement on the shores of the Great Salt Lake in Utah. Within 10 years, about 100 Mormon settlements had been established in what are now California, Idaho, Nevada, Utah, and Wyoming. One of the most remarkable chapters in the westward movement occurred from 1856 to 1860, when about 3,000 Mormons walked across the Great Plains to Utah, pushing their few belongings in handcarts. The Mormons survived in the desert because they successfully irrigated the parched land. By 1852, they had dug about 1,000 miles (1,600 kilometers) of irrigation ditches. See **Mormons** (The Mormons in Utah).

California. Reports of fertile valleys and a mild climate attracted a steady stream of pioneers to California during the early 1840's. In 1848, gold was discovered along the American River at Sutter's Mill, near what is now Sacramento. News of the discovery spread rapidly, and by 1849, eager gold seekers began pouring into California. The gold rush attracted "Forty-Niners" from all parts of the world. The population of California exploded from about 15,000 in early 1848 to more than 100,000 by the end of 1849. During that time, San Fran-

Oil painting on canvas (1865) by A. D. O. Bowere; National Cowboy Hall of Fame

Eager prospectors flocked to California after the discovery of gold in 1848. Many miners remained in the Far West, greatly contributing to the permanent settlement of the area.

cisco, the gateway to the gold fields, grew tremendously. It changed from a small town to a bustling city almost overnight.

Most people heading for California followed the Oregon Trail across the Rockies and then branched off to the south along the California Trail. Others chose more southerly routes, such as the Santa Fe, Gila River, and

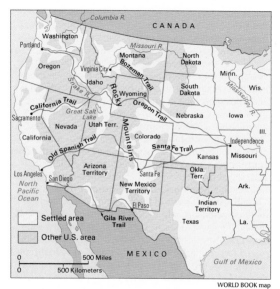

By 1890, settlements had spread throughout the Great Plains and Far West, though large areas were thinly populated. That year, the government reported that no frontiers were left.

Old Spanish trails. Some sailed the Atlantic Ocean south to the Isthmus of Panama, where they crossed over land to the Pacific Ocean and continued the sea voyage to San Francisco. From 1848 to 1855, more than 100,000 people traveled to the mining frontiers by the Panama route. Gold seekers also reached California by sailing around the southern tip of South America.

According to western tradition, miners caught up in gold fever either struck it rich or died in poverty. However, most prospectors did not fit that image. The majority searched for gold for several years and then returned home to their former occupation. Some stayed on in California and became farmers, ranchers, and merchants, greatly contributing to the permanent settlement of the area. Thus, gold rushes helped develop mining regions, though they did not last long in any one area. The process was repeated as prospectors carried their search elsewhere. Gold and silver rushes occurred in Nevada and Colorado in 1859. Gold rushes also drew miners to what is now Montana in 1862 and to what is now South Dakota in 1875.

Settling the Great Plains

The vast Great Plains between the Missouri River and the Rockies remained unsettled until the 1860's. But as the government gained control of Indian lands on the Plains, cattle ranchers and farmers rushed in. By 1890, the conquest of the West had drawn to a close.

The last Indian wars. After the Civil War ended in 1865, the U.S. Army began to round up the last Indian tribes that freely roamed the western plains. Land-hungry pioneers and expanding railroads wanted to move into the Great Plains from the east. Prospectors searching for gold and silver advanced from the west. But the

Plains Indians fought fiercely to keep their hunting grounds and to avoid being confined on reservations.

A series of bitter Indian wars occurred from the 1860's until 1890. The Sioux rose up in the mid-1860's, when the government built forts to protect the Bozeman Trail. That route, used by miners, ran through Sioux hunting grounds in Wyoming. Fighting broke out again after the discovery of gold in 1874 brought miners into Sioux territory in the Black Hills of South Dakota. To the south, some members of the Arapaho, Cheyenne, Comanche, Kiowa, and other Plains Indian tribes rebelled against moving to reservations in 1868. Indian hostilities in the south erupted again in 1871 and reached a climax in the Red River War of 1874-1875.

One by one, the various Plains Indian tribes were forced to sign treaties that opened their lands to white settlement. The Indians were then resettled on cramped reservations. The last major battle between the Plains Indians and whites occurred in 1890. That year, the U.S. Army massacred more than 200 Sioux at Wounded Knee Creek in South Dakota.

Cattle frontiers. The Great Plains opened to settlers as the government defeated the Plains Indians. Ranchers moved in first. Ranching started in Texas, and it soon turned the Great Plains into a vast cattle empire.

The westward expansion of the railroads contributed to the rise of the cattle industry. Railroads provided transportation to markets in the East. By 1867, the railroad had extended west to Abilene, Kans., which became the first of the western cattle towns. That year, 35,000 cattle arrived in Abilene. By 1871, more than 600,000 cattle entered Abilene. Texas ranchers hired cowboys to drive their herds to the railroads. The cowboys followed the Chisholm Trail, the Western Trail, and other cattle trails north. Herds of livestock soon rumbled into such Kansas cattle towns as Ellsworth, Newton,

Wichita, Caldwell, and perhaps the most famous of all, Dodge City.

These boisterous cattle towns gave rise to many western legends about gunfighters and such law officers as Wild Bill Hickok, Wyatt Earp, and Bat Masterson. Although cowboys engaged in much merrymaking after the long cattle drives, reports of violence in these communities have been greatly exaggerated. From 1870 to 1885, only 45 violent deaths were recorded in all of the cattle towns together.

Ranching and the railroads quickly spread from Texas north and west into Colorado, Wyoming, Montana, and Oregon. In 1869, the Union Pacific and Central Pacific railroads met at Promontory, Utah, providing the nation with its first transcontinental railroad. Many people in the East and in Europe invested money in ranching after hearing reports of the easy money to be made in the cattle industry. However, the resulting overproduction of cattle, the rising costs of ranching, and the severe winter of 1886-1887 combined to bring an end to the cattle boom in the mid-1880's.

Homesteading on the Great Plains. Farmers known as *homesteaders* followed the cattle ranchers onto the Great Plains. The Homestead Act, passed by Congress in 1862, encouraged farmers to move west. This act gave 160 acres (65 hectares) of free land to any person who had lived on the land and improved it for five years. Many farmers came to the Great Plains because they no longer believed the Great American Desert image. The westward expansion of the railroad also was an important factor. The railroads offered land for sale and provided transportation for the western farmer's products.

Inventions of the 1870's also contributed to the successful settlement of the Great Plains. The lack of trees and water on the Plains presented difficulties for the western farmer. But barbed wire, first sold in 1874, pro-

Capture and Death of Sitting Bull (1890), a lithograph by Kurz and Allison; Denver Public Library

Advancing settlers fought the Indians for control of the Great Plains after the end of the Civil War in 1865. By 1890, the U.S. Army had defeated most of the Plains Indians.

vided a cheap substitute for the wood fence. Improved windmills allowed settlers to bring up water from far underground, and they became common sights on small farms by the 1890's. In addition, improvements in farm machinery produced more efficient plows and other machines that enabled the Plains farmer to cultivate large areas.

Closing of the frontier. The surge of eager homesteaders across the Great Plains left only the Indian Territory untouched. But white settlers demanded that the government make this area—now Oklahoma—available to them. In 1889, the government opened a large section of the Indian Territory that was not assigned for reservations. A wild land rush followed as thousands of pioneers scrambled for the best lots. Similar land rushes occurred in following years as more and more of the Indian Territory was opened to white settlement. But the conquest of the West had drawn to a close. In 1890, the Bureau of the Census declared in a report that no frontiers remained in the United States. The population west of the Mississippi River had grown remarkably—from 6,877,000 in 1870 to 16,775,000 in 1890.

Results of the westward movement

Patterns of migration. For almost 300 years, the westward movement influenced American history. However, the westward flow of people was not constant. Migration halted when Indian hostilities or wars with other nations made the frontiers unsafe. But once peace was restored, pioneers resumed their westward march. People also tended to migrate during prosperous times, when money was available. During periods of depression, migration often slowed to a trickle. Sometimes, as in the case of the Great Plains, technology spurred settlement. The invention of barbed wire and improvements in the windmill and in farm machinery helped open the Great Plains to settlers.

The frontier influence. The frontier was more than a place on a map. It was an experience that shaped many American institutions and ideas. The frontier environment presented challenges that produced creative solutions. For example, frontier settlements were much less complex than the established communities of the East. As a result, pioneers set up simple forms of government that met frontier needs. Similarly, the elaborate social customs of the East gave way to the simpler pleasures of barn dances and cornhusking contests.

The frontier experience promoted democracy. Established leaders rarely migrated from the East, and so the frontier brought a wide range of people into government. Class lines also blurred in frontier societies. It became difficult to distinguish a permanent upper or lower class because anyone might strike it rich or suffer a setback. The frontier's abundant resources were equally available to all.

The frontier experience also encouraged the development of certain "American" characteristics. Frontiers were isolated places, and so pioneers had to make many items they might otherwise have traded for or bought. They built their own houses and barns and produced their own food. They made their own candles, clothing, furniture, pots, tools, and other necessities. As jacks of all trades, pioneers became inventive and self-reliant. In addition, frontiers offered opportunities for success to those who worked hard. As a result, pioneers tended to be optimistic about the future and concerned with material wealth. Boastfulness and self-confidence emerged as frontier traits as well.

Unfortunately, the pioneers also became extremely wasteful because they lived among such plentiful natural resources. Pioneers cut down vast areas of forests, lost large amounts of gold and other minerals in careless mining operations, and exhausted the soil.

The continual pursuit of a better life made Americans more restless than their European ancestors. The French historian Alexis de Tocqueville remarked that in America "a man builds a house to spend his old age, and he sells it before the roof is on. . . . He brings a field into tillage and leaves other men to gather the crops; he embraces a profession and gives it up; he settles in a place, which he soon afterwards leaves to carry his changeable longings elsewhere." As people moved from place to place, they lost their attachment to a specific region. They began to identify more with the nation as a whole and to see themselves as "Americans." In that way, the westward movement promoted nationalism. Many historians believe that such frontier traits as nationalism, inventiveness, and optimism survive in the American character today. Jerome O. Steffen

Related articles in *World Book.* See the *History* section of the various state articles, such as **Texas** (History). See also:

Leaders of the westward movement

Austin	Houston, Samuel
Boone, Daniel	Lee, Jason
Bridger, James	Lewis, Meriwether
Carson, Kit	Long, Stephen Harriman
Chouteau	McLoughlin, John
Clark, George Rogers	Pike, Zebulon Montgomery
Clark, William	Putnam, Rufus
Colter, John	Sevier, John
Crockett, David	Smith, Jedediah Strong
Fargo, William	Sublette, William Lewis
Frémont, John Charles	Whitman, Marcus
Gist, Christopher	Young, Brigham

Early trails

Boston Post Road	Natchez Trace
Bozeman Trail	National Road
Braddock's Road	Oregon Trail
Chisholm Trail	Santa Fe Trail
El Camino Real	Wilderness Road
Mohawk Trail	

Other related articles

Astoria	Northwest Ordinance
Colonial life in America	Northwest Territory
Donner Pass	Ohio Company
Forty-Niner	Pioneer life in America
Franklin, State of	Public lands
French and Indian wars	Scout
Gold rush	Turner, Frederick
Homestead Act	Jackson
Hudson's Bay Company	United States, History
Indian wars	of the (Expansion;
Lewis and Clark expedition	pictures)
Louisiana Purchase	Watauga Association
Mexican War	Western frontier life
North West Company	

Outline

I. The first frontiers
    A. The earliest settlements
    B. The Old West

C. Regional conflict
D. The French and Indian War (1754-1763)
E. The Proclamation of 1763
F. Crossing the Appalachians
G. The Revolutionary War (1775-1783)

II. **Reaching the Mississippi River**
A. The Ordinance of 1785
B. The Northwest Ordinance
C. Indian conflicts
D. The Old Northwest
E. The Old Southwest

III. **Exploring and settling the Far West**
A. The Louisiana Purchase   E. The Oregon Trail
B. Exploration   F. The Southwest
C. The Santa Fe Trail   G. Utah
D. Texas   H. California

IV. **Settling the Great Plains**
A. The last Indian wars
B. Cattle frontiers
C. Homesteading on the Great Plains
D. Closing of the frontier

V. **Results of the westward movement**
A. Patterns of migration
B. The frontier influence

Questions

Who were the "mountain men"?
What were the ordinances of 1785 and 1787?
Why did Indian wars break out on the Great Plains?
What American characteristics developed on the frontier?
How did the War of 1812 affect westward migration?
What routes did the Forty-Niners follow to California?
Why was the Erie Canal important to both the East and the West?
What inventions aided the settlement of the Great Plains?
Why did Great Britain issue the Proclamation of 1763?
What land did the United States gain as a result of the Mexican War?

Additional resources

Level I

Fradin, Dennis B. *Pioneers.* Childrens Press, 1984.
Freedman, Russell. *Children of the Wild West.* Clarion, 1983.
Levenson, Dorothy. *Homesteaders and Indians.* Watts, 1971.
Steele, William O. *Westward Adventure: The True Stories of Six Pioneers.* Harcourt, 1962.
Stein, R. Conrad. *The Story of the Homestead Act.* Childrens Press, 1978.

Level II

Billington, Ray A., and Ridge, Martin. *Westward Expansion: A History of the American Frontier.* 5th ed. Macmillan, 1982.
Brown, Dee. *The Westerners.* Holt, 1974.
Lavender, David S. *The American Heritage History of the Great West.* Bonanza, 1982. First published in 1965.
Merk, Frederick. *History of the Westward Movement.* Knopf, 1978.
The Reader's Encyclopedia of the American West. Ed. by Howard R. Lamar. T. Y. Crowell, 1978.

Wet milling. See Corn (The wet-milling industry).

Wetland is an area of land where the water level remains near or above the surface of the ground for most of the year. Wetlands support a variety of plant and animal life and occur throughout the world.

There are several kinds of wetlands. The major types include *bogs, fens, marshes,* and *swamps.* Bogs and fens are found primarily in northern climates. Bogs are characterized by acidic soils and the heavy growth of mosses, particularly sphagnum moss. Grasses and sedges characterize fens, where the soil is neither highly acidic nor basic. Both bogs and fens contain large amounts of partially decayed plant life called *peat.* Some bogs and fens have trees and shrubs, but woody plants are absent from others. Marshes and swamps generally occur in warmer climates. Marshes are dominated by grasses, reeds, rushes, sedges, and other nonwoody plants. Swamps, on the other hand, include many trees and shrubs.

A number of shorebirds and waterfowl make their homes in wetlands. These areas also provide food and shelter for such mammals as mink, moose, and muskrats. The wet areas are valuable ecologically in other ways as well. For example, they help control floods because they hold back water. In addition, wetlands store large amounts of water for long periods.

Many people consider wetlands to be waste areas. For this reason, more than 35 per cent of the wetlands in the United States had been drained and destroyed by the 1970's. Since the early 1970's, however, there has been an increasing awareness of the ecological value of wetlands. In the United States, various programs have been undertaken to preserve remaining wetlands, especially coastal salt marshes.   Robert Leo Smith

See also **Bog; Marsh; Peat; Peat moss; Swamp.**

Wettin. See Windsor (family).

Weyden, Rogier van der. See Van der Weyden, Rogier.

Weyerhaeuser, *WY ur HOW zur,* **Frederick** (1834-1914), was the leading American lumberman of his time. He came to the United States from Germany at the age of 18. In 1856, he went to work for a lumber firm in Rock Island, Ill. Four years later, Weyerhaeuser and his brother-in-law, Frederick Denkmann, bought the mill. In 1870, they joined 16 other lumber firms and formed the Mississippi River Logging Company.

The new company floated rafts of logs down northern tributaries to the Mississippi. There, the logs were cut into lumber, which the firm sold in the Midwest. Through the years, Weyerhaeuser and his associates bought more and more woodland in the Midwest. In 1900, they incorporated the Weyerhaeuser Timber Company to purchase large areas of timberland in the Pacific Northwest. Weyerhaeuser became president of the firm. He was born in Niedersaulheim, near Mainz, in what is now West Germany.   Barry W. Poulson

Weyler y Nicolau, *WEH ee lehr ee NEE koh LAH oo,* **Valeriano,** *VAH lay RYAH noh* (1838-1930), a Spanish general, was appointed governor of Cuba in 1896. His cruel methods aroused such a storm of protest in the United States that the Spanish government recalled him in 1897. Weyler put down revolts in Cuba in 1868, fought in Spain against Spanish rebels known as *Carlists,* and served as minister of war. Weyler was born on the island of Majorca. He had the title Marquis of Tenerife.

J. Cary Davis

Weymouth, *WAY muhth,* Mass. (pop. 55,601), is on an inlet of Massachusetts Bay, about 12 miles (19 kilometers) southeast of Boston (see **Massachusetts** [political map]). Industries in Weymouth produce electronic equipment, furniture, and sheet metal. The Abigail Adams House, birthplace of the wife of President John Adams, stands in Weymouth. The town is the second oldest settlement in Massachusetts. Only Plymouth is older. Weymouth was founded in 1622 and incorporated in 1635. Weymouth claims it originated the New England town meeting form of government (see **Town meeting**).   Laurence A. Lewis

James Hudnall

A mother whale and her calf remain close together for at least a year. This baby humpback whale is resting on its mother's back as she swims along just beneath the surface of the water.

Whale

Whale is a huge sea animal that looks much like a fish. But whales are not fish. They belong instead to the group of animals called *mammals*. Other mammals include chimpanzees, dogs, and human beings. Like these mammals, whales have a highly developed brain and so are among the most intelligent of all animals.

Most whales are enormous creatures. One kind, the blue whale, is the largest animal that has ever lived. Blue whales may grow up to 100 feet (30 meters) long and can weigh more than 220 short tons (200 metric tons). However, some kinds of whales are much smaller. Belugas and narwhals, for example, grow only 10 to 15 feet (3 to 5 meters) long.

Whales have the same basic shape as fish, but they differ from fish in many ways. The most visible difference is the tail. Fish have *vertical* (up and down) tail fins, but whales have sideways tail fins. Fish breathe by

Michael A. Bigg, the contributor of this article, is Head of Marine Mammal Research at the Pacific Biological Station.

means of gills, which absorb dissolved oxygen from water. Whales, on the other hand, have lungs and must come to the surface to breathe. But they can hold their breath for long periods. One kind of whale, the sperm whale, can hold its breath up to 75 minutes.

Like other mammals, whales give birth to live young and feed them with milk produced by the mother's body. Most fish, however, lay eggs and do not feed their offspring. Whales are also *warm-blooded*—that is, their body temperature remains about the same regardless of the temperature of their surroundings. Almost all fish are *cold-blooded*. Their body temperature changes with changes in the temperature of the water.

Down through the ages, whales have gradually lost some of the characteristics of mammals. For example, hair covers the bodies of most mammals. But whales have only a few stiff hairs on the head. Most mammals also have four legs. A whale has no hind legs. The only traces of them that remain are two tiny hipbones. In addition, the front legs have developed into flippers, which help a whale steer and keep its balance.

People have hunted whales since prehistoric times. In early days, people killed whales for their meat and for whale oil, which they used as a fuel for lamps and for cooking. Today, people in Japan, as well as native peoples on several other Pacific islands and in Arctic regions, still eat whale meat. Whale oil and other parts of whales are used to make a variety of products, such as cosmetics, fertilizer, glue, medicines, and soap.

During the 1900's, whaling fleets have killed huge numbers of whales and so have seriously endangered the survival of some kinds of whales. For this reason, the International Whaling Commission limits the number of whales that may be killed each year. The International Whaling Commission also completely prohibits the killing of certain kinds of whales. The United States government forbids the import of whale products.

Whales belong to a group of mammals called *cetaceans* (pronounced *see TAY shuhnz*). This name comes from a Latin word meaning *large sea animal.* Scientists have identified at least 75 kinds of cetaceans. They divide the various kinds into two major groups—*baleen whales,* which do not have teeth, and *toothed whales,* which have teeth. This article discusses the chief kinds of whales in each group. It also describes the bodies of whales and the life of whales. Finally, it traces the history of whaling and looks at the future of whales.

Kinds of baleen whales

Baleen whales have no teeth. Instead, they have hundreds of thin plates in the mouth. A whale uses these plates to strain out food from the water. The plates are called *baleen* or *whalebone* and consist of the same material as human fingernails. The baleen hangs from the whale's upper jaw. The inside edges of the plates have brushlike fibers that filter out the food. Baleen whales feed mainly on *plankton*—drifting masses of tiny plants and animals.

There are 10 kinds of baleen whales. Scientists divide them into three groups: (1) right whales; (2) gray whales; and (3) rorquals.

Right whales have a thick, solid body and an unusually large head. The head of most right whales makes up about a third of the total body length. Right whales swim slowly, averaging about 3 miles (4.8 kilometers) per hour. They feed by swimming into a mass of plankton with their mouths open. Water flows through the baleen, and the plankton becomes entangled in the baleen fibers. There are three main kinds of right whales: (1) bowhead whales; (2) black right whales; and (3) pygmy right whales.

Bowhead whales, also called *Greenland whales,* have the longest baleen of all baleen whales. They have a

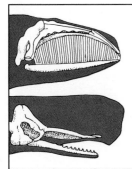

WORLD BOOK illustration by Marion Pahl

Baleen consists of thin plates that hang from the upper jaw of baleen whales. Baleen is made of the same type of material as human fingernails.

Peglike teeth grow from the lower jaw of nearly all species of toothed whales. Some species have teeth in the upper jaw as well.

William A. Watkins, Woods Hole Oceanographic Institution

A baleen whale has no teeth. Instead, it has hundreds of thin plates called *baleen.* It uses these plates to filter out food from the water. Baleen whales form one of the two major groups of whales. Toothed whales make up the other group.

highly arched mouth suited to the huge baleen, which may grow as long as 13 feet (4 meters). Bowhead whales are black with white areas on the tail and the tip of the lower jaw. They measure up to 60 feet (18 meters) long and live only in the Arctic Ocean.

Black right whales usually are called simply *right whales.* Compared with bowhead whales, they have shorter baleen and a less highly arched mouth. They are black, and some have white areas on the belly. Right whales live in all the oceans and may grow up to 60 feet (18 meters) long. They have a calluslike area called a *bonnet* on the snout.

Pygmy right whales, the smallest of all baleen whales, grow no longer than 20 feet (6 meters). Pygmy right whales live south of the equator and are seldom seen by people.

Gray whales live in the North Pacific Ocean. In spite of their name, they may be black or dark gray. Their skin is dotted with white blotches, some of which are shellfish called *barnacles.* Gray whales have a series of low humps on the lower back. The animals may measure up to 50 feet (15 meters) long. Gray whales eat small animals that live on the sandy ocean bottom. The whales suck up the sand and use their baleen to strain out the animals. They also feed on plankton and small fish.

Rorquals are baleen whales that have long grooves on the throat and chest. These grooves may number from 10 to 100 and are 1 to 2 inches (2.5 to 5 centimeters) deep. They enable a rorqual to open its mouth extremely wide and gulp enormous quantities of food and water. As the whale closes its mouth, its tongue forces the water out of the mouth through the baleen. The food becomes trapped inside the baleen and is swallowed by the whale. All rorquals have a *dorsal,* or back, fin, and so they are sometimes called *finback whales.* Most of them have a long, streamlined shape and can swim faster than other whales.

There are six kinds of rorquals. They are (1) blue whales; (2) Bryde's (pronounced *BROO dahs*) whales; (3) fin whales; (4) humpback whales; (5) minke whales; and (6) sei (*say*) whales.

Blue whales are the largest animals that have ever

Some kinds of whales

The illustrations on this page and the following page show some of the major kinds of baleen and toothed whales. Baleen whales include nearly all the extremely large types of whales. Among toothed whales, only the sperm whale can compare in size with baleen whales. Unlike baleen whales, the various kinds of toothed whales differ greatly in both size and appearance.

Baleen whales

Blue whale
Balaenoptera musculus
Up to 100 feet
(30 meters) long

Gray whale and calf
Eschrichtius robustus
Up to 50 feet
(15 meters) long

Sei whale
Balaenoptera borealis
Up to 55 feet
(17 meters) long

Black right whale
Balaena glacialis
Up to 60 feet
(18 meters) long

Fin whale
Balaenoptera physalus
Up to 80 feet
(24 meters) long

WORLD BOOK illustration by Harry McNaught

Bowhead whale
Balaena mysticetus
Up to 60 feet
(18 meters) long

Minke whale
Balaenoptera acutorostrata
Up to 30 feet
(9 meters) long

Humpback whale
Megaptera novaeangliae
Up to 50 feet
(15 meters) long

Toothed whales

Sperm whale
Physeter macrocephalus
Up to 60 feet
(18 meters) long

Killer whale
Orcinus orca
Up to 30 feet
(9 meters) long

Baird's beaked whale
Berardius bairdii
Up to 40 feet
(12 meters) long

Pilot whale
Globicephala melaena
Up to 28 feet
(8.5 meters) long

Narwhal
Monodon monoceros
Up to 15 feet
(5 meters) long

Beluga
Delphinapterus leucas
Up to 15 feet
(5 meters) long

lived. They may grow up to 100 feet (30 meters) long and can weigh more than 220 short tons (200 metric tons). They are dull blue. But some of them have growths of tiny yellowish, or sulfur-colored, plants called *diatoms* on the belly. For this reason, blue whales are sometimes called *sulfur-bottom whales.* Blue whales live in all the oceans but are rare. They feed almost entirely on small shrimplike animals called *krill,* which are part of the plankton.

Bryde's whales live only in tropical and subtropical seas. They are bluish-gray with a white belly and may reach 45 feet (14 meters) in length. Unlike other rorquals, Bryde's whales eat mainly small fish and *squid,* an octopuslike animal.

Fin whales are black on top and whitish below. They have cream-colored baleen in the front of the mouth and bluish-gray in the back. The lower jaw is white on the right side and black on the left. Fin whales grow up to 80 feet (24 meters) long and live in all the oceans. Fin whales that live south of the equator eat krill, but those in the Northern Hemisphere also eat anchovies, herring, and other small fish.

Humpback whales grow no longer than 50 feet (15 meters) and are chubby compared with other rorquals. The humpback whale's most outstanding feature is its exceptionally long flippers, which may be a third as long as its body. The body is black on top and white underneath. Wartlike knobs cover the head and flippers. In spite of its name, the humpback whale has no hump on its back. Humpback whales live in all the oceans and often swim in coastal waters. They feed chiefly on krill but also eat small fish.

Minke whales, the smallest of the rorquals, measure no more than 30 feet (9 meters) long. They are blue-gray on top and white below. Minke whales dwell in all the seas. Those that live in the Southern Hemisphere feed on krill, but those in the Northern Hemisphere eat mainly small fish.

Sei whales look much like small fin whales, except that the lower jaw is black on both sides. They may grow up to 55 feet (17 meters) long. Sei whales live in all the oceans, but the greatest numbers dwell in the wa-

Bruce Coleman Inc.

Toothed whales use their teeth only to capture prey, not to chew it. All toothed whales swallow their food whole.

ters around Antarctica. They feed on krill and other plankton animals.

Kinds of toothed whales

Unlike baleen whales, toothed whales have teeth. There are about 65 kinds of toothed whales. They differ greatly in size, in shape, and in the number of teeth they have. Some toothed whales eat fish, and others eat such animals as cuttlefish and squid.

Scientists divide the various kinds of toothed whales into five groups: (1) sperm whales; (2) beaked whales; (3) belugas and narwhals; (4) dolphins and porpoises; and (5) river dolphins. Most people do not consider dolphins and porpoises to be whales. But scientists classify them as toothed whales because they have the same basic body features as other toothed whales.

Sperm whales, also called *cachalots* (*KASH uh lahts*), are by far the largest toothed whales. They grow up to 60 feet (18 meters) long and range in color from blue-gray to black. Sperm whales have an enormous, square-shaped head. It makes up about a third of the total body length. The lower jaw is long and extremely thin. It has 16 to 30 peglike teeth on each side. The upper jaw has no visible teeth.

Almost all sperm whales live only in tropical and *temperate* (mild) waters, though a few males spend the summer in polar seas. They dive to great depths for food, which consists mainly of cuttlefish and squid. They also eat certain fishes, such as barracuda and sharks. The sperm whale has a small relative, the pygmy sperm whale, which grows only about 12 feet (3.7 meters) long.

Beaked whales have a beaklike snout and only two or four teeth in the lower jaw. They have no upper teeth. Some kinds of beaked whales grow only about 15 feet (5 meters) long, and others reach 40 feet (12 meters). Beaked whales live in all the oceans and feed mainly on squid and fish.

Belugas and narwhals measure 10 to 15 feet (3 to 5 meters) long. Narwhals and most belugas live in the Arctic, but some belugas are found farther south. Belugas and narwhals eat mostly fish and squid. Belugas are milk-white when fully grown and are often called *white whales.* They have 32 to 40 teeth. Narwhals are grayish on top and whitish underneath and have dark spots over the entire body. They have only two teeth. The teeth of female narwhals remain buried in the upper jaw. Among most males, the left tooth develops into a spiral tusk up to 9 feet (2.7 meters) long.

Dolphins and porpoises live in all the oceans. Most porpoises grow 4 to 6 feet (1.2 to 1.8 meters) long, making them the smallest cetaceans. Dolphins range from about 7 to 30 feet (2.1 to 9 meters) long. The largest dolphins include killer whales and pilot whales. For more information on dolphins and porpoises, see **Dolphin; Killer whale; Pilot whale; River dolphin.**

River dolphins, unlike other cetaceans, do not live in the sea. They live in the muddy waters of such rivers as the Amazon in South America and the Ganges in India. They measure about 8 feet (2.4 meters) and have a long beak and poorly developed eyesight.

The bodies of whales

Several features of the whale body suggest that whales are closely related to hoofed mammals, particu-

The body of a female fin whale

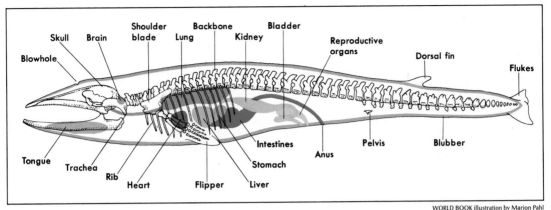

WORLD BOOK illustration by Marion Pahl

larly split-hoofed mammals, such as cattle and deer. Some scientists believe that whales developed from primitive meat-eating mammals. The oldest whale fossil yet discovered dates from about 45 million years ago. However, scientists think that whales probably began to develop as early as 70 million years ago.

Whales basically have the same body features as other mammals. But whales have many special characteristics suited to living in water. Also, living in water enables them to reach enormous sizes. A land animal can grow only so big before its bones and muscles can no longer support its body weight. But the *buoyancy* (lift) of water helps support a whale's body and makes it possible for whales to grow far larger than any land animal.

Body shape. Whales have a highly streamlined shape, which enables them to swim with a minimum of resistance. Their shape resembles that of fish. But a whale's powerful tail fins, called *flukes,* are horizontal instead of vertical like the tail fins of a fish. A whale propels itself by moving its flukes up and down. Most fish swim by swinging their tail fins from side to side.

The ancestors of whales lived on land and had four legs. But after these animals moved into the sea, their body features gradually changed. Over millions of years, the front legs developed into flippers and the hind legs disappeared. A whale uses its flippers to help in steering and in keeping its balance.

Skeleton. A whale's backbone, ribcage, and shoulder blades resemble those of other mammals. The absence of hind legs, however, distinguishes the whale from most other mammals. Two small bones buried in the hip

muscles are all that remain of the whale's hind legs.

Almost all mammals have seven neck vertebrae. But in whales, these vertebrae are greatly compressed into a short length or joined together into one bone. This feature keeps the head from moving about as a whale swims. It also contributes to the whale's streamlined shape by joining the head directly to the body.

Skin and blubber. Whales have smooth, rubbery skin that slips easily through the water. Most mammals are covered with hair, which holds warm air next to the body. Whales, however, do not have a coat of hair to provide them with insulation. A few bristles on the head are all the hair that whales have.

Beneath the skin, whales have a layer of fat called *blubber,* which keeps them warm. Actually, rorquals have more difficulty getting rid of excess heat than keeping warm. Their blubber, therefore, never grows more than about 6 inches (15 centimeters) thick. In contrast, right whales may have a layer of blubber up to 20 inches (50 centimeters) thick. If food is scarce, whales can live off their blubber for a long time. Blubber is lighter than water, and so it also increases the buoyancy of whales.

Respiratory system. Like all other mammals, whales have lungs. They must therefore come to the surface regularly to breathe. Baleen whales usually breathe every 5 to 15 minutes, but they can go as long as 40 minutes without breathing. A sperm whale can hold its breath up to 75 minutes.

Whales can go for long periods without breathing for several reasons. Their muscles store much more oxygen than do the muscles of other mammals. Human beings,

WORLD BOOK illustration by Marion Pahl

A rapid forward roll enables a whale to surface, breathe, and begin a new dive in one continuous motion. This movement gives the whale only about two seconds to exhale and inhale. Many kinds of whales throw their *flukes* (tail fins) clear of the water when beginning a deep dive.

Jen and Des Bartlett, Bruce Coleman Inc.

Impressive leaps from the water are performed by some species of whales. Scientists call this behavior *breaching.* The right whale shown above is breaching off the coast of Argentina.

for example, store only about 13 per cent of their oxygen supply in the muscles, compared with about 41 per cent for whales. During a dive, a whale's body greatly reduces the blood flow to the muscles but keeps a normal flow to the heart and brain. The heartbeat also slows, which helps save oxygen. After a dive, a whale must take several breaths to recharge its tissues with oxygen before diving again.

When a whale comes up to breathe, it rolls forward as it breaks the surface. This movement gives the whale only about two seconds to blow out and breathe in up to 2,100 quarts (2,000 liters) of air. Whales breathe through nostrils, called *blowholes,* at the top of the head. Toothed whales have one blowhole, but baleen whales have two. Powerful muscles and valves open the blowholes wide for whales to breathe, and then the openings snap tightly shut.

When a whale exhales, it produces a cloud called a

blow or *spout.* The blow consists chiefly of water vapor. It may also include mucus and oil droplets. Experts can identify the species of a whale by the height and shape of its blow. Blows range in height from about 6 feet (1.8 meters) in humpback whales to 25 feet (8 meters) in sperm whales. Right whales have a double V-shaped blow, and rorquals have a pear-shaped one. Sperm whales blow forward and to the left.

Senses. Whales have no sense of smell, and most species have poor eyesight. Studies indicate that some kinds of toothed whales may have a limited sense of taste, but most whales cannot taste. However, all whales have well-developed senses of touch and hearing. Their keen hearing provides them with most of their information about their surroundings. They can hear an extremely wide range of sounds, including low- and high-pitched sounds far beyond the range of human hearing. Unlike people, whales can also tell from what direction a sound is coming underwater.

Toothed whales produce sounds within the *nasal sac system,* a series of air-filled pouches around the blowhole. The whales locate underwater objects by listening for the echoes produced when objects reflect the sounds. From the echoes, they determine the distance to an object and the direction in which it lies. This method of navigation is called *echolocation.* Biologists do not know for sure whether baleen whales echolocate, but some experts believe that they do.

The life of whales

Reproduction. Most kinds of whales mate during a specific season. The male, called a *bull,* and the female, called a *cow,* engage in playful courting as part of the mating process. During the courting, the whales may stroke each other with their flippers. Humpback and right whales may also make spectacular leaps from the water. Humpback whales sometimes hold each other with their long, curved flippers.

The pregnancy period varies from species to species, but in most kinds of whales it lasts 10 to 12 months. A

Paul Thomas, Black Star

A visible cloud called a *spout* is produced when a whale exhales through its *blowhole,* or nostril, *left.* Toothed whales have one blowhole. Baleen whales have two.

A whale's short, wide nasal passage, *below,* helps the whale breathe quickly.

WORLD BOOK illustration by Marion Pahl

The birth of a whale, such as that of a bottle-nosed dolphin shown above, occurs tailfirst. In many cases, other female whales help the mother while she gives birth.

A newborn whale begins swimming immediately, but it depends on its mother for food and protection. As soon as it is born, the mother helps it to the surface to take its first breath.

female sperm whale, however, carries her baby 16 months. In almost all cases, a whale has only one baby, called a *calf,* at a time. Twins rarely occur. One or more females may help the mother during birth. Whales are already giant animals at birth. Newborn blue whales, for example, average about 2 short tons (1.8 metric tons) in weight and 23 feet (7 meters) in length. As soon as the baby is born, the mother nudges it to the surface to take its first breath.

The mother whale is highly protective of her baby and stays close to it for at least a year. Like all other mammals, whales nurse their young. The female has special breast muscles that pump milk into the baby's mouth. Whale milk is highly concentrated and much richer in fat, protein, and minerals than the milk of land mammals. This rich food helps the calves grow amazingly fast. Baby blue whales gain about 200 pounds (91 kilograms) per day. Young blue and fin whales nurse up to seven months. Other whales nurse for nearly a year.

Group life. Toothed whales appear to be more socially organized than baleen whales. Bottle-nosed whales and many species of dolphins swim in herds of 100 to 1,000. Sperm whales form several kinds of smaller groups. A "harem" school consists of one adult male and several females and their young. Females with young calves form "nursery" groups. "Bachelor" schools are composed of playful young males.

Some types of baleen whales, such as blue and sei whales, live mostly in family groups. Such a family consists of a male, a female, and one or two offspring. Baleen whales sometimes gather in large groups to feed. Humpback whales migrate in groups—mothers and their young first, males and nonpregnant females next, and pregnant females last.

Whales communicate with one another by making a wide variety of sounds called *phonations.* Whales can easily hear these sounds over great distances. Microphones have picked up the deep moans of bowhead whales at a distance of 50 miles (80 kilometers). The best-known whale sounds are the songs of humpback whales. Each song consists of a series of sounds that

lasts 7 to 30 minutes and is then repeated. All humpback whales produce basically the same song. The song changes gradually over the life of each individual. Scientists do not yet know what information whales communicate through phonations.

Migrations. Most kinds of baleen whales migrate between polar and tropical regions. The cold waters of the Arctic and Antarctic have the richest concentrations of plankton. The whales spend the summer in these areas, feeding and storing up large reserves of blubber. As winter approaches, the polar waters freeze over and the whales move to warmer seas near the equator. There they mate and the females that are already pregnant give birth. The warm waters provide a comfortable environment for the babies, which lack a thick layer of blubber to keep them warm.

In the tropics, adult whales live mostly off their blubber because food is scarce. Mother whales convert part of their blubber into milk for the babies. By late spring, the young whales are large enough to move with the group to the polar feeding area.

Two kinds of baleen whales do not migrate. Bryde's whales live in the tropics the year around, and bowhead whales never leave the Arctic. Most species of toothed whales also do not migrate. Belugas and narwhals stay in Arctic waters. Most sperm whales live only in tropical or temperate seas. A few males spend the summer in polar waters.

Life span. The life span of whales ranges from 15 years for the common porpoise to 60 or more years for sperm whales. Human hunters account for many whale deaths. But aside from people, whales have almost no natural enemies. Killer whales, which are dolphins, occasionally attack young whales, small dolphins, and weak or diseased baleen whales. However, most whales that escape the hunter's harpoon probably live to old age and die of natural causes.

Some whales die after stranding themselves on a beach. In some cases, a whale swims ashore alone. In other instances, an entire school of whales becomes stranded. Only toothed whales beach themselves in

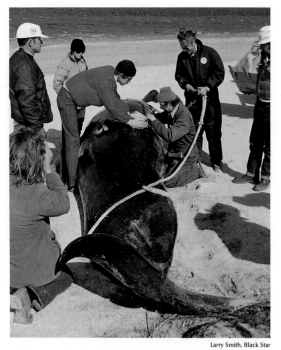

Scientists examine a beached whale that died after stranding itself ashore. Studies of beached whales and of whales killed by whalers provide most of our knowledge about whale anatomy.

groups. People often return beached whales to the sea, but most swim back onto the beach. Stranded whales cannot live long. Out of water, the whales may overheat, become crushed by their own weight, or drown when the tide covers their blowholes.

Scientists do not know for certain what causes beachings, but they have proposed a number of explanations. Some suggest that parasites in the whales' ears or brains interfere with the animals' ability to echolocate. Others suggest that gently sloping beaches reflect sounds over the heads of the whales. As a result, the whales are not warned that they are swimming onto a beach. Still other scientists think that a variety of these and other causes may be responsible for beachings.

The early days of whaling

The first whalers. People began to hunt whales in prehistoric times. At first, they simply killed and ate whales that had stranded on beaches. People who lived in what is now Norway were probably the first whalers to seek out and kill whales in the sea. Norwegian rock carvings about 4,000 years old show a variety of whaling scenes. The earliest written record of Norwegian whaling dates from about A.D. 890. However, this record does not reveal what methods the whalers used or the types of whales they hunted.

The Basque people of southern France and northern Spain established the first large whaling industry. During the 900's, the Basques began to hunt baleen whales in the Bay of Biscay, which lies west of France and north of Spain. They first hunted near the shore from small open boats. The whalers maneuvered their boat close enough to a whale so that one of them could

harpoon it. A rope connected the harpoon to the boat. In time, the whale became exhausted. The whalers then killed it with sharp lances and towed the body to shore for processing.

During the 1200's, the Basques began to equip large sailing ships for whaling voyages. Each ship carried several small whaleboats from which the whalers set out to kill whales. After killing a whale, the whalers brought it alongside the ship. Then with long-handled knives, they peeled off the blubber in strips as the body turned over and over in the water. The crew used ropes to lift the blubber onto the ship. The whalers removed the baleen from the whale and discarded the rest of the body.

The whalers stored blubber and baleen on the ship until they had a full load. The ship then returned to shore, where the blubber was cooked to make oil. The Basques burned whale oil in lamps and used baleen in such articles as corsets, dress hoops, and whips.

The Basques chiefly hunted one type of whale, which became known as the *right whale.* The Basques considered it the right, or correct, whale to hunt because it swims slowly, floats when dead, and has great quantities of baleen. After right whales became scarce in the Bay of Biscay, the Basque whalers ventured farther out to sea. During the 1500's, their voyages even carried them as far as the coast of Newfoundland.

The growth of European whaling. Many European nations began whaling during the 1600's. Dutch and English explorers reported that the Arctic waters were filled with whales. These reports attracted whalers from many countries, including Denmark, England, Germany, and the Netherlands. Bowhead whales were especially plentiful around Svalbard, a group of islands north of Norway. Svalbard became the main center of Arctic whaling. The Dutch and the English in particular developed profitable whaling industries there. At first, they employed Basques to kill and cut up the whales, but they soon learned to do these jobs themselves. By 1720, whalers had killed all the whales around Svalbard and moved on to other areas of the Arctic.

American whaling. The first American whalers were Indians, who hunted from shore in much the same way as the early Basques. During the early 1600's, the American colonists began to hunt right whales off the Atlantic coast. The colonists used baleen from these whales in making such products as corsets, fishing rods, and umbrellas. In 1712, a ship hunting for right whales was carried far from land by a storm. The ship came upon a school of sperm whales, killed one, and brought it back to port. This chance event began the sperm-whaling industry in America.

Shore-based whaling for right whales declined during the 1700's, but sperm whaling developed into a major industry by the end of the century. Nantucket and New Bedford, Mass., became the chief American whaling ports. By 1770, Americans were hunting sperm whales throughout the Atlantic Ocean. American sperm whaling expanded into the South Pacific Ocean about 1790.

Whalers obtained three valuable substances from sperm whales. The most important was *sperm oil,* which came from the head and the blubber. People used the oil as a fuel for lamps and as a lubricant. Whalers also took another oil called *spermaceti* from the sperm whale's head. This oil became the chief ingredient in candles. The third substance, called *ambergris,* came from the intestines of sperm whales. It was used as a base for expensive perfumes. Whalers found ambergris in only a few of the whales they killed. Nevertheless, the substance brought them much income because perfume manufacturers paid extremely high prices for it.

American whalers used basically the same methods as European whalers. However, the Americans cooked the blubber on board ship instead of storing it and carrying it back to land for processing. They extracted the oil by *trying out* (cooking) the blubber in large iron pots called *try pots.* Unlike blubber, the oil did not spoil during long voyages through the tropics. It also required much less storage space than blubber.

The American sperm-whaling industry had its greatest prosperity from about 1820 to 1850. During this period, it employed more than 70,000 persons and killed about 10,000 whales annually. The whaling fleet consisted of over 730 ships, which sailed all the oceans. Much whaling took place in the Pacific Ocean, and San Francisco became a major whaling port. By this time, many voyages lasted as long as four to five years. Whaling ships sent their whale oil home by cargo ship from time to time and continued whaling.

The decline of American sperm whaling began with the California gold rush in 1849. Many crew members of whaling ships deserted to seek their fortunes prospecting for gold. But the American Civil War (1861-1865) dealt the most severe blow to the whaling industry. During the war, Southern ships sank many whaling vessels. Whaling began to revive after the war, but the birth of the U.S. petroleum industry posed a new threat. Petroleum products soon replaced sperm oil as a fuel for lamps and spermaceti as a base for candles. American sperm whaling declined throughout the late 1800's and

early 1900's. After 1925, all that remained of the industry were a few shore-based whaling operations along the Pacific coast.

Modern whaling

Hunting techniques. During the 1860's, a Norwegian whaling captain named Svend Foyn invented a new type of harpoon and a gun to fire it. His harpoon was tipped with a bomb that would explode inside the whale and cause death much sooner than an ordinary harpoon. Foyn mounted the harpoon gun on the bow of another of his inventions—a steam-powered whaling boat. This *catcher boat* could travel much faster than the sailing ships and small open boats that whalers had used previously. Foyn's boat and harpoon enabled whalers to hunt rorquals, whose great speed and power had formerly protected them from whalers. About 1900, whalers began to hunt the enormous rorqual populations in the waters surrounding Antarctica.

By 1925, whalers also had developed the *factory ship.* A factory ship was a huge vessel that was served by a fleet of catcher boats and was equipped to process a wide variety of whale products. A modern factory ship fleet included up to 12 diesel-powered catcher boats and a crew of about 400. Spotters in airplanes or helicopters helped the whalers in their search for whales. In addition, the ships had sonar to trace whales underwater. These advanced techniques enabled the crew of a catcher boat to track down and kill any whale that they spotted. After harpooning a whale, the whalers pumped air into its body cavity to keep it afloat. Later, the catcher boats or special *buoy boats* towed the whales to the factory ship. An iron claw was attached to the whale's flukes, and the animal was hauled onto the ship.

Modern whaling techniques proved highly effective. As a result, more whales were killed during the

Detail of *Panorama of a Whaling Voyage Round the World* (about 1847), a painting by Benjamin Russell and Caleb P. Purrington; New Bedford Whaling Museum, New Bedford, Mass.

American whaling flourished throughout the first half of the 1800's. The scene above shows hunters killing right whales off the northwest coast of North America in the 1840's.

Modern whaling vessels enabled whalers to kill and process whales efficiently. In the picture at the left, taken during the 1970's, a Soviet *factory ship* tows a dead whale to be processed on board. *Catcher boats,* such as the one on the right, were used to chase down and kill the whales.

Matt Herron, Black Star

first 40 years of the 1900's than during the preceding four centuries. The number of whales killed worldwide peaked in 1962, when whalers killed more than 66,000. Excessive killing, however, greatly reduced the world's whale populations and jeopardized the survival of some species. The whale catch thus declined sharply in the late 1960's and the 1970's. By 1980, the whale catch had decreased to about 15,000. By 1988, all commercial whaling had ceased.

Processing whale products. Processing began after a whale had been hauled aboard a factory ship or to a shore-based factory. First, workers called *flensers* used long knives to cut slits along the whale's body. The flensers then peeled off the whale's blubber and cut it up. The blubber then was placed in cookers, which re-

Steve McCutcheon

Eskimo whale hunters, *above,* strip a whale of its meat and blubber. Only Eskimos and other peoples who have traditionally relied on whales for food are legally permitted to hunt whales.

moved the oil. After the blubber was peeled off, workers called *lemmers* cut up the rest of the body. They cut the meat to be sold as human food into large chunks and froze it. The bones, the rest of the meat, and some internal organs were cooked to make such products as cattle feed and fertilizer.

Today, whales killed for scientific purposes are sometimes later used in making various products, including cosmetics, glue, medicines, and soap. In addition, people in Japan eat the meat of whales killed for scientific use.

The future of whales

Many of the larger kinds of whales face an uncertain future. Whalers have killed so many blue, bowhead, humpback, and right whales that those species have been threatened with extinction. Overhunting has also greatly reduced the number of fin and sei whales.

In 1946, the major whaling countries formed the International Whaling Commission (IWC) to protect whales from overhunting and to regulate the whaling industry. For many years, the IWC established unrealistically high *quotas* (limits) on the number of whales that could be killed. During the 1960's, the commission began to set reduced quotas and banned the hunting of several whale species. IWC quotas declined further during the 1970's, and in 1979 the commission limited the use of factory ships.

In 1982, the IWC voted for a *moratorium* (temporary halt) on commercial whaling, beginning with the 1985 and the 1986 hunting seasons. By 1988, all nations had halted commercial whaling. Several nations, however, have continued to kill whales for purposes of scientific research, a practice that has stirred controversy. The

IWC planned to determine by 1990 whether whale numbers had grown enough to support renewed hunting.

The United States has strongly opposed commercial whaling. In 1971, the U.S. government ordered an end to commercial U.S. whaling and outlawed the importation of whale products. Federal law also calls for *sanctions* (penalties) against any nation that disregards IWC rules.

Public opinion in the United States, Canada, and some European countries has been strongly opposed to commercial whaling. For example, in 1973, antiwhaling groups agreed to *boycott* (refuse to buy) products from Japan and the Soviet Union until those countries stopped commercial whaling. Public opinion also played a major role in the passage of the IWC moratorium on commercial whaling.

The IWC permits native peoples who have traditionally depended on whales for food to continue hunting whales. These peoples include Eskimos of Alaska, Greenland, and the Soviet Union. They eat whale blubber, meat, and skin. The IWC regulates which whales these people may hunt and the hunting methods used.

Most biologists believe that all species of whales have been saved for the present. However, complete protection of endangered species must continue for a long time to allow them to recover from years of extreme overhunting. Even with protection, some species may not be able to recover. For example, the right whale has been fully protected since 1935, but it has not yet made a significant comeback.

Every year, the number of people in the world increases about $1\frac{1}{2}$ per cent, and so the demand for food rises constantly. This fact may threaten the survival of whales. If the population does not level off, people may have to compete with whales for food in the sea. Some nations have already begun experimental fishing for krill, the main food of whales in Antarctic waters.

Scientific classification. Whales belong to the order Cetacea, which is divided into two suborders. Toothed whales form the suborder Odontoceti. Baleen whales make up the suborder Mysticeti.   Michael A. Bigg

Related articles in *World Book* include:

Ambergris	Killer whale
Antarctica (Animal life)	Krill
Blubber	Narwhal
Cetacean	Pilot whale
Colonial life in America (picture:	River dolphin
Colonial whaling)	Sperm whale
Dolphin	Spermaceti
Greenpeace	

Outline

I. **Kinds of baleen whales**
  A. Right whales
  B. Gray whales
  C. Rorquals
II. **Kinds of toothed whales**
  A. Sperm whales
  B. Beaked whales
  C. Belugas and narwhals
  D. Dolphins and porpoises
  E. River dolphins
III. **The bodies of whales**
  A. Body shape
  B. Skeleton
  C. Skin and blubber
  D. Respiratory system
  E. Senses
IV. **The life of whales**
  A. Reproduction
  B. Group life
  C. Migrations
  D. Life span
V. **The early days of whaling**
  A. The first whalers
  B. The Basque people
C. The growth of European whaling
D. American whaling
VI. **Modern whaling**
  A. Hunting techniques
  B. Processing whale products
VII. **The future of whales**

Questions

Why can whales grow far larger than any land animal?
What are the two major groups of whales?
In what ways do whales differ from fish?
How do whales communicate with one another?
What functions does blubber serve for a whale?
Why do beached whales die?
What events led to the decline of American whaling?
How has the International Whaling Commission acted to protect whales from the threat of extinction?
What were some uses of whale products?

Reading and Study Guide

See *Whale* in the Research Guide/Index, Volume 22, for a *Reading and Study Guide.*

Additional resources

Level I
Bunting, Eve. *The Sea World Book of Whales.* Harcourt, 1986. First published in 1980.
McGowen, Tom. *Album of Whales.* Macmillan, 1980.
Patent, Dorothy Hinshaw. *All About Whales.* Holiday House, 1987.

Level II
Baker, Mary L. *Whales, Dolphins, and Porpoises of the World.* Doubleday, 1987.
Minasian, Stanley M. and others. *The World's Whales: The Complete Illustrated Guide.* Smithsonian Books, 1984.
Watson, Lyall. *Sea Guide to Whales of the World.* Dutton, 1981.

Whale shark. See Shark (Kinds; picture).

Whaling. See Whale (The early days of whaling; Modern whaling).

Wharton, Edith (1862-1937), was an American author. She became known for her psychological examination of the moral and social values of middle-class and upper-class society. Much of Wharton's fiction explores contrasts in the traditional cultural values of specific regions of the United States and Europe. Wharton also described the gradual erosion of these values from generation to generation.

Wharton's best-known works focus on New York City during the 1800's and early 1900's. She won the 1921 Pulitzer Prize for fiction for her novel *The Age of Innocence* (1920). The book provides a satirical view of aristocratic society in New York City during the 1870's. Her other works about New York City include the novels *The House of Mirth* (1905) and *The Custom of the Country* (1913) and a book of stories, *Old New York* (1924).

Perhaps Wharton's most popular work is the short novel *Ethan Frome* (1911). It tells a starkly realistic story of New England farming people.

Wharton was born in New York City into a socially prominent and wealthy family. Her maiden name was Edith Newbold Jones. She began writing as a child but quit shortly after marrying Edward Wharton in 1885. She later returned to writing, partly as a reaction against her unintellectual socialite environment. In 1911, Wharton settled permanently in France. She became a close friend of the American author Henry James, who strongly influenced her work. She wrote a vivid description of James in her autobiography, *A Backward Glance* (1934).   John B. Vickery

A field of ripened wheat is golden-brown. Wheat fields cover more of the world's farmland than any other food crop.

J. C. Allen & Son

Wheat

Wheat is the world's most important food crop. Hundreds of millions of people throughout the world depend on foods made from the *kernels* (seeds or grains) of the wheat plant. The kernels are ground into flour to make breads, cakes, cookies, crackers, macaroni, spaghetti, and other foods.

Wheat is a member of the grass family. It belongs to the group of grasses called *cereals* or *cereal grains.* Other important cereals include rice, corn, barley, sorghum, oats, millet, triticale, and rye.

Wheat covers more of the earth's surface than any other food crop. The leading wheat-producing countries include China, the Soviet Union, the United States, India, France, and Canada. The world's farmers grow about 570 million short tons (517 million metric tons) of wheat a year. This amount could fill a freight train stretching around the world about $2\frac{1}{2}$ times.

Long before the beginnings of agriculture, people gathered wild wheat for food. Scholars believe that about 11,000 years ago people in the Middle East took the first steps toward agriculture. Wheat was one of the first plants they grew. In time, farmers raised more grain than they needed to feed themselves. As a result, many people did not have to produce their own food and were freed to develop other useful skills. These changes led to the building of towns and cities, the expansion of trade, and the development of the great civilizations of ancient Egypt, India, and Mesopotamia.

Early farmers probably selected kernels from their best wheat plants to use as seeds for planting the next crop. In this way, certain desired qualities were passed on from one generation of wheat to the next. Such practices resulted in the gradual development of improved kinds of wheat. During the 1900's, scientists have developed many new wheat varieties that produce large amounts of grain and can resist cold, disease, insects, and other crop threats. As a result, wheat production has risen dramatically.

Uses of wheat

Food for people. Wheat is the most important food for more than a third of the world's people. In many areas of the world, wheat appears in some form at nearly every meal. Wheat is eaten chiefly in bread and other foods prepared from wheat flour. People also eat wheat in macaroni, spaghetti, and other forms of *pasta* and in breakfast cereal.

Wheat flour is excellent for baking because it contains a protein substance called *gluten* that makes dough elastic. This elasticity allows dough containing yeast to rise. About two-thirds of all the wheat flour milled is used by commercial bakers to bake bread, buns, cakes, cookies, crackers, pies, rolls, and other goods. In addition, wheat flour and baking mixes containing wheat flour are sold for use at home.

To produce wheat flour, millers grind the wheat kernels into a fine powder. Wheat kernels are rich in *nutri-*

Lavoy I. Croy, the contributor of this article, is Professor of Agronomy at Oklahoma State University.

ents (nourishing substances), including protein, starch, vitamin E, and the B vitamins—niacin, riboflavin, and thiamine. The kernels also contain such essential minerals as iron and phosphorus.

Whole wheat flour is made from the entire kernel. It therefore contains the nutrients found in all parts of the kernel. To produce white flour, however, millers grind only the soft, white inner part of the kernel, which is called the *endosperm*. The endosperm contains the gluten and nearly all the starch in the kernel. But white flour lacks the vitamins and minerals found in the *bran*—the kernel's tough covering—and the *germ,* which is the *embryo* (undeveloped stage) of a new wheat plant inside the kernel. In the United States, Canada, and many other countries, millers and bakers add B vitamins and iron to most white flour to increase its food value. Such flour is called *enriched flour.* See **Flour.**

Pasta. Wheat is the chief ingredient in macaroni, spaghetti, and other forms of pasta. Most pasta is made from *semolina*—the coarsely ground grain of durum wheat. Manufacturers of pasta products add water and other ingredients to the semolina to form a thick paste or dough. They force this paste through machines that form it into macaroni, noodles, spaghetti, and other shapes. See **Pasta.**

Breakfast foods. Many breakfast foods are made with wheat. Ready-to-eat breakfast cereals containing wheat include bran flakes, puffed wheat, shredded wheat biscuits, and wheat flakes. Cooked breakfast cereals made with wheat include cracked wheat, farina, malted cereals, rolled wheat, and whole wheat meal.

Livestock feed. Some wheat germ and bran that remain after white flour is milled are used in feeds for poultry and other livestock. Farm animals also eat wheat when it is economical to feed it to them.

Other uses. Wheat is also the source of certain substances that are used to improve the nutritional value or

Food value of whole-grain wheat

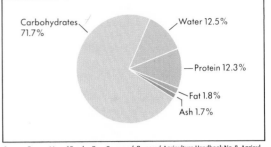

Carbohydrates 71.7%
Water 12.5%
Protein 12.3%
Fat 1.8%
Ash 1.7%

Source: *Composition of Foods—Raw, Processed, Prepared,* Agriculture Handbook No. 8, Agricultural Research Service, U.S. Department of Agriculture. Data are for hard, red winter wheat.

flavor of foods. Vitamin-rich wheat germ and wheat germ oil are added to some breakfast cereals, specialty breads, and other foods. Glutamic acid obtained from wheat is used in making *monosodium glutamate* (*MSG*). Monosodium glutamate is a salt that has little flavor of its own, but it brings out the flavor of other foods. See **Monosodium glutamate.**

The stems of wheat plants are dried to make straw, which can be woven into baskets and hats, made into strawboard for boxes, or used as fertilizer. Industry uses the outer coatings of wheat kernels to polish metal and glass. Adhesives made from wheat starch hold layers of plywood together. Alcohol made from wheat is used as a fuel and in manufacturing synthetic rubber and other products.

The wheat plant

Young wheat plants have a bright green color and look like grass. The mature plants grow 2 to 5 feet (0.6 to 1.5 meters) tall. They turn golden-brown when ripe.

Structure. The main parts of a mature wheat plant are the roots, stem, leaves, and head. Wheat has two

WORLD BOOK photo by Ralph J. Brunke

Foods made with wheat are a major part of the diet for over a third of the world's people. Such foods include bread, cake, breakfast cereal, cookies, crackers, and pasta.

J. C. Allen & Son

Feed for farm animals often contains wheat. The feed may include the wheat germ and bran that remain after white flour is milled, or it may contain wheat unsuitable for milling.

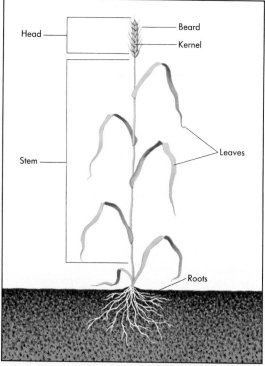

WORLD BOOK diagram by James Teason

The wheat plant grows up to 5 feet (1.5 meters) high and turns golden-brown when ripe. The head of the plant holds from 30 to 50 kernels of grain. Many kinds of wheat have bristly hairs, called *beards* or *awns,* which extend from the head.

types of roots, primary and secondary. Three to five primary roots grow out of the seed, about $1\frac{1}{2}$ to 3 inches (3.8 to 7.6 centimeters) below the surface of the soil. These roots usually live for only six to eight weeks. As the stem begins to grow out of the soil, the secondary roots form just below the surface. They are thicker and stronger than the primary roots and anchor the plant securely in the soil. Most of the root system lies in the upper 15 to 20 inches (38 to 50 centimeters) of soil. But if the soil is loose, the root system may extend as deep as 7 feet (210 centimeters).

Most wheat plants have a main stem and several additional stalks, called *tillers.* Each leaf of a wheat plant has a sheath and a blade. The sheath wraps around the stem or tiller. The blade, which is long, flat, and narrow, extends from the top of the sheath. Each blade is on the opposite side of the stem from the blade that is just below it.

A wheat head, also called a *spike,* forms at the top of each main stem and tiller. The head is composed of a many-jointed stem. The head carries clusters of flowers, called *spikelets,* which branch off from each joint. Each primary spikelet contains a wheat kernel wrapped in a husk. Many kinds of wheat have bristly hairs, called *awns* or *beards,* which extend from the spikelets. A typical wheat spike bears 30 to 50 kernels.

A wheat kernel is usually $\frac{1}{8}$ to $\frac{3}{8}$ inch (3 to 9 millimeters) long. It has three main parts—the bran, the endosperm, and the germ. The bran, or seed coat, covers the surface of the kernel. The bran has several layers and makes up about 14 per cent of the kernel. Inside the bran are the endosperm and the germ. The endosperm forms the largest part of the kernel—about 83 per cent. The germ makes up only about 3 per cent of the kernel. It is the part of the seed that grows into a new plant after sowing.

Growth and reproduction. A wheat kernel begins to absorb moisture and swell shortly after planting. The primary roots appear, and the stem starts growing toward the surface of the soil. One to two weeks later, the young plant appears above the ground. In less than a month, leaves appear and the tillers and secondary roots begin to grow.

In spring when conditions are favorable, stems *elongate* (lengthen) from the leaf sheaths. Heads appear on the tillers soon afterward. A few days after the spike emerges from the sheath, the flowers are pollinated and develop into wheat kernels. Usually, each wheat flower pollinates itself. Occasionally, however, pollen from one flower is carried by the wind and fertilizes another flower.

Wheat becomes fully ripe about 30 to 60 days after flowering, depending on the weather. During the ripening period, the kernels increase in size and gradually harden. The entire plant becomes dry and turns golden-brown. Ripe kernels may be white, red, yellow, or even purple, depending on the variety of wheat.

Kinds of wheat

There are several ways of classifying wheat. Wheats can be broadly grouped into winter wheats and spring wheats. Scientists classify wheat according to its species and variety. In addition, the government in many wheat-producing countries has introduced market classes to simplify wheat sales.

Winter wheats and spring wheats are grouped by their growing season. The kind of wheat planted depends primarily on the climate. Winter wheats are grown in milder climates than spring wheats. In general, winter wheats produce higher yields.

Winter wheat is planted in the fall and harvested the following spring or summer. It reaches the stage when

Cross section of kernel of wheat

WORLD BOOK illustration by Emily McGowan

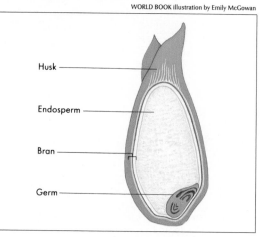

Husk

Endosperm

Bran

Germ

tillers form and then stops growing as cold weather arrives. The plants resume growing when warm weather returns in the spring. Winter wheat needs such a period of cold weather, with short days and long nights, to flower. If winter wheat is planted in the spring, it ordinarily will not *head* (produce a crop).

Spring wheat is grown in areas with extremely cold weather. It is planted in the spring of the year and becomes fully ripe that summer.

Species of wheat. Scientists have identified about 30 species of wheat, based on differences in such traits as appearance and growth patterns. Only three of these species—*common wheat, club wheat,* and *durum wheat* —are commercially important in the United States. Moreover, some scientists consider club wheat to be a part of common wheat, not a separate species. Scientists also disagree about the classification of several other species.

Common wheat is also called *bread wheat.* It is the most widely grown wheat species in the world. The kernels of common wheat may be red, *amber* (yellowish-brown), white, purple, or blue. They range in texture from hard to soft. Common wheat includes both winter and spring wheats. It is grown on the prairies of the central United States and Canada and in most major wheat-producing areas of the world.

Club wheat is closely related to common wheat. Its kernels are white or red and are usually soft in texture. In the United States, club wheat is grown mainly in the Pacific Northwest. Club wheat may be of the winter or spring type.

Durum wheat has hard kernels that are white, red, amber, or purple. Ground durum wheat holds together well when made into a paste. For this reason, durum wheat is used in pasta products. In North America, most durum wheat is of the spring wheat type and is grown in Minnesota, the Dakotas, and southern Canada.

Some species of wheat

Common name	Latin name	Common name	Latin name
Club	*Triticum compactum*	Persian	*T. carthlicum*
		Polish	*T. polonicum*
Common or Bread	*T. aestivum*	Shot	*T. sphaerococcum*
Cone, Poulard, or Rivet	*T. turgidum*	Spelt	*T. spelta*
		Wild einkorn	*T. boeoticum*
Durum	*T. durum*		
Einkorn	*T. monococcum*	Wild emmer	*T. dicoccoides*
Emmer	*T. dicoccon*		

Varieties of wheat. Each wheat species is divided into many varieties. These varieties differ in such characteristics as grain yield; growing time; grain protein content; and the ability to resist cold, drought, disease, and insect pests.

More than 40,000 varieties of wheat have been produced in the world. Scientists keep seeking new varieties with the most desirable combination of characteristics. In laboratories at agricultural experiment stations, seed companies, and universities, scientists breed new varieties by a process called *crossing.* In crossing, pollen from one variety is used to fertilize plants of another variety. The offspring form a new variety with some characteristics of both parent varieties. The offspring with the most desirable characteristics are grown for several generations to ensure that the new variety is pure and has acceptable characteristics.

Commercial classes of wheat. The United States Department of Agriculture (USDA) divides wheat into seven market classes based on such qualities as the color and texture of the kernels. These classes are (1) hard red winter wheat, (2) soft red winter wheat, (3) hard red spring wheat, (4) durum wheat, (5) red durum wheat, (6) white wheat, and (7) mixed wheat.

The USDA market classes help the government regu-

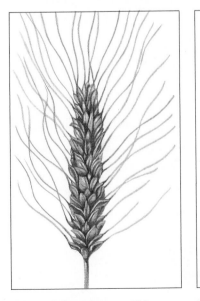

WORLD BOOK illustrations by Paul D. Turnbaugh

Common wheat, the most widely grown wheat species, includes both winter and spring types.

Club wheat has a short, thick head that is usually nonbearded. It includes both winter and spring types.

Durum wheat is usually bearded and has hard kernels. Most durum wheat in North America is spring wheat.

late the quality of wheat sold in the United States. They also help milling companies and exporters select the grain they purchase. Each class has different characteristics and uses. In general, hard wheats have more protein than soft wheats do. Hard red wheats make excellent bread flour. Soft red wheats are used for cakes, cookies, and pastries. Durum wheats are purchased to make pasta products. White wheats are soft and best suited for breakfast foods and pastries. Mixed wheats consist of wheats from two or more classes.

How wheat is grown

Wheat grows in a wide range of climates and soils. But a good wheat crop requires suitable weather and proper soil. To achieve the highest yields, wheat farmers must use high-quality seed that is free from disease. Farmers also must plant and harvest the wheat at just the right time. In addition, they must protect the growing crop from damage caused by diseases and pests.

The basic steps for growing wheat are much the same all over the world. However, wheat farms differ in size and levels of *mechanization* (work done by machinery). In many nonindustrial countries, wheat farmers use animals to pull their plows across small plots. They also may plant and harvest their crops by hand. In industrialized countries, nearly all the wheat is grown on large farms with the aid of tractors and specialized machinery. This section describes how wheat is grown on a large, mechanized farm.

Climate conditions. Fairly dry and mild climates are the most favorable for growing wheat. Extreme heat or cold, or very wet or very dry weather will destroy both spring and winter wheat. Weather conditions, including temperatures and rainfall, influence when wheat is planted. Planting seeds too early or too late reduces the yield. Late planting of winter wheat also increases the chance of damage from cold.

Farmers plant winter wheat in time for the young plants to become hardy enough to survive the winter

cold. Winter wheat is planted as early as September 1 in Montana and as late as November 1 in Texas, where cold weather arrives much later. In northern winter wheat areas, farmers may plant wheat in *furrows* (narrow channels) a few inches deep. These furrows fill with blowing snow, which acts like a blanket and protects the plants from extreme cold.

Spring wheat is exposed to fewer weather hazards because it has a far shorter growing period than winter wheat does. Farmers in northern Nebraska and South Dakota may plant spring wheat in early March. Farmers to the north—in Minnesota and North Dakota—may wait until mid-April to plant spring wheat.

Soil conditions. Wheat grows best in the kinds of soil called *clay loam* and *silt loam* (see **Loam**). The soil should contain much decayed *organic* (plant and animal) matter to provide food for the wheat plants. If the soil lacks some nutrients, a farmer may add these in the form of fertilizer.

In many parts of the world, farmers grow wheat on the same land every year. After many years, such land may lack the nutrients needed to produce a good crop. In addition, erosion by wind or water can remove nutrients from the soil. Farmers commonly have samples of soil tested to determine if the soil has the necessary nutrients. Such tests also indicate the amount of acid in the soil. If soil becomes too acid, wheat will not grow well and may not even sprout. Farmers can add fertilizer and lime to the soil to restore nutrients and reduce acidity.

Some farmers do not plant wheat on the same land every year. They may plant wheat in rotation with such crops as clover, corn, oats, soybeans, or timothy. This practice returns nutrients to the soil and helps control diseases and pests. In regions with little rainfall, farmers may plant a field every other year. Between wheat crops, they leave the field *fallow* (unplanted) so that it can store moisture.

Preparing the soil. Wheat farmers prepare fields for the next crop by plowing. They begin plowing as soon

Shostal

Plowing the field is the first step in preparing the soil for planting wheat. The plow turns and loosens the earth to aid in planting. Plowing also makes it easier for the seeds to sprout and grow.

Grant Heilman

Planting wheat requires from $\frac{1}{2}$ bushel to 2 bushels of seeds per acre (1.2 to 4.9 bushels per hectare). A machine called a *drill, left,* drops the seeds into the ground and covers them with soil.

as possible after harvest. Plowing breaks up the soil surface and allows moisture to soak into the ground where it is stored for the next crop. It also buries weeds and the remains of the previous crop. This plant matter releases nutrients as it decays. In areas that suffer from erosion, farmers use a plow that loosens the soil but leaves plants on the surface. These plants help reduce erosion.

Just before planting wheat, farmers prepare the seedbed with a device called a *spring-tooth harrow.* Harrows have sharp metal spikes that break up chunks of earth into small pieces that can pack closely around the wheat seeds.

Planting. Farmers use a tractor-drawn machine called a *drill* to plant wheat seed. The drill digs furrows just deep enough to plant the seeds. At the same time, it drops the seeds, one by one, into the furrows and covers the seeds with soil. Some drills also drop a small amount of fertilizer with the seed. Drills can be set to plant the desired number of seeds per acre. Seeding rates range from about $\frac{1}{2}$ bushel per acre (1.2 bushels per hectare) in dry regions to about 2 bushels per acre (4.9 bushels per hectare) in moist regions. With a large drill, a farmer can plant more than 200 acres (81 hectares) of wheat a day.

Care during growth. Growing wheat can suffer damage from diseases, insect pests, and weeds. Wheat farmers employ various practices to help prevent such damage.

Controlling diseases. The most destructive wheat disease is *rust.* This disease is caused by a fungus that grows on the wheat plant and produces small, rust-colored spots on the leaves, stems, and heads. The spots later turn brown. The fungi draw food and water from the wheat plant. This action may prevent the kernels from developing. There are two types of rust, leaf rust and stem rust. To protect their wheat crops, farmers often destroy nearby barberry plants, on which the stem rust fungus must live during some stages of its growth. Some varieties of wheat are resistant to certain kinds of

rust. Breeders continue to develop more varieties of wheat that can resist rust. See **Rust.**

Another serious fungus disease that harms wheat kernels is *smut.* The two main kinds that attack wheat are *bunt* (also called *stinking smut*) and *loose smut.* Wheat kernels infected with bunt fill with a black mass of smut spores. These infected kernels are called *smut balls.* When smut balls break, they release a rotten, fishy odor. If smut balls break during harvesting, the spores spread and contaminate thousands of other kernels. If infected kernels are sown, the next crop also will be damaged. In wheat plants infected with loose smut, black smut spores replace both the kernels and the husks. Wind carries these spores to other wheat plants, spreading the disease. Farmers can control both kinds of smut by treating the seeds before planting or by spraying their crop with a chemical that kills the spores. Some varieties of wheat can resist smut infection. See **Smut.**

Several other diseases attack wheat, but in most cases they do not cause widespread damage. They include *flag smut, glume blotch, leaf blotch, scab, take-all, black chaff,* and *mosaic.*

Controlling insect pests. Insects damage about 10 per cent of the United States wheat crop every year. More than 100 different kinds of insects attack wheat. Some, including grasshoppers and locusts, eat the stems and leaves of the wheat plant. Wireworms, cutworms, and some other insects eat the roots and seeds or cut the wheat stem at the surface of the soil. Still other insects, including Hessian flies, suck sap from the stems. Insects that damage wheat also include army worms, cereal leaf beetles, greenbugs, jointworms, wheat stem sawflies, and wheat stem maggots. Grain weevils and Angoumois grain moths attack stored wheat grain.

Some varieties of wheat are resistant to Hessian flies and wheat stem sawflies. Farmers can control other insect pests by using insecticide sprays. Planting winter wheat after the Hessian flies that hatch in the fall have died also helps farmers to reduce the crop damage caused by this insect pest.

J. C. Allen & Son

Harvesting wheat is often done with a machine called a *combine*. The combine cuts the stalks and *threshes* the wheat—that is, separates the kernels from the rest of the plant.

Controlling weeds. Weeds rob wheat plants of moisture and nourishment. This loss reduces grain yields. Certain weeds can spoil a wheat crop. For example, wild garlic and wild onions give wheat an odor that makes it unfit for use as flour. Other weeds that cause serious damage to wheat crops include Canada thistle, cheat, field bindweed, Russian thistle, wild morning glory, wild mustard, and wild oats. Careful preparation of the seedbed helps prevent the growth of weeds. If weeds become a problem among growing wheat plants, farmers may apply chemicals that have been approved for such use by government agencies.

Harvesting. Farmers harvest their wheat as soon as possible after it has ripened, before bad weather can damage the crop. Wheat is ready for harvest when moisture makes up no more than 14 per cent of the weight of the kernel. To check for ripeness, farmers may take a sample to a grain storage elevator for moisture testing. Farmers also may test the grain by biting a kernel or breaking it with their fingernails. When ready for harvest, the kernels are hard and brittle and break with a sharp, cracking sound.

Large mechanized farms use huge, self-powered machines called *combines* to harvest wheat. Combines cut the stalks and *thresh*—that is, separate the kernels from the rest of the plant. In North America, large teams of

Harvesttime around the world

Harvesting the world's wheat crop takes place all year. Each month, wheat is gathered and threshed somewhere in the world, as shown below.
January: Argentina, Australia, Chile, and New Zealand.
February: Burma, Chile, New Zealand, and Uruguay.
March: India and upper Egypt.
April: Lower Egypt, India, Iran, Mexico, and Morocco.
May: Algeria, China, Japan, Spain, and Southwestern United States.
June: China, southern France, Greece, Italy, Portugal, Spain, Tunisia, Turkey, and the United States south of about 40° north latitude.
July: Bulgaria, East Germany, southern England, France, Hungary, Romania, Soviet Union, Northern United States, West Germany, and Yugoslavia.
August: Belgium, Canada, Denmark, northern England, the Netherlands, central Soviet Union, and Northern United States.
September and October: Parts of Canada, northern Soviet Union, Scandinavian countries, and Scotland.
November: Argentina, Brazil, Venezuela, and South Africa.
December: Argentina and Australia.

combines follow the wheat harvest north from Texas to Canada. These combine teams move from field to field, operating day and night to harvest the wheat on time.

Where wheat is grown

China and the Soviet Union consistently lead the world in wheat production, followed by the United States. In some years China ranks first, and in other years the Soviet Union ranks first. Some countries produce more wheat than their own people consume. Farmers in these countries depend heavily on export sales. The United States leads all other countries in exports of wheat and wheat flour. Argentina, Australia, Canada, and France also export large amounts of wheat. China and the Soviet Union are the world's leading importers of wheat.

In China, farmers grow wheat in many areas of the country, primarily on the North China Plain in the east. Most of China's farmers plant winter wheat. In some irrigated fields, they plant such crops as corn, cotton, or soybeans between the rows of wheat before the wheat is ready for harvest.

In the Soviet Union, wheat is the most important crop by far. It is planted on nearly a fifth of the total cropland. The country's main wheat-growing region is a level prairie in the southwest with deep, fertile soils. This Black Earth Belt extends about 2,000 miles (3,200 kilometers) from the Danube River Basin across northern Kazakhstan and into southwestern Siberia. The chief kinds of wheat grown in the Soviet Union are hard red winter and hard red spring wheats.

In the United States, the many varieties of wheat are planted at different times and in different areas, depending on the climate. In the southern Great Plains—Texas, Oklahoma, Kansas, Colorado, and Nebraska—farmers grow hard red winter wheat. In Minnesota and the northern Great Plains—South Dakota, North Dakota, and Montana—farmers plant hard red spring wheat. Winters in this region are often too cold for winter wheat. Spring durum wheat is also grown widely in the northern Great Plains. Smaller amounts of winter durum wheat are planted in Arizona and California.

Wheat-producing areas of the world

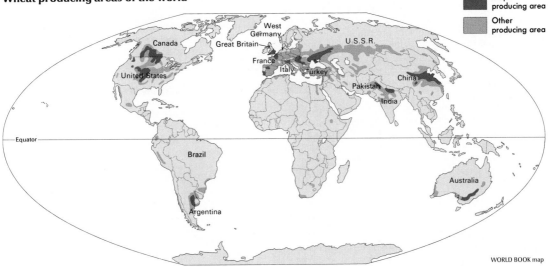

Major producing area
Other producing area

WORLD BOOK map

In the Midwest and the East—in such states as Missouri, Illinois, Indiana, Ohio, and Pennsylvania—farmers commonly plant soft red winter wheat. White wheat is grown in Michigan and New York.

In the Western United States, the chief wheat-producing areas are the Columbia River Valley and the uplands of Washington, Oregon, and Idaho. This region has deep, fertile soils that hold water well. Most of the wheat grown is white wheat. White wheat also is grown in California.

In Canada, most wheat is grown in the Prairie Provinces—Saskatchewan, Alberta, and Manitoba. Nearly all of the crop is hard red spring wheat, though some other wheats, especially durum, are also grown.

In other countries. In South America, the primary wheat-growing area is the *Pampa*—a fertile plain in Argentina. Hard red winter wheat is grown on huge, mechanized plantations in the Pampa.

After the Soviet Union, France and Great Britain rank as the leading wheat producers in Europe. Much wheat also is grown in West Germany and Italy.

India, Turkey, and Pakistan follow China as the leading wheat-producers in Asia. Farmers plant winter wheat across much of northern India just after the summer rains stop. In Australia, farmers grow wheat in the southern part of the country. Nearly all of Australia's crop is white spring wheat.

Marketing wheat

Transporting and storing wheat. After the harvest, most farmers haul their wheat by truck to a country grain elevator for storage. Each truck empties its load of grain into a pit. A conveyor belt then scoops up the grain, carries it to the top of the elevator, and dumps it into a tall storage bin. Country elevators dry and clean the grain they receive and provide farmers with marketing information. Country elevators assign the grain to one of six grades, based on its weight and quality. The grades have different uses, and wheat is marketed on the basis of its grade. Country elevators receive most of their wheat directly from farmers, but some of the wheat

may come from smaller country elevators.

From the country elevator wheat travels by truck or railroad boxcar to a terminal elevator located in a large grain market or shipping center. Different lots may be combined at the terminal elevator to produce blends needed by flour mills. If the grain is to be exported, the United States Department of Agriculture inspects and grades it. Terminal elevators commonly hold from 1 million to 10 million bushels of wheat, though some can hold much more. See **Grain elevator.**

From the terminal elevator, some wheat is loaded into huge ships for export. Much of the remainder is carried by truck, rail, or barge to mills for grinding into flour. The rest is shipped to other processors to be used in

Leading wheat-growing countries

Bushels of wheat grown in a year

China	3,223,000,000 bushels
Soviet Union	3,123,000,000 bushels
United States	2,105,000,000 bushels
India	1,675,000,000 bushels
France	1,008,000,000 bushels
Canada	968,000,000 bushels
Turkey	696,000,000 bushels
Australia	448,000,000 bushels
Pakistan	442,000,000 bushels
Great Britain	435,000,000 bushels

One bushel equals 60 pounds (27 kilograms). Figures are for 1987.
Source: *FAO Production Yearbook, 1987,* Food and Agriculture Organization of the United Nations.

animal feed or other industrial products. For a description of flour milling, see **Flour** (How white flour is milled).

Buying and selling wheat. In the United States, milling companies buy some wheat directly from farmers. Most often, however, country elevators buy the farmers' wheat. Most wheat stored in grain elevators is sold through a *commodity exchange* or *grain exchange.* The Chicago Board of Trade and the Kansas City Board of Trade are two large grain exchanges. An exchange itself does not buy or sell any wheat. It is an organized market where people who want to buy a *commodity* (good) meet those who want to sell it. These traders include farmers, representatives of grain elevators and flour mills, and exporters. In addition, some traders are *speculators*—that is, they buy and sell a commodity in the hope of making a profit without actually exchanging the commodity itself.

Buyers may purchase wheat already in storage. The larger exchanges also have a *futures market* where traders make contracts to buy and sell wheat at a specified price and future date. The futures market helps milling companies and other processors by assuring them a steady supply of grain at prices determined well in advance of delivery. See **Commodity exchange.**

A government agency, the Canadian Wheat Board (CWB), markets wheat in Canada. The CWB represents farmers, consumers, and the government. It buys and sells wheat at prices established by the government, establishes quotas for purchases from wheat farmers, and regulates exports. Wheat farmers are paid when they deliver their crop to a country elevator. The farmers' wheat is then pooled and sold by the wheat board. The farmers may receive an additional payment after the crop has been sold. Under this system, all farmers re-

Leading wheat-growing states and provinces

Bushels of wheat grown in a year

State/Province	Bushels
Saskatchewan	565,522,000 bushels
Kansas	366,300,000 bushels
North Dakota	269,120,000 bushels
Alberta	219,985,000 bushels
Montana	151,220,000 bushels
Manitoba	146,883,000 bushels
Oklahoma	129,600,000 bushels
Washington	114,285,000 bushels
South Dakota	106,704,000 bushels
Minnesota	102,588,000 bushels

One bushel equals 60 pounds (27 kilograms). Figures are for 1987. Sources: *Crop Production, 1987 Summary,* U.S. Department of Agriculture; Statistics Canada.

ceive the same price for wheat of similar quality, and they are guaranteed a fair share of the market.

Controlling wheat production. Worldwide wheat production varies greatly from year to year, depending on weather and the amount of land planted. In years of high production, many countries may harvest more wheat than they can use. They can either store the sur-

Wheat-producing areas in North America

Wheat is grown in large quantities in the United States and Canada. Spring wheat is raised in the northern Great Plains states and in the Prairie Provinces. Severe winters prevent planting in both these regions in the fall. The winter wheat belt extends from the southern Great Plains states through the Eastern United States.

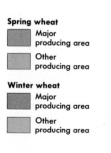

Spring wheat

　Major producing area

　Other producing area

Winter wheat

　Major producing area

　Other producing area

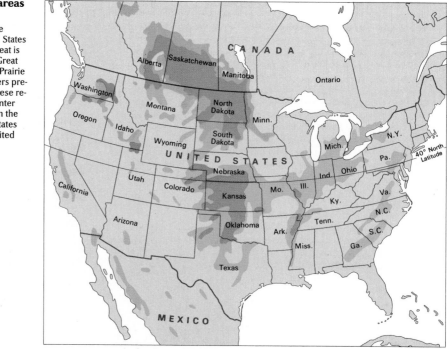

WORLD BOOK map

Grant Heilman

A country elevator stores wheat after it has been harvested. The elevator cleans the wheat and grades its quality. Grain is bought or sold on the basis of its grade.

plus or sell it to countries that need wheat. As countries try to unload their surplus, the price of wheat tends to drop. Sometimes, the price falls far below the farmers' cost of growing the wheat. If wheat prices remain low, farmers may decide to plant less wheat or switch to another crop. Then, in years of low production, there may be too little wheat to feed the people.

In many countries, the government has farm programs aimed at matching production levels with expected market demand, thus preventing large surpluses or shortages. Some governments support wheat prices by guaranteeing to buy surplus wheat at a "target" price if the market price falls below that price. The government may store the surplus wheat and sell it later when the price rises.

Other government programs aim at increasing or reducing the acreage planted, depending on the country's needs. The United States, for example, has a wheat surplus year after year. From 1962 to 1973 and again in the late 1970's, the U.S. government tried to limit the amount of land planted in wheat by paying farmers to leave fields unplanted. It offered a payment-in-kind (PIK) program in 1983 and 1984. Under this program, farmers who restricted their acreage could receive payment in surplus wheat that the government had stored from previous years. Farmers could sell this wheat or store it. A modified PIK program began in 1986. This new program allowed farmers to receive payment in other commodities besides wheat.

History

Origins. Scientists believe that wild relatives of wheat first grew in the Middle East. Species from that region— wild einkorn, wild emmer, and some wild grasses—are the ancestors of all cultivated wheat species. At first, people probably simply gathered and chewed the kernels. In time, they learned to toast the grains over a fire and to grind and boil them to make a porridge. Frying such porridge resulted in flat bread, similar to pancakes. People may have discovered how to make yeast bread after some porridge became contaminated by yeast.

Wheat was one of the first plants to be cultivated. Scientists think that farmers first grew wheat about 11,000 years ago in the Middle East. Archaeologists have found the remains of wheat grains dating from about 9,000 B.C. at the Jarmo village site near Damascus, Syria. They also have found bone hoes, flint sickles, and stone grinding tools that may have been used to plant, harvest, and grind grains.

The cultivation of wheat and other crops led to enormous changes in people's lives. People no longer had to wander continuously in search of food. Farming provided a handier and more reliable supply of food and enabled people to establish permanent settlements. As grain output expanded, many people were freed from food production and could develop other skills. With the improvement of agricultural and processing methods, people in some areas grew enough grain to feed people in other lands. In this way, trade developed. Thriving cities replaced tiny villages. These changes helped make possible the development of the great ancient civilizations.

The spread of wheat farming. By about 4,000 B.C., wheat farming had spread to much of Asia, Europe, and northern Africa. New species of wheat gradually developed as a result of the accidental breeding of cultivated wheats with wild grasses. Some of the new wheats had qualities that farmers preferred, and so those kinds began to replace older wheats. Emmer and einkorn were cultivated widely until durum wheat appeared about 500 B.C. By about A.D. 500, common wheat and club wheat had developed.

Wheat was brought to the Americas by explorers and settlers from many European countries. In 1493, Christopher Columbus introduced wheat to the New World on his second trip to the West Indies. Wheat from Spain reached Mexico in 1519 and Argentina by 1527. Spanish

Dale Wittner, West Stock

At a grain exchange, traders buy and sell wheat and other crops. The traders include farmers, representatives of grain elevators and flour mills, and exporters.

missionaries later carried wheat with them to the American Southwest. In Canada, French settlers began growing wheat in Nova Scotia in 1605.

English colonists planted wheat at Jamestown, Va., in 1611 and at Plymouth Colony in New England in 1621. But the New England colonists had less luck with wheat than with the corn the Indians gave them. Colonists from the Netherlands and Sweden had more success growing wheat in New York, New Jersey, Delaware, and Pennsylvania.

Wheat farming moved westward with the pioneers. Wheat grew well on the Midwestern prairies, where the climate was too harsh for many other crops. Large shipments of wheat traveled to markets in the East by canal and railroad. By the 1860's, Illinois, Indiana, Iowa, and Ohio had become leading wheat-producing states.

The introduction of winter wheat gave the U.S. wheat industry a major boost. In the 1870's, members of a religious group called the Mennonites immigrated from Russia to Kansas. They brought with them a variety of winter wheat called Turkey Red, which was extremely well suited to the low rainfall on the Great Plains. Turkey Red and varieties that were developed from it soon were planted on nearly all the wheat farms in Kansas and nearby states. Many present-day varieties of wheat grown in the United States can be traced to Turkey Red.

The mechanization of wheat farming. From the beginnings of agriculture until the early 1800's, there was little change in the tools used for wheat farming. For thousands of years, farmers harvested wheat by hand with a sickle or a scythe. The stalks were then tied into bundles and gathered into piles to await threshing. To thresh the grain, livestock trampled the stalks or

farmers beat the stalks with a hinged stick called a *flail.* After the grain was loosened from the stalks, the wheat was tossed into the air. The chaff blew away, leaving the kernels behind. This process was called *winnowing.* Much grain spoiled because it took so long to harvest and thresh it.

Machines that were developed in the 1800's made wheat farming far more efficient. The American inventor Cyrus McCormick patented the first successful reaping machine in 1834. By the 1890's, most reapers had an attachment that tied the stalks in bundles. Also in 1834, two brothers from Maine, Hiram and John Pitts, built a threshing machine. The thresher could do in a few hours the work that once took several days. A combined harvester-thresher, or combine, was developed in the 1830's by Hiram Moore and John Haskall of Michigan. However, most farmers continued to use separate reapers and threshers. During the 1920's, a shortage of farm labor coupled with improvements in combines led more farmers to use them.

Until the late 1800's, most farm equipment was powered by farm animals or human labor. During the 1880's, steam engines gradually replaced the animals that pulled most farm machinery in the United States. By the early 1920's, internal-combustion engines were used to power tractors and other farm machines.

Mechanization has greatly reduced the amount of human labor needed to grow wheat. Before 1830, it took a farmer more than 64 hours to prepare the soil, plant the seed, and cut and thresh 1 acre (0.4 hectare) of wheat. Today, it takes less than 3 hours of labor. Mechanization has also enabled farmers to cultivate much larger areas. Using hand tools, a farm family can grow

A steam-powered threshing machine, *above,* was used by wheat farmers of the late 1800's and early 1900's. The machine separated the kernels from the stalks and blew the husks from the kernels. Threshers were so expensive that a group of farmers bought and shared one machine.

WORLD BOOK photo by Ted Streshinsky

New varieties of wheat have enabled many countries to increase grain production. American agricultural scientist Norman E. Borlaug, *above in yellow cap,* won the 1970 Nobel Peace Prize for research that led to high-yield wheat varieties.

about 2.5 acres (1 hectare) of wheat. But with modern machinery, the same family can farm about 1,000 acres (405 hectares).

Breeding new varieties of wheat. Some of the most important advances in the history of wheat have resulted from the scientific breeding of wheat during the 1900's. By developing new varieties of wheat, plant breeders have greatly increased the yield of wheat per acre or hectare of land. Some varieties have higher yields because they can resist diseases or pests. Others mature early, enabling the grain to escape such dangers as early frosts and late droughts. Breeders have also developed plants with strong stalks that can support a heavy load of grain. Many high-yield varieties require large amounts of fertilizers or pesticides.

During the mid-1900's, agricultural scientists led a worldwide effort to boost grain production in developing countries. This effort was so successful that it has been called the *Green Revolution.* Its success depended primarily on the use of high-yield grains. In 1970, American agricultural scientist Norman E. Borlaug was awarded the Nobel Peace Prize for wheat research that led to the development of these varieties. See **Borlaug, Norman E.**

The Green Revolution reduced the danger of famine in many developing countries. It helped these countries become less dependent upon imported wheat for their growing population. It also helped focus attention on obstacles to increasing the world's food supply. For example, water supplies are often limited and soils are of poor quality. Many farmers cannot afford irrigation systems or the large amounts of fertilizers and pesticides the new grains require. In some developing countries,

grain can be damaged or spoiled by insects, rodents, poor transportation, and poor distribution systems. Finally, in many countries, the population is growing faster than the food supply, offsetting the gains achieved by the Green Revolution.

Scientific classification. Wheat belongs to the grass family, Gramineae. It makes up the genus *Triticum.*　　Lavoy I. Croy

Related articles in *World Book* include:

Enemies of wheat

Army worm	Grasshopper	Mosaic disease
Chinch bug	Hessian fly	Rust
Grain weevil	Locust	Smut

Growing and harvesting wheat

Agriculture	McCormick, Cyrus Hall
Alberta (picture)	North Dakota (picture)
Combine	Oklahoma (picture)
Dry farming	Reaper
Farm and farming	Saskatchewan (picture)
Grain elevator	Threshing machine
Kansas (picture)	

Products from wheat

Bran	Gluten
Bread	Pasta
Flour	Starch
Food (picture)	

Other related articles

Borlaug, Norman E.	Grain
Commmodity exchange	Grass
Food supply	Triticale

Outline

I. Uses of wheat
  A. Food for people
  B. Livestock feed
  C. Other uses
II. The wheat plant
  A. Structure
  B. Growth and reproduction
III. Kinds of wheat
  A. Winter wheats and   C. Varieties of wheat
     spring wheats   D. Commercial classes of
  B. Species of wheat   wheat
IV. How wheat is grown
  A. Climate conditions   D. Planting
  B. Soil conditions   E. Care during growth
  C. Preparing the soil   F. Harvesting
V. Where wheat is grown
  A. In China   D. In Canada
  B. In the Soviet Union   E. In other countries
  C. In the United States
VI. Marketing wheat
  A. Transporting and storing wheat
  B. Buying and selling wheat
  C. Controlling wheat production
VII. History

Questions

What part of the wheat kernel is used in making white flour?
Why do some farmers plant wheat in rotation with other crops?
What are *tillers*?
Which three major wheat-farming machines were developed during the 1830's?
What are the three leading wheat-producing countries?
When and where do scientists think people first grew wheat?
What was the *Green Revolution*?
How many kernels does a typical head of wheat have?
What is a *grain exchange*?
How is the development of ancient civilizations linked to the history of wheat?

Wheat germ. See **Wheat** (Food for people).

Wheatley, Phillis (1753?-1784), was the first important black American poet. She was born in Africa and was taken to Boston on a slave ship at the age of about 8. John Wheatley, a Boston tailor, bought her at an auction and made her a servant for his wife.

The Wheatleys taught Phillis to read and write. They also encouraged her to study geography, history, and Latin. Phillis started to write poetry when she was about 14, and her poems soon began to be published. A book of her verse called *Poems on Various Subjects, Religious and Moral* was published in London in 1773.

Wheatley was deeply religious, and some of her poems express her happiness about being brought from Africa into a Christian society. She also wrote about issues of her time, especially in "To the Right Honorable William, Earl of Dartmouth" (1772). In this poem, Wheatley contrasted the demand of the American Colonies for independence from Great Britain with her status as a slave.   Clark Griffith

Wheatstone, Sir Charles (1802-1875), was a British physicist and inventor. Wheatstone became best known for his work on electrical measuring devices, including the "Wheatstone bridge," which he did not invent but improved, and also for his work in electrical telegraphy (see **Telegraph** [Development]; **Wheatstone bridge**).

Wheatstone experimented on the speed of electricity in wires, and suggested that electricity be used to send messages. With W. F. Cooke, he patented an electrical telegraph in 1837, about the same time that Samuel Morse developed his telegraph in the United States. Wheatstone's device was widely used in Great Britain. He also invented a cryptographic machine and studied arc spectra analysis of metals.

Wheatstone was born in Gloucester. He became professor of experimental philosophy at King's College, London, in 1834.   Robert E. Schofield

Wheatstone bridge is a type of electric circuit used to determine an unknown *resistance* (see **Electric circuit** [Circuit mathematics]). It consists of four resistors whose arrangement is usually represented by the figure of a diamond.

Two of the circuit's resistors have known resistances. They come together at an angle and form the top half of the diamond. In the lower half, a resistor representing an unknown resistance is connected to a variable resistor that can be adjusted to a known resistance. A device called a *galvanometer*, which measures current, is connected to the top and bottom corners of the diamond to bridge the two halves of the circuit. The other corners are connected to a battery, which produces a current through the resistors. The variable resistor is adjusted until the voltage at the top and bottom corners of the circuit are equal. At this point, the galvanometer shows no current flow, and the circuit is said to be *balanced*. The unknown resistance can then be determined by using the following formula:

$$R_x = \left(\frac{R_2}{R_1} \right) R_v$$

The unknown resistance (R_x) is found by multiplying the ratio of the two known resistances (R_1 and R_2) by the variable resistance (R_v).   Robert B. Prigo

Wheel and axle is a mechanical device used in lifting loads. It is one of the *six simple machines* developed in ancient times and ranks as one of the most important inventions in history. The simplest wheel and axle has a cylinder and a large wheel, fastened together and turning on the same axis. The wheel and axle is a first-class lever (see **Lever**). The center of the axle (the cylinder) corresponds to the fulcrum. The radius of the axle corresponds to the load arm. The radius of the wheel corresponds to the force, or effort, arm to which force is applied. Sometimes a crank is used instead of a wheel.

The advantage of a wheel and axle is that it can lift heavy weights for us with only little effort on our part. The following law gives the ratio between the two: *The force applied multiplied by the radius of the wheel equals the load multiplied by the radius of the axle.* To reduce this to a formula, let *F* stand for force; *R* for the radius of the wheel; *L* for the load; and *r* for the radius of the axle.

$$F \times R = L \times r, \text{ or } \frac{L}{F} = \frac{R}{r}$$

The mechanical advantage of a machine is always the ratio of the load (*L*) to the force (*F*) (see **Machine** [Mechanical advantage]). Let us use an example in which the radius of the wheel (*R*) is 10 inches, the radius of the axle (*r*) is 1 inch, and the load (*L*) is 20 pounds. If there were no friction, the formula would be $\frac{20}{F} = \frac{10}{1}$. Since $10F = 20$, the force needed would be the same as that normally used to lift a mere 2 pounds. The mechanical advantage, the ratio of *L* to *F*, would be $\frac{20}{2}$, or 10.

Uses of the wheel and axle. In the ordinary windlass used for raising water from a well, a crank replaces the wheel. The hand applies the effort to the crank. The weight of the bucket of water is the load. In a grindstone, the radius of the wheel is usually longer than the crank handle, because speed is needed as well as force. Sometimes teeth or cogs may be placed around the edge of the wheel, as in a cogwheel, or on the sprocket wheel of a bicycle.   W. David Lewis

See also **Ratchet; Windlass; Work.**

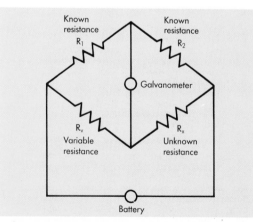

A **Wheatstone bridge** is an electric circuit used to measure an unknown resistance. A battery produces a flow of current through the circuit, and a variable resistor is adjusted until the galvanometer shows no current flow. The unknown resistance then can be calculated using a mathematical formula.

Wheelbarrow is a device for moving loads too heavy to lift by hand. It consists of a tub or box mounted on a wheel with two handles that extend under the body and join on the axle of the wheel. The wheelbarrow is an application of the principle of the lever, and is the kind known as a second-class lever (see **Lever**). The longer the handles of a wheelbarrow, the less force required to lift a given load. Wheelbarrows now usually have rubber tires, and may be made of wood or light metals such as aluminum.   Allen S. Hall, Jr.

Wheeler, Burton Kendall (1882-1975), an American statesman, served in the United States Senate as a Montana Democrat from 1923 until 1947. In 1924, he ran unsuccessfully for Vice President on the Progressive Party ticket (see **Progressive Party**). He helped expose the scandals during the presidential administration of Warren G. Harding. Wheeler was an extreme isolationist before World War II. In 1962, he published his autobiography, *Yankee from the West.* He was born in Hudson, Mass.   Harvey Wish

Wheeler, Earle Gilmore (1908-1975), a general in the U.S. Army, was Chairman of the Joint Chiefs of Staff from 1964 to 1970. He served as chief of staff for the U.S. Army from 1962 until his appointment as chairman by President Lyndon B. Johnson. Wheeler was with the 63rd Division during campaigns in Europe in World War II. He also held high staff positions in Europe with United States and North Atlantic Treaty Organization (NATO) forces after the war. Wheeler was born in Washington, D.C., and was graduated from the U.S. Military Academy.   Maurice Matloff

Wheeler, Joseph (1836-1906), was an American soldier. He served in campaigns against the Indians, before he joined the Confederate Army in 1861. During the Civil War, he made a brilliant record as a cavalry general at the Battle of Shiloh and in campaigns in Tennessee and Georgia. After the war, Wheeler practiced law in Alabama, and served several terms as a Democratic U.S. congressman between 1881 and 1900. He commanded U.S. forces during the Spanish-American War and in the Philippine Insurrection of 1900. He was born near Augusta, Ga., and was graduated from the U.S. Military Academy. A statue of him represents Alabama in Statuary Hall.   Arthur A. Ekirch, Jr.

Wheeler, William Almon (1819-1887), served as Vice President of the United States from 1877 to 1881 under President Rutherford B. Hayes. He also served as a Republican from New York in the U.S. House of Representatives from 1861 to 1863 and from 1869 to 1877. As a congressman, he devised the Wheeler Adjustment in 1874 to settle a disputed election in Louisiana.

Wheeler showed that he had strict principles by opposing the Salary Grab Act of 1873. Congress, however, voted itself the disputed pay increase. Wheeler refused to profit from the additional income. He bought government bonds, and then had the bonds canceled.

Wheeler was born in Malone, N.Y. He was a successful lawyer and businessman.   Irving G. Williams

See also **Vice President of the United States** (picture).

Wheeling (pop. 43,070; met. area pop. 185,566) is an industrial city on the Ohio River in northern West Virginia (see **West Virginia** [political map]). The city has an area of about 11 square miles (28 square kilometers). It includes Wheeling Island in the Ohio River. Wheeling is the seat of Ohio County. The Wheeling metropolitan area includes Belmont County in Ohio.

Wheeling lies on a level plain, which rises to steep hills, along the Ohio River. A scenic plaza was built in the heart of the business district. Two bridges connect Wheeling Island with the rest of the city. Wheeling Downs, which features dog races, occupies one end of the island. Wheeling has two principal parks and several neighborhood parks. Oglebay Park, a 1,400-acre (567-hectare) recreational area, lies outside the city.

Wheeling has about 40 public schools. Other educational institutions include Wheeling College; West Virginia Northern Community College; Mount de Chantal Academy for Girls; and Linsly Institute, a preparatory school for boys. West Liberty State College is located near Wheeling.

Wheeling lies near West Virginia's great coal- and natural-gas-producing region, and these minerals furnish power for many of the city's industries. Wheeling's most important products include iron and steel, aluminum, bronze, tin plate, metal stampings, plastics, glass, chemical products, and garments. The city is also a coal shipping center. Tourism is the most important industry in Wheeling, attracting visitors with its parks, historic sites, and local events. Wheeling has two modern hospitals and serves as a medical center for the surrounding region.

Colonel Ebenezer Zane and his brothers founded Wheeling in the winter of 1769-1770. They came from the south branch of the Potomac Valley in Virginia to settle a claim at the city's present site. Other settlers soon joined them, and in 1774 they erected Fort Fincastle. In 1776, they changed the fort's name to Fort Henry in honor of Patrick Henry. The town of Wheeling was laid out in 1793, incorporated in 1806, and first chartered as a city in 1836. The National Road, now U.S. Highway 40, reached the Ohio River at Wheeling in 1818.

For many years, the city served as a center of trade in the upper Ohio Valley. In 1852, it became the first city on the Ohio River below Pittsburgh to be reached by a railroad from the east. During the Civil War (1861-1865), Wheeling was the headquarters of Virginians who opposed secession from the Union. Union supporters organized the state of West Virginia in Wheeling on June 20, 1863, and the city served as the state capital from 1863 to 1870 and from 1875 to 1885. Wheeling has a city-manager form of government.   Harry Hamm

Wheelwright, William (1798-1873), an American businessman, devoted most of his life to developing transportation and communication in South America. In 1823 his ship was wrecked near Buenos Aires, and he decided to settle in South America. He was appointed U.S. Consul at Guayaquil, Ecuador, in 1824. He later moved to Valparaíso, Chile, and in 1840 set up a steamship line to serve the western coast of South America. Wheelwright discovered coal and copper deposits in Chile and built the first railroad in South America, from the mines to the coast. He built other railroads in Chile and Argentina, and developed the port of La Plata. He also built the continent's first telegraph line. He was born in Newburyport, Mass.   John B. McFerrin

Whelk is a large sea snail with a sturdy spiral shell. There are many *species* (kinds) of whelks. Most species are edible. The *waved whelk* lives in 6 to 500 feet (1.8 to 150 meters) of water off the coasts of northern Europe and off the northeastern coast of North America. It grows up to 3 inches (8 centimeters) long. The *knobbed whelk* of the U.S. Atlantic coast reaches 8 inches (20 centimeters) in length. See also **Shell** (picture).

Scientific classification. Waved whelks are in the family Buccinidae. They are *Buccinum undatum.* Knobbed whelks are in the family *Melongenidae.* They are *Busycon carica.*

M. Patricia Morse

Whetstone is any abrasive stone, natural or artificial, that is used for grinding and sharpening. Artificial abrasives, such as silicon carbide and aluminum oxide, are most often used. At one time a fine-grained variety of quartz, called *novaculite,* was used for grindstones. Its uniform hard grains made it capable of grinding quickly and withstanding wear.   Frederick H. Pough

Whig Party was a name applied to political parties in England, Scotland, and America. *Whig* is a short form of the word *whiggamore,* a Scotch word once used to describe people from western Scotland who opposed King Charles I of England in 1648.

In the late 1600's, Scottish and English opponents of the growing power of royalty were called Whigs. The Whig Party maintained a strong position in English politics until the 1850's, when the Whig progressives adopted the term Liberal. See **Great Britain** (History).

In the American Colonies, the Whigs were those people who resented British control, and favored independence from Great Britain. The term was probably first used in New York City about 1768. The Whigs supported the American Revolutionary War. British loyalists, called *Tories,* opposed the Whigs in the struggle (see **Tory Party**). The terms *Whig* and *Tory* fell into disuse after the colonies won their independence.

The Whig Party of the 1800's began to take shape about 1832. Political groups that opposed Andrew Jackson and his theories started to combine and unify themselves into a political party. These groups included the National Republicans, certain conservative factions of the Democratic-Republican Party, and some former members of the Anti-Masonic Party. Some of the political leaders of the Whig Party included such well-known National Republicans as Henry Clay, Daniel Webster, and John Quincy Adams. Soon many wealthy Southern cotton planters joined in protest against the democratic, leveling doctrines of the Jacksonians. In the north and east, many factory owners also joined the group because it supported a protective tariff. First as the National Republicans and later under the name of Whigs, these groups advocated new and broader activities for both state and national governments.

The first program of the Whigs followed Henry Clay's "American System." It included a proposal for a high protective tariff to encourage the growth of American industry. Clay wanted to distribute to the states money received from the sale of federal lands, so that they would construct new transportation systems of canals and highways. Clay argued that Western and Southern farmers and Eastern manufacturers formed a natural and interdependent economic unit that would furnish markets for each other, if they were connected with good transportation facilities.

When Jackson and his followers came out against the United States Bank, Clay immediately supported it. The Whigs soon adopted an advanced financial program calling for federal control of the banking system in the interest of sound currency. They also wanted to insure a supply of credit adequate to meet the increasing demands from expanding commercial interests in the East and from the moving frontier in the West. Clay opposed Jackson with this program in the presidential election of 1832, but was defeated. In 1836 the Whig Party nominated William Henry Harrison, Hugh White, and Daniel Webster for the presidency. But the Democratic candidate, Martin Van Buren, won easily.

In the 1840's, many able men joined the party. They included Horace Greeley, editor of the New York *Tribune;* William H. Seward of New York; and Edward Everett, the Whigs' most brilliant orator.

The Whigs nominated William Harrison as their presidential candidate in 1840. He won the election, but died after serving only one month in office. Vice President John Tyler followed Harrison as President. Tyler had received the nomination for Vice President mainly to attract the Southern votes. Actually, Tyler was not a Whig, and opposed the Whig program. His opposition as President weakened the Whig strength.

In 1844, the Whigs renominated Henry Clay for the presidency, but he lost again. One reason for his defeat lay in his refusal to take a position on slavery. This cost Clay many Northern Whig votes. In the election of 1844, the Whigs for the first time presented a real political program. The program included a high tariff, regulated currency, and a single term for the presidency.

Decline of the Whigs. The Whigs managed to win the presidency with the popular Zachary Taylor in 1848. Four years later they tried to repeat the victory with General Winfield Scott. But the Democratic candidate, Franklin Pierce, defeated him. In 1856, a Whig convention backed Millard Fillmore, the unsuccessful Know-Nothing candidate for the presidency.

The Whig Party had already begun to break into sectional groups over the question of slavery. The Kansas-Nebraska Bill of 1854 split the party still further. Most Northern Whigs joined the new Republican Party. Many Southern Whigs returned to the Democratic Party. The remaining Whigs joined the Constitutional Union Party by 1860.   Donald R. McCoy

See also the separate articles for the various Whig leaders mentioned in this article, such as **Clay, Henry.**

Whin. See Furze.

Whiplash is a term commonly used to describe a type of injury to the neck. This kind of injury results from a sudden blow that throws the head rapidly backward and forward. Such a blow can damage the muscles and ligaments that hold the bones in the neck. A whiplash injury typically causes pain and stiffness in the neck, and often in the shoulders. It frequently produces severe headaches. Most whiplash injuries occur in car accidents. Raised headrests and the use of safety belts greatly reduce the chance of such injuries.

In many cases of whiplash, the victim does not experience pain until several hours after the injury occurs. The pain generally is most severe during the next several days. Wearing a padded collar to stabilize the neck, use of heat and massage, and taking mild pain medicines can help reduce the discomfort. Emotional upset due to

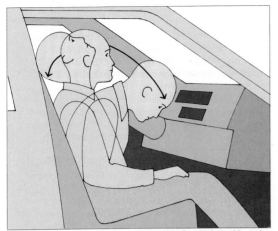

WORLD BOOK illustration by David Cunningham

Whiplash most often occurs as the result of a car accident. When the car is struck from the front or the rear, the sudden force throws the head rapidly backward and forward.

whiplash injury can make the condition worse, so doctors often reassure victims that the pain will diminish.

In most cases of whiplash injury, X rays do not show damage to the muscles and ligaments of the neck. As a result, it is difficult to determine the exact cause of the pain and the amount of disability that the injury produces.   Richard D. Penn

Whippet is a medium-sized hound with great speed. The whippet's lean, muscular form gives it the appearance of a small greyhound. A whippet weighs from 18 to 23 pounds (8 to 10 kilograms) and stands $17\frac{1}{2}$ to $22\frac{1}{2}$ inches (44 to 57 centimeters) high. Whippets have a short coat that may be any color or combination of colors. The dogs have a long, lean head, arched muscular back, and a long, tapering tail. Whippets are popular dogs for hunting rabbits and for racing. The dogs are able to run as fast as 35 miles (56 kilometers) per hour. See also **Dog** (picture: Hounds).
     Critically reviewed by the American Whippet Club

Whipping post is a post to which persons are tied when being whipped as a form of punishment. Such beatings once took place in public. Most villages in England and the American Colonies had whipping posts in their public squares. The posts were often set up with another device called the *stocks* (see **Stocks**).

Today, few persons are sentenced to be whipped. Fines and prison terms have replaced physical beating as forms of punishment in most countries. British law allowed whipping until 1948, and Canada abolished the whipping penalty in 1972. Delaware, the last state of the United States that allowed physical beating, prohibited the punishment in 1972. Whipping is still a legal punishment in some countries, including Singapore, South Africa, and such Muslim nations as Iran, Pakistan, and Saudi Arabia.   Marvin E. Wolfgang

Whipple, William (1730-1785), was a New Hampshire signer of the Declaration of Independence. He served as a delegate to the provincial congress in 1775, and to the Continental Congress in 1775-1776, and 1778. He fought as a brigadier general in the Revolutionary War. Whipple served in the state assembly from 1780 to 1784, and

as financial receiver for New Hampshire from 1782 to 1784. He was an associate justice of the superior court from 1782 until his death. Whipple was born in Kittery, Me.   Richard B. Morris

Whippoorwill is a North American bird named for its odd, whistling call, which sounds like "whip-poor-will, whip-poor-will." The whippoorwill lives in the eastern, central, and southern parts of the United States. It also is found as far north as southeastern Canada and as far south as Mexico and Honduras. The whippoorwill spends the winter along the Gulf Coast, in Mexico, and in Central America.

The whippoorwill is about 10 inches (25 centimeters) long. Its spotted, brown feathers make the bird hard to see in the heavily wooded areas in which it lives. During

Ron Willocks, Animals Animals

A whippoorwill has spotted brown feathers that blend with its woodland habitat and help protect the bird from enemies.

the day, the whippoorwill usually rests on the ground or perches lengthwise on a log. It flies mostly at night. Soft feathers help the whippoorwill fly silently. The bird uses its wide mouth rimmed with long bristles to catch flying insects. The female whippoorwill lays her two eggs among the leaves on the ground. The white eggs are delicately marked with lilac and brown. The whippoorwill and its relatives, the *chuck-will's widow* and the *poorwill,* often help farmers. These birds eat insects, including those that harm crops.

Scientific classification. The whippoorwill belongs to the goatsucker family, Caprimulgidae. It is *Caprimulgus vociferus.*
     Bertin W. Anderson

See also **Bird** (picture: Birds' eggs).

Whirligig. See Water beetle.

Whirlpool is a mass of water which spins around and around rapidly and with great force. A whirlpool may form in water for several reasons. It may occur when the water current strikes against a bank which has a peculiar form. It may also occur when opposing currents meet, and it may be caused by the action of the wind. Rocks or tides may get in the way of an ocean current. Whirlpools often form as a result.

There are several well-known whirlpools. One is the whirlpool in the gorge below Niagara Falls. This whirlpool was caused by the wearing away of a side basin out of the line of the river's course. The Maelstrom, which is off the coast of Norway, is formed by rocks and tides that oppose the current. The Charybdis, between

Sicily and Italy, is formed by winds, which act against the tidal currents. During storms the whirlpools become violent and dangerous to ships.   Eldred D. Wilson

See also **Maelstrom; Niagara River** (Description).

Whirlwind is a whirling mass of air. Whirlwinds include cyclones, dust devils, hurricanes, tornadoes, typhoons, and waterspouts. For more information about these types of whirlwinds, see the separate articles on each of them in *World Book.*

Whiskey is a strong alcoholic beverage made from such grains as barley, corn, rye, and wheat. It is one of the leading alcoholic beverages in the United States. Only beer and wine are more popular.

Whiskey is made by a process called *distilling.* Distillers first grind the grain and cook it in water, forming a mash. Then they mix in a mash of malt and water, which changes the starch in the grain to sugar. Next, yeast is added and the mixture *ferments.* Fermentation changes the sugar to ethyl alcohol. The mash then is heated, giving off alcohol vapors. Distillers collect the vapors and cool them. The cooling vapors liquefy as whiskey.

Whiskey ages about 2 to 12 years in oak barrels, where it develops flavor and an amber color. Before distillers bottle the whiskey, they add distilled water, diluting most beverages to between 80 and 100 *proof.* Proof signifies the percentage of alcohol in a beverage. In the United States, proof equals twice the amount of alcohol. Therefore, a beverage that is 100 proof is 50 per cent alcohol.

Whiskeys differ according to the grain used, the proof of the beverage, and the aging time. The most common whiskeys made in the United States are *blended whiskey, bourbon, Tennessee whiskey,* and *rye.* Blended whiskey is at least 20 per cent straight whiskey, blended with other whiskeys or with pure ethyl alcohol and water. Bourbon is made from a mash of mostly corn. Tennessee whiskey is similar to bourbon but is filtered through charcoal before aging. Rye is made from a mash of mostly rye grains. Any whiskey that is made in the United States except blended whiskey may be labeled "bottled in bond" if it has aged at least four years and is not less than 100 proof.

Imported whiskeys include *Canadian whisky, Irish whiskey,* and *Scotch whisky.* Canadian whisky is a blend usually made from corn and rye, with some wheat and barley malt. Irish whiskey and Scotch whisky are made mostly from barley. Scotch whisky, also called *Scotch,* tastes smoky because it is made from malt that has been dried over peat fires.   F. A. Meister

See also **Alcoholic beverage; Distilling.**

Whiskey Rebellion of 1794 was brought about by a federal tax in 1791 on United States whiskey makers. The rebellion was led by farmers in western Pennsylvania. These farmers found it profitable to turn much of their corn and rye crop into whiskey. They could ship whiskey to markets more easily and profitably than they could ship the bulky grain, because early roads and transportation facilities were poor.

The federal tax law permitted government agents to enter homes and collect money from small whiskey producers. Farmers throughout the Union immediately protested against this. In 1792, the Congress of the United States removed the tax from the smallest stills. This change satisfied Virginia and North Carolina farmers,

but whiskey makers in Pennsylvania still refused to pay the tax.

In the summer of 1794, the federal government ordered certain Pennsylvania ringleaders arrested. A series of bitter fights between United States marshals and the rebel farmers resulted. Several persons were killed or wounded before President George Washington sent in troops to stop the rebellion. Two rebel leaders were convicted of treason. However, they were later pardoned. The Whiskey Rebellion tested the use of federal power to enforce a federal law within a state.
     Richard Hofstadter

See also **Washington, George** (Whiskey Rebellion).

Whiskey Ring was an association of whiskey manufacturers and high government officials that was active during the 1870's in the United States. The conspirators banded together to cheat the United States government of taxes imposed on distilled liquors. The Whiskey Ring was one of the great political scandals of the Ulysses S. Grant Administration.

The association was formed in St. Louis, Mo., and soon spread to other cities. Many distillers were forced to join the ring in order to save their businesses. The illegal profits were divided among the conspiring government officials, some of whom held important positions. One of these government officials was the chief clerk in the Department of the Treasury. Another one, General Orville E. Babcock, was President Grant's private secretary.

The Treasury Department soon realized that it was losing millions of dollars in liquor revenue. It tried to trace the loss, but investigation was difficult. The thieves had friends in the Treasury Department who warned them of government activities. But Secretary of the Treasury Benjamin H. Bristow finally found evidence against the lawbreakers in 1875. Many persons were convicted, but the leaders escaped with light punishment.   John Donald Hicks

Whistle is a device that makes a sound when air or steam is blown through it. Most whistles consist of a tube with a sharp edge or lip. The air or steam is blown in one end of the tube and goes into a swirling motion when it strikes the lip. This motion first compresses and then expands the air, causing a sound.

Steam whistles are seldom used today. Steam locomotives used steam whistles. But today's diesel locomotives use various types of air horns, some of which sound like steam whistles. Police officers and sports officials blow small air whistles.   Paul J. Scheips

Whistler, James Abbott McNeill (1834-1903), was a famous American artist. He spent most of his life in Europe. Whistler's paintings, flamboyant manner, clever wit, and quarrelsome nature made him an international celebrity.

Whistler's best-known painting is *Arrangement in Gray and Black No. 1: Portrait of the Artist's Mother* (1872), commonly called *Whistler's Mother.* Its flattened forms, *monochrome* (single-color) tone, and unsymmetrical composition are characteristic of Whistler's style. He was influenced by Japanese artists who used similar techniques in woodcuts.

Whistler named many of his paintings for types of musical compositions, such as nocturnes and symphonies. He believed paintings, like music, should be ab-

Whistler's Mother ranks among the world's most famous portraits. The formal name of the painting is *Arrangement in Gray and Black No. 1: Portrait of the Artist's Mother*. Whistler painted the picture in London in 1872. He posed his mother against a gray wall. The small painting on the wall and the curtain enhance the harmony of the composition.

The Louvre, Paris (Art Resource)

stract. They should not describe objects or tell stories, but respond to the imagination of the artist. Whistler also felt forms in a painting are more important than the subject.

The English art critic John Ruskin criticized one of Whistler's most abstract paintings, *Nocturne in Black and Gold—The Falling Rocket* (about 1874). Ruskin declared that Whistler had flung "a pot of paint in the public's face." Whistler sued Ruskin for libel and defended his theories on art in court. He won the case but received less than a penny in damages. The cost of the lawsuit forced Whistler into bankruptcy. Nevertheless, it gave desirable publicity to his belief that art should be created for its own sake rather than for a moral purpose. Whistler included excerpts from his defense in a book of his collected writings, *The Gentle Art of Making Enemies* (1890).

In addition to his paintings, Whistler became well known for his prints and interior decorations. Whistler created about 440 etchings, including many illustrations of Venice and the River Thames (see **Etching** [picture: An etching by James Whistler]). The most famous example of Whistler's interior decoration is the Peacock Room, which he designed for a house in London. The room is now in the Freer Gallery in Washington, D.C.

Whistler was born in Lowell, Mass. In 1843, he moved with his family to St. Petersburg (now Leningrad), Russia, where his father directed the construction of a railroad. He returned to the United States in 1849. In 1851, Whistler entered the U.S. Military Academy at West Point. He was expelled three years later for academic reasons. From November 1854 to February 1855, Whistler worked as a chartmaker for the U.S. Coast and Geodetic Survey, where he received fine training in the technique of etching. In 1855, Whistler went to Paris to study art. He moved to London in 1859 and died there.

Alison McNeil Kettering

See also **Etching** (picture).

White. See **Color.**

White is the family name of two popular American journalists, father and son.

William Allen White (1868-1944) was a country editor who became known as the *Sage of Emporia*. He made his small-town newspaper, the *Emporia* (Kans.) *Gazette,* one of the most famous papers in the world. In 1923, he won the Pulitzer Prize for editorial writing. He also was awarded a Pulitzer Prize in 1947, after his death, for his autobiography.

White was born in Emporia, Kans., and was educated at Emporia College and at the University of Kansas. In 1890, he left college and took a job on the El Dorado (Kans.) *Republican.* After various newspaper jobs in Kansas, he returned to Emporia in 1895 and became owner and editor of the *Gazette.* A year later, White wrote an editorial entitled "What's the Matter with Kansas?" This editorial made him famous overnight. The Republican Party reprinted the article and used it in the campaign to elect William McKinley as President of the United States. From that time on, White's editorials played an important part in the political affairs of the country.

William Lindsay White (1900-1973), the son of William Allen White, won fame during World War II as a war correspondent and an author of books about the war. He was born in Emporia, and graduated from Harvard University. After graduating from college, he worked with his father on the *Gazette.* In 1935, White joined the staff of the *Washington Post,* and two years later left to work for *Fortune* magazine. In 1940, White became a member of the staff of the *Reader's Digest.*

John Eldridge Drewry

White, Alfred Holmes (1873-1953), pioneered in the development of engineering as a profession in the United States. He was associated with the University of Michigan. His books, *Technical Gas and Fuel Analysis* (1913) and *Engineering Materials* (1939), became important texts. His work with the American Institute of Engineers and the Society for the Promotion of Engineering Education set the standards for the American engineering education program. White was born in Peoria, Ill.

Herbert S. Rhinesmith

White, Bill (1934-   ), became president of the National Baseball League in 1989. In that position, White was the highest-ranking black executive of a major American professional sports league.

White has spent his entire adult life in professional baseball. He played in the National League for 13 seasons, beginning with the New York (now San Francisco) Giants in 1956. He spent most of his playing career as a first baseman for the St. Louis Cardinals, retiring in 1969. In 1971, White became a broadcaster of New York Yankees games, a job he held until he was named National League president.

White was born in Lakewood, Fla. His full name is William DeKova White.   Thomas H. Barnidge

White, Byron Raymond (1917-   ), became an associate justice of the Supreme Court of the United States in 1962. President John F. Kennedy appointed him to succeed Justice Charles E. Whittaker, who had retired. White was deputy attorney general at the time.

White has sided with liberals in supporting school desegregation and *affirmative action* (see **Affirmative action**). However, he has taken conservative positions on a number of other issues. For example, White opposed court decisions that strengthened safeguards designed to assure that people accused of a crime are treated fairly. He has also objected to the belief that the U.S. Constitution guarantees individuals a right to privacy. Thus, White opposed decisions that declared certain state laws against abortion invalid. He also wrote a majority opinion upholding a state law that made homosexual acts a crime.

White was born in Fort Collins, Colo. He graduated from the University of Colorado in 1938 and from Yale Law School in 1946. He won national fame and the nickname "Whizzer" as an all-American halfback at Colorado. He later played professional football to help finance his law studies.

After law school, White served as a law clerk to Chief Justice Fred M. Vinson. He joined a Denver law firm in 1947 and became a partner in 1950. He was appointed deputy attorney general in 1961.   Owen M. Fiss

See also **Supreme Court of the U.S.** (picture).

White, E. B. (1899-1985), was an American author. He was known chiefly as an essay writer, but he also wrote poetry and children's books. His essays, which deal with both serious and light subjects, have a clear, witty style. White wrote in an informal, personal manner.

White wrote three children's books. *Stuart Little* (1945) tells of a mouse with human parents, and *Charlotte's Web* (1952) concerns a girl, a pig, and a spider (see Lit-

erature for children [picture: *Charlotte's Web*]). *The Trumpet of the Swan* (1970) is about a swan without a voice. In these books, which deal with friendship and love, the animals talk and act like people. Several collections of White's writings have been published, including *Letters of E. B. White* (1976), *Essays of E. B. White* (1977), and *Poems and Sketches of E. B. White* (1981).

Photoworld from FPG

E. B. White

Elwyn Brooks White was born in Mount Vernon, N.Y. He started writing for *The New Yorker* magazine in 1925 and strongly influenced its literary style. Many of his works tell of his life in Maine, where he lived. In 1963, White received the Presidential Medal of Freedom. He received a Pulitzer Prize special citation in 1978 for his writings.   Marcus Klein

White, Edward Douglass (1845-1921), served as chief justice of the United States from 1910 to 1921. In 1894, he was appointed an associate justice of the Supreme Court of the United States. White became best known for his dissent in the case declaring the national income tax unconstitutional, and for his antitrust decisions requiring the dissolution of the Standard Oil and American Tobacco companies. He was born in Lafourche Parish, La. A statue of White represents Louisiana in the United States Capitol.   Jerre S. Williams

White, Edward Higgins, II (1930-1967), in 1965 became the first United States astronaut to leave his craft while in outer space. The spacewalk lasted 21 minutes and took place on June 3, 1965, during a four-day flight made by White and James A. McDivitt. White and astronauts Virgil Grissom and Roger Chaffee died on Jan. 27, 1967, when a flash fire swept through their Apollo spacecraft. The fire occurred during a test at Cape Kennedy (now Cape Canaveral), Fla.

White was born on Nov. 14, 1930, in San Antonio, Tex. He graduated from the U.S. Military Academy in 1952 and went into the Air Force. In 1959, he earned a master's degree in aeronautical engineering from the University of Michigan.   William J. Cromie

White, Hugh Lawson (1773-1840), an American statesman and jurist, was a candidate for President of the United States in 1836. In that year, Martin Van Buren ran as Andrew Jackson's hand-picked successor on the Democratic ticket. The Whigs hoped to defeat Van Buren by running Daniel Webster, William Henry Harrison, and White. The plan failed, and White carried only two states, Georgia and Tennessee.

White was born in Iredell County, North Carolina. He moved to Tennessee, where he practiced law and became a judge, state senator, and U.S. attorney. He was a U.S. senator from 1825 to 1840.   Richard N. Current

White, John. See Lost Colony.

White, Margaret Bourke-. See Bourke-White, Margaret.

White, Patrick (1912-   ), an Australian novelist, won the 1973 Nobel Prize for literature. He became the first Australian writer to receive this high award.

White writes in a complex, flowery style. He often uses the *stream of consciousness* technique, which describes in detail the thoughts that flow through the mind of the characters.

The major characters in White's novels are emotionally isolated from other people. In his first novel, *Happy Valley* (1939), White wrote an ironic account of life in a dreary Australian village. He gained international recognition with his fourth novel, *The Tree of Man* (1955), which tells the story of an Australian family. *Voss* (1957), a historical novel, describes an explorer's expedition across Australia in the mid-1800's. White's other novels include *The Aunt's Story* (1948), *Riders in the Chariot* (1961), *The Eye of the Storm* (1973), and *A Fringe of Leaves* (1977). White wrote an autobiography, *Flaws in the Glass* (1982). He also has written plays, poetry, and short stories. Patrick Victor Martindale White was born in London, England.   Thomas A. Erhard

White, Paul Dudley (1886-1973), an American physician, was regarded as one of the world's great authorities on heart diseases. He served as president of the American Heart Association from 1942 to 1944, and became president of the International Society of Cardiology in 1954. He headed many committees and foreign missions, and was a consultant of governments. He acted as a consultant to President Dwight D. Eisenhower. White was born in Boston.   Noah D. Fabricant

White, Peregrine (1620-1703), was the first English child born in New England, on the *Mayflower* in Cape Cod Bay. His father, William, died soon afterwards. His mother, Susanna White, then married Edward Winslow, becoming both the first mother and the first bride in Plymouth. Peregrine became a captain of militia and settled in Marshfield.   Bradford Smith

White, Stanford (1853-1906), was a leading American architect. He was a partner in McKim, Mead, and White, one of the largest and best-known American architectural firms of the late 1800's and early 1900's. White helped found the firm in 1879 with Charles Follen McKim and William Rutherford Mead. White's works were especially noted for their ornamentation and rich texture.

White designed a wide range of buildings, including country houses, churches, city housing projects, and office buildings. He also collaborated with the American sculptor Augustus Saint-Gaudens on a number of monuments. White's major designs include the Tiffany Building (1906), the Washington Arch (1889-1895), the Judson Memorial Church (1891), and the campus of what is now the Bronx Community College of the City University of New York (1892-1901). All these projects were built in New York City.

White was born in New York City. He began his career as an assistant to the American architect Henry Hobson Richardson. White was shot to death by Harry K. Thaw, the jealous husband of Evelyn Nesbit, one of White's friends. White's murder and Thaw's trial created a sensation in the United States.   Leland M. Roth

White, Walter Francis (1893-1955), was an American civil rights leader. White served as secretary of the National Association for the Advancement of Colored People (NAACP) from 1931 until his death. He fought to eliminate the lynching of blacks during the 1920's and 1930's. White's book *Rope and Faggot* (1929) was a powerful at-

tack on lynching. White received the Spingarn Medal in 1937 for promoting the rights of blacks.

White was born in Atlanta. He described his struggles against racial prejudice in his autobiography, *A Man Called White* (1948). White also wrote two novels that dealt with race relations, *Fire in the Flint* (1924) and *Flight* (1926).   Edwin H. Cady

White ant. See Termite.

White blood cell. See Blood.

White cliffs of Dover. See England (Surface features; picture).

White-eye is the name of a group of small, active songbirds found mainly in Africa, southern Asia, Australia, and New Zealand. The birds get their name from the circle of bright white feathers that surround the eyes of most species in the group. Their other feathers are dull shades of green, yellow, gray, and tan. White-eyes

WORLD BOOK illustration by John Dawson

Indian white-eyes live in southern Asia. Like most species of white-eyes, they have white feathers around the eyes. White-eyes huddle close together on branches when resting.

average from 4 to $5\frac{1}{2}$ inches (10 to 14 centimeters) in length and have long, thin bills.

There are about 85 species of white-eyes. They live in open, shrubby, and sparsely wooded areas. These birds are usually found in flocks. The flocks continually move from tree to tree, feeding on insects, berries, fruits, and flower nectar. White-eyes seem to enjoy touching each other. They huddle close together on branches when resting, and members of the flock will often *preen* (groom) each other with their bills.

White-eyes build cuplike nests of tightly woven plant fibers, usually in the forks of branches. The female white-eye lays from 2 to 4 eggs, which normally hatch in 11 to 13 days. Often, several adult white-eyes feed the young.

For small birds, white-eyes have been exceptionally successful at reaching oceanic islands and establishing themselves there. Most of the islands in the Indian Ocean have at least one species of white-eye. Although white-eyes are useful to people because they eat insect pests, they also can be a nuisance because they destroy fruit crops.

Scientific classification. White-eyes make up the white-eye family, Zosteropidae.   David M. Niles

White gold. See Gold (Jewelry); Platinum.

William R. Wilson

The north portico of the White House faces Pennsylvania Avenue in Washington, D.C.

White House is the official residence of the President of the United States. The President lives and works in the world-famous mansion in Washington, D.C. The White House contains the living quarters for the Chief Executive's family and the offices in which the President and staff members conduct official business of the United States. Some of the most important decisions in history have been made there.

The 132-room White House stands in the middle of a beautifully landscaped 18-acre (7-hectare) plot at 1600 Pennsylvania Avenue (see **Washington, D.C.** [map]). The building was popularly known as the *White House* in the 1800's. However, its official name was first the *President's House* and then *Executive Mansion* until 1901. That year, President Theodore Roosevelt authorized *White House* as the official title.

The White House is one of the most popular tourist attractions in the United States. Every year, more than $1\frac{1}{2}$ million visitors go through parts of the mansion that are open to the public. Certain rooms in the White House are open to the public Tuesday through Saturday between 10 a.m. and noon. Tourists may take special tours by obtaining passes from members of Congress from their state. The building is closed to the public on Sundays, Mondays, and holidays.

Outside the White House

The main building is 175 feet (53 meters) long and 85 feet (26 meters) high. A wide curved *portico* (porch) with Ionic columns two stories high stands on the mansion's south side. A square portico on the north side is the main entrance. Two long, low galleries extend from the building's east and west sides. The terraced roof covering them forms a promenade on the first floor. Facilities for the White House press corps are under the west terrace. A theater is under the east terrace.

The east and west wings stand at the end of the terraces. The west (executive) wing contains the offices of the President and the presidential staff, and the Cabinet room. The east wing includes the offices of the President's military aides.

The south lawn, often called the President's Park, contains many trees and shrubs planted by former occupants of the White House. For example, the south portico is shaded by magnificent magnolia trees planted by President Andrew Jackson.

Inside the White House

Public rooms. Tourists enter the White House through the east wing. Most visitors are shown only five rooms on the first floor of the mansion, but these rooms represent the elegance and beauty of the entire interior.

The State Dining Room at the west end of the main building can accommodate as many as 140 dinner guests at one time. It was remodeled in 1902.

The Red Room is furnished in the style of the period from 1810 to 1830. The walls are hung with red silk.

The Blue Room is the main reception room for guests of the President. Its furnishings represent the period from 1817 to 1825. President James Monroe, who occupied the White House during these years, ordered much of the furniture now in this oval room.

Drawing by Robert W. Nicholson, National Geographic Society;
copyrighted by the White House Historical Association

These models show the back of the White House and the main rooms of the building's interior.

Ground floor
1. Library
2. Ground Floor Corridor*
3. Vermeil Room
4. China Room

5. Diplomatic Reception Room
6. Map Room

First floor
7. East Room*

8. Green Room*
9. Blue Room*
10. South Portico
11. Red Room*
12. State Dining Room*

13. Family Dining Room
14. Cross Hall*
15. Entrance Hall*

*Open to the public

Lorenzo S. Winslow, Architect

This model shows the original main building and the two wings added later.
1. East wing
2. Movie theater for family
3. Main building
4. White House press facilities
5. President's office
6. Executive wing

Inside the White House

The Diplomatic Reception Room, *above,* serves as the entrance to the White House for official functions. The wallpaper in this oval room was printed in France in 1834.

The Red Room, *above,* is furnished in the American Empire style, popular between 1810 and 1830. The walls are hung with red silk edged with gold trim. The Red Room serves as a parlor.

The State Dining Room, *left,* is the scene of the President's official banquets. Its tables can accommodate 140 guests for a state dinner.

The Blue Room, *above,* is an oval drawing room. It serves as the main reception room for guests of the President. President James Monroe ordered many of the furnishings in the room.

The Green Room, *above,* is decorated in the style popular between 1800 and 1814. A light green silk material covers the walls. The Green Room, like the Red Room, is a parlor.

All photographs by the National Geographic Society; copyrighted by the White House Historical Association

The library, *left,* is decorated chiefly in the style of the early 1800's. The crystal chandelier once belonged to the family of American novelist James Fenimore Cooper. The carpet was made in the mid-1800's in Tabriz, Iran.

The Green Room has been restored in the style of the years between 1800 and 1814. Its walls are covered with a light green silk moire. Its furniture is in the style of Duncan Phyfe, a noted American furniture maker of the late 1700's and early 1800's.

The East Room is the largest room in the White House, 79 feet (24 meters) long and $36\frac{3}{4}$ feet (11.2 meters) wide. Guests are entertained in the East Room after formal dinners. It is at the end of the first floor. The East Room was remodeled in 1902.

Private rooms. The President, the President's family, their guests, and the President's staff use many other rooms in the White House every day. The ground floor contains the Diplomatic Reception Room, used as the entrance for formal functions; the kitchen; the library; and offices of the White House physician and curator.

The second floor contains the living quarters of the President and the President's family. The Lincoln Bedroom, the Treaty Room, and the Queen's Room are also on that floor. The third floor contains guest rooms and staff quarters. The White House also has a private bowling alley, swimming pool, and movie theater.

History of the White House

The original building was begun in 1792. It was designed by James Hoban, an Irish-born architect. Hoban's design was selected in a competition sponsored by the federal government. It showed a simple Georgian mansion in the classical Palladian style of Europe in the 1700's. He modeled the design after Leinster House, the meeting place of the Irish Parliament, in Dublin, Ireland.

1807

1814

1848

The White House changed appearance several times during the 1800's. It was almost completely rebuilt following a fire in 1814. The photograph of the White House about 1860 was taken by Mathew Brady, the famous Civil War photographer. It may be the first photograph of the White House.

From the Book *The White House* by Amy La Follette Jensen, published by McGraw-Hill Book Co., Inc.; Brady-Handy Collection

1860

President and Mrs. John Adams became the first occupants of the White House in 1800. But work on the White House had not yet been completed, and they suffered many inconveniences. Mrs. Adams used the East Room to dry the family laundry.

The White House became more comfortable and beautiful during the Administration of Thomas Jefferson. With the aid of architect Benjamin H. Latrobe, Jefferson carried out many of the original White House plans, and added terraces at the east and west ends.

A new building. British forces burned the mansion on Aug. 24, 1814, during the War of 1812. President James Madison and his wife, Dolley, were forced to flee. The White House was rebuilt and President and Mrs. James Monroe moved into it in 1817. The north and south porticos were added in the 1820's.

President Theodore Roosevelt had the building repaired in 1902. He rebuilt the east terrace and added the executive wing adjacent to the west terrace.

President Franklin D. Roosevelt enlarged the west wing. An indoor swimming pool was added there. The east wing was also expanded.

Rebuilding and redecorating. The White House underwent extensive repairs from 1948 to 1952, during the presidency of Harry S. Truman. Workers used concrete and steel to strengthen the dangerously weakened structure of the Executive Mansion. The third floor was converted into a full third story, and a second-story balcony was added to the south portico for the President's private use. The basement was expanded, and the total number of rooms was increased from 125 to 132.

But the historic rooms familiar to the American public remained basically unchanged until the Administration of John F. Kennedy. In 1961, Mrs. Kennedy appointed a Fine Arts Committee to restore the White House interior to its original appearance. The White House Historical Association was chartered in 1961 to publish guide books on the mansion and to acquire historic furnishings for the White House. A library committee was formed to stock the White House library with books representing American thought throughout U.S. history.

More major changes in the building's historic rooms occurred during the Administration of Richard M. Nixon. Beginning in 1970, Mrs. Nixon continued Mrs. Kennedy's efforts to restore the White House interior in an early 1800's *motif* (theme).   Clement E. Conger

Related articles. See the section on Life in the White House in articles on the Presidents. Other related articles in *World Book* include:

Blair House	Secret Service, United States
President of the United States (The life of the President; pictures)	White House hostesses

Additional resources

Aikman, Lonnelle. *The Living White House.* 7th ed. White House Historical Assn., 1982.

Bruce, Preston, and others. *From the Door of the White House.* Norton, 1984. Suitable for younger readers. Recollections of 20 years on the White House staff.

Sandak, Cass R. *The White House.* Watts, 1981. For younger readers.

White House Historical Assn. *The White House: An Historic Guide.* 15th ed. The Assn., 1982.

White House conference is a national meeting that the President of the United States calls to discuss issues facing the American people. Community leaders, concerned citizens, and various experts attend the conferences, which may last three or four days, to discuss the topics and recommend action. White House conferences have dealt with such issues as child care, drug abuse, the economy, education, family life, and nutrition. Other topics have included aging, civil rights, the handicapped, highway safety, and libraries. Each conference reports to the President, and the President usually speaks at a major session of the conference.

In organizing most White House conferences, the President appoints a governing committee and an executive director, who heads the conference staff and directs the selection of delegates. The President will sometimes request that governors call state conferences on a particular issue before a large national conference is held. Recommendations from state conferences are forwarded to the national meeting.

There have been more than 60 White House conferences, most of which have been held since 1945. President Theodore Roosevelt called the first conference in 1908 to discuss conservation of natural resources. The next year, he authorized the Conference on Dependent Children. This conference of 216 delegates led to the formation in 1912 of the Children's Bureau, now part of the Department of Health and Human Services.

Some topics have become the subject of repeated and expanded conferences. Besides Roosevelt, Presidents Woodrow Wilson, Herbert Hoover, Franklin D. Roosevelt, Harry S. Truman, Dwight D. Eisenhower, Richard M. Nixon, and Ronald Reagan all held conferences on children and youth. Conferences on aging occurred in 1950, 1961, 1971, and 1981.   Thomas E. Cronin

White House hostesses include the women who receive and entertain the President's guests at the White House, in place of the President's wife. Thomas Jefferson was the first President to come to the White House without a wife. During Jefferson's years as President, the role of hostess was filled by Dolley Madison, the wife of Secretary of State James Madison, and by Jefferson's daughter Martha Randolph.

Andrew Jackson's chief hostess was his wife's niece, Emily Donelson; and for Martin Van Buren, his daughter-in-law, Angelica Singleton Van Buren. The wife of William Henry Harrison was too ill to travel to Washington, D.C. She sent their daughter-in-law, Jane Irwin Harrison, to serve as hostess. John Tyler's wife died shortly after he became President. His daughter-in-law, Priscilla Cooper Tyler, and later his daughter Letitia Tyler Semple, officiated until he remarried in 1844.

The wife of Zachary Taylor refused to attend social affairs. Her daughter, Betty Bliss, presided for her. Millard Fillmore's daughter, Mary Abigail, served in place of her invalid mother. Harriet Lane, niece of James Buchanan, a bachelor, served as his hostess. Martha Johnson Patterson, the daughter of Andrew Johnson, presided in place of his invalid wife. Hostess for Chester Arthur was his sister Mary Arthur McElroy. Rose Cleveland, Grover Cleveland's sister, was his hostess until he married in 1886. After the death of Woodrow Wilson's first wife, his daughter Margaret officiated until he remarried in 1915.

Kathryn K. Sklar

See also the section on *Life in the White House* in articles on those Presidents mentioned above.

White magic. See Magic (Kinds of magic).

White Mountains are part of the Appalachian Mountain system. They stretch in a southwestern direction from Maine into New Hampshire. The White Mountains received their name because their rocky summits appear white when they reflect sunlight. For location, see **New Hampshire** (physical map).

The White Mountains cover about 1,000 square miles (2,590 square kilometers). Few people live in the area because of the rugged terrain and lack of good farmland. The mountains include a number of ranges. The Presidential Range in New Hampshire is the most important. Chief mountains in this range bear the names of early U.S. Presidents. Mount Washington (6,288 feet, or 1,917 meters) is the highest peak in New Hampshire. Sixty-eight other peaks are over 3,900 feet (1,190 meters).

Deep canyons called "notches" cut through the White Mountains. The best known of these are the Carter, Crawford, Dixville, Franconia, Kinsman, and Pinkham. The famous Old Man of the Mountains, or Great Stone Face, is a feature of Profile Mountain in Franconia Notch. Wind and rain have carved a natural profile of a man's face on this cliff. Nathaniel Hawthorne immortalized the profile in his story "The Great Stone Face."

Since 1911, much of the White Mountains area has

Shostal

The Old Man of the Mountains, or Great Stone Face, is a feature of Profile Mountain in the White Mountains. This natural granite formation resembles a side of a man's face.

been included in a national forest. State forests have helped preserve two of the notches. Crawford was established in 1911, and Franconia in 1925.

A nonprofit organization, called Mt. Washington Observatory, Inc., keeps daily records of temperature, wind velocity, and radioactive "fallout" in the mountains. On April 12, 1934, the observatory recorded a wind of 231 miles (372 kilometers) per hour, the highest wind velocity ever recorded on earth. Since 1955, Mount Washington has been a testing site for cloud seeding to produce rainfall.   J. Duane Squires

See also **Mount Washington; New Hampshire** (pictures).

White paper is a British government report or policy statement on an important subject. It is a common name for *command papers* (documents technically submitted to the House of Commons on "command of the Crown"). The British called these documents *white papers* because many were prepared hastily and submitted without the traditional blue cover used for longer documents. The U.S. government does not use the term officially. But certain U.S. documents are popularly referred to as "white papers."   Robert E. Dowse

White Sands Missile Range, New Mexico, is the main missile testing site of the United States Army. The range covers about 2 million acres (800,000 hectares) in south-central New Mexico. This area is almost as large as the states of Connecticut and Rhode Island combined. The range extends 120 miles (193 kilometers) from north to south, and 40 miles (64 kilometers) from east to west. The headquarters of the range are located 27 miles (43 kilometers) east of Las Cruces.

The Army established the White Sands Proving Ground in 1945 and renamed it in 1958. The United States tested its first missiles there in 1945, shortly before the end of World War II. They were V-2 missiles captured from the Germans. The first atomic bomb was exploded in July 1945 at Trinity Site, on the eastern side of the range.   Thomas S. Grodecki

White Sands National Monument is in southern New Mexico. It contains great deposits of wind-blown gypsum sand. In bright light, the sands resemble a vast snowfield. The monument was established in 1933. For its area, see **National Park System** (table: National monuments).

White Sea, called *Beloye More* in the Soviet Union, is an arm of the Arctic Ocean. It reaches into the northern part of the Soviet Union. For location, see **Union of Soviet Socialist Republics** (terrain map). The Onega, Dvina, and Mezen' rivers flow into the White Sea. Onega and Archangel are the largest cities on this sea. The sea is icebound from September until June, but shipping is heavy in summer. The Dvina, Volga, and Dnepr rivers link the sea to the Caspian and Black seas. The Norwegian explorer Ottar discovered the White Sea in the A.D. 800's.   John D. Isaacs

White Sea-Baltic Canal. See **Canal** (table).

White shark. See **Shark** (Kinds of sharks).

White Sulphur Springs, W. Va. (pop. 3,371), named for its mineral springs, is a famous health resort. It lies about 120 miles (193 kilometers) east of Charleston, the state capital. For location, see **West Virginia** (political map). The city has a mayor-council government.

Settlers first came to the region about 1750. Fashionable people of the Old South visited the springs as early as 1779. After the resort became famous, its *President's Cottage* served as the summer home of Presidents Martin Van Buren, John Tyler, and Millard Fillmore. During the Civil War, soldiers fought the Battle of Dry Creek near the resort.   Rebecca Sarver

White walnut. See **Butternut**.

White whale. See **Whale** (Belugas and narwhals).

Whitefield, *HWIHT feeld,* **George** (1714-1770), was an Anglican preacher and evangelist. In Great Britain, Whitefield played an important part in the founding of Methodism. In the American Colonies, he became a leader of a series of religious revival movements called the Great Awakening (see **Great Awakening**).

Whitefield was born in Gloucester, England. While studying at Oxford University in the early 1730's, he was influenced by Charles and John Wesley, the founders of Methodism. Whitefield experienced a religious conversion in 1735 that changed his life. He was ordained an Anglican deacon in 1736 and became known for his bold, dramatic, and severely challenging preaching. Some Anglican ministers accused him of disrupting their congregations and refused to let him preach in their churches. Whitefield began to preach outdoors and attracted large crowds. His success influenced John Wesley to begin outdoor preaching, which became typical of the Methodists.

Between 1738 and 1770, Whitefield visited America seven times. There he angered some ministers who resented his attacks on the lack of interest in the spiritual life. These ministers also denied their pulpits to Whitefield, so he again turned to outdoor preaching, with great success. His preaching made him one of the best known religious figures in colonial America.
    Mark A. Noll

Whitefish is the name of a group of fishes that live in fresh water. Whitefish are found in many lakes and streams in the northern regions of North America, Europe, and Asia. They are related to trout and salmon, but they have larger scales than those fish. They also have smaller teeth than trout and salmon. Some whitefish are toothless. Whitefish are among the most important freshwater food fishes.

The *lake whitefish,* which lives in North American lakes and rivers, is the most valuable species. It has a long body, a cone-shaped snout, and a forked tail. It lacks teeth, and its upper jaw projects beyond the lower jaw. Most lake whitefish weigh about 4 pounds (1.8 kilograms). In the past, however, individuals weighing up to 20 pounds (9 kilograms) were caught in the Great Lakes. Lake whitefish feed on insects and shellfish and usually live in deep water.

The *lake herring,* also called *cisco,* also is a type of whitefish. It is found in the Great Lakes and is a valuable food fish. It is more abundant than the lake whitefish. Another excellent food fish is the *mountain whitefish.* It lives in mountain lakes and streams in the Western United States. The *round whitefish* lives in the lakes of New England and the Adirondacks, in the Great Lakes, and in rivers and streams in northern Canada. This fish also is commercially valuable.

Scientific classification. Whitefish belong to the trout family, Salmonidae. The lake whitefish is *Coregonus clupeaformis,* and the lake herring is *C. artedii.* The mountain whitefish is *Prosopium williamsoni,* and the round whitefish is *P. cylindraceum.*
    David W. Greenfield

See also **Fish** (picture: Fish of temperate fresh waters).

Whitehead, Alfred North (1861-1947), was an English mathematician and philosopher. His writings did much to narrow the gap between philosophy and science. Whitehead's works reflect his firsthand knowledge of science, his philosophical insight, and his imaginative writing style. He thought scientific knowledge, though precise, is incomplete. It must be supplemented, he said, by philosophical principles and insights of poets.

Whitehead was born in Ramsgate. He taught at Cambridge University and London University until 1924, when he joined the faculty of Harvard University. Whitehead's writings on mathematics, logic, and the theory of knowledge laid the groundwork for his philosophical classic, *Process and Reality* (1929). This book explains that process and growth are the fundamental ideas which lead us to understand God, nature, and our own experiences. Whitehead also wrote *Principia Mathematica* (with Bertrand Russell, 1910-1913) and *Science and the Modern World* (1925).   John E. Smith

Whitehorse (pop. 15,199) is the capital and chief distribution and communication center of the Yukon Territory. Whitehorse lies on the west bank of the Yukon River, 111 miles (179 kilometers) north of Skagway, Alaska. It is located on the Alaska Highway. Whitehorse's economy centers on mining, tourism, transportation, and government services. The city has regional headquarters of the Royal Canadian Mounted Police and many federal government departments. Mining products are shipped from Whitehorse to outside markets. Lake trout and grayling swim in neighboring streams and lakes. The region has bears, moose, and other game animals. For the location of Whitehorse, see **Yukon Territory** (map).

Airlines link Whitehorse with cities in Canada and the United States. A dam built above Whitehorse Rapids in 1959 to furnish power has created a lake in Miles Canyon. Many gold seekers came past Whitehorse in the rush of 1897-1898. Whitehorse was named for the Yukon River rapids, which resemble the mane of a white horse.

Patricia M. Living

Whiteman, Paul (1890-1967), was a famous American orchestra conductor. He was often called the "King of Jazz." In 1919, Whiteman introduced "symphonic jazz." Later he conducted the first performances of such compositions as George Gershwin's *Rhapsody in Blue* (1924) and Ferde Grofé's *Grand Canyon Suite* (1931), both of which show jazz influences. Whiteman was born in Denver, Colo., and played first viola in the Denver Symphony Orchestra while in his teens. After World War I, he formed his own orchestra and toured the United States and Europe. In the 1930's, Whiteman became a popular conductor on radio programs. In 1943, he became musical director of the Blue Network, which later became the American Broadcasting Company. See also **Grofé, Ferde.**   Gerald Bordman

Whitewash is a white mixture made from whiting, glue, water, common salt, flour, and unslaked lime. It is used instead of paint to put a coating on basement walls, the walls of lighthouses, fences, and other spots where a clear white is desired and where paint is too expensive to be practical. Whitewash is applied with a brush. A heavy coating over rough mortar plaster closes the pores against moisture and dirt.   Edward W. Stewart

Whiting. See Chalk.

Whitman, Marcus (1802-1847), was an American pioneer, doctor, and missionary among the Indians. Appointed as a Presbyterian missionary physician to Oregon by the American Board for Foreign Missions, he visited the Pacific Northwest with Samuel Parker in 1835. He returned there in 1836, with his wife, the Reverend Henry Spalding and his wife, and W. H. Gray. They established two missions, one near the site of the present city of Walla Walla, Wash.

They drove their wagon as far as Fort Boise, and thus were credited with opening that part of the wagon road to Oregon. In the winter of 1842, Whitman rode to the East to gain further missionary support, and to try to en-

courage emigration to Oregon. He also hoped to interest the United States government in settling the area.

The new settlers of 1847 brought with them an epidemic of measles that caused the death of many Indian children. The missionaries' medicine did not help them. In 1847, a band of Cayuse Indians, who probably believed their children were poisoned, attacked the mission. They killed Whitman, his wife, and 12 other persons, and burned all the mission buildings. Whitman was born in Rushville, N.Y. He practiced medicine for eight years before becoming a missionary. A statue of Whitman in the U.S. Capitol represents the state of Washington.   Thomas D. Clark

See also **Whitman, Narcissa; Whitman Mission National Historic Site.**

Whitman, Narcissa (1808-1847), was a missionary teacher to the Indians of the Pacific Northwest. Born in Prattsburg, N.Y., she married the missionary Marcus Whitman in 1836. She was one of the first two white women to journey overland to the Northwest. The couple began a mission among the Cayuse Indians at Waiilatpu, in what is now Washington. Indians massacred the Whitmans and 12 other people on Nov. 29, 1847. See also **Whitman, Marcus.**   Earle E. Cairns

Whitman, Walt (1819-1892), was an American poet who wrote *Leaves of Grass.* This collection of poems is considered one of the world's major literary works.

Whitman's poems sing the praises of the United States and of democracy. The poet's love of America grew from his faith that Americans might reach new worldly and spiritual heights. Whitman wrote: "The chief reason for the being of the United States of America is to bring about the common good will of all mankind, the solidarity of the world."

Whitman may have begun working on *Leaves of Grass* as early as 1848. The book's form and content were so unusual that no commercial publisher would publish it. In 1855, he published the collection of 12 poems at his own expense. In the preface, Whitman wrote: "The United States themselves are essentially the greatest poem." Between 1856 and 1882, Whitman published five more revised and enlarged editions of his book. He believed that *Leaves of Grass* had grown with his own emotional and intellectual development.

His work. Beginning students of Whitman will find it easiest to study the poems separately. They should try to understand each poem's imagery, symbolism, literary structure, and unity of theme.

"Song of Myself," the longest poem in *Leaves of Grass,* is considered Whitman's greatest. It is a lyric poem told through the joyful experiences of the narrator, simply called "I," who chants the poem's 52 sections. Sometimes "I" is the poet himself—"Walt Whitman, an American." In other passages, "I" speaks for the human race, the universe, or a specific character being dramatized. Like all Whitman's major poems, "Song of Myself" contains symbols. For example, in the poem he describes grass as a symbol of life—"the babe of vegetation," "the handkerchief of the Lord/A scented gift and remembrancer designedly dropt."

"Out of the Cradle Endlessly Rocking" tells of a man reminiscing over a boyhood experience in which a mockingbird lost its mate in a storm at sea. The memory of the bird's song teaches the man the meaning of death and thus the true vocation of a poet: to celebrate death as merely part of the cycle of birth, life, death, and rebirth.

Whitman wrote "When Lilacs Last in the Dooryard Bloom'd" on the death of Abraham Lincoln. Lincoln died in April, a time of rebirth in nature. As his coffin is transported from Washington, D.C., to Springfield, Ill., it passes the young wheat, "every grain from its shroud in the dark-brown fields uprisen." Whitman says that each spring the blooming lilac will remind him not only of the death of Lincoln, but also of the eternal return to life. The evening star Venus symbolizes Lincoln, who has "droop'd in the western sky."

In "Passage to India," Whitman sees modern achievements in transportation and communication as symbols of universal brotherhood. First, individuals are to be united with themselves and then with God, the "Elder Brother."

A group of Civil War poems called "Drum Taps" describes battlefield scenes and Whitman's emotions during wartime. "O Captain! My Captain!," another poem on Lincoln's death, is Whitman's most popular poem, but differs from his others in rhyme and rhythm. The "Children of Adam" poems defend the sacredness of sex. The "Calamus" poems praise male companionship.

Whitman wrote in a form similar to *thought-rhythm,* or *parallelism.* This form is found in Old Testament poetry. It is also found in sacred books of India, such as the *Bhagavad-Gita,* which Whitman may have read in translation. The rhythm of his lines suggests the rise and fall of the sea he loved so much. This structure is better suited to expressing emotion than to logical discussion.

In general, Whitman's poetry is idealistic and romantic while his prose is realistic. His best prose is in a book of essays, mostly autobiographical, called *Specimen Days* (1882). Whitman's essay "Democratic Vistas" (1871) deals with his theory of democracy and with the creation of a democratic literature.

His life. Walter Whitman was born in West Hills, Long Island, New York, and grew up in Brooklyn. He worked as a school teacher, printer, and journalist in the New York City area. He wrote articles on political questions, civic affairs, and the arts. Whitman loved mixing in crowds. He attended debates, the theater, concerts, lectures, and political meetings. He often rode on stagecoaches and ferries just to talk with people.

During the Civil War, Whitman was a government clerk and a volunteer assistant in the military hospitals in Washington, D.C. After the war, he worked in several government departments until he suffered a stroke in 1873. He spent the rest of his life in Camden, N.J., where he continued to write poems and articles. See **Camden.**

Whitman believed that the vitality and variety of his life reflected the vitality and variety of American democracy during his time. Most critics accept this view of the man and his poems. However, some insist Whitman was not a prophetic spokesman, but simply a powerful and unusual lyric poet.   Jerome Loving

Additional resources

Kaplan, Justin. *Walt Whitman: A Life.* Simon & Schuster, 1986. First published in 1980.
Whitman, Walt. *Complete Poetry and Collected Prose.* Ed. by Justin Kaplan. Library of America, 1982.
Zweig, Paul. *Walt Whitman: The Making of the Poet.* Basic

Ewing Galloway

Walt Whitman received literary acclaim from English writers long before American critics recognized him as a great poet.

Books, 1985. First published in 1984.

Whitman massacre. See Whitman, Marcus.

Whitman Mission National Historic Site is in southeastern Washington. It includes the site of an Indian mission and school established in 1836 by Marcus Whitman and his wife. The mission was a landmark on the Oregon Trail, and the school was the first mission school in the Pacific Northwest. The mission was made a national monument in 1936 and became a national historic site in 1963. For area, see **National Park System** (table: National historic sites).

Critically reviewed by the National Park Service

Whitney, Eli (1765-1825), an American inventor, is best known for his cotton gin. This invention provided a fast, economical way to separate the cotton seeds from the fibers. Whitney's cotton gin made cotton growing profitable and quickly helped the United States become the world's leading cotton grower. Whitney also became a manufacturer of muskets and other weapons.

Early life. Whitney was born in Westborough, Mass. Even as a boy, he had mechanical skill. He made a violin when he was 12 and established a nail-making business when he was still a teen-ager. From 1783 to 1789, Whitney taught at a grammar school. He entered Yale College in 1789 and graduated three years later.

In 1792, Whitney went to Savannah, Ga., to teach and study law. But he found that someone had taken the teaching job he expected to get. He then met Catherine Littlefield Greene, the widow of a hero of the Revolutionary War in America, General Nathanael Greene. She invited Whitney to be her guest while he studied law. Whitney wanted to be "worth his keep" and began fixing things around the house. His mechanical skill impressed her. One night, guests discussing green-seed cotton said they could not grow it profitably because of the time it took to clean. Mrs. Greene said, "Mr. Whitney can make a machine to clean it." By April 1793, Whitney had built the cotton gin. It could clean as much cotton in a day as 50 people could working by hand.

The cotton gin. In 1794, Whitney obtained a patent for his cotton gin. With the financial backing of a partner, Phineas Miller, Whitney began to make cotton gins in New Haven, Conn. But soon the business had problems. It could not make cotton gins fast enough to meet the demand. In addition, other manufacturers had been producing imitations of Whitney's cotton gin. Whitney sued them. He won after years of court trials. However, the life of his patent had almost expired, and the U.S. Congress refused to grant his appeal for a renewal.

Brown Bros.

Eli Whitney

Arms manufacturer. During the years he fought for his patent, Whitney also made arms for the U.S. government. In 1798, the Department of the Treasury gave him a contract to produce 10,000 muskets.

Whitney probably knew about existing French and American techniques for the mass production of muskets. As a result, he built a number of machines to help produce standard, interchangeable parts for the arms he was making. Some scholars credited him for the invention of a milling machine that made standard parts for weapons and that led to mass production. But no evidence exists that he invented such a machine or that he perfected the manufacture of interchangeable parts. However, Whitney was the best-known promoter of the "interchangeable system."   R. Douglas Hurt

See also **Agriculture** (picture: The cotton gin); **Cotton gin; Mass production.**

Additional resources

Green, Constance M. *Eli Whitney and the Birth of American Technology.* Little, Brown, 1965. A standard work on Whitney's influence and significance. First published in 1956.
Latham, Jean Lee. *The Story of Eli Whitney.* Harper, 1962. For younger readers. First published in 1953.
Mirsky, Jeannette, and Nevins, Allan. *The World of Eli Whitney.* Collier, 1962. First published in 1952.

Whitney, Mount. See Mount Whitney.

Whittaker, Charles Evans (1901-1973), was a justice of the Supreme Court of the United States from 1957 to 1962, when he resigned because of poor health. President Dwight D. Eisenhower nominated him as a U.S. District Judge in 1954, and two years later he became a judge of the U.S. Court of Appeals for the Eighth Circuit. Whittaker was born in Doniphan County, Kansas. As a youth, he trapped animals and sold their pelts to earn $700 for his law studies.   Merlo J. Pusey

Whittier, John Greenleaf (1807-1892), was an American poet. His best-known poems fall into two groups— those attacking slavery, and those praising the charms of New England country life. Whittier's simple, direct, and

sentimental style has made his poems popular with both young readers and adults.

Whittier was born in Haverhill, Mass. His parents were Quaker farmers. Whittier's poetry shows the influence of his Quaker religion and rural New England background, and he is often called the "Quaker poet." The Scottish poet Robert Burns also influenced Whittier. Like Burns, Whittier wrote many ballads on rural themes. But Whittier's poetry lacks the wit of Burns's work.

From 1833 to 1863, Whittier was active in politics and the antislavery movement. He called for the abolition of slavery in newspaper articles and while serving in the Massachusetts legislature in 1835. The abolitionist cause also dominated his poetry. In "The Moral Warfare" (1838)

Brown Bros.

John Greenleaf Whittier

and "Massachusetts to Virginia" (1843), he attacked the injustices of slavery. He also condemned what he considered the hypocrisy of a nation that was founded on ideals of freedom but allowed slavery.

Whittier's finest political poem is "Ichabod" (1850), a lyric. It criticizes Senator Daniel Webster of Massachusetts for his role in the passage of the Compromise of 1850. Whittier objected to the compromise because it required that runaway slaves be returned to their owners. But Whittier used a dignified, restrained tone that makes "Ichabod" seem less an attack on Webster than an expression of sympathy for him.

In two ballads, "Skipper Ireson's Ride" (1857) and "Telling the Bees" (1858), Whittier showed his interest in the people, customs, legends, and settings of New England. These features appear in his masterpiece, "Snow-Bound" (1866). This long poem tells of a family marooned in their farmhouse during a blizzard. Whittier's affectionate descriptions of Quaker life, combined with his simple style and organization, made "Snow-Bound" extremely popular.   Clark Griffith

See also **Frietchie, Barbara; Liberty Party.**

Additional resources

Critical Essays on John Greenleaf Whittier. Ed. by Jayne K. Kribbs. G. K. Hall, 1980.
Pickard, John B. *John Greenleaf Whittier: An Introduction and Interpretation.* Barnes & Noble, 1961.
Pickard, Samuel T. *Life and Letters of John Greenleaf Whittier.* 2 vols. Haskell House, 1969. Reprint of 1907 revised edition. A standard biography.

Whittington, Dick, was an English folk hero. The character was based on Richard Whittington (mid-1300's-1423), an English merchant and mayor of London. The real Whittington was born into a prominent family, probably in Gloucestershire. He grew rich in London as a cloth merchant and was Lord Mayor three times.

Legends about Whittington appeared after 1600. They portrayed him as a poor country orphan. A kind London merchant hires him to wash pots in his kitchen, where the cook mistreats the boy. To earn money, Dick sends his cat to be sold by the merchant on a trading voyage.

By luck, the cat is sold for a huge sum to a king of Barbary, who is plagued by mice and rats. Meanwhile, Dick runs away to escape the cook. Outside London, he hears church bells that seem to say "Turn again, Whittington/ Lord Mayor of London." Dick returns, collects his fortune from the sale of the cat, marries the merchant's daughter, and becomes a merchant and mayor.

David S. Chamberlain

Whittle, Sir Frank (1907-   ), became one of the leading pioneers in the development of the turbojet engine. His company, Powerjets, Limited, produced the Whittle engine, which powered Britain's first jet plane in 1941. It became the model for the first U.S. turbojets.

Whittle was born in Coventry, England, the son of an inventor. He entered Leamington College on a scholarship at the age of 11, and joined the Royal Air Force at 16. Whittle distinguished himself in a mechanics course and was assigned to officers' flight training. He became interested in light turbine engines and received his first patent in 1930 after the Air Ministry rejected his jet engine proposals. Whittle's basic patents lapsed in 1935 because he did not have enough money to pay patent fees. Later that year, a group of engineers became interested in his work and, with the government and Whittle, formed Powerjets, Ltd., to produce engines. Whittle was knighted in 1948.   Robert B. Hotz

Whitworth, Sir Joseph (1803-1887), was a British mechanical engineer and inventor. He invented measuring machines and found a method of milling and testing plane surfaces. He introduced a system of standard measures, gauges, and screw threads. His experiments in ordnance established principles of gun design that were adopted by all major countries except his own. Whitworth was born in Stockport, England. He founded a company that became a leader in tool design and manufacture.   Robert E. Schofield

WHO. See World Health Organization.

Who, The, became one of the most popular British groups in the history of rock music. The Who originally consisted of guitarist Peter Townshend (1945-   ), principal vocalist Roger Daltrey (1945-   ), bass player John Entwistle (1946-   ), and drummer Keith Moon (1947-

Mickey Adain, Star File

The Who became one of the most popular and influential British groups in the history of rock music. It originally consisted of, *left to right*, John Entwistle, bass player; Roger Daltrey, vocalist; Keith Moon, drummer; and Peter Townshend, guitarist. The Who became famous for its energetic concert performances.

1978). Kenny Jones became the drummer after Moon's death from a drug overdose. Townshend composed most of The Who's music.

The Who was formed in London in the early 1960's. The group soon became famous for its energetic concert performances, which often ended with the performers destroying their instruments and equipment on stage. In the late 1960's, The Who was among the first rock groups to record "concept albums" tied together by a story line or theme. The album *The Who Sell Out* (1967) was the group's first concept album. Probably the most popular of these albums, the rock opera *Tommy,* was released in England in 1968 and in the United States in 1969. It was made into a film starring Daltrey in 1975.

In 1979, The Who was featured in two motion pictures. One was *Quadrophenia,* based on a 1973 Who album of the same name. The other was *The Kids Are Alright,* a history of the group.   Jerry M. Grigadean

Wholesaler. See Trade (The use of markets); **Careers** (Marketing and distribution).

Wholistic medicine. See Holistic medicine.

Whooper. See Whooping crane.

Whooping cough, *HOO pihng,* also called *pertussis,* is a serious, highly contagious disease of the respiratory system. The name *whooping cough* comes from the high-pitched, whooping noise victims make when they try to catch their breath after severe coughing attacks. Whooping cough occurs worldwide, mainly among infants and young children. It is caused by a bacterium called *Bordetella pertussis.*

From the 1950's through the 1970's, the number of cases and the severity of whooping cough declined sharply in the United States and many other countries. These changes resulted from the widespread use of pertussis vaccine and from improvements in the standard of living and in health care. In the early and mid-1980's, however, the percentage of young children in the United States who received the vaccine declined. As a result, the number of cases of whooping cough in the United States nearly doubled from 1982 to 1985.

Symptoms of whooping cough progress through three stages. These stages, in order of development, are (1) the catarrhal stage, (2) the paroxysmal stage, and (3) the convalescent stage.

During the catarrhal stage, symptoms resemble those of the common cold. Victims have trouble breathing, due to an increase of mucus in the nose and throat. They cough and have a fever. At this stage, the disease is highly contagious. It spreads through the spray of bacteria-filled droplets from the victim's nose and mouth. The catarrhal stage generally lasts from one to two weeks.

The paroxysmal stage, during which the "whoop" occurs, is the most serious phase of the disease. It generally lasts from two to three weeks. In this stage, severe coughing *paroxysms* (attacks) occur first at night, then later during both the day and night. Victims often vomit thick globs of mucus following these coughing spells. The attacks can lead to inadequate oxygen circulation, which can cause convulsions. Other complications may include pneumonia or collapse of the lungs. Victims of whooping cough, especially infants under 6 months of age, may die during the paroxysmal stage.

During the *convalescent* (recovery) stage, coughing and vomiting of mucus begin to lessen. Victims show general improvement and finally return to a normal state of health. Full recovery may take weeks or months.

Treatment and prevention. Physicians use the antibiotic erythromycin to treat whooping cough. If given in the catarrhal stage, this drug can halt the illness or lessen its severity. After the paroxysmal stage begins, treatment centers on helping the patient breathe freely and on limiting the number of severe coughing attacks.

Immunization of infants and young children with pertussis vaccine protects them from whooping cough. For a recommended schedule of whooping cough immunizations, see **Immunization** (table: Recommended immunization for children in the United States). Physicians prescribe erythromycin to help prevent the development of whooping cough in unvaccinated people who have been exposed to the disease.   Hugh C. Dillon, Jr.

Whooping crane is one of the rarest birds of North America. It is a symbol of wildlife conservation. Whooping cranes, also called *whoopers,* are named for their loud, buglelike call. Whooping cranes are the tallest birds in North America. They stand about 5 feet (1.5 meters) tall and have long legs and a long neck. The adults are white, with black-tipped wings and a patch of bare, red skin on their heads. Whoopers less than a year old are rust colored. See **Crane** (picture).

Wild whooping cranes breed in marshy areas of Wood Buffalo National Park in the Northwest Territories of Canada. They make nests of piles of grasses or other plants. The female usually lays two eggs, but only one chick survives in most cases. Whoopers migrate about 2,500 miles (4,000 kilometers) to Aransas National Wildlife Refuge in Texas for the winter. Their food in winter includes clams, crabs, and crayfish, but scientists know little about what they eat the rest of the year.

Whoopers once nested between Louisiana and Canada. They began to die out during the 1800's, when increasing numbers of settlers disturbed their habitats. By 1941, only 15 whoopers remained in the flock that migrated between Canada and Texas. Another 6 whoopers lived in Louisiana, but these died out by 1948.

Wild whooping cranes are protected by international law. Their breeding and wintering grounds are protected, and the birds are closely watched during their migrations. Laws also prohibit the shooting of whooping cranes. This protection helped increase the flock wintering in Texas to more than 130 birds by the late 1980's.

In a further effort to save the species, biologists remove one egg from some of the nests of wild whoopers in Canada. Some of these eggs were used to start a captive flock of whooping cranes. Someday the offspring from this flock may be released to increase the wild population of whoopers. Beginning in 1975, biologists transferred some whooper eggs to the nests of sandhill cranes at Grays Lake National Wildlife Refuge in Idaho. The sandhill cranes act as foster parents by hatching and raising the young whooping cranes. This new flock of whoopers, which numbered about 15 birds in the late 1980's, migrates to Bosque del Apache National Wildlife Refuge in New Mexico. Biologists hope that the Idaho-New Mexico flock eventually will begin breeding.

Scientific classification. Whooping cranes belong to the crane family, Gruidae. They are species *Grus americana.*

Eric G. Bolen

See also **Bird** (Endangered species).

Additional resources

Johnsgard, Paul A. *Cranes of the World.* Indiana Univ. Press, 1983.
McClung, Robert M. *America's Endangered Birds: Programs and People Working to Save Them.* Morrow, 1979.
McNulty, Faith. *The Whooping Crane: The Bird That Defies Extinction.* Dutton, 1966. *Peeping in the Shell: A Whooping Crane Is Hatched.* Harper, 1986. For younger readers.

Wichita, *WIHCH uh TAW* (pop. 279,835; met. area pop. 442,401), is the largest city in Kansas. It serves as a major manufacturing center and as the distribution center for a large farm region that produces dairy products, grain, and livestock. Wichita is called the *Air Capital of the World.* It ranks as the world's largest producer of general aviation aircraft, which includes small planes used for business, recreation, and flight training.

Wichita lies in south-central Kansas where the Arkansas and the Little Arkansas rivers meet. For location, see **Kansas** (political map). White settlers first came to the area to trade with the Wichita Indians. The city's name came from that tribe.

The city covers about 112 square miles (290 square kilometers) and is the county seat of Sedgwick County. About two-thirds of Wichita lies east of the Arkansas River, and about a third lies west of the river. The city's main business and industrial districts are in the area east of the river.

Century II, a cultural-convention center completed in 1969, covers 5 acres (2 hectares) east of the river in the heart of downtown Wichita. This project includes an auditorium, a concert hall, convention and exhibition halls, and a theater. The A. Price Woodard, Jr., Memorial Park, with its fountains, trees, waterfalls, and an outdoor amphitheater, lies between Century II and the river. Expo Hall, which provides additional convention space, was completed in 1986. Wichita's old city hall, completed in 1892, still stands in the downtown area. Its architectural design and towers attract many tourists. Today, the building houses the Wichita Historical Museum.

Karl Kummels, Shostal

Wichita is the largest city in Kansas. The domed Century II cultural-convention center, *right,* in downtown Wichita includes a concert hall, exhibition halls, and a theater.

Economy. Wichita ranks as the largest manufacturing center in Kansas. There are more than 500 manufacturing plants in the Wichita metropolitan area. The production of civilian aircraft, including small planes and commercial jets, is the major industry. Wichita also ranks as the petroleum capital of Kansas. Oil fields lie just outside the city, and many oil companies have offices or refineries in Wichita. Other industries produce chemicals, camping and recreational equipment, metal products, and plastics.

Wichita ranks high among the nation's cities as a meat processor. The city lies in a rich, wheat-growing area, and Wichita's flour mills grind more wheat than any other Kansas city. Wichita is also a regional medical center. The city has six hospitals, including one operated by the Department of Veterans Affairs.

Four railroads serve the city, and truck lines also operate there. Wichita Mid-Continent Airport is southwest of the downtown area of the city. The Col. James J. Jabara Airport lies northeast of the city. Wichita has one daily newspaper, the *Eagle-Beacon.* Four television stations and 13 radio stations broadcast from the area.

Education and cultural life. Wichita's public school system includes about 100 elementary schools and 8 high schools. The city also has about 20 parochial and private schools.

Wichita State University is the third largest college in the state. The university is known for its Institute of Logopedics, the world's largest center for helping people with speech and hearing handicaps. Friends University and Kansas Newman College (formerly Sacred Heart College) are also in Wichita. The city's public library system consists of a central library and several branches. The Wichita Symphony Orchestra performs at the Century II Concert Hall. The Wichita Community Theatre stages nine productions a year.

Historic Wichita Cow Town, which consists of about 40 restored buildings, traces the city's history from 1868 to 1880. The Wichita Historical Museum also offers exhibits on local history. The city has three art museums—the Wichita Art Association, the Wichita Art Museum, and the Ulrich Gallery at Wichita State University. The Wichita Art Museum houses the famous Roland P. Murdock Collection, one of the nation's largest collections of American art.

Wichita's public park system includes 70 parks and covers more than 3,000 acres (1,200 hectares). Pawnee Prairie, the largest park in the city, covers 700 acres (280 hectares) and includes a golf course. The Sedgwick County Zoo lies on the northwest border of the city.

Government. Wichita has a council-manager form of government. The voters elect five commissioners to four-year terms, and the commissioners choose one of their group as mayor. The mayor presides at commission meetings, but has the same duties as the other commissioners. The five commissioners appoint a city manager, who serves as the administrative head of the city government.

History. The Wichita Indians once lived in what is now the Wichita area. Whites first settled there in 1866 and traded with the Indians. In 1870, the whites incorporated their settlement as a town. The Atchison, Topeka, and Santa Fe Railroad (now The Atchison, Topeka, and Santa Fe Railway Company) began to serve Wichita in

1872, and the town soon became an important shipping point for cattle. Cowboys drove Texas longhorn cattle along the Chisholm Trail, fattened them on Kansas grass, and shipped them from Wichita to distant markets.

During the late 1880's, Wichita became known for its cowboys, dance halls, gambling, and saloons. Wyatt Earp, the famous frontier lawman, served as a peace officer in the town in the mid-1870's. Although Wichita gained attention for lawlessness, the people also built churches, a library, schools, and some industry, including a brick plant and a meat-packing plant.

Wichita received a city charter in 1886. The population of the community grew from 4,911 in 1880 to 23,853 in 1890. Much of this growth resulted from land speculation.

The discovery of oil in the Wichita area during the early 1900's brought further growth. The city's population rose from 24,671 in 1900 to 111,110 in 1930. In 1919, Wichita's first airplane manufacturing company built its factory. Wichita soon became the nation's aircraft production center. The city won fame for its pioneers in the industry, including Walter H. Beech, Clyde V. Cessna, and Lloyd C. Stearman.

The prospering aircraft and oil industries helped Wichita avoid hard times during the 1930's. The rest of the Kansas region suffered during those years from dust storms and the Great Depression.

During World War II (1939-1945), Wichita's three airplane factories produced more military aircraft than any other U.S. city. After the war, Wichita continued to rank among the leading producers of jet bombers for the Air Force. In 1951, McConnell Air Force Base opened in Wichita. Aircraft production soared again during the Korean War (1950-1953).

The city's economy grew during the early 1960's, when another aircraft corporation built a plant there. This plant helped Wichita become the world's largest producer of general aviation aircraft. Since the late 1960's, the city's aircraft industry has suffered periodically as the demand for planes has dropped. The reduced demands have resulted from slumps in the entire U.S. economy.

Important developments in Wichita during the 1970's included construction of a new 14-story City Hall, completed in 1975, and the Mid-America All Indian Center, which opened in 1976. A coliseum was completed in the city in 1978. It is used for such events as circuses, concerts, rodeos, and hockey and soccer games. In 1979, the privately funded Foundation for Wichita Development, Inc., was established to help renew the downtown area. Many homes and business buildings in and near downtown have been restored as a result of the organization's efforts.   Betty Wells Cox

For the monthly weather in Wichita, see **Kansas** (Climate). See also **Kansas** (pictures).

Wichita Falls, *WIHCH uh TAW,* Tex. (pop. 94,201; met. area pop. 121,082), is headquarters for independent oil producers and a center for services and trade in north-central Texas and southwestern Oklahoma. The city lies on the Wichita River near the Texas-Oklahoma border. For location, see **Texas** (political map).

Wichita Falls serves as a center of government, agriculture, and industry. It is the home of the North Texas Oil and Gas Association. The oil and gas industry provides many of the jobs in Wichita County. Wichita Falls has more than 125 manufacturing firms. They produce electrical components, glass, jet aircraft parts, jeans, and plastic pipe. The city is the home of Midwestern State University and Sheppard Air Force Base.

Wichita Falls was founded in 1882. It was named for the Wichita Indians and the falls of the Wichita River. The first major oil deposit in north Texas was discovered near Wichita Falls in 1910, and the community became a boom town several years later. In 1978, the city began a long-term project to renew the downtown area. The project has resulted in the completion of hotels, a community center, a farmers' market, and several other improvements. Many vacant buildings have been remodeled for use as offices. Wichita Falls is the county seat of Wichita County. It has a council-manager form of government.   Lois Luecke

Wicker is a small, flexible branch or twig, usually of willow, that can be woven to make baskets, furniture, and other objects. The term *wicker* also refers to any basketlike furniture or accessory. Some wicker objects are woven from such plant materials as bamboo, cane, rattan, and reed, and from artificial fibers.

Wicker furniture is made by weaving the material around a sturdy frame. Wicker is loosely woven and allows air to circulate, making such furniture especially suitable for hot areas. Wicker is also lightweight and extremely durable. Some pieces have lasted more than 100 years. Wicker furniture was originally used outdoors, but today it is popular indoors as well.

Wicker chairs were made in ancient Egypt. During the 1800's, wicker chairs and tables became popular in Europe and the United States. Each piece was handmade and took several days to complete. As the costs of labor and materials rose, manufacturers sought less expensive ways of making wicker objects. They developed an artificial fiber from specially treated twisted paper. They also began to weave wicker on looms. Today, however, some wicker objects are still made by hand, mostly in Asian countries.   Jim L. Bowyer

Wiclif, John. See Wycliffe, John.

Widgeon. See Wigeon.

Wien, the official name for Vienna. See Vienna.

Wiener. See Sausage.

Wiener, *WEE nuhr,* **Norbert** (1894-1964), a mathematician and logician, had an important role in developing high-speed electronic computers. He adopted the word *cybernetics,* and used it as the title of a book he published in 1948. Wiener did mathematical work at the Aberdeen (Md.) Proving Ground during World War I (1914-1918), and helped develop high-speed electronic computers during World War II (1939-1945). He won the National Medal of Science in 1964. Wiener was born in Columbia, Mo. He graduated from Tufts University at the age of 14, and received a Ph.D. from Harvard University at 18. He taught at the Massachusetts Institute of Technology from 1919 to 1960.   Phillip S. Jones

See also **Cybernetics.**

Wiesbaden, *VEES BAHD uhn* (pop. 266,623), is a resort city 6 miles (10 kilometers) northeast of Mainz in West Germany. It lies in a valley on the southern slope of the Taunus Mountains (see **Germany** [political map]). In 1945, it became the capital of the newly created state of Hesse. Many mineral springs in and around Wiesbaden attract visitors. The tourist trade is an important source of income. The springs in the area were known to the Romans, and many relics of the Roman period have been discovered there. The city's Latin name was *Aquae Mattiacorum,* meaning *waters of the Mattiaci* (a German tribe). Its German name, *Wiesbaden,* means *baths on the meadows.*   Frank Ahnert

Wiesel, *wee ZEHL,* **Elie,** *EHL ee* (1928-   ), an American author, became a leading spokesman for people who survived Nazi concentration camps during World War II (1939-1945). He was a prisoner at camps where the Nazis murdered millions of European Jews. Wiesel dedicated his life to describing the horrors he witnessed and to helping victims of oppression and racism. He won the 1986 Nobel Peace Prize.

Eliezer Wiesel was born in Sighet, Romania. In 1944, he was sent with his family and the town's other Jews to a camp at Auschwitz (now Oświęcim), Poland, near Krakow. He was later sent to a camp at Buchenwald, Germany, near Weimar. Wiesel's parents and a sister died at these camps. After Buchenwald was liberated in 1945, Wiesel settled in France. He later studied philosophy at the University of Paris, became a journalist, and moved to the United States. In 1976, Wiesel became a professor of humanities at Boston University. President Jimmy Carter appointed him chairman of the President's Commission on the Holocaust in 1979. In 1980, Wiesel was named head of the U.S. Holocaust Memorial Council.

Wiesel's first book, *Night* (1958), is a memoir of his experiences in the concentration camps. *Dawn* (1960) and *The Accident* (1961) are novels about survivors of the Holocaust. Wiesel's other books include *The Jews of Silence* (1966), *A Beggar in Jerusalem* (1968), and *The Testament* (1980).   Michael Berenbaum

Wiesenthal, *VEE zehn TAHL,* **Simon** (1908-   ), is an Austrian Jew who helped bring more than 1,100 Nazi war criminals to justice. He is the founder and director of the Jewish Documentation Center in Vienna, Austria. The center, established in 1961, collects evidence about the murders of more than 6 million Jews and millions of other persons by the Nazis during World War II (1939-1945). It also gathers information on the present location of Nazis who have avoided capture. Wiesenthal helped bring to trial such former Nazi officers as Adolf Eichmann, who directed the removal of Jews to concentration camps, and Karl Silberbauer, who arrested Anne Frank (see **Frank, Anne**).

Wiesenthal was born in Buchach, near Lvov, in what is now the Soviet Union. He was trained as an architect and engineer. Nearly all his relatives were killed by the Nazis during the war, while he worked as a slave laborer in several concentration camps. After the war, Wiesenthal dedicated his life to the memory of those who died and vowed to bring the guilty to justice.   Leon A. Jick

Wig is a false covering of hair for the head. The name comes from the word *periwig.* The custom of wearing wigs dates back to ancient times. Egyptian mummies have been found with them. The ancient Greeks and Romans wore them. In the 1600's, the French made wigs fashionable. Wigs then became large and heavy, and expensive. Usually they were powdered white. Wigs were worn by nobles, courtiers, ministers, judges, doctors, and professional people. English judges began wearing wigs in the days of Queen Anne and still wear them today. Wigs were fashionable in colonial America and became popular in the 1960's and 1970's. They are also worn by people who are bald. Quality wigs are made of the best grade of human hair. Wigmakers also make *toupees* (small hairpieces used to cover bald spots).

Mary Evans

See also **Hairdressing** (with pictures); **Colonial life in America** (Clothing); **London** (picture: London lawyers).

Wigeon, *WIHJ uhn,* also spelled *widgeon,* is a duck found in North America and in Europe. The *American wigeon,* also called the *baldpate,* has a distinctive call—*whew, whew, whew.* The crown and forehead of the male are white. The *European wigeon* lives in the northern part of Europe, and occasionally in the United States. Both species are about 19 inches (48 centimeters) long. The female lays 7 to 12 creamy-white eggs in ground nests near water. See also **Bird** (picture: Birds of inland waters and marshes).

Scientific classification. Wigeons are in the family Anatidae. The American is classified as *Anas americana.* The European is *A. penelope.*   Joseph J. Hickey

Wiggin, Kate Douglas (1856-1923), was an American writer of books for children. She is best remembered for her novel *Rebecca of Sunnybrook Farm* (1903). Rebecca Randall, the bright young heroine, leaves Sunnybrook Farm to live with her mother's sisters after her father's death. The novel's characters, places, and events are taken from Wiggin's childhood and later life in Maine. Her other notable children's novels include *The Birds' Christmas Carol* (1887) and *Mother Carey's Chickens* (1911). Wiggin also wrote books for adults and an autobiography, *My Garden of Memory* (1923).

Wiggin was born in Philadelphia. In 1878, she helped establish in San Francisco the first free kindergarten west of the Rocky Mountains.   Virginia L. Wolf

Wigglesworth, Michael (1631-1705), was a Puritan pastor, doctor, and poet of colonial New England. He is best known for his somber poem *The Day of Doom: or, A Poetical Description of the Great and Last Judgment* (1662). Wigglesworth believed that many people were disobeying God and that God judged both individuals and nations. He wrote *The Day of Doom* as a warning to the New England colonists. His crude but dramatic ballad presented theology to the colonists in a form they could easily read and memorize. *The Day of Doom* became a best seller.

Wigglesworth was born in England and moved to America with his parents at the age of 7. In 1656, he settled in Malden, Mass., and served as minister and physician.   Mark A. Noll

Wight, *wyt,* **Isle of,** lies off the southern coast of England (see **England** [map]). A strait called *The Solent* separates the island from the mainland county of Hampshire. Ferries and hovercraft provide transportation between the island and the mainland. The island covers 147 square miles (381 square kilometers), and has a population of 119,800.

The Isle of Wight is famous for its mild, sunny climate and its scenery, which attracts tourists. The island's administrative center is Newport. Cowes, its leading port, is known for its sailing and yacht races. Many people work on farms or in light industry.   D. Ian Scargill

Wigner, Eugene Paul (1902-   ), is an American physicist. He worked with Enrico Fermi when Fermi produced the first nuclear chain reaction in 1942. Wigner developed many practical uses for nuclear energy. He won the Atomic Energy Commission's Enrico Fermi Award in 1958, and shared the 1959 Atoms for Peace Award with Leo Szilard. He shared the 1963 Nobel Prize in physics with J. Hans Jensen and Maria Goeppert Mayer. Wigner was born in Budapest, Hungary, and became a U.S. citizen in 1937. He became a professor of mathematical physics at Princeton University in 1938. See also **Szilard, Leo.**   Aaron J. Ihde

Wigwam is the name for a kind of dwelling used by the Algonquian-speaking Indians of the eastern woodlands. In the East, the foundation was usually made of light poles tied together with bark, forming an oval-shaped dome. The covering was layers of bark or reed mats, laid on like shingles. Other wigwams had a rectangular frame and gabled roof. Some northern Algonquians used a cone-shaped tent.   W. Roger Buffalohead

See also **Indian, American** (picture: Indian ways of life [Eastern woodlands]).

Wilberforce, Samuel (1805-1873), was an important figure in the Anglican Church in England. He held several major church offices, including bishop of Oxford, dean of Westminster, and Chaplain of the House of Lords. Wilberforce played a mediating role during a conflict between two groups within the church—the Anglo-Catholics and the Evangelicals. Anglo-Catholics wanted to reestablish ties with Roman Catholicism without accepting the authority of the pope. The Evangelicals stressed conversion, strict morality, and social action. As Chaplain of the House of Lords, Wilberforce used his considerable influence in an attempt to bring about prison reform and measures dealing with the abuse of women and children.

Wilberforce was born in Clapham, near London. He was ordained a priest in 1829. His father, William, an English statesman, played a crucial role in the abolition of slavery in British territories.   Robert L. Ferm

Wilberforce, William (1759-1833), was a leader in the fight to abolish the slave trade and slavery in the British Empire. In 1780, he entered Parliament and became a leading Tory, noted for his eloquence. In 1789, Wilberforce led a campaign against the British slave trade. A bill to end this trade passed in the House of Commons in 1792 but failed in the House of Lords. When such a bill finally became law in 1807, Wilberforce turned against the foreign slave trade. He retired from Parliament in 1825 but continued to support the campaign against the foreign slave trade. After 1823, Wilberforce supported the emancipation of the slaves in Britain's colonies. He was born in Hull, England, and studied at Cambridge University.   Howard Temperley

Wilberforce University is a private coeducational liberal arts university in Wilberforce, Ohio. It is affiliated with the African Methodist Episcopal Church. The university has divisions of business and economics, humanities, natural science, and social science. Courses lead to the bachelor's degree. All Wilberforce students alternate periods of study on the campus with periods of work at approved off-campus jobs. Wilberforce was founded in 1856 and is the oldest predominantly black private university in the United States. For enrollment, see **Universities and colleges** (table).

Critically reviewed by Wilberforce University

Wilbur, Richard (1921-   ), is an American poet. He won Pulitzer Prizes in poetry for *Things of This World* in 1957 and *New and Collected Poems* in 1989. He was co-winner of the 1971 Bollingen Prize for poetry for *Walking to Sleep.* Wilbur received a one-year appointment as poet laureate of the United States in 1987.

Wilbur often uses myth and philosophy to illuminate ordinary experience. His poems see the dark side of human failure redeemed by a respect for intelligence, artistry, and "the things of this world." Wilbur's poems are frequently formal in style, have a musical quality, and are witty and mentally stimulating. From his first published work, *The Beautiful Changes* (1947), to *Advice to a Prophet* (1961), Wilbur attempted to show how the mind and the senses can enrich our understanding of the world.

Wilbur was born in New York City. He wrote a children's book, *Loudmouse* (1963), and skillfully translated *The Misanthrope, The School for Wives, Tartuffe,* and *The Learned Ladies,* four comedies by the French playwright Molière. *Responses* (1976) is a collection of Wilbur's essays and literary criticism.   Bonnie Costello

Wild animal. See Animal; Wildlife conservation.
Wild ass. See Donkey; Onager.
Wild barley is a troublesome weed related to the grass family. It grows in various parts of the North American continent. It has a slender, rounded stem that grows about 2 feet (61 centimeters) tall. The spikes of the flowers develop a bristly beard around them. Because this beard somewhat resembles a squirrel's tail, the name *squirreltail* has been given to wild barley.

Wild barley is a pest because it grows rapidly and kills off other plants. Also, the seeds of wild barley cling to the wool of sheep and irritate their hides. When animals eat the leaves and flowers of the plant, the leaves and flowers sometimes stick in their throats and cause them to choke. A fungus that grows on wild barley produces the poisonous drug ergot (see **Ergot**).

Scientific classification. Wild barley is in the grass family, Gramineae. It is *Hordeum jubatum.*   Frank Thone

Wild boar. See Boar, Wild.
Wild canary. See Goldfinch.
Wild carrot, also called *Queen Anne's lace,* is a carrot

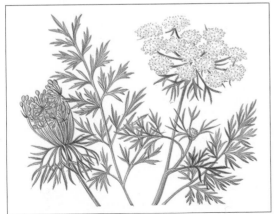

The wild carrot is also known as *Queen Anne's lace* because of the plant's lacy clusters of small white or yellowish flowers.

that grows wild. The cultivated carrot that people eat has a European and Asiatic origin. In North America, many carrot plants grow wild as common weeds. The name *Queen Anne's lace* was given the plants because of their lacy clusters of small white or yellowish flowers. The wild carrot is either an annual or a biennial. It grows to 3 feet (91 centimeters) tall. Its roots resemble the domestic carrot but should not be eaten.

Scientific classification. The wild carrot belongs to the parsley family, Umbelliferae. It is *Daucus Carota,* variety *Carota.*
Theodor Just

Wild flower. See Flower.
Wild ginger. See Ginger.
Wild rice is a cereal grain that grows on an aquatic grass. It is not related to rice. The stalks of wild rice grow from 4 to 8 feet (1.2 to 2.4 meters) high. The grain, which is high in protein and vitamins, is obtained from the heads of the stalks. Wild rice grows naturally in the shallow lakes of Minnesota, Wisconsin, and central Canada. The plant also is cultivated commercially in artificial paddies. Indians harvested wild rice by bending the heads of the plant over the edge of a boat. They beat the grains loose with sticks. Today, most of the crop is harvested mechanically.

Scientific classification. Wild rice belongs to the grass family, Gramineae. It is classified as *Zizania aquatica.*
Richard A. Havens

Wild rose. See Eglantine; Rose.
Wildcat is a name generally given to small, wild members of the cat family. The true wildcat lives in Europe, Asia, and Africa. It is an extremely vicious animal and generally larger and stronger than the domestic cat. It has yellowish to grayish fur and black streaks around the body, legs, and tail.

Two species of wildcats live in North America. They have longer bodies, longer legs, and shorter tails than domesticated cats. They prowl mainly at night. Their ears have tufts of fur on them, and their coats vary in color and thickness. One species, called the *Canada lynx,* has a long, gray coat. It ranges across the Northern United States, Alaska, and Canada. The other species, often called the *bobcat,* has short, yellowish-brown fur, covered with dark spots and other markings. It ranges from southern Canada south through Mexico. A variety of wildcat called the *Egyptian cat* is believed to be the ancestor of the common house cat.

Scientific classification. Wildcats belong to the cat family, Felidae. The European species is *Felis silvestris.* Bobcats are *Lynx rufus.* The Canada lynx is *L. canadensis.*   Duane A. Schlitter

See also **Bobcat; Serval.**
Wildcat bank was the name for unstable banking institutions that issued paper money called *wildcat currency.* They operated under state charters, particularly in the South, during the early and middle 1800's. Wildcat banks became especially numerous and irresponsible after President Andrew Jackson's successful struggle against the Second Bank of the United States.

The Bank of the United States used its influence to restrain state banks from issuing more paper money, or *wildcat currency,* than their assets would justify. In 1833, Jackson succeeded in withdrawing government deposits from the Bank of the United States. His victory so crippled the Bank that it could no longer restrain the state banks. Many banks, especially in the South and

West, then issued unreasonably large amounts of paper money, and lent it freely on the flimsiest security.

As a result, this caused a money inflation, followed by a period of wild speculation in Western land. The situation finally alarmed Jackson, who then issued his famous *Specie Circular,* ordering government agents to accept nothing but gold and silver in payment for public lands. In consequence, many of the wildcat banks were unable to meet the demands made on them and failed abruptly. These bank failures contributed to the serious financial panic in 1837.   James C. Curtis

See also **Jackson, Andrew** (The money surplus).

Wildcatting. See Gas (Exploring for gas).

Wilde, *wyld,* **Oscar** (1854-1900), was an author, playwright, and wit. He preached the importance of style in both life and art and attacked Victorian narrow-mindedness and complacency.

Wilde was born in Dublin, Ireland. His full name was Oscar Fingal O'Flahertie Wills Wilde. At 20, Wilde left Ireland to study at Oxford University where he distinguished himself as a scholar and wit. He soon became a well-known public figure, but the period of his true achievement did not begin until he published *The Happy Prince and Other Tales* in 1888. In these fairy tales and fables, Wilde found a literary form well-suited to his talents. Wilde's only novel, the ingenious *Picture of Dorian Gray* (1890), is an enlarged moral fable. It describes a man whose portrait ages and grows ugly as a reflection of his moral corruption while his actual appearance remains the same. The book seems to show the destructive side of a devotion to pleasure and beauty similar to Wilde's own.

Wilde's plays taken together are his most important works. *Lady Windermere's Fan* (1892), *A Woman of No Importance* (1893), and *An Ideal Husband* (1895) combine then current fashionable drama of social intrigue with witty high comedy. In each play, Wilde brings together an intolerant young idealist and a person who has committed a social sin in the past. They meet in a society where appearances are everything. The effect is always to educate the idealists to their own weaknesses and to show the need for tolerance and forgiveness.

In *The Importance of Being Earnest* (1895), his masterpiece, Wilde departed from his standard formula by combining high comedy with farce. Thematically, he unites his own concern with style with society's concern with appearances. He ridicules social hypocrisy and the Puritan idea of earnestness and sincerity. The result is a satirical fantasy on surfaces in which apparently trivial matters such as a name are treated with extravagant seriousness. Wilde also wrote *Salomé* in French (1893), a one-act Biblical tragedy.

In 1895, Wilde was at the peak of his career and had three hit plays running at the same time. But in that year he was accused of having homosexual relations with Lord Alfred Douglas by Douglas' father, the Marquess of

Brown Bros.
Oscar Wilde

Queensberry. As a result, Wilde became involved in a hopeless legal dispute and he was sentenced to two years in prison at hard labor. From his prison experiences came his best poem, *The Ballad of Reading Gaol* (1898), and a remarkable autobiographical document sometimes called *De Profundis.*

Wilde left England after his release. Ruined in health, finances, and creative energy, but with his wit intact, he died in France three years later.   Martin Meisel

Additional resources

Ellmann, Richard. *Oscar Wilde.* Knopf, 1988.
Miller, Robert K. *Oscar Wilde.* Ungar, 1982.
Nicholls, Mark. *The Importance of Being Oscar: The Wit and Wisdom of Oscar Wilde Set Against His Life and Times.* St. Martin's, 1980.
The Portable Oscar Wilde. Ed. by Richard Aldington and Stanley Weintraub. Rev. ed. Penguin, 1981.

Wildebeest. See Gnu.

Wilder, *WYL duhr,* **Billy** (1906-   ), is a leading motion-picture director, producer, and writer. His movies combine technical skill, keen dialogue, and a rather cynical realism about human behavior. Wilder often works with other writers on his scripts. Wilder's films vary in tone. They include the grim *Double Indemnity* (1944), *The Lost Weekend* (1945), and *Sunset Boulevard* (1950); the serio-comic *The Apartment* (1960); the satirical *One, Two, Three* (1961), *The Fortune Cookie* (1966), and *Some Like It Hot* (1959); and the sophisticated *Sabrina* (1954) and *Love in the Afternoon* (1957). Wilder won Academy Awards for his directing of *The Lost Weekend* and *The Apartment*, and he shared three awards for best screenplay.

Wilder was born Samuel Wilder in Vienna, Austria. He came to the United States in 1934 and became a U.S. citizen in 1940.   Howard Thompson

Wilder, *WYL duhr,* **Laura Ingalls,** *IHNG guhlz* (1867-1957), was an American author of books for children. She is best known for her series of nine novels called the "Little House" books. Most of the series is loosely based on her experiences growing up in the Midwest in the 1870's and 1880's. The series has been praised as a vivid literary saga of the American frontier. The "Little House" stories have a chronological pattern and follow Laura from her childhood wilderness home to her final home with her husband, Almanzo Wilder. The stories show the importance of a closely knit family, and they are filled with humor and tenderness.

Laura Ingalls was born in Pepin, Wis. She lived a rugged pioneer life with her family as they moved from place to place. She described her childhood in the first "Little House" book, *Little House in the Big Woods* (1932). In 1885, she married Almanzo Wilder, who came from an old established family in northern New York. *Farmer Boy* (1933) is the story of his childhood. *These Happy Golden Years* (1943) unites the families with the marriage of Laura and Almanzo.

Harper & Bros.
Laura Ingalls Wilder

The other books in the series are *Little House on the Prairie* (1935), *On the Banks of Plum Creek* (1937), *By the Shores of Silver Lake* (1939), *The Long Winter* (1940), *Little Town on the Prairie* (1941), and *The First Four Years* (published in 1971, after the author's death). *West from Home* (1974) is a collection of letters Laura wrote to Almanzo in 1915 while she was visiting her daughter in San Francisco. Jill P. May

See also **Laura Ingalls Wilder Award.**

Wilder, Thornton Niven (1897-1975), was an American playwright and novelist. He won Pulitzer Prizes in both fields—in 1928 for his novel *The Bridge of San Luis Rey* (1927) and in 1938 and 1943 for the plays *Our Town* (1938) and *The Skin of Our Teeth* (1942).

Wilder achieved his first success with *The Bridge of San Luis Rey,* a short novel that describes how fate influences human existence. He based two novels, *The Woman of Andros* (1930) and *The Ides of March* (1948), on ancient Roman sources. In the novel *Heaven's My Destination* (1935), Wilder created an ironic portrait of an American salesman. Wilder's longest and most complex novel, *The Eighth Day* (1967), deals with life in a Midwestern American city about 1900. Wilder's essays and other nonfiction were collected in *American Characteristics* (published in 1979, after his death).

Wilder began writing for the stage in 1915. In a 1941 essay, he wrote that ". . . the theater carries the art of narration to a higher power than the novel or the epic poem." Two collections of his early one-act plays were published as *The Angel That Troubled the Waters* (1928) and *The Long Christmas Dinner* (1931). Wilder's masterpiece is *Our Town* (1938), a sensitive drama about life and death in a New England village. He revised his 1938 farce *The Merchant of Yonkers* under the title *The Matchmaker* (1955). This comedy, in turn, was adapted into the musical *Hello, Dolly!* (1964). In *The Skin of Our Teeth,* Wilder wrote an expressionist fantasy about humanity's ability to survive even its own follies. Wilder was born in Madison, Wis. Barbara M. Perkins

Wilderness, Battle of the. See Civil War (Battle of the Wilderness).

Wilderness Road was an important pioneer road. In March 1775, 30 axmen led by Daniel Boone began to cut a trail. Their route began at the Block House in Virginia, passed through the Powell River Valley, crossed the Cumberland Mountains through Cumberland Gap, and ended in central Kentucky. Boone and his followers built a settlement called *Boonesborough* at the trail's end near present-day Lexington. Another branch of the Wilderness Road led to Harrodsburg.

The road was the only usable route through the mountains to Kentucky. It was a rocky trail menaced by unfriendly Indians. By 1800, about 200,000 settlers had traveled the road. W. Turrentine Jackson

See also **Boone, Daniel** (The Wilderness Road).

Wildlife conservation is the wise management of natural environments for the protection and benefit of plants and animals. Some species of plants and animals have become extinct because of natural causes. However, in modern times, the activities of human beings and human population growth have increased the danger for wildlife. As a result, some species have declined greatly in numbers and others are now extinct. Thus, human beings created the need for conservation.

Throughout history, wildlife has suffered because of human beings and their activities. The invention of increasingly efficient weapons, such as the bow and arrow and, later, the rifle and shotgun, enabled people to kill game with growing ease. With the help of these advances, hunters have killed off some kinds of animals. People also have cleared forests, drained swamps, and dammed rivers to clear the way for agriculture and industry. These activities have seriously harmed or destroyed many habitats for wild plants and animals. In addition, human pollution of the environment has affected a number of wild species.

Various species had become extinct even before people appeared on the earth. In the past, however, other species developed and replaced those that died off, and the total variety of life did not diminish. Today, human activities kill off species with no hope for their replacement, and so the variety of life decreases.

Since about 1600, many kinds of wildlife have become extinct. In North America, such species include the Carolina parakeet, the passenger pigeon, the California grizzly bear, and a birch that once grew in Virginia.

Beginning in the late 1800's, growing concern for the world's vanishing wildlife has led to increased conservation action. The governments of many nations have passed protective laws and set aside national parks and other reserves for wildlife. Such efforts have saved the American bison, the pronghorn, the California big tree, and many of the rare plants found on such islands as the Hawaiian and Galapagos islands.

However, several hundred species of animals and thousands of species of plants still face the danger of extinction. Such animals include the Asiatic lion, the Bengal tiger, the blue whale, the orangutan, the mountain gorilla, the whooping crane, the California condor, the ivory-billed woodpecker, and all the Asian rhinoceroses. Plants that are facing extinction include the black cabbage tree, the Ozark chestnut, the St. Helena redwood, and several kinds of California manzanitas.

Values of wildlife conservation

If people ignore the need for wildlife conservation, today's endangered species will soon become extinct. Many other species will also face extinction. If this happens, human beings will lose much of great value that cannot be replaced. Wildlife is important to people for four main reasons: (1) beauty, (2) economic value, (3) scientific value, and (4) survival value.

Beauty. Every kind of animal and plant differs from every other kind and thus contributes in a special way to the beauty of nature. Most people feel that such beauty enriches their life. It also heightens the enjoyment of camping and other forms of outdoor recreation.

Economic value. Wild species of animals and plants provide many valuable substances, such as wood and other plant products, fibers, meat and other foods, and skins and furs. The financial value of wild species is important to the economies of many nations. In industrialized nations, the recreational viewing of animals at zoos and wildlife refuges is also a source of revenue.

Scientific value. The study of wildlife provides valuable knowledge about various life processes. Such study has helped scientists understand how the human body functions and why people behave as they do. Scientists have also gained medical knowledge and discovered important medical products by studying wildlife. In addition, by observing the effect of environmental pollution on wild animals, scientists have learned how pollution affects human life.

Survival value. Every species of wildlife plays a role in helping maintain the balanced, living systems of the earth. These systems must continue to function if life is to survive. Thus, the loss of any species can threaten the survival of all life, including human beings.

Classifications of scarce wildlife

Wildlife biologists use three main classifications for animals and plants that face possible extinction: (1) endangered, (2) threatened, and (3) rare.

Endangered species face the most serious threat of extinction. They require direct human protection for survival. The California condor is endangered because only about 25 birds of this species still exist, all of them in captivity. Wildlife biologists captured the last wild California condor in 1987 after the U.S. Fish and Wildlife Service had decided that the birds must be completely protected from human interference.

Threatened species are generally abundant in some areas, but they face serious dangers nevertheless. These dangers may result from unfavorable changes in the environment. They also may be due to extensive hunting, fishing, or trapping, or even to collecting by hobbyists. The gray wolf, a threatened species, is plentiful in some places. But its overall numbers worldwide are being steadily reduced by hunting, trapping, and poisoning.

Rare species have small populations. They live in protected environments, and their numbers are not decreasing. The Torrey pine tree is classified as rare. It grows only in two small areas of southern California, but human actions do not threaten or endanger its survival.

Methods of wildlife conservation

The method used to protect wildlife depends on the source of the danger to the threatened species. In many cases, wildlife can be helped by ensuring that their environment provides enough food, water, and shelter. This method, called *habitat management,* involves such action as soil conservation, good forestry practices, and water management.

Many species of wildlife have been threatened by human destruction of their habitat. For example, some swamps and marshes have been drained and converted into farmland. Poor farming practices also may destroy land, or the spread of cities and industries may pave over former wildlife habitats. Pollution may poison the air, water, plants, and animals. To save wildlife habitats, people must control pollution and set aside areas in which wild animals and plants can survive.

An animal threatened by too much hunting can be protected by laws that forbid or regulate such killing. These laws may specify when a certain species may be hunted or how many of the species may be killed. Laws can also protect plants endangered by over-collection. If an entire habitat requires protection, the area may be made a national park or wildlife refuge. In some cases, predatory animals that kill an endangered species must be controlled until the endangered animal has increased in numbers. On the other hand, a species may

become too numerous. When this happens, the animal may threaten its own survival—or the survival of other species—by eating too much of the food supply. This problem has occurred with elk and hippopotamuses in national parks. The numbers of such a species must then be reduced, either by controlled hunting or by restoring its natural enemies where they have become scarce.

If a species can no longer survive in its natural environment, it may be raised in captivity and then released into a protected area. This method saved the Hawaiian goose. Likewise, conservationists hope to save the whooping crane. In one program, scientists place whooping crane eggs in the nests of the more common sandhill crane. The sandhill cranes hatch the eggs and raise the young whoopers. Conservationists hope that when these whooping cranes begin to reproduce, they will establish new breeding populations of whoopers. A species threatened by disease may be helped by sanitation measures in its habitat. Rare plants can be maintained in botanical gardens, or their seeds can be saved in seed banks for future planting.

The success of wildlife conservation depends on a knowledge of the *ecology* of a species. In other words, it requires an understanding of the way in which a species lives, and how it relates to everything, both living and nonliving, in its environment. See **Ecology.**

History

Early efforts. The first wildlife conservation probably occurred among prehistoric peoples. These peoples may have limited their hunting to preserve the supply of wild animals they needed for food. Rulers of ancient civilizations set up the first game reserves—as their personal hunting grounds—and medieval European kings continued this practice. These kings also forbade hunting by anyone other than a member of the ruling class. But such action resulted from a ruler's love of hunting as a sport, rather than any awareness of the need for conservation. Certain forests were protected for religious reasons, and others were preserved for their value in providing timber to build ships.

During the 1600's and 1700's, the British colonies in America passed laws to protect wildlife. But most colonists ignored these laws. Effective wildlife conservation in the United States began in the late 1800's. Congress established Yellowstone National Park, the world's first national park, in 1872. In 1903, President Theodore Roosevelt established Pelican Island, in Florida, as the nation's first federal wildlife refuge. Also in the late 1800's, many states began to pass—and enforce—game laws. Beginning in the 1890's, millions of acres of forests were protected by the national forest system.

Congress set up the National Park System in 1916 under the direction of the National Park Service, an agency of the Department of the Interior. In 1940, the government created the Fish and Wildlife Service in the same department to strengthen the wildlife conservation program. The service manages the federal wildlife refuges, which in 1966 were organized into the National Wildlife Refuge System. Many private wildlife conservation organizations have been founded since 1900. These organizations include the National Audubon Society and the National Wildlife Federation.

Wildlife protection has a long history in Europe. In

Italy, for example, what is now Gran Paradiso National Park has been a wildlife sanctuary since 1856. Canada created its first national park, Banff National Park, in 1887. Australia set up its first national park in 1879. In 1898, the Sabi Game Reserve (now Kruger National Park) was established in what is now South Africa. This reserve was the beginning of the extensive network of national parks and game reserves that covers Africa. The first Asian and South American national parks were created during the early 1900's. Governments have also established wildlife refuge systems and have passed laws for the protection of wildlife.

International cooperation in wildlife conservation began on a worldwide scale after the birth of the United Nations (UN) in 1945. The Food and Agriculture Organization of the United Nations (FAO) and the United Nations Educational, Scientific and Cultural Organization (UNESCO), set up wildlife conservation programs. In 1948, UNESCO helped establish the International Union for the Conservation of Nature and Natural Resources (IUCN) to support worldwide conservation. As part of this international program, the IUCN started to gather information on the endangered species of the world. It publishes this data in its *Red Data Book.* In 1961, the IUCN helped set up the World Wildlife Fund. This fund raises money for conservation programs.

Wildlife conservation today. There are more than 1,200 national parks, wildlife reserves, and similar protected areas throughout the world. In addition, most countries have laws that protect wildlife. In the United States, the National Park System has more than 330 protected areas, and the National Wildlife Refuge System includes more than 400 refuges.

State and federal laws also protect wildlife in the United States. For example, the Endangered Species Act of 1973 protects rare wildlife from being hunted, collected, or otherwise threatened. Among other things, the act prohibits federal projects, such as the construction of dams, that would destroy an area where an endangered species lives. In 1978, the act was amended to permit the exemption of certain federal projects.

In the United States, a specialized profession has developed to serve the needs of wildlife conservation. Many universities have programs to educate ecologists and wildlife and fishery biologists. These specialists manage natural environments on public and private lands for the benefit of plants and animals.

But in spite of the many conservation efforts, the future remains uncertain for the world's wildlife. The continued growth of the human population, the destruction of wildlife habitats, and the spread of environmental pollution present an increasing threat to the survival of wild species.   Leigh H. Fredrickson

Related articles in *World Book* include:

Audubon Society, National	Fishing industry
Balance of nature	(Fishery conservation)
Bird (Bird study and	Izaak Walton League
protection)	Leopold, Aldo
Conservation (Wildlife	National Wildlife
conservation)	Federation
Elephant (Protecting elephants)	National Wildlife
Extinct animal	Refuge System
Fish and Wildlife Service	Sierra Club

See also *Wildlife conservation* in the Research Guide/Index, Volume 22, for a *Reading and Study Guide.*

Additional resources

Burt, Olive W. *Rescued! America's Endangered Wildlife on the Comeback Trail.* Messner, 1980. For younger readers.
Dasmann, Raymond F. *Wildlife Biology.* 2nd ed. Wiley, 1981.
Jordan, W. J., and Hughes, J. *Care of the Wild: Family First Aid for All Wild Creatures.* Rawson Associates, 1983.
The Last Extinction. Ed. by Les Kaufman and Kenneth Mallory. MIT Press, 1986.
Rensberger, Boyce. *The Cult of the Wild.* Doubleday, 1977.
Stuart, Gene S. *Wildlife Alert! The Struggle to Survive.* National Geographic Society, 1980. For younger readers.

Wildlife management. See Wildlife conservation; Conservation (Careers).

Wiley, Harvey W. See Pure food and drug laws (History).

Wilhelm, *VIHL hehlm,* or in English, William, was the name of two German emperors.

Wilhelm I (1797-1888) became king of Prussia and the first emperor of modern Germany. During the revolution of 1848, Wilhelm became unpopular because he opposed constitutional reform. He was forced to leave the country, but he soon came back and put down an uprising in Baden.

In 1858, Wilhelm became regent in place of his brother, Frederick William IV, who was suffering from mental disorders. He was proclaimed king of Prussia and given the title Wilhelm I in 1861. He supported the policies of his prime minister, Otto von Bismarck, who brought about three wars while unifying the German states into one empire (see **Bismarck, Otto von**). During the Franco-Prussian War in 1871, Wilhelm became *Kaiser* (emperor) of a united Germany (see **Franco-Prussian War; Germany** [The unification of Germany]).

Bettmann Archive

Wilhelm I

Wilhelm was born in Berlin, the second son of Frederick William III, king of Prussia. He was trained as a soldier from his early youth, and he fought in the war of 1814 and 1815 against Napoleon I. See also **Prussia.**

Wilhelm II (1859-1941) was the last emperor of Germany. The Hohenzollern dynasty, which had ruled Prussia since 1701, ended with him (see **Hohenzollern**). Wilhelm was the Kaiser of World War I (1914-1918). Although he received blame for the war, historians now believe that Russia and Austria were equally guilty in starting the war.

Wilhelm, the grandson of Wilhelm I, was born in Berlin. He was the oldest son of Emperor Frederick III and Princess Victoria, daughter of Queen Victoria of England. George V of England and Nicholas II of Russia, who fought against him during World War I, were his cousins. His education emphasized military training, and made him friendly to the aristocratic military class. Wilhelm had a paralyzed left arm. He hid this weakness and ruled as the most powerful figure in Germany.

Wilhelm came to the throne in 1888 after the 100-day reign of his father (see **Frederick III** [of Prussia]). Bismarck was still chancellor and prime minister, but Wilhelm dismissed him in 1890. Under Wilhelm's reign, Germany became prosperous. He encouraged manufacturing and trade. He gained colonies in Africa and in the Pacific Ocean, and he built up the army and the navy until they were among the world's greatest. His program of colonial, naval, and foreign trade expansion brought Germany into conflict with Britain.

In 1890, Wilhelm broke the old Prussian alliance with Russia. This diplomatic blunder forced Germany in 1914 to fight a two-front war and led that nation to ultimate defeat (see **Germany** [History]). Early in November 1918, several revolts broke out and the German Navy mutinied. On November 7, the prime minister demanded that Wilhelm give up his throne. Wilhelm abdicated two days later. He fled to the Netherlands, which was neutral. For more than 20 years he lived in comfortable exile at Doorn.   Gabriel A. Almond

See also **Germany** (picture: Emperor Wilhelm II).

Wilhelmina, *WIHL hehl MEE nuh* (1880-1962), became queen of the Netherlands in 1890 when her father, William III, died. Her mother, Queen Emma, ruled as regent until 1898. In 1901 Wilhelmina married Henry, duke of Mecklenburg-Schwerin.

When the Germans invaded the Netherlands in 1940, they tried to capture Wilhelmina. But she escaped to London and directed the Netherlands forces against both Germany and Japan. After the war, her people joyfully welcomed her home. She celebrated her Golden Jubilee in August 1948, and then gave up her throne to her daughter, Juliana (see **Juliana**). She became the princess of the Netherlands. She was born at The Hague, the Netherlands.   Jane K. Miller

Wilkes, Charles (1798-1877), was an American explorer and naval officer. From 1838 to 1842, he led a United States Navy expedition that proved Antarctica was a continent. Wilkes was also a key figure in the Trent Affair, a naval incident that almost made Great Britain an ally of the Confederacy in the Civil War (1861-1865).

Wilkes was born in New York City. In 1840, the Wilkes expedition sailed more than 1,500 miles (2,400 kilometers) along the coast of Antarctica. Wilkes became the first person to recognize Antarctica as a continent and not just a huge ice pack. In 1842, the Navy court-martialed Wilkes on numerous charges, but found him guilty only of illegally whipping members of his crew. He served on special duty from 1843 to 1861, mainly writing reports on his expedition's findings.

The Trent Affair began in November 1861, when Wilkes seized Confederate diplomatic agents James Mason and John Slidell from the British ship *Trent* near Cuba. This act violated the principle of freedom of the seas. Northerners considered Wilkes a hero, but the U.S. government in time released the two agents. See **Trent Affair.**   Gabor S. Boritt

Wilkes-Barre, *WIHLKS BAIR ee* or *WIHLKS BAIR uh* (pop. 51,551), is a manufacturing and service center in eastern Pennsylvania. It lies in the Wyoming Valley on the east bank of the Susquehanna River (see **Pennsylvania** [political map]). Wilkes-Barre and nearby Scranton form a metropolitan area with a population of 728,796. The city is the home of King's and Wilkes colleges. Wilkes-Barre's most important industries include printing and publishing; data processing operations; and the manufacture of aircraft and missile parts, clothing, electronic equipment, fabricated steel, glass products, and graphic arts supplies.

Connecticut colonists made the first settlement on the site of Wilkes-Barre in 1769. The settlement was twice destroyed by fire and rebuilt. Wilkes-Barre became a city in 1871. In 1972, a tropical storm struck the Wyoming Valley, including Wilkes-Barre, and caused about $1 billion in damages. The city has a mayor-council form of government and is the seat of Luzerne County.   Paul L. Golias

Wilkins, Sir Hubert (1888-1958), was an Australian explorer, scientist, aviator, and photographer. He became famous for his air explorations in the Arctic and Antarctic.

Wilkins learned to live in the Arctic while on an expedition under explorer Vilhjalmur Stefansson from 1913 to 1916. Wilkins led a natural history expedition into northwestern Australia for the British Museum between 1923 and 1925. In 1928, after two unsuccessful attempts, he and Carl Ben Eielson became the first to fly an airplane

U.S. Army
Sir Hubert Wilkins

across the Arctic Ocean from Point Barrow, Alaska, to Spitsbergen in the Arctic Ocean, a distance of 2,200 miles (3,540 kilometers). King George V of Britain knighted Wilkins that year.

Later in 1928, Wilkins led an Antarctic expedition, and made the first Antarctic airplane flights while surveying the Antarctic Peninsula. In 1931, he tried, but failed, to reach the North Pole by submarine. He managed explorer Lincoln Ellsworth's Antarctic expeditions from 1933 to 1936, and served as a United States government adviser from 1942 to 1958.

George Hubert Wilkins was born in Mount Bryan East, in the state of South Australia.   John Edwards Caswell

Wilkins, Mary Eleanor. See Freeman, Mary Eleanor Wilkins.

Wilkins, Maurice Hugh Frederick (1916-   ), is a British biophysicist. He shared the 1962 Nobel Prize for physiology or medicine with biologists James D. Watson of the United States and Francis H. C. Crick of Great Britain. Wilkins performed X-ray studies on *deoxyribonucleic acid* (DNA), the substance that transmits genetic information from one generation to the next. This work led Watson and Crick to create a model of the molecular structure of DNA.

Wilkins worked on the World War II Manhattan Project that developed the atomic bomb. He turned to biophysics research after the war. Working at King's College in London, Wilkins became an authority on the structure of nucleic acids. Wilkins was born in Pongaroa, New Zealand.   Irwin H. Herskowitz

Wilkins, Roy (1901-1981), was a noted black American leader and was often called "Mr. Civil Rights." He served as executive secretary of the National Association for the Advancement of Colored People (NAACP) from 1955 to 1977. He helped direct the fight for equal rights and opportunities for blacks. In 1964, he won the Spingarn Medal for his work in civil rights.

Wilkins was born in St. Louis, Mo., the grandson of a slave. He graduated from the University of Minnesota. Wilkins worked for a black newspaper, the *Kansas City Call,* before joining the NAACP in 1931. He edited the NAACP magazine *The Crisis* from 1934 to 1949.　　Carl T. Rowan

NAACP

Roy Wilkins

Will, in law, is a document that disposes of a person's property after the person's death. The person who makes the will is called the *testator,* if a man, and the *testatrix,* if a woman. Personal property left by will is called a *bequest,* or a *legacy.* Real estate left by will is called a *devise.*

Most wills are prepared by lawyers, who can make sure that the formal legal requirements for wills are satisfied. Wills must be in writing and signed by the testator or testatrix and, usually, two or three witnesses.

Each state of the United States and each province of Canada has laws governing wills. Some laws require that a will be witnessed. Other laws do not. The number of witnesses required may also vary. Many states do not allow witnesses to get any benefits under a will. Some states accept a *holographic* will, or one prepared in a person's own handwriting and unwitnessed.

A person may die *intestate* (without a valid will). The person's property then descends, according to state law, to the individual's spouse and relatives. If the person is not survived by a spouse or relatives and leaves no valid will, the individual's property may *escheat* (transfer) to the state in which the person lived.

Administration. People may dispose of their property in any way they choose. But in most states, the spouse of the testator or testatrix cannot be completely disinherited. In Louisiana, the children of the testator or testatrix must also receive a share of the estate. The will usually names some person as an *executor.* The executor must see that the provisions of the will are carried out. If no executor has been named, the court that has jurisdiction over estates may appoint an *administrator,* whose duties are the same as those of an executor. For the faithful performance of their duties, executors must give a *bond* (written pledge to pay money) or provide for *surety* (a person who agrees to pay if the executor cannot). If an executor does not faithfully carry out the provisions of the will, the bond is forfeited. Usually, the giving of a bond may be waived if the will so provides.

Estate plan. It is desirable that people who own considerable property have an estate plan in which the will is only a part. If a person owns more than a certain amount of property upon death, both the government of the state where the person lives and the U.S. government will collect an estate tax. A properly drawn estate plan may save many thousands of dollars that otherwise would have to be paid in estate taxes.

Codicil is an addition made after a will has been prepared that changes the will in some way. People may alter or destroy their wills at any time. Such alteration will be legal provided that the will maker is of sound mind and the alteration was not caused by undue influence from parties interested in the change. The codicil must be made according to the formalities required by state law just as the will must be. If the will must be witnessed by two people, then the codicil must be witnessed by two people.　　William M. McGovern

See also **Executor; Legacy; Probate.**

Will-o'-the-wisp is a ghostly, bluish light sometimes seen over marshes and graveyards. Scientists believe it is caused by the natural burning of *methane* (marsh gas) produced by decaying plants. Will-o'-the-wisp is also called *jack-o'-lantern, foxfire,* and *ignis fatuus,* a Latin term that means *foolish fire.* Will-o'-the-wisp often seems to move away or vanish when approached. It was once thought to be a spirit that enjoyed misleading travelers. People who followed such a light would suddenly find themselves hopelessly lost in a swamp. In several English legends, the hero turns one of his garments inside out to magically end the power of will-o'-the-wisp. Other traditions speak of will-o'-the-wisp as the soul of a dead person. See also **Methane.**　　Alan Dundes

Willamette River, *wih LAM iht,* rises in the Cascade and Coast mountains of west-central Oregon. It flows northward for about 190 miles (306 kilometers), and empties into the Columbia River (see **Oregon** [physical map]). The Willamette Valley is the richest farming area in Oregon. Oceangoing ships can sail up the river for 12 miles (19 kilometers) to Portland, Oregon's largest city. A canal around Willamette Falls allows small boats to go up the river to Harrisburg, about 90 miles (140 kilometers) south of Portland.　　Richard M. Highsmith, Jr.

Willard, Emma Hart (1787-1870), was the first American woman publicly to support higher education for women. Her efforts advanced that movement in the United States. She also wrote a volume of poems that included "Rocked in the Cradle of the Deep" (1830).

Willard was born in Berlin, Conn., and started teaching school there at the age of 16. In 1809, she married John Willard, who helped her establish a girls' boarding school at Middlebury, Vt. Later, she founded a girls' seminary at Waterford, N.Y. It was later moved to Troy, N.Y. The school, the Troy Female Seminary, later became famous as the Emma Willard School. Willard strongly supported the establishment of public schools, and she educated hundreds of teachers in her schools for girls.

Wayne Davis

Emma Willard

Claude A. Eggertsen

Willard, Frances Elizabeth Caroline (1839-1898), was an American educator and social reformer. She organized the temperance movement on the plan by which it attained national prohibition (see **Prohibition**). She served as president of the Woman's Christian Temperance Union (W.C.T.U.) from 1879 until her death, and made the W.C.T.U. a national organization (see **Woman's**

Christian Temperance Union). In 1883, Willard founded a world temperance union. She was also a strong advocate of woman suffrage.

Willard was born on Sept. 28, 1839, at Churchville, N.Y. She served as president of the Evanston (Ill.) College for Ladies. When it merged with Northwestern University, she became the dean of the Woman's College.

Brown Bros.

Frances E. Willard

A statue of Frances Willard represents the state of Illinois in Statuary Hall in the United States Capitol in Washington, D.C. Louis Filler

Willemstad, *VIHL uhm STAHT* or *WIHL uhm STAHT* (pop. 50,000), is the capital of the Netherlands Antilles. It lies on the southwest coast of the island of Curaçao (see **Venezuela** [political map]). St. Anna Bay divides the city into two sections, Punda and Otrabanda.

Willemstad has two of the oldest Jewish landmarks in the Western Hemisphere—a cemetery established in 1659 and a temple built in 1732. Many houses in Willemstad are built in traditional Dutch style, and many are painted in pastel colors.

Arawak Indians were the first inhabitants of what is now Willemstad. The city was founded by the Dutch in 1634. Since 1915, it has been a center for the refining and shipping of crude oil. Willemstad is the southeast Caribbean's center for warehousing, shipping, banking, and property investment. Gustavo A. Antonini

Willet is a large shore bird of North and South America. The willet is often called the *duck snipe,* and has 10 or more other common names. The *eastern willet* breeds along the Atlantic Coast between Virginia and the Bahama Islands, and migrates in winter as far south as Peru. It is rarely seen in Europe. The *western willet* ranges from Manitoba to Texas, and migrates south to the area around the Caribbean Sea in winter.

The willet measures about 16 inches (41 centimeters) long, and appears gray or white-colored below, and dark gray above. Its extended wings display striking black and white markings. Its long bill is straight and slender. The bird nests in a clump of weeds or grass in marshes close to the shore. The female lays four greenish-white or brownish-olive eggs that are speckled brown and purple.

Scientific classification. The eastern willet belongs to the sandpiper family, Scolopacidae. It is *Catoptrophorus, semipalmatus semipalmatus.* The western willet is *C. semipalmatus inornatus.* Herbert Friedmann

William was the name of four kings of England.

William I, the Conqueror (1027?-1087), was the first Norman king of England. He was born at Falaise, France. He was the son of Robert I, Duke of Normandy, and inherited Normandy at about the age of 8 in 1035. During his youth, there were many disorders. In 1047, William put down a great rebellion at the battle of Val-ès-dunes, which he won with the aid of his lord, King Henry of France. From that time on, William ruled Normandy with an iron hand.

In 1051, King Edward the Confessor of England promised William succession to the English throne as his nearest adult heir. In 1064, Edward's brother-in-law Harold was shipwrecked on the Norman coast and taken prisoner. Harold promised to support William's claim to the throne in return for freedom. But Harold won the throne in 1066 through a deathbed grant by Edward and election by the nobles (see **Harold** [II] of England).

William immediately invaded England. His expedition had the pope's blessings, because William was expected to depose the Anglo-Saxon archbishop of Canterbury and introduce ecclesiastical reforms. Before William could sail, the king of Norway invaded northern England. King Harold hurried north and defeated the Norwegian invaders at Stamford Bridge. William landed before Harold could return to defend the coast. The Normans destroyed the Anglo-Saxon army and killed Harold at the Battle of Hastings (see **Hastings, Battle of; Norman Conquest**).

On Christmas Day, 1066, William was crowned king. William then suppressed local rebellions. He took lands from those who resisted him, and gave them to his followers to hold in return for their military service to him. To emphasize the legitimacy of his crown, William confirmed the laws of Edward the Confessor and retained all the powers of the Anglo-Saxon monarchy. He levied *Danegeld,* the only national tax on landed property in all of Europe at that time. At Salisbury in 1086, he made all the landholders, even the vassals of his barons, swear allegiance directly to him as king.

William was devout, firm in purpose, and unchanging in gaining his ends. His greatest monument is *Domesday Book,* an exhaustive survey of the land, the principal landholders, the farm population, and the material and financial resources of his realm (see **Domesday Book**).

See also **Flag** (picture: Historical flags of the world).

Additional resources

Brooks, Janice Y. *Kings and Queens: The Plantagenets of England.* Thomas Nelson, 1975. Suitable for younger readers. Biography of William I is on pages 13-32.
Douglas, David C. *William the Conqueror: The Norman Impact upon England.* Univ. of California Press, 1964.

William II (1057?-1100), son of William I, became king in 1087. He was called Rufus, meaning *red,* because of his ruddy complexion. Lustful for power and completely illiterate, he ruled with violence rather than strength. The clergy denounced his brutality and his infringements on church rights.

In 1088, several powerful Norman barons revolted against William. He put down the revolt and strengthened his position. Later, he gained control of Normandy by financing the crusading ventures of his brother Robert, Duke of Normandy. He also invaded Scotland and brought it under his control in 1097.

William's reign was marked by a bitter quarrel with the Roman Catholic Church. William kept the see of Canterbury vacant after the archbishop died in 1089, in order to collect its revenues for himself. When he fell seriously ill in 1093, he welcomed the election of Anselm as archbishop to atone for his sins. But when he recovered his health, he forced Anselm into exile. An arrow shot by a fellow hunter killed William while he was hunting. The clergy refused to give him a church funeral. Robert S. Hoyt

William III (1650-1702), known as **William of Orange,** was king of England, Scotland, and Ireland. He was born in The Hague, the son of the Prince of Orange and Mary, the daughter of Charles I of England. He gained fame by his opposition to King Louis XIV of France.

When Louis invaded the Netherlands in 1672, the Dutch chose William as their leader. William was defeated time and again, but continued to fight. Once he was forced to open the dikes and flood the land. This stopped the French for a while, and William had time to build up an alliance against them. In 1677, he married his cousin Mary. Her father, James, Duke of York, later became James II of England.

William hoped to gain the support of England. He became friendly with those opposed to King James II, who was a Roman Catholic. When James's son was baptized a Catholic, the Protestants turned to William and Mary. Both William and Mary were related to the royal family, and both were Protestant. Leading politicians invited William to invade England with Dutch forces to restore English liberties.

William landed in England with an army of 14,000 men in 1688. No blood was shed in this "Glorious Revolution," and James escaped to France. William and Mary became rulers of England in 1689, after they promised to obey the terms of the Declaration of Rights (later called the Bill of Rights). Although they ruled jointly, William made the decisions. In 1690, William defeated James and a French and Irish army at the Battle of the Boyne in Ireland. The Protestants of Ulster, Ireland, backed William and they are still known as *Orangemen* today.

William was one of the ablest kings of England, but he was not popular. The people did not understand his ways, and he did not understand the English political system. He let Parliament limit his power in order to gain its support against France. He proved to be a good soldier and a clever diplomat in the struggle with France over Louis XIV's attempt to annex the Spanish Empire. He made alliances in 1701 with nearly all Europe against Louis, but he died soon after the War of the Spanish Succession began.

See also **Bill of rights** (English Bill of Rights).

William IV (1765-1837) was the son of King George III and Charlotte of Mecklenburg-Strelitz. He succeeded his brother George IV and ruled from 1830 to his death. Three of England's greatest reforms were passed during his reign—the Reform Bill of 1832, the abolition of slavery in England's colonies, and factory reform (see **Great Britain** [The era of reform]). Willard M. Wallace

William, of Germany. See **Wilhelm.**

William I (1772-1843) was the first king of the present-day kingdom of the Netherlands. He was the son of William V, Prince of Orange, the last Netherlands governor, or *stadthouder,* who lost his throne to the French in 1795. William I joined the Prussian Army against Napoleon I, and in 1806 lost the German duchy of Nassau. He regained Nassau in 1815, but then he traded it for the duchy of Luxembourg at the Congress of Vienna.

The congress made William king of the new Kingdom of the Netherlands, which included Belgium and the Grand Duchy of Luxembourg. In 1830, Belgium demanded its independence, which was recognized in 1839. Because of trouble within the country, William gave up the Netherlands throne in 1840, in favor of his son William II. Jane K. Miller

William I, Prince of Orange (1533-1584), was the father of the Dutch Republic. He was called *William the Silent* because of his cautious nature.

William was born in Dillenburg, near Wetzlar, Germany. His parents were Lutherans, but William became a Roman Catholic to please Emperor Charles V, who had taken a liking to him. He put William in command of troops on the French frontier in 1555.

In 1556, Charles gave the throne to his son Philip II. Philip tried to increase control of the Low Countries (Belgium and the Netherlands). When he also tried to stamp out the Protestant religion there, William joined the Protestant Church. He led a rebellion against Spain in 1568. Although William tried hard to unite all the Low Countries in the revolt, he did not succeed. In 1579, the seven northern provinces formed a league which later became the Dutch Republic. In 1581, Philip put a price on William's head, and three years later an insane assassin killed him. Jane K. Miller

William and Mary, College of, is a coeducational, state-supported university in Williamsburg, Va. It was founded in 1693 by King William III and Queen Mary II of England, and is the second oldest institution of higher education in the United States. Harvard University, founded in 1636, is the oldest. In 1779, the college of William and Mary became the first college in the United States to offer professional training in law.

Courses at William and Mary lead to bachelor's, master's, and doctor's degrees. The Marshall-Wythe School of Law offers the Master of Law and Taxation and the Doctor of Jurisprudence degrees. Richard Bland College, a two-year branch campus, is in Petersburg, Va.

The university lists many famous Americans among its former students. They include Thomas Jefferson, James Monroe, John Tyler, and John Marshall. George Washington received his surveyor's license from William and Mary in 1749. He served as its chancellor from 1788 until his death in 1799. Some of the oldest buildings at William and Mary are the Sir Christopher Wren, built in 1695; the Brafferton, built in 1723; and the President's house, built in 1732.

Phi Beta Kappa, an honorary scholastic society, was founded at William and Mary in 1776 (see **Phi Beta Kappa**). The honor system was founded there in 1779. William and Mary was the first college in the United States to have an elective system of study (1779), a school of modern languages (1779), and a school of modern history (1803). For enrollment, see **Universities and colleges** (table).

Critically reviewed by the College of William and Mary

William of Ockham, *AHK uhm* (1284?-1347?), also spelled *Occam,* was an English philosopher and theologian. He was the most influential scholastic thinker of the 1300's (see **Scholasticism**). His attitudes toward knowledge, logic, and scientific inquiry played a major part in the transition from medieval to modern thought.

Ockham believed that the primary form of knowledge came from experience gained through the senses. He based scientific knowledge on such experience and on self-evident truths—and on logical propositions resulting from those two sources.

In his writings, Ockham stressed the Aristotelian principle that "entities must not be multiplied beyond what is necessary." This principle became known as *Ockham's Razor.* In philosophy, according to Ockham's Razor, a problem should be stated in its basic and simplest terms. In science, the simplest theory that fits the facts of a problem is the one that should be selected.

Ockham was born in southern England. He joined the Franciscans and eventually became prominent in that religious order. Ockham studied at Oxford University and then taught theology. In 1324, Pope John XXII called him to Avignon, France, to answer charges of *heresy* (teaching false doctrine). Ockham remained there four years. In 1328, he fled to the protection of Louis of Bavaria, an enemy of the pope.   William J. Courtenay

William the Conqueror. See **William (I) of England.**
William the Silent. See **William I, Prince of Orange.**
Williams, Daniel Hale (1856-1931), an American doctor, pioneered in surgery on the human heart. In 1893, he became the first surgeon to repair a tear in the *pericardium* (sac around the heart). Williams, a black, helped improve medical opportunities for members of his race. In 1891, he founded Provident Hospital in Chicago, the country's first interracial hospital and training school for black nurses and interns. Later, he established a nursing school for blacks at Freedman's Hospital in Washington, D.C. He established surgical clinics at Meharry Medical College, Nashville, Tenn.

Williams was born in Hollidaysburg, Pa. He graduated from Chicago Medical College (now Northwestern University Medical School) in 1883 and began his Chicago practice. He was the only black original member of the American College of Surgeons, which was founded in 1913.   Daniel J. Kevles

Williams, Emlyn (1905-1987) was a Welsh actor and playwright. He wrote more than 20 plays and performed in over 150 plays and motion pictures. Williams also gained wide recognition for his concert readings from the works of the English author Charles Dickens and the Welsh poet Dylan Thomas.

Williams became best known for his autobiographical play *The Corn Is Green* (1938). This drama depicts his life as a poor boy in a Welsh village. It ends with the boy winning a university scholarship through the encouragement of a devoted teacher. Williams also wrote *Night Must Fall* (1935), a popular suspense thriller. Williams' performance as the charming but insane young murderer in this drama also brought him fame as an actor. His other plays include *A Murder Has Been Arranged* (1930), *The Light of Heart* (1940), *Accolade* (1950), and *Someone Waiting* (1953).

George Emlyn Williams was born in Mostyn, near Prestatyn. He wrote two autobiographies. *George: An Early Autobiography* (1961) describes his childhood and his years at Oxford University. *Emlyn* (1973) tells about his early career in the theater.   Mardi Valgemae

Williams, Hank (1923-1953), was a country and western singer and composer. His songs helped country music spread from the rural South and Southwest to other regions of the United States. Williams' best-known songs include "Cold, Cold Heart" (1951), "Jambalaya" (1952), and "Your Cheatin' Heart" (1953).

Hiram Williams was born in Georgiana, Ala. He taught himself to play the guitar when he was 8 years old. At 13, he formed his own band, the Drifting Cowboys. The band began to perform on radio the next year.

In 1947, Williams moved to Nashville, Tenn., the recording and broadcasting center of country music. There he achieved his greatest popularity through recordings and radio performances, particularly on the "Grand Ole Opry" program. Williams died of a heart ailment at the age of 29 while traveling to a performance. Williams' son, Hank Williams, Jr., also became a leading country music singer and composer.   Burt Korall

See also **Country music** (picture).
Williams, Ralph Vaughan. See Vaughan Williams, Ralph.
Williams, Roger (1603?-1683), was a clergyman, a founder of the colony of Rhode Island, and a strong supporter of religious and political liberty. He believed that people had a right to complete religious freedom, rather than mere religious toleration that could be denied at the government's will. Williams helped establish a complete separation of church and state for Rhode Island. This example contributed greatly to a similar system of separation that was later adopted by framers of the Constitution of the United States.

Early life. Williams was born in London, the son of a merchant tailor. As a youth, he became a scribe for Sir Edward Coke, a noted English lawyer and judge. Coke helped Williams enter Cambridge University, where he received a bachelor's degree in 1627. In 1629, Williams became a chaplain in the household of a wealthy family. But Williams was a religious nonconformist—that is, he did not agree with principles of England's official church, the Church of England. At the time, King Charles I and William Laud, bishop of London, were persecuting those who dissented from the Church of England. As a result, Williams began to associate with nonconformists who were anxious to settle in New England, an area of English colonies in America. In 1629, Williams married Mary Barnard. They had six children.

In Massachusetts. Williams and his wife came to the Massachusetts Bay Colony in America in 1631. Williams refused an invitation to become the minister of the church in Boston because he opposed its ties to the Church of England. In 1634, he became the minister of the church at nearby Salem. There, many people favored his desire to have a church that was independent of the Church of England and of the colonial government.

By this time, Williams had gained a reputation as a troublesome person. He argued that the royal charter did not justify taking land that belonged to the Indians, and he declared that people should not be punished for religious differences. Officials of Massachusetts Bay Colony acted to send Williams back to England. But he fled into the wilderness in January 1636. The Narragansett Indians provided Williams with land beyond the borders of Massachusetts, and he founded Providence, later the capital of Rhode Island.

In Rhode Island. Williams established a government for Providence based on the consent of the settlers and on complete freedom of religion. In 1643, American colonists organized the New England Confederation without including the Providence settlement or other settlements in Rhode Island. The Confederation repeatedly denied membership to the Rhode Island settlements because of disagreement with their system of government and of religious freedom. To safeguard Rhode Island liberties and lands, Williams went to England in 1643 and secured a charter from the English government. Under this charter, Rhode Island adopted a system of government that included frequent elections, a flexible constitution, and local home rule. Williams went to England again in 1651 to save the colony from a rival claim.

Williams' most famous work, *The Bloudy Tenent of Persecution* (1644), was published during his first visit to England and upheld his argument for the separation of church and state. He wrote it as part of a long dispute with John Cotton, a Puritan leader of Massachusetts Bay Colony. In the work, Williams explained his belief that the church had to be spiritually pure to prepare corrupt and fallen human beings for eternity, and that governments were for earthly purposes only.

From 1654 to 1657, Williams was president of the Rhode Island colony. In 1657, he contributed to Rhode Island's decision to provide refuge for Quakers who had been banished from other colonies, even though he disagreed with their religious teachings.

Williams earned his living by farming and trading with the Indians. He went on missionary journeys among them and compiled a dictionary of their language. Williams was a close friend of the Indians. But he acted as a captain of the Providence militia and fought against the Indians during King Philip's War (1675-1676).

For most of his life, Williams, an intensely religious man, was a "seeker" after "truth" without a church he could call his own. He died in 1683 and was buried with military honors. Rhode Island placed a statue of him in the U.S. Capitol.   Craig W. Horle

See also **Rhode Island** (History).

Additional resources

Garrett, John. *Roger Williams: Witness Beyond Christendom, 1603-1683.* Macmillan, 1970.
Gilpin, W. Clark. *The Millenarian Piety of Roger Williams.* Univ. of Chicago Press, 1979.

Williams, Roy Lee (1915-1989), served as president of the Teamsters Union, the largest labor union in the United States, from 1981 to 1983. Many of the approximately 2 million Teamsters are truckdrivers.

Williams was born in Ottumwa, Iowa. He became a truckdriver in 1935. Williams began his union career in 1948 as business agent for the Teamsters in Wichita, Kans. He served as president of Joint Council 56, a regional Teamsters organization, from 1953 to 1981. In 1976, the Teamsters president, Frank Fitzsimmons, appointed Williams to serve also as director of the union's 14-state Central Conference. Williams was elected Teamsters president after Fitzsimmons died.

Williams' supporters praised his ability to bargain for advantageous contracts for Teamsters members. Critics believed Williams had close ties to criminals and pointed to grand jury *indictments* (charges of criminal activity) that were brought against him. He had been indicted four times. In 1982, Williams was found guilty of attempting to bribe Senator Howard W. Cannon of Nevada. He was sentenced to 55 years in prison. In 1985, his sentence was changed to 10 years. He was released from prison in 1988 after serving about three years of the sentence.   Warren Van Tine

Williams, Ted (1918-   ), was one of the greatest hitters in baseball history. Williams batted .406 in 1941 and

UPI/Bettmann Newsphotos

Ted Williams was one of the greatest hitters in baseball history. Williams had a lifetime batting average of .344 during the 19 seasons he played as an outfielder with the Boston Red Sox.

was the last player to reach .400 in the major leagues. Williams won six American League batting titles and had a lifetime batting average of .344. He led the American League in home runs four times, in runs batted in four times, and in runs scored six times. In addition, Williams had a career total of 2,019 walks, second only to Babe Ruth.

Theodore Samuel Williams was born in San Diego, Calif. He was an outfielder with the Boston Red Sox for 19 seasons from 1939 through 1960. His career was interrupted twice by military service as a Marine Corps pilot. He missed the 1943, 1944, and 1945 seasons during World War II and most of the 1952 and 1953 seasons during the Korean War. Williams was elected to the National Baseball Hall of Fame in 1966. From 1969 through 1972, he was manager of the Washington Senators and the Texas Rangers.   Dave Nightingale

See also **Baseball** (picture).

Williams, Tennessee (1911-1983), was an American playwright whose dramas portray the loneliness and isolation of life. He is best known for two plays, *The Glass Menagerie* (1945) and *A Streetcar Named Desire* (1947). In both plays, Williams portrayed the confrontation between a sensitive and poetic individual and the brutality and coarseness of modern life.

In *The Glass Menagerie,* a narrator, Tom Wingfield, recreates his memories of his sister, Laura, and of his mother, Amanda. Laura, a cripple, escapes into a fantasy world of old phonograph records and the glass animals in her "menagerie." Amanda's harsh practicality is balanced by romanticized memories of her Southern girlhood. Tom dreams of adventure and finally runs away from his family to join the merchant marines.

© Alex Gotfryd

Tennessee Williams

Special Report
WILLIAMS, TED
2003 Year Book, p. 156

In *A Streetcar Named Desire,* Blanche DuBois, an aging Southern belle who lives in a world of illusion, seeks shelter from her troubled past. She goes to live in New Orleans with her sister Stella and Stella's husband, Stanley Kowalski. Eventually, Kowalski brutally rapes Blanche. He is a symbol of harsh realism and a new working class South without traditional Southern courtesy and refinement. The play won a Pulitzer Prize in 1948.

Williams' play *Cat on a Hot Tin Roof* (1955) won a Pulitzer Prize in 1955. His other plays include *Summer and Smoke* (1948), *The Rose Tattoo* (1951), *Sweet Bird of Youth* (1959), and *The Night of the Iguana* (1961).

Thomas Lanier Williams was born in Columbus, Miss. He chose Tennessee as a pen name. Williams also wrote poetry, fiction, and memoirs.   Albert Wertheim

Williams, William (1731-1811), was a signer of the Declaration of Independence. He was a delegate to the Continental Congress from 1776 to 1778, and a delegate to the Congress of the Confederation in 1783 and 1784. He helped frame the Articles of Confederation. He also served in the Connecticut convention that ratified the United States Constitution in 1788. He was born in Lebanon, Conn.   Richard B. Morris

Williams, William Carlos (1883-1963), was an American poet. Of all modern American poets, he is probably the closest in spirit and technique to Walt Whitman. Like Whitman, Williams tried to reveal the essential worth of every object and every experience. Like Whitman, he favored a kind of free verse based on what he called the "variable foot." The meter was determined by the nature of the subject matter rather than the requirements of conventional literary form.

Williams was born in Rutherford, N.J. He received his M.D. from the University of Pennsylvania Medical School in 1906 and specialized in the care of children in Rutherford for over 40 years. It was medicine, Williams observed in his *Autobiography* (1951), that "gained me entrance to . . . the secret gardens of the self. . . . I was permitted by my medical badge to follow the poor, defeated body into those gulfs and grottos."

Williams felt poetry should "see the thing itself without forethought and without afterthought but with great intensity of perception." His concentration on the individuality of his subject matter produced a hard, clear poetry quite different from the indirect, intellectual work of his close friend Ezra Pound and the imaginative richness of another friend, Wallace Stevens.

Williams' *Pictures from Breughel* won the 1963 Pulitzer Prize for poetry. *Paterson* (1946-1958), a long major poem, is designed to provide a complex picture of the history and people of an American city. His *Selected Essays* were published in 1954. *Many Loves,* a collection of his plays, appeared in 1961. *The Collected Poems of William Carlos Williams, Volume One: 1909-1939,* was published in 1987.   Elmer Borklund

Williamsburg, Va. (pop. 9,870), is a historic city that lies on a peninsula between the James and York rivers (see **Virginia** [political map]). Today, Williamsburg is a famous tourist attraction because the city's Historic Area looks much as it did during colonial times. More than 80 original buildings, including many homes, have been restored to appear as they did in the 1700's. In addition, over 400 structures have been reconstructed on their original foundations, including public buildings.

Williamsburg was the capital of the Virginia Colony from 1699 to 1776 and of the Commonwealth of Virginia from 1776 to 1780. During colonial times, the city ranked with Boston, New York City, and Philadelphia as a cultural, political, and social center.

Many principles of self-government were established in Williamsburg. In 1765, the famous statesman Patrick Henry delivered a noted speech against the Stamp Act in the Williamsburg Capitol. There, the colonists adopted the Virginia Declaration of Rights in 1776. This document included the guarantees of liberty that became models for the Bill of Rights, the first 10 amendments to the United States Constitution.

Early days. English colonists founded the Williamsburg settlement in 1633. They chose the site because it had fewer mosquitoes and better soil drainage for crops than did the area around Jamestown, Va., the first permanent English settlement in America. The colonists called their community Middle Plantation because it lay in the middle of the peninsula. They built a fence of stakes 6 miles (10 kilometers) long across the peninsula for protection against the Indians. The College of William and Mary, the second oldest university in the United States, was founded in Middle Plantation in 1693.

In 1699, the colonists renamed their settlement Williamsburg in honor of King William III of England. Also in 1699, the capital of the Virginia Colony was moved to Williamsburg after a fire destroyed Jamestown. Williamsburg received a city charter in 1722.

Williamsburg ranked as the most important city in the Virginia Colony. Twice each year, plantation owners and their families gathered in Williamsburg to attend sessions of the General Court, Virginia's highest court. On these occasions, called *publick times,* Virginians also conducted business and attended auctions, balls, fairs, horse races, and other social events. The colony's first newspaper, the *Virginia Gazette,* was published in Williamsburg in 1736. In 1773, the first public mental institution in the American Colonies was opened in the city.

Virginia became one of the first colonies to vote for independence from Great Britain. It passed the Virginia Resolution for American Independence in Williamsburg in May 1776. In 1780, during the Revolutionary War, the Virginians moved their capital from Williamsburg to Richmond. The westward shift of Virginia's population made the more central location desirable. The people also feared that British warships might attack Williamsburg from the James River.

Williamsburg declined in importance and population after the Revolutionary War. Its economy came to depend largely on the College of William and Mary. In 1862, during the Civil War, the Battle of Williamsburg was fought east of the city. The city changed little during the 1800's and early 1900's.

Restoration. In 1926, philanthropist John D. Rockefeller, Jr., became interested in restoring and preserving the colonial appearance of the city. The idea came from W. A. R. Goodwin, minister of Williamsburg's Bruton Parish Church. Rockefeller provided the money that set up The Colonial Williamsburg Foundation.

Williamsburg today. Today, the Historic Area of Williamsburg covers more than 170 acres (69 hectares). Eleven major historic buildings and many colonial craft

Duke of Gloucester Street is lined with restored homes and shops that show how Williamsburg looked during the 1700's. The street is in the city's large Historic Area.

Colonial Williamsburg Foundation

The interiors of several restored homes in Colonial Williamsburg are open to visitors.

A blacksmith shop is one of several colonial craft shops in Williamsburg. Workers in colonial costume re-create many traditional crafts for visitors.

WORLD BOOK map

Williamsburg

VIRGINIA

Williamsburg

Williamsburg lies between the James and York rivers in eastern Virginia. The map at the right shows the city's restored area in yellow and the major points of interest.

Historic Area
■ Important building
□ Other building

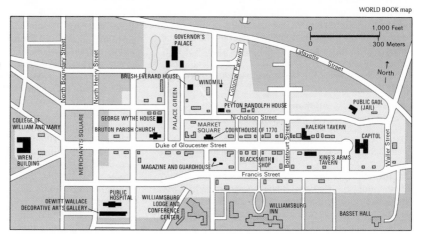

Eric Carle, Shostal

The Governor's Palace is one of Williamsburg's chief attractions. The city's visitors may ride in a horse-drawn carriage.

shops are open to the public daily. Guides in colonial costume escort visitors through the buildings, and craftworkers demonstrate such colonial skills as barrelmaking, cabinetmaking, and blacksmithing. The furnishings of the homes, public buildings, and shops make up one of the finest collections of American and English antiques in the United States. The DeWitt Wallace Decorative Arts Gallery displays furniture, ceramics, silver, paintings, prints, textiles, and costumes.

Williamsburg attracts more than a million visitors a year. Among the tourist attractions near Williamsburg is Carter's Grove, a plantation mansion completed in 1755. The Colonial National Historical Park includes much of Jamestown Island, several historic Yorktown homes, the Yorktown battlefield, and a scenic parkway that connects these sites with Williamsburg. Jamestown, Williamsburg, and Yorktown form what is often called the "historic triangle" of Virginia. Also near Williamsburg is Busch Gardens/The Old Country, an entertainment park.

Williamsburg covers about 9 square miles (23 square kilometers), almost five times its area in colonial times. Many modern housing developments surround the city. Williamsburg has a council-manager form of government. The people elect the five members of the council to two-year terms. A city manager hired by the council supervises public services. Williamsburg is the seat of James City County.   Will Molineux

See also **Colonial life in America** (pictures); **Virginia** (picture).

Additional resources

Goodwin, Rutherford. *Williamsburg in Virginia.* Rev. ed. Colonial Williamsburg, 1968.
Lewis, Taylor B., and others. *A Window on Williamsburg.* 2nd ed. CBS Publishing, 1983. Primarily photographs with supplementary text.

Williamson, Hugh (1735-1819), a scientist, writer, doctor, and politician, was a North Carolina signer of the Constitution of the United States. Williamson was one of the most outspoken delegates at the Constitutional Convention of 1787. He played a key role in set-

tling the dispute between large and small states over representation in Congress. Later, Williamson helped win *ratification* (approval) of the Constitution by North Carolina.

Williamson was born in West Nottingham Township, in Chester County, Pa., and educated at the College of Philadelphia. Although first trained as a minister, he later studied medicine in Scotland and the Netherlands. He began his medical practice in Philadelphia and soon joined the scientific circle surrounding Benjamin Franklin. He assisted Franklin in several experiments with electricity.

Williamson defended the rebellious acts of the New England Colonies to the British in his essay *The Plea of the Colonies* (1775). During the Revolutionary War in America (1775-1783), Williamson won distinction as an army doctor.

In 1782, Williamson was elected to the North Carolina legislature. He served in the Congress of the Confederation from 1782 to 1785 and from 1787 to 1789, and in the U.S. House of Representatives from 1789 to 1793. He then retired to New York, where he devoted his time to scientific work and writing.   Joan R. Gundersen

Willingdon, Marquess of, *MAHR kwihs* (1866-1941), a British colonial official, served as governor general of Canada from 1926 to 1931. He was the first Canadian governor general to represent the British monarch rather than the British government.

Willingdon was born at Ratton, near Eastbourne, East Sussex. His given and family name was Freeman Freeman-Thomas. In 1900, he was elected to the British Parliament as a Liberal. He became an earl in 1931 and a marquess in 1936. In 1913, Willingdon was sent to India, where he served as governor of Bombay until the end of 1918 and as governor of Madras from 1919 to 1924. He was *viceroy* (ruler) of India from 1931 to 1936. Willingdon did much to improve economic, political, and social conditions in India.   Jacques Monet

Willkie, Wendell Lewis (1892-1944), was the Republican candidate for President of the United States in 1940 when Franklin D. Roosevelt ran for a third term. Willkie was defeated, but he polled over 22 million votes. His running mate for the vice presidency was Senator Charles L. McNary of Oregon.

Willkie's political career was one of the most unusual in American history. Most of his life he had been a loyal member of the Democratic Party, but he became a Republican in the middle 1930's. Willkie rose to political prominence without the aid of a regular political machine, and most of his advisers were political amateurs. The chant "We want Willkie" from the galleries at the 1940 Republican National Convention forced many unwilling Republican leaders to give Willkie their party's nomination for President of the United States.

His life. Willkie was born on Feb. 18, 1892, in Elwood, Ind. His first name was originally Lewis and

Harris & Ewing

Wendell L. Willkie

his middle name Wendell. But when he enlisted in the Army during World War I, the Army mistakenly reversed them and he accepted the change. He studied law at Indiana University.

In 1929, he became legal adviser to the Commonwealth and Southern Electric Utilities Company. Four years later, he was elected the company's president. He fought a long legal battle against the Tennessee Valley Authority. But when in 1939 the U.S. Supreme Court refused to consider the constitutionality of the authority's activities, he sold the properties of the Tennessee Electric Power Company, a subsidiary of Commonwealth and Southern, to the TVA for $78 million.

His public career. Willkie became prominent for his opposition to the New Deal of President Roosevelt. He favored many of its social reforms, but opposed its business regulations. He favored removing controls and changing the tax system to encourage business expansion. He largely agreed with Roosevelt's foreign policy.

After the United States entered World War II, Willkie rallied his followers in a program of national unity. Roosevelt sent him on a number of visits to other countries as his unofficial envoy. After Willkie returned from an airplane trip around the world in 1942, he wrote the book *One World* (1943). In it, he outlined his ideas for international cooperation. Willkie entered the Wisconsin primary in 1944 as a candidate for the Republican nomination for President. He was defeated and retired from politics.   Harvey Wish

See also **Roosevelt, Franklin D.** (Election of 1940).

Willow is a large group of graceful trees and shrubs that usually have slender branches and narrow leaves. There are about 300 *species* (kinds) of willows, and about 80 of them are native to North America. The smallest willow is a tiny shrub about 1 inch (2.5 centimeters) high that grows in Arctic regions and above the timberline on mountains. The largest willows grow more than 120 feet (37 meters) high.

Willows usually grow near water. Sometimes they are planted in damp regions so that their roots take up water and dry the soil. The roots interlace to form a tough network that holds the soil together and prevents soil erosion. Willows also are planted to provide shade and to protect fields from winds.

The twigs of the willow are soft and slender, and they bend easily. Because of this, the wood is used to make baskets and wicker furniture. The wood of some willows also produces a high grade of charcoal that once was used to make gunpowder. The bark yields a chemical that the human body converts to a *salicylate,* a group of compounds to which aspirin belongs. In the past, people in various parts of the world used willow bark to relieve pain and fever. Most willows have long, narrow leaves that taper to a point and have finely toothed edges. Some willows have small, oval-shaped leaves.

In early spring, willows produce upright clusters of tiny, yellowish-green flowers. These flower clusters are called *catkins* because they resemble a cat's tail. The female flower develops a flask-shaped pod that splits open and releases tiny seeds with white, silky hairs.

The *black willow* is an important tree in the Eastern United States. Most willow lumber comes from the black willow. The wood is used mainly for boxes, crates, and wicker furniture. This willow has rough, dark bark.

© Pat Lynch, Photo Researchers

The willow typically has slender branches and narrow leaves. The black willow, *above,* is an important source of lumber.

Wicker furniture and baskets are also made from young shoots of the shrubby *basket willow.* The basket willow was brought to North America from Europe and now grows in the Northeastern United States.

The *white willow* is a popular decorative tree. The underside of its leaves appears white and silky. The *crack willow* gets its name from the fact that its brittle twigs break off in high winds. The *weeping willow,* thought to be native to China, has graceful, drooping branches. The *pussy willow* develops furry catkins, and its twigs are often used as decorations.

Scientific classification. Willows belong to the willow family, Salicaceae. They are genus *Salix.* The black willow is *S. nigra;* basket willow is *S. viminalis;* weeping willow is *S. babylonica;* white willow is *S. alba;* crack willow is *S. fragilis;* pussy willow is *S. discolor.*   Linda B. Brubaker

See also **Catkin; Osier; Pussy willow; Tree** (Familiar broadleaf and needleleaf trees [picture]).

Willow herb. See **Fireweed.**

Wills, Helen Newington (1906-   ), won more major tennis championships than any other woman in the world. She won the United States women's title seven times and the British championship at Wimbledon eight times. She was noted for her ability to hit the ball harder than any woman she faced and for poise that earned her the name "Little Miss Poker Face." She won her first U.S. women's tournament in 1923, and retired after winning at Wimbledon in 1938. She was born in Centerville, Calif. After marrying Frederick Moody in 1929, she played as Helen Wills Moody.   Pat Harmon

See also **Tennis** (picture; tables).

Willys, John North (1874-1935), was an American automobile manufacturer. He purchased the Overland Automobile Company in 1907 and from it organized the Willys-Overland Company. The company made such automobiles as the Overland, Willys-Knight, and Whippet.

By 1917, Willys' holdings included the car company and airplane, truck, and plow companies. But he lost control of his giant corporation in 1920. He reorganized the firm, and regained control in 1924. Willys was born in Canandaigua, N.Y. He was U.S. ambassador to Poland from 1930 to 1932. Smith Hempstone Oliver

Wilmington, Del. (pop. 70,195; met. area pop. 523,221), is the largest city and the chief manufacturing center of the state. Wilmington is called the *Chemical Capital of the World* because the city's metropolitan area is the home of several leading chemical firms. They include the Du Pont Company, one of the world's largest manufacturers of chemical products. The city lies in northeast Delaware, where the Brandywine and Christina rivers join the Delaware River (see **Delaware** [political map]). Wilmington has a mayor-council form of government.

Description. Wilmington, the county seat of New Castle County, covers 16 square miles (41 square kilometers). Many tourists visit the Fort Christina Monument and State Park, Old Swedes Church, and the Quaker Hill restoration area. The Delaware Center for the Performing Arts presents concerts, plays, and other productions. Several museums are in or near Wilmington. The Hagley Museum features exhibits of industries of the 1800's, including the original Du Pont gunpowder mills. The Henry Francis du Pont Winterthur Museum has a collection of Early American furniture. Three Du Pont family estates are open to the public. Other museums include the Delaware Art Museum and the Delaware Museum of Natural History. Wilmington is the home of Goldey Beacom College. Wilmington College and two campuses of Delaware Technical and Community College are near the city.

Wilmington has about 20 manufacturing plants. The chemical companies employ about a third of the workers of the area. Service industries, including banks and insurance companies, employ another third. Other industries produce automobiles, dyed fabrics, and military equipment. The city's port is a center for exporting and importing automobiles, bananas, lumber, and mineral products. Oceangoing ships dock there. Delaware Bay links the Delaware River and the Atlantic Ocean.

History. Leni-Lenape Indians lived in what is now the Wilmington area before the white settlers arrived. In 1638, Swedish colonists arrived and planned to set up a fur-trading and shipping center along the river they named the Christina. The colonists chose a site with a natural wharf, and there they built Fort Christina. Dutch forces seized the settlement in 1655. The English captured it in 1664 and, in 1739, they named the settlement Wilmington in honor of the Earl of Wilmington.

In 1802, Éleuthère Irénée du Pont, a French chemist, built some gunpowder mills near Wilmington. They grew into the Du Pont Company. Many other firms also set up offices in the city during the 1800's and 1900's.

In 1976, a six-block mall was completed in downtown Wilmington. A civic center was finished the next year. The mall includes Old Town Hall, five houses built in the 1700's, a performing-arts center, and stores and office buildings. In the early 1980's, Wilmington began two riverfront redevelopment projects. The projects included construction of new buildings and the conversion of old mills into townhouses. David D. Oyler

See also **Delaware** (Visitor's guide; pictures).

Wilmot Proviso, *WIHL muht pruh VY zoh.* President James K. Polk asked Congress in August 1846 to appropriate $2 million to negotiate a peace with Mexico, then at war with the United States. The President hoped to purchase new territory for the United States from Mexico. David Wilmot, a Democratic representative from Pennsylvania, offered an amendment to the bill in the House of Representatives. This amendment, called the *Wilmot Proviso,* declared that slavery should be forbidden in any territory obtained with the $2 million.

The House of Representatives approved the amendment on Feb. 15, 1847. But the Senate, where Southern representation was stronger, refused to pass it. For several years, the Wilmot Proviso was offered unsuccessfully as an amendment to many bills. The proviso led to bitter debate over the issue of slavery in the territories. The issue was settled in 1862, when Congress banned slavery in any U.S. territory. Norman A. Graebner

Wilson, Sir Angus (1913-), is a British author of novels and satirical short stories. His books deal with the deceptions that occur in human relationships, both public and private. Wilson uses masses of detail to create a realistic atmosphere.

The heroes of Wilson's novels *Hemlock and After* (1952), *Anglo-Saxon Attitudes* (1956), and *The Middle Age of Mrs. Eliot* (1958) are all middle-aged or elderly. They are frustrated and confused and are bogged down in everyday detail. Wilson enlivens these dreary characters with brilliant, witty dialogue and sharp observations on society. His other novels include *The Old Men at the Zoo* (1961), *No Laughing Matter* (1967), *As If by Magic* (1973), and *Setting the World on Fire* (1980). *Death Dance* (1969) is a collection of 25 short stories.

Wilson wrote several literary studies, including *The World of Charles Dickens* (1970) and *The Strange Ride of Rudyard Kipling* (1978). His criticism appears in *Diversity and Depth in Fiction* (1984). His travel essays were published as *Reflections in a Writer's Eye* (1986). Angus Frank Johnstone-Wilson was born in Bexhill-on-Sea, England. He was knighted in 1981. Frederick R. Karl

Wilson, Edmund (1895-1972), an American author, wrote about a wide variety of subjects. He became known for important works in such fields as literary criticism, Biblical studies, history, literature, and political science.

Wilson's many books reflect his broad interests. He learned Russian to do research on *Travels in Two Democracies* (1936) and, later, *A Window on Russia* (1972). He mastered Hebrew to do research for *Scrolls from the Dead Sea* (1955). Some of his books reflect his broad knowledge of cultural, social, and historical subjects. They include *To the Finland Station* (1940), *Apologies to the Iroquois* (1960), and *Patriotic Gore: Studies in the Literature of the American Civil War* (1962).

Wilson's first work of literary criticism, *Axel's Castle* (1931), is a study of the symbolist movement in literature. *The Wound and the Bow* (1941) examines the writings of noted European and American authors. Wilson also wrote numerous essays and reviews for magazines. Many were collected in *Classics and Commercials* (1950), *The Shores of Light* (1952), and *American Earthquake* (1958). Wilson wrote one novel, *I Thought of Daisy* (1929). Wilson's *Letters on Literature and Politics: 1912-1972* was published in 1977.

Wilson was born in Red Bank, N.J. Many of his essays and reviews first appeared in *The New Yorker* magazine. At his death, Wilson left over 2,000 pages of notes. Four volumes of these notes were published as *The Twenties* (1975), *The Thirties* (1980), *The Forties* (1983), and *The Fifties* (1986).   Victor A. Kramer

Wilson, Ethel (1890-1980), was a Canadian author. Most of her novels and short stories are gentle, sympathetic treatments of people from humble backgrounds. Most of her novels are set in or around Vancouver, B.C. She described the city, its people, and the surrounding wilderness landscape with wit and understanding. Her first novel was *Hetty Dorval* (1947). Her other novels include *The Innocent Traveller* (1949), *The Equations of Love* (1952), and *Love and Salt Water* (1956). Wilson's best-known novel, *Swamp Angel* (1954), tells the story of a middle-aged woman escaping a monotonous marriage to seek renewed contact with nature.

Wilson was born in Port Elizabeth, South Africa, and was raised in England and Vancouver. In 1937, she began to write short stories, which were collected in *Mrs. Golightly and Other Stories* (1961) and in *Ethel Wilson: Stories, Essays and Letters* (1987).   Laurie R. Ricou

Wilson, Henry (1812-1875), served as Vice President of the United States from 1873 to 1875 under President Ulysses S. Grant. He was a Republican U.S. senator from Massachusetts from 1855 to 1873. He helped found the Republican Party. He served in both houses of the Massachusetts legislature, but was defeated when he ran for governor in 1853. He was chairman of the Senate Military Affairs Committee during the Civil War, and a "Radical Republican" during Reconstruction (see **Reconstruction**). He was implicated in the Credit Mobilier scandal of 1872 (see **Credit Mobilier of America**).

Wilson was born Jeremiah Jones Colbaith in Farmington, N.H., but changed his name. He moved to Natick, Mass., in 1833, and became a shoe manufacturer. He was called the *Natick Cobbler*.   Irving G. Williams

See also **Vice President of the United States** (picture).

Wilson, James (1742-1798), a prominent Pennsylvania lawyer, was one of six people who signed both the Declaration of Independence and the Constitution of the United States. At the 1787 Constitutional Convention in Philadelphia, his influence was probably surpassed only by that of Virginia delegate James Madison. Wilson spoke 168 times at the convention. He also demonstrated his understanding of political theory in dealing with convention issues. Wilson argued for a strong national government whose authority would be based in the will of the people. He favored direct election of the chief executive and of both houses of the legislature. Wilson was largely responsible for Pennsylvania's *ratification* (approval) of the Constitution.

Wilson was born in Carskerdo, near St. Andrews, Scotland. He moved to America in 1765 and became a successful lawyer in Carlisle, Pa. Wilson was elected to the Second Continental Congress, which adopted the Declaration of Independence in 1776. He served in the Congress of the Confederation in 1783, 1785, and 1786. Wilson was appointed to the Supreme Court of the United States in 1789. In the 1793 case of *Chisholm v. Georgia,* he asserted the right of the court to decide cases brought against states. Bad investments left him unable to pay his many debts.   Richard D. Brown

Wilson, Lanford (1937-   ), is a leading American playwright. Most of his dramas use a few people—frequently members of one family—to represent the world in general. They often imply that people are not always successful at making the best of bad circumstances.

Wilson won a Pulitzer Prize in 1980 for *Talley's Folly* (1979), a love story about Matt Friedman, a 42-year-old Jew, and Sally Talley, a 31-year-old non-Jew from a bigoted family. *The Fifth of July* (1978) also deals with members of the Talley family. *Balm in Gilead* (1965) is a realistic portrait of life in an all-night New York diner. *The Hot l Baltimore* (1973) describes the residents of a run-down New York City hotel. *Lemon Sky* (1970) tells how a father-son conflict leads to a family's disintegration. *Angels Fall* (1982) describes the reactions of people who are brought together inside a New Mexico mission church after a nuclear accident. In *Burn This* (1987), a dancer is seduced by the crude brother of her deceased roommate.

Wilson was born in Lebanon, Mo., the background for several of his plays. Many of his early dramas were performed in a New York City coffee house from 1963 to 1966.   Gerald Bordman

Wilson, Lord (1916-   ), served as prime minister of Great Britain from 1964 to 1970 and from 1974 to 1976. He was also the leader of Britain's Labour Party from 1963 to 1976. Wilson was prime minister during times of great economic difficulty. His country faced inflation, strikes, low industrial production, and a deficit in its balance of payments. To try to solve these problems, Wilson's government devalued the British pound, raised taxes, and put a ceiling on prices and wages.

Wilson was born in Huddersfield, Yorkshire, England. His full name was James Harold Wilson, but he was commonly known as Harold Wilson. Wilson graduated from Oxford University in 1937 and taught economics there for two years. During World War II (1939-1945), he served as an economist for the government. He was first elected to the House of Commons of Parliament in 1945. Also in 1945, Wilson became parliamentary secretary for the Ministry of Works. In 1947, he was named secretary of overseas trade. Later in 1947, he became president of the Board of Trade. He held that post until 1951. In 1954, he became a member of the Labour Party's parliamentary committee. Wilson became the party's leader in 1963. The Labour Party won the parliamentary elections in 1964, and Wilson became prime minister. His term ended in 1970, when the Conservative Party won the parliamentary elections.

The Labour Party regained power in the 1974 elections, and Wilson became prime minister again. He resigned as prime minister and Labour Party leader in 1976. He was knighted that year and became Sir Harold Wilson. Wilson was in the House of Commons until 1983. He was then named a baron and became Lord Wilson and a member of the House of Lords.   Richard Rose

Lionel Cherruault, Camera Press
Lord Wilson

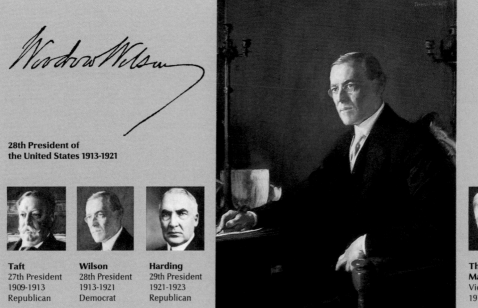

**28th President of
the United States 1913-1921**

Taft
27th President
1909-1913
Republican

Wilson
28th President
1913-1921
Democrat

Harding
29th President
1921-1923
Republican

**Thomas R.
Marshall**
Vice President
1913-1921

Oil painting on canvas (1921) by Edmund Charles Tarbell; National Portrait Gallery, Smithsonian Institution, Washington, D.C.

Wilson, Woodrow (1856-1924), led the United States through World War I and gained lasting fame as a champion of world peace and democracy. Wilson was one of the most remarkable men in American history. Before reaching the height of popularity as a world statesman, he had achieved success in two other careers. First, as a scholar, teacher, and university president, he greatly influenced the course of education. Then, as a political leader, he brought successful legislative reforms to state and national government. Wilson would have won a place in history even if he had been active in only one of his three careers.

Wilson was first of all a scholar. Even his physical appearance was like the popular idea of a scholar. He was thin, of medium height, and wore glasses. His high forehead, firm mouth, and jutting jaw all gave signs of thoughtfulness and strength. He was also a strong leader as a teacher, university president, and statesman. He was by nature somewhat headstrong and ready to fight. He was often unforgiving toward persons who disagreed with him. In his letters, Wilson often said he was not able to establish close friendships. But in truth, he had a great capacity for warm friendship. His energy, magnetic personality, and high ideals won for him the loyalty of many friends and political supporters.

Historians consider Wilson one of the three or four most successful Presidents. They agree that, as a spokesman for humanity in a world crisis, he stood for integrity, purity of purpose, and responsibility. Not even Wil-

son's enemies suggested he was weak or stupid. They knew he was honest, and that not even friendship could turn him aside from what he thought was right.

A minority of the voters elected Wilson to the presidency in 1912. That year the Republicans split their votes between President William Howard Taft and former President Theodore Roosevelt. In 1916, the people reelected Wilson, partly because "He kept us out of war." Three months later, German submarines began unrestricted attacks on American ships. Wilson went before Congress and called for war. After the war ended in 1918, the President fought for a peace treaty that included a League of Nations. Wilson saw his dream of U.S. leadership of the League crumble in 1920 when Warren G. Harding was elected President. Harding opposed American membership in the new organization.

In many ways, the Wilson era separated an old America from the modern nation of today. In 1910, when Wilson was elected governor of New Jersey, a majority of Americans lived on farms or in rural regions. By 1920, toward the end of Wilson's presidency, farmers had become a minority group in the United States. In 1910, Americans drove fewer than 500,000 automobiles. By 1920, more than 8 million cars, many of them Model T Fords, crowded the highways. Throughout this brief period of 10 years, the speeding-up in the nation's way of life could be seen in many ways. The electrical industry grew rapidly, skyscrapers rose in large cities, machinery revolutionized farm life, and good roads began to crisscross the country.

The period also brought great social changes. From 1910 to about 1914, Americans lived largely in a world of unchanging moral values and romantic ideals. These were reflected in the popularity of such books as Zane

Arthur S. Link, contributor of this article, is Shelby Cullom Davis Professor of American History at Princeton University and editor of The Papers of Woodrow Wilson.

World War I raged through Europe from 1914 to 1918.

The peace conference in 1919 led to the Treaty of Versailles.

The world of President Wilson

Major labor reforms were announced in 1914 by automobile manufacturer Henry Ford. He initiated the 8-hour workday and established a minimum wage of $5 a day, double what skilled laborers had been earning.

Three amendments to the U.S. Constitution were ratified during Wilson's presidency. Amendment 17, ratified in 1913, provided for the direct election of U.S. senators by the voters of a state, rather than by state legislators. Amendment 18, ratified in 1919, instituted Prohibition. Women gained the right to vote as a result of Amendment 19, ratified in 1920.

The Panama Canal opened for shipping in 1914, though the official opening was delayed until 1920.

The first transcontinental telephone line was established between New York City and San Francisco in 1915.

Silent movies became a major form of entertainment. *The Birth of a Nation,* produced in 1916, was the first screen epic. Such movie stars as Charlie Chaplin, Douglas Fairbanks, Mary Pickford, and Buster Keaton enjoyed great popularity.

The Russian Revolution of 1917 toppled Czar Nicholas II and eventually led to the establishment of a Communist government under V. I. Lenin.

The Black Sox baseball scandal created a stir in 1920. Eight members of the Chicago White Sox were accused of purposely losing the 1919 World Series against the Cincinnati Reds, in return for money from gamblers.

Fears of Communism swept the nation around 1920. Police arrested many innocent people during the "Red Scare."

Grey's *Riders of the Purple Sage* and Jean Webster's *Daddy Long Legs.* New currents began to stir the mainstream of American culture about 1914. One was the development of motion pictures, which became popular during Wilson's administration. Another was the increasing popularity of jazz music, which first appeared on phonograph records in 1917. World War I revolutionized social life in America. It began a wave of far-reaching social changes, including the prohibition of liquor, giving women the right to vote, and the migration of blacks from the South to the North.

Early years

Childhood. Woodrow Wilson was probably born on Dec. 29, 1856, at Staunton, Va. Confusion exists over the date because the family Bible shows it as "12 ¾ o'clock" at night on December 28. Wilson's mother said he was born "about midnight on the 28th." Wilson himself used December 28. He was the third of the four children of Joseph Ruggles Wilson and Janet "Jessie" Woodrow Wilson. The Wilsons named their second son Thomas

Important dates in Wilson's life

1856	(Dec. 29) Born at Staunton, Va.
1885	(June 24) Married Ellen Louise Axson.
1902	(June 9) Named president of Princeton University.
1910	(Nov. 8) Elected governor of New Jersey.
1912	(Nov. 5) Elected President of the United States.
1914	(Aug. 6) Ellen Wilson died.
1915	(Dec. 18) Married Edith Bolling Galt.
1916	(Nov. 7) Reelected President.
1919	(Sept. 26-Oct. 2) Suffered collapse and stroke.
1920	(Dec. 10) Awarded Nobel Prize for peace.
1924	(Feb. 3) Died in Washington, D.C.

Woodrow for his maternal grandfather. As a child, he was called "Tommy," but he dropped the name Thomas soon after being graduated from college.

Wilson's father, a Presbyterian minister, had grown up in Ohio. James Wilson, his grandfather, was a Scotch-Irish immigrant who had become a well-known Ohio newspaperman and legislator. Wilson's mother was born in Carlisle, England, near Scotland. Her Scottish father, also a Presbyterian minister, brought his family to the United States when Janet was 9.

An atmosphere of religious piety and scholarly interests dominated Wilson's early years. From the time of his birth, he lived among people who were deeply religious, believed in Presbyterian doctrines, and stressed

Woodrow Wilson Birthplace Foundation

Wilson's birthplace in Staunton, Va., is a national historic site. The Wilsons moved to Georgia before Woodrow was 2.

the importance of education. Before Wilson was 2, his family moved to Augusta, Ga., where his father became pastor of a church. Between the ages of 4 and 8, Wilson lived in an atmosphere colored by the Civil War. His earliest memory was of a passer-by shouting in great excitement that Abraham Lincoln had been elected President and that war would follow. Years later, Wilson wrote about General William Sherman's famous march through Georgia saying, "I am painfully familiar with the details of that awful march." During the war, Joseph Wilson, a strong Southern sympathizer, turned his church into a hospital for wounded Confederate soldiers.

Education. Wilson did not begin school until he was 9, mainly because the war had closed many schools. But his father taught the boy much at home. On weekdays, the minister would take him to visit a corn mill, a cotton gin, or some other plant. During the war, they visited ammunition factories and iron foundries. After these trips, Wilson always had to discuss what he had seen, because his father believed the exact expression of ideas was necessary for clear understanding. At home, the Wilsons read the Bible together every day, and gathered to sing hymns on Sunday evenings.

In 1870, Wilson's father became a professor in the Presbyterian theological seminary at Columbia, S.C. Three years later, when Wilson was 17, he entered Davidson College at Davidson, N.C. The school still suffered from the effects of the war. Davidson students had to carry their own water and firewood, as well as perform other chores. Wilson did well, and he enjoyed his freshman year at Davidson. But he withdrew at the end of the year because he wanted to attend Princeton University (then called College of New Jersey) at Princeton, N.J. His father was offered a post in a large church in Wilmington, N.C., and could now afford to send his son to Princeton. Wilson stayed home for a year to learn shorthand and to further prepare himself for his studies.

In September 1875, Wilson enrolled in the college at Princeton. While there, he practiced public speaking, became a leader in debating, and read the lives of great American and British statesmen. During his senior year, he served as managing editor of the college newspaper, the *Princetonian*. In 1879, Wilson was graduated 38th in a class of 106. He planned a career in public life.

In October, Wilson entered the University of Virginia Law School at Charlottesville, Va. He felt that law would provide the best path to the career he desired. Wilson took an active part in the university's debating societies. He withdrew from school in 1880 because of ill health.

Beginning career

Lawyer. In 1882, Wilson established a law office in Atlanta, Ga. He attracted few clients, and spent much of his time reading, writing newspaper articles, and studying political problems. By the spring of 1883, Wilson realized that he was not suited to be a lawyer. He decided to become a college teacher, and began graduate study in history and political science at Johns Hopkins University in Baltimore, Md.

Graduate student. At Johns Hopkins, Wilson came into contact with brilliant, thoughtful men. He worked hard to improve his writing style and to master history and political science. In 1885, Wilson published his first book, *Congressional Government, A Study in American*

Politics. Educators, lawmakers, and students praised his analysis of the federal government and of American legislative practices. Wilson later presented this study as his doctoral thesis, and Johns Hopkins awarded him the Ph.D. degree in June, 1886.

Wilson's family. In 1883, Wilson made a business trip to Rome, Ga. There he met and fell in love with Ellen Louise Axson (May 15, 1860-Aug. 6, 1914), the daughter of a Presbyterian minister. They were married on June 24, 1885.

Mrs. Wilson became the most influential person in her husband's life. She appreciated his talents and greatness, and sympathized with his ideals. Mrs. Wilson had many literary and artistic interests. But she devoted most of her time to making a comfortable home where her husband could relax from the cares of his work.

The Wilsons had three daughters: Margaret Wilson (1886-1944), Jessie Woodrow Wilson (1887-1933), and Eleanor Randolph Wilson (1889-1967). Wilson was tender and affectionate, and enjoyed nothing more than rollicking with his children or telling them stories at the dinner table. Like his father, Wilson spent many evenings reading Scott, Dickens, or Wordsworth aloud to his family. He often played charades with his daughters, and once dressed up in a velvet curtain, feather scarf, and one of his wife's hats to look like an old lady.

Teacher. In the autumn of 1885, Wilson began a three-year period as associate professor of history at Bryn Mawr College, a woman's school in Bryn Mawr, Pa. He then became professor of history and political economy at Wesleyan University in Middletown, Conn. Wilson also coached football at Wesleyan, and developed one of the school's greatest teams. He told his players: "Go in to win. Don't admit defeat before you start." In 1889, Wilson published *The State,* one of the first textbooks in comparative government. This book is considered his most important scholarly work. In 1890, Princeton University invited him to become professor of jurisprudence and political economy.

University president

At Princeton, Wilson's reputation as a scholar and teacher grew steadily. He worked constantly to express

Culver

Wilson and his first wife had three daughters. *Left to right* are Margaret, Mrs. Ellen Wilson, Eleanor, Jessie, and Wilson.

his thoughts precisely in writing. He also became a popular and distinguished lecturer. On June 9, 1902, the Princeton trustees unanimously elected Wilson president of the university. Never before had anyone but a clergyman held this position. As soon as Wilson took office, he announced his intention to change Princeton from "a place where there are youngsters doing tasks to a place where there are men thinking." But his belief that "the object of a university is simply and entirely intellectual" found little support among students devoted largely to social events and athletics.

Wilson helped to reorganize the university's undergraduate course program. He introduced a new method of teaching which he called the *Preceptorial System.* He believed that this system, using individual instruction by tutors, would bring students and teachers into a closer relationship. He also believed it would help students organize scattered information from their undergraduate programs and from general reading.

Wilson's educational reforms won high praise from the few who understood them. But what brought the president of Princeton to public attention was his fight to reform the eating-clubs. These organizations somewhat resembled the fraternities of other schools. Some of the clubs had restricted their memberships and become exclusive. Wilson felt that the clubs were undemocratic and detracted from the intellectual life of Princeton. He wanted to replace them by rebuilding the university with separate colleges, each arranged in a quadrangle around a central court. Each college would have its own dormitories, eating hall, master, and tutors. Wilson felt this arrangement, which became known as the *Quad Plan,* would stimulate intellectual life.

At first, many Princeton students, including members of the clubs, approved Wilson's idea. But the alumni disliked it because they enjoyed coming back to their clubs at reunions and football games. Bitter feelings were aroused. Finally, the board of trustees asked Wilson to withdraw his proposal. Twenty years later, Harvard and Yale both adopted a form of Wilson's Quad Plan. Thus, Wilson proved himself an educator ahead of his time.

Wilson suffered a second defeat in the development of plans for Princeton's graduate school. He tried to integrate this school with the undergraduate college. He believed such a move would make the graduate school more responsive to his authority and establish it as the center of intellectual life on the campus. Andrew West, Dean of the Graduate College, opposed Wilson's plan. The two men even battled over the location of a proposed new building for the graduate school. The bitter fight ended in defeat when a graduate died and left a sum thought to be several million dollars to the graduate school on condition that West remain in charge.

Wilson's struggles at Princeton attracted wide public notice. Newspapers reported the argument over the Quad Plan as a fight by Wilson for democracy and against snobbery. He was pictured as a man who favored the common people against the rich and powerful. Such a picture distorted Wilson's main objectives, but it made him politically appealing.

Governor of New Jersey

James Smith, Jr., the Democratic party boss in New Jersey, began to think of Wilson as a possible candidate

As president of Princeton from 1902 to 1910, Wilson gained nationwide attention for his efforts at educational and social reforms. He was viewed as a strong supporter of democracy.

for governor. The party's record was so bad that it needed a candidate whose honesty was above question. At this same time, Colonel George B. M. Harvey, a party leader and the editor of *Harper's Weekly,* also became interested in Wilson. Smith and Harvey together could almost control the nomination for governor, and they offered it to Wilson.

They timed their offer well. Because of his disappointments at Princeton, Wilson was ready to change careers. As a scholar in the field of government, he knew the facts of machine politics. He suspected that Smith planned to use him for some purpose of his own. But Wilson wanted to run for governor as the first step toward the White House, and Smith badly needed Wilson. The two men agreed, therefore, not to attempt to control each other.

On Oct. 20, 1910, Wilson resigned from Princeton to campaign for governor. The power and eloquence of his campaign speeches stirred voters throughout the state. He was elected by the largest majority received by a Democrat in New Jersey up to that time.

Political reformer. Wilson at once made it clear that he wanted nothing to do with the political practices of the Democratic machine headed by Smith. Smith, who had previously served in the U.S. Senate, decided to run for that office again. At that time, Senators were elected by the state legislatures. If no candidate received a majority of the votes in each house of a legislature, both houses met in joint session to elect a Senator. Wilson's victory had given the Democrats a majority in the joint session of the New Jersey legislature. When Smith refused to withdraw, Wilson endorsed a rival candidate who won. A reporter wrote that Wilson had "licked the gang to a frazzle."

Meanwhile, Wilson was pushing a series of reforms through the legislature. These laws changed New Jersey from one of the most conservative states into one of the most progressive. During its first session, the legislature enacted the most important proposals of Wilson's campaign. It passed a primary-election law, a corrupt-practices act, a public-utilities act, and an employers' liability law. At Wilson's urging, it also passed various school-reform laws, and enacted a law permitting cities to adopt the commission form of government. Wilson did not hesitate to break long-established customs in his political fights. He hired a superintendent of schools from outside the state. He frequently asked the advice of members of the legislature, and turned up unexpectedly at some of their private meetings. He sometimes appealed directly to the people, over the heads of legislators and officials.

Presidential candidate. Wilson's reforms in New Jersey brought him national attention at an opportune time. The progressive wing of the Democratic party was seeking a presidential candidate to replace William Jennings Bryan, who had been defeated three times. By 1911 Wilson had clearly become a candidate for the nomination. He started speaking on national issues throughout the country, and progressive Democrats began to support him. Most importantly, Wilson won the confidence of Bryan, the party's official leader.

The Democratic national convention met at Baltimore in June 1912. Champ Clark of Missouri, Speaker of the House of Representatives, received a majority of the delegates' votes on the 10th ballot. Not since 1844 had a candidate who had gained a majority failed to go on and receive the two-thirds vote then necessary for nomination. But Wilson's followers stayed with him. On the 14th ballot, Bryan swung his support to Wilson. The old progressive rose dramatically in the crowded convention hall to explain his vote. He pointed out that Charles Francis Murphy, the boss of New York City's Tammany Hall machine, had thrown his support to Clark. He said he could never vote for Clark as long as the Speaker had Tammany's support. From this point on (although not because of Bryan's change of vote), Wilson gained slowly until the 46th ballot, when he won the nomination. The convention nominated Governor Thomas R. Marshall of Indiana for Vice President.

Wilson's nomination meant almost certain election, because the Republican party was badly split. Conservative Republicans had renominated President William Howard Taft. Progressive Republicans then formed a new Progressive party that nominated former President Theodore Roosevelt. In a series of campaign speeches, later published as *The New Freedom,* Wilson stirred the public with his understanding of national problems.

The popular vote, overwhelmingly for Wilson and Roosevelt, was a clear endorsement of a liberal reform program. Wilson received 435 electoral votes; Roosevelt, 88; and Taft, 8.

Wilson's first Administration (1913-1917)

Inauguration. During his inauguration on March 4, 1913, Wilson noticed that a wide space had been cleared in front of the speaker's platform. He motioned

President-elect Wilson rode to his inauguration in 1913 in a horse-drawn carriage, with President Taft at his side.

to the police holding back the crowd and ordered: "Let the people come forward." His supporters said the phrase expressed the spirit of his administration.

In his inaugural address, the President accepted the challenge of the November landslide that had also swept a Democratic Congress into office. "No one can mistake the purpose for which the nation now seeks to use the Democratic party," he declared. "It seeks to use it to interpret a change in its plans and point of view." Among the laws that needed to be changed, Wilson named those governing tariffs, industry, and the banking system.

Wilson was the last President to ride to his inauguration in a horse-drawn carriage. Neither he nor his wife liked large social affairs, so the Wilsons did not give an inaugural ball. On March 15, only 11 days after his inauguration, Wilson held the first regular presidential press conference. He felt that the people were entitled to reports on the progress of his administration.

Legislative program. Wilson called Congress into special session on April 7, 1913, to consider a new tariff bill. For the first time since the presidency of John Adams, the President personally delivered his legislative requests to Congress. In October, Congress passed Wilson's first important reform measure, the Underwood Tariff Act. This law lowered rates on imports, and removed all tariffs from wool, sugar, iron ore, steel rails, and many other items. After signing the bill, Wilson remarked: "I have had the accomplishment of something like this at heart ever since I was a boy."

Wilson's first election

Place of nominating convention	Baltimore
Ballot on which nominated	46th
Progressive opponent	Theodore Roosevelt
Republican opponent	William Howard Taft
Electoral vote*	435 (Wilson) to:
	88 (Roosevelt)
	8 (Taft)
Popular vote	6,293,152 (Wilson) to:
	4,119,207 (Roosevelt)
	3,486,333 (Taft)
Age at inauguration	56

*For votes by states, see **Electoral College** (table).

On June 23, as Congress debated the tariff bill, Wilson presented his program for reform of the banking and currency laws. He spoke of this reform as "the second step in setting the business of this country free." Representative Carter Glass of Virginia introduced a bill to establish a central banking system. It was designed to provide a new currency and to help the flow of capital through 12 reserve banks, under the direction of a Federal Reserve Board. Congress debated the bill hotly for six months. In December, it passed the Federal Reserve Act basically in the form the President had recommended. Amendments also provided for exclusive governmental control of the Federal Reserve Board and for short-term agricultural credit through the new reserve banks. This act is regarded as the most effective banking and currency bill in the nation's history. See **Federal Reserve System.**

Wilson also asked for a series of other reforms. In 1914, Congress established the Federal Trade Commission to investigate and stop unfair trade practices (see **Federal Trade Commission**). That same year, it passed the Clayton Antitrust Act which increased the power of the federal government to police unfair practices of big business. In 1916, Wilson led Congress in adopting a series of reform measures. The Adamson Act established the eight-hour working day for railroad employees. The Child Labor Act, which limited children's work hours, began a new program of federal regulation of industry. Heavy taxes were placed on wealth. A tariff commission was established to "take the tariff out of politics." Other programs were started to improve rural education and rural roads.

Foreign affairs demanded much of the President's attention. He persuaded Congress to repeal the Panama Tolls Act, which had allowed American ships to use the Panama Canal toll-free when sailing between U.S. coastal ports. Wilson believed this law violated a treaty with Great Britain. The President also refused to approve a bankers' loan to China, and put himself on record against "dollar diplomacy." Wilson insisted that his party live up to its campaign promise of preparing the Philippines for independence. In 1916, Congress passed the Jones Bill, which greatly increased Philippine self-gov-

Vice President and Cabinet

Vice President	*Thomas R. Marshall
Secretary of state	*William Jennings Bryan
	*Robert Lansing (1915)
	Bainbridge Colby (1920)
Secretary of the treasury	*William Gibbs McAdoo
	Carter Glass (1918)
	David F. Houston (1920)
Secretary of war	Lindley M. Garrison
	Newton D. Baker (1916)
Attorney general	James C. McReynolds
	*Thomas W. Gregory (1914)
	A. Mitchell Palmer (1919)
Postmaster general	Albert S. Burleson
Secretary of the Navy	Josephus Daniels
Secretary of the interior	Franklin K. Lane
	John B. Payne (1920)
Secretary of agriculture	David F. Houston
	Edwin T. Meredith (1920)
Secretary of commerce	William C. Redfield
	Joshua W. Alexander (1919)
Secretary of labor	William B. Wilson

*Has a separate biography in *World Book.*

Puck, March 5, 1913

Revolutionary turmoil in Mexico was a problem Wilson inherited from Taft, as shown in this 1913 cartoon.

ernment and made many reforms in the administration of the islands.

Crisis in Mexico. Relations between the United States and Mexico were frequently troubled during Wilson's first Administration. In 1913, the President told Congress that there could be no peace in Mexico while Victoriano Huerta ruled as dictator. Wilson declared that the United States "can have no sympathy with those who seek to seize the powers of government to advance their own personal interests or ambition." Wilson tried unsuccessfully to negotiate for Huerta's retirement. Then the President permitted the dictator's enemies, who had begun a revolution, to obtain arms in the United States. Wilson let the Mexican groups fight it out for a while. But when Huerta's forces arrested 14 American sailors who had gone ashore at Tampico, Mexico, the President struck hard. He refused to accept Huerta's apology, and demanded that Huerta publicly salute the American flag in Tampico. When Huerta refused, Wilson in April 1914 ordered American forces to occupy the Mexican port of Veracruz. Eighteen Americans were killed in the action.

At this point, Wilson accepted an offer of the ABC powers (Argentina, Brazil, and Chile) to arbitrate the dispute. A peaceful settlement was worked out. Huerta fled from Mexico, and Venustiano Carranza, the leader of the anti-Huerta rebels, became acting president of Mexico. Pancho Villa, one of Carranza's chief generals, then quarreled with his leader and led a revolution against him. Carranza's soldiers drove Villa into northern Mexico. From there, Villa's troops raided Columbus, N. Mex. Many Americans called for war, but Wilson would not yield to their pressure. "Watchful waiting" became his policy. He sent troops under General John J. Pershing to patrol the border. Then, in 1916, he ordered Pershing to pursue Villa deep into Mexico. Carranza warned that he would resist any further invasion. Fighting did occur, and only a series of dramatic events in the late spring of

1916 averted open war. In 1917, Wilson officially recognized the Mexican government that had been established by a new constitution. But relations were never cordial with Mexico during the rest of the Wilson era. See **Mexico** (The revolution of 1910; The constitution of 1917).

Caribbean problems. Both Wilson and Secretary of State William Jennings Bryan spoke out against taking more land for the United States by the use of force. But their policies toward many small nations of Latin America and the Caribbean area did not differ much from those of previous Presidents. In 1914, Wilson and Bryan took over most of the control of revolution-torn Nicaragua. They sent troops in 1915 to occupy Haiti. A year later, the Dominican Republic was placed under American military government.

World War I begins. In August 1914, the outbreak of World War I stunned people everywhere. Most Americans joined in a single cry: "Let's stay out of it." Wilson proclaimed the neutrality of the United States. He said the nation "must be neutral in fact as well as in name . . . we must be impartial in thought as well as in action."

But neutrality became easier to think about than to maintain. On May 7, 1915, a German submarine torpedoed and sank the British passenger liner *Lusitania,* killing 128 Americans. This incident enraged some Americans, but Wilson remained calm. He began negotiations with the Germans and got them to order their submarines not to attack neutral or passenger ships. Angry men and women called Wilson "a human icicle" who did nothing to avenge the loss of American lives. But most Americans approved the President's fight for peace and neutrality.

UPI/Bettmann Newsphotos

Wilson's reelection campaign reminded voters of the various reforms his first Administration had achieved, and stressed the peace issue with such slogans as "He kept us out of war."

Life in the White House. With the help of her three daughters, Mrs. Wilson put her greatest efforts into making the White House as much like a private home as possible. She had little interest in entertaining, and often sat silently through dinner parties. She devoted herself to welfare work and to small groups interested in literature and art.

Then family life changed radically. Within an eight-month period, from November 1913 to July 1914, two of the President's daughters were married, and Mrs. Wilson became ill. After a short illness, the President's wife died on Aug. 6, 1914. Wilson was so saddened by her death that he nearly lost his will to live. Wilson's unmarried daughter, Margaret, and his first cousin, Helen Woodrow Bones, became hostesses for the President.

Remarriage. In March 1915, Wilson met Mrs. Edith Bolling Galt (Oct. 15, 1872-Dec. 28, 1961), widow of a Washington jeweler. He fell in love with the charming Mrs. Galt almost at once, and sent long letters and flowers to her every day. They were married in Mrs. Galt's home in Washington on Dec. 18, 1915.

The second Mrs. Wilson was an intelligent and strong-minded woman. Wilson again found the happiness and security he had known with his first wife.

Election of 1916. In June 1916, the Democrats renominated Wilson and Marshall. The Republicans had healed the split in their party, and chose a ticket of Supreme Court Justice Charles Evans Hughes and former Vice President Charles W. Fairbanks. The war in Europe overshadowed all other issues in the campaign. Democrats sought votes for Wilson with the slogan, "He kept us out of war." Wilson himself appealed to those who favored peace, but he also stressed the reforms his administration had accomplished.

On election night, the outcome was confused because of delays in receiving the election returns. Wilson went to bed believing Hughes had won. Many newspapers carried stories of Wilson's "defeat." But the final count in California gave the state to Wilson by about 3,400 votes. This insured his reelection.

Wilson's second Administration (1917-1921)

Declaration of war. During the next three months, Wilson devoted all his efforts to halting the fighting in

Historical Pictures Service

Wilson's second wife was Edith Bolling Galt, a widow whom he married in December 1915, 16 months after the death of his first wife. Edith was a loving and devoted companion to him.

Wilson's second election

Place of nominating convention	St. Louis
Ballot on which nominated	1st
Republican opponent	Charles Evans Hughes
Electoral vote*	277 (Wilson) to 254 (Hughes)
Popular vote	9,126,300 (Wilson) to 8,546,789 (Hughes)
Age at second inauguration	60

*For votes by states, see **Electoral College** (table).

Europe. But in February 1917, the Germans began unlimited submarine warfare against all merchant shipping, including American ships. The President immediately broke off diplomatic relations with Germany. Later that month, British agents uncovered a German plot to start a war between Mexico and the United States. German submarines began to attack American ships without warning in March, and enraged Americans demanded war.

Wilson decided the United States could no longer remain neutral. On the evening of April 2, the President drove to the Capitol with an escort of cavalry. As he stepped before a joint session of Congress, his face was tense and white. He spoke in a voice heavy with feeling. He said actions by Germany were "in fact nothing less than war against the government and people of the United States." Thunderous applause greeted the President's words. Wilson asked Congress to declare war against Germany, declaring that "the world must be made safe for democracy."

Four days later, on April 6, 1917, Congress passed a joint resolution declaring war on Germany. For a complete discussion of the United States in the war, see **World War I** (The United States enters the war).

War leader. The President proved himself as great a leader in war as he had been in peace. His many speeches in support of the American and Allied cause

Library of Congress

Wilson asked for a declaration of war in a speech before a joint session of Congress on April 2, 1917. Four days later, Congress passed a joint resolution declaring war on Germany.

stirred free people everywhere. Wilson stated the great issues of the war, and defined the aims for which the democracies fought. He also pointed out the necessity of making a better world after the war. The American people rallied with great loyalty and patriotism. A crusading spirit, almost hysterical in its intensity, swept the nation. People sang "I'm a Yankee Doodle Dandy," "Over There," and other popular war songs. Well-known film stars, such as Mary Pickford, Douglas Fairbanks, and Charlie Chaplin, drew huge crowds to purchase Liberty bonds at rallies.

The Fourteen Points. Wilson delivered his most important speech on Jan. 8, 1918. In this address to Congress, the President named Fourteen Points to be used as a guide for a peace settlement. Five of the points established general ideals. Eight points dealt with immediate political and territorial problems. The fourteenth point called for an association of nations to help keep world peace. The Fourteen Points are summarized as follows:

1. Open covenants of peace openly arrived at, with no secret international agreements in the future.
2. Freedom of the seas outside territorial waters in peace and in war, except in case of international action to enforce international treaties.
3. Removal of all possible economic barriers and establishment of equal trade conditions among nations.
4. Reduction of national armaments to the lowest point consistent with domestic safety.
5. Free, open-minded, and absolutely impartial adjustment of all colonial claims.
6. Evacuation of German troops from all Russian territory, an opportunity for Russia independently to determine its own political development and national policy, and a welcome for Russia into the society of free nations.
7. Evacuation of German troops from Belgium and the rebuilding of that nation.
8. Evacuation of German troops from all French territory and the return of Alsace-Lorraine to France.
9. Readjustment of Italian frontiers along the clearly recognizable lines of nationality.

Highlights of Wilson's Administration

1913	Wilson signed a bill creating an independent Department of Labor.
1913	Amendment 17 to the Constitution, providing for the election of U.S. Senators by popular vote instead of by state legislatures, became law.
1913	Congress passed the Underwood Tariff Act and established the Federal Reserve System.
1914	Congress passed the Clayton Antitrust Act and created the Federal Trade Commission.
1914	Wilson emphasized U.S. neutrality, following the outbreak of World War I in Europe.
1917	Congress approved the purchase of the Virgin Islands from Denmark.
1917	(April 6) Congress declared war against Germany.
1918	(Jan. 8) Wilson set forth the Fourteen Points.
1918	(Oct. 6–Nov. 11) Wilson negotiated the armistice with Germany.
1919	(Jan. 18–June 28) Wilson helped draft the Versailles Treaty at the Paris Peace Conference.
1919	Amendment 18 to the Constitution, banning the manufacture, sale, and transportation of alcoholic beverages, became law.
1920	Congress rejected the Versailles Treaty and American membership in the League of Nations.
1920	Amendment 19 to the Constitution, giving women the right to vote, became law.

National Archives

Paris streets were mobbed with people waiting for Wilson to arrive for the peace conference of 1919. In France, Britain, and Italy, Wilson was hailed as a just and honorable leader.

UPI/Bettmann Newsphotos

The "Big Four" Allied leaders gathered at the peace conference. *Left to right* are David Lloyd George of Britain, Vittorio Orlando of Italy, Georges Clemenceau of France, and Wilson.

10. Limited self-government for the peoples of Austria-Hungary.

11. Evacuation of German troops from Romania, Serbia, and Montenegro, and independence guaranteed for the Balkan countries.

12. Independence for Turkey, but an opportunity to develop self-government for other nationalities under Turkish rule, and guarantees that the Dardanelles be permanently opened as a free passage to ships of all nations.

13. Independence for Poland.

14. "A general association of nations must be formed under specific covenants for the purpose of affording mutual guarantees of political independence and territorial integrity to great and small states alike."

Wilson's speech did much to undermine German morale during the final months of the war. It also gave the Germans a basis upon which to appeal for peace. On Nov. 9, 1918, only 10 months after the President had stated his Fourteen Points, Kaiser Wilhelm II gave up control of the German government. Two days later, an armistice negotiated by Wilson was proclaimed.

The peace settlement. After the armistice had been signed, Wilson decided to lead the United States delegation to the peace conference at Paris. He wanted to make certain that his Fourteen Points would be carried out. The President also thought the United States should be represented by its political leader, as were Great Britain, France, and the other powers. Wilson appointed a peace delegation that included no member of the U.S. Senate and no influential Republicans. He was criticized for this, and later it helped cause the Senate to reject the treaty agreed upon at Paris.

Wilson knew the United States would be the only country represented at the peace table that wanted nothing for itself. He also believed he would be the only representative of the great powers who really cared about establishing an association of nations to prevent war. The President was determined to use his power and prestige to have the final peace settlement include a plan for a League of Nations.

Wilson was the first President to cross the Atlantic Ocean while in office. He landed at Brest, France, on Dec. 13, 1918, and the next morning rode through the streets of Paris. Never had the people of Paris given a

Quotations from Wilson

The following quotations come from some of Woodrow Wilson's speeches and writings.

Uncompromising thought is the luxury of the closeted recluse.
Speech at the University of Tennessee, June 17, 1890

Big business is not dangerous because it is big, but because its bigness is . . . created by privileges and exemptions . . .
Acceptance speech, Democratic National Convention, 1912

Liberty is its own reward.
Speech in New York City, Sept. 9, 1912

We can afford to exercise the self-restraint of a really great nation which realizes its own strength and scorns to misuse it.
Message to Congress, Aug. 27, 1913

There must be, not a balance of power but a community of power; not organized rivalries but an organized, common peace. . . . It must be a peace without victory. . . . Victory would mean peace forced upon the loser . . . accepted in humiliation. . . . It would leave . . . a bitter memory upon which terms of peace would rest, not permanently, but only as upon quicksand. Only a peace between equals can last.
Speech to the Senate, January 1917

There is one choice we cannot make . . . we will not choose the path of submission . . . The world must be made safe for democracy.
Speech before Congress, April 2, 1917

To conquer with arms is to make only a temporary conquest; to conquer the world by earning its esteem is to make a permanent conquest.
Speech to Congress, Nov. 11, 1918

. . . people call me an idealist. Well, that is the way I know I am an American. America is the only idealistic nation in the world.
Speech in Sioux Falls, S.D., Sept. 8, 1919

king or emperor such a joyous reception. Banners welcomed "Wilson le Juste." From France, Wilson went to England where he stayed at Buckingham Palace. In Rome, he met with Pope Benedict XV, and became the first President to talk with a pope while in office. Everywhere he went in Europe, great crowds cheered him as the hope of humanity.

At the Paris Peace Conference, held from January to June, Wilson obtained only part of the treaty provisions he wanted. In order to win support for the League and other provisions in the Fourteen Points, he compromised on several major issues. Wilson's concessions weakened his moral position in the eyes of the world, although they insured establishment of the League of Nations. See **World War I** (The peace settlement); **League of Nations; Versailles, Treaty of.**

Opposition to the League. In February 1919, Wilson returned to the United States briefly to discuss the League and the peace treaty with the Senate. The Constitution required two-thirds approval by the Senate for the United States to adopt the treaty, which included the League. The President also hoped to quiet rising criticism throughout the country. Wilson's position was no longer strong politically. He had asked for the election of Democrats to Congress in 1918 as an indication of personal trust. But the voters had chosen more Republicans than Democrats.

Wilson soon discovered that he could not win Senate ratification of the League without some amendments to satisfy his critics at home. He went back to Paris in March 1919, and the conference delegates accepted several of these provisions. Wilson returned to the United States early in July with the text of the treaty. He found public debate on the peace terms in full swing, with mounting congressional opposition to the treaty and the League of Nations.

American opinion on the treaty was split into three groups. The isolationists, led by Senators William E. Borah, Hiram W. Johnson, and James A. Reed, stood firmly against any League. They argued that the United States should not interfere in "European affairs." The sec-

Brown Brothers

In retirement, Wilson lived a quiet life as a semi-invalid. He is shown above leaving his Washington home after his last public address, a speech to a group of friends on Armistice Day, 1923.

ond group consisted of Wilson and his followers, who urged that the treaty be ratified with no important changes or compromises. The men in the largest group, led by Senator Henry Cabot Lodge, took a middle ground between Wilson and the isolationists. They were ready to ratify the treaty with important changes. Some of these men, including Lodge, demanded changes that would reduce or eliminate America's obligations to the League.

Wilson's collapse. The President decided to take his case for the League to the American people—the method that had worked successfully for him in the past. On September 4, Wilson began a speaking tour through the Midwest and the Far West. His doctor had advised him against the trip, because his strenuous labors over the past several years had weakened his health. On September 25, Wilson spoke at Pueblo, Colo., urging approval of the League. That night, as his train sped toward Wichita, Kans., Wilson collapsed from fatigue and nervous tension. He canceled the remainder of his tour and returned to Washington. On October 2, the President suffered a paralytic stroke.

Wilson was an invalid for the rest of his life, but he did not give up the presidency. The Constitution did not then state clearly who inherits executive power when a President becomes severely ill but does not die or resign. After October, Wilson left his bed only for simple recreation or for purely formal tasks. These greatly taxed his strength, and his wife guided his hand when he signed official documents. Wilson did not call a meeting of the Cabinet until April 13, 1920. Before that, the Cabinet met unofficially and carried on much of the routine work of government during Wilson's long illness.

From his sickbed, the President helplessly watched the losing fight for his treaty. Senator Lodge, chairman of the Senate Foreign Relations Committee, presented the treaty for vote in November 1919. He and his com-

UPI/Bettmann Newsphotos

Wilson toured the nation in 1919 to win public support for the League of Nations. But his collapse on September 25 cut short his efforts. He suffered a stroke in October.

mittee had added 14 reservations. The most important one declared that the United States assumed no obligation to support the League of Nations unless Congress specifically approved by joint resolution. Claiming that this reservation would destroy the League, Wilson instructed Senate Democrats to vote against approval of the treaty containing the Lodge reservations. As a result, the treaty failed to win two-thirds approval. The treaty came up for vote again in March 1920, but once more it failed.

Wilson insisted that the treaty and the League should be the chief issue of the 1920 presidential campaign. The Democratic platform endorsed the League, and the Republican platform opposed it. In the election, Warren G. Harding, the Republican nominee, overwhelmingly defeated James M. Cox, his Democratic opponent. As far as the United States was concerned, the League of Nations was dead.

On Dec. 10, 1920, Wilson was awarded the 1919 Nobel Peace Prize for his work in founding the League of Nations and seeking a fair peace agreement.

Last years

For almost three years after his term ended in March 1921, Wilson lived in quiet retirement in Washington. He formed a law partnership with Bainbridge Colby, his third Secretary of State. Although Wilson had regained partial use of his arms and legs, his physical condition did not permit any actual work. He saw an occasional motion picture or play, listened to books and magazines read aloud to him, and sometimes invited friends for lunch.

Wilson was confident that future events would prove him correct regarding the League and the peace terms. In his last public speech, to a group of friends outside his home on Armistice Day, 1923, he said: "I cannot refrain from saying it: I am not one of those who have the least anxiety about the triumph of the principles I have stood for. I have seen fools resist Providence before and I have seen their destruction, as will come upon these again—utter destruction and contempt. That we shall prevail is as sure as that God reigns."

Wilson continued to bear the crushing blows of defeat with dignity and calm. But he told his friends he was "tired of swimming upstream." On Feb. 3, 1924, he died in his sleep. Two days later, Wilson was buried in Washington Cathedral. He is the only President interred in Washington, D.C.   Arthur S. Link

Related articles in *World Book* include:

Bryan, William Jennings
Fourteen Points
House, Edward Mandell
League of Nations
Marshall, Thomas Riley
Nobel Prizes (picture)
President of the U.S.

Roosevelt, Theodore (Later years)
Versailles, Treaty of
World War I (The United States enters the war; The peace settlement)

Outline

I. **Early years**
  A. Childhood   B. Education
II. **Beginning career**
  A. Lawyer
  B. Graduate student
  C. Wilson's family
  D. Teacher
III. **University president**
IV. **Governor of New Jersey**
  A. Political reformer   B. Presidential candidate
V. **Wilson's first Administration (1913-1917)**
  A. Inauguration   F. World War I begins
  B. Legislative program G. Life in the White House
  C. Foreign affairs   H. Remarriage
  D. Crisis in Mexico   I. Election of 1916
  E. Caribbean problems
VI. **Wilson's second Administration (1917-1921)**
  A. Declaration of war   D. The peace settlement
  B. War leader   E. Opposition to the League
  C. The Fourteen Points   F. Wilson's collapse
VII. **Last years**

Questions

Why was Wilson's election to the presidency in 1912 almost certain following his nomination?
What were Wilson's main reforms at Princeton University?
What brought Wilson to national attention as a presidential prospect?
What were the most important achievements in domestic affairs during his first Administration?
What was one of Wilson's most valuable techniques for winning legislation that he wanted?
Why was Wilson's family life so important to him?
Why did Wilson personally attend the Paris Peace Conference in 1919?
Why do historians regard Wilson as one of the nation's greatest Presidents?
What were his three main careers?
In what connection did Wilson make the statement: "Let the people come forward"?

Reading and Study Guide

See *Wilson, Woodrow,* in the Research Guide/Index, Volume 22, for a *Reading and Study Guide.*

Additional resources

Ambrosius, Lloyd E. *Woodrow Wilson and the American Diplomatic Tradition: The Treaty Fight in Perspective.* Cambridge, 1987.
Clements, Kendrick A. *Woodrow Wilson, World Statesman.* Twayne, 1987.
Cooper, John Milton, Jr., *The Warrior and the Priest: Woodrow Wilson and Theodore Roosevelt.* Harvard, 1983.
Link, Arthur S. *Wilson.* 5 vols. Princeton, 1947-1965. These volumes cover the years 1856 to 1917.

Wilson cloud chamber is a device that makes the paths of electrically charged atomic particles visible. Scientists examine these paths to determine the charge, mass, and velocity of the particles. Particles whose paths may be observed in a Wilson cloud chamber include *alpha rays* and *beta rays* from radioactive materials, and *cosmic rays* from outer space (see **Radioactivity; Cosmic rays**). The Wilson cloud chamber was invented in 1912 by Charles T. R. Wilson, a British physicist.

A simple cloud chamber consists of a container fitted with a piston. The chamber contains air or some other gas that is highly concentrated with water vapor, alcohol vapor, or both. When electrically charged particles pass through the gas, they knock electrons off molecules that lie in their path, changing these molecules into ions. Vapor collects around the ions to form droplets that make visible streaks in the cloud chamber. These streaks, also called *tracks,* thus represent the paths of the charged particles. The tracks disappear quickly, but scientists may photograph them through a glass wall or window provided for this purpose.

In order for tracks to form, the gas in a cloud chamber must become *supersaturated*—that is, its relative humidity must be greater than 100 per cent. Saturated gas becomes supersaturated when it cools. Saturated gas in a cloud chamber is cooled by moving the piston outward. The gas cools because the piston's movement results in a reduction of pressure within the chamber. Vapor in the gas then condenses on the ions to form droplets. In many cloud chambers, the movement of the piston is triggered by a signal from *electronic counters,* which can detect electrically charged particles.

Scientists often build cloud chambers between the poles of an electromagnet. The magnet causes charged particles in the chamber to move along curved paths. From these curves, scientists can determine the momentum of a particle.   Robert H. March

See also **Bubble chamber; Spark chamber.**

Wilt, in plants, is a condition in which the leaves and stems droop and die. It is usually a symptom of plant diseases which cause the cells to collapse. A plant wilts if it needs water. Disease bacteria that cause wilting stop up the channels that carry water in the plant. Many fungi that attack plants may cause wilting, sometimes by secreting poisons into the plant tissues.

Many root diseases bring about wilting. *Fusarium* is a fungus that wilts asters, potatoes, tomatoes, cotton, flax,

Wirt Wills, Photo/Nats

Wilt is usually caused by bacterial or fungal diseases. The photos above, *from left to right,* show the progression of wilt.

and other plants. *Sclerotinia,* another fungus, wilts many garden vegetables. Dutch elm disease also is caused by a fungus. This disease produces wilt in elm trees and kills many elms every year.

Control of wilt depends on the disease that causes it. Generally, one should destroy the diseased plants, and practice crop rotation. Fungicides also may be applied to the soil. Some of the newer varieties of plants produced by scientists resist wilt.   Jerry T. Walker

See also **Dutch elm disease.**

Wimbledon. See Tennis.

Wimsey, Lord Peter. See Sayers, Dorothy.

Winch is a crank that is used to give rotary motion to a machine. It is also the name of a device that has a crank attached to a drum around which rope is wound. The rope is attached to a heavy object. By turning the crank, a person can *winch* (move) the object to a desired position or height. See also **Crane.**

Winchell, Walter (1897-1972), an American newspaperman and commentator, became important for making the gossip column a regular newspaper feature. Critics accused him of snooping, but his column became widely read and imitated. In his column, Winchell used a type of jargon that has been widely copied. He coined colorful words and phrases, such as "lohengrined" and "middle-aisled" for "married."

Winchell was born in New York City. He played in vaudeville before beginning to write for *The Vaudeville News* in 1920. He became nationally known in 1929 through his syndicated column about Broadway. He also appeared on radio and television. He retired in 1969.
     Paul Molloy

Winchester was the chief town of England in Anglo-Saxon times. It is the chief town in the district of Winchester, which has a population of about 93,700. It is a religious, service, and light industrial center. It is also the administrative center of the county of Hampshire. Winchester is one of the most prosperous towns in Great Britain. It lies on the River Itchen in southern England (see **England** [map]).

Both Alfred the Great and the Danish King Canute were buried at Winchester. After the Normans conquered England in 1066, Winchester continued to rival London as a trade and political center. William of Wykeham completed Winchester's famous cathedral in the 1300's. This cathedral, which is 556 feet (169 meters) long, is the longest church in England. William also founded Winchester College, one of the leading English public schools.   D. A. Pinder

Winchester College at Winchester, England, is one of the oldest and most prominent public schools in the country. William of Wykeham, bishop of Winchester, founded it in 1382, and it was opened in 1394. The motto of the school is "Manners Makyth Man." The college was originally established for 70 poor scholars, but greater numbers were gradually admitted. It flourished until the 1700's, when a decline began. William Stanley Goddard, who became headmaster in 1796, saved the school by his reforms. Winchester College was one of the first public schools to introduce courses in science and mathematics.   P. A. McGinley

Winckelmann, *VIHNG kuhl MAHN,* **Johann Joachim,** *YOH hahn YOH ah kihm* (1717-1768), was a German scholar who has been called the father of both archaeology and art history. His work was the first systematic study of ancient Greek and Roman art. Winckelmann showed that art objects can reveal as much important information about the history of a culture as writings do. His belief in Greek art as an ideal greatly influenced many writers and artists of his time.

Winckelmann was born in Stendal, Prussia (now in East Germany). As a boy, he learned Greek and Latin so he could read Homer and other ancient writers. Winckelmann later studied theology and medicine, but he earned his living as a teacher and a librarian.

In 1754 and 1755, Winckelmann studied art in Dresden. He then moved to Italy, where he did most of the work for which he became known. His reports of the excavations at the ancient Roman towns of Pompeii and Herculaneum were widely read. Art historians still use his principal work, *Geschichte der Kunst des Altertums* (*The History of Ancient Art,* 1764).   Richard G. Klein

Wind is air moving across the earth's surface. Wind may blow so slowly and gently that it can hardly be felt. Or it may blow so fast and hard that it smashes buildings and pushes over large trees. Strong winds can whip up great ocean waves that damage ships and flood land. Wind can blow away soil from farmland so crops cannot grow. Sharp grains of dust carried by wind wear away rock and change the features of land.

Wind is also a part of weather. A hot, moist day may suddenly turn cool if a wind blows from a cool area. Clouds with rain and lightning may form where the cool air meets the hot, moist air. Later, another wind may blow the clouds away and allow the sun to warm the land again. Wind can carry a storm great distances.

Winds are named according to the direction *from* which they blow. For example, an *east* wind blows from east to west. A *north* wind blows from north to south.

Causes of wind

Wind is caused by the uneven heating of the *atmosphere* (the air around the earth) by energy from the sun. The sun heats the surface of the earth unevenly. Air above hot areas expands and rises. Air from cooler areas then flows in to replace the heated air. This process is called *circulation.* The circulation over the entire earth is the *general circulation.* The smaller-scale circulations that cause day-to-day wind changes are known as *synoptic-scale circulations.* Winds that occur only in one place are called *local winds.*

General circulation produces average winds that occur over large sections of the earth's surface. These winds, called *prevailing winds,* vary with differences in latitude. Near the equator, heated air rises to about 60,000 feet (18,000 meters). Surface air moving in to replace the rising air produces two belts of prevailing winds. These belts lie between the equator and about 30° north and south latitude. The winds there are called *trade winds* because sailors once relied on them in sailing trading ships.

The trade winds do not blow straight toward the equator. Instead, they blow somewhat from east to west. The westward part of their motion is caused by the spinning of the earth. The earth and the air around it rotate eastward together. Each point on the earth's surface travels around a complete circle in 24 hours. Points near the equator travel around larger circles than points near 30° north or south latitude, because the earth is larger at the equator. So, the points that are near the equator travel faster.

As air moves toward the equator, it reaches faster-moving points on the earth's surface. Because these surface points are moving eastward faster than the air, a person standing on the earth feels a wind blowing westward against him.

There are no prevailing winds near the equator and up to about 700 miles (1,100 kilometers) on either side of it, because the air rises there instead of moving across the earth. This calm belt is called the *doldrums.* Often the trade winds *converge* (come together) in a narrow zone which is called the *intertropical convergence zone* (ITCZ).

Some of the air that rises at the equator returns to the earth's surface at about 30° north and south latitude. Air moving downward there produces no wind. These areas are called the *horse latitudes,* possibly because many horses died on sailing ships that were stalled by the lack of wind there.

Two other kinds of prevailing winds result from the general circulation in the atmosphere. The *prevailing westerlies* blow somewhat from west to east in two belts between latitudes of about 30° and 60° north and south of the equator. These winds result from surface air moving away from the equator and reaching slower-moving points nearer the poles. Prevailing westerlies carry weather eastward across the northern United States and southern Canada. The *polar easterlies* blow somewhat from east to west in two belts between the poles and about 60° north and south latitude. Surface air moving away from the poles moves westward across faster-moving points nearer the equator.

General circulation of air around the earth

Prevailing winds result from the general circulation of air around the earth, shown at the right. In this drawing, the circulation has been greatly simplified. At the equator, air is heated by the sun and rises, as shown by the blue arrows. In the upper atmosphere, this air flows away from the equator. When the air returns to the earth's surface, it flows across the surface, as shown by the black arrows. This moving surface air produces the six belts of prevailing winds around the earth. The turning of the earth causes the winds to blow toward the east in belts where the air moves away from the equator. In belts where the air moves toward the equator, the prevailing winds blow toward the west.

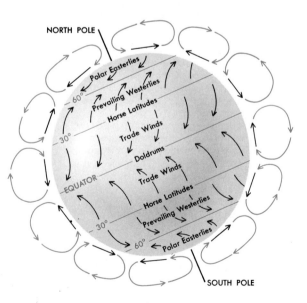

Synoptic-scale circulations are air motions around relatively small regions of high and low pressure in the atmosphere. These regions form within the larger general circulation. Air flows toward low-pressure regions called *lows* or *cyclones*. Air flows away from high-pressure regions called *highs* or *anticyclones*. Viewed from above, the wind moves clockwise around a high and counterclockwise around a low in the Northern Hemisphere. These directions are reversed in the Southern Hemisphere.

Highs and lows generally move with the prevailing winds. As they pass a given spot on the earth, the wind direction changes. For example, a low moving eastward across Chicago produces winds that shift from southeast to northwest.

Local winds arise only in specific areas on the earth. Local winds that result from the heating of land during summer and the cooling of land during winter are called *monsoons*. They blow from the ocean during summer and toward the ocean during winter. Monsoons control the climate in Asia, producing wet summers and dry winters. A warm, dry, local wind that blows down the side of a mountain is called a *chinook* in the western United States and a *foehn* in Europe. These three local winds, as well as the harmattan and the sirocco, are discussed in articles listed in the *Related articles* at the end of this article.

Measuring wind

Two features of wind, its speed and its direction, are used in describing and forecasting weather.

Wind speed is measured with an instrument called an *anemometer*. Several kinds of anemometers are used today. The most common kind has three or four cups attached to spokes on a rotating shaft. The spokes turn the shaft as the wind blows. The wind speed is indicated by the speed of the spinning shaft.

In the United States, wind speeds are stated in miles per hour or in *knots* (nautical miles per hour). But in many other countries, they are stated in kilometers per hour.

Wind direction is measured with an instrument called a *weather vane*. A weather vane has a broad, flat blade that is attached to a spoke pivoted at one end. Wind blowing on the blade turns the spoke so that the blade lines up in the direction of the wind. The wind direction may be indicated by an arrow fastened to the spoke, or by an electric meter remotely controlled by the weather vane.

Wind directions are often indicated by using the 360 degrees of a circle. On this circle, north is indicated by 0°. An east wind blows from 90°, a south wind blows from 180°, and a west wind blows from 270°. Winds at various altitudes often differ in speed and direction. For example, smoke from a chimney may be blown northward while clouds higher in the sky are blown eastward.

Winds high above the earth's surface are measured by sending up helium-filled balloons. A balloon moves with the same speed and in the same direction as the wind. The balloon's motion is measured by sight or by radar. The balloon's altitude is sometimes determined by noting the atmospheric pressure, as measured by an attached barometer. Cloud motions determined from satellites are also used to estimate winds, especially over the ocean, where few balloons are launched.

The Beaufort wind scale is a series of numbers, ranging from 0 to 17, that are used to indicate wind speeds. The scale was devised in 1805 by British Rear Admiral Sir Francis Beaufort. Beaufort defined the numbers in terms of the effect of various winds on sailing vessels. For example, in a standard version of the scale published in 1874, the number 2 indicated a wind defined as "That in which a well-conditioned man-of-war, with all sail set, and clean full, would go in smooth water from 1 to 2 knots." Wind indicated by the number 12 was "That which no canvas could withstand."

Today, the Beaufort scale is defined in terms of wind speeds measured 10 meters (about 33 feet) above the ground. The scale is sometimes used to estimate wind speeds. Margaret A. LeMone

Related articles in *World Book* include:

Air	Doldrums	Hurricane	Storm
Anemometer	Dune	Jet stream	Tornado
Calms, Regions of	Dust devil	Monsoon	Trade wind
Chinook	Erosion	Norther	Waterspout
Climate	Foehn	Prevailing westerly	Weather
Cloud	Harmattan	Sirocco	Weather vane
Cyclone	Horse latitudes	Squall	Wind chill

Wind Cave National Park is a park in the rolling hills of southwestern South Dakota which surrounds one of the most unusual caves in the United States. Strong currents of wind that blow alternately in and out of the mouth of the cave suggested its name. In the

Beaufort wind scale

Beaufort number	Name	Miles per hour	Kilometers per hour	Effect on land
0	Calm	less than 1	less than 1	Calm; smoke rises vertically.
1	Light air	1-3	1-5	Weather vanes inactive; smoke drifts with air.
2	Light breeze	4-7	6-11	Weather vanes active; wind felt on face; leaves rustle.
3	Gentle breeze	8-12	12-19	Leaves and small twigs move; light flags extend.
4	Moderate breeze	13-18	20-28	Small branches sway; dust and loose paper blow about.
5	Fresh breeze	19-24	29-38	Small trees sway; waves break on inland waters.
6	Strong breeze	25-31	39-49	Large branches sway; umbrellas difficult to use.
7	Moderate gale	32-38	50-61	Whole trees sway; difficult to walk against wind.
8	Fresh gale	39-46	62-74	Twigs broken off trees; walking against wind very difficult.
9	Strong gale	47-54	75-88	Slight damage to buildings; shingles blown off roof.
10	Whole gale	55-63	89-102	Trees uprooted; considerable damage to buildings.
11	Storm	64-73	103-117	Widespread damage; very rare occurrence.
12-17	Hurricane	74 and above	more than 117	Violent destruction.

cave, the wind is quiet, and the temperature remains a cool 53° F. (12° C). The cave was formed as water slowly dissolved away layers of limestone.

Wind Cave has a series of strange boxwork and frostwork formations which are not found elsewhere in the United States. The boxwork formations are calcite crystal structures, which vary from bright yellow through pink and rich browns to deep blue. The frostwork is made up of many tiny white crystals along the ceilings and walls. Electric lights in the cave make the boxwork shine and the frostwork gleam.

Tom Bingham, a Black Hills pioneer, is credited with discovering the cave in 1881. While deer hunting, he heard a strange whistling sound coming from a clump of brush. He discovered an opening in the rock, about 10 inches (25 centimeters) in diameter, from which a strong draft came. This opening is a few steps from the present entrance to the cave, which was built later.

The land around Wind Cave was made a national park in 1903. The park is located about 10 miles (16 kilometers) north of Hot Springs, S. Dak. For the area of the park, see **National Park System** (table: National parks). The surface area is a wildlife preserve for buffalo, deer, prairie dogs, pronghorn, and other animals.

Critically reviewed by the National Park Service

Wind chill is an estimate of the relationship between wind speed and temperature, with respect to the physical effects of the wind on living things. Wind blowing toward a person's body makes the person feel as though the temperature is lower. The faster the wind blows, the faster the body loses heat. Therefore, the feeling of cold increases as the speed of the wind increases. For example, when the temperature is 10° F. and the wind is blowing at 10 mph, the wind chill temperature is equal to −9° F. This means that with a 10 mph wind at 10° F.

Equivalent wind chill temperatures

The chart below illustrates the danger of frostbite at various air temperatures and wind speeds. The pale blue range indicates little danger. In the middle blue range, danger increases, and in the dark blue range, people face a high danger of frostbite.

Air temperature (°F.)	Wind speed in miles per hour								
	0	5	10	15	20	25	30	35	40
	Equivalent wind chill temperatures								
35	35	32	22	16	12	8	6	4	3
30	30	27	16	9	4	1	-2	-4	-5
25	25	22	10	2	-3	-7	-10	-12	-13
20	20	16	3	-5	-10	-15	-18	-20	-21
15	15	11	-3	-11	-17	-22	-25	-27	-29
10	10	6	-9	-18	-24	-29	-33	-35	-37
5	5	0	-15	-25	-31	-36	-41	-43	-45
0	0	-5	-22	-31	-39	-44	-49	-52	-53
-5	-5	-10	-27	-38	-46	-51	-56	-58	-60
-10	-10	-15	-34	-45	-53	-59	-64	-67	-69
-15	-15	-21	-40	-51	-60	-66	-71	-74	-76
-20	-20	-26	-46	-58	-67	-74	-79	-82	-84
-25	-25	-31	-52	-65	-74	-81	-86	-89	-92

people lose as much heat and feel as cold as they do when the temperature is −9° F. and the wind is calm.

Wind chill is not an exact measurement of cold because temperature and wind are not the only conditions that make people feel cold. Someone who is thin or whose clothes are damp will lose more heat and feel colder than another person. But wind chill temperatures can give a better idea of how cold it feels than a thermometer reading alone. Wind chill measurements were developed from experiments performed in Antarctica in 1939. The chart in this article is part of a table published by the U.S. National Weather Service. That agency reports wind speeds in miles per hour and temperatures in degrees Fahrenheit.   William C. Mahaney

Wind erosion. See **Dust storm; Erosion.**

Wind instrument. See **Music** (Musical instruments).

Wind tunnel is a ground-based testing facility used to study the effects of wind, or airflow, on aircraft and other vehicles and structures. Wind tunnels are built in many shapes and for different purposes. Some of them are very large and can test full-sized experimental aircraft. But most wind tunnels test scaled-down models.

Most wind tunnels have a long segment called the *test section* through which a stream of air is blown at an object at a uniform speed. Air pressure and temperature can be controlled as well. The air is generally blown by electric fans, but other devices, such as pressurized tanks, may be used. A large nozzle in front of the test section accelerates the air to the desired speed. After the wind passes through the test section, a duct called a *diffuser* slows down the airflow. The vehicle or structure being tested is secured by supports that extend from the ground or from behind the object. The supports are fastened to measuring devices outside the test section that record the force of the airflow on the vehicle or structure. Instruments also can measure surface pressure at many places on the object.

Wind tunnels in which the air speed is close to the speed of sound—that is, about 760 miles (1,225 kilometers) per hour—are called *transonic* tunnels. In *subsonic* tunnels, the air travels slower than the speed of sound. Wind tunnels in which air travels faster than the speed of sound are *supersonic* tunnels. In *hypersonic* tunnels, air speeds are more than five times as fast as the speed of sound.

Highly compressed air or other gases may be blown through wind tunnels to simulate various flight conditions. In some wind tunnels, very high or low temperatures can be achieved, enabling experts to study such subjects as aircraft icing and automobile performance in arctic or tropical climates.   Allen Plotkin

See also **Aerodynamics; Airplane** (Design and testing); **Wright brothers.**

Wind turbine. See **Windmill.**

Wind vane. See **Weather vane.**

Windermere, *WIHN duhr MEER,* is the largest lake in England. This beautiful body of water lies in the county of Cumbria, in northwestern England. It forms part of the famous English Lake District (see **Great Britain** [political map]). The scenery surrounding Windermere inspired English poets William Wordsworth, Robert Southey, and Samuel Coleridge. Wooded hills rise as much as 1,000 feet (300 meters) high around the lake. The small islands in the center of the lake form a picturesque group. Windermere covers 5.69 square miles (14.7 square kilometers), and is from 30 to 200 feet (9 to 61 meters) deep, or deeper. Its greatest width is 1 mile (1.6 kilometers), and it is about 10½ miles (16.9 kilometers) long. The River Leven flows from Windermere into Morecambe Bay.   John W. Webb

Windflower. See Anemone.

Windhoek, *VIHNT hook* (pop. 104,100), is the capital and largest city of Namibia. It lies on a dry plateau near the center of the country. For location, see **Namibia** (map). Windhoek serves as the commercial and administrative center of Namibia. The white government of neighboring South Africa rules Namibia. Although most of Windhoek's people are blacks, its whites dominate the city economically and politically. Windhoek has white suburbs and one major black living area. A small technical college is in the city.

German soldiers established Windhoek in the late 1880's, when Germany occupied the surrounding area. South Africa conquered Namibia during World War I (1914-1918), and has continued to control it despite international protests.   Robert I. Rotberg

Windhover. See Kestrel.

Windlass, *WIND lus,* is a simple machine used to lift weights and pull loads. It was once commonly used to hoist water from wells. The windlass is a form of the wheel and axle which raises a heavy load by the application of a small amount of force. The simple windlass consists of a cylinder which can be turned by a crank. A rope or chain is wound around this cylinder. A bucket fastened to the end of the rope or chain was lowered into a well and raised again by turning the crank. Modern forms of the windlass include drums and cables of cranes and elevators. Most modern forms are turned by machines rather than by hand.   Allen S. Hall, Jr.

See also **Wheel and axle.**

Windmill is a machine that is operated by wind power. Windmills are used chiefly to provide power to pump water or generate electricity. Modern windmills used to produce electricity are often called *wind turbines.*

Most windmills have a wheel of blades or sails that is turned by the wind. In most cases, the wheel is set on a horizontal shaft. The shaft is mounted on a tower, mast, or other tall structure. The shaft is turned by the movement of the wheel, and it transmits power, through a series of gears, to a vertical shaft. The vertical shaft then carries power to a water pump, electric generator, or other device.

Windmills probably originated in the A.D. 600's in Iran. These windmills had sails that revolved around a vertical axis. They were used chiefly to grind grain.

By the 1100's, windmills had spread to Europe. About this time, inventors discovered that windmills produced more power if the sails or blades turned on a horizontal shaft. This discovery eventually led to the development of *Dutch windmills.* These windmills were widely used in the Netherlands to drain water from the land. They had four long arms with cloth sails or wooden slats or shutters mounted on them.

During the 1800's and early 1900's, many *American windmills* were built throughout the United States to pump water and generate electricity. The wheel of these windmills had numerous curved blades of wood or steel, and was mounted on a horizontal shaft. A vane on the end of the shaft opposite the wheel moved the wheel to face the wind. During the 1930's, the U.S. government started building a large number of central generating plants to bring electricity to rural areas. Thus, the use of windmills to produce electricity declined.

During the 1970's, shortages of oil for generating electricity led to renewed interest and research in wind power. The U.S. government has sponsored the building and testing of a number of wind turbines. One type has two long propellerlike blades, and can generate more than 2 megawatts of electricity in a moderate wind. Researchers also have developed the *Darrieus wind turbine.* This device, which resembles an eggbeater, has two or three long curved blades attached to a vertical shaft.   David Gordon Wilson

See also **Turbine** (Wind turbines; History).

© Adam Woolfitt, Woodfin Camp, Inc.   © Tony Freeman

Windmills are machines operated by wind power. The windmill at the left provides power to pump water for cattle. Windmills called *wind turbines, right,* drive generators to make electricity.

Additional resources

Baker, T. Lindsay. *A Field Guide to American Windmills.* Univ. of Oklahoma Press, 1985.

Cross, Mike. *Wind Power.* Gloucester Press, 1985. For younger readers.

Johnson, Gary L. *Wind Energy Systems.* Prentice-Hall, 1985.

McDonald, Lucile S. *Windmills: An Old-New Energy Source.* Elsevier, 1981. For younger readers.

Window is an opening in a wall or door to admit light and air into a closed space. The term may also refer to the glass placed over such an opening. One or more flat sheets of glass called *panes* cover most windows. Bars known as *mullions* hold the panes in place. The panes and mullions fit into a frame called a *sash.*

Some windows are designed to be permanently closed. There are two basic types of movable windows—*hinged* or *casement windows* and *double-hung windows.* Some hinged or casement windows have two sashes, one hinged to each side of the window. The sashes open inward or outward like a door. This was the first type of movable window. A double-hung window consists of two sashes hung one above the other. The lower sash slides upward on a track to let in air. The double-hung window was invented in the Netherlands about 1680 and rapidly became very popular.

Most windows are placed flat in a wall surface, but there are also other designs. *Dormer windows* are cut through the roof of a building. *Bay windows, bow windows,* and *oriel windows* project out from a wall.

Until the 1800's, only small panes of glass could be manufactured. The invention of improved machinery in the 1850's permitted the production of large panes. This development had a major impact on the appearance and design of buildings. During the early and middle 1900's, huge panes of glass, often mirrored or tinted, became popular for large buildings. They are too large and heavy to be opened. But advancements in heating and air-conditioning have made such windows practical.

In early times, people who lived in warm climates left windows uncovered. In cold climates, people put animal skins over windows for protection from the weather. People in the Far East used paper to cover windows.

During the Middle Ages, craftworkers invented stained glass for use in church windows. A stained-glass window consists of pieces of colored glass arranged to form figures and decorative patterns. Metal bands hold the pieces in place. Stained-glass windows made in tall, thin, pointed shapes are called *lancet* windows. Stained-glass windows made in a circular shape are called *rose windows.*   William J. Hennessey

See also **Glass** (Kinds of glass; Recipes for making glass); **Stained glass; Tracery.**

Windpipe. See Trachea.

Windsor, *WIHN zuhr,* is the name of the present royal family of Great Britain. In 1960, Queen Elizabeth II announced that future generations, except for princes and princesses, will bear the surname *Mountbatten-Windsor* in honor of her husband Philip Mountbatten. The name *Windsor,* adopted in 1917, was taken from Windsor Castle, a royal residence. The new name was chosen to replace *Saxe-Coburg-Gotha,* which was abandoned during World War I (1914-1918) because of its German origin.

The first British king of the line preceding the Wind-

sors was George I of Hanover. The family name of Hanover originated from the Electorate of Hanover, in Germany, which the British kings also ruled. The last Hanoverian king was William IV, Victoria's uncle. The laws of Hanover did not permit a woman ruler, and when Victoria became Queen of Great Britain, the Electorate of Hanover passed from the British royal family to Ernest Augustus, brother of William IV.

Saxe-Coburg was a duchy in Saxony held by the Wettin family. One of the daughters of Duke Francis, ruler of the duchy, married the Duke of Kent, son of George III of England. She was Victoria's mother.

In 1826 the Saxon lands were redivided. Ernest, son of Duke Francis, exchanged Saalfeld for Gotha and founded the house of Saxe-Coburg-Gotha. Ernest had two sons, Ernest II and Albert, who were first cousins of Victoria. Albert married Victoria in 1840. Victoria's children took their father's name, and Edward VII, her son, was the first English king to bear the name of Saxe-Coburg-Gotha. His son George V was the first to use the name of Windsor.   Charles Loch Mowat

See also **Edward** (VII; VIII); **Elizabeth II; George,** of England; **Victoria; Windsor Castle.**

Windsor, *WIHN zuhr,* Ont. (pop. 193,111; met. area pop. 253,988), is the southernmost city of Canada. It is the chief port of entry between Canada and the United States. Windsor lies on the southwest bank of the Detroit River, opposite Detroit (see **Ontario** [political map]). The location of the city on one of the world's busiest inland waterways makes Windsor a major transportation center. Windsor leads all other Canadian cities in the production of automobiles and automotive products.

About 1750, French explorers established the first permanent white settlement in what is now the Windsor area. English settlers came to the area during the 1790's. In 1836, they named the area for Windsor, England.

Description. Windsor covers 47 square miles (122 square kilometers). The city is the home of the St. Clair College of Applied Arts and Technology and the University of Windsor. Windsor's attractions include the Art Gallery of Windsor, the Hiram Walker Historical Museum, Cleary Auditorium, and Memorial Convention Hall. The Windsor Light Opera Association and the Windsor Symphony perform in the Cleary Auditorium. Windsor has 47 acres (19 hectares) of riverfront parks.

Economy. Windsor's leading industry is the manufacture of transportation equipment, chiefly automobiles and automotive parts. This industry employs more than 25 per cent of the city's workers. Windsor produces about 25 per cent of Canada's automotive products and is sometimes called the *City That Put Canada on Wheels.* Many of Windsor's people work in Detroit offices and hospitals. They commute via the bridge and a tunnel that connect the two cities. Other leading Windsor industries include chemicals, food and beverages, and metal products. The city's docks can handle oceangoing ships.

Government and history. Windsor has a council-manager government. The city council consists of a mayor and 10 aldermen, all of whom are elected to three-year terms. The council appoints a city manager.

Huron and Iroquois Indians lived in what is now the Windsor area before French explorers claimed it in the mid-1600's. The French government gave land to people who established a village there in the mid-1700's. English settlers arrived in the 1790's. A log ferryboat connected the village with Detroit, and in 1812 the people named their community The Ferry. They later changed its name to Richmond. In 1836, a dispute arose over whether to call it The Ferry, Richmond, or South Detroit. The people compromised by renaming it Windsor, the name of a borough near Richmond, England.

Windsor received a city charter in 1892. The Ford Motor Company produced the first Canadian-made Ford there in 1904. Two other U.S. automakers, the Chrysler and General Motors corporations, established plants in the city in 1920. Windsor annexed the towns of East Windsor, Sandwich, and Walkerville in 1935. The city's population reached 100,000 that year. During the mid-1960's, Windsor annexed all or part of four other communities—Ojibway, Riverside, Sandwich East, and Sandwich West.

Windsor's Main Library opened in 1973. A number of expansion projects were also completed during the 1970's. These projects involved such institutions as Metropolitan General Hospital, the St. Clair College of Applied Arts and Technology, and the University of Windsor. In 1983, the Ouellette Avenue Mall was completed in Windsor's downtown section.   Carl Morgan

Windsor, Duchess of. See Edward (VIII).
Windsor, Duke of. See Edward (VIII).
Windsor Castle is the chief residence of the rulers of Great Britain. The castle stands in Windsor, which is about 21 miles (34 kilometers) west of London. William the Conqueror chose the site and built a castle there. Edward III tore this castle down and began the present structure. Later kings added to the castle until it now covers about 24 acres (10 hectares). Windsor Castle

stands in the Little Park, which joins the Great Park south of Windsor. Queen Victoria and her husband are buried in the Little Park.

The most important feature of the castle is the round *keep* (tower), which dates from the time of Edward III. The keep is 80 feet (24 meters) high, and can be seen from far away. Four other towers also rise from the castle walls.

The section west of the central tower is called the Lower Ward. It contains Saint George's Chapel, begun by Edward IV and finished by Henry VIII. In the chapel vault lie the bodies of Henry VIII, Charles I, William IV, George V, George VI, and other English rulers. The beautiful Albert Memorial Chapel also stands in the Lower Ward. Henry III began construction of this chapel, Henry VII rebuilt it, and Queen Victoria completed it in memory of her husband. King Edward VII was buried there in 1910. The Upper Ward, to the east of the central tower, contains the royal apartments and great state rooms. These were built chiefly during the 1800's.   G. Holmes Perkins

Windsurfing is a common term for two similar water sports—*sailsurfing* and *sailboarding.* Both sports use a *sailboard,* which is a surfboard with a sail attached to a mast at the board's center. A sailsurfer rides like a surfer. A sailboarder sprints across flat water like a sailor. Therefore, sailsurfing needs waves, and sailboarding needs wind.

Most sailsurfing boards are no more than 7 feet (2.1 meters) long. A sailboard measures 10 to 12 feet (3.0 to 3.7 meters) long. The mast is attached to either kind of board by a universal joint. The universal joint allows the rider to turn the sail in any direction and thus steer the

F. Jalain, Explorer

Windsor Castle is the chief residence of the rulers of Great Britain. It stands in the town of Windsor, near London. The most notable architectural feature of the castle is the round *keep* (tower), which is shown at the far left.

© Darrell Jones, The Stock Market

Windsurfing includes the sport called *sailboarding, above,* in which individuals race wind-driven surfboards across flat water.

board. The sailboard was first patented in 1969.

Robert Sadler Clark

Windward Islands are a group of islands that lie in the southeastern West Indies. They stretch around the eastern end of the Caribbean Sea to South America (see **West Indies** [map]). The islands are so named because they are exposed to northeast trade winds. The Windward group includes Martinique, St. Lucia, Grenada, St. Vincent, and the Grenadine chain. Martinique is a French possession. St. Lucia is an independent nation. Grenada and part of the Grenadines form the independent nation of Grenada. St. Vincent and the rest of the Grenadines make up an independent nation called St. Vincent and the Grenadines.

The Windward Islands cover about 950 square miles (2,460 square kilometers), and have a population of about 715,000. Most of the people are of black African descent. The chief products include arrowroot, bananas, cocoa, cotton, mace, nutmeg, and sugar.

Arawak Indians were the first known inhabitants of the Windward Islands. Europeans settled there in the early 1600's. Between 1763 and 1814, the islands, except for Martinique, became British colonies. Grenada became an independent nation in 1974. St. Lucia and St. Vincent and the Grenadines became independent nations in 1979. Gustavo A. Antonini

See also **Grenada; Martinique; Saint Lucia; Saint Vincent and the Grenadines.**

Wine is an alcoholic beverage most often made from the juice of grapes. Wine also can be made from many other fruits, including apples and pears, and even from such plants as dandelions. Many wines retain the flavor and aroma of the fruit from which they were made. For thousands of years, people have used wine to complement their meals and to celebrate joyful occasions. They have also used wine in cooking and medicine and in religious ceremonies.

Types of wine. Wines can be divided into four categories: (1) table wines, (2) sparkling wines, (3) fortified wines, and (4) flavored wines. Alcohol makes up from 7 to 14 per cent of the volume of most wines. However, fortified wines have a higher alcohol content, ranging from 18 to 24 per cent.

Table wines are the most commonly produced type

of wine. They are most often served with a meal. They may be grouped by color into red, white, and *rosé* (pink) wines. Crushed grapes produce a light green or yellow juice. The juice is tinted by contact with grape skins. In general, red and rosé wines are made from red or purple grapes, and white wines from white grapes. But a type of white wine called *blanc de noir* is made from red grapes. The grape skins have little contact with the juice, giving blanc de noir a paler color than rosé.

Wine drinkers describe a wine that lacks sweetness as *dry.* Most red table wines are dry. But white wines and rosé wines range from dry to sweet. Some white wines can be very sweet.

Sparkling wines, such as the champagne types, contain bubbles of carbon dioxide gas. People enjoy drinking sparkling wines on festive occasions.

Fortified wines have brandy or wine alcohol added to them. They tend to be sweeter than most other wines. For this reason, some people prefer to drink fortified wines with dessert or after a meal, while others choose to drink dry sherry or white port before dinner. The most popular fortified wines are port and sherry.

Flavored wines contain flavoring substances. For example, vermouth is a white wine flavored with herbs. Wine coolers are wines flavored with fruit juices. Most flavored wines are served alone or before a meal.

Where wine comes from. Most of the world's wine comes from grapes belonging to the species *Vitis vinifera,* which originated in the Middle East. Vinifera grapes are also known as European grapes. These grapes thrive in the vineyards of Europe and on the West Coast of the United States. Vinifera grapes produce their best wine when grown in regions that are cool but not cold. In the Eastern United States and in Canada, vinifera grapes have been crossbred with species native to North America, chiefly *Vitis labrusca* and *Vitis riparia.* These hybrid grapes can withstand cold climates better than European grapes can. But in many cases, hybrid grapes keep some of the flavor of the native grapes.

Robert Tixador, Agence Top

Wine is made from the juice of crushed grapes. Many European winemakers use a mechanical press like the one shown above to crush the grapes. The juice runs out the bottom of the press.

Wine Institute

Grape juice becomes wine through the process of fermentation, which takes place in a large vat. Carbon dioxide escapes from the juice, causing a bubbling action, *above.*

David Moore, Colorific

Wine is aged in storage casks after it has fermented. Aging may take months or years, depending on the wine. A worker uses a device called a *wine thief* to take the wine from a cask to test it, *above.*

Grape species are made up of many varieties. In the United States, many wines take the name of the variety of grapes from which they are principally made. Such wines are often called *varietals.* Examples of varietal wines include Cabernet Sauvignon, Chardonnay, and Pinot Noir. According to U.S. law, a varietal made from vinifera grapes must contain at least 75 per cent of the variety after which it is named.

Most European wines are classified by the region they come from, such as Burgundy or Bordeaux in France or the valley of the Rhine River in West Germany. Wines called *generics* sometimes take the name of a region in Europe, even though they may show little resemblance to wines from that region. A generic wine is usually a blend of several varieties of grapes.

Most nations produce some wine. The countries most famous for their wine include France, Italy, the United States, and West Germany. Spain and Portugal also produce well-known wines. Today, many countries in North and South America produce wines that resemble European wines. Wineries throughout the world emphasize varietal wines, and they seek new grape-growing regions that will produce distinctive wines.

Wines from France are famous because of French growing conditions and winemaking methods. The country's chief winemaking regions include Bordeaux, in southwestern France; Burgundy, in east-central France; and Champagne, east of Paris.

In the Bordeaux region, Cabernet Sauvignon and Merlot grapes go into making dry red wines. White Bordeaux wines come from Sémillon and Sauvignon Blanc grapes. Pinot Noir grapes form the basis of the red wines of Burgundy. White Burgundy wines come from Chardonnay grapes. Chardonnay and Pinot Noir grapes also form the basis of champagne, a sparkling wine of the Champagne region.

Wines from Italy. Grapevines grow throughout Italy. The red wines of the Piedmont region in northwestern Italy are known as Barolo and Barbaresco. They come from Nebbiolo grapes. Cortese grapes, also grown in the region, produce a crisp white wine called Gavi. Chianti, probably the most familiar Italian wine, comes mainly from Sangiovese grapes native to the regions of Tuscany and Umbria in central Italy.

Wines from the United States. California produces about 90 per cent of the wine made in the United States. New York, Washington, Oregon, Virginia, and several other states also make wine. California wines are made from the same varieties of vinifera grapes as are European wines. California's chief grape-growing regions include the Napa and Sonoma valleys north of San Francisco Bay; the central coast; and the San Joaquin Valley, in the middle of the state.

Wines from West Germany. West Germany's distinctive white wines are produced mainly from Riesling grapes. Sylvaner grapes are also used to make white wine. Riesling and Sylvaner wines come from all of the country's winemaking regions, particularly those along the Rhine River and two of its tributaries, the Moselle (or Mosel) and Nahe rivers.

Wine styles from other countries include port and sherry. Port is a fortified wine that may be dark red or white. It was first made from grapes grown in the Douro Valley in northern Portugal. Sherry, a fortified white wine, ranges from pale gold to brown and from dry to sweet. The first sherry wines came from grapes grown in Jerez in southwestern Spain.

How wine is made. Winemaking requires a series of steps. Decisions made by the winemaker during each step influence the final "character" of the wine. A winemaker must first decide which grapes to use and when to harvest them. After the grapes are crushed, the juice is converted into wine through a process called *fermentation.* Wine is then aged until it is ready for drinking.

Harvesting the grapes. Grape growers harvest their crop as soon as the grapes have ripened, usually in the fall. Winemakers commonly measure ripeness by the amount of sugar in the grapes. They may also consider

Leading wine-producing countries

Amount of wine produced in a year	
Italy	●●●●●●●●●●●●●●●●●●●●●●
	1,934,000,000 gallons (7,320,000,000 liters)
France	●●●●●●●●●●●●●●●●●●●●●◑
	1,870,000,000 gallons (7,079,000,000 liters)
Spain	●●●●●●●●●●◑
	1,004,000,000 gallons (3,800,000,000 liters)
Soviet Union	●●●●●◑
	528,300,000 gallons (2,000,000,000 liters)
Argentina	●●●●●◑
	501,900,000 gallons (1,900,000,000 liters)
United States	●●●●◑
	447,800,000 gallons (1,695,000,000 liters)
Portugal	●●●
	269,500,000 gallons (1,020,000,000 liters)
Romania	●●◑
	264,200,000 gallons (1,000,000,000 liters)
West Germany	●●◑
	228,500,000 gallons (865,000,000 liters)
Yugoslavia	●◑
	160,600,000 gallons (608,000,000 liters)

Figures are for 1987. Source: *Production Yearbook, 1987,* Food and Agriculture Organization of the United Nations.

the grapes' acid content, flavor, and aroma. Workers pick grapes by hand or with mechanical harvesters that shake the fruit from the vine. The grapes then go to the winery for processing.

The grape harvest is sometimes called the *vintage.* In some years, a favorable climate produces grapes of especially high quality. Those vintage years are considered superior.

Preparing the juice. At the winery, a machine called a *crusher* breaks the grapes and removes them from their stems. The crushed grapes and their juice are called *must.* The length of contact between the juice and the skin affects the color of red wines and the taste of all wines. To make white wine, winemakers separate the skins and pulp from the juice. The juice then enters a tank or barrel for fermentation. In making red wine, the seeds and skins go into the fermentation tank with the juice. Stirring the mixture from time to time ensures that the color is extracted from the skins.

Fermentation is the chemical change in which yeast converts the sugar in grapes into alcohol. Some yeast grows naturally on the skins of grapes. Some European winemakers allow this yeast to conduct the fermentation. In the United States and most other countries, winemakers add selected yeasts to the must to begin fermentation. During fermentation, the yeast grows and changes sugars called *glucose* and *fructose* into ethanol, a type of alcohol, and carbon dioxide gas. The carbon dioxide is released as bubbles. The yeast also produces various by-products that may add to the wine's flavor and aroma.

Fermentation also releases heat. Most wineries refrigerate the must to keep its temperature constant during fermentation. Winemakers usually ferment juice for white wine at about 59° F. (15° C) and juice for red wine at about 86° F. (30° C). The temperature of the must influences the rate of fermentation, the retaining of grape aromas, and the formation of yeast by-products. It also determines the rate at which the color and flavor of the grape skins transfer into the wine. The fermentation of red wine takes from 4 to 6 days. White-wine fermentations last from 12 to 18 days.

Most red table wines and some white table wines undergo a second fermentation, by bacteria. This fermentation, called the *malolactic fermentation,* lowers a wine's acid content by converting a substance called *malic acid* into *lactic acid.*

Clarifying and aging the wine. A new wine appears cloudy after fermentation. Winemakers *clarify* (clear) the wine by removing particles of yeast and other unwanted substances. Such particles may be filtered out, allowed to settle naturally, or separated from the wine by a machine called a *centrifuge.* Wine may be further clarified, or *fined,* by adding certain solutions that reduce the content of unstable or unpleasant components.

After clarification, wine goes into wooden barrels or stainless steel tanks for aging. Wooden barrels contribute their own flavor to the wine. The size of the barrel, the age of the wood, the storage temperature and humidity, and the length of storage time all influence the extent of the aging process. Many wineries hold wine at a temperature close to freezing for one or more days so that a salt called potassium bitartrate will *precipitate* (separate) out of the wine. This prevents the salt from forming crystals in the wine after bottling.

Although some wines are soon ready for drinking, others must age a few years to soften harsh flavors and allow desirable flavors to develop. Wine is bottled after some aging, and it continues to age slowly in the bottle.

Fortified wines, such as port and sherry, are made by adding brandy to fermenting must. The brandy halts the fermentation by killing the yeast before all the sugar has turned into alcohol. The wine that results generally is sweet. Drier fortified wines are achieved by adding brandy near or at the end of fermentation. Sparkling wines are usually made by a second yeast fermentation of a table wine. This fermentation may take four to eight weeks. The bubbles of carbon dioxide produced by the fermentation are trapped in the wine.

History. The earliest references to wine date back about 5,000 years to civilizations in ancient Egypt and Babylon (now part of Iraq). Egyptian picture writing shows people harvesting and crushing grapes and storing wine in clay vessels. The Bible tells of winemaking in Palestine. The ancient Greeks and Romans dealt extensively with wine in their paintings and writings. The Romans planted grapevines in regions they conquered, including what are now Austria, France, and Germany.

From about A.D. 500 to 1400, the spread of Christianity in Europe encouraged the growing of grapes to make the wines used in religious ceremonies. After the 1500's, European explorers and settlers introduced vinifera grapes to the lands now known as Argentina, Australia, Brazil, Chile, Mexico, New Zealand, South Africa, the Soviet Union, and the United States.   Roger Boulton

See also **Grape; Europe** (picture: Grapes).

Wing. See Airplane (The wing); **Aerodynamics; Bee** (Wings); **Bird** (How birds move); **Helicopter** (Lift); **Insect** (Wings).

Wingate's Raiders were a group of Allied soldiers who fought behind Japanese lines in Burma during World War II. British Brigadier General Orde Charles

Wingate organized the group, known as *Chindits,* from British, Burmese, and Nepalese troops in 1942. In 1943, the group secretly entered Japanese-held territory, where it operated against enemy communications. The force suffered heavy losses, and its first campaign had only limited success. Wingate was promoted to major general, and he led a second similar campaign early in 1944.

Wingate died in an airplane crash in March 1944, but the Raiders continued to fight in Burma. Members of the group cut railroad lines, blew up bridges and highways, and destroyed Japanese military installations. They also supported the Allied advance into Burma led by U.S. General Joseph W. Stilwell.　　James L. Stokesbury

See also **Commando.**

Winged bull is a fabulous beast that originated in Assyria. It had the head of a man and the winged body of a bull. The beast appeared in ancient paintings and in the minor arts, but the most important examples are statues of gigantic size. The earliest ones date from about 1000 B.C. They were placed in pairs in the entrances of palaces to frighten evil spirits and enemies of the state. The bulls were often represented with five legs so that when viewed from the side they appear to be walking, while from the front they are standing still.　　Warren G. Moon

Winged lion is an imaginary creature in ancient cultures, especially in Babylonia and Assyria. The creature had the head of a man, the wings of an eagle, and the body of a lion. Most winged lions were sculptures that stood in pairs, often of huge size, in the gateways or entrances to a city or to the king's palace. The figures were intended to terrify enemies and evil spirits. The winged lion is also found in ancient paintings and in the minor arts. See also **Assyria** (picture: A winged lion).

Warren G. Moon

Winged Victory is a beautiful ancient Greek statue that was discovered by a French archaeologist in 1863. The statue was broken, and 118 pieces were found scattered on a hillside on the Greek island of Samothraki (Samothrace). The statue portrays Nike, the Greek goddess of victory. Her drapery is blown against her body by the wind as she brings the message of victory, conquest, and success from the gods. She has wings to represent her great speed and her gift of flight. The rhythms of the composition are turbulent, perhaps symbolizing the difficult road to victory.

The sculptor of the Winged Victory is unknown, but scholars have dated the statue to about 180 B.C. It now stands in the Louvre in Paris. For a picture of the Winged Victory, see **Europe.**　　Warren G. Moon

Winkelried, *VIHNG kuhl REET,* **Arnold von,** *AHR nawlt fuhn,* is the legendary national hero of Switzerland. He was supposed to have brought victory to the Swiss in the battle of Sempach against the Austrians in 1386. According to legend, the Swiss were beginning to retreat when Winkelried, a Swiss soldier, dashed boldly into the Austrian ranks and seized with his bare hands as many enemy spears as he could reach. As he fell, pierced by the spears, he created a gap in the Austrian ranks. The Swiss rushed through the opening, and won the battle in hand-to-hand fighting.　　Arthur M. Selvi

Winkle, Rip Van. See Rip Van Winkle.

Winnebago, Lake. See Lake Winnebago.

Winnebago Indians, *WIHN uh BAY goh,* were an eastern woodland tribe. The language of the Winnebago resembled that of the Sioux in many ways (see **Sioux Indians**). Tribal traditions say that at one time the Winnebago lived near the Missouri River, but that they were forced east and settled near Green Bay in Wisconsin.

The Winnebago hunted buffalo, caught fish, and raised corn and squash. They built long lodges with arched roofs and arbors over the entrances. Chiefs, who were sometimes women, inherited their rank. Important tribal ceremonies included the Medicine Dance, organized around a secret society, and the Winter Feast, a war ceremony.

The Winnebago were nearly destroyed by the Illinois sometime before 1670. But small groups continued to live along Lake Winnebago and elsewhere in southern Wisconsin and northern Illinois. They were friendly to most nearby tribes, and to the French. During the Revolutionary War and the War of 1812, the Winnebago sided with Great Britain. Some Winnebago lived in a village, now called Prophetstown, on the Rock River in Illinois. The town was named after their leader, Wabokieshiek (White Cloud), who was called the Prophet. The Winnebago ceded their lands in Wisconsin and Illinois to the federal government in the 1830's. They were moved to Minnesota, then to South Dakota, and finally to Nebraska. Some of the Winnebago refused to leave Wisconsin and Minnesota, and they still live there.

Robert E. Powless

Winnemucca, *WIHN uh MUHK uh,* **Sarah** (1844?-1891), was an American Indian who won fame for her criticism of the government's mistreatment of her people. Winnemucca, a member of the Paiute tribe, began to speak out against the government as early as 1870. She later established two schools for Indian children.

Winnemucca, called *Thoc-me-tony* (Shell Flower) by the Paiutes, was born near Humboldt Sink in what is now Nevada. During the late 1860's and the 1870's, she served as an interpreter, guide, and scout for various government officials. In the 1870's, she protested such abuses of the Paiutes as seizure of their lands and an Army attack on a Paiute settlement.

In 1880, Winnemucca met on her people's behalf with President Rutherford B. Hayes. The next year, she lectured in Boston and other Eastern cities on the government's mistreatment of the Paiutes. She also wrote a book called *Life Among the Paiutes: Their Claims and Wrongs* (1883). In 1881, Winnemucca opened a school for Indian children at Vancouver Barracks, an Army post in the Washington Territory (now Washington). She later founded a school for Paiute children near Lovelock, Nev.

W. Roger Buffalohead

Winnetka Plan, *wuh NEHT kuh,* is a teaching plan designed to provide individualized instruction. It was developed in the public elementary and junior high schools of Winnetka, Ill., after World War I. It influenced widely the growth of the progressive education movement. According to the plan, teachers deal with each pupil individually so that pupils can develop their own particular abilities at their own rate of speed. Pupils work alone in their regular studies, but take part in many group activities in which their achievements are not measured.　　Douglas Sloan

Winnie-the-Pooh. See Milne, A. A.

The Winnipeg Art Gallery, *left,* helps make the city one of the leading cultural centers of Canada. Winnipeg is the capital of Manitoba and ranks as Canada's fourth largest city, behind Montreal, Toronto, and Calgary.

The Winnipeg Art Gallery (Ernest Mayer)

Winnipeg, *WIHN uh PEHG,* is the capital of Manitoba, and Canada's fourth largest city. Only Montreal, Toronto, and Calgary have more people. Winnipeg is Canada's main grain market and one of the nation's leading centers of culture, finance, industry, and trade. More than half of Manitoba's people live in the city.

Winnipeg lies about 60 miles (97 kilometers) north of the Canadian-United States border and almost midway between the Atlantic and Pacific oceans. The city's central location makes it the chief transportation center linking eastern and western Canada. Winnipeg is also the principal distribution point for goods traveling west from eastern Canada. The city has the nickname *Gateway to the West.* It was named after Lake Winnipeg, about 40 miles (64 kilometers) to the north. The word *Winnipeg* comes from the Cree Indian words *win nipee,* meaning *muddy water.*

The city covers 221 square miles (572 square kilometers). It lies at the junction of the Red and Assiniboine rivers. Main Street, once an important settlers' trail, is Winnipeg's chief north-south street. Portage Avenue, the beginning of the old overland route to Edmonton, Alta., is the main east-west street. The 34-story Richardson Building, Winnipeg's tallest structure, rises at Main and Portage. The city's chief public buildings are located in the nearby Civic Centre. The Manitoba Legislative Building stands on the Mall in a park on the north bank of the Assiniboine River.

Winnipeg's metropolitan area covers 892 square miles (2,310 square kilometers). The Winnipeg metropolitan area ranks as Canada's seventh largest metropolitan area in population.

The people. More than 80 per cent of Winnipeg's people were born in Canada, and about half have British ancestors. The next largest ethnic groups in the city are the French, Germans, and Ukrainians.

A large number of Indians and *métis* (people of mixed Indian and white ancestry) live in Winnipeg. Most of the people in these groups moved to the city from rural areas. Many have little or no education or employment skill and find it hard to get jobs. They live in the city's poorest sections. The Indian and Métis Friendship Centre provides a place for advice, companionship, and recreation. But the low standard of living of many Indians and métis remains a major problem in Winnipeg.

Economy. The Winnipeg metropolitan area ranks as one of Canada's leading manufacturing centers. About a fifth of the workers in the metropolitan area are employed in manufacturing. More than 1,000 factories in the metropolitan area produce goods worth more than $1 billion yearly. The area's chief products include buses, cement, clothing, farm machinery, furniture, metal products, processed foods, and rockets and airplane parts.

Winnipeg lies in a rich wheat-growing region, and

Facts in brief

Population: 594,551. *Metropolitan area population*—625,304.
Area: 221 sq. mi. (572 km²). *Metropolitan area*—892 sq. mi. (2,310 km²).
Altitude: 760 ft. (232 m) above sea level.
Climate: *Average temperature*—January, 0° F. (−18° C); July, 68° F. (20° C). *Average annual precipitation* (rainfall, melted snow, and other forms of moisture)—23inches (58 centimeters). For the monthly weather in Winnipeg, see **Manitoba** (Climate).
Government: Mayor-council. *Terms*—3 years for the mayor and 29 councillors.
Founded: 1870. Incorporated as a city in 1873.

the Winnipeg Commodity Exchange is Canada's major grain market. The Canadian Wheat Board and many grain companies have their main offices in Winnipeg. The Winnipeg Stock Exchange helps make the city a major financial center.

The city is also an important transportation center. Canada's two transcontinental railroads have their western headquarters in Winnipeg, and a U.S. railroad serves the city. The Trans-Canada Highway and Manitoba's main highways pass through Winnipeg. Winnipeg International Airport is one of Canada's busiest airports.

Winnipeg is Canada's largest and most important trading point between Toronto and Vancouver, B.C. But the rapid development of such cities as Calgary and Edmonton in Alberta lessened Winnipeg's importance as a distribution point. The city met this problem by seeking more industry. Winnipeg's older industries worked to modernize their plants and to expand their markets.

Education. Winnipeg's public school system has about 180 elementary schools and 55 high schools, with a total enrollment of approximately 115,000. The city also has about 30 parochial and private schools. Property taxes provide the chief source of revenue for the public schools. But rapidly rising school costs have become a heavy burden for many property owners. To ease this problem, the provincial government has taken over a larger share of the school expenses.

The University of Manitoba, which was founded in Winnipeg in 1877, has more than 20,000 students. The University of Winnipeg is located in the downtown area.

Cultural life. Winnipeg is one of the chief cultural centers of Canada. The world-famous Royal Winnipeg Ballet and the Winnipeg Symphony Orchestra perform in Concert Hall. The hall is part of the Manitoba Centennial Centre, which also includes the Manitoba Theatre Centre, the Museum of Man and Nature, and a planetar-

ium. The Winnipeg Art Gallery attracts many visitors.

City of Winnipeg Libraries, the public library system, operates 22 branches. The Winnipeg Centennial Library is the main branch. The city has two daily newspapers, the *Winnipeg Free Press* and the *Winnipeg Sun.* Four television stations and 11 radio stations serve Winnipeg, including one French-language television station and one multi-language radio station.

Winnipeg has about 300 parks, squares, and athletic fields. Assiniboine Park, covering 375 acres (152 hectares), is the largest park. It includes beautiful gardens and a zoo with more than 750 animals and birds. The Winnipeg Blue Bombers of the Canadian Football League play their home games in Winnipeg Stadium. The Winnipeg Jets of the National Hockey League compete in the Winnipeg Arena.

Ross House, western Canada's first post office, is in downtown Winnipeg. It opened in 1855. Lower Fort Garry, north of Winnipeg, is the only stone fur-trading post still standing in North America.

Government. Winnipeg has a mayor-council government. The people in each of Winnipeg's 29 *wards* (voting areas) elect one councillor to the city council. The councillors serve three-year terms. They also elect a mayor to a three-year term as administrative head of the government. A five-member board of commissioners, including a chief commissioner, supervises various departments of the government. Property taxes provide about two-thirds of Winnipeg's revenue.

History. The Assiniboine and Cree Indians lived in what is now the Winnipeg area before the first whites arrived. In 1738, Sieur de la Vérendrye, a French-Canadian fur trader, became the first white person to reach what is now Winnipeg. He built Fort Rouge at the junction of the Red and Assiniboine rivers and traded for furs with the Indians. See **La Vérendrye, Sieur de.**

City of Winnipeg

MANITOBA

Winnipeg.

Winnipeg, a major transportation center, lies in southern Manitoba at the junction of the Red and Assiniboine rivers. The map shows the city and major points of interest.

City boundary
Built-up area
Nonbuilt-up area
Main road
Other road
Rail line
• Point of interest

WORLD BOOK map

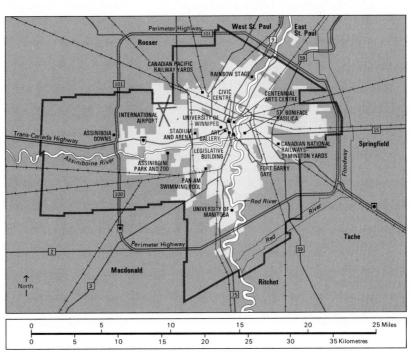

During the early 1800's, the Winnipeg area became the center of fur-trade rivalry between the North West Company and the Hudson's Bay Company. In 1812, Scottish and Irish farmers established the area's first permanent settlement along the Red River (see **Manitoba** [The Red River Colony]). The Hudson's Bay Company absorbed its chief rival in 1821. That year, the company enlarged Fort Gibraltar, a post at the site of present-day Winnipeg, and renamed it Fort Garry. It rebuilt the fort in 1835 and called it Upper Fort Garry. A trading post north of Winnipeg was known as Lower Fort Garry. Upper Fort Garry became the center of the Red River settlement.

In 1870, Manitoba entered the Dominion of Canada. The Red River settlement was renamed Winnipeg that same year, and it became the capital of the new province. It was incorporated as a city in 1873. By then, it had about 1,900 people. In 1878, Manitoba's first railroad linked Winnipeg and St. Paul, Minn. The Canadian Pacific Railway (now CP Rail) connected Winnipeg with eastern Canada in 1881. The government's offer of free land in western Canada helped Winnipeg's population reach 16,694 by 1884.

During the early 1900's, large numbers of Europeans settled in Winnipeg. Industry grew rapidly in the city during this period, and Winnipeg became the manufacturing center of western Canada. By 1914, the city's population had climbed to 203,000. The opening of the Panama Canal in 1914 slowed Winnipeg's expansion. Companies in eastern Canada could now send their products to the West more cheaply by ship through the canal than by railroad. Winnipeg's economy continued to suffer during the Great Depression of the 1930's.

During World War II (1939-1945), sharp increases in the demand for livestock, lumber, metals, and wheat brought prosperity back to Winnipeg. Between 1946 and 1950, about 200 industries began in Winnipeg. The city's population fell during the 1960's, partly because of a trend toward suburban living. In 1960, Winnipeg was Canada's fourth largest city. By 1967, it ranked eighth.

In 1960, the Manitoba legislature established the Metropolitan Corporation of Greater Winnipeg to administer a number of services for Winnipeg and 11 of its suburbs. These services included planning and zoning, public transportation, and water supply. Each municipality in the corporation also had its own governing council to administer local affairs.

During the 1960's, officials of the metropolitan agency and those of the local governing councils often challenged each other's jurisdiction over various matters. Partly because of these disputes, the Manitoba legislature in 1971 combined Winnipeg and the suburbs into one municipality, the unified city of Winnipeg. The merger took effect on Jan. 1, 1972. As a result of the merger, Winnipeg became Canada's third largest city. By 1981, it had fallen to fourth.

A downtown building boom that began in the late 1960's continued into the 1970's. Tall apartment and office buildings and hotels replaced many old structures. New construction included the Winnipeg Convention Centre, which opened in 1975, and a system of enclosed walkways above the streets.

In 1981, the city, provincial, and federal governments launched the Core Area Initiative. Through this program, the governments provided funds to improve education, social services, and economic development in the inner city. As part of this program, workers renovated historic office and warehouse buildings in the downtown area known as the Exchange district. Construction of a shopping and residential development on Portage Avenue began in 1986. The project was completed in 1987.   John Dafoe

Winnipeg, Lake. See Lake Winnipeg.

Winnipeg River is part of the Saskatchewan-Nelson river system that empties into Hudson Bay. The Winnipeg River is 140 miles (225 kilometers) long. It rises in western Ontario and flows west in a winding course, draining the Lake of the Woods. It empties into Lake Winnipeg, near the city of Winnipeg. Hydroelectric generating stations on the river supply some of Winnipeg's power needs. In pioneer days, the Winnipeg River was on the fur-trade route to the Northwest. See **Manitoba** (physical map).   John S. Brierley

Winslow, Edward (1595-1655), was a founder of Plymouth Colony. He joined the Pilgrims in Leiden, The Netherlands, and came to Plymouth on the *Mayflower*. Winslow and Susanna White became the first couple to marry in the new colony. Winslow arranged the first treaty with the Indian chief Massasoit, and explored and traded with the Indians. Winslow served as an assistant for 20 years and governor of the colony for three. Winslow left Plymouth in 1646 and served in Oliver Cromwell's government in England. He was born in Droitwich, England.   Bradford Smith

Winston-Salem, N.C. (pop. 131,885), has one of the largest tobacco-manufacturing plants in the world and one of the largest leaf-tobacco markets. The city lies in northwestern North Carolina, about 45 miles (72 kilometers) from the Blue Ridge Mountains (see **North Carolina** [political map]). With Greensboro and High Point, the city forms a metropolitan area with 851,851 people. Winston-Salem plants produce men's and boys' knitwear, hosiery, electronic equipment, and tobacco products. Salem College, Wake Forest University, and several other schools are in the city.

A group of Moravians founded Salem in 1766. Winston was founded in 1849. Winston and Salem consolidated in 1913. The city has a council-manager form of government.   Stephen S. Birdsall

Winter is the coldest season of the year. The Northern Hemisphere, the northern half of the earth, has winter weather during December, January, February, and early March. In the Southern Hemisphere, winter weather begins in late June and lasts until early September. For dates of the first day of winter and information about the position of the earth and sun during winter, see **Season.**

During winter, the polar region is especially cold because the sun does not rise there for weeks or months at a time. Cold, dry air moves south from this region, bringing cold weather. Storms move from west to east along the southern edge of the cold air. In the United States, winter storms produce large snowfalls in some areas. The most snow falls in the western mountains and in much of the northern region east of the Rocky Mountains. Many winter storms bring rain to warmer southern areas. The lowest winter temperatures usually occur in the middle of all continents.   John E. Kutzbach

See also **December; January; February; March.**

Winter sports. See Biathlon; Bobsledding; Curling; Hockey; Ice skating; Iceboating; Skiing; Tobogganing.
Winterberry is a shrub related to the holly. Many winterberries grow on swampy land in the Eastern United States. The shrub is sometimes called *black alder,* or *deciduous holly.* It grows 6 to 12 feet (2 to 4 meters) tall. Its bright red berries appear in November.

Scientific classification. Winterberry belongs to the holly family, Aquifoliaceae. It is *Ilex verticillata.*   J. J. Levison

Wintergreen is a hardy woodland plant that bears white flowers. It grows in almost all parts of the Northern Hemisphere and received its name because its leaves remain green all winter. The name also applies to other plants of this type. The wintergreen is a low-growing shrub with creeping, or subterranean, stems. Its

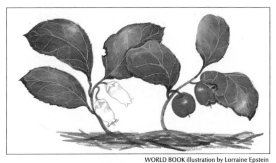

WORLD BOOK illustration by Lorraine Epstein
The wintergreen has white blossoms and red berries.

glossy oval leaves cluster at the top of short, erect reddish branches. Its attractive flowers are shaped like urns. They cannot be seen easily because the plant's leaves hide them. The plant produces a bright red berry. Wintergreen provides a pleasant-smelling, pleasant-tasting oil. Wintergreen oil serves as a flavoring for candy, medicine, chewing gum, and tooth powder.

Scientific classification. Wintergreen is in the heath family, Ericaceae. It is *Gaultheria procumbens.*   J. B. Hanson

Winthrop is the family name of two American colonial leaders, father and son.

John Winthrop (1588-1649) was a Puritan governor of the Massachusetts Bay Colony. He was born in Edwardstone, Suffolk, England, of well-to-do country people. In 1602, he went to Cambridge University. He married at 17, practiced law, and became devoutly religious. In 1629, he became governor of the Massachusetts Bay Company, and in 1630, he sailed to Salem on the *Arbella.* About a thousand settlers followed him. Taking over the government from John Endecott, Winthrop soon settled Boston. He helped establish a Congregational church, and led the colony through the first hard winter. He was governor almost continuously until his death.

Winthrop's principles were high, and he tended to be aristocratic. In any community, he said, "the best part is always the least, and of that part the wiser part is always the lesser." He took part in all the major affairs of the colony, such as forming the New England Confederation. A statue of him represents Massachusetts in the U.S. Capitol.

John Winthrop, Jr. (1606-1676), was a colonial governor of Connecticut. He came to America in 1631. In 1633,
he founded the town of Ipswich, Mass. He represented Massachusetts Bay Colony in England in 1634. He returned to govern a new colony in Saybrook, Conn. In 1646, Winthrop founded what is now New London, Conn., and later he served as governor of Connecticut. He was born in Groton, England.   Bradford Smith
WIPO. See World Intellectual Property Organization.
Wire is a long, thin, flexible metal rod that has a uniform cross section. Only *ductile* metals, or metals that can be easily drawn out, can be used for making wire. The chief ductile metals are copper, steel, brass, tungsten, gold, silver, and aluminum.

How wire is made. From early ages until the 1300's, wire was made by hammering metal into plates. These plates were then cut into strips and rounded by beating. Then crude methods of "drawing" wire were introduced. Machine-drawn wire was first made in England in the mid-1800's. Today, all wire is machine-made. Steel or iron *billets,* 2-inch (5-centimeter) square blocks of metal, are heated and run through rollers that press them into smaller, longer shapes. They come out as long rods about $\frac{1}{4}$ inch (6 millimeters) in diameter. The rods are cast into coils and cleansed in sulfuric acid and water.

Pulling the rods through a series of tungsten carbide dies draws them out to form wire. The die has a funnel-like shape with a round opening smaller than the rod. The rod, which is pointed at one end by hammering, may be run into the die as thread runs through the eye of a needle. As soon as the pointed end passes through the die, it is seized with a pair of pincers, which are operated either mechanically or by hand, and drawn far enough to be attached to an upright drum. The drum rotates, pulling the wire through the die. The wire winds on the drum. Fine wire is drawn through a series of dies of continuously decreasing diameters. Drawn wire tends to harden, and so it is softened and made less brittle by being heated in a furnace. For drawing the finest kinds of wire, extremely hard dies made of diamonds are used.

Sizes of wire. The size of wire differs according to its gauge, or diameter. *American,* or *Brown and Sharpe,* is the standard gauge used in the United States for copper and other nonferrous wire. This gauge varies from No. 000000, which equals 0.58 inch (15 millimeters) in diameter, to No. 51, which is 0.000878 inch (0.022301 millimeter). A number of other U.S. standards are used. Sometimes the *imperial* gauge of England is used. France and Germany use gauges based on the millimeter. The *steel wire gauge* is the standard gauge for steel wire in the United States. Wire may be drawn through specially shaped dies to be made square, oval, flat, or triangular. However, most wire is round.

Uses of wire. Manufacturers make telegraph, telephone, and electric-power wires of copper, which is unusually ductile and one of the best conductors of electricity. The extremely thin wires used in telescopes are made of platinum. People find other uses for wire in making nails, fences, watch springs, screens, and strings for musical and scientific instruments. Wire is also used in making automobile springs, bolts, fasteners, nuts, paper clips, screws, and staples. Magnet wire is used in generators and motors. Wire netting, gauze, and cloth are woven from wire. Wire ropes and cables consist of a number of single wires twisted together. Large suspen-

How wire is made

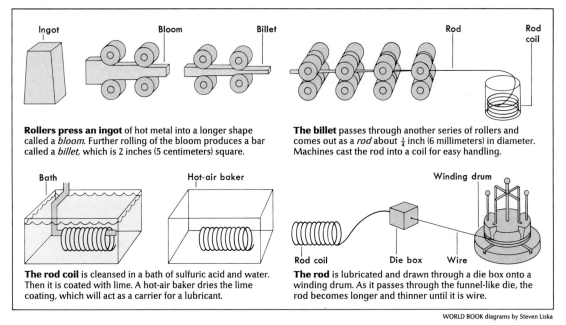

Rollers press an ingot of hot metal into a longer shape called a *bloom*. Further rolling of the bloom produces a bar called a *billet,* which is 2 inches (5 centimeters) square.

The billet passes through another series of rollers and comes out as a *rod* about $\frac{1}{4}$ inch (6 millimeters) in diameter. Machines cast the rod into a coil for easy handling.

The rod coil is cleansed in a bath of sulfuric acid and water. Then it is coated with lime. A hot-air baker dries the lime coating, which will act as a carrier for a lubricant.

The rod is lubricated and drawn through a die box onto a winding drum. As it passes through the funnel-like die, the rod becomes longer and thinner until it is wire.

WORLD BOOK diagrams by Steven Liska

sion bridges are supported by steel-wire cables, which consist of many separate wires that have been bunched together. Wire ropes are used in mining and oil drilling. *Optical fibers* are a type of wire made from glass. These wires are used for high-speed data transmission.

I. Melvin Bernstein

Related articles in *World Book* include:

Annealing
Barbed wire
Copper (Copper wire)

Ductility
Fiber optics
Wire glass

Wire fox terrier is a popular breed of small, sturdy dogs. A wire fox terrier has a rough, wiry, white coat, usually with patches of black or tan, or both black and tan. Its head is long and narrow with small ears that fall forward in a V shape. Its tail is short and erect. Wire fox terriers weigh about 15 to 19 pounds (7 to 9 kilograms).

Libwyre Kennel

The wire fox terrier makes a good pet.

The American Kennel Club recognized the wire fox terrier as a breed in 1985. Until then, wire fox terriers and smooth fox terriers were regarded as a single breed, called *fox terriers* (see **Smooth fox terrier**).

The wire fox terrier was developed in northern England in the late 1800's. It originally was used in fox-hunting to drive the fox from its hiding place. Wire fox terriers have remarkable endurance, excellent eyesight, and a keen sense of smell. They are friendly and good-tempered and make good pets. They also are excellent watchdogs.   Critically reviewed by the American Fox Terrier Club

Wire glass consists of sheets of glass from $\frac{1}{4}$ to $\frac{3}{4}$ inch (6 to 19 millimeters) thick that contain a wire mesh embedded during the manufacturing process. The wire mesh strengthens the glass and holds it in place after breakage occurs. It has been used widely for windows and doors. The invention of wire glass is attributed to two men, Frank Shuman of Philadelphia and Leon Appert of France. They achieved practically the same result by different processes. The *Appert process* consists of rolling one sheet of glass and laying the meshed wire on it, then rolling another sheet of glass on the top and pressing the wire and the sheets of glass into one solid sheet. The *Shuman process* consists of rolling one sheet of glass, into which the wire netting is pressed and rolled. Wire glass can also be made by placing the wire on a casting table and holding it in position while glass is poured around it. One surface of wire glass is always smooth, and the other may have various designs to diffuse light and obscure vision. Wire glass is usually $\frac{1}{4}$ inch (6 millimeters) thick. In many applications, wire glass is being replaced with a type of plastic that is less likely to break upon impact.   Peter J. Vergano

Wire service. See News service.

Wirehaired pointing griffon is a hunting dog that originated in France and the Netherlands in the late 1800's. A good retriever, it shows where game is by

The wirehaired pointing griffon is a hunting dog.

pointing its body toward the game. It has a rough, steel-gray coat, with splashes of chestnut. The dog works deliberately, locating game by scent on the wind. Owners usually *dock* (cut off) about two-thirds of the tail. The dog stands 19 to 23 inches (48 to 58 centimeters) high at the shoulder and weighs from 50 to 60 pounds (23 to 27 kilograms).   Critically reviewed by the American Kennel Club

Wireless. See **Radio** (History; picture: Guglielmo Marconi).

Wirephoto. See **Telephoto.**

Wiretapping usually means the interception of telephone conversations by a listening device connected to the telephone wire or placed nearby. The message may be heard live, or it may be recorded or transmitted to another location.

Wiretapping is sometimes used as part of an investigative procedure called *audio surveillance.* The term *wiretapping* sometimes refers to the use of any electrical or electronic device to eavesdrop on private conversations. However, the interception of nontelephone conversations is usually called *bugging* or *electronic eavesdropping.*

Sophisticated methods and devices permit eavesdropping in almost any situation. Some types of microphones may be attached to a wall or a door so that conversations can be overheard through the partition. Directional microphones may be beamed or focused to pick up conversations from long distances. Even greater distances can be overcome by concealed miniature microphones and transmitters that send messages to a radio receiver.

In most countries, the right of people to speak freely in their homes and businesses and in public places—without fear of eavesdroppers—is considered extremely important. Many nations, states, and provinces have passed laws restricting or prohibiting various types of electronic surveillance. But much illegal eavesdropping continues, both by individuals and by governments.

In the United States, the problem of wiretapping and electronic eavesdropping has become a confusing and controversial legal issue. There is much disagreement about (1) the constitutionality of electronic surveillance by law enforcement agencies and (2) methods of con-

trolling government eavesdropping if it is permitted. However, many Americans oppose wiretapping and bugging by either governments or private individuals.

The wiretapping controversy began in 1928, when the Supreme Court of the United States ruled that wiretapping did not violate the Fourth Amendment to the Constitution. This amendment sets forth restrictions on search and seizure.

In 1934, Congress passed the Federal Communications Act, which prohibits the interception and public disclosure of any wire or radio communication. On the basis of this law, the Supreme Court ruled in 1937 that evidence obtained by wiretapping cannot be used in a federal court. Following this ruling, federal officials argued that the 1934 law did not prohibit wiretapping by the government so long as the evidence was not used in court. Since 1940, U.S. Presidents have claimed constitutional power to order wiretaps in matters of national security.

In 1968, Congress passed a law permitting federal, state, and local government agencies to use wiretapping and bugging devices in certain crime investigations. Before undertaking such surveillance, an agency would have to obtain a court order. The law stated that nothing in it was intended to limit the President's constitutional authority to order wiretapping without court warrants in national security cases.

In the late 1960's and early 1970's, the executive branch broadly interpreted the national security provisions of the 1968 law. It conducted electronic surveillance without court approval on a number of domestic radicals it considered subversive. In 1972, the Supreme Court ruled that such surveillance without a court warrant was unconstitutional. Also in 1972, wiretapping of the Democratic Party's national headquarters became a main issue in the Watergate Scandal. Members of a committee working for the reelection of President Richard M. Nixon, a Republican, were involved in this wiretapping. See **Watergate.**   George T. Felkenes

See also **Warrant.**

Wireworm is the name given to the hard-skinned *lar-*

The wireworm causes great damage to farm crops.

vae (young) of click beetles. Wireworms received their name because they look somewhat like a piece of wire. They usually live in the soil or in decaying wood for two or three years. They often do great damage to crops by eating the roots of plants. Wireworms appear yellowish or brownish in color and measure from $\frac{1}{4}$ to $\frac{1}{2}$ inch (6 to 13 millimeters) long. They have three pairs of legs. Farmers sometimes rotate their crops or apply insecticides to the soil to help reduce the number of wireworms. See also **Click beetle.**

Scientific classification. Wireworms are in the beetle order, Coleoptera. They form the click beetle family, Elateridae.
     David J. Shetlar

Cows graze on a Wisconsin farm amid the state's rolling countryside. Farmers in Wisconsin raise thousands of herds of dairy cattle, earning the state the nickname of *America's Dairyland.*

Wisconsin *The Badger State*

Wisconsin is a Midwestern state of the United States that has long been famous for its dairy products. Thousands of herds of milk cows graze on the rich, green pastures of the rolling Wisconsin countryside. They make Wisconsin the nation's leading milk producer. The state also produces about a third of the country's cheese and about a fourth of its butter. This tremendous output of dairy products has earned Wisconsin the title of *America's Dairyland.* The processing of milk into butter, cheese, and other dairy products is a leading manufacturing activity in Wisconsin. Manufacturing is more important to Wisconsin's economy than it is to the economies of most other states.

Wisconsin is one of the leading states in the manufacture of machinery, food products, and paper products. The cities of southeastern Wisconsin produce construction cranes, engines, machine tools, and other machinery. Besides dairy products, the state's food products include canned and frozen vegetables, sausages, and beer. Northern Wisconsin has many paper mills.

Most of Wisconsin's workers are employed in service

The contributors of this article are Gary C. Meyer, Associate Professor of Geography at the University of Wisconsin at Stevens Point; and Benjamin D. Rhodes, Professor of History at the University of Wisconsin at Whitewater.

industries, which include education, finance, health care, and trade. The state's public university system is one of the largest in the nation. Milwaukee ranks as one of the Midwest's chief financial centers. Madison, Milwaukee, and La Crosse have major medical centers. Ports along Lake Michigan and Lake Superior handle both foreign and domestic trade.

The natural beauty and recreational resources of Wisconsin attract millions of vacationers every year. Wisconsin has about 15,000 lakes to delight swimmers, fishing enthusiasts, and boaters. Hikers and horseback riders follow paths through the deep, cool north woods of Wisconsin. Hunters shoot game animals in the forests and fields. In winter, sports fans enjoy skiing, tobogganing, and iceboating.

Wisconsin has won fame as one of the nation's most progressive states. An important reform movement called *Progressivism* started in Wisconsin during the early 1900's. The state began many educational, social, political, and economic reforms that were later adopted by other states and the federal government. Many of these reforms were sponsored by the La Follettes, one of the most famous families in American political history.

Wisconsin led the way to direct primary elections, regulation of public utilities and railroads, pensions for teachers, minimum-wage laws, and workers' compensa-

Buck Miller, Black Star

Grand Avenue Mall, in downtown Milwaukee, attracts many shoppers. Milwaukee is the largest city in Wisconsin.

tion. Wisconsin also was the first state to end the death penalty for crime.

The first schools for training rural teachers were established in Wisconsin, as were the first vocational schools. The University of Wisconsin was one of the first universities to offer correspondence courses. The nation's first kindergarten began in Wisconsin. Wisconsin established the first library for state legislators.

Wisconsin has been a leader in the development of farmers' institutes and cooperatives, dairy farmers' associations, and cheese-making federations. The Republican Party was founded in Wisconsin. One of the nation's first hydroelectric plants was installed in Wisconsin. Wisconsin was the first state to adopt the number system for marking highways. It passed the first law requiring safety belts in all new automobiles bought in the state.

Wisconsin is an Indian word. It has several possible meanings, including *gathering of the waters, wild rice country,* and *home land.* Wisconsin has been nicknamed the *Badger State,* and its people are known as *Badgers.* This nickname was first used for Wisconsin lead miners in the 1820's. Some of these miners lived in caves that they dug out of the hillsides. They reminded people of badgers burrowing holes in the ground.

Madison is the capital of Wisconsin. Milwaukee is the state's largest city.

Interesting facts about Wisconsin

WORLD BOOK illustrations by Kevin Chadwick

The first practical typewriter was invented by Christopher Latham Sholes, with the help of Carlos Glidden and Samuel W. Soule, in Milwaukee in 1867.

The first kindergarten in the United States was opened in 1856 in Watertown by Mrs. Carl Schurz. Schurz had been a pupil

First kindergarten

of Friedrich Frobel, the father of the kindergarten movement, who started his first kindergarten in Germany in 1837.

The world's first plant to produce electricity from water power began operating in Appleton in 1882. The plant was built on the Fox River.

Malted milk was invented by William Horlick in 1887 in Racine.

The first woman commissioned by Congress to create a work of sculpture was Vinnie Ream of Madison. She was commissioned to produce a statue of Abraham Lincoln when she was only 18 years old. Her statue of him still stands in the U.S. Capitol Rotunda.

Malted milk

Mercury Marine

Workers assemble outboard motors at a plant in Fond du Lac. Manufacturing is Wisconsin's leading economic activity.

Wisconsin in brief

Symbols of Wisconsin

The state flag, adopted in 1913, bears the state seal. The name *Wisconsin* and the year it became a state, *1848,* were added in 1981. On the state seal, adopted in 1881, a sailor and a miner support a shield with symbols of agriculture, mining, navigation, and manufacturing. A small United States coat of arms symbolizes Wisconsin's loyalty to the Union. The badger above the shield represents Wisconsin's nickname—the *Badger State.*

State flag

State seal

Wisconsin (brown) ranks 26th in size among all the states and 10th in size among the Midwestern States (yellow).

General information

Statehood: May 29, 1848, the 30th state.
State abbreviations: Wis. (traditional); WI (postal).
State motto: *Forward.*
State song: "On, Wisconsin!" Words by J. S. Hubbard and Charles D. Rosa; music by William T. Purdy.

The State Capitol is in Madison, Wisconsin's capital since 1848. Territorial capitals were Belmont (1836), Burlington, now in Iowa (1837-1838), and Madison (1838-1848).

Land and climate

Area: 56,153 sq. mi. (145,436 km²), including 1,727 sq. mi. (4,472 km²) of inland water but excluding 10,062 sq. mi. (26,060 km²) of Lake Michigan and Lake Superior.
Elevation: *Highest*—Timms Hill, 1,952 ft. (595 m) above sea level. *Lowest*—581 ft. (177 m) above sea level along the shore of Lake Michigan.
Record high temperature: 114° F. (46° C) at Wisconsin Dells on July 13, 1936.
Record low temperature: −54° F. (−48° C) at Danbury on Jan. 24, 1922.
Average July temperature: 70° F. (21° C).
Average January temperature: 14° F. (−10° C).
Average yearly precipitation: 31 in. (79 cm).

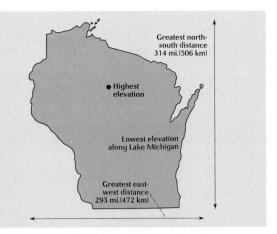

Greatest north-south distance 314 mi.(506 km)

● Highest elevation

Lowest elevation along Lake Michigan

Greatest east-west distance 293 mi.(472 km)

Important dates

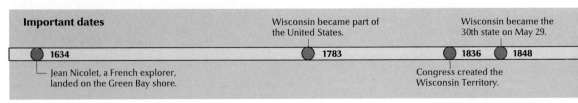

Wisconsin became part of the United States.

Wisconsin became the 30th state on May 29.

| 1634 | 1783 | 1836 | 1848 |

Jean Nicolet, a French explorer, landed on the Green Bay shore.

Congress created the Wisconsin Territory.

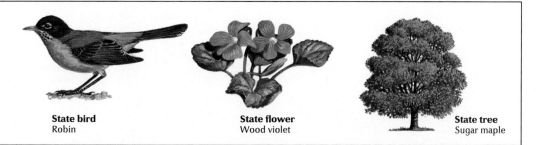

State bird
Robin

State flower
Wood violet

State tree
Sugar maple

People

Population: 4,705,642 (1980 census)
Rank among the states: 16th
Density: 84 persons per sq. mi. (32 per km²), U.S. average 67 per sq. mi. (26 per km²)
Distribution: 64 per cent urban, 36 per cent rural

Largest cities in Wisconsin

Milwaukee	636,297
Madison	170,616
Green Bay	87,899
Racine	85,725
Kenosha	77,685
West Allis	63,982

Source: U.S. Bureau of the Census.

Population trend

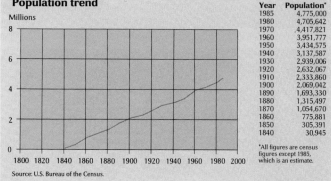

Millions

Source: U.S. Bureau of the Census.

Year	Population*
1985	4,775,000
1980	4,705,642
1970	4,417,821
1960	3,951,777
1950	3,434,575
1940	3,137,587
1930	2,939,006
1920	2,632,067
1910	2,333,860
1900	2,069,042
1890	1,693,330
1880	1,315,497
1870	1,054,670
1860	775,881
1850	305,391
1840	30,945

*All figures are census figures except 1985, which is an estimate.

Economy

Chief products

Agriculture: milk.
Manufacturing: machinery, food products, paper products, electrical equipment, fabricated metal products.
Mining: crushed stone, sand and gravel.

Gross state product

Value of goods and services produced in 1986, $76,922,000,000. *Services* include community, business, and personal services; finance; government; trade; and transportation, communication, and utilities. *Industry* includes construction, manufacturing, and mining. *Agriculture* includes agriculture, fishing, and forestry.

Source: U.S. Bureau of Economic Analysis.

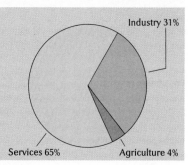

Industry 31%

Services 65%

Agriculture 4%

Government

State government

Governor: 4-year term
State senators: 33; 4-year terms
State representatives: 99; 2-year terms
Counties: 72

Federal government

United States senators: 2
United States representatives: 9
Electoral votes: 11

Sources of information

For information about tourism in Wisconsin, write to: Wisconsin Department of Development, Tourism Development, 123 West Washington Avenue, P. O. Box 7970, Madison, WI 53707. The Office of the Governor handles requests for information about the state's economy, government, or history. Write to: Office of the Governor, State Capitol, Box 7863, Madison, WI 53707.

The state legislature set up a teacher's pension and established a commission to settle labor disputes.

The legislature created a state university system—the University of Wisconsin System.

1901   1911   1932   1971

Robert M. La Follette, Sr., became governor, and the progressive era began.

Wisconsin passed the first state unemployment-compensation act.

The Wisconsin Division of Tourism

The University of Wisconsin at Madison is the largest of 13 universities in the extensive University of Wisconsin system. Agriculture Hall, *left,* is one of the main buildings on the Madison campus.

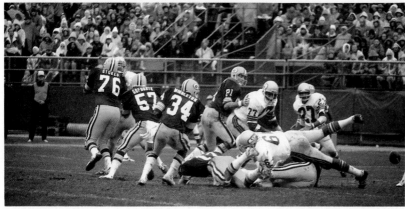

Michael Philip Manheim from Marilyn Gartman

The Green Bay Packers are Wisconsin's National Football League franchise. The Packers play home games at Milwaukee County Stadium and at Lambeau Field in Green Bay.

Population density

About two-thirds of the people of Wisconsin live in urban areas. Most of the urban population is concentrated in the southeastern part of the state.

Persons per sq. mi.	Persons per km²
More than 100	More than 40
50 to 100	20 to 40
25 to 50	10 to 20
Less than 25	Less than 10

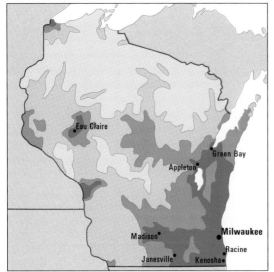

WORLD BOOK map; based on U.S. Bureau of the Census data.

Population. The 1980 United States census reported that Wisconsin had 4,705,642 people. The population had increased 7 per cent over the 1970 figure, 4,417,821. The U.S. Bureau of the Census estimated that by 1985 the state's population had reached about 4,775,000.

About two-thirds of the people live in urban areas. Almost a third live in the metropolitan area of Milwaukee. The state has 13 metropolitan areas, 11 of which lie entirely within the state (see **Metropolitan area**). Two metropolitan areas lie mainly in Minnesota. They are Minneapolis-St. Paul and Duluth. For the populations of these metropolitan areas, see the *Index* to the Wisconsin political map.

Milwaukee, Wisconsin's largest city, is a leading center of manufacturing. Madison, the state's capital, is Wisconsin's second largest city. It is home to the oldest and largest campus of the University of Wisconsin. Other large Wisconsin cities are Green Bay, Racine, and Kenosha. All are important manufacturing and shipping centers. See the articles on Wisconsin cities in the *Related articles* at the end of this article.

About 97 of every 100 Wisconsinites were born in the United States. Most of those born in other lands came from Canada, Germany, Italy, Mexico, Poland, and Yugoslavia. Milwaukee is a leading U.S. center of German-American culture. Immigrants from Norway, Switzerland, Great Britain, and Finland have also made important contributions to the state's development.

The Milwaukee Public Museum is one of the finest natural history museums in the United States. These visitors are looking at one of the museum's life-sized replicas of dinosaurs.

Wisconsin Division of Tourism

Universities and colleges

Wisconsin has 28 universities and colleges that offer bachelor's or advanced degrees and are accredited by the North Central Association of Colleges and Schools. Locations shown below refer to the schools' mailing addresses. For enrollments and further information, see **Universities and colleges** (table).

Name	Location	Name	Location
Alverno College	Milwaukee	Mount Mary College	Milwaukee
Beloit College	Beloit	Mount Senario College	Ladysmith
Cardinal Stritch College	Milwaukee	Northland College	Ashland
Carroll College	Waukesha	Northwestern College	Watertown
Carthage College	Kenosha	Ripon College	Ripon
Columbia College of Nursing	Milwaukee	St. Francis Seminary School	
Concordia College	Mequon	of Pastoral Ministry	Milwaukee
Edgewood College	Madison	St. Norbert College	De Pere
Institute of Paper Chemistry	Appleton	Silver Lake College	Manitowoc
Lakeland College	Sheboygan	Viterbo College	La Crosse
Lawrence University	Appleton	Wisconsin, Medical College of	Milwaukee
Marian College of Fond du Lac	Fond du Lac	Wisconsin School of Professional	
Marquette University	Milwaukee	Psychology	Milwaukee
Milwaukee Institute of Art and Design	Milwaukee	Wisconsin, University of	*
Milwaukee School of Engineering	Milwaukee	Wisconsin Lutheran College	Milwaukee

*For campuses and founding dates, see **Universities and colleges** (table).

Schools. Michael Frank, a newspaper editor in Southport (now Kenosha), led the movement for free schools in Wisconsin. In 1845, he started Wisconsin's first public school. The state Constitution, adopted in 1848, provided free schooling for all children between the ages of 4 and 20. In 1856, Mrs. Carl Schurz opened the nation's first kindergarten in Watertown.

A 1911 Wisconsin law required all cities and towns with populations of 5,000 or more to establish vocational schools. This was the first law of its kind in the United States. Today, the Milwaukee Vocational School ranks as one of the largest trade schools in the United States. In 1891, the University of Wisconsin established one of the first correspondence schools in the nation.

Wisconsin's public schools are directed by the superintendent of public instruction, who is elected to a four-year term. School attendance is required of children from ages 6 through 17. In districts with a vocational school, attendance is required until age 18 or the completion of 12th grade. For the number of students and teachers in Wisconsin, see **Education** (table).

Libraries. Wisconsin has about 370 public libraries, all of which take part in the state's 17 regional library systems. Wisconsin also has many college and university libraries and other special libraries serving industry, institutions, and government. The State Law Library was founded in Madison in 1836. State support for free public libraries began in 1872. A reference library for legislators is in the state Capitol. It was founded in 1901, and was the first of its kind in the nation.

Today, the State Department of Public Instruction is responsible for the promotion and development of library service in the state. The largest libraries in the state are the Milwaukee Public Library and the University of Wisconsin Library in Madison. Each has over two million books. The State Historical Society in Madison has one of the nation's largest collections of books, newspapers, and manuscripts on U.S. history.

Museums. The Milwaukee Public Museum is Wisconsin's largest museum. It is among the finest natural history museums in the nation. The State Historical Society in Madison features exhibits on the state's history. Wisconsin has some highly specialized museums, including the Dard Hunter Paper Museum in Appleton; the Circus World Museum in Baraboo; the Farm and Craft Museum in Cassville; and the Experimental Aircraft Association Museum in Oshkosh. Old World Wisconsin near Eagle, honors the ethnic groups that settled the state. The Leigh Yawkey Woodson Art Museum, in Wausau, is known for its bird collection. Wisconsin has art museums in Beloit, Madison, Milwaukee, and Oshkosh; and on university campuses.

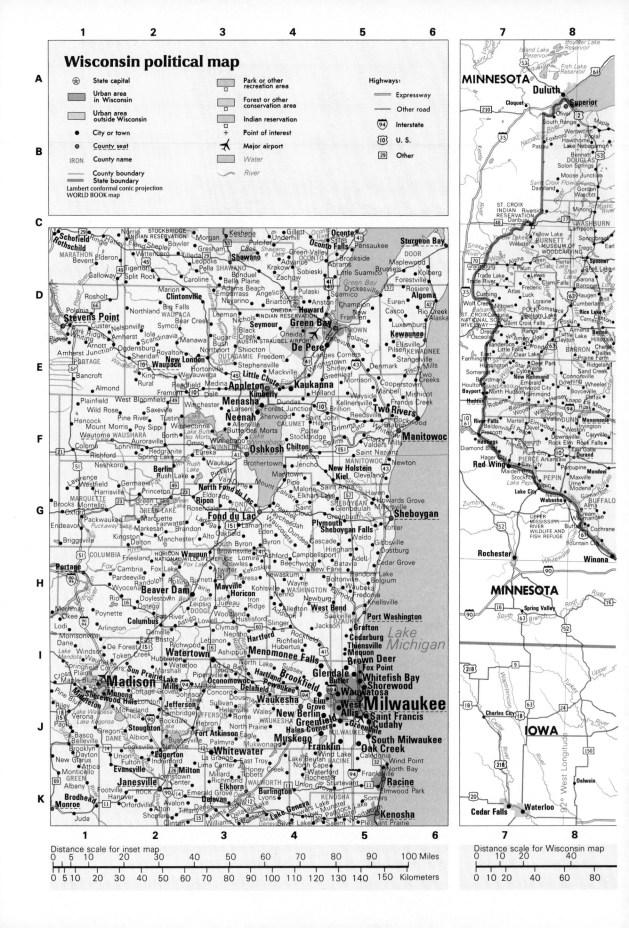

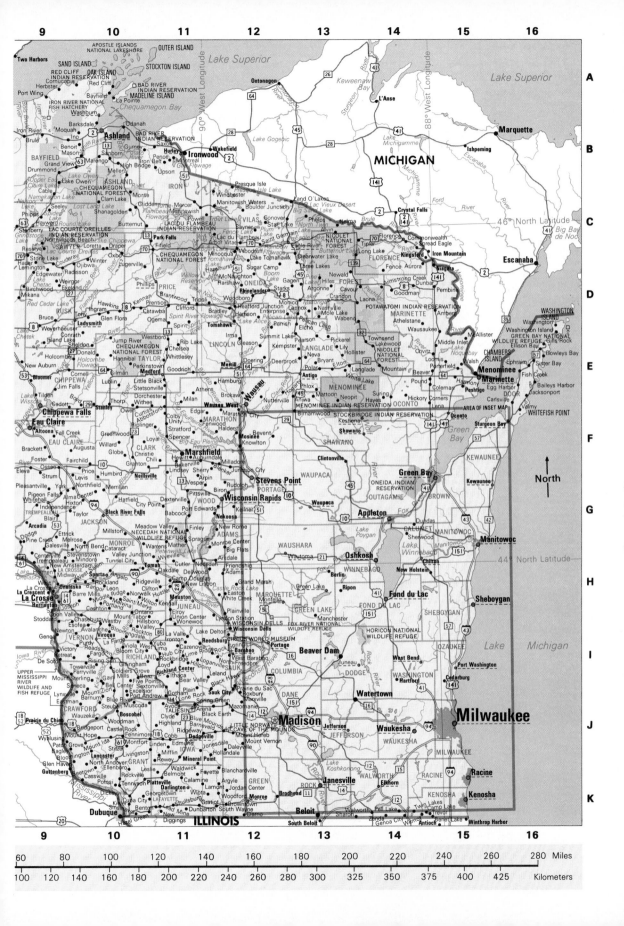

Wisconsin map index

Metropolitan areas

Appleton-Oshkosh 291,369
Duluth (Minn.) 266,650 (222,229 in Minn.; 44,421 in Wis.)
Eau Claire 130,392
Green Bay 175,280
Janesville-Beloit 139,420
Kenosha 123,137
La Crosse 91,056
Madison 323,545
Milwaukee 1,397,143
Minneapolis-St. Paul (Minn.) 2,137,133 (2,093,871 in Minn.; 43,262 in Wis.)
Racine 173,132
Sheboygan 100,935
Wausau 111,270

Counties

Adams 13,457 G 12
Ashland 16,783 B 10
Barron 38,730 E 8
Bayfield 13,822 B 9
Brown 175,280 G 15
Buffalo 14,309 G 8
Burnett 12,340 C 8
Calumet 30,867 G 14
Chippewa 52,127 E 9
Clark 32,910 F 10
Columbia 43,222 I 12
Crawford 16,556 J 9
Dane 323,545 J 12
Dodge 75,064 I 13
Door 25,029 E 16
Douglas 44,421 B 8
Dunn 34,314 F 8
Eau Claire 78,805 F 9
Florence 4,172 C 14
Fond du Lac 88,964 H 14
Forest 9,044 D 13
Grant 51,736 J 10
Green 30,012 K 12
Green Lake 18,370 H 13
Iowa 19,802 J 11
Iron 6,730 B 11
Jackson 16,831 G 10
Jefferson 66,152 J 13
Juneau 21,037 H 11
Kenosha 123,137 K 15
Kewaunee 19,539 F 15
La Crosse 91,056 H 9
Lafayette 17,412 K 11
Langlade 19,978 E 13
Lincoln 26,555 E 11
Manitowoc 82,918 G 15
Marathon 111,270 F 11
Marinette 39,314 D 14
Marquette 11,672 H 12
Menominee 3,373 E 13
Milwaukee 964,988 J 15
Monroe 35,074 G 10
Oconto 28,947 F 14
Oneida 31,216 D 12
Outagamie 128,799 G 14
Ozaukee 66,981 I 15
Pepin 7,477 G 8
Pierce 31,149 F 7
Polk 32,351 D 7
Portage 57,420 G 12
Price 15,788 D 11
Racine 173,132 K 14
Richland 17,476 I 11
Rock 139,420 K 13
Rusk 15,589 D 9
St. Croix 43,262 E 7
Sauk 43,469 I 12
Sawyer 12,843 C 9
Shawano 35,928 F 13
Sheboygan 100,935 H 15
Taylor 18,817 E 10
Trempealeau 26,158 G 9
Vernon 25,642 I 9
Vilas 16,535 C 12
Walworth 71,507 K 14
Washburn 13,174 C 8
Washington 84,848 I 14
Waukesha 280,203 J 14
Waupaca 42,831 G 13
Waushara 18,526 G 13
Winnebago 131,772 H 13
Wood 72,799 G 11

Cities and villages

Abbotsford 1,901 F 11
Abrams D 4
Adams 1,744 H 12
Adell 545 H 5
Afton K 2
Albany 1,051 K 1
Albion J 2
Algoma 3,656 D 6
Allens Grove K 3
Allenton H 4
Allouez* 14,882 G 15
Alma 848 °G 8
Alma Center 454 G 10
Almena 526 D 8
Almond 477 E 1
Alpha D 7
Alto G 3
Altoona 4,393 F 9
Amberg D 15
Amery 2,404 E 7
Amherst 701 E 1
Amherst Junction 225 E 1
Angelo H 10
Aniwa 273 E 13
Anston D 4
Antigo 8,653 °E 13
Appleton 58,913 °G 14
Arbor Vitae C 12
Arcadia 2,109 G 9
Arena 451 J 11
Argonne D 13
Argyle 720 K 12
Arkansaw F 8
Arlington 440 I 1
Armstrong Creek D 14
Arnott E 1
Arpin 361 G 11
Ashford H 4
Ashippun I 3
Ashland 9,115 °B 10
Ashwaubenon* 14,486 G 15
Athelstane D 14
Athens 988 E 11
Auburndale 641 F 11
Augusta 1,560 F 9
Auroraville F 2
Avalon K 2
Avoca 505 J 11
Babcock G 11
Bagley 317 J 9
Baileys Harbor E 16
Bakerville F 11
Baldwin 1,620 E 7
Balsam Lake 749 °D 7
Bancroft E 1
Bangor 1,012 H 10
Baraboo 8,081 °I 12
Barneveld 579 J 11
Barron 2,595 °E 8
Barronett D 8
Basco J 1
Batavia H 5
Bay City 543 F 7
Bayfield 778 A 10
Bayside* 4,724 J 15
Bear Creek 454 D 3
Beaver Dam 14,149 I 13
Beechwood H 4
Beetown K 10
Beldenville F 7
Belgium 892 H 5
Bell Center 124 I 10
Belleville 1,302 J 1
Belmont 826 K 11
Beloit 35,207 K 13
Beloit North* 5,457 K 13
Benton 983 K 11
Berlin 5,478 H 13
Bevent F 12
Big Bend* 1,345 J 14
Big Falls 107 D 2
Birchwood 437 D 9
Birnamwood 688 F 13
Biron 698 G 12
Black Creek 1,097 E 3
Black Earth 1,145 J 12
Black River* 1,046 H 15
Black River Falls 3,434 °G 10
Blair 1,142 G 9
Blanchardville 803 K 12
Blenker F 11
Bloom City I 10
Bloomer 3,342 E 9
Bloomingdale I 10
Bloomington 743 J 10
Blue Mounds 387 J 12
Blue River 412 J 10
Boardman E 7
Boaz 161 I 10
Bohners Lake* 1,507 K 14
Boltonville H 4
Bonduel 1,160 D 3
Boscobel 2,662 J 10
Boulder Junction C 12
Bowler 339 C 2
Boyceville 862 E 8
Boyd 660 F 10
Brackett F 9
Branch F 5
Brandon 862 G 3
Briggsville G 1
Brill D 8
Brillion 2,907 F 5
Bristol K 5
Brodhead 3,153 K 12
Brokaw 298 E 12
Brookfield 34,035 J 4
Brooklyn 627 J 1
Brooks G 1
Brothertown F 4
Brown Deer 12,921 I 5
Browns Lake* 1,648 K 14
Browntown 284 K 12
Bruce 905 D 9
Brule B 9
Brussels D 6
Buffalo 894 G 8
Burlington 8,385 K 4
Burnett H 3
Butler 2,059 I 4
Butte des Morts F 3
Butternut 438 C 10
Byron G 4
Cable 227 C 9
Cadott 1,247 F 9
Calamine K 11
Caledonia J 5
Cambria 680 H 2
Cambridge 844 J 2
Cameron 1,115 D 8
Camp Douglas 589 H 11
Camp Lake 2,060 K 14
Campbellsport 1,740 H 4
Canton D 9
Caroline D 2
Cascade 615 G 5
Casco 484 D 6
Cashton 827 H 10
Cassville 1,270 K 10
Cataract H 10
Catawba 205 D 10
Cato F 5
Cavour D 13
Cazenovia 259 I 11
Cecil 445 C 3
Cedar Grove 1,420 H 5
Cedarburg 9,005 I 15
Centerville H 9
Centuria 711 D 7
Chaseburg 279 I 9
Chelsea E 11
Chenequa* 532 J 14
Chetek 1,931 E 9
Chili F 11
Chilton 2,965 °H 14
Chippewa Falls 12,270 °F 9
Clarks Mills F 5
Clarno K 12
Clayton 425 E 8
Clear Lake 899 E 8
Clearwater Lake C 13
Cleveland 1,270 G 5
Clifton H 11
Clinton 1,751 K 2
Clintonville 4,567 F 13
Clyman 317 I 3
Cobb 409 J 11
Cochrane 512 G 8
Colby 1,496 F 11
Coleman 852 E 15
Colfax 1,149 E 8
Collins F 5
Coloma 367 F 1
Columbus 4,049 I 2
Combined Locks* 2,573 G 14
Commonwealth C 14
Como* 1,376 K 14
Comstock D 8
Concord J 3
Connorsville E 8
Conover C 12
Conrath 86 E 10
Cooksville J 2
Coon Valley 758 H 10
Cooperstown E 5
Cornell 1,583 E 9
Cornucopia A 9
Cottage Grove 888 J 2
Couderay 114 D 9
Crandon 1,969 °D 13
Crivitz 1,041 E 15
Cross Plains 2,156 I 1
Cuba City 2,129 K 10
Cudahy 19,547 J 5
Cumberland 1,983 D 8
Curtiss 127 F 11
Cushing D 7
Custer D 1
Cylon E 7
Dale E 3
Daleyville J 12
Dallas 477 E 8
Dalton G 2
Danbury C 7
Dane 518 I 1
Darien 1,152 K 3
Darlington 2,300 °K 11
Dayton J 1
Deer Park 232 E 7
Deerfield* 1,466 J 13
De Forest 3,367 I 1
Delafield 4,083 J 4
Delavan 5,684 K 3
Delavan Lake 2,082 K 3
Denmark 1,475 E 5
De Pere 14,892 E 4
De Soto 318 I 9
Diamond Bluff F 7
Dickeyville 1,156 K 10
Dodge G 9
Dodgeville 3,458 °J 11
Dorchester 613 E 11
Dousman 1,153 J 3
Downing 242 E 8
Downsville F 8
Doylestown 294 H 2
Dresser 670 E 7
Drummond B 9
Dunbar D 14
Dundee G 4
Durand 2,047 °F 8
Dyckesville D 5
Eagle 1,008 J 3
Eagle River 1,326 °C 13
Earl C 8
East Troy 2,385 K 4
Eastman 371 J 10
Easton H 12
Eau Claire 51,509 °F 9
Eau Galle F 8
Eden 534 G 4
Edgar 1,194 F 11
Edgerton 4,335 J 2
Edmund J 11
Egg Harbor 238 E 16
Eland 230 C 2
Elcho D 13
Elderon 191 D 1
Eldorado G 3
Eleva 593 F 9
Elk Mound 737 F 8
Elkhart Lake 1,054 G 5
Elkhorn 4,605 °K 14
Ellison Bay E 16
Ellisville E 5
Ellsworth 2,143 °F 7
Elm Grove 6,735 J 4
Elmwood 885 F 8
Elmwood Park 483 K 5
El Paso F 7
Elroy 1,504 H 11
Elton E 13
Embarrass 496 D 3
Emerald E 8
Emerald Grove K 2
Endeavor 335 G 1
Enterprise D 12
Ephraim 319 E 16
Ettrick 462 G 9
Eureka F 3
Evansville 2,835 K 1
Evergreen* 1,842 F 12
Excelsior J 10
Exeland 219 D 9
Fairchild 577 F 10
Fairwater 298 G 2
Fall Creek 1,148 F 9
Fall River 850 H 2
Falun D 7
Fence D 14
Fennimore 2,212 J 10
Fenwood 165 F 11
Ferryville 227 I 9
Fifield C 11
Fish Creek E 16
Florence °C 14
Fond du Lac 35,863 °H 14
Fontana 1,764 K 3
Footville 794 K 2
Forest Junction F 4
Forestville 455 D 6
Fort Atkinson 9,785 J 3
Foster F 9
Fountain City 963 G 8
Fox Lake 1,373 H 2
Fox Point 7,649 I 5
Francis Creek 538 F 5
Franklin 16,871 J 5
Franksville K 5
Frederic 1,039 D 7
Fredonia 1,437 H 5
Freedom E 4
Fremont 510 E 2
French Island* 4,118 H 9
Friendship 744 °H 12
Friesland 267 H 2
Fulton J 2
Galesville 1,239 H 9
Galloway D 1
Gays Mills 627 I 10
Genoa 283 I 9
Genoa City 1,202 K 14
Germania G 1
Germantown* 10,729 J 14
Gibbsville G 5
Gillett 1,356 C 4
Gills Rock E 16
Gilman 436 E 10
Gilmanton G 8
Gleason E 12
Glen Flora 83 D 10
Glen Haven K 9
Glenbeulah 423 G 5
Glendale 13,882 I 5
Glenwood City 950 E 8
Glidden C 10
Goodman D 14
Gordon C 8
Gotham J 11
Grafton 8,381 I 5
Grand Marsh H 12
Grand View B 9
Granton 399 F 10
Grantsburg 1,153 °D 7
Gratiot 280 K 11
Green Bay 87,899 °G 15
Green Lake 1,208 °H 13
Green Valley C 4
Greenbush G 4
Greendale 16,928 J 5
Greenfield 31,353 J 5
Greenleaf E 4
Greenwood 1,124 F 10
Gresham 534 C 3
Grimms F 5
Gurney B 10
Hager City F 7
Hales Corners 7,110 J 5
Hamburg E 11
Hammond 991 E 7
Hancock 419 F 1
Hannibal E 10
Hanover K 2
Harrisville G 1
Hartford 7,159 I 14
Hartland 5,559 I 4
Hatfield G 10
Hatley 300 C 1
Haugen 251 D 8
Hawkins 407 D 10
Hayton F 4
Hayward 1,698 °C 9
Hazel Green 1,282 K 10
Hazelhurst D 12
Heafford Junction D 12
Hebron J 3
Helenville J 3
Herbster A 9
Hersey E 8
Hewitt 470 F 11
Highland 860 J 11
Hilbert 1,176 F 4
Hiles D 13
Hillpoint I 11
Hillsboro 1,263 I 11
Hillsdale E 8
Hingham H 5
Hixton 364 G 10
Holcombe E 9
Holland E 4
Hollandale 271 J 11
Hollister E 13
Holmen 2,411 H 9
Honey Creek K 4
Horicon 3,584 H 3
Hortonville 2,016 E 3
Houlton E 7
Howard 8,240 D 4
Howards Grove 1,838 G 5
Hubertus I 4
Hudson 5,434 °E 7
Humbird G 10
Hurley 2,015 °B 11
Hustisford 874 I 3
Hustler 170 H 11
Independence 1,180 G 9
Indianford J 2
Ingram 61 D 10
Iola 957 E 2
Irma E 12
Iron Belt B 11
Iron Ridge 766 H 3
Iron River B 9
Ironton 206 I 11
Irvington F 8
Ithaca I 11
Ixonia I 3
Jackson 1,817 I 4
Jacksonport E 16
Janesville 51,071 °K 13
Jefferson 5,647 °J 13
Jericho F 4
Jim Falls E 9
Johnson Creek 1,136 J 3
Johnstown Center K 2
Juda K 1
Jump River E 10
Junction City 523 F 12
Juneau 2,045 °I 13
Kaukauna 11,310 E 4
Kekoskee 224 H 3
Kellner G 12
Kellnersville 369 E 5
Kendall 486 H 11
Kennan 194 D 10
Kenosha 77,685 °K 15
Keshena °F 14
Kewaskum 2,381 H 4
Kewaunee 2,801 °G 15
Kiel 3,083 G 5
Kieler K 10
Kimberly 5,881 E 4
King E 2
Kingston 328 G 2
Knapp 419 F 8
Knellsville H 5
Knowles H 3
Kohler 1,651 G 5
Krakow D 4
Lac La Belle 289 I 3
La Crosse 48,347 °H 9
Ladysmith 3,826 °D 9
La Farge 746 I 10
Lake Beulah J 4
Lake Delton 1,158 I 12
Lake Geneva 5,612 K 4
Lake Mills 3,670 I 2
Lake Nebagamon 780 B 8
Lake Tomahawk D 12
Lake Wazeecha* 2,176 G 12
Lake Wissota* 1,788 E 9

Lakewood		E 14
Lamartine		G 3
Lancaster	4,076.°	J 10
Land O' Lakes		C 13
Langlade		E 13
Lannon*	987	J 15
Laona		D 14
La Pointe		A 10
Larsen		F 3
La Valle	412	I 11
Lead Mine		K 11
Lebanon		I 3
Lena	585	F 15
Leopolis		D 3
Lewis		D 7
Lily		E 13
Lima Center		K 13
Lime Ridge	191	I 11
Linden	395	J 11
Little Chute	7,907	E 4
Little Suamico		D 5
Livingston	642	J 11
Lodi	1,959	I 1
Loganville	239	I 11
Lohrville	336	F 2
Lomira	1,446	H 3
London		J 2
Lone Rock	577	J 11
Long Lake		C 13
Loretta		C 10
Lowell	326	I 3
Loyal	1,252	F 10
Lublin	142	E 10
Luck	997	D 7
Luxemburg	1,040	D 5
Lyndon Station	375	H 11
Lynxville	174	J 9
Lyons		K 4
Mackville		E 4
Madison	170,616.°	J 12
Maiden Rock	172	F 7
Manawa	1,205	E 2
Manchester		H 13
Manitowish Waters		C 11
Manitowoc	32,547.°	G 15
Maple Bluff	1,351	I 1
Maplewood		D 6
Marathon City	1,552	F 12
Marengo		B 10
Maribel	363	E 5
Marinette	11,965.°	E 15
Marion	1,348	D 2
Markesan	1,446	G 2
Marquette	204	G 2
Marshall	2,363	I 2
Marshfield	18,290	F 11
Martell		F 7
Marytown		G 4
Mason	102	B 10
Mather		G 11
Mattoon	382	E 13
Mauston	3,284.°	H 11
Mayville	4,333	H 3
Mazomanie	1,248	J 12
McFarland	3,783	J 1
Medford	4,035.°	E 11
Medina		E 3
Mellen	1,046	B 10
Melrose	507	G 10
Melvina	117	H 10
Menasha	14,728	F 4
Menomonee Falls	27,845	I 4
Menomonie	12,769.°	F 8
Mequon	16,193	I 5
Mercer		C 11
Merrill	9,578.°	E 12
Merrillan	587	G 10
Merrimac	365	H 1
Merton*	1,045	J 14
Middleton	11,848	I 1
Midway		H 9
Mifflin		J 11
Mikana		D 9
Milan		E 11
Milford		I 3
Milladore	250	F 12
Millersville		G 5
Millston		G 10
Milltown	732	D 7
Milton	4,092	K 2
Milwaukee	636,297.°	J 15
Mindoro		H 9
Mineral Point	2,259	J 11
Minocqua		C 12
Minong	557	C 8
Mishicot	1,503	E 6
Modena		G 8
Mole Lake		D 13
Mondovi	2,545	F 8
Monico		D 13
Monona	8,809	J 1
Monroe	10,027.°	K 12
Monroe Center		H 11
Montello	1,273.°	H 12
Montfort	616	J 10
Monticello	1,021	K 1
Montreal	887	B 11
Morrison		E 5
Morrisonville		I 1
Mosinee	3,015	F 12
Mount Calvary	585	G 4
Mount Hope	197	J 10
Mount Horeb	3,251	J 12
Mount Ida		J 10
Mount Morris		F 2
Mount Sterling	223	I 10
Mount Vernon		J 12
Mountain		E 14
Mukwonago	4,014	J 4
Muscoda	1,331	J 10
Muskego	15,277	J 4
Nashotah*	513	J 14
Navarino		D 3
Necedah	773	H 11
Neenah	22,432	F 3
Neillsville	2,780.°	G 10
Nekoosa	2,519	G 11
Nelson	389	G 8
Nelsonville	199	E 1
Neopit	1,065	E 13
Neosho	575	I 3
Neshkoro	386	F 2
New Amsterdam		H 9
New Auburn	466	E 9
New Berlin	30,529	J 4
New Diggings		K 11
New Fane		H 3
New Glarus	1,763	J 1
New Holstein	3,412	H 14
New Lisbon	1,390	H 11
New London	6,210	E 3
New Munster		K 4
New Richmond	4,306	E 7
Newald		D 13
Newburg	783	H 5
Newville		I 1
Niagara	2,079	D 15
Nichols	267	D 3
Norrie		C 2
North Bay	219	K 5
North Bend		H 9
North Cape		K 4
North Fond du Lac	3,844	G 3
North Freedom	616	I 10
North Hudson	2,218	E 7
North Lake		I 4
North Prairie	938	J 4
Northwoods Beach		C 9
Norwalk	517	H 10
Oak Creek	16,932	J 5
Oakdale		H 11
Oakfield	990	G 3
Oconomowoc	9,909	I 3
Oconomowoc Lake*	524	J 14
Oconomowoc Lake South*		J 14
Oconto	4,505.°	F 15
Oconto Falls	2,500	C 4
Odanah		B 10
Ogdensburg	214	E 2
Ogema		D 11
Ojibwa		D 9
Okauchee*	3,958	J 14
Okee		H 1
Oliver	253	B 8
Omro	2,763	F 3
Onalaska	9,249	H 9
Oneida		E 4
Ontario	398	H 10
Oostburg	1,647	H 5
Oregon	3,876	J 1
Orfordville	1,143	K 1
Osceola	1,581	E 7
Oshkosh	49,620.°	H 14
Osseo	1,474	F 9
Owen	998	F 10
Oxford	432	G 1
Packwaukee		G 1
Paddock Lake	2,207	K 4
Palmyra	1,515	J 3
Paoli		J 1
Pardeeville	1,594	H 1
Park Falls	3,192	C 11
Park Ridge	643	D 1
Patch Grove	259	J 10
Patzau		B 8
Peebles		G 4
Pelican Lake		D 13
Pell Lake	1,826	K 14
Pella		D 3
Pembine		D 15
Pence		B 11
Pensaukee		C 5
Pepin	890	G 8
Perkinstown		E 10
Peshtigo	2,807	E 15
Pewaukee	4,637	I 4
Pewaukee West*		J 14
Phelps		C 13
Phillips	1,522.°	D 11
Phlox		E 13
Pickerel		E 13
Pickett		G 3
Pigeon Falls	338	G 9
Pine Bluff		J 1
Pine Creek		G 9
Pine River		F 2
Pipe		G 4
Pittsville	810	G 11
Plain	676	I 11
Plainfield	813	F 1
Platteville	9,580	K 11
Pleasant Prairie		K 5
Plover	5,310	E 1
Plum City	505	F 8
Plymouth	6,027	G 5
Poland		E 5
Polar		E 13
Polonia		D 1
Poplar	569	B 8
Port Edwards	2,077	G 11
Port Washington	8,612.°	I 15
Port Wing		A 9
Portage	7,896.°	I 12
Poskin		D 8
Potosi	736	K 10
Potter		F 4
Potter Lake*	1,068	K 14
Pound	407	E 15
Powers Lake	1,162	K 4
Poy Sippi		F 2
Poynette	1,447	H 1
Prairie du Chien	5,859.°	J 9
Prairie du Sac	2,145	I 12
Prairie Farm	387	E 8
Prentice	605	D 11
Prescott	2,654	F 7
Presque Isle		C 12
Princeton	1,479	G 2
Pulaski	1,875	D 4
Pulcifer		C 4
Racine	85,725.°	K 15
Radisson	280	D 9
Randolph	1,691	H 2
Random Lake	1,287	H 5
Readfield		E 3
Readstown	396	I 10
Red Cliff		A 10
Redgranite	976	F 2
Reedsburg	5,038	I 11
Reedsville	1,134	F 5
Reeseville*	649	J 13
Reserve		C 9
Retreat		I 9
Rewey	233	J 11
Rhinelander	7,873.°	D 12
Rib Lake	945	E 11
Rib Mountain, see Wausau West [-Rib Mountain]		
Rice Lake	7,691	D 8
Richfield		I 4
Richland Center	4,997.°	I 11
Richwood		I 3
Ridgeland	300	E 8
Ridgeway	503	J 1
Ringle		C 1
Rio	785	H 1
Rio Creek		D 6
Riplinger		F 11
Ripon	7,111	H 13
River Falls	9,019	F 7
River Hills*	1,642	I 15
Roberts	833	E 7
Rochester	746	K 4
Rock Elm		F 8
Rock Falls		F 8
Rock Springs	426	I 11
Rockbridge		I 11
Rockdale	200	J 2
Rockfield		I 4
Rockland	383	H 10
Rockwood		F 5
Rolling Prairie		H 3
Rome		J 3
Rosendale	725	G 3
Rosholt	520	D 1
Rothschild	3,338	C 1
Roxbury		J 12
Royalton		E 2
Rudolph	392	G 12
Rural		E 2
Rusk		F 8
St. Anna		G 4
St. Cloud	560	G 4
St. Croix Falls	1,497	D 7
St. Francis	10,095	J 5
St. Germain		C 12
St. Joseph		H 10
St. Nazianz	738	F 5
Salem		K 4
Sanborn		B 10
Sand Creek		E 8
Sarona		D 8
Sauk City	2,703	J 12
Saukville	3,494	H 5
Saxeville		F 2
Saxon		B 11
Sayner		C 12
Scandinavia	292	E 2
Schofield	2,226	C 1
Seneca		I 10
Sextonville		I 11
Seymour	2,530	D 4
Sharon	1,280	K 13
Shawano	7,013.°	F 14
Sheboygan	48,085.°	H 15
Sheboygan Falls	5,253	G 5
Sheboygan South*		H 15
Sheldon	292	E 10
Shell Lake	1,135.°	D 8
Sherry		F 11
Sherwood	372	F 4
Shiocton	805	E 3
Shopiere		K 2
Shorewood	14,327	I 5
Shorewood Hills	1,837	I 1
Shullsburg	1,484	K 11
Silver Lake	1,598	K 4
Sinsinawa		K 10
Siren	896	D 7
Sister Bay	564	E 16
Slinger	1,612	I 4
Sobieski		D 4
Soldiers Grove	622	I 10
Solon Springs	590	B 8
Somers		K 5
Somerset	860	E 7
South Byron		H 3
South Milwaukee	21,069	J 5
South Range		B 8
South Wayne	495	K 11
Sparta	6,934.°	H 10
Spencer	1,754	F 11
Spooner	2,365	D 8
Spread Eagle		C 14
Spring Green	1,265	J 11
Spring Lake		F 2
Spring Valley	987	F 8
Springbrook		C 9
Stanley	2,095	F 10
Star Prairie	420	E 7
Stephensville		E 3
Stetsonville	487	E 11
Steuben	175	J 10
Stevens Point	22,970.°	G 12
Stiles		C 5
Stitzer		J 10
Stockbridge	567	F 4
Stockholm	104	G 7
Stoddard	762	I 9
Stone Lake		C 9
Stoughton	7,589	J 2
Stratford	1,385	F 11
Strum	944	G 9
Sturgeon Bay	8,847.°	F 16
Sturtevant	4,130	K 5
Suamico		D 5
Sugar Camp		D 12
Sullivan	434	J 3
Summit Lake		E 13
Sun Prairie	12,931	I 2
Superior	29,571.°	A 8
Superior*	580	B 8
Suring	581	E 14
Sussex	3,482	I 4
Symco		D 2
Taycheedah		G 4
Taylor	411	G 9
Tennyson	476	K 10
Theresa	766	H 4
Thiensville	3,341	I 5
Thorp	1,635	F 10
Three Lakes		D 13
Tichigan Lake*	1,066	K 14
Tiffany		K 2
Tigerton	865	D 2
Tilleda		C 2
Tipler		C 14
Tisch Mills		E 6
Token Creek		I 1
Tomah	7,204	H 10
Tomahawk	3,527	D 12
Tony	146	D 10
Townsend		E 14
Trego		C 8
Trempealeau	956	H 9
Trevor		K 15
Troy Center*		K 14
Tunnel City		H 10
Turtle Lake	762	E 8
Tustin		F 2
Twin Lakes	3,474	K 14
Two Rivers	13,354	F 6
Underhill		C 4
Union Center	216	I 11
Union Grove	3,517	K 5
Unity	418	F 11
Upson		B 11
Valders	973	F 5
Valley Junction		H 11
Valmy		F 16
Van Dyne		G 3
Verona	3,336	J 1
Vesper	554	G 11
Victory		I 9
Viola	696	I 10
Viroqua	3,716.°	I 10
Wabeno		D 13
Waldo	416	G 5
Waldwick		K 11
Wales	1,992	J 4
Walworth	1,607	K 14
Warrens	300	G 10
Wascott		C 8
Washburn	2,080.°	B 10
Washington Island		E 16
Waterford	2,051	K 4
Waterloo	2,393	I 2
Watertown	18,113	J 14
Waubeka		H 5
Waukau		F 3
Waukesha	50,365.°	J 14
Waumandee		G 8
Waunakee	3,866	I 1
Waupaca	4,472.°	G 13
Waupun	8,132	H 3
Wausau	32,426.°	F 12
Wausau West[-Rib Mountain]	6,005	F 12
Wausaukee	648	E 15
Wautoma	1,629.°	H 12
Wauwatosa	51,308	J 5
Wauzeka	580	J 10
Wayne		H 4
Wayside		E 5
Webster	610	C 7
Wentworth		B 8
West Allis	63,982	J 5
West Baraboo	846	I 12
West Bend	21,484.°	I 14
West La Crosse		H 9
West Lima		I 10
West Milwaukee*	3,535	J 15
West Salem	3,276	H 9
Westboro		E 11
Westby	1,797	I 10
Westfield	1,033	G 1
Weston*	8,775	F 12
Weyauwega	1,549	E 2
Weyerhaeuser	313	D 9
Wheeler	231	E 8
White Creek		H 12
White Lake	309	E 13
Whitefish Bay	14,930	I 5
Whitehall	1,530.°	G 9
Whitelaw	649	F 5
Whitewater	11,520	J 3
Whiting	2,050	E 1
Wild Rose	741	F 1
Willard		F 10
Williams Bay	1,763	K 3
Wilmot		K 14
Wilson	155	F 8
Wilton	465	H 10
Winchester		C 11
Winchester		F 3
Wind Lake		J 4
Wind Point	1,695	K 5
Windsor		I 1
Winnebago	1,433	F 3
Winneconne	1,935	F 3
Winter	376	D 10
Wiota		K 11
Wisconsin Dells	2,521	I 12
Wisconsin Rapids	17,995.°	G 12
Withee	509	F 10
Wittenberg	997	C 2
Wonewoc	842	I 11
Woodford		K 12
Woodland		H 3
Woodman	116	J 10
Woodruff		C 12
Woodville	725	F 7
Woodworth		K 5
Wrightstown	1,169	E 4
Wyalusing		J 9
Wyeville	163	H 11
Wyocena	548	H 1
Yuba	72	I 11
Zachow		D 4
Zenda		K 14

*Does not appear on map; key shows general location.

°County seat.

Source: 1980 census. Places without population figures are unincorporated areas.

Wisconsin's natural beauty has made it a favorite vacation spot with tourists in all seasons. Millions of people visit the state each year. Vacationers enjoy Wisconsin's sparkling lakes, rolling hills, quiet valleys, and cool, pine-scented breezes. In spring and summer, hikers and cyclists enjoy the countryside. The winters are ideal for cross-country skiing, skating, and snowmobiling. The state is host to the Birkebeiner, North America's largest cross-country ski race. The National Snowmobile Derby takes place at Eagle River.

The city of Milwaukee offers a wide range of ethnic and music festivals. Summerfest, a music festival, offers live music of every type. Summer theaters in the state offer plays of all types, from off-Broadway to Shakespeare. During one week each August, Wittman Field in Oshkosh becomes the busiest airport in the United States, as the Experimental Aircraft Association holds its annual Fly-In.

Many communities in Wisconsin stage curling matches during the winter months, and others hold snowmobile derbies. Winnebago Indians perform colorful ceremonial dances at the Wisconsin Dells every evening from June to September. Many annual events celebrate the state's rich ethnic heritage and diversity.

Cameramann International, Ltd. from Marilyn Gartman

Door County, a popular vacation area

Places to visit

Apostle Islands, offshore from Bayfield, offer "deep-sea" fishing for trout and salmon. Anglers come from all parts of the country to try their luck.

Cave of the Mounds, between Mount Horeb and Blue Mounds, has hundreds of colorful stone formations in the cavern's 14 rooms.

Circus World Museum, in Baraboo, has a large collection of equipment used by U.S. circuses. Displays include items used by the Ringling brothers, who started their world-famous circus in Baraboo in 1884. Circus acts perform daily each summer.

Door County, on Door Peninsula, is a popular vacation spot. Tourists enjoy the picturesque countryside and visit the area's many resorts, beaches, fruit orchards, and arts and crafts shops.

House on the Rock is a 22-room home 11 miles (18 kilometers) north of Dodgeville. It sits atop a huge rock that rises 450 feet (137 meters). It has six fireplaces, seven pools, and many antiques and music boxes.

Little Norway, near Mount Horeb, was built in 1926. It preserves a Norwegian homestead of the early 1800's. The 160-acre (65-hectare) tract has several picturesque houses with Scandinavian pioneer furnishings.

Old World Wisconsin, near Eagle, is an outdoor museum that contains a number of houses and other structures built by Wisconsin immigrants of the 1800's.

Taliesin, near Spring Green, was the country estate of the American architect Frank Lloyd Wright. Tours of public buildings on the estate are available during the summer months.

Wisconsin Dells, in Adams, Columbia, Juneau, and Sauk counties, is one of the state's most beautiful regions. The Wisconsin River has cut a channel 7 miles (11 kilometers) long and 100 feet (30 meters) deep through soft sandstone. Weird formations have been carved out of the rock. They have such names as Devil's Elbow, Grand Piano, and Fat Man's Misery.

Parklands. The Ice Age National Scientific Reserve consists of several separate areas in southern and northwestern Wisconsin. The reserve is designed to preserve the features left on the land by the glaciers that once covered these parts of Wisconsin. The state also has a number of recreation areas managed by the National Park Service. For information on these areas, see the map and tables in the *World Book* article on **National Park System.**

National forests. Wisconsin has two national forests, both of which were established in 1933. Chequamegon National Forest lies in north-central Wisconsin. This forest has more than 170 lakes within its borders. Nicolet National Forest, in northeastern Wisconsin, has over 260 lakes. Both national forests offer hunting, fishing, and skiing.

State parks and forests. Wisconsin has 49 state parks, 9 state forests, and 10 state trails. For information on the state parks and forests, write to Wisconsin Division of Tourism, Box 7970, Madison, WI 53707.

Annual events

January-March
Ski-jumping tournaments in Middleton and Westby (January and February); World Championship Snowmobile Derby in Eagle River (January); American Birkebeiner Cross-Country Race at Telemark (February).

April-June
Syttende Mai Norwegian Festival in Stoughton, Westby, Woodville, and Grantsburg (May); Great Wisconsin Dells Balloon Rally in Wisconsin Dells (late May-early June); Fyr Bal Fest in Ephraim (June); Heidi Festival in New Glarus (June), Walleye Weekend in Fond du Lac (June).

July-September
Summerfest in Milwaukee (July); Sports car races at Road America near Elkhart Lake (July); Holland Festival in Cedar Grove (July); Lumberjack World Championship in Hayward (July); Cherry Harvest in Door County (July); Experimental Aircraft Association Fly-In in Oshkosh (July); Wisconsin State Fair in Milwaukee (August).

October-December
World Dairy Exposition in Madison (October); Fall Festival in Sister Bay (October); Holiday Folk Fair in Milwaukee (November).

Cameramann International, Ltd. from Marilyn Gartman

Experimental Aircraft Association Fly-In in Oshkosh

Joseph Rupp, West Stock

Rock climbing in Devil's Lake State Park

Wisconsin Division of Tourism

Ski-jumping tournament in Middleton

Hillstrom Stock Photo

A sightseeing boat in the Wisconsin Dells

Land and climate

Gene Ahrens, Shostal

The Mississippi River forms much of Wisconsin's western border with Minnesota and Iowa. Near Prairie du Chien, *above,* the river is broad and dotted with many islands.

Wisconsin is a land of rolling hills, ridges, fertile plains and valleys, and beautiful lakes. A series of glaciers that began about a million years ago traveled over most of present-day Wisconsin. The glaciers scraped hilltops, filled in valleys, and changed most of the surface. As the ice melted and the glaciers wasted away, they left thick deposits of earth materials. These deposits blocked drainage of the water, causing lakes, marshes, and streams with falls and rapids. Glaciers do not appear to have touched southwestern Wisconsin. Much of this portion of the state is rough, with steep-sided ridges and deep valleys.

Land regions. Wisconsin has five major land regions. They are (1) the Lake Superior Lowland, (2) the Northern Highland, or Superior Upland, (3) the Central Plain, (4) the Western Upland, and (5) the Eastern Ridges and Lowlands, or Great Lakes Plains.

The Lake Superior Lowland is a flat plain that slopes gently upward toward the south from Lake Superior. The plain ends from 5 to 20 miles (8 to 32 kilometers) inland at a steep cliff.

The Northern Highland covers most of northern Wisconsin. It slopes gradually downward toward the south. The region is a favorite vacationland because of its heavily forested hills and hundreds of small lakes. Timms

Hill, the state's highest point, rises 1,952 feet (595 meters) above sea level in Price County.

The Central Plain curves across the central part of the state. Glaciers covered the eastern and northwestern parts of this region. Much of the southern portion was not touched by glaciers. In this southern portion, the Wisconsin River has carved the scenic gorge called the Wisconsin Dells.

The Western Upland is one of the most attractive parts of Wisconsin. Steep slopes and winding ridges, untouched by glaciers, rise in the southwestern part of the region. Limestone and sandstone bluffs of breathtaking beauty stand along the Mississippi River.

The Eastern Ridges and Lowlands region extends from the Green Bay area southward to Illinois. Gently rolling plains of glacial material partly cover limestone ridges that run from north to south. This region is the richest agricultural section of Wisconsin. It has the state's largest areas of high-grade soil, and its longest growing season.

Shoreline of Wisconsin extends 381 miles (613 kilometers) along Lake Michigan and 292 miles (470 kilometers) along Lake Superior. Bluffs and sandy beaches line the Lake Michigan shore. Lake Superior's shoreline also has sandy beaches, but fewer rugged bluffs. Wisconsin's largest ports include Ashland, Green Bay, Manitowoc, Milwaukee, and Superior.

Rivers, waterfalls, and lakes. An east-west *divide* cuts across northern Wisconsin. This ridge of land separates short rivers that enter Lake Superior—such as the Bad, Montreal, and Nemadji rivers—from the longer rivers that flow southward—such as the Flambeau and St. Croix. A north-south divide runs down the eastern third

Land regions of Wisconsin

WORLD BOOK map

Map index

Apostle Islands ....A 3	Chippewa R. ....D 2	Lake Du Bay ....D 4	Military Ridge ....E 3	Spirit River
Baraboo Range ....E 4	Door Peninsula ....D 6	Lake Geneva ....F 5	Mississippi R. ....F 3	Flowage ....C 4
Baraboo R. ....E 3	Eau Claire R. ....D 2	Lake Koshkonong ......F 5	Outer Island ....A 3	Stockton Island ....B 3
Bayfield Ridge ....B 2	Flambeau R. ....C 2	Lake Mendota ....E 4	Pecatonica R. ....F 4	Superior Upland ....B 2
Big Eau Pleine	Fox R. ....D 5	Lake Michigan ....F 6	Penokee Range ....B 3	The Dells (cliffs) ....E 4
Reservoir ....D 4	Green Bay ....D 6	Lake Pepin ....D 1	Peshtigo R. ....C 5	Timms Hill (highest
Black R. ....D 3	Green Lake ....E 5	Lake Poygan ....D 5	Petenwell Lake ....D 4	point in Wisconsin) ....C 3
Blue Hills ....C 2	High Falls	Lake Superior ....A 4	Puckaway Lake ....E 4	Turtle Flambeau
Brute R. ....C 5	Reservoir ....C 5	Lake Winnebago ....D 5	Rainbow Flowage ....C 4	Flowage ....B 3
Caldron Falls	Holcombe Flowage .....C 2	Lake Wisconsin ....E 4	Rib Mountain ....D 4	Washington Island ......C 7
Reservoir ....C 5	Lac Courte Oreilles .....C 2	Lake Wissota ....D 2	Rock R. ....E 5	Willow Reservoir ....C 4
Castle Rock Lake ....E 4	La Crosse R. ....E 3	Madeline Island ....B 3	St. Croix R. ....C 1	Wisconsin R. ....E 3
Chequamegon Bay ......B 3	Lake Chippewa ....C 2	Menominee R. ....C 6	Shawano Lake ....D 5	Wolf R. ....D 5

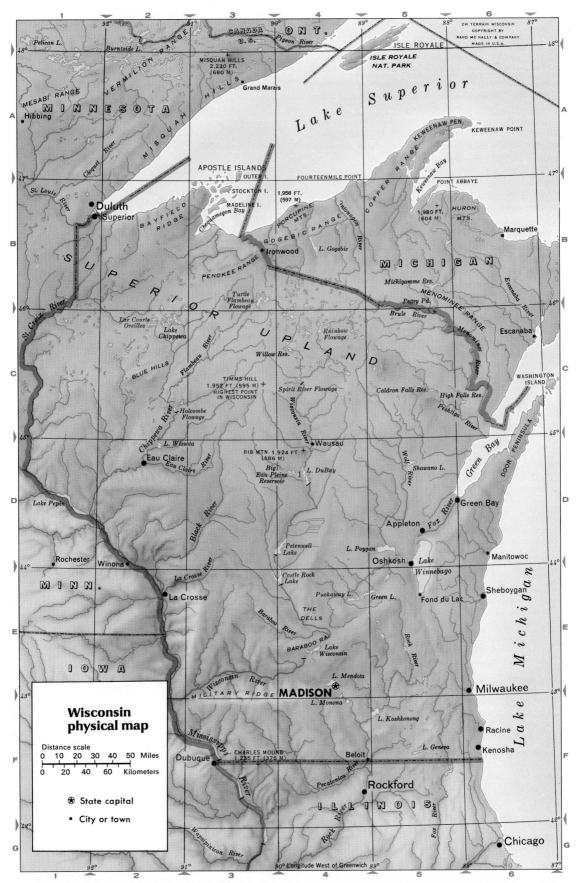

Wisconsin
physical map

Distance scale
0 10 20 30 40 50 Miles
0   20   40   60 Kilometers

✳ State capital
• City or town

Specially created for *The World Book Encyclopedia* by Rand McNally and World Book editors

of the state. West of this divide, the rivers flow into the Mississippi. These rivers include the Black, Chippewa, La Crosse, St. Croix, and Wisconsin. Streams east of the divide empty into Lake Michigan directly or through Green Bay. These rivers include the Fox, Menominee, Milwaukee, Oconto, and Peshtigo.

Wisconsin has hundreds of waterfalls. The highest is Big Manitou Falls in Pattison State Park, in the extreme northwest. The falls, located on the Black River, drop more than 165 feet (50 meters).

Wisconsin has about 15,000 lakes. Lake Winnebago, the state's largest lake, covers 215 square miles (557 square kilometers). Green Lake, more than 237 feet (72 meters) deep, is the deepest lake. Other large natural lakes include Butte des Morts, Geneva, Koshkonong, Mendota Pepin, Poygan, Puckaway, and Shawano. The chief artificially created lakes include Beaver Dam, Castle Rock, Chippewa, Du Bay, Flambeau, Petenwell, Wisconsin, and Wissota.

Average monthly weather

	Milwaukee					Green Bay				
	Temperatures				**Days of rain or snow**		**Temperatures**			**Days of rain or snow**
	F°		**C°**				**F°**		**C°**	
	High	Low	High	Low			High	Low	High	Low	
Jan.	29	15	−2	−9	10	Jan.	25	8	−4	−13	10
Feb.	32	17	0	−8	9	Feb.	26	9	−3	−13	9
Mar.	41	26	5	−3	11	Mar.	37	20	3	−7	11
Apr.	53	36	12	2	11	Apr.	52	32	11	0	11
May	64	45	18	7	13	May	65	44	18	7	12
June	75	55	24	13	11	June	75	54	24	12	11
July	81	61	27	16	9	July	81	59	27	15	10
Aug.	79	61	26	16	9	Aug.	79	57	26	14	10
Sept.	72	53	22	12	8	Sept.	70	50	21	10	9
Oct.	60	42	16	6	8	Oct.	58	39	14	4	8
Nov.	45	30	7	−1	10	Nov.	41	26	5	−3	9
Dec.	33	19	1	−7	10	Dec.	27	13	−3	−11	11

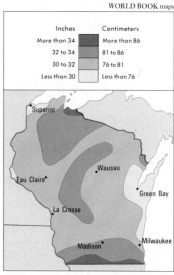

William Carter, Bruce Coleman Inc.

Horicon Marsh, north of Horicon, is a stopping place for thousands of Canada geese, ducks, and other waterfowl during their spring and fall migrations.

Plant and animal life. Forests cover almost half of Wisconsin. The state's softwood trees include balsam fir, hemlock, pine, spruce, tamarack, and white cedar. Hardwood trees include ash, aspen, basswood, elm, maple, oak, and yellow birch.

Blueberries, huckleberries, Juneberries, wild black currants, and other shrubs grow in parts of northern

Average January temperatures
Much of the state has long, severe winters. The southeastern section has the mildest temperatures in wintertime.

Average July temperatures
The southern and southwestern parts of the state have the warmest summers. The far north has the coolest summers.

Average yearly precipitation
Most of Wisconsin gets a fairly even amount of precipitation. The far north receives the heaviest snowfall.

WORLD BOOK maps

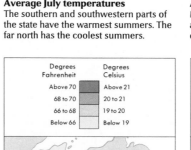

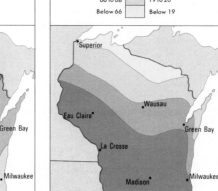

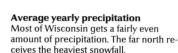

and central Wisconsin. Pink trailing arbutus blossoms over rocks and under trees in early spring. More than 20 kinds of violets bloom in all sections. In autumn, the Wisconsin countryside is a blaze of color. The red and gold tree leaves blend with brilliant asters, fireweeds, and goldenrods.

Bears, coyotes, deer, and foxes are found in Wisconsin's deep forests. Fur-bearing animals include beavers and muskrats. Badgers, gophers, and prairie mice scurry through the underbrush. Other animals found in Wisconsin include chipmunks, porcupines, raccoons, and woodchucks.

Wisconsin's northern lakes and streams abound with such game fish as bass, muskellunge, pickerel, pike, sturgeon, and trout. Game birds include ducks, geese, jacksnipes, partridges, pheasants, ruffed grouse, and woodcocks. Loons and other waterfowl breed on the northern lakes. The marshes shelter bitterns, black terns, and coots. Other birds include chickadees, nuthatches, robins, snipes, swallows, warblers, and wrens.

Climate. Wisconsin usually has warm summers and long, severe winters. Lake Michigan and Lake Superior make summers somewhat cooler and winters slightly milder along the shores. Average January temperatures range from 12° F. (−11° C) in the northwest to 22° F. (−6° C) in the southeast. Danbury recorded the state's lowest temperature, −54° F. (−48° C), on Jan. 24, 1922. Average July temperatures range from 69° F. (21° C) in the north to 73° F. (23° C) in the south. The state's record high, 114° F. (46° C), was set at Wisconsin Dells on July 13, 1936.

Wisconsin's *precipitation* (rain, melted snow, and other forms of moisture) averages about 31 inches (79 centimeters) a year. Annual snowfall averages from over 100 inches (250 centimeters) in northern Iron County to about 30 inches (76 centimeters) in southern Wisconsin.

Economy

Service industries, taken together, make up about two-thirds of Wisconsin's *gross state product*—the total value of all goods and services produced in a state in a year. However, manufacturing is the single most important economic activity. It accounts for more than a fourth of the gross state product.

Natural resources of Wisconsin include rich soil, plentiful water, minerals, and vast forests.

Soil. Southeastern, southern, and western Wisconsin are the state's best agricultural areas. These areas have mostly gray-brown forest soils. They also have scattered sections of dark prairie soils. In northern Wisconsin, soils are less fertile and often contain too much acid.

Water. Wisconsin has 1,690 square miles (4,377 square kilometers) of inland water in addition to its outlying waters of Lake Michigan and Lake Superior. These two Great Lakes and the Mississippi River provide inexpensive transportation. Wisconsin's thousands of lakes help make the state a popular vacationland. Rainfall is abundant, and little water is needed for irrigation.

Minerals. Almost every Wisconsin county has sand and gravel. Stone, including dolomite and granite, is also valuable. Dolomite is found mainly in the southern part of the state and granite in the central and northern sections. Iron ore is found in Jackson County, and there are large deposits also in Ashland and Iron counties. Deposits of lead and zinc are found in Grant, Iowa, and Lafayette counties. Sulfide deposits containing large amounts of copper and zinc are in Forest, Oneida, and Rusk counties. Few of the metal ore deposits have been developed because they are expensive to mine. The state's other minerals include peat and quartzite.

Forests cover almost half the state. Hardwood trees make up about 80 per cent of the forests. Most of the woodlands have second-growth trees. The most valuable hardwoods found in Wisconsin include ash, aspen, basswood, elm, maple, oak, and yellow birch. Softwoods include balsam fir, hemlock, pine, spruce, tamarack, and white-cedar.

Service industries account for 65 per cent of the gross state product. Most of Wisconsin's service industries are concentrated in its 13 metropolitan areas.

Finance, insurance, and real estate together form the leading service industry in terms of Wisconsin's gross state product. The large sums of money involved in the buying and selling of homes and other property make real estate the largest part of this industry. Milwaukee ranks as one of the Midwest's major financial centers. It is the home of Wisconsin's two largest banking companies, Firstar and Marshall & Ilsley. One of the biggest insurance companies in the United States, Northwestern Mutual Life, is also based in Milwaukee. Madison and Green Bay are also important centers of finance.

Wholesale and retail trade ranks second among the service industries in terms of Wisconsin's gross state product. This industry is also the leading employer among service industries. Wholesale trade companies buy goods from producers and sell them to other businesses. Important wholesale trade products in Wisconsin include farm products, groceries, and machinery.

Production and workers by economic activities

Economic activities	Per cent of GSP* produced	Employed workers Number of persons	Per cent of total
Manufacturing	28	514,500	24
Finance, insurance, & real estate	18	108,100	5
Wholesale & retail trade	15	477,200	22
Community, social, & personal services	14	434,900	20
Government	10	325,600	15
Transportation, communication, & utilities	8	93,700	4
Agriculture	4	141,400	7
Construction	3	68,000	3
Mining	†	1,900	†
Total	100	2,165,300	100

*GSP = gross state product, the total value of goods and services produced in a year.
†Less than one-half of 1 per cent.
Figures are for 1986.
Sources: *World Book* estimates based on data from U.S. Bureau of Economic Analysis, U.S. Bureau of Labor Statistics, and U.S. Department of Agriculture.

Cameramann International, Ltd.

Dairy products are a major part of Wisconsin's economy. Swiss cheese is made at this factory in Monroe. Wisconsin ranks among the nation's top producers of milk, cheese, and butter.

Roundy's, one of the leading U.S. wholesale grocery companies, has its headquarters in Pewaukee. Retail trade businesses sell goods to consumers. The major types of retail businesses in Wisconsin include automobile dealerships, discount stores, and food stores.

Community, social, and personal services rank third in gross state product. This industry consists of a variety of businesses, including doctors' offices and private hospitals, law firms, hotels and resorts, and repair shops. Many resort areas lie along the shores of Wisconsin's lakes and in the northern woods.

Government is Wisconsin's fourth-ranking service industry. Government services include public schools and hospitals, military establishments, and Indian reservations. The public school system employs many people. The University of Wisconsin is one of the largest university systems in the nation. Its medical center, located near the Madison campus, is one of the state's leading health care facilities. Several Indian reservations lie in the northern part of the state.

Transportation, communication, and utilities make up the remaining service industries in Wisconsin. Many shipping and trucking companies are based in Milwaukee. Telephone companies form the most important part of the communications sector. Utilities include electric, gas, and water service. For more information, see the headings *Transportation* and *Communication* in this section of the article.

Manufacturing accounts for 28 per cent of Wisconsin's gross state product. Goods made in the state have a *value added by manufacture* of about $29 billion yearly. This figure represents the increase in value of raw materials after they become finished products.

Machinery is Wisconsin's leading manufactured product in terms of value added by manufacture. Southeastern Wisconsin is one of the leading U.S. centers of machinery production. The main types of machinery made in the state include engines and turbines, power cranes and other construction machinery, heating and cooling equipment, and metalworking machinery.

Food products are the state's second-ranking manufactured product. Wisconsin produces more butter than any other state. Its cheese factories make about a third of the cheese produced in the United States. Wisconsin also ranks high among the states in the production of ice cream and evaporated and dried milk. Plants that process dairy products are located throughout most of the state. Cudahy, Green Bay, and Madison have large meat-packing plants. Factories in Green Bay and other cities can huge amounts of the state's vegetable and fruit crops. Wisconsin is a leader in canning peas, sweet corn, beets, snap beans, lima beans, cranberries, and sour cherries. It is also a leader in the production of beer. Milwaukee, La Crosse, and many other cities in Wisconsin produce beer.

Paper products are third in value. Paper products include typing paper, cardboard boxes, tissue paper, paper bags, and adhesive tape. The state's leading paper-producing areas are the lower Fox River Valley and the upper Wisconsin River Valley. Fort Howard Paper Company has its headquarters in Green Bay.

The production of electrical equipment is the fourth most important manufacturing activity in Wisconsin.

Wisconsin Division of Tourism

Paper mills operate in Wisconsin mainly in the lower Fox River Valley and the upper Wisconsin River Valley. Wisconsin is a leading manufacturer of paper and paperboard products.

Farm, mineral, and forest products

This map shows where the state's leading farm, mineral, and forest products are produced. The major urban areas (shown on the map in red) are the state's important manufacturing centers.

WORLD BOOK map

Chief electrical products include distributing equipment, household appliances, industrial controls, and motors and generators. Johnson Controls, a leading manufacturer of environmental controls for buildings, is based in Milwaukee. The Appleton-Oshkosh and Racine areas are also electrical equipment centers.

Fabricated metal products, including knives and hardware, metal cans, and metal forgings and stampings, rank next in value. Manitowoc, Milwaukee, and Racine make large amounts of metal products.

Other types of products manufactured in Wisconsin include, in order of value, printed materials, transportation equipment, and wood products. The state's major cities produce newspapers and large quantities of printed materials for businesses. Motor vehicles and motor vehicle parts are the main types of transportation equipment made in Wisconsin. The northern part of the state has many sawmills.

Agriculture contributes 4 per cent of the gross state product. The state has about 82,000 farms. Farms and pastures cover about half of Wisconsin.

Dairying is the most important type of farming in Wisconsin. The dairy industry started about 1870. It was encouraged through the efforts of many people, especially William Dempster Hoard. Hoard helped organize the Wisconsin Dairymen's Association in 1872. The association did much to improve and promote Wisconsin dairy products. Later, it urged farmers to work together and to market their products cooperatively. Today, about 500 farm cooperatives have headquarters in Wisconsin (see **Cooperative**).

Wisconsin leads the states in milk production, and milk provides 60 per cent of Wisconsin's farm income. The largest concentration of dairy cattle within the state lies in the region between Green Bay and Monroe. The region around Eau Claire also has many dairy farms.

Beef cattle and hogs rank as Wisconsin's second and third most important livestock products, after milk. Southwestern Wisconsin has the largest concentration of cattle and hog farms. Southeastern Wisconsin is the most important region for egg and chicken farms.

Farmers in all regions of the state raise hay for livestock feed. Corn is fed to hogs, and oats, hay, and corn are fed to cattle. Other field crops raised in Wisconsin include barley, soybeans, tobacco, and wheat.

Wisconsin is an important producer of vegetables and fruits. It leads the states in the production of beets, green peas, and snap beans. Wisconsin is also a chief producer of cabbages, cucumbers, lima beans, potatoes, and sweet corn. Most of the vegetables raised in the state are sent to canneries. Wisconsin ranks among the leading states in growing cranberries. The state's farmers also raise raspberries, strawberries, and other small fruits.

Mining accounts for less than 1 per cent of the gross state product. Two mineral products, crushed stone and sand and gravel, account for most of the state's mining income. Both of these products are used primarily in the construction industry.

Electric power. Plants that burn coal provide about 70 per cent of the electric power generated in Wisconsin. Nuclear plants supply about 25 per cent. Most of the remaining power comes from hydroelectric plants. One of the first hydroelectric plants in the nation was built in Appleton on the Fox River in 1882.

Transportation. Many of Wisconsin's first settlers traveled up the Mississippi River in flat-bottomed boats called *bateaux.* Later settlers came by steamboat up the Mississippi River, by ship on Lake Michigan, and overland by wagon. Mississippi River traffic declined with the growth of railroads. Great Lakes transportation increased following the opening of the St. Lawrence Seaway in 1959.

The first railroad in Wisconsin was opened in 1851. It

ran between Milwaukee and Waukesha, a distance of about 20 miles (32 kilometers). Today, six railroads provide freight service in Wisconsin. Passenger trains serve about 10 cities.

Milwaukee has Wisconsin's busiest airport. Madison and Green Bay also have major airports.

Wisconsin has about 108,000 miles (174,000 kilometers) of roads and highways. About 95 per cent are surfaced. In 1917, Wisconsin became the first state to adopt the number system for highways. Other states soon adopted the system.

Wisconsin's major ports are at Superior, Green Bay, and Milwaukee. Superior shares port facilities with Duluth, Minn. Green Bay handles mostly U.S. cargo. International cargo passes mainly through Milwaukee.

A canal located at Sturgeon Bay links Green Bay and Lake Michigan. An automobile ferry operates between Kewaunee and Ludington, Mich.

Communication. Wisconsin's first newspaper, the *Green-Bay Intelligencer,* was founded in 1833. Today,

Wisconsin publishers issue about 325 newspapers, of which about 35 are dailies. Daily newspapers with the largest circulations include the *Green Bay Press Gazette,* the *Milwaukee Journal,* the *Milwaukee Sentinel,* and the *Wisconsin State Journal* of Madison. Wisconsin publishers also issue about 180 periodicals.

In 1853, the Wisconsin Press Association was founded. It was the nation's first state news service. The association, now the Wisconsin Newspaper Association, collects and distributes news among member newspapers. It has a membership of about 240 weekly papers and 38 dailies.

The history of radio in Wisconsin dates from 1909. That year, University of Wisconsin scientists conducted wireless experiments. The university radio station was licensed as 9XM in 1916, and the station became WHA in 1922. The state's first television station, WTMJ-TV, started broadcasting from Milwaukee in 1947. Wisconsin now has about 260 radio stations and about 40 television stations.

Government

Constitution. Wisconsin is still governed under its original Constitution, adopted in 1848. Only six other states are governed under older constitutions. An amendment to Wisconsin's Constitution may be proposed in either house of the state Legislature. The amendment then must be approved by a majority of each house in two successive legislative sessions. Next, it must be approved by a majority of the persons who vote on the amendment. The Constitution may also be amended by a constitutional convention. A proposal to call such a convention must be approved by a majority of the Legislature and by a majority of the persons voting on the proposal.

Executive. The governor of Wisconsin holds office for a four-year term and can serve an unlimited number of terms.

The lieutenant governor, secretary of state, attorney general, treasurer, and state superintendent of public instruction are also elected by the people to serve four-year terms. The governor of Wisconsin appoints about 20 full-time state officers and numerous part-time officers who serve as members of state boards and commissions.

Legislature consists of a Senate of 33 members and an Assembly of 99 members. Voters in each of Wisconsin's 33 senatorial districts elect one senator to a four-year term. One representative from each of 99 districts is elected to the Assembly. Representatives serve two-year terms.

Regular sessions of the Legislature begin in January of odd-numbered years. There is no time limit on the legislative sessions. The governor may call special sessions of the Legislature. Such sessions also have no time limit.

Courts. The highest court in Wisconsin is the state Supreme Court. It has seven justices, elected to 10-year terms. The justice who has been on the court for the longest time serves as the chief justice. Other Wisconsin courts include an appellate court and circuit courts. The people elect the judges of these courts to six-year terms.

Wisconsin Legislature

The Wisconsin Legislature consists of an Assembly of 99 members and a Senate of 33 members. The Assembly meets in chambers in the State Capitol in Madison, *above.*

All Wisconsin judges are elected on *nonpartisan ballots* (ballots without political party labels). In 1966, Wisconsin abolished the office of justice of the peace.

Local government. Wisconsin has 72 counties. A board of elected supervisors governs each county in the state. The supervisors select one of their members as head of the board. Other county officials in Wisconsin include the sheriff, treasurer, surveyor, coroner, and district attorney. Eight Wisconsin counties elect a county executive.

Wisconsin law allows cities and villages to operate under the mayor, manager, or commissioner form of government. A few cities and villages have the manager form. All the rest have the mayor-council form of government.

Revenue. Taxation brings in more than 60 per cent of the state government's *general revenue* (income). Much of the rest comes from federal grants and other U.S. government programs. Individual and corporation income taxes provide about half of the state's tax revenue. A general sales tax is another leading source of revenue in Wisconsin. Motor-fuel taxes and motor-vehicle license fees are used for highway construction and maintenance. Other important sources of revenue include taxes on property and public utilities.

Politics. The majority of the voters in Milwaukee, Madison, and other urban centers in the state are Democrats. Republican strength lies mainly in Wisconsin's rural areas. Throughout most of its history, Wisconsin has strongly favored the Republican Party. In fact, a meeting at a Ripon schoolhouse in 1854 contributed to the founding of the party. About three times as many Republicans as Democrats have served as governor of the state. Republicans also dominated the state legislature and Wisconsin's congressional delegations until the late 1950's. Then the state began sending more Democrats than Republicans to Congress. Since 1958, Democrats have also won the governorship several times. In the state legislature, Democrats have controlled the Assembly since 1971 and the Senate since 1975.

In presidential elections, Wisconsin has supported the Republican candidate more than twice as often as the Democratic candidate. In the 1924 presidential election, Wisconsin cast its votes for a native son, Senator Robert M. La Follette, Sr., who ran unsuccessfully as a Progressive. For the state's voting record in presidential elections since 1848, see **Electoral College** (table).

The governors of Wisconsin

	Party	Term		Party	Term
Nelson Dewey	Democratic	1848-1852	Francis E. McGovern	Republican	1911-1915
Leonard J. Farwell	Whig	1852-1854	Emanuel L. Philipp	Republican	1915-1921
William A. Barstow	Democratic	1854-1856	John J. Blaine	Republican	1921-1927
Arthur MacArthur	Democratic	1856	Fred R. Zimmerman	Republican	1927-1929
Coles Bashford	Republican	1856-1858	Walter J. Kohler, Sr.	Republican	1929-1931
Alexander W. Randall	Republican	1858-1862	Philip F. La Follette	Republican	1931-1933
Louis P. Harvey	Republican	1862	Albert G. Schmedeman	Democratic	1933-1935
Edward Salomon	Republican	1862-1864	Philip F. La Follette	Progressive	1935-1939
James T. Lewis	Republican	1864-1866	Julius P. Heil	Republican	1939-1943
Lucius Fairchild	Republican	1866-1872	Walter S. Goodland	Republican	1943-1947
Cadwallader C. Washburn	Republican	1872-1874	Oscar Rennebohm	Republican	1947-1951
William R. Taylor	Democratic	1874-1876	Walter J. Kohler, Jr.	Republican	1951-1957
Harrison Ludington	Republican	1876-1878	Vernon W. Thomson	Republican	1957-1959
William E. Smith	Republican	1878-1882	Gaylord A. Nelson	Democratic	1959-1963
Jeremiah McLain Rusk	Republican	1882-1889	John W. Reynolds	Democratic	1963-1965
William D. Hoard	Republican	1889-1891	Warren P. Knowles	Republican	1965-1971
George W. Peck	Democratic	1891-1895	Patrick J. Lucey	Democratic	1971-1977
William H. Upham	Republican	1895-1897	Martin J. Schreiber	Democratic	1977-1979
Edward Scofield	Republican	1897-1901	Lee S. Dreyfus	Republican	1979-1983
Robert M. La Follette, Sr.	Republican	1901-1906	Anthony S. Earl	Democratic	1983-1987
James O. Davidson	Republican	1906-1911	Tommy G. Thompson	Republican	1987-

History

Indian days. The Winnebago, Dakota, and Menominee Indians lived in the Wisconsin region when the first white explorers came in the early 1600's. These Indians were skilled craftworkers. They lived in lodges made of bark, saplings, and rushes. They fished and hunted, and grew corn, beans, and squash. The Winnebago lived in the area between Green Bay and Lake Winnebago. The Dakota lived in the northwestern part of the region. The Menominee lived west and north of Green Bay.

Many other tribes moved into the Wisconsin area during the later 1600's. Some had been driven from their eastern homes by white people. Others fled into the region to escape the warring Iroquois League. The Chippewa came from the northeast and settled along the southern shore of Lake Superior. Other tribes came from the Michigan region. The Sauk settled west of Green Bay, the Fox along the Fox River, and the Ottawa along the southern shore of Lake Superior. The Kickapoo made their home in the south-central area, and the Huron in the northwestern section. Bands of Miami and Illinois Indians spread along the upper Fox River. The Potawatomi camped in what is now Door County. See **Indian, American** (table of tribes).

Exploration and settlement. In 1634, the French explorer Jean Nicolet became the first white person to set foot in the Wisconsin area. He landed on the shore of Green Bay while seeking a water route to China. Nicolet stepped ashore wearing a colorful robe and firing two pistols. He was disappointed when Winnebago Indians, not Chinese officials, greeted him. Nicolet returned to New France (Quebec), and reported that America was far vaster than anyone had imagined.

About 25 years later, Pierre Esprit Radisson and Médard Chouart, Sieur des Groseilliers, explored the Wisconsin area while searching for furs. The first missionary to the Wisconsin Indians, Father René Ménard, arrived about 1660. He established a Roman Catholic mission near present-day Ashland. Father Claude Jean Allouez came to Wisconsin about 1665 and set up several missions. With the help of Father Louis André, he established a center for missionary work on the site of present-day De Pere. Other French explorers and missionaries who visited the area included Louis Jolliet, Father Jacques Marquette, and Robert Cavelier, Sieur de la Salle.

Struggle for control. From the time of Nicolet's visit, the French had friendly relations with most of the Wisconsin Indian tribes. But in 1712, a long war broke out between the French and the Fox Indians. Both wanted control of the Fox and Wisconsin rivers, the region's chief water route. After many bloody battles, the French finally defeated the Fox in 1740. But the long war had weakened France's defenses in the region. France also lost the friendship of many former Indian allies.

In 1754, the French and Indian War began. This war was fought between Great Britain and France over rival claims in America. Britain won the war. Under the terms of the 1763 Treaty of Paris, France lost Canada and almost all its possessions east of the Mississippi River. Control of the Wisconsin region thus passed to the British. See **French and Indian wars** (The French and Indian War).

English fur traders took over the fur-trading posts of the French. In 1774, the British passed the Quebec Act. Under this act, Wisconsin became part of the province of Quebec. The Quebec Act was one of the causes of the revolt by the American colonies against Britain in 1775. The 1783 Treaty of Paris ended the American Revolutionary War. Under the treaty, Britain gave up all its territory east of the Mississippi and south of the Great Lakes. The Wisconsin region then became part of the United States.

Territorial days. Wisconsin formed part of the Indiana Territory from 1800 to 1809, part of the Illinois Territory from 1809 to 1818, and part of the Michigan Territory from 1818 to 1836. Settlement of southwestern Wisconsin began during the 1820's. This region had rich deposits of lead ore. In the 1820's, the demand for lead for use in making paint and shot rose sharply. Lead miners from nearby states and territories poured into the region, and the population boomed. Some of the miners lived in shelters they dug out of the hillsides. These miners were nicknamed *Badgers,* which, in time, became the nickname of all Wisconsinites.

The Indians made their last stand in Wisconsin against white people in the Black Hawk War of 1832. The Sauk Indians of northwestern Illinois had been pushed across the Mississippi River into Iowa by the arrival of white settlers. Black Hawk, a Sauk leader, wanted to return to his homeland and grow corn. In April 1832, he led a thousand Indians back across the Mississippi. The white settlers panicked, and volunteer militia and regular troops were called out. Black Hawk's Indians retreated into Wisconsin, where several bloody battles were fought. When the war ended in August, only about 150 Indians were left.

On April 20, 1836, Congress created the Wisconsin Territory. The territorial legislature met temporarily in Belmont and later in Burlington (now in Iowa). The first meeting in Madison, the capital of the territory and later of the state, took place in 1838. The Wisconsin Territory included parts of present-day Minnesota, Iowa, and North and South Dakota. President Andrew Jackson appointed Henry Dodge as the first territorial governor. Congress created the Iowa Territory in 1838. Wisconsin's western boundary then became the Mississippi

River, with a northward extension to Lake of the Woods in present-day Minnesota. About a third of the present state of Minnesota remained part of Wisconsin until 1848.

Statehood. Wisconsin joined the Union as the 30th state on May 29, 1848. Its boundaries were set as they are today. The people had already approved a constitution. They elected Nelson Dewey, a Democrat, as the first governor. In 1840, 30,945 white persons lived in Wisconsin. By 1850, the population had soared to 305,391. Newcomers came from other parts of the United States and from other countries. All saw opportunities for a better life in frontier Wisconsin.

In 1854, Wisconsin citizens became aroused over the introduction of the Kansas-Nebraska Bill in Congress. This bill was designed to allow the new territories of Kansas and Nebraska to decide for themselves whether they wished to permit slavery. Most Wisconsinites opposed slavery and did not want it extended to new territories. A group of Wisconsinites held a protest meeting against the bill in Ripon in February 1854. This meeting contributed to the development of the Republican Party. See **Kansas-Nebraska Act.**

The Republican Party quickly became a powerful force in the North. Wisconsin's first Republican governor, Coles Bashford, took office in 1856. For the next hundred years, except for brief periods, the Republicans controlled the state government.

During the Civil War (1861-1865), Wisconsin generals at various times commanded the Iron Brigade, one of the Union's outstanding fighting groups. The brigade consisted largely of Wisconsin regiments.

In 1871, Wisconsin was struck by the worst natural disaster in its history—the great Peshtigo forest fire. The summer and fall of 1871 were extremely dry, and many small fires broke out at various places in northeastern Wisconsin. Then, on the night of October 8, northeastern Wisconsin erupted in flame. The fire wiped out the town of Peshtigo and several villages. The fire also spread into Michigan. About 1,200 persons were killed, 900 more than the number of persons killed in the Great Chicago Fire, which occurred that same night. The fire destroyed more than $5 million worth of property.

The Progressive Era. During the 1890's, a split developed in the Republican Party in Wisconsin. The party had been controlled by political bosses who represented lumber and railroad interests. Robert M. La Follette, Sr., a Madison lawyer and former U.S. congressman, began to lead a movement to overthrow the rule by bosses.

La Follette won the Wisconsin governorship in 1900. He was reelected in 1902 and 1904. Under "Fighting Bob," the state made important social, political, and economic reforms. La Follette's program was called *Progressivism.* La Follette set up a "brain trust" of University of Wisconsin professors and experts on government to advise him on state problems. The brain trust was part of the "Wisconsin Idea." This was the theory that the state should be served by its best minds and its best experts in legislation and administration. Measures adopted under La Follette included an inheritance tax, a railroad property tax, regulation of railroad rates and service, and a direct primary law (see **Primary election**). La Follette entered the U.S. Senate in 1906 and served

Historic Wisconsin

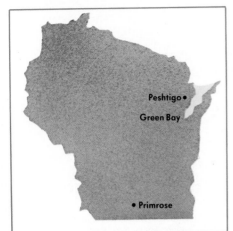

Peshtigo•
Green Bay

• Primrose

Jean Nicolet, the first explorer to enter Wisconsin, landed at Green Bay in 1634 while seeking a Northwest Passage to China.

The Black Hawk War was fought in Wisconsin in 1832. Chief Black Hawk and his Sauk Indians were defeated after many bloody battles.

"Battling Bob" La Follette of Wisconsin ran for President as the nominee of the Progressive Party in 1924.

The Peshtigo forest fire swept through northeastern Wisconsin on the night of Oct. 8, 1871. About 1,200 people were killed, 900 more than the number who died in the Great Chicago Fire, which occurred the same night.

The University of Wisconsin System, created in 1971, merged state facilities that include 13 universities, 14 two-year campuses, and an extension system. Administrative offices are in Madison.

WORLD BOOK illustrations by Kevin Chadwick

Important dates in Wisconsin

1634 Jean Nicolet, a French explorer, landed on the Green Bay shore.
c. 1670 Fathers Claude Jean Allouez and Louis André founded a missionary center at De Pere.
1673 Louis Jolliet and Father Jacques Marquette traveled through the Wisconsin region.
1740 The French defeated the Fox Indians.
1763 England received the Wisconsin region from France under terms of the Treaty of Paris.
1783 Wisconsin became part of the United States.
1836 Congress created the Wisconsin Territory.
1848 Wisconsin became the 30th state on May 29.
1871 About 1,200 persons were killed in a forest fire that destroyed Peshtigo and nearby villages.
1872 William D. Hoard and others organized the Wisconsin Dairymen's Association.
1901 Robert M. La Follette, Sr., became governor, and the Progressive era began.

1911 The state legislature set up a teachers' pension, established a commission to settle labor disputes, and passed other progressive legislation.
1924 Robert M. La Follette, Sr., was defeated as the Progressive Party candidate for President of the United States.
1932 Wisconsin passed the first state unemployment-compensation act.
1958 Gaylord Nelson became the first Democrat to win election as governor since 1932.
1964 Wisconsin became the first state to have its legislative districts reapportioned by its supreme court.
1971 The state legislature created a state university system—the University of Wisconsin System.
1987 Wisconsin adopted a state lottery to increase government revenues.

there until 1925. See **La Follette** (Robert Marion La Follette, Sr.).

In 1911, the Wisconsin legislature passed the Workmen's Compensation Act to protect workers injured in accidents. That same year, the legislature established the Wisconsin Industrial Commission to enforce industrial safety codes. Both measures were inspired by Professor John R. Commons of the University of Wisconsin. Other progressive reforms approved by the 1911 legislature included a state income tax law, the state life insurance fund, and forest and waterpower conservation laws.

In 1924, La Follette ran for President as the Progressive Party candidate. President Calvin Coolidge, a Republican, won the election. La Follette received the electoral votes of only one state—Wisconsin. But he got almost 5 million popular votes. La Follette died in 1925, and his eldest son, Robert, Jr., was elected to fill his Senate seat. Young La Follette served in the Senate for 21 years.

The 1930's. In 1930, Philip F. La Follette, the youngest son of Robert M. La Follette, Sr., was elected governor. La Follette, a Republican, lost the governorship in 1932. But he was reelected in 1934 and 1936 as a Progressive. Much of the legislation enacted under La Follette sought to relieve the suffering caused by the Great Depression of the 1930's. In 1932, under his administration, the first state unemployment-compensation act was passed.

In the spring of 1938, La Follette tried to organize a new national third party, the National Progressives of America. But he won little support. The voters rejected La Follette in 1938 and elected Julius P. Heil, a Republican, to the governorship of the state. Heil worked to cut government costs. He did away with many agencies that La Follette had set up while in office. Heil was reelected in 1940.

The mid-1900's. After World War II (1939-1945), Wisconsin agriculture, long the state's top-ranking industry, began to decline in importance to the economy. At the same time, the importance of manufacturing increased. Heavy beef imports from other countries, in addition to low milk prices, hurt agriculture in the state. Changes in the American diet, with emphasis on low-calorie foods, lowered the demand for dairy products. Between 1951 and 1969, the number of Wisconsin dairy farms fell from about 132,000 to 63,000. A number of cheese factories, creameries, and other processing plants closed. Many small farms merged, and the use of farm machinery increased. All these changes reduced the need for farmworkers in Wisconsin, and the population began to shift from farms to cities.

In politics, La Follette Progressivism declined. After 21 years in the U.S. Senate, Robert M. La Follette, Jr., lost the 1946 primary election to Republican Joseph R. McCarthy. McCarthy won election to the Senate that year. He later became one of the most controversial figures in American politics because of his unsupported charges that Communists dominated the U.S. Department of State.

After 26 years of Republican or Progressive control of the state government, Democrat Gaylord A. Nelson won the governorship in 1958. He was reelected in 1960. In 1962, Nelson ran for the U.S. Senate and defeated Re-

State Historical Society of Wisconsin

The Treaty of Butte des Morts was signed on this site in 1827. The treaty adjusted the boundaries of territories held by Chippewa, Menominee, and Winnebago Indians in Wisconsin.

publican Alexander Wiley, who had been a senator since 1939. Nelson won reelection to the senate in 1968 and in 1974.

In 1962, Wisconsin voters elected another Democratic governor, John W. Reynolds. But in 1964, they chose Republican Warren P. Knowles. Knowles was reelected in 1966 and 1968. Also in 1964, the voters elected Bronson La Follette, grandson of Robert M. La Follette, Sr., as state attorney general.

During the 1960's, Governors Nelson and Reynolds battled with the Republican-controlled legislature over *reapportionment* (redivision) of the state's legislative and congressional districts. The Wisconsin Constitution requires that the districts be redrawn every 10 years, if necessary, to provide fair representation. Both Nelson and Reynolds vetoed reapportionment bills passed by the legislature. They said the bills did not make the districts equal in terms of population. In 1963, the legislature passed a bill that reapportioned the state's 10 congressional districts. Reynolds signed this bill, but he and the legislature could not agree on a bill for the legislative districts. Finally, in 1964, the Wisconsin Supreme Court drew up a reapportionment plan. This was the first time any state supreme court had reapportioned a state legislature. The court's plan went into effect with the 1964 elections.

In 1969, the state assembly cut Governor Knowles's recommended welfare program for Wisconsin's urban areas. A group of protesters occupied the assembly chamber for 11 hours until they were removed by police.

The need for money to pay for education, public welfare, and other programs resulted in state tax increases during the 1960's. The state legislature also passed a law, in 1961, that established the first sales tax in Wisconsin's history. In 1963, the legislature increased the number of items covered by the sales tax.

During the mid-1900's, Wisconsin expanded its educational facilities. Between 1956 and 1970, the University of Wisconsin opened 15 new branches throughout the state.

Recent developments. Officials of the University of Wisconsin tightened their control over student activities in the 1970's. In 1969, following several student disorders on the Madison campus, the state legislature passed laws to control such disturbances. These laws established fines and imprisonment for campus misconduct. In 1971, the state legislature merged the University of Wisconsin and Wisconsin State University to form a state university system called the University of Wisconsin System.

Manufacturing, with the help of the Wisconsin Department of Development, remains strong in the state.

But agriculture continues to be vital to the economy of Wisconsin. Although dairying still provides the most agricultural income, income from crops is increasing. However, farms in Wisconsin continue to decrease in number and increase in size.

Wisconsin today faces a number of other challenges. These problems include increasing costs for education, welfare, control of water pollution, and the purchase of land for recreational purposes. The state is also concerned with problems related to agriculture, such as the huge debt of its farmers and the need to develop exports. In 1987, Wisconsin adopted a state lottery as a means of increasing government revenues.

Gary C. Meyer and Benjamin D. Rhodes

Study aids

Related articles in *World Book* include:

Biographies

Andrews, Roy Chapman	Nicolet, Jean
Berger, Victor L.	O'Keeffe, Georgia
Catt, Carrie Chapman	Proxmire, William
Ferber, Edna	Raskin, Ellen
Gale, Zona	Ringling brothers
Jolliet, Louis	Schurz (family)
Kennan, George F.	Slayton, Donald Kent
La Follette (family)	Turner, Frederick J.
Laird, Melvin R.	Welles, Orson
Lunt, Alfred	Wilder, Thornton N.
Marquette, Jacques	Wright, Frank Lloyd
McCarthy, Joseph R.	

Cities

La Crosse	Milwaukee
Madison	

History

Northwest Territory	Westward movement
Republican Party	Winnebago Indians

Physical features

Great Lakes	Wisconsin River
Mississippi River	

Outline

I. People
 A. Population
 B. Schools
 C. Libraries
 D. Museums
II. Visitor's guide
 A. Places to visit
 B. Annual events
III. Land and climate
 A. Land regions
 B. Shoreline
 C. Rivers, waterfalls, and lakes
 D. Plant and animal life
 E. Climate
IV. Economy
 A. Natural resources
 B. Service industries
 C. Manufacturing
 D. Agriculture
 E. Mining
 F. Electric power
 G. Transportation
 H. Communication
V. Government
 A. Constitution
 B. Executive
 C. Legislature
 D. Courts
 E. Local government
 F. Revenue
 G. Politics
VI. History

Questions

What was the greatest natural disaster in Wisconsin's history?
How many state constitutions has Wisconsin had in its history?
What per cent of the cheese produced in the United States does Wisconsin produce?
How did Wisconsin receive the nickname the *Badger State*?
In what Wisconsin city was the Republican Party founded?
What was the "Wisconsin Idea"?
What are Devil's Elbow, Grand Piano, and Fat Man's Misery?
Why was Jean Nicolet disappointed when he landed on the Green Bay shore in 1634?
What role did Mrs. Carl Schurz play in the history of education?
What are some of the reforms Wisconsin began that other states later adopted?

Additional resources

Level I

Carpenter, Allan. *Wisconsin.* Rev. ed. Childrens Press, 1978.
Derleth, August W. *Wisconsin.* Coward, 1967.
Fradin, Dennis B. *Wisconsin in Words and Pictures.* Childrens Press, 1977.
Thompson, Kathleen. *Wisconsin.* Raintree, 1986.

Level II

The Atlas of Wisconsin. Ed. by Arthur H. Robinson, and others. Univ. of Wisconsin Press, 1974.
Blei, Norbert. *Door Way: The People in the Landscape.* Ellis Press, 1981. Stories from Door County.
Current, Richard N. *Wisconsin: A Bicentennial History.* Norton, 1977.
Derleth, August W. *The Wisconsin: River of a Thousand Isles.* Univ. of Wisconsin Press, 1985. First published in 1942.
The History of Wisconsin. State Historical Society of Wisconsin, 1973-. Multivolume work, publication in progress. Titles in this series include *From Exploration to Statehood,* by Alice E. Smith (1973), *The Civil War Era, 1848-1873,* by Richard N. Current (1976), *The Late Nineteenth Century, 1873-1893,* by Robert C. Nesbit (1985), and *Continuity and Change, 1940-1965,* by William F. Thompson (1988).
Nesbit, Robert C. *Wisconsin: A History.* Univ. of Wisconsin Press, 1973.
Ozanne, Robert W. *The Labor Movement in Wisconsin: A History.* State Historical Society of Wisconsin, 1985. First published in 1984.
Thelen, David P. *Robert M. La Follette and the Insurgent Spirit.* Univ. of Wisconsin Press, 1986. First published in 1976.

University of Wisconsin

Bascom Hall, on the University of Wisconsin-Madison campus, contains the main administrative offices, the business school library, faculty offices, and many classrooms.

Wisconsin, University of, is a coeducational state-supported educational system. Its official name is the University of Wisconsin System. It consists of 13 universities, 13 two-year campuses, and an extension system. The Wisconsin State Universities and the University of Wisconsin merged to form the system in 1971. The administrative offices are in Madison. Each university in the system is called the University of Wisconsin (UW) and has its location or campus name in its title.

UW-Madison has colleges of agricultural and life sciences, engineering, and letters and science; and schools of allied health professions, business, education, family resources and consumer sciences, journalism and mass communications, law, library science, medicine, music, natural resources, nursing, pharmacy, social work, and veterinary medicine. It grants bachelor's, master's, and doctor's degrees.

UW-Eau Claire has schools of arts and sciences, business, education, and nursing. It grants bachelor's and master's degrees.

UW-Green Bay has programs in business administration, humanities and fine arts, and natural sciences. It grants bachelor's and master's degrees.

UW-La Crosse has colleges of arts, letters, and sciences, business administration, education, and health, physical education, and recreation. It grants bachelor's and master's degrees.

UW-Milwaukee has colleges of engineering and applied science and of letters and science. It has schools of allied health, architecture and urban planning, business administration, education, fine arts, library and information science, nursing, and social welfare. It grants bachelor's, master's, and doctor's degrees.

UW-Oshkosh has colleges of business administration, education and human services, letters and science, and nursing. It grants bachelor's and master's degrees.

UW-Parkside, located between Kenosha and Racine, has colleges of behavioral science, business and management sciences, education, and natural science. It grants bachelor's and master's degrees.

UW-Platteville has divisions of agriculture, arts and sciences, business, industry and commerce, education, and engineering. It grants bachelor's and master's degrees.

UW-River Falls has colleges of agriculture, arts and sciences, and education. It grants bachelor's and master's degrees.

UW-Stevens Point has colleges of fine arts, letters and science, natural resources, and professional studies. It grants bachelor's and master's degrees.

UW-Stout at Menomonie has schools of education and human services, home economics, industry and technology, and liberal studies. It grants bachelor's and master's degrees.

UW-Superior has divisions of business and economics, education, fine and applied arts, humanities and social services, and sciences and mathematics. It grants bachelor's and master's degrees.

UW-Whitewater has colleges of the arts, business and economics, education, and letters and science. It grants bachelor's and master's degrees.

For enrollments, see **Universities and colleges** (table). Critically reviewed by the University of Wisconsin System

Wisconsin Dells. See Dalles; Wisconsin (Places to visit); Wisconsin River.

Wisconsin River is a beautiful stream that rises in Lac Vieux Desert on the Michigan-Wisconsin boundary. It flows south to Portage, Wis., and then turns westward. The Wisconsin empties into the Mississippi River below Prairie du Chien. It is about 430 miles (692 kilometers) long. The river was an important waterway in pioneer days. Today, there are a number of power dams and reservoirs along the river, and the upper Wisconsin River Valley is a leading paper-producing area.

Near the town of Wisconsin Dells, the Wisconsin River forms one of the most scenic spots in North America. Here the stream has cut through the sandstone rock to a depth of about 150 feet (46 meters). It forms canyon walls cut in unusual shapes. Gary C. Meyer

Wisdom tooth. See Teeth (Permanent teeth).

Wise, Isaac Mayer (1819-1900), a prominent American rabbi, is generally considered the pioneer of Reform Judaism in America. He founded the Hebrew Union College in Cincinnati for the training of rabbis, and was its president from the time of its organization in 1875 until his death. Wise also helped organize the Union of American Hebrew Congregations in 1873, and the Central Conference of American Rabbis in 1889. He served as president of the Conference for 11 years. He was born at Steingrub, Bohemia, and came to the United States in 1846. Clifton E. Olmstead

Wise, John (1652-1725), was a Congregational minister of colonial Massachusetts. He vigorously opposed actions by both church and government that he believed would deprive colonists of their rights and privileges.

In 1687, Wise led a protest against what he felt was an unfair tax levied by Sir Edmund Andros, the English colonial governor. In the early 1700's, Wise opposed an attempt by some Massachusetts clergymen, led by Increase and Cotton Mather, to organize themselves into associations. These associations would have taken over many functions previously controlled by individual churches. Wise argued that the associations would reduce the ability of local church members to direct their own affairs. His opposition led to the plan's defeat.

Wise was born in Roxbury, Mass. From 1680 until his death, he served as minister of a Congregational church in Ipswich, Mass. Mark A. Noll

Wise, Stephen Samuel (1874-1949), was one of the best-known American Jewish leaders. He became noted for his liberalism and his wide activities in political and social life. He was born in Budapest, Hungary, and came to the United States in 1875. He was educated at the College of the City of New York and Columbia University. He founded the Free Synagogue in New York City in 1907, and served as its rabbi until his death. In 1922, he founded the Jewish Institute of Religion and served as its first president. He also helped organize the American Jewish Congress.

Wise was a champion of Zionism, and established the first section of the Federation of American Zionists (see **Zionism**). He wrote many books, including *How to Face Life* (1917) and *Child Versus Parent* (1922). He also edited the magazine *Opinion.*　Clifton E. Olmstead

Wisteria, *wihs TIHR ee uh,* is the name of a group of thick-growing vines that bear large clusters of flowers.

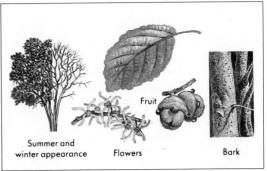

WORLD BOOK illustrations by John D. Dawson

Witch hazel has clusters of feathery, golden flowers.

Derek Fell

A wisteria is a thick-growing vine that produces clusters of showy flowers. The flowers droop from a screen of foliage. The plant is often grown to cover walls and verandas.

Wisterias belong to the pea family. The *Chinese wisteria* is often seen growing around homes in the United States. It is native to China. Other species of wisterias are native to the eastern part of the United States.

Wisterias are twining, climbing vines and may grow over 35 feet (11 meters) tall. The flowers may be bluish-lavender, pink, or white and resemble pea blossoms. The flower clusters are 1 to 2 feet (30 to 61 centimeters) long and drop from a heavy screen of foliage. The lacy leaves consist of 9 to 15 leaflets. Wisteria is an easy plant to grow in deep soil with plenty of moisture. Wisteria pods and seeds contain a poison that can cause severe stomach upset if eaten.

Scientific classification. Wisterias belong to the pea family, Leguminosae, or Fabaceae. The Chinese wisteria is *Wisteria sinensis.*　Fred T. Davies, Jr.

Witan. See Witenagemont.
Witch. See Witchcraft.
Witch hazel, *HAY zuhl,* is a shrub or small tree used to make a soothing lotion. Witch hazel grows in the eastern United States and Canada. Its jointed, twisting branches point in all directions. The forked twigs have been used for divining rods, and the name witch hazel comes from this use by superstitious people. It is also called *tobaccowood, spotted alder,* or *winterbloom.*

After the leaves have died, in October or November, witch hazel bears its flowers. They grow in feathery, golden clusters. The fruits do not ripen until the next year. Then the seeds shoot from their small woody capsules to a distance of several yards or meters.

Witch hazel lotion, or *hamamelin,* is a tonic and healing astringent, applied on the skin or taken internally. It is made by distilling the bark and leaves in alcohol. Doctors prescribe it for bruises, sprains, hemorrhoids, ulcers, bleeding, and skin troubles.

Scientific classification. Witch hazel makes up the witch hazel family, Hamamelidaceae. It is *Hamamelis virginiana.*
W. Dennis Clark

Witchcraft is the use of supposed magic powers, generally to harm people or to damage their property. A witch is a person believed to have received such powers from evil spirits. From earliest times, people in all parts of the world have believed in witches. According to some scholars, more than half the people in the world today think witches can influence their lives.

Through the centuries, witchcraft as practiced in countries with a European culture has differed from witchcraft elsewhere. European witchcraft is anti-Christian and involves an association with the Devil. For example, a person wanting to be a witch might sell his or her soul to the devil in exchange for magic powers.

On the other hand, witchcraft in Africa and the West Indies and among the Indians of North America does not involve the Devil. Most of the time, such non-European witchcraft seeks to harm people. But it may also be used to help people. For example, a person in love may ask a witch for a love *potion* (drink) to give the loved one. Drinking the potion will supposedly make the loved one return the giver's love.

The word *witch* comes from the Anglo-Saxon word *wicca,* meaning *wise one* or *magician.* Originally, a witch was either a man or a woman who supposedly had supernatural powers. Through the years, however, only women came to be considered witches. Men with similar powers were called *sorcerers, warlocks,* or *wizards.*

The powers of witches

People who believe in witchcraft think a witch can harm people in various ways. By giving someone a magic potion, for example, a witch can make that person fall in love against his or her will. In another form of

Woodcut by Francesco Guazzo from *Compendium Maleficarum,* The Newberry Library, Chicago

WORLD BOOK illustration

The Devil holds court at the initiation of several witches, *left,* in this artist's portrayal of a witch's rejection of God and dedication to Satan. The star with a goat's face, *above,* a symbol used in witchcraft, represents Satan.

witchcraft, the witch makes a small wax or wooden image of the victim. The witch may put something from the victim's body into the image, such as fingernail clippings or hair. The witch then destroys the image by cutting it, burning it, or sticking pins into it. The victim supposedly suffers severe pain or even death.

Sometimes a witch casts a spell by reciting a magic formula. The spell makes the victim suffer. The witch usually mutters the victim's name while casting the spell. In some societies, people use false names so that witches can have no power over them.

People once blamed witches for any unexplained misfortune, such as illness, a sudden death, or a crop failure. Many persons accused witches of marrying demons and bearing monster children. Witches might make cows go dry by stealing their milk or cast a spell on a churn to prevent butter from forming. People also thought witches could raise storms and turn people into beasts. In addition, witches could ride through the air on a broom, and make themselves invisible. In ancient times, many people believed that witches and warlocks assembled on October 31 to worship their master, the devil. Today, children dress up as witches and goblins on this date to celebrate Halloween (see **Halloween**).

Witchcraft has led to many widely believed superstitions. For example, many people in southern Europe and the Near East fear a power called the *evil eye.* This power enables witches to cause harm or bring bad luck to others by merely looking at them. According to another superstition, a black cat brings bad luck if it crosses a person's path. This superstition came from the belief that every witch had a personal demon called a *familiar.* Many familiars, which lived with and served their witches, existed in the form of a black cat or some other animal.

History

Ancient times. A number of witches appear in ancient Greek and Latin literature. In the epic poem, the *Odyssey,* the witch Circe had the power to turn people into animals. Medea, another famous witch, used magic spells to help the Greek hero Jason obtain the Golden Fleece. See **Circe; Medea.**

The Old Testament includes several references to witches and witchcraft. For example, the commandment "Thou shalt not suffer a witch to live" appears in Exodus (22: 18). Hundreds of years later, witch-hunters accepted such Biblical statements as proof that witches existed. They also used the statements to justify the persecution of persons accused of witchcraft.

From the 1400's through the 1700's. Some scholars regard witchcraft as an extremely old system of organized religious worship. They trace it back to pre-Christian times in many parts of Europe. From the 1400's through the 1700's, church authorities tried to stamp out witchcraft. But people in many parts of the world continued to practice witchcraft as a religion.

Church persecution of witches occurred in England, France, Germany, Italy, Scotland, and Spain. In 1431, Joan of Arc, the French national heroine, was condemned to death as a witch by the English and was burned at the stake. From 1484 to 1782, according to some historians, the Christian church put to death about 300,000 women for practicing witchcraft. Many of these women suffered such terrible torture that they confessed to being witches simply to avoid further torment.

People used many kinds of tests to determine whether a woman was a witch. For example, they looked for moles, scars, or other marks on the woman's body where a pin could be stuck without causing pain. Such *devil's marks* were said to be places where the devil had touched the accused woman. Devil's marks also included birthmarks. In another test, people tied the suspected woman's arms and legs and threw her into deep water. If she floated, she was considered guilty of being a witch. If she sank, she was innocent.

During the 1600's and 1700's, an almost hysterical fear of witchcraft swept most of Europe. Thousands of persons were tried and executed as witches. The courts allowed gossip and rumor to be used as evidence. Many children testified against their own parents.

The American colonists brought the belief in witchcraft from England. Suspected witches suffered persecution in Connecticut, Massachusetts, and Virginia. The most famous witch hunt in American history occurred in Salem, Mass. Many historians believe that Cotton

The Witches' Sabbath (1823), an oil painting by Francisco Goya; the Prado, Madrid, Spain (MAS)

Witches assemble at a Witches' Sabbath to worship their master, the Devil.

Mather, a colonial preacher, did much to stir up public feeling against the supposed evil deeds of witches. In 1692, the Massachusetts colonists executed 19 people as witches and one person was pressed to death for refusing to plead to the witchcraft charge. In addition, about 150 others were imprisoned. See **Mather; Salem** (Mass.).

Witchcraft today. Belief in witchcraft exists in many societies today. Such societies include those of the Hopi and Navajo Indians of the southwestern United States, the Maori of New Zealand, and many peoples of southern Africa. In the West Indies and elsewhere, the beliefs and practices of *voodoo* closely resemble those of witchcraft (see **Voodoo**). Some groups believe a person may inherit witch powers from a parent. Such people do not have to deal with evil spirits to become witches.

Witchcraft may serve as a means of social control among the members of a community. For example, a person who becomes too rich or powerful may be accused by neighbors of using witchcraft. The fear of being called a witch could keep such a person from acquiring too much wealth or power.

During the mid-1900's, a new interest in witchcraft occurred in Europe and the United States. As a result, witchcraft as an organized religion has attracted large numbers of believers. These people meet regularly in local *covens* (groups of 13 or fewer members). Witchcraft festivals called Witches' Sabbaths take place four times a year, one in each season. The most important festival occurs on Halloween.

Books, motion pictures, and television shows have done much to lessen the fear of witches and witchcraft. Today, many witches are portrayed as attractive, slightly unusual persons whose supernatural activities do harm to no one.   Alan Dundes

See also **Evil eye; Hecate; Magic; Sewall, Samuel.**

Additional resources

Ashley, Leonard R. *The Wonderful World of Magic and Witch-craft.* Dembner, 1986.

Hoyt, Charles A. *Witchcraft.* Southern Illinois Univ. Press, 1981. The background and history of witchcraft.

McHargue, Georgess. *Meet the Witches.* Lippincott, 1984. For younger readers.

Russell, Jeffrey B. *A History of Witchcraft: Sorcerers, Heretics, and Pagans.* Peter Smith, 1983. First published in 1980.

Witenagemot, *WIHT uh nuh guh* моднт, means *a meeting of the witan* (or *wise men*) of Anglo-Saxon Eng-

land. The witan were royal counselors, including bishops, abbots, earls, and the *thanes,* or followers, who held household offices or important positions in local government. The king could summon any thane he wished to attend the witenagemot.

The king consulted his witan before taking important steps, such as issuing laws, granting lands, making war or peace, appointing bishops or earls, or granting privileges to churches or monasteries. The witan also functioned as a royal court, giving judgment in important lawsuits. The witan could assume extraordinary powers, such as dethroning a king or choosing a new king in a disputed succession. The Norman conquerors of England in 1066 replaced the witenagemot with the *curia regis* (king's court).   Robert S. Hoyt

Withdrawal illness. See **Drug addiction.**

Witherspoon, John (1723-1794), was a leader in American political, religious, and educational life. He served in the Continental Congress and signed the Declaration of Independence. Witherspoon was born in Scotland. He was a Presbyterian minister before coming to America in 1768 to become president of the College of New Jersey (now Princeton University). After the Revolutionary War, he continued his duties as college president.   Richard B. Morris

Witness is a person who gives testimony in a judicial, legislative, or administrative proceeding. Such testimony is given under oath, or, if the witness's religion forbids an oath, under affirmation. A witness may also be a person who signs a legal instrument, such as a will or deed, that another person executes in the presence of the witness.

A court witness is ordered to appear in court by a *subpoena,* which compels the person to attend and to give evidence. A person who fails to appear is liable to punishment for *contempt of court.* A witness who testifies untruthfully is guilty of the crime of *perjury,* and can be severely punished. Witnesses may legally refuse to testify against themselves or their spouses.

The question of who is suitable to serve as a witness is regulated by *rules of evidence.* The law considers certain people as unsuitable to give legal testimony. People who are insane and people who are too young to understand the nature of a binding oath are included in this class.   Jack M. Kress

See also **Evidence; Oath; Perjury; Subpoena; Trial.**

Wittgenstein, *VIHT guhn SHTYN,* **Ludwig,** *LOOT vihk* (1889-1951), was one of the most important philosophers of the 1900's. His ideas greatly influenced two philosophical movements called *logical positivism* and *linguistic analysis.*

Wittgenstein believed that most philosophical problems result because philosophers think most words are names. For example, philosophers have asked, "What is time?" and they have been puzzled because they could not find anything named *time.* Wittgenstein said this is the wrong way to find out what time is. All that is necessary is to determine how the word *time* is used in a sentence. In the sentence, "It is time to go home," we know what *time* means, and so its meaning is not a problem. The word *time* has no meaning except for its use in such a sentence. Wittgenstein claimed that this way of viewing language "dissolves" the traditional problems of philosophy. His approach to language has greatly influenced scholars in many fields.

Wittgenstein was born in Vienna, Austria. He studied at Cambridge University in England and later taught there. He gained recognition for his books *Tractatus Logico-Philosophicus* (1921) and *Philosophical Investigations* (published in 1953, after his death).   W. T. Jones

Wizard. See Witchcraft.

Wizard of Oz. See Baum, L. Frank.

WMO. See World Meteorological Organization.

Wobblies. See Labor movement (The Industrial Workers of the World); Industrial Workers of the World.

Wodehouse, *WUD hows,* **P. G.** (1881-1975), was an English writer famous for his humorous novels and short stories. Nearly all his tales are set in England during the early 1900's. Wodehouse created many types of funny characters, including silly young men, emptyheaded young women, domineering older female relatives, and self-important businessmen. Two of his best-known characters are the dim-witted aristocrat Bertie Wooster and Wooster's valet, Jeeves. Wodehouse's clever, complex plots are filled with unlikely events.

Wodehouse wrote about 100 novels and books of short stories. He also worked with such famous composers as Jerome Kern and George Gershwin. He wrote lyrics for Kern's musical comedy *Leave It to Jane* (1917) and Gershwin's *Rosalie* (1928).

Pelham Grenville Wodehouse was born in Guildford, England, near London. The Nazis arrested him in France as an enemy alien in 1940, during World War II, and later detained him in Berlin. In 1941, while in German custody, Wodehouse made some controversial radio broadcasts in which he joked about his imprisonment. Many people in England considered him a traitor, but he was not formally accused. Wodehouse never returned to England. He moved to New York City in 1947 and became a United States citizen in 1956. Queen Elizabeth II knighted him in 1975.   John B. Vickery

Woden. See Odin.

Wöhler, *WUR luhr or VUR luhr,* **Friedrich,** *FREE drihk* (1800-1882), a German chemist, in 1828 became the first person to make an organic substance (in this case urea) from inorganic chemicals. His experiments destroyed the belief that organic substances could be formed only in the living bodies of plants or animals.

Wöhler isolated the element beryllium, and was the first person to measure the specific gravity of aluminum (see **Aluminum** [The first aluminum]). His method of preparing phosphorus was similar to that still used after World War I. Wöhler's studies on cyanates and uric acid were of fundamental importance to science.

Wöhler was born at Eschersheim, near Frankfurt, West Germany. In 1825, he became a chemistry instructor at the Polytechnic School in Berlin. Wöhler later became professor of chemistry at the University of Göttingen.   K. L. Kaufman

See also **Chemistry** (picture).

Wolcott, *WUL kuht,* is a family name of three Connecticut patriots who were active in early American politics.

Roger Wolcott (1679-1767) was colonial governor of Connecticut from 1750 to 1754. He was second in command at the Battle of Louisbourg in 1745. Wolcott wrote *Poetical Meditations* (1725), the first poetry book published in Connecticut. He was born in Windsor, Conn.

Oliver Wolcott (1726-1797), the son of Roger Wolcott, was a Connecticut signer of the Declaration of Independence. He served in the Continental Congress from 1775 to 1778 and again in 1780 and 1781. Wolcott was a member of the Congress of the Confederation from 1781 to 1784. He commanded 14 Revolutionary War regiments that helped defend New York in 1776. He was governor of Connecticut from 1796 until his death. Born in Windsor, Wolcott graduated from Yale College.

Oliver Wolcott, Jr. (1760-1833), the son of Oliver Wolcott, succeeded Alexander Hamilton as secretary of the Treasury in 1795. He resigned in 1800 after he and Hamilton became involved in a political attack against President John Adams. Wolcott was governor of Connecticut from 1817 to 1827. He was born in Litchfield, and graduated from Yale.   Richard B. Morris

Wolf is one of the largest members of the dog family. Wolves are expert hunters and prey chiefly on large hoofed animals, such as caribou, deer, elk, and moose. Many people fear wolves. They believe wolves attack human beings, and the animal's eerie howl frightens them. But wolves avoid people as much as possible.

Almost all wolves belong to a species called the *gray wolf.* There are two chief types of gray wolves, the *timber wolf* and the *tundra wolf.* The timber wolf lives in wooded, subarctic regions. The tundra wolf, also called the *Arctic wolf* or *white wolf,* makes its home on the treeless plains of the Arctic. Some zoologists believe that there is a separate species of wolves called the *red wolf.* This animal once lived throughout the Southern States. By the late 1980's, however, only about 80 red wolves remained, almost all of them in captivity.

Wolves can live in almost any climate, though they are seldom found in deserts or tropical forests. In ancient times, they roamed throughout the northern half of the world. But wherever large numbers of people settled, they destroyed wolves. As a result, wolves have disappeared from many areas. Today, most wolves live in sparsely populated northern regions, such as Alaska, Minnesota, Canada, China, and Russia. Small numbers of wolves still inhabit wilderness areas of Greece, India, Mexico, Spain, and other countries.

The body of a wolf

Wolves look much like large German shepherd dogs. But a wolf has longer legs, bigger feet, a wider head,

Leonard Lee Rue III, Keystone

The timber wolf lives in forests of northern Asia, Europe, and North America. Most timber wolves have fur that is brown or gray or a mixture of those colors, but some have jet black coats.

Warren Garst, Van Cleve Photography

Young wolves learn some hunting skills by scuffling with one another. They begin to hunt with the pack when they are about 6 months old. This family of wolves includes a black pup.

and a long bushy tail. Most adult male wolves weigh from 75 to 120 pounds (34 to 54 kilograms). They measure from 5 to 6½ feet (1.5 to 2 meters) long, including the tail, and are about 2½ feet (76 centimeters) tall at the shoulder. Female wolves are smaller than the males.

The fur of a wolf varies in color from pure white on the Arctic plains to jet black in the subarctic forests. Most wolves have gray fur. Wolves of the northern and Arctic regions grow long, thick winter coats that protect them from the bitter cold.

A wolf has excellent vision, a keen sense of smell, and fine hearing. These three senses help the animal locate prey. A wolf can see and smell a deer more than a mile (1.6 kilometers) away.

A wolf has 42 teeth, including four fangs at the front of the mouth that are used to wound, grab, and kill prey. The fangs may measure up to 2 inches (5 centimeters) long from root to tip. The small front teeth are used to nibble and pull at skin. The sharp side teeth cut easily through tough muscle. The flat back teeth crush thick bone so it can be swallowed.

The wolf has a large stomach and can eat as much as 20 pounds (9 kilograms) of food at one time. However, a wolf can go without food for two weeks or longer.

The life of a wolf

Wolves live in family groups called *packs.* Most packs have about 8 members, but some may have more than 20. Zoologists believe the members of a pack remain together because they have strong affection for one another. Some wolves leave the pack and become *lone wolves.* A lone wolf travels alone until it finds a mate. These two may have pups and form their own pack.

Habits. Each wolf pack has a social order called a *dominance hierarchy.* Every member of the pack has a certain rank in the hierarchy. High-ranking members, called *dominant wolves,* dominate low-ranking members, known as *subordinate wolves.* A dominant wolf and a subordinate wolf show their rank almost every time they meet. The dominant wolf stands erect, holds its tail aloft, and points its ears up and forward. It may show its teeth and growl. The subordinate wolf crouches, holds its tail between its legs, and turns down its ears. It may also whine. See **Dominance** (picture).

A pack lives within a specific area called a *territory.* Studies indicate that the size of the territory depends mainly on the availability of prey. If prey is scarce, the territory may cover more than 200 square miles (520 square kilometers). If prey is plentiful, the area may be as small as 30 square miles (77 kilometers).

Wolves claim a territory by marking it with their scent. The leader of the pack urinates on rocks, trees, and other objects along the boundaries of the area. Other wolves then know where the territory is located. A pack does not allow other wolves to hunt in its territory. If wolves from another pack trespass, they may be attacked.

Young. Wolves mate during the winter. The female carries her young inside her body for about 65 days. She then gives birth to 1 to 11 pups in a sheltered area called a *den.* The den may be in a cave, a hollow log, an abandoned beaver lodge, or underground.

Wolf pups weigh about 1 pound (0.5 kilogram) at birth and are blind, deaf, and helpless. At first, they live only on the mother's milk. When they are about 3 weeks old, they begin to eat meat and to leave the den for short periods. Adult wolves provide the pups with meat. An adult eats much meat after killing an animal. To get some of this meat, the pups lick the mouth of the adult wolf. The adult coughs up the meat, and the pups eat it.

Wolf pups leave the den permanently when they are about 2 months old. They move to an unsheltered area called a *rendezvous site* and remain there during the summer while the adults hunt and bring back food. In the fall, the pups and the adults begin to hunt together as a pack.

How wolves hunt. Wolves eat almost any animal they can catch. Many of the animals they hunt, such as caribou and elk, are faster and stronger than wolves. Therefore, wolves must be quick, tireless, and clever to catch them.

Wolves hunt at any time of the day or night. When the members of a pack gather to begin a hunt, they greet each other with howls. Their howling may become very loud, and it warns other wolves to stay out of the pack's territory.

Wolves roam through their territory until they find prey. They move in on an animal by traveling toward it in the opposite direction that the wind is blowing. This method prevents the animal from smelling the wolves. The wolves quietly inch closer to their prey, perhaps in single file. Then they break into a run, and the chase begins.

Wolves hunt and chase many more animals than they can catch. If wolves can catch their prey, they attack the rump or sides of the animal. They try to wound the animal and make it bleed until it weakens. Then they grab the victim by the throat or snout. Wolves can usually kill a large animal in only a few minutes. But the entire hunt may take several hours. The wolves may give up the chase if the animal is very strong, such as a healthy moose. They also may abandon the hunt if the animal is exceptionally fast.

Sick, injured, or aged animals that lag behind their herds make easy targets for wolves. The wolf helps strengthen the herds of its prey by killing such animals. An old or unhealthy animal can be a burden to its herd. For example, an aged caribou eats food that other caribou need to raise their young. A sick elk may infect other members of the herd. By eliminating such animals, wolves perform an important natural function.

Wolves and people

Many people despise the wolf because it kills other animals. Wolves provoke farmers and ranchers by destroying sheep, cows, and other livestock. Many hunters dislike the wolf because it kills game animals, such as antelope and deer. These hunters mistakenly think that

Rolf O. Peterson

A wolf pack chases a moose through the snow. But the wolves may not be able to kill their prey after cornering it. Many animals are too strong for even a group of hungry wolves to kill.

wolves wipe out game in certain areas.

Folklore also has contributed to the wolf's bad reputation. In many old sayings, the animal is a symbol of badness or evil. For example, "to keep the wolf from the door" means to prevent hunger or poverty. "A wolf in sheep's clothing" describes a person who acts friendly but has evil intentions. Fables and other folk tales pass on the misleading notion that wolves attack people. In the story of Little Red Riding Hood, a wolf threatens to eat a little girl.

Hatred and fear of wolves have led people to destroy large numbers of them. In the United States, organized hunts have killed thousands of wolves. *Bounties* (rewards) have been offered for their pelts. In the mid-1980's, from 6,000 to 10,000 wolves lived in Alaska. There were only about 1,300 wolves elsewhere in the United States, most of them in Minnesota. The United States government has classified the wolf as an endangered species in every state except Alaska and Minnesota. The wolf is classified as a threatened species in Minnesota.

Scientific classification. Wolves belong to the family Canidae. The gray wolf is *Canis lupus.* The red wolf is *C. rufus.*

L. David Mech

Additional resources

McConoughey, Jana. *The Wolves.* Crestwood, 1983. For younger readers.
Murie, Adolph. *The Wolves of Mount McKinley.* Univ. of Washington Press, 1985. First published in 1944.

Wolf fish. See Wolffish.

Wolfe, James (1727-1759), was the British general whose success in the Battle of Quebec in 1759 won Canada for the British Empire. His victory against the French came after several discouraging failures, due in part to his poor judgment. His greatness as a general has sometimes been exaggerated because of his dramatic death at the moment of victory.

Before the attack on Quebec, Wolfe moved his troops up the Saint Lawrence River to a landing well above the city. The troops moved down the river during the night of Sept. 12-13, 1759, to a point much nearer Quebec. They landed there, and then climbed a steep bluff on the north side of the river to the plains outside the city walls. When General Montcalm, the French commander, discovered the British in the morning, he decided to fight on the site Wolfe had chosen.

The Battle of Quebec lasted less than 15 minutes. Wolfe was wounded twice, but he continued in command until a third bullet struck his lungs. He died just as the French troops were breaking. General Montcalm was also mortally wounded, and he lived only a few hours after the battle (see **Montcalm, Marquis de; Quebec, Battle of**).

Wolfe was born in the County of Kent, England. He joined the army when he was 14, and served in Flanders and Scotland. He was a brigadier in the French and Indian War, which began in 1754. He served under Lord Jeffery Amherst in the Battle of Louisbourg in 1758 (see **Amherst, Lord Jeffery; Louisbourg**).

Wolfe returned to England after that battle. William Pitt, who was then directing England's foreign affairs, chose Wolfe to command the expedition against Quebec. Wolfe's success there, at the cost of his life, permitted the British to seize Montreal in 1760 and to complete

***The Death of General
Wolfe,*** a famous painting by
Benjamin West, shows Wolfe's
death at the moment of victory
in the Battle of Quebec.

Oil painting on canvas (1770); Gift of the Duke of Westminster, National Gallery of Canada, Ottawa

the conquest of Canada (see **Canada, History of** [British
conquest and rule]).   W. B. Willcox

Wolfe, Thomas Clayton (1900-1938), was an American author who won fame for his autobiographical novels. Wolfe claimed that all great art was necessarily autobiographical. The story of his childhood and youth
assumes a symbolic significance in his novels. His central character, under whatever name he appears, is a
sensitive, worthwhile person who is, in essence, the author. Through this character, Wolfe treated a theme that
is important to his work—the development of the artist
in America.

Wolfe was born in Asheville, N.C. He graduated from
the University of North Carolina in 1920 and then entered the Harvard University graduate school. Wolfe
wrote two plays at Harvard but considered them failures
and turned to writing novels. He taught English at New
York University between 1924 and 1930.

Maxwell E. Perkins, an editor at Scribner's publishers,
was the most important influence in Wolfe's career.
Wolfe wrote long rambling works, and Perkins helped
him cut and organize the material. Wolfe's first novel
was *Look Homeward, Angel* (1929). It was followed by a
sequel, *Of Time and the River* (1935). After Wolfe's
death, Edward Aswell, an
editor at Harper publish-
ers, edited his two other
novels—*The Web and the
Rock* (1939) and *You Can't
Go Home Again* (1940). The
character of Eugene Gant
in the first two novels is
modeled on Wolfe as a
young man. The other two
novels also draw on
Wolfe's personal experi-
ences. They concern a
character called George
Webber.

Pinchot

Thomas Wolfe

Wolfe's writing has been criticized for its apparent
lack of discipline and artistic control. Some critics believe that each novel is a torrent of undigested details
and that Perkins' editing is responsible for whatever
form the novels have. Wolfe seemed to support this
view in *The Story of a Novel* (1936), in which he critically
examined his own writings. However, later critics have
stressed that Wolfe was more than a reporter. They note
that he chose details and emphasized elements that
make each of the episodes in his novels a dramatic unit.

Although Wolfe has been frequently criticized for ex-
cesses in language, at his best he wrote powerful prose
that is often close to poetry. *The Notebooks of Thomas
Wolfe* (1970) describes Wolfe's struggle to become a
mature writer. *The Complete Short Stories of Thomas
Wolfe* was published in 1987.   Noel Polk

Additional resources

Donald, David Herbert. *Look Homeward: A Life of Thomas
    Wolfe.* Little, Brown, 1987.
Evans, Elizabeth. *Thomas Wolfe.* Ungar, 1984.

Wolfe, Tom (1931-   ), is an American journalist, essayist, novelist, and social commentator. Much of his
work is an example of New Journalism, which mixes detailed reporting with controversial opinion.

Wolfe has written about many aspects of modern life
and the arts. His first book, *The Kandy-Kolored Tanger-
ine-Flake Streamline Baby* (1965), is a collection of essays
about modern American life styles. *Radical Chic & Mau-
Mauing the Flak Catchers* (1970) is a controversial description of a fund-raiser for the radical Black Panther
Party at the home of symphony conductor Leonard
Bernstein. *The Right Stuff* (1979) describes the selection,
training, and daily lives of the first seven American astronauts. *The Painted Word* (1975) criticizes the preten-
tions Wolfe saw in modern art. *From Bauhaus to Our
House* (1981) attacks modern architecture. *The Bonfire of
the Vanities* (1987) is a novel about the very wealthy and
the very poor in New York City.

Thomas Kennerly Wolfe, Jr., was born in Richmond, Va. He has been a newspaper reporter and an editor for *New York* and *Esquire* magazines, where much of his writing first appeared.　Barbara M. Perkins

Wolffish live in the North Atlantic and the North Pacific. The wolffish gets its name from its terrifying appearance. This savage fish will try to attack anyone who captures it. It has powerful jaws and its bite can be extremely painful. It is reddish or grayish and has no pelvic fins. The Atlantic wolffish grows about 3 feet (91 centimeters) long. The North Pacific wolffish, called the *wolf eel,* may reach 8 feet (2.4 meters). The fish spawns large eggs that cluster in a ball.

The wolffish uses its broad, strong front teeth to crush the shells of the animals it eats. Its flesh tastes

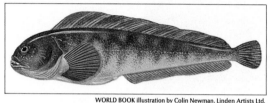

WORLD BOOK illustration by Colin Newman, Linden Artists Ltd.
The Atlantic wolffish has powerful jaws and teeth.

much like that of the cod. It is a favorite food fish in Iceland. Its strong, durable skin makes a good leather used for pouches, bookbindings, and other articles.

Scientific classification. The Atlantic wolffish is in the family Anarhichadidae. It is classified as *Anarhichas lupus.* The wolf eel belongs to the family Anarhichthyidae. It is *Anarrhichthys ocellatus.*　Leonard P. Schultz

See also **Fish** (picture: Fish of coastal waters).

Wolfhound is the name of a family of dogs made up of three breeds—the *Irish wolfhound,* the *borzoi* or *Russian wolfhound,* and the *Scottish deerhound.* The Irish dog is the largest of all dogs, although not the heaviest. It was the companion of kings in ancient Ireland, and is still used for hunting.

The borzoi resembles the greyhound except for its long, luxuriant coat. This breed of wolfhound was developed by the Russian czars. The czars used these dogs to

WORLD BOOK photo
The Irish wolfhound belongs to the wolfhound family.

chase after and destroy wolves.

The Scottish deerhound descended from the staghound and other large breeds once used for stalking deer. It is a large, striking dog, though smaller than the Irish wolfhound.

Critically reviewed by the American Kennel Club

See also **Borzoi; Dog** (picture: Hounds); **Irish wolfhound; Scottish deerhound.**

Wolfram. See Tungsten.

Wolfram von Eschenbach, VAWL frahm fuhn EHSH uhn BAHK (1170?-1220?), was a German knight and poet. His rhymed poem *Parzival* is considered a masterpiece of medieval literature.

Parzival is about a courageous boy who finds his way through ignorance and guilt to manhood and wisdom. During years of wandering, Parzival grows in purity and humility until finally God judges him worthy of the *Grail,* a holy stone that transmits God's will by means of a mysterious inscription. Wolfram based his poem on a French romance by Chrétien de Troyes. Richard Wagner based his opera *Parsifal* on Wolfram's masterpiece. Wolfram also wrote short poems and two unfinished verse epics—*Titurel* and *Willehalm.*

Little is known of Wolfram's life. He was born into a noble family in Bavaria and probably served as a knight under powerful lords.　James F. Poag

Wolframite, WUL fruh myt, is one of the two most important ores of tungsten. It consists of iron, manganese, oxygen, and tungsten, and its chemical symbol is $(Fe,Mn)WO_4$. Tungsten is a chemical element that is important in the production of electronic equipment and industrial tools (see **Tungsten**). The other chief tungsten ore is scheelite.

Wolframite is a black to brownish mineral that occurs in crystals. It is often found with quartz and in veins that run in and around granite. Australia, Bolivia, China, Korea, and the Soviet Union have major wolframite deposits.　Robert B. Cook

Wollongong, WOOL uhn GAWNG (pop. 206,803), is an important industrial city along the southeast coast of Australia. Part of the state of New South Wales, it lies 51 miles (82 kilometers) south of Sydney, Australia's largest city. For the location of Wollongong, see **Australia** (political map). Wollongong has many historic buildings in the Georgian and Victorian styles of architecture that date from the 1840's. The city also has modern residential and commercial areas. It is the home of the University of Wollongong.

Wollongong's major industries include steel and iron production and coal mining. Wollongong is also a shipping center for products produced in the area.

Wollongong was first settled by Europeans in 1815. It became a town in 1859 but did not receive the status of a city until 1942.　Alan Fitzgerald

Wollstonecraft, WUL stuhn kraft, **Mary** (1759-1797), a British author, was best known for her book *A Vindication of the Rights of Woman* (1792). This book was one of the first to claim that women should have equality with men. Wollstonecraft said that men considered women morally and mentally inferior to themselves. She argued that women could live happy, creative lives if they had better educational opportunities. She based her book on the democratic principles of the French Revolution (1789-1799) and on her own experiences.

Wollstonecraft was born in London. She educated herself by studying books at home. For a brief period, she and her sisters ran a school. From this experience, she wrote *Thoughts on the Education of Daughters* (1787). In this pamphlet, she criticized the cruel treatment of young girls that was common at the time. She also wrote other essays as well as stories and translations.

Mary Wollstonecraft

In 1797, Wollstonecraft married William Godwin, a British political reformer. Their daughter, Mary Wollstonecraft Shelley, wrote the famous horror novel *Frankenstein* (1818). Cynthia F. Behrman

Wolsey, *WUL zee,* **Thomas Cardinal** (1475?-1530), was an English statesman and a cardinal of the Roman Catholic Church. He was the most powerful person in England for many years.

Wolsey was born at Ipswich, where his father was a butcher. He was educated at Magdalen College, Oxford University. Several years after his graduation, he was elected a fellow of the college. In 1498, he was ordained a priest, and became rector of Limington, in Somerset. He later became chaplain to the archbishop of Canterbury, and then chaplain to the English governor of Calais. Wolsey's Oxford friends and his own driving ambition helped his rapid rise to political power. By 1507 he had become chaplain to King Henry VII. The king often used Wolsey in diplomatic missions, and rewarded him in 1509 by making him dean of Lincoln.

When Henry VIII became king in 1509, Wolsey's affairs prospered. He became canon of Windsor in 1511 and received high church positions. He also became a member of the Privy Council in 1511, and soon was the controlling figure in all matters of state. In 1514, he was made bishop of Lincoln, and then archbishop of York. Pope Leo X made him a cardinal in 1515. Wolsey loved display and wealth. He lived in royal splendor and reveled in his power. Wolsey's ambition was to become pope.

Cardinal Wolsey spent his great abilities as a statesman and administrator mainly in managing England's

Oil painting (about 1600) by Sampson Strong; Christ Church College, Oxford, England

Thomas Cardinal Wolsey was the most powerful religious and political leader in England during the early 1500's.

foreign affairs for Henry VIII. Despite the many enemies his greed and ambition earned him, he held Henry VIII's confidence until Henry decided to divorce his wife, Catherine of Aragon, and marry Anne Boleyn (see **Henry VIII**). Wolsey disapproved of this, and was slow in arranging the divorce. The delay angered the king, and made Wolsey an enemy of Anne Boleyn and her friends.

His fall was sudden and complete. Stripped of office and property, he was permitted to remain archbishop of York. But shortly afterward, he was accused of treason and ordered to London. In great distress, he set out for the capital. He fell ill and died on the way. "If I had served God," the cardinal said remorsefully, "as diligently as I have done the king, He would not have given me over in my grey hairs." Paul M. Kendall

Wolverine, *WUL vuh REEN,* is a fur-bearing animal that lives in the northern woods and *tundras* (cold, treeless

The wolverine lives in North America, northern Europe, and Asia. It is one of the most powerful animals of its size.

plains) of Europe, Asia, and North America. It is sometimes called the *glutton*. Adult wolverines measure about 3½ feet (110 centimeters) long and weigh up to 55 pounds (25 kilograms). They are somewhat bearlike in appearance, with a heavy body and short legs. The wolverine's long coat ranges from dark-brown to black, with a band of lighter-colored fur along its sides to the top of a bushy tail. The animal is extremely powerful for its size.

During the summer, wolverines feed chiefly on small and medium-sized mammals, birds, and plants. During the winter, they hunt reindeer and caribou. A wolverine kills such large prey by jumping on the animal's back and holding on until the animal falls. The wolverine will tear apart the body and hide the pieces until it can return to eat them. Wolverines also feed on the remains of reindeer and caribou that have been killed by wolves, bears, or other animals.

The wolverine is rare today. In the past, it was ruthlessly hunted for its fur and because it sometimes kills game animals and livestock.

Scientific classification: The wolverine belongs to the weasel family, Mustelidae. It is *Gulo gulo.*   Gary A. Heidt

Wolverine State. See Michigan.

Woman. See Human being; Women's movements.

Woman suffrage is the right of women to vote. Today, women in nearly all countries have the same voting rights as men. But they did not begin to gain such rights until the early 1900's, and they had to overcome strong opposition to get them. The men and women who supported the drive for woman suffrage were called *suffragists.*

In the United States

During colonial times, the right to vote was limited to adult males who owned property. Many people thought property owners had the strongest interest in good government and so were best qualified to make decisions. Most women could not vote, though some colonies gave the vote to widows who owned property.

By the mid-1700's, many colonial leaders were beginning to think that all citizens should have a voice in government. They expressed this belief in such slogans as "No Taxation Without Representation" and "Government by the Consent of the Governed."

After the United States became an independent nation, the Constitution gave the states the right to decide who could vote. One by one, the states abolished property requirements and, by 1830, all white male adults could vote. Only New Jersey gave women the vote, but in 1807, that state also limited voting rights to men.

Beginnings of the movement. Changing social conditions for women during the early 1800's, combined with the idea of equality, led to the birth of the woman suffrage movement. For example, women started to receive more education and to take part in reform movements, which involved them in politics. As a result, women started to ask why they were not also allowed to vote.

One of the first public appeals for woman suffrage came in 1848. Two reformers, Lucretia Mott and Elizabeth Cady Stanton, called a women's rights convention in Seneca Falls, N.Y., where Stanton lived. The men and women at the convention adopted a Declaration of Sen-

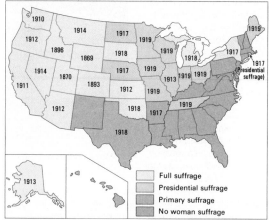

WORLD BOOK map

Woman suffrage existed in three forms before it became law throughout the United States in 1920—voting in all elections, voting only in presidential elections, or voting only in primary elections. The dates shown are the years in which these states granted women the right to vote.

timents that called for women to have equal rights in education, property, voting, and other matters. The declaration, which used the Declaration of Independence as a model, said, "We hold these truths to be self-evident: that all men and women are created equal. . . ."

Suffrage quickly became the chief goal of the women's rights movement. Leaders of the movement believed that if women had the vote, they could use it to gain other rights. But the suffragists faced strong opposition.

Most people who opposed woman suffrage believed that women were less intelligent and less able to make political decisions than men. Opponents argued that men could represent their wives better than the wives could represent themselves. Some people feared that women's participation in politics would lead to the end of family life.

Growth of the movement. The drive for woman suffrage gained strength after the passage of the 15th Amendment to the Constitution, which gave the vote to black men but not to any women. In 1869, suffragists formed two national organizations to work for the right to vote. One was the National Woman Suffrage Association, and the other was the American Woman Suffrage Association.

The National Woman Suffrage Association, led by Stanton and another suffragist named Susan B. Anthony, was the more radical of the two organizations. Its chief goal was an amendment to the Constitution giving women the vote. In 1872, Anthony and a group of women voted in the presidential election in Rochester, N.Y. She was arrested and fined for voting illegally. At her trial, which attracted nationwide attention, she made a stirring speech that ended with the slogan "Resistance to Tyranny Is Obedience to God."

The American Woman Suffrage Association, led by the suffragist Lucy Stone and her husband, Henry Blackwell, was more conservative. Its main goal was to induce individual states to give the vote to women. The two organizations united in 1890 to form the National

American Woman Suffrage Association. The Woman's Christian Temperance Union and other organizations also made woman suffrage a goal.

During the early 1900's, a new generation of leaders brought a fresh spirit to the woman suffrage movement. Some of them, including Carrie Chapman Catt and Maud Wood Park, were skilled organizers who received much of their support from middle-class women. These leaders stressed organizing in every congressional district and lobbying in the nation's capital. Other leaders, including Lucy Burns, Alice Paul, and Stanton's daughter Harriot E. Blatch, appealed to young people, radicals, and working-class women. This group of leaders devoted most of their efforts to marches, picketing, and other active forms of protest. Paul and her followers even chained themselves to the White House fence. The suffragists were often arrested and sent to jail, where many of them went on hunger strikes.

Action by individual states. In 1869, the Territory of Wyoming gave women the right to vote. The Utah Territory did so a year later. Wyoming entered the Union in 1890 and became the first state with woman suffrage. Colorado adopted woman suffrage in 1893, and Idaho in 1896. By 1920, 15 states—most of them in the West—had granted full voting privileges to women. Twelve other states allowed women to vote in presidential elections, and two states let them vote in primary elections.

The 19th Amendment. A woman suffrage amendment was first introduced in Congress in 1878. It failed to pass but was reintroduced in every session of Congress for the next 40 years.

During World War I (1914-1918), the contributions of women to the war effort increased support for a suffrage amendment. In 1918, the House of Representatives held another vote on the issue. Spectators packed the galleries, and several congressmen came to vote despite illness. One congressman was brought in on a stretcher. Representative Frederick C. Hicks of New York left his wife's deathbed—at her request—to vote for the amendment. The House approved the amendment, but the Senate defeated it. In 1919, the Senate finally passed the amendment and sent it to the states for approval.

By late August 1920, the required number of states had ratified what became the 19th Amendment to the U.S. Constitution. The amendment says, "The right of citizens of the United States to vote shall not be denied or abridged by the United States or by any state on account of sex."

In other countries

In 1893, New Zealand became the first nation to grant women full voting rights. In 1902, Australia gave women the right to vote in national elections. Other countries that enacted woman suffrage during the early 1900's included Canada, Finland, Germany, Great Britain, and Sweden. In the mid-1900's, China, France, India, Italy, Japan, and other nations gave women the vote. By the mid-1980's, only seven nations—all of them in the Middle East—still denied women the vote. They were Bahrain, Kuwait, Oman, Qatar, Saudi Arabia, the United Arab Emirates, and Yemen (Sana).   Anne Firor Scott

Related articles in *World Book* include:

Anthony, Susan B.
Blatch, Harriot E. S.
Catt, Carrie Chapman
Davis, Paulina Wright
Duniway, Abigail J. S.
Kelley, Florence
League of Women Voters
Lockwood, Belva A. B.
Mansfield, Arabella Babb
McClung, Nellie
Morris, Esther H.
Mott, Lucretia C.
Pankhurst, Emmeline G.
Paul, Alice
Rose, Ernestine P.
Shaw, Anna Howard
Spencer, Anna G.
Stanton, Elizabeth Cady
Stone, Lucy
Thomas, Martha Carey
Willard, Frances E. C.
Woodhull, Victoria C.

Additional resources

Flexner, Eleanor. *Century of Struggle: The Woman's Rights Movement in the United States.* Rev. ed. Harvard, 1975.
Scott, Anne Firor and A. M. *One Half the People: The Fight for Woman Suffrage.* Univ. of Illinois Press, 1983. First published in 1975.
Stein, R. Conrad. *The Story of the Nineteenth Amendment.* Childrens Press, 1982. For younger readers.

Woman's Christian Temperance Union (WCTU)

is a nonprofit organization that works to lessen social problems. The organization's official name is the National Woman's Christian Temperance Union. It is also commonly called the WCTU. One of the WCTU's chief aims is to educate people, especially youths, on the harmful effects of alcohol, other narcotic drugs, and tobacco. The WCTU has helped enact state laws requiring public schools to teach about such effects.

The WCTU's broad programs also promote good citizenship, child welfare, and world peace. In addition, the WCTU takes leading roles in other areas that deal with humanitarian concerns. These areas include child abuse and equal justice for women, minority groups, and all other classes of people.

The WCTU has branches in all the states of the United States and in Puerto Rico and the Virgin Islands. It was founded in 1874. The WCTU developed out of the Women's Temperance Crusade of 1873. During this campaign, women church members went into saloons, sang hymns, prayed, and asked the saloonkeepers to stop selling liquor. The Temperance Crusade swept over 23 states, and resulted in the closing of thousands of places that sold liquor throughout the nation.

Members of the Temperance Crusade attending the Chautauqua Sunday School Assembly in 1874 issued the call which resulted in the organization of the National Woman's Christian Temperance Union in November 1874 at Cleveland, Ohio. The WCTU's first president was Annie Wittenmyer, and the second was the noted educator and reformer, Frances E. Willard (see **Willard, Frances E.**).

The organization grew rapidly, and its influence increased with its growth. It worked through schools, churches, and other groups. Finally the Eighteenth Amendment to the Constitution of the United States (passed in 1919) prohibited the manufacture, import, export, and sale of alcoholic beverages. This amendment remained in force from 1920 until 1933, when the Twenty-first Amendment repealed it. See **Prohibition.**

In 1883, Willard founded the first international organization for women, called the World's Woman's Christian Temperance Union. It is made up of women's temperance groups in 72 countries and has about 1 million members. The WCTU has national headquarters at 1730 Chicago Avenue, Evanston, IL 60201.

Critically reviewed by the Woman's Christian Temperance Union

See also **American Council on Alcohol Problems.**

Woman's Relief Corps, National, is the oldest woman's patriotic organization in the United States. In July 1883, it was voted the official auxiliary of the Grand Army of the Republic, an organization of veterans of the Union Army in the Civil War. The Woman's Relief Corps has about 15,000 members, and is the only existing patriotic organization that was founded solely on the basis of loyal womanhood, regardless of kinship.

The Woman's Relief Corps' aims were to aid and memorialize the Grand Army of the Republic, and to perpetuate the memory of its dead. The organization also works to assist veterans of all U.S. wars. Members promote patriotism and take part in child welfare work. Headquarters are at 629 S. Seventh Street, Springfield, IL 62703.

Critically reviewed by the National Woman's Relief Corps

Womb. See Uterus.

Wombat is a stocky, burrowing animal of Australia. There are two main kinds of wombats. *Common,* or *forest, wombats* feed on grass, leaves, and roots in woodlands. *Plains wombats* graze in grasslands. Wombats measure up to 4 feet (1.2 meters) long and weigh from 30 to 75 pounds (14 to 34 kilograms). They have brown fur. The common wombat's fur is much thicker and coarser than that of the plains wombat. The plains wom-

Eric Worrell, Photographic Library of Australia

Wombats are stocky, burrowing animals of Australia. The *common wombat, above,* has thick brown fur and small ears.

bat has a hairy nose, but the common wombat's nose is hairless. Plains wombats also have larger ears than common wombats do.

Wombats are *marsupials.* Female marsupials give birth to tiny, poorly developed offspring. Like most marsupials, young wombats are carried in a pouch on the mother's belly until they develop more completely.

Scientific classification. Wombats belong to the marsupial family Vombatidae. Common wombats are *Vombatus ursinus.* The hairy-nosed wombat, the main plains wombat, is *Lasiorhinus latifrons.*   Michael L. Augee

Women's American ORT is the largest affiliate of the worldwide *Organization for Rehabilitation through Training,* or *ORT.* Women's American ORT has about 145,000 members in the United States. The worldwide ORT is a nonprofit agency founded in 1880 to free underprivileged and uprooted Jewish people from dependence upon charity by teaching them skills and

trades. It maintains over 800 installations in 22 countries on 5 continents. About 116,000 people a year use its high school credit courses, its short-term apprenticeship and adult-training courses, or its junior colleges. Courses are geared to the labor needs of the countries in which the schools are located. The ORT program is financed by governments, local communities, the American Jewish Joint Distribution Committee, and by affiliated ORT groups. Headquarters are at 315 Park Avenue S., New York, NY 10010.

Critically reviewed by Women's American ORT

Women's Bureau is an agency of the United States Department of Labor. It develops policies and programs to improve the welfare and status of women in the work force. The bureau is chiefly a fact-finding, service, and promotional agency. It does not administer any laws.

The Women's Bureau conducts research and develops programs to find ways of improving job opportunities for women and girls, especially in fields that have not traditionally been open to them. It encourages improved vocational counseling, better job-training programs, and continuing education for women. It works for the expansion of child care and other supportive services. The bureau also promotes legislation to improve the status of women and to eliminate sex discrimination in the workplace. It conducts or sponsors various studies and publishes its findings.

The bureau provides information and assistance to individuals; employers; labor unions; schools; employment agencies; federal, state, and local government agencies; and international organizations. Congress established the Women's Bureau in 1920.

Critically reviewed by the Women's Bureau

Women's Clubs, General Federation of, is an international organization of about 10 million women who belong to women's clubs in about 35 countries. This total includes more than 600,000 members in more than 12,000 clubs in the United States.

The General Federation of Women's Clubs was founded in 1890. In that year, Sorosis of New York, one of the oldest clubs in the United States, invited delegates from other clubs to a general convention. This meeting set up the framework for the general federation. International headquarters are at 1734 N Street NW, Washington, DC 20036.

Critically reviewed by the General Federation of Women's Clubs

Women's Equal Rights Amendment. See Equal Rights Amendment.

Women's International Bowling Congress (WIBC) regulates women's organized bowling competition. It has nearly 4 million members and ranks as the largest women's sports organization in the world. Its members include both amateur and professional bowlers.

The WIBC establishes and enforces rules for leagues and tournaments, gives awards for outstanding achievements, and promotes interest in bowling. It conducts the annual WIBC Championship Tournament; the Queens Tournament, an event for only the top women bowlers; and a national amateur championship tournament to qualify women for international competition.

The WIBC was founded in 1916. It has headquarters at 5301 S. 76th Street, Greendale, WI 53129.

Critically reviewed by the Women's International Bowling Congress

Bettmann Archive

© Penelope Breese, Gamma/Liaison

Women's movements have led to greater social, economic, and political rights for women. In the early 1900's, *left,* women marched for the right to vote. Since the 1960's, women have demonstrated for equal pay and job opportunities, and for child-care and other social programs, *right.*

Women's movements

Women's movements are group efforts, chiefly by women, that seek to improve women's lives or the lives of others. Probably the best-known women's movements are those that have engaged in political efforts to change the roles and status of women in society. Such political movements by women on their own behalf are often referred to as *feminist movements* (see **Feminism**). Women's groups also have worked to help others, primarily through religious and charitable activities. Whether political, religious, or charitable, women's movements have sought to achieve greater social, economic, and political involvement for women.

Throughout history, women have usually had fewer rights and a lower social status than men. The traditional role of wife and mother dominated, and most women's lives centered around their households. Women's movements first developed during the 1800's in the United States and Europe and then spread to other parts of the world. The first women's movements arose largely in response to the coming of modern urban and industrial society. The industrial age brought about great economic and political changes, creating upheaval in women's traditional roles and causing women to question their status and situation. This first wave of women's movements concentrated primarily on gaining voting rights for women.

A second wave of women's movements emerged during the 1960's, another period of great political and social change in many areas of the world. These contemporary women's movements have sought greater equality for women in the family, in the workplace, and in political life.

Women's movements have enabled large groups of women to question and determine their rights and responsibilities. The specific goals and methods of these movements have varied from one time and place to another, depending on local customs regarding the treatment of women, on national political values, and on economic conditions. But in almost every case, women's movements have won greater freedom for women to act as self-sufficient individuals, rather than as dependent wives or daughters.

Women's status through the ages

Origins of women's traditional roles. Throughout history, most societies have held women in an inferior status compared to that of men. This situation was often justified as being the natural result of biological differences between the sexes. In many societies, for example, people believed women to be naturally more emotional and less decisive than men. Women were also held to be less intelligent and less creative by nature. But research shows that women and men have the same range of emotional, intellectual, and creative characteristics. Many sociologists and anthropologists maintain that various cultures have taught girls to behave according to negative *stereotypes* (images) of femininity, thus keeping alive the idea that women are naturally inferior.

There are, of course, certain physical differences between the sexes. From earliest times, the fact that women were the childbearers helped establish a division of tasks between women and men. In every society, only women bear children and nurse infants, leading to a tradition of women assuming most of the responsibility for child care. Men, by contrast, have been free to work at greater distances from their families. In early societies, this division of labor did not necessarily suggest inequality. But in more developed societies, a division of labor between women who worked mainly in the home and men who worked outside the home could give men economic superiority. A woman who stayed home came to depend on someone else—usually a man—to earn money for the necessities of life.

Women also differ physically from men in being, on average, smaller and less powerfully muscled. These physical differences helped define certain physically demanding or dangerous jobs as "men's work."

Eventually, the division of tasks that originally had been determined by physical differences became a matter of tradition. Consequently, even after machinery canceled out the advantage of male strength and after birth control gave women the means to regulate their childbearing, women continued to face barriers to entering many occupations.

The remainder of this section traces the status of women through history. It focuses on Western societies, because it is in these societies that women's movements first arose and have had their greatest impact to date.

In ancient societies, the lives of most women centered around their households. For example, in the Greek city-state of Athens from about 500 to 300 B.C., women raised children and managed the spinning, weaving, and cooking in the household. Wealthy women supervised slaves in these tasks, but they also did some of the work themselves. Respectable Athenian women seldom left their homes. Only men could purchase goods or engage in soldiering, lawmaking, and public speaking. The societies of ancient Egypt and of the Greek city-state of Sparta provided a rare contrast. Both Egyptian and Spartan women could own property and engage in business.

In ancient Rome, as in Athens, women's primary role was to manage household affairs. Women could not hold public office. Men dominated as head of the household. But the Romans developed a system of government based on the authority and leadership of a noble class that included not only statesmen and military leaders, but also the *matrons* (married women) of leading Roman families. For example, the Roman matron Cornelia, who lived during the 100's B.C., achieved fame and respect for her managerial skill, patriotism, and good works. In time, such upper-class women gained greater control over their property and over marriage decisions. However, even these women could not vote or hold public office.

During the Middle Ages, which began in the A.D. 400's and lasted about a thousand years, women's lives continued much as before. Like the Roman matrons, medieval noblewomen managed large households and supervised servants, oversaw gardens, attended to clothing and furnishings, and entertained guests. Many other women worked as cooks and servants, or worked in the pastures and fields of large estates.

However, two new roles for women did appear during the Middle Ages—the nun and the woman active in trade, either as an artisan or as a merchant. Convents flourished during the early Middle Ages. They offered primarily upper-class women an alternative to marriage and provided education, spiritual development, and control over extensive land. Beginning in the 1200's, women found increasing opportunities for independence as artisans and merchants in the medieval cities of England, France, Germany, and other western European lands.

From the Renaissance to the 1800's, fundamental changes in religious and political outlook took root, as leading thinkers began to emphasize the rights of the individual. The Renaissance was a period of great cultural and intellectual activity that spread throughout Europe from the 1300's to about 1600. The most significant intellectual movement of the Renaissance was *humanism,* which stressed the importance of human beings and their nature and place in the universe. Some humanists questioned certain traditional ideas about women, and favored better education and a more responsible family role for women.

The Reformation, the religious movement of the 1500's that gave rise to Protestantism, also encouraged a reassessment of women's roles. Protestant leaders permitted ministers to marry and began to picture marriage as a mutual relationship of spiritually equal partners. Husbands had less control over the lives of their wives. Protestants also began to view marriage and divorce as matters of individual choice rather than as the fulfillment of obligations to such authorities as parents and the church.

The Age of Reason—another period of great intellectual activity—swept Europe in the 1600's and 1700's. During this era, educated women participated in intellectual and political debates. In Paris, gatherings called *salons* promoted conversation and discussion among learned men and women. The salons widened these women's view of society and their possible roles in it.

Women's roles as workers also expanded during the Age of Reason. In western Europe and the American Colonies, women worked as innkeepers, landowners, midwives, printers, servants, teachers, and textile workers. But rural occupations continued to employ the largest group of female, and male, workers. Rural women toiled as laborers on large farms and in their own small gardens and cottages. Both urban and rural women engaged in knitting, sewing, and other home industries that made crucial contributions to household income.

The rise of women's movements

Forces of change. Several developments during the late 1700's and early 1800's set the stage for the rise of women's movements. The thinkers of the Age of Reason questioned established political and religious authority and stressed the importance of reason, equality, and liberty. The new intellectual atmosphere helped justify women's rights to full citizenship. On the eve of the French Revolution (1789-1799), the Marquis de Condorcet, a French philosopher, spoke in favor of women's right to vote. The British author Mary Wollstonecraft argued for women's rationality and equality with men in her book *A Vindication of the Rights of Woman* (1792).

In the American Colonies, the Revolutionary War (1775-1783), fought in the name of liberty and equality, raised the hopes of some women. Women supported the war with their sewing and farming, and by boycotting British goods and engaging in other forms of protest. Although neither the American nor the French revolutions increased women's rights, these conflicts gave new prominence to the idea of equality.

The spread of industrialization during the 1800's also affected women. The Industrial Revolution moved men's, women's, and children's work out of the home and into factories (see **Industrial Revolution**). Factory jobs offered working-class women an opportunity to earn wages. But if a woman was married, her husband legally controlled her earnings.

Industrialization had a different effect on middle-class women in small towns and cities. With the separation of work and home, these women lost a sense of useful involvement in productive work. They became regarded as "ladies" whose place was in the home, while their husbands provided the family income. Many of these women turned to such pursuits as needlework and craftwork—and to religious and charitable activities, as well.

The beginnings of women's movements. Before women's movements emerged, women began to form many kinds of groups based on common interests. After the French Revolution, for example, various women's political clubs took shape in both France and Great Britain. In the United States, women formed temperance societies, which campaigned to abolish alcoholic beverages, and missionary societies, which supported the spread of Christianity.

In the United States and Britain, two major types of women's movements gradually developed: (1) "social," or "domestic," women's movements and (2) "equal rights" feminist groups. Women's social movements carried out religious, charitable, and social activities. Equal rights feminists primarily worked to remove educational and political barriers to women and to change women's roles.

Before the Civil War (1861-1865), many American women's movements were of the social type. These included societies to promote temperance, to aid poor women and orphans, and to send missionaries to the Indians or to foreign lands. Women formed similar religious and charitable associations in Britain before 1860 and in other Western countries during the late 1800's.

Fewer groups were centered on gaining equal rights for women. But such groups had a clear goal to improve women's situation through such reforms as better education for girls, support for women's property rights, and voting rights for women.

Women's educational opportunities gradually expanded throughout the 1800's. In 1821, American teacher Emma Willard founded the Troy Female Seminary (now the Emma Willard School) in Troy, N.Y. Willard's school was one of the first institutions to offer girls a high-school education. In 1833, Oberlin Collegiate Institute (now Oberlin College) opened as the first coeducational college in the United States. By 1900, some major European and American universities were accepting women for advanced study and professional training.

Women's efforts to secure legal rights, particularly property rights, also brought reform. In the United States, many states enacted property laws during the 1840's and 1850's. Such laws allowed married women to make contracts, to own property, to control their own earnings, and to have joint custody of their children. For example, in 1848 a New York law gave married women the right to retain control of their own real estate and personal property. The new laws especially aided widowed, deserted, and mistreated wives. Similar legislation passed in Britain and other Western countries during the middle and late 1800's.

In 1848, social reformers Lucretia Mott and Elizabeth Cady Stanton organized the first women's rights convention in the United States in Seneca Falls, N.Y. The convention adopted a Declaration of Sentiments, which called for women to receive "all the rights and privileges which belong to them as citizens of the United States." National women's rights conventions met almost every year from 1850 until the onset of the Civil War in 1861. The delegates discussed the rights of women regarding divorce, guardianship of children, property control, voting, and other concerns.

Many of the equal rights feminists were also leaders in the movement to abolish slavery. During the Civil War, most women reformers devoted their efforts to supporting war activities.

The right to vote. The issue of *suffrage* (the right to vote) became increasingly important to women during the 1800's. In the United States, the cause of woman suffrage was championed by two key organizations: the National Woman Suffrage Association (NWSA) and the American Woman Suffrage Association (AWSA). Stanton and women's rights leader Susan B. Anthony led the NWSA, founded in 1869. The more radical organization of the two, the NWSA demanded equal education, equal employment opportunities, and voting rights for women immediately. Women's rights leader Lucy Stone, her husband, Henry Blackwell, and other reformers formed the AWSA, also in 1869. The more moderate AWSA supported gradual advances, such as limited suffrage for women in local elections.

In 1890, the two organizations joined to form the National American Woman Suffrage Association (NAWSA). *Suffragists* (supporters of woman suffrage) held conventions, waged state-by-state campaigns, and distributed literature to win support for their cause. New methods of campaigning used by British women suffragists—especially parades and outdoor speeches—spurred the drive for suffrage. Support from both social and equal rights women's movements proved necessary to the final suffrage victory. Women's social movements—temperance organizations, missionary societies, and progressive reformers—realized that they needed the vote to reach their goals. Equal rights feminists appealed to women laborers and to professional and college-educated women, all of whom had an interest in securing political power and more responsible and better-paying jobs. In 1920, the United States adopted the 19th Amendment to the Constitution, granting American women the right to vote.

Suffrage movements also arose in other Western countries during the 1800's and early 1900's. In 1893, New Zealand became the first nation to grant women full voting rights. Australia gave women the right to vote in federal elections in 1902. Swedish women with property could vote in city elections in 1862. Sweden granted women full suffrage in 1921. In Britain, the suffrage movement began in the 1860's, though women did not win full voting rights until 1928. See **Woman suffrage.**

Birth control also emerged as a woman's issue during the early 1900's. At that time, the distribution of birth control information was illegal in the United States. A number of social reformers supported birth control as a way to relieve poverty. Margaret Sanger, a trained nurse, led the birth control movement in the United States. By the 1920's, her work had helped make it possible for doctors to give out birth control information legally.

Decline after 1920. By 1920, the first wave of women's movements had peaked in the United States. With suffrage finally granted, many women assumed that the need for women's movements had disappeared. As a result, a period of relative inactivity followed. The NAWSA became the League of Women Voters and worked to educate women voters about current political issues. A few women, such as Frances Perkins, who served as secretary of labor under President Franklin D.

Roosevelt, were appointed to high public office.

In some countries, including Belgium, France, and Italy, the struggle for woman suffrage continued into the 1940's. But they, too, experienced little feminist activity after women gained the right to vote.

During World War II (1939-1945), several million American women took factory production jobs to aid the war effort. But after the war ended, these women were urged to leave the work force to make room for the returning servicemen. Society encouraged women to become full-time housewives. Devotion to home and family and the rejection of a career emerged as the ideal image for women. This view of womanhood, described by American author Betty Friedan in her book *The Feminine Mystique* (1963), all but replaced any organized struggle for women's rights until the 1960's.

Contemporary women's movements

In Western societies, a new wave of women's movements emerged during the 1960's. Civil rights protests in the United States, student protests around the world, and women's rebellion against the middle-class housewife's role contributed to this second wave of women's movements. It began with women's examination of their personal lives and developed into a program for social and political change. Women's groups discovered discrimination in the workplace, where women received less pay and fewer promotions than men. They also uncovered barriers to women seeking political office and to female students striving for high academic achievement.

Women's organizations. Two types of women's groups appeared in the United States during the 1960's. One type consisted of the small, informal women's liberation groups, which were first formed by female students active in the civil rights movement and in radical political organizations. These groups tended to be leaderless and focused on members' personal experiences. They emphasized self-awareness and open discussion to combat discrimination and to establish greater equality between men and women in marriage, child-rearing, education, and employment.

Large, formal organizations developed alongside the small women's liberation groups. These organizations, known as women's rights groups, campaigned for the passage and strict enforcement of equal rights legislation. President John F. Kennedy's Commission on the Status of Women, established in 1961, discovered a number of legal barriers to women's equality. It reported on laws that barred women from jury service, excluded women from certain occupations, and, in general, kept women from enjoying their full rights as citizens. In 1966, a number of feminist leaders formed the National Organization for Women (NOW) to fight sexual discrimination. NOW has since grown into the largest group in the U.S. women's movement.

Other women's rights organizations also appeared. The Women's Equity Action League, founded in 1968, monitored educational programs to detect inequalities in faculty pay and promotion. It also drew attention to what was called the "chilly classroom climate," an environment that discouraged discussion and participation by female students. The National Women's Political Caucus, formed in 1971, focused on finding and supporting women candidates for political office.

Other Western nations experienced a similar revival of women's movements. In Canada, for example, both women's liberation groups and women's rights organizations formed in the 1960's. The National Action Committee on the Status of Women, founded in 1972, is the largest women's organization in Canada.

Legal gains. The second wave of women's movements brought about many important legal gains for women. In the United States, several laws passed during the 1960's and 1970's aimed at providing equal rights for women. The Equal Pay Act of 1963 requires equal pay for men and women doing the same work. Title VII of the Civil Rights Act of 1964 prohibits job discrimination on the basis of sex as well as on the basis of color, race, national origin, and religion. Title IX of the Education Amendments of 1972 bans discrimination on the basis of sex by schools and colleges receiving federal funds. This law applies to discrimination in all areas of school activity, including admissions, athletics, and educational programs. The Equal Credit Opportunity Act took effect in 1975. It prohibits banks, stores, and other organizations from discriminating on the basis of sex or marital status in making loans or granting credit.

Court rulings have also expanded women's legal rights in the United States. Undoubtedly the most controversial such ruling was the 1973 Supreme Court decision in *Roe v. Wade,* which established women's unrestricted right to abortion during the first three months of pregnancy. NOW and a number of other women's groups have consistently opposed attempts at limiting women's legal access to abortion. Other women, however, favor tighter restrictions on the availability of abortion. See **Abortion.**

Not all efforts to broaden women's rights have been successful. In 1972, Congress passed the Equal Rights Amendment (ERA) and sent it to the states for ratification. The proposed amendment read: "Equality of rights under the law shall not be denied or abridged by the United States or any state on account of sex." Supporters of the ERA argued that the amendment would provide specific constitutional guarantees of equal treatment under the law, regardless of sex. Opponents, which included political activist Phyllis Schlafly and many other women, warned that passage of the ERA would require women to serve in the military and would deprive them

© Joseph Rodriquez, Black Star

The establishment of day-care centers, like this one in Sweden, is a goal of today's women's movements. Such child care programs help women obtain equal employment opportunities.

of the right to financial support from their husbands. The amendment failed to become part of the Constitution because only 35 of the necessary 38 states had approved it by the 1982 deadline.

Since the 1970's, women's groups in the United States have increasingly pushed for the enactment of social welfare legislation. Such laws provide benefits through family and community programs. Women need such programs if they are to have equal employment opportunities. Social welfare bills may concern preschool child care; before- and after-school programs for children; and parental leave from work for pregnancy, childbirth, or the care of sick or dependent family members. France, Sweden, and other European countries have instituted a number of such social welfare programs for their citizens.

In the Soviet Union and Eastern Europe. Many of the countries that underwent Communist revolutions or take-overs granted women equal rights and benefits in one stroke, often long before such rights were obtained by women in Western societies. For example, women have had maternity leave, government-funded child care, equal pay for equal work, equal education, and the right to hold any political office in the Soviet Union since 1918 and in East Germany since 1949. Party members from these countries argue that they have no need for Western-style women's movements.

Critics, however, note that the "double burden" of employment and household responsibilities still falls heavily on women in Communist societies. Women's employment appears to have had less effect on men's roles in these countries than in Western nations. Husbands rarely help with shopping, cooking, and other household tasks. In addition, many labor-saving conveniences remain much scarcer in the Soviet Union and Eastern Europe than in Western societies. Sexism continues to exist in other areas as well. For example, although women hold about half of the political offices in the Soviet Union, they fill largely ceremonial and local-level positions.

In developing nations in Africa, Asia, and Latin America, few organized women's movements have emerged. In addition, vast cultural differences make it difficult to determine the direction women's movements may take in such nations. For instance, Muslim women in the Middle East and northern Africa come from a tradition where men's and women's activities have been strictly segregated and women have lived largely in seclusion. Women in eastern and western Africa, on the other hand, have a long history of social independence as food producers and traders.

Yet despite cultural differences, women in developing countries share some common concerns. Many women in these nations question whether modern economic development benefits them. During the 1970's and 1980's, several reports on the effects of economic development described women's loss of involvement in food production. Western experts often gave men the money and machinery to improve agricultural production, though women were traditionally the farmers. Men used the scarce resources to buy expensive equipment to produce and transport cash crops. As a result, women directed their efforts away from growing food for family use and the local market. Instead, they grew carnations, strawberries, and other cash crops that would bring in more money. Food shortages resulted, and families suffered from hunger.

Women working in industry in developing nations also faced problems. Foreign-owned factories employed thousands of women in such industries as food processing, electronics, and textiles. But the women received low pay and little job security. In addition, they endured poor working conditions and heavy demands for high productivity and obedience.

The United Nations sponsored several conferences to examine women's living conditions around the world during its Decade for Women (1975-1985). At these conferences, women from the developing world expressed concern about food shortages, the poverty of women and children, and other issues. They have continued to stress the need for greater consideration of women's lives when working for economic development.

Impact of women's movements

Contemporary women's movements have had an impact on several levels of society in such Western countries as Canada, Sweden, and the United States. Women's groups have changed many people's views about male and female roles. These changes have affected the workplace, the family, and the way women live their lives. Through the vote, women's groups have influenced election results and government. They have also influenced legislation. Information about the legislative impact of women's movements appears in the section *Contemporary women's movements.*

On women's lives. The most notable single change in women's lives may be their growing participation in the paid labor force. In the United States, the percentage of employed women rose from 28 per cent in 1940 to 57 per cent in 1989. The contemporary women's movement contributed to an increasing acceptance of careers for all women, including mothers with young children. Such changes were associated in part with a growing expectation that women would combine employment with their roles as wife and mother. The proportion of married women with children under 18 and a job rose dramatically, from 18 per cent in 1950 to 66 per cent in 1988.

However, long-standing differences between the sexes in job opportunities and in earnings showed little sign of disappearing, even in such progressive nations as Sweden. The majority of women's work opportunities still fell within a narrow range of occupations, such as nursing, teaching, retail sales, and secretarial work. Largely because of lower pay in these "women's" jobs, women working full-time and year-round continued to earn less than men. For example, in the United States, such women earned about 70 per cent of what men earned in 1988. Furthermore, working women throughout the world continued to face the "double burden" of being the primary homemaker while holding down a job outside the home.

On attitudes and values. Certain broad cultural changes have taken place that reflect new attitudes toward the roles of men and women. They also point to a growing equality between the sexes. Textbook publishers have adopted guidelines to eliminate language that uses male forms to represent everyone. For example,

© James A. Sugar, Black Star

A woman commercial pilot holds a traditionally male job. Women's movements have changed attitudes about female and male roles, thereby increasing career opportunities for women.

fireman becomes *fire fighter,* and *policeman* becomes *police officer.* Women as well as men serve as anchors for television news shows. Several women have held the highest political office in their country, including Margaret Thatcher of Great Britain, Golda Meir of Israel, Benazir Bhutto of Pakistan, and Corazon Aquino of the Philippines. In the United States, the number of women in law and medicine has risen dramatically since 1970. In high schools and colleges, women's studies courses in history, literature, and sociology have brought new attention to women's lives.

Changing attitudes about the roles of women and men have also affected the way people conduct their everyday lives. For example, many men now take a more active role in parenting. More husbands now join their wives in natural childbirth classes. Some men have taken parental leave from work or chosen to work part-time when they become new fathers.

Notable differences in outlook still exist between the sexes, however. In the early 1980's, U.S. elections revealed for the first time a "gender gap," where women followed a different voting pattern than men. Women's votes showed greater support for candidates favoring social programs and domestic spending, while more men voted for candidates favoring defense spending. A similar voting pattern has emerged in other countries, including Canada, Great Britain, and Sweden.

The final outcome of these changing attitudes and values has yet to be seen. But it appears likely that the blurring of distinctions between women's and men's roles and the trend toward greater equality of the sexes will continue.   Janet Zollinger Giele

Related articles in *World Book* include:

Leaders in women's movements

See the biographies listed at the end of **Woman suffrage.** See also the following articles:

Adams, Abigail S.
Beecher, Catharine Esther
Blackwell, Antoinette B.
Bloomer, Amelia J.
Dickinson, Anna E.
Friedan, Betty
Gilman, Charlotte P.
Goldman, Emma
Grimke (family)
Heckler, Margaret M.
Howe (Julia Ward)

Mill (Harriet Taylor)
Murphy, Emily G.
O'Reilly, Leonora
Sanger, Margaret
Steinem, Gloria
Terrell, Mary C.
Truth, Sojourner
Walker, Mary E.
Wells-Barnett, Ida Bell
Willard, Emma H.
Wright, Frances

Other related articles

Abortion
Alimony
Birth control
Careers (table: Annual
  income)
Civil Rights Act of 1964
Divorce
Equal Rights Amendment
Feminism

Marriage
National Organization
  for Women
Planned Parenthood
  Federation of America
Roe v. Wade
Woman suffrage
Women's Bureau

Outline

I. Women's status through the ages
  A. Origins of women's traditional roles
  B. In ancient societies
  C. During the Middle Ages
  D. From the Renaissance to the 1800's
II. The rise of women's movements
  A. Forces of change   C. The right to vote
  B. The beginnings of   D. Birth control
    women's movements   E. Decline after 1920
III. Contemporary women's movements
  A. In Western societies
  B. In the Soviet Union and Eastern Europe
  C. In developing nations
IV. Impact of women's movements
  A. On women's lives
  B. On attitudes and values

Questions

Why did women's movements experience a decline after 1920?
What is the chief concern of women in developing nations?
How did the National Woman Suffrage Association and the American Woman Suffrage Association differ?
Why do party members from the Soviet Union and Eastern Europe say they do not need a women's movement?
What was the role of women in ancient Athens?
How does social welfare legislation benefit women?
What two types of women's groups emerged in the United States during the 1960's?
How did the Industrial Revolution affect the lives of middle-class women?
What is the "double burden" that most women carry?
How do the Civil Rights Act of 1964 and the Education Amendments of 1972 affect women?

Reading and Study Guide

See *Women's movements* in the Research Guide/Index, Volume 22, for a *Reading and Study Guide.*

Additional resources

American Woman, 1987-88: A Report in Depth. Ed. by Sara E. Rix for the Women's Research and Education Institute of the Congressional Caucus for Women's Issues. Norton, 1987. Additional report published annually.
Boulding, Elise. *The Underside of History: A View of Women Through Time.* Westview, 1976. *Women in the Twentieth Century World.* Sage, 1977.
Changing Patterns: Women in Canada. Ed. by Sandra Burt and others. McClelland (Toronto), 1988.
Jones, Jacqueline. *Labor of Love, Labor of Sorrow: Black Women, Work, and the Family from Slavery to the Present.* Vintage, 1986. First published in 1985.

Tuttle, Lisa. *Encyclopedia of Feminism.* Facts on File, 1986.
Women: A World Report. Comp. by the New Internationalist
Publication Staff. Oxford, 1985.

Women's rights. See Women's movements.

Wonder, Stevie (1950-   ), is an American composer, singer, and musician. A child prodigy, he recorded his first hit, "Fingertips" (1963), at the age of 13. Wonder has since matured into one of the most highly praised artists in popular music. He often uses his music as a force for social progress.

Wonder's compositions range in style from the rhythmic soul music of "Superstition" (1972) to the social realism of "Living for the City" (1973). He also wrote melodic ballads such as "You Are the Sunshine of My Life" (1973). Wonder has incorporated Jamaican and African rhythms into his music.

Tony Korody, Sygma
Stevie Wonder

Wonder paid tribute to the American composer Duke Ellington with the song "Sir Duke" (1977), one of his biggest hits.

Wonder was born in Saginaw, Mich. His given and family name is Stevland Morris. Wonder has been blind almost from birth. He first played the harmonica and later progressed to the keyboards. Since the early 1970's, Wonder's mastery of synthesizers and other instruments has made him almost a one-man band in the recording studio.   Don McLeese

Wonders of the world. See Seven Wonders of the Ancient World.

Wood is a tough substance under the bark of trees, shrubs, and certain other plants. The physical properties of wood, plus its chemical composition, make it one of the most valuable natural resources. Wood is used in making thousands of products, including baseball bats, furniture, lumber, musical instruments, railroad ties, cellophane, charcoal, and paper.

Wood's physical properties make it especially useful for construction work. It is tough, strong, and easy to handle. Wood also insulates well, does not rust, and resists high heat better than steel. However, wood shrinks and swells, depending on how much moisture it loses or absorbs.

Every piece of wood has a distinctive—and different—pattern called the *figure.* The figure is a highly desirable feature of wood used for furniture, cabinets, and other fine wood products.

This article discusses the physical and chemical properties of wood. For additional information on wood and its many uses, see the *World Book* articles on **Forest products, Lumber,** and **Tree.**

Kinds of wood. There are two general kinds of wood, *softwood* and *hardwood.* These terms refer to the type of tree from which wood comes. They do not indicate the hardness of wood.

Softwood comes from cone-bearing trees, called *conifers.* Most conifers have needlelike, evergreen leaves. Common softwoods include Douglas-fir, hemlock, pine,

Some types of wood   Wood is classified as *softwood* or *hardwood.* Softwoods can be easily sawed, planed, or bored, and so they are used chiefly for structural work. Hardwoods have beautiful grain patterns and are widely used for furniture, floors, and paneling. Some of the most popular hardwoods are shown below.

Chester B. Stem, Inc. (WORLD BOOK photos)

Beech   Birch   Cherry   Elm

Hickory   Mahogany   Maple   Oak

Red gum   Rosewood   Sycamore   Walnut

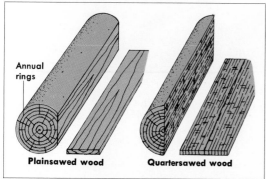

Annual
rings

Plainsawed wood   **Quartersawed wood**

WORLD BOOK diagram by David Cunningham

Wood patterns are determined partly by the way logs are cut. Plainsawed wood is cut along the edges of a tree's annual rings, and quartersawed wood is cut through the rings.

and redwood. They can be easily sawed, planed, chiseled, and bored, and so they are good for construction purposes. They also supply most of the pulpwood used to make cellophane and paper products.

Hardwood comes from broad-leaved trees. Most of these trees are *deciduous*—that is, they lose their leaves every autumn. Birch, elm, mahogany, maple, and oak are common hardwoods. The rich and distinctive figures of these woods add to the beauty of furniture, cabinets, paneling, and floors.

The composition of wood. Wood consists of tiny, tube-shaped cells that form layers of permanent tissue around a plant stem. The walls of wood cells contain three chief substances—*cellulose, lignin,* and *hemicellulose.* Cellulose makes up about half of wood by weight and gives wood its strength and structure. Lignin holds the fibers of wood together. Hemicellulose resembles both cellulose and lignin. Wood also contains substances called *extractives.* They include fats, gums, oils, and coloring matter.

The proportion of cellulose, lignin, hemicellulose, and extractives varies among different kinds of wood. The cellular structure also differs. These variations make some wood heavy and some light, some stiff and some flexible, and some plain and some colorful.

Manufacturers obtain several useful chemicals and by-products from wood. For example, cellulose is used in making explosives, fabrics, paints, paper, and many other products. Lignin has a variety of uses, especially in making animal feeds, plastics, and artificial vanilla. The extractives of certain woods provide oils, pitch, turpentine, and tar. Hemicellulose has few uses.

Wood figures are determined chiefly by the growth process of the tree. They result from combinations of color, luster, texture, and grain.

The color comes mainly from extractives. Uneven distribution of the extractives produces a *pigment figure,* found especially in ebony, rosewood, and walnut. Luster is the way wood reflects light. Many woods, including birch and pearwood, require a coat of varnish or another clear finish to bring out their luster. The texture of wood results from the structure of the cells. For example, beech, satinwood, and sycamore have small, closely spaced cells, which produce a fine texture. The grain depends on the arrangement and direction of the cells.

The grains of ash, birch, mahogany, and walnut give these woods a wavy *fiddleback figure.* Maple trees have a *bird's eye figure,* which looks like a knot.

The figure is also determined by the way wood is sawed. There are two ways of cutting wood, *plainsawing* and *quartersawing.* Plainsawing produces oval and curved figures. These patterns increase the beauty of such woods as cedar, cherry, and walnut. Quartersawing gives wood a striped appearance. Mahogany, oak, and sycamore have rich figures when they are quartersawed.

In some woods, the figure depends on the part of the tree from which the wood is cut. For example, tree stumps and wartlike outgrowths called *burls* have attractive patterns. The most popular stumpwood is American walnut. Cherry and walnut have highly prized burls.

Harry E. Troxell

Related articles. For more information on the uses of wood, see **Forest products, Lumber,** and **Tree** with their lists of *Related articles.* See also the following articles:

Cellulose	Plywood	Veneer
Furniture	Stain	Wallboard
Lignin	Varnish	Woodworking

Wood, Grant (1891-1942), was an American artist known for his paintings of the rural Midwest. He was a leading figure in a movement known as *regionalism,* which dominated American art during the 1930's. Wood primarily portrayed the people and landscapes of Iowa, where he was born and lived most of his life. Wood believed that artists should remain in their home communities and paint from personal experience based on their local heritage.

Wood's paintings show the influence of German and Flemish painters of the 1400's and 1500's in their realism, precise details, and enamellike surfaces. His compositions feature simple geometric shapes with sharp contours. Wood's most famous painting is *American Gothic* (1930), which portrays a typical Midwest farm couple. This work is reproduced in **Painting** (The 1900's). In *The Midnight Ride of Paul Revere* (1931), Wood made fun of the legendary ride by changing the setting from New England to a hilly Iowa landscape. Wood's *Arbor Day* (1932) praises the values of domestic life in rural America. Wood was born near Anamosa, Iowa.

Bess L. Hormats

Wood, Leonard (1860-1927), was an American soldier and colonial administrator. As military governor of Cuba from 1899 to 1902, he prepared the island for independence. He built roads and schools, and helped stamp out yellow fever by cleaning up swamps and mosquito-ridden areas, making Cuba a more healthful place to live.

Wood was born in Winchester, N.H. After graduating from Harvard Medical School, he joined the Army Medical Corps. He commanded the *Rough Riders,* a famous volunteer regiment in which Theodore Roosevelt also served, during the Spanish-American War (see **Rough Riders**). Wood commanded the United States forces in the Philippines from 1906 to 1909, and served as chief of staff from 1910 to 1914. He urged military preparedness during World War I. In 1920, a movement among Republicans to nominate Wood for the presidency failed. He served as governor general of the Philippines from 1921 until his death. Nelson M. Blake

Wood alcohol. See Methanol.

Wood-block print. See Block printing; Hokusai (picture); Japanese print.
Wood-burning stove. See Heating (Local heating systems).
Wood carving. See Woodcarving.
Wood duck is a colorful water bird that lives in forests of southern Canada and throughout wooded areas of the United States. Most wood ducks are found in the eastern half of North America, but some live along the Pacific Coast. The lowland forests along the Mississippi River provide excellent habitats for wood ducks.

Male wood ducks are the most colorful North American ducks. Their upper feathers glitter with green, blue, and purple. Underneath, the feathers are red, yellow, and white. Females are brown above and yellowish-brown and whitish below. Both males and females have crests extending back from the top of their heads. Wood ducks are about 20 inches (51 centimeters) long.

Wood ducks frequent ponds, swamps, and other wetlands near woods. They feed in shallow water on acorns, seeds, and insects. Wood ducks nest in tree cavities formed by woodpeckers and natural decay. Each female lays 10 to 15 eggs.

Wood ducks nearly became extinct in the early 1900's because of overhunting and the clearing of their forest habitats by people. Since then, conservation efforts have helped to increase the number of these birds.

Scientific classification. The wood duck is a member of the family Anatidae. It is *Aix sponsa.*   Eric G. Bolen

See also **Duck** (picture: A wood duck and her ducklings).

Wood louse, also called *sow bug,* is a small *invertebrate* (animal without a backbone) that lives on land. It belongs to a group of mostly marine animals known as *isopods.* Like its marine relatives, a wood louse has a flat, oval body that is divided into a number of segments. Special muscles enable the animal to roll up into a ball when disturbed.

Most wood lice live in dark, damp, humid places, such as under stones and in bark. They come out only at night to feed. A few species live in the desert. They burrow deep into the sand to avoid daytime heat.

WORLD BOOK illustration by John F. Eggert
Wood louse

Scientific classification. The wood louse belongs to the subphylum Crustacea and the order Isopoda. The most common species are in the genera *Oniscus* and *Porcellio.*

P. A. McLaughlin

Wood nymph, an insect. See Butterfly (Satyrs and wood nymphs; pictures).
Wood pewee, *PEE wee,* is a small bird related to the flycatcher. It nests in the summer in Canada and the eastern United States, and spends the winters in Central and South America. It is also called the *Eastern pewee.* The *Western pewee* resembles the wood pewee, but has a different song.

The wood pewee looks somewhat like the phoebe,

WORLD BOOK illustration by Trevor Boyer, Linden Artists Ltd.
The wood pewee sings at daybreak and at twilight.

but has a grayer brown coloring, and white bars on its wings (see Phoebe). The wood pewee's plaintive call sounds somewhat like *pee a wee.* The pewee sings at the first sign of daybreak, and also in the early evening.

The wood pewee builds one of the daintiest nests. It weaves various plant fibers together tightly and covers the outside with lichens. The bird places its nest on a horizontal limb of a tree. The female lays two to four eggs, colored a creamy-white and speckled with brown. The wood pewee is useful to human beings because it eats many insect pests.

Scientific classification. The wood pewee belongs to the flycatcher family, Tyrannidae. It is classified as *Contopus virens.*

Arthur A. Allen

Wood pulp. See Paper; Forest products; Lumber (Introduction); Tree (Wood products).
Wood sorrel. See Shamrock.
Wood thrush. See Thrush.
Wood tick. See Tick; Rocky Mountain spotted fever.
Woodbine. See Honeysuckle; Virginia creeper.
Woodcarving is the act of creating figures or designs in wood by cutting or chiseling. Woodcarving is both a hobby and an art form. Some carving is performed on machines with cutters mounted on high-speed spindles. This article describes woodcarving by hand.

Most woodcarving is done with chisels of various sizes and shapes. Chisels have flat cutting edges. Other tools called *gouges,* have cutting edges that vary in shape from almost flat to deeply U-shaped. *Parting tools* have V-shaped cutting edges.

Woodcarvers can use a variety of methods. In *chip carving,* they cut patterns or designs into a wooden surface by removing small triangular slices of wood with a chisel or a knife or both. In *line* or *scratch carving,* carvers cut lines into the wood with a U-shaped gouge or a V-shaped parting tool. In *relief carving,* woodcarvers cut background wood away, leaving designs that project from the surface, which looks three-dimensional. Another woodcarving technique, *carving in the round,* involves making a free-standing object that can be viewed from any side, such as a statue or a bowl.

A number of woodcarvers have gained fame as artists. One of the best known was Grinling Gibbons, who worked in England during the late 1600's and early 1700's. Gibbons carved many beautiful interior decorations for chapels and libraries. Wilhelm Schimmel was a noted American woodcarver of the 1800's. Schimmel, a

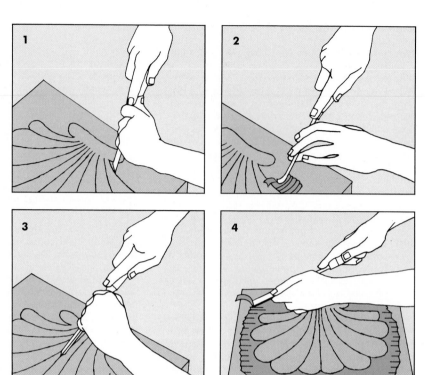

Woodcarving tools include a variety of chisels and other cutting implements. A woodcarver uses the slanted cutting edge of a *skew chisel* to cut the outline of a design into a smooth surface (picture 1). A *bend gouge* with a U-shaped cutting edge is used to cut away wood that lies near the edge of the design (picture 2). A carver deepens lines in the design with the V-shaped cutting edge of a *parting tool* (picture 3). The background area can be cut away with a *straight chisel* (picture 4).

wandering folk artist, became especially famous for his crudely carved figures of eagles.   Harold L. Enlow

Related articles in *World Book* include:

Folk art	Knife (picture: Kinds of knives)
Furniture	Relief
Indian, American (Arts and crafts)	Sculpture (The sculptor at work; pictures)

Woodchuck, also called *ground hog,* is an animal that belongs to the squirrel family. Woodchucks are a kind of marmot (see **Marmot**). They live in Canada, and in the Eastern and Midwestern United States. According to an old superstition, a person can tell when spring will come by watching what a woodchuck does on Ground-Hog Day (See **Ground-Hog Day**).

Several subspecies of woodchucks live in North America. The woodchuck of Canada and the eastern

Leonard Lee Rue III, Tom Stack & Assoc.

The woodchuck, also known as the *ground hog,* lives in Canada and the Eastern and Midwestern United States. Adult woodchucks eat grasses and other green plants.

United States is typical. It is about 2 feet (61 centimeters) long, including its bushy tail, and has a broad, flat head. Its coarse fur is grayish-brown on the upper parts of its body and yellowish-orange on the under parts.

Woodchucks dig complex burrows or dens that contain several compartments and may have several entrances. In winter, the woodchuck hibernates in a special den that has only one entrance.

When a woodchuck goes to look for food, it first sits up on its haunches at the entrance to its burrow. It looks and listens for any sign of danger. This habit makes the woodchuck an easy target for hunters. Woodchucks eat such plants as alfalfa and clover. Some farmers consider woodchucks pests because they destroy crops.

Woodchucks eat large amounts of food in the fall before hibernating. The extra food is changed to fat in their bodies, and the woodchucks live on this fat during their winter sleep. Female woodchucks give birth to four or five young in the spring.

Scientific classification. The woodchuck belongs to the squirrel family, Sciuridae. It is *Marmota monax.*

Charles A. Long

Woodcock is the name of several species of birds in the snipe family. These birds live in moist woods and sheltered bogs in many parts of the world. The *American woodcock* lives in the eastern United States and southern Canada. It is about 11 inches (28 centimeters) long, and has a heavy body. It has short legs and tail, and a long bill with a sensitive tip. The woodcock uses its bill to search for earthworms in the mud.

The American woodcock flies south to Missouri, New Jersey, and the Gulf Coast in winter. It comes north again in spring, appearing by the first of March. It lives on the ground in the woods, and makes nests of dry leaves. The female lays four tannish and reddish-brown eggs. Woodcocks are wood brown with black bars. These colors make the bird blend with its background in the thickets and help protect it from enemies.

On spring evenings, the cock performs its courtship flight for the hen. As it circles high in the air, the cock makes whistling sounds with its wing feathers and utters various voice calls. After the young hatch, a parent woodcock may carry them between its thighs during flight.

Scientific classification. Woodcocks belong to the family Scolopacidae. The American woodcock is *Philohela minor.*

Alfred M. Bailey

Woodcock, Leonard (1911-   ), was an American labor leader and diplomat. He served as president of the United Automobile Workers (UAW), one of the largest labor unions in the United States, from 1970 to 1977. From 1979 to 1981, Woodcock was U.S. ambassador to China.

Woodcock was a Detroit factory worker before he became a union organizer of the Congress of Industrial Organizations (CIO) in 1938. He joined the UAW staff in 1940. From 1947 to 1955, Woodcock held many leadership posts in the union. In 1955, he became a UAW vice president and the union's chief negotiator with the General Motors Corporation. In the early 1970's, Woodcock led a drive to establish national health insurance in the United States. He served on the U.S. Pay Board in 1971 and 1972. In 1977, President Jimmy Carter appointed Woodcock chief of the U.S. Liaison Office in Beijing, China. Woodcock was named ambassador to China in 1979, after the United States and China established full diplomatic ties. He was born in Providence, R.I.

Abraham J. Siegel

Woodcut is a print or design made from a block of wood. The block itself is also called a woodcut. Since the 1400's, artists have produced woodcuts that rank among the masterpieces of printmaking.

Artists make most woodcuts from pine blocks. The artist alters the surface by removing parts of the wood using chisels, gouges, and knives. The cutaway sections appear white in the final print, and the uncut parts produce the desired image. The artist coats the uncut parts, which stand in relief, with ink. A sheet of paper is then placed over the inked block and rubbed with the back

of a spoon or with some similar implement. The rubbing transfers the inked image onto the paper. To make colored woodcuts, the artist uses colored ink and a number of separate blocks, generally one for each color. Each block makes up a portion of the picture. The artist must cut the blocks so they appear in the correct *registration* (relationship to each other) in the completed woodcut.

Woodcuts were first used in Europe in the Middle Ages to print patterns on textiles. By the 1400's, artists made woodcuts to portray religious subjects, to decorate and illustrate books, and to make playing cards. In the late 1400's and early 1500's, the German artist Albrecht Dürer created woodcuts that achieved new heights of expression and technical skill. For examples of early woodcuts, see **Bookplate, Card game, Literature for children** (picture: *The New England Primer*), and **Switzerland** (picture: The Battle of Sempach).

During the 1700's and 1800's, Japanese artists produced many outstanding woodcuts known as *ukiyo-e.* These prints influenced such European artists as Edgar Degas, Edouard Manet, Henri de Toulouse-Lautrec, and Vincent van Gogh. The Europeans admired the Japanese woodcuts for their bold, flat shapes of brilliant color; delicate flowing lines; and superb composition. For examples of Japanese woodcuts, see **Japanese print, Drama** (Asian drama), **Hokusai,** and **Sharaku.**

During the early 1900's, expressionist artists created many fine woodcuts (see **Expressionism**). These artists included Ernst Ludwig Kirchner of Germany and Edvard Munch of Norway.   Andrew J. Stasik, Jr.

See also **Baskin, Leonard; Bewick, Thomas; Dürer, Albrecht; Ward, Lynd K.**

Wooden, John (1910-   ), was one of the greatest coaches in college basketball history. He coached the University of California at Los Angeles (UCLA) to a record 10 National Collegiate Athletic Association (NCAA) championships from 1964 to 1975. In that period, his teams won 335 games and lost 22. His teams won a record seven straight NCAA championships from 1967 to 1973. From 1971 to 1974, UCLA won 88 consecutive games, a college basketball record. He coached many all-Americans, including Kareem Abdul-Jabbar, Gail Goodrich, Bill Walton, and Sidney Wicks.

John Robert Wooden was born in Martinsville, Ind.,

Making a woodcut

Cutting

Inking

© Peter Gonzalez

Printing

An artist creates a woodcut by cutting away portions of a block of wood with sharp tools, *left.* To make a print of the picture, the uncut, raised surfaces of the block are coated with ink, *center,* and a sheet of paper is placed over the block. The paper is then rubbed with the back of a spoon or some similar object. The rubbing transfers the inked image onto the paper, *right.*

and graduated from Purdue University. He won all-America honors as a guard on the Purdue basketball team in 1930, 1931, and 1932. Wooden was basketball coach at UCLA from 1948 to 1975. He is the only man elected to the Naismith Memorial Basketball Hall of Fame as both a player and a coach.   Nick Curran

Wooden horse. See Trojan War.

Woodhull, Victoria Claflin (1838-1927), was the first woman to run for President of the United States. In 1872, she was the candidate of the new Equal Rights Party. Women's voting rights groups admired her stand in favor of allowing women to vote. But they rejected her candidacy because she also spoke for the right of women to have love affairs, whether married or not.

Bettmann Archive
Victoria C. Woodhull

In 1870, Woodhull and her sister Tennessee Claflin established the first stock brokerage firm owned by women, near Wall Street in New York City. That same year, the two sisters founded a weekly newspaper. Both ventures did very well for several years.

Victoria Woodhull was born in Homer, Ohio, near Utica. She received little formal education. Woodhull and Claflin moved to England in 1877.   Miriam Schneir

Woodpecker is a bird that uses its long, chisellike bill for drilling into trees. Woodpeckers bore holes in bark and wood to find food and build nests. These small- to medium-sized birds live in almost all parts of the world.

Body. Woodpeckers have several features that are especially useful to their way of life. Strong feet and sharp claws enable the birds to climb up and down tree trunks and to cling to bark. Most woodpeckers have two front toes and two hind toes, an arrangement that helps them to climb without falling backwards. Stiff tail feathers brace the birds against the tree trunk. Strong neck muscles propel the bird's head rapidly back and forth while it drills. Muscles on the head act as shock absorbers, protecting the skull from the impact of the drilling.

M. Vinciguerra, N.A.S.

WORLD BOOK illustration by Marion Pahl

The woodpecker's tongue

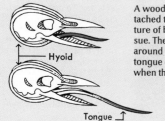

Hyoid

Tongue

A woodpecker's tongue is attached to the *hyoid,* a structure of bone and elastic tissue. The hyoid, which loops around the skull, pushes the tongue out of the mouth when the bird is feeding.

The male pileated woodpecker, *left,* is often mistaken for the ivory-billed woodpecker. It is found in eastern North America and in parts of the Northwest. Both sexes have a high crest on the head.

Ivory-billed woodpecker
Campephilus principalis
Once found in southeastern United States, now known only in Cuba
Body length: 20 inches (51 centimeters)

Green woodpecker
Picus canus
Found in Eurasian forests
Body length: 12 inches
(30 centimeters)

Hairy woodpecker
Dendrocopos villosus
Found in North America
Body length: 10 inches
(25 centimeters)

WORLD BOOK illustrations
by Guy Coheleach

Many woodpeckers have black and white or brown and white feathers, and many are banded or spotted. Most of the males have some red feathers on their head. Some woodpeckers also have yellow or green feathers.

Habits. Woodpeckers use their bill to probe bark and wood for the adult insects and insect larvae they eat. They draw the food out with an extremely long, sticky tongue that has a barbed tip. Some woodpeckers also catch insects on the ground or in the air. In addition, many woodpeckers eat fruit and nuts. The wood-boring insects that woodpeckers eat are available the year around. For this reason, few woodpeckers migrate.

For their nests, woodpeckers dig holes in the trunks of trees. The nest may extend 6 to 18 inches (15 to 45 centimeters) below the entrance hole. It has no lining except for some wood chips. A female woodpecker lays from two to eight pure-white eggs.

A woodpecker's call consists of a series of harsh notes. The birds also drum with their bills on dead branches or on anything hollow. They use this sound to advertise their presence and defend their territory. Except for nesting pairs, most woodpeckers live alone.

Kinds. There are about 200 species of woodpeckers, but only about 23 species live in North America. Their habitat ranges from evergreen forests to arid deserts.

The large *ivory-billed woodpecker* once lived in the swampy forests of the southeastern United States. Logging has destroyed most of its habitat, and for many years it was feared to be extinct. In 1986, at least two ivory-billed woodpeckers were sighted in Cuba. Some people mistake the male *pileated woodpecker* for the ivory-bill because both birds have red crests on their heads. However, the pileated woodpecker remains fairly common in North American forests. The *acorn woodpecker* of the western United States drills holes for storing acorns, which it eats when other food is scarce. The *redheaded woodpecker* of the eastern and midwestern United States is distinguished by its bright-red head and neck. This bird damages telephone and telegraph poles in areas where few trees grow.

The only woodpeckers that damage trees are *sapsuckers.* They do so by boring many holes in bark to reach the sap they feed on. *Flickers* are among the most common North American woodpeckers. They feed mainly on the ground and are especially fond of ants.

Scientific classification. Woodpeckers belong to the woodpecker family, Picidae. The ivory-billed woodpecker is *Campephilus principalis;* the pileated is *Dryocopus pileatus;* the acorn is *Melanerpes formicivorus;* and the redheaded is *M. erythrocephalus.*   Richard C. Banks

See also **Bird** (picture: Birds of the desert); **Flicker; Sapsucker.**

Woodrat, also called *pack rat* or *trade rat,* is a native of North and Central America. It looks much like the house rat but has larger ears, softer fur, and a hairy, instead of a naked, scaly, tail. The woodrat also has cleaner habits. It will not live in sewers and garbage dumps. Some western woodrats live in the mountains and build their nests on rock ledges. Others live on the deserts in clumps of cactus and scrubby growth. They make their nests in piles of sticks and cactus. A female has one or two litters (3 to 6 young) a season.

Woodrats are curious about everything that goes on around them. They pick up and hide or carry home small articles that catch their fancy, such as silverware, nails, buckles, brightly colored stones, and even manure. This is why they got the name *pack rats.* Sometimes the animal will drop and leave behind something it is carrying, in order to "pack off" a more attractive article. This accounts for its being called *trade rat.*

Scientific classification. Woodrats belong to the family Cricetidae. They make up the genus *Neotoma.* A typical species is *N. floridana.*   Clyde Jones

See also **Rat.**

Woods, Granville T. (1856-1910), was a black American inventor who obtained more than 50 patents. He made his most significant invention, a railway telegraph system, in 1887. This system allowed crew members on moving trains to communicate with one another and with railroad stations. It made rail traffic safer by helping to avoid train collisions.

Woods was born in Columbus, Ohio. He was mostly self-taught, but also took college engineering courses and worked as a railroad engineer. Woods received his first patent, for an improved steam boiler furnace, in 1884. His inventions included an egg incubator, an automatic air brake, a *galvanic* (electric) battery, a telephone transmitter, and devices for telegraphs and railway systems. Woods sold many inventions to such large companies as General Electric, Westinghouse Air Brake, and American Bell Telephone.   Raymond W. Smock

Woods Hole Oceanographic Institution is a private, nonprofit research center for marine science on Cape Cod, at Woods Hole, Mass. It has a variety of laboratories onshore, and several research vessels, including a small deep-diving submarine, for exploring the oceans. Scientists at the institution pursue research in such fields as marine biology, chemistry, geology and geophysics, physics, and engineering. The institution awards doctor's degrees and offers programs for advanced undergraduates and postdoctoral students.

Critically reviewed by the Woods Hole Oceanographic Institution

Woodson, Carter Goodwin (1875-1950), is widely regarded as the leading writer on black history of his time. A black American, Woodson devoted his life to bringing the achievements of his race to the world's attention. His founding of the Association for the Study of Negro Life and History (now the Association for the Study of Afro-American Life and History) in 1915 has been called the start of the black history movement. The association began publishing *The Journal of Negro His-*

Bruce Coleman Inc.

A woodrat has soft fur and a hairy tail.

tory, a scholarly magazine, in 1916. The best known of Woodson's 16 books is *Negro in our History* (1922). Many scholars consider it one of the finest full-length works on black history.

Woodson was born in New Canton, Va. His parents were former slaves. Woodson received a Ph.D. degree in history from Harvard University. He won the Spingarn Medal in 1926.   Richard Bardolph

See also **Black History Month.**

Woodsworth, James Shaver (1874-1942), was a Methodist minister and one of Canada's leading social reformers of the 1900's. He recommended many of the social welfare programs that Canada has adopted since World War II ended in 1945, including old age pensions and unemployment relief.

Woodsworth was born near Toronto, Ont. In the early 1900's, he became known for his dedication to helping needy farmers and workers. Woodsworth strongly opposed violence, and during World War I (1914-1918), he spoke out against Canada's military draft. He participated in the Winnipeg general strike of 1919, in which about 30,000 workers in Winnipeg, Man., struck for various rights. In 1921, Woodsworth won election to the Canadian Parliament as a member of the Manitoba Independent Labour Party. Woodsworth served there until his death.

In 1933, Woodsworth helped found the Co-operative Commonwealth Federation, Canada's former socialist party. He led the party (now the New Democratic Party) until 1940. Woodsworth was the only member of the House of Commons who voted against Canada's entry into World War II in 1939.   Richard Allen

Woodward, Robert Burns (1917-1979), an American chemist, won the 1965 Nobel Prize in chemistry for his work in synthetic organic chemistry. This field involves producing artificially chemical compounds found in nature. Woodward developed methods for making such organic compounds as chlorophyll, cholesterol, cortisone, quinine, and strychnine. He also determined the molecular structures of Aureomycin, Terramycin, and other complex organic compounds.

Woodward was born in Boston and earned a Ph.D. degree in chemistry from the Massachusetts Institute of Technology. He taught at Harvard University from 1941 until his death.   O. Bertrand Ramsay

Woodwind instrument. See **Music** (Musical instruments [Wind instruments]; illustration); **Orchestra** (The musicians; illustration).

Woodworking is the forming and shaping of wood to make useful and decorative objects. It is one of the oldest crafts and ranks as a popular hobby and an important industry. A skilled woodworker with a well-equipped home workshop can build items as simple as a birdhouse or as complicated as decorative furniture. Tools for a workshop can be purchased at hardware and department stores. Lumber retail stores and hobby shops sell a wide variety of wood.

The construction industry employs carpenters who construct the wooden framework of buildings. Other kinds of woodworkers include *finish carpenters* and *cabinetmakers.* Finish carpenters do the inside trim work around windows, cabinets, and other features that must fit exactly. Cabinetmakers design, shape, and assemble furniture, built-in cabinets, and stairways.

This article discusses woodworking as a hobby. For details on woodworking in industry, see **Carpentry.**

The history of woodworking goes back to about 8,000 B.C., when people first used an ax as a woodworking tool. In the Middle Ages, woodworkers and other craftworkers formed organizations called *guilds.* The guilds were similar in some ways to today's labor unions.

In 1873, electric power was used to drive machine tools for the first time. Through the years came the development of the power tools now used for woodworking. The first practical hand drill was patented in 1917. By 1925, woodworkers could buy electric portable saws for their home workshop. Today, power tools can be used in most woodworking operations, but many people enjoy shaping wood with hand tools instead.

Steps in woodworking

Woodworking projects, together with plans for their construction, can be found in books, magazines, and manuals in bookstores and public libraries. This article includes plans for building a desk rack to hold a set of *World Book.* There are five main steps in woodworking: (1) planning and design, (2) cutting, (3) drilling, (4) fastening, and (5) sanding and finishing.

Planning and design. Careful planning can prevent mistakes and save time and materials. A scale drawing of the object being built should be made before starting any woodworking project. This drawing includes the exact measurements of the object. The craftworker marks the measurements on the wood with a pencil and lists all the steps to be followed in the project.

A woodworking *tape* and *rule* are used to measure dimensions. A *square* can also be used for measuring and for making straight lines and angles. Various *gauges* make marks and parallel lines for the woodworker to follow when cutting joints and attaching hinges.

The parts of the finished object will fit together properly if the drawing has been prepared correctly and if measuring and construction have been done accurately. A well-designed object is both attractive and the right size for its purpose. For example, a birdhouse must have an entrance large enough for the birds that will use it.

Cutting wood to the right size and shape can be done with a variety of hand and power tools, including *saws, chisels,* and *planes.* The largest and most familiar handsaws are the *crosscut saw* and the *ripsaw.* Crosscut saws cut across the grain of the wood, and ripsaws cut with the grain.

Power tools can do a job far more quickly, easily, and accurately than hand tools. For example, a *toothed disk blade* has a toothed disk that spins at great speed. Different blades can be attached for a variety of cutting operations, such as crosscutting and ripping. A circular saw can also cut joints to connect sections of wood.

A common hand tool for cutting joints is the *backsaw,* which has a thin rectangular blade for fine work. The blade has a metal bar along its back to make it stiff. Chisels, which can cut deeply into the surface of wood, can be used for making joints or for trimming and carving. A *portable electric router* has attachments called *bits* that can be used to trim or shape wood and to make joints and decorative cuts. A hand tool called a *coping saw* consists of a metal frame that holds a narrow blade used for cutting curves in wood. *Jigsaws* and *saber saws,* power tools that cut curves, have a thin blade that moves up and down at great speed.

Mechanical planes, called *jointers,* and hand planes have sharp blades that smooth and shape wood. A *wood-turning lathe* shapes wood into rounded forms by rapidly spinning it against a cutting edge held by the operator. A *file* shapes wood in places where a sharper cutting tool does not fit. Files can also sharpen tools.

Drilling enables a woodworker to connect sections of wood with *screws, metal plates,* and *hinges.* Drilling may also be required when constructing some *joints.*

Braces and *hand drills* have bits to make holes of different sizes for various purposes. *Portable electric drills* and *drill presses* also use bits to drill holes. They have attachments for sanding and other purposes.

Fastening. Sections of wood are fastened together with metal fasteners, such as *screws* and *nails,* and with *adhesives.* Tools for fastening include *screwdrivers* and *hammers.* Screwdrivers insert screws that connect sections of wood and hold hinges and metal plates. Hammers are used to drive in nails and a variety of other types of metal fasteners.

Basic tools for woodworking Hobbyists use many of the woodworking tools pictured below. Although power tools can be used in any woodworking operation, many people prefer to shape wood with hand tools.

WORLD BOOK illustrations by Dick Keller and William Graham

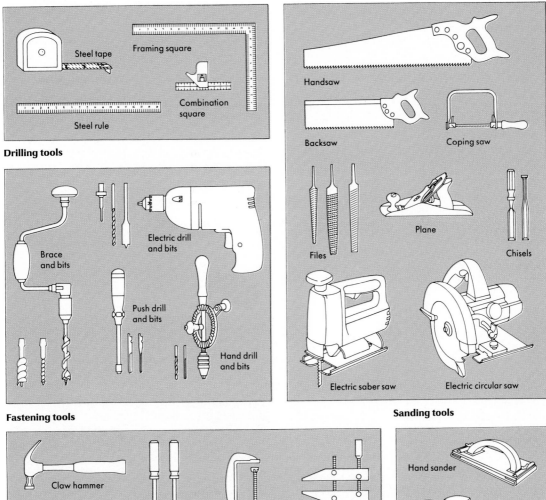

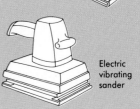

How to build a *World Book* desk rack

Materials 1- by 3-in. board, 55 in. long
1- by 10-in. board, 17 in. long
8 flat-head wood screws
size 12, 2 in. long

Tools Pencil   Crosscut saw
Rule   Coping saw
Square   Drill and bits
Screwdriver   Sandpaper

Making the supports and end pieces

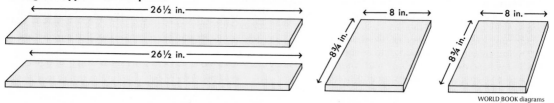

WORLD BOOK diagrams

With a crosscut saw, cut the 1- by 3-inch board into two 26½-inch lengths. These sections will serve as the back and bottom supports of the *World Book* desk rack. Next, use the crosscut saw to cut the 1- by 10-inch board into two sections. Each section should measure 8 inches wide and 8¾ inches high. These sections will be the end pieces of the desk rack.

Marking the end pieces

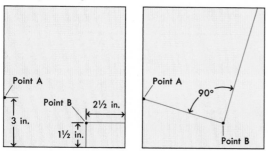

With a pencil, mark points A and B on each end piece according to the measurements given in the diagram at the left above. Draw a line from A to B. Place a square along the line and extend the line upward to form a 90° (right) angle, as shown in the diagram at the right above.

Locating the supports

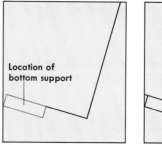
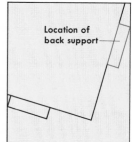

Place the end of the bottom support against the line that connects points A and B, as shown in the diagram at the left above. Draw lines around the edge of the support. Place the end of the back support against the other line, as shown in the diagram at the right above. Draw lines around the support's edge.

Drilling the holes

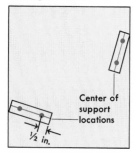

Draw a line through the center of each of the rectangles you have marked on the end pieces, as shown in the diagram at the far left. On the lines, mark the locations of the screw holes ½ inch from the ends of the rectangles. Drill holes slightly larger than the screws you will use. Next, draw lines through the center of each of the ends of the supports, as shown in the diagram at the left. Mark the lines with the locations of the screw holes, as shown, and drill holes smaller than the screws you will use.

Cutting the feet

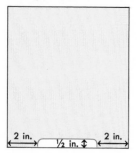

Before assembling, use a coping saw to cut out the feet of the end pieces, as shown in the diagram at the left.

WORLD BOOK photo by Steven Spicer

To complete the desk rack, first sand all edges, rough surfaces, and tool marks. After assembling the pieces, you may finish the rack by staining and varnishing it or by painting it.

Gluing is one of the oldest methods of fastening sections of wood, and a variety of adhesives are used in woodworking. *Polyvinyl resin emulsion glue,* or white glue, can be applied directly from the bottle. It should not be used if it will come in contact with water or high temperatures. *Urea-formaldehyde resin glue* and *resorcinol formaldehyde resin glue* both must be mixed by the user. Urea glue can resist cold water for short periods, but it cannot withstand high temperatures. Resorcinol glue is waterproof and heat resistant.

After gluing, wood should be put into *clamps* for as long as 12 hours. The length of time depends on the temperature, the kind of wood, and the type of glue. Clamping holds the wood in place and spreads the glue into the pores.

Sanding and finishing. Sanding removes tool marks and makes wood surfaces smooth for finishing. Sanding should not begin until the wood has been cut to its final size. Most *abrasive paper* manufactured for use by hand has rough particles of the minerals *flint* or *garnet.* Aluminum oxide is a common sanding material used in such machines as a *portable belt sander* or a *vibrating sander.* Portable belt sanders work better than vibrating sanders on large wood surfaces.

Woodworkers use a variety of *finishes* to protect wood and to bring out the beauty of the grain. A *stain* is a dye that colors wood without hiding the pattern and feel of the grain. *Paint* covers the grain of the wood and provides a color of its own. Varnish, shellac, and lacquer add a hard, glossy finish while exposing the beauty of the wood. *Wax* protects varnish and has a smooth, shiny finish when polished. *Enamel* is a type of glossy paint.

Tool care and safety

Tools are made to be safe when used correctly. They can be preserved—and accidents can be prevented—by using the right tools for the job and keeping them clean and sharp. A woodworker must use extra pressure with a dull tool, and injury could result if the tool slips. Many tools can be sharpened on the rough surface of an *oilstone.* A broken or damaged tool does not work properly and should not be used.

Whenever possible, wood should be held in a vise or by clamps, so that both hands are free to handle the tool being used. Floors should be kept clean of such substances as sawdust and finishing materials, which are slippery and also could catch fire. Safety glasses should always be worn during cutting and boring operations in order to protect the eyes from flying particles of wood. Loose clothing and jewelry that could get caught in a machine should not be worn in a woodworking area.

A craftworker can prevent accidents by holding a portable power tool until all the moving parts have stopped. A machine should never be left running unless the person operating it is present. In addition, a machine should be disconnected when not in use. The hazard of receiving an electric shock can be reduced by connecting *ground wires* to machines that have not been previously grounded.

Wood for woodworking

Woodworkers classify wood as *hardwood* or *softwood,* depending on the type of tree from which it comes. Most hardwood trees are *deciduous*—that is,

they lose their leaves every autumn. Most softwood, or *coniferous,* trees have narrow, pointed leaves and stay green the year around. This classification system does not indicate the hardness of wood, because various softwoods are harder than some hardwoods. However, the two types of wood have other characteristics that are important to the woodworker.

Hardwoods have beautiful grain patterns and can be used to make fine furniture. Some hardwoods have large pores and must be treated with a paste or liquid called *filler* before being covered with a finish. Wood to be finished with paint does not need a fancy grain to be attractive because the paint covers the pattern. Hardwoods used in woodworking include birch, mahogany, maple, oak, and walnut.

Most softwoods can easily be sawed, planed, chiseled, or bored. They are used mainly for structural work, but such softwoods as Douglas-fir, ponderosa pine, redcedar, and white pine can be used for woodworking and furniture.

Hardwood or softwood can also be used to make a type of manufactured board called *plywood.* Plywood consists of an odd number of thin layers of wood glued together. It is lightweight and strong and can be purchased in many sizes and wood patterns.   Alva H. Jared

See also **Plywood; Saw; Wood; Woodcarving.**

Additional resources

Level I
Lasson, Robert. *If I Had a Hammer: Woodworking with Seven Basic Tools.* Dutton, 1974.
Meyer, Carolyn. *Saw, Hammer, and Paint: Woodworking and Finishing for Beginners.* Morrow, 1973.
Weiss, Harvey. *Hammer & Saw: An Introduction to Woodworking.* Harper, 1981.

Level II
Feirer, John L. *The Woodworker's Reference Guide and Sourcebook.* Scribner, 1983.
Scharff, Robert. *Complete Book of Wood Finishing.* 2nd ed. McGraw, 1974.
Scott, Ernest. *Working in Wood: The Illustrated Manual of Tools, Methods, Materials, and Classic Constructions.* Putnam, 1980.

Woody nightshade. See Bittersweet.
Woof. See Weaving.
Wool is a fiber that comes from the fleece of sheep and some other animals. It is made into durable fabrics used in manufacturing blankets, clothing, rugs, and other items. Wool fabrics clean easily, and they resist wrinkles and hold their shape well. Wool also absorbs moisture and insulates against both cold and heat. All these features make wool popular for coats, sweaters, gloves, socks, and other clothing.

Wool fibers are nearly cylindrical in shape. Overlapping scales on the surface make the fibers mat and interlock under heat, moisture, and pressure. This property of wool fibers is called *felting.* Felting increases the strength and durability of wool fabrics. It also enables wool to be made into felt. See **Fiber** (picture: Wool and nylon fibers).

The Wool Products Labeling Act of 1939 established guidelines in the United States for defining and labeling wool products. This law defines wool as the fiber from the fleece of sheep. It also includes such fibers as alpaca, from alpacas; camel's hair; cashmere, from Cashmere goats; mohair, from Angora goats; and vicuña, from vicuñas.

Grant Heilman

Sheep shearers use power clippers to remove a fleece. An expert shearer can clip 200 or more sheep a day. In most parts of the world, sheep are sheared once a year.

physical condition of the animal and by the climate in which it lives. The fleece of a healthy sheep is covered by an oily substance called *yolk.* Yolk consists of wool grease and *suint* (dried perspiration). It protects the sheep from rain and keeps the fleece from becoming matted.

Young sheep produce the best wool. The softest and finest wool, called *lamb's wool,* comes from 6- to 12-

Worldwide production of raw wool totals about $6\frac{1}{4}$ billion pounds (2.8 billion kilograms) annually. The leading wool-producing nations are Australia, the Soviet Union, New Zealand, China, and Argentina, in that order. Every state in the United States produces some wool. Texas is the leading producer, followed by California, Wyoming, Colorado, and South Dakota, in that order. The United States uses more wool than it produces, and so it imports some wool.

Sources of wool. Almost all wool comes from sheep. These animals—and their wool—are classified into five groups, depending on the quality of the fleece. The five classes of wool, listed here in order of quality, are (1) fine wool, (2) crossbred wool, (3) medium wool, (4) long wool, and (5) coarse wool, or carpet wool.

Fine-wooled sheep include the Merino and other breeds with Merino ancestry, such as the Debouillet and the Rambouillet. These sheep produce the finest wool, which is used in making high-quality clothing.

Crossbred-wooled sheep, such as the Columbia and Corriedale, are crossbreeds of fine- and long-wooled breeds. Their wool is used for rugged clothing.

Medium-wooled sheep provide wool used in making industrial and upholstery fabrics. Cheviot, Dorset, Hampshire, Oxford, Shropshire, Southdown, and Suffolk sheep are in this group.

Long-wooled sheep include the Cotswold, Leicester, Lincoln, and Romney. They produce wool used for carpets and industrial fabrics.

Coarse-wooled sheep include the Karakul and Scottish Blackface. The wool of these animals is used mostly for carpets and handicraft yarns.

Types of wool are determined by the quality of a sheep's fleece. The quality depends on the age and

Leading wool-producing states

Wool clipped from sheep each year

Texas	17,500,000 pounds (7,900,000 kilograms)
California	9,400,000 pounds (4,300,000 kilograms)
Wyoming	8,000,000 pounds (3,600,000 kilograms)
Colorado	6,700,000 pounds (3,000,000 kilograms)
South Dakota	6,400,000 pounds (2,900,000 kilograms)
Utah	5,400,000 pounds (2,450,000 kilograms)
Montana	5,200,000 pounds (2,360,000 kilograms)
New Mexico	5,000,000 pounds (2,300,000 kilograms)
Iowa	3,300,000 pounds (1,500,000 kilograms)
Idaho	3,200,000 pounds (1,450,000 kilograms)

Figures are for 1984.
Source: *Agricultural Statistics 1985,* U.S. Department of Agriculture.

Leading wool-producing countries

Wool clipped from sheep each year

Australia	1,607,000,000 lbs. (729,000,000 kg)
Soviet Union	1,021,000,000 lbs. (463,000,000 kg)
New Zealand	800,000,000 lbs. (363,000,000 kg)
China	412,000,000 lbs. (187,000,000 kg)
Argentina	342,000,000 lbs. (155,000,000 kg)
South Africa	241,000,000 lbs. (109,000,000 kg)
Uruguay	201,000,000 lbs. (91,000,000 kg)
Turkey	139,000,000 lbs. (63,000,000 kg)
Great Britain	113,000,000 lbs. (51,000,000 kg)
United States	101,000,000 lbs. (46,000,000 kg)

Figures are for 1984. Source: *Production Yearbook 1984,* FAO.

month-old sheep. *Hog wool,* also called *hogget wool,* is the first fleece sheared from a sheep that is 12 to 14 months old. After a sheep has been sheared for the first time, its wool is called *wether wool.*

Lower quality wool comes from dead or diseased sheep. Sheep that have been slaughtered for their meat provide *pulled wool,* sometimes called *skin wool* or *slipe wool. Dead wool* is taken from sheep that have died of disease or have been killed by other animals. Aged sheep have matted and tangled fleeces that provide *cotty wool.* Fleeces soiled by manure or dirt are called *tag locks* in the United States and *stain pieces* in England and Australia.

The United States Federal Trade Commission, which administers the Wool Products Labeling Act, classifies wool into two categories. *Virgin wool,* or *new wool,* has never been spun into yarn or made into felt. Some fabrics are made of fibers that have been reclaimed from previously spun or woven wool. *Recycled wool* is the name given to these products. Fabrics made from recycled wool are sometimes called *shoddy.*

Processing of wool involves four major steps: (1) shearing, (2) sorting and grading, (3) making yarn, and (4) making fabric.

Shearing. Most sheep shearers use power shears, and experts can clip 200 or more animals a day. They remove the fleece in one piece so the various parts can be easily identified for sorting and grading. Different parts of a fleece vary in quality. For example, the best wool comes from the shoulders and sides of the sheep.

In most parts of the world, sheep are sheared once a year, in spring or early summer. But in some regions, the fleeces may be cut off twice yearly.

Sorting and grading. Workers remove any stained, damaged, or inferior wool from each fleece and sort the rest of the wool according to the quality of the fibers.

Wool fibers are judged not only on the basis of their strength, but also by their (1) *fineness* (diameter), (2) length, (3) *crimp* (waviness), and (4) color.

In the United States, the fineness of wool fibers is determined by comparing them to the fineness of Merino wool. In England, fineness depends on the number of fibers per inch. In Australia, the diameter of the fibers is generally measured in units called *microns.* A micron equals a millionth of a meter (.000039 inch).

Fiber length is important in determining what processes will be used to make yarn and fabric. *Carding length fibers,* also called *clothing length fibers,* measure less than $1\frac{1}{2}$ inches (3.8 centimeters) long. *French combing length fibers* range from $1\frac{1}{2}$ to $2\frac{1}{2}$ inches (3.8 to 6.4 centimeters) in length. *Combing length fibers* are more than $2\frac{1}{2}$ inches (6.4 centimeters) long.

The natural crimp of wool provides the fibers with elasticity. This property enables wool fabrics to hold their shape after being stretched or twisted. The best wool fibers have many evenly spaced waves.

The color of most wool ranges from white to dark ivory. White wool is the most desirable because manufacturers may have to bleach darker wool before it can be dyed.

Making yarn. The wool is scoured with detergents to remove the yolk and such impurities as dust and sand. Wool grease from the yolk is processed into lanolin, a substance used in hand creams and other cosmetics.

After the wool dries, it is *carded.* The carding process involves passing the wool through rollers that have thin wire teeth. The teeth untangle the fibers and arrange them into a flat sheet called a *web.* The web is then formed into narrow ropes known as *slivers.*

After carding, the processes used in making yarn vary slightly, depending on the length of the fibers. Carding length fibers are used in making *woolen yarn.* Comb-

Making wool yarn involves several steps. Carding machines, *left,* untangle the fibers and arrange them into a sheet called a *web.* Webs are formed into narrow ropes called *slivers, center.* Slivers are stretched into thinner strands, and spinning machines twist them into yarn, *right.*

Burlington Industries, Inc.

Wool fabrics are woven by large power looms, *above.* After a fabric has been made, it goes through various finishing processes to give it the desired appearance and strength.

ing length and French combing length fibers are made into *worsted yarn.* The processes used for the two kinds of yarn are similar. But worsted slivers go through an additional step called *combing,* which removes impurities and short fibers.

After carding or combing, the slivers are stretched and slightly twisted to form thinner strands called *roving.* Spinning machines then twist the roving into yarn. Woolen yarn is bulky and fuzzy, with fibers that lie in different directions. Worsted yarn is smooth and highly twisted, and its fibers are parallel.

Making fabric. Wool manufacturers knit or weave yarn into a variety of fabrics. They use woolen yarns in making flannel, homespun, melton, Saxony, Shetland, and tweed fabrics. Worsted yarns are used for such fabrics as broadcloth, crepe, gabardine, serge, sharkskin, twill, and whipcord. Almost all wool fabrics except felt are made from yarn (see **Felt**).

Wool may be dyed at various stages of the manufacturing process. If the fibers are dyed before spinning, the process is called *stock dyeing* or *top dyeing.* If they are dyed after being spun into yarn, it is called *yarn dyeing, package dyeing,* or *skein dyeing.* If the dyeing does not take place until the fabric has been made, it is known as *piece dyeing.* Most fabrics with fancy designs are stock dyed or yarn dyed. Piece dyeing is used for solid-colored fabrics. See **Dye**.

All wool fabrics undergo finishing processes to give them the desired appearance and feel. The finishing of fabrics made of woolen yarn begins with *fulling.* This process involves wetting the fabric thoroughly with water and then passing it through rollers. Fulling makes

the fibers interlock and mat together. It shrinks the material and gives it additional strength and thickness. Worsteds go through a process called *crabbing,* in which the fabric passes through boiling water and then cold water. This procedure strengthens the fabric.

Some wool fabrics tend to shrink when dry-cleaned. To prevent such shrinkage, some manufacturers preshrink the fabric. One popular process, called London Shrinking, uses water and pressure to shrink the fabric. After the various finishing processes, the fabric is made into clothing and other products.

History. About 10,000 years ago, people in central Asia began to raise sheep for food and clothing. The art of spinning wool into yarn developed about 4000 B.C. and encouraged trade among the nations in the region of the Mediterranean Sea. Merino sheep were developed in Spain by A.D. 100. Spain was the only source of these sheep until the 1700's.

The first wool factory in England was established about A.D. 50 in Winchester by the Romans. The wool industry soon played a major part in the nation's economy. By 1660, the export of wool fabrics accounted for about two-thirds of England's foreign trade.

In the early 1500's, Spanish explorers brought sheep to what is now the United States. England discouraged the wool industry's growth in the American Colonies so colonists would have to rely on English goods. But the colonists smuggled sheep from England. By the 1700's, spinning and weaving were flourishing in America.

In 1797, the British brought 13 Merino sheep to Australia and started the country's Merino sheep industry. Spain first sold Merino sheep to the United States in the early 1800's. Americans bred these animals with descendants of the sheep that had been brought from England. In the 1800's, many pioneers brought sheep with them while traveling to the West. As a result, the production of wool and wool fabrics spread to nearly all parts of the United States. Ira Block

Related articles in *World Book* include:

Alpaca	Cashmere goat	Llama	Vicuña
Camel	Goat	Mohair	Weaving
Cashmere	Lanolin	Sheep	Worsted

Wool wax. See Lanolin.

Woolf, Virginia (1882-1941), was a major British novelist, critic, and essayist. She was one of the leading figures in the literary movement called *modernism.* Other modernists included James Joyce, Gertrude Stein, Ezra Pound, and T. S. Eliot. Woolf used a literary technique called *stream of consciousness* to reveal the inner lives of her characters and at the same time to criticize the social system of the day. See **Novel** (New directions in the novel).

Woolf's most famous novel, *To the Lighthouse* (1927), examines the life of an upper-middle class British family. It shows the fragility of human relationships and the collapse of social values. Some readers believe the portrait of Mr. Ramsay in this novel resembles Woolf's father, the critic Leslie Stephen.

Woolf's other fiction includes the novels *Jacob's Room* (1922) and *Mrs. Dalloway* (1925), in which she studies the world of characters tragically affected by World War I. *Orlando* (1928) and *Flush* (1933) are fanciful biographies. In *The Waves* (1931), interior monologues reveal the personalities of the six central characters.

Unlike other modernists, whose politics were rightwing and often profascist, Woolf was a feminist, socialist, and pacifist. She expressed her socialist-feminist theories in the essays *A Room of One's Own* (1929) and *Three Guineas* (1938). Her last novels, *The Years* (1939) and *Between the Acts* (1941), are as experimental as her earlier work.

Virginia Stephen was born in London. In 1912, she married editor and writer Leonard Woolf. She belonged to the Bloomsbury Group, an informal group of intellectuals (see **Bloomsbury Group**). With her husband, Woolf founded the Hogarth Press, which published works of noted modern writers. Her reputation has soared with the publication of several volumes of letters and diaries and her critical essays.   Jane Marcus

Woolley, Mary Emma (1863-1947), was an outstanding American educator. She served as president of Mount Holyoke College from 1901 to 1937 and was president of the American Association of University Women from 1927 to 1933. Woolley was also active in world peace movements and public affairs. In 1932, she became the first woman to represent the United States at an international disarmament conference. Woolley was born in Norwalk, Conn.   Albert E. Van Dusen

Woolley, Sir Leonard (1880-1960), was a British archaeologist. He became known for his discoveries at Ur, a city in ancient Sumer (now part of Iraq). His findings revealed achievements of the Sumerians, who created one of the earliest civilizations over 5,000 years ago.

Between 1922 and 1934, Woolley directed excavations at Ur. He discovered geological evidence for a great flood, possibly the Flood described in the Bible. He also uncovered the royal cemetery, whose tombs contained bodies buried with objects made of precious metals.

Woolley, whose full name was Charles Leonard Woolley, was born in London and graduated from Oxford University. He led excavations in Great Britain, Italy, Turkey, Syria, and Iraq. He wrote more than 25 books, including *Spadework: Adventures in Archaeology* (1953) and *Excavations at Ur: A Record of 12 Years' Work* (1954). He was knighted in 1935.   Richard G. Klein

Woolly mammoth. See **Mammoth.**

Woolly monkey is a type of large monkey that lives in the Amazon River basin of South America. There are two species—the *common woolly monkey,* also called *Humboldt's woolly monkey,* and the *yellow-tailed woolly monkey.*

Woolly monkeys have thick, soft, dark fur. They live in groups of about 12 animals. They move through the trees, feeding mostly on fruit. Woolly monkeys spend most of their time sleeping, but they are playful when awake. They are known to greet each other by "kissing."

Adult woolly monkeys weigh from 10 to 20 pounds (4.5 to 9 kilograms). They measure 15 to 23 inches (38 to 58 centimeters) long, not including their 22- to 27-inch (56- to 69-centimeter) long tail, which can be used to grasp objects. The underside of the tail has no fur near the end. This area has ridges similar to human fingerprints and rough skin.

Woolly monkeys are threatened by the destruction of their rain forest home and by hunters who kill them for their meat. The yellow-tailed woolly monkey is extremely rare.

Scientific classification. Woolly monkeys belong to the New World monkey family, Cebidae. The common woolly mon-

key is *Lagothrix lagothricha,* and the yellow-tailed is *L. flavicauda.*   Roderic B. Mast and Russell A. Mittermeier

See also **Monkey** (pictures).

Woolman, John (1720-1772), was a colonial American writer and Quaker minister. He worked to abolish slavery, relieve poverty, obtain better treatment for Indians, and end war.

Woolman was born on a farm near what is now Rancocas, N.J. He worked as a clerk until he was 22 years old, when he became a minister and a tailor. Woolman preached while traveling on foot from New England to North Carolina. He convinced Philadelphia Quakers at their yearly meeting in 1758 to resolve not to keep or deal in slaves. This resolution was the first of its kind in the American Colonies.

When he was about 36 years old, Woolman began to write an account of his life and religious beliefs. His *Journal,* published in 1774, is noted for its sensitive descriptions of his feelings. Woolman also wrote essays condemning slavery and calling for better conditions for the poor.   Edward W. Clark

Woolworth is the family name of two American businessmen who were brothers.

Frank Winfield Woolworth (1852-1919) was the principal founder in 1912 of the F. W. Woolworth Company, a chain of five-and-ten-cent stores. When he died, the chain had more than 1,000 stores. In 1913, he built the Woolworth Building in New York City. It was the tallest building in the world at that time.

Woolworth was born in Rodman, N.Y., and he clerked in the village grocery store there. In 1878, while working for the firm of Moore & Smith in Watertown, N.Y., he suggested putting slow-moving goods on a counter and selling them for 5 cents. The venture was so successful that it was continued with new goods. Six store chains grew out of the five-cent counter experiment. All were united in 1912 to form the F. W. Woolworth Company.

Charles S. Woolworth (1856-1947) was cofounder of the F. W. Woolworth Company. He served as vice president until 1919 and as chairman of the board until 1944, when he retired. He was born in Rodman, N.Y. Woolworth founded 15 stores, which he and his brother united with 581 other stores in 1912 to form the F. W. Woolworth Company.   W. H. Baughn

Worcester, *WUS tuhr* (pop. 161,799; met. area pop. 402,918), is a leading New England industrial center and the second largest city of Massachusetts. Worcester lies about 40 miles (64 kilometers) west of Boston, the largest city (see **Massachusetts** [political map]).

In 1673, settlers from eastern Massachusetts founded the village of Quinsigamond on what is now the site of Worcester. In 1684, King Charles II of England canceled the Massachusetts Bay Colony's charter. This action so angered the people of Quinsigamond that they renamed their village Worcester. According to tradition, this name honored the Battle of Worcester (1651), in which Charles suffered a great defeat in the English Civil War.

Worcester, the county seat of Worcester County, covers 38 square miles (98 square kilometers). The city has about 375 manufacturing plants. Worcester's chief products include machinery and machine tools; fabricated metals; printed materials; and chemicals, plastics, and abrasives. Airlines, railroad freight lines, and passenger trains serve the city.

The College of the Holy Cross, the oldest Roman Catholic college in New England, was founded in Worcester in 1843. The city is also the home of Assumption College, Central New England College of Technology, Clark University, the University of Massachusetts Medical School, and Worcester Polytechnic Institute.

The Worcester Art Museum is known for its art objects from many periods of history. The Higgins Armory has an outstanding display of medieval and Renaissance armor. The American Antiquarian Society owns the largest collection of early American publications, including newspapers, sheet music, and children's books. The Worcester Science Center includes Gage Planetarium and a science museum and zoo. Also in Worcester are Mechanics Hall, the site of many cultural events; Centrum Civic Center; and Worcester Center, a three-level shopping complex.

Nipmuc Indians lived near what is now the site of Worcester before whites built a village there in 1673. Indians destroyed that settlement and another built in 1684. The whites settled Worcester permanently in 1713 and incorporated it as a town in 1722.

During the Revolutionary War in America (1775-1783), Worcester became the home of the *Massachusetts Spy,* a newspaper famous for its support of the colonists.

Manufacturing became important in Worcester after 1828, when the Blackstone Canal linked the town with Narragansett Bay, an arm of the Atlantic Ocean. Worcester received a city charter in 1848. Through the years, the growing number of industrial jobs in Worcester attracted thousands of immigrants.

The city's population reached a peak of 203,486 in 1950. Since then, many middle-income families have left Worcester and moved to the suburbs. A number of companies have also moved their factories from the city. Worcester has a council-manager form of government.

Barry J. Parsons

Word processing. See Typewriter (Kinds); **Office work** (Recording information); **Computer** (Creating and displaying words and pictures).

Worden, Alfred Merrill (1932-   ), a United States astronaut, was the command module pilot on the Apollo 15 mission. This mission was the first manned moon trip devoted primarily to scientific exploration.

During the Apollo 15 mission, from July 26 to Aug. 7, 1971, Worden orbited the moon in the command module *Endeavour* for six days. He took photographs, operated automatically recording instruments, and launched an 80-pound (36-kilogram) subsatellite into lunar orbit. While Worden orbited the moon, astronauts David R. Scott and James B. Irwin explored the moon. During the return to earth, Worden left the spacecraft for 20 minutes and took the first "walk" in deep space.

Worden was born in Jackson, Mich. He entered the Air Force after graduating from the United States Military Academy in 1955. Worden was an astronaut from 1966 until 1972, when he took an administrative job in the space program.   William J. Cromie

Words. See Dictionary; Etymology; Language; Pronunciation; Semantics; Slang; Spelling; Vocabulary.

Wordsworth, William (1770-1850), is considered by many scholars to be the most important English romantic poet. *Lyrical Ballads* (1798), a collection of poems by Wordsworth and Samuel Taylor Coleridge, is regarded as beginning the romantic movement in England.

In the preface to the second edition of *Lyrical Ballads* (1800), Wordsworth outlined ideas about poetry that have since been identified with romanticism. He argued that serious poems could describe "situations from common life," and be written in the ordinary language "really used by men." He believed such poems could clarify "the primary laws of our nature." He also insisted that poetry is the imaginative expression of emotions coming from actual personal experience.

Wordsworth has often been praised for his descriptions of nature. But he rightly claimed that his primary interest was the "mind of man." His finest poems, including "Michael," the "Lucy" lyrics, "The Solitary Reaper," and "Resolution and Independence," dramatize how imagination creates spiritual values out of the memory of sights and sounds in nature.

Early life. Wordsworth was born in Cockermouth, which is now in the county of Cumbria. His mother died in 1778 and his father died in 1783. Relatives provided for his education. Wordsworth entered Cambridge University in 1787, the year he wrote his first significant poem. During a summer vacation in 1790, he visited France, then in turmoil because of the French Revolution. After graduating from Cambridge in 1791, he returned to France and became a supporter of the revolution. He returned to England in December 1792. Although liberal in

Detail of a pencil and chalk drawing (1798) by Robert Hancock; National Portrait Gallery, London

William Wordsworth

his youth, he became politically and religiously conservative. He was appointed poet laureate in 1843.

Wordsworth met Coleridge about 1795, and *Lyrical Ballads* appeared in 1798. Most of its poems were by Wordsworth, including his famous "Tintern Abbey."

Later career. Wordsworth married Mary Hutchinson in 1802. They had five children. Wordsworth was deeply saddened by the death of his brother John in 1805. His sadness was reflected in his poem "Elegiac Stanzas Suggested by a Picture of Peele Castle" (1806). By 1806, Wordsworth had completed one of the most famous poems in English literature, "Ode: Intimations of Immortality." In this piece, Wordsworth praised childhood and urged individuals to rely on their intuition.

Wordsworth's masterpiece is his long autobiographical poem, *The Prelude: Growth of a Poet's Mind.* He wrote it between 1798 and 1805, but continued to revise it for the rest of his life. It was published in 1850, shortly after his death. In its best passages, it achieves a remarkable combination of simplicity and grandeur. Wordsworth wrote most of his best poetry before 1807. But he wrote several important works later, notably *The Excursion* (1814). This long poem discusses virtue, education, and religious faith. Wordsworth wrote 523 sonnets, and many of them compare with those of William Shakespeare and John Milton.   Karl Kroeber

See also **Bryant, William C.; Romanticism; Poetry** (Rhythm and meter).

Additional resources

Davies, Hunter. *William Wordsworth: A Biography.* Atheneum, 1980.
McCracken, David. *Wordsworth and the Lake District: A Guide to the Poems and Their Places.* Oxford, 1984.
Moorman, Mary Trevelyan. *William Wordsworth: A Biography.* 2 vols. Oxford, 1957-1965.
Noyes, Russell. *William Wordsworth.* G. K. Hall, 1971.

Work, in physics, is the result of a force moving an object through a measurable distance against a resistance. Two factors determine the amount of work done. One factor is the amount of force applied. The other factor is the distance the object moves. In physics, work is accomplished only when the force is sufficient to move the object. In other words, work is measured by what is done, not by the effort applied in attempting to move an object. People do work only when lifting, pushing, or sliding an object from one place to another. They do no work when holding an object without moving it, even though they may become tired.

Scientists and engineers measure work in units that represent the measurement of both force and distance. In the customary system of measurement, force is measured in such units as pounds or tons, and distance is measured in feet, inches, miles, or yards. Work can be measured as the product of any distance unit and any force unit. For example, one foot-pound equals the work done when a force of one pound moves something a distance of one foot. If a 50-pound object is lifted 4 feet, the work done is 200 foot-pounds. If, however, a 4-pound object is lifted 50 feet, the work done is still 200 foot-pounds. The foot-pound is the commonly used unit of work in the customary system.

In the metric system, the unit of force is the newton, and the unit of distance is the meter. Thus, work is measured in newton-meters. Another name for the newton-meter is *joule.* One foot-pound equals 1.35 newton-meters or joules. People who use the metric system also sometimes measure force in *dynes* and distance in centimeters. When these two units are used, work is measured in *dyne-centimeters,* or *ergs.* One dyne-centimeter or erg equals $\frac{1}{10,000,000}$ of a joule.

Work is always done by some agent, such as a person or a machine. The agent produces the force that causes motion. This motion is always produced against some form of resistance. For example, an automobile produces motion against the friction of the road and wind.

The units used to measure work are also used to measure energy. Energy is the ability of something to do work (see **Energy**). The rate at which work is done is called *power.* In measuring power, the amount of time needed to do the work is considered along with force and distance. Power is measured in a unit called the *watt.* One watt equals one joule per second. See **Power; Watt.**   Robert L. Weber

See also **Foot-pound; Joule; Dyne; Thermodynamics.**
Work school. See **Alternative school** (Features of alternative schools).
Work-study. See **Cooperative education.**
Workers' compensation provides pay and medical help for workers who are injured on the job, and pensions to the dependents of such workers in cases where death occurs. Loss of income due to accidents on the job has been a major problem of workers since the in-troduction of machine methods to industry. Today, most major countries have laws or private programs for workers' compensation.

The first workers' compensation laws were passed in Germany in 1883. Austria passed similar laws in 1887. Norway, Finland, France, Denmark, and Great Britain passed such laws in the 1890's. During the early 1900's, most other European nations passed workers' compensation laws.

Employers' liability laws preceded workers' compensation laws. They made an employer responsible for injuries to workers caused by defective machinery or by negligence on the part of management. In 1880, Britain adopted one of the first such laws.

In the United States, Maryland passed the first state compensation law in 1902. But the U.S. Supreme Court declared the Maryland law and other compensation acts of that decade unconstitutional. The growth of workers' compensation coverage increased greatly after Congress passed the Federal Employees' Compensation Act of 1916. This law provided benefits for certain federal civilian workers, or their survivors, in connection with injuries or death on the job.

Ten states passed workers' compensation laws in 1911. Wisconsin was the first. In 1948, the last of the then 48 states enacted a workers' compensation program. Alaska and Hawaii had such laws when they became states in 1959.

The state workers' compensation laws differ widely in provisions and administration. In general, the laws provide compensation and medical care for injured workers, and death benefits and pensions for the dependents of workers killed on the job. Employers bear the cost of workers' compensation benefits. In most states, the costs of administering the programs are financed by assessments against employers or insured carriers. However, in a few states, such costs are financed by general fund appropriations. Most state laws provide training in new jobs for workers who cannot continue in their old work because of injuries. The federal government and all states have laws covering compensation for occupational diseases. Workers' compensation laws exclude most farm workers and domestic servants, and some workers in small firms. State workers' compensation programs are administered by the states, but the level of state agency involvement varies considerably among the states. The Office of Workers' Compensation Programs in the Department of Labor administers federal compensation laws.

In the early 1980's, the total premiums paid for workers' compensation policies were about $20 billion a year and about 80 million workers were covered. An average company spent an amount equal to about 2 per cent of its payroll on workers' compensation protection. Total workers' compensation premiums amounted to more than $20 billion a year. Approximately $3 billion in additional benefits were paid by federal programs.   Paul L. Burgess

Working class. See **Social class.**
Working dog. See **Dog** (table: Breeds of purebred dogs; pictures); **Dog guide; Sheepdog.**
Works Progress Administration. See **New Deal** (The Second Hundred Days); **Roosevelt, Franklin Delano** (The New Deal); **Adult education.**

J. P. Laffont, Sygma

A United Nations (UN) General Assembly session brings together delegates from nearly all the world's nations. The UN works to settle disputes among countries and to maintain world peace.

World

World is the planet earth viewed especially as the home of human beings and other living things. The earth is just one of countless heavenly bodies in the universe. But it is the only one known to support life.

From the very beginning of their life on the earth, people have had to adapt to conditions in the world to survive. The earliest human beings lived by hunting and gathering wild plants. They made clothing from animal hides and furs and used branches and other natural materials to build shelters. About 10,000 years ago, some people began to raise plants and animals after food became scarce. People who farmed could settle in one place and produce enough food to feed many others. Villages grew up, and people developed methods of living in large groups. New occupations and forms of government became necessary. Over the years, people created more advanced technology and increasingly complicated forms of social life. They built great cities, developed civilizations, and found ways to control many powerful natural forces.

The world's surface consists of water and land. Air surrounds the surface and extends to outer space. Water—chiefly the great oceans—covers about 70 per cent of the world's surface. All living things must have water to live, just as they must have air. People also use water for irrigation, industry, power, and transportation. In addition, the oceans, lakes, and rivers provide fish and other foods.

Kevin R. Cox, the contributor of this article, is Professor of Geography at Ohio State University.

The oceans separate huge land masses called *continents.* Most of the world's countries lie on the continents. Others are on islands. Each country has its own political and economic systems. However, countries cooperate with one another in many ways. For example, they make trade agreements and sign treaties designed to reduce the likelihood of war.

The physical features of a country strongly influence where the people of that country live. People can most easily grow food on plains or in river valleys, where the soil is rich and deep. Mountainous regions generally are not suitable for crop farming because the soil is thin and easily washed away by rainfall. Many of the world's biggest cities began as important trading centers on seacoasts, lakeshores, and riverbanks. Thus, the majority of the world's people live on flat, fertile plains and in large cities that border major water transportation routes.

About $5\frac{1}{4}$ billion people live in the world. They are distributed unevenly over the land. Many areas are heavily populated. Other areas have no people at all. The population is increasing far more rapidly in some countries than in others.

All the world's people belong to the same species, *Homo sapiens,* which means they have a common ancestry. But many groups of people have lived apart for such a long time that they have developed certain physical variations. Members of the same group, or *race,* resemble one another more than they resemble members of other races. In some cases, physical appearance—such as the color of the skin or the shape of the eyes—can identify members of a race. However, many scientists use blood groups and other characteristics of body chemistry in comparing races.

Race has often been confused with cultural differences among people, such as differences in language or religion. Racial and cultural differences have been a basis of discrimination and prejudice. At times, these differences have served as an excuse for slavery, violence, and war.

This article provides an overview of the world as the home of human beings. It briefly describes the world's nations, people, and surface features. *World Book* contains a wealth of information about the world we live in. For information on the world as a planet, see the article **Earth**. The history of the world is traced in the article **World, History of the**. See also the *Related articles* listed at the end of this article.

Nations of the world

In 1990, the world had 170 independent countries and 47 dependencies. An independent country controls its own affairs. Dependencies are controlled in some way by independent countries. In most cases, an independent country is responsible for the dependency's foreign relations and defense, and some of the dependency's local affairs. However, many dependencies have complete control of their local affairs. About 5¼ billion people live in independent countries. Only about 15 million people live in dependencies.

The largest nation in the world in area is the Soviet Union. It covers 8,649,500 square miles (22,402,000 square kilometers). Each of the next four largest nations—Canada, China, the United States, and Brazil—covers more than 3 million square miles (7.8 million square kilometers). The five smallest independent countries, in descending order, are San Marino, Tuvalu, Nauru, Monaco, and Vatican City. Each of these countries covers less than 25 square miles (65 square kilometers). Vatican City has an area of only $\frac{1}{6}$ square mile (0.4 square kilometer).

Throughout history, the political map of the world has changed repeatedly. The most important changes have resulted from major wars. During ancient times, such military leaders as Alexander the Great and Julius Caesar conquered many different groups of people and established vast empires. Numerous empires rose and fell during later periods of history, and boundaries changed again and again.

Beginning about 1500, many European nations established colonies in North America, South America, Asia, Africa, and Australia. Most national boundaries established by the ruling countries remained after the colonies gained their independence.

World War I (1914-1918) and World War II (1939-1945) resulted in many important changes on the world map. World War I led to the formation of a number of new nations in Europe. These nations included Austria, Czechoslovakia, Hungary, and Yugoslavia. After World War II, several nations gained or lost territory, and many new nations were established in Asia. In Africa, a strong movement for independence swept the continent. More than 45 African colonies have gained independence since the 1950's.

How nations are grouped. The nations of the world may be grouped in various ways. They may be grouped by region, such as the *Far East,* the *Middle East,* and *Central America.* People often call the countries of the Eastern Hemisphere the *Old World* and those of the Western Hemisphere the *New World.* Countries are also often identified by continent, such as *African* or *Asian.*

The Soviet Union and the other Communist countries of Europe and Asia are known as the *Eastern bloc* or the *Communist World.* The United States, Canada, and other countries that oppose Communism are called the *Western bloc* or the *Free World.* Most countries have not committed themselves to either group. These *neutral,* or *nonaligned,* nations are often called the *Third World.* The term *First World* refers to the industrial countries of the Western bloc, and *Second World* to the Soviet Union and the Communist countries of the Eastern bloc.

Economists generally divide the nations of the world into two groups—*developed nations* and *developing nations.* Developed nations have a wide variety of industries and, in general, are wealthier than developing nations. Developing nations have long depended on agriculture and have few industries. Most of them are poor. Developed nations include the United States, Canada, Japan, Australia, and most countries in Western Europe. More than 120 countries are considered to be developing nations. The majority are Third World countries and are in Africa, Asia, and Latin America.

Most industrial nations, both Communist and non-Communist, lie in the Northern Hemisphere. Most Third World nations lie in the Southern Hemisphere. For this reason, many people use the terms *North* for the developed nations and *South* for the developing nations.

Relations between the Eastern and Western bloc nations have tended to be hostile. The Third World has become a major area of the conflict between them as they struggle for influence among the nonaligned nations. The two blocs try to gain influence by offering economic and military assistance to Third World nations.

Forms of government. Nearly all governments claim to be democracies. But governments differ greatly in how closely they fulfill the democratic ideal of government by the people. In a democracy, the people elect representatives to make laws and to govern according to those laws. The people may run for office and remove officials who behave improperly. Nations and governments can be classified as being more or less demo-

Interesting facts about the world

Area of the world's surface is about 196,951,000 square miles (510,100,000 square kilometers).

Population of the world in 1990 totaled about 5,288,000,000.

Largest continent is Asia, which covers 16,956,000 square miles (43,917,000 square kilometers).

Smallest continent is Australia, which covers 2,966,150 square miles (7,682,300 square kilometers).

Largest country is the Soviet Union, which covers 8,649,500 square miles (22,402,000 square kilometers).

Smallest country is Vatican City. It has an area of only $\frac{1}{6}$ square mile (0.4 square kilometer).

Most populous country is China, which had about 1,100,000,000 people in 1990.

Least populous country, Vatican City, had only about 1,000 citizens in 1990.

Highest point in the world, Mount Everest in Asia, rises 29,028 feet (8,848 meters) above sea level.

Lowest point on land is the shore of the Dead Sea in Asia. It lies 1,310 feet (399 meters) below sea level.

Deepest point in the world's oceans is Challenger Deep, 36,198 feet (11,033 meters) below the surface of the Pacific Ocean southwest of Guam in the Mariana Trench.

cratic, depending on the extent to which the people may take part in the process of government.

Democratic nations may be republics or constitutional monarchies. For example, the United States is a republic in which the President serves as head of state and head of government. Great Britain is a constitutional monarchy. A king or queen serves as head of state, and a prime minister serves as head of government. Other countries with democratic governments include Canada, Australia, New Zealand, Japan, and most countries of Western Europe.

Many countries that claim to be democracies actually have an *authoritarian* government. In such countries, relatively few people have power, and most citizens play a limited role in making decisions. Authoritarian governments may rule by persuasion, force, or both. Communist Party organizations control authoritarian governments in the Soviet Union, China, the countries of Eastern Europe, and some other nations. Dictators supported by the army rule many authoritarian countries in Latin America and Africa. Nearly two-thirds of the world's people live under authoritarian governments.

Economic systems. Every country has an economic system to determine how to use its resources. The three major economic systems today are (1) capitalism, (2) Communism, and (3) mixed economies.

Capitalism is based on *free enterprise*—that is, most of the resources needed for production are privately owned. Individuals and private firms determine what to produce and sell. They also decide how to use their income. Capitalism is practiced in the United States, Canada, Australia, New Zealand, and many countries of Western Europe.

Communism is based on government ownership of most productive resources. The government also decides what goods to produce and how to distribute income. The government may provide housing and medical care for the people. The Soviet Union and the nations of Eastern Europe have a Communist system. Other Communist nations include China, Cuba, and North Korea.

Mixed economies combine both private control and government control. Under a mixed economy, the government may own such industries as banks, railroads, and steel. However, other industries are privately owned. The government does some economic planning, but it also allows much private choice. Great Britain, Norway, Sweden, Denmark, and certain Latin-American countries have mixed economies.

Cooperation among nations. Every nation depends on other nations in some ways. The interdependence of the entire world and its peoples is called *globalism*. Nations trade with one another to earn money and to obtain manufactured goods or the natural resources that

(Text continued on page 415.)

Independent countries of the world*

Name	Area In sq. mi.	Area In km²	Rank in area	Population†	Rank in population	Capital	Map key	
Afghanistan	251,773	652,090	38	15,885,000	50	Kabul	D	13
Albania	11,100	28,748	122	3,248,000	107	Tiranë	C	11
Algeria	919,595	2,381,741	10	25,174,000	33	Algiers	D	10
Andorra	180	465	156	49,000	163	Andorra	C	10‡
Angola	481,354	1,246,700	21	10,000,000	65	Luanda	F	10
Antigua and Barbuda	171	442	158	86,000	160	St. John's	E	6
Argentina	1,073,400	2,780,092	8	32,361,000	29	Buenos Aires	G	6
Australia	2,966,150	7,682,300	6	16,365,000	49	Canberra	G	16
Austria	32,377	83,855	105	7,493,000	78	Vienna	C	10
Bahamas	5,385	13,878	135	251,000	148	Nassau	D	6
Bahrain	265	688	153	516,000	137	Manama	D	12
Bangladesh	55,598	143,998	87	116,000,000	8	Dhaka	D	14
Barbados	166	430	159	260,000	147	Bridgetown	E	7
Belgium	11,783	30,519	120	9,895,000	67	Brussels	C	10
Belize	8,867	22,965	129	182,000	151	Belmopan	E	5
Benin	43,484	112,622	93	4,737,000	95	Porto-Novo	E	10
Bhutan	17,950	46,500	114	1,513,000	124	Thimphu	D	14
Bolivia	424,165	1,098,581	26	7,311,000	80	La Paz; Sucre	F	6
Botswana	224,607	581,730	42	1,283,000	126	Gaborone	G	11
Brazil	3,286,488	8,511,965	5	150,557,000	6	Brasília	F	7
Brunei	2,226	5,765	142	277,000	146	Bandar Seri Begawan	E	15
Bulgaria	42,823	110,912	96	8,985,000	71	Sofia	C	11
Burkina Faso	105,869	274,200	66	8,996,000	70	Ouagadougou	E	9
Burma	261,218	676,552	37	41,279,000	24	Rangoon	D	14
Burundi	10,747	27,834	124	5,450,000	91	Bujumbura	F	11
Cameroon	183,569	475,442	47	11,236,000	60	Yaoundé	E	10
Canada	3,849,674	9,970,610	2	26,279,000	31	Ottawa	C	4
Cape Verde	1,557	4,033	144	378,000	140	Praia	E	8
Central African Republic	240,535	622,984	40	2,911,000	112	Bangui	E	10
Chad	495,755	1,284,000	19	5,674,000	89	N'Djamena	E	10
Chile	292,258	756,945	35	13,185,000	55	Santiago	G	6
China	3,696,032	9,572,678	3	1,100,258,000	1	Beijing	D	14
Colombia	440,831	1,141,748	25	31,863,000	30	Bogotá	E	6
Comoros	863	2,235	147	518,000	136	Moroni	F	12
Congo	132,047	342,000	56	2,183,000	119	Brazzaville	F	10
Costa Rica	19,730	51,100	112	3,017,000	110	San José	E	5
Cuba	42,804	110,861	97	10,279,000	63	Havana	D	5
Cyprus	3,572	9,251	141	701,000	135	Nicosia	D	11
Czechoslovakia	49,373	127,876	90	15,659,000	51	Prague	C	10
Denmark	16,632	43,077	115	5,119,000	93	Copenhagen	C	10
Djibouti	8,958	23,200	128	337,000	144	Djibouti	E	12
Dominica	290	751	150	98,000	158	Roseau	E	6
Dominican Republic	18,816	48,734	113	7,172,000	82	Santo Domingo	E	6
Ecuador	109,484	283,561	65	10,782,000	61	Quito	F	6
Egypt	386,662	1,001,449	28	53,522,000	21	Cairo	D	11
El Salvador	8,124	21,041	130	5,655,000	90	San Salvador	E	5
Equatorial Guinea	10,831	28,051	123	411,000	138	Malabo	E	10
Ethiopia	471,778	1,221,900	23	48,630,000	22	Addis Ababa	E	11

See footnotes at end of table on page 414.

(Table continued on next page.)

Independent countries of the world* (continued)

Name	Area In sq. mi.	Area In km²	Rank in area	Population†	Rank in population	Capital	Map key	
Fiji	7,056	18,274	132	772,000	133	Suva	F	1
Finland	130,559	338,145	57	4,981,000	94	Helsinki	B	11
France	210,026	543,965	44	56,236,000	19	Paris	C	10
Gabon	103,347	267,667	68	1,172,000	128	Libreville	F	10
Gambia	4,361	11,295	138	820,000	132	Banjul	E	9
Germany, East	41,828	108,333	99	16,645,000	48	East Berlin	C	10
Germany, West	96,005	248,651	70	60,471,000	14	Bonn	C	10
Ghana	92,100	238,537	73	15,020,000	53	Accra	E	9
Great Britain	94,248	244,100	72	57,293,000	16	London	C	9
Greece	50,962	131,990	88	10,053,000	64	Athens	D	11
Grenada	133	344	161	96,000	159	St. George's	E	6
Guatemala	42,042	108,889	98	9,117,000	69	Guatemala City	E	5
Guinea	94,926	245,857	71	6,871,000	86	Conakry	E	9
Guinea-Bissau	13,948	36,125	118	985,000	130	Bissau	E	9
Guyana	83,000	214,969	77	868,000	131	Georgetown	E	7
Haiti	10,714	27,750	125	5,777,000	88	Port-au-Prince	E	6
Honduras	43,277	112,088	94	5,144,000	92	Tegucigalpa	E	5
Hungary	35,920	93,032	102	10,545,000	62	Budapest	C	10
Iceland	39,800	103,000	100	250,000	149	Reykjavik	B	9
India	1,269,219	3,287,263	7	853,532,000	2	New Delhi	D	13
Indonesia	741,101	1,919,443	14	180,594,000	5	Jakarta	F	16
Iran	636,300	1,648,000	16	56,800,000	17	Teheran	D	12
Iraq	169,235	438,317	51	18,048,000	44	Baghdad	D	12
Ireland	27,136	70,283	109	3,637,000	103	Dublin	C	9
Israel	8,019	20,770	131	4,585,000	96	Jerusalem	D	11
Italy	116,320	301,268	63	57,380,000	15	Rome	C	10
Ivory Coast	124,504	322,463	61	12,053,000	58	Abidjan	E	9
Jamaica	4,244	10,991	139	2,520,000	115	Kingston	E	6
Japan	145,830	377,801	55	123,749,000	7	Tokyo	D	16
Jordan	35,475	91,880	103	3,065,000	109	Amman	D	11
Kampuchea	69,898	181,035	82	6,993,000	85	Phnom Penh	E	15
Kenya	224,081	580,367	43	25,081,000	35	Nairobi	E	11
Kiribati	277	717	152	69,000	162	Tarawa	F	1
Korea, North	46,540	120,538	91	22,965,000	39	Pyongyang	C	16
Korea, South	38,625	99,106	101	43,650,000	23	Seoul	D	16
Kuwait	6,880	17,818	133	2,096,000	120	Kuwait	D	12
Laos	91,430	236,800	75	4,070,000	101	Vientiane	E	15
Lebanon	4,015	10,400	140	2,947,000	111	Beirut	D	11
Lesotho	11,720	30,355	121	1,757,000	122	Maseru	G	11
Liberia	43,000	111,370	95	2,552,000	114	Monrovia	E	9
Libya	679,362	1,759,540	15	4,356,000	97	Tripoli	D	10
Liechtenstein	62	160	165	28,000	166	Vaduz	C	10‡
Luxembourg	998	2,586	146	367,000	142	Luxembourg	C	10
Madagascar	226,658	587,041	41	11,969,000	59	Antananarivo	F	12
Malawi	45,747	118,484	92	8,198,000	75	Lilongwe	F	11
Malaysia	127,317	329,749	59	17,344,000	46	Kuala Lumpur	E	15
Maldives	115	298	163	215,000	150	Male	E	13
Mali	478,841	1,240,192	22	8,278,000	74	Bamako	E	9
Malta	122	316	162	350,000	143	Valletta	D	10
Mauritania	397,956	1,030,700	27	2,021,000	121	Nouakchott	D	9
Mauritius	788	2,040	148	1,105,000	129	Port Louis	G	12
Mexico	756,067	1,958,201	13	88,560,000	11	Mexico City	D	4
Monaco	0.73	1.9	169	29,000	165	Monaco	C	10‡
Mongolia	604,250	1,565,000	17	2,185,000	118	Ulan Bator	C	15
Morocco	177,117	458,730	49	25,169,000	34	Rabat	D	9
Mozambique	308,642	799,380	32	15,627,000	52	Maputo	F	11
Nauru	8	21	168	9,000	168	—	F	18
Nepal	56,827	147,181	86	19,157,000	43	Kathmandu	D	14
Netherlands	14,405	37,310	117	14,765,000	54	Amsterdam	C	10
New Zealand	103,883	269,057	67	3,402,000	106	Wellington	G	18
Nicaragua	50,200	130,000	89	3,606,000	104	Managua	E	5
Niger	489,200	1,267,000	20	7,905,000	84	Niamey	E	10
Nigeria	356,669	923,768	30	112,765,000	10	Lagos	E	10
Norway	149,405	386,958	54	4,213,000	99	Oslo	B	10
Oman	82,030	212,457	78	1,469,000	125	Muscat	E	12
Pakistan	307,374	796,095	33	113,163,000	9	Islamabad	D	13
Panama	30,193	78,200	107	2,421,000	117	Panama City	E	5
Papua New Guinea	178,704	462,840	48	3,824,000	102	Port Moresby	F	17
Paraguay	157,048	406,752	52	4,278,000	98	Asunción	G	7
Peru	496,225	1,285,216	18	22,330,000	40	Lima	F	6
Philippines	116,000	300,000	64	62,446,000	13	Manila	E	16
Poland	120,728	312,683	62	38,441,000	26	Warsaw	C	10
Portugal	34,340	88,941	104	9,903,000	66	Lisbon	D	9
Qatar	4,416	11,437	137	369,000	141	Doha	D	12
Romania	91,700	237,500	74	23,279,000	38	Bucharest	C	11
Rwanda	10,169	26,338	127	7,222,000	81	Kigali	F	11
St. Christopher and Nevis	101	261	164	48,000	164	Basseterre	E	6‡
St. Lucia	238	616	155	143,000	154	Castries	E	6
St. Vincent and the Grenadines	150	388	160	117,000	156	Kingstown	E	6
San Marino	24	61	166	23,000	167	San Marino	C	10‡
São Tomé and Principe	372	964	149	123,000	155	São Tomé	E	10
Saudi Arabia	830,000	2,149,690	12	12,939,000	56	Riyadh	D	12
Senegal	75,750	196,192	79	7,360,000	79	Dakar	E	9
Seychelles	175	453	157	71,000	161	Victoria	F	12
Sierra Leone	27,699	71,740	108	4,146,000	100	Freetown	E	9
Singapore	239	618	154	2,704,000	113	Singapore	E	15
Solomon Islands	10,639	27,556	126	329,000	145	Honiara	F	18
Somalia	246,201	637,657	39	7,106,000	83	Mogadishu	E	12
South Africa	471,445	1,221,037	24	36,696,000	27	Cape Town; Pretoria; Bloemfontein	G	11
Spain	194,897	504,750	46	39,623,000	25	Madrid	C	9
Sri Lanka	25,333	65,610	110	16,779,000	47	Colombo	E	14
Sudan	967,500	2,505,813	9	23,797,000	37	Khartoum	E	11
Suriname	63,037	163,265	85	408,000	139	Paramaribo	E	7

See footnotes at end of table on page 414.

(Table continued on page 414.)

Political map of the world

This map shows each continent in a different color. The names of continents and independent nations are printed in capital letters.

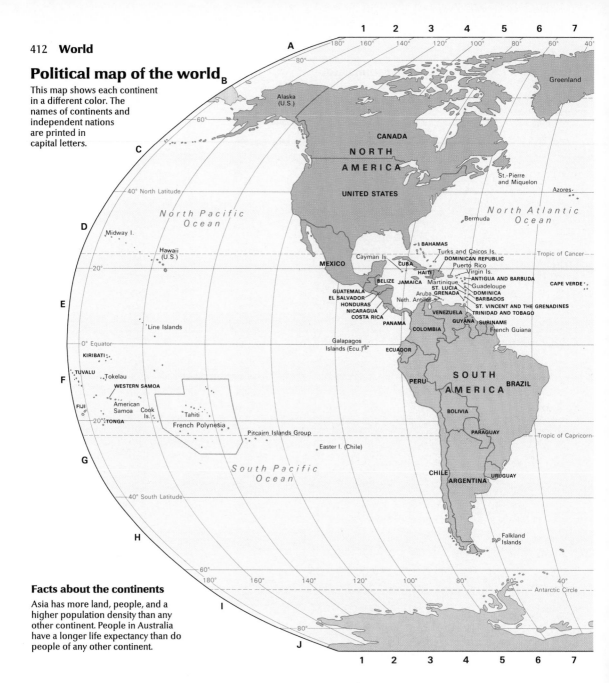

A 1 2 3 4 5 6 7
180° 160° 140° 120° 100° 80° 60° 40°
80°

B Greenland

Alaska (U.S.)

60°

CANADA

C NORTH AMERICA

St.-Pierre and Miquelon

40° North Latitude

UNITED STATES

Azores

North Pacific Ocean

North Atlantic Ocean

D Midway I.

Bermuda

Hawaii (U.S.)

20°

Tropic of Cancer

BAHAMAS

Turks and Caicos Is.

MEXICO Cayman Is. CUBA DOMINICAN REPUBLIC

Puerto Rico

Virgin Is.

HAITI Martinique ANTIGUA AND BARBUDA

BELIZE JAMAICA ST. LUCIA GRENADA Guadeloupe DOMINICA CAPE VERDE

GUATEMALA Aruba BARBADOS

E EL SALVADOR Neth. Antilles ST. VINCENT AND THE GRENADINES

HONDURAS VENEZUELA TRINIDAD AND TOBAGO

NICARAGUA GUYANA SURINAME

COSTA RICA French Guiana

PANAMA COLOMBIA

Line Islands

Galapagos Islands (Ecu.) ECUADOR

0° Equator

KIRIBATI

F TUVALU Tokelau

WESTERN SAMOA PERU SOUTH BRAZIL

AMERICA

American Samoa Cook BOLIVIA

FIJI Is. Tahiti

20° TONGA French Polynesia PARAGUAY

Pitcairn Islands Group Tropic of Capricorn

G Easter I. (Chile)

South Pacific Ocean CHILE URUGUAY

ARGENTINA

40° South Latitude

H

Falkland Islands

60°

I 180° 160° 140° 120° 100° 80° 60° 40°

Antarctic Circle

80°

J 1 2 3 4 5 6 7

Facts about the continents

Asia has more land, people, and a higher population density than any other continent. People in Australia have a longer life expectancy than do people of any other continent.

Area

Asia	17,006,000 sq. mi. (44,045,000 km²)
Africa	11,683,000 sq. mi. (30,259,000 km²)
North America	9,358,000 sq. mi. (24,237,000 km²)
South America	6,888,000 sq. mi. (17,840,000 km²)
Antarctica	5,400,000 sq. mi. (14,000,000 km²)
Europe	4,061,000 sq. mi. (10,517,000 km²)
Australia	2,966,000 sq. mi. (7,682,000 km²)

Population

Asia	3,172,000,000
Europe	693,000,000
Africa	643,000,000
North America	427,000,000
South America	297,000,000
Australia	16,000,000
Antarctica	(no permanent population)

Sources: Area and population figures are 1990 estimates based on the latest figures from official government and United Nations sources. Life expectancy figures are UN estimates for 1985-1990.

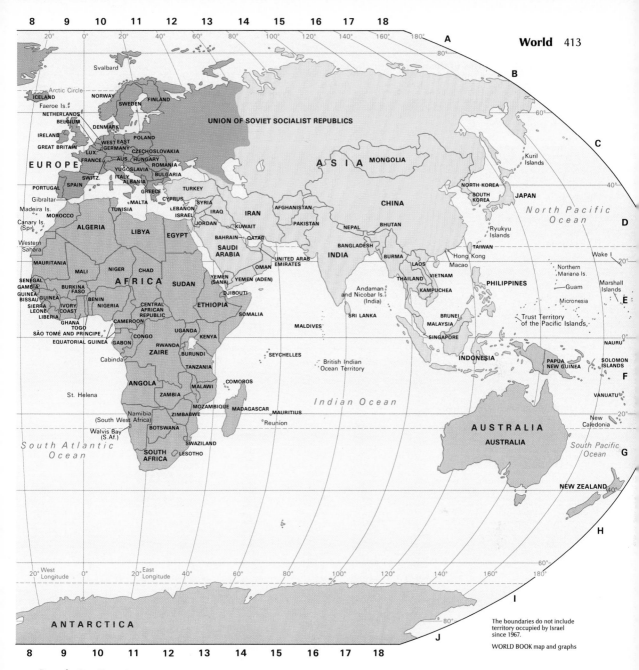

The boundaries do not include territory occupied by Israel since 1967.

WORLD BOOK map and graphs

Population Density

Asia	187 persons per sq. mi. (72 per km²)
Europe	171 persons per sq. mi. (66 per km²)
Africa	55 persons per sq. mi. (21 per km²)
North America	46 persons per sq. mi. (18 per km²)
South America	43 persons per sq. mi. (17 per km²)
Australia	6 persons per sq. mi. (2 per km²)
Antarctica	(no permanent population)

Life Expectancy

Region	Life Expectancy
Australia	75.0 years
Europe	73.6 years
North America	71.9 years
South America	65.4 years
Asia	60.1 years
Africa	51.8 years
Antarctica	(no permanent population)

Independent countries of the world* (concluded)

Name	Area In sq. mi.	In km²	Rank in area	Population†	Rank in population	Capital	Map key	
Swaziland	6,704	17,364	134	779,000	134	Mbabane	G	11
Sweden	170,250	440,945	50	8,346,000	73	Stockholm	B	10
Switzerland	15,943	41,293	116	6,509,000	87	Bern	C	10
Syria	71,498	185,180	81	12,471,000	57	Damascus	D	11
Taiwan	13,900	36,000	119	20,454,000	41	Taipei	D	16
Tanzania	364,900	945,087	29	25,955,000	32	Dar es Salaam	F	11
Thailand	198,115	513,115	45	55,760,000	20	Bangkok	E	15
Togo	21,925	56,785	111	3,451,000	105	Lomé	E	9
Tonga	289	748	151	101,000	157	Nukualofa	F	1
Trinidad and Tobago	1,980	5,128	143	1,283,000	127	Port-of-Spain	E	6
Tunisia	63,170	163,610	84	8,095,000	76	Tunis	D	10
Turkey	300,948	779,452	34	56,549,000	18	Ankara	D	11
Tuvalu	10	26	167	8,000	169	Funafuti	F	1
Uganda	91,074	235,880	76	17,593,000	45	Kampala	E	11
Union of Soviet Socialist Republics	8,649,500	22,402,000	1	288,239,000	3	Moscow	C	13
United Arab Emirates	32,278	83,600	106	1,731,000	123	Abu Dhabi	D	12
United States	3,618,770	9,372,571	4	250,372,000	4	Washington, D.C.	C	4
Uruguay	68,500	177,414	83	3,130,000	108	Montevideo	G	7
Vanuatu	4,706	12,189	136	164,000	153	Port-Vila	F	18
Vatican City	0.17	0.44	170	1,000	170	—	C	10‡
Venezuela	352,145	912,050	31	19,744,000	42	Caracas	E	6
Vietnam	127,242	329,556	60	67,084,000	12	Hanoi	E	15
Western Samoa	1,093	2,831	145	170,000	152	Apia	F	1
Yemen (Aden)	128,587	333,038	58	2,486,000	116	Aden	E	12
Yemen (Sana)	75,300	195,000	80	7,993,000	77	Sana	E	12
Yugoslavia	98,766	255,804	69	23,853,000	36	Belgrade	C	10
Zaire	905,365	2,344,885	11	35,330,000	28	Kinshasa	F	11
Zambia	290,586	752,614	36	8,459,000	72	Lusaka	F	11
Zimbabwe	150,804	390,580	53	9,700,000	68	Harare	G	11

*Each country listed has a separate article in *World Book*.
†Populations are 1990 estimates based on the latest figures from official government and United Nations sources.
‡Not on map; key shows general location.

Dependencies in the world*

Name	Area In sq. mi.	In km²	Population†	Capital	Map key	
American Samoa (United States)	76	197	37,000	Pago Pago	F	1
Anguilla (Great Britain)	35	91	7,000	The Valley (unofficial)	E	6‡
Aruba (Netherlands)	75	193	63,000	Oranjestad	E	6
Azores (Portugal)	905	2,344	249,500	Angra do Heroismo; Horta; Ponta Delgada	D	8
Bermuda (Great Britain)	21	54	72,000	Hamilton	D	6
British Indian Ocean Territory (Great Britain)	30	78	2,000	—	F	13
Cayman Islands (Great Britain)	100	259	19,000	Georgetown	D	5
Channel Islands (Great Britain)	75	195	138,000	St. Helier; St. Peter Port	C	9‡
Cook Islands (New Zealand)	93	240	17,200	Avarua	F	2
Faeroe Islands (Denmark)	540	1,399	46,000	Tórshavn	B	9
Falkland Islands (Great Britain)	4,700	12,170	2,000	Stanley	H	7
French Guiana (France)	35,135	91,000	73,000	Cayenne	E	7
French Polynesia (France)	1,544	4,000	137,000	Papeete	F	2
Gaza Strip (§)	146	378	556,000	Gaza	D	11‡
Gibraltar (Great Britain)	2.3	6	35,000	Gibraltar	D	9
Greenland (Denmark)	840,004	2,175,600	56,000	Godthåb	B	7
Guadeloupe (France)	658	1,704	328,000	Basse-Terre	E	6
Guam (United States)	212	549	120,000	Agana	E	17
Hong Kong (Great Britain)	1,126	2,916	5,705,000	Victoria	D	15
Macao (Portugal)	6	16	302,000	Macao	D	15
Madeira Islands (Portugal)	308	797	258,238	Funchal	D	9
Man, Isle of (Great Britain)	227	588	70,000	Douglas	C	9‡
Marshall Islands (United States)	70	181	34,000	Majuro	E	18
Martinique (France)	425	1,102	329,000	Fort-de-France	E	6
Micronesia, Federated States of (United States)	271	702	88,000	Kolonia	E	17
Midway Island (United States)	2	5	468	—	D	1
Montserrat (Great Britain)	38	98	13,000	Plymouth	E	6‡
Namibia, or South West Africa (South Africa)	317,818	823,145	1,874,000	Windhoek	G	10
Netherlands Antilles (Netherlands)	310	800	185,000	Willemstad	E	6
New Caledonia (France)	7,366	19,079	161,000	Nouméa	G	18
Niue Island (New Zealand)	100	259	2,500	—	F	1‡
Norfolk Island (Australia)	14	36	2,000	—	G	18‡
Northern Mariana Islands (United States)	184	477	19,000	Saipan	E	17
Pacific Islands, Trust Territory of the (United States)	192	497	13,000	Koror	E	17
Pitcairn Islands Group (Great Britain)	2	5	60	—	G	3
Puerto Rico (United States)	3,515	9,103	3,282,000	San Juan	E	6
Reunion (France)	970	2,512	564,000	Saint-Denis	G	12
St. Helena Island Group (Great Britain)	160	414	7,900	Jamestown	F	9
St-Pierre and Miquelon (France)	93	242	6,000	St.-Pierre	C	7
South West Africa. See Namibia						
Tokelau (New Zealand)	4	10	2,000	—	F	1
Turks and Caicos Islands (Great Britain)	166	430	9,000	Grand Turk	D	6
Virgin Islands (Great Britain)	59	153	11,000	Road Town	E	6
Virgin Islands (United States)	132	342	111,000	Charlotte Amalie	E	6
Wake Island (United States)	3	8	300	—	E	18
Wallis and Futuna Islands (France)	106	275	12,000	Mata-Utu	F	1‡
West Bank(#)	2,263	5,860	1,053,000	—	D	13‡
Western Sahara (**)	102,700	266,000	180,000	—	D	9

*The dependencies listed are controlled in some way by the country shown in parentheses.
†Populations are 1990 and earlier estimates based on the latest figures from official government and United Nations sources.
‡Not on map; key shows general location.
§Occupied by Israel; formerly administered by Egypt.
#Occupied by Israel; claimed by the Palestine Liberation Organization.
**Occupied by Morocco; claimed by Morocco and by the Polisario Front.

they lack. Nations with similar interests and political beliefs may pledge to support one another in case of war. Developed countries provide developing nations with financial aid and technical assistance. Such aid strengthens trade as well as defense ties.

A number of international organizations promote cooperation among countries. The United Nations (UN) is the largest such organization. Nearly all independent countries are UN members. The UN works mainly to try to settle disputes among nations and to maintain world peace. It also has programs intended to aid needy people and to improve health and education, particularly in developing nations.

Many international organizations are designed to encourage economic progress among member nations. Such groups stimulate trade among members by eliminating tariffs and other trade barriers within the organization. These groups include the European Economic Community (EEC), the European Free Trade Association (EFTA), the Latin American Free Trade Association (LAFTA), and the Central American Common Market.

International military alliances provide for military cooperation among the members, who pledge to support one another in case of attack. The North Atlantic Treaty Organization (NATO) is a military alliance of 13 Western European nations, Turkey, the United States, and Canada. The Warsaw Pact is an alliance of the Soviet Union and other Communist countries of Eastern Europe.

People of the world

Population. In 1990, the world's population totaled about 5¼ billion. The yearly rate of population growth

Growth of the world's population

The world's population grew slowly before A.D. 1. It then almost doubled by the year 1000. At its present rate of growth, the world's population doubles about every 40 years. At that rate, the world will have over 6 billion people by the year 2000.

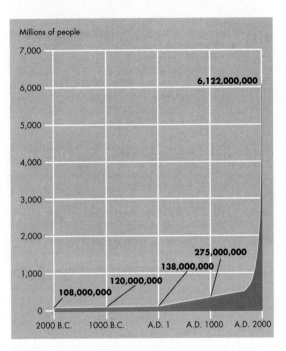

Where the people of the world live This map shows how the world's population is distributed. About three-fourths of all people live in Asia and Europe. Regions with severe climates, such as desert areas, are thinly populated. The map also shows the location of some of the world's largest metropolitan areas.

WORLD BOOK map

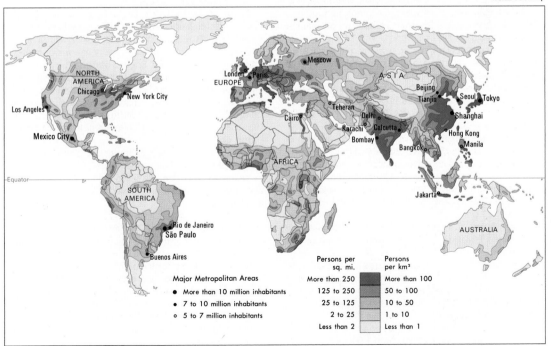

Traditional farming practices survive in many parts of the world that lack modern machinery. These women in Senegal are threshing peanuts by hand, as their ancestors did years ago.

during the late 1980's was 1.7 per cent. At that rate, the world's population would double every 41 years.

If all the world's people were distributed evenly over the land, about 100 people would live on every square mile (39 on every square kilometer). However, the world's people are not distributed evenly, and so the *population density* (the average number of people in a specific area) varies greatly. Some regions, including Antarctica and certain desert areas, have no permanent settlers at all.

The most densely populated regions of the world are in Europe and in southern and eastern Asia. North America has heavy concentrations of people in the northeastern and central regions and along the Pacific coast. Africa, Australia, and South America have densely populated areas near the coasts. The interiors of those continents are thinly settled.

Just as the population density varies from one part of the world to another, so does the rate of population growth. Developing countries generally have higher average rates of increase than developed nations. Africa has a population growth rate of 3.0 per cent yearly, the highest of all continents. South America's rate of increase—2.1 per cent—is also high. Asia's rate is 1.8 per cent, North America's is 0.8 per cent, and Australia's is 1.2 per cent. Europe has the lowest rate of increase, only 0.2 per cent.

The world's largest country in terms of population is China, which has more than a billion people. India ranks second largest, followed in descending order by the Soviet Union, the United States, Indonesia, and Brazil. More than half the world's people live in these six nations. Vatican City has the smallest population of any of the world's nations. It has only about 1,000 people.

The growth and change of the world's population throughout history are described in the article **Population**. See also the articles on individual countries, states, and provinces for population details.

Races. Classifying the world's people by race varies greatly according to the classifier and the purposes of classification. Many scholars recognize nine *geographical races,* which include hundreds of *local races*. The geographical races are (1) African, (2) American Indian, (3) Asian, (4) Australian, (5) European, (6) Indian, (7) Melanesian, (8) Micronesian, and (9) Polynesian.

The African race consists mainly of a large group of local races in Africa south of the Sahara. American blacks are chiefly of African origin. Most American Indians live in the Western United States and in South America. Members of the Asian racial group include Chinese, Japanese, Koreans, and most peoples of southeastern Asia. Australians, also called *Australian Aborigines,* are a group of local races in Australia. The European race includes the "white" populations of Europe, the Middle East, Australia, New Zealand, North America, South America, South Africa, and Africa north of the Sahara. Most members of the Indian geographical race live in India, Pakistan, and Bangladesh. Melanesians, Micronesians, and Polynesians live on different groups of islands in the Pacific Ocean.

The main characteristics of the major races are described in the article **Races, Human**. The article also tells how races developed, changed, and spread to different parts of the world.

Languages. There are about 3,000 spoken languages in the world. However, only 12 are widely used. Each of these languages is spoken by over 100 million people. More people speak Chinese than any other language. English ranks second, followed by Russian, Spanish, Hindi, Arabic, Bengali, Portuguese, Japanese, German, Malay-Indonesian, and French.

Beginning in the 1500's, England, Spain, Portugal, and France established colonies in various parts of the world. For this reason, English, Spanish, Portuguese, and French are now spoken in many nations outside their countries of origin. English became the chief language of such nations as the United States, Australia, and New Zealand. It is also one of the main languages in Canada and South Africa. Spanish became the chief language throughout most countries of Latin America. Portuguese became the main language of Brazil, Mozambique, and Angola.

French, like English, is an important language of Canada. Most people in the province of Quebec speak French. French is also widely spoken in Algeria, Chad and some other countries in western Africa, Morocco, and Vietnam.

For information about the development of the world's languages, see **Language**. See also the articles on individual countries for the most widely used languages in those nations.

Religions. The peoples of the world practice thousands of religions, but only eight religions have followers that number in the millions. Christianity has more than a billion members, more than any other religion. Islam has more than 500 million members. The six other major religions are Buddhism, Confucianism, Hinduism, Shinto, Taoism, and Judaism.

Christianity originated in the Middle East. Today, most Christians live in Europe and North and South America. Islam also began in the Middle East and is now the chief religion throughout most of the area. It is also the major faith in northern Africa, Malaysia, Indonesia, Pakistan, and Bangladesh. Hinduism has most of its followers in India, where the religion originated. Buddhism, which also developed in India, is the major religion of Sri Lanka and the mainland of southeastern Asia. It also has many followers in such countries as Japan and South Korea. Shinto is the native religion of Japan.

Confucianism and Taoism are native religions of China. The Communist government of China discourages them and all other religions. But Chinese people in Taiwan still practice Confucianism and Taoism. Judaism originated in the Middle East. Today, the largest number of Jews live in the United States, Israel, and the Soviet Union. Thousands of local traditional religions are practiced by ethnic groups in Africa, Asia, Australia, North America, South America, and the Pacific Islands.

For a description of the major religions, see **Religion** and the separate articles on the various faiths. See also the *Religion* section of the country and continent articles.

Problems among the world's people. Through the years, human beings have made great progress in providing for their basic needs. Modern methods of producing food, clothing, and shelter have helped many people live more comfortably. Education has become available to more and more people, and scientists have discovered cures for many diseases.

But serious problems still face the world's people. Millions of people in developing countries lack adequate food, clothing, shelter, medical care, and education. Many people in developed countries, especially in large cities, suffer from poverty, unemployment, and discrimination. New problems have also developed. Numerous nations face the growing problem of environmental pollution. In addition, the threat of nuclear war has become a worldwide concern.

Physical features of the world

The surface area of the world totals about 196,951,000 square miles (510,100,000 square kilometers). Water covers about 139,692,000 square miles (361,800,000 square kilometers), or about 70 per cent of the world's surface. Only about 30 per cent consists of land, which covers about 57,259,000 square miles (148,300,000 square kilometers).

The physical geography of a specific region includes the region's surface features and climate. It also includes the soil, mineral deposits, plant and animal life, and other natural resources. Physical geography thus helps determine the economy of a region and how people in the region live.

This section describes the two major surface features of the world: (1) water and (2) land.

Water. Oceans, lakes, and rivers make up most of the water that covers the surface of the world. The water surface consists chiefly of three large oceans—the Pacific, the Atlantic, and the Indian. The Pacific Ocean is the largest. It covers about 63,800,000 square miles (165,200,000 square kilometers), or about a third of the world's surface. The Atlantic Ocean is about half as large as the Pacific, and the Indian Ocean is slightly smaller than the Atlantic. These three oceans come together around Antarctica. The Atlantic and the Pacific meet again near the North Pole, where they form the Arctic Ocean.

The world's largest lake is the Caspian Sea, a body of salt water that lies between Asia and Europe east of the Caucasus Mountains. The Caspian covers about

(Text continued on page 420.)

Physical map index

Aconcagua (mountain)	G	6
Aleutian Islands	C	1
Alps (mountains)	C	10
Amazon River	F	7
Amur River	C	16
Andes Mountains	F	6
Antarctic Peninsula	I	6
Appalachian Mountains	D	5
Arabian Peninsula	D	12
Arabian Sea	E	13
Aral Sea	C	13
Arctic Circle	B	9
Arctic Ocean	A	1
Asia Minor	D	11
Atacama Desert	G	6
Atlas Mountains	D	9
Azores (islands)	D	8
Baffin Island	B	6
Balkan Peninsula	C	11
Baltic Sea	C	10
Bay of Bengal	E	14
Bering Sea	C	1
Black Sea	C	11
Borneo (island)	E	15
Brazilian Highlands	F	7
British Isles	C	9
Canary Islands	D	9
Cape Agulhas	G	11
Cape Horn	H	6
Cape of Good Hope	G	11
Caribbean Sea	E	6
Caspian Sea	D	12
Caucasus Mountains	D	12

Congo River	F	10
Coral Sea	F	17
Danube River	C	11
Darling River	G	17
Deccan Plateau	E	13
East China Sea	D	16
Ethiopian Highlands	E	11
Galapagos Islands	F	5
Ganges River	D	13
Gobi Desert	C	15
Gran Chaco (plain)	G	7
Great Basin (desert)	D	4
Great Bear Lake	B	4
Great Dividing Range	G	17
Great Lakes	C	5
Great Plains	C	4
Great Slave Lake	B	4
Great Victoria Desert	G	16
Guiana Highlands	E	7
Gulf of Alaska	C	2
Gulf of Mexico	D	5
Hainan (island)	E	15
Hawaiian Islands	D	2
Himalaya (mountains)	D	13
Hispaniola (island)	E	6
Hokkaido (island)	C	17
Honshu (island)	D	16
Huang He River	D	15
Hudson Bay	C	5
Iberian Peninsula	C	9

Indian Ocean	F	13
Indochina	E	15
Indus River	D	13
Java (island)	F	15
Kalahari Desert	G	11
Kamchatka Peninsula	C	18
Kerguelen Islands	H	13
Kilimanjaro (mountain)	F	11
Labrador Sea	C	7
Labrador Peninsula	C	6
Lake Baikal	C	15
Lake Balkhash	C	13
Lake Chad	E	10
Lake Nyasa	F	11
Lake Tanganyika	F	11
Lake Victoria	F	11
Lake Winnipeg	C	5
Lena River	B	16
MacKenzie River	B	3
Madagascar (island)	F	12
Madeira Islands	D	9
Malay Peninsula	E	15
Mediterranean Sea	D	10
Mekong River	D	15
Melanesia (islands)	F	17
Mesopotamia	D	12
Micronesia (islands)	E	17
Mississippi River	D	5
Mount Elbrus	C	12
Mount Everest	D	14
Mount Kosciusko	G	17
Mount McKinley	C	2
Murray River	G	17
New Guinea (island)	F	17

New Siberian Islands	B	17
Niger River	E	10
Nile River	D	11
North Atlantic Ocean	D	7
North European Plain	C	10
North Pacific Ocean	D	2
North Sea	C	10
Novaya Zemlya (islands)	B	12
Ob River	B	13
Orinoco River	E	6
Pampa (plain)	G	6
Panama Canal	E	6
Paraná River	G	7
Patagonia (plateau)	H	6
Peninsula of Lower California	D	4
Persian Gulf	D	12
Philippines (islands)	E	16
Plateau of Tibet	D	14
Polynesia (islands)	F	2
Queen Elizabeth Islands	B	4
Red Sea	D	11
Rocky Mountains	C	4
Ross Sea	J	1
Sahara (desert)	D	10
Sahel (plain)	E	10
Sakhalin (island)	C	17
Scandinavia	B	10
Sea of Japan	C	16
Sea of Okhotsk	C	17
Severnaya Zemlya (islands)	B	14
Seychelles (islands)	F	12

Siberia	C	14
Sonoran Desert	D	4
South Atlantic Ocean	G	9
South China Sea	E	15
South Georgia Island	H	8
South Pacific Ocean	G	3
Suez Canal	D	11
Sulawesi (island)	F	16
Svalbard (island)	B	10
Taiwan (island)	D	16
Taklimakan Desert	D	14
Tasmania (island)	H	17
Tian Shan (mountains)	C	13
Tierra del Fuego (islands)	H	6
Ural Mountains	C	12
Vancouver Island	C	3
Vinson Massif (mountain)	I	5
Volga River	C	12
Weddell Sea	I	7
West Indies (islands)	E	6
West Siberian Plain	C	14
Yangtze River	D	15
Yellow Sea	D	16
Yenisey River	B	14
Yucatán Peninsula	D	5
Yukon River	B	2
Zambezi River	F	11

Physical map of the world

This map shows the world's chief physical features. Areas shown in shades of green generally have fertile soil and sufficient rainfall. Most of the world's people live in these areas.

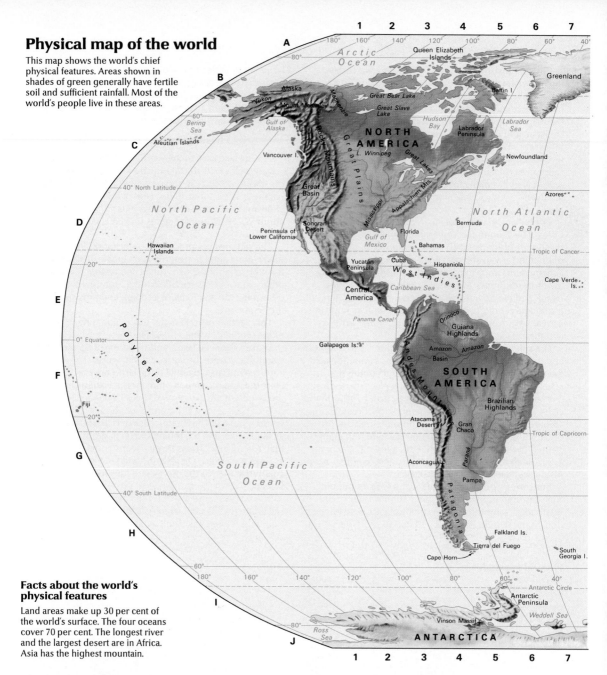

Column numbers: 1 2 3 4 5 6 7

Row letters: A B C D E F G H I J

Arctic Ocean
Queen Elizabeth Islands
Greenland
Alaska
Baffin I.
Yukon
Great Bear Lake
Mount McKinley
Mackenzie
Great Slave Lake
Hudson Bay
Labrador Sea
Labrador Peninsula
Bering Sea
Gulf of Alaska
Rocky Mountains
NORTH AMERICA
Aleutian Islands
Vancouver I.
L. Winnipeg
Great Lakes
Newfoundland
Great Plains
Great Basin
Mississippi
Appalachian Mts.
Azores
North Pacific Ocean
North Atlantic Ocean
Sonoran Desert
Bermuda
Peninsula of Lower California
Florida
Tropic of Cancer
Hawaiian Islands
Gulf of Mexico
Bahamas
Yucatán Peninsula
Cuba
Hispaniola
West Indies
Cape Verde Is.
Central America
Caribbean Sea
Panama Canal
Orinoco
Guiana Highlands
Galapagos Is.
Amazon
Amazon Basin
Polynesia
SOUTH AMERICA
Andes Mountains
Brazilian Highlands
Fiji
Atacama Desert
Gran Chaco
Tropic of Capricorn
Aconcagua
Paraná
South Pacific Ocean
Pampa
Patagonia
Falkland Is.
South Georgia I.
Tierra del Fuego
Cape Horn
Antarctic Circle
Antarctic Peninsula
Weddell Sea
Vinson Massif
Ross Sea
ANTARCTICA

Facts about the world's physical features

Land areas make up 30 per cent of the world's surface. The four oceans cover 70 per cent. The longest river and the largest desert are in Africa. Asia has the highest mountain.

The world's surface

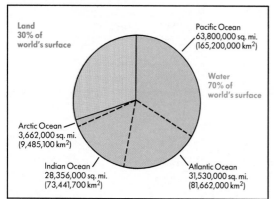

Land 30% of world's surface

Water 70% of world's surface

Pacific Ocean
63,800,000 sq. mi.
(165,200,000 km²)

Arctic Ocean
3,662,000 sq. mi.
(9,485,100 km²)

Indian Ocean
28,356,000 sq. mi.
(73,441,700 km²)

Atlantic Ocean
31,530,000 sq. mi.
(81,662,000 km²)

Longest river on each continent

Africa	Nile	4,145 mi. (6,671 km)
South America	Amazon	4,000 mi. (6,437 km)
Asia	Yangtze	3,915 mi. (6,300 km)
North America	Mississippi	2,348 mi. (3,779 km)
Australia	Murray-Darling	2,310 mi. (3,718 km)
Europe	Volga	2,194 mi. (3,531 km)
Antarctica	(no rivers)	

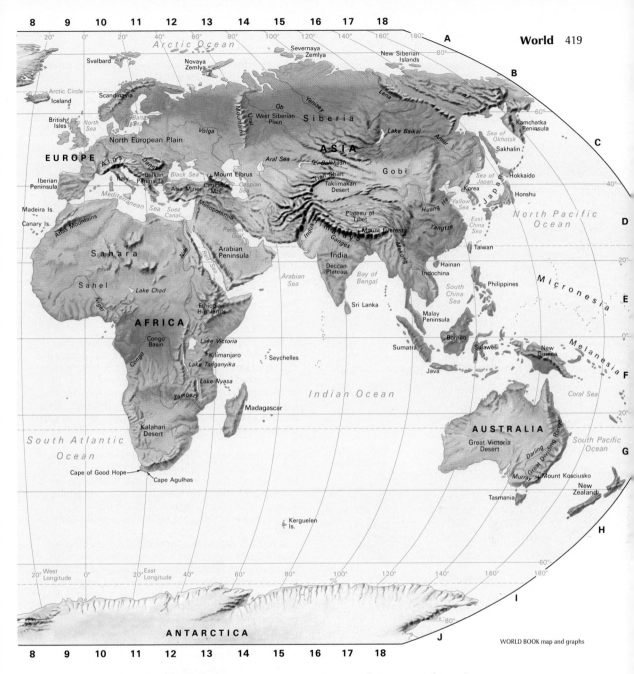

Highest mountain on each continent

Continent	Mountain	Elevation
Asia	Everest	29,028 ft. (8,848 m)
South America	Aconcagua	22,831 ft. (6,959 m)
North America	McKinley	20,320 ft. (6,194 m)
Africa	Kilimanjaro	19,340 ft. (5,895 m)
Europe	Elbrus	18,481 ft. (5,633 m)
Antarctica	Vinson Massif	16,864 ft. (5,140 m)
Australia	Kosciusko	7,310 ft. (2,228 m)

Largest desert on each continent

Africa	Sahara	3,500,000 sq. mi. (9,000,000 km²)
Asia	Gobi	500,000 sq. mi. (1,300,000 km²)
Australia	Great Victoria	250,000 sq. mi. (650,000 km²)
South America	Atacama	140,000 sq. mi. (360,000 km²)
North America	Sonoran	120,000 sq. mi. (310,000 km²)
Europe	(no deserts)	
Antarctica	(no deserts)	

WORLD BOOK map and graphs

J. L. Atlan, Sygma

Making barren land productive through modern techniques increases the world's food supply. This irrigation project in Libya enables farmers to raise crops in the desert. The project spreads water from an underground source over circular plots.

wells to irrigate crops. Oceans, lakes, and rivers supply us with fish and other foods.

Water is also a source of power. The force of falling water from rivers, waterfalls, and dams can be used to generate hydroelectricity. In such countries as Brazil and Norway, hydroelectric power stations supply nearly all the electricity used in industry and homes.

The waters of the world also serve as major transportation routes. Every day, thousands of cargo ships cross the oceans, sail along seacoasts, and travel on inland waters. A nation's location along a seacoast can have a powerful influence on its progress and prosperity. The United States, Great Britain, Japan, and some other leading trading nations have long coastlines. Many of the world's major cities border important water transportation routes.

Land. The land area of the world consists of seven continents and many thousands of islands. Asia is the largest continent, followed by Africa, North America, South America, Antarctica, Europe, and Australia. Geographers sometimes refer to Europe and Asia as one continent called *Eurasia.*

The world's land surface includes mountains, plateaus, hills, valleys, and plains. Relatively few people live in mountainous areas or on high plateaus. Most such regions are too cold, rugged, or dry for comfortable living or for crop farming and other human activities. The soil is poor and easily washed away by rain. However, some mountain valleys and high grassy plateaus serve as grazing land for cattle, sheep, and other livestock. The majority of the world's people live on plains or in hilly regions. Most plains and hilly regions have excellent soil and an abundant water supply. They are good regions for farming, manufacturing, and trade. Many areas unsuitable for farming, particularly mountainous regions, have plentiful mineral resources. Some desert areas, especially in the Middle East, have large deposits of petroleum.

A region's natural resources influence its economic development. The Pampa, a grassy plain in central Argentina, has excellent pastureland for raising cattle and rich soil for growing wheat. Beef and wheat make up Argentina's leading exports. Great Britain lacks enough good farmland to support all its people, but large deposits of coal and iron ore have helped make the country an industrial power. Such countries as the United States, Canada, and the Soviet Union have a variety and abundance of natural resources, which have helped make them become economic giants.

Threats to the environment. For centuries, people have used the world's natural resources to make their lives more comfortable. However, these resources are not always used wisely. Many problems have thus resulted that threaten the environment.

Many water supplies have become polluted by sewage, industrial chemicals, and other wastes. The burning of fuel in motor vehicles, factories, and furnaces has caused air pollution in numerous cities. Forest regions have been stripped of large areas of trees, resulting in soil erosion and the destruction of animal life. Certain farming practices, including the use of chemical fertilizers and pesticides, have polluted the soil. Many farmers plant the same crop in a field year after year, which reduces the soil's fertility.

143,630 square miles (372,000 square kilometers). The world's largest body of fresh water is the Great Lakes in North America. These five lakes—Erie, Huron, Michigan, Ontario, and Superior—are interconnected, and so they are often referred to as one body of water. Together, they cover about 94,510 square miles (244,780 square kilometers).

The longest river in the world is the Nile in Africa, which flows 4,145 miles (6,671 kilometers). The second longest river, the Amazon in South America, has a length of 4,000 miles (6,437 kilometers). The Mississippi is the longest river in the United States. It flows 2,348 miles (3,779 kilometers).

All living things need water to stay alive. People obtain drinking water from rivers, freshwater lakes, and wells. We also require water for our way of life. We use water in our homes for cleaning and cooking. The manufacture of almost all our products requires water. In dry regions, farmers draw water from rivers, lakes, and

Since the mid-1900's, people have become increasingly aware of the need to protect their environment. Local and national governments have passed laws to control the use of natural resources. But it takes many years to renew a water supply, grow a forest, or replace a layer of topsoil. People must practice conservation continuously to repair damage that has already occurred and to prevent future problems.   Kevin R. Cox

Related articles in *World Book.* For detailed information about the physical world, see **Earth** and its list of *Related articles.* For the story of human history and progress, see **World, History of the;** and **Prehistoric people.** See also the lists of *Related articles* at the end of these articles. See also the following articles:

Continents

Africa	Australia	North America
Antarctica	Europe	South America
Asia		

Countries

See the separate article on each country and dependency listed in the *Nations of the world* section of this article.

Regions

Arctic	Far East	Pacific Islands
Balkans	Latin America	Southeast Asia
Central America	Middle East	

Geography

Climate	Mountain	River
Desert	Ocean	Volcano
Geography	Plain	Water
Island	Plateau	Waterfall
Lake	Rain	Weather

Government and economics

Capitalism	Law
Communism	Multinational corporation
Democracy	Poverty
Economics	Public health
Foreign aid	Socialism
Government	Standard of living
Gross national product	Trade
International trade	World government

Organizations, agreements, and programs

See **United Nations** and the international organizations listed in its *Related articles.* See also the following articles:

Agency for International Development
ANZUS
Arab League
Asian Development Bank
Bank for International Settlements
Colombo Plan
Europe, Council of
European Community
European Free Trade Association
European Monetary System
European Organization for Nuclear Research
European Space Agency
General Agreement on Tariffs and Trade
International Air Transport Association
International Bureau of Weights and Measures
International Confederation of Free Trade Unions
International Council of Scientific Unions
International Energy Agency
North Atlantic Treaty Organization
Organization for Economic Cooperation and Development
Organization of African Unity
Organization of American States
Organization of Petroleum Exporting Countries
Strategic Arms Limitation Talks
Warsaw Pact

Other related articles

Agriculture	International relations
Anthropology	Invention
Art and the arts	Irrigation
Civilization	Language
Clothing	Manufacturing
Communication	Medicine
Conservation	Natural resources
Culture	Olympic Games
Developing country	Peace
Education	Population
Energy supply	Races, Human
Environmental pollution	Religion
Food	Science
Food supply	Shelter
Geopolitics	Technology
Human being	Third World
Industry	Transportation
International law	War

Outline

I. Nations of the world
  A. How nations are grouped
  B. Forms of government
  C. Economic systems
  D. Cooperation among nations

II. People of the world
  A. Population
  B. Races
  C. Languages
  D. Religions
  E. Problems among the world's people

III. Physical features of the world
  A. Water
  B. Land
  C. Threats to the environment

Questions

How does the geography of a region help determine how people in the region live?

How does an independent country differ from a dependency?

Why do the human races have distinct differences?

What three oceans make up most of the water surface of the world?

Which of the world's languages is spoken by the largest number of people?

What are the three major economic systems practiced in the world today?

How do people use the world's water supplies?

What has caused the most important changes in the world's political map throughout history?

Why do most of the world's people live on plains or in hilly regions?

How do international organizations help countries cooperate with one another?

Additional resources

Level I

Lands and Peoples. Ed. by William Shapiro. 6 vols. Rev. ed. Grolier, 1983.

National Geographic Society. *Far-Out Facts.* The Society, 1980. *More Far-Out Facts.* 1982. Physical, social, and historical facts about the world.

Worldmark Encyclopedia of the Nations. 5 vols. 6th ed. Wiley, 1984.

Level II

Atlas of Man. Ed. by John Gaisford. St. Martin's, 1978. A geographic guide to the peoples of the world.

Gregor, Arthur S. *Life Styles: An Introduction to Cultural Anthropology.* Scribner, 1978.

Loraine, John A. *Global Signposts to the 21st Century.* Univ. of Washington Press, 1979. Contemporary issues and what they mean for the world's future.

Pei, Mario. *Talking Your Way Around the World.* 3rd ed. Harper, 1971. Profiles of the world's major languages.

Political Handbook of the World. Ed. by Arthur S. Banks and William Overstreet. McGraw. Published annually.

Ancient Egypt   Art Resource   The Golden Age of Greece   Photoresources   The Middle Ages   Giraudon from Art Resource

The history of the world is a dramatic story that began about 5,500 years ago with the invention of writing. It traces human progress from the first civilizations to the space age.

World history

World, History of the. People have probably lived on the earth about 2 million years. But the story of world history begins only about 5,500 years ago with the invention of writing. The period before people began to write is usually called *prehistory*.

Archaeologists have pieced together the story of prehistory by studying what the people left behind, including artwork, tools, ruins of buildings, fossils, and even their own skeletons. Such objects provide the main evidence of what prehistoric people were like and how they lived. For a description of life in prehistoric times, see the *World Book* article **Prehistoric people**.

The first traces of writing date from about 3500 B.C. From then on, people could record their own history. By writing down their experiences, they could tell future generations what they were like and how they lived. From these documents, we can learn firsthand about the rise and fall of civilizations and the course of other important events. The history of the world—from the first civilizations to the present—is based largely on what has been written down by peoples through the ages.

The development of agriculture about 9,000 B.C.

brought about a great revolution in human life. Prehistoric people who learned to farm no longer had to roam in search of food. Instead, they could settle in one place. Some of their settlements grew to become the world's first cities. People in the cities learned new skills and developed specialized occupations. Some became builders and craftworkers. Others became merchants and priests. Eventually, systems of writing were invented. These developments gave rise to the first civilizations.

For hundreds of years, the earliest civilizations had little contact with one another and so developed independently. The progress each civilization made depended on the natural resources available to it and on the inventiveness of its people. As time passed, civilizations advanced and spread, and the world's population rose steadily. The peoples of various civilizations began to exchange ideas and skills. Within each civilization, groups of people with distinctive customs and languages emerged. In time, some peoples, such as the Romans, gained power over others and built huge empires. Some of these empires flourished for centuries before collapsing. Great religions and later science and scholarship developed as people wondered about the meaning of human life and the mysteries of nature.

About 500 years ago, one civilization—that of west-

SCALA from Art Resource

The Renaissance

AP/Wide World

World War I

NASA

The space age

ern Europe—started to exert a powerful influence throughout the world. The Europeans began to make great advances in learning and the arts, and they came to surpass the rest of the world in scientific and technological achievements. The nations of Europe sent explorers and military forces to distant lands. They set up overseas colonies, first in the Americas and then on other continents, and conquered other regions. As a result, Western customs, skills, political ideas, and religious beliefs spread across much of the world.

Today, the many peoples of the world continue to be separated by different cultural traditions. But they also have more in common than ever before. Worldwide systems of communications and transportation have broken down barriers of time and distance and rapidly increased the exchange of ideas and information between peoples. However far apart people may live from one another, they are affected more and more by the same political and economic changes. In some way, almost everyone can now be affected by a war or a political crisis in a faraway land or by a rise in petroleum prices in distant oil-producing countries. The separate cultures of the world seem to be blending into a common world culture. Much of world history is the story of the way different civilizations have come closer together.

About this article

John Morris Roberts, the contributor of this article, is Warden of Merton College of Oxford University in Oxford, England. He is the author of numerous historical works. They include History of the World, The French Revolution, *and* Revolution and Improvement: The Western World 1775-1847.

The article traces the history of the world from ancient times to the present. The outline below gives the major sections of the article. Each section of the text includes a reference page that provides a time line of major developments of the period, a map, and a table of important dates. World Book also has many separate articles on important events and people in world history. Cross-references within this article refer the reader to other World Book articles for additional details on key topics. The Study aids *section at the end of the article includes a listing of related articles. The section also provides a listing of selected outside resources for further reading on world history.*

Article outline

I. Early centers of civilization
II. The advance of civilization
III. The world from 500 to 1500
IV. The spread of Western civilization
V. The world since 1900
VI. Study aids

The civilization of ancient Egypt began to develop in the Nile River Valley about 3100 B.C. Agriculture thrived in the valley, where floodwaters of the Nile deposited rich soil year after year. The farming scenes shown above were painted on a tomb during the 1400's B.C.

For hundreds of thousands of years, prehistoric people lived by hunting, fishing, and gathering wild plants. Even small groups of people had to roam over large areas of land to find enough food. A group usually stayed in one place only a few days. The discovery of agriculture gradually ended the nomadic way of life for many people. After prehistoric men and women learned to raise crops and domesticate animals, they no longer had to wander about in search of food. They could thus begin to settle in villages.

Agriculture was developed at different times in different regions of the world. People in the Middle East began to grow cereal grasses and other plants about 9000 B.C. They also domesticated goats and sheep at about that time, and they later tamed cattle. In southeastern Asia, people had begun raising crops by about 7000 B.C. People who lived in what is now Mexico probably learned to grow crops about 7000 B.C.

The invention of farming paved the way for the development of civilization. As prehistoric people became better farmers, they began to produce enough food to support larger villages. In time, some farming villages developed into the first cities. The plentiful food supplies enabled more and more people to give up farming for other jobs. These people began to develop the arts, crafts, trades, and other activities of civilized life.

Agriculture also stimulated technological and social changes. Farmers invented the hoe, sickle, and other tools to make their work easier. The hair of domestic animals and fibers from such plants as cotton and flax were used to make the first textiles. People built ovens to bake the bread they made from cultivated grain and learned to use hotter ovens to harden pottery. The practice of agriculture required many people to work together to prepare the fields for planting and to harvest

the crops. New systems of government were developed to direct such group activities.

The changes brought about by agriculture took thousands of years to spread widely across the earth. By about 3500 B.C., civilization began. It started first in Southwest Asia. Three other early civilizations developed in Africa and in south and east Asia. All these early civilizations arose in river valleys, where fertile soil and a readily available water supply made agriculture easier than elsewhere. The valleys were (1) the Tigris-Euphrates Valley in the Middle East, (2) the Nile Valley in Egypt, (3) the Indus Valley in what is now Pakistan, and (4) the Huang He Valley in northern China.

While civilization was developing in the four valleys, people in most other parts of the world were still following their old ways of life. Little cultural progress was being made in such regions as northern and central Europe, central and southern Africa, northern and southeastern Asia, and most of North America. In parts of Central and South America, the people were developing some new ways of life. But advanced civilizations did not appear there until hundreds of years later.

The Tigris-Euphrates Valley. One of the most fertile regions of the ancient world lay between the Tigris and Euphrates rivers in southern Mesopotamia (now Iraq). Silt deposited by the rivers formed a rich topsoil ideal for growing crops. By the 5000's B.C., many people had settled in villages in the lower part of the Tigris-Euphrates Valley, an area later called Sumer.

The Sumerians lived by farming, fishing, and hunting the wild fowl of the river marshes. They built dikes to control the flooding of the Tigris and Euphrates rivers and irrigation canals to carry water to their fields. By about 3500 B.C., some Sumerian farm villages had grown into small cities, which marked the beginning of

Major developments

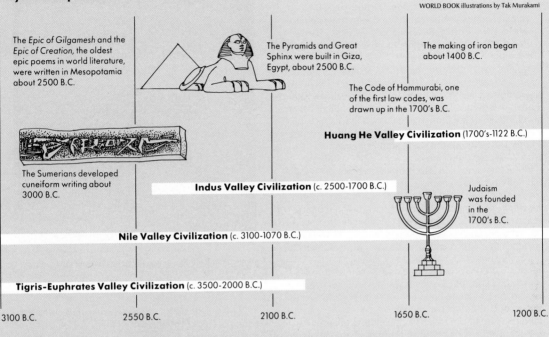

The *Epic of Gilgamesh* and the *Epic of Creation*, the oldest epic poems in world literature, were written in Mesopotamia about 2500 B.C.

The Pyramids and Great Sphinx were built in Giza, Egypt, about 2500 B.C.

The making of iron began about 1400 B.C.

The Code of Hammurabi, one of the first law codes, was drawn up in the 1700's B.C.

Huang He Valley Civilization (1700's-1122 B.C.)

The Sumerians developed cuneiform writing about 3000 B.C.

Indus Valley Civilization (c. 2500-1700 B.C.)

Judaism was founded in the 1700's B.C.

Nile Valley Civilization (c. 3100-1070 B.C.)

Tigris-Euphrates Valley Civilization (c. 3500-2000 B.C.)

3100 B.C.   2550 B.C.   2100 B.C.   1650 B.C.   1200 B.C.

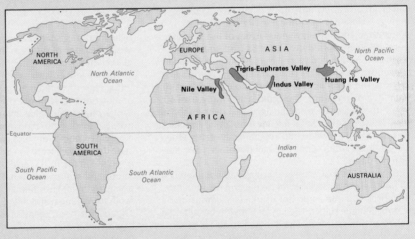

The earliest civilizations arose in four river valleys in Asia and Africa between about 3500 B.C. and the 1700's B.C. The fertile soil of the valleys supported flourishing farming villages. Civilization began when such villages developed into cities.

Important dates

c. 9000 B.C. The development of agriculture began with the growing of crops and the domestication of animals in the Middle East.

c. 3500 B.C. A number of small cities, centers of the world's first civilization, appeared in Sumer, the lower part of the Tigris-Euphrates Valley.

c. 3500 B.C. The Sumerians invented the first form of writing. It was later simplified to produce wedge-shaped *cuneiform* writing, which spread throughout the Middle East.

c. 3100 B.C. King Menes of Upper Egypt united Lower and Upper Egypt.

c. 2500 B.C. The Indus Valley civilization began to flourish in the cities of Moen-jo-Daro and Harappa in what is now Pakistan.

c. 2500-1100 B.C. The Minoan civilization on the island of Crete rose and fell.

2300's B.C. Sargon of Akkad conquered the Sumerians and united all Mesopotamia under his rule, creating the world's first empire.

1700's B.C. The Shang dynasty began its rule in the Huang He Valley of China.

c. 1792-1750 B.C. Babylonia flourished under King Hammurabi.

1500's-c. 1100 B.C. The city of Mycenae was the leading political and cultural center on the Greek mainland.

c. 1595 B.C. The Hittites, a warlike people from what is now central Turkey, conquered the Babylonians.

c. 1500 B.C. The Aryans of central Asia began migrating to India.

the world's first civilization. A number of these cities developed into powerful city-states by about 3200 B.C.

The Sumerians produced one of the greatest achievements in world history. By about 3500 B.C., they had invented the first form of writing. It consisted of picture-like symbols scratched into clay. The symbols were later simplified to produce *cuneiform*, a system of writing that used wedge-shaped characters (see **Cuneiform**). Archaeologists have found thousands of clay tablets with Sumerian writings. These tablets show the high level of development of the Sumerian culture. They include historical and legal documents; letters; economic records; literary and religious texts; and studies in mathematics, astronomy, and medicine.

The Sumerians used baked bricks to build great palaces and towering temples called *ziggurats* in their cities. They believed that their gods lived on the tops of the ziggurats. Sumerian craftworkers produced board games, beautifully designed jewelry, metalware, musical instruments, decorative pottery, and stone seals engraved with pictures and inscriptions. The Sumerians invented the potter's wheel and were among the first people to brew beer and make glass. Their system of counting in units of 60 is the basis of the 360-degree circle and the 60-minute hour. For more information on the Sumerian civilization, see **Sumer**.

The Sumerian city-states had no central government or unified army and continually struggled among themselves for power. As time passed, they were increasingly threatened by neighboring Semitic peoples, who were attracted by the growing wealth of the Tigris-Euphrates Valley. During the 2300's B.C., a Semitic king, Sargon of Akkad, conquered Sumer. Sargon united all Mesopotamia under his rule, creating the world's first empire. The Akkadians combined Sumerian civilization with their own culture. Their rule lasted more than 60 years. Then invaders from the northeast overran the empire. These invaders soon left Mesopotamia, and Sumer was once again divided into separate city-states. One city-state, Ur, briefly controlled all the others. See **Sargon of Akkad**.

By about 2000 B.C., the Sumerians had completely lost all political power to invading Semites. Mesopotamia then broke up into a number of small kingdoms under various Semitic rulers. The city of Babylon became the center of one kingdom. The Babylonian rulers gradually extended their authority over all Mesopotamian peoples. The greatest Babylonian king was Hammurabi, who ruled from about 1792 to 1750 B.C. Hammurabi developed one of the first law codes in history. The famous Code of Hammurabi contained nearly 300 legal provisions, including many Sumerian and Akkadian laws. It covered such matters as divorce, false accusation, land and business regulations, and military service. See **Babylonia; Hammurabi**.

The Nile Valley. The civilization of ancient Egypt began to develop in the valley of the Nile River about 3100 B.C. Agriculture flourished in the valley, where the floodwaters of the Nile deposited rich soil year after year. Beyond the Nile Valley lay an uninhabited region of desert and rock. Egyptian culture thus developed with little threat of invasions by neighboring peoples.

Karachi Museum (SCALA from Art Resource)

A stone seal from the Indus Valley civilization has a carved figure of an animal and some writing. The seal, which is about 4,000 years old, was uncovered at Mohenjo-Daro, Pakistan.

During the 3000's B.C., Egypt consisted of two large kingdoms. Lower Egypt covered the Nile Delta. Upper Egypt lay south of the delta on the two banks of the river. About 3100 B.C., according to legend, King Menes of Upper Egypt conquered Lower Egypt and united the two kingdoms. Menes also founded the first Egyptian *dynasty* (series of rulers in the same family). The rulers of ancient Egypt were believed to be divine.

The ancient Egyptians borrowed little from other cultures. They invented their own form of writing—an elaborate system of symbols known as *hieroglyphics* (see **Hieroglyphics**). They also invented *papyrus*, a paperlike material made from the stems of reeds. The Egyptians developed one of the first religions to emphasize life after death. They tried to make sure their dead enjoyed a good life in the next world. The Egyptians built great tombs and *mummified* (embalmed and dried) corpses to preserve them. They filled the tombs with clothing, food, furnishings, and jewelry for use in the next world. The most famous Egyptian tombs are gigantic pyramids in which the kings were buried. The pyramids display the outstanding engineering and surveying skills of the Egyptians. The government organized thousands of workers to construct the pyramids, as well as temples and palaces, in the Egyptian cities. The cities served chiefly as religious and governmental centers for the surrounding countryside. Most of the people lived in villages near the cities.

Over the years, huge armies of conquering Egyptians expanded the kingdom's boundaries far beyond the Nile Valley. At its height in the 1400's B.C., Egypt ruled Syria, Lebanon, Palestine, and part of the Sudan. As a powerful state at the junction of Asia and Africa, Egypt played an important role in the growth of long-distance trade. Egyptian caravans carried goods throughout the vast desert regions surrounding the kingdom. Egyptian ships sailed to all the major ports of the ancient world.

From other lands, the Egyptians acquired gems, gold, ivory, leopard skins, fine woods, and other rich materials, which they used to create some of the most magnificent art of ancient times.

Although the ancient Egyptians had contacts with other cultures, their way of life changed little over thousands of years. Their civilization gradually declined, and the Egyptians found it harder and harder to resist invaders who had greater vigor and better weapons. Egyptian records from the 1200's and 1100's B.C. describe constant attacks by "sea peoples." These peoples may have come from islands in the Aegean Sea or from lands along the east coast of the Mediterranean Sea. After 1000 B.C., power struggles between rival Egyptian dynasties further weakened the kingdom.

For a detailed description of life in ancient Egypt, see **Egypt, Ancient.**

The Indus Valley. Historians have only partly translated the writings left behind by the ancient civilization that arose in the valley of the Indus River and its tributaries. As a result, they have had to rely almost entirely on archaeological findings for information about the Indus culture. The ruins of two large cities—Mohenjo-Daro and Harappa—tell much about the Indus Valley civilization. The remains of hundreds of small settlements have also been discovered in the valley. Some of these settlements were farming villages, and others were seaports and trading posts.

Mohenjo-Daro and Harappa probably had more than 35,000 inhabitants each by about 2500 B.C. The people of the Indus Valley had a well-developed system of agriculture that provided food for the large population. They dug ditches and canals to irrigate their farms. The Indus cities had brick buildings and well-planned streets laid out in rectangular patterns. Elaborate brick-lined drainage systems provided sanitation for the towns. Craftworkers made decorated furniture, fine jewelry, metal utensils, toys, and stone seals engraved with animal and human forms. Inscriptions on these seals provide the only traces of Indus writing known at present.

Palace of St. Michael and St. George, Corfu, Greece (Photoresources)

A bronze ceremonial vessel shows the skill of an ancient Chinese artist. The vessel dates from the Shang dynasty, which arose in the valley of the Huang He during the 1700's B.C.

Archaeologists have discovered that standardized sizes of bricks and uniform weights and measures were used throughout the Indus Valley. These findings suggest that an effective central government may have ruled the entire region. The Indus settlements traded with one another and with foreign cultures. Traces of seals used on goods from the Indus Valley have been found as far away as Mesopotamia. The Indus people probably also traded with people of central Asia, southern India, and Persia.

Between 2000 and 1750 B.C., the Indus Valley civilization began to decay. Scholars do not know why. Overuse of the land along the riverbanks or natural disasters may have severely damaged the territory. Or the people may have been unable to defend themselves against invaders who came into the valley through mountain passes to the northwest. By about 1700 B.C., the Indus civilization had disappeared.

For more information on what archaeologists have discovered about the ancient Indus Valley culture, see **Indus Valley civilization.**

The Huang He Valley. The earliest written records of Chinese history date from the Shang dynasty, which arose in the valley of the Huang He during the 1700's B.C. The records consist largely of writings scratched on animal bones and turtle shells. The bones and shells, known as *oracle bones*, were used in religious ceremonies to answer questions about the future. After a question was written on an oracle bone, a small groove or hole was made in the bone. The bone was then heated so that cracks ran outward from the groove or hole. By studying the pattern of the cracks, a priest worked out the answer to the question.

Thousands of oracle bones have been found. They provide much information about the ancient Chinese. Many of the bones record astronomical events, such as eclipses of the sun and moon, and the names and dates of rulers. The system of writing used by the Shang people had more than 3,000 characters. Some characters on the oracle bones closely resemble those of the present-day Chinese language.

Little remains of the cities of the Shang period. Most of the buildings were made of mud or wood and have long since crumbled away. However, the foundations of pounded earth survive and indicate that some of the cities were fairly large and surrounded by high walls. The people of the Shang period cast beautiful bronze vessels. They also carved marble and jade and wove silk. The Shang people had many gods. They attached great importance to ties of kinship and worshiped the spirits of their ancestors. They believed that their ancestors could plead with the gods on their behalf.

The Shang people were governed by a king and a hereditary class of aristocrats. The king and the nobility carried out religious as well as political duties. However, only the king could perform the most important religious ceremonies. The Shang leaders organized armies of as many as 5,000 men and equipped them with bronze weapons and horse-drawn war chariots. They used their armies to control the other peoples of the Huang He Valley. The Shang ruled much of the valley for about 600 years. See **Shang dynasty.**

Temple of Poseidon (400's B.C.), Paestum, Italy (Photoresources)

Greek civilization was the first advanced civilization on the European mainland. It became the most magnificent civilization of ancient times and spread to other lands. Greek colonists built many temples, such as this one in southern Italy, in regions they settled.

From about 1200 B.C. to A.D. 500, Mesopotamia and Egypt were increasingly affected by the gradual growth of a new civilization on the islands and shores of the Aegean Sea. The most magnificent civilization of ancient times—that of the Greeks—eventually developed in the Aegean region. For a time, the Greeks dominated much of the ancient world. Later, the lands of the Greeks, as well as Mesopotamia and Egypt, became part of the Roman Empire. The combined arts, philosophies, and sciences of ancient Greece and Rome provided much of the foundation of later European culture.

As the civilizations of ancient times grew and spread, they began to have certain features in common. By about A.D. 500, for example, all the major civilizations had learned how to make iron. The spread of such knowledge was helped by trade, conquest, and migration. Traders carried the products of one culture to other cultures. The soldiers of invading armies often settled in the conquered lands, where they introduced new ways of life. Groups of people migrated from one region to another, bringing the customs, ideas, and skills of their homelands with them.

The most important migrations in ancient times were made by peoples belonging to the Indo-European language groups. The Indo-European peoples once lived in what is now the southern part of the Soviet Union. Sometime before 2000 B.C., large numbers of them began moving into Europe, the Middle East, and across the highlands of Persia to India. Many of the migrations resulted in the destruction of old states and the creation of new ones.

Middle Eastern civilizations. For several hundred years following 1200 B.C., various Indo-European and Semitic peoples struggled for power in the Middle East.

One of the Semitic peoples, the Hebrews, founded a kingdom in what is now Israel about 1020 B.C. The Hebrews, also called Jews, established the first religion based on the belief in one God. The Hebrew faith, called Judaism, had a lasting influence on human history. Both Christianity, the most widespread religion of modern times, and Islam, the religion of the Muslims, developed from Judaism. See **Jews.**

During the 700's B.C., much of the Middle East was conquered by the Assyrians, a northern Mesopotamian people. The cities of Nineveh and Assur on the upper Tigris River were the chief centers of their empire. The Assyrians were a rough, warlike people who often treated their subject peoples cruelly. Conquered rulers were replaced by brutal Assyrian governors who acted on orders from the central government in Nineveh. For more information, see **Assyria.**

In 612 B.C., the Babylonians and an Indo-European people called the Medes joined forces and destroyed Nineveh. The Assyrian Empire thus ended. The Medes then established the Median Empire, which included the area north of Mesopotamia (see **Media**). In Mesopotamia and to the west, the New Babylonian Empire, sometimes called the Chaldean Empire, came into being. Under its most famous ruler, Nebuchadnezzar II, Babylon became one of the most magnificent cities of the ancient world. Nebuchadnezzar probably built the Hanging Gardens, one of the Seven Wonders of the Ancient World (see **Seven Wonders of the Ancient World** [with picture]).

About 550 B.C., the Persians, led by Cyrus the Great, overthrew the Medes and established the Persian Empire. Cyrus went on to conquer Babylonia, Palestine, Syria, and all Asia Minor. Cyrus' son Cambyses added

Major developments

WORLD BOOK illustrations by Tak Murakami

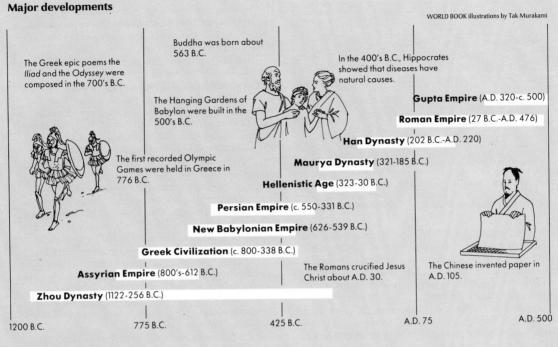

The Greek epic poems the *Iliad* and the *Odyssey* were composed in the 700's B.C.

Buddha was born about 563 B.C.

The Hanging Gardens of Babylon were built in the 500's B.C.

In the 400's B.C., Hippocrates showed that diseases have natural causes.

Gupta Empire (A.D. 320-c. 500)

Roman Empire (27 B.C.-A.D. 476)

Han Dynasty (202 B.C.-A.D. 220)

The first recorded Olympic Games were held in Greece in 776 B.C.

Maurya Dynasty (321-185 B.C.)

Hellenistic Age (323-30 B.C.)

Persian Empire (c. 550-331 B.C.)

New Babylonian Empire (626-539 B.C.)

Greek Civilization (c. 800-338 B.C.)

Assyrian Empire (800's-612 B.C.)

The Romans crucified Jesus Christ about A.D. 30.

The Chinese invented paper in A.D. 105.

Zhou Dynasty (1122-256 B.C.)

| 1200 B.C. | 775 B.C. | 425 B.C. | A.D. 75 | A.D. 500 |

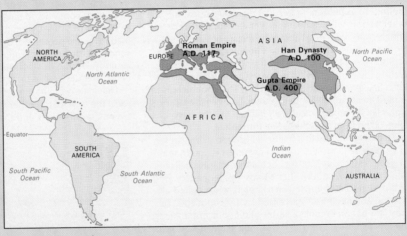

Powerful empires emerged as civilization advanced and spread between 1200 B.C. and A.D. 500. The Roman Empire covered much of Europe and the Middle East, and the north coast of Africa. The Han dynasty of China and the Gupta dynasty of India also ruled huge empires.

WORLD BOOK map

Important dates

1020 B.C. The Hebrews founded a kingdom in what is now Palestine.

800's B.C. The Etruscans settled in west-central Italy.

750-338 B.C. Athens, Corinth, Sparta, and Thebes were the chief city-states of Greece.

c. 550 B.C. Cyrus the Great established the Persian Empire.

509 B.C. The people of Rome revolted against their Etruscan rulers and established a republic.

338 B.C. Philip II of Macedonia conquered the Greeks.

331 B.C. Alexander the Great defeated the Persians at Arbela, opening the way to his conquest of northern India.

221-206 B.C. The Qin dynasty established China's first strong central government.

202 B.C. The Han dynasty began its 400-year rule of China.

146 B.C. The Romans conquered Greece.

55-54 B.C. Julius Caesar led the Roman invasion of Britain.

27 B.C. Augustus became the first Roman emperor.

c. A.D. 250 The Maya Indians developed an advanced civilization in Central America and Mexico.

313 Constantine issued the Edict of Milan, which granted freedom of worship to Christians of the Roman Empire.

320 India began its golden age under the Gupta dynasty.

395 The Roman Empire split into the East Roman, or Byzantine, Empire and the West Roman Empire.

476 The Germanic chieftain Odoacer overthrew Romulus Augustulus, the last emperor of the West Roman Empire.

British Museum, London (Photoresources)

Assyrian King Ashurbanipal and his queen are shown feasting in the royal garden on this stone carving. The carving, found at the king's palace in Nineveh, dates from the 600's B.C.

Egypt to the empire in 525 B.C. The Persians built excellent roads throughout their vast empire. They divided the empire into provinces, each governed by a Persian official. Unlike the Assyrians, the Persians allowed the conquered peoples to keep their own religions and traditions. See **Persia, Ancient.**

The Persian Empire lasted more than 200 years. Under Persian rule, Medes, Babylonians, Jews, and Egyptians were united for the first time. Although they still had different traditions and customs, they could no longer be thought of as belonging to separate civilizations. Another people who came under Persian control were the Phoenicians, who lived along the coasts of what are now Syria, Lebanon, and Israel. The Phoenicians were great explorers and traders who helped spread civilization among the peoples living in coastal areas along the Aegean Sea and in what is now Turkey. The Phoenicians invented an alphabet that became the basis of the Greek alphabet. All other Western alphabets, in turn, have been taken from the Greek. See **Phoenicia.**

The Greeks. The first major civilization in the region of Greece began to develop on Crete, an island in the Aegean Sea, about 3000 B.C. Scholars call this civilization the *Minoan* culture after Minos, the legendary king of the island (see **Minos**). The Minoans were skilled artists and architects and active traders. By about 2000 B.C., they had begun to build a series of magnificent palaces, the most elaborate of which was the Palace of Minos in the town of Knossos.

The Minoans traded with peoples in the Middle East, Sicily, and Greece. Their trade routes provided an important link between Middle Eastern civilizations and mainland Europe. Minoan culture flourished for about 500 years. It began to decline after 1450 B.C., when fire destroyed nearly all the towns on Crete. By about 1100 B.C., the culture had disappeared.

The most important early culture on the mainland of Greece centered on the southern city of Mycenae. The people of Mycenae were probably descendants of Indo-European peoples who had been migrating to Greece since about 2000 B.C. By the 1500's B.C., the Mycenaean culture had become rich and powerful. Mycenae was the leading political and cultural center on the Greek mainland until it collapsed in the early 1100's B.C. About

this time, barbarian peoples from the north began moving into Greece. Later Greeks called these people the Dorians. Historians are not sure what part the Dorians played in the fall of Mycenae.

Greek civilization developed between about 800 and 500 B.C. The first recorded Olympic Games were held for Greek athletes in 776 B.C., and the first surviving Greek inscriptions date from about 50 years later. The ancient Greeks settled in independent communities called *city-states.* Between 750 and 338 B.C., the chief city-states were Athens, Corinth, Sparta, and Thebes. The city-states were never united politically, and the people were divided into various groups. However, the Greeks were tied together by a common culture and language, and they thought of themselves as distinct from other peoples. The first democratic governments were established in the Greek city-states. Neither slaves nor women could vote, but more people took part in government in Greece than in any earlier civilization.

Greek culture gradually spread to other lands. The Greeks established many towns and trading posts in Sicily and in what are now southern Italy and Turkey. Greek colonists also founded settlements as far away as present-day Portugal, France, Libya, and India. Many Greeks served as craftworkers, teachers, and soldiers in the courts of foreign rulers.

In 479 B.C., the Greeks defeated the Persians after a long war. Greek civilization then entered its Golden Age. Architects constructed masterpieces of classical beauty. Lasting works of art, literature, drama, history, and philosophy were produced. Greek scientists made great advances in mathematics, medicine, physics, botany, and zoology. During this period, Athens became the cultural center of the Greek world.

The achievements and growing power of Athens were the envy of the other Greek city-states. Hostility between the Athenians and their fellow Greeks led to the

Delphi Museum, Greece (Photoresources)

An ancient Greek dish portrays the god Apollo, patron of musicians and poets and the ideal of manly beauty. Greek culture thrived in the 400's B.C., the Golden Age of Greek civilization.

Photoresources

A famous Roman aqueduct, the Pont du Gard near Nîmes, France, stands as a reminder of one of the world's greatest empires. At its peak of power, in the A.D. 100's, the Roman Empire covered about half of Europe, much of the Middle East, and the north coast of Africa.

bitter Peloponnesian War (431-404 B.C.). Athens lost the war. The victorious city-states soon started to quarrel among themselves, and Greece began to decline in power. In 338 B.C., Philip II of Macedonia conquered the Greek city-states. His son, Alexander the Great, succeeded him in 336 B.C. Until his death in 323 B.C., Alexander expanded his empire through conquests of much of the civilized world from Egypt to India. Alexander deeply admired Greek traditions and achievements. He introduced Greek ideas and the Greek way of life into all the lands he conquered.

After Alexander died, his empire was divided among his generals. They continued to preserve Greek culture. The period after Alexander's death became known as the Hellenistic Age in Greece and the Near East. It lasted until the Romans took control, ending in Greece in 146 B.C. Egypt, the last major stronghold of the Hellenistic world, fell to the Romans in 30 B.C. See **Alexander the Great; Hellenistic Age.**

For a detailed description of life in ancient Greece, see **Greece, Ancient.**

The Romans. By the 500's B.C., Greek traders and colonists had established many settlements in Italy and Sicily. They carried Greek civilization directly to the mixed group of peoples living there, most of whom were descendants of Indo-European immigrants. These peoples included the Etruscans, who had settled in west-central Italy during the 800's B.C. In 509 B.C., the people of Rome, one of the cities under Etruscan control, revolted. The Romans gained their independence and declared Rome a republic.

For hundreds of years, Roman conquerors expanded the republic. By 290 B.C., Rome controlled most of Italy. It soon became one of the most powerful states of the western Mediterranean. During the 200's and 100's B.C., Rome defeated its only major rival, the former Phoenician colony of Carthage, in a series of struggles called the Punic Wars (see **Punic Wars**). As a result of the wars, Sicily and Spain became Roman provinces. Rome also expanded into the eastern Mediterranean. In 148 B.C., the Romans made Macedonia their first eastern province. Two years later, they conquered Greece. In 55 and 54 B.C., the Roman general Julius Caesar invaded Britain. Other conquests followed until the original city of Rome had grown into an enormous empire. At its height, in A.D. 117, the empire covered about half of Europe, much of the Middle East, and the entire north coast of Africa.

Roman territory included all the Greek lands of the Hellenistic Age. The Romans imitated Greek art and literature, made use of Greek scientific knowledge, and based their architecture on Greek models. Educated people throughout the Roman Empire spoke Greek. By imitating Greek accomplishments, the Romans preserved and passed on much Greek culture that otherwise might have been lost.

The Romans also contributed their own achievements to the civilization they developed. They were superb engineers who constructed massive aqueducts and bridges, vast systems of roads, and monumental arches. The Romans developed an excellent legal system. Their legal code forms the basis of civil law in numerous

Detail of a mosaic (about 986-994) in Hagia Sophia, Istanbul, Turkey (Photoresources)

Constantine the Great was the first Roman emperor to become a Christian. He came to the throne in A.D. 306 and formed close ties between the Christian church and the Roman Empire.

European and Latin-American countries, and many of its principles and terms are part of English and American common law. Latin, the language of the Romans, was the official language of the empire. It became the basis of French, Italian, Spanish, and other Romance languages of today.

The Romans excelled in the art of government. One of their most important achievements was the empire itself, which provided a stable framework of government for many peoples with widely different customs. The Romans showed great respect for these customs and won the good will of many of the peoples they governed. Rome was a republic until 27 B.C., when Augustus took supreme power. Augustus and his successors retained republican titles and forms of government, but Rome actually became a monarchy ruled by emperors.

During the A.D. 100's and 200's, Rome was increasingly threatened by barbarian invaders in both the east and the west. As a result, the army became more and more powerful and began to play a major role in choosing Rome's emperors. One of the most important emperors the army helped bring to power was Constantine the Great, who came to the throne in 306. In 313, Constantine granted Christians of the Roman Empire freedom of worship. Christ had been born during the reign of the Emperor Augustus and was crucified by the Roman authorities in about A.D. 30, during the rule of Tiberius. The Romans had at times persecuted the Christians. However, after Constantine granted Christians legal recognition, a strong link was formed between the Christian church and the Roman Empire. Emperor Theo-

dosius I proclaimed Christianity the official religion of the empire in the late 300's.

A period of great disorder followed Constantine's death in 337. In 395, the Roman Empire split into two parts—the West Roman Empire and the East Roman, or Byzantine, Empire. The West Roman Empire soon fell to Germanic tribes, but the Byzantine Empire was to thrive for many years. For more information on the rise and fall of the Roman Empire, see **Rome, Ancient.**

Achievements in India. About 1500 B.C., bands of Aryans, an Indo-European people, began migrating to India. The Aryans came from the plains of central Asia through the mountain passes of the Hindu Kush. By 1000 B.C., they had taken over most of the valley of the upper Ganges River in northern India.

The Aryans never invaded southern India, but their influence gradually extended over the entire country and greatly affected Indian culture. Sanskrit, the language developed by the Aryans, is the basis of languages still spoken in India. Hinduism, the religion of most Indians today, is rooted in Indo-European beliefs. The division of present-day Indian society into social classes called *castes* dates from the divisions of early Aryan society into four classes. These classes were priests and scholars; rulers and warriors; merchants and professionals; and laborers and servants. See **Caste.**

At various times in its history, the Aryan territory was divided into many states. In one state, a prince named Siddhartha Gautama was born about 563 B.C. Gautama abandoned a life of luxury to seek religious enlightenment. He became a great religious teacher known to his followers as *Buddha* (Enlightened One). Gautama's teachings are the foundation of Buddhism, one of the world's major religions. See **Buddhism.**

By about 300 B.C., much of India was united for the first time under one dynasty, the Maurya. The Maurya Empire reached its peak under Emperor Asoka, who ruled during the 200's B.C. From his capital at Pataliputra (now Patna) in northern India, Asoka controlled almost

Borromeo from Art Resource

A Hindu stone temple built during the A.D. 500's stands at Aihole, India, near Belgaum. It reflects a style of architecture that became popular under the Gupta dynasty.

Fred Ward, Black Star

The Great Wall of China was built to keep out invaders from the north. Emperor Shi Huangdi began major work on it in the 200's B.C. by linking walls built by earlier rulers. By the A.D. 1600's, it reached its present length, almost 4,000 miles (6,400 kilometers).

The Avery Brundage Collection (Gemini Smith)

A jade ornament of a bearded man dates from the Han dynasty, which ruled China from 202 B.C. to A.D. 220.

all India and part of central Asia. Asoka supported Buddhism, which spread and prospered during his reign. He sent Buddhist missionaries to Ceylon (now Sri Lanka) and other countries. See **Asoka; Maurya Empire.**

The Maurya dynasty ended with the assassination of its last emperor in 185 B.C. For most of the next 500 years, India was divided into small political units under no one ruler. In A.D. 320, a new dynasty, the Gupta, came to power in northern India. The Gupta dynasty lasted about 200 years. During the Gupta period, Indian civilization enjoyed a golden age of peace, good government, and cultural development. Beautiful cities arose, and universities were founded. Sanskrit literature, particularly drama, flourished during the Gupta era. The Gupta emperors were Hindus, but Buddhism also thrived under their rule. See **Gupta dynasty.**

Achievements in China. About 1122 B.C., the Zhou people of western China overthrew the Shang and established their own dynasty. The Zhou ruled until 256 B.C. The Zhou kings introduced the idea that they had been appointed to rule by Heaven. All later Chinese dynasties adopted that idea. From its beginning, the Zhou dynasty directly controlled only part of northern China. The rest of the kingdom consisted of semi-independent states. As time passed, the lords of these states grew increasingly powerful and so weakened the dynasty. In 771 B.C., the Zhou were forced to abandon their capital, near what is now Xi'an, and move eastward to Luoyang.

For hundreds of years after the Zhou moved their capital, fighting raged among the states for control of all China. Efforts to restore order to Chinese society led to the birth of Chinese philosophy during this period. The great philosopher Confucius stressed the importance of moral standards and tradition and of a well-ordered society in which people performed the duties of their stations in life. See **Confucianism.**

In 221 B.C., the Qin (also spelled Ch'in) state in northwestern China defeated all its rivals. The Qin created the first unified Chinese empire controlled by a strong central government. The name *China* came from the name of their dynasty. The first Qin emperor, Shi Huangdi, standardized weights and measures and the Chinese writing system. He also built extensive irrigation projects. To keep out barbarian invaders, he ordered major construction on the Great Wall of China.

The Qin dynasty lasted only until 206 B.C. The Han dynasty gained control of China in 202 B.C. Under the Han emperors, Confucianism became the philosophical basis of government. Candidates for government jobs had to take a civil service examination based on Confucian ideals. Art, education, and science thrived during the Han period. Sometime before A.D. 100, Buddhism was introduced into China from India. In A.D. 105, the Chinese invented paper.

Han China expanded southwest to what is now Tibet. Han warriors also conquered parts of Indochina and Korea and overcame nomadic tribes in the north and west. Political struggles among the Han leaders led to the collapse of the dynasty in A.D. 220. For the next 400 years, China was again divided into warring states. See **Han dynasty.**

September by the Limbourg brothers, from the Duc de Berry's illuminated manuscript of the 1400's *Très Riches Heures;* Musée Condé, Chantilly, France (Giraudon from Art Resource)

European life in the Middle Ages centered on control of the land. Lords owned most of the land, which was farmed by their peasants. The lords lived in mighty castles like the one above.

Various parts of the world gradually came more closely into contact with one another during the period from 500 to 1500. In fact, some regions came into contact with other regions for the first time. However, the various regions still remained largely independent of one another during most of that time, and their histories continued to progress along separate lines.

Great changes occurred in the old areas of civilization during the 1,000-year period. In western Europe, a number of separate states eventually arose from the disorder that followed the fall of the West Roman Empire. The East Roman, or Byzantine, Empire continued to survive and flourish. A new world religion, Islam, sprang up in Arabia and spread to many other parts of the world. Meanwhile, China continued to preserve its special way of life under a series of dynasties. Partly under influence from China, another Oriental civilization appeared, that of Japan. In the Americas, civilizations developed without any outside influences.

In European history, the period between about 500 and 1500 is often referred to as the *Middle Ages* or the

medieval period. The word *medieval* comes from the Latin words *medium*, meaning *middle*, and *aevum*, meaning *age*. The terms *Middle Ages* and *medieval period* made sense to later Europeans who looked back on those years as a distinct period in the middle of their history between the civilizations of ancient Greece and Rome and the start of modern times. But the terms cannot be applied to world history as a whole because the histories of many parts of the world have no connection with ancient Greece and Rome.

Medieval Europe. By A.D. 400, many barbarian invaders and immigrants from the east had settled within the West Roman Empire. In 476, a Germanic chieftain named Odoacer overthrew the last emperor, Romulus Augustulus. By that time, Germanic conquerors had carved kingdoms out of all the West Roman provinces. The framework of government created by the Romans had disappeared.

Roman culture was not completely destroyed, however. Many Germanic rulers adopted some Roman customs and converted to Christianity. The Christian church became the most important civilizing force among the Germanic peoples. Its missionaries introduced the barbarians to Roman ideas of government and justice. Cathedrals and monasteries provided the main centers of learning and philosophy. The monks and the clergy helped continue the reading and writing of Latin and preserved many ancient manuscripts.

For hundreds of years after the fall of the West Roman Empire, the Germanic kings had great difficulty defending themselves against invaders. The invaders included Arabs from the south, Vikings from the north, and Magyars and Avars from the east. During these troubled times, a new military and political system known as *feudalism* developed in western Europe. Under this system, powerful lords—who owned most of the land—gave some of their holdings to less wealthy noblemen in return for pledges of allegiance. These lesser nobles, called *vassals*, swore to fight for the lord when he needed their help. Peasants worked the fields of the lords and their vassals. By the 900's, most of western Europe was divided into feudal states. The feudal lords completely controlled their estates. Kings ruled only their own lands and vassals. See **Feudalism.**

During the 1000's, many lords established strong governments and achieved periods of peace under the feudal system. Trade revived along the old land routes and waterways used by the Romans. Towns sprang up and prospered along the trade routes. The peasants learned better farming methods and gained new farmland by clearing forests and draining swamps. The population rose. Learning and the arts thrived as trade brought increasing contact with the advanced Byzantine and Islamic civilizations. During the 1100's and 1200's, the first European universities were established.

The people of the medieval towns often supported the kings against the feudal lords. The townspeople agreed to pay taxes to the kings in return for protection and freedom. During the 1300's and 1400's, some kings became increasingly powerful and began to extend their authority over the feudal lords. By 1500, France, England, Spain, and Portugal had become unified nation-

Major developments

WORLD BOOK illustrations by Tak Murakami

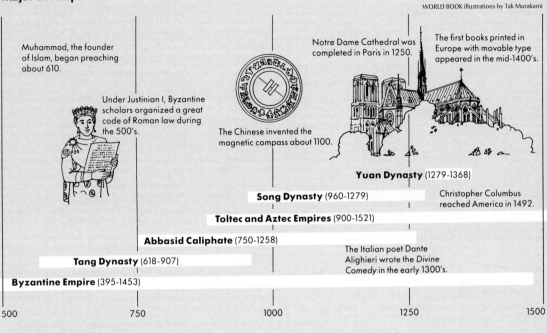

Muhammad, the founder of Islam, began preaching about 610.

Under Justinian I, Byzantine scholars organized a great code of Roman law during the 500's.

The Chinese invented the magnetic compass about 1100.

Notre Dame Cathedral was completed in Paris in 1250.

The first books printed in Europe with movable type appeared in the mid-1400's.

Yuan Dynasty (1279-1368)

Song Dynasty (960-1279)

Christopher Columbus reached America in 1492.

Toltec and Aztec Empires (900-1521)

Abbasid Caliphate (750-1258)

The Italian poet Dante Alighieri wrote the *Divine Comedy* in the early 1300's.

Tang Dynasty (618-907)

Byzantine Empire (395-1453)

500   750   1000   1250   1500

Between 500 and 1500, new civilizations appeared in Africa and the Americas. In the Middle East, the Muslim Arabs rose to power and conquered a huge empire by the mid-700's. In the 1200's, Mongol warriors swept through Asia, creating one of the largest empires in history.

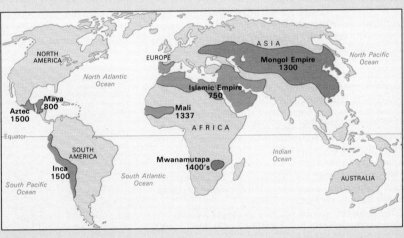

WORLD BOOK map

Important dates

527-565 The Byzantine Empire reached its greatest extent under Emperor Justinian I.

622 Muhammad, founder of Islam, fled from Mecca to Medina. His flight, called the Hegira, marks the beginning of the Islamic calendar.

700's-mid-1000's The Ghana Empire, the first great black empire in western Africa, flourished as a trading state.

732 Charles Martel and the Franks defeated invading Muslims in fighting in west-central France. The victory prevented the Muslims from overrunning Europe.

750 The Abbasids became the caliphs of the Islamic world.

800 Pope Leo III crowned Charlemagne, ruler of the Franks, emperor of the Romans.

c. 988 Vladimir I converted the Russians to Christianity.

1054 Rivalries between the church in Rome and the church in Constantinople resulted in their separation as the Roman Catholic Church and Eastern Orthodox Churches, respectively.

1192 Yoritomo became the first shogun to rule Japan.

1215 English barons forced King John to grant a charter of liberties called Magna Carta.

1279 The Mongols gained control of all China.

1300's The Renaissance began in Italy.

1368 The Ming dynasty began its nearly 300-year rule of China.

1453 The Ottoman Turks captured Constantinople (Istanbul) and overthrew the Byzantine Empire.

Detail of a painting (1400's) by Jean Mielot (Bettmann Archive)

Medieval monks like the one above copied many valuable manuscripts written by ancient Greek and Roman scholars. Their work helped preserve knowledge of ancient times.

states ruled by monarchs. For more information about medieval Europe, see **Middle Ages.**

The Byzantine Empire was a continuation of the East Roman Empire. Its capital and military stronghold was Constantinople (now Istanbul, Turkey). The Byzantine rulers kept Roman governmental and legal traditions. However, the East Roman provinces had always been more influenced by Greek culture than by Latin culture. As a result, the Byzantines helped preserve ancient Greek language, literature, and philosophy.

Christianity flourished in the Byzantine Empire. The Byzantine church was the chief civilizing force among the Slavic peoples of southeastern Europe and Russia. Byzantine missionaries converted the Slavs to Christianity and invented a script in which the Slavic languages were written down. The church in Constantinople was united with the church in Rome for many years. But rivalries developed between the churches, and they drifted apart. The Western church eventually became known as the Roman Catholic Church. The Eastern Orthodox Churches developed out of Byzantine Christianity. See **Eastern Orthodox Churches**.

The Byzantine Empire reached its greatest extent under Emperor Justinian, who came to the throne in 527. His empire included Italy, much of southeastern Europe, part of Spain, much of the Middle East, and lands along the north coast of Africa. At the command of Justinian, Byzantine scholars collected and organized the many laws of the ancient Romans. The resulting code of laws, called the *Justinian Code*, clarified the laws of the times and is today the basis of the legal systems of many countries (see **Justinian Code**). Art and architecture flourished during Justinian's reign. The Byzantines constructed domed cathedrals with ornately decorated interiors. One of these cathedrals is the magnificent Hagia Sophia built by Justinian in Constantinople. See **Byzantine art; Hagia Sophia.**

For hundreds of years, the Byzantine Empire protected western Europe from attacks from the east by barbarians, Persians, and such Muslim invaders as the

Arabs and Ottoman Turks. Beginning in the 1000's, however, the Byzantine emperors fought a losing battle against the Muslims. By 1400, the Ottoman Turks had taken much of southeastern Europe and all the Asian territories of the Byzantines. In 1453, the Ottomans captured Constantinople. This conquest brought to an end the last remnants of the old Roman Empire. See **Byzantine Empire.**

The Islamic world. In the 600's, Islam, a new religion based on the teachings of Muhammad, began in Arabia. Muhammad was born about 570 and grew up in Mecca, a major trading center on the Arabian Peninsula. At that time, most Arabs believed in nature gods and prayed to idols and spirits. But Muhammad urged the Arabs to worship one God. The Meccans rejected Muhammad's teachings and persecuted him and his followers. In 622, Muhammad and his disciples fled to the city of Medina (then called Yathrib). Muhammad's flight, called the Hegira, marks the beginning of the Islamic calendar. The people of Medina accepted Muhammad as God's messenger. By 630, Muhammad and his followers had captured Mecca.

After Muhammad's death in 632, authority to head the Islamic community passed to religious leaders later called *caliphs*. The first caliphs were members of Muhammad's family. Under their leadership, Islam became a great conquering force. The Muslim armies defeated the tribes of southern Arabia and then spread north to Palestine, Syria, Mesopotamia, and Persia. In 661, the caliphate passed to another family, the Umayyads, who established their capital at Damascus. The Umayyad ca-

SCALA from Art Resource

The Basilica of St. Mark in Venice, Italy, is one of the outstanding examples of Byzantine architecture in western Europe. The Roman Catholic church was built during the 1000's.

Illumination by an unknown Persian artist; Metropolitan Museum of Art, New York City (Werner Forman Archive)

A Muslim pharmacist is shown preparing a drug in an illustration from a medical book of the 1200's. Muslims, followers of Islam, contributed greatly to advances in science and the arts.

liphs led the Muslim Arabs to new victories. By the early 700's, the Arabs had conquered Cyprus, Rhodes, Sicily, northern Africa, and Afghanistan. Muslim forces had also pushed into Spain and India and reached the borders of China.

In 750, the Abbasids became the caliphs of the expanding Islamic world. They moved the capital to Baghdad. Under the Abbasids, Islamic civilization reached its greatest heights. Baghdad became a huge city, rivaling Constantinople in wealth and population. Islamic art and architecture flourished, and many Islamic academies and universities were founded. As a result of their conquests, the Muslims had come into contact with Persian astronomy, history, and medicine; Indian mathematics; and Greek science and philosophy. The Arabs became learned in these fields and made significant contributions of their own in mathematics, medicine, astronomy, and other sciences. They also developed literature of their own in Arabic. Many ancient Greek texts were translated into Arabic and eventually introduced into western Europe.

The Abbasid caliphate declined during the 900's as peoples from central Asia began invading the Middle East. Some of these peoples were Turks who had been converted to Islam. During the early 1300's, the Ottoman Turks, who had settled in Anatolia (now Turkey), became the military leaders of the Islamic world. After the Ottomans seized Constantinople in 1453, they made the city the capital of their empire. By 1700, the Ottoman Empire covered southeastern Europe, southern Russia, part of northern Africa, and much of the Middle East. See **Ottoman Empire.**

For more details on the history of the Islamic world, see **Muslims.**

China. From 500 to 1500, Chinese civilization still owed little to the outside world. Land travelers found it hard to reach China, and few travelers came by sea. Isolation helped make Chinese society extremely stable and self-sufficient. During the Tang dynasty (618-907) and

the Song dynasty (960-1279), China enjoyed great prosperity and cultural accomplishment.

The Tang and Song rulers continued to use the system of civil service examinations based on Confucianism that had begun hundreds of years earlier during Han times. Successful candidates for government office thus shared a common body of beliefs and a respect for traditional ways. Cities and towns grew rapidly during the Tang and Song periods. The Tang capital at Chang'an (now Xi'an) had more than a million people. The Tang and Song emperors continued to extend the Grand Canal system, which had already linked the rice-growing lower Yangtze Valley with the north by the early 600's. Literature, history, and philosophy flourished under the Tang and Song dynasties. During the Tang period, the Chinese invented block printing. Chinese inventions during the Song period included gunpowder, the magnetic compass, and movable type for printing. See **Tang dynasty; Song dynasty.**

During the 1200's, Mongol warriors swept into China from the north. The Mongol leader Kublai Khan established the Yuan dynasty, which lasted from 1279 to 1368. The Mongol period marked the first time that all China had come under foreign rule. Kublai Khan encouraged commerce and cultural exchange with other civilized peoples. During Yuan times, Europeans became increasingly interested in China as a result of the reports of travelers and traders. Rebellions drove the Mongols from China during the mid-1300's. In 1368, Chinese rule was reestablished under the Ming dynasty, which held power until 1644. See **Mongol Empire.**

The rise of Japanese civilization. The development of Japanese civilization was greatly influenced by the neighboring Chinese culture. During the 500's, Confucianism, Buddhism, and knowledge of ironmaking reached Japan from China. The Japanese borrowed the Chinese system of writing and adopted some Chinese ideas of government and administration. Japanese government, like Chinese government, centered on an emperor. Beneath the emperor, Japanese society was divided into various *clans* (related families).

During the late 700's and early 800's, the Fujiwaras, an aristocratic clan, rose to power in Japan. The Fujiwaras

Denver Art Museum, Marion G. Hendrie Collection

A Chinese block print from 975 symbolizes China's technological progress despite its isolation. The Chinese invented block printing during the Tang dynasty, which ruled from 618 to 907.

Detail of *The Tale of the Heiji War Scroll* (mid-1200's), an ink painting with colors on paper by an unknown Japanese artist; Museum of Fine Arts, Boston (Gemini Smith)

Rival Japanese clans fought for control of the country's government during the 1100's. Members of the Minamoto family helped kidnap a Taira family emperor in 1160, *left*, but failed to gain power. Minamoto leaders finally won control of Japan in 1185. They later established a military government known as the *shogunate*.

gained control over the emperor and his court by intermarrying with the imperial family. Under the Fujiwaras, the court nobility enjoyed a life of splendor and luxury. The people of Japan began to cast off Chinese cultural influences. Some of the first masterpieces of Japanese literature were written during the Fujiwara era. The Japanese also produced fine ceramics and lacquerware and developed such arts as flower arranging, landscape gardening, and silk weaving. Japanese exports gradually began to appear in the markets of China and southeastern Asia. The Fujiwara clan ruled Japan about 300 years. During that time, the emperors lost all real power, though they still officially reigned.

During the 1000's, civil wars between rival noblemen brought an end to Fujiwara rule. Another powerful clan, the Minamoto, seized control of the imperial court in 1185. The Minamoto leaders established a form of military government called the *shogunate*. The emperor remained in retirement, and a Minamoto *shogun* (military commander) ruled in his name (see **Shogun**). The Minamoto shogunate collapsed in the early 1300's, when Japan was again torn by violent civil wars. The wars slowed the growth of cities and towns and weakened

the nation. But Japan remained safe from attack by foreign powers because of its isolated island position. The Mongols tried to invade Japan in 1274 and 1281, but both attempts failed because of typhoons in the Sea of Japan. See **Japan** (History).

The age of invasions of India. After the Gupta Empire fell in about 500, India broke up into many small kingdoms. From then until the early 1500's, India suffered repeated invasions from the northwest. In the early 700's, Muslim invaders from Arabia swept across northwestern India but were eventually overcome by Indian forces. During the late 1100's, Muslim Turks from central Asia conquered the Indus Valley. By 1206, they had established a *sultanate* (government by a sultan) in Delhi. The Delhi sultanate soon controlled all northern India. During the sultanate, many Muslims came to India to serve as soldiers, government officials, merchants, and priests. Muslim holy men converted many Indians to Islam. See **Delhi sultanate.**

In 1398, a Mongol army raided India and captured Delhi. The Mongols soon withdrew, however. The sultanate regained Delhi, but the rest of the sultanate territory was split into kingdoms. In 1526, Babar, a Muslim

Eliot Elisofon, National Museum of African Art, Timbuktu, Mali

The Sankore Mosque in Timbuktu, Mali, became an important Islamic house of worship in the Mali Empire. During the 1200's, the Mali Empire replaced the Ghana Empire as the most powerful state in western Africa. The Mali Empire flourished until the 1400's.

British Museum, London (Photoresources)   Lee Boltin

Early civilizations in the Americas were developed by the Maya Indians in Mexico and Central America and by the Inca Indians in Peru. The jade carving of a Maya official at the far left dates from about 900. The silver cup at the left was made by an Inca artist in about 1500.

prince from what is now Afghanistan, invaded India and defeated the forces of the last sultan of Delhi. Babar founded the Mogul Empire and made himself emperor. By the time Babar died in 1530, the Mogul Empire stretched from Kabul in Afghanistan to the mouth of the Ganges River in what is now Bangladesh. See **Babar; Mogul Empire.**

African civilizations. The Muslim Arabs completed their conquest of northern Africa by 710. For hundreds of years, the Islamic faith and culture spread to other parts of Africa. Camel caravans that crossed the Sahara brought northern Muslims into contact with western Africa. Muslim traders who sailed the Indian Ocean converted the peoples living along the east coasts of what are now Somalia, Kenya, and Tanzania. Black African empires developed and prospered along some of the major trade routes.

Islamic records provide information about the Ghana Empire, the first great black empire in western Africa. The empire flourished from the 700's to the mid-1000's. The Arabs called Ghana the "land of gold" because Ghanaian traders supplied them with gold from regions south of the empire. During the 1200's, an even bigger empire, the Islamic Mali Empire, arose as the most powerful state in western Africa. One of Mali's cities, Timbuktu, became an important center of trade and Muslim culture. The Mali Empire began to break up during the 1400's. See **Ghana Empire; Mali Empire.**

Islamic influence did not extend into southern Africa. Much of the south was originally settled by black peoples who spoke Bantu languages. About the time of Christ, these peoples began migrating southward from what is now the border region between Nigeria and Cameroon. Their migrations lasted over 1,000 years.

On the east coast of Africa, the Bantu peoples came into contact with traders from the Persian Gulf region who wanted to buy gold, copper, iron, ivory, and slaves. Several large trading empires developed in southeastern Africa, but little is known about them. One empire, the Mwanamutapa Empire, arose during the 1400's in what are now Mozambique and Zimbabwe. The city of Zimbabwe served as the empire's capital. During the late 1400's, the Changamire Empire conquered the

Mwanamutapa and took over the capital. Massive towers and walls from a royal residence and burial place built during Changamire times still stand on the site of the city. See **Zimbabwe** (History).

Civilizations in the Americas. The first civilizations in the Americas arose in Central America and in what are now Mexico and Peru. The Maya Indians of Central America and Mexico developed one of the most advanced early cultures. Between about 250 and 900, the Maya built large religious centers that consisted of palaces, pyramids, temples, and terraces. The Maya studied astronomy, invented an accurate yearly calendar, and developed an advanced form of writing. For reasons still unknown to scholars, Maya civilization began to decline during the 900's, and many Maya sites were abandoned. See **Maya.**

From about 900 to 1200, the Toltec Indians were the dominant people in the central Mexican highlands. The Toltec were a warlike tribe that occupied much of the old Maya territory. They spread the worship of a feathered serpent god, Quetzalcóatl, throughout their empire. By the early 1400's, the Aztec replaced the Toltec as the most powerful people in central Mexico. The Aztec built a magnificent capital city, Tenochtitlan, on the site of present-day Mexico City and established a mighty empire. The Aztec devoted much of their time to religious practices. Human sacrifice was the central feature of their religion. The Aztec waged war on neighboring peoples mainly to obtain prisoners to sacrifice to their gods. See **Toltec Indians; Aztec.**

By the 1200's, civilization had made great advances in Peru. Peruvian farmers were using bronze tools, and Peruvian stonemasons had become master builders. The people used *quipu*, a cord with knotted strings of various lengths and colors, to keep records and send messages. During the 1300's and 1400's, the Inca Indians gained control of the Peruvian civilization. By the early 1500's, the Inca ruled an empire that stretched between what are now southern Colombia and central Chile. A vast network of roads linked the distant provinces of the empire. Conquered peoples were forced to help build and maintain the roads, to raise crops for the Inca, and to serve in the Inca army. See **Inca.**

Detail from *The Return of the Ambassadors* (1490's) by Vittore Carpaccio
Accademia, Venice (SCALA from Art Resource)

People of the Renaissance developed bold new ideas that led to major achievements in architecture, painting, sculpture, and literature in western Europe from the 1300's through the 1500's. Venice, Italy, *above,* an early center of the Renaissance, attracted many visitors.

Great changes occurred in the course of world history between 1500 and 1900. The world's population rose dramatically, from about 450 million in 1500 to more than 1½ billion by 1900. Cities and towns grew steadily. Western, or European, civilization began to lead the world in cultural, economic, and technological progress. A world in which civilizations developed largely independently of one another gradually gave way to the dominance of Western civilization.

A number of factors contributed to the wide expansion of Western influence. A great age of European exploration during the 1400's and 1500's led to the founding of European colonies in Africa, Asia, and the Americas. Thousands of Europeans migrated to these colonies. Industrialization began in Europe during the 1700's, and the continent soon became the manufacturing center of the world. The European nations established more and more colonies overseas to serve as markets for their manufactured products and as sources of raw materials for industry. Growing trade with these colonies brought increasing wealth and power to the continent. Political rivalries among the European states

also encouraged them to expand their empires abroad. Advances in technology, such as better ships and weapons, helped the Europeans conquer new territories.

The Europeans often introduced their arts and technology and their systems of law, government, and education into the areas where they settled. Thus, the ideas and skills of Western civilization became more widespread than those of any other civilization in history.

The Renaissance. European culture during the Middle Ages largely reflected the powerful influence of Christianity and the Roman Catholic Church. But during the late Middle Ages—between 1300 and 1500—scholars and artists began to develop a new way of looking at life. They became less concerned with religion and concentrated, instead, on understanding people and the world. This new outlook became known as *humanism.* Humanist scholars pioneered in the revival of classical studies—the literature, history, and philosophy of ancient Greece and Rome. They believed that by returning to the classics, they could begin a new golden age of culture. See **Humanism.**

The humanist philosophy formed the intellectual

Major developments

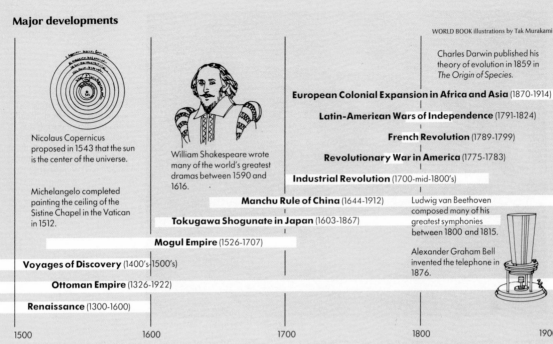

WORLD BOOK illustrations by Tak Murakami

Nicolaus Copernicus proposed in 1543 that the sun is the center of the universe.

Michelangelo completed painting the ceiling of the Sistine Chapel in the Vatican in 1512.

William Shakespeare wrote many of the world's greatest dramas between 1590 and 1616.

Charles Darwin published his theory of evolution in 1859 in *The Origin of Species.*

European Colonial Expansion in Africa and Asia (1870-1914)

Latin-American Wars of Independence (1791-1824)

French Revolution (1789-1799)

Revolutionary War in America (1775-1783)

Industrial Revolution (1700-mid-1800's)

Manchu Rule of China (1644-1912)

Tokugawa Shogunate in Japan (1603-1867)

Mogul Empire (1526-1707)

Voyages of Discovery (1400's-1500's)

Ottoman Empire (1326-1922)

Renaissance (1300-1600)

Ludwig van Beethoven composed many of his greatest symphonies between 1800 and 1815.

Alexander Graham Bell invented the telephone in 1876.

1500   1600   1700   1800   1900

European colonial empires

had spread over much of the world by the late 1800's. The largest empires of the period belonged to Great Britain, France, and Germany.

- Belgium
- France
- Germany
- Great Britain
- Italy
- Netherlands
- Portugal
- Spain

WORLD BOOK map

Important dates

1500's The Reformation led to the birth of Protestantism.

1519-1521 Ferdinand Magellan commanded the first globe-circling voyage, completed in 1522 after his death.

1521 The Spanish conquistador Hernando Cortés defeated the Aztec Indians of Mexico.

1526 Babar, a Muslim prince, invaded India and founded the Mogul Empire.

1588 The Royal Navy of England defeated the Spanish Armada, establishing England as a great naval power.

1644-1912 The Manchus ruled China as the Qing dynasty.

1776 The 13 American Colonies adopted the Declaration of Independence, establishing the United States of America.

1789 The French Revolution began.

1815 Napoleon Bonaparte was defeated in the Battle of Waterloo, ending his attempt to rule Europe.

1853-1854 Commodore Matthew Perry visited Japan and opened two ports to U.S. trade, ending Japan's isolation.

1858 Great Britain took over the rule of India from the East India Company after the Sepoy Rebellion.

1865 Union forces defeated the Confederates in the American Civil War after four years of fighting.

1869 The Suez Canal opened.

1871 Germany became united under the Prussian king, who ruled the new empire as Kaiser Wilhelm I.

1898 The United States took control of Guam, Puerto Rico, and the Philippines following the Spanish-American War.

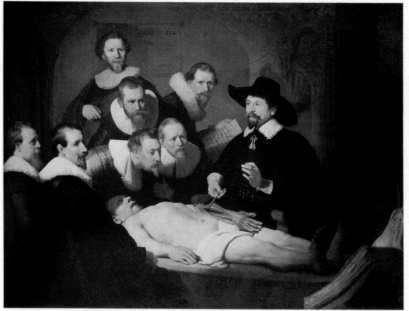

The study of the body led to important medical discoveries in Europe during the 1600's. The Dutch artist Rembrandt portrayed this study in his famous painting *Anatomy Lesson of Professor Tulp.*

core of the Renaissance, a 300-year period of great advancement in the arts and learning in Europe. The Renaissance began in Italy in the early 1300's and spread throughout most of Europe during the 1400's and 1500's. Renaissance thinkers stressed that the duty of intellectuals was to concentrate on human problems, not to seek an understanding of religious questions. Writers of the period described human feelings and situations that people could easily understand. Renaissance artists tried to capture the dignity and majesty of human beings in lifelike paintings and sculptures. Architects designed many nonreligious buildings that incorporated elements of classical style. Many world masterpieces of architecture, literature, painting, and sculpture were created during the Renaissance. See **Renaissance.**

Other changes that occurred during the Renaissance affected the Christian church itself. During the early 1500's, a religious movement called the Reformation led to the birth of Protestantism. The Reformation followed many earlier attempts by religious reformers to correct abuses that had developed within the Roman Catholic Church. Beginning in 1517, Martin Luther, a German monk and theology professor, became the leader of the reform movement. Luther's criticisms gradually led him and his followers to break completely with the Catholic Church.

By the mid-1500's, the Reformation had resulted in the establishment of Protestant churches in nearly half the European countries. Many Protestant groups developed, which helped create a mood of religious toleration in many parts of Europe. The Protestant movement led to the Counter Reformation, a reform and renewal movement in the Catholic Church. The Counter Reformation removed many bad practices within the church and greatly strengthened the authority of the pope. See **Reformation; Counter Reformation.**

The spread of new ideas during the Renaissance was made faster and easier by the invention of movable type in Europe in the mid-1400's. Most of the first printed books were classic Greek and Roman texts or religious books, particularly the Bible. But the Renaissance stimulated a renewed interest in scientific research and in the study of the natural world, and so books on scientific subjects began to appear by the late 1500's. During the 1600's, scientists developed the modern scientific method, with its emphasis on experimentation and careful observation. The invention of such instruments as the microscope and telescope contributed to a rapid growth in scientific knowledge. By 1700, new discoveries had revolutionized such fields as anatomy, astronomy, chemistry, and physics.

The great age of exploration. A remarkable wave of European exploration had begun in the early 1400's. Portuguese explorers in search of an eastward sea route to Asia started to sail down the west coast of Africa. They gradually developed better navigational charts and improved the rigging of their sailing ships. By 1473, a Portuguese ship had crossed the equator, and another one had reached the Cape of Good Hope at the southern tip of Africa by 1487. Christopher Columbus, an Italian navigator in the service of Spain, reached America in 1492. In 1497 and 1498, a Portuguese explorer, Vasco da Gama, made the first voyage from Europe around Africa to India.

During the 1500's and 1600's, Europeans continued to gain geographical knowledge. In the early 1500's, Ferdinand Magellan, a Portuguese navigator in the service of Spain, set out on an expedition to sail around the world. Magellan was killed on the journey, but one of his ships completed the voyage. Sailors from France, England, and the Netherlands led the search for shorter routes to Asia—either a Northwest Passage across North America or a Northeast Passage north of Europe. Explorers slowly began to work their way through the land mass of America. See **Exploration** (The great age of European discovery).

The discovery of new territories provided opportunities for the expansion of European commerce. By 1700, Europeans were trading throughout the world, and some European nations had acquired colonial empires. The colonies provided Europeans with bananas, coffee, cotton fabrics, hard woods, spices, and other products. New crops, such as potatoes and tobacco, were introduced into Europe from America. A flourishing slave trade developed with Africa. In addition, a continuous flow of gold and silver from the New World enabled Europeans to increase their trade with India and China, where demand for the precious metals was high.

The colonization of America. The search for gold drew many of the first Spanish explorers and *conquistadors* (conquerors) to the New World. The most famous conquistador was Hernando Cortés. In 1519, he landed in Mexico, marched his army to the Aztec capital at Tenochtitlan, and took the Aztec emperor captive. The Aztec rebelled in 1520. They were finally defeated in 1521. Cortés then claimed Mexico for Spain. In 1533, another Spaniard, Francisco Pizarro, conquered the wealthy empire of the Inca Indians in Peru. See **Cortés, Hernando; Pizarro, Francisco.**

Except for members of the Spanish clergy, few Spaniards had respect for the Indians and their ways of life. They made the Indians give them a fortune in gold and other riches and forced them to work in their mines and on their plantations. Millions of Indians died of mistreatment or of diseases brought by the Spaniards.

Spanish rule rapidly expanded in the Americas. By 1700, Spain controlled Mexico, Central America, and most of South America. The Spaniards established cities and universities throughout their territory. European government, the Spanish language, and the Catholic Church became dominant in most of Latin America. The population of the colonies rose as more settlers arrived and the Indians acquired some resistance to European diseases. Many Spaniards and Indians intermarried, producing the beginning of a population of mixed ancestry. However, the ruling class of the colonies consisted only of people of unmixed European ancestry.

Much of Latin America had been colonized before the first lasting English settlement was established at Jamestown, Va., in 1607. By 1733, there were 13 English colonies, with a total population of about a million, along the Atlantic coast of North America. Many colonists were drawn to the New World by its economic opportunities, such as the availability of plentiful land. Some settlers, including Puritans, Quakers, and Roman Catholics, came to the English colonies to escape persecution for their religious beliefs. Most of the colonists were English. But other European immigrants also came. In 1624, for example, the Dutch settled New Netherland, which included parts of what are now Connecticut, Delaware, New Jersey, and New York. Farther north, French colonists settled throughout the St. Lawrence River Valley.

The English colonists were soon able to grow enough food to support themselves. They also produced tobacco and other valuable exports to pay for imports from England. But unlike the Spanish colonies, the English colonies had no silver or gold. In addition, the English settlers in North America did not find highly advanced Indian societies like those in Mexico and Peru. At first, the Indians and the settlers had friendly relations. But as more and more settlers claimed greater amounts of Indian hunting grounds, wars broke out between the two groups. See **Indian wars** (Colonial days).

The Islamic empires. Parts of Europe and Asia remained under control of the Ottoman Turks until the early 1900's. The Ottoman Empire never had a strong central government. Ottoman governors ruled the prov-

From the *Vallard Atlas*; The Huntington Library

An atlas printed in 1547 included this map of the Caribbean region. The map is fairly accurate, but it shows the region upside down. A great age of European exploration began during the 1400's. By 1700, the general outlines of most of the world's major land masses were known.

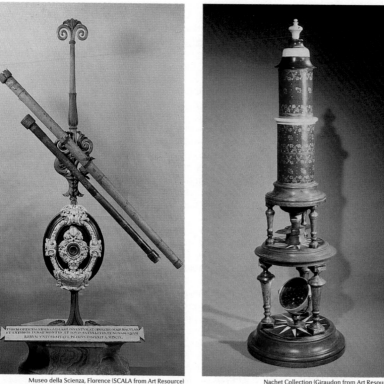

New scientific devices,
such as the telescope and the
microscope, contributed to a
rapid growth of knowledge
during the 1600's and 1700's.
At the far left are telescopes
used by the Italian astronomer Galileo, who made revolutionary discoveries in astronomy. At the left is a Dutch
microscope made during the
1700's. It has three reflecting
mirrors.

Museo della Scienza, Florence (SCALA from Art Resource)

Nachet Collection (Giraudon from Art Resource)

inces of the empire. Their chief tasks included collecting
taxes and raising armies. But they interfered as little as
possible in the lives of the conquered peoples. For example, Christians and Jews could practice their faiths as
long as they paid their taxes. The subject peoples thus
continued to be divided into separate communities and
felt no loyalty to their Ottoman rulers. This lack of unity
weakened the empire.

The Ottomans could not control some areas of their
empire. Mesopotamia was especially difficult to govern.
For nearly 200 years, this valley between the Tigris and
Euphrates rivers was the site of warfare between the Ottomans and another Islamic power, Persia. A new
dynasty, the Safavid, had been established in Persia in
the early 1500's. The greatest Safavid king was Shah
Abbas, who came to the throne in 1587. He successfully
fought the Ottomans and Uzbek tribes from Turkestan.
Shah Abbas and his successors strongly supported the
development of the arts. Isfahan, which became the Safavid capital in 1598, was known as one of the world's
most beautiful cities. The Safavid dynasty began to decline after Shah Abbas died in 1629. It ended in 1722,
when armies from Afghanistan invaded Persia and captured Isfahan.

In addition to fighting the Ottomans, the Safavid rulers fought another great Islamic power, the Mogul Empire of India. The Mogul Empire reached its height
under Akbar, who ruled from 1556 to 1605. Akbar controlled most of northern and central India plus Afghanistan. He ruled wisely, and his religious tolerance won
the loyalty of many Hindus. The empire weakened under

Akbar's successors. Serious trouble developed during
the reign of Aurangzeb, who became emperor in 1658.
Aurangzeb placed a special tax on Hindus and destroyed many of their temples. He also tried to force
non-Muslims to convert to Islam. Partly as a result of Aurangzeb's policies and costly wars with Persia, the
Mogul Empire began breaking up soon after his death
in 1707. See **Akbar; Aurangzeb.**

At first, the spread of European influence had little effect on the Islamic world, though trade gradually increased between the European nations and the Islamic
empires. But as the Islamic powers declined, the Europeans took advantage of the situation and began to assume control of Islamic lands. By 1900, European nations dominated most of the Islamic world. The French
established themselves in northern Africa, and the
Dutch took Indonesia. Britain occupied Egypt and the
Sudan, set up an empire in India, and ruled Malaya. During the 1900's, Italy seized Turkish territories in northern
Africa and along the eastern shores of the Mediterranean Sea.

Developments in China and Japan. The Ming
dynasty, which had come to power in China in 1368,
began to decline during the 1500's. Rebellions in outlying provinces troubled the empire, and Indochina and
other distant dependencies slipped out of its control.
The Ming emperors looked down on all things foreign
and regarded the European traders who visited China as
inferiors. But some rights were granted to the Europeans as the dynasty weakened. The Portuguese were allowed to establish a permanent settlement at Macao, on

the southeast coast of China, in 1557. A European community later grew up in the port city of Canton, a major center of foreign trade with China.

In 1644, the Ming asked the Manchus, a barbarian people from Manchuria, for help in putting down rebellions within the empire. The Manchus then invaded China—but only to establish their own dynasty, the Qing, on the throne. The Manchus ruled China until 1912. They had great respect for Chinese civilization and did little to change Chinese life or government. The Manchu rulers pushed back Russian advances in the Amur River Valley, established imperial control over Tibet, regained parts of Indochina, and added Korea to their territory. During the 1700's, the Qing empire enjoyed stability and prosperity. Contacts with Europeans multiplied, and Christian missionaries were welcomed at the Manchu capital, Beijing. The Manchus admired the Europeans' scientific knowledge and their skills in mapmaking and the manufacture of guns, but they did not wish to imitate European ways of life. Chinese culture remained largely cut off from the rest of the world.

Japan was even more isolated than China. The Tokugawa family seized power in Japan in 1603 and established the Tokugawa shogunate. The Tokugawas ruled for more than 250 years. They were determined to end the civil wars that had troubled the country for years and restore order to Japanese society. Under Tokugawa rule, Japan was divided into about 250 regions, each headed by a lord who swore allegiance to the shogun.

European traders and Christian missionaries had begun arriving in Japan during the 1500's. But the Tokugawa rulers feared that the missionaries might soon bring European armies with them to conquer Japan. In the early 1600's, they ordered all missionaries to leave the country. They also tried to force all Japanese converts to give up their new faith. Those who refused were persecuted or killed. By 1640, Christianity had been al-most eliminated. The Tokugawa government also believed that contact with the outside world must end to keep order in Japan. During the 1630's, it therefore cut ties with other nations. All European traders except the Dutch had to leave the country. The Dutch were permitted a small trading station on the tiny island of Deshima in the harbor at Nagasaki. The Tokugawa shogunate allowed one Dutch ship to come to the trading station each year.

The rise of democracy and nationalism. During the 1700's and 1800's, most countries in the Western world were affected by two powerful political forces—democracy and nationalism. During this period, many peoples won the right to take part in their governments. Nationalistic feelings—particularly the desire of people who shared a common culture to be united as a nation—led to the formation of many new states.

In some areas, the movement toward democracy and nationalism triggered revolts against existing political systems. One of the most important revolts was the Revolutionary War in America. Relations between Great Britain and its colonies in America began to break down in the mid-1700's. The colonists, who had enjoyed a large measure of self-government, wanted even greater freedom. They deeply resented efforts by the British government to tighten its control over the colonies. The Revolutionary War began on April 19, 1775. On July 4, 1776, the colonists issued the Declaration of Independence, in which they declared their freedom from British rule and the formation of a new nation, the United States of America. The Revolutionary War ended with Britain's defeat. In 1783, Britain acknowledged the independence of the colonies. The United States Constitution, adopted in 1788, officially established the new nation as a republic. See **Declaration of Independence; Revolutionary War in America.**

Another major revolution occurred in France. The

Color engraving; Bettmann Archive

The French Revolution began on July 14, 1789, with an attack on the Bastille, *left.* This famous prison in Paris had come to symbolize the hated government of King Louis XVI. The French revolutionaries issued a great document—the Declaration of the Rights of Man and of the Citizen. The revolution lasted 10 years.

Smoking factory chimneys signaled the start of the Industrial Revolution in Europe during the 1700's. The rise of industrialism reshaped Western civilization and changed the lives of millions of people in many parts of the world.

French Revolution lasted from 1789 to 1799. It began when King Louis XVI called a meeting of the States-General, the French national assembly, to solve the state's financial problems. Commoners in the States-General revolted and seized control of the government, declaring themselves the legal National Assembly of France. The Assembly adopted the Declaration of the Rights of Man and of the Citizen. The document set forth the principles of human liberty and the rights of individuals. The French nobles gave up most of their titles and special privileges. In 1792, the revolutionaries established the First French Republic. See **Rights of Man, Declaration of the; French Revolution.**

During the French Revolution, Napoleon Bonaparte, a professional soldier, began to attract notice as a successful general. In 1799, he overthrew the revolutionary government and seized control of France. Napoleon made himself emperor in 1804. Under his leadership, the French came to control most of western Europe. But Napoleon lost much of his army when he invaded Russia in 1812. In 1815, allied European forces crushed Napoleon in the Battle of Waterloo, ending his attempt to rule Europe. See **Napoleon I.**

In 1814 and 1815, European political leaders met at the Congress of Vienna. By that time, the ideas of the French Revolution had spread throughout Europe. The great rulers at the congress feared the effects of these ideas and wanted to smother democratic and nationalistic feelings among their subjects. They restored monarchies in France, Spain, and several other countries where they had been overthrown by Napoleon. But the congress failed to halt the spread of democracy and nationalism in the long run. See **Vienna, Congress of.**

By the late 1800's, nearly every European nation had a constitution, and at least some had democratic institutions. Germany and Italy, which had been divided into many small states, were each united as a nation under a constitutional monarchy. Many new nations with constitutional governments appeared in southeastern Europe as the Ottoman Empire began to crumble. The United States had survived the crisis of the Civil War (1861-

1865), when its unity as a nation had been at stake. By 1900, many people believed that democracy and nationalism would continue to spread and eventually solve all the world's political problems. But in some areas, these forces had already started to create new problems. Nationalism posed serious threats for Russia and Austria-Hungary, which governed peoples of many different nationalities. Quarrels among the new nations of southeastern Europe also threatened to disrupt peace.

The Industrial Revolution. During the 1700's and 1800's, the spread of power-driven machinery helped bring about a rapid growth of industry. Large factories began to replace homes and small workshops as manufacturing centers. The use of the new machinery and the development of factories led to an enormous increase in the production of goods. As industrial nations began to export their manufactured products and to import the raw materials needed for their factories, a worldwide system of markets took shape. The Industrial Revolution began in Great Britain. By the mid-1800's, industrialization had become widespread in western Europe and the northeastern United States. Such countries as Russia and Japan were also beginning to develop their industries. See **Industrial Revolution.**

The Industrial Revolution transformed human life more dramatically than any other event since the development of agriculture. Before the Industrial Revolution, most Europeans lived in farm areas. Towns and villages served chiefly as market centers for the farmers. But as factories appeared, towns grew into industrial cities. People streamed into the cities to take factory jobs. Better systems of transportation and communication became necessary to link the growing cities. Many railroads, roads, and waterways were built. The invention of the telegraph by 1837 furnished a fast means of long-distance communication.

Industrialization brought many social changes. The middle class prospered and grew rapidly. Members of the middle class owned most of the factories, hired the workers, and operated the banks, mines, and railroads. They believed that business should be regulated by supply and demand, largely without government control. This idea forms the basis of *capitalism*, an economic system in which the chief means of production are privately owned. During the early 1800's, Britain began to develop the first capitalist economy. Capitalism soon spread to other industrial nations. See **Capitalism.**

Often, early factory workers were poorly paid and had to work long hours under unhealthful conditions. They could not form labor unions, and their working conditions were not regulated by law. In the growing industrial cities, housing could not keep up with the migration of workers from rural areas. Severe overcrowding resulted, and many people lived in extremely unsanitary conditions that led to outbreaks of disease. Unemployed workers rioted and destroyed machinery in an attempt to gain revenge against the factories they blamed for their joblessness. Employed workers joined in riots, went on strike, and formed illegal trade unions to fight for their rights.

Some people believed that the evils of industrialization resulted from capitalism. Socialism became the chief rallying point for many such people. The socialists wanted to put all industrial production under the control of the workers. From that basic idea, Karl Marx, a German writer and social philosopher, developed the theories of communism. Marx believed that workers would be driven by the march of history to rise up against the wealthy and to establish socialist economic systems and classless societies. By 1900, many European socialists had accepted Marx's ideas and belonged to political parties whose aim was the overthrow of the capitalist system. See **Communism** (Origins of Communism); **Marx, Karl** (Marx's theories).

During the 1800's, workers in many countries won the right to form labor unions. Laws regulating working conditions were passed in the United States and Great Britain during the 1840's. Great Britain and Germany pioneered in social legislation that provided accident, sickness, and unemployment insurance for industrial employees. By the late 1800's, most industrial nations had laws that regulated working conditions and raised the workers' standards of living.

Imperialism. The Industrial Revolution contributed to a great rise in *imperialism* (colonial expansion) during the 1800's. The industrialized nations acquired more and more colonies as they eagerly sought raw materials for their factories, markets for their manufactured goods, and opportunities for investment. Africa was one of the main areas of colonial expansion. By the late 1800's, Belgium, France, Germany, Great Britain, Italy, Portugal, and Spain had divided up almost all of Africa. Only Ethiopia and Liberia remained independent.

European nations also took over large sections of southeastern Asia and many islands in the South Pacific Ocean. The only major Asian nations that remained independent were China, Japan, and Siam (now Thailand). However, China's government had weakened, and the country had given up Indochina and many of its other outlying dependencies to Western nations. After the British defeated the Chinese in the Opium War in 1842, China lost all real control over the presence of foreigners in its territory. Many Chinese ports were opened to

BBC Hulton from Bettmann Archive

A tiger hunt in India was a popular sport among the British during the 1800's. India was then the largest single part of the British Empire, which covered about a fourth of the world's land.

foreign residence and trade. Japan began to develop into an industrial and military power in the 1860's and successfully resisted imperialist interference. By the early 1900's, Japan had become strong enough to seize parts of Chinese territory and to win a war against Russia over control of southern Manchuria and Korea.

In Latin America, a series of wars of independence during the early 1800's freed many colonies from European rule (see **Latin America** [The wars of independence]). The United States, backed by Great Britain, acted to protect the new Latin-American republics against European attempts to reestablish colonial rule. In 1823, U.S. President James Monroe issued the Monroe Doctrine, which warned European powers not to interfere in the affairs of the Western Hemisphere.

The United States itself expanded into new areas during the 1800's. As a result of the Mexican War (1846-1848), it gained Mexican territory that now covers California, Nevada, Utah, and parts of four other states. In 1867, the United States purchased Alaska from Russia. Spain surrendered Guam, Puerto Rico, and the Philippines to the United States after losing the Spanish-American War in 1898.

Imperialism affected the colonial peoples in various ways. In some areas, it brought economic development and raised living standards by introducing Western agricultural, industrial, and medical techniques. Colonial rule also ended local wars in numerous lands. However, many imperialist nations took advantage of their colonies by exporting natural resources without providing economic benefits in return to most of the people. Colonial administrations often cared little about local customs and destroyed old ways of life. As time passed, injustices under the imperialistic system triggered nationalistic feelings, resistance movements, and demands for self-government among the colonial peoples.

Walking in space, *left,* was one of the most exciting achievements of the United States space program. The space age began in the mid-1900's and opened a new chapter in the history of exploration. Space travel has contributed to many advances in science and technology.

Since 1900, the world has changed faster than ever before. The population has continued to rise rapidly. The world had about $1\frac{3}{4}$ billion people in 1900, about $2\frac{1}{2}$ billion in 1950, and about 5 billion in the late 1980's. Industrial output has soared as more and more countries have become industrialized, and international trade has expanded enormously. Advances in science and technology have altered basic ways of life to an extent that would never have been dreamed possible during the 1800's. In 1957, the space age began when the Soviet Union launched the first artificial satellite to circle the earth. In 1969, two U.S. astronauts became the first human beings to walk on the moon. See **Space travel.**

The great colonial empires of the 1800's have disappeared, and many new nations have emerged. Europe no longer dominates international affairs. Instead, the United States and the Soviet Union have become the world's superpowers and the leaders of two competing political systems—democracy and Communism. China and Japan have also developed into world powers.

Differences in beliefs and customs continue to divide the many peoples of the world. But at the same time, people throughout the world increasingly share similar experiences and problems. Many of the same political and economic forces operate around the globe, and events in one country can now quickly affect distant nations. The development of one world culture—which began with the spread of Western culture during the 1700's and 1800's—continues to be an important trend.

The world wars. War—fought on a greater scale than ever before—overshadowed world developments in the first half of the 1900's. World War I raged from 1914 to 1918, and World War II from 1939 to 1945.

World War I resulted chiefly from the competition for colonial and economic power among European nations, the desire of national groups to gain independence, and the secret military alliances among the nations of Europe. In the war, the Allies, which included France, Great Britain, Russia, and Italy, fought the Central Powers, which included Germany, Austria-Hungary, and the Ottoman Empire. The United States joined the Allies in 1917. In November 1917 (October on the old Russian calendar), a revolution in Russia established a Communist dictatorship there, and Russia withdrew from the war. The Allies gained victory in 1918. The Treaty of Versailles, signed in 1919, ended the war with Germany (see **Versailles, Treaty of**). The Allies signed separate treaties with the other Central Powers. See **World War I.**

World War I was fought at a terrible cost. Millions of men, women, and children were killed, and whole cities were destroyed. The economic damage was huge. The war brought many changes in the political map of Europe. For example, Austria-Hungary and the Ottoman Empire split into national states. In Germany, the monarchy collapsed, and a republic was established.

Under the Treaty of Versailles, Germany was forced to disarm, give up much of its territory, and pay war damages to the Allies. Many of the German people felt that they had been treated too harshly. Adolf Hitler, head of the Nazi Party, won their support by promising to rebuild Germany into a mighty empire. In 1933, he became dictator of Germany. See **Hitler, Adolf.**

In 1938, German forces seized Austria and part of Czechoslovakia. In March 1939, they took the rest of Czechoslovakia. On September 1, Germany invaded Poland, and World War II began. In the war, Germany, Italy, Japan and other Axis powers fought the Allies, which included France, Great Britain, the Soviet Union, Canada, China, and the United States. The United States entered the war in 1941, after Japan attacked U.S. military bases at Pearl Harbor in Hawaii. The war in Europe ended with Germany's surrender in May 1945. In August 1945, U.S. planes dropped the first atomic bombs used in warfare on the Japanese cities of Hiroshima and Nagasaki. The next month, Japan signed the terms of surrender. See **World War II.**

Major developments

WORLD BOOK illustrations by Tak Murakami

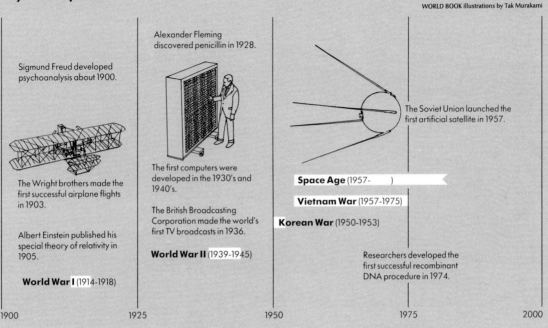

Sigmund Freud developed psychoanalysis about 1900.

Alexander Fleming discovered penicillin in 1928.

The Soviet Union launched the first artificial satellite in 1957.

The Wright brothers made the first successful airplane flights in 1903.

The first computers were developed in the 1930's and 1940's.

Albert Einstein published his special theory of relativity in 1905.

The British Broadcasting Corporation made the world's first TV broadcasts in 1936.

World War II (1939-1945)

World War I (1914-1918)

Space Age (1957-   )

Vietnam War (1957-1975)

Korean War (1950-1953)

Researchers developed the first successful recombinant DNA procedure in 1974.

1900   1925   1950   1975   2000

The wealth of nations can be compared on the basis of each country's *gross national product* (GNP). The GNP is the value of all goods and services produced by a country in a year. The developing countries of Africa and Asia have the lowest GNP per person.

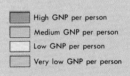

High GNP per person

Medium GNP per person

Low GNP per person

Very low GNP per person

WORLD BOOK map
Map is based on U.S. government
GNP estimates for 1982.

Important dates

1914 The assassination of Archduke Francis Ferdinand of Austria-Hungary started World War I.

1917 The Bolsheviks (Communists) seized power in Russia.

1933 Adolf Hitler became dictator of Germany.

1939 Germany invaded Poland, starting World War II.

1941 The Japanese attacked Pearl Harbor, and the United States entered World War II.

1945 The United Nations was established.

1945 The first atomic bombs used in warfare were dropped by U.S. planes on Hiroshima and Nagasaki.

1945 World War II ended in Europe on May 7 and in the Pacific on September 2.

1949 The Chinese Communists conquered China.

1950 North Korean Communist troops invaded South Korea, starting the Korean War.

1957 The Vietnam War started when South Vietnamese rebels known as the Viet Cong attacked the U.S.-backed South Vietnamese government.

1962 The Soviet Union agreed to U.S. demands that its missiles be removed from Cuba, ending a serious Cold War crisis.

1969 U.S. astronauts made the first manned moon landing.

1975 The Vietnam War ended when South Vietnam surrendered to the Viet Cong and North Vietnam.

1979 Soviet troops invaded Afghanistan to support the leftist Afghan government against rebel tribes.

1989 The Soviet Union completed withdrawal of its troops from Afghanistan.

Christopher Morris, Black Star

The Berlin Wall, built by the Communists in 1961, divides Germany's largest city. It has become a symbol of the Cold War between the Communist world and the non-Communist world.

The cost of World War II, both financially and in terms of human suffering and loss of life, was even greater than that of World War I. The political effects were also more sweeping. Europe lay in ruins. Germany, once the strongest European nation, was occupied by Allied military forces. The major European nations were too weak to hold on to their colonies. The United States and the Soviet Union emerged from the war as the world's leading powers. Out of the horror of World War II came attempts by nations to settle their disputes peacefully. A new international organization, the United Nations (UN), was established near the end of the war to provide a meeting place where countries could try to work out their political differences. See **United Nations.**

The rise of Communism. The Communist movement, which achieved its first major success in Russia in 1917, expanded significantly after World War II. During the late 1940's, Soviet-controlled Communist governments were established in most countries of Eastern Europe. Germany became a divided country in which Communists controlled East Germany and freely elected representatives governed West Germany. In 1949, Chinese Communists established the People's Republic of China. Several other Asian nations also came under Communist control.

Alarmed by Communist expansion, the United States and its allies began giving military and economic aid to non-Communist countries and pledged to help nations threatened by Communist take-over. The struggle between the Communist world, led by the Soviet Union, and the non-Communist world, led by the United States, became known as the Cold War. See **Cold War.**

Tensions between Communist and non-Communist nations increased during the 1950's and 1960's. The Korean War (1950-1953) broke out when troops from

Communist-ruled North Korea invaded South Korea (see **Korean War**). Cold War incidents occurred from time to time in the divided German city of Berlin. In 1961, for example, the Communists built a wall between democratic West Berlin and Communist-controlled East Berlin to prevent East Germans from escaping. Probably the most serious Cold War incident was the Cuban missile crisis of 1962. Communists had come to power in Cuba in 1959. In October 1962, the United States learned that the Soviet Union had installed missiles in Cuba that could launch nuclear attacks on American cities. The crisis passed after the Soviet Union agreed to President John F. Kennedy's demands to remove the missiles. The Vietnam War, which began in 1957, became a major contest between Communist and non-Communist forces. The war ended in 1975 in a Communist victory. See **Berlin; Cuba** (The Cuban Missile Crisis); **Vietnam War.**

The birth of new nations. Large-scale colonialism ended during the 1950's and 1960's. After World War II, the European nations had neither the money nor the will to continue to rule their colonies. In addition, nationalistic feelings and demands for self-government had been growing among colonial peoples in Africa and Asia. Between 1950 and 1980, over 45 African colonies gained their freedom. Most European colonies in Asia and the Middle East also became independent.

The formation of so many new nations led to a big increase in the membership of the UN and greatly affected the balance of power in the organization. Many former colonies became part of a group of economically developing countries called the Third World. Most Third World countries do not regularly support either side in the conflict between Communist and non-Communist nations. See **Third World.**

The end of colonialism has made international politics much less stable. In numerous cases, the ruling powers had given the colonial peoples too little training in self-government. As a result, leaders in many of the new nations have found it difficult to handle crises in political, economic, and social affairs. Large areas of the world once governed peacefully by imperialist powers have been torn by conflicts among the new nations. For example, disputes have occurred periodically between India and Pakistan, areas once ruled by the British. Fighting between Arabs and Jews has broken out frequently in Middle Eastern lands that were once part of the Ottoman Empire.

Many of the new nations had hoped that an end to colonial exploitation would automatically bring economic well-being. Instead, they continue to face such grave problems as rapid population growth, poverty, illiteracy, disease, and food shortages. Most of the former colonies have found it almost impossible to develop their economies without investment from wealthier countries. But such investment has often led to renewed political interference from the countries that are providing aid.

Scientific and technological achievements. During the 1900's, advances in science and technology have changed the world in many dramatic ways. Airplanes, automobiles, communications satellites, computers, lasers, plastics, refrigerators, and television are only a few of the inventions that have transformed human life in this century. Research into the structure of the atom has expanded scientists' view of the universe and led to the discovery of nuclear energy as a source of power. Unmanned space probes have explored other planets and sent back data on them. Antibiotics and other new drugs have helped control most infectious diseases. Agricultural output has soared as scientists have developed better varieties of plants and highly efficient fertilizers and pesticides. The rapid medical progress and increases in food supplies have enabled millions of people to live healthier and longer lives.

In a number of cases, the scientific and technological achievements of the 1900's have created new problems. Breakthroughs in nuclear research, for instance, have led to the development of powerful weapons of mass destruction. The rapid growth of industrial technology has created such serious side effects as environmental pollution and fuel shortages (see **Technology** [Side effects of technology]). Increases in life expectancy have contributed to overpopulation in many of the world's developing countries, where birth rates have remained high as death rates have declined.

The interdependence of nations. In some ways, the world today seems more divided than it has ever been. Although no war has broken out directly between major world powers since World War II ended in 1945, fighting has been going on in one part of the globe or another almost every day since then. The struggle between Communist and non-Communist nations continues, and rivalries between the Soviet Union and the United States have made the threat of nuclear war a worldwide concern. The gulf between developing and developed countries is also much greater than it has ever been. About 60 per cent of the people in the Third World live in extreme poverty, while resources are consumed in huge quantities in developed countries simply to provide luxuries.

In spite of all the divisions in the world today, peoples and nations are tied together more closely than ever before. Electronic communications and worldwide systems of transportation make it possible for ideas and information to be shared quickly by peoples around the globe. Exchanges between cultures are more rapid and widespread than at any time in the past. Nations have become increasingly interdependent as such problems as pollution and the reduction of natural resources have grown too big for any one government to handle. Many countries belong to international economic or political organizations. Some developed countries have established programs that provide developing nations with financial aid and technical assistance.

The breakdown of barriers between cultures began with the spread of European civilization. Westernization, more than any other force, has shaped much of the modern world and laid the foundation for the development of a common world culture. Today, many peoples throughout the world recognize the interdependence of nations and the need for international cooperation. The growing unity of human experience offers some hope that nations can settle their differences peacefully and avoid another world war.   John Morris Roberts

Related articles in *World Book.* See the *History* section of the country articles, such as **Argentina** (History), and the separate articles **Canada, History of; United States, History of the.** See also:

History of continents or regions
See the *History* section of the following articles:

Africa	Central America	Middle East
Asia	Europe	Pacific Islands
Balkans	Latin America	

Early centers of civilization
Aegean civilization	Hittites	Nubia
Babylonia	Indus Valley civiliza-	Sumer
Egypt, Ancient	tion	Troy
	Mesopotamia	

The advance of civilization
Aksum	Jews	Palestine
Assyria	Kush	Parthia
Carthage	Kushan Empire	Persia, Ancient
Chaldea	Lydia	Phoenicia
Etruscans	Macedonia	Phrygia
Greece, Ancient	Nok	Rome, Ancient

The world from 500 to 1500
Aztec	Hundred Years' War	Mali Empire
Benin	Inca	Maya
Byzantine Empire	Kanem	Middle Ages
Crusades	Knights and knight-	Mongol Empire
Feudalism	hood	Muslims
Ghana Empire	Kongo	Songhai Empire
Holy Roman Empire		Vikings

The spread of Western civilization
Age of Reason	New France	Revolutionary War
Exploration	Ottoman Empire	in America
French Revolution	Reformation	Seven Years' War
Fur trade	Renaissance	Thirty Years' War
Industrial Revolution	Revolution of 1848	Vienna, Congress of

The world since 1900
Cold War	Nuclear energy	Vietnam War
Foreign aid	Space travel	World War I
Korean War	United Nations	World War II

Other related articles
Archaeology	Government	Religion
Architecture	History	Science
Civilization	Indian, American	Sculpture
Classical music	Law	Slavery
Colonialism	Literature	Socialism
Communism	Painting	War
Culture	Population	World
Democracy	Prehistoric people	Writing

Outline
I. Early centers of civilization
  A. The Tigris-Euphrates Valley
  B. The Nile Valley
  C. The Indus Valley
  D. The Huang He Valley

II. The advance of civilization
  A. Middle Eastern civilizations
  B. The Greeks
  C. The Romans
  D. Achievements in India
  E. Achievements in China

III. The world from 500 to 1500
  A. Medieval Europe
  B. The Byzantine Empire
  C. The Islamic world
  D. China
  E. The rise of Japanese civilization
  F. The age of invasions of India
  G. African civilizations
  H. Civilizations in the Americas

IV. The spread of Western civilization
  A. The Renaissance
  B. The great age of exploration
  C. The colonization of America
  D. The Islamic empires
  E. Developments in China and Japan
  F. The rise of democracy and nationalism
  G. The Industrial Revolution
  H. Imperialism
V. The world since 1900
  A. The world wars
  B. The rise of Communism
  C. The birth of new nations
  D. Scientific and technological achievements
  E. The interdependence of nations

Questions

How did the invention of farming pave the way for the development of civilization?

In what ways was early Japanese civilization influenced by Chinese culture?

Why did large-scale colonialism end after World War II?

What major contributions did the Aryans make to present-day civilization in India?

What military and political system developed in western Europe after the fall of the West Roman Empire?

How have advances in science and technology transformed human life during the 1900's?

What were some of the important accomplishments of the Sumerians? Of the Egyptians?

How did European leaders at the Congress of Vienna try to halt the spread of democracy and nationalism?

How was Greek culture preserved in the Roman Empire?

What factors contributed to the spread of Western civilization after 1500?

Additional resources

Level I

Arnold, Guy. *Datelines of World History.* Watts, 1983.
Herman, David. *The Julian Messner Young Readers' Guide to Dates & Events.* Messner, 1986.
Picture History of the World. Ed. by Frances M. Clapham. Putnam, 1986.
van Loon, Hendrik W. *The Story of Mankind.* Rev. ed. Liveright, 1984.
Ventura, Piero. *There Once Was a Time.* Putnam, 1987.

Level II

Brinton, Crane, and others. *A History of Civilization.* 3 vols. 6th ed. Prentice-Hall, 1984.
The Columbia History of the World. Ed. by John A. Garraty and Peter Gay. Harper, 1972.
Discovery of Lost Worlds. Ed. by Joseph J. Thorndike. Scribner, 1979.
Durant, Will and Ariel. *The Story of Civilization.* 11 vols. Simon & Schuster, 1935-1975.
Evans, Harold. *Front Page History: Events of Our Century that Shook the World.* Salem House, 1984.
Grun, Bernard. *The Timetables of History: A Horizontal Linkage of People and Events.* 2nd ed. Simon & Schuster, 1982.
Macmillan Concise Dictionary of World History. Ed. by Bruce Wetterau. Macmillan, 1983.
McNeill, William H. *A World History.* 3rd ed. Oxford, 1979.
Nisbet, Robert. *History of the Idea of Progress.* Basic Books, 1979.
The Times Atlas of World History. Rev. ed. Hammond, 1984.
Unstead, R. J. *A History of the World.* A & C Black, 1983.
Wedgwood, Cicely V. *The Spoils of Time: A World History from the Dawn of Civilization Through the Early Renaissance.* Doubleday, 1985.

World Bank is an international organization that provides loans to countries for development projects. It lends money to member governments and their agencies and to private organizations in the member nations. The World Bank is a specialized agency of the United Nations. Its official name is the International Bank for Reconstruction and Development. About 150 countries are members. The World Bank gets its loan funds from member countries and by borrowing in the world money market.

The World Bank operates through a board of governors and about 20 executive directors chosen by members. The bank makes loans to members that cannot obtain money from other sources at reasonable terms. These loans help members develop their national economies. The bank encourages private investment in member countries. It also provides many technical assistance services for members. The bank was founded at an economic conference held in Bretton Woods, N.H., in 1944. It began operating in 1946. The bank's headquarters are in Washington, D.C.

The International Development Association is an organization that was established in 1960 as an affiliate of the World Bank. This association makes loans to less developed member countries on a long-term basis at no interest.   Critically reviewed by

International Bank for Reconstruction and Development

Related articles in *World Book* include:

Bretton Woods	International Finance
Food supply (Food supply	Corporation
programs)	International Monetary Fund
International Development	
Association	

World Book Encyclopedia. See Encyclopedia (World Book).

World Community of Islam in the West. See Black Muslims.

World Council of Churches is a worldwide organization of about 300 Protestant, Anglican, Old Catholic, and Orthodox churches. The council works to promote cooperation and unity among all the churches of the world. The churches that belong to the council have about 400 million members in more than 100 countries.

The Roman Catholic Church, though not a member of the council, works with the organization in a number of programs. The council has also opened discussions with such non-Christian groups as Buddhists and Muslims.

The council's activities include education; worldwide missionary and evangelical work; aid to refugees, the sick, and underprivileged; and the promotion of world peace and social and interracial justice. It has sponsored studies on the future of human society in an age of scientific and technical progress. It has also studied the role Christians should play in improving government, courts, prisons, and other social institutions.

The World Council of Churches was founded in 1948 in Amsterdam, the Netherlands. Member churches elect six presidents and a 145-member central committee. This group meets annually to set council policies. The council has its headquarters in Geneva, Switzerland, and an office at 475 Riverside Drive, New York, NY 10027.

   Critically reviewed by World Council of Churches

World Court. See International Court of Justice.
World Cup. See Skiing (Skiing as a sport).
World government. Some people believe that a single authority should dispense justice and maintain law and order for the whole world. They would like to see a world government make the major decisions concerning security and the welfare of individuals that sep-

Special Report
WORLD CUP
2007 Year Book, p. 350

arate national governments now make. World government could come about through conquest, just as the Romans conquered the lands around the Mediterranean Sea. But people who favor world government think of it as the result of persuasion and agreement.

Some people began dreaming of a world government as early as the 1300's. The devastation caused by World War I (1914-1918) and World War II (1939-1945) led to further interest in world government. Some people viewed the formation of the United Nations in 1945 as a step toward a more orderly system of world government.

Supporters of world government believe that war is inevitable as long as separate national governments exist. They point out that war has become a threat to the survival of the whole human race. They argue that countries should give a world government the right to make the final decisions regarding war and peace. Some schemes for world government foresee a federal system, in which subdivisions of the world would continue to perform some governmental functions. Most advocates are unwilling to wait for international organizations to grow slowly into a world government. They want the change to come peacefully, but all at once.

People who favor world government are active in most countries of the Western world. But many people oppose the idea. Critics of world government ask how the peoples of the world could reach agreement on such a topic in the face of acute present conflicts. They point out that, if the conflicts between East and West die down, making agreement on world government attainable, the need for such a government is also diminished.

Some other problems that must be solved include finding leaders for a world government, keeping it from becoming tyrannical, and avoiding civil wars, often bloodier than international ones. Michael P. Sullivan

World Health Organization (WHO) is a specialized agency of the United Nations. It helps build better health systems throughout the world, especially in developing countries.

WHO establishes standards in a variety of fields, such as food, biological and pharmaceutical goods, diagnostic procedures, and environmental health protection. It also helps name and classify diseases. Prevention of disease is a key goal of WHO. The agency works with governments to provide safe drinking water, adequate sewage disposal, and immunization against childhood diseases. WHO also identifies important research goals and organizes researchers all over the world to achieve these goals.

WHO has about 165 members. Its principal organs are the World Health Assembly, the Executive Board, and the Secretariat. The World Health Assembly meets once a year and consists of national delegations. The Executive Board advises the World Health Assembly and implements its policies. The Secretariat, headed by a director-general, consists of workers at WHO's headquarters in Geneva, Switzerland, and around the world. WHO also has six regional offices in various parts of the world. It was founded in 1948.

Critically reviewed by the World Health Organization

World Hockey Association. See Hockey.
World Intellectual Property Organization is an international agency that works to protect legal rights in artistic and literary works, inventions, trademarks, and other original creations. Such rights are known as *intellectual property.* The organization promotes international agreements concerning copyright, patents, trademarks, and other original creations. It also furnishes technological information and other assistance to developing countries. The organization, known as WIPO, is a specialized agency of the United Nations (UN). WIPO has a membership of more than 110 countries. Its headquarters are in Geneva, Switzerland.

WIPO administers two treaties that were established in the 1880's. One protects copyright. The other protects patents, trademarks, and other original creations. Administrative agencies of the two treaties joined in 1893 and were replaced by that of WIPO when it was founded in 1967. The agency became part of the UN in 1974.

Critically reviewed by the World Intellectual Property Organization

World Jewish Congress is an international association of Jewish organizations from more than 70 countries. These groups work together to promote unity among Jews and to maintain Jewish cultural, religious, and social customs. The congress stresses the importance of Israel as the center of Jewish heritage. It issues publications on various economic, political, and social matters. The association also sponsors the Institute of Jewish Affairs in London, which conducts research into various problems facing Jews.

The association tries to protect the rights of Jews throughout the world. For example, it attempted to rescue Jews from Nazi persecution before and during World War II (1939-1945). The congress later set up relief and rehabilitation programs for the victims. During the 1970's, the congress helped arrange the release of thousands of Jews from the Soviet Union.

The World Jewish Congress was founded in 1936. The organization has its headquarters in New York City.

Critically reviewed by the World Jewish Congress

World map. See World.
World Medical Association is an organization of national medical associations from about 45 countries. Organized in 1947, it has adopted an international code of medical ethics and several other ethical declarations and statements. Headquarters are at 28, Avenue de Alpes, 01210 Ferney-Voltaire, France.

Critically reviewed by the World Medical Association

World Meteorological Organization (WMO) is a specialized agency of the United Nations (UN). It sponsors such programs as the World Weather Watch program for the rapid exchange of observations to forecast the weather. The program consists of networks of weather stations in all parts of the world, satellites and computers, and a worldwide telecommunications system. The WMO's technical cooperation program helps developing countries set up or improve their meteorological services. The organization also offers advice on how weather conditions affect natural resources and such activities as farming and air and sea transportation.

The organization was founded in 1873 as the International Meteorological Organization. In 1951, it changed its name and became part of the United Nations. WMO headquarters are in Geneva, Switzerland.

Critically reviewed by the World Meteorological Organization

World Series. See Baseball (Major leagues).
World trade. See International trade.

Bettmann Archive

Bettmann Archive

Soldiers headed for the battlefront at first welcomed the outbreak of World War I. The German soldiers at the left received flowers as they marched off to France. The French cavalrymen at the right confidently rode off to drive the Germans back. Each side expected quick victory.

World War I

World War I (1914-1918) involved more countries and caused greater destruction than any other war except World War II (1939-1945). An assassin's bullets set off the war, and a system of military *alliances* (agreements) plunged the main European powers into the fight. Each side expected quick victory. But the war lasted four years and took the lives of nearly 10 million troops.

Several developments led to the awful bloodshed of the Great War, as World War I was originally called. War plants kept turning out vast quantities of newly invented weapons capable of extraordinary slaughter. Military drafts raised larger armies than ever before, and extreme patriotism gave many men a cause they were willing to die for. Propaganda whipped up support for the war by making the enemy seem villainous.

On June 28, 1914, an assassin gunned down Archduke Francis Ferdinand of Austria-Hungary in Sarajevo, the capital of Austria-Hungary's province of Bosnia. The killer, Gavrilo Princip, had ties to a terrorist organization in Serbia (now part of Yugoslavia). Austria-Hungary believed that Serbia's government was behind the assassination. It seized the opportunity to declare war on Serbia and settle an old feud.

The assassination of Francis Ferdinand sparked the outbreak of World War I. But historians believe that the war had deeper causes. It resulted chiefly from the growth of extreme national pride among various European peoples, an enormous increase in European armed forces, a race for colonies, and the formation of military alliances. When the fighting began, France, Great Britain, and Russia—who were known as the Allies—backed Serbia. They opposed the Central Powers, made up of Austria-Hungary and Germany. Other

Edward M. Coffman, the contributor of this article, is Professor of History at the University of Wisconsin-Madison and the author of The War to End All Wars: The American Military Experience in World War I.

nations later joined the Allies or the Central Powers.

Germany won early victories in World War I on the main European battlefronts. On the Western Front, France and Britain halted the German advance in September 1914. The opposing armies then fought from trenches that stretched across Belgium and northeastern France. The Western Front hardly moved for $3\frac{1}{2}$ years in spite of fierce combat. On the Eastern Front, Russia battled Germany and Austria-Hungary. The fighting seesawed back and forth until 1917, when a revolution broke out in Russia. Russia soon asked for a truce.

The United States remained neutral at first. But many Americans turned against the Central Powers after German submarines began sinking unarmed ships. In 1917, the United States joined the Allies. U.S troops gave the Allies the manpower they needed to win the war. In the fall of 1918, the Central Powers surrendered.

World War I had results that none of the warring nations had foreseen. The war helped topple emperors in Austria-Hungary, Germany, and Russia. The peace treaties after the war carved new nations out of the defeated powers. The war left Europe exhausted, never to regain the controlling position in world affairs that it had held before the war. The peace settlement also created conditions that helped lead to World War II.

Causes of the war

The assassination of Archduke Francis Ferdinand triggered World War I. But the war had its origins in developments of the 1800's. The chief causes of World War I were (1) the rise of nationalism, (2) a build-up of military might, (3) competition for colonies, and (4) a system of military alliances.

The rise of nationalism. Europe avoided major wars in the 100 years before World War I began. Although small wars broke out, they did not involve many countries. But during the 1800's, a force swept across the continent that helped bring about the Great War. The force was *nationalism*—the belief that loyalty to a person's nation and its political and economic goals comes before any other public loyalty. That exaggerated form

Destruction and death, instead of quick victory, awaited the warring nations in the long and brutal conflict. After fierce fighting in Belgium, the city of Ypres lay in ruins, *left.* Many men, like the French soldier on the right, met death in a trench along the Western Front.

of patriotism increased the possibility of war because a nation's goals inevitably came into conflict with the goals of one or more other nations. In addition, nationalistic pride caused nations to magnify small disputes into major issues. A minor complaint could thus quickly lead to the threat of war.

During the 1800's, nationalism took hold among people who shared a common language, history, or culture. Such people began to view themselves as members of a national group, or nation. Nationalism led to the creation of two new powers—Italy and Germany—through the uniting of many small states. War had a major role in achieving national unification in Italy and Germany.

Nationalist policies gained enthusiastic support as many countries in Western Europe granted the vote to more people. The right to vote gave citizens greater in-

The warring nations

The table below indicates the date on which each of the Allies and Central Powers entered World War I. More than 20 countries eventually joined the war on the Allied side. However, not all of them sent troops.

The Allies

Belgium (Aug. 4, 1914)
Brazil (Oct. 26, 1917)
British Empire
  (Aug. 4, 1914)
China (Aug. 14, 1917)
Costa Rica
  (May 23, 1918)
Cuba (April 7, 1917)
France (Aug. 3, 1914)
Greece (July 2, 1917)
Guatemala
  (April 23, 1918)
Haiti (July 12, 1918)
Honduras (July 19, 1918)
Italy (May 23, 1915)
Japan (Aug. 23, 1914)
Liberia (Aug. 4, 1917)
Montenegro
  (Aug. 5, 1914)

Nicaragua (May 8,1918)
Panama (April 7, 1917)
Portugal (March 9, 1916)
Romania (Aug. 27, 1916)
Russia (Aug. 1, 1914)
San Marino
  (June 3,1915)
Serbia (July 28, 1914)
Siam (July 22, 1917)
United States
  (April 6, 1917)

The Central Powers

Austria-Hungary
  (July 28, 1914)
Bulgaria (Oct. 14, 1915)
Germany (Aug. 1, 1914)
Ottoman Empire
  (Oct. 31, 1914)

terest and greater pride in national goals. As a result, parliamentary governments grew increasingly powerful.

On the other hand, nationalism weakened the eastern European empires of Austria-Hungary, Russia, and Ottoman Turkey. Those empires ruled many national groups that clamored for independence. Conflicts among national groups were especially explosive in the Balkans—the states on the Balkan Peninsula in southeastern Europe. The peninsula was known as the "Powder Keg of Europe" because tensions there threatened to ignite a major war. Most of the Balkans had been part of the Ottoman Empire. First Greece and then Montenegro, Serbia, Romania, Bulgaria, and Albania won independence in the period from 1821 to 1913. Each state quarreled with neighbors over boundaries. Austria-Hungary and Russia also took advantage of the Ottoman Empire's weakness to increase their influence in the Balkans.

Rivalry for control of the Balkans added to the tensions that erupted into World War I. Serbia led a movement to unite the region's Slavs. Russia, the most powerful Slavic country, supported Serbia. But Austria-Hungary feared Slavic nationalism, which stirred unrest in its empire. Millions of Slavs lived under Austria-Hungary's rule. In 1908, Austria-Hungary greatly angered Serbia by adding the Balkan territories of Bosnia and Hercegovina to its empire. Serbia wanted control of those lands because many Serbs lived there.

A build-up of military might occurred among European countries before World War I broke out. Nationalism encouraged public support for military build-ups and for a country's use of force to achieve its goals. By the late 1800's, Germany had the best-trained army in the world. It relied on a military draft of all able-bodied young men to increase the size and strength of its peacetime army. Other European countries followed Germany's lead and expanded their standing armies.

At first, Great Britain remained unconcerned about Germany's military build-up. Britain, an island country, relied on its navy for defense—and it had the world's strongest navy. But in 1898, Germany began to develop a naval force big enough to challenge the British navy.

Important dates during World War I

1914

June 28	Archduke Francis Ferdinand was assassinated.
July 28	Austria-Hungary declared war on Serbia. Several other declarations of war followed during the next week.
Aug. 4	Germany invaded Belgium and started the fighting.
Aug. 10	Austria-Hungary invaded Russia, opening the fighting on the Eastern Front.
Sept. 6-9	The Allies stopped the Germans in France in the First Battle of the Marne.

1915

Feb. 18	Germany began to blockade Great Britain.
April 25	Allied troops landed on the Gallipoli Peninsula.
May 7	A German submarine sank the liner *Lusitania.*
May 23	Italy declared war on Austria-Hungary, and an Italian Front soon developed.

1916

Feb. 21	The Germans opened the Battle of Verdun.
May 31-June 1	The British fleet fought the German fleet in the Battle of Jutland.
July 1	The Allies launched the Battle of the Somme.

1917

Feb. 1	Germany resumed unrestricted submarine warfare.
April 6	The United States declared war on Germany.
June 24	American troops began landing in France.
Dec. 15	Russia signed an armistice with Germany, ending the fighting on the Eastern Front.

1918

Jan. 8	President Woodrow Wilson announced his Fourteen Points as the basis for peace.
March 3	Russia signed the Treaty of Brest-Litovsk.
March 21	Germany launched the first of its final three offensives on the Western Front.
Sept. 26	The Allies began their final offensive on the Western Front.
Nov. 11	Germany signed an armistice ending World War I.

Germany's decision to become a major seapower made it a bitter enemy of Great Britain. In 1906, the British navy launched the *Dreadnought,* the first modern battleship. The heavily armed *Dreadnought* had greater firepower than any other ship of its time. Germany rushed to construct ships like it.

Advances in *technology*—the tools, materials, and techniques of industrialization—increased the destructive power of military forces. Machine guns and other new arms fired more accurately and more rapidly than earlier weapons. Steamships and railroads could speed the movement of troops and supplies. By the end of the 1800's, technology enabled countries to fight longer wars and bear greater losses than ever before. Yet military experts insisted that future wars would be short.

Competition for colonies. During the late 1800's and early 1900's, European nations carved nearly all of Africa and much of Asia into colonies. The race for colonies was fueled by Europe's increasing industrialization. Colonies supplied European nations with raw materials for factories, markets for manufactured goods, and opportunities for investment. But the competition for colonies strained relations among European countries. Incidents between rival powers flared up almost every year. Several of the clashes nearly led to war.

A system of military alliances gave European powers a sense of security before World War I. A country hoped to discourage an attack from its enemies by entering into a military agreement with one or more other countries. In case of an attack, such an agreement guaranteed that other members of the alliance would come to the country's aid or at least remain neutral.

Although military alliances provided protection for a country, the system created certain dangers. Because of its alliances, a country might take risks in dealings with other nations that it would hesitate to take alone. If war

World War I battlefronts

The fighting in World War I spread from Western Europe to the Middle East. The key battles were fought along the Western Front, which stretched across Belgium and France, and along the Eastern Front, which seesawed across Russia and Austria-Hungary.

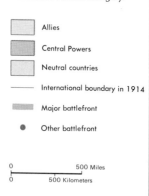

	Allies
	Central Powers
	Neutral countries
——	International boundary in 1914
	Major battlefront
●	Other battlefront

0 ————— 500 Miles
0 ————— 500 Kilometers

came, the alliance system meant that a number of nations would fight, not only the two involved in a dispute. Alliances could force a country to go to war against a nation it had no quarrel with or over an issue it had no interest in. In addition, the terms of many alliances were kept secret. The secrecy increased the chances that a country might guess wrong about the consequences of its actions.

The Triple Alliance. Germany was at the center of European foreign policy from 1870 until the outbreak of World War I. Chancellor Otto von Bismarck, Germany's prime minister, formed a series of alliances to strengthen his country's security. He first made an ally of Austria-Hungary. In 1879, Germany and Austria-Hungary agreed to go to war if either country were attacked by Russia. Italy joined the agreement in 1882, and it became known as the Triple Alliance. The members of the Triple Alliance agreed to aid one another in the case of an attack by two or more countries.

Bismarck also brought Austria-Hungary and Germany into an alliance with Russia. The agreement, known as the Three Emperors' League, was formed in 1881. The three powers agreed to remain neutral if any of them went to war with another country. Bismarck also persuaded Austria-Hungary and Russia, which were rivals for influence in the Balkans, to recognize each other's zone of authority in the region. He thus reduced the danger of conflict between the two countries.

Germany's relations with other European countries worsened after Bismarck left office in 1890. Bismarck had worked to prevent France, Germany's neighbor on the west, from forming an alliance with either of Germany's two neighbors to the east—Russia and Austria-Hungary. In 1894, France and Russia agreed to *mobilize* (call up troops) if any nation in the Triple Alliance mobilized. France and Russia also agreed to help each other if either were attacked by Germany.

The Triple Entente. During the 1800's, Great Britain had followed a foreign policy that became known as "splendid isolation." But Germany's naval build-up made Britain feel the need for allies. The country therefore ended its isolation. In 1904, Britain and France settled their past disagreements over colonies and signed the Entente Cordiale (Friendly Agreement). Although the agreement contained no pledges of military support, the two countries began to discuss joint military plans. In 1907, Russia joined the Entente Cordiale, and it became known as the Triple Entente.

The Triple Entente did not obligate its members to go to war as the Triple Alliance did. But the alliances left Europe divided into two opposing camps.

Beginning of the war

World War I began in the Balkans, the site of many small wars. In the early 1900's, the Balkan states fought the Ottoman Empire in the First Balkan War (1912-1913) and one another in the Second Balkan War (1913). The major European powers stayed out of both wars. But they did not escape the third Balkan crisis.

The assassination of an archduke. Archduke Francis Ferdinand, heir to the throne of Austria-Hungary, hoped that his sympathy for Slavs would ease tensions between Austria-Hungary and the Balkans. He arranged to tour Bosnia with his wife, Sophie. As the couple rode

UPI/Bettmann Newsphotos
Archduke Francis Ferdinand of Austria-Hungary, *far right,* was shot to death on June 28, 1914, shortly after this photo was taken. His assassination triggered the outbreak of World War I.

through Sarajevo on June 28, 1914, an assassin jumped on their automobile and fired two shots. Francis Ferdinand and Sophie died almost instantly. The murderer, Gavrilo Princip, was linked to a Serbian terrorist group called the Black Hand.

The assassination of Francis Ferdinand gave Austria-Hungary an excuse to crush Serbia, its long-time enemy in the Balkans. Austria-Hungary first gained Germany's promise of support for any action it took against Serbia. It then sent a list of humiliating demands to Serbia on July 23. Serbia accepted most of the demands and offered to have the rest settled by an international conference. Austria-Hungary rejected the offer and declared war on Serbia on July 28. It expected a quick victory.

How the conflict spread. Within weeks of the archduke's assassination, the chief European powers were drawn into World War I. A few attempts were made to prevent the war. For example, Great Britain proposed an international conference to end the crisis. But Germany rejected the idea, claiming that the dispute involved only Austria-Hungary and Serbia. However, Germany tried to stop the war from spreading. The German *kaiser* (emperor), Wilhelm II, urged Czar Nicholas II of Russia, his cousin, not to mobilize.

Russia had backed down before in supporting its ally Serbia. In 1908, Austria-Hungary had angered Serbia by taking over Bosnia and Hercegovina, and Russia had stepped aside. In 1914, Russia vowed to stand behind Serbia. Russia first gained a promise of support from France. The czar then approved plans to mobilize along Russia's border with Austria-Hungary. But Russia's military leaders persuaded the czar to mobilize along the German border, too. On July 30, 1914, Russia announced it would mobilize fully.

Germany declared war on Russia on Aug. 1, 1914, in response to Russia's mobilization. Two days later, Germany declared war on France. The German army swept into Belgium on its way to France. The invasion of neutral Belgium caused Britain to declare war on Germany on August 4. By the time the war ended in November 1918, few areas of the world had remained neutral.

The Western Front. Germany's war plan had been prepared in 1905 by Alfred von Schlieffen. Schlieffen was chief of the German General Staff, the group of officers who provided advice on military operations. The Schlieffen Plan assumed that Germany would have to fight both France and Russia. It aimed at a quick defeat of France while Russia slowly mobilized. After defeating France, Germany would deal with Russia. The Schlieffen Plan required Germany to strike first if war came. Once the plan was set in motion, the system of military alliances almost assured a general European war.

The Schlieffen Plan called for two wings of the German army to crush the French army in a pincers movement. A small left wing would defend Germany along its frontier with France. A much larger right wing would invade France through Belgium; encircle and capture France's capital, Paris; and then move east. As the right wing moved in, the French forces would be trapped between the pincers. The success of Germany's assault depended on a strong right wing. However, Helmuth von Moltke, who had become chief of the General Staff in 1906, directed German strategy at the outbreak of World War I. Moltke changed the Schlieffen Plan by reducing the number of troops in the right wing.

Belgium's army fought bravely but held up the Germans for only a short time. By Aug. 16, 1914, the right wing of the German army could begin its pincers motion. It drove back French forces and a small British force in southern Belgium and swept into France. But instead of swinging west around Paris according to plan, one part of the right wing pursued retreating French troops east toward the Marne River. This maneuver left the Germans exposed to attacks from the rear.

Meanwhile, General Joseph Joffre, commander in chief of all the French armies, stationed his forces near the Marne River east of Paris and prepared for battle. Fierce fighting, which became known as the First Battle of the Marne, began on September 6. On September 9, German forces started to withdraw.

The First Battle of the Marne was a key victory for the Allies because it ended Germany's hopes to defeat France quickly. Moltke was replaced as chief of the German General Staff by Erich von Falkenhayn.

The German army halted its retreat near the Aisne River. From there, the Germans and the Allies fought a series of battles that became known as the Race to the Sea. Germany sought to seize ports on the English Channel and cut off vital supply lines between France and Britain. But the Allies stopped the German advance to the sea in the First Battle of Ypres in Belgium. The battle lasted from mid-October until mid-November.

By late November 1914, the war reached a *deadlock* along the Western Front as neither side gained much ground. The battlefront extended more than 450 miles (720 kilometers) across Belgium and northeastern France to the border of Switzerland. The deadlock on the Western Front lasted nearly $3\frac{1}{2}$ years.

The Eastern Front. Russia's mobilization on the Eastern Front moved faster than Germany expected. By late August 1914, two Russian armies had thrust deeply into the German territory of East Prussia. The Germans learned that the two armies had become separated, and they prepared a battle plan. By August 31, the Germans had encircled one Russian army in the Battle of Tannenberg. They then chased the other Russian army out of East Prussia in the Battle of the Masurian Lakes. The number of Russian *casualties*—that is, the number of men killed, captured, wounded, or missing—totaled about 250,000 in the two battles. The victories made heroes of the commanders of the German forces in the east—Paul von Hindenburg and Erich Ludendorff.

Austria-Hungary had less success than its German ally on the Eastern Front. By the end of 1914, Austria-Hungary's forces had attacked Serbia three times and been beaten back each time. Meanwhile, Russia had

The Western Front: 1914-1917

Fighting began in August 1914, when Germany invaded Belgium and France. The two sides were locked in trench warfare along the Western Front by year's end. The Western Front remained deadlocked for nearly $3\frac{1}{2}$ years.

Allies

Central Powers

Neutral countries

International boundary in 1914

Farthest German advance into France – September 1914

Trench line after November 1914

→ Allied forces

→ German forces

✳ Major battle

0   50   100 Miles
0   50   100 Kilometers

London
North Sea
NETHERLANDS
GREAT BRITAIN
Dover
Ostend
Antwerp
Ghent
Strait of Dover
Calais
Passchendaele July-Nov. 1917
Battles of Ypres Oct.-Nov. 1914 April 1915
Brussels
Cologne
Rhine R.
Lys R.
BELGIUM
Liège
Start of invasion of Belgium and France Aug. 4, 1914
English Channel
Mons
Namur
Vimy Ridge April 1917
Battle of the Somme July-Nov. 1916
Somme R.
Hindenburg Line April 1917
Meuse R.
Moselle R.
LUXEMBOURG
Le Havre
Nivelle's Offensive April-May 1917
Aisne R.
Longwy
Verdun Feb.-July 1916
GERMANY
Saar
Seine R.
Marne
Paris
First Battle of the Marne Sept. 1914
R.
Nancy
Alsace-Lorraine
Strasbourg
Troyes
Seine R.
FRANCE
Moselle R.
Orléans
Loire R.
Rhine R.
Basel
SWITZERLAND

Weapons of World War I

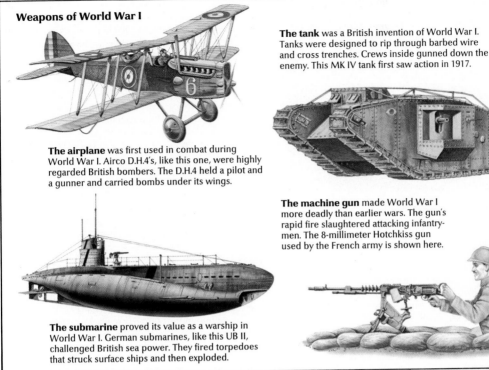

The airplane was first used in combat during World War I. Airco D.H.4's, like this one, were highly regarded British bombers. The D.H.4 held a pilot and a gunner and carried bombs under its wings.

The tank was a British invention of World War I. Tanks were designed to rip through barbed wire and cross trenches. Crews inside gunned down the enemy. This MK IV tank first saw action in 1917.

The machine gun made World War I more deadly than earlier wars. The gun's rapid fire slaughtered attacking infantrymen. The 8-millimeter Hotchkiss gun used by the French army is shown here.

The submarine proved its value as a warship in World War I. German submarines, like this UB II, challenged British sea power. They fired torpedoes that struck surface ships and then exploded.

WORLD BOOK illustrations by Tony Gibbons, Linden Artists Ltd.

captured much of the Austro-Hungarian province of Galicia (now part of Poland and the Soviet Union). By early October, a humiliated Austro-Hungarian army had retreated into its own territory.

Fighting elsewhere. The Allies declared war on the Ottoman Empire in November 1914, after Turkish ships bombarded Russian ports on the Black Sea. Turkish troops then invaded Russia. Fighting later broke out in the Ottoman territories on the Arabian Peninsula and in Mesopotamia (now mostly Iraq), Palestine, and Syria.

Britain stayed in control of the seas following two naval victories over Germany in 1914. The British then kept Germany's surface fleet bottled up in its home waters during most of the war. As a result, Germany relied on submarine warfare.

World War I quickly spread to Germany's overseas colonies. Japan declared war on Germany in late August 1914 and drove the Germans off several islands in the Pacific Ocean. Troops from Australia and New Zealand seized other German colonies in the Pacific. By mid-

1915, most of Germany's empire in Africa had fallen to British forces. However, fighting continued in German East Africa (now Tanzania) for two more years.

The deadlock on the Western Front

By 1915, the opposing sides had dug themselves into a system of trenches that zigzagged along the Western Front. From the trenches, they defended their positions and launched attacks. The Western Front remained deadlocked in trench warfare until 1918.

Trench warfare. The typical *front-line trench* was about 6 to 8 feet (1.8 to 2.4 meters) deep and wide enough for two men to pass. Dugouts in the sides of the trenches protected men during enemy fire. *Support trenches* ran behind the front-line trenches. Off-duty soldiers lived in dugouts in the support trenches. Troops and supplies moved to the battlefront through a network of *communications trenches*. Barbed wire helped protect the front-line trenches from surprise attacks. Field artillery was set up behind the support trenches.

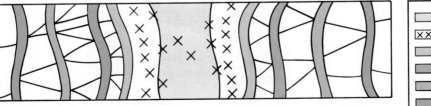

No man's land
☒☒ Barbed wire
Firing trench
Cover trench
Support trench
Reserve trench
Communications trench

A network of trenches snaked along the Western Front. No man's land separated opposing sides. Firing and cover trenches protected front-line soldiers from enemy fire. Communications trenches linked front lines with support and reserve troops at the rear.

Gas masks were worn by soldiers on the Western Front for protection against poisonous fumes. Germany was first to use poison gas, in April 1915 during the Second Battle of Ypres.

Between the enemy lines lay a stretch of ground called "no man's land." No man's land varied from less than 30 yards (27 meters) wide at some points to more than 1 mile (1.6 kilometers) wide at others. In time, artillery fire tore up the earth, making it very difficult to cross no man's land during an attack.

Soldiers generally served at the front line from a few days to a week and then rotated to the rear for a rest. Life in the trenches was miserable. The smell of dead bodies lingered in the air, and rats were a constant problem. Soldiers had trouble keeping dry, especially in water-logged areas of Belgium. Except during an attack, life fell into a dull routine. Some soldiers stood guard. Others repaired the trenches, kept telephone lines in order, brought food from behind the battle lines, or did other jobs. At night, patrols fixed the barbed wire and tried to get information about the enemy.

Enemy artillery and machine guns kept each side pinned in the trenches. Yet the Allies repeatedly tried to blast a gap in the German lines. Allied *offensives* (assaults) followed a pattern. First, artillery bombarded the enemy front-line trenches. The infantry then attacked as commanders shouted, "Over the top!" Soldiers scrambled out of trenches and began the dash across no man's land with fixed bayonets. They hurled grenades

into enemy trenches and struggled through the barbed wire. But the artillery bombardment seldom wiped out all resistance, and so enemy machine guns slaughtered wave after wave of advancing infantry. Even if the attackers broke through the front line, they ran into a second line of defenses. Thus, the Allies never cracked the enemy's defensive power.

Both the Allies and the Central Powers developed new weapons, which they hoped would break the deadlock. In April 1915, the Germans first released poison gas over Allied lines in the Second Battle of Ypres. The fumes caused vomiting and suffocation. But German commanders had little faith in the gas, and they failed to seize that opportunity to launch a major attack. The Allies also began to use poison gas soon thereafter, and gas masks became necessary equipment in the trenches. Another new weapon was the flame thrower, which shot out a stream of burning fuel.

The Battle of Verdun. As chief of the German General Staff, Falkenhayn decided in early 1916 to concentrate on killing enemy soldiers. He hoped that the Allies would finally lack the troops to continue the war. Falkenhayn chose to attack the French city of Verdun. He believed that France would defend Verdun to the last man. Fierce bombardment began on February 21.

Joffre, commander of the French armies, felt that the loss of Verdun would severely damage French morale. Through spring and summer, the French forces held off the attackers. As Falkenhayn predicted, France kept pouring men into the battle. However, Falkenhayn had not expected the battle to take nearly as many German lives as French lives. He halted the unsuccessful assault in July 1916. The next month, Hindenburg and Ludendorff—the two German heroes of the Eastern Front—replaced Falkenhayn on the Western Front. Hindenburg became chief of the General Staff. Ludendorff, his top aide, planned German strategy.

General Henri Pétain had organized the defense of Verdun and was hailed a hero by France. The Battle of Verdun became a symbol of the terrible destructiveness of modern war. French casualties totaled about 315,000 men, and German casualties about 280,000. The city itself was practically destroyed.

The Battle of the Somme. The Allies planned a major offensive for 1916 near the Somme River in

A cry of "Over the top!" signaled the start of an assault. At the command, troops scrambled out of their trenches to begin the dash toward enemy trenches. The Canadian soldiers shown here were following an officer over the top during the Battle of the Somme in France in July 1916.

France. The Battle of Verdun had drained France. Thus, the Somme offensive became mainly the responsibility of the British under General Douglas Haig.

The Allies attacked on July 1, 1916. Within hours, Britain had suffered nearly 60,000 casualties—its worst loss in one day of battle. Fierce fighting went on into the fall. In September, Britain introduced the first primitive tanks. But the tanks were too unreliable and too few in number to make a difference in the battle. Haig finally halted the useless attack in November. At terrible cost, the Allies had gained about 7 miles (11 kilometers). The Battle of the Somme caused more than 1 million casualties—over 600,000 Germans, over 400,000 British, and nearly 200,000 French. In spite of the tragic losses at Verdun and the Somme, the Western Front stood as solid as ever at the end of 1916.

The war on other fronts

During 1915 and 1916, World War I spread to Italy and throughout the Balkans, and activity increased on other fronts. Some Allied military leaders believed that the creation of new battlefronts would break the deadlock on the Western Front. But the war's expansion had little effect on the deadlock.

The Italian Front. Italy had stayed out of World War I during 1914, even though it was a member of the Triple Alliance with Austria-Hungary and Germany. Italy claimed that it was under no obligation to honor the agreement because Austria-Hungary had not gone to war in self-defense. In May 1915, Italy entered World War I on the side of the Allies. In a secret treaty, the Allies promised to give Italy some of Austria-Hungary's territory after the war. In return, Italy promised to attack Austria-Hungary.

The Italians, led by General Luigi Cadorna, hammered away at Austria-Hungary for two years in a series of battles along the Isonzo River in Austria-Hungary. Italy suffered enormous casualties but gained very little territory. The Allies hoped that the Italian Front would help Russia by forcing Austria-Hungary to shift some troops away from the Eastern Front. Such a shift occurred, but it did not help Russia.

The Dardanelles. After World War I began, the Ottoman Empire closed the waterway between the Aegean Sea and the Black Sea. It thereby blocked the sea route

The Italian Front

Italy entered the war against Austria-Hungary in May 1915. In spite of many bitter battles, the Italians gained very little territory. But they wore down the armies of Austria-Hungary.

WORLD BOOK map

to southern Russia. French and British warships attacked the Dardanelles, a strait that formed part of the waterway, in February and March 1915. The Allies hoped to open a supply route to Russia. However, underwater mines halted the assault.

In April 1915, the Allies landed troops on the Gallipoli Peninsula on the west shore of the Dardanelles. Troops from Australia and New Zealand played a key role in the landing. Ottoman and Allied forces soon became locked in trench warfare. A second invasion in August at Suvla Bay to the north failed to end the standstill. In December, the Allies began to evacuate their troops. They had suffered about 250,000 casualties in the Dardanelles.

Eastern Europe. In May 1915, the armies of Germany and Austria-Hungary broke through Russian lines in Galicia, the Austro-Hungarian province that Russia

Robert Hunt Library

Robert Hunt Library

Atop a rocky peak near Austria-Hungary's border, Italian troops prepared to do battle, *far left.* They first had to hoist artillery into position, *near left.* The rugged Alps hampered Italy's efforts to advance into Austria-Hungary.

had invaded in 1914. The Russians retreated about 300 miles (480 kilometers) before they formed a new line of defense. In spite of the setback, Czar Nicholas II staged two offensives to relieve the pressure on the Allies on the Western Front. The first Russian offensive, in March 1916, failed to pull German troops away from Verdun.

The second Russian offensive began in June 1916 under General Alexei Brusilov. Brusilov's army drove Austria-Hungary's forces back about 50 miles (80 kilometers). Within a few weeks, Russia captured about 200,000 prisoners. To halt the assault, Austria-Hungary had to shift troops from the Italian Front to the Eastern Front. The Russian offensive nearly knocked Austria-Hungary out of the war. But it also exhausted Russia. Each side suffered about a million casualties.

Bulgaria entered World War I in October 1915 to help Austria-Hungary defeat Serbia. Bulgaria hoped to recover land it had lost in the Second Balkan War. In an effort to aid Serbia, the Allies landed troops in Salonika, Greece. But the troops never reached Serbia. By November, the Central Powers had overrun Serbia, and Serbia's army had retreated to Albania.

Romania joined the Allies in August 1916. It hoped to gain some of Austria-Hungary's territory if the Allies won the war. By the end of 1916, Romania had lost most of its army, and Germany controlled the country's valuable wheat fields and oil fields.

The war at sea. Great Britain's control of the seas during World War I caused serious problems for Germany. The British navy blockaded German waters, preventing supplies from reaching German ports. By 1916, Germany suffered a shortage of food and other goods.

Germany combated British seapower with its submarines, called *U-boats.* In February 1915, Germany declared a submarine blockade of the British Isles and warned that it would attack any ship that tried to get through the blockade. Thereafter, U-boats destroyed great amounts of goods headed for Britain.

On May 7, 1915, a U-boat torpedoed without warning the British passenger liner *Lusitania* off the coast of Ireland. Among the 1,198 passengers who died were 128 Americans. The sinking of the *Lusitania* led U.S. President Woodrow Wilson to urge Germany to give up unrestricted submarine warfare. In September, Germany agreed not to attack neutral or passenger ships.

The warships that Britain and Germany had raced to build before World War I remained in home waters during most of the war. There, they served to discourage an enemy invasion. The only major encounter between the two navies was the Battle of Jutland. It was fought off the coast of Denmark on May 31 and June 1, 1916. Admiral Sir John Jellicoe commanded a British fleet of 150 warships. He faced a German fleet of 99 warships under the command of Admiral Reinhard Scheer. In spite of Britain's superior strength, Jellicoe acted cautiously. He feared that he could lose the entire war in a day because the destruction of Britain's fleet would give Germany control of the seas. Both sides claimed victory in the Battle of Jutland. Although Britain lost more ships than Germany, it still ruled the seas.

The war in the air. Great advances in aviation were made by the Allies and the Central Powers during World War I. Each side competed to produce better airplanes than the other side. Airplanes were used mainly

The Eastern Front

The Eastern Front swung back and forth until Russia agreed to stop fighting late in 1917. Under the Treaty of Brest-Litovsk, Russia gave much territory to Germany. To the south, the Central Powers had crushed Serbia in 1915 and Romania in 1916.

▢	Allies
▨	Central Powers
▢	Neutral countries
——	International boundary in 1914
━━	Farthest advance westward by Allies
━━	Farthest advance eastward by Central Powers
→	Allied forces
→	Forces of the Central Powers
✳	Major battle

0   250 Miles
0   250 Kilometers

Robert Hunt Library

On the seas, Germany tried to starve Britain into surrender by sinking cargo ships headed for its ports. The ship shown here was torpedoed by the German submarine in the foreground.

to observe enemy activities. The pilots carried guns to shoot down enemy planes. But a pilot risked shooting himself if a bullet bounced off the propeller.

In 1915, Germany developed a machine gun timed to fire between an airplane's revolving propeller blades. The invention made air combat more deadly and led to *dogfights*—clashes between enemy aircraft. A pilot who shot down 5 or more enemy planes was called an *ace*. Many aces became national heroes. Germany's Baron Manfred von Richthofen, who was known as the Red Baron, shot down 80 planes, more than any other ace. Other famous aces included Billy Bishop of Canada, René Fonck of France, Edward Mannock of Great Britain, and Eddie Rickenbacker of the United States.

Aerial bombing remained in its early stages during World War I. In 1915, Germany began to bomb London and other British cities from airships called *zeppelins*. But bombing had little effect on the war.

The final stage

Allied failures. During 1917, French and British military leaders still hoped that a successful offensive could win the war. But German leaders accepted the deadlock on the Western Front and improved German defenses. In March 1917, German troops were moved back to a strongly fortified new battle line in northern France. It was called the Siegfried Line by the Germans and the Hindenburg Line by the Allies. The Siegfried Line shortened the Western Front and placed German artillery and machine guns to best advantage. It also led to the failure of an offensive planned by France.

General Robert Nivelle had replaced Joffre as commander in chief of French forces in December 1916. Nivelle planned a major offensive near the Aisne River and predicted he would smash through the German line within two days. Nivelle's enthusiasm inspired the French troops. Germany's pullback to the Siegfried Line did not shake Nivelle's confidence.

In April 1917, shortly before Nivelle's offensive began, Canadian forces seized a hill called Vimy Ridge. Many Allied troops had fallen in earlier attempts to dislodge

the Germans from that height in northern France.

Nivelle's offensive opened on April 16, 1917. By the end of the day, it was clear that the assault had failed. But fighting continued into May. Mutinies broke out among the French forces after Nivelle's offensive collapsed. The troops had had enough of the pointless bloodshed and the horrid conditions on the Western Front. They no longer had faith in their leaders. Men who had fought bravely for almost three years refused to go on fighting. Pétain, the hero of Verdun, replaced Nivelle in May 1917. Pétain improved the soldiers' living conditions and restored order. He promised that France would remain on the defensive until it was ready to fight again. Meanwhile, any further offensives on the Western Front remained Britain's responsibility.

General Haig was hopeful that a British offensive near Ypres would lead to victory. The Third Battle of Ypres, also known as the Battle of Passchendaele, began on July 31, 1917. For more than three months, British troops and a small French force pounded the Germans in an especially terrible campaign. Heavy Allied bombardment before the infantry attack began had destroyed the drainage system around Ypres. Drenching rains then turned the water-logged land into a swamp where thousands of British soldiers drowned. Snow and ice finally halted the disastrous battle on November 10. In late November, Britain used tanks to break through the Siegfried Line. But the failure at Ypres had used up the troops Britain needed to follow up that success.

In 1917, first France and then Britain thus saw their hopes for victory shattered. Austria-Hungary drove the Italians out of its territory in the Battle of Caporetto in the fall. A revolution in Russia made the Allied situation seem even more hopeless.

Imperial War Museum from Keystone

Military aviators played an important role in World War I. Pilots, such as these members of the British Royal Flying Corps, fought enemy planes in aerial battles called *dogfights*.

War-weary Russian soldiers retreated in disorder in the summer of 1917 after learning that the Germans had smashed through their battle line. By year's end, Russia had quit fighting.

The Russian Revolution. The Russian people suffered greatly during World War I. By 1917, many of them were no longer willing to put up with the enormous casualties and the severe shortages of food and fuel. They blamed Czar Nicholas II and his advisers for the country's problems. Early in 1917, an uprising in Petrograd (now Leningrad) forced Nicholas from the throne. The new government continued the war.

To weaken Russia's war effort further, Germany helped V. I. Lenin, a Russian revolutionary then living in Switzerland, return to his homeland in April 1917. Seven months later, Lenin led an uprising that gained control of Russia's government. Lenin immediately called for peace talks with Germany. World War I had ended on the Eastern Front.

Germany dictated harsh peace terms to Russia·in a peace treaty signed in Brest-Litovsk, Russia, on March 3, 1918. The Treaty of Brest-Litovsk forced Russia to give up large amounts of territory, including Finland, Poland, the Ukraine, Bessarabia, and the Baltic States—Estonia, Livonia (now Latvia), and Lithuania. The end of the fighting on the Eastern Front freed German troops for use on the Western Front. The only obstacle to a final German victory seemed to be the entry of the United States into the war.

The United States enters the war. At the start of World War I, President Wilson had declared the neutrality of the United States. Most Americans opposed U.S. involvement in a European war. But the sinking of the *Lusitania* and other German actions against civilians drew American sympathies to the Allies.

Several events early in 1917 persuaded the United States government to enter World War I. In February, Germany returned to unrestricted submarine warfare, which it assumed might bring the United States into the war. But German military leaders believed that they could still win the war by cutting off British supplies.

They expected their U-boats to starve Britain into surrendering within a few months, long before the United States had fully prepared for war.

Tension between the United States and Germany increased after the British intercepted and decoded a message from Germany's foreign minister, Arthur Zimmermann, to the German ambassador to Mexico. The message, known as the "Zimmermann note," revealed a German plot to persuade Mexico to go to war against the United States. The British gave the message to Wilson, and it was published in the United States early in March. Americans were further enraged after U-boats sank several U.S. cargo ships.

On April 2, Wilson called for war, stating that "the world must be made safe for democracy." Congress declared war on Germany on April 6. Few people expected that the United States would make much of a contribution toward ending the war.

Mobilization. The United States entered World War I unprepared for battle. Strong antiwar feelings had hampered efforts to prepare for war. After declaring war, the government worked to stir up enthusiasm for the war effort. Government propaganda pictured the war as a battle for liberty and democracy. People who still opposed the war faced increasingly unfriendly public opinion. They could even be brought to trial under wartime laws forbidding statements that might harm the successful progress of the war.

During World War I, U.S. government agencies directed the nation's economy toward the war effort. President Wilson put financier Bernard M. Baruch in charge of the War Industries Board, which turned factories into producers of war materials. The Food Administration, headed by businessman Herbert Hoover, controlled the prices, production, and distribution of food. Americans observed "meatless" and "wheatless" days in order that food could be sent to Europe.

Manpower was the chief contribution of the United States to World War I. The country entered the war with a Regular Army of only about 126,000 men. It soon organized a draft requiring all men from 21 through 30 years old to register for military service. The age range was broadened to 18 through 45 in 1918. A lottery determined who served. Many men enlisted voluntarily, and women signed up as nurses and office workers. The

A propaganda poster urged Americans to buy war bonds by showing the enemy as a vicious killer. *Hun* was a scornful term applied to Germans during World War I.

American gunners crawled through a war-torn area of northeastern France in the fall of 1918 during the last assault of World War I. The area lay between the Meuse River and the Argonne Forest. Almost a million U.S. troops took part in the assault, known as the Meuse-Argonne offensive.

National Archives

U.S. armed forces had almost 5 million men and women by the end of the war. Of that number, about $2\frac{3}{4}$ million men had been drafted. Few soldiers received much training before going overseas because the Allies urgently needed them.

Before U.S. help could reach the Western Front, the Allies had to overcome the U-boat threat in the Atlantic. In May 1917, Britain began to use a *convoy system,* by which cargo ships went to sea in large groups escorted by warships. The U-boats proved no match for the warships, and Allied shipping losses dropped sharply.

American troops in Europe. The soldiers sent to Europe by the U.S. Army made up the American Expeditionary Forces (AEF). General John J. Pershing, commander of the AEF, arrived in France in mid-June 1917. The first troops landed later that month. Pershing told U.S. military authorities that he needed 3 million American troops, a third of them within the next year. The American officials were shocked. They had planned to send only 650,000 troops in that time. In the end, about 2 million Americans served in Europe.

Britain, France, and Italy knew well how desperately they needed U.S. manpower by the fall of 1917. In November, the Allies formed the Supreme War Council to plan strategy. They decided to make their strategy defensive until U.S. troops reached the Western Front. The Allies wanted Americans to serve as replacements and fill out their battered ranks. But Pershing was convinced that the AEF would make a greater contribution by fighting as an independent unit. The argument was the major wartime dispute between the Europeans and their American ally. Pershing generally held firm, though at times he lent troops to France and Britain.

The last campaigns. The end of the war on the Eastern Front boosted German hopes for victory. By early 1918, German forces outnumbered the Allies on the Western Front. In spring, Germany staged three offensives. Ludendorff counted on delivering a crushing blow to the Allies before large numbers of American troops reached the front. He relied on speed and surprise.

Germany first struck near St.-Quentin, a city in the Somme River Valley, on March 21, 1918. By March 26, British troops had retreated about 30 miles (50 kilometers). In late March, the Germans began to bombard Paris with "Big Berthas." The enormous guns hurled shells up to 75 miles (120 kilometers). After the disaster at St.-Quentin, Allied leaders met to plan a united defense. In April, they appointed General Ferdinand Foch of France to be the supreme commander of the Allied forces on the Western Front.

A second German offensive began on April 9 along the Lys River in Belgium. British troops fought stubbornly, and Ludendorff called off the attack on April 30. The Allies suffered heavy losses in both assaults, but German casualties were nearly as great.

Germany attacked a third time on May 27 near the Aisne River. By May 30, German troops had reached the Marne River. American soldiers helped France stop the German advance at the town of Château-Thierry, less than 50 miles (80 kilometers) northeast of Paris. During June, U.S. troops drove the Germans out of Belleau Wood, a forested area near the Marne. German forces crossed the Marne on July 15. Foch ordered a counterattack near the town of Soissons on July 18.

The Second Battle of the Marne was fought from July 15 through Aug. 6, 1918. It marked the turning point of World War I. After winning the battle, the Allies advanced steadily. On August 8, Britain and France attacked the Germans near Amiens. By early September, Germany had lost all the territory it had gained since spring. In mid-September, Pershing led U.S. forces to easy victory at St.-Mihiel.

The last offensive of World War I began on Sept. 26, 1918. About 900,000 U.S. troops participated in heavy fighting between the Argonne Forest and the Meuse River. Ludendorff realized that Germany could no longer overcome the superior strength of the Allies.

The fighting ends. The Allies won victories on all fronts in the fall of 1918. Bulgaria surrendered on September 29. British forces under the command of General Edmund Allenby triumphed over the Ottoman army in Palestine and Syria. On October 30, the Ottoman Empire signed an armistice. The last major battle between Italy and Austria-Hungary began in late October in Italy. Italy, with support from France and Great Britain, defeated Austria-Hungary near the town of Vittorio Veneto. Austria-Hungary signed an armistice on November 3.

Germany teetered on the edge of collapse as the war continued through October. Britain's naval blockade had nearly starved the German people, and widespread discent led to riots and rising demands for peace. Kaiser Wilhelm gave up his throne on November 9 and fled to the Netherlands. An Allied delegation headed by Foch met with German representatives in a railroad car in the Compiègne Forest in northern France.

In the early morning on Nov. 11, 1918, the Germans accepted the armistice terms demanded by the Allies. Germany agreed to evacuate the territories it had taken during the war; to surrender large numbers of arms, ships, and other war materials; and to allow the Allied powers to occupy German territory along the Rhine River. Foch ordered the fighting to stop on the Western Front at 11 a.m. World War I was over.

Consequences of the war

Destruction and casualties. World War I caused immeasurable destruction. Nearly 10 million soldiers died as a result of the war—far more than had died in all the wars during the previous 100 years. About 21 million men were wounded. The enormously high casualties resulted partly from the destructive powers of new weapons, especially the machine gun. Military leaders contributed to the slaughter by failing to adjust to the changed conditions of warfare. In staging offensives,

The Western Front: 1918

Germany staged three assaults from March to June of 1918. With American help, the Allies halted the German advance outside Paris in June. Thereafter, the Allies steadily drove the Germans back. An armistice ended the fighting on Nov. 11, 1918.

WORLD BOOK map

they ordered soldiers armed with bayonets into machine-gun fire. Only in the last year of the war did generals successfully use tanks and new tactics.

Germany and Russia each suffered about $1\frac{3}{4}$ million battle deaths during World War I—more than any other country. France had the highest percentage of battle deaths in relation to its total number of servicemen. It lost about $1\frac{1}{3}$ million soldiers, or 16 per cent of those mobilized. No one knows how many civilians died of disease, starvation, and other war-related causes. Some historians believe as many civilians died as soldiers.

Property damage in World War I was greatest in France and Belgium. Armies destroyed their farms and villages as they passed through them or, even worse, dug in for battle. The fighting wrecked factories, bridges, and railroad tracks. Artillery shells, trenches, and chemicals made barren the land along the Western Front.

Economic consequences. World War I cost the fighting nations a total of about $337 billion dollars. By 1918, the war was costing about $10 million an hour. Nations raised part of the money to pay for the war through income taxes and other taxes. But most of the money came from borrowing, which created huge debts. Governments borrowed from citizens by selling war bonds. The Allies also borrowed heavily from the United States. In addition, most governments printed extra money to meet their needs. But the increased money supply caused severe inflation after the war.

The problem of war debts lingered after World War I ended. The Allies tried to reduce their debts by demanding *reparations* (payments for war damages) from the Central Powers, especially Germany. Reparations worsened the economic problems of the defeated countries and did not solve the problems of the victors.

World War I seriously disrupted economies. Some businesses shut down after workers left for military service. Other firms shifted to the production of war materials. To direct production toward the war effort, governments took greater control over the economy than ever before. Most people wanted a return to private enterprise after the war. But some people expected government to continue to solve economic problems.

The countries of Europe had poured their resources into World War I, and they came out of the war exhausted. France, for example, had lost nearly one-tenth of its work force. In most European countries, many returning soldiers could not find jobs. In addition, Europe lost many of the markets for its exports while producing war goods. The United States and other countries that had played a smaller role in the war emerged with increased economic power.

Political consequences. World War I shook the foundations of several governments. Democratic governments in Britain and France withstood the stress of the war. But four monarchies toppled. The first monarch to fall was Czar Nicholas II of Russia in 1917. Kaiser Wilhelm II of Germany and Emperor Charles of Austria-Hungary left their thrones in 1918. The Ottoman sultan, Muhammad VI, fell in 1922.

The collapse of old empires led to the creation of new countries in the years after World War I. The prewar territory of Austria-Hungary formed the independent republics of Austria, Hungary, and Czechoslovakia, as well as parts of Italy, Poland, Romania, and Yugosla-

National Archives

Cheering the end of World War I, a joyful crowd streamed through the streets of a French town on Nov. 11, 1918. The long, horrible war had taken the lives of nearly 10 million soldiers.

via. Russia and Germany also gave up territory to Poland. Finland and the Baltic States—Estonia, Latvia, and Lithuania—gained independence from Russia. Most Arab lands in the Ottoman Empire were placed under the control of France and Britain. The rest of the Ottoman Empire became Turkey. European leaders took national groups into account in redrawing the map of Europe and thus strengthened the cause of nationalism.

World War I gave the Communists a chance to seize power in Russia. Some people expected Communist revolutions to break out elsewhere in Europe. Revolutionary movements gained strength after the war, but Communist governments did not take hold.

Social consequences. World War I brought enormous changes in society. The death of so many young men affected France more than other countries. During the 1920's, France's population dropped because of a low birth rate. Millions of people were uprooted by the war. Some fled war-torn areas and later found their houses, farms, or villages destroyed. Others became refugees as a result of changes in governments and national borders, especially in central and eastern Europe.

Many people chose not to resume their old way of life after World War I. Urban areas grew as peasants settled in cities instead of returning to farms. Women filled

Military casualties in World War I (1914-1918)*

	Dead	Wounded
The Allies		
Belgium	14,000	44,700
British Empire	908,400	2,090,200
France	1,385,000†	4,266,000
Greece	5,000	21,000
Italy	650,000	947,000
Portugal	7,200	13,800
Romania	335,700†	120,000
Russia	1,700,000	4,950,000
Serbia and Montenegro	48,000	143,000
United States	116,516‡	234,428‡
The Central Powers		
Austria-Hungary	1,200,000	3,620,000
Bulgaria	87,500	152,400
Germany	1,773,000	4,216,000
Ottoman Empire	325,000	400,000

*Except for the United States, all figures are approximate.
†Includes missing.
‡Official U.S. government figure.
Source: *World War I: An Outline History* by Hanson W. Baldwin. Copyright © 1962 Hanson W. Baldwin. Reprinted by permission of Harper & Row, Publishers, Inc., and Curtis Brown, Ltd.

jobs in offices and factories after men went to war, and they were reluctant to give up their new independence. Many countries granted women the vote after the war.

The distinction between social classes began to blur as a result of World War I, and society became more democratic. The upper classes, which had traditionally governed, lost some of their power and privilege after having led the world into an agonizing war. Men of all classes had faced the same danger and horror in the trenches. Those who had bled and suffered for their country came to demand a say in running it.

Finally, World War I transformed attitudes. Middle- and upper-class Europeans lost the confidence and optimism they had felt before the war. Many people began to question long-held ideas. For example, few Europeans before the war had doubted their right to force European culture on the rest of the world. But the destruction and bloodshed of the war shattered the belief in the superiority of European civilization.

The peace settlement

The Fourteen Points. In January 1918, 10 months before World War I ended, President Woodrow Wilson of the United States proposed a set of war aims called the Fourteen Points. Wilson believed that the Fourteen Points would bring about a just peace settlement, which he termed "peace without victory." In November 1918, Germany agreed to an armistice. Germany expected that the peace settlement would be based on the Fourteen Points.

Eight of Wilson's Fourteen Points dealt with specific political and territorial settlements. The rest of them set forth general principles aimed at preventing future wars. The last point proposed the establishment of an international association—later called the League of Nations—to maintain the peace. See **Wilson, Woodrow** (The Fourteen Points).

The Paris Peace Conference. In January 1919, representatives of the victorious powers gathered in Paris to draw up the peace settlement. They came from 32 nations. Committees worked out specific proposals at the Paris Peace Conference. But the decisions were made by four heads of government called the Big Four. The Big Four consisted of Wilson, Britain's Prime Minister David Lloyd George, France's Premier Georges Clemenceau, and Italy's Premier Vittorio Orlando.

The Paris Peace Conference largely disregarded the lofty principles of the Fourteen Points. The major European Allies had sacrificed far more than the Americans and wanted to be paid back. Wilson focused his efforts on the creation of the League of Nations. He yielded to France and Britain on many other issues.

In May 1919, the peace conference approved the treaty and presented it to Germany. Germany agreed to it only after the Allies threatened to invade. With grave doubts, German representatives signed the treaty in the Palace of Versailles near Paris on June 28, 1919. The date was the fifth anniversary of the assassination of Archduke Francis Ferdinand.

In addition to the Treaty of Versailles with Germany, the peacemakers drew up separate treaties with the other Central Powers. The Treaty of St.-Germain was signed with Austria in September 1919, the Treaty of Neuilly with Bulgaria in November 1919, the Treaty of Trianon with Hungary in June 1920, and the Treaty of Sèvres with the Ottoman Empire in August 1920.

Provisions of the treaties that officially ended World War I stripped the Central Powers of territory and arms and required them to pay reparations. Germany was punished especially severely. One clause in the Treaty of Versailles forced Germany to accept responsibility for causing the war.

Under the Treaty of Versailles, Germany gave up territory to Belgium, Czechoslovakia, Denmark, France, and Poland and lost its overseas colonies. France gained control of coal fields in Germany's Saar Valley for 15 years. An Allied military force, paid for by Germany, was to occupy the west bank of the Rhine River for 15 years. Other clauses in the treaty limited Germany's armed forces and required the country to turn over war materials, ships, livestock, and other goods to the Allies. A total sum for reparations was not set until 1921. At that time, Germany received a bill for about $33 billion.

The Treaty of St.-Germain and the Treaty of Trianon reduced Austria and Hungary to less than a third their former area. The treaties recognized the independence of Czechoslovakia, Poland, and a kingdom that later became Yugoslavia. Those new states, along with Italy and Romania, received territory that had belonged to Austria-Hungary. The Treaty of Sèvres took Egypt, Lebanon, Mesopotamia, Palestine, Syria, and Transjordan away from the Ottoman Empire. Bulgaria lost territory to Greece and Romania. Germany's allies also had to reduce their armed forces and pay reparations.

The postwar world. The peacemakers found it impossible to satisfy the hopes and ambitions of every nation and national group. The settlements they drew up disappointed both the victors and the defeated powers.

In creating new borders, the peacemakers considered the wishes of national groups. However, territorial claims overlapped in many cases. For example, Romania gained a chunk of land with a large Hungarian population, and parts of Czechoslovakia and Poland had many Germans. Such settlements heightened tensions between countries. In addition, some Arab nations were bitter because they had failed to gain independence.

Certain borders created by the peace settlements made little economic sense. For example, the new countries of Austria and Hungary were small and weak and unable to support themselves. They had lost most of their population, resources, and markets. Austria's largely German population had wanted to unite with Germany. But the peace treaties forbade that union. The peacemakers did not want Germany to gain territory from the war.

Among the European Allies, Britain entered the postwar world the most content. The nation had kept its empire and control of the seas. But Britain worried that the balance of power it wanted in Europe could be upset by a severely weakened Germany and a victory by the Communists in a civil war in Russia. France had succeeded in imposing harsh terms on Germany—its traditional foe—but not in safeguarding its borders. France had failed to obtain a guarantee of aid from Britain and the United States in the event of a German invasion. Finally, Italy had gained less territory than it had been promised and felt it deserved.

In the United States, the Senate reflected public opinion and failed to approve the Treaty of Versailles. It thereby rejected President Wilson. The treaty would have made the United States a member of the League of Nations. Many Americans were not yet ready to accept

Europe and the Near East after World War I

World War I led to changes in many borders. Austria-Hungary and the Ottoman Empire split into national states. Russia and Germany gave up territory. Although several states won independence, most Arab lands in the Ottoman Empire were placed under French and British rule.

- German Empire
- Austria-Hungary
- Russian Empire
- Ottoman Empire
- —— International boundary of newly created country
- —— Other international boundary

0   500 Miles
0   500 Kilometers

WORLD BOOK map

the responsibilities that went along with their country's new power. They feared that the League of Nations would entangle the country in European disputes.

The Treaty of Versailles imposed harsher terms than Germany had expected. The responsibility of having accepted those terms weakened Germany's postwar government. During the 1930's, a strongly nationalist movement led by Adolf Hitler gained power in Germany. Hitler promised to ignore the Treaty of Versailles and to avenge Germany's defeat in World War I. In 1939, Germany invaded Poland. World War II had begun.

Edward M. Coffman

Related articles in *World Book.* See the *History* section of articles on the countries that took part in World War I. See also the following articles:

Battle areas

Alsace-Lorraine	Jutland, Battle of	Verdun, Battles of
Balkans	Saar	Vimy Ridge,
Flanders Field	Siegfried Line	Battle of

Allied military biographies

Albert I	Kitchener, Horatio H.
Allenby, Lord	March, Peyton C.
Bishop, Billy	Mitchell, Billy
Byng, Julian H. G.	Pershing, John J.
Foch, Ferdinand	Pétain, Henri Philippe
Haig, Earl	Piłsudski, Józef
Jellicoe, Sir John R.	Rickenbacker, Eddie
Joffre, Joseph J. C.	York, Alvin C.

Allied civilian biographies

Asquith, Herbert H.	Nicholas II (of Russia)
Baruch, Bernard M.	Orlando, Vittorio E.
Borden, Sir Robert L.	Poincaré, Raymond
Clemenceau, Georges	Venizelos, Eleutherios
Hoover, Herbert C.	Wilson, Woodrow
Lloyd George, David	

Central Powers biographies

Hindenburg, Paul von	Wilhelm (II)
Ludendorff, Erich F. W.	Zeppelin, Ferdinand von

Other biographies

Ataturk, Kemal	Constantine (I) (of	Lenin, V. I.
Cavell, Edith L.	Greece)	Mata Hari
	Lawrence, T. E.	

Forces, materials, and weapons

Air force	Camouflage
Air Force, United States	Chemical-biological-radiolog-
Aircraft, Military	ical warfare
Airship	Machine gun
Army	Navy
Army, United States	Navy, United States
Artillery	Submarine
Automobile (World War I)	Tank
Aviation	

Treaties

Saint Germain, Treaty of	Trianon, Treaty of
Sèvres, Treaty of	Versailles, Treaty of

Other related articles

American Legion	Stars and Stripes
American Legion Auxiliary	Triple Alliance
Fourteen Points	Triple Entente
League of Nations	United States, History of the
Lusitania	Unknown Soldier
Mandated territory	Veterans Day
Neutrality	War aces
Red Cross	War crime
Refugee	War debt

Outline

I. Causes of the war
  A. The rise of nationalism
  B. A build-up of military might
  C. Competition for colonies
  D. A system of military alliances
II. Beginning of the war
  A. The assassination of an archduke
  B. How the conflict spread
  C. The Western Front
  D. The Eastern Front
  E. Fighting elsewhere
III. The deadlock on the Western Front
  A. Trench warfare
  B. The Battle of Verdun
  C. The Battle of the Somme
IV. The war on other fronts
  A. The Italian Front   D. The war at sea
  B. The Dardanelles   E. The war in the air
  C. Eastern Europe
V. The final stage
  A. Allied failures
  B. The Russian Revolution
  C. The United States enters the war
  D. The last campaigns
  E. The fighting ends
VI. Consequences of the war
  A. Destruction and casualties
  B. Economic consequences
  C. Political consequences
  D. Social consequences
VII. The peace settlement
  A. The Fourteen Points
  B. The Paris Peace Conference
  C. Provisions of the treaties
  D. The postwar world

Questions

What were the four chief causes of World War I?
What country first used poison gas in World War I? What country first used tanks?
Which World War I heads of government made up the Big Four?
Which countries formed the Triple Entente? The Triple Alliance? How did the two alliances differ?
How did Germany combat British naval power during World War I?
What was the chief contribution made by the United States to World War I?
What was the Schlieffen Plan in World War I?
Why was the First Battle of the Marne a key Allied victory?
Why did French troops mutiny in 1917?
How did Germany try to weaken Russia's war effort in 1917?

Reading and Study Guide

See *World War I* in the Research Guide/Index, Volume 22, for a *Reading and Study Guide.*

Additional resources

Barnett, Correlli. *The Great War.* Putnam, 1980.
Coffman, Edward M. *The War to End All Wars: The American Military Experience in World War I.* Univ. of Wisconsin Press, 1986. First published in 1968.
Kennedy, David M. *Over Here: The First World War and American Society.* Oxford, 1980.
The Marshall Cavendish Illustrated Encyclopedia of World War I. Ed. by Peter Young and Mark Dartford. 12 vols. Rev. ed. Cavendish, 1984.
Stokesbury, James L. *A Short History of World War I.* Morrow, 1981.
Taylor, A. J. P. *Illustrated History of the First World War.* Putnam, 1964.
Terraine, John. *To Win a War: 1918, The Year of Victory.* Doubleday, 1981.
Tuchman, Barbara W. *The Guns of August.* Macmillan, 1962.

Süddeutscher Verlag   Imperial War Museum

The fighting fronts in World War II spread to nearly every part of the globe. In Europe and northern Africa, they included cities and desert wastes. Little remained standing in Tournai, Belgium, *left*, after a German bombing raid. Tank warfare kept armies on the run in Egypt, *right*.

World War II

World War II (1939-1945) killed more people, destroyed more property, disrupted more lives, and probably had more far-reaching consequences than any other war in history. It brought about the downfall of Western Europe as the center of world power and led to the rise of the Soviet Union. The development of the atomic bomb during the war opened the nuclear age.

The exact number of people killed because of World War II will never be known. Military deaths probably totaled about 17 million. Civilian deaths were even greater as a result of starvation, bombing raids, massacres, epidemics, and other war-related causes. The battlegrounds spread to nearly every part of the world. Troops fought in the steaming jungles of Southeast Asia, in the deserts of northern Africa, and on islands in the Pacific Ocean. Battles were waged on frozen fields in the Soviet Union, below the surface of the Atlantic Ocean, and in the streets of many European cities.

World War II began on Sept. 1, 1939, when Germany invaded Poland. Germany's dictator, Adolf Hitler, had built Germany into a powerful war machine. That machine rapidly crushed Poland, Denmark, Luxembourg, the Netherlands, Belgium, Norway, and France. By June 1940, Great Britain stood alone against Hitler. That same month, Italy joined the war on Germany's side. The fighting soon spread to Greece and northern Africa. In June

1941, Germany invaded the Soviet Union. Japan attacked United States military bases at Pearl Harbor in Hawaii on Dec. 7, 1941, bringing the United States into the war. By mid-1942, Japanese forces had conquered much of Southeast Asia and had swept across many islands in the Pacific.

Germany, Italy, and Japan formed an alliance known as the Axis. Six other nations eventually joined the Axis. The United States, Great Britain, China, and the Soviet Union were the major powers fighting the Axis. They were called the Allies. The Allies totaled 50 nations by the end of the war.

During 1942, the Allies stopped the Axis advance in northern Africa, the Soviet Union, and the Pacific. Allied forces landed in Italy in 1943 and in France in 1944. In 1945, the Allies drove into Germany from the east and the west. A series of bloody battles in the Pacific brought the Allies to Japan's doorstep by the summer of 1945. Germany surrendered on May 7, 1945, and Japan on Sept. 2, 1945.

An uneasy peace took effect as a war-weary world began to rebuild after World War II. Much of Europe and parts of Asia lay in ruins. Millions of people were starving and homeless. Europe's leadership in world affairs had ended. The United States and the Soviet Union had become the world's most powerful nations. But their wartime alliance broke down soon after the war. New threats to peace arose as the Soviet Union sought to spread Communism in Europe and Asia.

Causes of the war

Many historians trace the causes of World War II to problems left unsolved by World War I (1914-1918). World War I and the treaties that ended it also created new political and economic problems. Forceful leaders in several countries took advantage of those problems

James L. Stokesbury, the contributor of this article, is Professor of History at Acadia University and the author of A Short History of World War II.

to seize power. The desire of dictators in Germany, Italy, and Japan to conquer additional territory brought them into conflict with democratic nations.

The Peace of Paris. After World War I ended, representatives of the victorious nations met in Paris in 1919 to draw up peace treaties for the defeated countries. The treaties, known together as the Peace of Paris, followed a long and bitter war. They were worked out in haste by countries with opposing goals and failed to sat-

Special Report
WORLD WAR II
1995 Year Book, p. 66

National Archives

Charles Kerlee from National Archives

Battlegrounds in Asia and the Pacific included tropical jungles and vast ocean spaces. Troops waded across muddy rivers and crawled through thick vegetation, *left,* in Southeast Asia and on Pacific islands. Planes based on aircraft carriers, *right,* did much of the fighting at sea.

isfy even the victors. Of all the countries on the winning side, Italy and Japan left the peace conference most dissatisfied. Italy gained less territory than it felt it deserved and vowed to take action on its own. Japan gained control of German territories in the Pacific and thereby launched a program of expansion. But Japan was angered by the peacemakers' failure to endorse the principle of the equality of all races.

The countries that lost World War I—Germany, Austria, Hungary, Bulgaria, and Turkey—were especially dissatisfied with the Peace of Paris. They were stripped of territory and arms and were required to make *reparations* (payments for war damages).

The Treaty of Versailles, which was signed with Germany, punished Germany severely. The German government agreed to sign the treaty only after the victorious powers threatened to invade. Many Germans particularly resented a clause that forced Germany to accept responsibility for causing World War I.

Economic problems. World War I seriously damaged the economies of European countries. Both the winners and the losers came out of the war deeply in debt. The defeated powers had difficulty paying reparations to the victors, and the victors had difficulty repaying loans from the United States. The shift from a wartime economy to a peacetime economy caused further problems. Many soldiers could not find jobs after the war.

Italy and Japan suffered from too many people and too few resources after World War I. They eventually tried to solve their problems by territorial expansion. In Germany, runaway inflation destroyed the value of money and wiped out the savings of millions of people. In 1923, the German economy neared collapse. Loans from the United States helped Germany's government restore order. By the late 1920's, Europe appeared to be entering a period of economic stability.

A worldwide business slump known as the Great Depression began in the United States in 1929. By the early 1930's, it had halted Europe's economic recovery. The Great Depression caused mass unemployment and spread poverty and despair. It weakened democratic governments and strengthened extreme political movements that promised to end the economic problems. Two movements in particular gained strength. The forces of Communism, known as the Left, called for revolution by the workers. The forces of fascism, called the Right, favored strong national government. Throughout Europe, the forces of the Left clashed with the forces of the Right. The political extremes gained the most support in countries with the greatest economic problems and the deepest resentment of the Peace of Paris.

Nationalism was an extreme form of patriotism that swept across Europe during the 1800's. Supporters of nationalism placed loyalty to the aims of their nation above any other public loyalty. Many nationalists viewed foreigners and members of minority groups as inferior. Such beliefs helped nations justify their conquest of other lands and the poor treatment of minorities within their borders. Nationalism was a chief cause of World War I, and it grew even stronger after that war.

Nationalism went hand in hand with feelings of national discontent. The more people felt deprived of national honor, the more they wished to see their country powerful and able to insist on its rights. Many Germans felt humiliated by their country's defeat in World War I and its harsh treatment under the Treaty of Versailles. During the 1930's, they enthusiastically supported a violently nationalistic organization called the Nazi Party. The Nazi Party declared that Germany had a right to become strong again. Nationalism also gained strength in Italy and Japan.

The Peace of Paris established an international organization called the League of Nations to maintain peace. But nationalism prevented the League from working effectively. Each country backed its own interests at the expense of other countries. Only weak countries agreed to submit their disagreements to the League of Nations for settlement. Strong nations reserved the right to settle their disputes by threats or, if tough talk failed, by force.

The rise of dictatorships. The political unrest and poor economic conditions that developed after World War I enabled dictatorships to arise in several countries, especially in those countries that lacked a tradition of democratic government. During the 1920's and 1930's, dictatorships came to power in the Soviet Union, Italy, Germany, and Japan. They held total power and ruled without regard to law. The dictatorships used terror and secret police to crush opposition to their rule. People who objected risked imprisonment or execution.

In the Soviet Union, the Communists, led by V. I. Lenin, had seized power in 1917. Lenin set up a dictatorship that firmly controlled the country by the time he died in 1924. After Lenin's death, Joseph Stalin and other leading Communists struggled for power. Stalin eliminated his rivals one by one and became the Soviet dictator in 1929.

In Italy, economic distress after World War I led to strikes and riots. As a result of the violence, a strongly nationalistic group called the Fascist Party gained many supporters. Benito Mussolini, leader of the Fascists, promised to bring order and prosperity to Italy. He vowed to restore to Italy the glory it had known in the days of the ancient Roman Empire. By 1922, the Fascists had become powerful enough to force the king of Italy to appoint Mussolini premier. Mussolini, who took the title *il Duce* (the Leader), soon began to establish a dictatorship.

In Germany, the Nazi Party made spectacular gains as the Great Depression deepened during the early 1930's. Many Germans blamed all their country's economic woes on the hated Treaty of Versailles, which forced Germany to give up territory and resources and pay large reparations. In 1933, Adolf Hitler, the leader of the Nazis, was appointed chancellor of Germany. Hitler,

who was called *der Führer* (the Leader), soon made Germany a dictatorship. He vowed to ignore the Versailles Treaty and to avenge Germany's defeat in World War I. Hitler preached that Germans were a "superior race" and that such peoples as Jews and Slavs were inferior. He began a campaign of hatred against Jews and Communists and promised to rid the country of them. Hitler's extreme nationalism appealed to many Germans.

In Japan, military officers began to hold political office during the 1930's. By 1936, they had strong control of the government. Japan's military government glorified war and the training of warriors. In 1941, General Hideki Tojo became premier of Japan.

Aggression on the march. Japan, Italy, and Germany followed a policy of aggressive territorial expansion during the 1930's. They invaded weak lands that could be taken over easily. The dictatorships knew what they wanted, and they grabbed it. The democratic countries responded with timidity and indecision to the aggression of the dictatorships.

Japan was the first dictatorship to begin a program of conquest. In 1931, Japanese forces seized control of Manchuria, a region of China rich in natural resources. Some historians consider Japan's conquest of Manchuria as the real start of World War II. Japan made Manchuria a puppet state called Manchukuo. In 1937, Japan launched a major attack against China. It occupied most of eastern China by the end of 1938, though the two countries had not officially declared war. Japan's military leaders began to speak about bringing all of eastern Asia under Japanese control.

The world at war:
1939-1945   Germany, Italy, Japan, and their Axis partners fought Great Britain, the Soviet Union, the United States, and the other Allies in World War II. This map shows the Allies and the lands controlled by the Axis nations at the height of their power. Few countries remained neutral.

World Book map

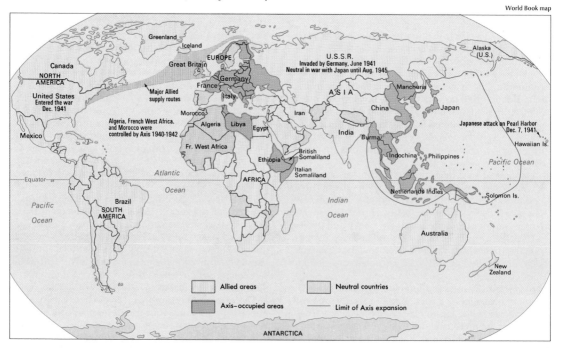

Italy looked to Africa to fulfill its ambitions for an empire. In 1935, Italian troops invaded Ethiopia, one of the few independent countries in Africa. The Italians used machine guns, tanks, and airplanes to overpower Ethiopia's poorly equipped army. They had conquered the country by May 1936.

Soon after Hitler took power, he began to build up Germany's armed forces in violation of the Treaty of Versailles. In 1936, Hitler sent troops into the Rhineland, a region of Germany along the banks of the Rhine River. Under the treaty, the Rhineland was to remain free of troops. In March 1938, German soldiers marched into Austria and united it with Germany. Many people in Germany and Austria welcomed that move.

The acts of aggression were easy victories for the dictatorships. The League of Nations proved incapable of stopping them. It lacked an army and the power to enforce international law. The United States had refused to join the League or become involved in European disputes. Great Britain and France were unwilling to risk another war so soon after World War I. The two powers knew they would bear the burden of any fighting.

The aggressors soon formed an alliance. In 1936, Germany and Italy agreed to support one another's foreign policy. The alliance was known as the Rome-Berlin Axis. Japan joined the alliance in 1940, and it became the Rome-Berlin-Tokyo Axis.

The Spanish Civil War. A civil war tore Spain apart from 1936 to 1939. In 1936, many of Spain's army offi-

AP/Wide World

Members of the Nazi Party marched in a rally in Nuremberg, Germany, in 1938. Their banners bore the Nazi emblem, the *swastika.* The Nazi Party gained control of Germany in 1933.

The warring nations

The Allies

Argentina (March 27, 1945)
Australia (Sept. 3, 1939)
Belgium (May 10, 1940)
Bolivia (April 7, 1943)
Brazil (Aug. 22, 1942)
Canada (Sept. 10, 1939)
Chile (Feb. 14, 1945)
China (Dec. 9, 1941)
Colombia (Nov. 26, 1943)
Costa Rica (Dec. 8, 1941)
Cuba (Dec. 9, 1941)
Czechoslovakia (Dec. 16, 1941)
Denmark (April 9, 1940)
Dominican Republic (Dec. 8, 1941)
Ecuador (Feb. 2, 1945)
Egypt (Feb. 24, 1945)
El Salvador (Dec. 8, 1941)
Ethiopia (Dec. 1, 1942)
France (Sept. 3, 1939)
Great Britain (Sept. 3, 1939)
Greece (Oct. 28, 1940)
Guatemala (Dec. 9, 1941)
Haiti (Dec. 8, 1941)
Honduras (Dec. 8, 1941)
India (Sept. 3, 1939)
Iran (Sept. 9, 1943)
Iraq (Jan. 16, 1943)
Lebanon (Feb. 27, 1945)
Liberia (Jan. 26, 1944)
Luxembourg (May 10, 1940)

Mexico (May 22, 1942)
Mongolian People's Republic (Aug. 9, 1945)
Netherlands (May 10, 1940)
New Zealand (Sept. 3, 1939)
Nicaragua (Dec. 8, 1941)
Norway (April 9, 1940)
Panama (Dec. 7, 1941)
Paraguay (Feb. 8, 1945)
Peru (Feb. 11, 1945)
Poland (Sept. 1, 1939)
San Marino (Sept 24, 1944)
Saudi Arabia (March 1, 1945)
South Africa (Sept. 6, 1939)
Soviet Union (June 22, 1941)
Syria (Feb. 26, 1945)
Turkey (Feb. 23, 1945)
United States (Dec. 8, 1941)
Uruguay (Feb. 22, 1945)
Venezuela (Feb. 16, 1945)
Yugoslavia (April 6, 1941)

The Axis

Albania (June 15, 1940)
Bulgaria (April 6, 1941)
Finland (June 25, 1941)
Germany (Sept. 1, 1939)
Hungary (April 10, 1941)
Italy (June 10, 1940)
Japan (Dec. 7, 1941)
Romania (June 22, 1941)
Thailand (Jan. 25, 1942)

Dates are those on which each country entered the war.

Lee Lockwood, Black Star

Two European dictators, Adolf Hitler of Germany, *left,* and Benito Mussolini of Italy, *right,* dreamed of powerful empires. Their actions plunged much of Europe and Africa into war.

AP/Wide World

The glorification of military power accompanied the rise of a dictatorship in Japan during the 1930's. This military band was showered with confetti as it marched through Tokyo in 1937.

cers revolted against the government. The army rebels chose General Francisco Franco as their leader. Franco's forces were known as Nationalists or Rebels. The forces that supported Spain's elected government were called Loyalists or Republicans. The Spanish Civil War drew worldwide attention. During the war, the dictatorships again displayed their might while the democracies remained helpless.

Hitler and Mussolini sent troops, weapons, aircraft, and advisers to aid the Nationalists. The Soviet Union was the only power to help the Loyalists. France, Britain, and the United States decided not to become involved. However, Loyalist sympathizers from many countries joined the International Brigades that the Communists formed to fight in Spain.

The last Loyalist forces surrendered on April 1, 1939, and Franco set up a dictatorship in Spain. The Spanish Civil War served as a military proving ground for World War II because Germany, Italy, and the Soviet Union

used it to test weapons and tactics. The war in Spain was also a rehearsal for World War II in that it split the world into forces that either supported or opposed Nazism and Fascism.

The failure of appeasement. Hitler prepared to strike again soon after Germany absorbed Austria in March 1938. German territory then bordered Czechoslovakia on three sides. Czechoslovakia had become an independent nation after World War I. Its population consisted of many nationalities, including more than 3 million people of German descent. Hitler sought control of the Sudetenland, a region of western Czechoslovakia where most of the Germans lived. Urged on by Hitler, the Sudeten Germans began to clamor for union with Germany.

Czechoslovakia was determined to defend its territory. France and the Soviet Union had pledged their support. As tension mounted, Britain's Prime Minister Neville Chamberlain tried to restore calm. Chamberlain wished to preserve peace at all cost. He believed that war could be prevented by meeting Hitler's demands. That policy became known as *appeasement.*

Chamberlain had several meetings with Hitler during September 1938 as Europe teetered on the edge of war. Hitler raised his demands at each meeting. On September 29, Chamberlain and French Premier Édouard Daladier met with Hitler and Mussolini in Munich, Germany. Chamberlain and Daladier agreed to turn over the Sudetenland to Germany, and they forced Czechoslovakia to accept the agreement. Hitler promised that he had no more territorial demands.

The Munich Agreement marked the height of the policy of appeasement. Chamberlain and Daladier hoped that the agreement would satisfy Hitler and prevent war—or that it would at least prolong the peace until Britain and France were ready for war. The two leaders were mistaken on both counts.

The failure of appeasement soon became clear. Hitler broke the Munich Agreement in March 1939 and seized the rest of Czechoslovakia. He thereby added Czechoslovakia's armed forces and industries to Germany's military might. In the months before World War II began, Germany's preparations for war moved ahead faster than did the military build-up of Britain and France.

Early stages of the war

During the first year of World War II, Germany won a series of swift victories over Poland, Denmark, Luxembourg, the Netherlands, Belgium, Norway, and France. Germany then attempted to bomb Britain into surrendering, but it failed.

The invasion of Poland. After Hitler seized Czechoslovakia, he began demanding territory from Poland. Great Britain and France pledged to help Poland if Germany attacked it. Yet the two powers could aid Poland only by invading Germany, a step that neither chose to take. Britain had only a small army. France had prepared to defend its territory, not to attack.

Great Britain and France hoped that the Soviet Union would help defend Poland. But Hitler and Stalin shocked

the world by becoming allies. On Aug. 23, 1939, Germany and the Soviet Union signed a *nonaggression pact* —in which they agreed not to go to war against each other. They secretly decided to divide Poland between themselves.

On Sept. 1, 1939, Germany invaded Poland and began World War II. Poland had a fairly large army but little modern equipment. The Polish army expected to fight along the country's frontiers. However, the Germans introduced a new method of warfare they called *blitzkrieg* (lightning war). The blitzkrieg stressed speed and surprise. Rows of tanks smashed through Poland's defenses and rolled deep into the country before the Polish army had time to react. Swarms of German dive bombers

Ullstein Bilderdienst

Germany's *blitzkrieg* (lightning war) overran Poland at the outbreak of World War II. In Tczew, the people deserted the streets as German armored vehicles rumbled through, *above.*

and fighter aircraft knocked out communications and pounded battle lines.

The Poles fought bravely. But Germany's blitzkrieg threw their army into confusion. On Sept. 17, 1939, Soviet forces invaded Poland from the east. By late September, the Soviet Union occupied the eastern third of Poland, and Germany had swallowed up the rest.

The Phony War. Great Britain and France declared war on Germany on Sept. 3, 1939, two days after the invasion of Poland. But the two countries stood by while Poland collapsed. France moved troops to the Maginot Line, a belt of steel and concrete fortresses it had built after World War I along its border with Germany. Britain sent a small force into northern France. Germany stationed troops on the Siegfried Line, a strip of defenses Hitler built in the 1930's opposite the Maginot Line. The two sides avoided fighting in late 1939 and early 1940. Journalists called the period the Phony War.

The conquest of Denmark and Norway. Valuable shipments of iron ore from Sweden reached Germany

by way of Norway's port of Narvik. Hitler feared British plans to cut off those shipments by laying explosives in Norway's coastal waters. In April 1940, German forces invaded Norway. They conquered Denmark on the way. Britain tried to help Norway, but Germany's airpower prevented many British ships and troops from reaching the country. Norway fell to the Germans in June 1940. The conquest of Norway secured Germany's shipments of iron ore. Norway also provided bases for German submarines and aircraft.

Chamberlain, the champion of appeasement, resigned after the invasion of Norway. Winston Churchill replaced him as Britain's prime minister on May 10, 1940. Churchill told the British people he had nothing to offer them but "blood, toil, tears, and sweat."

The invasion of the Low Countries. The Low Countries—Belgium, Luxembourg, and the Netherlands—hoped to remain neutral after World War II began. However, Germany launched a blitzkrieg against them on May 10, 1940. The Low Countries immediately requested Allied help. But Luxembourg surrendered in one day, and the Netherlands in five days. British and French forces rushed into Belgium and fell into a German trap. As the Allied forces raced northward, the main German invasion cut behind them through the Belgian Ardennes Forest to the south. The Germans reached the English Channel on May 21. They had nearly surrounded Allied forces in Belgium.

King Leopold III of Belgium surrendered on May 28, 1940. His surrender left the Allied forces trapped in Belgium in great danger. They were retreating toward the French seaport of Dunkerque on the English Channel. Britain sent all available craft to rescue the troops. The rescue fleet included destroyers, yachts, ferries, fishing vessels, and motorboats. Under heavy bombardment, the vessels evacuated about 338,000 troops from May 26 to June 4. The evacuation of Dunkerque saved most of Britain's army. But the army left behind all its tanks and equipment. The remaining Allied troops in Dunkerque surrendered on June 4, 1940.

AP/Wide World   Keystone

The evacuation of Dunkerque rescued about 338,000 Allied soldiers in 1940. While the Germans attacked, every available British vessel, including small craft like those above, ferried the troops to safety. At the right, soldiers waded out to a ship.

World War II in Europe and northern Africa: 1939-1942

Germany's powerful war machine brought much of Europe under Axis control during the early stages of the war. By November 1942, Axis-controlled territory extended from Norway to northern Africa and from France to the Soviet Union. That month, Allied forces invaded northern Africa.

WORLD BOOK map

The fall of France. France had expected to fight along a stationary battlefront and had built the Maginot Line for its defense. But German tanks and aircraft went around the Maginot Line. The Germans passed north of the Maginot Line as they swept through Luxembourg and Belgium and into northern France in May 1940. They launched a major assault against France on June 5. The blitzkrieg sent French forces reeling backward. As France neared collapse, Italy declared war on France and Great Britain on June 10.

German troops entered Paris on June 14, 1940. The French government had already fled the capital. Paul

Reynaud had become premier of France in March. Reynaud wanted to fight on. But many of his generals and cabinet officers believed that the battle for France was lost. Reynaud resigned, and a new French government agreed to an *armistice* (truce) on June 22.

Under the terms of the armistice, Germany occupied the northern two-thirds of France and a strip of western France along the Atlantic Ocean. Southern France remained in French control. The town of Vichy became the capital of unoccupied France. Marshal Henri Pétain, a French hero of World War I, headed the Vichy government. He largely cooperated with the Germans. Then in

Important dates in Europe and northern Africa: 1939-1942

1939
Sept. 1   Germany invaded Poland, starting World War II.
Sept. 3   Britain and France declared war on Germany.

1940
April 9   Germany invaded Denmark and Norway.
May 10   Germany invaded Belgium and the Netherlands.
June 10   Italy declared war on France and Great Britain.
June 22   France signed an armistice with Germany.
July 10   Battle of Britain began.

1941
April 6   Germany invaded Greece and Yugoslavia.
June 22   Germany invaded the Soviet Union.
Sept. 8   German troops completed the blockade of Leningrad, which lasted until January 1944.

1942
Aug. 25   Hitler ordered his forces to capture Stalingrad.
Oct. 23   Britain attacked the Axis at El Alamein in Egypt.
Nov. 8   Allied troops landed in Algeria and Morocco.

Mauritius, Black Star

After France fell, victorious German soldiers paraded down the Champs Élysées, the famous Paris boulevard. France's surrender in June 1940 left Britain alone to fight Germany.

November 1942, German troops occupied all France.

One of the French generals, Charles de Gaulle, had escaped to Britain after France fell. In radio broadcasts to France, he urged the people to carry on the fight against Germany. The troops who rallied around de Gaulle became known as the Free French forces.

The Battle of Britain. Hitler believed that Great Britain would seek peace with Germany after the fall of France. But Britain fought on alone. Hitler made preparations to cross the English Channel and invade southern England. Before the Germans could invade, however, they had to defeat Britain's Royal Air Force (RAF). The Battle of Britain, which began in July 1940, was the first battle ever fought to control the air.

In August 1940, the German air force, the Luftwaffe, began to attack RAF bases. Germany's aircraft out-numbered those of the RAF. But radar stations along England's coast provided warning of approaching German planes and helped the RAF intercept them.

Each side greatly overestimated the number of enemy planes it had shot down. By September 1940, the Luftwaffe mistakenly believed it had destroyed the RAF. The Germans then halted their strikes against RAF bases and began to bomb London and other civilian targets. They hoped to weaken civilian morale and force Britain to surrender. Air raids known as the Blitz took place nearly every night through the fall and the winter. In May 1941, Germany finally gave up its attempts to defeat Britain from the air.

Hitler's decision to end the attacks on the RAF enabled Britain to rebuild its air force. Britain's survival was immensely important later in the war because the country served as a base for the Allied *liberation* (freeing) of Europe from Nazi rule.

BBC Hulton from Bettmann Archive

UPI/Bettmann Newsphotos

The bombing of London, called the Blitz, began in September 1940 and caused much ruin, *left.* Londoners sought safety in subway tunnels during the nightly raids, *above.* In May 1941, Germany stopped trying to bomb Britain into surrendering.

World War II had become a global conflict by the end of 1941. Fighting spread to Africa, the Balkan Peninsula of southeastern Europe, and the Soviet Union. The Axis and the Allies also battled each other at sea. In December 1941, the United States entered the war.

Fighting in Africa. The Italians opened battlefronts in Africa at about the time of the Battle of Britain. Mussolini expected easy victories over the small British forces in British Somaliland (now northern Somalia) and Egypt. In August 1940, the Italians pushed eastward from Ethiopia and overran the forces in British Somaliland. The following month, Italian forces that were stationed in Libya invaded Egypt.

For two years, the fighting seesawed back and forth across Libya and Egypt. Britain fought to keep the Axis out of Egypt. Axis control of Egypt would have cut Britain off from oil fields in the Middle East and from the Suez Canal, the shortest sea route to Britain's empire in Asia. Britain struck back at the Italians in December 1940, sweeping them out of Egypt and back into Libya. However, an Italian invasion of Greece then drew part of Britain's force from Africa and ended the advance.

Early in 1941, Hitler sent tank units trained in desert warfare to help the Italians in northern Africa. The tank units, known as the Afrika Korps, were led by General Erwin Rommel. Rommel's clever tactics earned him the nickname "The Desert Fox." During the spring, Rommel recaptured the Libyan territory the Italians had lost and drove into Egypt. The British again pushed the Axis forces back into Libya. In May 1942, Rommel broke through British lines and reached El Alamein, only 200 miles (320 kilometers) from the Suez Canal.

However, the Germans did not save Mussolini's empire in eastern Africa. By May 1941, Britain had defeated the Italians in British Somaliland and Ethiopia.

Fighting in the Balkans. Hitler used threats to force Bulgaria, Hungary, and Romania into joining the Axis. Those countries supplied Germany with food, petroleum, and other goods. Yugoslavia's government signed an agreement with the Axis in March 1941. But Yugoslavia's armed forces rebelled and overthrew the government. An enraged Hitler ordered that Yugoslavia be crushed. German troops began to pour into the country on April 6. Yugoslavia surrendered 11 days later. During that time, Hitler had to rescue Mussolini's troops elsewhere on the Balkan Peninsula.

Mussolini had tired of playing Hitler's junior partner, and he badly wanted a victory to boost his standing. In October 1940, Italian forces based in Albania invaded Greece. They expected to defeat the poorly equipped Greek army easily. The Greeks fought fiercely, though they were greatly outnumbered. By December, they had driven the Italians out of Greece and had overrun part of Albania. Britain sent a small force to help Greece. But in April 1941, a much larger German force came to the aid of the Italians. By the end of April, the Axis controlled Greece.

British troops in Greece withdrew to the island of Crete in the Mediterranean Sea. On May 20, 1941, thousands of German paratroopers descended on Crete and seized an airfield. More German troops then landed. The first airborne invasion in history gave Germany an important base in the Mediterranean by the end of May.

The defeats in the Balkans were serious blows to Britain. However, some historians believe that the detours into Yugoslavia and Greece were costly for Hitler because they delayed his invasion of the Soviet Union. Hitler confidently predicted victory over the Soviet Union within eight weeks, and he had failed to prepare for a winter war.

Süddeutscher Verlag   Ullstein Bilderdienst

In the Battle of the Atlantic, German submarines, called *U-boats,* sank ships headed for Britain. Britain's survival depended on shipments across the Atlantic from North America. At the left, a U-boat surfaced to look for targets. At the right, a U-boat officer prepared to launch a torpedo.

The invasion of the Soviet Union. Germany and the Soviet Union proved to be uneasy partners. Hitler viewed the Soviet Union as Germany's chief enemy. He feared Soviet ambitions to expand in eastern Europe. Hitler also wanted control of Soviet wheat fields and oil fields. His 1939 nonaggression pact with Stalin served merely to keep the Soviet Union out of the war while Germany overran western Europe.

Stalin distrusted Hitler, and he sought to obtain more naval bases and to strengthen Soviet borders. In November 1939, the Soviet Union invaded Finland. The Finns surrendered in March 1940 after a fierce fight. In the summer, the Soviet Union seized the countries of Estonia, Latvia, and Lithuania along the Baltic Sea.

Germany's invasion of the Soviet Union, which was code-named Operation Barbarossa, began on June 22, 1941. It took the Soviet Union by surprise. German tanks smashed through Soviet battle lines. During the first few weeks of the campaign, the German armies encircled and killed or captured hundreds of thousands of Soviet troops. As the Germans advanced, the Soviet people destroyed factories, dams, railroads, food supplies, and anything else that might be useful to the enemy. The Germans appeared headed for victory by late July. They then began to make mistakes.

Hitler's generals wanted to press on to Moscow. But Hitler overruled them. Instead, he reinforced the German armies heading north toward Leningrad and south toward the Crimean Peninsula on the Black Sea. While the Germans wasted time transferring forces, Stalin brought in fresh troops. The German advance slowed in September, though the Germans took the city of Kiev in the south. Heavy rains fell in October, and German tanks and artillery bogged down in mud.

By November 1941, the Germans had surrounded Leningrad and had begun to encircle Moscow. They reached the suburbs of Moscow by early December. The temperature then plunged to $-40°$ F. $(-40°$ C). An unusually severe Soviet winter had begun early. German troops lacked warm clothing and suffered from frostbite. Their tanks and weapons broke down in the bitter cold. Winter had saved the Soviet Union.

The Battle of the Atlantic. Britain's survival in World War II depended on shipments of food, war materials, and other supplies across the Atlantic Ocean from North America. Throughout the war, Germany tried to destroy such shipments, while Britain struggled to keep its Atlantic shipping lanes open.

Germany's surface fleet was far too weak to challenge Britain's Royal Navy in battle during World War II. But individual German battleships attacked British cargo vessels. The Royal Navy hunted down and sank such raiders one by one. The biggest operation was against the powerful German battleship *Bismarck.* In May 1941, a fleet of British warships chased, trapped, and finally sank the *Bismarck* about 400 miles (640 kilometers) off the coast of France. Afterward, Germany rarely allowed its large warships to leave harbor.

The greatest threat to British shipping came from German submarines, called *Unterseeboote* or *U-boats.* U-boats prowled the Atlantic, torpedoing any Allied cargo ships they spotted. The conquest of Norway and of France gave Germany excellent bases for its U-boats. To combat the U-boats, Britain began to use a *convoy system.* Under that system, cargo ships sailed in large groups escorted by surface warships. But Britain had few such ships available for escort duty.

From 1940 to 1942, Germany appeared to be winning the Battle of the Atlantic. Each month, U-boats sank thousands of tons of Allied shipping. But the Allies gradually overcame the U-boat danger. They used radar and an underwater detection device called *sonar* to locate German submarines. Long-range aircraft bombed U-boats as they surfaced. Shipyards in North America stepped up their production of warships to accompany convoys. By mid-1943, the Allies were sinking U-boats faster than Germany could replace them. The crisis in the Atlantic had passed.

The United States enters the war

After World War II began in Europe in 1939, President Franklin D. Roosevelt announced the neutrality of the United States. Canada declared war on Germany almost at once. As part of the British Commonwealth of Nations, it entered the war on Sept. 10, 1939, one week after Great Britain did.

The majority of people in the United States thought that their country should stay out of World War II. Yet most Americans hoped for an Allied victory. Roosevelt and other *interventionists* urged all aid "short of war" to nations fighting the Axis. They argued that an Axis victory would endanger democracies everywhere. *Isolationists,* on the other hand, opposed U.S. aid to warring nations. They accused Roosevelt of steering the nation into a war it was not prepared to fight.

All the countries in North and South America eventually declared war on the Axis. But only Brazil, Canada, Mexico, and the United States sent troops. The United States played a key role in the final Allied victory.

The arsenal of democracy. Roosevelt hoped to defeat the Axis powers by equipping the nations fighting them with ships, tanks, aircraft, and other war materials. Roosevelt appealed to the United States to become what he called "the arsenal of democracy."

At the start of World War II, U.S. neutrality laws forbade the sale of arms to warring nations. Congress soon changed the laws to help Britain and France. A new law permitted warring nations to buy arms for cash. But by late 1940, Britain had nearly run out of funds for arms. Roosevelt then proposed the Lend-Lease Act, which would permit him to lend or lease raw materials, equipment, and weapons to any nation fighting the Axis. Congress approved the act in March 1941. In all, 38 nations received a total of about $50 billion in aid under Lend-Lease. More than half the aid went to the British Empire and about a fourth to the Soviet Union.

Japan attacks. Japan, not Germany, finally plunged the United States into World War II. By 1940, Japanese

The attack on Pearl Harbor by Japanese planes on Dec. 7, 1941, drew the United States into World War II. The air raid crippled the U.S. Pacific Fleet. Within hours, four of the eight battleships moored at Pearl Harbor had gone to the bottom, and almost 200 planes had been destroyed.

Bettmann Archive

forces were bogged down in China. The Chinese government, led by Chiang Kai-shek, had fled to central China. But China refused to give up. To force China to surrender, Japan decided to cut off supplies reaching China from Southeast Asia. Japan also wanted the rich resources of Southeast Asia for itself. Japan's military leaders spoke of building an empire, which they called the Greater East Asia Co-Prosperity Sphere.

The United States opposed Japan's expansion in Southeast Asia. In 1940, Japanese troops occupied northern Indochina (today part of Laos and Vietnam). In response, the United States cut off important exports to Japan. Japanese industries relied heavily on petroleum, scrap metal, and other raw materials from the United States. Tension rose after Japan seized the rest of Indochina in 1941. Roosevelt then barred the withdrawal of Japanese funds from American banks.

General Hideki Tojo became premier of Japan in October 1941. Tojo and Japan's other military leaders realized that only the United States Navy had the power to block Japan's expansion in Asia. They decided to cripple the U.S. Pacific Fleet with one forceful blow.

On Dec. 7, 1941, Japanese aircraft attacked without warning the U.S. Pacific Fleet at anchor in Pearl Harbor in Hawaii. The bombing of Pearl Harbor was a great success for Japan at first. It disabled much of the Pacific Fleet and destroyed many aircraft. But in the long run, the attack on Pearl Harbor proved disastrous for Japan. It propelled enraged Americans to arms.

The United States, Canada, and Great Britain declared war on Japan on Dec. 8, 1941. The next day, China declared war on the Axis. Germany and Italy declared war on the United States on December 11. World War II had become a global conflict.

The Allies Attack in Europe and Northern Africa

Allied defeats in Europe ended late in 1941. Soviet forces held off the German advance in eastern Europe in 1942 and won a major victory at Stalingrad in 1943. The Allies invaded northern Africa in 1942 and forced Italy to surrender in 1943. Allied troops swarmed ashore in 1944 in northern France in the largest seaborne invasion in history. Allied attacks from the east and the west forced Germany to surrender in 1945.

The strategy. Churchill, Roosevelt, and Stalin—the leaders of the three major Allied powers—were known during World War II as the Big Three. The Big Three and their military advisers planned the strategy that defeated the Axis. Churchill and Roosevelt conferred frequently on overall strategy. Stalin directed the Soviet war effort but rarely consulted his allies.

Roosevelt relied heavily on his military advisers, the Joint Chiefs of Staff. They consisted of General of the

Army Henry H. Arnold, commanding general of the Army Air Forces; General of the Army George C. Marshall, chief of staff of the Army; Fleet Admiral Ernest J. King, chief of naval operations; and Fleet Admiral William D. Leahy, Roosevelt's chief of staff. Churchill had a similar advisory body.

The main wartime disagreement among the Big Three concerned an Allied invasion of western Europe. Stalin constantly urged Roosevelt and Churchill to open a second fighting front in western Europe and thus draw German troops from the Soviet front. Both Roosevelt and Churchill supported the idea but disagreed on where and when to invade. The Americans wanted to land in northern France as soon as possible. The British argued that an invasion of France before the Allies were fully prepared would be disastrous. Instead, Churchill favored invading Italy first. His view won out.

Roosevelt and Churchill first met in August 1941 aboard ship off the coast of Newfoundland. They issued the Atlantic Charter, a statement of the postwar aims of the United States and Great Britain. After the Japanese attacked Pearl Harbor, Roosevelt and Churchill conferred in Washington, D.C. The two leaders felt that Germany was a nearer and a more dangerous enemy than Japan. They decided to concentrate on defeating Germany first.

In January 1943, Roosevelt and Churchill met in Casablanca, Morocco. They agreed to invade the Mediterranean island of Sicily after driving the Germans and Italians from northern Africa. At the conference, Roosevelt announced that the Allies would accept only *unconditional* (complete) surrender from the Axis powers. Churchill supported him.

Roosevelt and Churchill first met with Stalin in November 1943 in Teheran, Iran. The Big Three discussed plans for a joint British and American invasion of France in the spring of 1944. They did not meet again until Germany neared collapse. In February 1945, Roosevelt, Churchill, and Stalin gathered at Yalta, a Soviet city on the Crimean Peninsula. They agreed that their countries would each occupy a zone of Germany after the war. France was to occupy a fourth zone. At the Yalta Conference, Stalin pledged to permit free elections in Poland and other countries in eastern Europe after the war. He later broke that pledge. Roosevelt died in April 1945, two months after the Yalta Conference.

On the Soviet front. Soviet forces struck back at the Germans outside Moscow in December 1941. The Soviet troops pushed the invaders back about 100 miles

National Archives

The Big Three set overall Allied strategy. They were Soviet leader Joseph Stalin, *left;* U.S. President Franklin D. Roosevelt, *center;* and British Prime Minister Winston Churchill, *right.*

(160 kilometers) from Moscow during the winter. The Germans never again came so close to Moscow as they had been in December 1941. However, the Soviet recovery was short lived.

In the spring of 1942, the Germans again attacked. They overran the Crimean Peninsula and headed eastward toward Soviet oil fields in the Caucasus region. Hitler ordered General Friedrich von Paulus to press on and to take the city of Stalingrad (now Volgograd). A savage five-month battle for Stalingrad began in late August. By September, German and Soviet soldiers were fighting hand to hand in the heart of the city.

Süddeutscher Verlag   Ullstein Bilderdienst

In the Soviet Union, winter weather and the determination of the army and the people slowed the German advance. German equipment broke down and had to be pushed through the snow, *left.* In the ruins of Stalingrad, *right,* Soviet soldiers fought the Germans building by building.

With winter approaching, Paulus asked permission to pull back from Stalingrad. Hitler ordered him to hold on and fight. Soviet troops counterattacked in mid-November. Within a week, they had trapped Paulus' army. The Luftwaffe promised to supply the army by air. But few supplies landed. Each day, thousands of German soldiers froze or starved to death. On Feb. 2, 1943, the last German troops in Stalingrad surrendered.

The Battle of Stalingrad marked a turning point in World War II. It halted Germany's eastward advance. About 300,000 German troops were killed or captured. An enormous number of Soviet soldiers also died.

In northern Africa. The Germans took a beating in northern Africa about the same time as their defeat at Stalingrad. In the summer of 1942, German and Italian forces led by Rommel faced the British at El Alamein, Egypt. General Harold Alexander and Lieutenant General Bernard L. Montgomery commanded the British forces in northern Africa.

Rommel attacked in late August 1942 at Alam el Halfa, south of El Alamein. The British halted the attack, partly because they had secretly learned of Rommel's battle plan. Churchill called for an immediate counterattack. But Montgomery refused to rush into battle before

World War II in Europe and northern Africa: 1943-1945   The Allies attacked the Axis in Europe after defeating it in northern Africa in May 1943. Italy surrendered in September 1943, two months after the invasion of Sicily. In June 1944, the Allies landed in northern France. Attacks from the east and west forced Germany to surrender in May 1945.

WORLD BOOK map

he was fully prepared. On October 23, Montgomery struck at El Alamein. He had broken through the enemy lines by early November. The Axis forces retreated toward Tunisia with the British in hot pursuit. The Battle of El Alamein, like the Battle of Stalingrad, marked a turning point in the war. In both battles, the Allies ended Hitler's string of victories.

Soon after the Battle of El Alamein, the Allies invaded French colonies in northern Africa. Allied troops commanded by Lieutenant General Dwight D. Eisenhower of the United States landed in Algeria and Morocco on Nov. 8, 1942. Vichy French forces in northern Africa fought back for a few days. They then joined the Allied side.

The Allies hoped to advance rapidly into Tunisia and thereby cut off the Axis forces from their home bases in Italy and Sicily. But Axis troops moved faster and seized Tunisia first. There, Rommel prepared for battle. American troops first engaged in combat with the Germans in February 1943 near Kasserine Pass in northern Tunisia. Rommel defeated the inexperienced Americans in hard fighting. But thereafter, the Allies steadily closed in. The last Axis forces in northern Africa surrendered in May. Rommel had already returned to Germany. By clearing the Axis forces from northern Africa, the Allies obtained bases from which to invade southern Europe.

The air war. Before World War II began, some aviation experts claimed that the long-range bomber was the most advanced weapon in the world. They believed that bombers could wipe out cities and industries and so destroy an enemy's desire and ability to go on fighting. Their theory was tested during World War II.

The first great air battle in history opened in 1940 between Germany's Luftwaffe and Britain's Royal Air Force. During the Battle of Britain, Marshal Hermann Goering, commander of the Luftwaffe, failed to defeat Britain from the air. RAF fighter planes, including Spitfires and Hurricanes, helped win the Battle of Britain by shooting down German bombers. By May 1941, the bombing of Britain had largely stopped. But RAF bombers pounded Germany until the end of the war.

Important dates in Europe and northern Africa: 1943-1945

1943

Feb. 2	The last Germans surrendered at Stalingrad.
May 13	Axis forces in northern Africa surrendered.
July 4	Germany opened an assault near the Soviet city of Kursk.
July 10	Allied forces invaded Sicily.
Sept. 3	Italy secretly surrendered to the Allies.
Sept. 9	Allied troops landed at Salerno, Italy.

1944

June 6	Allied troops landed in Normandy in the D-Day invasion of northern France.
July 20	A plot to assassinate Hitler failed.
Dec. 16	The Germans struck back at U.S. troops in the Battle of the Bulge.

1945

April 30	Hitler took his life in Berlin.
May 7	Germany surrendered unconditionally to the Allies in Reims, France, ending World War II in Europe.

Imperial War Museum

The air war against Germany was aimed at destroying its ability to keep on fighting. Bombers like this American B-17 struck factories, railroads, and other industrial targets.

At first, Britain's bombing campaign was costly and ineffective. The RAF relied on *area bombing* in the hope of hitting a target by plastering the area with bombs. It favored nighttime raids, which were safer than daytime raids. But pilots often missed their targets in the dark. In 1942, Britain turned to *saturation bombing* of German cities. About 900 bombers battered Cologne on May 30, 1942, in the first such massive raid.

The United States joined the air war against Germany in 1942. The American B-17 bomber carried a better bombsight than British planes. B-17's were known as Flying Fortresses because of their heavy armor and many guns, and they could take much punishment. For those reasons, the Americans favored *pinpoint bombing* of specific targets during daytime rather than area bombing at night. From 1943 until the end of the war, bombs rained down on Germany around the clock.

In spite of the massive bombardment, German industries continued to increase production, and German morale failed to crack. The air war achieved its goals during the last 10 months of World War II. In that time, nearly three times as many bombs fell on Germany as in all the rest of the war. By the end of the war, Germany's cities lay in ruins. Its factories, refineries, railroads, and canals had nearly ceased to operate. Hundreds of thousands of German civilians had been killed. Millions more were homeless. The bomber had finally become the weapon its supporters had foreseen.

Germany's air defenses rapidly improved during World War II. The Germans used radar to spot incoming bombers, and they used fighter aircraft to shoot them down. In 1944, Germany introduced the first jet fighter, the Messerschmitt Me-262. The fast plane could easily overtake the propeller-driven fighters of the Allies. But Hitler failed to use jet fighters effectively, which kept Germany from gaining an advantage in the air war.

In 1944, Germany used the first guided missiles against Britain. The V-1 and V-2 missiles caused great

AP/Wide World

The campaign in Italy was a slow and bitter struggle against strongly defended German posts. The U.S. infantrymen above belonged to the 92nd Division, a black unit that served in Italy.

damage and took many lives. But the Germans introduced the weapons too late to affect the war's outcome.

The invasion of Italy. The Allies planned to invade Sicily after driving the Axis forces out of northern Africa. Axis planes bombed Allied ships in the Mediterranean Sea from bases in Sicily. The Allies wanted to make the Mediterranean safe for their ships. They also hoped that an invasion of Sicily might knock a war-weary Italy out of the war.

Allied forces under Eisenhower landed along Sicily's south coast on July 10, 1943. For 39 days, they engaged in bitter fighting with German troops over rugged terrain. The last Germans left Sicily on August 17.

Mussolini fell from power on July 25, 1943, after the invasion of Sicily. The Italian government imprisoned Mussolini, but German paratroopers later rescued him. Italy's new premier, Field Marshal Pietro Badoglio, began secret peace talks with the Allies. Badoglio hoped

to prevent Italy from becoming a battleground. Italy surrendered on September 3. However, Field Marshal Albert Kesselring, Germany's commander in the Mediterranean region, was determined to fight the Allies for control of Italy.

Allied forces led by Lieutenant General Mark W. Clark of the United States landed at Salerno, Italy, on Sept. 9, 1943. They fought hard just to stay ashore. Another Allied force had already landed farther south. The Allies slowly struggled up the Italian Peninsula in a series of head-on assaults against well-defended German positions. By early November, the Allies had nearly reached Cassino, about 75 miles (120 kilometers) south of Rome. But they failed to pierce German defenses there. Some of the most brutal fighting of World War II occurred near Cassino.

In January 1944, the Allies landed troops at Anzio, west of Cassino, in an effort to attack the Germans from behind. However, German forces kept the Allies pinned down on the beaches at Anzio for four months. Thousands of Allied soldiers died there.

The Allies finally broke through German defenses in Italy in May 1944. Rome fell on June 4. The Germans held their positions in northern Italy through the fall and winter. But in the spring, the Allies swept toward the Alps. German forces in Italy surrendered on May 2, 1945. Mussolini had been captured and shot by Italian resistance fighters on April 28.

D-Day. Soon after the evacuation of Dunkerque in 1940, Great Britain started to plan a return to France. In 1942, the United States and Britain began to discuss a large-scale invasion across the English Channel. That summer, the Allies raided the French port of Dieppe on the channel. The raiders met strong German defenses and suffered heavy losses. The Dieppe raid convinced the Allies that landing on open beaches had a better chance of success than landing in a port.

Throughout 1943, preparations moved ahead for an

U.S. Coast Guard

Hitting the beach, Allied infantrymen swarmed ashore along the Normandy coast of northern France on D-Day—June 6, 1944. It was the largest seaborne invasion in history. Hitler had boasted that German defenses along the coast could resist any attack. But he was wrong.

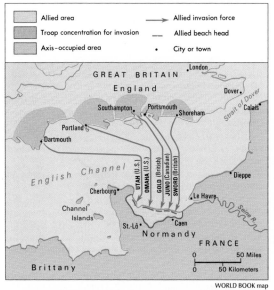

WORLD BOOK map

The Normandy invasion on June 6, 1944, brought Allied forces ashore on five beaches, shown with their code names. Within a week, the Allies held the area outlined in blue.

U.S. Army

Talking to his men, General Dwight D. Eisenhower, commander of the Normandy invasion, wished paratroopers luck before they dropped behind German lines in France on D-Day.

invasion of northern France the following year. The invasion plan received the code name Operation Overlord. The Allies assembled huge amounts of equipment and great numbers of troops for Overlord in southern England. General Dwight D. Eisenhower was selected to command the invasion.

The Germans expected an Allied invasion along the north coast of France in 1944. But they were unsure where. A chain of fortifications, which the Germans called the Atlantic Wall, ran along the coast. Hitler placed Rommel in charge of strengthening German defenses along the English Channel. Rommel brought in artillery, mined the water and the beaches, and strung up barbed wire. The Germans concentrated their troops near Calais, at the narrowest part of the English Channel. But the Allies planned to land farther west, in a region of northern France called Normandy.

Eisenhower chose Monday, June 5, 1944, as D-Day—the date of the Normandy invasion. Rough seas forced him to postpone D-Day until June 6. During the night, about 2,700 ships carrying landing craft and 176,000 soldiers crossed the channel. Minesweepers had gone ahead to clear the water. Paratroopers dropped behind German lines to capture bridges and railroad tracks. At dawn, battleships opened fire on the beaches. At 6:30 A.M., troops from the United States, Britain, Canada, and France stormed ashore on a 60-mile (100-kilometer) front in the largest seaborne invasion in history.

D-Day took the Germans by surprise. But they fought back fiercely. At one landing site, code-named Omaha Beach, U.S. troops came under heavy fire and barely managed to stay ashore. Nevertheless, all five Allied landing beaches were secure by the end of D-Day. The Allies soon had an artificial harbor in place for unloading more troops and supplies. A pipeline carried fuel

across the channel. By the end of June 1944, about a million Allied troops had reached France.

The Allied forces advanced slowly at first. The Americans struggled westward to capture the badly needed port of Cherbourg. British and Canadian soldiers fought their way to Caen. The battle for Cherbourg ended on June 27. Caen, which the British hoped to capture on D-Day, fell on July 18. Near the end of July, the Allies finally broke through German lines into open country.

The drive to the Rhine. On July 25, 1944, Allied bombers blasted a gap in the German front near St.-Lô, about 50 miles (80 kilometers) southeast of Cherbourg. The U.S. Third Army under Lieutenant General George S. Patton plowed through the hole. The battlefield had opened up. During August, the Allies cleared the Germans out of most of northwestern France. Allied bombers hounded the retreating Germans.

Patton's army rolled eastward toward Paris. On Aug. 19, 1944, Parisians rose up against the occupying German forces. Hitler ordered the city destroyed. But his generals delayed carrying out the order. American and Free French forces liberated Paris on August 25.

In mid-August 1944, Allied forces landed in southern France. They moved rapidly up the Rhône River Valley. Meanwhile, Patton raced eastward toward the German border and the Rhine River. In late August, his tanks ran out of fuel. To the north, British forces led by Field Marshal Bernard L. Montgomery swept into Belgium and captured Antwerp on September 4. The Allies planned a daring airborne operation to carry them across the Rhine. On September 17, about 20,000 paratroopers dropped behind German lines to seize bridges in the Netherlands. But bad weather and other problems hampered the operation. It became clear that victory over Germany would have to wait until 1945.

Robert Capa, Magnum

Wild with joy, Parisians welcomed Allied troops as they rode down the Champs Élysées on Aug. 26, 1944. Paris had been freed the day before, after over four years of Nazi occupation.

Germany's generals knew they were beaten. But Hitler pulled his failing resources together for another assault. On Dec. 16, 1944, German troops surprised and overwhelmed the Americans in the Ardennes Forest in Belgium and Luxembourg. However, the Germans lacked the troops and fuel to turn their thrust into a breakthrough. Within two weeks, the Americans stopped the German advance near the Meuse River in Belgium. The Ardennes offensive is also known as the Battle of the Bulge because of the bulging shape of the battleground on a map.

The Soviet advance. The Soviet victory in the Battle of Stalingrad ended Germany's progress in eastern Europe. After January 1943, Soviet soldiers slowly pushed the Germans back. Soviet forces had improved by 1943, and they greatly outnumbered the opposing German armies. Supplies poured into the Soviet Union from Britain and the United States, and Soviet factories had geared up for wartime production.

Nevertheless, the Germans returned to the offensive in July 1943 near the Soviet city of Kursk. They massed about 3,000 tanks for the assault. Soviet forces lay waiting for them. In one of the greatest tank battles in history, Soviet mines, tanks, antitank guns, and aircraft blew apart many German tanks. Hitler finally called off the attack to save his remaining tanks.

Soviet troops moved slowly forward during the summer and fall of 1943. In January 1944, a Soviet offensive ended the siege of Leningrad, which had begun in September 1941. About a million Leningraders died during the siege, mostly from lack of food and heat. But the city never surrendered.

In June 1944, soon after the Normandy invasion, Stalin's armies attacked along a 450-mile (720-kilometer) front. By late July, Soviet troops had reached the outskirts of Warsaw. Poland's Home Army rose up against German forces in Warsaw on August 1. But Soviet troops refused to come to Poland's aid. Stalin permitted the Germans to destroy the Home Army, which might have resisted his plans to set up a Communist govern-

ment in Poland after the war. The Home Army surrendered after two months. More than 200,000 Poles died during the Warsaw uprising. Soviet forces entered Warsaw in January 1945.

Meanwhile, Soviet troops drove into Romania and Bulgaria. The Germans pulled out of Greece and Yugoslavia in the fall of 1944 but held out in Budapest, the capital of Hungary, until February 1945. Vienna, Austria's capital, fell to Soviet soldiers in April. By then, Soviet troops occupied nearly all of eastern Europe.

Victory in Europe. The Allies began their final assault on Germany in early 1945. Soviet soldiers reached the Oder River, about 40 miles (65 kilometers) east of Berlin, in January. Allied forces in the west occupied positions along the Rhine by early March.

British and Canadian forces cleared the Germans out of the Netherlands and swept into northern Germany. American and French forces raced toward the Elbe River in central Germany. Hitler ordered his soldiers to fight to the death. But large numbers of German soldiers surrendered each day.

As they advanced, the Allies discovered horrifying evidence of Nazi brutality. Hitler had ordered the imprisonment and murder of millions of Jews and members of other minority groups in concentration camps. The starving survivors of the death camps gave proof of the terrible suffering of those who had already died.

The capture of Berlin, then Germany's capital, was left to Soviet forces. By April 25, 1945, Soviet troops had surrounded the city. From a *bunker* (shelter) deep underground, Hitler ordered German soldiers to fight on. On April 30, however, Hitler committed suicide. He remained convinced that his cause had been right but that the German people had proven unworthy of his rule.

Grand Admiral Karl Doenitz briefly succeeded Hitler as the leader of Germany. Doenitz arranged for Germany's surrender. On May 7, 1945, Colonel General Alfred Jodl, chief of staff of the German armed forces, signed a statement of unconditional surrender at Eisenhower's headquarters in Reims, France. World War II had ended in Europe. The Allies declared May 8 as V-E Day, or Victory in Europe Day.

Imperial War Museum

Survivors of a Nazi death camp—some too weak to stand—provided proof of Nazi savagery. The Nazis imprisoned and murdered millions of Jews, Slavs, and members of other groups.

The Spitfire was an outstanding British fighter plane of World War II. Spitfires were noted for their speed, ability to make tight turns, and rapid climbing rate. Thus, they could outmaneuver most German fighters. In 1940, Spitfires helped defeat Germany in the Battle of Britain. A Spitfire IA is shown at the left.

The B-17 was a widely used U.S. bomber of World War II. B-17's became famous for daytime raids over Germany. They were called Flying Fortresses because of their heavy armor and many guns. The B-17G, *right,* carried 13 machine guns.

The DUKW, nicknamed "Duck," was an American six-wheeled truck that traveled over water and land. Ducks carried men and supplies from transport ships to enemy shores in *amphibious* (seaborne) landings. They were first used in the invasion of Sicily in July 1943 and later in amphibious operations in the Pacific.

The tank played a key role in combat in World War II. Germany, in particular, made use of the tank's mobility and firepower. In early victories, Germany massed its tanks and smashed through enemy battle lines in surprise attacks. The German Tiger, *right,* was a heavy tank that could outgun almost all Allied tanks.

The aircraft carrier was a floating airfield that became the backbone of the U.S. Navy during World War II. Carrier-based planes took part in many battles in the Pacific and helped defeat Japan. The irregular pattern on the U.S.S. *Wasp, below,* made it hard for enemy submarines to determine the ship's course.

WORLD BOOK illustrations by Tony Gibbons

The attack on Pearl Harbor on Dec. 7, 1941, left the U.S. Pacific Fleet powerless to halt Japan's expansion. During the next six months, Japanese forces swept across Southeast Asia and the western Pacific Ocean. Japan's empire reached its greatest size in August 1942. It stretched northeast to the Aleutian Islands of Alaska, west to Burma, and south to the Netherlands Indies (now Indonesia). The Allies halted Japan's expansion in the summer of 1942. They nibbled away at its empire until Japan agreed to surrender in August 1945.

Early Japanese victories. On Dec. 8, 1941, within hours of the attack on Pearl Harbor, Japanese bombers struck the British colony of Hong Kong on the south coast of China and two U.S. islands in the Pacific Ocean—Guam and Wake. The Japanese invaded Thailand the same day. Thailand surrendered within hours and joined the Axis. Japanese troops took Hong Kong, Guam, and Wake Island by Christmas.

From Thailand, Japanese forces soon advanced into Malaya (now part of Malaysia) and Burma. Great Britain then ruled that region. The British wrongly believed that soldiers could not penetrate the thick jungles of the Malay Peninsula. They expected an assault by sea instead. But Japanese troops streamed through the jungles and rapidly overran the peninsula.

By late January 1942, the Japanese had pushed British forces back to Singapore, a fortified island off the tip of the Malay Peninsula. The Japanese stormed the island on February 8, and Singapore surrendered a week later. Japan captured about 85,000 soldiers, making the fall of Singapore Britain's worst military defeat ever.

Japan's next target was the petroleum-rich Netherlands Indies, south of Malaya. Allied warships protected those islands. Japan's navy mauled the ships in February 1942 in the Battle of the Java Sea. The Netherlands Indies fell in early March.

Meanwhile, Japanese forces had advanced into southern Burma. China sent troops into Burma to help Britain hold onto the Burma Road. Weapons, food, and other goods traveled over that supply route from India to China. In April 1942, Japan seized and shut down the Burma Road. The Japanese had driven Allied forces from most of Burma by mid-May.

Only the conquest of the Philippines took longer than Japan expected. Japan had begun landing troops in the Philippines on Dec. 10, 1941. American and Philippine forces commanded by U.S. General Douglas MacArthur defended the islands. In late December, MacArthur's forces abandoned Manila, the capital of the Philippines, and withdrew to nearby Bataan Peninsula. Although suffering from malnutrition and disease, they beat back Japanese attacks for just over three months.

President Roosevelt ordered MacArthur to Australia, and he left the Philippines in March 1942. He promised the Filipinos, "I shall return." On April 9, about 75,000 exhausted troops on Bataan surrendered to the Japanese. Most of them were forced to march about 65 miles (105 kilometers) to prison camps. Many prisoners died of disease and mistreatment during what became known as the Bataan Death March. Some soldiers held out on Corregidor Island, near Bataan, until May 6. By then, the Japanese were victorious everywhere.

Japan's string of quick victories astonished even the Japanese. It terrified the Allies. The fall of the Netherlands Indies left Australia unprotected. The capture of Burma brought the Japanese to India's border. Australia and India feared invasion. Japanese planes bombed Darwin on Australia's north coast in February 1942.

The tide turns. Three events in 1942 helped turn the tide against Japan. They were (1) the Doolittle raid, (2) the Battle of the Coral Sea, and (3) the Battle of Midway.

The Doolittle raid. To show that Japan could be beaten, the United States staged a daring bombing raid on the Japanese homeland. On April 18, 1942, Lieutenant Colonel James H. Doolittle led 16 B-25 bombers in a surprise attack on Tokyo and other Japanese cities. The bombers took off from the deck of the *Hornet,* an aircraft carrier more than 600 miles (960 kilometers) east of Japan. The raid did very little damage. But it alarmed Japan's leaders, who had believed that their homeland was safe from Allied bombs. To prevent future raids, the Japanese determined to capture more islands to the south and the east and so extend the country's defenses. They soon found themselves in trouble.

UPI/Bettmann Newsphotos
American soldiers in the Philippines had to march to prison camps after they were captured by the Japanese in April 1942. Many died during what is known as the Bataan Death March.

Important dates in the Pacific: 1941-1942

1941	
Dec. 7	Japan bombed U.S. military bases at Pearl Harbor in Hawaii.
Dec. 8	The United States, Great Britain, and Canada declared war on Japan.
1942	
Feb. 15	Singapore fell to the Japanese.
Feb. 26-28	Japan defeated an Allied naval force in the Battle of the Java Sea.
April 9	U.S. and Philippine troops on Bataan Peninsula surrendered.
April 18	U.S. bombers hit Tokyo in the Doolittle raid.
May 4-8	The Allies checked a Japanese assault in the Battle of the Coral Sea.
June 4-6	The Allies defeated Japan in the Battle of Midway.
Aug. 7	U.S. marines landed on Guadalcanal.

The Battle of the Coral Sea. In May 1942, a Japanese invasion force sailed toward Australia's base at Port Moresby on the south coast of the island of New Guinea. Port Moresby lay at Australia's doorstep. American warships met the Japanese force in the Coral Sea, northeast of Australia. The Battle of the Coral Sea, fought from May 4 to 8, was unlike all earlier naval battles. It was the first naval battle in which opposing ships never sighted one another. Planes based on aircraft carriers did all the fighting. Neither side won a clear victory. But the battle halted the assault on Port Moresby and temporarily checked the threat to Australia.

The Battle of Midway. Japan next sent a large fleet to capture Midway Island at the westernmost tip of the Hawaiian chain. The United States had cracked Japan's naval code and thus learned about the coming invasion. Admiral Chester W. Nimitz, commander of the U.S. Pacific Fleet, gathered the ships that had survived the raid on Pearl Harbor and the Battle of the Coral Sea. He prepared to ambush the Japanese.

The Battle of Midway opened on June 4, 1942, with a Japanese bombing raid on Midway. Outdated U.S. bombers flew in low and launched torpedoes against Japanese warships. But Japanese guns downed most of the slow-moving planes. American dive bombers swooped in next. They pounded enemy aircraft carriers while their planes refueled on deck. During the three-day battle, the Japanese lost 4 aircraft carriers and more than 200 planes and skilled pilots. Japan sank 1 U.S. aircraft carrier and shot down about 150 U.S. planes.

The Battle of Midway was the first clear Allied victory over Japan in World War II. Aircraft carriers had become the most important weapon in the war in the Pacific. Japan's naval power was crippled by the loss of 4 of its 9 aircraft carriers.

Although Japan failed to capture Midway, it seized two islands at the tip of Alaska's Aleutian chain on June 7, 1942. The Americans drove the Japanese out of the Aleutians in the spring and summer of 1943.

The South Pacific. After the Battle of Midway, the Allies were determined to stop Japanese expansion in the South Pacific. In the battles that followed, American

World War II in Asia and the Pacific: 1941-1942

After Japan attacked Pearl Harbor on Dec. 7, 1941, its forces rapidly advanced across Southeast Asia and the Western Pacific Ocean. This map shows key battles in that campaign and the greatest extent of Japan's empire. The Allies halted Japan's expansion in the summer of 1942.

WORLD BOOK map

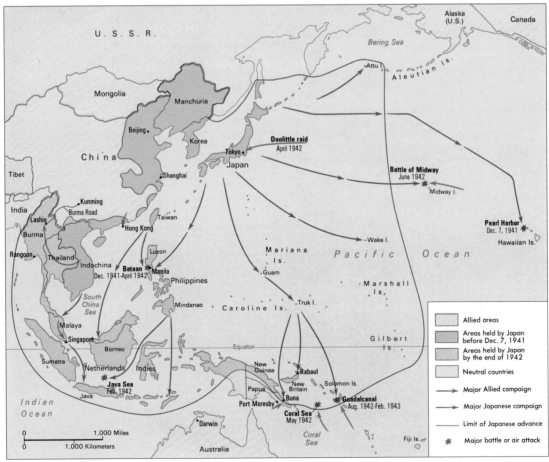

soldiers and marines fought many jungle campaigns on Pacific islands. The jungle itself was a terrifying enemy. Heavy rains drenched the troops and turned the jungle into a foul-smelling swamp. The men had to hack their way through tangled, slimy vegetation and wade through knee-deep mud. The Japanese hid everywhere, waiting to shoot unsuspecting servicemen. Scorpions and snakes were a constant menace. Malaria and other tropical diseases took a heavy toll.

The Americans also encountered Japan's strict military code in the South Pacific. The code required Japanese soldiers to fight to the death. Japanese soldiers believed that surrender meant disgrace, and the Allies rarely captured them alive. When cornered, the Japanese sometimes charged at Allied troops in nighttime suicide attacks. Rather than admit defeat, Japan's military leaders took their lives by stabbing themselves in the abdomen according to the tradition of *hara-kiri.*

The Allies developed two major campaigns against Japan in the South Pacific. One force under MacArthur checked the Japanese on New Guinea. Another force under Nimitz battled the Japanese in the Solomon Islands northeast of Australia. MacArthur and Nimitz aimed at taking the port of Rabaul on New Britain. Rabaul was Japan's chief base in the South Pacific. Japanese aircraft and warships attacked Allied ships from Rabaul, and Japan supplied other islands in the South Pacific from that base.

New Guinea. In the summer of 1942, Japanese troops began an overland drive across New Guinea's rugged, jungle-covered mountains to the Australian base of Port Moresby on the south coast. An Allied force made up chiefly of Australians quickly counterattacked. By November, the Japanese had been pushed back across the mountains. MacArthur then attacked Japanese positions along the north coast in a series of brilliant operations that combined air, sea, and land forces. Brutal fighting continued on New Guinea until mid-1944.

Guadalcanal. On Aug. 7, 1942, U.S. marines invaded the island of Guadalcanal in the first stage of a campaign in the Solomon Islands. The Japanese were building an air base on Guadalcanal from which to attack Allied

ships. The invasion took the Japanese by surprise. But they fought back, and a fierce battle developed.

The six-month battle for Guadalcanal was one of the most vicious campaigns of World War II. Each side depended on its navy to land supplies and troop reinforcements. In a series of naval battles, the Allies gained control of the waters surrounding Guadalcanal. They then cut off Japanese shipments. Until that time, Allied supplies had been short, and the marines had depended on rice captured from the enemy. By February 1943, the starving Japanese had evacuated Guadalcanal.

After taking Guadalcanal, American forces led by Admiral William F. Halsey worked their way up the Solomon Islands. In November 1943, the Americans reached Bougainville at the top of the island chain. They defeated the Japanese there in March 1944.

Rabaul. In the summer of 1943, Allied military leaders canceled the invasion of Rabaul. Instead, American bombers pounded the Japanese base, and aircraft and submarines sank shipments headed for Rabaul. About 100,000 Japanese defenders waited there for an attack that never came. The Allies spared many lives by isolating Rabaul rather than capturing it.

Island hopping in the Central Pacific. From late 1943 until the fall of 1944, the Allies hopped from island to island across the Central Pacific toward the Philippines. During the island-hopping campaign, the Allies became expert at *amphibious* (seaborne) invasions. Each island they captured provided a base from which to strike the next target. But rather than capture every island, the Allies by-passed Japanese strongholds and invaded islands that were weakly held. That strategy, known as *leapfrogging,* saved time and lives. Leapfrogging carried the Allies across the Gilbert, Marshall, Caroline, and Mariana islands in the Central Pacific.

Admiral Nimitz selected the Gilbert Islands as the first major objective in the island-hopping campaign. American marines invaded Tarawa in the Gilberts in November 1943. The attackers met heavy fire from Japanese troops in concrete bunkers. But they inched forward and captured the tiny island after four days of savage fighting. About 4,500 Japanese soldiers died defending

Department of Defense

Hugging the ground to avoid enemy gunfire, U.S. marines crawled over the sandy shores of Tarawa in the Gilbert Islands in November 1943. Lessons learned in the costly battle for Tarawa helped the Allies improve their seaborne landing techniques.

the island. Only 17 remained alive. More than 3,000 marines were killed or wounded in the assault. The Allies improved their amphibious operations because of lessons they had learned at Tarawa. As a result, fewer men died in later landings.

In February 1944, U.S. marines and infantrymen leaped north to the Marshall Islands. They captured Kwajalein and Enewetak in relatively smooth operations. Allied military leaders meanwhile had decided to bypass Truk, a key Japanese naval base in the Caroline Islands west of the Marshalls. They bombed Truk instead and made it unusable as a base.

The Americans made their next jump to the Mariana Islands, about 1,000 miles (1,600 kilometers) northwest of Enewetak. Bitter fighting for the Marianas began in June 1944. In the Battle of the Philippine Sea on June 19 and 20, Japan's navy once again attempted to destroy the U.S. Pacific Fleet. During the battle, which was fought near the island of Guam, the Allies massacred Japan's navy and destroyed its airpower. Japan lost 3 aircraft carriers and about 480 airplanes, or more than three-fourths of the planes it sent into battle. The loss of so many trained pilots was also a serious blow to Japan.

By August 1944, American forces occupied Guam, Saipan, and Tinian—the three largest islands in the Marianas. The occupation of the Marianas brought Nimitz' forces within bombing distance of Japan. Tojo resigned as Japan's prime minister in July 1944 after the loss of Saipan. In November, American B-29 bombers began using bases in the Marianas to raid Japan.

A final hop before the invasion of the Philippines took U.S. forces to the Palau Islands in September 1944. The islands lie between the Marianas and the Philippines. The attackers met stiff resistance on Peleliu, the chief Japanese base in the Palaus. About 25 per cent of the Americans were killed or injured in a month-long fight.

The liberation of the Philippines. The campaigns in New Guinea and the Central Pacific brought the Allies within striking distance of the Philippine Islands. MacArthur and Nimitz combined their forces to liberate the Philippines. Allied leaders decided to invade the island of Leyte in the central Philippines in the fall of 1944.

The Allies expected the Japanese to fight hard to hold the Philippines. They therefore assembled the largest landing force ever used in the Pacific campaigns. About 750 ships participated in the invasion of Leyte, which began on Oct. 20, 1944. It had taken MacArthur more than $2\frac{1}{2}$ years and many brutal battles to keep his pledge to return to the Philippines.

While Allied troops poured ashore on Leyte, Japan's navy tried yet again to crush the Pacific Fleet. The Battle for Leyte Gulf, which was fought from Oct. 23 through 26, 1944, was the the greatest naval battle in history in total tonnage. In all, 282 ships took part. The battle ended in a major victory for the United States. Japan's navy was so badly damaged that it was no longer a serious threat for the rest of the war.

During the Battle for Leyte Gulf, the Japanese unleashed a terrifying new weapon—the *kamikaze* (suicide pilot). Kamikazes crashed planes filled with explosives onto Allied warships and died as a result. Many kamikazes were shot down before they crashed. But others

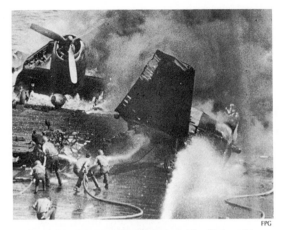

FPG

An attack by a Japanese *kamikaze* (suicide pilot) set this aircraft carrier aflame. In a last desperate effort to win the war, kamikazes crashed their planes onto Allied ships.

caused great damage. The kamikaze became one of Japan's major weapons during the rest of the war.

The fight for Leyte continued until the end of 1944. On Jan. 9, 1945, the Allies landed on the island of Luzon and began to work their way toward Manila. The city fell in early March. The remaining Japanese troops on Luzon pulled back to the mountains and went on fighting until the war ended.

About 350,000 Japanese soldiers died during the campaign in the Philippines. American casualties numbered nearly 14,000 dead and about 48,000 wounded or missing. Japan was clearly doomed to defeat after losing the Philippines. But it did not intend to surrender.

The China-Burma-India theater. While fighting raged in the Pacific, the Allies also battled the Japanese on the Asian mainland. The chief *theater of operations* (area of military activity) involved China, Burma, and India. By mid-1942, Japan held much of eastern and southern China and had conquered nearly all Burma. The Japanese had closed the Burma Road, the overland supply route from India to China. China lacked equipment and trained troops and barely managed to go on fighting. But the Western Allies wanted to keep China in the war because the Chinese tied down hundreds of thousands of Japanese troops. For three years, the Allies flew war supplies over the world's tallest mountain system, the Himalaya, from India to China. The route was known as "the Hump."

China. By 1942, five years after Japan had invaded China, the opposing armies were near exhaustion. Japanese troops staged attacks especially to capture China's food supplies for themselves and to starve the country into surrender. As a result, millions of Chinese people died from lack of food during the war.

A struggle between China's Nationalist government, headed by Chiang Kai-shek, and Chinese Communists further weakened the country's war effort. At first, the Nationalist forces and the Communists had joined in fighting the Japanese invaders. But their cooperation gradually broke down as they prepared to fight each other after the war.

World War II in Asia and the Pacific: 1943-1945

From 1943 to August 1945, the Allies worked their way across the Pacific toward Japan. Allied forces on the Asian mainland recaptured Burma. This map shows the Allied route and gives the dates of key battles in the Pacific campaign. Japan still held much territory when it surrendered.

WORLD BOOK map

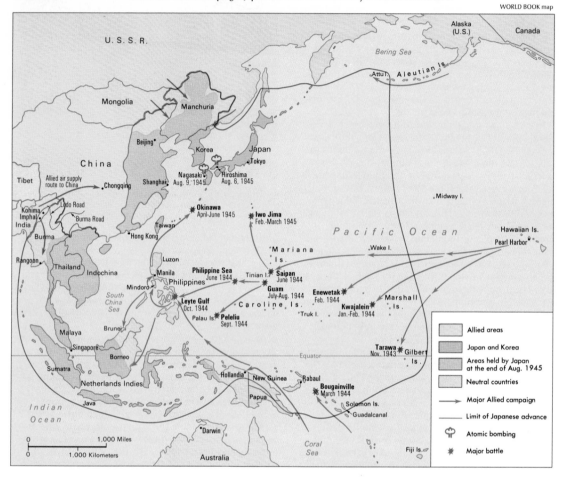

The United States sent military advisers as well as equipment to China. Colonel Claire L. Chennault, for example, trained pilots and established an air force in China. By the end of 1943, his pilots controlled the skies over China. But they could not help exhausted Chinese troops on the ground. Major General Joseph W. Stilwell served as Chiang's chief of staff and trained the Chinese army. Stilwell also commanded the U.S. forces in China and Burma.

Burma. The Allied campaign in Burma was closely linked to the fighting in China. From 1943 until early 1945, the Allies fought to recapture Burma from the Japanese and reopen a land route to China. But rugged jungle, heavy rains, and a shortage of troops and supplies hampered the Allies in Burma.

Admiral Louis Mountbatten of Great Britain became supreme Allied commander in Southeast Asia in August 1943. He directed several successful offensives in Burma in late 1943 and in 1944. By the end of 1944, Allied forces had battled their way through the jungles of northern Burma. They opened a supply route across northern

Burma to China in January 1945. Rangoon, Burma's capital, fell to the Allies in May. The Allies finally regained Burma after a long, horrible campaign.

India. India became an important supply base and training center for Allied forces during World War II. Japan's conquest of Burma in 1942 placed India in great danger. In early 1944, Japanese troops invaded India and encircled the towns of Imphal and Kohima just inside India's border. The British supplied the towns by air. The attackers finally began to withdraw from India late in June. Thousands of Japanese soldiers died of disease and starvation during the retreat.

Closing in on Japan. Superiority at sea and in the air enabled the Allies to close in on Japan in early 1945. By then, Japan had lost much of its empire, most of its aircraft and cargo ships, and nearly all its warships. Hundreds of thousands of Japanese soldiers remained stranded on Pacific islands by-passed by the Allies. American B-29 bombers were pounding Japan's industries, and American submarines were sinking vital supplies headed for Japan.

Important dates in the Pacific: 1943-1945

1943

Nov. 20	U.S. forces invaded Tarawa.

1944

June 19-20	A U.S. naval force defeated the Japanese in the Battle of the Philippine Sea.
July 18	Japan's Prime Minister Tojo resigned.
Oct. 20	The Allies began landing in the Philippines.
Oct. 23-26	The Allies defeated Japan's navy in the Battle of Leyte Gulf in the Philippines.

1945

March 16	U.S. marines captured Iwo Jima.
June 21	Allied forces captured Okinawa.
Aug. 6	An atomic bomb was dropped on Hiroshima.
Aug. 8	The Soviet Union declared war on Japan.
Aug. 9	An atomic bomb was dropped on Nagasaki.
Aug. 14	Japan agreed to surrender unconditionally.
Sept. 2	Japan signed surrender terms aboard the battleship U.S.S. *Missouri* in Tokyo Bay.

U.S. Air Force

Allied flights over the Himalaya, the world's tallest mountains, supplied China with war materials from 1942 to 1945. The dangerous air route from India to China was called "the Hump."

In January 1945, Major General Curtis E. LeMay took command of the air war against Japan. LeMay ordered more frequent and more daring raids. American bombers increased their accuracy by flying in low during nighttime raids. They began to drop *incendiary* (fire-producing) bombs that set Japanese cities aflame. A massive incendiary raid in March 1945 destroyed the heart of Tokyo. By the end of the month, about 3 million people in Tokyo were homeless.

Japan's military leaders went on fighting, though they faced certain defeat. The Allies decided they needed more bases to step up the bombing campaign against Japan. They chose the Japanese islands of Iwo Jima and Okinawa.

Iwo Jima lies about 750 miles (1,210 kilometers) south of Japan. About 21,000 Japanese troops were stationed there. They prepared to defend the tiny island from fortified caves and underground tunnels. Allied aircraft began bombarding Iwo Jima seven months before the invasion. American marines landed on Feb. 19, 1945, and made slow progress. The Japanese hung on desperately

until March 16. About 25,000 marines—about 30 per cent of the landing force—were killed or wounded in the campaign for Iwo Jima.

Okinawa, the next stop on the Allied route toward Japan, lies about 350 miles (565 kilometers) southwest of Japan. Allied troops began to pour ashore on Okinawa on April 1, 1945. Japan sent kamikazes to attack the landing force. By the time the battle ended on June 21, kamikazes had sunk at least 30 ships and damaged more than 350 others. The capture of Okinawa cost the Allies about 50,000 casualties. About 110,000 Japanese died, including many civilians who chose to commit suicide rather than be conquered.

By the summer of 1945, some members of Japan's government favored surrender. But others insisted that Japan fight on. The Allies planned to invade Japan in November 1945. American military planners feared that the invasion might cost as many as 1 million U.S. lives. Some Allied leaders believed that Soviet help was needed to

AP/Wide World

Supplies poured ashore on Iwo Jima after U.S. marines secured beaches on the Japanese island in February 1945. The battle for Iwo Jima was one of the bloodiest campaigns of World War II.

An atomic blast demolished the center of Hiroshima, Japan, *above,* on Aug. 6, 1945. Japan agreed to surrender after a second atomic bomb was dropped on Nagasaki on August 9.

Japan's surrender on Sept. 2, 1945, ended World War II. General of the Army Douglas MacArthur, *far left,* signed for the Allies, and General Yoshijiro Umezu, *right,* for the Japanese army.

defeat Japan, and they had encouraged Stalin to invade Manchuria. However, the Allies found another way to end the war.

The atomic bomb. In 1939, the German-born scientist Albert Einstein had informed President Roosevelt about the possibility of creating a superbomb. It would produce an extremely powerful explosion by splitting the atom. Einstein and other scientists feared that Germany might develop such a bomb first. In 1942, the United States set up the Manhattan Project, a top-secret program to develop an atomic bomb. The first test explosion of an atomic bomb occurred in the New Mexico desert in July 1945.

Roosevelt died in April 1945, and Vice President Harry S. Truman became President of the United States. Truman met with Churchill and Stalin in Potsdam, Germany, in July, shortly after Germany's defeat. At the Potsdam Conference, Truman learned of the successful test explosion of the atomic bomb and informed the other leaders of it. The United States, Britain, and China then issued a statement threatening to destroy Japan unless it surrendered unconditionally. In spite of the warning, Japan went on fighting.

On Aug. 6, 1945, an American B-29 bomber called the *Enola Gay* dropped the first atomic bomb used in warfare on the Japanese city of Hiroshima. The explosion killed from 70,000 to 100,000 people, it is estimated, and destroyed about 5 square miles (13 square kilometers). After Japanese leaders failed to respond to the bombing, the United States dropped a larger bomb on Nagasaki on August 9. It killed about 40,000 people. Later, thousands more died of injuries and radiation from the two bombings. Meanwhile, on August 8, the Soviet Union declared war on Japan and invaded Manchuria. Soviet troops raced south toward Korea.

Victory in the Pacific. Although Japan's emperors had traditionally stayed out of politics, Hirohito urged the government to surrender. On August 14, Japan agreed to end the war. Some of the country's military leaders committed suicide.

On Sept. 2, 1945, representatives of Japan signed the official statement of surrender aboard the U.S. battleship *Missouri,* which lay at anchor in Tokyo Bay. Representatives of all the Allied nations were present. Truman declared September 2 as V-J Day, or Victory over Japan Day. World War II had ended.

The secret war

Throughout World War II, a secret war was fought between the Allies and the Axis to obtain information about each other's activities and to weaken each other's war effort. Codebreakers tried to decipher secret communications, and spies worked behind enemy lines to gather information. Saboteurs tried to disrupt activities on the home front. Many people in Axis-held territories joined undercover *resistance groups* that opposed the occupying forces. All the warring nations used propaganda to influence public opinion.

The Ultra secret. Soon after the outbreak of World War II, Britain obtained, with the help of Polish spies, one of the machines Germany used to code secret messages. In an outstanding effort, British mathematicians

and codebreakers solved the machine's electronic coding procedures. Britain's ability to read many of Germany's wartime communications was known as the Ultra secret. Ultra helped the Allies defeat Germany.

The Ultra secret played an important role in battle. During the 1940 Battle of Britain, for example, Ultra supplied advance warning of where and when the Luftwaffe planned to attack. Ultra also helped Montgomery defeat the Germans in Egypt in 1942 by providing him with Rommel's battle plan. The British carefully guarded the Ultra secret. They were extremely cautious about using their knowledge so that Germany would not change its coding procedures. The Germans never discovered that Britain had broken their code.

Spies and saboteurs were specially trained by the warring nations. Spies reported on troop movements, defense build-ups, and other developments behind enemy lines. Spies of Allied nations also supplied resistance groups with weapons and explosives. Saboteurs hampered the enemy's war effort in any way they could. For example, they blew up factories and bridges and organized slowdowns in war plants.

Germany had spies in many countries. But its efforts at spying were less successful in general than those of the Allies. The U.S. government set up a wartime agency called the Office of Strategic Services (OSS) to engage in spying and sabotage. The OSS worked closely with a similar British agency, the Special Operations Executive. The Soviet Union operated networks of spies in Allied nations as well as in Germany and Japan.

Resistance groups sprang up in every Axis-occupied country. Resistance began with individual acts of defiance against the occupiers. Gradually, like-minded people banded together and worked in secret to overthrow the invaders. The activities of resistance groups expanded as the war continued. Their work included publishing and distributing illegal newspapers, rescuing Allied aircrews shot down behind enemy lines, gathering information about the enemy, and sabotage.

In such countries as France, Yugoslavia, and Burma, resistance groups engaged in *guerrilla warfare.* They organized bands of fighters who staged raids, ambushes, and other small attacks against the occupation forces.

All resistance movements suffered many setbacks. But they also achieved outstanding successes. For example, the French resistance interfered with German efforts to turn back the Allied invasion of Normandy in 1944. Norwegian resistance workers destroyed a shipment of *heavy water* headed for Germany. Heavy water is a substance needed in the production of an atomic bomb. Yugoslavia had the most effective resistance movement of all—the Partisans. With Allied help, the Partisans drove the Germans out of Yugoslavia in 1944.

Even in Germany itself, a small underground movement opposed the Nazis. In July 1944, a group of German army officers planted a bomb intended to kill Hitler. However, Hitler escaped the explosion with minor injuries. He ordered the plotters arrested and executed.

The risks of joining the resistance were great. A resistance worker caught by the Nazis faced certain death. The Germans sometimes rounded up and executed hundreds of civilians in revenge for an act of sabotage against their occupation forces.

Propaganda. All the warring nations used propaganda to win support for their policies. Governments aimed propaganda at their own people and at the enemy. Radio broadcasts reached the largest audiences. Motion pictures, posters, and cartoons were also used for propaganda purposes.

The Nazis skillfully used propaganda to spread their beliefs. Joseph Goebbels directed Germany's Ministry of Propaganda and Enlightenment, which controlled publications, radio programs, motion pictures, and the arts in Germany and German-occupied Europe. The ministry worked to persuade people of the superiority of German culture and of Germany's right to rule the world.

... we here highly resolve that these dead shall not have died in vain ...

REMEMBER DEC. 7th!

Bettmann Archive

A U.S. government poster reminded Americans of the event that plunged them into war—Japan's attack on Pearl Harbor. All warring nations used propaganda techniques to stir patriotism.

After the war began to go badly for the Axis, the Germans claimed that they were saving the world from the evils of Communism.

Mussolini stirred the Italians with dreams of restoring Italy to the glory of ancient Rome. Italy's propaganda also ridiculed the fighting ability of Allied soldiers.

Japan promised conquered peoples a share in the Greater East Asia Co-Prosperity Sphere, which would unite all eastern Asia under Japanese control. Using the slogan "Asia for the Asians," the Japanese claimed that they were freeing Asia from European rule.

Nightly newscasts beamed by the British Broadcasting Corporation (BBC) to the European mainland provided truthful information about the day's fighting. The Nazis made it a crime for people in Germany and German-held lands to listen to BBC broadcasts.

The U.S. government established the Office of War Information (OWI) to encourage American support for the war effort. The agency told Americans that they were fighting for a better world. In 1942, the Voice of America, a government radio service, began broadcasting to Axis-occupied countries.

The warring countries also engaged in *psychological warfare* intended to destroy the enemy's will to fight. American planes dropped leaflets over Germany that told of Nazi defeats. The Axis nations employed a few traitors who broadcast radio programs to weaken the morale of Allied soldiers. For example, Mildred Gillars, an American known as "Axis Sally," made broadcasts for Germany. Another American, Iva D'Aquino, who was called "Tokyo Rose," broadcast for Japan. Such broadcasts merely amused most troops.

National Archives

"Rosie the Riveter" became the humorous yet respectful name for the millions of American women who worked in defense plants during the war. This "Rosie" worked on an airplane assembly line.

World War II affected the civilian populations of all the fighting nations. But the effects were extremely uneven. Much of Europe and large parts of Asia suffered widespread destruction and severe hardship. The United States and Canada, which lay far from the battlefronts, were spared most of the horror of war. North America, in fact, prospered during World War II.

In the United States and Canada, most people fully backed the war effort. Nearly all Americans and Canadians despised Nazism and wished to defeat it. Americans sought also to avenge the bombing of Pearl Harbor.

Producing for the war. Victory in World War II required an enormous amount of war materials, including huge numbers of ships, tanks, aircraft, and weapons. The United States and Canada built many plants to manufacture war goods. They also turned old factories into war plants. For example, automobile factories began to produce tanks and aircraft.

The United States astonished the world with its wartime output. Roosevelt called for the production of 60,000 aircraft during 1942—a goal many industrialists believed was impossible to achieve. Yet U.S. war plants turned out nearly 86,000 planes the following year. Shipbuilding gains were just as impressive. For example, the time needed to build an aircraft carrier dropped from 36 months in 1941 to 15 months in 1945.

Canada also greatly expanded its output during World War II. Wartime expansion made Canada a leading industrial power by the war's end.

Millions of women in the United States and Canada joined the labor force during World War II, after men left for combat. Women worked in shipyards and aircraft factories and filled many jobs previously held only by men. The number of working women in the United States climbed from about 15 million in 1941 to about 19 million in 1945. Canadian women replaced men on farms as well as in factories. They helped raise the crops that fed Allied troops.

New opportunities opened up for American blacks

during World War II. In 1941, Roosevelt created the Fair Employment Practices Committee to prevent job discrimination in U.S. defense industries. Large numbers of Southern blacks moved to the North to work in war plants.

Mobilizing for the war. The United States introduced its first peacetime draft in September 1940. Under the draft law, all men aged 21 through 35 were required to register for military service. The draft was later extended to men 18 through 45. More than 15 million American men served in the armed forces during World War II. About 10 million were drafted. The rest volunteered. About 338,000 women served in the U.S. armed forces. They worked as mechanics, drivers, clerks, and cooks and also filled many other noncombat positions.

Canada also expanded its armed forces greatly during World War II. At the outbreak of the war, the Canadian government promised not to draft men for service overseas. Canada relied on volunteers for overseas duty until November 1944. By then, it suffered from a severe shortage of troops and began to send draftees overseas. More than a million Canadians, including about 50,000 women, served in the armed forces during the war.

Financing the war. The U.S. and Canadian governments paid for the costs of World War II in several ways. In one major method, they borrowed from individuals and businesses by selling them war bonds, certificates, notes, and stamps. The United States government raised nearly $180 billion from such sales. Canada's government also raised several billion dollars.

Taxes also helped pay for World War II. Income increased tremendously during the war years. As a result, revenue from income taxes soared. In the United States, the tax rate on the highest incomes reached 94 per cent.

AP/Wide World

Government rationing helped assure the fair distribution of scarce goods in the United States and Canada. Ration books enabled citizens to buy limited amounts of meat and other items.

AP/Wide World

The wartime confinement of Japanese Americans in relocation camps was a denial of their rights. It resulted from distrust of all Japanese after the attack on Pearl Harbor.

The government also taxed entertainment and such luxury goods as cosmetics and jewelry. Corporations paid extra taxes on higher-than-normal profits. Canadians also paid increased taxes during the war.

In spite of greater borrowing and higher taxes, the U.S. and Canadian governments spent more than they raised to pay for the war. In the United States, the national debt increased from about $49 billion in 1941 to $259 billion in 1945. Canada's national debt rose from $4 billion in 1939 to $16 billion in 1945.

Government controls over civilian life in the United States and Canada expanded during World War II. In both countries, the national government established various agencies to direct the war effort on the home front. The agencies helped prevent skyrocketing prices, severe shortages, and production foul-ups. The War Production Board, for example, controlled the distribution of raw materials needed by U.S. industries. The Office of Price Administration limited price increases in the United States. It also set up a *rationing program* to distribute scarce goods fairly. Each family received a book of ration coupons to use for purchases of such items as sugar, meat, butter, and gasoline.

Canada's government had even greater wartime powers. For example, the National Selective Service controlled Canada's work force. It forbade men of military age to hold jobs it termed "nonessential." Such jobs included driving a taxi or selling real estate. Canada's Wartime Prices and Trade Board determined wages and prices and set up a rationing program.

Treatment of enemy aliens. During World War II, the U.S. government classified more than a million newly arrived immigrants from Germany, Italy, and Japan as *enemy aliens.* However, only the Japanese were treated unjustly. After the bombing of Pearl Harbor, some Americans directed their rage at people of Japanese ancestry. In 1942, anti-Japanese hysteria led the U.S. government to move about 110,000 West Coast residents of Japanese ancestry to inland relocation camps. They lost their homes and their jobs as a result. About two-thirds of them were citizens of the United States. Canada also relocated about 21,000 people of Japanese ancestry during the war.

In Germany, most of the people greeted the start of World War II with little enthusiasm. But Germany's string of easy victories from 1939 to mid-1941 stirred support for the war. By the summer of 1941, the Germans did not expect the war to last much longer.

Civilian life. Food, clothing, and other consumer goods remained plentiful in Germany during the early years of the war. Imports poured in from Nazi-occupied countries of Europe. The Allied bombing of Germany got off to a slow start and did little damage at first.

Germany's situation had changed by late 1942. The armed forces bogged down in the Soviet Union, and there were fewer reports of German victories to cheer the people. Allied bombs rained down day and night on German cities. Consumer goods became increasingly scarce. Yet the people continued to work hard for the war effort.

The Nazi terror. Hitler's dreaded secret police, the Gestapo, ruthlessly crushed opposition to the Nazi Party. The Gestapo arrested anyone suspected of opposing Nazism in Germany and in German-held territories.

To free German men for combat, the Gestapo recruited workers from occupied countries. Millions of Europeans were eventually forced to work long hours under terrible conditions in German war plants. Many died of mistreatment or starvation.

The Nazis brutally persecuted several groups, including Jews, Gypsies, and Slavs. By 1942, Hitler had started a campaign to murder all European Jews. The Nazis rounded up Jewish men, women, and children from occupied Europe and shipped them in boxcars to concentration camps. About 6 million Jews died in concentration camps during World War II. Many were mowed down by firing squads or killed in groups in gas chambers. Others died of lack of food, disease, or torture. The Nazis also slaughtered many Poles, Gypsies, and members of other groups.

In other countries, conditions on the home front depended on the nearness of the fighting and on the length of the war effort. Conditions were especially difficult in the Soviet Union, where fierce fighting went on for nearly four years. Stalin ordered retreating Soviet soldiers to burn everything in their path that German troops could use for food or shelter. But that *scorched-earth policy* also caused great hardships for the Soviet people. Millions of Soviet civilians died of famine and other war-related causes. In the Ukraine and areas occupied by the Soviet Union, many of the people at first welcomed the conquering German troops. They believed that the Germans would deliver them from Stalin's harsh rule. But the cruelty of the Nazi occupation forces turned the people against them. During World War II, civilians and soldiers in the Soviet Union fought the Germans with a hatred and determination seldom matched elsewhere in Europe.

The civilian population of Great Britain also united wholeheartedly behind the war effort. The people worked long hours in war plants and accepted severe shortages of nearly all goods. Prime Minister Churchill inspired the British people with his stirring words.

Life was especially hard in the countries under Nazi rule. Germany looted the conquered lands to feed its own people and fuel its war effort. Opponents of Nazism lived in constant fear of Gestapo brutality.

Japan came closest to collapse of all the warring nations. As the Allies closed in, they deprived Japan of more and more of the raw materials needed by the country's industries. American bombers pounded Japan's cities, and American submarines sank Japanese cargo ships. By 1945, hunger and malnutrition were widespread in Japan. But the Japanese people remained willing to make enormous sacrifices for the war effort.

Consequences of the war

Deaths and destruction. World War II took more lives and caused more destruction than any other war. Altogether, about 70 million people served in the armed forces of the Allied and Axis nations. About 17 million of them lost their lives. The Soviet Union suffered about $7\frac{1}{2}$ million battle deaths, more than any other country. The United States and Great Britain had the fewest battle deaths of the major powers. About 400,000 American and about 350,000 British military personnel died in the war. Germany lost about $3\frac{1}{2}$ million servicemen, and Japan about $1\frac{1}{4}$ million.

Aerial bombing during World War II rained destruction on civilian as well as military targets. Many cities lay in ruins by the end of the war, especially in Germany and Japan. Bombs wrecked houses, factories, and transportation and communication systems. Land battles also spread destruction over vast areas. After the war, millions of starving and homeless people wandered among the ruins of Europe and Asia.

No one knows how many civilians died as a direct result of World War II. Bombing raids destroyed many of the records needed to estimate those deaths. In addition, millions of people died in fires, of diseases, and of other causes after such essential services as fire fighting and health care broke down in war-torn areas.

The Soviet Union and China suffered the highest toll of civilian deaths during World War II. As many as 20 million Soviet civilians and as many as 10 million Chinese civilians may have died. Many of the deaths resulted from famine.

Displaced persons. World War II uprooted millions of people. By the war's end, more than 12 million *displaced persons* remained in Europe. They included orphans, prisoners of war, survivors of Nazi concentration and slave labor camps, and people who had fled invading armies and war-torn areas. Others were displaced by changes in national borders. For example, many Germans moved into Poland, Czechoslovakia, and other lands in eastern Europe that the Nazis took over. After the war, those countries expelled German residents.

To help displaced persons, the Allies established the United Nations Relief and Rehabilitation Administration (UNRRA). UNRRA began operating in 1944 in areas freed by the Allies from Nazi occupation. The organization set up camps for displaced persons and provided them with food, clothing, and medical supplies. By 1947, most of the displaced persons had been resettled. However, about a million people still remained in camps. Many had fled from countries in eastern Europe and refused to return to homelands that had come under Communist rule.

New power struggles arose after World War II ended. The war had exhausted the leading prewar powers of Europe and Asia. Germany and Japan ended the war in complete defeat, and Great Britain and France were severely weakened. The United States and the Soviet Union emerged from the war as the world's leading powers. Their wartime alliance soon collapsed as the Soviet Union sought to spread Communism in Europe and Asia. The struggle between the Communist world, led by the Soviet Union, and the non-Communist world, led by the United States, is known as the Cold War.

The United States had fought the Axis to preserve democracy. After the war, Americans found it impossible to return to the policy of isolation their country had followed before the war. Americans realized that they needed strong allies, and they helped the war-torn nations recover.

World War II had united the Soviet people behind a great patriotic effort. The Soviet Union came out of the war stronger than ever before, in spite of the severe destruction it had suffered. Before the war ended, the Soviet Union had absorbed three nations along the Baltic Sea—Estonia, Latvia, and Lithuania. It had also taken parts of Poland, Romania, Finland, and Czechoslova-

Keystone

The human suffering caused by World War II was enormous. Cities lay in ruins, and millions of people had to be resettled. These homeless Germans reflected the widespread despair.

kia by mid-1945. At the end of the war, Soviet troops occupied most of eastern Europe. In March 1946, Churchill warned that an "Iron Curtain" had descended across Europe, dividing eastern Europe from western Europe. Behind the Iron Curtain, the Soviet Union helped Communist governments take power in Bulgaria, Czechoslovakia, Hungary, Poland, and Romania.

Communism also gained strength in the Far East. The Soviet Union set up a Communist government in North Korea after the war. In China, Mao Zedong's Communist forces battled Chiang Kai-shek's Nationalist armies. Late in 1949, Chiang fled to the island of Taiwan, and China joined the Communist world.

By 1947, Communists threatened to take control of Greece, and the Soviet Union was demanding military bases in Turkey. That year, President Truman announced that the United States would provide military and economic aid to any country threatened by Communism. American aid helped Greece and Turkey resist Communist aggression.

In 1948, the United States set up the Marshall Plan to help war-torn nations in Europe rebuild their economies. Under the plan, 18 nations received $13 billion in food, machinery, and other goods. The Soviet Union forbade countries in eastern Europe to participate in the Marshall Plan.

The nuclear age opened with the development of the atomic bomb during World War II. Many people believed that weapons capable of mass destruction would make war unthinkable in the future. They hoped that the world would learn to live in peace. But a race to develop ever more powerful weapons soon began.

At the end of World War II, only the United States knew how to build an atomic weapon. In 1946, the United States proposed the creation of an international

Military casualties in World War II (1939-1945)

	Dead	Wounded
The Allies		
Australia	23,365	39,803
Belgium	7,760	14,500
Canada	37,476	53,174
China	2,200,000	1,762,000
France	210,671	390,000
Great Britain*	329,208	348,403
Poland	320,000	530,000
Soviet Union	7,500,000	5,000,000
United States	405,399	671,278
The Axis		
Austria	380,000	350,117
Bulgaria	10,000	21,878
Finland	82,000	50,000
Germany	3,500,000	7,250,000
Hungary	140,000	89,313
Italy	77,494	120,000
Japan	1,219,000	295,247
Romania	300,000	(†)

*Including colonials.
†Figure unavailable.
Source: James L. Stokesbury, author of *A Short History of World War II.*

agency that would control atomic energy and ban the production of nuclear weapons. But the Soviet Union objected to an inspection system, and the proposal was dropped. Stalin ordered Soviet scientists to develop an atomic bomb, and they succeeded in 1949. During the early 1950's, the United States and the Soviet Union each tested an even more destructive weapon, the hydrogen bomb.

People have feared a nuclear war since the nuclear age began. At times, Cold War tensions have threatened to erupt into war between the two superpowers. But the terrifying destructiveness of nuclear weapons may well have kept them from risking a major war.

Establishing the peace

Birth of the United Nations (UN). Out of the horror of World War II came efforts to prevent war from ever again engulfing the world. In 1943, representatives of the United States, Great Britain, the Soviet Union, and China met in Moscow. They agreed to establish an international organization that would work to promote peace. The four Allied powers met again in 1944 at Dumbarton Oaks, an estate in Washington, D.C. The delegates decided to call the new organization the United Nations. In April 1945, representatives from 50 nations gathered in San Francisco, Calif., to draft a charter for the United Nations. They signed the charter in June, and it went into effect on October 24.

Peace with Germany. Before World War II ended, the Allies had decided on a military occupation of Germany after its defeat. They divided Germany into four zones, with the United States, the Soviet Union, Great Britain, and France each occupying a zone. The four powers jointly administered Berlin.

At the Potsdam Conference in July 1945, the Allies set forth their occupation policy. They agreed to abolish Germany's armed forces and to outlaw the Nazi Party. Germany lost territory east of the Oder and Neisse riv-

ers. Most of the region went to Poland. The Soviet Union gained the northeastern corner of this territory.

The Allies brought to trial Nazi leaders accused of war crimes. The trials exposed the monstrous evils inflicted by Nazi Germany. Many leading Nazis were sentenced to death. The most important war trials took place in the German city of Nuremberg from 1945 to 1949.

Soon after the occupation began, the Soviet Union stopped cooperating with its Western Allies. It blocked all efforts to reunite Germany. The Western Allies gradually joined their zones into one economic unit. But the Soviet Union forbade its zone to join.

The city of Berlin lay deep within the Soviet zone of Germany. In June 1948, the Soviet Union sought to drive the Western powers from Berlin by blocking all rail, water, and highway routes to the city. For over a year, the Western Allies flew in food, fuel, and other goods to Berlin. The Soviet Union finally lifted the Berlin blockade in May 1949, and the airlift ended in September.

The Western Allies set up political parties in their zones and held elections. In September 1949, the three Western zones were officially combined as the Federal

Republic of Germany. It is also known as West Germany. In May 1955, the Western Allies signed a treaty ending the occupation of West Germany, and granting the country full independence. But the treaty was not a general peace treaty because the Soviet Union refused to sign it.

The Soviet Union set up a Communist government in its zone. In October 1949, the Soviet zone became the German Democratic Republic, also called East Germany. Soviet control over East Germany remains strong, though the country became officially independent in 1955.

Peace with Japan. The military occupation of Japan began in August 1945. Americans far outnumbered other troops in the occupation forces because of the key role their country had played in defeating Japan. General MacArthur directed the occupation as supreme commander for the Allied nations. He introduced many reforms designed to rid Japan of its military institutions and transform it into a democracy. A Constitution drawn up by MacArthur's staff took effect in 1947. The Constitution transferred all political rights from the Japanese emperor to the people. In addition, the Constitution granted voting rights to women, and denied Japan's right to declare war.

The Allied occupation forces brought to trial 25 Japanese war leaders and government officials who were accused of war crimes. Seven of these individuals were executed. The other people who were tried received prison sentences.

In September 1951, the United States and most of the other Allied nations signed a peace treaty with Japan. The treaty took away Japan's overseas empire. But it permitted Japan to rearm. The Allied occupation of Japan ended soon after the nations signed the peace treaty. However, a new treaty permitted the United States to keep troops in Japan. China's Nationalist government signed its own peace treaty with Japan in 1952, and the Soviet Union and Japan also signed a separate peace treaty in 1956.

Peace with other countries. Soon after World War II ended, the Allies began to draw up peace treaties with Italy and four other countries that had fought with the Axis—Bulgaria, Finland, Hungary, and Romania. The treaties limited the armed forces of the defeated countries and required them to pay war damages. The treaties also called for territorial changes. Bulgaria gave up territory to Greece and Yugoslavia. Czechoslovakia gained land from Hungary. Finland lost territory to the Soviet Union. Italy gave up land to France, Yugoslavia, and Greece. The country also lost its empire in Africa. Romania gained territory from Hungary, but in turn it lost land to Bulgaria and the Soviet Union.

James L. Stokesbury

Study aids

Related articles in *World Book*. See the *History* section of articles on countries that took part in World War II. Additional related articles in *World Book* include:

Battles

Bataan Peninsula	Midway Island
Chinese-Japanese wars	Okinawa
Corregidor	Pearl Harbor Naval Base
Dunkerque	Russo-Finnish wars
Guam	Saipan
Iwo Jima	Stalingrad, Battle of
Manila Bay	Wake Island

Allied military leaders

Alexander of Tunis, Earl	McNaughton, Andrew G. L.
Arnold, Henry H.	Montgomery, Bernard L.
Bradley, Omar N.	Mountbatten, Louis
Chennault, Claire L.	Nimitz, Chester W.
Clark, Mark W.	Patton, George S., Jr.
Clay, Lucius D.	Ridgway, Matthew B.
Doolittle, James H.	Roosevelt, Theodore, Jr.
Eisenhower, Dwight D.	Spaatz, Carl
Halsey, William F., Jr.	Spruance, Raymond A.
Hobby, Oveta C.	Stilwell, Joseph W.
King, Ernest J.	Taylor, Maxwell D.
LeMay, Curtis E.	Wainwright, Jonathan M.
MacArthur, Douglas	Zhukov, Georgi K.
Marshall, George C.	

Axis military leaders

Doenitz, Karl	Keitel, Wilhelm
Goering, Hermann W.	Rommel, Erwin
Heydrich, Reinhard	Yamamoto, Isoroku
Jodl, Alfred	Yamashita, Tomoyuki

Allied political figures

Attlee, Clement R.	Chiang Kai-shek
Beneš, Eduard	Churchill, Sir Winston L. S.
Chamberlain (Neville)	Daladier, Édouard

De Gaulle, Charles A. J. M.	Roosevelt, Franklin D.
Eden, Anthony	Stalin, Joseph
Haile Selassie I	Stimson, Henry L.
Hull, Cordell	Tito, Josip Broz
Knox, Frank	Truman, Harry S.
Molotov, Vyacheslav M.	

Axis political figures

Bormann, Martin	Mussolini, Benito
Eichmann, Adolf	Pétain, Henri P.
Goebbels, Joseph	Quisling, Vidkun A. L.
Hess, Rudolf	Ribbentrop, Joachim von
Himmler, Heinrich	Rosenberg, Alfred
Hirohito	Speer, Albert
Hitler, Adolf	Tojo, Hideki
Laval, Pierre	

Other biographies

Bonhoeffer, Dietrich	Mauldin, Bill
Frank, Anne	Miller, Dorie
Kaiser, Henry J.	Pyle, Ernie
Krupp (family)	Wallenberg, Raoul

Conferences and treaties

Munich Agreement	San Francisco Conference
Pan-American Conferences	Teheran Conference
Potsdam Conference	Yalta Conference

Forces, materials, and weapons

Air force	Aviation	Convoy
Air Force, United	Bazooka	Fifth column
States	Blitzkrieg	Flying Tigers
Aircraft, Military	Bomb	Guided missile
Aircraft carrier	Bulldozer	Helmet
Airplane	Camouflage	Hostage
Ammunition	Coast Guard, United	Intelligence
Amphibious warfare	States	service
Army	Commando	
Army, United States		

Jeep
Jet propulsion
Kamikaze
Lend-Lease
Marine Corps,
  United States
Mine warfare
Minesweeper
Navy

Navy, United States
Nuclear weapon
Propaganda
PT boat
Radar
Rationing
Remote control
Rocket
Savings bond

Sniperscope
Sonar
Submarine
Tank
Torpedo
War aces
War correspond-
  ent
Warship

Organizations

American Legion
American Legion Auxiliary
AMVETS
Red Cross
Strategic Services, Office of

United Nations
United Service Organizations
Veterans of Foreign Wars of
  the United States

Other related articles

Alaska Highway
Atlantic Charter
Azores
Bismarck (ship)
Burma Road
Concentration camp
D-Day
Draft, Military
Four Freedoms
Gestapo
Graf Spee
Hiroshima
Holocaust
Jews (The Holocaust)
Korean War
Lidice

Maquis
Neutrality
Nuremberg Trials
Partisan
Polish Corridor
Refugee
Stars and Stripes
V-E Day
V-J Day
Underground
United States, History of the
Unknown Soldier
War crime
War debt
World War I
Yank

Outline

I. Causes of the war
  A. The Peace of Paris
  B. Economic problems
  C. Nationalism
  D. The rise of dictatorships
  E. Aggression on the march
  F. The Spanish Civil War
  G. The failure of appeasement

II. Early stages of the war
  A. The invasion of Poland
  B. The Phony War
  C. The conquest of Denmark and Norway
  D. The invasion of the Low Countries
  E. The fall of France
  F. The Battle of Britain

III. The war spreads
  A. Fighting in Africa
  B. Fighting in the Balkans
  C. The invasion of the Soviet Union
  D. The Battle of the Atlantic

IV. The United States enters the war
  A. The arsenal of democracy
  B. Japan attacks

V. The Allies attack in Europe and northern Africa
  A. The strategy
  B. On the Soviet front
  C. In northern Africa
  D. The air war
  E. The invasion of Italy
  F. D-Day
  G. The drive to the Rhine
  H. The Soviet advance
  I. Victory in Europe

VI. The war in Asia and the Pacific
  A. Early Japanese victories
  B. The tide turns
  C. The South Pacific
  D. Island hopping in the Central Pacific
  E. The liberation of the Philippines
  F. The China-Burma-India theater
  G. Closing in on Japan
  H. The atomic bomb
  I. Victory in the Pacific

VII. The secret war
  A. The Ultra secret
  B. Spies and saboteurs
  C. Resistance groups
  D. Propaganda

VIII. On the home front
  A. In the United States
    and Canada
  B. In Germany
  C. In other countries

IX. Consequences of the war
  A. Deaths and destruction
  B. Displaced persons
  C. New power struggles
  D. The nuclear age

X. Establishing the peace
  A. Birth of the United Nations (UN)
  B. Peace with Germany
  C. Peace with Japan
  D. Peace with other countries

Questions

Why did Japan decide to cripple the U.S. Pacific Fleet at anchor in Pearl Harbor?

Which two battles marked a turning point for the Allies in the war against Germany?

What was *appeasement*? When did it become clear that that policy had failed?

What terrifying new weapon did Japan introduce in 1944 during the Battle for Leyte Gulf?

What was the largest seaborne invasion in history?

Which two leaders shocked the world by becoming allies in 1939?

How did the United States help the Allies before it entered World War II?

How was the Battle of the Coral Sea unlike all earlier naval battles?

How did the bombing campaigns against Germany by the United States and Great Britain differ?

What was the Ultra secret? How did it help Great Britain win the Battle of Britain?

Reading and Study Guide

See *World War II* in the Research Guide/Index, Volume 22, for a *Reading and Study Guide.*

Additional resources

Anderson, Karen. *Wartime Women: Sex Roles, Family Relations, and the Status of Women During World War II.* Greenwood, 1981.

Arnold-Forster, Mark. *The World at War.* Stein & Day, 1973.

Buchanan, Albert R. *Black Americans in World War II.* ABC-Clio, 1977.

Churchill, Winston. *The Second World War.* 6 vols. Houghton, 1948-1953.

Daniels, Roger. *Concentration Camps North America: Japanese in the United States and Canada During World War II.* Krieger, 1981. First published in 1971 as *Concentration Camps USA: Japanese Americans and World War II.*

Liddell Hart, Basil H. *History of the Second World War.* Putnam, 1979. First published in 1971.

Lukacs, John A. *The Last European War: September 1939-December 1941.* Doubleday, 1976. *1945, Year Zero.* 1978.

The Rand McNally Encyclopedia of World War II. Ed. by John Keegan. Abingdon, 1979. First published in 1977.

Sherwin, Martin J. *A World Destroyed: The Atomic Bomb and the Grand Alliance.* Random House, 1975.

Stokesbury, James L. *A Short History of World War II.* Morrow, 1980.

Terkel, Studs. *"The Good War": An Oral History of World War Two.* Random House, 1984.

World War II. 39 vols. Time-Life Books, 1976-1983. Each of the books in this series focuses on a different aspect of the war, such as *Prelude to War* (1976) and *The War in the Desert* (1977).

World's Columbian Exposition. See Chicago (A city reborn).

World's fair is an international exposition that features exhibits dealing with commerce, industry, and science. Most fairs also offer entertainment and cultural activities and promote tourism in a region or country. Exhibitors include nations and private companies.

A world's fair runs for several months and attracts millions of visitors. Most fairs have been held in Europe and the United States. But fairs have also been held in Africa, Australia, Canada, India, Japan, and New Zealand.

The first world's fair was the Great Exhibition of 1851 in London. A huge glass and iron hall called the Crystal Palace housed exhibits of art, handicrafts, and machinery. New products on display included the reaper and the Colt revolver. By the 1980's, more than 80 fairs had been held throughout the world.

World's fairs are regulated by the Bureau of International Expositions (B.I.E.). The B.I.E. has established regulations that govern the frequency and duration of officially approved events. Under B.I.E. rules, only one major fair can be held each decade and it can last for no longer than six months. But the B.I.E. also approves smaller events that can be held more often.

Through the years, world's fairs have become a showcase for new inventions, new types of foods, and new kinds of art. Alexander Graham Bell's newly invented telephone was displayed at the Centennial Exposition in Philadelphia in 1876. Visitors at the 1904 Louisiana Purchase Exposition in St. Louis saw early types of automobiles and several new foods, including iced tea and the ice cream cone. Visitors to the New York World's Fair in 1939 and 1940 could see early versions of television.

A number of famous structures have been designed for world's fairs. The Eiffel Tower was erected for a world's fair in Paris in 1889. The Museum of Science and Industry in Chicago is housed in a building constructed for the World's Columbian Exposition in 1893. The Space Needle was built for the Century 21 world's fair in Seattle, Wash., in 1962.

Early world's fairs offered general exhibits. Modern fairs have concentrated on specific themes. The Century 21 fair emphasized exhibits about the dawn of the space age. The 1975 fair in Okinawa, Japan, featured exhibits about the world's ocean environment. The 1982 fair in Knoxville, Tenn., dealt with the world's energy needs. The 1986 fair in Vancouver, Canada, centered on transportation. The 1988 fair in Brisbane, Australia, explored leisure in the age of technology.   Michael R. Pender

See also **Architecture** (The Industrial Revolution); **Chicago** (picture: The World's Columbian Exposition).

Worm is any of several kinds of animals that have a soft, slender body and no backbone or legs. There are thousands of kinds of worms. The largest species measure many feet or meters long, and the smallest ones cannot be seen without a microscope. Some worms live in water or soil. Many of these free-living worms eat small plants and animals, and others feed on decaying matter. Still other worms live as parasites in various animals and plants. They cause a number of diseases.

Many people believe that such wormlike animals as caterpillars and grubs are worms. But these animals are insects in their *larval* (juvenile) stage and do not resemble worms after they mature.

Most kinds of worms have a well-developed sense of touch. They also have special organs that respond to chemicals in their surroundings. Many species have a sense of sight, with eyes or eyespots on the head.

Some common worms There are several thousand kinds of worms. The illustrations below show representatives of each of the four major groups of worms. The sizes listed are approximate because many species can stretch to unusually great lengths. For example, bootlace worms are normally no more than 6½ feet (2 meters) long. But scientists measured one bootlace worm that was stretched to nearly 90 feet (27 meters). The illustrations are not drawn to scale.

WORLD BOOK illustrations by Patricia J. Wynne

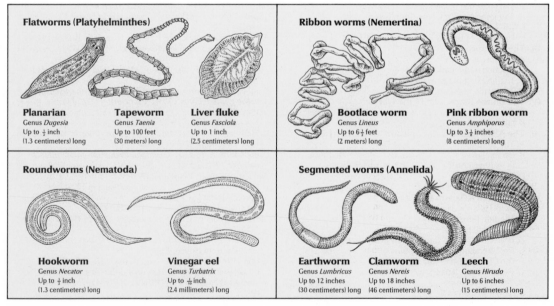

Flatworms (Platyhelminthes)

Planarian	**Tapeworm**	**Liver fluke**
Genus *Dugesia*	Genus *Taenia*	Genus *Fasciola*
Up to ½ inch	Up to 100 feet	Up to 1 inch
(1.3 centimeters) long	(30 meters) long	(2.5 centimeters) long

Ribbon worms (Nemertina)

Bootlace worm	**Pink ribbon worm**
Genus *Lineus*	Genus *Amphiporus*
Up to 6½ feet	Up to 3¼ inches
(2 meters) long	(8 centimeters) long

Roundworms (Nematoda)

Hookworm	**Vinegar eel**
Genus *Necator*	Genus *Turbatrix*
Up to ½ inch	Up to 1/16 inch
(1.3 centimeters) long	(2.4 millimeters) long

Segmented worms (Annelida)

Earthworm	**Clamworm**	**Leech**
Genus *Lumbricus*	Genus *Nereis*	Genus *Hirudo*
Up to 12 inches	Up to 18 inches	Up to 6 inches
(30 centimeters) long	(46 centimeters) long	(15 centimeters) long

There are four main groups of worms: (1) flatworms, or *Platyhelminthes;* (2) ribbon worms, or *Nemertina;* (3) roundworms, or *Nematoda;* and (4) segmented worms, or *Annelida.* The study of parasitic worms is called *helminthology.*

Flatworms are the simplest kinds of worms. Some look like oval leaves, and others resemble ribbons. Flatworms include both free-living and parasitic species.

Most free-living flatworms live in the sea. But many freshwater species, called *planarians,* live among algae and stones along the shores of lakes and ponds. They eat tiny animals. *Flukes* and *tapeworms* are parasitic flatworms that infect human beings and many other animals. In human beings, they cause serious blood and intestinal disorders.

Ribbon worms resemble flatworms, but many species are larger. Most ribbon worms live in the sea. One, the *bootlace worm,* grows several feet or meters long. Ribbon worms are also called *proboscis worms.* They have a long *proboscis* (tubelike structure) that they shoot out from their head to capture prey. They feed on animals, including other worms and mollusks.

Roundworms make up the largest group of worms. There are more than 10,000 species. Roundworms have a long, cylindrical body that resembles a piece of thread. Some, including *filariae, hookworms,* and *trichinae,* are parasites that cause disease in human beings and other animals and in plants. Free-living roundworms live in water or on land and eat small plants and animals.

Segmented worms are the most highly developed worms. Their body consists of segments that give the worms a ringed appearance. This group includes *polychaete worms, oligochaete worms,* and *leeches.*

Polychaete worms, the largest group of segmented worms, live in the sea and along the shore. Many of these worms have *tentacles* (feelers) on their head and a pair of leglike projections called *parapodia* on each body segment. The parapodia are used in crawling. They have many *setae* (bristles) that help the worms grip the surface on which they are moving. Many polychaete worms live among algae or burrow in mud or sand. Some live in tubes attached to the sea floor. A worm makes its tube from sand or from material secreted by its body. Some polychaete worms eat small plants and animals. Others feed on plant and animal remains.

Oligochaete worms include earthworms and many freshwater species. They have a few setae but no parapodia. Most of these worms eat decaying plant matter.

Leeches make up the smallest group of segmented worms. They grow from $\frac{3}{4}$ to 8 inches (2 to 20 centimeters) long and have a flat body with a sucker at each end. Most leeches live in water and feed on the blood of fish and other water creatures.   Robert D. Barnes

Related articles in *World Book* include:

Earthworm	Hookworm	Nematoda	Roundworm
Eelworm	Horsehair	Pinworm	Tapeworm
Filaria	worm	Planarian	Trichina
Flatworm	Leech	Ribbon worm	Vinegar eel
Fluke	Lobworm		

Worms, *vawrms* (pop. 71,827), is a historic town and river port in southern West Germany. It lies on the west bank of the Rhine River (see **Germany** [political map]).

Worms has a magnificent cathedral that is a fine example of Romanesque architecture. The cathedral dates from the 1000's. A monument dedicated to the Protestant reformer Martin Luther stands in the city. It honors Luther's appearance before the Diet of Worms in 1521. The *diet* (assembly) issued the Edict of Worms, which proclaimed Luther a heretic. Worms is also the site of what may be Europe's oldest Jewish cemetery. The cemetery dates from the 1000's. Worms produces the famous Liebfraumilch wine. Its other economic activities include shipping and the manufacture of chemicals, furniture, leather goods, machinery, and textiles.

Roman soldiers built a fort on the site of what is now Worms in 14 B.C. During the Middle Ages, officials of the Holy Roman Empire held nearly 100 diets in Worms.
Melvin Croan

Worms, Edict of, was a decree that declared Reformation leader Martin Luther a heretic and cast him and his followers outside the protection of the law. The decree was issued by a *diet* (assembly) of princes, nobles, and clergy at Worms, Germany, in May 1521.

The edict was an important instance of a civil body issuing a condemnation for the religious charge of heresy. Succeeding diets debated whether it should be enforced, and leagues of Roman Catholic and Protestant states were formed to defend each side of the question. The conflict did not end until the truce provided by the Peace of Augsburg in 1555.   Dale A. Johnson

See also **Luther, Martin** (Reformation leader); **Reformation** (Martin Luther).

Wormwood is a large group of plants that give off pleasant odors. Often the term applies to an entire group of about 250 different kinds of plants of the genus *Artemisia.* The wormwood shrub grows mostly in the Northern Hemisphere and is most abundant in arid regions. The most important wormwood in commercial use is a perennial plant that grows in Europe and North Africa. This kind of wormwood supplies an essential oil

E. Foster, Bruce Coleman Inc.

The leaves of the wormwood yield a valuable oil.

used in the manufacture of absinthe and medicine. Europeans grow common wormwood, or *mugwort,* for seasoning and medicinal purposes. People in eastern Canada and the northeastern United States consider this plant a weed. Several kinds of shrubby wormwoods are called *sagebrush* in the western United States.

Scientific classification. Wormwood is in the composite family, Compositae. Wormwood yielding oil for absinthe is *Artemisia absinthium.* Common wormwood is *A. vulgaris.* Common sagebrush is *A. tridentata.*   Harold Norman Moldenke

Worry. See Anxiety.

Worship. See Religion; Colonial life in America (Why the colonists came to America); **Freedom of religion; God; Idolatry; Prayer; Sun worship.**

Worsted, *WUR stihd* or *WUS tihd,* is a smooth, shiny, strong wool yarn. It is named for Worstead, England, where it was first made. It is spun from long wool that has been combed to lay the fibers parallel. The word *worsted* also describes cloth woven with worsted yarns. Worsted cloths look smooth and hard. Poplin and serge fabrics are often worsted. See also **Serge.**

Wotan. See Odin.

Wouk, *wohk,* **Herman** (1915-   ), is a popular American novelist and playwright. His most successful books are based on his experiences serving in the United States Navy during World War II (1939-1945).

Wouk won the 1952 Pulitzer Prize for fiction for *The Caine Mutiny* (1951). This novel tells about the conflict between Philip Queeg, the unstable captain of an American minesweeper in the Pacific Ocean, and his rebellious junior officers. *The Caine Mutiny* became known for the sharply drawn characters of Queeg and Willie Keith, one of the officers. Wouk adapted part of the novel into a play, *The Caine Mutiny Court-Martial* (1954).

In *The Winds of War* (1971) and *War and Remembrance* (1978), Wouk describes the effects of World War II on Victor Henry, an American naval officer, and his family. The two novels mingle fictional characters with historical figures against a background of major events of the period.

Wouk's other novels include *Aurora Dawn* (1947), *The City Boy* (1948), *Marjorie Morningstar* (1955), *Youngblood Hawke* (1962), *Don't Stop the Carnival* (1965), and *Inside, Outside* (1985). His other plays are *The Traitor* (1949) and *Nature's Way* (1957). He discusses Judaism in *This Is My God* (1959). Wouk was born in New York City.

Barbara M. Perkins

Wound. See First aid (First aid for bleeding).

Wounded Knee, Battle of. See South Dakota (Territorial days).

Wovoka, *woh VOH kuh* (1856?-1932), founded the Ghost Dance religion of the western American Indians. While sick with a fever in 1889, he dreamed that he was lifted into the sky where the Great Spirit talked to him. He also saw all the old-time Indians living a happy life. The Great Spirit taught him some songs and a new dance, and told him to teach the Indians to stop fighting and to lead a good life. Then no one would ever grow old, be sick, or go hungry. All the dead Indians and the buffalo would come back to life.

Wovoka was a Paiute Indian, born in Nevada. His father had been a prophet before him. Adopted as a boy by a white settler named David Wilson, he was also known as Jack Wilson.   E. Adamson Hoebel

WPA was the Works Progress Administration. See **New Deal** (The Second Hundred Days); **Roosevelt, Franklin D.** (The New Deal); **Adult education.**

Wrangel Island, *RANG guhl,* lies in the Arctic Ocean, about 90 miles (140 kilometers) north of the northeastern corner of Siberia. For location, see **Union of Soviet Socialist Republics** (terrain map). It covers 2,819 square miles (7,301 square kilometers), and has a population of about 50. It is part of the Soviet Union. Wrangel Island is barren, granite rock locked in by ice most of the year. Lichen and grass grow in the summer. Birds, polar bears, seals, and walruses live there. The people fish, hunt, and trap furs. There is also a meteorological station on the island.

Wrangel Island was named for the Russian explorer Baron Ferdinand von Wrangel, who searched for the island in 1823 after Siberian natives had reported its existence. But Wrangel never found the island. American whalers discovered it in 1867, and named it for Wrangel. Claimed by the United States, Canada, and the Soviet Union, the island was finally left to the Soviet Union in 1924. The Soviet Union sent settlers there in 1926.

Theodore Shabad

Wrangell-St. Elias National Park, *RANG guhl SAYNT uhl EYE uhs,* is the largest national park in the United States. Located in southeastern Alaska, it covers 8,945,000 acres (3,620,000 hectares), or about 14,000 square miles (36,000 square kilometers). It is so vast that few tourists have ever visited its remote parts. For location, see **Alaska** (political map).

Wrangell-St. Elias National Park includes the country's greatest collection of mountains that stand more than 16,000 feet (4,880 meters) high. The tallest of these mountains, Mount St. Elias, rises 18,008 feet (5,489 meters). The park also has the largest group of glaciers in North America. Animals that live in the park include black bears, grizzly bears, caribou, moose, Dall's sheep, mountain goats, minks, sea otters, and trumpeter swans. The area was established as a national monument in 1978 and became a national park in 1980.

Critically reviewed by the National Park Service

Wren is the name of a group of small, energetic birds found in most parts of the world. Wrens are extremely protective of their nests. Some wrens are known to enter nearby nests of other birds and pierce the eggs. Wrens eat insects and seeds that they find in underbrush and tangled root growths. They sing melodiously, but can also make harsh, chattering sounds. There are 63 types of wrens, most of which live in Asia and the Americas. Only one kind lives in Europe.

A wren has a slender bill and rounded wings. Most wrens are brown and may be striped, spotted, or streaked with black or white. Wrens have short tails that they often hold upward.

The *house wren,* commonly known as the *jenny wren,* is the most familiar wren in North America. It is about 5 inches (13 centimeters) long. It often lives in cities, where many people build birdhouses for it. Gardeners value the house wren because it eats insects. The female house wren lays six to eight eggs a year. The eggs are white and speckled with brownish red.

The largest wren in North America is the *cactus wren,* which grows to 8½ inches (22 centimeters) long. This wren lives in dry regions of the Southwestern United

Bewick's wren
Thryomanes bewickii
Found from southern Canada
to Mexico
Body length 5½ inches (14 centimeters)

Karl Maslowski, Photo Researchers

The house wren often builds its nest in a backyard birdhouse.
The entrance is about the size of a quarter.

Riverside wren
Thryothorus semibadius
Found in Costa Rica and Panama
(Body length 5½ to 5¾ inches)

Winter wren
Troglodytes troglodytes
Found in the Northern Hemisphere
(Body length 4 to 5 inches)

Band-backed wren
Campylorhynchus zonatus
Found from Mexico to western Panama
and western Ecuador
(Body length 7¾ to 8¼ inches)

Sedge wren
Cistothorus platensis
Found in North and South America
(Body length 4 inches)

Rock wren
Salpinctes obsoletus
Found from southwestern
Canada and the West-
ern United States to
northwestern Costa Rica
(Body length 5 to 6 inches)

**Long-billed marsh
wren**
Telmatodytes palustris
Found from southern Canada
to central Mexico
(Body length 4 to 5½ inches)

WORLD BOOK illustrations by Guy Tudor

Wren's Greenwich Hospital is typical of the architect's style in its repetition of columns and arches. The buildings, which are located in Greenwich, a borough of London, now house the Royal Naval College.

Eric Crichton, Bruce Coleman Ltd.

States and northern Mexico. Its back, wings, and tail are heavily streaked, and it has a broad stripe over each eye. The *rock wren* lives in the western section of the United States. It builds its nest under rocks in the dry foothills of the Rocky Mountains. Most rock wrens are gray-brown with cinnamon coloring near the tail. The *Carolina wren* lives in the southern part of the United States. Its back is rust-brown, and its belly is dull yellow. Most Carolina wrens nest around farm buildings.

Other wrens common in the United States are the Bewick's wren, winter wren, marsh wren, and sedge wren. The *Bewick's wren* lives near people's homes. It has a white-edged tail and white stripes over its eyes. The *winter wren* nests in the Northern United States and in Canada. Its songs echo through evergreen forests in these regions. The *marsh wren* builds its nest in cattail marshes. The *sedge wren* prefers grassy marshes and meadows. The marsh wren, which is more common, has a gurgling song. The sedge wren's song is like the sound made by striking two pebbles together rapidly.

Scientific classification. Wrens are in the wren family, Troglodytidae. The house wren is *Troglodytes aedon,* and the cactus wren is *Campylorhynchus brunneicapillus.*

Edward H. Burtt, Jr.

See also **Bird** (pictures: Birds of forests and woodlands; Birds of brushy areas; Birds' eggs).

Wren, Sir Christopher (1632-1723), was an English architect, scientist, and mathematician. After the Great Fire of London in 1666, he redesigned part or all of 55 of the 87 churches that had been destroyed. The most famous one is St. Paul's Cathedral (1710). The grace and variety of many of Wren's church spires are still a feature of the London skyline. His other major buildings include the churches of St. Bride (about 1678) and St. James (about 1684), Chelsea Hospital (about 1691), and Greenwich Hospital (about 1715).

Wren was born in the village of East Knoyle in the county of Wiltshire. His early interests and training were in science and mathematics. From 1641 to 1646, he attended Westminster School in London, where the poet John Dryden and the philosopher John Locke were fellow students. Wren received his B.A. degree from Oxford University in 1651 and his M.A. degree there in 1653. In 1657, Wren was appointed professor of astronomy at Gresham College in London. His lectures helped

spread his reputation among European scientists.

In 1661, King Charles II appointed Wren to the important architectural position of assistant surveyor general. In 1663, Wren attracted attention with his proposal for a unique roofing system over the Sheldonian Theatre in Oxford. Unlike other English architects of his day, Wren never went to Italy to gain firsthand knowledge of classical architecture. He did visit France in 1665, and the architecture he saw there probably influenced his work.

Wren was a founding member of the Royal Society in 1660. According to a biography written by his son, Wren was responsible for 53 inventions, experiments, and theories. J. William Rudd

For a picture of the exterior of St. Paul's Cathedral, see **Architecture** (Baroque); for a picture of the interior of this cathedral, see **London** (Places to visit). See also **England** (The arts); **London** (Churches).

Additional resources

Downes, Kerry. *The Architecture of Wren.* Universe Books, 1982.
Whinney, Margaret D. *Christopher Wren.* Praeger, 1971.

Wrestling, *REHS lihng,* is a sport in which two opponents try to *pin* (hold) each other's shoulders to a mat on the floor. Wrestlers use maneuvers called *holds* to grasp their opponents and control their movements.

Successful wrestling demands strength, speed, coordination, balance, physical conditioning, and knowledge of body leverage. A clever wrestler can often defeat a stronger and heavier opponent.

There are more than 50 kinds of wrestling. Each has its own rules. Some kinds do not require a pin for victory. In Japanese *sumo,* for example, a wrestler tries to throw his opponent to the ground or force him outside a 15-foot (4.6-meter) circle.

Amateur wrestling

Amateur wrestling is a popular sport in schools in the United States and Canada. Every year, students in elementary school through college take part in wrestling matches. National and world championship competitions are held annually. Every four years, wrestlers compete in the Summer Olympic Games. Wrestlers from Western Hemisphere nations also meet at four-year intervals in the Pan American Games.

The Fédération Internationale de la Lutte Amateur

(FILA) governs international amateur wrestling. USA Wrestling governs the sport in the United States. Although amateur wrestling traditionally is a sport for boys and men, FILA established separate competition for women's freestyle wrestling in 1988.

Chief forms of wrestling. The two most popular forms of wrestling in the world are *Greco-Roman* and *freestyle.* Freestyle is the older of the two forms and the most popular in North America. It resembles the style practiced by the ancient Greeks. The Greco-Roman style developed after the Romans conquered Greece and modified the Greeks' style. Greco-Roman is the more popular form throughout Europe. International competition, including the Olympics, is held in both.

Most of the rules and procedures in the two styles are the same. The main difference concerns the use of the legs. In freestyle, wrestlers may use the legs to grasp an opponent's arms or legs, or to trip or tackle an opponent's legs. In Greco-Roman, a wrestler cannot attack an opponent's legs or attack with his own legs. The legs may be used only for support, so upper body strength and leverage are the chief factors.

Some international meets feature competition in a style called *sambo,* or *sombo,* which originated in the Soviet Union in the 1930's. Sambo is a blend of several forms of wrestling and the martial arts, especially judo.

High school and intercollegiate wrestling. There are 13 weight classes in high school wrestling in the United States. There are 10 intercollegiate classes. A wrestler may weigh no more than the weight in his class, though he may weigh less. The high school weight classes range from 103 pounds to a heavyweight class of no more than 275 pounds. Intercollegiate classes range from 118 pounds to no more than 275 pounds.

High school matches are divided into three periods of two minutes each. Intercollegiate matches begin with a three-minute period. The remaining two periods last two minutes each. Matches take place on a cushioned mat with a wrestling area at least 32 feet (9.75 meters) square or 32 feet in diameter. At least 5 feet (1.5 meters) of mat must surround the wrestling area. The first period begins with the wrestlers standing and facing each

other. The second period begins with one wrestler having a choice of top position, bottom position, or neutral position, or the wrestler can defer the choice to the opponent. For a description of these positions, see the illustrations of wrestling holds and positions that appear in this article.

Wrestlers receive points for skillfully executing various holds and maneuvers. They may also win points if their opponent commits a technical error, uses an illegal hold, or breaks a rule. The match ends when a wrestler gains a fall by holding his opponent's shoulders to the mat. The opponent's shoulders must be held for two seconds in a high school match and for one second in an intercollegiate match. If no fall occurs, the wrestler with the most points wins by a *decision.* The referee is sometimes assisted by a second referee.

International competition. There are 10 weight classes in both freestyle and Greco-Roman wrestling in international competition, including the Olympics. They range from 105.5 pounds to a class of no more than 286 pounds. The participants in each class are divided by lot into two *pools* (groups). Competition in each pool is conducted as a separate tournament. The winners of the pools meet in the championship finals.

Each match consists of one five-minute period. The wrestlers start the match on their feet, facing each other.

How points are scored

Individual match points

Near fall	2 or 3 points
Takedown	2 points
Reversal	2 points
Time advantage (1 minute)	1 point
Escape	1 point

Dual meet points

Fall	6 points
Forfeit	6 points
Default	6 points
Disqualification	6 points
Decision (by 15 or more points)	5 points
Decision (by 8 to 14 points)	4 points
Decision (by less than 8 points)	3 points
Draw	2 points

© Sylvain Legrand, Agence Vandystadt from Photo Researchers

A wrestling match is a test of strength and skill between the two opponents. Each wrestler tries to win the match by *pinning* (holding) his opponent's shoulders to the mat for a specified time. The referee, *right,* watches for a pin, awards points for skillful maneuvers, and penalizes wrestlers for illegal holds or tactics.

**Wrestling holds
and positions**   These illustrations show some basic holds and positions college wrestlers use. Most wrestling holds and positions are used to pin an opponent or to control his movements.

A match begins when the wrestlers approach each other from opposite sides of the mat. Each wrestler tries to outmaneuver his opponent in an effort to pin his shoulders.

The starting position, also called the referee's position, begins the second and third periods. One starting position is shown on the left, with the offensive man on top and the defensive man on the bottom. In the *optional starting position,* shown on the right, the offensive man is behind the defensive man. The wrestlers reverse positions to begin the third period.

A take down is awarded when one wrestler puts his opponent on the mat from a *neutral position*—that is, from a position in which neither wrestler had control.

University of Iowa

A ride is one of several methods by which a wrestler controls the movements of his opponent. An offensive wrestler rides his opponent by controlling a leg and an arm.

An escape occurs when the wrestler on the bottom gains a neutral position and the top wrestler has lost control of his opponent. The referee awards the escaping wrestler 1 point.

A near fall is a position in which the offensive wrestler has his opponent in a controlled pinning position for two seconds. The referee awards either 2 or 3 points.

A fall ends a match. To gain a fall, a wrestler must pin his opponent's shoulders to the mat while the referee counts a specific amount of time, 1 second in college competition.

Three officials direct each match. At least two of them must agree on a decision.

Professional wrestling

Professional wrestling has become more of an entertainment spectacle than a sport. Showmanship often replaces skill. Most matches take place in a roped and padded ring similar to a boxing ring. Many wrestlers wear fantastic costumes and use unusual names. Many matches pair a "hero" against a "villain," and they often appear to be violently attacking each other.

History

Wrestling dates back to prehistoric times. In French caves, drawings and carvings 15,000 to 20,000 years old show wrestlers in various positions. Wrestling was introduced into the Olympic Games in Greece in 708 B.C. In America, Indians wrestled before Europeans arrived in the New World.   Dan Gable

See also **Olympic Games** (table; wrestling).

Wright, Frances (1795-1852), was a lecturer and journalist who worked to promote human rights in the United States. She supported women's rights, the abolition of slavery, and public education for children.

Wright was born in Scotland and came to the United

States in 1824. In 1828 and 1829, she toured the country, lecturing to large, working-class audiences. Wright argued that depriving women of equal rights lowered the quality of life for all people. She shocked audiences by claiming that women had a right to receive information on birth control and to seek divorces. Wright criticized organized religions because she believed they discouraged people from thinking for themselves.

In 1825, Wright founded Nashoba, a model community near Memphis in which slaves worked to buy their freedom. Nashoba failed and closed in 1827. Wright then joined a community founded by the Welsh-born social theorist Robert Owen in New Harmony, Ind. Wright and Owen's son, Robert D. Owen, edited the New Harmony *Gazette,* a magazine. From 1829 to 1832, they edited the magazine *Free Enquirer* in New York City.

June Sochen

Bettmann Archive

Frances Wright

Wright, Frank Lloyd (1867-1959), was one of America's most influential and imaginative architects. During his career of almost 70 years, he created a striking variety of architectural forms. His works ranged from buildings typical of the late 1800's to ultramodern designs, such as his plan for a skyscraper 1 mile (1.6 kilometers) high.

Wright became internationally famous as early as 1910, but he never established a style that dominated either American or European architecture. His influence was great but generally indirect. It was spread as much by his speeches and writings as by his buildings and designs. His *Autobiography* (1932, revised 1943 and 1977), one of the great literary self-portraits of the 1900's, provides insights into his philosophy of architecture.

Early career. Wright was born in Richland Center, Wis. He studied engineering briefly at the University of Wisconsin in the mid-1880's. In 1887, Wright moved to Chicago, where he became a draftsman for Joseph Lyman Silsbee, a noted Midwestern architect. Wright designed his first building while working for Silsbee.

Later in 1887, Wright joined the staff of the famous Chicago architects Dankmar Adler and Louis Sullivan. He soon became their chief draftsman. Wright left Adler and Sullivan in 1893 to establish his own practice. Wright's work after 1893 reflected Sullivan's influence, especially in attempts to harmonize a building's form with its function. See **Sullivan, Louis H.**

Wright's first distinctive buildings were homes designed in his famous *prairie style.* In a typical prairie house, spaces inside the home expand into the outdoors through porches and terraces. Because of their low, horizontal form, the homes seem to grow out of the ground. This effect was emphasized by Wright's use of wood and other materials as they appear in nature.

Wright designed many prairie houses in and around Chicago. The Willits House (1902) in Highland Park, Ill., was shaped like a cross, with the rooms arranged so they seemed to flow into one another. The Robie House (1909-1910) in Chicago looks like a series of horizontal layers floating over the ground.

Wright's nonresidential designs of the early 1900's included the Larkin Soap Company administration building (1904-1906) in Buffalo, N.Y., and Unity Temple (1906-1908) in Oak Park, Ill. The core of the Larkin building was a skylighted court. Unity Temple was one of the first public buildings in the United States whose concrete construction formed part of its exterior. In most earlier concrete buildings, the concrete had been covered with some other materials.

Karsh, Ottawa

Frank Lloyd Wright

In 1910, a German publishing firm published a luxurious volume of illustrations of Wright's drawings and plans. A second volume appeared in 1911. These books and later publications of Wright's works strongly influenced the development of architecture in Europe from about 1913 through the 1920's. European architects were especially impressed by Wright's complex use of cubic shapes.

During the 1920's, Wright designed several houses in southern California that are noted for the use of precast concrete blocks. He also planned the Imperial Hotel complex (1915-1922) in Tokyo. The hotel was designed to withstand the earthquakes common in Japan and was one of the few undamaged survivors of a severe earthquake that struck Tokyo in 1923.

Later career. In 1932, Wright founded the Taliesin Fellowship. This fellowship was made up of architectural students who paid to live and work with Wright. The students worked during the summer at Taliesin, Wright's home near Spring Green, Wis. During the winter, they worked at Taliesin West, Wright's home in Scottsdale, Ariz.

Wright's projects of the 1930's included the Kaufmann "Fallingwater" house (1936-1937) at Bear Run near Uniontown, Pa., and the Johnson Wax Company administration building (1936-1939) in Racine, Wis. The Kaufmann house was dramatically perched over a waterfall and became a symbol for the general public of far-out modern architecture. The Johnson Wax building featured a smooth, curved exterior of brick and glass. The design expressed the streamlined style in automobiles and other products of the late 1930's. A laboratory tower designed by Wright was added later.

During his final years, Wright designed two of his most famous projects—the Guggenheim Museum (completed in 1960) in New York City and the Marin County (Calif.) Civic Center. The interior of the museum is dominated by a spiral ramp that runs from the floor almost to the ceiling. The civic center is a series of long structures that connects three hills. About nine buildings are planned for the center, which is expected to be com-

Ed Kumler, Tom Stack & Assoc.

Wright's Marin County Civic Center was one of his final and most imaginative designs. This series of long structures connects several hills near San Francisco.

Special Report
WRIGHT, FRANK LLOYD
2002 Year Book, p. 68

WORLD BOOK photo by Dan Miller

Wright's Robie House is an example of his prairie style. He tried to blend the structure with its natural surroundings.

pleted by the year 2000.   Leland M. Roth

For additional pictures of Wright's work, see **Architecture** (Frank Lloyd Wright); **Florida** (People); **Furniture** (Organic design); **United States** (The arts). For a *Reading and Study Guide,* see *Wright, Frank Lloyd,* in the Research Guide/Index, Volume 22.

Additional resources

Gill, Brendan. *Many Masks: A Life of Frank Lloyd Wright.* Putnam, 1987.
Heinz, Thomas A. *Frank Lloyd Wright.* St. Martin's, 1982.
Twombly, Robert C. *Frank Lloyd Wright: His Life and His Architecture.* Wiley, 1979.

Wright, James Claude, Jr. (1922-   ), a Texas Democrat, served as Speaker of the United States House of Representatives from 1987 to 1989. Wright resigned as Speaker and as a member of Congress after the House Committee on Standards of Official Conduct accused him of breaking a number of House ethics rules. One charge was that Wright had accepted about $145,000 worth of gifts from a Texas real estate developer who was in a position to benefit directly from legislation over which Wright had influence. The committee also accused Wright of earning more income from outside sources than House rules permitted. According to the committee, the extra income was disguised as earnings from the sale of Wright's book *Reflections of a Public Man* (1984). Wright denied he had broken any House rules. But he resigned as Speaker and gave up his seat in Congress. Before becoming Speaker, Wright had served as majority leader of the House since 1976.

Wright was born in Fort Worth, Tex., and attended Weatherford College and the University of Texas. He left the university in 1941, during World War II, to enlist in the Army Air Forces. From 1947 to 1949, Wright was a member of the Texas House of Representatives. Then, at the age of 26, he was elected mayor of Weatherford, Tex. He was mayor until 1954, when he won election to the U.S. House of Representatives.

In Congress, Wright supported generous spending for defense and highway construction. He was also a strong supporter of water conservation.
Nancy Dickerson

Wright, Richard (1908-1960), is often considered the most important black American writer of his time. He earned a reputation for artistic excellence and outspoken criticism of racial discrimination.

Wright gained his reputation as a result of four books written early in his career. *Uncle Tom's Children* (1938), in its first edition, consists of four stories set in the South about black males who are victims of racial violence. Wright's first novel, *Native Son* (1940), tells the story of Bigger Thomas, a 19-year-old Chicago black who accidentally commits murder. Bigger is pursued, tried, and sentenced to death. The novel condemns the racial injustice that creates an environment forcing Bigger into crime. Wright warns that this environment threatens to produce new Biggers. Wright's *12 Million Black Voices* (1941) is a pictorial history of blacks in the United States. *Black Boy* (1945) is Wright's story of his childhood and youth in Mississippi and Tennessee.

Wright also wrote poetry, as well as nonfiction about his ideas and experiences. *White Man, Listen!* (1957) is a collection of some of his important essays. Wright explains why he abandoned Communism in an essay in an anthology of writings by former Communists called *The God That Failed* (1949). He continued his autobiography in *American Hunger* (published in 1977 after his death). Wright was born near Natchez, Miss.   Darwin T. Turner

Additional resources

Fabre, Michel. *The Unfinished Quest of Richard Wright.* Morrow, 1973. *The World of Richard Wright.* University Press of Mississippi, 1985.
Walker, Margaret. *Richard Wright, Daemonic Genius: A Portrait of the Man, A Critical Look at His Work.* Warner Books, 1988.

Wright, Willard H. See Van Dine, S. S.

Wright brothers—Wilbur (1867-1912) and Orville (1871-1948)—invented and built the first successful airplane. On Dec. 17, 1903, they made the world's first flight in a power-driven, heavier-than-air machine near Kitty Hawk, N.C. With Orville at the controls, the plane flew 120 feet (37 meters) and was in the air 12 seconds. The brothers made three more flights that day. The longest, by Wilbur, was 852 feet (260 meters) in 59 seconds.

Besides the Wrights, four men and one boy witnessed the flights. One of the men snapped a picture of the plane just as Orville piloted it into the air. Only a few newspapers mentioned the event, and their stories were inaccurate. The Wrights continued to fly from a pasture near their hometown of Dayton, Ohio, but local newspapers remained uninterested. The Wrights issued a statement about their achievement to the press in January 1904. It received little attention. Octave Chanute, an American civil engineer, reported their success in an article appearing in the March 1904 issue of *Popular Science Monthly.* The first eyewitness report of a flight by the Wrights appeared in a magazine called *Gleanings in Bee Culture* in January 1905.

Despite some factual and accurate stories, the Wrights' achievement was practically unknown for five years. Most people at that time remained doubtful about flying machines. In any case, the Wrights preferred to work quietly, perfecting their airplane and developing flight technique. They believed that airplanes would eventually be used to transport passengers and mail. They also hoped airplanes might serve to prevent war.

Early life. Wilbur Wright was born April 16, 1867, on a farm 8 miles (13 kilometers) from New Castle, Ind., and Orville Wright was born Aug. 19, 1871, in Dayton, Ohio. Their father was a bishop of the United Brethren Church. The boys went through high school, but neither received a diploma. Wilbur did not bother to go to the

Orville Wright

Underwood & Underwood

Wilbur Wright

commencement exercises, and Orville took special subjects rather than a prescribed course in his final year. Mechanics fascinated them even in childhood. To earn pocket money they sold homemade mechanical toys. Orville started a printing business, building his own press. They later launched a weekly paper, the *West Side News,* with Wilbur as editor. Wilbur was 25 and Orville 21 when they began to rent and sell bicycles. Then they began to manufacture them, assembling the machines in a room above their shop.

Flying experiments. After reading about the death of pioneer glider Otto Lilienthal in 1896, the brothers became interested in flying. They began serious reading on the subject in 1899, and soon obtained all the scientific knowledge of aeronautics then available.

On the advice of the Weather Bureau (now the National Weather Service) in Washington, D.C., the Wrights selected for their experiments a narrow strip of sand called Kill Devil Hill, near the settlement of Kitty Hawk, N.C. In 1900, they tested their first glider that could carry a person. The glider measured 16 feet (5 meters) from wing tip to wing tip. They returned to Kitty Hawk in 1901 with a larger glider. They showed that they could control sidewise balance by presenting the tips of the right and left wings at different angles to the wind. But neither the 1900 nor the 1901 glider had the lifting power they had counted on.

The Wrights concluded that all published tables of air pressures on curved surfaces must be wrong. They set up a 6-foot (1.8-meter) wind tunnel in their shop and began experiments with model wings. They tested more than 200 wing models in the tunnel. From the results of their tests, the brothers made the first reliable tables of air pressures on curved surfaces. These tables made it possible for them to design a machine that could fly.

The brothers built a third glider and took it to Kitty Hawk in the summer of 1902. This glider, based on their new figures, had aerodynamic qualities far in advance of any tried before. With it, they solved most of the problems of balance in flight. They made nearly 1,000 glides in this model, and, on some, covered distances of more than 600 feet (180 meters). Their basic patent, applied for in 1903, relates to the 1902 glider.

First airplane. Before leaving Kitty Hawk in 1902, the brothers started planning a power airplane. By the fall of 1903, they completed building the machine at a cost of less than $1,000. It had wings $40\frac{1}{2}$ feet (12 meters) long and weighed about 750 pounds (340 kilograms) with the pilot. They designed and built their own lightweight gasoline engine for the airplane.

The Wrights went to Kitty Hawk in September 1903, but a succession of bad storms and minor defects delayed their experiment at Kill Devil Hill until December 17. They had reason to be sure of their eventual success because their gliders had proven their airplane's design and control system to be sound. The brothers had also become skilled pilots. Their understanding of aerodynamics and ability as pilots set them apart from most others who tried and failed to fly powered airplanes.

The Wrights continued their experiments at a field near Dayton in 1904 and 1905. In 1904, they made 105 flights, but totaled only 45 minutes in the air. Two flights lasted five minutes each. On Oct. 5, 1905, the machine flew 24.2 miles (38.9 kilometers) in 38 minutes 3 seconds. When the Wrights first offered their machine to the U.S. government, they were not taken seriously. But by 1908 they closed a contract with the U.S. Department of War for the first military airplane. Meanwhile, they resumed experimental flights near Kitty Hawk that newspapers reported at great length.

Immediately after these trials, Wilbur went to France, where he aroused the admiration and enthusiasm of thousands. He made flights to altitudes of 300 feet (91 meters) and more. He arranged with a French company for the construction of his machine in France. When he returned to the United States, he made demonstration flights from Governors Island, N.Y., around the Statue of Liberty, up to Grant's Tomb, and back.

While Wilbur was in France, Orville made successful flights in the United States. On the morning of Sept. 9, 1908, he made 57 complete circles at an altitude of 120 feet (37 meters) over the drill field at Fort Myer, Va. He remained in the air 1 hour 2 minutes and set several records the same day. On September 17, however, while he was flying at 75 feet (23 meters), a blade of the right-hand propeller struck and loosened a wire of the rear rudder. The wire coiled about the blade and snapped it

Culver

The Wright brothers' first airplane reached a speed of about 30 miles (48 kilometers) per hour on its first flight in December 1903.

across the middle. The machine became difficult to manage and plunged to the earth. Orville suffered a broken thigh and two broken ribs. His passenger, Lieutenant Thomas E. Selfridge, died within three hours of a fractured skull. This accident was the most serious in the Wright brothers' career. Orville reappeared at Fort Myer the next year, fully recovered. He completed official tests with no evidence of nervousness.

In August 1909, the Wrights closed a contract with some wealthy men in Germany for the formation of a German-Wright Company. Later that year, they formed the Wright Company in New York City to manufacture airplanes. They earned some money but were troubled with imitators, infringements on their patents, conflicting claims, and lawsuits. From 1910 to 1912, the Wrights gave flying lessons to several people who later became aviation leaders and famous exhibition pilots.

After Wilbur's death. Wilbur died of typhoid fever on May 30, 1912, just as the airplane was beginning to make great advances. Orville worked on alone, and in 1913 won the Collier Trophy for a device to balance airplanes automatically. He sold his interest in the Wright Company and retired in 1915.

Orville continued work on the development of aviation in his own shop, the Wright Aeronautical Laboratory. In 1929, he received the first Daniel Guggenheim Medal for his and Wilbur's contributions to the advancement of aeronautics. He died on Jan. 30, 1948. Wilbur was elected to the Hall of Fame for Great Americans in New York City in 1955, and Orville in 1965.

Orville sent the original plane flown near Kitty Hawk to the Science Museum in London in 1928. The Science Museum sent the plane to the United States in 1948, and it is now in the National Air and Space Museum in Washington, D.C. Basic principles of that plane are used in every airplane. The Kill Devil Hill Monument National Memorial in North Carolina became the Wright Brothers National Memorial in 1953.   Roger E. Bilstein

See also **Air Force, U.S.** (picture); **Aircraft, Military** (picture); **Airplane** (The Wright brothers; pictures); **Glider** (History; picture).

Additional resources

Combs, Harry, and Caidin, Martin. *Kill Devil Hill: Discovering the Secret of the Wright Brothers.* Houghton, 1979.
Reynolds, Quentin. *The Wright Brothers: Pioneers of American Aviation.* Random House, 1981. First published in 1950. For younger readers.

Wrist is the joint that connects the hand and the forearm. A person uses the wrist to move the hand up, down, and sideways. The word *wrist* also refers to an area of the upper part of the hand. This area includes eight small bones called *carpals.*

The carpal bones extend across the hand in two rows of four bones each. Strong tissues called *ligaments* bind the carpals in place, but they also permit movement. Three carpals of the upper row join the *radius,* one of the two bones of the forearm, to form the wrist joint. The *ulna,* the other bone of the forearm, does not connect with the carpals. It forms a joint with the radius just above the wrist. This joint permits the wrist to rotate and thus helps turn the palm of the hand up and down.

Cordlike tissues called *tendons* extend through the carpal area and connect the finger bones with muscles in the arm. When these arm muscles contract, they pull

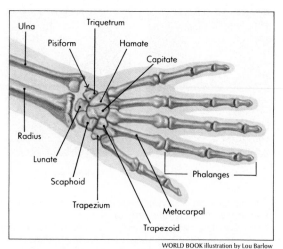

WORLD BOOK illustration by Lou Barlow

The wrist includes eight small, irregularly shaped bones located between the ulna and radius, the bones of the forearm, and the metacarpals, the bones of the palm.

the tendons and make the fingers move. The tendons on the palm side of the carpals bend the fingers. Those on the back of the hand straighten the fingers.

A fall on an outstretched arm may fracture one of the carpals, called the *scaphoid* bone, or the radius's lower end. Either injury is called a broken wrist. Many athletes suffer such fractures.   J. Donald Opgrande

See also **Carpal tunnel syndrome; Hand.**

Writ is generally used in its legal meaning to describe the written orders of a court of law. Many kinds of orders have specific names. For instance, if a court orders the sheriff to seize property which has been wrongfully taken, it gives the sheriff a *writ of replevin.* A *writ of habeas corpus* is designed to protect people taken into custody unlawfully. A *writ of error* is an order to a court to send records of a proceeding to a superior or appellate court, so that the judgment may be examined for errors of law. Early English-speaking people called anything in writing a writ. Even today, some people call the Bible the *Holy Writ.*   Paul C. Giannelli

Related articles in *World Book* include:

Attachment	Mandamus
Certiorari, Writ of	Subpoena
Habeas corpus	Summons
Injunction	

Writ of assistance was a general search warrant that permitted customs officers to enter premises in the daytime, using force if necessary, to search for goods imported illegally. The writs did not specify the place to be searched and were good for an unlimited time. But they expired six months after the death of a king. Writs were authorized for English customs officials in 1662. Courts in the American Colonies first issued them in the 1750's. The colonists strongly criticized the writs in the years before the Revolutionary War in America (1775-1783).

In 1761, James Otis of Boston tried to persuade the Superior Court of Massachusetts that writs of assistance violated "the fundamental principles of law." He failed. The controversy over such writs led to the prohibition of general warrants in the Fourth Amendment to the Constitution of the United States.   Pauline Maier

Writing, as a career, attracts more people than any other field in the arts. Writing offers various personal rewards. It enables people to express themselves, as well as to entertain, inform, and influence others. A writer needs only a few tools—paper, a typewriter, and pencils—and may achieve fame and wealth. But most authors spend hundreds of hours perfecting their skills before they can sell any of their works.

There are two main kinds of writers, *staff writers* and *free-lance writers.* Staff writers are professional writers who work for a salary. Many earn a living as newspaper reporters or columnists. Others work as *technical writers,* who express the complex ideas of engineers and scientists in words that a nonexpert can understand. Many staff writers prepare documents for public agencies. Others work as editors for book publishers, magazines, or newspapers.

Free-lance writers have no employer and earn no salary. They get paid only if a publisher buys their work. Free-lancers write most books—both fiction and nonfiction—dramas, poems, screenplays, and short stories, as well as many magazine and newspaper articles. Many staff writers create free-lance material in addition to their regular work.

This article discusses the chief types of free-lance writing and tells how to submit works for publication. For some information on how to write, see the *World Book* article on **Composition.**

Preparing for a writing career. A person who wants to be a writer should set aside some time to write every day. Learning to express ideas clearly and effectively in writing takes a great deal of practice. Many experienced writers sharpen their skills and develop new material in a private journal. A journal can also serve as a storehouse for information, observations, and ideas.

Beginning writers should also study the many kinds of writing encountered every day. News items, textbooks, cookbooks, repair manuals, essays, short stories, novels, and plays each use a particular method of organizing and presenting material. A beginner who carefully analyzes how each piece of writing works can develop a flexible approach to writing.

Successful authors write about subjects they know and understand. They gather information from experience, observation, reading, and interviews. They first write their material in rough form. Then they revise and refine it. Some authors spend weeks or months polishing an article, poem, or short story. Editors help revise the work. Beginners may ask a teacher to point out problems and suggest revisions in grammar, style, organization, and other elements of writing.

High schools and colleges offer many learning opportunities for young writers. Most students learn about composition and literature in English courses. They may also take creative writing and journalism courses to sharpen their writing abilities. Many students work on literary magazines, newspapers, and yearbooks published by their school. These young people may write stories, edit articles, and gain other valuable writing experience.

Beginners can also gain experience and recognition by entering various writing contests. Civic organizations in most communities sponsor essay contests on a wide range of topics. So do companies whose products appeal especially to young people. Entrants who express their ideas in a clear, convincing style may win a prize and have their picture appear in the local newspaper. Such rewards give a beginner confidence and provide encouragement to continue writing. Many well-known magazines also offer cash awards to promising young authors whose works they publish.

Free-lance markets include book publishers, magazines, and newspapers. A reference book called *Writer's Market* lists the name, address, editorial needs, and policies of more than 5,000 magazines, publishers, and other literary markets. It also provides general information about methods of preparing a manuscript and the legal rights of authors and publishers. *Writer's Market* is revised annually and can be found in most public libraries. Articles in such monthly magazines as *The Writer* and *Writer's Digest* also offer helpful tips on how to write and sell manuscripts.

Some magazines welcome free-lance material. Many editors send a free copy of their magazine and a list of editorial guidelines to anyone who requests them. These materials can help free-lancers decide whether the content and style of their work would appeal to readers of a publication.

Some writers hire a *literary agent* to find markets for their works. An agent reads a client's manuscript and suggests ways to improve it. The agent then tries to sell the manuscript to a publisher. If the manuscript is sold, the agent receives a commission of 10 to 15 per cent of the author's income for that piece of writing. Beginning writers should try to sell their own works. Many agents work only with writers who have been recommended by editors or professional authors.

Nonfiction ranks as the largest market for free-lance writers. Book publishers buy about 10 times as many nonfiction manuscripts as novels. In most magazines, nonfiction articles greatly outnumber poems and short stories. Nonfiction articles range in length from a few hundred words to a book-length piece. Long articles may be *serialized* (published in installments) in several issues of a magazine.

Several kinds of publications accept nonfiction from free-lancers. General-interest magazines contain articles on current, popular subjects that appeal to a wide audience. Such magazines attract many professional writers. Readers of specialized publications share a common interest, such as a hobby, a political viewpoint, a specialized technical subject, or membership in a professional organization. Many beginners succeed in selling articles to these magazines, which attract relatively few well-known writers.

Writers should choose a topic that readers want to know more about. Then they can select the *format* (kind of presentation) best suited for their subject and a particular magazine. A free-lancer who writes about money might offer an article called "How to Find a Part-Time Job" to *Seventeen.* Another article, called "Stretching Your Food Dollars," might be sent to *Family Circle.* A writer should always use reliable sources so that the article presents accurate information.

Payment for nonfiction material varies widely. Specialized publications with a relatively small readership usually offer lower payments than general-interest magazines with large readerships. Payment for a magazine article ranges from less than $100 to several thousand dollars. Book publishers usually pay authors a *royalty* (commission) of 10 to 15 per cent of the book's price for each copy sold.

Fiction sold by free-lance writers includes short stories of various kinds—adventure and confession tales, mysteries, romances, science fiction, and westerns. Markets include many general-interest publications and fiction and literary magazines.

A writer who wants to sell a novel should study the catalogs and books of various publishers. These materials help the writer determine which publishers are most likely to buy a particular kind of work. Some writers submit an entire manuscript to a publisher. Most editors respond within two months. Other writers prefer to submit only the first few chapters of a novel, plus a one- or two-page summary of the plot. This method usually brings a response in about a month.

Poetry is one of the most challenging and lowest-paying types of writing. A poet whose works appear in a literary magazine may win honor and recognition. But top general-interest magazines only pay about $3 per line for poetry. Some magazines pay poets by giving them copies of the issue in which their work appears. Literary and poetry magazines publish more poetry than any other type of publication. Some newspapers, religious magazines, and trade journals also publish poetry. A poet should study several issues of poetry magazines to determine the preferred length, style, and subject matter for each publication.

Scriptwriting. Writing scripts for plays, movies, or television can bring great financial rewards. However, scriptwriting is an extremely competitive field in which relatively few people succeed. Most plays produced on Broadway in New York City are written by established authors. Some off-Broadway and regional theaters have special programs to encourage the work of talented young playwrights. But most beginners have their works performed in school or community theaters. Many play producers and theaters list their interests and needs in *Writer's Digest* and such specialized publications as *The Dramatists Guild Quarterly, Information for Playwrights,* and *Scriptwriter News.*

Most professional and amateur productions pay the scriptwriter a percentage of the total box-office receipts as royalties. Royalties of 5 to 10 per cent are common. Other forms of payment include buying the rights to the material and payment per performance.

Many motion-picture screenplays and television scripts are written by free-lance writers. Free-lancers should hire an agent to sell such material because movie and television producers rarely deal directly with an author. The size of the royalty depends on the writer's professional reputation and the quality of the script. Such publications as *Daily Variety, The Hollywood Reporter,* and *Scriptwriter News* help writers by reporting trends in the film and television industries.

Literature for children includes adventure stories, mysteries, and articles about folklore, nature, science, and famous people. Many children's magazines also buy quizzes, puzzles, and riddles. Articles and stories published in children's magazines are usually no more than 1,500 words long. Authors usually receive payment of about 4 cents per word or a single payment that is gen-

erally less than $100. Free-lance authors write nearly all of the approximately 2,500 juvenile books published yearly in the United States. Most publishing firms that specialize in children's books prefer to receive complete manuscripts.

Preparing and submitting a manuscript. All manuscripts should be neatly typed on white, high-quality paper that measures $8\frac{1}{2}$ by 11 inches (22 by 28 centimeters). The typist should doublespace and leave a margin of about $1\frac{1}{4}$ inches (3.2 centimeters) at the top, bottom, and sides of every page. The number of each page should be at the center of the top margin. The author's name and address appear in the upper left-hand corner of the title page. The title and the author's *by-line* should be centered about halfway down the page. A by-line is the author's name as the author wants it to appear in the published article or book.

A writer may enclose a *cover letter* that briefly describes his or her qualifications for writing about the subject. Some editors prefer that a free-lancer send a *query letter* that summarizes the manuscript before submitting the entire work. The writer should always enclose a stamped, self-addressed envelope for the editor to use to return the manuscript.   Carl H. Klaus

Related articles in *World Book* include:

Autobiography	Fiction	Novel
Biography	Literature	Poetry
Book	Literature for chil-	Publishing
Criticism	dren	Science fiction
Detective story	Magazine	Short story
Drama	Motion picture	Television (Writ-
Essay	(Development)	ers)

Additional resources

Messenger, William E., and De Bruyn, Jan. *The Canadian Writer's Handbook.* 2nd ed. Prentice-Hall (Scarborough, Ont.), 1986.
The Writer's Handbook. Ed. by Sylvia K. Burack. The Writer. New editions published frequently.

Writing is a system of human communication by means of visual symbols or signs. The most primitive stages of "writing," or marking on objects, date almost from the time of the earliest human beings. However, the first fully developed system of writing appeared only about 5,500 years ago.

Counting devices have been used in all parts of the world. Such devices include sticks, pebbles, clay tokens, and strings. For example, a shepherd could record the exact number of sheep in his flock by cutting one notch in a stick for each sheep. He could also keep pebbles or clay tokens of about the same size and shape to represent the different kinds of animals in his care. The Inca of Peru tied knots in strings of various lengths and colors to keep accounts. These methods of counting could not easily be adapted to real writing.

Rock drawings conveyed a clearer meaning, but were not so useful for counting. A simple rock drawing was found near a dangerously steep trail in New Mexico. The design shows a mountain goat and a man riding a horse. The mountain goat stands on all fours, but the horse and rider are upside down. The design warns a horseman that a mountain goat can climb the rocky trail, but that his horse cannot.

Ideographs. The characteristic feature of this Indian drawing, and of any primitive drawing, is that it expresses a group of ideas without any clear connection with any language. Any other person can understand it, whether or not he or she speaks the language of the person who drew it. This way of expressing ideas, not necessarily in words, is called *ideography.* Pictures drawn for the purpose of communication differ only slightly from pictures drawn for artistic purposes. Communication pictures are simplified and stereotyped, and they have no details that are not needed as part of the communication.

Logographs. Human beings took the decisive step in developing real writing when they learned to express ideas indirectly. They did this by using signs that stood for the words in their language, not the ideas the words stood for. This kind of writing is called *logography.* To see how it works, take such a message as "The king killed a lion." In ideography, the message would include two drawings, one showing a man with the insignia of his office, such as a crown, holding a spear in his hand, and the other showing a lion. Logography, or word writing, would express the same message by signs that stand for the words themselves. One picture, of a man wearing a crown, stands for the word "king." A spear stands for the word "kill," and a drawing of a lion stands for "lion." If the king had killed three lions, the phrase "three lions" would be expressed in word writing by two signs, one standing for the numeral "three" and the other for "lion." In ideography, the message would have to contain pictures of three lions.

Early in the development of this kind of writing, the pictures became *conventional,* or simplified and formal. They often showed only a part for the whole, such as a crown for the word "king." But pictures cannot represent words like "the" or "a," nor can they represent grammatical endings like the "-ed" of "killed."

The Sumerians, who lived in southern Mesopotamia, were the first people to reach the stage of a primitive writing, about 3500 B.C. They kept records with such simple entries as "10 arrows" and the sign for a personal name, or "5 cows" and the sign for another name. They could easily use signs for numbers and for items such as arrows or cows. But they had difficulty in writing names and abstract ideas.

Phonetization. To overcome these problems, the Sumerians found that they could use word-symbols of objects that were easy to picture, like "arrow," to stand for words that sounded similar, but were hard to picture. The sign for "arrow" could also stand for "life," because the word *ti* means both things in Sumerian. This principle of *phonetization,* often called the *rebus* principle, is the most important single step in the history of writing (see **Rebus**). If the arrow sign could stand for both "arrow" and "life," because they are both pronounced *ti,* why not use the arrow sign for the sound *ti* wherever it occurs, regardless of its meaning? The Sumerian language was made up largely of one-syllable words, so it was not difficult for the people to work out a *syllabary* of about one hundred phonetic signs.

Sumerian writing is called *logo-syllabic,* or word-syllabic. It uses both *logograms,* or word signs, and *syllabograms,* or syllabic signs. Logograms expressed most of the words in the language, and syllabograms expressed rare and abstract words and proper names. Sumerian writing gradually developed the wedgelike appearance we call *cuneiform.* The Babylonians and Assyrians took cuneiform from the Sumerians, and the

Hittites and other peoples learned it from them (see **Cuneiform**).

The Egyptians developed another important word-syllabic writing, *hieroglyphic,* about 3000 B.C. It resembled Sumerian in using word-signs, but differed in the choice of syllabic signs. The Sumerians regularly indicated differences in vowels in their syllabic signs, but the Egyptians did not. The Hittites also had a writing of their own, *hieroglyphic Hittite,* that was related to some of the systems used in the lands around the Aegean Sea. See **Hieroglyphics.**

The Chinese, perhaps about 1500 B.C., began the most highly developed word writing in the world. The peoples of the Middle East usually had only a few hundred word signs, but the Chinese may have as many as 50,000. They use some of these signs for the syllables in proper names or in foreign words.

The alphabet. The older word-syllable systems were gradually simplified. From the complicated Egyptian system, the Semites of Syria, especially the Phoenicians, developed simple systems of from 22 to 30 signs, each standing for a consonant followed by any vowel. The Japanese worked out a syllabic system with symbols for an initial consonant and different vowels. They also used many word symbols borrowed from Chinese. The alphabet was the next step. The Greeks were the first to evolve a system of vowel signs, creating the first alphabetic system of writing.   I. J. Gelb

Related articles. See the articles on letters of the alphabet. See also the following articles:

Aegean civilization	Egypt, Ancient (The	Manuscript
Alphabet	people)	Pictograph
Babylonia	Hittites	Rune
Chinese language	Inca	Sumer

Wrocław, *VRAWTS lahf* (pop. 637,200), is a city that lies in southwestern Poland on the Oder River. For location, see **Poland** (political map). Wrocław serves as a rail center and river port. Leading products of Wrocław include computers, machinery, and textiles. The city has two universities and a cathedral that dates from the 1100's. Wrocław became part of Poland in the 900's. Austria took over the city in 1526 and Prussia seized it in 1742. Wrocław became part of Germany in 1871. The city's German name was *Breslau.* When World War II ended in 1945, Poland again gained control of the city.

Adam Bromke

Wryneck, also called *snakebird,* is a small, mottled-brown bird of Europe. Three of its species also live in Africa. The bird nests in the hollows of trees. When the wryneck is disturbed, it thrusts its head and neck out of its nest and hisses. Its name comes from the twisting motion of its neck when it does this. The wryneck has a cone-shaped beak and a horny-tipped tongue.

Scientific classification. The European wrynecks belong to the woodpecker family, Picidae. They are *Jynx torquilla.*

Arthur A. Allen

WORLD BOOK illustration by Trevor Boyer, Linden Artists Ltd.

European wryneck

Wu, *woo,* **Chien-shiung,** *chehn shung* (1912?-   ), an American experimental physicist, helped disprove the law of the conservation of parity (see **Parity** [In physics]). For about 30 years, most physicists had accepted this law as a universal principle. But in 1957, Wu did an experiment that showed it to be incorrect.

The law stated, in part, that electrons called *beta particles,* which are emitted by a radioactive nucleus, would fly off in any direction, regardless of the spin of the nucleus. Using atoms of cobalt-60, Wu showed that beta particles were more likely to be emitted in a particular direction that depended on the spin of the cobalt nuclei. Her experiment confirmed a theory proposed in 1956 by two Chinese-born American physicists, Tsung Dao Lee and Chen Ning Yang. Lee and Yang shared the 1957 Nobel Prize in physics for their theory.

Wu was born in Liuhe, China, near Shanghai. She moved to the United States in 1936 and received a Ph.D. degree from the University of California at Berkeley. Wu became a professor of physics at Columbia University in 1957.   Stanley Goldberg

Wu Daozi, *woo dow dzuh* (A.D. 700's), was a famous Chinese painter. His name is also spelled *Wu Tao-tzu.* He painted chiefly religious subjects on the walls of Buddhist and Taoist temples in the Chinese capital of Chang'an (now Xian). He usually worked on a very large scale in black and white. His murals were destroyed, and we can only imagine his style from descriptions and inferior copies. He was born near Luoyang, in Henan.

Robert A. Rorex

Wu Tao-tzu. See Wu Daozi.

Wuchang. See Wuhan.

Wuhan, *woo hahn* (pop. 3,340,000), is the collective name for the adjacent cities of Hankou, Hanyang, and Wuchang in Hubei Province of China (see **China** [political map] for the location of Wuhan). The cities are considered a single political and economic unit. Wuchang lies on the south bank of the Yangtze River. Hankou and Hanyang are on the north bank. The Han River separates Hankou and Hanyang. The Han River bridge and ferries provide transportation between these two cities. The Yangtze bridge links Wuchang with Hanyang. Wuhan, an industrial center, was the birthplace of the Chinese Revolution in 1911.   Parris H. Chang

Wundt, *voont,* **Wilhelm,** *VIHL hehlm* (1832-1920), a German philosopher, became known as the father of modern psychology. He founded one of the first laboratories for experimental psychology in 1879. He believed the ways of studying psychology included both laboratory experimentation and *introspection* (self-observation). He was born in Neckarau, in Baden. See also **Psychology** (History).   Kenneth E. Clark

Wupatki National Monument, *wu PAT kee,* is in northern Arizona. It contains prehistoric dwellings, built by farming Indians. The Hopi Indians are believed to be partially descended from the Indians who built these dwellings. The monument was established in 1924. For its area, see **National Park System** (table: National monuments).   Critically reviewed by the National Park Service

Wyandotte Cave. See Indiana (Places to visit).

Wyatt, *WY uht,* **Sir Thomas** (1503?-1542), was an English poet. His most important works are lyrics he wrote for lute accompaniment. Wyatt was active during the first phase of the English Renaissance. He adapted

works by many writers, including the Italian Renaissance poet Luigi Alamanni. Wyatt and Henry Howard, Earl of Surrey, are credited with introducing Petrarch's sonnet techniques into English literature. Wyatt is usually linked in literary history with the Earl of Surrey because their poems were first published together in *The Book of Songs and Sonnets* (1557), usually called *Tottel's Miscellany.* See **Surrey, Earl of.**

Wyatt was born in Kent. He received a good education, and traveled on the European continent as a diplomat for King Henry VIII. Wyatt wrote a satire on court life called *Mine Owne John Poins.*   John N. King

Wycherley, *WIHCH uhr lee,* **William** (1640?-1716), an English playwright, ranks with Sir George Etherege and William Congreve as a leading author of witty satires called *comedies of manners* during the Restoration period of English literature. Many of Wycherley's plays are brutally satiric and his attitude toward people is often venomous and cynical.

Wycherley's first plays, *Love in a Wood* (1671) and *The Gentleman Dancing Master* (1672), are light comedies of intrigue. *The Country Wife* (1675) best reveals Wycherley's attitude toward his society and toward humanity. Most of the characters are fools, *cuckolds* (husbands of unfaithful wives), or comically shrewd seekers of sexual pleasures. *The Plain Dealer* (1676) is based partly on plays by Shakespeare and Molière, but it is more savage in its presentation of humanity. Wycherley was born in the county of Shropshire.   Albert Wertheim

Wycliffe, *WIHK lihf,* **John** (1328?-1384), was a leading English philosopher in religion and politics during the late Middle Ages. His challenges to religious and political practices remained influential long after Wycliffe's death.

Wycliffe was educated at Oxford University and became a *master* (professor) there at Balliol College in 1360. At one time, he served as a parish priest, but he was best known as a professor of philosophy.

Wycliffe felt driven to become a reformer because of conditions in Europe during his time. A form of bubonic plague called the *black death* killed about a fourth of Europe's population during the 1300's. The Hundred Years' War between England and France began in 1337. Throughout the 1300's, violent struggles for power occurred between the popes and clergy on one side, and the kings and their nobles on the other. Both sides seemed corrupt and dominated by self-interest, and neither apparently cared about the common people.

The conditions in Europe raised many questions in people's minds. Was the pope lord over kings? Could a civil government punish a wicked bishop or priest? Could a civil government tax the church, or could the church demand that the government support it? Could church rulers or civil rulers make laws merely because they wished to, or did their laws have to be fair? Wycliffe dealt with these issues in his lectures and books. His chief political idea was summarized in the statement, "Dominion is founded in grace." He meant that unjust rulers could not claim that people must obey them because obedience was God's will. After Wycliffe applied this idea to the popes and bishops, he was tried several times in church courts. Each time, the English royal family saved him from condemnation.

By about 1371, Wycliffe had become a writer for the

Dry-brush tempera (1954); collection of Mr. and Mrs. Joseph E. Levine

Teel's Island by **Andrew Wyeth** shows how the artist created a haunting mood of isolation out of a commonplace subject. Wyeth painted the scene while visiting a friend on an island in Maine.

royal family and its supporters against the bishops and their followers. He evidently felt that there was more hope of reform from the royal family. Wycliffe tried to show that the claim to authority by popes and bishops was founded on false ideas of the superiority of priests over lay people. He denied the doctrine of transubstantiation, which he regarded as the basis of the clergy's claim to superiority. According to this doctrine, priests changed bread and wine into the body and blood of Jesus Christ during the Mass. In Wycliffe's later writings, he declared that the Bible, not the church, was the authority for Christian beliefs.

Wycliffe's followers, with his help and inspiration, translated the Bible into English about 1382. They completed an improved version about 1388, after his death. Wycliffe's followers, called *Lollards,* were severely persecuted in England (see **Lollards**). The upper classes felt that Wycliffe's ideas encouraged the poor to demand better lives.

Wycliffe's writings influenced a number of reformers, including John Hus of Bohemia. Many early English Protestants regarded the teachings of Wycliffe as forerunners of those of the Reformation. They considered him the first great English reformer.   Peter W. Williams

Wyeth, Andrew (1917-   ), probably ranks as the most popular American painter of his time. He is best known for his realistic and thoughtful pictures of people and places in rural Pennsylvania and Maine.

Wyeth's paintings show uncrowded rural scenes that are reminders of earlier American life. His works include pictures of old buildings with bare windows and cracked ceilings, and abandoned boats on deserted beaches. Such scenes portray the remains of past activity rather than the accomplishments of the present. Wyeth also depicts the people he knows. In 1986, he revealed a group of works representing a neighbor named Helga. She had been one of his favorite subjects for 15 years. An example of his portraits, *Albert's Son,* appears in the **Painting** article.

Wyeth paints in a style that follows the tradition of Thomas Eakins and Winslow Homer, two realistic American painters of the late 1800's. His work is often extremely detailed. Wyeth paints in *egg tempera,* a me-

dium that allows him to represent tiny details and gives his pictures a smooth, delicate surface. He also uses a water color technique called *dry brush.*

Wyeth was born in Chadds Ford, Pa., near Philadelphia. His father, N. C. Wyeth, was a noted illustrator of children's books (see **Literature for children** [picture: Great illustrators of the 1900's]). He gave Andrew an appreciation of disciplined drafting skills. Andrew Wyeth's son Jamie is also a painter.   Pamela A. Ivinski

Wyler, William (1902-1981), was a motion-picture director whose films have a high artistic quality and wide popular appeal. He won Academy Awards for his directing in three films: *Mrs. Miniver* (1942), *The Best Years of Our Lives* (1946), and *Ben-Hur* (1959). His other important films include *Dodsworth* (1936), *Dead End* (1937), *Wuthering Heights* (1939), *The Letter* (1940), *The Little Foxes* (1941), *The Heiress* (1948), *Roman Holiday* (1953), *The Desperate Hours* (1955), *Friendly Persuasion* (1956), *Collector* and *Funny Girl* (1968).

Wyler was born in Mulhouse, France. He was a film publicist in Europe before coming to Hollywood in 1920 as an assistant director. He became a director and a United States citizen in 1928.   Howard Thompson

Wylie, Elinor (1885-1928), was an American poet. Her style is noted for its rich, exact vocabulary and its brilliant word pictures. Wylie experimented widely in traditional verse forms, and was equally skilled using such forms as blank verse and the sonnet. Her goal as a poet was the refinement of verse technique.

Wylie had a short but brilliant literary career. She became known in 1921 with the publication of her first major collection, *Net to Catch the Wind.* She wrote three more volumes of poetry: *Black Armour* (1923), *Trivial Breath* (1928), and *Angels and Earthly Creatures* (published in 1929, after her death). Wylie also wrote four novels, all with historical backgrounds. The best known is *Jennifer Lorn* (1923).

Wylie was born in Somerville, N.J. Her maiden name was Elinor Hoyt. She wrote under the name of her second husband, Horace Wylie. In 1923, she married her third husband, William Rose Benét. After her death, Benét edited Wylie's *Collected Poems* (1932) and *Collected Prose* (1933).   Bonnie Costello

John M. Burnley, Bruce Coleman Inc.

The Teton Mountains rise sharply from a beautiful valley called Jackson Hole in northwestern Wyoming. The Grand Teton peak, *center,* rises to a height of 13,770 feet (4,197 meters). The majestic mountains are a feature of Grand Teton National Park.

Wyoming *The Equality State*

Wyoming is a state of the United States that is famous for the beauty of its mountains. The peaks of the Rocky Mountains tower over the landscape. They provide the setting for the nation's largest and the world's oldest national park—Yellowstone. Wyoming also has the first national monument in the United States, Devils Tower, and the first national forest, Shoshone. Another famous scenic wonder, Grand Teton National Park, includes some of the West's most beautiful mountains. Millions of tourists visit Wyoming each year to enjoy its scenery and historic places.

Not all of Wyoming is mountainous. Between the mountain ranges in the state lie broad, flat, treeless basins. Some are dotted with rugged, lonely towers of

The contributors of this article are Ronald E. Beiswenger, Professor of Geography at the University of Wyoming; and Robert W. Righter, Associate Professor of History at the University of Wyoming.

rock called *buttes.* In the eastern part of the state, a flat, dry plain stretches westward toward the mountains.

Much of Wyoming's wealth comes from its land. About 80 per cent of the state's land is used for grazing. Thousands of oil wells dot the prairies. Visitors may see a white-face steer cropping the grass near a pumping oil well. Petroleum, natural gas, coal, and other minerals make Wyoming an important mining state.

Most of Wyoming's workers are employed in service industries. Service industries include such activities as education, health care, and retail trade.

The federal government owns almost half the land in Wyoming. Since the state depends mostly on its land, this makes the government especially important in Wyoming's economy. Federal agencies control grazing, logging, and mining activities that take place on the government land. The U.S. Air Force operates a nuclear missile base just outside Cheyenne, the state capital.

Wyoming has attracted travelers since the earliest days of white settlement. Three of the great pioneer

Interesting facts about Wyoming

The world's largest bronze bust, a likeness of Abraham Lincoln, is located near Laramie. University of Wyoming sculptor Robert Russin created the bust, which weighs 3 short tons (3.2 metric tons). It is 12 feet (3.8 meters) tall and rests on a stone base 30 feet (9 meters) high.

Independence Rock is a granite boulder located near Casper. It rises to a height of 193 feet (59 meters) and covers 27 acres (11 hectares). The rock is called the "Register of the Desert." More than 5,000 pioneers have carved their names on the rock, some as long ago as the early 1800's.

It took four treaties for the United States to get the land that makes up Wyoming, more than for any other state.

Independence Rock

WORLD BOOK illustrations by Kevin Chadwick

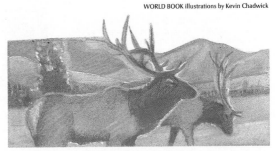

The National Elk Refuge

The National Elk Refuge, near Jackson, was established in 1912. It was the first big-game refuge created before the animals to be protected were considered endangered. The refuge covers about 25,000 acres (10,000 hectares). From 7,000 to 8,000 elk feed there each winter. The first national forest, Shoshone, and the first national park, Yellowstone, are also in Wyoming.

Wyoming Travel Commission

Ranchers round up cattle on a Wyoming range. Ranching ranks as the leading agricultural activity in the state. About 50 per cent of Wyoming's land is used to graze cattle and sheep.

trails of the United States cross Wyoming. The California, Mormon, and Oregon trails all took the covered wagons through South Pass. This pass became famous as the easiest way for the pioneers to travel across the mountains.

Millions of people have crossed Wyoming, but relatively few have stayed. The 1980 United States census reported that Wyoming had fewer people than any other state except Alaska. According to Census Bureau estimates, Alaska passed Wyoming in population in 1985, leaving Wyoming last among the states. Wyoming's largest city, Casper, has only about 51,000 people.

The word *Wyoming* comes from a Delaware Indian word meaning *upon the great plain.* Wyoming is nicknamed the *Equality State* because Wyoming women were the first in the nation to vote, hold public office, and serve on juries. In 1870, Wyoming's Esther H. Morris became the nation's first woman justice of the peace. In 1924, Wyoming voters elected the first woman governor, Nellie Tayloe Ross.

Wyoming Travel Commission

Frontier Days, Wyoming's most popular annual event, takes place during late July in Cheyenne. The festival has been held each year since 1897. Cheyenne is the capital of Wyoming.

Wyoming in brief

Symbols of Wyoming

The state flag, adopted in 1917, shows the seal on a buffalo to represent the branding of livestock. The red border symbolizes Indians and the blood of the pioneers. On the state seal, adopted in 1893, the woman and the motto symbolize equal rights in Wyoming, the first state to grant unrestricted civil and political rights to women. A cowboy and a miner represent the state's important livestock and mining industries.

State flag

State seal

Wyoming (brown) ranks ninth in size among all the states and fourth among the Rocky Mountain States (yellow).

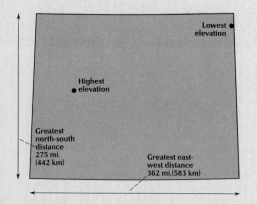

The State Capitol is in Cheyenne, the capital of Wyoming since 1869.

General information

Statehood: July 10, 1890, the 44th state.
State abbreviations: Wyo. (traditional); WY (postal).
State motto: *Equal Rights.*
State song: "Wyoming." Words by Charles E. Winter; music by G. E. Knapp.

Land and climate

Area: 97,809 sq. mi. (253,326 km²), including 820 sq. mi. (2,125 km²) of inland water.
Elevation: *Highest*—Gannett Peak, 13,804 ft. (4,207 m) above sea level. *Lowest*—Belle Fourche River in Crook County, 3,100 ft. (945 m) above sea level.
Record high temperature: 114° F. (46° C) at Basin on July 12, 1900.
Record low temperature: −63° F. (−53° C) at Moran on Feb. 9, 1933.
Average July temperature: 67° F. (19° C).
Average January temperature: 19° F. (−7° C).
Average yearly precipitation: 13 in. (33 cm).

Lowest elevation

Highest elevation

Greatest north-south distance 275 mi. (442 km)

Greatest east-west distance 362 mi. (583 km)

Important dates

	Robert Stuart discovered South Pass, which became an important pioneer route across the Rocky Mountains.
	The Union Pacific Railroad entered Wyoming.

1807   1812   1834   1867   1872

John Colter explored the Yellowstone area.

William Sublette and Robert Campbell established Fort William (later Fort Laramie).

Yellowstone became the first national park.

State bird
Meadowlark

State flower
Indian paintbrush

State tree
Cottonwood

People

Population: 469,557 (1980 census)
Rank among the states: 49th
Density: 5 persons per sq. mi. (2 per km²), U.S. average 67 per sq. mi. (26 per km²)
Distribution: 63 per cent urban, 37 per cent rural
Largest cities in Wyoming

Casper	51,016
Cheyenne	47,283
Laramie	24,410
Rock Springs	19,458
Sheridan	15,146
Green River	12,807

Source: U.S. Bureau of the Census.

Population trend

Thousands

Year	Population*
1985	509,000
1980	469,557
1970	332,416
1960	330,066
1950	290,529
1940	250,742
1930	225,565
1920	194,402
1910	145,965
1900	92,531
1890	62,555
1880	20,789
1870	9,118

*All figures are census figures except 1985, which is an estimate.

Source: U.S. Bureau of the Census.

Economy

Chief products

Agriculture: beef cattle.
Manufacturing: chemicals, petroleum products.
Mining: petroleum, coal, natural gas.

Gross state product

Value of goods and services produced in 1986, $11,673,000,000. *Services* include community, business, and personal services; finance; government; trade; and transportation, communication, and utilities. *Industry* includes construction, manufacturing, and mining. *Agriculture* includes agriculture, fishing, and forestry.

Source: U.S. Bureau of Economic Analysis.

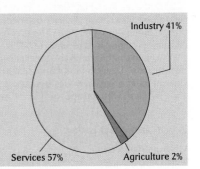

Industry 41%
Services 57%
Agriculture 2%

Government

State government

Governor: 4-year term.
State senators: 30; 4-year terms.
State representatives: 64; 2-year terms.
Counties: 23

Federal government

United States senators: 2
United States representatives: 1
Electoral votes: 3

Sources of information

Tourism: Wyoming Travel Commission, I-25 and College Drive, Cheyenne, WY 82002
Economy: Economic Development and Stabilization Board, Herschler Building, Cheyenne, WY 82002
Government: Legislative Service Office, Capitol, Cheyenne, WY 82002
History: State Archives Museum and Historical Department, Barrett Building, Cheyenne, WY 82002

Wyoming became the 44th state on July 10.

The first U.S. operational intercontinental ballistic missile base opened near Cheyenne.

| 1883 | 1890 | 1925 | 1960 |

The state's first oil well was drilled in the Dallas Field near Lander.

Nellie Tayloe Ross became the first woman governor in the United States.

People

Population. The 1980 United States census reported that Wyoming had 469,557 people. The population had increased about 42 per cent over the 1970 figure, 332,416. The percentage increase was one of the highest among the states. The U.S. Bureau of the Census estimated that by 1985 the state's population had reached about 509,000.

About three-fifths of Wyoming's people live in cities. Most of the cities are small compared with those in other states. Casper, the largest city, and Cheyenne, the capital and second largest city, both have only about 50,000 people. The next three cities, in order of size, are Laramie, Rock Springs, and Sheridan. About a fourth of the state's people live in cities and towns along a single major highway and rail line in southern Wyoming. See the separate articles on the cities of Wyoming listed in the *Related articles* at the end of this article.

Wyoming has two metropolitan areas, the Casper metropolitan area and the Cheyenne metropolitan area. For their populations, see the *Index* to the political map of Wyoming.

About 98 out of 100 people in Wyoming were born in the United States. Wyoming has about 7,000 Indians. Over half of them live on the Wind River reservation near Riverton.

Schools. The first school in Wyoming was founded at Fort Laramie in 1852. William Vaux, the chaplain of the fort, started the school. In 1860, a school was built at Fort Bridger, and its students began studying that year. In 1869, the territorial legislature passed a law providing tax support for schools. There were district schools in many communities after 1870. The first high school in Wyoming opened in Cheyenne in 1875.

Wyoming's public school system is supervised by an elected state superintendent of public instruction. A nine-member board of education makes school policies. The governor, with the approval of the senate, appoints

Population density

Wyoming is one of the most sparsely populated states. About 60 per cent of the people live in urban areas, but most cities are small compared with those of other states.

	Persons per sq. mi.	Persons per km²
More than 10		More than 4
5 to 10		2 to 4
2 to 5		1 to 2
Less than 2		Less than 1

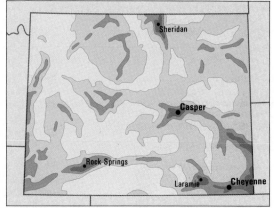

WORLD BOOK map; based on U.S. Bureau of the Census data.

board members to six-year terms. Most of the money for Wyoming's schools comes from property taxes. Income from state-owned land also supports the schools.

Children are required to attend school either from age 7 through 15, or until they complete the eighth grade. Wyoming has one of the highest percentages in the United States of people who can read and write. For the number of students and teachers in Wyoming, see **Education** (table).

The University of Wyoming is the state's only univer-

Wyoming map index

Metropolitan area

Casper 71,856
Cheyenne 68,649

Counties

Albany ....29,062..I	14
Big Horn ....11,896..B	10
Campbell ......24,367..D	14
Carbon ....21,896..I	11
Converse ......14,069..F	14
Crook ....5,308..B	15
Fremont ....38,992..F	7
Goshen ....12,040..I	16
Hot Springs .....5,710..E	9
Johnson ....6,700..D	12
Laramie ....68,649..J	15
Lincoln ....12,177..H	5
Natrona ....71,856..F	11
Niobrara ....2,924..F	15
Park ....21,639..C	8
Platte ....11,975..H	15
Sheridan ......25,048..B	11
Sublette ....4,548..G	6
Sweetwater ...41,723..J	8
Teton ....9,355..D	6
Uinta ....13,021..J	5
Washakie ....9,496..D	10
Weston ....7,106..D	15

Cities and towns

Acme ....B	11
Afton ....1,481..G	5
Aladdin ....B	16
Albany ....J	13
Albin ....128..J	16
Alcova ....G	12
Alpine Junction ....F	5
Altvan ....J	15
Amesville ....F	5
Arapahoe ....F	9
Archer I	15

Arlington I	13
Arminto ....F	11
Arvada ....B	13
Aspen Tunnels ....J	5
Atlantic City ....G	8
Auburn ....F	5
Ayers ....H	15
Baggs ....433..K	10
Bairoil ....H	10
Banner ....B	12
Barnum ....E	11
Basin ....1,349.°C	10
Beckton ....B	11
Beckwith ....H	5
Bedford ....F	5
Bentonite Spur ....B	16
Beulah ....B	16
Big Horn ....B	11
Big Piney ....530..G	6
Big Sandy ....G	7
Big Trails ....D	11
Bill ....E	14
Bitter Creek I	9
Bondurant ....K	2
Bonneville ....E	10
Bordeaux ....H	15
Bosler I	14
Bosler Junction I	14
Boulder ....G	7
Boxelder ....G	13
Brookhurst ....F	13
Buckhorn C	16
Buffalo ....3,799.°C	12
Buford ....J	14
Burgess Junction ......B	10
Burlington C	9
Burns ....268..J	16
Burntfork ....K	6
Burris ....E	9
Byron ....633..B	9
Calpet ....H	6
Canyon Junction ......F	2
Carlile C	15
Carpenter ....J	16

Carter ....J	5
Casper ....51,016.°F	12
Cassa ....G	15
Centennial ....J	13
Cheyenne ....47,283.°J	15
Chugwater ....282..I	15
Church Butte ....J	6
Clareton ....D	15
Clark ....B	8
Clay Spur ....D	15
Clearmont ....191..B	12
Cody ....6,790.°C	8
Cokeville ....515..H	5
Colony ....B	16
Colter ....D	10
Colter Bay I	2
Cora ....F	6
Cow Creek ....E	15
Cowley ....455..B	9
Coyote Springs I	12
Creston I	10
Creston Junction I	10
Crooks Gap ....G	10
Crowheart ....E	8
Curtis ....H	15
Dale Creek ....J	14
Daniel ....F	6
Daniel Junction ....F	6
Dayton ....701..B	11
Deaver ....178..B	9
Devils Tower ....B	15
Diamond I	15
Diamondville ...1,000..I	5
Dixon ....82..K	10
Donkey Creek C	15
Douglas ....6,030.°G	14
Dubois ....1,067..E	7
Duncan ....E	7
Durkee ....D	10
Duroc I	16
Dwyer ....H	15
East Thermopolis ...359..E	9
Echeta C	13
Eden ....H	7

Edgerton ....510..E	13
Edson I	12
Egbert ....J	16
Elk I	2
Elk Mountain ....338..I	12
Elkol I	5
Elmo I	12
Emblem C	9
Encampment .....611..J	12
Ervay ....F	11
Esterbrook ....G	14
Ethete ....F	8
Etna ....F	5
Evanston ....6,421.°J	5
Evansville ....2,335..F	13
Fairview ....G	5
Farrah ....B	16
Farson ....H	7
Farthing I	14
Ferris ....H	11
Fletcher Park ....H	14
Fontenelle ....H	6
Fort Bridger ....J	6
Fort Fred Steele I	11
Fort Laramie ....356..H	16
Fort Washakie ....F	8
Four Corners C	16
Fox Farm° .....2,850..J	15
Foxpark ....J	13
Frannie ....138..B	9
Freedom ....F	5
Freeland ....G	12
Frewen I	10
Frontier I	5
Garland ....B	9
Garrett ....H	14
Gebo ....D	9
Gibson ....H	15
Gillette ....12,134.°C	14
Glendo ....367..G	15
Glenrock ....2,736..F	13
Golden Prairie ....J	16
Goose Egg ....G	12
Granger ....177..I	6

Granite Canyon ....J	15
Grant Village ....G	2
Grass Creek ....D	9
Green River .....12,807.°I	7
Greybull ....2,277..C	10
Grover ....F	5
Grovont ....J	2
Guernsey ....1,512..H	15
Hamilton Dome ....D	9
Hampshire ....E	15
Hampton I	6
Hanna ....2,288..I	12
Harriman ....K	14
Hartville ....149..H	15
Hat Creek ....F	16
Hawk Springs I	16
Heldt ....H	16
Hermosa ....J	14
Highlight ....D	14
Hiland ....F	11
Hillsdale ....J	16
Hoback Junction ......K	2
Horse Creek ....J	14
Horton C	16
Howell ....J	14
Hudson ....514..F	9
Hulett ....291..B	15
Huntley ....H	16
Hyattville C	10
Jackson ....4,511.°E	5
James Town I	7
Jay Em ....G	16
Jeffrey City .....1,882..G	10
Jelm ....J	13
Jerome ....D	15
Kane ....B	9
Kaycee ....271..D	12
Kearny C	12
Keeline ....G	15
Kelly ....J	2
Kemmerer .....3,273.°I	5
Kinnear ....F	8
Kirby ....129..D	9
Kirtley ....F	16

sity. It is accredited by the North Central Association of Colleges and Schools. The university was founded in Laramie in 1886, and is state supported. Wyoming also has seven community colleges.

Libraries and museums. In 1886, Wyoming's territorial legislature passed laws providing for a system of free county libraries. Today, each of Wyoming's 23 counties has a public county library. The Wyoming Territorial Library was established in Cheyenne in 1871. It is now called the Wyoming State Library. The chief libraries at the University of Wyoming include the William Robertson Coe Library and a geological library.

Wyoming has about 90 museums. Most of these museums feature pioneer and Indian relics. Outstanding collections in the state include the exhibits at the Wyoming State Museum and the Cheyenne Frontier Days Old West Museum, both in Cheyenne; the Fort Caspar Museum in Casper; the Fort Bridger State Museum in Fort Bridger; and the Wyoming Pioneers' Memorial Museum in Douglas.

Other museums have exhibits about particular areas or points of interest. For example, the Fort Laramie National Historic Site has relics from the days of the old pioneer wagon trains. The Jackson Hole Museum in Jackson, has displays about the area's early days. The National Park Service operates the Fur Trade Museum at Moose. The National Park Service also operates the Colter Bay Museum, which has a fine collection of Indian art. This museum is located in Grand Teton National Park.

The Buffalo Bill Historical Center in Cody displays possessions of the famous hunter and showman, Buffalo Bill Cody. Also in the center are the Whitney Gallery of Western Art, which features paintings and sculpture by famous Western artists; the Plains Indian Museum; and the Winchester Museum, which has a collection of more than 5,000 firearms.

The University of Wyoming Geological Museum has fine collections of fossils, minerals, and rocks. It also features exhibits about prehistoric times.

University of Wyoming, in Laramie, is the state's only university. Robert Russin's sculpture *The Family, center,* stands on the main quadrangle of the campus.

University of Wyoming

Name	Map	Name	Map	Name	Map	Name	Map	Name	Map
La Barge ....302..H	6	Meriden I	16	Parkman ....B	11	Salt Wells I	8	Trotter ....B	8
La Grange ....232..I	16	Merna ....F	6	Patrick Draw I	9	Sand Draw ....G	9	Ucross ....B	12
Lake Junction ....G	2	Midvale ....F	9	Pavillion ....287..F	8	Saratoga ....2,410..J	12	Ulm ....B	12
Lamont..................H	11	Midwest ....638..E	13	Pedro ....D	16	Savageton ....D	13	Upton ....1,193..C	15
Lance Creek ....F	15	Milford ....F	8	Piedmont ....J	5	Savery ....K	11	Urie ....J	6
Lander ....7,867.°F	8	Millis ....J	5	Pine Bluffs ....1,077..J	16	Seely ....B	15	Uva ....H	15
Laramie .... 24,410.°J	14	Mills ....2,139..F	12	Pinedale ....1,066.°F	7	Seminoe Dam ....H	12	Valley C	7
Leefe I	5	Moneta ....F	10	Point of Rocks I	8	Shawnee ....G	15	Van Tassell ....10..G	16
Leiter ....B	12	Moorcroft ....1,014..C	15	Powder River ....F	11	Shell C	10	Verne I	6
Leo ....H	12	Moose ....J	2	Powell ....5,310..B	8	Sheridan .... 15,146.°B	11	Verona ....B	12
Leroy ....J	5	Moran Junction I	2	Prospector\-Rawhide		Shoshoni ....879..F	9	Veteran ....H	16
Lightning Flat ....B	15	Morrisey ....E	16	Village* ....1,100..C	4	Sibylee ....H	15	Wakeley ....B	11
Linch ....E	13	Morton ....F	8	Quealy I	8	Sinclair ....586..I	11	Walcott I	12
Lindbergh ....J	16	Morton ....F	14	Ragan ....J	5	Skull Creek C	16	Waltman ....F	11
Lingle ....475..H	16	Moskee C	16	Ralston ....B	8	Smoot ....G	5	Wamsutter ....681..I	10
Little America I	7	Mountain Home ....K	13	Ranchester ....655..B	11	South Cole Creek ....E	13	Wapiti C	7
Little Medicine ....G	13	Mountain View .....628..J	6	Raven ....D	15	South Pass City ....G	8	Warren* ....3,627..J	15
Lonetree ....J	6	Mountain View ....F	12	Rawhide Village, see		South Superior .....586..I	8	Wendover ....H	15
Lost Cabin ....E	10	Moyer I	5	Prospector\-Rawhide		South Torrington ....H	16	Wertz Dome ....H	11
Lost Springs ....9..G	15	Muddy Gap ....H	11	Village]		Split Rock ....G	10	West Thumb ....G	2
Lovell ....2,447..B	9	Natrona ....F	12	Rawlins .... 11,547.°I	11	Spotted Horse ....B	13	Weston ....B	14
Lucerne ....D	9	Neiber ....D	10	Recluse ....B	13	Story ....B	11	Westvaco I	7
Lusk ....1,650.°F	16	New Fork ....G	7	Red Buttes ....J	14	Stroner ....B	15	Wheatland ....5,816.°H	15
Lyman ....2,284..J	6	Newcastle ....3,596.°D	16	Redbird ....E	16	Sundance ....1,087.°C	16	Whitman ....F	16
Lysite ....E	10	Node ....J	16	Reliance I	8	Sunrise ....G	15	Wildcat ....B	13
Madison Junction ....F	1	Norris Junction ....F	2	Riner I	10	Superior I	8	Willow Island ....F	7
Mammoth ....B	5	Nowood ....E	11	Riverside ....55..I	12	Sussex ....D	12	Willwood ....B	8
Manderson ....174..C	10	O'Donnell ....B	8	Riverton ....9,247..F	9	Sweetwater		Wilson ....J	1
Manville ....94..F	15	Old Faithful ....G	1	Riverview ....J	6	Station ....G	9	Winchester ....D	9
Marbleton ....537..G	6	Opal I	6	Robertson ....J	6	Table Rock I	9	Wind River ....F	8
Marse ....H	5	Orchard Valley ...3,327..J	15	Rochelle ....E	15	Ten Sleep ....407..D	11	Winkleman ....F	8
Mayoworth ....D	12	Orin ....G	14	Rock River ....415..I	13	Teton Village ....J	1	Wolf ....B	11
McFadden I	13	Oriva C	13	Rock Springs ....19,458..I	8	Thayne ....256..F	5	Woods	
McKinley ....G	14	Orpha ....F	14	Rockypoint ....B	14	Thermopolis .....3,852.°E	9	Landing ....J	13
McKinnon ....K	6	Osage ....D	16	Ross ....E	13	Thornton C	15	Worland ....6,391.°D	10
Meadow Creek ....E	13	Oshoto ....B	15	Rozet C	14	Tie Siding I	14	Wright ....1,117..D	14
Meadowdale ....J	15	Otto C	9	Ryan Park I	12	Tipton I	9	Wyarno ....B	12
Medicine Bow ......953..I	13	Pahaska C	6	Saddle String C	12	Torrington ....5,441.°H	16	Wyodak ....B	14
Meeteetse ....512..C	8	Paradise Valley ....G	12	Sage I	5	Tower		Wyoming I	14
		Parkerton ....F	13	St. Stephens ....F	9	Junction ....E	2	Yoder ....110..H	16

°County seat.
*Does not appear on map; key shows general location.
Source: 1980 census. Places without population figures are unincorporated areas.

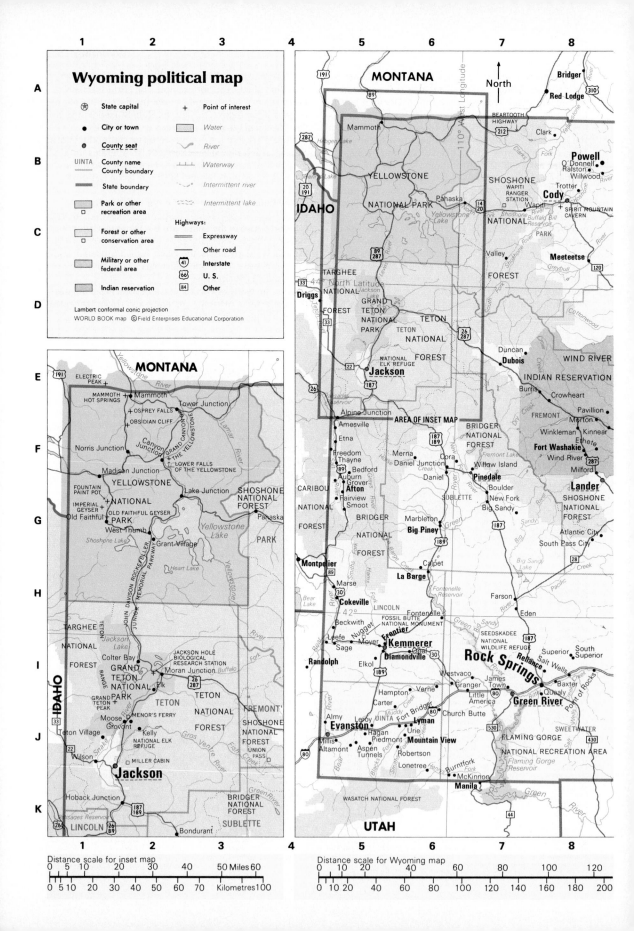

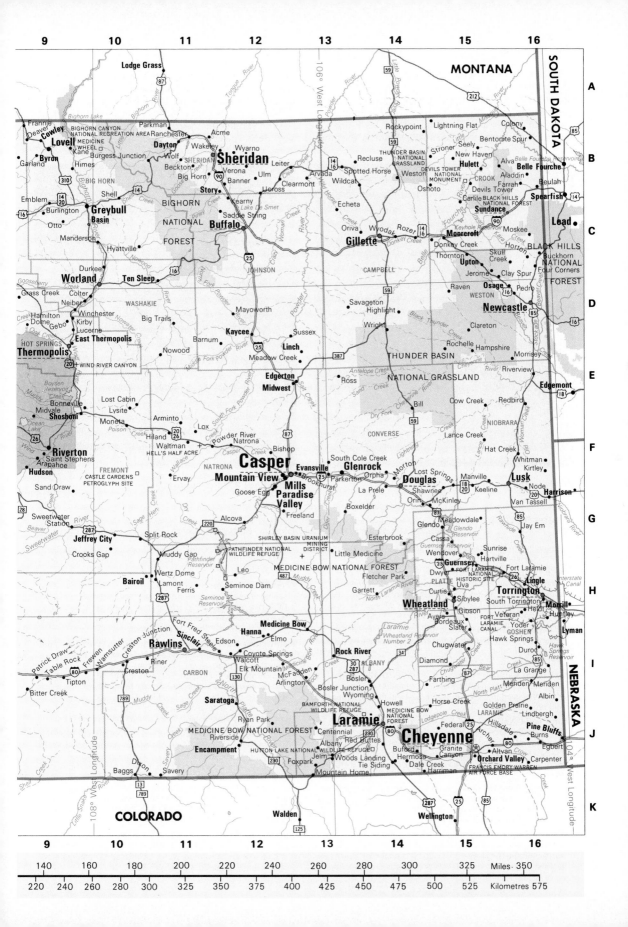

Wyoming's tourist attractions rank among the most spectacular in the nation. Each year, several million people visit the state. Yellowstone and Grand Teton national parks are the chief attractions. They have beautiful mountain scenery and many kinds of animals. Wilderness trails challenge the hiker's skill. Visitors also come to Wyoming to hunt big game animals or to fish in the lakes and streams. In 1904, the Eaton Ranch, near Sheridan, became the first dude ranch in the West.

Wyoming's most popular annual event is the Frontier Days celebration in Cheyenne, which has been staged since 1897. The celebration is held for 10 days in July.

Artstreet

Devils Tower National Monument

Larry Beck

Green River Rendezvous in Pinedale

Places to visit

Following are brief descriptions of some of Wyoming's many interesting places to visit:

Devils Tower National Monument, in northeastern Wyoming, is a volcanic tower that stands 865 feet (264 meters) above its base, which is 415 feet (126 meters) high. In 1906, President Theodore Roosevelt established Devils Tower as the nation's first national monument.

Fort Laramie National Historic Site, near the town of Fort Laramie, was a fur trading center and later a military post. The fort helped protect pioneer wagon trains on the Oregon Trail. A number of the original buildings have been restored.

Fossil Butte National Monument, 10 miles (16 kilometers) west of Kemmerer, has the fossilized remains of fishes and plants that lived in the water which covered the area about 50 million years ago.

Grand Teton National Park lies in northwestern Wyoming. The majestic Teton Mountains rise sharply from the floor of a beautiful valley called Jackson Hole. Several lakes lie along the east side of the mountains. Visitors can see many kinds of wild animals, which are protected there. See **Grand Teton National Park.**

Hell's Half Acre, west of Casper, is a rugged 320-acre (129-hectare) depression where wind and water have created unusual rock gullies, ridges, and towers. The canyon is located near the South Fork of the Powder River.

Wildlife refuges. Wyoming has six major wildlife refuge areas where visitors can watch animals and birds in their natural surroundings. The largest area is the National Elk Refuge near Jackson. Jackson Hole Wildlife Park is near Moran Junction.

Federal waterfowl refuges include Pathfinder near Leo, Bamforth, and Hutton Lake near Laramie, and Seedskadee near Green River.

Wind River Canyon, south of Thermopolis, offers motorists a scenic drive between the Bridger and Owl Creek mountains. Cliffs rise 2,000 feet (610 meters) above the river. The canyon walls are interesting because of the rock formations exposed where the river cut through the mountains.

Yellowstone National Park, in northwestern Wyoming, is the nation's largest and the world's oldest national park. Its spectacular beauty and unusual attractions were recognized by early explorers. Yellowstone became a national park in 1872, and the earliest tourists faced danger from Indians. The most notable features of the park include the world's largest geyser area, spectacular towering waterfalls, hot springs, deep canyons, and excellent fishing. See **Yellowstone National Park.**

National forests. Ten national forests in Wyoming provide timber and serve as recreation areas. Shoshone, in northwestern Wyoming, is the largest forest. Other forests entirely in Wyoming are Bighorn near Sheridan, Bridger near Pinedale, Medicine Bow near Laramie, and Teton near Jackson.

Wyoming shares five of its national forests with bordering states. The Black Hills forest is shared with South Dakota, Caribou with Idaho and Utah, Targhee with Idaho, and Ashley and Wasatch with Utah.

State parks. Wyoming has set aside a number of historic sites, parks, and recreation areas. For information on the state parks and facilities in Wyoming, write to Director, Wyoming Recreation Commission, Cheyenne, WY 82002.

Annual events

January-April

Cutter (horse-drawn sleigh) races near Afton, Big Piney, Jackson, Pinedale, and Saratoga (January); Wyoming State Winter Fair in Lander (January).

May-August

Days of '49 in Greybull (June); Pioneer Days in Lander (July 1-4); Rodeos in Buffalo, Cody, Sheridan, and other towns (July 4); Jubilee Days in Laramie (second week of July); Green River Rendezvous in Pinedale (second Sunday in July); Indian Sun Dances in Ethete and Fort Washakie (late July); Central Wyoming Fair and Rodeo in Casper (late July or early August); Grand Teton Music Festival in Teton Village (July and August); Indian pageant in Thermopolis (early August); Wyoming State Fair in Douglas (late August).

September-December

Old Timers Rodeo in Lander (early September); Evanston Cowboy Days (Labor Day).

Wyoming Travel Commission

Frontier Days Rodeo in Cheyenne

Tom Stack & Associates

Indian dance at Frontier Days

John Running, Black Star

Old Faithful geyser in Yellowstone National Park

Geri Wright, Bruce Coleman Inc.

Cutter race in Jackson Hole

Land regions. Wyoming lies where the Great Plains meet the Rocky Mountains. The Continental Divide winds through Wyoming from the northwest corner to the south-central edge of the state (see **Continental Divide**). Water on the east side of the divide flows to the Atlantic Ocean. Water on the west side goes into the Pacific Ocean. Wyoming has an average elevation of 6,700 feet (2,042 meters), and is higher than any other state except Colorado. Wyoming has three major land regions: (1) the Great Plains, (2) the Rocky Mountains, and (3) the Intermontane Basins.

The Great Plains cover the eastern part of the state. This region is part of the vast interior plain of North America that stretches from Canada to Mexico. In Wyoming, short, tough grass covers much of the land and provides good grazing for cattle and sheep. Cottonwoods and thickets of brush grow along the rivers. Little rain falls on the plains, but irrigation has turned portions of this region into valuable farmland.

A portion of the famous Black Hills lies in the northeastern part of the state. About a third of the Black Hills area is located in Wyoming, and the rest is in South Dakota.

The Rocky Mountains sweep across Wyoming in huge ranges, most of which extend from north to south. In the north, the Bighorn Mountains form the front range of the mountain area. The Laramie Range stretches north from Colorado. Between these two front ranges lies a wide plateau. In the 1800's, pioneers traveled westward on trails through this area. The Absaroka Range rises along the east side of Yellowstone National Park. The rugged Wind River Range to the south includes nine peaks that tower above 13,000 feet (3,960 meters). Among them is the highest mountain in Wyoming, 13,804-foot (4,207-meter) Gannett Peak. The Granite Mountains extend eastward from near the southern tip of the Wind River Range. The Gros Ventre, Salt River, Snake River, Teton, and Wyoming ranges are near the western border. The scenic Teton Mountains rise nearly straight up for more than 1 mile (1.6 kilometers) from the Jackson Hole Valley. Other major mountain ranges include the Medicine Bow and Sierra Madre in southern Wyoming.

There is one special link between the flat land of the plains and the heights of the mountains. It is in southeastern Wyoming, where a narrow finger of land rises gently from the plains to a point high in the Laramie Mountains. Along the slope are major rail and highway routes that quickly bring a traveler from the plains to the mountains. This slope, sometimes called the *Gang Plank,* is only about 100 yards (91 meters) wide.

The Intermontane Basins include several fairly flat areas between Wyoming's mountain ranges. The word *intermontane* means *between mountains.* The major basins include the Bighorn and Powder River basins in the north, and the Wind River basin in central Wyoming. The Green River, Great Divide, and Washakie basins are in southwestern Wyoming.

The basins are mostly treeless areas that get less rainfall than the mountains. Short grasses and other low plants make most of the basins good areas for grazing sheep and cattle. The Great Divide Basin is an exception. It lies along the Continental Divide, but has no drainage of water either to the Atlantic or the Pacific. The divide splits and runs around the 3,000 square miles (7,800 square kilometers) of this basin. The little rain that falls there soaks quickly into the dry ground. Part of the Great Divide Basin and the area to the south of it are sometimes called the *Red Desert.* A few pronghorns and wild

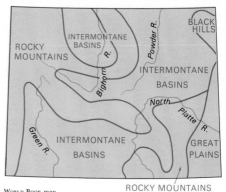

WORLD BOOK map

Land regions of Wyoming

Map index

Absaroka Range	B	3	
Absaroka Ridge	D	2	
Alkali Creek	E	4	
Aspen Mts.	E	3	
Atlantic Peak	D	3	
Bald Knoll (Mountain)	D	2	
Bear Lodge Mts.	B	8	
Bear Mountain	E	6	
Bear River Divide	E	2	
Beartooth Basin	B	3	
Beartooth Pass	B	3	
Beartooth Range	A	3	
Belle Fourche R.	C	7	
Big Sandy Reservoir	D	3	
Bighorn Basin	B	4	
Bighorn Canyon Nat'l. Rec. Area	B	4	
Bighorn Mts.	B	5	
Bighorn R.	B	4	
Black Butte	B	5	
Boysen Reservoir	C	4	
Bridger Basin	E	2	
Bridger Mts.	C	4	
Bridger Peak	E	5	
Buffalo Bill Reservoir	B	3	
Cheyenne R.	C	8	
Chugwater Creek	E	8	
Clear Creek	B	6	
Cloud Peak	B	5	
Continental Divide	D	4	

Crazy Woman Creek	B	6	
Crow Creek	E	8	
Devils Tower Nat'l. Mon.	B	8	
Doubletop Peak	C	2	
Downs Mountain	C	3	
Elk Mountain	E	6	
Ferris Mts.	D	5	
Flaming Gorge Nat'l. Rec. Area	E	3	
Flaming Gorge Res.	E	3	
Francs Peak	C	3	
Freezeout Mts.	D	6	
Fremont Peak	C	3	
Gannett Peak (highest point in Wyoming)	C	3	
Glendo Reservoir	D	7	
Grand Teton (Mountain)	C	2	
Grand Teton Nat'l. Park	C	2	
Granite Pass	B	5	
Granite Peak	D	4	
Granite Mountains*	D	5	
Great Divide Basin	E	4	
Great Plains	B	7	
Green Mts.	D	5	
Green R.	E	3	
Green River Basin, see Bridger Basin			

Greybull R.	B	4	
Gros Ventre Range	C	2	
Gros Ventre R.	C	2	
Hams Fork	E	2	
Hazelton Peak	B	5	
Henrys Fork	E	3	
Horse Creek	E	8	
Hunt Mountain	B	5	
Index Peak	B	3	
Indian Peak	B	3	
Jackson Lake	C	2	
Keyhole Reservoir	B	8	
Lake Mountain	E	6	
Lance Creek	C	8	
Laramie Basin	D	6	
Laramie Mts.	D	6	
Laramie Peak	D	7	
Laramie R.	D	7	
Little Missouri R.	B	8	
Little Powder R.	B	7	
Little Snake R.	E	5	
Lizard Head Peak	D	3	
Lodgepole Creek	E	8	
Mather Peaks	B	5	
Medicine Bow Mts.	E	6	
Medicine Bow Peak	E	6	
Medicine Bow R.	D	6	
Missouri Buttes	B	8	
Mt. Crosby	C	3	
Mt. Isabel	D	2	

Mt. McDougall	D	2	
Mt. Sheridan	B	2	
Muddy Creek	E	5	
Needle Mountain	B	3	
North Platte R.	D	6	
Nowood Creek	B	4	
Old Faithful Geyser	B	2	
Owl Creek	C	4	
Owl Creek Mts.	C	4	
Palisades Reservoir	C	1	
Pathfinder Reservoir	D	6	
Pine Ridge	D	8	
Pinnacle Buttes	C	3	
Pole Mountain	E	7	
Powder R.	B	6	
North Fork	C	6	
Middle Fork	C	6	
South Fork	C	6	
Powder River Basin*	B	6	
Powder River Pass	B	5	
Ptarmigan Mountain	B	3	
Pumpkin Buttes	C	7	
Rattlesnake Hills	D	5	
Rocky Mts.	C	2	
Salt River Range	C	2	
Sandy Creek	D	3	
Seminoe Reservoir	E	6	
Shirley Basin*	D	6	
Shoshone Basin	C	4	
Shoshone Lake	B	2	

Shoshone R.	B	4	
North Fork	B	3	
South Fork	B	3	
Sierra Madre (Mts.)	E	6	
Snake R.	C	2	
Snake River Range	C	1	
South Pass	D	4	
Sweetwater R.	D	4	
Teton Mts.	C	2	
Togwotee Pass	C	2	
Tongue R.	A	6	
Trout Peak	B	3	
Tump Range	E	2	
Twin Mts.	E	7	
Wapiti Range	B	3	
Washakie Basin*	E	4	
Washakie Needles	C	3	
Wiggins Peak	C	3	
Wild Horse Creek	B	7	
Wind R.	C	3	
Wind River Basin	C	4	
Wind River Range	C	3	
Wyoming Basin	E	3	
Wyoming Peak	D	2	
Wyoming Range	C	2	
Yellowstone Lake	B	2	
Yellowstone Nat'l. Park	B	2	
Yellowstone Plateau	B	2	
Yellowstone R.	B	2	

*Does not appear on the map; key shows general location.

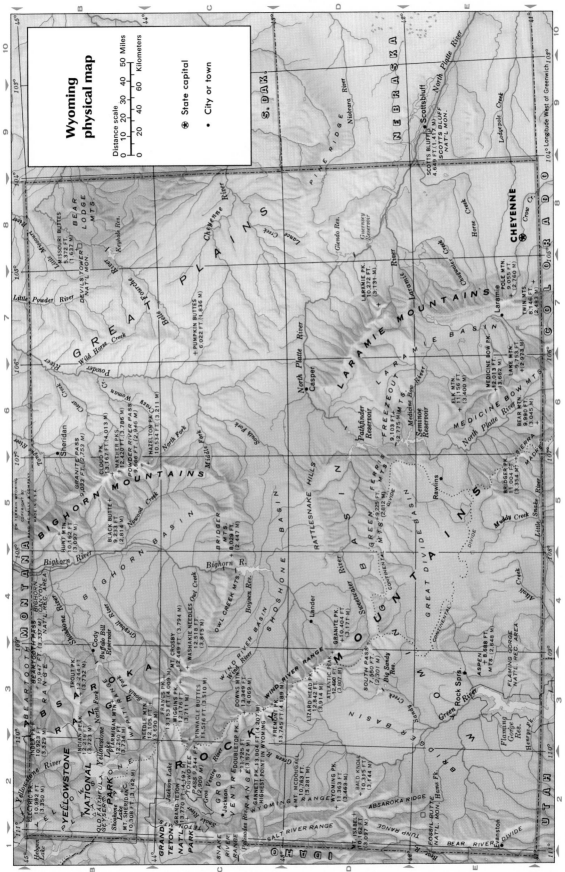

Wyoming physical map

Distance scale

| | | | | | |
|0|10|20|30|40|50 Miles|

| | | | | |
|0|20|40|60 Kilometers|

⊛ State capital

• City or town

Specially created for *The World Book Encyclopedia* by Rand McNally and World Book editors

David R. Frazier

Yellowstone Lower Falls tumbles 308 feet (94 meters) into the Grand Canyon of Yellowstone National Park. The beautiful canyon reaches a depth of about 2,000 feet (610 meters).

horses feed on the thinly scattered plant growth and sagebrush. Sometimes sheep are grazed there.

Rivers and lakes. Parts of three great river systems start in the mountains of Wyoming. These three river systems are the Missouri, the Colorado, and the Columbia.

The tributaries of the Missouri flow both north and east. The Yellowstone, Clarks Fork, Bighorn, Tongue, and Powder rivers flow north. The Cheyenne, Niobrara, and North Platte rivers flow east.

The Green River, the major source of the Colorado River, rises in the Wind River Mountains and flows south across western Wyoming into Utah. The Snake River is part of the Columbia River system. This river starts in the Absaroka mountains in Yellowstone Park. It flows into Grand Teton National Park, then turns west into Idaho. The Snake leaves Wyoming through a magnificent canyon that cuts through three mountain ranges. The Snake River is joined by the Salt River and eventually reaches the Columbia. Bear River, in the southwestern corner of Wyoming, flows into the Great Salt Lake of Utah.

Average monthly weather

	Cheyenne					Sheridan				
	Temperatures				Days of rain or snow		Temperatures				Days of rain or snow
	F.°		C°				F.°		C°		
	High	Low	High	Low			High	Low	High	Low	
Jan.	37	14	3	−10	7	Jan.	33	7	1	−14	8
Feb.	40	16	4	−9	6	Feb.	36	11	2	−12	9
Mar.	44	20	7	−7	9	Mar.	43	20	6	−7	12
Apr.	54	29	12	−2	10	Apr.	56	31	13	−1	11
May	63	37	17	3	13	May	66	40	19	4	13
June	74	47	23	8	11	June	75	48	24	9	11
July	83	54	28	12	11	July	86	55	30	13	7
Aug.	81	53	27	12	10	Aug.	84	53	29	12	7
Sept.	72	43	22	6	7	Sept.	73	43	23	6	8
Oct.	60	33	16	1	6	Oct.	61	32	16	0	7
Nov.	47	23	8	−5	6	Nov.	46	21	8	−6	8
Dec.	40	17	4	−8	5	Dec.	37	12	3	−11	8

Average January temperatures

Wyoming's winters are cold and dry. The western and south-central parts have the coldest temperatures.

Average July temperatures

The state has mild and sunny summers. The eastern and central sections generally have the warmest temperatures.

Average yearly precipitation

Precipitation varies widely in Wyoming. The Bighorn Basin is dry but the northwestern mountains get heavy snows.

WORLD BOOK maps

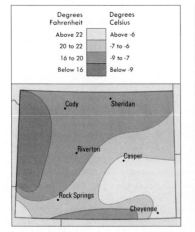

Degrees Fahrenheit	Degrees Celsius
Above 22	Above -6
20 to 22	-7 to -6
16 to 20	-9 to -7
Below 16	Below -9

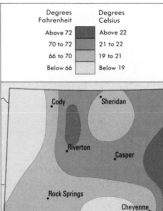

Degrees Fahrenheit	Degrees Celsius
Above 72	Above 22
70 to 72	21 to 22
66 to 70	19 to 21
Below 66	Below 19

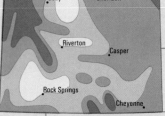

Inches	Centimeters
More than 24	More than 61
12 to 24	30 to 61
8 to 12	20 to 30
Less than 8	Less than 20

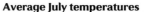

Many of the rivers have cut beautiful canyons, and some plunge over steep cliffs in spectacular waterfalls. The most interesting canyons include the Laramie River Canyon, the Grand Canyons of the Snake and the Yellowstone, Platte River Canyon, Shoshone River Canyon, and the Wind River Canyon. The most dramatic waterfalls are the Upper and Lower falls of the Yellowstone River.

Wyoming has hundreds of clear, cold, mountain lakes. Among the largest are Fremont, Jackson, Shoshone, and Yellowstone lakes. The major artificially created lakes include Alcova, Boysen, Buffalo Bill, Glendo, Guernsey, Keyhole, Pathfinder, and Seminoe reservoirs. Two new dams outside the state formed major lakes in Wyoming. Yellowtail Dam in Montana created a large lake in the northeastern part of Wyoming. Flaming Gorge Dam in Utah backs up water of the Green River 30 miles (48 kilometers) inside Wyoming.

Plant and animal life. Forests cover nearly a sixth of Wyoming's land. The chief commercial trees are Douglas-fir, Engelmann spruce, lodgepole pine, and ponderosa pine. Other trees include alpine fir, aspen, and cottonwood.

Bluegrass, wheat grass, tufted fescues, and redtops grow on much of the state's approximately 50 million acres (20 million hectares) of grazing lands. Cactus and sagebrush are found in the drier regions. Areas of Wyoming with poor soil produce greasewood brush, which is used as firewood. Mountain wild flowers found in the state include the arnica, buttercup, evening star, five-finger, flax, forget-me-not, goldenrod, saxifrage, sour dock, and windflower.

Wyoming's most common larger animals include black bears, elk, mule deer, and pronghorns. Moose are common in the state's northwestern forests, and mountain sheep live among the rocky peaks of the higher mountains. Grizzly bears, lynxes, and mountain lions are seen from time to time. Some of the smaller fur-bearing animals in Wyoming include beavers, martens, raccoons, and otters.

Pronghorns are common in the open areas of the basins. Other animals in the basin areas include badgers, cottontail and jack rabbits, coyotes, foxes, skunks, and wildcats. Game birds include ducks, geese, grouse, pheasants, sage hens, and wild turkeys. Wyoming also is the home of bald and golden eagles. The bald eagle builds its nest in tall pines near mountain streams or lakes. The golden eagle usually chooses a home farther from water.

Climate. Wyoming has a dry, sunny climate. Winters are cold and the summers are warm. The dry air makes the climate more comfortable than the temperatures would indicate. Differences in altitude create large differences in temperature in various parts of the state. At Casper, in central Wyoming, the average January temperature is 22° F. (−6° C), and the average July temperature is 71° F. (22° C). Near Yellowstone Lake, at a higher elevation, the January average is 12° F. (−11° C), and the July average is 59° F. (15° C). In the high mountains, freezing temperatures can occur any time of the year.

Wyoming's highest recorded temperature was 114° F. (46° C) at Basin on July 12, 1900. Moran, near Elk, had the lowest temperature, −63° F. (−53° C), on Feb. 9, 1933.

The average annual *precipitation* (rain, melted snow, and other forms of moisture) ranges from about 5 inches (13 centimeters) at Hyattville in the Bighorn Basin to about 50 inches (130 centimeters) in the Yellowstone Park area. Snowfall varies from 15 to 20 inches (38 to 51 centimeters) in the Bighorn Basin to about 260 inches (660 centimeters) in the northwestern mountains.

On the Great Plains, and in some open areas of southern Wyoming, the wind blows during the afternoons, usually from the west or southwest. If dry snow is on the ground, the wind may whip it into a *ground blizzard.* A person cannot see straight ahead in the swirling snow, even though the sky may be blue and the sun shining.

Economy

Service industries, taken together, make up over half of Wyoming's *gross state product*—the total value of all goods and services produced in a state in a year. However, Wyoming's economy depends almost entirely on its land. The land provides the state's most important product—petroleum. Petroleum, coal, natural gas, and other mineral products account for more than a fourth of the gross state product. Wyoming's land provides grazing for cattle and sheep. Most of the state's manufacturing plants process the products of Wyoming's mines, farms, and forests. Millions of tourists come to Wyoming to enjoy its scenic beauty. They spend about $800 million annually.

Government plays an important part in Wyoming's economy. The federal government owns half the state's land. The government controls grazing, logging, and mining in this huge area, which includes national forests and parks, Indian lands, and other public lands.

Natural resources. Wyoming's most important natural resources are mineral deposits, grazing land, scenery, wildlife, and water.

Soil. Wyoming does not have large areas of fertile soil. Much of the state has sandy soil formed from sandstone rock that lies beneath the surface. The most fertile soils of Wyoming are those deposited in the major river valleys by floodwaters. Wind-blown dirt called *loess* also has formed fertile soil in some areas.

Minerals. Wyoming's reserves of bentonite, coal, petroleum, trona, and uranium rank among the nation's largest. The mineral reserves are found mostly in the basin areas of the state.

Much of the petroleum and natural-gas reserves occur in an underground region called the *Overthrust Belt.* This region lies beneath southwestern Wyoming and parts of neighboring states. About 40 per cent of Wyoming has coal under it. However, much of the coal is too deep—and thus too costly—to mine under present economic conditions. Trona, a white mineral containing sodium carbonate, is found in southwestern Wyoming. The state's largest uranium deposits are in the Powder River, Shirley, and Wind River basins. Bentonite is a clay used in oil drilling. The largest bentonite reserves are in the northeast and north-central sections. Wyoming also has gemstones, particularly agate and jade. Other mineral resources include building stone, gold, gypsum, limestone, and zeolites.

Forests cover about 10 million acres (4 million hectares), or nearly a sixth of Wyoming's land. Most of the forests grow in the mountain areas. About two-fifths of the forests are available for commercial use. About $2\frac{2}{3}$ million acres (1.1 million hectares) have been set aside in parks and other reserves. The federal government controls about 75 per cent of the commercial forest land. The chief commercial trees are lodgepole pine, Engelmann spruce, and ponderosa pine. Other trees include alpine fir, aspen, cottonwood, and Douglas-fir.

Service industries account for 57 per cent of the gross state product of Wyoming. Most of the service industries are concentrated in Casper, Cheyenne, and Laramie, the state's largest cities.

Finance, insurance, and real estate provide a larger share of the gross state product than any other service industry in Wyoming. Real estate is the most important part of this industry because of the large sums of money involved in the selling and leasing of buildings. Casper and Cheyenne are the leading financial centers. The state's largest bank is the First Interstate Bank of Casper.

Transportation, communication, and utilities rank second among Wyoming service industries in terms of the gross state product. Pipeline companies are a major part of the transportation sector. Pipelines carry Wyoming's large oil and gas output to processing and distribution sites. Railroad companies transport other minerals and farm goods. Telephone companies are the most important part of the communications sector. Utility companies supply electric, gas, and water service. More information about transportation and communication in Wyoming appears later in this section.

Government ranks third in gross state product. Government services employ more people than any other economic activity in Wyoming. Government includes public schools and hospitals and military establishments. Many people are employed in Wyoming's public schools and universities. State government offices are based in Cheyenne. Warren Air Force Base lies just outside Cheyenne. The base is the control center for a large network of long-range nuclear missiles. The federal government also operates Yellowstone National Park, which provides hundreds of seasonal jobs.

Wholesale and retail trade form the fourth-ranking service industry in Wyoming. Wholesale trade involves buying goods from producers and selling the goods to other businesses. The wholesale trade of petroleum and machinery is most important in Wyoming. Retail trade involves selling goods to consumers. Automobile dealerships, food stores, and restaurants are examples of leading types of retail businesses.

Community, social, and personal services rank last in importance among service industries in Wyoming. This industry consists of a variety of businesses, including doctors' offices and private hospitals, hotels and ski resorts, law firms and engineering companies, and repair shops. The growth of tourism in Wyoming has benefited the state's hotels and ski resorts.

Mining provides 26 per cent of Wyoming's gross state product. This is one of the highest percentages of any state. Petroleum, coal, and natural gas are the state's leading mineral products. Changes in the prices of any

of these mineral products have a large impact on Wyoming's overall economy.

Large petroleum deposits lie in several parts of Wyoming. The leading oil-producing counties are Campbell, Park, and Uinta. Each of these counties lies in a different area. The oil companies that produce the most petroleum in Wyoming are Amoco and Marathon.

Only Kentucky mines more coal than Wyoming. Almost all of Wyoming's coal is obtained from surface mines. These mines provide a variety of coal called *sub-bituminous.* Campbell County provides most of Wyoming's coal. Sweetwater and Converse counties produce most of the remaining coal.

Natural gas, like petroleum, is found in several parts of the state. Southwestern Wyoming is the leading area for natural gas production.

Among Wyoming's other mineral products, sodium carbonate is the most important. It is used to make glass, soap, and paper. All of the sodium carbonate comes from Sweetwater County. Wyoming is also a major producer of bentonite and other clays. The state also produces crushed stone, gypsum, and sand and gravel.

Manufacturing accounts for 3 per cent of Wyoming's gross state product, a lower percentage than in any other state. Goods manufactured in the state have a *value added by manufacture* of about $400 million a year. Value added by manufacture represents the increase in value of raw materials after they become finished products.

The production of chemicals and related products is Wyoming's most important manufacturing industry. Fertilizer is the state's chief chemical product. Basin and Cheyenne have fertilizer factories.

Petroleum refining ranks second among manufacturing activities in Wyoming in terms of value added by manufacture. Casper and Sinclair have large oil refineries. Refineries also are located near Cheyenne, La Barge, and Newcastle.

Other products manufactured in Wyoming include

Production and workers by economic activities

Economic activities	Per cent of GSP* produced	Employed workers	
		Number of persons	Per cent of total
Mining	26	19,400	9
Finance, insurance, & real estate	14	8,000	4
Transportation, communication, & utilities	13	14,000	6
Government	12	53,100	25
Construction	12	16,200	8
Wholesale & retail trade	10	44,400	21
Community, social, & personal services	8	33,200	16
Manufacturing	3	7,900	4
Agriculture	2	16,000	7
Total	100	212,300	100

*GSP = gross state product, the total value of goods and services produced in a year.
Figures are for 1986.
Sources: *World Book* estimates based on data from U.S. Bureau of Economic Analysis, U.S. Bureau of Labor Statistics, and U.S. Department of Agriculture.

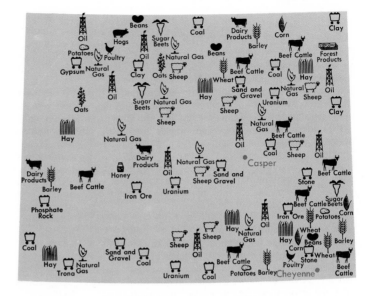

Farm, mineral, and forest products

This map shows where the leading farm, mineral, and forest products are produced. The urban areas (shown in red) are the important manufacturing centers.

WORLD BOOK map

machinery, printed materials, and wood products. Cheyenne and Torrington produce machinery. Newspapers are the most important kind of printed material. Afton, Cheyenne, Laramie, and many other cities have sawmills.

Agriculture contributes 2 per cent of the gross state product. Farms and ranches cover about half of Wyoming. The state has about 8,700 farms and ranches.

Ranching is by far the most important agricultural activity in Wyoming. Beef cattle provide about two-thirds of the total income from farm products. Most beef cattle are raised in eastern Wyoming. Other livestock products in Wyoming include milk, sheep, and wool. Wyoming ranks third to Texas and California in the production of sheep and wool. About half of Wyoming's land is used to graze cattle and sheep. This includes vast amounts of federal government land leased to ranchers.

Wyoming's most valuable field crops are grown on about $1\frac{1}{2}$ million acres (607,000 hectares) of irrigated land. The leading crops, in order of value, are hay, barley, wheat, sugar beets, corn, and beans. Hay is grown chiefly as feed for livestock, especially cattle. Little of the hay is marketed. Certified seed potatoes, which must be unusually free of disease, are raised in Goshen and Laramie counties. Farmers use dry farming methods on the Great Plains (see **Dry farming**). The most important crops raised on these farms include hay, and wheat and other grains.

Electric power. Coal-burning power plants generate about 95 per cent of the state's electric power. Major plants operate near Gillette and in Glenrock, Kemmerer, Rock Springs, and Wheatland. Water power provides the rest of Wyoming's electricity. The largest hydroelectric plants are at Alcova, Fremont Canyon, Glendo, Kortes, and Seminoe dams.

Transportation. Wyoming has about 38,000 miles (61,000 kilometers) of roads and highways. About 60 per cent of them are surfaced. Casper has the state's busiest airport. Wyoming's first railroad was the Union Pacific. It was built across the territory in 1867 and 1868. Today, three rail lines provide Wyoming with freight service to other states. No passenger trains serve Wyoming.

Communication. The first newspaper in Wyoming was the *Daily Telegraph,* published at Fort Bridger in 1863. Today, Wyoming has about 50 newspapers, including 10 dailies. Newspapers with the largest circulations include the *Casper Star Tribune,* and the *Wyoming State Tribune* and *Wyoming Eagle,* both of Cheyenne. The state's first radio station, KDFN (now KTWO), began broadcasting at Casper in 1930. The first television station was KFBC-TV (now KYCU-TV) in Cheyenne, which started operating in 1954. Today, the state has about 65 radio stations and 9 TV stations.

David R. Frazier

Drilling for oil is the most important mining activity in Wyoming. The state ranks among the nation's leading producers of both petroleum and natural gas.

Constitution. Wyoming is still governed under its original Constitution, which was adopted in 1889. *Amendments* (changes) to the Constitution must be approved by a majority of the people voting in that particular election. Amendments may be proposed by a two-thirds vote of both houses of the legislature, or by a constitutional convention. Such a convention must be approved by two-thirds of the members of each house of the legislature, and by a majority of the voters.

Executive. The people of Wyoming elect the governor to a four-year term. This official may be reelected an unlimited number of times.

Much of the governor's power lies in the right to appoint other important state officials. For example, the governor appoints the attorney general and the heads of the budget and personnel departments.

The voters elect four other high state officials to four-year terms. These are the secretary of state, auditor, treasurer, and superintendent of public instruction. All four of these officials may be reelected an unlimited number of times.

Wyoming does not have a lieutenant governor. If the governor of Wyoming dies in office or resigns, the secretary of state serves as governor until a new governor is elected.

Legislature consists of a 30-member senate and a 64-member house of representatives. Senators are elected to four-year terms, and representatives are elected to two-year terms.

The two houses of the Legislature meet each year. General sessions of the Legislature begin on the second Tuesday of January in odd-numbered years. Budget sessions begin on the third Monday in February in even-numbered years. The Legislature may not meet more than 40 legislative days in any year or more than 60 days in each two-year period. The governor may call special legislative sessions.

Courts. The highest court in Wyoming is the Supreme Court. This court has five justices who are appointed to serve eight-year terms. These justices elect one of their number to serve as the chief justice. The Supreme Court usually hears only appeals from the lower courts.

Most major civil and criminal trials in the state are held in district courts. Wyoming has nine judicial districts, each with either one or two district judges. District judges are appointed to six-year terms. The governor appoints all judges of the Supreme Court and district courts. The governor chooses them from nominees of the Wyoming Judicial Nominating Commission. Other courts in the state include county courts, police courts, municipal courts, and justice-of-the-peace courts.

Local government. Wyoming has 23 counties, each governed by a board of three or five commissioners. The commissioners are elected to four-year terms. Most Wyoming cities have the mayor-council form of government. Exceptions are the cities of Casper and Laramie, which employ city managers. By state law, a community must have at least 4,000 residents to be classified as a city. Wyoming's cities are called first class cities. Communities with populations between 150 and 4,000 are called towns.

Revenue. Taxation provides slightly more than half of the state government's *general revenue* (income). Sales

Wyoming State Capitol

The Wyoming House of Representatives meets in the State Capitol in Cheyenne. Its 64 members serve two-year terms. The Wyoming Senate has 30 members who serve four-year terms.

The governors of Wyoming

	Party	Term		Party	Term
Francis E. Warren	Republican	1890	Alonzo M. Clark	Republican	1931-1933
Amos W. Barber	Republican	1890-1893	Leslie A. Miller	Democratic	1933-1939
John E. Osborne	Democratic	1893-1895	Nels H. Smith	Republican	1939-1943
William A. Richards	Republican	1895-1899	Lester C. Hunt	Democratic	1943-1949
DeForest Richards	Republican	1899-1903	Arthur Griswold Crane	Republican	1949-1951
Fenimore Chatterton	Republican	1903-1905	Frank A. Barrett	Republican	1951-1953
Bryant B. Brooks	Republican	1905-1911	C. J. Rogers	Republican	1953-1955
Joseph M. Carey	Democratic	1911-1915	Milward L. Simpson	Republican	1955-1959
John B. Kendrick	Democratic	1915-1917	J. J. Hickey	Democratic	1959-1961
Frank L. Houx	Democratic	1917-1919	Jack R. Gage	Democratic	1961-1963
Robert D. Carey	Republican	1919-1923	Clifford P. Hansen	Republican	1963-1967
William B. Ross	Democratic	1923-1924	Stanley K. Hathaway	Republican	1967-1975
Frank E. Lucas	Republican	1924-1925	Edward J. Herschler	Democratic	1975-1987
Nellie Tayloe Ross	Democratic	1925-1927	Mike Sullivan	Democratic	1987-
Frank C. Emerson	Republican	1927-1931			

taxes, severance taxes, and property taxes, in that order, bring in the most money. Most of the rest of the state government's revenue comes from federal grants and other U.S. government programs.

Politics. In state and local elections, Republicans have won two-thirds of the contests since 1890, but Democrats often win major offices. The cities of south-ern Wyoming are a major source of Democratic strength. Republicans usually get more votes from the northern counties, which are largely rural.

In presidential elections, Wyoming has voted for Re-publican candidates more than twice as often as for Democratic candidates. For Wyoming's electoral votes and voting record, see **Electoral College** (table).

History

Indian days. The first people who lived in the Wyo-ming area were Indian hunters of at least 11,000 years ago. Later, huge herds of buffaloes roamed the prairies. This rich source of meat attracted many Indians to the area. When white people arrived they found Arapaho, Bannock, Blackfeet, Cheyenne, Crow, Shoshone, Sioux, and Ute Indians living in what is now Wyoming.

Exploration. French trappers may have entered the Wyoming region in the mid-1700's. However, explora-tion of the area did not begin until after 1800. The United States bought most of the region from France in 1803, as part of the Louisiana Purchase. After that, Amer-ican trappers came to the area to find furs. In 1807, a trapper named John Colter became the first white man to travel across the Yellowstone area. Five years later, in 1812, a party of fur traders from Oregon crossed the area from west to east. The group, led by Robert Stuart, discovered a relatively easy way across the mountains through South Pass. This route became important in pio-neer travel to the West.

During the 1820's and 1830's, the fur trade became more highly organized. General William Ashley estab-lished an annual *rendezvous* (gathering) of trappers. At these gatherings, Ashley's fur company traded ammuni-tion, food, and other supplies for furs. The first rendez-vous took place in 1825 on the Green River, near the present Wyoming-Utah border. The yearly rendezvous became important to the trappers not only for trading, but also for exchange of news and as an enjoyable so-cial event.

A trapping and trading party of more than a hundred men came to the Wyoming area in 1832. The group was led by Captain Benjamin L. E. de Bonneville. Bonneville's party discovered an oil spring in 1833 in the Wind River Basin. In 1834, traders William Sublette and Robert Campbell established Fort William in what is now east-ern Wyoming. This fort, later called Fort Laramie, was the area's first permanent trading post. Jim Bridger, one of the great western trappers and scouts, founded Fort Bridger in southwestern Wyoming in 1843.

After trading posts were established, the rendezvous became less important. The last of these colorful gather-ings was held in 1840.

In 1842 and 1843, Lieutenant John C. Frémont ex-plored the Wind River Mountains. His party was guided by the famous scout Kit Carson. After Frémont made his report, Congress voted in 1846 to establish forts along the Oregon Trail to protect settlers moving west. In 1849, the government bought Fort William. This fort, also known as Fort John, was renamed Fort Laramie by the army.

At various times, parts of what is now Wyoming were in the territories of Louisiana, Missouri, Nebraska, Ore-gon, Washington, Idaho, Utah and Dakota. Part of south-ern Wyoming, south of the 42nd parallel, belonged to Spain from the 1500's to the 1800's. Mexico claimed it in the early 1800's, but lost it to the Republic of Texas in 1836. This area became part of the United States in 1845 when Texas joined the Union.

The great trails. By the mid-1840's, pioneers were streaming west through the Wyoming area on three fa-mous trails. These were the California Trail, the Mormon Trail to Utah, and the Oregon Trail to the Pacific North-west. All three trails took South Pass through the moun-tains. Beyond South Pass, the Oregon Trail turned north-west, and the Mormon and California trails went southwest. Settlers moving across southern Wyoming used the Overland (Cherokee) Trail, which joined other

Emigrant Train Fording Medicine Bow Creek, Rocky Mountains (1870), an oil painting on canvas by Samuel Colman; Bennington Museum, Bennington, Vt. (Gail McCullough)

Pioneers traveling west passed through Wyoming in great numbers during the mid-1800's. This painting de-picts a wagon train crossing the Medicine Bow River in southeastern Wyoming.

trails at Fort Bridger. Thousands of settlers traveled through Wyoming, but few of them stayed.

The Plains Indians often assisted early wagon trains by pointing out grazing lands and watering areas. The various tribes often traded with the travelers.

Indian and settler conflicts. By 1849, the Sioux and other tribes were becoming alarmed at the growing number of settlers crossing traditional Indian land. The white settlers killed or frightened away the game. Their carelessness with fire caused roaring blazes on the prairie, and their diseases killed or crippled countless Indians. Fighting broke out between the Indians and the settlers, and the United States Army often had to step in. The conflicts resulted in the deaths of many more Indians than settlers.

Gold was discovered in Montana in the 1860's, and settlers began moving north up the Bozeman Trail to Montana. This trail crossed the Powder River Basin, a different area of the Indian land. The tribes fought with new fury.

To keep the Bozeman Trail open, the army built Fort Phil Kearny near the Bighorn Mountains in the summer of 1866. The Sioux hated this fort. Led by Red Cloud, they put war parties around it in what was called the *Circle of Death.* During the first six months, about 150 men were killed. Captain W. J. Fetterman and 81 of his men died in a single battle. Finally, in 1868, Red Cloud and other Indian leaders signed a treaty. The army agreed to give up Fort Phil Kearny and two other forts and leave northeastern Wyoming to the Indians. In return, the Indians agreed not to interfere with the construction of the Union Pacific Railroad through southern Wyoming.

A troubled peace lasted until 1874, when prospectors discovered gold in the Black Hills. Thousands of white people violated the treaty by moving into the area. The Sioux considered the Black Hills sacred, and they fought the new invasion. Sioux and Cheyenne warriors won two bitter battles with U.S. soldiers in what is now Montana. However, the Indian force broke up to flee from other troops. Some Indians went to Canada, and others agreed to move to reservations. Serious Indian fighting ended in the summer of 1876, and Wyoming settlers finally had peace.

Territorial progress. Even before the Indian troubles ended, southern Wyoming was developing rapidly. The foundations for Wyoming's minerals industry had been laid long before the area became a territory. In 1833, the Bonneville party greased its wagon axles at a spot where oil seeped from the ground in the Wind River Basin. Jim Bridger sold oil at his fort, and pioneers mixed it with flour to use as axle grease.

Gold was found at South Pass in 1842. However, the discovery aroused little interest. In 1867, a more promising gold strike attracted many prospectors to the area. Several boom towns, such as Atlantic City and South Pass City, sprang up.

The Union Pacific Railroad entered the area in 1867. Towns were founded as the "end of track" moved west. Cheyenne, Laramie, Rawlins, Rock Springs, Green River, and Evanston grew up in turn. Towns also appeared along the route of the great trails. In 1868, Congress created the Territory of Wyoming. President Ulysses S. Grant appointed Brigadier General John A. Campbell as the first governor of the territory.

On Dec. 10, 1869, the territorial legislature granted women the right to vote, hold office, and serve on juries. The new law was the first of its kind in the United States. Women first served on juries in 1870, in Laramie. That same year, Esther H. Morris of South Pass City became the nation's first woman justice of the peace.

Wyoming's tourist industry got its start during the territorial days. In 1872, Congress created Yellowstone National Park, the nation's first national park. The park immediately attracted tourists.

In 1883 and 1884, interest in oil was revived because of profitable drilling elsewhere. The first successful well was drilled in 1883 in the Dallas Field, near Lander. Plans were made for exploration of several areas near Casper, but the industry developed slowly, and several years passed before oil activity prospered.

Ranching supported the new territory's economy. Large numbers of cattle were driven north from Texas to Wyoming. Wealthy ranchers controlled huge areas of the territory and ruled the affairs of the territorial government.

By 1885, however, cattle prices had dropped. In addi-

Bureau of American Ethnology, Smithsonian Institution

Wind River Indian Reservation was presented to the Shoshoni Indian Chief Washakie in 1868 by the U.S. government. The Shoshoni received the reservation in return for their friendliness to white people and their help in fighting tribes hostile to settlers. W. H. Jackson took this picture in 1870. His photographs form a vivid record of Wyoming history during the late 1800's.

Historic Wyoming

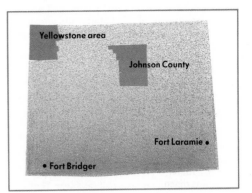

Yellowstone was established as the first national park in 1872. John Colter discovered the area in 1807.

The Johnson County War broke out in 1892 when ranchers joined to stop rustlers they suspected of looting their herds. The ranchers killed two men.

Fort Laramie and Fort Bridger offered protection and supplies for weary pioneers. Thousands of travelers crossed the state in covered wagons on overland trails between 1840 and 1870.

The Treaty of Fort Laramie in 1868 brought temporary peace with the Sioux when they agreed to limit their lands.

Nellie Tayloe Ross was elected governor of Wyoming in 1925, becoming the first woman governor in the U.S.

Important dates in Wyoming

WORLD BOOK illustrations by Kevin Chadwick

1807 John Colter explored the Yellowstone area.

1812 Robert Stuart discovered South Pass across the Rocky Mountains.

1833 Captain Benjamin L. E. de Bonneville mapped the Wyoming area and discovered oil east of the Wind River Mountains.

1834 William Sublette and Robert Campbell established Fort William (later Fort Laramie).

1843 Scout Jim Bridger established Fort Bridger.

1867 The Union Pacific Railroad entered Wyoming.

1868 Congress created the Territory of Wyoming. Its first coal mines began operation in Carbon and Sweetwater counties.

1869 The Wyoming territorial legislature gave women the right to vote and hold elective office.

1872 Yellowstone became the first national park.

1883 Wyoming's first oil well was drilled in the Dallas Field.

1890 Wyoming became the 44th state on July 10.

1892 The Johnson County War broke out after a dispute over cattle rustling.

1906 President Theodore Roosevelt made Devils Tower the first national monument.

1910 Engineers completed Shoshone (now Buffalo Bill) Dam.

1925 Nellie Tayloe Ross became the first woman governor in the United States.

1929 Grand Teton became a national park.

1938-1939 Engineers completed Alcova and Seminoe dams.

1951-1952 Major uranium deposits were found in several parts of Wyoming.

1960 The United States first operational intercontinental ballistic missile base opened near Cheyenne.

1965 Minuteman missile installations were completed near Cheyenne.

1988 Fires damaged large areas of Yellowstone National Park.

tion, there was a severe shortage of grass for grazing. In 1887, thousands of cattle died in the howling blizzards and freezing temperatures of a bitterly cold winter. Many ranchers were ruined financially and lost much of their political power.

Statehood. Wyoming became the 44th state of the Union on July 10, 1890. Francis E. Warren, a Republican, became the first state governor on September 11. He resigned in November after being elected to the U.S. Senate. Settlers flocked to Wyoming, and trouble started almost immediately. Many settlers built homes on the prairie and tended small herds of cattle. Powerful cattlemen who had used the range for years grew angry when the settlers began fencing their small ranches. Many of the cattlemen who had financial problems blamed their hardship on the small ranchers. They accused these small outfits of fencing the land and *rustling* (stealing) cattle from established ranches to build their herds. The Wyoming Stock Growers Association, an organization controlled by the "cattle barons," hired detectives to protect its interests.

The Johnson County War. Violence broke out in north-central Wyoming in 1892. The established cattlemen were convinced that their herds were being looted. They had no proof to identify the rustlers, but they had strong suspicions. The operators of the large ranches prepared a list of suspects and decided to kill the men on the list. They brought in about 25 gunmen from Texas and made up a force of about 55 men. This force, called the Invaders, raided the Kaycee Ranch near Buffalo and killed two men.

Information about the killings reached Buffalo, the seat of Johnson County, and a group of armed men was formed to stop the Invaders. The two forces met on the TA Ranch, but federal troops arrived in time to prevent a bloody battle. The Invaders were taken to Cheyenne for trial. However, important witnesses failed to appear at the trial. The Invaders were released, and the "war" ended.

Trouble again broke out on the range in the early 1900's. Cattlemen and sheepmen argued over grazing rights. The cattlemen claimed that their animals would not feed on land that had been grazed by sheep. A feud developed as the number of sheep increased. The climax came when cattlemen killed three sheepmen near Ten Sleep in 1909. But tempers cooled, and sheep became an important Wyoming product.

Progress as a state. After 1900, Wyoming's population grew rapidly. The Homestead acts of 1909, 1912, and 1916 provided large areas of free land for settlers under certain conditions. The construction of dams along major streams brought irrigation water to some areas of the prairie. Crops grown on this land increased the agricultural wealth of the state. In 1906, President Theodore Roosevelt made Devils Tower the first national monument. Tourism became more important as railroads and improved roads made it easier for people to reach such scenic areas as Yellowstone National Park and Jackson Hole.

Wyoming's first oil boom came in 1912 in the Salt Creek Field north of Casper. Oil companies built pipelines and refineries to handle the crude oil. By 1918, Casper had become a bustling center of business and finance.

In 1924, Wyoming voters elected the United States' first woman governor, Nellie Tayloe Ross. In 1933, Ross became the first woman director of the U.S. Mint.

Wyoming suffered less than most of the other states during the Great Depression of the 1930's. The state's economy was helped by increasing oil production and by various government construction projects. These included the Kendrick Project, which provided both irrigation water and new hydroelectric capacity. The project, on the North Platte River, included Alcova, Kortes, and Seminoe dams.

The mid-1900's. Wyoming's economy boomed during World War II (1939-1945). The war brought great demands for the state's coal, lumber, meat, and oil. Economic development continued after the war, and tourism increased.

New industrial growth in Wyoming resulted from the mining of two minerals, trona and uranium. Sodium carbonate, the key ingredient of trona, has many uses in the chemical industry.

Oil drilling in southwestern Wyoming had shown that trona lay over 1,500 feet (457 meters) under the surface of the earth in the Green River Basin. A mine shaft was sunk there in 1947, and mining of trona began. Output increased rapidly during the 1950's. During the 1960's, two chemical companies built huge plants near the town of Green River to be used for the mining of trona and the production of sodium carbonate.

The first major uranium discovery in Wyoming occurred in 1951. Large deposits of uranium were found in the Powder River area. After the findings were published early in 1952, uranium was discovered in many areas throughout the state. By the late 1950's, Wyoming ranked third among the states in known uranium reserves.

Many companies expanded their operations in Wyoming during the 1960's. A steel company built a new iron ore processing plant near Sunrise. Another firm revived the ghost town of Atlantic City by opening an iron mine and building a processing plant there. Trona operations near Green River continued to grow. Oil and natural gas exploration also expanded, with the greatest activity in the Powder River Basin. A group of oil companies experimented with the production of oil from oil shale.

Two electric power companies built generating plants—located at Glenrock and Kemmerer—that use Wyoming's huge coal deposits as fuel. Coal production, which had dropped during the 1950's, rose again in 1959.

In 1960, Wyoming became the headquarters of the first operational long-range missile squadron in the United States. This squadron ranks as one of the largest missile installations in the world. The control center for the missile squadron is Francis E. Warren Air Force Base in Cheyenne.

Recent developments. Between 1970 and 1980, Wyoming's population grew by about 42 per cent, one of the highest rates in the nation. Large numbers of people moved to Wyoming to work in the state's rapidly developing mining industries. The sudden population growth caused housing shortages and other problems in Wyoming's mining communities. During the 1970's, the state legislature approved new taxes on minerals to provide funds to help communities deal with their problems.

During the 1980's, however, Wyoming began to experience an economic decline. Important uranium discoveries in Canada and Australia reduced the demand for Wyoming's uranium. Also, the nuclear energy industry, which uses uranium, has continued to develop slowly in the United States. Many Wyoming uranium mines and mills closed down. Americans also became more conservation-minded and reduced their use of coal and oil. Also, a drop in oil prices in 1986 contributed to rising unemployment in Wyoming. Today, state leaders are trying to find ways to broaden Wyoming's economy and make it less dependent on mineral production.

The 1980 United States census reported that Wyoming ranked 49th and Alaska 50th among the 50 states in population. But according to Census Bureau estimates, Alaska passed Wyoming in 1985, leaving Wyoming last in population.   Ronald E. Beiswenger and Robert W. Righter

Study aids

Related articles in *World Book* include:

Biographies

Bridger, James
Laramie, Jacques
Morris, Esther H.
Pollock, Jackson

Ross, Nellie Tayloe
Simpson, Alan K.
Spotted Tail
Washakie

Cities

Casper   Cheyenne   Laramie

History

Bozeman Trail
Homestead Act
Indian, American
Indian wars (Death on the Plains)
Oregon Trail
Pony express
Western frontier life

Physical features

Black Hills
Devils Tower National Monument
Fossil Butte National Monument
Grand Teton National Park
Great Plains
Rocky Mountains
Teton Range
Yellowstone National Park
Yellowstone River

Other related articles

Cowboy
Ranching
Wyoming, University of

Outline

I. **People**
  A. Population
  B. Schools
  C. Libraries and museums
II. **Visitor's guide**
  A. Places to visit
  B. Annual events
III. **Land and climate**
  A. Land regions
  B. Rivers and lakes
  C. Plant and animal life
  D. Climate
IV. **Economy**
  A. Natural resources
  B. Service industries
  C. Mining
  D. Manufacturing
  E. Agriculture
  F. Electric power
  G. Transportation
  H. Communication
V. **Government**
  A. Constitution
  B. Executive
  C. Legislature
  D. Courts
  E. Local government
  F. Revenue
  G. Politics
VI. **History**

Questions

What three famous pioneer routes crossed Wyoming in the mid-1800's? How did the passage of the pioneers disturb the Plains Indians?

What part of what is now Wyoming once belonged to the Republic of Texas?

What was the first U.S. national park? How did its establishment affect Wyoming?

Why was the construction of the Union Pacific Railroad during the 1860's important to the development of cities in Wyoming?

Why was the result of Wyoming's election for governor in 1924 so unusual?

What is Wyoming's leading mineral product?

What Wyoming tourist attraction became the first U.S. national monument?

Why is Wyoming nicknamed the *Equality State*?

Who were the Invaders?

What was a fur trappers' *rendezvous*?

Additional resources

Level I

Burt, Nathaniel. *War Cry of the West: The Story of the Powder River.* Holt, 1964.

Carpenter, Allan. *Wyoming.* Rev. ed. Childrens Press, 1979.

Fradin, Dennis B. *Wyoming in Words and Pictures.* Childrens Press, 1980.

Kirk, Ruth. *Yellowstone: The First National Park.* Atheneum, 1974.

Thompson, Kathleen. *Wyoming.* Raintree, 1988.

Level II

Bragg, William F. *Wyoming: Rugged but Right.* Pruett, 1979. Collection of 60 episodes from Wyoming history. *Wyoming: Wild and Wooly.* 1983.

Brown, Robert H. *Wyoming: A Geography.* Westview, 1980.

Calkins, Frank. *Jackson Hole.* Knopf, 1973.

Larson, Taft A. *Wyoming: A Bicentennial History.* Norton, 1977. *History of Wyoming.* 2nd ed. Univ. of Nebraska Press, 1978.

Miller, Donald C. *Ghost Towns of Wyoming.* Pruett, 1982.

Murray, Robert A. *Military Posts of Wyoming.* Old Army Press, 1974. *The Bozeman Trail: Highway of History.* Pruett, 1988.

Olson, Ted. *Ranch on the Laramie.* Little, Brown, 1972. The author's memories of Wyoming life on the ranch before World War I.

Righter, Robert W. *Crucible for Conservation: The Creation of Grand Teton National Park.* Colorado Associated, 1982.

Smith, Helena H. *The War on Powder River.* Univ. of Nebraska Press, 1967. First published in 1965.

Trenholm, Virginia C. *The Arapahoes: Our People.* Univ. of Oklahoma Press, 1986. First published in 1970.

Woods, L. Milton. *The Wyoming Country Before Statehood.* Worland, 1971.

Wyoming, University of, is a state-supported coed-ucational school in Laramie, Wyo. It has colleges of agri-culture, arts and sciences, commerce, education, engi-neering, health sciences, and law; a graduate school; and Army and Air Force ROTC units. Courses at the uni-versity lead to bachelor's, master's, and doctor's de-grees.

The University of Wyoming is noted for its geology program, its American Studies program, and its large manuscript and printed collections on Western history. The school has a science camp in the Medicine Bow Mountains, a biological research station at Jackson, and five agricultural substations in the state. The university was founded in 1886. For enrollment, see **Universities and colleges** (table).

Critically reviewed by the University of Wyoming

Wyoming Valley is a section of northeastern Pennsyl-vania 3 to 4 miles (5 to 6 kilometers) wide and about 20 miles (32 kilometers) long. It lies along the north branch of the Susquehanna River near Wilkes-Barre. The valley has rich deposits of *anthracite* (hard coal).

The Wyoming Valley is a historic gateway to central Pennsylvania from New England and New York. Many settlers entered the valley during colonial days. In the 1770's, it became the center of a boundary controversy between Connecticut and Pennsylvania. Congress set-tled the dispute in favor of Pennsylvania. In 1778, the Wyoming Valley was the scene of a bloody massacre (see **Wyoming Valley Massacre**).

Wyoming Valley Massacre, one of many tragedies of the American Revolutionary War, occurred in what is now Luzerne County, Pennsylvania. In 1778, it was an in-corporated county in the colony of Connecticut. At that time, most of the inhabitants of the Wyoming Valley be-lieved in the American cause of independence from Great Britain. However, some residents of the Wyoming Valley were Tories, and they remained loyal to Great Britain.

As the war went on, the Tories were driven out of the community, and joined other Tory and Indian bands. In the summer of 1778, these bands attacked Wyoming Valley. The inhabitants fled for safety to Forty Fort, near the site of the present city of Wilkes-Barre, Pa. About 300 men defended the fort. An army of 800 fighters, led by a British officer, opposed them. Six hundred of the at-tackers were Indians.

On July 3, the two groups met in a hard-fought battle. The attackers defeated the settlers, and killed more than two-thirds of them. The Indians tortured many of them to death. The survivors were left to find their way to the nearest settlements, and many of them died before they could reach help. The attackers completely destroyed the village and left the rest of the valley in ruins.

John R. Alden

Wyss family, *vees,* wrote *The Swiss Family Robinson,* a popular children's adventure story about a ship-wrecked family. Johann David Wyss (1743-1818), a Swiss pastor, made up the story to tell his four young sons. He wrote it down for the family, and he and his son Johann Emmanuel (1782-1837) illustrated it. Years later, another son, Johann Rudolf (1781-1830), rediscovered the story. He revised it and, in 1812 and 1813, had it published. He and his father are each sometimes considered the au-thor.

In *The Swiss Family Robinson,* the Robinson family struggles to survive alone on an island. They learn that they must work together, rather than separately. Young readers especially enjoy the book because the four Rob-inson sons behave—and misbehave—like real children. The book shows the influence of *Robinson Crusoe* (1719), a novel about a shipwrecked sailor on an island. This novel, by the English author Daniel Defoe, was ex-tremely popular at the time. See **Robinson Crusoe.**

Johann Rudolf Wyss was a professor and a scholar of Swiss folklore. He wrote the words to a popular Swiss patriotic song. He, Johann Emmanuel Wyss, and their fa-ther were all born in Bern.   Marilyn Fain Apseloff

Wyszyński, *vih SHIHN skee,* **Stefan Cardinal** (1901-1981), was the head of the Roman Catholic Church in Po-land from 1948 until his death. He became an arch-bishop in 1948 and a cardinal in 1953. Several months after Wyszyński became a cardinal, Poland's Communist government imprisoned him for opposing its antireli-gious policies.

Wyszyński led the oppo-sition to the government from 1956, when he was released from prison, until his death. However, he fol-lowed a policy of compro-mise. For example, he spoke out for religious freedom and other per-sonal rights. But he avoided open conflict with the Communists, especially when he thought it might lead to Russian interven-tion in Poland. During the

Keystone
Cardinal Wyszyński

1970's, his policies helped improve relations between the church and the government.

Wyszyński was born in Zuzela, near Warsaw. He was ordained a priest in 1924 and earned a doctorate in soci-ology from Catholic University in Lublin. Wyszyński took part in the resistance movement against the Nazi occu-pation of Poland during World War II (1939-1945).

Adam Bromke

Wythe, *wihth,* **George** (1726-1806), an American statesman, was a signer of the Declaration of Independ-ence. He was also a well-known lawyer and judge, and a patron of Thomas Jefferson and other distinguished Vir-ginians (see **Jefferson, Thomas** [Education]). He wrote the original Virginia protest against the Stamp Act in 1764. It was so fiery that it had to be rewritten in a softer tone. He participated in the Constitutional Convention of 1787.

Wythe served in the Second Continental Congress in 1775 and 1776. Later he helped draft the Virginia consti-tution. He became a judge of the court of chancery of Virginia in 1778, and, in 1786, he became chancellor of the state.

Wythe was born at Back River, Va., and attended the College of William and Mary. He was admitted to the bar in 1757, and entered the Virginia House of Bur-gesses a year later. In 1779, Wythe was appointed to the nation's first law professorship. The professorship was established that year at William and Mary by Thomas Jefferson.   Clarence L. Ver Steeg

X is the 24th letter of our alphabet. It probably developed from a letter called *samekh* used by the Semites, who once lived in Syria and Palestine. Historians are not sure what symbol the Semites used for this letter. About 1000 B.C., the Phoenicians developed a symbol that looks like a support for their letter *samekh.* The Greeks later took this symbol into their alphabet. It could represent the sounds of *kh* or *ks.*

Uses. *X* or *x* is about the 23rd most frequently used letter in books, newspapers, and other printed material in English. *X,* used alone or in combination with other letters, often stands for the word *Christ,* as in *Xmas. X* is the Roman numeral for *ten. X* is used in physical science and in mathematics to denote an unknown quantity, or a quantity that was at first unknown, as in *X ray.* In arithmetic problems, *x* is the sign of multiplication. In describing measurements, *x* represents the word *by,* as in *9' x 12',* or *nine by twelve feet.*

Pronunciation. In English, *x* has six sounds: *ks,* as in *six; gz,* as in *examine; ksh,* as in *luxury; gzh,* as in *luxurious; sh,* as in *anxious;* and *z,* as in *xylophone.* In some cases, such as *luxury,* the *x* is not voiced. In *luxurious,* the *x* is voiced. In Spanish, *x* may be pronounced as the English *s* or as the English *h.* In most other European languages, *x* has the same sounds as it has in English. See **Pronunciation.**   Marianne Cooley

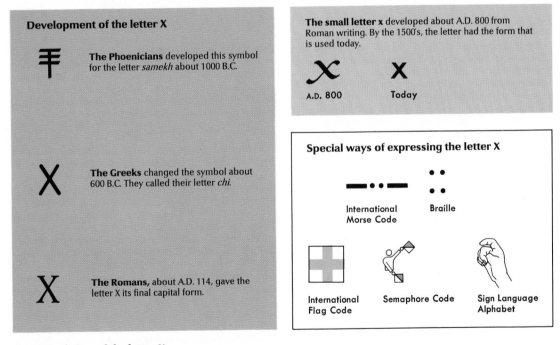

Development of the letter X

The Phoenicians developed this symbol for the letter *samekh* about 1000 B.C.

The Greeks changed the symbol about 600 B.C. They called their letter *chi.*

The Romans, about A.D. 114, gave the letter X its final capital form.

The small letter x developed about A.D. 800 from Roman writing. By the 1500's, the letter had the form that is used today.

A.D. 800   Today

Special ways of expressing the letter X

International Morse Code

Braille

International Flag Code

Semaphore Code

Sign Language Alphabet

Common forms of the letter X

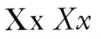

Handwritten letters vary from person to person. *Manuscript* (printed) letters, *left,* have simple curves and straight lines. Cursive letters, *right,* have flowing lines.

Roman letters have small finishing strokes called *serifs* that extend from the main strokes. The type face shown above is Baskerville. The italic form appears at the right.

Sans-serif letters are also called *gothic letters.* They have no serifs. The type face shown above is called Futura. The italic form of Futura appears at the right.

Computer letters have special shapes. Computers can "read" these letters either optically or by means of the magnetic ink with which the letters may be printed.

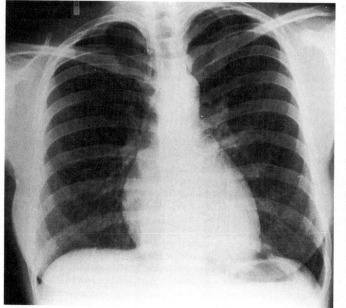

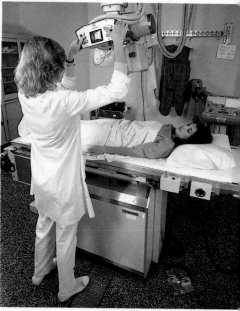

Saint Mary of Nazareth Hospital Center

© Larry Mulvehill, Photo Researchers

A chest X ray, *left,* reveals the shadows of the heart, the lungs, and the ribs. It can help physicians detect lung disease, broken bones, and other abnormal conditions inside a patient's body. X-ray pictures are produced by an X-ray machine, *right,* operated by a technologist.

X rays are one of the most useful forms of energy. They were discovered in 1895 by Wilhelm K. Roentgen, a German physicist. Roentgen called the rays *X rays* because at first he did not understand what they were. *X* is a scientific symbol for the unknown.

Scientists now know that X rays are a kind of *electromagnetic radiation,* which also includes visible light, radio waves, and gamma rays. X rays and visible light, for example, have many characteristics in common. X rays travel at the speed of light—186,282 miles (299,792 kilometers) per second. Both X rays and light travel in straight lines in the form of related electric and magnetic energy, called *electromagnetic waves.* In addition, X rays darken photographic film in much the same way that light does.

However, X rays and light differ in terms of *wavelength,* the distance between two crests of an electromagnetic wave. The wavelengths of X rays are much shorter than those of light. For this reason, X rays can penetrate deeply into many substances that do not transmit light. The penetrating power and other characteristics of X rays make them extremely useful in medicine, industry, and scientific research.

X rays can cause biological, chemical, and physical changes in substances. If the rays are absorbed by a plant or animal, they may damage or even destroy living tissue. For this reason, X rays can be dangerous. In human beings, an overdose of X rays may produce cancer, skin burns, a reduction of the blood supply, or other serious conditions. Dentists and *radiologists* (physicians who work with X rays) must take special care not to overexpose their patients or themselves to the rays.

In nature, X rays are produced by the sun, other stars, pulsars, and certain other heavenly bodies. Most X rays

from sources in space are absorbed by the atmosphere before they reach the earth.

Machine-made X rays are produced chiefly with *X-ray tubes,* a principal part of X-ray machines. Devices that accelerate atomic particles also produce X rays. Such devices include *betatrons* and *linear accelerators* (see **Betatron; Linear accelerator**).

Use of X rays

In medicine, X rays are widely used to make *radiographs* (X-ray pictures) of the bones and internal organs of the body. Radiographs help physicians detect abnormalities and disease conditions, such as broken bones or lung disease, inside a patient's body. Dentists take X-ray pictures to reveal cavities and impacted teeth (see **Teeth** [Dental checkups; picture]).

A radiograph is made by passing a beam of X rays through the patient's body onto a piece of photographic film. The bones absorb more of the rays than do muscles or other organs, and so the bones cast the sharpest shadows on the film. Other parts of the body allow more X rays through than the bones do and cast shadows of varying density. The shadows of the bones show up clearly as light areas on a radiograph, and the organs are seen as darker areas. Radiologists can see a patient's organs actually functioning by means of an X-ray device called a *fluoroscope.* The rays cause a special screen in the fluoroscope to *fluoresce* (glow) when they strike it. See **Fluoroscopy; Fluorescence.**

Sometimes a harmless substance is injected into the body to make certain organs stand out clearly on a radiograph or fluoroscopic image. For example, a doctor may give a patient a solution of barium sulfate to swallow before making an intestinal X ray. The barium sulfate absorbs X rays, and so the intestines show up clearly on the X-ray image.

X rays are widely used to treat cancer. They kill cancer cells more readily than they kill normal cells. A cancerous tumor can be exposed to a limited dose of X rays. In many cases, the X rays eventually destroy the tumor but do less damage to nearby healthy tissue.

X rays also serve other purposes in medicine. For example, they are used to sterilize such medical supplies as plastic or rubber surgical gloves and syringes. These materials would be damaged by exposure to intense heat and cannot be sterilized by boiling.

In industry, X rays are used to inspect products made of various kinds of materials, including aluminum, steel, and other cast metals. Radiographs reveal cracks and other defects in these products that are not visible on the surface. X rays are also used to check the quality of many mass-produced products, such as transistors and other small electronic devices. Some metal detection devices work by means of X rays. They include the scanners used at airports to check for weapons in luggage.

Manufacturers treat certain kinds of plastics with X rays. The rays cause a chemical change in these substances that makes them stronger. Powerful X rays have been used to help control an insect pest called the *blowfly*. Male blowflies cannot produce young after being exposed to X rays. In addition, X rays have been used to cause *mutations* (changes in cell structure) in barley. Mutated barley has produced new varieties of the grain. Some of these varieties can be raised in poor soil that cannot support regular barley.

In scientific research. X rays have been used to analyze the arrangement of atoms in many kinds of substances, particularly crystals. The atoms in crystals are arranged in planes, with regular spacing between each plane. When a beam of X rays travels through a crystal, the planes of atoms act as tiny mirrors that *diffract* (spread out) the rays into a regular pattern. Each type of crystal has a different diffraction pattern. Scientists have learned much about the arrangement of atoms in crystals by studying the various diffraction patterns. The study of how crystals diffract X rays is known as *X-ray crystallography*. Scientists also use X rays to help analyze the structure and makeup of many complex chemical substances, such as enzymes and proteins.

Archaeologists have used X rays to examine ancient objects that are covered by a heavy crust of dirt or corrosion. This method allows researchers to see an image of the object without attempting to remove the crust, which could damage the specimen. X rays also are used to reveal a painting covered by other paintings.

Characteristics of X rays

Electromagnetic radiation with short wavelengths has higher energy than radiation with long wavelengths. X rays have some of the shortest wavelengths and highest energies among all the kinds of electromagnetic radiation. The wavelengths of X rays range from about $\frac{1}{100}$ of an *angstrom unit* to 100 angstrom units. An angstrom unit equals about $\frac{4}{1,000,000,000}$ of an inch (0.00000001 centimeter). By comparison, the wavelengths of visible light range from about 4,000 to 7,000 angstrom units. The *World Book* article on **Electromagnetic waves** has a diagram that compares X rays with other kinds of electromagnetic radiation.

Many of the special characteristics of X rays result from their short wavelengths and high energy. The behavior of X rays can be compared with the behavior of visible light. For example, X rays can penetrate matter more deeply than light can because their energy is much higher than the energy of light. Also, X rays cannot be reflected easily by a mirror, as light can. Because of their high energy, X rays usually penetrate the mirror instead of being reflected by its surface.

X rays do not *refract* (bend) much when they travel from one material into another, as light does when it travels from air into a glass lens. Light is refracted by a lens because the light waves interact with the electrons in the atoms of the lens. But X rays have such short wavelengths that they pass through many substances without interacting with the electrons.

X rays are absorbed by a substance when they strike electrons in the atoms of the substance. The number of electrons in an atom equals its *atomic number* (see **Atom** [The atomic number]). Therefore, substances that have atoms of a high atomic number generally absorb more X rays than do substances with atoms of a low atomic number. Lead, which has an atomic number of 82, absorbs more X rays than most substances do. It is

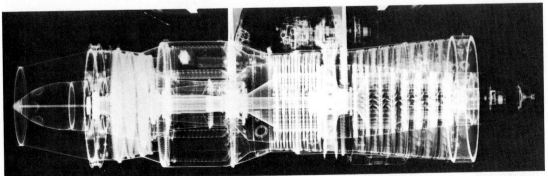

Eastman Kodak Company

X rays have many industrial uses because of their tremendous penetrating power. They can be used to check the construction of a jet airplane engine, *above.* An X-ray picture of this kind can uncover cracks and other structural defects that may not be visible on the surface.

often used to make X-ray shields. Beryllium, which has an atomic number of 4, absorbs relatively few X rays. X-ray absorption also depends on the density of the substance and on other complex factors. High-density substances absorb more X rays than do low-density substances.

If the X rays absorbed by a substance have enough energy, they knock electrons out of the atoms of the substance. Whenever an electrically neutral atom gains or loses electrons, it becomes an electrically charged particle called an *ion*. This process is called *ionization*. Ionization causes the many kinds of biological, chemical, and physical changes that make X rays both useful and dangerous.

How X rays are produced

X rays are produced whenever high-energy electrons suddenly give up energy. Machines produce the rays by accelerating electrons to extremely high speeds and then crashing them into a piece of solid material called a *target*. There, the electrons rapidly slow down because they collide with atoms in the target, and part of their energy is changed into X rays. Physicists call such X rays *bremsstrahlung*—from the German word for *braking radiation*.

Some of the high-energy electrons knock other electrons out of their normal positions in the atoms of the target. When these dislodged electrons fall back into place, or are replaced by others, other X rays may be produced. Physicists call such X rays *characteristic X rays*. Bremsstrahlung has a wide range of wavelengths, but each characteristic X ray has a particular wavelength, depending on the electronic structure of the atom it came from (see **Atom** [How scientists study atoms]).

X rays are produced by high-vacuum X-ray tubes for many medical and industrial uses. Such tubes consist of an airtight glass container with two electrodes—one positive and one negative—sealed inside (see **Electrode**). The *cathode* (negative electrode) has a small coil of wire. The *anode* (positive electrode) consists of a block of metal. In most X-ray tubes, the anode and cathode consist of tungsten or a similar metal that can withstand high temperatures.

When an X-ray tube is in operation, an electric cur-

rent flows through the cathode, causing it to glow white-hot. The heat releases electrons from the cathode. At the same time, an extremely high voltage is applied across the cathode and the anode. This high voltage forces the free electrons to travel at extremely high speeds toward the anode, which serves as the target. The electrons move easily through the space between the cathode and the target because the tube contains almost no air to block their motion. When the electrons strike the target, X rays and heat are produced.

The X rays are given off in many directions from the target. But most of them are absorbed by the *tube housing,* a metal case that surrounds the tube. One side of the housing has a small window through which a narrow beam of X rays escapes. The beam can be aimed at whatever object is to be X-rayed. The tube housing has a lead lining to absorb stray X rays. It also may contain oil or water to insulate and cool the tube.

The voltage across the cathode and target of an X-ray tube determines the energy, or penetrating power, of the rays it produces. A high voltage slams the electrons into the target at a higher energy level than does a low voltage. The X rays become more penetrating as the speed of the electrons increases. The voltage can be either raised or lowered by means of a control box.

The voltage in most X-ray tubes ranges from about 20,000 to 250,000 volts. Such voltages produce X rays powerful enough for most medical purposes. However, voltages of 300 million electronvolts (300 MeV) or higher can be achieved in betatrons and linear accelerators. X rays produced by these machines are used for medical and other scientific research.

History

After Roentgen discovered X rays in 1895, he experimented with them and soon demonstrated most of their characteristics. The discovery caused a sensation among scientists and the public. Within a few months, doctors were using X rays to examine broken bones.

In 1896, the American inventor Thomas A. Edison improved the fluoroscope so it could be used to view X-ray images. During the next 17 years, various scientists and inventors refined the X-ray tube. In 1913, the American physicist William D. Coolidge devised a way to

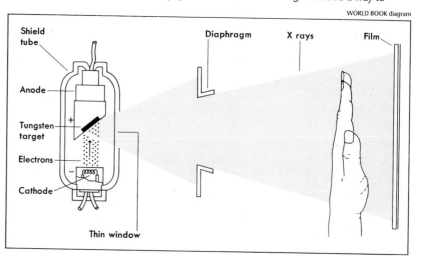

WORLD BOOK diagram

How an X-ray machine works

An electric current flows through the cathode, causing it to become extremely hot. The heat releases electrons from the cathode. At the same time, a high voltage is applied across the cathode and the anode. This voltage forces the electrons to travel at high speeds toward the tungsten target. X rays are produced when the electrons strike the target.

Shield tube

Anode

Tungsten target

Electrons

Cathode

Thin window

Diaphragm

X rays

Film

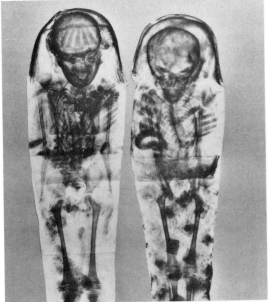

Field Museum of Natural History, Chicago

An x-ray image can help archaeologists examine ancient objects like these mummies. The image above reveals the skeletons of a boy and a girl under their heavy cloth wrappings.

make a more efficient X-ray tube. Modern X-ray tubes are basically the same as the type developed by Coolidge.

In the 1970's, radiologists began to use new processes for recording X-ray pictures. One process, called *xeroradiography,* records the image on a sheet of clear plastic instead of on photographic film. Xeroradiography is less expensive and requires less X-ray exposure than the old process. In another process, called *digital imaging,* detectors measure the X rays that pass through the body and send this information to a computer. The computer converts the data into an image that is displayed on a television screen. The image is stored on a magnetic disk.

Digital imaging is used in the *computerized tomographic scanner,* or *CT scanner,* an X-ray machine that makes a cross-sectional view of a patient's body. The CT scanner shoots a pencil-thin beam of X rays through the body from many angles. Detectors measure the rays that pass through, and a computer converts the many views into a single, cross-sectional image. CT scanners enable physicians to see detailed pictures of various organs and tissues with greatly improved contrast.

John W. Poston

Related articles in *World Book* include:

Angiography	Radiation
Betatron	Roentgen, Wilhelm K.
Bragg, Sir William	Siegbahn, Karl, M. G.
Computerized tomography	Synchrotron
Gamma rays	Telescope (Other telescopes)
Laue, Max T. F. von	
Magnetic resonance imaging	

Additional resources

Grey, Vivian. *Roentgen's Revolution: The Discovery of the X Ray.* Little, Brown, 1973.

Laws, Priscilla W. *X Rays: More Harm Than Good? How You Can Protect Yourself from Unnecessary Radiation by Understanding the Uses and Misuses of Diagnostic X-Rays.* Rodale, 1977.

Xavier, *ZAY vee uhr,* **Saint Francis** (1506-1552), was a Jesuit missionary. He is called the "Apostle of the Indies." Most of his work was done in Asia.

Saint Francis Xavier was born Francisco de Xavier near Sangüesa, Spain. His study in Paris brought him acquaintance with Ignatius of Loyola, with whom he helped to found the Society of Jesus. He accompanied Ignatius to Italy, doing hospital and missionary work, and was ordained a priest in 1537. He remained in Rome as secretary to the Jesuit society until 1540.

The next year, Xavier was sent by John III of Portugal to spread Christianity in the Portuguese possessions in India. He landed in Goa, on the Malabar Coast, in 1542. His preaching in Travancore, in Melaka, and in Japan gained many converts to the Roman Catholic Church. In 1551, the Vatican named him provincial of the province of India. He planned a mission to China, but died on the island of Shangchuan while trying to gain admission to the mainland. His body lies in a shrine in Goa. He was declared a saint in 1622.

Many miracles were credited to Xavier. He was one of the greatest missionaries and explorers in the Far East, and his converts numbered hundreds of thousands. Wherever he worked, he left well-organized Christians. His feast day is December 3.   James A. De Jong

See also **Japan** (Foreign relations); **Jesuits.**

Xenon, *ZEE nahn* or *ZEHN ahn,* is a chemical element that makes up about 1 part in 20 million of the earth's atmosphere. The British chemists Sir William Ramsay and Morris W. Travers discovered xenon in 1898. Industry uses xenon in filling flash lamps and other powerful lamps. Xenon is also used to make *bubble chambers,* which are instruments used by physicists to study nuclear particles.

Xenon is a colorless, odorless, tasteless gas. It is obtained from liquid air. It does not react readily with other substances. Xenon is classed as a *noble gas* (see **Noble gas**). The chemical symbol for xenon is Xe. Xenon has an atomic number of 54, and an atomic weight of 131.29. It may be condensed to a liquid that boils at −107.1° C and freezes at −111.9° C. It forms compounds with two chemical elements, fluorine and oxygen.

Frank C. Andrews

See also **Ramsay, Sir William.**

Xenophon, *ZEHN uh fuhn* (430?-355? B.C.), was a Greek soldier, historian, and writer. His most important contributions are books about the Greek philosopher Socrates and about Greek history.

Xenophon was born in Athens of a noble family. He studied under Socrates but was more interested in military subjects than in philosophy. In 401 B.C., Xenophon and other Greek adventurers fought in the Battle of Cunaxa in Persia. The Greeks formed part of an army led by the Persian prince Cyrus the Younger, who wanted to seize the throne of Persia from his brother Artaxerxes II. Cyrus was killed in the battle, and all the Greek commanders were killed soon afterward. Thus, the remaining Greeks—about 10,000—were stranded without a commander in a strange country. They chose Xenophon to lead their retreat. Xenophon described this 1,500-mile (2,400-kilometer) march in his book *Anabasis.*

After returning home, Xenophon became a close friend and admirer of King Agesilaus of Sparta, under whom he served in Asia and in Greece. The Spartans rewarded Xenophon by granting him an estate near Olympia in Elis. The Eleans later drove him from his estate. Xenophon then moved to Corinth, where he died.

Xenophon's book *Hellenica* is the major source for Greek history from 411 to 362 B.C. His *Memorabilia* and *Apology* tell much about Socrates. Xenophon's *Constitution of Sparta* and his eulogy of Agesilaus are vital to the understanding of Sparta. Donald Kagan

Xerography. See **Photocopying** (Electrostatic photocopying).

Xerox Corporation, *ZIHR ahks,* a leading United States company, ranks as one of the world's largest industrial organizations. It developed the first automatic copier that makes dry copies of printed or written materials on ordinary paper. The corporation also develops various information products and systems and provides financial services.

The corporation was founded in 1906 as The Haloid Company, a manufacturer of photocopying and photographic papers. After World War II ended in 1945, it began work on *xerography,* a process that makes copies without ink or pressure (see **Photocopying** [Electrostatic photocopying]). This process was perfected in 1959 and soon revolutionized office work. The corporation, which has headquarters in Stamford, Conn., adopted its present name in 1961. For the sales, assets, and number of employees of the Xerox Corporation, see **Manufacturing** (table). Critically reviewed by the Xerox Corporation

Xerxes I, *ZURK seez* (519?-465 B.C.), ruled the Persian Empire from 486 B.C. until his death. He succeeded his father, Darius I, and spent several years trying to achieve his father's goal of conquering Greece. But Xerxes failed to defeat Greece, and his military struggles against it greatly weakened the influence and power of the Persian Empire.

Stone relief sculptures from Persepolis (Ronald Sheridan)

Xerxes I ruled the Persian Empire from 486 to 465 B.C. In the sculpture shown above, Xerxes stands directly behind his father, the Persian ruler Darius I, who is seated on a throne.

During the early years of his reign, Xerxes put down revolts in the Persian provinces of Babylonia and Egypt. Then he began to assemble a huge land and sea force to invade Greece. This force included more than 180,000 men drawn from all over the empire, which then stretched as far west as Libya and as far east as the Indus River in what is now Pakistan.

In 480 B.C., Xerxes led his army against a Greek force in a mountain pass at Thermopylae, northwest of Athens. The Greeks, led by troops from Sparta, held back the Persians until a traitor told Xerxes of another way through the mountains. The Persians attacked the Greeks from the rear and defeated them. The people of Athens then abandoned their great city. Xerxes burned many temples and other buildings in Athens.

Soon afterward, the Greeks and Persians fought in the Bay of Salamis. The Greeks had fewer ships but were better trained than the Persians for maneuvering in the small bay. Xerxes watched from a hillside on shore as the Greeks crushed his fleet. Then he fled to his western capital in Asia Minor (now Turkey).

In 479 B.C., Persian forces attacked the Greeks at Plataea, west of Athens, and were again defeated. In 467 or 466 B.C., Greek soldiers and seamen defeated Persian forces again at the mouth of the Eurymedon River, on the southern coast of Asia Minor. As a result, a group of Persian nobles murdered Xerxes. Jack Martin Balcer

See also **Navy** (Famous sea battles); **Thermopylae.**

Xhosa, *KOH suh,* are a black people whose ancestors moved into southern Africa by the 1500's. More than half of the approximately 5 million Xhosa live in two regions, the Ciskei and the Transkei, assigned to them by the Republic of South Africa. The South African government gave both regions limited independence in the 1970's.

Most Xhosa once tended cattle and raised crops for a living. The wealth of each group depended on how many cattle it owned. The Xhosa did not kill their cattle for food, though some of the animals were sacrificed during religious ceremonies.

Xhosa men traditionally practiced *polygamy,* the custom of having more than one wife at a time. A typical household consisted of a man, his wives and unmarried children, and his married sons and their families. Members of the household lived in a cluster of small cone-shaped houses with thatched roofs. During the 1900's, this traditional way of life has mostly disappeared.

Large numbers of British and Dutch settlers migrated to southern Africa during the 1800's, and the Xhosa were defeated in war by the British in the late 1800's. Their defeat, loss of grazing land, and poverty forced many Xhosa to migrate to towns or farms where they worked for white people. Today, large numbers of Xhosa live in urban areas, and many others work on white-owned farms. The Xhosa and other nonwhite groups in South Africa suffer severe discrimination under a policy of segregation called *apartheid* or *separate development.*

Wade C. Pendleton

See also **Apartheid; Transkei.**

Xi Jiang, *shee jee ahng,* also spelled *Hsi Chiang,* is the most important stream of southern China. It rises on the border of Yunnan and Guizhou provinces and flows southeast for about 1,650 miles (2,655 kilometers). The northern part is called the Hongshui River. The Xi Jiang empties into the South China Sea. Guangzhou, one of

China's largest cities, is on the delta formed by the Xi Jiang and smaller rivers. Steamships can sail 230 miles (370 kilometers) up the Xi Jiang to the city of Wuzhou.

Xiamen, *shee ah muhn* (pop. 510,656), is a seaport on the coast of Fujian Province in southeast China (see **China** [political map]). Xiamen is also known as *Amoy* (pronounced *uh moy*). The name Amoy is based on the pronunciation of the city's name in the South Fujian dialect. Xiamen has a fine harbor and was once the center of China's tea trade.

During the 1600's, traders from Portugal traded with Xiamen, but the Chinese drove them out because they mistreated the people. In 1842, a treaty with Great Britain opened Xiamen and four other ports to British trade. British citizens and other foreigners living in Xiamen gained special rights. In 1943, Great Britain and the United States gave up these special privileges, and other countries followed their example. Before World War II (1939-1945), Xiamen had a flourishing trade. In the early 1980's, the Chinese government set up the Xiamen Special Economic Zone to attract foreign investment. Trade began to flourish once again.

Opposite Xiamen is Gulangyu, an island where many wealthy Chinese have their homes. From the port of Xiamen, numerous Chinese from Fujian have gone to various countries in Southeast Asia. Most of the "overseas Chinese" in Southeast Asia speak the South Fujian dialect.   Parris H. Chang

See also **Treaty port.**

Xinjiang, *shihn jee ahng,* also spelled *Sinkiang,* is a region in western China that shares a 2,000-mile (3,200-kilometer) border with the Soviet Union (see **China** [political map]). The Chinese government rules Xinjiang, but calls it an *autonomous* (self-governing) region.

Much of Xinjiang is a desolate, thinly populated land of deserts and mountains. The region covers about 17 per cent of China's land but has only about 1 per cent of the country's population. Most of Xinjiang's 13 million people live on or near natural or artificially created oases.

A majority of the region's people are non-Chinese in origin. Turkic people called Uygurs make up about half of the population. Other groups include Kazakhs and

Kirghiz. Xinjiang was on the Silk Road, an old trade route that connected the Middle East and Europe with China. Many Middle Eastern people settled in Xinjiang, and Middle Eastern influences became strong. Islam—the chief religion of the Middle East—is also the chief religion of Xinjiang. The language and clothing of the people, and the region's architecture and music, also show Middle Eastern influences.

Herding and farming are important economic activities in Xinjiang. Herders raise cattle, sheep, goats, and other animals. Farmers grow corn, cotton, fruits, rice, and wheat. Xinjiang has vast mineral resources, including coal, iron ore, oil, and uranium. Ürümqi, Xinjiang's capital, has factories that make farm machinery and cement.

China first ruled Xinjiang during the Han dynasty (202 B.C.-A.D. 220). After periods of Uygur and Mongol rule, Xinjiang came under Chinese control again during the Manchu (Qing) dynasty (1644-1912). In 1884, China made it a province. Since the mid-1900's, several border disputes with the Soviet Union have caused tension in Xinjiang.   Norma Diamond

See also **Turkestan.**

Xmas. See **Christmas** (introduction).

Xochimilco. See **Lake Xochimilco.**

Xunzi, *shyoon dzuh* (340?-245? B.C.), also spelled *Hsun Tzu,* was an influential Chinese philosopher best known for his belief that human nature is basically evil. He considered himself a follower of the philosophy of Confucianism. However, his view of human nature differed from that of most Confucianists.

According to Xunzi, the evil tendencies of human beings can be controlled only through education and moral guidance. He believed that people can be taught to perform good deeds and obey the moral laws of their society. Xunzi emphasized the importance of cultural traditions and their role in maintaining social order. His ideas are presented in the book *Xunzi* (or *Hsun-tzu*), most of which he wrote himself.

Xunzi was born in the state of Zhao, in what is now Shanxi Province. Nothing is known of his early life. From about 278 to 265 B.C., he was the most honored philosopher in the state of Qi, which had an academy of schol-

Gerald Cubitt, Bruce Coleman Ltd.

A Xhosa boy, *left,* herds cattle in the Transkei region of South Africa. Some of the Xhosa still farm for a living. Many others have moved into urban areas. More than half of the approximately 5 million Xhosa live in the Transkei and the nearby Ciskei region.

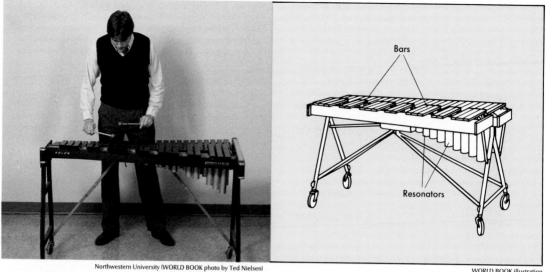

Northwestern University (WORLD BOOK photo by Ted Nielsen)   WORLD BOOK illustration

The xylophone is a percussion instrument. It has two rows of bars arranged like a piano keyboard on a frame. A musician stands behind it and strikes the bars with mallets, creating a hard, brittle sound. A metal tube called a *resonator* lies beneath each bar and amplifies the sound.

ars. He held government posts in Qi and several other states.   David R. Knechtges

See also **Confucianism** (Early Confucianism).

Xylem. See **Stem; Tree** (Trunks and branches; picture).

Xylophone, *ZY luh fohn,* is a percussion instrument that consists chiefly of a number of bars arranged on a frame like the keys of a piano. Most xylophones have 44 bars with a range of $3\frac{1}{2}$ octaves. The majority of xylophones have bars made of rosewood, but some have plastic bars. A musician strikes the instrument's bars with a mallet to produce a hard, brittle sound. A hollow metal tube called a *resonator* lies beneath each bar. The resonators amplify the sounds that are produced when the bars are struck. Variations in tone quality may be produced by using different types of plastic or rubber mallets.

No one knows exactly where or when the xylophone originated, but prehistoric peoples used some form of the instrument. During the 1500's in Europe, the xylophone was called the *Strohfiedel* because the bars were placed on belts made of straw. The German word *stroh* means *straw.* The word *fiedel* means *fiddle.* Musicians now play the xylophone in bands, orchestras, and small musical groups.   John H. Beck

XYZ Affair was the name given to a controversial exchange of diplomatic proposals between France and the United States in 1797. Relations between the two nations were strained at the time, and the exchange included outrageous demands from France. The three French agents who made these demands became known as X, Y, and Z. The XYZ Affair led to fighting at sea between the United States and France, though war was never declared.

The XYZ incident occurred while France was at war with Great Britain. The British had captured many French ships during that war. As a result, France depended on American ships to carry on the trade between France and the United States. But the French be-

came enraged at the Americans in 1796, when the U.S.-British Jay Treaty took effect. This treaty failed to guarantee American rights to trade with France. The French then began to seize American ships and cargoes. The French government also refused to receive the United States minister, General Charles Cotesworth Pinckney, who had been appointed by President George Washington.

The next President, John Adams, tried to avoid war by sending a special mission to France. He appointed two distinguished political leaders, John Marshall and Elbridge Gerry, to join Pinckney and settle the dispute. The French foreign minister, Prince Talleyrand, tried to stall the negotiations. He believed that a political dispute in the United States between the pro-French Republicans (later called Democratic-Republicans) and the pro-British Federalists was weakening the American ambassadors' bargaining position. Talleyrand appointed three agents to deal with the Americans sent by Adams. The agents told the Americans that before Talleyrand would see them, they would have to pay him a bribe of $250,000, loan France $12 million, and apologize for pro-British policies.

Adams reported France's demands to Congress. Republican Party congressmen asked to see the letters sent home by the American ambassadors as proof that the French had acted badly. Adams gave them the correspondence but substituted the letters X, Y, and Z for the actual names of the French agents. Thus, these events became known as the XYZ Affair.

Adams then asked Congress for money to prepare for war and gave American ships permission to fire on French ships. In 1800, after two years of naval conflict, a second American mission to France obtained a peace settlement.   Jerald A. Combs

See also **Adams, John** (Difficulties with France); **Gerry, Elbridge; Marshall, John; Pinckney, Charles C.; Talleyrand.**

Yy

Y is the 25th letter of our alphabet. It came from a symbol used by the Semites, who once lived in Syria and Palestine. They named it *waw,* their word for *hook,* and adapted an Egyptian *hieroglyphic,* or picture symbol. *Waw* was also the origin of *F, U, V,* and *W.* The Greeks later took the symbol into their alphabet, and gave it its capital Y form. They called it *upsilon.* The Romans used the letter when writing words taken from Greek. See **Alphabet.**

Uses. *Y* or *y* is about the 17th most frequently used letter in books, newspapers, and other printed material in English. *Y* represents the word *young* in many abbreviations, such as *YMCA* for *Young Men's Christian Association.* In archaic words, such as *ye* in *Ye Olde Tea Shoppe, y* represents a discarded Anglo-Saxon character called *thorn.* The thorn resembled *y* in appearance, and had the sound of *th.* In chemistry, *Y* represents the metallic element *yttrium.*

Pronunciation. *Y* or *y* may be either a vowel or a consonant. In English, a person pronounces the consonant *y* by placing the front of the tongue near the hard palate, and then gliding the tongue into position to make the sound of the vowel that follows. The velum, or soft palate, is closed, and the vocal cords vibrate. As a vowel, the letter *y* may have the sound of long *i* as in *my* and *fly;* that of short *i* as in *myth* and *nymph;* that of *u* as in *myrtle;* or that of long *e* as in *baby.* See **Pronunciation.** Marianne Cooley

Development of the letter Y

The ancient Egyptians drew this symbol of a supporting pole about 3000 B.C. The Semites adapted the symbol and named it *waw,* their word for *hook.*

The Phoenicians used this symbol of a hook in their alphabet about 1000 B.C.

The Greeks changed the symbol and added it to their alphabet about 600 B.C. They called their letter *upsilon.*

The Romans, about A.D. 114, used the letter when they wrote words borrowed from Greek.

The small letter y developed during the A.D. 300's from Roman writing. By the 1500's, the letter had the form that is used today.

y y y

A.D. 300   1500   Today

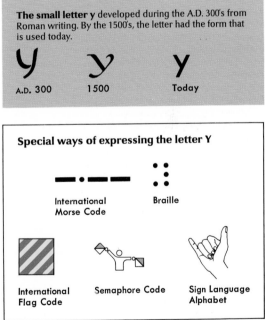

Special ways of expressing the letter Y

International Morse Code

Braille

International Flag Code

Semaphore Code

Sign Language Alphabet

Common forms of the letter Y

Handwritten letters vary from person to person. *Manuscript* (printed) letters, *left,* have simple curves and straight lines. Cursive letters, *right,* have flowing lines.

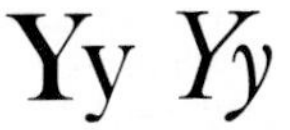

Yy *Yy*

Roman letters have small finishing strokes called *serifs* that extend from the main strokes. The type face shown above is Baskerville. The italic form appears at the right.

Yy Yy

Sans-serif letters are also called *gothic letters.* They have no serifs. The type face shown above is called Futura. The italic form of Futura appears at the right.

Computer letters have special shapes. Computers can "read" these letters either optically or by means of the magnetic ink with which the letters may be printed.

Y-Indian Guides is a national program of father-and-son clubs sponsored by the Young Men's Christian Association (YMCA). The program aims at fostering understanding and companionship between boys who are 6 to 8 years old and their fathers.

Knowledge of American Indian culture and traditions forms a basic part of the Y-Indian Guide program. Each club, called a *tribe,* has from six to nine father-son teams that meet in homes twice a month. Members plan and conduct their own activities. The tribes are organized into larger groups called *nations,* which go on camp-outs, short outings, and other events together.

Boys who are 9 to 11 years old and their fathers may join Y-Trail Blazers. This program emphasizes mental and spiritual growth, outdoor activities, physical fitness, service projects, and vocational exploration.

Critically reviewed by the YMCA of the USA

Y-Indian Maidens is a program of clubs in the United States for girls 6 to 8 years old and their mothers. The clubs, sponsored by the Young Men's Christian Association (YMCA), encourage companionship and understanding between mother and daughter.

The program's theme is based on American Indian culture. Each club, called a *tribe,* has from six to nine mother-daughter teams. Activities of the tribes include learning crafts, songs, and stories; outings; and service projects.   Critically reviewed by the YMCA of the USA

Y-Indian Princesses is a program of clubs in the United States for girls 6 to 8 years old and their fathers. It encourages companionship and understanding between father and daughter. The Young Men's Christian Association (YMCA) sponsors the Y-Indian Princesses.

American Indian culture forms a basic part of the program. Each club, called a *tribe,* has from six to nine father-daughter teams. They learn crafts, ceremonies, games, songs, and stories. Other activities include camping, service projects, and outings.

Critically reviewed by the YMCA of the USA

Y-Teens is a program for members of the Young Women's Christian Association who are of junior high or high school age. The program aims to serve the educational, health, recreational, and social needs of teen-age women. Members work to promote understanding among all people and to end racism.

Y-Teens began as the Little Girls' Christian Association in Oakland, Calif., in 1881. It was a model for other girls' clubs throughout the United States. In 1918, the program became known as Girl Reserves, and its name was changed to Y-Teens in 1947. The program operates in all U.S. states except Alaska. Headquarters are at 726 Broadway, New York, NY 10003.

Critically reviewed by the Young Women's Christian Association

Yablonovyy Mountains, YAHB *luh nuh VOY,* lie east of Lake Baikal in Siberia. The name of the range is also spelled *Yablonoi* (pronounced YAHB *luh NOY*). For location, see **Union of Soviet Socialist Republics** (terrain map). The range extends northeast from northern Mongolia for about 1,000 miles (1,600 kilometers) until it joins the Stanovoy Mountains. The Yablonovyy range is the dividing line between the rivers that flow into the Arctic Ocean and those that flow into the Pacific. Mount Sokhondo (8,199 feet, or 2,499 meters) is the highest peak. Some of the largest tin mines in the Soviet Union are in the Yablonovyy Mountains.   Theodore Shabad

Yacht, *yaht,* is a vessel, usually a small one, that is used only for pleasure. A yacht may be any kind of vessel, from a small sailing craft to a steam-powered ocean-going ship. Modern yachts originated in the Netherlands, where they were called *jaght boats,* or *hunting boats.* For more information on yachts, see **Boating.** See also **Sailing.**   Patience Wales

Yahweh. See **Jehovah.**

Yak, *yak,* is the wild ox of Asia. It inhabits the cold, dry plateaus of Tibet, often more than 16,000 feet (4,870 meters) above sea level. The wild yak stands over 6 feet (1.8 meters) high at the shoulders. But it carries its head low with the nose almost touching the ground. It may weigh from 1,100 to 1,200 pounds (499 to 544 kilograms). The yak is covered with black or brownish-black hair. The hair is especially long and silky on shoulders, flanks, and tail. The yak is agile in spite of its bulk and its heavy forequarters. It can slide down icy slopes, swim swift rivers, and cross steep rock slides. If forced to defend itself, it charges furiously. Excessive hunting has resulted in the killing of so many wild yaks that the animal is in danger of extinction.

The domestic yak, often called the *grunting ox* be-

Lynn M. Stone, Animals Animals

The yak of Asia is a relative of the American bison. Although big and bulky, the yak is agile.

cause of the sounds it makes, is the result of many generations of careful breeding. It is often white or piebald instead of black like the wild yak. Smaller and much more docile than the wild yak, it is useful in many ways. As a pack animal, it can carry a heavy load 20 miles (32 kilometers) a day. In Tibet, the yak carries travelers and mail. It provides rich milk. Its flesh is dried or roasted for food. The soft hair of the domestic yak is used to make cloth, and the coarser hair for mats and tent coverings. Saddles, whips, boots, and other articles are made from the hide. The bushy tail of the domestic yak is used as a fly chaser at ceremonial processions in India, and as an ornament for a tomb or shrine.

Scientific classification. The yak belongs to the bovid family, Bovidae. It is *Bos grunniens.*   C. Richard Taylor

Yakima, YAK *uh muh,* Wash. (pop. 49,826; met. area pop. 172,508), is a food-processing and shipping center. It lies in the Yakima Valley of south-central Washington, about 140 miles (225 kilometers) southeast of Seattle. For location, see **Washington** (political map). Many irrigated valley farms furnish fruits, potatoes, hops, wheat, poultry, and dairy products for the city's processing and packing plants. The manufacture of agricultural chemicals, packing boxes, and lumber are major industries in Yakima. The city is the eastern gateway to the recreational areas of the Cascade Mountains. Yakima is the name of the confederation of 14 Indian tribes that live on the nearby 1-million-acre (400,000-hectare) Yakima reservation. Yakima is the seat of Yakima County. It has a council-manager government.   Spencer Hatton

Yale, Elihu, *EHL uh ʜʏoo* (1649-1721), was an official of the East India Company and a benefactor of Yale University. During 27 years' service in India, from 1672 to 1699, he acquired a large fortune and became governor of Fort Saint George in Madras.

After returning to England, Yale made many gifts to churches, schools, and missionary societies. He gave books and other valuable goods to the Collegiate School which was founded in 1701 by the Congregationalists in Connecticut. In 1718, in recognition of his generosity, the trustees changed the name of the school to Yale College. Yale was born in Boston, but was taken to England at the age of three. He joined the East India Company in 1670.   Robert H. Bremner

Yale, Linus, *LY nuhs,* **Jr.** (1821-1868), an inventor and manufacturer, is best known for his inventions of locks. He began to assist his father in developing bank locks in 1849. He gained a wide reputation as an authority on these complicated devices, and held a number of patents. In 1861, Yale introduced the first of several combination safe locks and key-operated cylinder locks which set the pattern for future development. In 1868, he established a lock factory. He was born in Salisbury, N.Y.

        Robert P. Multhauf

See also **Lock.**

Yale University is a coeducational, privately endowed, nonsectarian school in New Haven, Conn. Chartered in 1701, Yale is the third oldest institution of higher learning in the United States. Only Harvard University and the College of William and Mary are older.

Yale graduates have always played a major role in American life. Many graduates have become leaders in government, business and industry, the arts, and community services. The presidents of about 90 U.S. universities and colleges graduated from Yale.

The Yale campus covers about 175 acres (71 hectares). Connecticut Hall, built in 1752, is the oldest building. This red brick building is the only structure left on the campus from colonial days. In recent years, famous American architects have constructed more than 25 buildings at Yale, including a science center.

Freshmen live on the *Old Campus,* the site of the original school. Sophomores, juniors, and seniors live in 12 residential colleges. Each college houses about 280 students and some faculty members. Each college has its own library, common rooms, and dining hall. The colleges compete with each other in several sports. The residence plan started in 1933 through the gifts of Edward S. Harkness, a Yale graduate.

The Yale library, containing more than 8 million volumes, is one of the largest libraries in the world. Yale's Beinecke Rare Book and Manuscript Library was dedicated in 1963. It is one of the largest buildings in the world devoted to rare books and manuscripts.

Yale News Bureau

Yale's Harkness Tower is part of the Memorial Quadrangle. The Gothic structure towers 201 feet (61 meters) in the air. The building was named for Charles W. Harkness, who was a graduate of Yale University and a benefactor of the school.

Yale's Peabody Museum of Natural History is one of the oldest university-related museums in the United States. It has many world-famous fossil exhibits. The Yale University Art Gallery is the oldest university art museum in the nation. The Yale Center for British Art has an excellent collection of British paintings and drawings, and related books and papers.

The *Yale Daily News,* established in 1878, is the oldest college daily newspaper in the United States. The *Yale Literary Magazine,* founded in 1836, was the first undergraduate magazine published in the United States.

Educational system. Yale has 12 divisions, each under the supervision of its own dean and faculty. The divisions of the university include Yale College; the graduate school; and the schools of art, architecture, divinity, drama, forestry, law, medicine, music, nursing, and organization and management.

The Corporation of Yale University governs the school. The corporation consists of the university president, the governor and lieutenant governor of Connecticut, and 16 *fellows* (trustees).

History. Yale was founded in 1701, when 10 Connecticut clergymen met in the village of Branford and made a gift of books to found a college. Later that year, the General Assembly of Connecticut approved a charter for the *Collegiate School.* From 1702 to 1707, classes met in the home of Rector Abraham Pierson at Killingworth (now Clinton).

Classes were held in Milford and then Saybrook before the school moved to New Haven in 1716. Two years later, the school's only college building was still unfinished due to lack of funds. Elihu Yale, a retired merchant in London, gave money to the school in 1718 (see **Yale, Elihu**). Yale is sometimes called *Old Eli*. The same year, the school adopted its present name in honor of Yale. The undergraduate school, known as Yale College, was open only to men until 1969. For the enrollment of the university, see **Universities and colleges** (table).

Critically reviewed by Yale University

See also **Connecticut** (picture); **Library** (picture: A rare book collection).

Yalta, *YAWL tuh* or *YAHL tah* (pop. 85,000), is a city in the Ukrainian Soviet Socialist Republic, a republic of the Soviet Union. It lies on the southern coast of the Crimean Peninsula, along the Black Sea. For location, see **Union of Soviet Socialist Republics** (political map). Yalta is a popular health resort and vacation area. It has a mild climate and mineral-rich sea air. The city is a busy seaport and a center for the production of wine, fruits, and tobacco.

Yalta was originally a Greek colony. The colony later fell under the control of Italy and then Turkey. Yalta became a part of Russia in 1783. In 1945, during World War II, Allied leaders met in the city for the Yalta Conference. For details, see **Yalta Conference.**

Jaroslaw Bilocerkowycz

Yalta Conference was one of the most important meetings of key Allied leaders during World War II (1939-1945). These leaders were President Franklin D. Roosevelt of the United States, Prime Minister Winston Churchill of Great Britain, and Premier Joseph Stalin of the Soviet Union. Their countries became known as the "Big Three." The conference took place at Yalta, a famous Black Sea resort in the Crimea, from Feb. 4 to 11, 1945. Through the years, decisions made at Yalta regarding divisions in Europe have stirred bitter debates.

When the meeting began, the Soviet Union held the strongest European military position. Soviet armies occupied much of Eastern Europe and were preparing to enter Berlin, Germany. The agenda at Yalta included the major problems in a postwar Europe.

The three leaders agreed on several points: (1) to accept the structure of a world peacekeeping organization that was to become the United Nations; (2) to reestablish order in Europe and to help the defeated countries create democratic governments; (3) to divide Germany into four zones that would be occupied by Great Britain, the United States, the Soviet Union, and France; (4) to support the Soviet-backed government and hold free elections in Poland, and to extend the Soviet Union's territory into Poland; and (5) to force Germany to give the Soviet Union equipment and other resources to make up for Soviet losses. In addition, the Soviet Union agreed to enter the war against Japan in exchange for control of the Kuril Islands, the southern half of Sakhalin Island, and two strategic ports.

After the war, critics said that President Roosevelt had "sold out" Eastern Europe and had given too much to the Soviet Union. However, most modern scholars believe that the conference produced a traditional and balanced settlement. They argue that the Soviet Union held the superior military and political position in Eastern Europe and yet made the greatest concessions at the conference. Stalin failed to win demands for huge sums of money from Germany to pay for tremendous war losses and for a shift of the German-Polish border westward. Most scholars also believe that the Soviet Union's domination of Eastern Europe resulted from earlier and later events, not decisions at Yalta.   Diane Shaver Clemens

Yalu River, *YAH LOO,* rises from the highest peak of the Changbai Shan, or Long White Mountains, of Manchuria. The river forms most of the boundary between North Korea and Manchuria as it flows 500 miles (800 kilometers) to the Yellow Sea. The river became important during the Korean War (1950-1953). Chinese Communists crossed the Yalu in mid-October, 1950, to aid North Korea in the war.   J. E. Spencer

Yam is a major food crop in many tropical countries. The edible part of the yam plant is its *tuber.* This enlarged portion of the plant's stem grows underground and stores food for the plant. The tuber contains a large amount of starch and water, and some sugar. Some tubers contain poisons that may cause illness if they are not destroyed by cooking. The tubers of some wild yams produce compounds called *saponins* that can be used to make cortisone and certain other drugs.

The word *yam* is commonly used to refer only to yam tubers. Some yams weigh as much as 100 pounds (45 kilograms) and measure as long as 6 feet (1.8 meters). Their flesh is white or yellow. Yams are often confused with sweet potatoes, because some sweet potatoes produce storage roots that are similar to yam tubers (see **Sweet potato**).

Yam plants are climbing vines. Their stems bear small green flower clusters. Yams require hot, moist weather and a long growing season. About 21 million short tons (19 million metric tons) of yams are grown for food each year. Western Africa produces about half of this crop. Yams also grow in India and in the countries of Southeast Asia and the Caribbean Sea. The United States grows no yams, because the weather is too cold and the growing season is too short.

Scientific classification. Yams belong to the yam family, Dioscoreaceae. Common edible yams include *Dioscorea alata* and *D. rotundata.*   Conrad K. Bonsi and Bobby R. Phills

Yam bean. See **Jicama.**

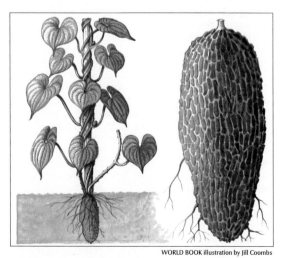

WORLD BOOK illustration by Jill Coombs
The yam is a major crop in many tropical countries.

Yamamoto, *YAH muh MOH toh,* **Isoroku,** *EE soh ROH koo* (1884-1943), commanded the Japanese combined fleet at the time of the attack on Pearl Harbor in 1941. He was one of Japan's great admirals, with a long and distinguished career in war and peace. He opposed the policies that led to war with the United States. But he sponsored the plans for the Pearl Harbor attack as Japan's only chance of victory. Yamamoto was born in Nagaoka. He was killed in 1943 when his plane was shot down in the South Pacific.   Marius B. Jansen

Yamashita, *YAH mah SHEE tah,* **Tomoyuki,** *TAW maw YOO kee* (1885-1946), a Japanese general in World War II, was executed for "violation of the laws of war." A brilliant field commander, Yamashita advanced rapidly in Korea and Manchuria. He became famous for the campaign against Malaya and Singapore in 1942. Later, he served in Manchuria until he took charge of the defense of the Philippines in 1944. Yamashita was born in Kōchi prefecture.   Marius B. Jansen

Yamato period, *YAH mah toh,* was the time in Japanese history from about A.D. 200 to 646. During this period, Japan's emperors ruled from the Yamato area, the area around what is now the city of Nara. They controlled much of central Japan and parts of southern Korea during the 200's and 300's. Japan's royal family traces its ancestry to the Yamato emperors, and so the entire nation is sometimes called *Yamato.*

Chinese culture and Buddhism greatly influenced the development of art, literature, and government in Japan during the Yamato period. Buddhism became popular among the rulers and the leading families of Japan. However, Shinto remained a chief religion. The Yamato period ended in 646, when the emperor began a program called the Taika Reform to establish a central government.   Tetsuo Najita

Yancey, *YAN sih,* **William Lowndes,** *lowndz* (1814-1863), an American statesman, was often called "The Orator of Secession." He served in the United States House of Representatives as a Democrat from Alabama from 1844 to 1846. After leaving Congress, Yancey devoted himself to arousing the South to defend its rights.

Yancey's "Alabama Platform" demanded that southerners have the right to take their slaves into western territories. He opposed the Compromise of 1850. In 1858, Yancey tried to organize a League of United Southerners to work for Southern rights in both the Democratic and Republican parties.

Yancey opposed Stephen A. Douglas' candidacy for the Democratic presidential nomination in 1860, and supported John C. Breckinridge. He drew up Alabama's Secession Ordinance. Later he was a Confederate commissioner to Europe and a Confederate senator from Alabama. Yancey was born in Warren County, Georgia. He practiced law and edited a newspaper in Greenville, S.C., before moving to Alabama.   W. B. Hesseltine

Yang, *yahng,* **Chen Ning** (1922-   ), a Chinese-born physicist, shared the 1957 Nobel Prize in physics with Tsung Dao Lee (see **Lee, Tsung Dao**). They received the award for their contributions to the laws of fundamental particles. They disproved the law of *conservation of parity,* which concerned the physical interactions of fundamental nuclear particles. Yang was born in Hefei, Anhui, China. He was a staff member at the Institute for Advanced Study in Princeton, N.J., from 1949 to 1965. He

became director of the Institute for Theoretical Physics at State University of New York at Stony Brook in 1965.
      Ralph E. Lapp

See also **Parity.**

Yangcheng. See Guangzhou.

Yangtze River, *yahng dzuh,* also called Yangtze Kiang, is the world's third longest river, and the longest and most important river in China. To most Chinese, the Yangtze is known as the *Chang Jiang,* or *long river.* It rises in the Tanggula Mountains of Qinghai Province, about 16,000 feet (4,880 meters) above sea level. The river flows east, southeast, and then south into the province of Yunnan. From here it flows northeast across Sichuan (Szechwan) Province. It then follows an irregular course east through central China and enters the East China Sea 3,915 miles (6,300 kilometers) from its source. The Yangtze and its branches drain about 706,000 square miles (1,829,000 square kilometers).

The high mountains at the Yangtze's source cause it to

Shostal

The Yangtze River is the longest river in China. Small boats carry people and goods on this important waterway.

flow rapidly for most of its length. The great gorges in its upper parts above Yizhang make it one of the most beautiful rivers in the world. Just above Yizhang is perhaps the largest potential hydroelectric site in the world. In places, mountains over 1 mile (1.6 kilometers) high form the river's banks. About half of China's ocean trade is distributed over the Yangtze and its branches. Ocean steamers reach Wuhan, 680 miles (1,090 kilometers) by river from the coast. Smaller boats can go 1,000 miles (1,600 kilometers) farther inland.

Thousands of Chinese live on the Yangtze on sailing craft called *junks.* Millions of Chinese live on the banks of this great river. Occasional summer floods temporarily drive many people from their homes. Among the great cities along the Yangtze River are Shanghai, Nanjing, Anqing, Yizhang, Chongqing, and Wuhan.
      J. E. Spencer

Yank was a weekly magazine for soldiers published during World War II by the United States Army. *Yank* was written and edited by a staff of enlisted personnel. *Yank* contained excellent features, and was credited with many exclusive stories on the course of the war. The first issue appeared on June 17, 1942. *Yank* was discontinued at the end of 1945. Over 2,600,000 soldiers read *Yank.* It was printed in 21 regional editions, which reached such distant places as Iran, India, Egypt, England, and France.   Earl F. English

Yankee. People of other countries often call any person from the United States a Yankee. In the southern United States, the word *Yankee* means a Northerner, or someone who comes from north of Mason and Dixon's line. But most of the people of the United States use the word *Yankee* to mean a New Englander.

People often say that someone is "shrewd as a Yankee" or "clever as a Yankee." The people of early New England had to develop great shrewdness and cleverness as they struggled to make homes and create industries in the rocky wilderness. "Yankee peddlers" roamed far and wide through early American communities, selling the articles made by Yankee craftworkers. These peddlers won a great reputation for getting high prices.

No one is certain where the word *Yankee* came from. Some dictionaries state that the English word *Yankee* comes from the Scottish word *yankie.* A *yankie* is a sharp and clever woman. Other dictionaries suggest that *Yankee* is an Indian pronunciation of the word *English,* or of the French word for *English,* which is *Anglais.* The word *Yankee* may have had a Dutch origin. Early Flemish people sometimes called people from the Netherlands *Jan Kees,* which was short for the common Dutch names *Jan* and *Cornelis.* Some authorities believe that the people of Flanders gave the same name to Netherlanders who lived in North America.

The first person to use the word Yankee very widely was a farmer of Cambridge, Mass., named Jonathan Hastings. He used the word in the early 1700's to express the idea of excellence, speaking of a "Yankee good horse," or "Yankee cider." Harvard students who hired horses from Hastings began to use the expression. The word was widely used during the Revolutionary War, when British soldiers made fun of New England troops by calling them Yankees. During the Civil War, Confederate soldiers called Federal troops "Yankees." When United States troops arrived in Paris in 1917, the French press hailed them as Yankees or Yanks. Europeans have continued to use the word as a name for American soldiers.

John R. Alden

See also **Yankee Doodle.**

Yankee Doodle is a song that has been popular in America since colonial days. The tune is an old one. It may have begun in southern Europe in the Middle Ages. About 1500, it was popular in Holland, where the harvesters sang it. The verses began with the meaningless words:

> Yanker dudel doodle down.

The song was sung to small children in England during Shakespeare's time. Later the tune was used for a rhyme that began:

> Lucy Locket lost her pocket,
>   Kitty Fisher found it;
> Nothing in it, nothing in it,
>   Save the binding round it.

Another English form of the Yankee Doodle tune was sung by the Cavaliers in the 1600's. They made up words to poke fun at Oliver Cromwell when he rode down from Canterbury to take charge of the Puritan forces.

> Yankee Doodle came to town
>   Upon a Kentish pony,
> He stuck a feather in his cap
>   And called it macaroni.

At that time, some people used the word *macaroni* to refer to the young men of London who dressed in odd Italian styles.

The words of "Yankee Doodle" known in the United States were written by an English army surgeon, Dr. Richard Schuckburgh. The song made fun of the untrained American troops during the French and Indian War in 1755. But the American troops liked "Yankee Doodle" and the song soon became popular. "Yankee Doodle" was well known all through the American colonies by the time of the Revolutionary War. The first printed notice of it in America appeared in the New York *Journal* on Oct. 12, 1768. The words of the song are:

> Father and I went down to camp,
>   Along with Captain Goodwin,
> And there we saw the men and boys,
>   As thick as hasty puddin'.
>
> Chorus: Yankee Doodle keep it up,
>   Yankee Doodle dandy,
>   Mind the music and the step,
>   And with the girls be handy.
>
> And there was Captain Washington,
>   Upon a slapping stallion,
> And giving orders to his men,
>   I guess there was a million.
>
> And then the feathers on his hat,
>   They looked so 'tarnal finy
> I wanted peskely to get,
>   To give to my Jemina.
>
> And then they had a swamping gun,
>   As big as a log of maple,
> On a deuced little cart,
>   A load for father's cattle.

"Yankee Doodle" was sung and played in every patriot camp. American soldiers often whistled it in battle. The British heard it so often during their retreat from Concord that General Gage is said to have exclaimed, "I hope I shall never hear that tune again!" But the British did hear it again. American bands played it as the British left after the surrender at Yorktown.   Raymond Kendall

Yankee terrier. See **American Staffordshire terrier.**

Yaoundé, *yah oon DAY* (pop. 313,706), is the capital of Cameroon. It lies on a plateau in the southern part of the country. For location, see **Cameroon** (map).

Yaoundé is in the most densely populated region of Cameroon. The city is important as the country's center of government, but it has little industry. The University of Yaoundé is the country's only university. The city has an international airport. Railroads connect Yaoundé with Douala, the country's largest city and leading port, and with many other cities.

The Germans founded Yaoundé in 1888. In 1922, the city became the capital of a French territory called East Cameroon. It remained the capital when Cameroon gained independence in 1960.   Immanuel Wallerstein

See also **Cameroon** (picture).

Yap Islands, *yap* or *yahp,* form an island group in the western Pacific Ocean. The group is part of the Caroline Islands. It lies about 1,000 miles (1,600 kilometers) east of the central Philippines and about 2,000 miles (3,200 kilometers) south of Yokohama, Japan. For location, see **Pacific Islands** (map). The Yap Islands include four large islands and 10 smaller islands. The main islands are Yap (the largest), Gagil-Tamil, Map, and Rumung. The island group covers 39 square miles (101 square kilometers) and has a population of about 5,200. The islands are composed of ancient crystalline rocks and have a rugged surface. Long, narrow channels separate the islands, and coral reefs surround them. One large break in the reefs allows small vessels to enter a natural harbor.

The people of the Yap Islands are Micronesians. Most of them make a living by farming. Taro, bananas, yams, coconuts, and tropical fruits are the main crops. Fishing is also important. Some people are employed by the government of the islands.

Spaniards first discovered and controlled Yap. In 1899, Spain sold the islands to Germany. In 1905, Yap became internationally important as a cable station between the United States, the Netherlands Indies (now Indonesia), and Japan.

After World War I ended in 1918, the League of Nations put Yap under Japanese mandate. The United States protested this action. In 1921, the United States and Japan signed a treaty by which the United States recognized the Japanese mandate. In return for this recognition, Japan granted the United States equal rights to cable and radio service through Yap, and also allowed United States citizens free entry there.

During World War II (1939-1945), the Japanese used the island group as a naval and air base. American troops occupied Yap after the war ended. In 1947, the United Nations made the United States trustee of the islands as part of the Trust Territory of the Pacific Islands. In 1980, the Yap Islands and other Caroline Islands formed the Federated States of Micronesia in an agreement with the United States. These islands became a self-governing political unit in free association with the United States in 1986.   Robert C. Kiste

See also **Caroline Islands; Pacific Islands, Trust Territory of the; Races, Human** (picture: Micronesian).

Yaqui Indians, *YAH kee,* are a tribe that lives in Mexico, Arizona, and California. They are noted for their religious ceremonies, which blend concepts of Roman Catholicism with ancient tribal customs. On holy days, the Yaqui perform ancient dances and rituals in honor of Jesus Christ, the Virgin Mary, and tribal patron saints.

The ancient Yaqui lived along the Yaqui River in northwestern Mexico. They raised beans, corn, and squash. They also hunted game and gathered wild plants. The Yaqui lived in small, scattered villages and had no central government.

Yaqui warriors defeated the Spanish invaders who entered their territory in 1533 and 1609. In 1610, the Yaqui made a treaty with the Spaniards and asked for Jesuit missionaries to settle in their villages. The Yaqui wanted the Jesuits to teach them how to raise wheat, fruit, and livestock. The Jesuits arrived in 1617, and the Yaqui lived prosperously for the next 120 years. They learned the Roman Catholic religion and blended it with their own culture. The Jesuits helped the Yaqui organize the villages into eight towns, which became centers of Yaqui religion and government.

In the 1730's, many Yaqui became dissatisfied with the Jesuits and the Spanish colonial government. Some of them sought independence. The tribe fought Spanish and Mexican troops in a series of bloody wars that lasted until the 1900's. During these wars, the Mexican government forced many Yaqui to leave their homeland and settle in other parts of Mexico. Some of the Yaqui fled Mexico to live in the United States. There are now about 40,000 Yaqui in Mexico and about 5,000 in the United States.   Don D. Fowler

Yard is a unit of length in the customary system of measurement used in the United States. It is equal to 3 feet, or 36 inches. One yard equals 0.9144 meter.

Yarmulka. See **Judaism** (Orthodox Judaism).

Yarn. See **Cotton** (Spinning); **Wool.**

Yates, Elizabeth (1905-   ), an American author, won the Newbery Medal in 1951 for *Amos Fortune, Free Man,* a biography of an American slave who purchased his freedom. Her other works include *High Holiday* (1938); *Once in the Year* (1947); *A Place for Peter* (1952); *An Easter Story* (1967); and *With Pipe, Paddle and Song* (1968). She was born in Buffalo, N.Y.

Yaw. See **Airplane** (Flying an airplane; diagram).

Yawning is the act of opening the mouth wide, or *gaping.* The usual yawn is due to drowsiness or fatigue. It is a sign that the body needs sleep. Yawning is an involuntary reflex. After the act has started, it is almost impossible to stop it. The mouth can be held closed, but the yawning muscles still contract.

People and animals yawn when oxygen is slowly cut off from them, and when the muscles are thoroughly relaxed. People who yawn often are probably not getting enough oxygen. They may need better ventilation, or exercise. They will generally stop yawning if they drink a beverage, or bathe their face with cold water. Scientists are not sure what part of the nervous system controls yawning, but it may be the *mesencephalon* (midbrain) in the brain. One purpose of yawning may be to awaken a person by stretching the muscles, helping the blood to circulate, and by increasing the amount of inhaled air.

Charles W. Cummings

Yaws, also called *frambesia, fram BEE zhuh,* is a disease that attacks chiefly children of humid tropical regions. Various kinds of *lesions* (skin eruptions) appear and disappear during the course of the disease, which may last several years. Yaws attacks the skin and bones, but it causes death in only rare cases.

Bacteria called *spirochetes* cause yaws. The spirochetes, which resemble those that cause syphilis, enter the body through a break in the skin. In most cases, a person catches yaws from contact with an infected individual. Three to four weeks after infection, a small, yellow-red, pimplelike lesion forms where the spirochetes entered the body. Other lesions, some of which resemble raspberries, break out weeks or months later. Painful sores often form on the soles of the feet and make walking difficult. Still later, tumorlike lesions may develop. The disease may gradually destroy the cartilage of the nose and cripple bones and joints. It can be cured by injections of penicillin.   Thomas H. Weller

Yazoo Fraud, *YAZ oo.* In 1795, Georgia's general assembly sold state-owned land on the Yazoo River to speculators. Most of the legislators were bribed. The people of Georgia became indignant, and the legislature passed a Rescinding Act in 1796. But the speculators refused to give up their bargain. The Supreme Court of the United States ruled in 1810 that the Rescinding Act was unconstitutional. However, by this time, Georgia had sold its western lands to the federal government. Congress appropriated over $4,200,000 to settle the Yazoo claims in 1814.   Albert B. Saye

Yeager, *YAY guhr,* **Charles Elwood** (1923-   ), was the first man to fly faster than the speed of sound. He accomplished this on Oct. 14, 1947, in a Bell X-1 rocket airplane. He set another speed record on Dec. 12, 1953, by flying $2\frac{1}{2}$ times the speed of sound in a Bell X-1A. Yeager was born in Myra, W. Va. During World War II (1939-1945), he served as a fighter pilot. In 1975, Yeager retired from the military with the rank of brigadier general. In 1986, he was named to the presidential commission investigating the explosion of the space shuttle *Challenger.*   Robert B. Hotz

Year is the time the earth takes to make one complete revolution around the sun. There are two different kinds of years which are used by astronomers. The *solar, equinoctial,* or *tropical* year is the time between two passages of the sun through the vernal equinox, which occurs in March. This year is 365 days, 5 hours, 48 minutes, and 46 seconds long. This year is used for all practical and astronomical purposes. It is the basis of our common or calendar year.

The *sidereal* year is made up of 365 days, 6 hours, 9 minutes, and 9.5 seconds. This is the time it takes the earth to return to the same place in its orbit, with reference to the fixed stars. The sidereal year is longer than the solar year because of the *precession of the equinoxes.* The sidereal year is seldom used except in the calculations of astronomers.

The calendar year is only 365 days long, and so we have to add an extra day every four years to correct the difference in time between the calendar year and the solar year. This fourth year is called *leap year,* and the extra day is February 29. Adding an extra day every fourth year makes the average calendar year 11 minutes, 14 seconds too long. So, the day is not added in the century years, except in those divisible by 400. The years 1700, 1800, and 1900 have had only 365 days. The year 2000 will contain 366 days.

Today, the *leap second* corrects for differences in the earth's rate of rotation from year to year. It is usually added to or subtracted from the last minute of the year. The leap second became a necessary part of the calendar year after scientists began measuring time intervals with atomic clocks (see **Atomic clock**).

The *lunar year* is made up of 12 lunar months. The ancient Greeks used this year. It contained 354 days.

In most Western nations, the calendar year begins on January 1. During the Middle Ages, however, most European nations considered March 25, Annunciation Day, to be the first day of the calendar year. By 1600, most of them had adopted the Gregorian calendar, which recognized January 1 as the beginning of the year.

The church calendar, which is used in the Roman Catholic and in most Protestant churches, is regulated partly by the solar and partly by the lunar year. This causes a difference between the fixed feast days, which always fall on the same day every year, and movable feasts such as Easter, whose dates vary from year to

year. The fixed feast days are determined by the solar year, and the movable feast days, by the lunar year.

In the early ancient Roman calendar, the year began on March 1. Later, the Romans used January 1 as the new year. The Jewish year begins near the autumnal equinox, around September 22. The Islamic year is based on the changing of the phases of the moon and lasts 354 days. Therefore, the beginning of the Islamic year continually falls earlier in the seasons. Thirty Islamic years make up a cycle during which there are 11 leap years at irregular intervals.   James Jespersen

Related articles in *World Book* include:

A.D.	Equinox
B.C.	Leap year
Calendar	Olympiad
Christian Era	Season

Yeast is a living substance that bakers put into dough to make it rise. It is also used in the production of beer, wine, and other alcoholic beverages. The yeasts used commercially consist of masses of microscopic, single-celled yeast organisms. There are more than 600 species of yeasts, but only a few are used commercially.

Until 1876, people made bread, beer, and wine without understanding the role that yeasts played in their production. That year, the French scientist Louis Pasteur reported that yeasts were living cells and that they played an important part in making beer.

Yeasts belong to a group of simple organisms known as *fungi,* which exist almost everywhere in nature, including the air. Yeasts reproduce rapidly, and they grow especially well in substances containing sugar. Yeast cells reproduce by *fission* (splitting in two) or by *budding.* In budding, part of the cell wall of the yeast swells and forms a new growth called a *bud.* The bud then breaks off and becomes an independent cell.

How yeast is used. Yeast fungi lack chlorophyll, the green matter that green plants use to make their own food. Therefore, yeasts must rely on other sources for food. They feed on sugar from a variety of natural sources, including fruit, grain, and nectar, and also from molasses. Yeast cells produce chemicals called *enzymes,* or *ferments,* that break down their food. Different species of yeasts produce different kinds of enzymes. Some break down sugar into alcohol and carbon dioxide. This process, called *fermentation,* plays an important part in making bread, beer, and wine.

In breadmaking, a commercial yeast called *baker's yeast* is used as a *leaven,* a substance that makes dough rise. Bread dough is made by mixing such basic ingredients as flour, water or milk, salt, and yeast. Flour provides only a small amount of the sugar needed for fermentation. Therefore, bakers add certain enzymes that convert some of the starch in the flour into sugar. Bakers may also hasten the fermentation process by adding sugar to the dough. The yeast then breaks down the sugar into alco-

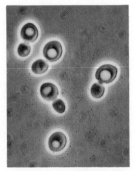

Anheuser-Busch, Inc.

Yeast cells

How yeast makes bread dough rise

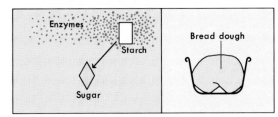

Enzymes are added to bread dough at the beginning of the breadmaking process. The enzymes convert starch into sugar.

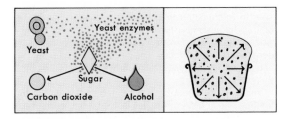

Yeast releases enzymes that break down the sugar into alcohol and carbon dioxide gas. The gas bubbles make the dough rise.

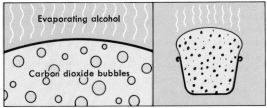

WORLD BOOK diagrams by Steven Liska

During baking, the alcohol evaporates. The gas bubbles remain trapped in the bread and give it a light, airy texture.

hol and carbon dioxide gas. Bubbles of gas are trapped by a substance in the dough called *gluten* (see **Gluten**). As the gas expands, the gluten stretches, causing the dough to rise. The alcohol produced by fermentation evaporates during the baking process. Baking also destroys the yeast.

The yeast used in winemaking acts on the sugar in grapes and other fruits to produce alcohol through fermentation. In most wines, the carbon dioxide gas is allowed to escape into the air. But it provides the bubbles for some champagnes and other sparkling wines.

Another type of commercial yeast, called *brewer's yeast,* cannot act directly on the grain used in the brewing of beer. Brewers must first convert the starch in the grain into sugar by means of a process called *malting.* The yeast is then added to convert the sugar to alcohol. Brewers use carbon dioxide to carbonate the beer.

Other uses of yeast fungi include the production of a dietary supplement called *single cell protein* (SCP). Some species of yeasts produce large amounts of a particular vitamin and are used in the commercial production of that vitamin. Other species, such as the yeasts used in brewing, can absorb and store vitamins from their food. People may eat these yeasts as vitamin supplements. Certain kinds of yeast fungi can produce large

amounts of such useful substances as fat, glycerol, industrial alcohol, and various enzymes. The yeasts are used in the commercial production of these substances.

How yeast is made. Before the commercial production of yeast in the 1880's, yeast fungi from the air leavened the bread that people baked. Homemakers prepared a dough and left it uncovered, and yeasts landed on it and began the fermentation process. Later, excess yeast from the beer and winemaking industries was used in breadmaking. This yeast is called *barm.* When the production of baker's yeast first became an industry, manufacturers grew yeast fungi on malted grain.

Today, baker's yeast is produced on molasses, which consists mostly of sugar. Baker's yeast is manufactured in two forms—as a moist, compressed cake and as dried grains. Cakes of yeast consist of live, active yeast cells. The yeast cells in dried yeast are alive but not active. Dried yeast must be mixed with warm water before the yeast fungi can grow. Yeast cakes must be refrigerated, but they spoil after about six weeks. Dried yeast need not be refrigerated, but it lasts longer under refrigeration.　　Martin W. Miller

See also **Bread; Brewing; Fermentation.**

Yeats, *yayts,* **William Butler** (1865-1939), an Irish poet and dramatist, won the 1923 Nobel Prize for literature. Many critics consider him the greatest poet of his time. Yeats led the Irish Literary Revival, a movement of the late 1800's and early 1900's that stimulated new appreciation of traditional Irish literature. The movement also encouraged the creation of works written in the spirit of Irish culture, as distinct from English culture.

Yeats developed elaborate theories about history as a recurring cycle of events. He expressed his personal views about history and life through the use of old Irish tales and the facts and legends of Irish history. His views also reflect his belief in the supernatural. Yeats published his theories in *A Vision* (1925), a book that is useful as a guide to some of his more difficult poems.

Yeats was born in Dublin and lived in London for part of his childhood. He spent many holidays in Sligo, a county in western Ireland that he loved and often wrote about. In 1898, he joined the authors Lady Gregory and Edward Martyn in establishing the Irish Literary Theatre. It was reorganized in 1904 as the Abbey Theatre, which became world famous.

The Irish Literary Theatre was founded partly to support Irish nationalism by encouraging the writing and production of plays about Irish life. The theater

Ewing Galloway

William Butler Yeats

performed most of Yeats's 26 plays, and he served until his death as one of the directors who managed the institution. The theater's first production was Yeats's *The Countess Cathleen,* written in 1891. This play was inspired in part by the author's love for Maud Gonne, a beautiful Irish nationalist leader. She became the subject of many of his plays and love lyrics.

Yeats's verse, unlike that of most poets, improved as

he grew older. He wrote much of his best work in the last 10 years of his life. His most important works were published in *Collected Plays* (1952) and *The Poems: A New Edition* (1984). *Memoirs,* containing autobiographical writings, was published in 1973.   Darcy O'Brien

Additional resources

Archibald, Douglas N. *Yeats.* Syracuse Univ. Press, 1983.
O'Donnell, William H. *The Poetry of William Butler Yeats: An Introduction.* Ungar, 1986.

Yellow. See Color.

Yellow daisy. See Black-eyed Susan.

Yellow-dog contracts were agreements between employers and employees in which workers promised not to join a union, assist a union, or take part in any group action against the employer. A yellow-dog contract, backed by court injunctions, was used by employers to oppose union organization in their plants.

The Norris-La Guardia Act of 1932 made it impossible to enforce yellow-dog contracts in federal courts. The National Labor Relations Act, passed in 1935, gave employees the right to join unions of their choice.

Daniel Quinn Mills

Yellow fever is a virus disease carried by certain mosquitoes. The virus damages many body tissues, but especially the liver. As a result of this damage, the liver cannot function properly and yellow bile pigments gather in the skin. These pigments make the skin look yellow and give the disease its name.

In most cases, the *Aëdes aegypti* mosquito carries the yellow fever virus from one person to another. Some monkeys and sloths may also be infected. When the mosquito bites an infected person or animal, the virus enters the insect's body, where it develops rapidly. After 9 to 12 days, the bite of the mosquito can produce yellow fever. A mosquito that becomes infected with the virus can transmit the disease for the rest of its life.

Symptoms. The first stage of yellow fever begins from three to six days after a person has been bitten. The victim develops a fever, headache, and dizziness, and the muscles ache. In many people, the disease progresses no further. But in others, the fever drops for a day or two and then rises steeply. The skin turns yellow and the patient's gums and stomach lining bleed.

Many patients recover from this stage. But some become delirious and go into a coma. Death follows the coma in most cases. Only from 2 to 5 per cent of all cases of yellow fever result in death, though the figure may be higher during an epidemic. Patients who recover have lifelong immunity to the disease.

Prevention. Yellow fever was once widespread throughout Central America, parts of South America, Africa, and some tropical islands. Occasional outbreaks of the disease continue to occur in jungle areas, especially in South America. However, yellow fever is under control in most urban areas. A U.S. Army physician, William Gorgas, developed mosquito control measures that eliminated the disease as a major health menace in the Panama Canal Zone. The disease can also be prevented with a vaccine developed in 1937 by Max Theiler, a South African research physician.

The conquest of yellow fever was one of the great achievements of modern medicine. In 1881, Carlos Finlay, a Cuban physician, suggested that a mosquito trans-

mitted the disease. Walter Reed, a U.S. Army doctor, proved that yellow fever was carried by a mosquito. Reed suggested that the cause was a microorganism. In 1927, three research physicians proved that the microorganism was a virus.   A. William Holmes

Related articles in *World Book* include:

Finlay, Carlos Juan	Panama Canal (Victory over
Gorgas, William C.	disease)
Lazear, Jesse W.	Reed, Walter
New Orleans (The *Paris of America*)	Tennessee (Reconstruction)

Yellow jacket is a type of small wasp with black-and-yellow markings. Some people mistakenly call yellow jackets "bees," but they actually are related to hornets. Like hornets, yellow jackets make their nests of paper. They form the paper by chewing up old wood and plant fibers. The nests consist of numerous hexagonal cells inside a thick paper covering. Most yellow jackets nest underground, but sometimes nests can be found hanging in trees or bushes, or within hollows in old stumps or the walls of buildings.

Yellow jackets eat primarily to feed their young. After feeding, the adult *regurgitates* (spits up) the food for the young. Most species of yellow jackets prey on living insects. They consume large numbers of flies, caterpillars, and other pests. Some species feed chiefly on dead animal matter, such as decaying fish and processed sandwich meats. Yellow jackets also feed on sweet, sugary substances, such as ripe fruit and soft drinks. Such feeding habits often make yellow jackets a major nuisance at picnics and campsites.

WORLD BOOK illustration by Oxford Illustrators Limited

Queen yellow jacket

Like honey bees and ants, yellow jackets live in communities made up of *queens* (mated females), *workers* (unmated females), and males. Males and queens do not sting, but workers will vigorously defend a nest if it is disturbed, often stinging repeatedly. People are sometimes stung when they run lawn mowers over hidden yellow jacket nests. Some people are strongly allergic to the proteins in a yellow jacket's *venom* (poison). If stung, they may require immediate medical attention.

Scientific classification. Yellow jackets belong to the family Vespidae. Two common North American species are *Vespula pennsylvanica* and *V. maculifrons.*   Robert W. Matthews

See also Hornet; Wasp.

Yellow journalism. See Journalism (The age of sensationalism); Outcault, Richard Felton.

Yellow-poplar, also called *tuliptree* and *tulip poplar,* is the tallest broadleaf tree in the eastern United States. In forests, it may grow 200 feet (61 meters) high, and its trunk may be 5 to 10 feet (1.5 to 3 meters) thick at the base. One of the most valuable of the North American hardwoods, the yellow-poplar grows from New England southward to Florida and westward to Arkansas. It is the state tree of Indiana and Tennessee.

© Yeager and Kay, Photo Researchers

A yellow-poplar blossom resembles a yellow tulip flower. The blossoms are an important source of nectar for bees.

The showy yellow blossoms of the yellow-poplar resemble tulips, and are an important source of nectar for bees. Its leaves are smooth, notched, long-stemmed, and graceful. The *sapwood* (outer wood) is whitish. The *heartwood* (inner wood) is sunshine-yellow to pale-tan. The wood is easily worked, and is used chiefly for furniture, veneer, boxes, and baskets.

Scientific classification. The yellow-poplar belongs to the magnolia family, Magnoliaceae. It is *Liriodendron tulipifera.*

T. Ewald Maki

See also **Tree** (Familiar broadleaf and needleleaf trees [picture]).

Yellow River. See Huang He.

Yellow Sea is an arm of the Pacific Ocean extending inland for about 400 miles (640 kilometers) between the east coast of China and Korea. The waters along the banks here are a yellow, muddy color, and the Chinese have named this part of the ocean the *Huang Hai* (Yellow Sea). The Yellow Sea gets its name from deposits of yellow earth (*huangtu*) brought to it by the Huang River. For location, see **China** (political map). The sea is about 300 feet (91 meters) deep in its deepest part. It covers 480,000 square miles (1,243,194 square kilometers).

Qingdao lies on the Chinese coast of the Yellow Sea, on the southern shore of the Shandong Peninsula. Lüshun and Luda are at the southern end of China's Liaodong Peninsula. The Korea Strait connects the Yellow Sea with the Sea of Japan. At the north, the Yellow Sea forms Laizhou Bay, the Bo Gulf, the Liaodong Gulf, and Korea Bay.　　Bostwick H. Ketchum

Yellowhammer is a popular name for the *yellow-shafted flicker,* a North American woodpecker. It is about 12 to 14 inches (30 to 36 centimeters) long and has a brown back and an ashy-gray head. The undersides of its wings have yellow patches. The yellowhammer ranges from the northern forests of Alaska and Canada south through the eastern United States to the Gulf of Mexico. It spends much of its time on the ground, searching for insects. It is the state bird of Alabama.

The *great crested flycatcher,* a North American bird, is sometimes called a *yellowhammer.* The name also refers to a species of bunting found in Europe and Asia.

Scientific classification. The yellow-shafted flicker, or yellowhammer, is a member of the woodpecker family, Picidae. It is classified as *Colaptes auratus auratus,* a subspecies of the common flicker.　　Sandra L. Vehrencamp

See also **Flicker; Bird** (picture: Birds of forests and woodlands [Yellow-shafted flicker]).

Yellowknife (pop. 11,753) is the capital and largest city of Canada's Northwest Territories. It lies on the shores of Yellowknife Bay, a projection at the northern end of Great Slave Lake. For location, see **Northwest Territories** (map). Yellowknife is a mining center. Its industries include gold mining, prospecting, transportation, and tourism. Yellowknife was founded in the mid-1930's and incorporated as a city in 1970.　　Annelies Pool

Yellowlegs is the name of two species of shore birds that have black and white markings and long yellow legs. The *greater yellowlegs* measures about 15 inches (38 centimeters) in length, and the *lesser yellowlegs* is a little over 10 inches (25 centimeters) long. Both can be seen along shores, ponds, and marshes during their flight north in spring. They nest in northern North America. In winter, they fly as far south as southern Chile in

WORLD BOOK illustration by John Dawson

The yellowlegs is named for its long yellow legs. In spring, it can be seen along shores, ponds, and marshes.

South America. Yellowlegs lay four buff or tan eggs. They have a flutelike whistle that hunters imitated to lure them to decoys. At one time they became rare because so many people hunted them. Now, federal laws protect them and they are again becoming common.

Scientific classification. Yellowlegs belong to the sandpiper family, Scolopacidae. The greater yellowlegs is classified as *Tringa melanoleuca;* the lesser yellowlegs is *T. flavipes.*

Fritz L. Knopf

Yellows. See Jaundice.

Yellowstone National Park, the oldest national park in the world, is famous for its many natural wonders. The park has more geysers and hot springs than any other area in the world. Yellowstone's scenic attractions include deep canyons, thundering waterfalls, sparkling lakes, and great expanses of evergreen forests broken by rolling meadows. Yellowstone is also the largest wildlife preserve in the United States. Bears, elk, and *bison* (American buffaloes) roam the park freely, and bald eagles, trumpeter swans, and white pelicans nest there.

Yellowstone lies in the northwest corner of Wyoming and spreads into Idaho and Montana. It covers 2,219,785

Special Report
YELLOWSTONE NAT'L PARK
2008 Science Year, p. 70

William S. Keller, Yellowstone National Park

Yellowstone's natural wonders include sparkling lakes and hot spring terraces. Yellowstone Lake, *left*, is the largest high-altitude lake in North America. The gently flowing waters of Minerva Terrace, *right,* deposit minerals that build up large rock terraces, one above the other.

acres (898,315 hectares). A series of high plateaus extends across the park, and mountains rise along Yellowstone's northern, eastern, and western boundaries. The highest point, Eagle Peak, rises 11,358 feet (3,462 meters) in the Absaroka Range in the east.

Most of Yellowstone's landscape was created by periodic volcanic eruptions more than 60,000 years ago. A large mass of molten rock still lies beneath the surface of the park. This rock, called *magma,* furnishes the heat for the park's geysers and hot springs. Yellowstone has more than 200 active geysers and thousands of hot springs.

The government established Yellowstone in 1872. The park was named for the yellow rocks that lie along the part of the Yellowstone River that is north of the park. More than 2 million people visit Yellowstone yearly. Most of them drive through the park, but many explore large wilderness areas that can be reached only by foot or on horseback. The park has more than 300 miles (480 kilometers) of roads and over 1,000 miles (1,600 kilometers) of trails.

Touring Yellowstone

There are five entrances into Yellowstone National Park—two from Wyoming and three from Montana. Each entrance road connects with the Grand Loop, a 143-mile (230-kilometer) road that leads to major points of interest. The Grand Loop consists of the southern Lower Loop and the northern Upper Loop.

The Lower Loop. The west entrance road joins the Lower Loop at Madison Junction. Southbound, the Lower Loop leads to several geyser basins. The Lower Geyser Basin includes the Fountain Paint Pots, a series of hot springs and bubbling pools of mud called *mudpots* or *paint pots.* The mudpots are formed by steam and other gases that rose from holes in the ground and changed the surrounding rock into clay. Minerals in the

Yellowstone National Park

	Park boundary
	State boundary
	Road
■	Point of interest

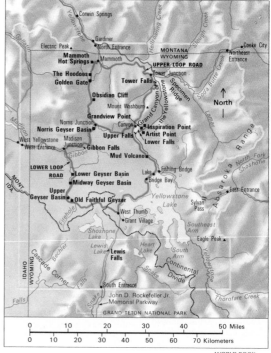

WORLD BOOK map

clay give the mud various colors. Great Fountain Geyser, also in the Lower Geyser Basin, erupts from the center of a large pool. The powerful bursts of water from this geyser sometimes spout 200 feet (61 meters) above the pool.

Grand Prismatic Spring, in Midway Geyser Basin, is the largest hot spring in Yellowstone. Its pool, which has a deep blue center ringed with pink, measures 370 feet (113 meters) in diameter. Small water plants called *algae* give the pool its color.

The Upper Geyser Basin has a large group of geysers. Old Faithful, the most famous geyser in the park, erupts on an average of every 73 minutes. The actual intervals between eruptions vary from about 33 to 120 minutes. The geyser sends a stream of boiling water more than 100 feet (30 meters) into the air (see **Wyoming** [picture]). Other geysers include Castle, Giantess, Grand, and Grotto. Morning Glory Pool, one of the basin's most beautiful hot pools, resembles the morning-glory flower in color and shape.

Yellowstone Lake, which lies 7,733 feet (2,357 meters) above sea level, is the largest high-altitude lake in North America. It measures about 20 miles (32 kilometers) long and 14 miles (23 kilometers) wide. The lake has a shoreline of more than 100 miles (160 kilometers). Geysers and hot springs occur along the shore at West Thumb. The Lower Loop follows the shoreline of Yellowstone Lake for 21 miles (34 kilometers), providing a view of the lake's islands and the rugged mountains of the Absaroka Range.

The Grand Canyon of the Yellowstone cuts across the landscape for about 20 miles (32 kilometers). This canyon reaches a depth of about 2,000 feet (610 meters) in some places. The Yellowstone River runs through the canyon, creating two waterfalls. The Lower Falls plunges 308 feet (94 meters) and the Upper Falls 109 feet (33 meters) into the canyon. Views of the canyon are especially beautiful from Artist Point, Grandview Point, and Inspiration Point. See **Yellowstone River.**

The Upper Loop leads north from Canyon with a climb through the mountains of the Washburn Range. Mount Washburn rises 10,243 feet (3,122 meters) on the east. Specimen Ridge, which can be seen from the road leading to the northeast entrance, has some of the park's most famous petrified forests. The trees of these forests were buried by lava ash during volcanic eruptions over 60,000 years ago. Minerals from the ash seeped into the trees and turned them into stone.

At Mammoth Hot Springs, beautiful terraces are formed by gently flowing waters. The waters deposit a form of limestone called *travertine,* building large terraces one above the other. Algae and bacteria give some of the terraces various colors. Minerva Terrace and Opal Terrace are among the most beautiful in the area. The terraces change continually through the years as the waters build them up. Some springs die, and the terraces become gray and lifeless. The Hoodoos are the remains of old hot-spring terraces broken up by landslides.

Obsidian Cliff is a mountain of black glass that was formed by molten lava. Rootless vegetation called *lichens* now cover the glass in many places.

Norris Geyser Basin consists of hundreds of geysers, hot springs, and pools. It is the hottest and most active thermal area in Yellowstone. The temperature of the water in some of the springs reaches more than 200° F. (93° C). Several of the geysers may erupt at the same time. Steamboat Geyser set a world record by hurling its water 400 feet (120 meters) into the air.

Plants and wildlife

Evergreen forests and mountain meadows cover most of Yellowstone. The most abundant tree is the lodgepole pine. Forests of Douglas fir, Engelmann spruce, limber pine, and subalpine fir grow in some areas. During the summer, the mountain meadows display a variety of wildflowers, including the fringed gentian, Indian paintbrush, monkey flower, and mountain bluebell.

More than 200 species of birds and over 40 kinds of other animals live in Yellowstone. Trumpeter swans, blue herons, white pelicans, bald eagles, and gulls feed on fish in the park's lakes and rivers. These fish include cutthroat trout, grayling, mountain whitefish, and rainbow trout.

Elk are the most common of the large animals in the park. Approximately 20,000 elk live in the park in summer. About half of them stay there through the winter, but the rest wander south to warmer areas. Yellowstone has about 2,000 bison. These animals were widely hunted in the United States during the 1800's. The protection provided by the park helped save them from being killed off completely. Other large animals in Yellowstone include black bears, grizzly bears, moose, mule deer, bighorn sheep, and cougars.

In Yellowstone, the balance of nature is maintained through natural controls such as disease, weather, and competition for food (see **Balance of nature**). For example, if the park's elk population becomes too large, many of the animals die during winters when food is scarce. In addition, park regulations protect the animal and plant life from human interference. The feeding of bears is prohibited not only because it is dangerous but because it disrupts their natural feeding habits.

Recreational activities

More than 1,000 miles (1,600 kilometers) of trails provide a wide choice of hiking routes through Yellowstone. Park naturalists offer free guided hikes and evening campfire programs. TW Services, Inc., has a program of bus tours, horseback trips, stagecoach rides, and cookouts in summer.

Fishing in the park's rivers and lakes is controlled by special regulations, and a permit is required. Hunting and the use of firearms are prohibited. Boats and canoes may be used on most of the lakes, but they are not allowed on the rivers. Visitors must obtain a permit to use any type of boat or canoe.

Campgrounds are located at Canyon, Madison Junction, Mammoth, Norris Junction, and other sites. A few major sites, including Canyon, Old Faithful, Mammoth, and Lake, have cottages, cabins, and hotels. Visitors who want to camp in the wilderness must have a permit.

During the winter, a heavy snow covers the park. All park roads, except the one connecting the north and northeast entrances, are closed. Snowmobiles may be used on the unplowed roads. Cross-country skiers and snowshoers can also travel over the trails through the park.

Information may be obtained by writing Superintendent, P.O. Box 168, Yellowstone National Park, WY 82190.

History

Yellowstone's landscape was shaped by the action of volcanoes and glaciers through millions of years. A large mass of magma, which lies about 2 miles (3.2 kilometers) below the surface of the park, has erupted more than 27 times during the past 2 million years.

A major volcanic eruption occurred in the Yellowstone area about 2 million years ago. About 600,000 years ago, another explosion of magma and gas created a huge crater about 40 miles (64 kilometers) long and 30 miles (48 kilometers) wide. Yellowstone Lake now occupies part of this crater. During the eruption, lava covered more than 1,000 square miles (2,600 square kilometers) and formed the broad plateaus that characterize Yellowstone today.

Glaciers once covered much of the area. The last ones melted about 10,000 years ago and filled Yellowstone Lake. Outflow from the lake drained northward and helped shape the Grand Canyon of the Yellowstone.

One Indian tribe, the Sheepeaters, are known to have lived in the area of the present-day park. Other tribes, including the Bannock, the Crow, and the Blackfeet, crossed the area to hunt bison and elk.

The government obtained the Yellowstone region in 1803 as part of the Louisiana Purchase. John Colter, a member of the Lewis and Clark expedition, was probably the first white person to see Yellowstone. He traveled alone on foot through the area in 1807 and 1808 (see **Colter, John**). Many other trappers explored the area during the 1830's and 1840's. They returned with stories of spouting geysers, hot springs, and mudpots.

In 1870, General Henry D. Washburn, the surveyor general of the Montana Territory, led an expedition to check out the reports of the trappers. In 1871, a government expedition led by Ferdinand V. Hayden, a geologist, documented the unusual features of the area.

In 1872, Congress passed a bill to establish the park and preserve its natural resources. Civilian superintendents administered the park for the first few years, but they were unable to stop widespread hunting and trapping there. The Army took over control of the park in 1886 and began to protect the wildlife. A detachment of cavalry occupied the park until 1916, when Congress established the National Park Service.

Today, the National Park Service manages Yellowstone. A superintendent, appointed by the director of the service and assisted by park rangers, naturalists, and a maintenance staff, administers the park. Park headquarters are at Mammoth.

In 1988, fires raged in Yellowstone. The fires burned large areas of forests and meadows.

Critically reviewed by Yellowstone National Park

Additional resources

Chase, Alston. *Playing God in Yellowstone: The Destruction of America's First National Park.* Harcourt, 1987. First published in 1986.

Haines, Aubrey L. *The Yellowstone Story: A History of Our First National Park.* 2 vols. Colorado Associated, 1977.

Yellowstone River rises near the Continental Divide in northwestern Wyoming and flows north into Yellowstone National Park. For location, see **Wyoming** (physical map). There it forms Yellowstone Lake, which covers 137 square miles (355 square kilometers) at an elevation of 7,731 feet (2,356 meters). The lake is the largest high-elevation lake in North America. North of the lake, the river plunges 109 feet (33 meters) over its upper falls and 308 feet (94 meters) over its lower falls into Yellowstone Canyon. Then it flows northeast across the Great Plains of Montana. The Yellowstone flows a total distance of 671 miles (1,080 kilometers) and joins the Missouri River on the Montana-North Dakota line. See also **Montana** (picture). John H. Garland

Yellowthroat is a common wood warbler that lives in North America. Yellowthroats grow about the size of a small wren. They live in wet grassy or marshy areas, where they can hide among the tall reeds. They have olive-green backs and bright orange-yellow throats. The male has a black mask on its face, with a white border above it. These birds nest on or near the ground. The female usually lays four eggs.

Scientists recognize 12 *races* (subspecies) of common yellowthroat. These groups differ slightly in color and size. Yellowthroats breed within an area stretching from Ontario and southeastern Alaska south to Mexico. They generally spend the winter in an area extending from the Gulf States into Central America.

Tom Edwards, Animals Animals

The yellowthroat is about as big as a small wren. It lives in wet areas among tall reeds, where it can hide easily.

Belding's yellowthroat is slightly larger, with solid yellow underparts and a yellow border on the black mask of the male. It lives in Baja California, Mexico.

Scientific classification. Yellowthroats are in the wood warbler family, Parulidae. The common yellowthroat is *Geothlypis trichas.* Belding's yellowthroat is *G. beldingi.*

George E. Hudson

Yemen (Aden) is an independent country on the southern edge of the Arabian Peninsula. It extends from the mouth of the Red Sea eastward along the Indian Ocean about 740 miles (1,191 kilometers) to the boundary of Oman. Three islands—Socotra in the Indian Ocean, and Kamaran and Perim in the Red Sea—are part of the country. About 90 per cent of its people are Arabs. The rest are Indians, Pakistanis, or East Africans.

Most of Yemen (Aden) is hot and dry. There are only a few fertile areas where the land can be farmed. Aden is the nation's capital and largest city. It is also an important port and oil center.

Yemen (Aden) gained independence from Great

Yemen (Aden)

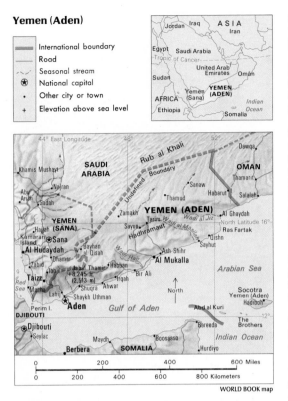

International boundary
Road
Seasonal stream
⊛ National capital
• Other city or town
+ Elevation above sea level

WORLD BOOK map

Britain on Nov. 30, 1967. The country's full name in Arabic, the official language, is Jumhuriyyat al-Yemen ash-Shaabiyyah al-dimugratiyyah (People's Democratic Republic of Yemen). The nation is often called Yemen (Aden), South Yemen, or Southern Yemen to distinguish it from Yemen (Sana)—its neighbor to the northwest.

Government. Yemen (Aden) is governed by the Yemeni Socialist Party (YSP), the country's only political party. The government is headed by a president. The president is also secretary of the YSP and chairman of the Presidium of the Supreme People's Council. The council is the country's legislative body. A 24-member Cabinet appointed by the Presidium helps carry out the government operations.

The country is divided into six areas called *governorates.* Each is headed by a governor. Yemen (Aden) is a member of the United Nations and the Arab League.

People. About 2,486,000 people live in Yemen (Aden). About 90 per cent are Arabs. The Arabs belong to various groups called tribes. The rest are Indians, Pakistanis, or East Africans. Almost all the people are Muslims of the Shafii sect.

The British brought Western ways of life to Aden, and some of the people there live much as Europeans do. They wear Western-style clothing, live in modern houses or apartments along broad streets, and shop in supermarkets. Others follow an older way of life. They live in thick-walled houses along narrow, twisting alleys, and they shop in open-air markets. Many men wear the striped *futa* (kilt). They also wear skullcaps, turbans, or tall round hats called *tarbooshes.* Women appear in public in veils and dark, shapeless clothing.

Each street in Aden's market district has its own trade.

Workers produce handicrafts in small, one-room shops. They make inlaid *jambiyas* (daggers), wooden chests, brassware, and jewelry.

Aden has many cafes where men sit and drink strong, bitter coffee. In the afternoon, many men meet in cafes and chew the leaves of a plant called the *khat* (also spelled *kat* or *qat*). These leaves contain a drug that gives people a feeling of contentment.

On the coast and on Socotra Island, the people live by fishing. The men spear fish near the shore from dugout canoes called *sambuqs,* or in deeper water from single-sail *dhows.* Inland are valleys and a few scattered oases where the people live by farming. Some farm families live in towns, such as Sayun, that have mud-brick houses standing three or four stories high. Others live in small villages close to the land they farm. Most of the families outside Aden have at least one member working as a trader or merchant in India, Java, or Sumatra.

In the desert, the people are herders. They travel constantly in search of water and food for their sheep and goats. Most of the men own nothing but their clothes and their curved jambiya. Women are unveiled. Many are tattooed on their faces and arms with tribal marks.

Rice, bread, lamb, and fish are the chief foods in Yemen (Aden). But most of the country's desert people live on bread and on ilb nuts, which they gather from wild thorn trees.

The British established the first public schools in Yemen (Aden). Today, the nation has about 900 elementary schools, 65 intermediate schools, 10 high schools, and 5 teacher training schools. The law requires all children to go to school for seven years. But some areas have no schools, and many children receive little or no education.

Land. Yemen (Aden) covers 128,587 square miles (333,038 square kilometers). The mainland part of the country has three regions: (1) the Coastal Plain, which is mostly sand but has a few fertile areas; (2) a dry, hilly plateau cut by deep valleys called *wadis* that have some rich farmland; and (3) the Empty Quarter, a stony desert that extends into Saudi Arabia. Socotra has a narrow coastal plain and a steep, rugged interior.

Yemen (Aden) is hot most of the year. Temperatures range from 61° to 106° F. (16° to 41° C) in Aden and climb to 130° F. (54° C) in the desert. Rainfall averages 3 inches (7.6 centimeters) a year.

Facts in brief

Capital: Aden.
Official language: Arabic.
Area: 128,587 sq. mi. (333,038 km²). *Coastline*—about 740 mi. (1,191 km).
Elevation: *Highest*—Jabal Thamir, 8,245 ft. (2,513 m). *Lowest*—sea level.
Population: *Estimated 1990 population*—2,486,000; density, 19 persons per sq. mi. (7 persons per km²); distribution, 57 per cent rural, 43 per cent urban. *1973 census*—1,590,275. *Estimated 1995 population*—2,896,000.
Chief products: *Agriculture*—barley, cotton, dates, millet, sorghum, wheat. *Industry*—dyeing, fishing, oil refining, ship refueling, tanning, weaving.
Flag: Red, white, and black horizontal stripes with a red star on a blue triangle at the mast. See **Flag** (picture: Flags of Asia and the Pacific).
Money: *Basic unit*—dinar.

Economy. Aden's oil refinery and port provide Yemen (Aden) with most of its income. The oil refinery can process about 50 million barrels of oil a year. Ships of many nations use the port for refueling, repairs, and transferring cargoes.

Outside of Aden, the economy is largely undeveloped. The country has few mineral resources. Agriculture is limited to the few areas with underground water for irrigation. Farmers grow three or four crops a year of millet, sorghum, sesame, wheat, and barley.

History. In ancient times, southern Arabia grew rich because it lay along important trade routes between Europe, Asia, and Africa. Cities were built and the land was irrigated. But fighting among local leaders and invasions from the north and east brought widespread destruction. In the 600's, the Prophet Muhammad's son-in-law, Ali, introduced Islam to the people.

Great Britain seized Aden in 1839, after people from the town robbed a wrecked British ship. Aden became an important refueling stop for British ships going to India by way of the Suez Canal and the Red Sea. Aden was a part of British India until 1937, when it became a British crown colony.

To protect Aden from Yemen, which claimed the town, Britain extended its control to the tribal states in the region around Aden. Britain signed treaties with the tribal leaders, promising protection and aid in return for loyalty. The region came to be known as the Aden Protectorate.

In 1959, six tribal states in the protectorate formed the Federation of the Arab Emirates of the South. Britain signed a treaty with the federation, promising to grant independence. The date for independence was later set for 1967. Meanwhile, the British controlled the federation's foreign policy and provided military protection and economic aid. In 1962, the name of the federation was changed to the Federation of South Arabia. By 1965, Aden and all but four of the tribal states in the protectorate had joined the federation.

In the early 1960's, Britain tried to form a representative government that would rule the federation after independence. But radical Arab nationalist leaders in Aden and tribal leaders in the protectorate both wanted to rule. The radicals began a terror campaign against the British and the tribal leaders. Two radical groups, the National Liberation Front (NLF) and the Front for the Liberation of Occupied South Yemen (FLOSY), also fought each other.

In late 1967, the federation government collapsed. Britain announced that it would withdraw its troops and give power to any group that could set up a government. The NLF emerged as the most powerful group in the federation. On Nov. 30, 1967, the last British troops were withdrawn, and the NLF formed a government and proclaimed the federation an independent country.

After independence, the NLF became the National Front, which merged with several smaller political groups in 1975 and formed the United Political Organization National Front (UPONF). In 1978, the groups that made up UPONF reorganized as the Yemeni Socialist Party (YSP). The leaders of Yemen (Aden) favor some political principles of Karl Marx, one of the founders of Communism. Yemen (Aden) has strong ties with the Soviet Union, Cuba, and East Germany, and it receives

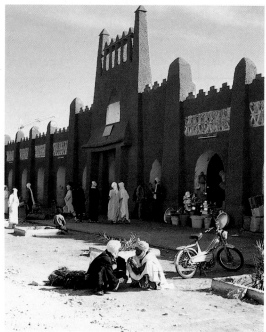

Robert Harding Picture Library

Aden is the capital of Yemen (Aden). The city has many streets lined with traditional Arab-style buildings.

much aid from these and other Communist countries.

The leaders of neighboring Yemen (Sana) oppose Communism. Border clashes took place between Yemen (Aden) and Yemen (Sana) from time to time during the 1970's. Yemen (Aden) was also involved in fighting with Oman, its eastern neighbor, during the 1970's. These clashes went badly for Yemen (Aden) and in the 1980's it adopted a more peaceful foreign policy.

In 1986, civil war broke out in Yemen (Aden) between the government and a group representing more extreme Marxist views than those held by the government. The extreme group overthrew the country's leaders and took control of the government.   Robert Geran Landen

See also **Aden; Arab League.**

Yemen (Sana) is a country in the southwestern corner of the Arabian Peninsula. It borders on the Red Sea on the west. Yemen (Sana) covers 75,300 square miles (195,000 square kilometers). Sana is its capital. See **Sana.**

The country's fertile high interior is the most beautiful and best cultivated part of Arabia. Almost as many people live there as in the rest of the peninsula.

Most people in Yemen (Sana) are farmers and craftworkers, but employment in modern businesses is growing. The country is famous for its Mocha coffee. Yemeni craftworkers have been famous for their textiles, leatherwork, and ironwork since ancient times.

The country's full name in Arabic, the official language, is Al-Jumhuriyah al Arabiyah al Yamaniyah (The Yemen Arab Republic). The country is often called Yemen (Sana), North Yemen, or Northern Yemen to distinguish it from Yemen (Aden)—its neighbor to the southeast.

Government. A president heads the government of Yemen (Sana). The president is elected to a five-year

Yemen (Sana)

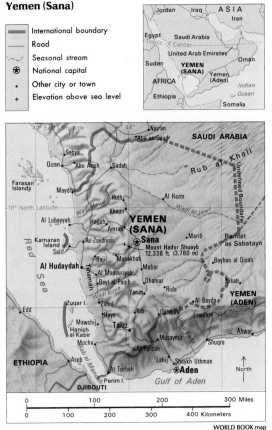

- International boundary
- Road
- Seasonal stream
- ⊛ National capital
- • Other city or town
- + Elevation above sea level

WORLD BOOK map

were chosen by God to govern, because they are descendants of Muhammad. The people in the southern part of Yemen (Sana), especially those in Taizz and the coastal ports, are Sunnites of the Shafii sect. This sect has a powerful merchant class that controls commerce. The division between the politically powerful Zaydis and the wealthy Shafiis has caused bitterness between them. The Zaydis emphasized a traditional style of education often limited to reading, writing, and studying Muslim law and tradition. But since the 1960's, steps have been taken to modernize education. The country's first university was founded in Sana in 1970.

Land. Yemen (Sana) has three land regions: a coastal plain, a cliff region, and a high interior.

The coastal plain, called the *Tihamah,* extends inland from the Red Sea for 20 to 50 miles (32 to 80 kilometers). It is hot and humid, but receives less than 10 inches (25 centimeters) of rain a year. Temperatures range from 68° to 130° F. (20° to 54° C). Few people live there.

A few rocky hills border the Tihamah on the east. Then, cliffs rise steeply. The cliffs get as much as 30 inches (76 centimeters) of rain a year. The rains have cut into the cliffs, forming short, steep valleys.

East of the cliffs is the high interior, called the *High Yemen.* Broad valleys and plateaus lie 6,000 feet (1,800 meters) above sea level. They are surrounded by steep mountains that rise as high as 12,336 feet (3,760 meters). The high altitude makes the region much cooler than the Tihamah. The High Yemen gets 10 to 15 inches (25 to 38 centimeters) of rain a year. East of the mountains, the land slopes to the desert in Saudi Arabia.

Economy of Yemen (Sana) depends on extensive foreign aid, on the wages sent home by the many Yemenis who work in other parts of Arabia, and on farming. The hills and highlands are the most productive part of Yemen (Sana) for farming. Farmers there raise such food grains as wheat, barley, and *dura* (a sorghum). They also raise a great variety of fruits, including citrus fruits, apricots, bananas, grapes, papayas, and pomegranates. They grow beans, lentils, onions, and tomatoes in gardens at the edges of towns and villages. People on the Tihamah raise dura and some dates and cotton. Since the early 1980's, the Yemenis have worked to turn desert areas into farmland by means of dams, irrigation, and other water and agricultural development projects.

term by the Constituent People's Assembly, a legislative body. The president appoints the 159 members of the Constituent People's Assembly. The Council of Ministers, led by a prime minister, assists the president. The president also appoints the members of the Council of Ministers.

People. Most of the people of Yemen (Sana) are Arabs and Muslims. The people belong to various groups called tribes. The Hashid, Khawlan, and Baqil are the largest and most powerful tribes. Many Yemenis, especially those in the cities, wear Western-style clothing. Many other Yemenis wear more traditional Arab clothing. The men's clothing includes cotton breeches or kilts, cotton shirts, and turbans. Many women wear long robes, black shawls, and veils. Sandals are common footwear for both men and women. In the high interior of Yemen (Sana), the people build mud or stone houses. Near the coast, many people live in straw huts. Many people in the cities live in one-story mud brick houses. Some city people reside in modern houses or apartment buildings.

The Muslims of Yemen (Sana) are divided into two main groups according to their beliefs. The largest group is the Shiites of the Zaydi sect. Many of them live in the high interior and Sana. The *imams,* who were the political and religious leaders of the country from A.D. 897 to 1962, were Zaydis. A group of Zaydis called the Sayyids served in the government, administered the courts, and collected taxes. The Zaydis claimed that they

Facts in brief

Capital: Sana.
Official language: Arabic.
Area: 75,300 sq. mi. (195,000 km²). *Coastline*—about 280 mi. (451 km).
Elevation: *Highest*—12,336 ft. (3,760 m). *Lowest*—sea level.
Population: *Estimated 1990 population*—7,993,000; density, 106 persons per sq. mi. (41 persons per km²); distribution, 75 per cent rural, 25 per cent urban. *1975 census*—5,237,893. *Estimated 1995 population*—9,266,000.
Chief products: *Agriculture*—coffee, fruits, grains, khat, vegetables. *Manufacturing*—building materials, handicrafts. *Mining*—petroleum.
National anthem: "Assalam Alwatani Al-Gumhuri" ("Republican National Anthem").
Flag: Red, white, and black horizontal stripes, with a green star in the center. These colors are traditional Arab colors. See Flag (picture: Flags of Asia).
Money: *Basic unit*—rial.

A. Tessore, Shostal

Sana is the capital of Yemen (Sana). The city is enclosed by a wall. Traffic enters and leaves through one of eight gates.

Khat (also spelled *kat* or *qat*) is the leading cash crop of Yemen (Sana). It is a woody shrub that grows in the highlands. Khat leaves contain a narcotic and produce a mild intoxication or *euphoria* (state of well-being) when they are chewed. Thousands of people in this part of Arabia chew khat. Coffee is another important cash crop. Coffee trees grow on terraces cut into the hills. Ancient *aqueducts* (water channels) carry water to the terraces.

Until the early 1980's, Yemen (Sana) had almost no industry. But large petroleum deposits were found in the northeastern part of the country, and petroleum mining became an important industry. Construction is a growing industry in Yemen (Sana). Construction projects include new hotels, office buildings, and roads.

Many goods in the country are still made by hand. The people weave and dye cloth, and make rope, glassware, harnesses, saddles, and pottery. They sell their goods in the village *bazaars* (marketplaces).

Trucks and automobiles provide most of the land transportation in Yemen (Sana). But many people still use camels, donkeys, and horses.

History. According to Arab tradition, Semitic people invaded what is now Yemen (Sana) about 2000 B.C. They brought farming and building skills to the herders who lived in Yemen. About 1400 B.C., an important trade route began forming. Caravans carrying pearls and spices passed through Yemen. Cities, castles, temples, and dams were built during this time. The Queen of Sheba ruled the Yemeni during the 900's B.C.

Yemen's prosperity ended after the time of Christ. Local chieftains fought among themselves, and Abyssinia (Ethiopia) invaded Yemen. The next 1,300 years were marked by fighting between Yemeni tribes and religious groups, and against invading Egyptians and Turks. Beginning in A.D. 897, an *imam* (ruler) was the political and religious leader of Yemen.

The Ottoman Empire, centered in Asia Minor (now Turkey), had varying degrees of control over Yemen from 1517 to 1918. The Treaty of Lausanne freed Yemen from the Turks in 1924.

On Sept. 26, 1962, a group of military officers sup-

ported by Egypt overthrew the imam and set up a republic. The imam's forces—called *royalists*—fought from their bases in the mountains to try to regain control of the government. They were supported by Saudi Arabia. But the republicans, supported by Egypt, ruled most of Yemen. The fighting between the republicans and royalists ended in 1970. The republicans then set up a new government that included republicans and royalists.

In 1974, army leaders took control of the government of Yemen (Sana). They are conservatives who oppose Communism. The leaders of neighboring Yemen (Aden) favor some political principles of Communism. Some clashes took place between Yemen (Sana) and Yemen (Aden) in the 1970's. Relations between the countries improved in the 1980's.   Robert Geran Landen

Yen is the monetary unit of Japan. Japanese coins in denominations of 5, 10, 50, 100, and 500 yen are commonly used. Paper money is printed in denominations of 1,000; 5,000; and 10,000 yen. The *sen* and *rin,* smaller denominations of the yen, were removed from circulation in 1954. But they are still used as units for circulation. For the value of the yen in dollars, see **Money** (table: Exchange rates).   R. G. Doty

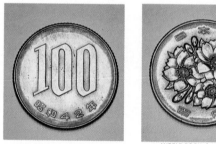

WORLD BOOK photo by James Simek

The yen is the monetary unit of Japan.

Yenisey River, *YEN uh SAY,* drains an area of more than 1 million square miles (2.6 million square kilometers) in Siberia. The Yenisey travels 2,543 miles (4,093 kilometers) from its origin in the Sayan Mountains of southern Siberia to its mouth on the Arctic coast. After the river leaves the Sayan Mountains, it flows in a general northerly direction. It enters the Arctic Ocean through an *estuary* (broad river mouth) about 200 miles (320 kilometers) east of the Bay of Ob. Ocean steamers go 400 miles (640 kilometers) up the river to Igarka, a lumber port. There are two large hydroelectric stations along the river.   Theodore Shabad

Yeoman, *YOH muhn,* was a *retainer* (dependent) of a feudal lord during the late Middle Ages in England. In the early 1400's, the name was used for officials in the households of nobles and for small freeholders and farmers on a feudal manor. By the Tudor period (1485-1603), yeomen had become an independent class of small landowners and farmers. They were superior in status to ordinary villagers and workers but ranked below gentlemen and squires. During the late 1700's, men of this class formed their own cavalry groups, called *yeomanry.* The yeomanry were officially organized by an Act of Parliament in 1794.

In 1485, King Henry VII organized the Yeomen of the Guard, who formed a bodyguard to the monarch of England. Today, the Yeomen still serve as royal bodyguards on formal occasions, but their duties are purely ceremonial. Officers of this group wear contemporary uniforms, but enlisted men wear colorful costumes—and carry weapons—that date back to the late 1400's and the 1500's. According to tradition, a visiting grand duke in 1669 was astonished by the large amounts of beef that the Yeomen Warders of the Tower of London consumed. He nicknamed them *beefeaters,* which they are still called today. See **Tower of London.**

An appointment to the Yeomen of the Guard is honorary. Members are chosen from the officers and enlisted men of Great Britain's regular armed forces. In the United States Navy, petty officers performing clerical work have the rating of yeoman.　　Richard P. Abels

See also **Great Britain** (picture).

Yerevan, YEHR uh VAHN (pop. 1,114,000), is the capital and largest city of Armenia—officially the Armenian Soviet Socialist Republic—in the Soviet Union. Its name is also spelled *Erevan.* Yerevan lies on the Razdan River in the southwestern part of the Soviet Union. For location, see **Armenia** (map).

Yerevan is an important cultural and scientific center. It has a university and several colleges, libraries, museums, theaters, and scientific research institutes. The city's products include chemicals, clothing, food, liquor, machinery, and synthetic rubber.

Archaeological evidence suggests that a fortress was built at what is now Yerevan in the 780's B.C. From the A.D. 1400's to the 1800's, Yerevan stood on the border of the rival Persian and Ottoman powers, and was frequently destroyed.　　Leslie Dienes

Yerkes, YUR keez, **Robert Mearns,** murnz (1876-1956), was an American psychologist known for his research on the behavior of apes. His most important book is *The Great Apes: A Study of Anthropoid Life* (1929), which his wife, the botanist Ada Watterson Yerkes, helped him write. The book describes the anatomy, behavior, and intelligence of chimpanzees, gorillas, and other apes. During 1923 and 1924, Yerkes raised two chimpanzees in his home. He wrote *Almost Human* (1925) and coauthored *Chimpanzee Intelligence and Its Vocal Expressions* (1925) based on this experience.

In 1929, with help from a foundation, Yerkes established an ape-breeding colony and research facility in Orange Park, Fla. He also became the center's first director. It is now in Atlanta, Ga., and is called the Yerkes Primate Research Center.

Yerkes was born in Breadysville, near Hatboro, Pa. During World War I (1914-1918), he helped develop intelligence tests for Army recruits. He taught psychology at Harvard University from 1902 to 1917 and at Yale University from 1924 to 1944.　　Donald Symons

Yerkes Observatory, YUR keez or YUR kuhs, is an astronomical observatory operated by the University of Chicago. It stands about 75 miles (122 kilometers) north of Chicago, at Williams Bay on Lake Geneva in Wisconsin. The observatory houses three major telescopes. Two are reflecting telescopes, one with a mirror 40 inches (102 centimeters) in diameter and the other with a mirror 24 inches (61 centimeters) in diameter. The third is a refracting telescope with a lens 40 inches (102 centimeters) in diameter. The refracting telescope, the largest of its kind in the world, is 63 feet (19 meters) long. A

dome 90 feet (27 meters) in diameter protects it.

Yerkes Observatory is famous for its accurate measurements of the distances of stars. These measurements were first made by the American astronomer Frank Schlesinger. The observatory also won fame for the advances in solar physics achieved by its first director, George E. Hale. In addition, Yerkes Observatory is noted for its studies of interstellar matter, stellar spectra, stellar photometry, and theoretical astrophysics. Hale founded the observatory in 1895 with a large donation from a Chicago businessman named Charles T. Yerkes.
　　Critically reviewed by Yerkes Observatory

See also **Hale, George Ellery.**

Yeti. See Abominable Snowman.

Yevtushenko, YEHV too SHEHNG koh, **Yevgeny,** yehv GEH nee (1933-　　), is a Soviet poet. Most of his works are directed toward people in the Soviet Union who grew up after the end of World War II in 1945. Yevtushenko is a master of technique and uses straightforward language.

Yevtushenko became famous in the West as one of the first Soviet writers to criticize Soviet society. He gained international fame with "Babi Yar" (1961), a tribute to Soviet Jews massacred by the Nazis in 1941 (see **Babi Yar**). The poem was remarkable for its open attack on anti-Semitism, a topic avoided by most Soviet writers. His other works include the long poem *Fuku* (1985); a novel in verse and prose, *Wild Berries* (1981); and *Almost at the End* (1987). He also wrote and directed an autobiographical film called *Kindergarten* (1983). Yevtushenko was born in Zima, near Irkutsk.　　Anna Lisa Crone

Yew is the name of a group of evergreen trees and shrubs. The leaves of yews are flat, pointed needles, dark-green on top and pale-green beneath. They spread apart in two rows along the stem. The bark is reddish-brown and scaly. Yews bear scarlet seeds that look like berries. The trunk of the yew may grow large, and yew trees sometimes live for hundreds of years.

The *English yew* grows in Europe, Asia, and Africa. There are a great many yews near the English Channel, where the chalky soil seems to further their growth. The famous English archers who defeated the French knights during the wars of the Middle Ages used long-bows made of yew wood. Yew trees often grew in English churchyards. Branches of the trees served as funeral decorations, and were twined into wreaths for the

The American yew is a shrub that is also called the *ground hemlock.* Its branches are often used as Christmas decorations.

heads of the mourners. For this reason, the yew often symbolizes sadness.

The yew has a tough elastic wood, and a grain almost as beautiful as that of mahogany. Yew is polished and made into tables. The heartwood has an orange-red color. The bark, needles, and seeds are poisonous.

Several different kinds of yews grow in America. One is the tall *western,* or *Pacific, yew.* The wood of this tree is valued for use in cabinetwork and for canoe paddles. The *Japanese yew* grows more in the form of a shrub. The *American yew,* or *ground hemlock,* is a low, straggling shrub. People often use the branches of the American yew for Christmas decorations.

Scientific classification. Yews belong to the yew family, Taxaceae. The English yew is *Taxus baccata,* the western yew is *T. brevifolia,* the Japanese yew is *T. cuspidata,* and the American yew is *T. canadensis.*　James D. Mauseth

See also **Conifer; Plant** (picture: Japanese yew).

Yi dynasty. See **Korea** (The Yi dynasty).

Yiddish language and literature. Yiddish is a language of the Jews. It developed during the A.D. 900's and 1000's from several languages, including German, Hebrew, Aramaic, French, and Italian. Yiddish, which uses the Hebrew alphabet, became the language of Western European Jews. As Jews migrated to Eastern Europe beginning in the 1300's, Yiddish absorbed elements of various Slavic languages. In the late 1800's, when thousands of European Jews settled on other continents, Yiddish came into contact with several more languages, especially English. Yiddish borrowed from English and also gave it many expressions.

Yiddish literature started in the late 1200's. Until about 1800, most Yiddish works were based on Jewish religious tradition. These writings included religious poetry, guides to rituals and customs, and poems on Biblical subjects. Works on ethics were written in Yiddish for people who could not read Hebrew, the language of Jewish study and prayer. Some Yiddish writers produced nonreligious works, such as verse romances and historical poems about local events.

Modern Yiddish literature began to develop in the 1800's during a Jewish cultural and literary movement called the *Haskalah* (Enlightenment). Reformers in the Haskalah tried to spread modern European culture among the Jews. They wrote Yiddish satires exposing what they considered religious superstition.

Three authors of the late 1800's and early 1900's rank as the first important figures in modern Yiddish literature. One was Sholom Aleichem, a humorist whose real name was Solomon Rabinowitz. The others were Mendele the Bookseller, the pen name of Shalom Jacob Abramovich, and Isaac Leibush Peretz. All these authors used the culture of a typical *shtetl* (Jewish town) as the setting for most of their works. Their novels, dramas, and short stories tell of social conflicts within the Jewish community. The works also describe the challenges facing Jewish tradition in the non-Jewish world.

After World War I (1914-1918), Yiddish literature flourished in Poland, the Soviet Union, and the United States. Outstanding writers of that period included Sholem Asch in Poland, David Bergelson in the Soviet Union, and Moishe Leib Halpern in the United States. During World War II (1939-1945), many Yiddish writers were among the more than 6 million Jews killed by the Nazis.

In 1952, the Soviet government executed a number of major Yiddish writers.

Today, the major centers of Yiddish literature are Israel and the United States. There are also Yiddish centers in Australia, Canada, South Africa, and several South American nations. In 1978, the Polish-born American author Isaac Bashevis Singer became the first Yiddish writer to receive the Nobel Prize for literature.

Ruth R. Wisse

See also **Asch, Sholem; Sholom Aleichem; Singer, Isaac Bashevis.**

Additional resources

Liptzin, Sol. *A History of Yiddish Literature.* Jonathan David, 1985. First published in 1972.
Never Say Die! A Thousand Years of Yiddish in Jewish Life and Letters. Ed. by Joshua A. Fishman. Mouton, 1981.

Yin and yang. See **Acupuncture; Medicine** (China and India).

YMCA. See **Young Men's Christian Association.**

Yo-yo is a small toy that has been popular in the United States and Europe since the 1930's. It consists of two round, flat pieces of wood or plastic joined at the center by a small peg. A string is attached to the peg and winds around it. The player ties the free end of the string to one finger. The yo-yo spins in and out of the hand as the string unwinds and rewinds. Players can perform tricks with the yo-yo because the string is looped around the peg rather than permanently attached. The loop permits the yo-yo to spin in place.

The word *yo-yo* originated in the Philippines and means "come back." People in the Philippines used the yo-yo as both a weapon and a toy. In the West, people have had toys like yo-yos for at least 3,000 years. In the late 1920's, the name *yo-yo* became associated with an improved yo-yo developed in the United States by Donald F. Duncan.　Rachel Gallagher

Yoga is a term that has two meanings. It is both (1) a school of thought in the Hindu religion and (2) a system of mental and physical exercise developed by that school. Followers of the yoga school, who are called *yogis* or *yogins,* use yoga exercise to achieve their goal of isolation of the soul from the body and mind. Many non-Hindus in Western countries practice some form of yoga exercise in hope of improving their health and achieving peace of mind. The word *yoga* means *discipline* in Sanskrit, the classical language of India.

According to the yoga school, every human being consists of *prakrti* and *purusha.* Prakrti includes a person's body, mind, and *ego* (conscious self). Purusha is pure, empty consciousness—the soul. The yoga school teaches that the soul is completely separate from the rest of a person, but that the person does not realize it. Human beings suffer because they wrongly believe that their soul is bound to their body and mind. The yoga school, through yoga exercise, aims to give people *prajna* (understanding) of the meaning of their soul. After a person has obtained this understanding, his or her soul will gain *moksha* (release) from the *samsara* (cycle of rebirth) in which Hindus believe.

A yogi, under the guidance of a *guru* (teacher), goes through eight stages of training on the way to moksha. The yogi learns: (1) disciplined behavior, called *yama;* (2) self-purification (*niyama*); (3) bodily postures, such as the

Shostal

Yoga includes exercises and postures that its followers believe help isolate the soul from the body and mind. The yogi shown above is meditating while sitting in the lotus position.

lotus position (*asana*); (4) control of breathing (*prana-yama*); (5) control of the senses (*pratyahara*); (6) fixing of the mind on a chosen object (*dharana*); and (7) meditation (*dhyana*). The eighth stage, called *samadhi*, is a state of concentration in which yogis realize that their soul is pure and free, and empty of all content. A yogi who has completed these eight stages has reached *kaivalya*. Kaivalya is total isolation of the soul from the body, from all other souls, and from all of nature.

In addition to the practices of the yoga school, other popular forms of yoga exist in the religious traditions of India. One form, called *bhakti-yoga*, involves the dedication of all actions and thoughts to a chosen god. Another form, *karma-yoga*, involves doing one's duty without caring about reward. A third form, *hatha-yoga*, stresses difficult bodily postures and breathing techniques, with better health as the main goal.

Various forms of yoga have become popular in the United States and Europe. One form, Transcendental Meditation, requires less mental concentration than does the yoga of Hinduism. Members of the Hare Krishna movement practice bhakti-yoga by devoting themselves to the supreme god Krishna. Hatha-yoga has been called a method of gaining perfect health. But research has shown that it provides little more than does any good athletic program.   Gerald James Larson

See also **Hinduism.**

Additional resources

Carr, Rachel E. *Wheel, Camel, Fish, and Plow, Yoga for You.* Prentice-Hall, 1981. For younger readers.
Hewitt, James. *The Complete Yoga Book: Yoga of Breathing, Yoga of Posture, and Yoga of Meditation.* Schocken, 1978.
Worthington, Vivian. *A History of Yoga.* Routledge & Kegan, 1982.

Yogurt, also spelled *yoghurt,* is a smooth, semisolid dairy product made from milk. It has a high acid content and thick curd. Yogurt ranks as a popular food in many parts of the world. People in Iran, Turkey, and some other countries of the Middle East have eaten yogurt for thousands of years. Yogurt consumption in the United States increased considerably in the 1970's and 1980's.

Yogurt may be made from the milk of buffaloes, cows, goats, or other cud-chewing animals. In the United States, commercial yogurt is made from cows' milk. Yogurt makers add two types of bacteria to milk to make yogurt. These bacteria, called *Lactobacillus bulgaricus* and *Streptococcus thermophilus,* multiply at carefully controlled temperatures and cause milk to *ferment* (ripen). During the fermentation process, the bacteria change *lactose* (milk sugar) into *lactic acid.* Lactic acid causes fluid milk to thicken, resulting in yogurt.

The high acid content of yogurt gives the product a sour taste that many people enjoy. However, many others prefer yogurt that has been sweetened with fruit flavoring. Yogurt has the same nutritional elements as milk. Some unflavored yogurt contains only a few calories per serving and is popular for low-calorie diets.

Some people make yogurt at home. They use commercial yogurt or bacteria from special laboratories to start fermentation. Several firms manufacture yogurt-making machines for home use.   Michael F. Hutjens

Yokohama, *YOH kuh HAH muh* (pop. 2,992,644), is a Japanese port and a major center of commerce and industry. Among the cities of Japan, only Tokyo has more people. Yokohama lies about 20 miles (32 kilometers) south of Tokyo, on the island of Honshu (see **Japan** [political map]). Yokohama is the capital of Kanagawa Prefecture. A prefecture is a political unit in Japan.

Yokohama covers 163 square miles (421 square kilometers) on the western shore of Tokyo Bay and on the slopes of the surrounding hills. Downtown Yokohama occupies a triangular plain. The plain is bordered by narrow streams on two sides and by the bay on the third side. Residential areas of the city lie among the hills.

Yokohama has a number of gardens, libraries, parks, and theaters. Universities in the city include Kanagawa University, Kanto Gakuin University, Yokohama Municipal University, and Yokohama National University.

The city faces such problems as air and water pollution and lack of space. Overcrowded harbor conditions led to the construction of a $111-million pier that opened in 1970. The pier has special loading and unloading machinery to speed the handling of cargo.

Yokohama is Japan's largest port in terms of cargo value. Ships leaving the city carry many products manufactured in Tokyo and other nearby industrial regions. Rail lines link Yokohama with such other major cities as Kobe, Osaka, and Tokyo. Shipbuilding is a major industry in Yokohama. The city's factories also make such products as automobiles, chemicals, electrical equipment, iron and steel, and machinery.

Until 1854, the area that is now Yokohama was little more than a seashore with a few houses. That year, Commodore Matthew C. Perry of the U.S. Navy signed an agreement with the Japanese opening Japan to trade with the United States. Traders from a number of countries established offices in Yokohama in 1859. In time, Yokohama became a major seaport.

The city has twice been almost destroyed. On Sept. 1, 1923, one of the worst earthquakes in history killed more than 23,000 Yokohamans. In 1945, during World War II, U.S. bombers dropped thousands of fire bombs on Yokohama. The war ended that same year, and the city was rebuilt a second time.

In 1973, a Yokohama law took effect that regulates new construction. It requires that no structure be built that allows sunlight to fall on the surrounding neighborhood less than four hours a day.   Kenneth B. Pyle

Yolk. See Egg.

Yom Kippur, *YOHM kih POOR,* is the Jewish day of atonement and the most important and sacred Jewish holy day. It falls in September or October, in the Jewish month of Tishri. It lasts from sunset on the ninth day of Tishri until three stars appear after the tenth day.

Jews observe Yom Kippur as a day of fasting and worship. On this day, devout Jews think of their sins, repent, and ask forgiveness from God and from other people. In ancient times, the high priest held a service in the Temple in Jerusalem and sacrificed certain animals as a ceremonial offering. The service, part of the process of repentence and atonement, was the main event of the day. Today, Jews fast, perform no work, and attend services in the synagogue or temple. The laws about Yom Kippur are found in Leviticus 16; 23: 26-32; 25: 9; and in Numbers 29: 7-11. See also **Scapegoat.**   B. Barry Levy

Yonkers, N.Y. (pop. 195,351), is an important manufacturing center that forms part of the New York City metropolitan area. Yonkers lies between the Bronx and Hudson rivers. For location, see **New York** (political map).

Yonkers covers 18 square miles (47 square kilometers). The city is the home of St. Joseph's College. Museums include Philipse Manor Hall and the Hudson River Museum. Yonkers has over 400 manufacturing plants. They employ about 20 per cent of the work force. The chief products include chemicals, corn syrup and molasses, and electronic parts for aircraft and spacecraft.

Manhattan Indians once lived in the area that is now Yonkers. In 1646, Adriaen Van der Donck, a Dutch nobleman, received a land grant that included the site. He built a sawmill near the junction of the Nepperhan and Hudson rivers, where he could use the Nepperhan's water power. Van der Donck was called *De Jonkheer* (young gentleman). The settlement around the mill was known as De Jonkheer's land and, later, as Yonkers.

In 1693, a merchant named Frederick Philipse gained possession of much of the Yonkers area. He rented land to farmers, and, by the 1800's, the community consisted chiefly of farmers. The Hudson River Railroad opened in 1849, which encouraged the development of new industries in the area. Elisha G. Otis opened an elevator manufacturing shop in Yonkers in 1853, and his business grew into a leading industry (see **Otis, Elisha Graves**). Yonkers became a village in 1855 and a city in 1872.

Industrial expansion continued in Yonkers in the early 1900's. The jobs created by the industries attracted many immigrants, and the city's population increased from 79,803 in 1910 to 204,297 in 1970. But between 1970 and 1980, the population decreased to 195,351. The Otis elevator factory closed in 1983. Yonkers has a council-manager form of government.   Gwen Hall

York was one of England's largest provincial cities from the Middle Ages until the Industrial Revolution of the 1700's and early 1800's. It stands at the junction of the rivers Ouse and Foss. For location, see **Great Britain** (political map). York is the largest city in the district of York, which has a population of about 102,200.

Romans founded York and called it *Eboracum.* York Minster Cathedral is one of the finest English churches. It was badly damaged by fire in 1984. Repairs of the damage were completed in 1988. The archbishop of York is second in authority to the archbishop of Canterbury in the Church of England. York's historic sites attract many tourists. The city is famous for its museums, which include the National Railway Museum and the Viking Museum.   M. Trevor Wild

York is a branch of the English royal family of Plantagenet. The House of York won the English throne from the House of Lancaster during the Wars of the Roses (1455-1485). Members belonging to the House of York ruled England from 1461 to 1485, with a brief interruption in the early 1470's. See **Wars of the Roses.**

Richard, duke of York, the leader of the Yorkist party, was descended, through his mother, from the third son of King Edward III. Henry VI, the reigning king, was descended from Edward III's fourth son, John of Gaunt, duke of Lancaster. Because he was descended from an older son, the duke of York claimed that he had a better right to the throne than Henry VI.

Open warfare broke out in 1455, when Henry VI was defeated at the first battle of St. Albans. In December 1460, the duke of York was killed at the Battle of Wakefield. But, the following year, King Henry's forces were decisively beaten, and York's eldest son was crowned Edward IV, the first Yorkist king. Edward lost his throne in 1470, but regained it in 1471 after the battles of Barnet and Tewkesbury. He ruled until 1483.

He was succeeded by his 12-year-old son, Edward V. Shortly afterward, the boy's uncle, Richard, duke of Gloucester, seized the crown as Richard III, and imprisoned Edward and his younger brother. The boys were never heard of again.

In 1485, Henry Tudor, earl of Richmond, a descendant of the House of Lancaster, defeated and killed Richard III at Bosworth Field. He was crowned Henry VII, first ruler of the Tudor dynasty. Henry married Edward IV's daughter, Elizabeth, and so at last united the rival houses of Lancaster and York.   Paul M. Kendall

See also **Edward** (IV; V); **Henry** (VI; VII) of England; **Lancaster; Richard** (III).

York, Alvin Cullum (1887-1964), an outstanding American soldier of World War I (1914-1918), killed more than 20 Germans and forced 132 others to surrender on Oct. 8, 1918. York was a member of a patrol sent to silence German machine-gun nests. He shot about 25 soldiers and forced a German major to order the entire group to surrender. York received the Congressional Medal of Honor for his deed. Marshal Ferdinand Foch called it "the greatest thing accomplished by any

United Press Int.

Alvin C. York

private soldier of all the armies of Europe." Although he became famous as Sergeant York, he was a corporal at the time of his incredible feat.

York was born in Fentress County, Tennessee, and grew up on a mountain farm. He developed amazing marksmanship with the rifle and pistol while a boy. He became deeply religious and sought exemption from the draft because he believed war was wrong. But he was denied exemption.   H. A. DeWeerd

York, Cape. See Cape York.

Yorkshire terrier is a breed of toy dog that weighs 4 to 7 pounds (1.8 to 3.2 kilograms). Weavers in northern England developed the breed in the 1850's. They wanted a dog bold enough to kill rats, but small enough to be carried in a pocket. The dog has long, silky hair. Its coat is steel-blue with golden-tan. See also **Dog** (picture: Toy dogs).   Critically reviewed by the Yorkshire Terrier Club of America

Yorktown, Va. (pop. 450), is a historic village on the York River (see **Virginia** [political map]). In 1781, Lord Cornwallis surrendered to General George Washington at Yorktown in the last major battle of the Revolutionary War. During the 1700's, Yorktown served as a major tobacco port. Today, several historic homes in Yorktown are part of Colonial National Historical Park. This park includes the Yorktown Battlefield; much of Jamestown Island; and Colonial Parkway, a drive that connects Jamestown and Yorktown and passes through historic Williamsburg.   Will Molineux

Yorktown, Battle of. See Revolutionary War in America (Surrender at Yorktown; picture).

Yoruba, *YOH ru bah,* are a group of people who inhabit southwestern Nigeria and parts of Benin and Togo. More than 17 million Yoruba live in these areas. They speak a language called Yoruba, which belongs to the Niger-Congo family of African languages.

Many Yoruba make their living mainly by farming. Large numbers of them live in cities and work on family-owned farms in surrounding areas. Many other Yoruba sell craftwork items, including handwoven cloth, metalwork, and pottery. Women control the sale of crafts, farm products, and imported goods in the lively local markets. Still other Yoruba work in technical jobs, in business, or in such professions as law and medicine.

The Yoruba practice several religions. Most Yoruba are Christians or Muslims. Others believe in the group's traditional religion. This religion centers on a supreme god and over 400 lesser gods and spirits called *orisha,* each with its own cult and priests.

Traditional Yoruba society included city-states, which consisted of towns, villages, and the surrounding farms and forests. Some city-states were ruled by a king called an *oba,* who was believed to be divine. Others were governed by chiefs or by the heads of large family groups. Some city-states became large kingdoms, the most powerful of which were Ife and Oyo.

From the late 1400's to the 1800's, Europeans sold many Yoruba as slaves to colonists in the Americas. During the late 1800's, the British conquered the Yoruba homeland. They established Christianity and European education among the Yoruba. During the 1900's, Yoruba farmers became important producers of cacao beans, from which chocolate is made. The Yoruba helped Nigeria win its independence in 1960, and have played leading roles in the nation since then. Yoruba civilization

also has influenced art, music, and religion in the Americas.   Dan R. Aronson

See also **Ife; Nigeria** (People; History).

Yosemite Falls, *yoh SEHM ih tee,* in California's Yosemite National Park, is one of the world's highest waterfalls. It is formed by Yosemite Creek as it plunges 2,425 feet (739 meters) down a rock wall of Yosemite Valley. Yosemite Falls has three parts: Upper Falls, 1,430 feet (436 meters) high; the intermediate cascade, 675 feet (206 meters); and Lower Falls, 320 feet (98 meters). See also **Waterfall** (picture; chart).   John W. Reith

Yosemite National Park, *yoh SEHM ih tee,* is a great wilderness in east-central California. It lies in the Sierra Nevada mountains, about 200 miles (320 kilometers) east of San Francisco (see **California** [political map]). It has about 700 miles (1,100 kilometers) of trails. Most of the trails lead to the "High Sierra," a region of sparkling lakes, rushing streams, and jagged mountain peaks. The Yosemite Museum in the park has a collection of Indian displays, and exhibits of the area's wildlife. For the area of the park, see **National Park System** (table: National parks).

More than 60 kinds of animals and more than 200 species of birds live in the forests and mountains. Bears and deer are numerous. Yosemite has more than 30 kinds of trees and more than 1,300 varieties of plants. There are three groves of the famous *Sequoiadendron giganteum* or *Big Trees.* The best known is the Mariposa Grove, 35 miles (56 kilometers) south of Yosemite Valley. It includes the Grizzly Giant Tree, whose base measures more than 34 feet (10 meters) in diameter.

In 1864, Congress gave Yosemite Valley to California for use as a public park and recreation area. John Muir, a naturalist, first saw the area in the 1860's. His enthusiastic reports of the beauties of the region aroused interest in the Yosemite Valley. Congress created Yosemite National Park in 1890. But the park did not include Yosemite Valley and the Mariposa Grove. California ceded these areas back to the federal government, and they were added to the park in 1906. The park has many tourist accommodations. Skiing is popular in the High Sierra. Other activities include horseback riding, fishing, golf, tennis, hiking, and swimming.

Yosemite Valley. Much of the park's most spectacular scenery is in the Yosemite Valley. The valley lies at a 4,000-foot (1,200-meter) elevation in the heart of the park. A group of explorers on their way to the Pacific Coast in the 1830's were probably the first white people to see the valley. But white people did not enter it until 1851. In that year, the Mariposa Battalion, a volunteer fighting force, set out to capture a group of Yosemite Indians. Tenaya, the Yosemite chief, had been leading raids on white settlers in the foothills of the Sierra Nevada. He was captured, but eventually was allowed to return to the valley, which was named for his tribe.

Millions of years ago, California's Sierra Nevada was formed by a gradual series of earth upheavals. As the mountains rose, the westward-flowing Merced River accelerated to torrential speed and carved the narrow, V-shaped Merced Canyon. Later, massive glaciers flowed down the canyon. The glaciers ground and polished the canyon to a smooth U-shaped valley, nearly 1 mile (1.6 kilometers) wide and almost 1 mile deep in places. Tributary streams did not carve their canyons as deep as

Gene Ahrens, Bruce Coleman Ltd.

Upper and Lower Yosemite Falls are a scenic attraction in Yosemite National Park. They rank among the 10 highest waterfalls in North America. The two falls and the cascade that connects them have a combined height of 2,425 feet (739 meters).

Merced Canyon. Glaciers sheared off these canyons, leaving them as "hanging valleys." Today, the world's greatest concentration of free, leaping waterfalls pours from these valleys.

Waterfalls. Bridalveil Fall is the first waterfall seen by most Yosemite visitors. It graces the southern wall of the valley with a 620-foot (189-meter) descent. The Illilouette Falls also tumbles over the side of the valley. Yosemite Falls is formed by Yosemite Creek, leaping free from its hanging valley 2,425 feet (739 meters) above the valley floor. The Upper Falls is 1,430 feet (436 meters) high, and the Lower Falls measures 320 feet (98 meters) high. The cascades between the two tumble another 675 feet (206 meters). The total height of Yosemite Falls is about $\frac{1}{2}$ mile (0.8 kilometer), about twice the height of the Empire State Building.

Vernal and Nevada falls pour over giant steps formed by glaciers. Vernal Falls, 317 feet (97 meters) high, is famous for the rainbows that sparkle in the heavy mist at its base. About 1 mile (1.6 kilometers) upstream is 594-foot (181-meter) Nevada Falls. It is so violent that the Indians called it *Yo-wipe* or *The Twisted Fall.*

Some of the park's falls burst forth during the high-water season in spring. These include the slender 1,612-foot (491-meter) Ribbon Falls, the erratic Sentinel Falls which drops 2,000 feet (610 meters), and the 1,170-foot (357-meter) Silver Strand Falls.

Rock masses. A number of rock masses rise sharply from the valley floor. The Half Dome rises to an elevation of about 8,800 feet (2,700 meters) at the head of the valley. El Capitan, which is a gigantic mass of unbroken granite, rises vertically about 3,600 feet (1,100 meters)

above the canyon. From Glacier Point, one can look down more than 3,000 feet (910 meters) into the valley. Cloud's Rest, the highest point in Yosemite Valley, stands about 9,900 feet (3,000 meters) above the valley floor.

Hetch Hetchy Valley lies in the northwestern part of the park. It was carved by the Tuolumne River and ancient glaciers in much the same manner as Yosemite Valley. A reservoir now covers the floor of the valley. The Grand Canyon of the Tuolumne River is above Hetch Hetchy, to the east. The river rushes through the canyon at great speed, dropping 4,000 feet (1,200 meters) in 4 miles (6 kilometers). It creates many cascades and waterfalls, including the Waterwheel Falls, a series of amazing pinwheels of water. Some of the pinwheels rise as high as 40 feet (12 meters). The pinwheels are formed when the river, cascading down a steep granite apron, strikes rocky obstructions.

The Tuolumne River flows through Tuolumne Meadows, a vast grassland. The meadows have an elevation of about 8,500 feet (2,590 meters). Tourists camp there and the area is also used as a base camp by mountain climbers. Tenaya Lake, near the meadows on Tioga Road, is the largest and is considered by many to be the most beautiful of the more than 300 lakes in Yosemite.

Transportation. Yosemite is a year-round park. Most roads remain open throughout the winter. However, snows close roads in the High Sierra region from about mid-autumn until late spring.

Critically reviewed by the National Park Service

Related articles in *World Book* include:

Bridalveil Fall	Nevada Falls	Sequoia
California (picture)	Ribbon Falls	Yosemite Falls
Muir, John		

Young, Andrew Jackson, Jr. (1932-   ), was the first black to serve as United States ambassador to the United Nations (UN). He held the post from 1977 to 1979. Young became known for his outspoken comments on world affairs. He strongly supported black majority rule in Africa. Young served as mayor of Atlanta, Ga., from 1981 to 1989.

Young was born in New Orleans. He graduated from Howard University and from the Hartford Theological Seminary. In 1955, Young was ordained a minister in what is now the United Church of Christ. He served as pastor of several churches in Alabama and Georgia.

In 1960, Young joined the Southern Christian Leadership Conference (SCLC), a civil rights organization led by Martin Luther King, Jr. Young became one of King's chief aides and served as executive director of the SCLC from 1964 to 1970. He was jailed in Selma, Ala., and St. Augustine, Fla., for taking part in civil rights demonstrations in those cities.

Young, a Democrat from Georgia, won election to the U.S. House of Representatives in 1972. He was the first black elected to Congress from the South since 1901. He held the seat until President

United Nations

Andrew Young, Jr.

Jimmy Carter appointed him to the UN. In 1978, Young received the Spingarn Medal for his work in domestic and international affairs.   Nancy Dickerson

Young, Brigham (1801-1877), led the Mormons from Illinois to what is now Utah, and established their church there. Young was the second president of the Mormon church, which is officially called the Church of Jesus Christ of Latter-day Saints. He became the Mormon leader in 1844, after Joseph Smith, the church founder, was shot to death.

Young was a stocky man, and a tireless worker. A strong will, engaging personality, and deep convictions made him an outstanding leader.

Early life. Young was born in Whitingham, Vt. His father, a farmer, had fought under George Washington during the Revolutionary War. In 1804, Young's father took the family to western New York. Young spent most of his early years on his father's farm. He attended school only about 12 days. As a young man, he worked as a painter, glazier, and carpenter. In 1829, Young settled in Monroe County, New York, near Joseph Smith's home. He studied Smith's religious teachings and was baptized into the church in 1832. In 1833, he joined the Mormon settlement at Kirtland, Ohio.

Mormon leader. The Kirtland community broke up and non-Mormons (called "gentiles" by the Mormons) drove them from Independence, Mo., in the 1830's. Young, Smith, and other church members then settled in Far West, Mo. Anti-Mormonism also developed there, and non-Mormons imprisoned Smith and other leaders on what Mormons believe were false charges in 1838. But Young led between 5,000 and 8,000 Mormons to safety in Illinois.

Young was one of the church's most successful missionaries. From 1839 to 1841, as a missionary in Great Britain, he converted many persons to his faith and arranged for them to come to the United States. Young was preaching in New England in 1844, when Joseph Smith was shot by a mob at Carthage, Ill. Young hurried back to Illinois. He made a powerful speech that rallied the church members. He was the undisputed leader of the Mormons from that time until his death.

Settles in Utah. Non-Mormons forced the Mormons to leave Illinois in 1846. Starting in mid-winter, Young led his followers on a long journey across the Mississippi River and through Iowa to the region near present-day Omaha, Nebr. But Young decided that there could be no lasting peace for his people until they were completely separated from the gentiles. So, in 1847, Young led an advance party of 148 Mormon settlers west to a previously planned refuge in the Great Basin. When the group arrived in the Great Salt Lake valley in what is now Utah, Young said, "This is the right place. Drive on." He supervised the migration of thousands of other Mormons to the valley. Young was formally elected president of the Mormon church in 1847.

Brigham Young

The Mormons prospered in Utah. Under Young's leadership, they developed irrigation techniques, and parts of the barren desert blossomed into rich and fruitful land. The United States government established the Territory of Utah in 1850 and appointed Young its first governor. Young still found time to direct missionary work and to establish hundreds of Mormon settlements in the West.

But the move to Utah did not end the Mormons' troubles. Gentiles came to the territory, and some who opposed them held political posts under the United States government. False reports circulated that the church was in rebellion against the government. These reports alarmed the federal government. In 1857, President James Buchanan replaced Young with a gentile governor and sent troops to Utah. The Mormons prepared to defend themselves, and the Utah War (also called the Mormon War) followed. However, no battles were fought between the Mormons and the federal troops. Although the Mormons raided some troop wagon trains as a delaying action, they then temporarily abandoned Salt Lake City to the army. The troops established a camp near the western mountains. During the winter of 1857 and 1858, Young and the federal troops discussed peace terms. The hostilities ended in 1858 when Young accepted the new governor and President Buchanan fully pardoned all concerned. Even though Young stepped down as governor, he remained the most powerful man in Utah until his death.

Young's place in history. Critics have accused Young of intolerance to opposition. Many people opposed his practice of polygamy. Young took a number of wives, 16 of whom bore him children. But Young's leadership and pioneering efforts rank him as one of the most important colonizers of the American West. Mormon history records that Young brought 100,000 people to the mountain valleys, founded more than 200 cities, towns, and villages, and established many schools and factories. A statue of Young represents Utah in Statuary Hall in Washington, D.C.

Critically reviewed by the Church of Jesus Christ of Latter-day Saints

See also **Mormons; Utah; Smith, Joseph; Latter Day Saints, Reorganized Church of Jesus Christ of.**

Additional resources

Arrington, Leonard J. *Brigham Young: American Moses.* Knopf, 1985.
Bringhurst, Newell G. *Brigham Young and the Expanding American Frontier.* Little, Brown, 1986.
West, Ray B. *Kingdom of the Saints: The Story of Brigham Young and the Mormons.* Viking, 1957.

Young, Cy (1867-1955), was one of the greatest right-handed pitchers in the history of baseball. Young won a record 511 major league games from 1890 through 1911. He also holds the record for the most innings pitched (7,356), the most complete games (753), and the most losses (313). Young pitched for the Cleveland Spiders, St. Louis Nationals, Boston Red Sox, Cleveland Indians, and Boston Braves.

Young was born in Gilmore, Ohio. His full name was Denton True Young. He was elected to the National Baseball Hall of Fame in 1937. At the end of each season, the Cy Young Award is given to the outstanding pitcher in the National League and the American League.

Dave Nightingale

Young, Edward (1683-1765), was an English poet. His later verse was part of a trend from the witty, imitative poetry of England's Augustan age, to the more passionate, imaginative poetry of the romantic period.

Two works established Young's reputation. *The Complaint: or Night Thoughts on Life, Death, and Immortality* (1742-1745) is a series of nine meditative blank verse poems defending Christianity against freethinkers. *Conjectures on Original Composition* (1759) is a critical essay claiming that originality in literature is superior to the imitation of ancient writers.

Young was born in Upham, near Winchester. In 1730, he became *rector* (clergyman in charge of a parish) at Welwin in Hertfordshire. Young held this position until his death.   Martin C. Battestin

Young, Ella Flagg (1845-1918), was the first woman to serve as superintendent of schools in a large city. She held this position in Chicago from 1909 to 1915. Her chief contribution was to introduce practical studies such as home economics and manual training. She was born in Buffalo, N.Y.   Claude A. Eggertsen

Young, John Watts (1930-   ), is a United States astronaut. He has made more space flights than any other astronaut. On March 23, 1965, Young and Virgil I. Grissom made the first flight in the Gemini program. They circled the earth three times and became the first space pilots to change their orbit.

Young and Michael Collins flew the Gemini 10 space mission from July 18 to 21, 1966. They performed two *rendezvous* (meetings) with unmanned spacecraft.

Young, Eugene A. Cernan, and Thomas P. Stafford went into orbit around the moon during the Apollo 10 space flight of May 18 to 26, 1969. Young remained in orbit in the command module while Cernan and Stafford flew to within 10 miles (16 kilometers) of the moon in the lunar module. This mission cleared the way for the first moon landing, two months later.

From April 16 to 27, 1972, Young commanded the Apollo 16 flight to the moon. He and Charles M. Duke, Jr., explored in the Descartes region of the moon's central highlands.

Young commanded the first space shuttle flight from April 12 to 14, 1981. He and Robert L. Crippen orbited the earth $36\frac{1}{2}$ times in the shuttle *Columbia* and then piloted the vehicle to a landing. He also commanded the ninth space shuttle flight from Nov. 28 to Dec. 7, 1983. During this flight, the astronauts aboard *Columbia* conducted scientific experiments in Spacelab, a European-built space laboratory.

Young was born in San Francisco. He graduated from the Georgia Institute of Technology in 1952. He joined the Navy that year and became a test pilot. He became an astronaut in 1962.   William J. Cromie

See also **Astronaut; Space travel** (picture: The commander and the pilot).

Young, Lester Willis (1909-1959), a tenor saxophonist, developed one of the most imitated styles in jazz history. More than any other jazz instrumentalist, Young was responsible for the transition from the "hot jazz" style in the 1930's to the more relaxed, behind-the-beat approach usually known as "cool." He did his best work while playing with the Count Basie band from 1936 to 1940.

Young was born in Woodville, Miss. He was nicknamed "Prez." He played with King Oliver, Walter Page, and Fletcher Henderson before joining Basie. In the 1940's and 1950's, Young often played on "Jazz at the Philharmonic" concert tours. The last years of his life were tragic. He had a nervous breakdown and was often hospitalized.   Leonard Feather

Young, Thomas. See **Color** (The three-component theory); **Interferometer; Light** (Interference).

Young, Whitney Moore, Jr. (1921-1971), was an American civil rights leader. He served as the executive director of the National Urban League from 1961 until his death. Young helped thousands of black Americans obtain jobs. He started on-the-job training programs, and established Head Start and tutoring centers.

Young was born in Lincoln Ridge, Ky. He graduated from Kentucky State College (now Kentucky State University) and earned a master's degree at the University of Minnesota. From 1947 to 1953, he worked for the Urban League in St. Paul and Omaha. Young was dean of the Atlanta University School of Social Work from 1954 to 1960. He taught at the University of Nebraska School of Social Work, and served on federal commissions concerned with social welfare or race relations. Young wrote several books, including *To Be Equal* (1964).

C. Eric Lincoln

Young Men's Christian Association (YMCA) is one of the largest nonprofit voluntary organizations in the world. It serves about 25 million members in more than 90 countries. The YMCA works to promote the values shared by Judaism and Christianity. It operates on the principles that all people are children of God, worthy of respect, and responsible for their own lives and actions. YMCA's believe that all people should join together to achieve equality and justice for one another. The World Alliance of YMCA's, an international YMCA organization, has headquarters in Geneva, Switzerland.

In the United States, about 13 million people participate annually at over 2,000 local YMCA branches, units, camps, and centers. Membership and services are open to people of all ages, religions, races, and incomes. Women and girls make up about 45 per cent of those involved in the YMCA. About half of those served are under the age of 18.

All YMCA branches share the same basic goals: (1) promoting healthy life styles, (2) strengthening the modern family, (3) developing leadership qualities in youth, (4) increasing international understanding, and (5) assisting in community development.

The association promotes its values through a variety of programs, such as health and fitness programs, child care, senior citizens' activities, and international education and exchange. Some YMCA's have residential and hotel facilities. YMCA's also offer employment, adventure, and leadership programs for teen-agers. The YMCA sponsors the National Youth Programs Using Minibikes and other programs to fight juvenile delinquency. Other activities include refugee resettlement programs and educational programs for the disabled.

Volunteer board members from the local community control each individual YMCA. The national headquarters, called the YMCA of the USA, works closely with local YMCA's to discover successful program ideas at the local level and spread these ideas nationally.

A number of widely adopted programs have grown

out of this discovery system. One is a health enhancement program in which local YMCA's work with corporations to provide health and exercise programs for employees. Another local innovation is the Home Team program, which encourages families to spend quality time together. Other programs that have expanded nationwide include Indian Guides, Indian Maidens, and Indian Princesses. These parent-child activity programs are designed to help strengthen the modern family.

The YMCA operates about 1,400 gymnasiums and pools, 1,000 health and fitness centers, 2,600 racquetball and handball courts, 1,000 tennis courts, 275 resident camps and conference centers, and 250 residences. There are special YMCA's for college students, military families, and railroad workers. The YMCA of the USA has national offices at 101 N. Wacker Drive, Chicago, IL 60606. It publishes a bimonthly color magazine, *Discovery YMCA.*

In Canada, more than 70 YMCA's provide programs for about 300 communities throughout the country. More than a million persons, almost half of whom are women and girls, take part in these programs. Most Canadian YMCA's provide programs in six areas: (1) adult education, (2) camping and outdoor education, (3) community and youth services, (4) guidance and counseling, (5) health and physical education, and (6) institutional services, such as residences and cafeterias.

Each YMCA is managed by its own board of directors or governors. In 1912, the existing YMCA's established the National Council of YMCA's of Canada in order to help individual YMCA's achieve their goals through collective action. The council's main office is at 2160 Yonge Street, Toronto, ON M4S 2A9.

History. The YMCA was founded in London in 1844 by a young British clerk named George Williams. Williams wanted to provide young clothing store clerks from the countryside with a place in London where they could read the Bible, relax, and find out about decent lodging. The YMCA movement traveled overseas to the United States and Canada in 1851. In that year, Thomas Sullivan, a missionary and retired sea captain, founded a YMCA in Boston. A group of young men formed a YMCA in Montreal at the same time.

Exercise and gymnastics became part of the American YMCA in the second half of the 1850's. The first YMCA swimming pool opened in Brooklyn, N.Y., in 1856. In 1891, a physical education instructor named James Naismith invented the game of basketball at the School for Christian Workers (now Springfield College) in Springfield, Mass. The school was associated with the YMCA. The original teams had nine players and used peach baskets as goals. In 1895, another physical education instructor, W. G. Morgan, invented volleyball at the Mount Holyoke, Mass., YMCA because he believed that basketball was too strenuous for businessmen.

The San Francisco YMCA admitted the association's first women members in 1874. The YMCA introduced the ideas of night school and junior college. It also assisted with the formation of other major voluntary groups, such as the Boy Scouts, Camp Fire, and the United Service Organizations (USO).

Critically reviewed by the YMCA of the USA

See also **HI-Y Club; Y-Indian Guides; Y-Indian Maidens; Y-Indian Princesses.**

Young Women's Christian Association (YWCA)

is the world's oldest and largest multiracial women's organization. The YWCA is open to women and girls of all faiths and backgrounds. The organization tries to meet its members' needs with a program that combines services and social action. It works to eliminate racism and to increase the power of women, minority groups, and young people. The YWCA provides services and training that help women become equal partners with men in the continual development of their nations.

The YWCA has more than $2\frac{1}{2}$ million members and participants in more than 80 countries, including the United States and Canada. This total includes men and boys, who may become YWCA associates. The organization employs approximately 23,000 national and local staff members, and it also has about 160,000 volunteer workers. The YWCA cooperates with, but is not related to, the Young Men's Christian Association (YMCA).

Programs. In the United States, the YWCA operates in all the states except Alaska. It conducts programs in more than 4,000 locations throughout the nation—in cities, towns, and rural communities; and on college campuses. Local YWCA's offer a wide range of activities and services. They feature child-care centers, classes on various subjects, discussion programs, food services, and health education. They also provide counseling, job placement services, leadership training programs, recreational activities, and residential facilities.

The YWCA of the United States sponsors programs to fight crime and delinquency. Many local YWCA's have a Y-Teen program for teen-age members (see **Y-Teens**).

In Canada, YWCA's provide services in nine provinces and in the Northwest Territories. Canadian YWCA's offer programs and services that are similar to those offered by YWCA's in the United States.

History. In 1855, a group of London women led by Emma Robarts organized a young women's association. Their purpose was to find housing for nurses who had returned from the Crimean War (1853-1856). At about the same time, another women's group in London organized prayer circles. The two groups united in 1877 as the Young Women's Christian Association.

In the United States, The Ladies' Christian Association, an organization similar to the London groups, was founded in New York City in 1858. The first Young Women's Christian Association was organized in Boston in 1866. The movement grew rapidly, especially in industrial cities, where the YWCA provided housing for single working women. Later, the YWCA became active on college campuses. The first student YWCA in the United States was founded in 1873 at Illinois State Normal University (now Illinois State University) in Normal, Ill. Separate organizations arose in the Midwest and in the East. In 1906, these groups united as the Young Women's Christian Associations of the United States of America. The YWCA of the United States has headquarters at 726-30 Broadway, New York, NY 10003.

The first YWCA in Canada was established in Saint John, N.B., in 1870. The organization's purpose was to help meet the needs of young working women. In 1893, local YWCA's established the national organization, the YWCA of Canada. The main office of the YWCA of Canada is at 80 Gerrard Street East, Toronto, ON M5B 1G6.

The YWCA's of both Canada and the United States are

members of the World Young Women's Christian Association. The association has headquarters in Geneva, Switzerland.

Critically reviewed by the Young Women's Christian Association

Youngstown (pop. 115,436) is an industrial city in northeastern Ohio (see **Ohio** [political map]). With Warren, it forms a metropolitan area with 531,350 people.

Youngstown has many parks and recreation areas. Mill Creek Park covers more than 2,300 acres (931 hectares) and is one of the nation's most beautiful natural parks. Youngstown institutions include the Youngstown Public Library and its branches, Youngstown State University, Butler Institute of American Art, Stambaugh Auditorium, Youngstown Symphony Center, and the Youngstown Playhouse.

Youngstown has foundries, machine shops, metal fabricators, and mill equipment suppliers. Its factories produce aluminum products, automotive parts, light bulbs, electronic equipment, office equipment, paints, paper products, plastics, rubber goods, and textile products.

Youngstown was settled in 1797 and named in honor of John Young of New York, who bought the site of the future city from the Connecticut Land Company. The town was incorporated in 1848. For many years, Youngstown was a leading steel-producing city in the United States. Its first steel mill was built in 1891. By the 1930's, Youngstown ranked third in steel production among U.S. cities. During the late 1970's, a number of economic factors made the production of steel in the Youngstown mills unprofitable. As a result, all the steel mills in the city closed between 1977 and 1981. Youngstown is the seat of Mahoning County and has a mayor-council form of government.   Richard J. Hopkins

Youth. See Adolescent.

Youth for Christ International is a nonprofit organization specializing in teen-age evangelism. Founded in 1944, it has more than 300 local groups in the United States, Canada, and about 60 other countries. Its local interdenominational groups sponsor youth rallies, high school clubs, and camps designed to supplement the work of local churches. The organization's world office is in Singapore. The U.S. headquarters are at 360 S. Main Place, Carol Stream, IL 60188.

Critically reviewed by Youth for Christ International

Youth hostel, *HAHS tuhl,* is an inexpensive overnight accommodation for travelers who belong to hosteling associations. The major association, the International Youth Hostel Federation, coordinates a system of more than 5,000 hostels in 62 countries. Its affiliate in the United States, American Youth Hostels, Incorporated, operates hostels in major urban areas and in or near U.S. national parks, state parks, and other scenic areas. Many hostels are located near one another, so members can easily tour an area by walking or cycling from one hostel to the next.

Many hostels occupy historic buildings. Generally, each hostel has dormitory-style sleeping quarters, a common kitchen, and a lounge for socializing and relaxing. Houseparents supervise each hostel, but visitors provide their own gear, prepare their own meals, and maintain their quarters themselves.

Youth hostels were originated by Richard Schirrmann, a German schoolteacher, in 1910. He founded hostels in the former state of Westphalia, Germany.

Greg Siple, American Youth Hostels, Inc.

Youth hostels in many parts of the world provide inexpensive lodging for travelers. Many youth hostel associations also sponsor bicycle trips, hikes, and other group activities. The cyclists shown above are resting at a hostel in Boston, Mass.

Schirrmann hoped to encourage people to spend more of their time outdoors. His plan became popular and quickly spread to most European countries.

The first youth hostel in North America was established in a tent in 1933 at Bragg Creek, Alberta, Canada, by two sisters, Mary and Catherine Barclay. They founded Canadian Youth Hostels. In the United States, Isabel and Monroe Smith introduced the first hostel, at Northfield, Mass., in 1934. The mailing address of American Youth Hostels, Incorporated, is P.O. Box 37613, Washington, DC 20013.

Critically reviewed by American Youth Hostels, Incorporated

Ypres, *EE pruh* (pop. 34,758), is a Belgian city in West Flanders, in the Dutch-speaking part of the country. For location, see **Belgium** (political map). The city's Dutch name is Ieper (pronounced *YAY puhr*). Linen and lace are made in Ypres from the flax of Flanders.

Ypres became famous as a center of the textile industry about 1300. At that time, its population was about 20,000, almost as great as London's. In World War I, Ypres was the scene of severe fighting, and it was almost destroyed. It was rebuilt, but again became a battleground during World War II.   Aristide R. Zolberg

Ytterbium, *ih TUR bee uhm,* is a soft silvery metal. Small amounts of ytterbium are used in metallurgical and chemical experiments. In 1878, the Swiss chemist Jean de Marignac gave the name *ytterbium* to a substance that he found in a mineral called *yttria.* In 1907, the French chemist Georges Urbain separated de Marignac's substance into two chemical elements, *lutetium* and *ytterbium.* Several minerals, such as monazite, gadolinite, and xenotime, contain ytterbium.

Ytterbium is a rare-earth element. Its chemical symbol is Yb and its atomic number is 70. Seven ytterbium isotopes are stable. Their average atomic weight is 173.04. The metal melts at 819° C, boils at 1196° C, and has a density of 6.973 grams per cubic centimeter at 25° C (see **Density**).   Larry C. Thompson

See also **Lutetium; Rare earth.**

Yttrium, *IHT ree uhm,* is a silvery-white metallic element. It has a number of important uses, particularly in the electronics industry. For example, the compound yttrium oxide forms the basis of the phosphors used in color televisions to reproduce red. This compound is also used to produce two kinds of crystals called *garnets.* One type of garnet acts as a microwave filter in radar, and the other serves as an imitation diamond. Yttrium is also used in lasers and in the manufacture of certain chemicals, glass, and ceramics.

Yttrium resembles the rare-earth elements and it occurs in nearly all rare-earth minerals (see **Rare earth**). The metal is obtained commercially from monazite sand.

Yttrium has the chemical symbol Y. Its atomic number is 39, and its atomic weight is 88.9059. The metal melts at 1522° C ($\pm$8° C) and boils at 3338° C. The Swedish chemist Carl Gustav Mosander discovered yttrium in 1843 in the mineral *yttria.*   R. Craig Taylor

Yuan, *yoo AHN,* is the Chinese word for *dollar.* In Taiwan, people refer to the *New Taiwan Dollar* as a *yuan.* China uses the yuan as its basic unit of currency. It is divided into 10 *chiao,* each worth 10 *fen.* In 1914, China established the yuan as a silver coin with 23.4934 grams of pure silver. The yuan usually circulates now as paper money with little silver backing.   R. G. Doty

Yuan dynasty. See **China** (Mongol rule; map).

Yucatán Peninsula, *yoo kuh TAN* or *yoo kuh TAHN,* includes the southeastern Mexican states of Campeche, Quintana Roo, and Yucatán; Belize; and part of El Petén, a department of Guatemala. The peninsula separates the Gulf of Mexico from the Caribbean Sea. It covers over 75,000 square miles (194,000 square kilometers).

The peninsula is a low, rolling tableland of coral and limestone covered by a thin layer of soil. It has a hot, humid climate. Tropical rain forests cover the lowlands. The chief cities include Mérida, capital of Yucatán; Campeche, capital of Campeche; and Progreso, Yucatán, the peninsula's chief port. Quintana Roo and Belize lie along the eastern coast of the peninsula. The state of Yucatán is in the peninsula's northern part. The state of Campeche lies south and west of Yucatán. Part of El Petén in Guatemala is inland in the peninsula's southern part.

Most of the people, called *Yucatecos,* are descendants of the Maya Indians who lived in Yucatán hundreds of years before the Spaniards arrived (see **Maya**). Ancient ruins of the Mayan civilization have been found at Chichén Itzá in Yucatán. Most Yucatecos are farmers. Northern Yucatán is one of the chief henequen-raising areas of the world. Henequen is used in making rope. Other crops of the Yucatán Peninsula include cacao, chicle, coffee, corn, cotton, sugar cane, and tobacco.

Francisco Fernández de Córdoba, a Spaniard, came to the peninsula in 1517. By 1542, Francisco de Montejo the Younger had set up Spanish rule over half of Yucatán and established the cities of Campeche and Mérida. Some of the Indians became slave laborers on henequen plantations. During the 1800's and 1900's, the Indians revolted several times against the Mexican government. They won most of the land in Campeche and Yucatán from the Mexican landlords. Salvador Alvarado and Felipe Carillo, who served as governors of Yucatán in the early 1900's, introduced many reforms.

See also **Belize.**

Yucca, *YUHK uh,* is the name of a group of shrubs or trees of the agave family. The yucca plant has a striking appearance. It is an evergreen plant, and does not shed its leaves each year.

Some yucca plants have short stems and others have tall woody and scaly trunks. The leaves of the yucca plants are usually pointed, stiff, and narrow, with sawlike or fibrous edges. They grow along the stem or in clusters at the end of a stem. The yucca plant has flowers shaped somewhat like bells. Certain varieties of the yucca have whitish-green flowers, while others have white or cream-colored flowers. These flowers grow in a cluster on a stem which springs up from the center of a cluster of leaves. Some of these flowers give off a strong fragrance when they open at night. The yucca has large fruits that may be either fleshy or dry. They contain many small, flat, black seeds. The yucca is pollinated by the female yucca moth, which carries pollen from one yucca to another. See **Flower** (Cross-pollination).

Yuccas grow most abundantly in the southern and southwestern parts of the United States. They also grow in the desert highlands and plateaus of Mexico. Most of the species are low shrubs. But in deserts of the southwestern United States, and in Mexico, there are several species that become large, picturesque trees. The Joshua Tree National Monument in California contains important collections of yucca trees. The popular northern species of yucca is called *Adam's needle.*

The Indians found many uses for yucca plants. They made rope, sandals, mats, and baskets from the leaf fibers. They ate the buds and flowers raw or boiled. The Indians dried the fleshy fruits and ate them during the winter. They also made a fermented drink from the fruits. The roots and stems of the yucca make a soap. Some kinds of yucca are known as *soapweed.* Yuccas serve as decorative plants in gardens throughout the United States. They are often grown as border plants.

Scientific classification. Yuccas belong to the agave family, Agavaceae. The Joshua tree is *Yucca brevifolia.* Another common species, *Y. baccata,* is found in the dry areas of the United States and Mexico. The soapweed, *Y. glauca,* is found from New Mexico to the Dakotas. The Adam's needle yucca is *Y. filamentosa.*   Philip W. Rundel

WORLD BOOK maps

The Yucatán Peninsula divides the Gulf of Mexico and the Caribbean Sea. It lies in southeastern Mexico, northern Guatemala, and Belize.

See also **Flower** (picture: Interesting facts about flowers); **Spanish bayonet.**

Shostal

Rugged mountains cover most of Yugoslavia. The mountains above tower over the town of Kotor, a historic seaport on the Adriatic Sea in southern Yugoslavia.

Yugoslavia

Yugoslavia, also spelled *Jugoslavia,* is a mountainous country in southeastern Europe. It lies on the Balkan Peninsula along the Adriatic Sea. Belgrade is the nation's capital and largest city.

The name *Yugoslavia* means *Land of the Southern Slavs.* The name comes from the fact that Slavic peoples make up most of the country's population. These peoples belong to six major nationality groups: Bosnian Muslims, Croats, Macedonians, Montenegrins, Serbs, and Slovenes. The country also has many other nationality groups, such as Albanians, Germans, Hungarians, Slovaks, and Turks.

Yugoslavia is organized into six basic federal units, called *socialist republics,* according to the historical boundaries of its major nationality groups. These republics are Bosnia and Hercegovina, Croatia, Macedonia, Montenegro, Serbia, and Slovenia. Serbia includes the *autonomous* (self-governing) provinces of Kosovo and Vojvodina. These two provinces have numerous ethnic minorities.

Yugoslavia's many nationality groups have given the country a rich variety of cultures. But differences in religion, language, and customs have also led to bitter disputes among the groups and made unity difficult. Yugo-

slavia has three major religions, three official languages, and two alphabets. But it has only one political party— the Communist Party.

After centuries of separate development, the regions that now make up Yugoslavia were united as an independent kingdom in 1918. In 1945, Yugoslavia became a Communist state under the leadership of Josip Broz Tito. However, the country developed its own form of Communism, independent of control by the Union of Soviet Socialist Republics (U.S.S.R.). Tito was Yugoslavia's top

Facts in brief

Capital: Belgrade.
Official languages: Serbo-Croatian (or Croato-Serbian), Slovenian, and Macedonian.
Official name: *Socijalistička Federativna Republika Jugoslavija* (Socialist Federal Republic of Yugoslavia).
Area: 98,766 sq. mi. (255,804 km²). *Greatest distances*— north-south, 415 mi. (668 km); east-west, 475 mi. (764 km). *Coastline*— 490 mi. (789 km) along the Adriatic Sea.
Elevation: *Highest*—Mount Triglav, 9,393 ft. (2,863 m) above sea level. *Lowest*—sea level.
Population: *Estimated 1990 population*—23,853,000; density, 242 persons per sq. mi. (93 per km²); distribution, 50 per cent rural, 50 per cent urban. *1981 census*—22,424,687. *Estimated 1995 population*—24,577,000.
Chief products: *Agriculture*—cattle, corn, grapes, hogs, potatoes, sugar beets, wheat. *Manufacturing*—automobiles, chemicals, clothing and textiles, food products, machinery, metal products, wood products.
National anthem: "Hej Sloveni" ("Hey Slavs").
Money: *Basic unit*—dinar. See **Money** (table).

Pedro Ramet, the contributor of this article, is Assistant Professor of International Studies at the University of Washington.

Special Report
YUGOSLAVIA
2000 Year Book, p. 434

leader until his death in 1980. He was also a spokesman of the Third World nations—those countries which side with neither the Communist powers nor the Western democracies.

Before the Communists gained control of Yugoslavia, most of the people were poor farmers. But the Communists have encouraged industrial growth and have worked to raise living standards. They developed an unusual system of economic self-management under which the workers themselves run the industries.

Government

Yugoslavia is a federation of socialist republics. The nation's Constitution was adopted in 1946, and it has been revised several times since. All Yugoslav citizens 18 or older may vote for delegates to local assemblies. These delegates, in turn, elect the members of higher legislative bodies. Political activity in Yugoslavia centers in the Socialist Alliance of the Working People of Yugoslavia and the Confederation of Trade Unions. The Communist Party controls both organizations.

The Communist Party is the only political party permitted in Yugoslavia. Its official name is the *League of Communists of Yugoslavia.* About 9 per cent of the Yugoslav people belong to the party. They play a major role at all levels of government. A 23-member Presidium directs the party's operations.

The national government of Yugoslavia is headed by a nine-member council called the *Presidency.* It is the country's chief policymaking body. The council has one representative from each republic and province. The council members take turns serving one-year terms as president of the council and as head of state.

Yugoslavia has a two-house legislature called the *Federal Assembly.* The 88 members of the Chamber of the Republics and Autonomous Provinces are elected by the assemblies of the republics and provinces. The Federal Chamber has 220 delegates. They are chosen by local assemblies. In addition to passing laws for the nation, the Federal Assembly elects the members of the cabinet, called the *Federal Executive Council.* Council members administer the departments of the national

Shostal

Parliament Building houses Yugoslavia's legislature, the Federal Assembly. The building stands in Belgrade, the capital.

Symbols of Yugoslavia. Yugoslavia's flag has stripes of blue, white, and red, the national colors. The red star stands for Communism. The coat of arms has six torches for the nation's six republics. The date is the start of Communist rule in Yugoslavia.

government. The president of the council, called the *premier,* is Yugoslavia's head of government. The Federal Executive Council has the chief responsibility for developing the country's economic plans. The Presidency is more concerned with foreign policy matters.

Republican government. The government of each republic and province is modeled on the federal system. Each has an assembly elected by local legislatures and an executive council chosen by the assembly.

Local government. Yugoslavia's republics and provinces are divided into more than 500 districts called *communes.* Each commune has an assembly and a communal council. Assembly delegates are elected by the residents of cities and towns; by members of social and political organizations; and by workers in individual factories, farms, and other places of work.

Courts. Yugoslavia has civil, criminal, and military courts at each level of government. Special economic courts called *self-management courts* settle disputes between business organizations.

The armed forces of Yugoslavia have about 250,000 men. They serve in the Yugoslav People's Army, which consists of air, ground, and naval forces and frontier guard units. Men are drafted at age 18 for 15 months of military service.

People

Ancestry and population. About 85 per cent of Yugoslavia's people belong to six Slavic nationality groups.

WORLD BOOK map

Yugoslavia is a country in southeastern Europe. It lies along the Adriatic Sea and forms part of the Balkan Peninsula.

Republics

Bosnia and Herce-			
govina	4,116,439	C	3
Croatia	4,578,109	B	2
Mace-			
donia	1,913,571	F	6
Montenegro	583,475	D	5
Serbia	9,278,861	D	6
Slovenia	1,883,764	B	2

Cities and towns†

Aleksinac*	67,104	D	6
Apatin	33,809	B	4
Aranđjel-			
ovac*	46,852	C	5
Bačka			
Palanka	57,803	B	5
Bačka			
Topola*	42,022	B	5
Banja Luka	183,324	C	3
Bar	32,241	E	4
Bečej	44,339	B	5
Belgrade (Beo-			
grad)	1,455,046	C	5
Bihać	65,679	C	2
Bijeljina	92,678	C	5
Bijelo			
Polje*	55,459	D	5
Bitola	138,149	F	6
Bjelovar	66,356	B	3
Bor	64,439	C	6
Brčko	82,912	C	4
Čačak	110,329	C	5
Čakovec*	116,664	A	3
Celje	63,843	A	2
Četinje	20,112	E	4
Čuprija	38,871	C	6
Đakovica	92,091	E	5
Đakovo	50,730	B	4
Derventa	56,583	B	4
Doboj	98,823	C	4
Dubrovnik	65,650	E	4
Foča	44,610	D	4
Gevgelija	31,804	F	7
Gnjilane*	84,196	E	6
Gornji			
Milanovac*	50,320	D	5
Gospić	31,034	C	2
Gostivar	102,057	E	6
Hercegnovi	23,011	E	4
Indija*	43,963	C	5
Ivangrad	49,627	D	5
Jajce	41,176	C	3
Jesenice	30,925	A	1
Kanjiza*	32,529	B	5
Karlovac	78,174	B	2
Kavadarci	39,687	F	7
Kičevo	52,407	F	6
Kikinda	69,566	B	5
Knin	43,503	C	3
Kniaževac*	48,876	C	7
Kočani	48,015	E	7
Konjic	43,861	D	4
Koper	41,887	B	1
Koprivnica	61,034	A	3
Kosovska			
Mitrovica	105,097	D	6
Kovin*	39,909	B	5
Kragujevac	163,945	C	6
Kraljevo	121,530	D	6
Kranj	66,096	A	1
Kruševac	132,605	D	6
Kula	49,732	B	5
Kumanovo	126,468	E	6
Leskovac	158,895	D	6
Livno	40,569	D	3
Ljubljana	303,469	A	1
Loznica	83,733	C	5
Maribor	183,757	A	2
Metković	20,379	D	4
Mladenovac	52,064	C	6
Mostar	109,894	D	4
Negotin	63,690	C	7
Nikšić	72,159	D	4
Niš	229,311	D	6
Nova			
Gorika*	56,599	B	1
Nova			
Gradiška	60,985	B	3
Novi Pazar	73,726	D	5
Novi Sad	257,577	B	5
Novo Mesto	55,072	B	2
Obrenovac*	62,135	B	5
Ogulin	31,012	B	2
Ohrid	64,622	F	6
Opatija	28,926	B	1
Orahovac*	61,048	C	6
Osijek	157,920	B	4
Pančevo	122,499	C	5
Paraćin	64,496	C	6
Peć	111,067	E	5
Pirot	69,393	D	7
Pljevlja	43,245	D	5
Požarevac	81,036	C	6
Priboj	35,184	D	5
Prijedor	108,470	B	3
Prilep	99,710	F	6
Priština	211,156	E	6
Prizren	134,689	E	6
Prokuplje*	55,781	D	6
Pula	77,057	C	1
Rijeka			
(Fiume)	191,504	B	1
Rovinj	18,061	B	1
Ruma	54,955	B	5
Šabac*	119,137	C	5
Sarajevo	447,687	D	4
Šenta	30,460	B	5
Šibenik	79,705	D	2
Šid	37,319	B	5
Sisak	84,138	B	3
Skopje	503,449	E	6
Slavonska			
Požega	71,388	B	4
Slavonski			
Brod	105,923	B	4
Smederevo	106,735	C	6
Smeder-			
evska			
Palanka	60,732	C	5
Sombor	98,919	B	5
Split	235,398	D	2
Srbobran	18,671	B	5
Sremska			
Mitrovica	84,815	B	5
Stara			
Pazova*	52,434	C	5
Štip	46,394	E	7
Struga	57,829	F	6
Strumica	87,273	F	7
Subotica	154,008	A	5
Svetozarevo	76,234	C	6
Tetovo	163,567	E	6
Titograd	132,086	E	5
Titov Veles	64,815	E	6
Titovo			
Užice	76,638	C	5
Travnik	64,134	C	4
Trbovlje	18,734	A	2
Tuzla	121,455	C	4
Uroševac	113,935	E	6
Valjevo	94,371	C	5
Varaždin	90,282	A	3
Velenje	38,455	A	2
Vinkovci	95,009	B	4
Virovitica	47,706	B	3
Vranje	82,218	E	6
Vrbas	45,608	B	5
Vršac	60,599	B	6
Vučitrn*	65,671	E	6
Vukovar	81,197	B	4
Zadar	114,386	C	2
Zagreb	763,293	B	2
Zaječar	76,692	C	7
Zenica	132,464	C	4
Zrenjanin	138,770	B	5

*Does not appear on map; key shows general location.
†Populations are for communes, which may include rural areas as well as the city or town.
Source: 1981 census.

These groups, in order of size, are Serbs, Croats, Bosnian Muslims, Slovenes, Macedonians, and Montenegrins. The chief non-Slavic ethnic groups in Yugoslavia are Albanians and Hungarians. Albanians outnumber both Macedonians and Montenegrins. Other nationalities in the country include Czechs, Germans, Gypsies, Italians, Slovaks, and Turks.

Groups of Slavs began to migrate to the Balkan Peninsula from what are now southern Poland and Russia during the A.D. 500's. Each Slavic group had its own leaders and culture. Relations among the various nationality groups—especially between Serbs and Croats—have always been tense.

Yugoslavia has a population of about 24 million. About 50 per cent of the people live in cities and towns. However, the percentage of urban dwellers is rising as more and more countrypeople move to the cities to seek jobs in industry. About $1\frac{1}{2}$ million people live in Belgrade, the capital and largest city. Zagreb, the next largest city, has about 750,000 people. Other major Yugoslav cities include Skopje, Sarajevo, Ljubljana, Novi Sad, Split, Niš, and Priština.

Languages. Yugoslavia has three official languages and two alphabets. One of the official languages exists in two different forms—Serbo-Croatian and Croato-Serbian. The other languages are Slovenian and Macedonian. All the languages are closely related. Serbo-Croatian is the most common language in Yugoslavia. Serbs, Montenegrins, and most Bosnians speak it. They write it in the Cyrillic alphabet. Croats speak Croato-Serbian, which they write in the Roman alphabet. Slovenian, which is used primarily in Slovenia, is written in Roman letters. Macedonian is used primarily in Macedonia and is written in Cyrillic letters.

Yugoslavia's other nationality groups also have their own languages. The Yugoslav Constitution guarantees citizens the right to use their native language in business, in the courts, and in schools. Many Yugoslavs speak more than one language.

Way of life. Yugoslavs have a higher standard of living than do the people of most other Eastern European countries. Many families own an automobile, a television set, and various other luxury items. Yugoslavs also have greater personal freedom than do the citizens of other Communist nations. For example, Yugoslavs may travel about their country freely. They also may travel abroad and even work in other countries. All citizens receive free medical care, and workers are given a pension on retirement.

Many city dwellers in Yugoslavia live in modern apartment buildings. Numerous others live in older apartments or houses. In most families, both the husband and the wife have a full-time job. Government day-care centers look after preschool children. Yugoslav cities have a severe housing shortage, largely because so many rural people keep moving to them. New apartment buildings are being constructed—but not fast enough to meet the demand.

Many rural families live in small stone or wooden houses. The size and style of the homes vary from region to region. About three-fourths of all rural homes in Yugoslavia have electricity.

In the cities, people wear Western-style clothing. Traditional costumes are more common in rural areas,

Jerry Frank, DPI

Belgrade is Yugoslavia's largest city. Modern buildings line the broad, busy streets of the downtown section.

mostly on holidays. But in Slovenia and Croatia, even countrypeople wear mainly Western-style clothes.

Food and drink. Each region of Yugoslavia has its own special foods. For example, Serbs like grilled meats, particularly a spicy meatball dish called *čevapčiči* (pronounced *cheh VAHP chee chee*). Fish stew and other seafood dishes are popular in the coastal areas. Macedonians eat many lamb dishes. Yugoslavia's national drink is plum brandy, called *šljivovica.* Yugoslavs also like wine and coffee.

Recreation. In the evening, many Yugoslavs take part in an old custom called the *korzo.* They stroll along the main street of their city or town and stop to chat with friends they meet. Coffee houses, called *kafanas,* are popular gathering places throughout Yugoslavia. Many city people enjoy motion pictures, concerts, operas, and stage plays.

Sports events, especially soccer games, draw huge

William Parker

Folk dancers in traditional costumes perform every Sunday in Cilipi, a village near Dubrovnik. Each of Yugoslavia's many nationality groups has preserved its rich folk traditions.

A rural fair in the republic of Serbia attracts people from neighboring villages and towns. Farmers come to the fair to buy and sell livestock and other products.

Richard Wilkie, Black Star

crowds. In winter, many people ski in the mountains of Slovenia and Bosnia. In summer, they enjoy fishing, swimming, and other water sports in the Adriatic Sea and in the country's many mountain lakes.

Religion is important in the lives of most Yugoslavs, but especially rural people. About 40 per cent of all Yugoslavs, including the majority of Macedonians, Montenegrins, and Serbs, belong to Eastern Orthodox churches. About 30 per cent of the people are Roman Catholics. They include most Croats and Slovenes. About 10 per cent of the Yugoslavs are Muslims. Most of them live in Bosnia and Macedonia.

The government tries to reduce the influence of religion in Yugoslavia. But it generally does not interfere with the religious practices of the people. However, religious organizations may not take part in politics.

Education. About 85 per cent of the Yugoslav people can read and write. Education is free. The law requires children from ages 7 through 14 to attend elementary

school. The students are taught in their native language. After completing elementary school, students may enter either a vocational school or a general secondary school. Yugoslavia has about 20 universities. Teachers are expected to support government policies.

The arts. Much of Yugoslavia's art reflects the rich folk traditions of the country's nationality groups. These traditions go back hundreds of years. They have been preserved in colorful costumes, dances, tales, songs, and handicrafts. Many modern Yugoslav writers, composers, and artists use elements of folk traditions in their works.

Until the 1800's, most of the people who lived in what is now Yugoslavia could not read or write. They handed down their culture orally from generation to generation. Religious writings were the only form of literature in most of the area before the 1800's. Then nonreligious literature began to develop. Most writers followed Western European and Russian styles, but many also bor-

Robert Frerck

The Coastal Region of Yugoslavia has many rocky cliffs and steep mountains that rise abruptly from the Adriatic Sea. The walled city shown here is Dubrovnik, which has been a major port for centuries. Dubrovnik is one of Yugoslavia's most popular tourist attractions.

rowed themes from folk stories and songs.

After the Communists came to power in 1945, they strictly controlled what Yugoslav authors could publish. But since the mid-1950's, writers have had greater freedom. Ivo Andrić, the best-known Yugoslav writer of the 1900's, won the 1961 Nobel Prize for literature. Other leading writers of the 1900's, include Ivan Cankar, Dobrica Ćosić, Oskar Davičo, Miroslav Krleža, and Oton Župančič.

Wall paintings decorate many Serbian churches built in the Middle Ages. These paintings are the most important examples of early Yugoslav art. Since the early 1800's, most Yugoslav painters have followed Western European styles. The so-called primitive paintings of untrained peasant artists have gained increasing praise from some art critics.

During the early 1900's, Ivan Meštrović became Yugoslavia's most famous sculptor. His highly patriotic and religious works can be seen in many parts of the world. Large commemorative sculptures stand throughout Yugoslavia. These sculptures memorialize events in the lives of the people of Yugoslavia during World War II (1939-1945).

The land

Yugoslavia occupies 98,766 square miles (255,804 square kilometers) on the Balkan Peninsula. Mountains cover most of the country. Yugoslavia has three main

land regions: (1) the Coastal Region, (2) the Interior Highlands, and (3) the Pannonian Plains.

The Coastal Region is a narrow, rocky strip of land along the Adriatic Sea. The region also includes more than 600 islands. In many areas, steep mountains and cliffs rise abruptly from the sea. The sharply indented coastline provides many excellent natural harbors. The region's beautiful scenery and sunny beaches attract millions of vacationists each year.

The Coastal Region is made up of a type of limestone that dissolves in water over a long period of time. Thus, the area has caves, sinkholes, and underground rivers. Such features are called *karst* landforms, named after an area of the Yugoslav coast. The Coastal Region has rocky cliffs and little fertile soil.

The Interior Highlands rise from the Coastal Region and consist of a number of mountain ranges. The mountain ranges extend from northwestern to southeastern Yugoslavia.

The Julian Alps lie in the northwest corner of the country. Mount Triglav, Yugoslavia's highest peak, rises 9,393 feet (2,863 meters) in this range. The Julian Alps have many ski resorts and are Yugoslavia's winter playground.

The Dinaric Alps parallel the Adriatic coast. Like the Coastal Region, the Dinaric Alps consist mostly of karst and have little fertile land. The area has many caves with fantastic rock formations. The cave at Postojna, near Lju-

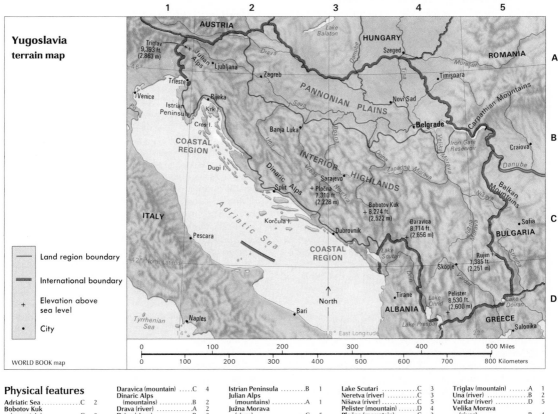

Yugoslavia
terrain map

Land region boundary

International boundary

+ Elevation above sea level

• City

WORLD BOOK map

0	100	200	300	400	500 Miles
0 100	200	300	400	500	600	700	800 Kilometers

Physical features

Adriatic Sea ....C 2	Daravica (mountain) .....C 4	Istrian Peninsula ....B 1	Lake Scutari ....C 3	Triglav (mountain) ....A 1
Bobotov Kuk	Dinaric Alps	Julian Alps	Neretva (river) ....C 3	Una (river) ....B 2
(mountain) ....C 3	(mountains) ....B 2	(mountains) ....A 1	Nišava (river) ....C 5	Vardar (river) ....D 5
Bosna (river) ....B 3	Drava (river) ....A 2	Južna Morava	Pelister (mountain) ....D 4	Velika Morava
Cres Island ....B 1	Drina (river) ....B 3	(river) ....C 5	Pločna (mountain) ....C 3	(river) ....B 4
Danube (river) ....A 3	Dugi Island ....B 2	Korčula Island ....C 2	Rujen (mountain) ....C 5	Vrbas (river) ....B 3
	Iron Gate	Krk Island ....B 2	Sava (river) ....B 3	Zapadna Morava
	Reservoir ....B 4	Lake Ohrid ....D 4	Tisa (river) ....A 4	(river) ....B 4

William Parker

Yugoslav farmers use both modern equipment and farm animals to work their fields. The government limits the size of private farms, which cover about 85 per cent of the farmable land.

bljana, is world famous. In eastern and southeastern Yugoslavia, mountain ranges extend into Romania, Bulgaria, and Greece.

The Interior Highlands are a barrier between the Coastal Region and the Pannonian Plains. In the past, the mountains often helped protect the country from invasion. But they also made communication and transportation difficult within Yugoslavia. Today, many roads and railroads cut through the mountains.

Earthquakes frequently strike the highlands. In 1963, a violent earthquake leveled most of Skopje. In 1979, a major earthquake badly damaged towns and villages in the southern Interior Highlands and caused even more damage in the southern Coastal Region.

The Pannonian Plains lie in north-central Yugoslavia. The region is mostly flat, with some low hills. It has the richest soil in Yugoslavia and is the country's chief agricultural area.

Rivers and lakes. Yugoslavia's most important river is the Danube. It enters the country from Hungary and flows through the Pannonian Plains. It then enters Romania through a gorge called the Iron Gate. The Danube's main tributaries in Yugoslavia are the Drava, Morava, Sava, and Tisa rivers. They serve as shipping routes, and many major cities lie along their banks. Other important Yugoslav rivers include the Bosna, Drina, Neretva, Nišava, and Vardar.

The Interior Highlands are dotted with hundreds of small, beautiful lakes that attract many tourists. Yugoslavia's largest lake, Lake Scutari, extends into Albania. Yugoslavia also shares Lake Ohrid with Albania, Lake Doiran with Greece, and Lake Prespa with both Albania and Greece.

Climate

The Coastal Region has a mild climate. In winter, the temperature rarely falls below freezing along most of the coast. But the northern area is often hit by strong, cold winds that blow in from the mountains. Summers are sunny, hot, and dry.

The Interior Highlands have exceptionally cold winters with much snow. Heavy rains fall in early summer. Summers are warm in the mountain valleys but cool at higher elevations.

The Pannonian Plains have cold winters with a freezing wind called a *košava*. Summers are dry and extremely hot. Temperatures often rise to about 100° F. (38° C). Heavy rains in spring and autumn frequently cause floods along the Danube and its tributaries. These floods sometimes do great damage.

Economy

Since World War II, the Communists have worked to develop Yugoslavia from an agricultural country into an industrial nation. The government introduced economic programs to encourage industrial growth and raise living standards. At first, the programs were developed and carried out by government agencies. But in the 1950's, the government began a system of *self-management*. Under this system, economic planning is done by workers in individual enterprises, such as factories and mines. A workers' council in each enterprise determines production goals, prices, and wages—all based on government guidelines.

Before World War II, agriculture accounted for half the value of all goods and services produced in Yugoslavia. About three-fourths of all workers were farmers. Today, agriculture accounts for about 15 per cent of the country's total production, compared with 50 per cent for industry and 35 per cent for service industries. Agriculture still employs about 30 per cent of all workers. But the number of farm workers is declining steadily as more and more of them seek higher-paying jobs in the cities.

Natural resources. Farmland covers about 58 per cent of Yugoslavia, and forests cover about 35 per cent. Yugoslav mines yield aluminum ore, antimony, coal, copper, iron ore, lead, and magnesium. Petroleum and natural gas are produced from wells in the Pannonian Plains and in the Adriatic Sea.

Power plants that use coal, oil, or natural gas generate more than 50 per cent of Yugoslavia's electric power. Hydroelectric plants provide about 40 per cent. A nuclear power plant near Zagreb generates the rest of the country's electricity.

Industry. Socialist factories produce about 85 per cent of Yugoslavia's industrial output. Privately owned businesses account for the rest. The government limits the size of private businesses.

Most of Yugoslavia's industries are in Slovenia and Croatia. They produce aluminum, automobiles, cement, chemicals, clothing, iron and steel, machinery, metal and wood products, processed foods, and textiles. Factories in the Pannonian Plains produce flour, refined sugar, textiles, and tobacco products. The coastal cities of Rijeka and Split are shipbuilding centers.

Craftworkers in small, privately owned shops make baskets, carpets, woodcarvings, and various other handicraft items. Yugoslavia's handicraft industry has grown rapidly with the increase in the number of foreign tourists. Many of these tourists prize handmade objects that reflect local cultures.

Agriculture. About 85 per cent of Yugoslavia's farmable land is privately owned. The government limits the size of private farms to 25 acres (10 hectares). Large farms are organized into *cooperative* and *state* farms. On cooperative farms, the workers decide what to produce and share the earnings. State farms are owned and operated by the government, and the workers receive a salary. Cooperative and state farms have modern equipment, but many private farmers use primitive methods and tools. As a result, cooperative and state farms account for a higher percentage of the nation's agricultural production, even though they employ only 5 per cent of the agricultural work force.

Yugoslavia's leading farm products include corn, sugar beets, and wheat, which grow chiefly on the Pannonian Plains. Farmers in the Interior Highlands grow barley, oats, and potatoes and raise cattle, hogs, and sheep. Tobacco and grapes, olives, plums, and other fruits are grown in the Coastal Region.

Trade. Yugoslavia's chief trading partners are the Soviet Union, Italy, and West Germany. The country's chief exports include aluminum, clothing and textiles, forest products, furniture, machinery, meat, metal goods, and motor vehicles. Its chief imports include chemicals, crude oil, iron and steel, and nonelectric machinery.

Yugoslavia spends more money on imports than it earns on exports. Income from the foreign tourist business partly makes up for this poor balance of trade. In addition, many Yugoslav citizens who work abroad send money home. Yugoslav cargo ships also bring in money by transporting goods for other countries. The total earnings from these three sources equal the value of Yugoslavia's exports.

Transportation. Yugoslavia has a good road network. The Adriatic Highway, along the coast, is one of Europe's most scenic routes. Yugoslavia has an average of about one automobile for every eight people. Buses carry many passengers throughout the country. Many people have motorcycles or bicycles. Yugoslavia's railway system links the major cities.

The government controls Yugoslavia's airlines. Belgrade and Zagreb have the largest airports. The country's leading seaports include Rijeka, Bar, Dubrovnik, and Split. The Danube River and its tributaries are major shipping routes.

Communication. Yugoslavia publishes about 25 daily newspapers. All of them operate under a *self-management system,* in which the employees have extensive

Shostal
Factory workers in Slovenia assemble parts for electronic equipment. Slovenia leads the other republics in industrial output. But industry is growing rapidly throughout the nation.

decision-making rights. The papers regularly differ among themselves in the opinions they express, and they sometimes criticize government policies. The largest newspapers are *Komunist* and *Večernje Novosti* of Belgrade and *Večernji List* of Zagreb. Many newspapers and magazines are published in local languages.

The government controls radio and television broadcasting. The country has an average of about one television set for every five people. Most families own one or more radios. Owners of radios and television sets pay an annual fee to help finance programs.

History

People have lived in what is now Yugoslavia for at least 100,000 years. The first settlers in recorded history were Illyrians and Thracians, who lived in the area about 3,000 years ago. The Greeks established colonies along the Adriatic Sea coast during the 600's B.C. Celtic tribes moved into the area 100 years later.

The Romans began to invade the Balkan Peninsula during the 300's B.C. By the time of Christ's birth, they had conquered the entire peninsula. In A.D. 395, the Roman Empire was divided into two parts. The West Roman Empire included what are now Croatia, Slovenia, and part of Bosnia. The East Roman, or Byzantine, Empire included what are now Macedonia, Montenegro, and Serbia. That division influenced the region's history to the present time. People in the areas ruled by the Byzantine Empire adopted the Eastern Orthodox faith and the Cyrillic alphabet. People in the other areas became Roman Catholics and used the Roman alphabet.

The Slavs. Groups of Slavs began to move into the Yugoslav area in the 500's. They migrated from what are now southern Poland and the Soviet Union and became known as *southern Slavs.* Each Slavic group formed its own independent state. For example, the Croats established Croatia, and the Serbs founded Serbia. But by 1400, foreign powers controlled nearly all the lands of the southern Slavs. Austria ruled Slovenia, and Hungary ruled Croatia. The Turks controlled Serbia, which included what are now Macedonia and Montenegro. The Turks also ruled Bosnia and Hercegovina. The Venetians controlled the coastal region of Dalmatia, which is now part of Croatia.

The movement for Slavic unity began in the early 1800's. Slovenia and Croatia were united from 1809 to 1815 under the rule of Emperor Napoleon I of France. This brief period of unity inspired the Slovenes and Croats to work for a single, independent nation of all southern Slavs. Serbia, which gained independence from Turkey in 1878, was also interested in such a union. But Austria-Hungary, which ruled Slovenia and Croatia, refused to grant them independence. In addition, the country extended its control of the area by gaining Bosnia and Hercegovina.

During the early 1900's, the movement to unite the southern Slavs became inflamed. On June 28, 1914, Gavrilo Princip, a Serbian patriot from Bosnia, assassinated Archduke Francis Ferdinand of Austria-Hungary in Sarajevo. Austria-Hungary believed that Serbia had planned the killing and declared war on it, which marked the start of World War I. Austria-Hungary was defeated in 1918. The southern Slavs were then free to form their own state.

A new nation called *the Kingdom of the Serbs, Croats, and Slovenes* was formed on Dec. 1, 1918. It consisted of Bosnia and Hercegovina, Croatia, Dalmatia, Montenegro, Serbia, and Slovenia. King Peter I of Serbia became king of the new nation. However, he was old and sick, and so his son Alexander served as regent. Peter died in 1921, and Alexander became king.

Problems soon developed in the kingdom. The Slovenes and Croats believed that the Serbs had too much power in the government. They demanded greater control over their local affairs. In addition, the many nationality groups made unity difficult.

The nation's Constitution, adopted in 1921, provided for a constitutional monarchy. But in 1929, King Alexander abolished the Constitution and began to rule as a dictator. He changed the name of the country to Yugoslavia and tried to unite the nationality groups by enforcing the use of only one language. He also created new political divisions that ignored the groups' historical boundaries. He banned political parties and restricted the press. Alexander's actions only worsened relations between the groups. He was assassinated in 1934 by Croatian terrorists. His 11-year-old son, King Peter II, was too young to rule. Alexander's cousin, Prince Paul, ruled in the boy's place. But Paul carried on Alexander's policies, and the disputes among the groups continued.

World War II began in 1939 as a struggle between the Axis powers, led by Germany and Italy, and the Allies, led by Great Britain and France. Yugoslavia was unprepared for war, and so its government wanted to be friendly with both sides. Under pressure from the Germans, the Yugoslav government joined the Axis on March 25, 1941. But the Yugoslav army rebelled. The army overthrew Paul's government, and 17-year-old Peter took the throne. On April 6, Germany invaded Yugoslavia. The Yugoslav armed forces surrendered 11 days later. Peter and government leaders fled to London and formed a government-in-exile.

German and other Axis troops occupied Yugoslavia. A resistance movement spread among the Yugoslav peo-

Important dates in Yugoslavia

1918 The Kingdom of the Serbs, Croats, and Slovenes was formed, uniting for the first time the regions that now make up Yugoslavia.

1929 King Alexander I changed the name of the country to Yugoslavia and began to rule as a dictator.

1934 Croatian terrorists assassinated Alexander I.

1941 The army overthrew the pro-German Yugoslav government. Germany and other Axis powers invaded Yugoslavia. Josip Broz Tito organized the *Partisans,* a resistance army.

1945 Yugoslavia became a republic under Communist rule and Tito's leadership.

1948 The Soviet Union broke off relations with Yugoslavia.

1955 Yugoslav and Soviet leaders reopened relations.

1974 A nine-member council, the Presidency, was created to provide leadership after Tito's retirement or death.

1980 Tito died.

ple. Some of them joined the *Partisans,* a group led by Josip Broz Tito and the Communist Party. Other Yugoslavs joined the *Chetniks,* a group that was led by Draža Mihailović. The Partisans wanted to establish a Communist government in Yugoslavia. The Chetniks supported the government of King Peter.

The two resistance groups fought each other, as well as the occupation forces. At first, the Allies provided the Chetniks with weapons and supplies. But they switched their support to the Partisans in 1943 because Tito's forces were more effective against the Axis.

Communist rule. The Partisans quickly gained the support of the Yugoslav people. The Communists set up a temporary government in Jajce in November 1943. Aided by Allied troops, the Partisans freed Belgrade from occupation in 1944. The Communists then began to govern from the capital. By the time World War II ended in Europe in May 1945, Tito and the Communists firmly controlled all Yugoslavia.

On Nov. 29, 1945, Yugoslavia became a republic. It was called the Federal People's Republic of Yugoslavia and was organized according to the present-day republics and provinces. The monarchy was abolished, and King Peter never returned to Yugoslavia. Opponents of the Communist government were either imprisoned or exiled. Mihailović was executed in 1946. The archbishop of Zagreb, Aloysius (or Alojzije) Stepinac, a Communist resister, was imprisoned the same year on false charges of having aided the enemies. The government permitted only one political party, the Communist Party, and took control of farms, factories, and other businesses.

Yugoslavia was a close Soviet ally, but Tito refused to let the Soviet Union control the country. In June 1948, Soviet dictator Joseph Stalin broke off relations with Yugoslavia. The Cominform, a group of Communist nations, expelled Yugoslavia and withdrew all aid. Yugoslavia turned to the United States and other Western nations for help. Beginning in 1951, the United States provided Yugoslavia with military and economic aid.

After the split with the Soviet Union, Yugoslavia began to develop its own type of Communist society. Yugoslavia's republics and provinces received greater control over local matters. A system of self-management, under which the workers run the industries in the country, began in about 1950. This approach became the

WORLD BOOK map

The formation of Yugoslavia began with the union of the territories dated 1918. Other territories were added in 1919, 1920, and 1947. The red line shows Yugoslavia's present borders.

basis of the Yugoslav economic system.

However, disagreements arose among Yugoslav Communist leaders. Some of them sided with the Soviet Union in the 1948 split and were imprisoned. Milovan Djilas, a high government official, was expelled from the party in 1954 for his writings, which criticized the Communist system.

In 1955, two years after Stalin's death, Soviet and Yugoslav leaders reopened relations. However, Tito refused to take sides in the Cold War between the Communist nations and the Western democracies. Instead, he became a leading speaker for the uncommitted nations of the world.

Recent developments. In 1971 and 1974, changes in the Yugoslav Constitution gave greater autonomy to the republics. But many Croats want complete independence. Since the 1960's, some Croatian groups have used terrorist methods to publicize their demands. In the early 1970's, several Croatian Communist leaders were expelled from the party for supporting the independence movement.

In 1974, a nine-member council called the *Presidency* was established to head the Yugoslav government. Tito remained the country's top leader as head of the council. The Presidency was formed to provide leadership after Tito's retirement or death. But many Yugoslavs feared a power struggle would then occur and would lead to increased Soviet influence in Yugoslavia. Tito died in May 1980. A system in which the members of the Presidency take turns serving one-year terms as head of the council went into effect. Yugoslavia's leaders continued Tito's independent course in foreign affairs.

The Yugoslav economy has declined since the late 1970's, and the country has experienced severe inflation and other economic problems. Yugoslavia's government has sought to build up the economies of the less developed regions of Kosovo, Macedonia, and Montenegro. But the efforts have failed, and a serious economic gap exists between the country's more developed and less developed regions. In the 1980's, many Yugoslavs took part in demonstrations to protest against government economic policies.

By the mid-1980's, the Yugoslavs were engaged in a wide-ranging debate about the future of their political system. Many people have called for major changes. For example, some seek the right to establish new political parties to oppose the Communist Party and give the voters a choice in elections.   Pedro Ramet

Related articles in *World Book* include:

Biographies

Alexander I	Peter II
Meštrović, Ivan	Stepinac, Aloysius Cardinal
Peter I	Tito, Josip Broz

Cities

Belgrade	Split
Sarajevo	Zagreb

History

Albania (History)	Hungary (History)	World War I
Austria-Hungary	Trieste	World War II
Balkans		

Republics

Bosnia and Hercegovina	Croatia

Macedonia	Serbia
Montenegro	Slovenia

Other related articles

Alps	Danube River
Dalmatia	Slavs

Outline

I. Government

A. The Communist Party	D. Local government
B. The national government	E. Courts
C. Republican government	F. The armed forces

II. People

A. Ancestry and population	E. Recreation
B. Languages	F. Religion
C. Way of life	G. Education
D. Food and drink	H. The arts

III. The land

A. The Coastal Region	C. The Pannonian Plains
B. The Interior Highlands	D. Rivers and lakes

IV. Climate

V. Economy

A. Natural resources	D. Trade
B. Industry	E. Transportation
C. Agriculture	F. Communication

VI. History

Questions

Who were the *Partisans*? The *Chetniks*?

What are the six main nationality groups in Yugoslavia?

What is the *korzo*?

How did the division of the Roman Empire influence Yugoslavia's history?

How does the Yugoslav economic system of self-management operate?

What does the name *Yugoslavia* mean?

What is Yugoslavia's chief agricultural region?

Who became the best-known Yugoslav writer of the 1900's?

What is a *cooperative farm*? A *state farm*?

Additional resources

Doder, Dusko. *The Yugoslavs*. Random House, 1978. Introduction to contemporary Yugoslavia.

Greene, Carol. *Yugoslavia*. Childrens Press, 1984. For younger readers.

Rusinow, Dennison I. *The Yugoslav Experiment, 1948-1974*. Univ. of California Press, 1977.

Singleton, Frederick B. *A Short History of the Yugoslav Peoples*. Cambridge, 1985.

Yukawa, *yoo KAH wah,* **Hideki,** *HEE deh kee* (1907-1981), a Japanese physicist, became famous for his contributions to theoretical nuclear physics. He won the 1949 Nobel Prize for physics. He was the first Japanese so honored. Yukawa received the award for a theory he worked out in 1935. The theory predicted the existence of a subatomic particle called a *meson* (see **Meson**).

Yukawa was born in Tokyo and studied at Kyoto University. He became a lecturer at Kyoto in 1932 and a professor there in 1939. From 1933 to 1936, he was a lecturer in nuclear physics at Osaka University.

Yukawa came to the United States in 1948 to act as a visiting professor and work at the Institute for Advanced Study in Princeton, N.J. He became professor of physics at Columbia University in 1950. In 1953, Yukawa became the first director of the Research Institute for Fundamental Physics at Kyoto University. Yukawa wrote books on advanced physics, but he was better known as an essayist.   R. T. Ellickson

See also **Anderson, Carl David.**

Yukon River, one of the longest rivers in North America, flows through Alaska and the Yukon Territory of Canada. The river rises in Canadian soil, but two-thirds of its course is in Alaska. Its total length, from its mouth on the Bering Sea to its headwaters in British Columbia, is 1,979 miles (3,185 kilometers). This is as far as the distance between Detroit and Los Angeles, or a little farther than the distance between Edmonton and Montreal in Canada. The Yukon drains over 330,000 square miles (855,000 square kilometers). About half of this area lies in Alaska.

The Yukon is navigable for almost its entire length. Before World War II, wood-burning stern-wheelers traveled from its mouth to Dawson in the Yukon Territory. The Yukon was the principal transportation route during the early mining days of Alaska and the famous Klondike Gold Rush. But decreased mining activities and the convenience of air transportation have made shipping by boat unprofitable. Villagers along the river still use boats to transport freight and other necessities. The Yukon is frozen up to seven months of the year. Many of the small tributaries contain gold-bearing gravels. The eastern part has hot springs.

The course of the Yukon. The Yukon River rises from a series of small lakes in northwest British Columbia. It flows northwest and joins the Pelly River at Fort Selkirk. The Yukon continues past Dawson, and crosses the United States-Canada border near Eagle, Alaska. The river continues to flow northwest to Ft. Yukon, where it begins flowing southwest. It then curves and flows northwest to the Bering Sea. The Yukon Valley is divided

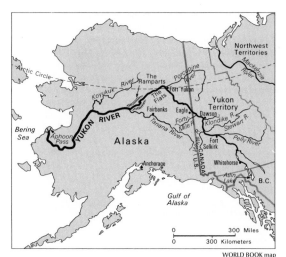

WORLD BOOK map

Location of the Yukon River

into two regions. They are the Upper Yukon and the Lower Yukon.

Upper Yukon. The principal tributaries of the Upper Yukon are the Selwyn, White, Stewart, Klondike, and Forty-Mile rivers. The first important discoveries of gold in this region were made on Forty-Mile Creek in 1895. But these were overshadowed a few years later by the richness of the Klondike field. Dawson, one of the largest settlements on the Upper Yukon, and the capital of the Yukon Territory until 1951, stands where the Klondike and Yukon rivers meet.

After flowing northwest for 450 miles (724 kilometers), the Yukon turns almost at right angles and flows southwest for 200 miles (320 kilometers) through the famous "Flats." These are level areas of sand bars and low islands, covered with spruce, willow, and birch. There the river channel constantly shifts, and at seasons of high water it increases from a normal width of 10 miles (16 kilometers) to more than 40 miles (64 kilometers). The "great bend" of the Yukon is about 3 miles (4.8 kilometers) north of the Arctic Circle.

The "Flats" end at the Ramparts, a gorge that extends 110 miles (177 kilometers) to the mouth of the Tanana River. In this part, the Yukon Valley is 1 to 3 miles (1.6 to 4.8 kilometers) wide. The Tanana, which is the Yukon's largest tributary entirely in Alaska, flows northwest for about 400 miles (640 kilometers), roughly parallel to and about 125 miles (201 kilometers) west of the Upper Yukon.

Lower Yukon. The Ramparts gorge ends at the mouth of the Tanana River. The Yukon River then enters a lowland about 25 miles (40 kilometers) wide. From this point to the sea, 800 miles (1,300 kilometers) away, the river valley is never less than 2 miles (3.2 kilometers) wide.

The Yukon delta covers nearly 9,000 square miles (23,000 square kilometers). The river has more than 20 outlets over 600 feet (180 meters) wide. But most of them are shallow and filled with sand bars. Steamers enter the delta through the Aphoon Pass, which is only 4 feet (1.2 meters) deep at low water.   Lyman E. Allen

Artstreet

A Yukon River cruise takes passengers through Miles Canyon, *above,* in the Yukon Territory of Canada. The river begins in British Columbia and flows across the Yukon Territory and Alaska.

Spectacular mountains and unspoiled wilderness areas make the Yukon Territory a popular spot for tourists. Outdoors enthusiasts enjoy hiking and fishing in the territory.

Yukon Territory, *YOO kahn,* is a region in northwest Canada. It is part of a vast subarctic region, with long, cold winters and short, warm summers. The Yukon Territory is sparsely populated due to its harsh climate and rugged terrain. The territory has rich mineral deposits and magnificent scenery. Many prospectors hurried to the territory during the Klondike Gold Rush in 1897 and 1898. Today, mining remains the most important industry. Tourism and government are also important.

The Yukon is one of Canada's two political units called *territories.* The other is the Northwest Territories. Whitehorse is the Yukon's capital and largest city.

The land and its resources

Location, size, and description. The Yukon Territory covers 186,661 square miles (483,450 square kilometers) in the shape of a rough triangle. The base rests on the border of British Columbia, and the peak on the Arctic Ocean. Alaska lies to the west of the territory, and the Northwest Territories lies to the east.

Ranges of the largest mountain system of North America almost entirely cover the Yukon. The Rockies form part of this system, but spread out into smaller chains in the southeast, near the Liard River. The highest peaks rise in the Saint Elias Mountains in the southwest. Mount Logan (19,524 feet, or 5,951 meters), in this range, is the highest point in Canada.

The territory derives its name from the Yukon River. The word *Yukon* probably had its origin in the Indian word *Youcon (greatest* or *big river).* The Yukon River drains more than half of the territory. Most of the rest is drained into the Mackenzie River through the Peel and Liard river systems.

Natural resources. The territory has large deposits of asbestos, coal, copper, gold, lead, nickel, silver, and zinc. Valuable forests of white spruce cover much of the land. Other trees include birch, fir, pine, and poplar.

Varieties of numerous fur-bearing animals live in the Yukon Territory. Animals of the region include bear, caribou, Dall (white) sheep, elk, moose, and mountain goats. Among the game birds are grouse, ptarmigan, and waterfowl. Rare gyrfalcons and peregrine falcons also live in the Yukon Territory. Grayling, northern pike, lake and rainbow trout, salmon, and whitefish swim in the territory's streams and lakes.

Climate. The territory's temperatures vary greatly. Average January temperatures are 5° F. (−15° C) at Whitehorse and −16° F. (−27° C) at Dawson. The coldest temperature ever recorded in North America was −81° F. (−63° C), at Snag Airport near the Alaska border on Feb. 3, 1947. Summer temperatures average from 50° F. (10° C) in the north to 60° F. (16° C) in the south. The territory's record high temperature, 95° F. (35° C), occurred in Dawson and Mayo on June 18, 1950. Annual snowfall varies from 40 inches (100 centimeters) in the north to more

Facts in brief

Capital: Whitehorse.

Government: *National*—members of the Senate, 1; members of the House of Commons, 1. *Territorial*—members of the legislative assembly, 16.

Area: 186,661 sq. mi. (483,450 km²), including 1,730 sq. mi. (4,481 km²) of inland water. *Greatest distances*— north-south, 666 mi. (1,072 km); east-west, 600 mi. (966 km).

Elevation: *Highest*—Mount Logan in the Saint Elias Mountains, 19,524 ft. (5,951 m) above sea level. *Lowest*—sea level, along the Beaufort Sea.

Population: *1986 census*—23,504; distribution, 64 per cent urban, 36 per cent rural; density, 13 persons per 100 sq. mi. (5 per 100 km²).

Chief products: *Fishing industry*—salmon, whitefish. *Fur industry*—beaver, lynx, marten, muskrat, wolverine. *Manufacturing*—lumber and wood products; printed materials; food products, clothing. *Mining*—zinc, gold, lead, silver. *Forestry*—logs and bolts.

Yukon Territory

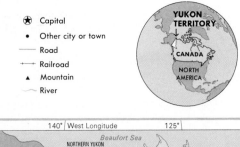

⊛	Capital
●	Other city or town
—	Road
+—+	Railroad
▲	Mountain
～	River

WORLD BOOK map

than twice as much in the south. Rainfall averages from 9 to 13 inches (23 to 33 centimeters) per year.

The people and their work

The 1986 census reported that the Yukon Territory had 23,504 people. Most Yukoners work for the territorial or federal government, or in other service industries such as tourism, transportation, and communication. Manufacturing, mining, fur trapping, fishing, and agriculture also provide jobs.

The people. Most of the people of the Yukon Territory are white, but the population also includes about 3,400 Indians. Almost all the people speak English. French is the native language of about 600 Yukoners. Tlingit, an Indian language, is spoken in some villages.

About two-thirds of the territory's people live in Whitehorse (pop. 15,199), the capital. Other Yukon communities and their populations include Dawson (896), Watson Lake (826), Faro (400), Ross River (352), and Haines Junction (340).

The people of the Yukon Territory must wear warm clothing in winter to protect themselves from the cold. Most people live in modern houses. Electricity, oil, and wood are used to heat houses. The burning of wood has caused air pollution problems in some suburbs of Whitehorse. Daily airline and trucking services bring perishable foods and other goods to the territory.

Mining is the leading economic activity. The territory's mining industry is based almost entirely on the production of metal ores. The value of Yukon mineral production often varies greatly from year to year because the price of metal ores is unstable. For example, in 1985, when metal prices were low, many Yukon mines were closed and total mineral production was valued at only about $60 million. But in 1986, metal prices rose and many mines reopened, causing the value of mineral production to rise to about $180 million.

Gold and zinc provide the most income for the Yukon's mining industry. Gold is found in the Klondike

Tourism Yukon

Whitehorse is the capital and largest city of the Yukon Territory. It lies on the Yukon River, near mountainous land that is rich in minerals. The city is also the distribution and communication center of the Yukon Territory.

River area. Zinc comes from a big mine near Faro. This mine also produces lead. Silver is mined near Keno Hill.

Tourism ranks as the second largest source of income in the Yukon Territory. It provides an annual income of about $80 million. Every year, more than 400,000 people travel across the Yukon on the Alaska Highway. The Yukon section is regarded by many to be the most scenic part of the highway. Tourists also visit the Yukon to see the scenes of the Klondike Gold Rush. Dawson has preserved many landmarks of that era.

Many visitors to the Yukon Territory have read the works of Robert William Service, who wrote his first famous poems in Whitehorse. Tourist attractions in Whitehorse include the MacBride Museum and the S.S. *Klondike,* an old Yukon paddlewheeler. Kluane National Park lies in southwestern Yukon. Northern Yukon National Park lies at the northern tip of the territory.

Manufacturing. The Yukon has several small manufacturing industries. Goods manufactured there have a *value added by manufacture* of about $3 million a year. This figure represents the increase in value of raw materials after they become finished products. Plants in Whitehorse refinish furniture, produce soft drinks, and make lenses for glasses. Indian style winter coats called *Yukon parkas* are also made in Whitehorse. Whitehorse also has several printing companies. Other industries in the Yukon make chemicals, jewelry, and such wood products as canoes, dogsleds, and snowshoes.

Fur industry. Fur trapping provides an annual income of about $1 million. The chief animals trapped are beavers, lynxes, martens, muskrats, and wolverines.

Fishing industry. A small amount of commercial fishing takes place on the Yukon River for chum and coho salmon. Whitefish and trout are caught in Lake Laberge and Teslin Lake.

Agriculture. Because of the short summer, agriculture is of little importance, except for the production of quick-growing vegetables. Excellent vegetables can be grown in greenhouses during the long hours of sun in the spring and summer.

Transportation and communication. Three airlines connect the Yukon Territory with Alaska, Alberta, British Columbia, and the Northwest Territories. The Alaska Highway extends for about 600 miles (970 kilometers) through the Yukon. The 450-mile (725-kilometer) Dempster Highway connects the Yukon with Inuvik in the Northwest Territories. Bus service provides connections to cities in Alaska, Alberta, and British Columbia. The White Pass & Yukon Route railway links Whitehorse with Skagway, Alaska.

The Canadian Broadcasting Corporation (CBC) has a radio station at Whitehorse. Automatic relays transmit its programs to the entire territory. A private radio station also serves Whitehorse. Live CBC television service reaches nearly all Yukon communities via communications satellite. Many communities also have cable television. Telephone and telegraph service are provided in most of the territory. Newspapers are published in Dawson, Haines Junction, and Whitehorse.

Education and social services

Education. The territorial government maintains public elementary schools (grades 1 through 7) at the population centers. There are public high schools (grades 8 through 12) in Carmacks, Dawson, Haines Junction, Mayo, Teslin, Watson Lake, and Whitehorse. Yukon College, in Whitehorse, is the only school of higher education. It was established in 1983.

Social services. Resident doctors live in Dawson, Elsa, Faro, Mayo, Watson Lake, and Whitehorse. Resident dentists have offices in Whitehorse and visit other settlements periodically. Dawson, Mayo, Watson Lake, and Whitehorse have hospitals. Other settlements are served by nursing stations.

Government

The Canadian government appoints a commissioner for the Yukon Territory. The commissioner's duties are similar to those of a provincial lieutenant governor. An official called the government leader is the actual head of the territorial government. The government leader is a member of the territory's 16-member elected Legislative Assembly and the leader of the majority political party. The assembly is the territory's lawmaking body. The government leader presides over an executive

Symbols of the Yukon Territory

The territorial flag

The territorial coat of arms

The floral emblem
Fireweed

On the coat of arms, the cross of St. George represents English explorers of the Yukon. The circle at the center of the cross symbolizes the fur trade. The red triangles with gold circles represent the Yukon's mineral-rich mountains. The wavy stripes represent its rivers. The malamute dog was important in Yukon history. The coat of arms was adopted in 1956, the territorial flag in 1967.

council, whose members direct the departments of the government. The territorial government deals with such local matters as education, public works, social services, and taxation. The people elect one representative to the Canadian House of Commons. The territory is also represented by one member in the Canadian Senate.

History

Indians have lived in the Yukon area since prehistoric times. In the 1840's, Robert Campbell, a British fur trader of the Hudson's Bay Company, became the first white person to explore the Yukon region. Campbell built a trading post on the Pelly River at Fort Selkirk in 1848. But Chilkat Indians looted and burned the post a short time later. The Yukon area was a part of the company's fur-trading empire until 1870, when the company began moving its operations to the Northwest Territories. The Yukon was made a district of the Northwest Territories in 1895. In 1898, it became a separate territory.

On Aug. 17, 1896, George W. Carmack and his Indian friends Skookum Jim and Tagish Charlie made a gold strike on Bonanza Creek. This led to the Klondike Gold Rush of 1897 and 1898. The creek is a tributary of the Klondike River, near the present site of Dawson. Thousands of prospectors poured into the Yukon when news of the rich discovery reached the rest of the world. Simple methods of hand mining produced $22,275,000 worth of gold in 1900. A fleet of gold dredges soon began digging gold. Dredges still dig gold from the rich deposits.

The miners in the Yukon were often rough and unruly. At the beginning of the gold rush, a detachment of the North-West Mounted Police entered the region to preserve order. The influx of prospectors increased the Yukon's political importance. In 1898, the Yukon became a territory, and Dawson became the capital.

At the height of the Klondike Gold Rush in 1898, an

Brown Bros.

Rugged miners packed their belongings in sleds and hurried to the gold fields during the Klondike Gold Rush in 1897.

estimated 35,000 people lived in the Yukon Territory. Records show that 7,080 boats passed down the Yukon River in 1898, carrying 28,000 people. About 5,000 people came by other routes.

After much of the surface ore had been exhausted by simple hand-mining methods, many prospectors sold their claims and drifted away from the Klondike area. Whitehorse had railroad service. Because of this, it became the distributing point for the entire territory, and grew more rapidly than Dawson. Whitehorse became the capital in 1951.

In 1979, the federal government transferred authority over a number of local matters from the commissioner to the elected council. These areas included education and taxation.   Patricia M. Living

Related articles in *World Book* include:

Alaska Highway	Service, Robert W.
Klondike	Whitehorse
Mount Logan	Yukon River

Yule is another word for Christmas. *Yuletide* means the Christmas season. The origin of the word *Yule* has not been established, but it probably goes back to a pre-Christian harvest festival held in November. Germanic tribes called Goths used the word *qiul* or *hiul* for *wheel.* Some scholars suggest that yule refers to the annual revolution, or wheel, of the sun. When Roman Christian culture advanced northward, the customs of the harvest festival became part of Christmas.

The burning of the Yule log was a popular custom that survived into Christmas times. On Christmas Eve, a huge log, often an oak, was brought in and lit with much celebrating. A torch from the previous year's log was used to light the new fire. Each night until the feast of Twelfth Night, the log would be burned for a while. The ashes and charcoal were used during the year to ward off evil and even to cure cattle diseases.   Robert J. Myers

Yuma, *YOO muh* (pop. 42,481), is a commercial center in southwestern Arizona. It lies on the Colorado River, near the place where Arizona, California, and Mexico meet (see **Arizona** [political map]).

Yuma has a hot, dry climate that once made farming in the area difficult. But irrigation systems built since the early 1900's have turned the desert that once surrounded the city into rich farmland. The area's major crops include alfalfa, citrus fruits, cotton, lettuce, and wheat. A U.S. Marine Corps air station and the Yuma Proving Ground—a U.S. Army testing area—are near Yuma. Agriculture, government and military agencies, and tourism each provide many jobs for Yuma's people.

Yuma was founded in 1854 at a popular spot for crossing the Colorado River. It was originally called Colorado City and, later, Arizona City. In 1873, it was renamed Yuma, after the Yuma Indians. In the late 1800's, Yuma served as a shipping center for goods entering Arizona by way of the Colorado River. From 1876 to 1909, it was the site of the Arizona Territorial Prison. The prison buildings still stand in Yuma, and the grounds now serve as a state historical park.

Yuma is the seat of Yuma County. It has a council-manager form of government. For the monthly weather, see **Arizona** (Climate).   Cathy Carrithers Richardson

Yurt. See **Mongolia** (The people; picture: On the Mongolian plains).

YWCA. See **Young Women's Christian Association.**

Zz

Z is the 26th and last letter in our alphabet. Historians believe that it came from a symbol used by the Semites, who once lived in Syria and Palestine. They named it *zayin* and adapted an Egyptian *hieroglyphic,* or picture symbol, for an arrowlike object. The Greeks later made the symbol the sixth letter of their alphabet, and called it *zeta.* They gave it the capital *Z* form that we use. The Romans used *z* only when writing words borrowed from Greek, and moved the letter to the end of their alphabet. In Canada and Great Britain, *z* is called *zed.* In some English dialects it is called *izzard.* See **Alphabet.**

Uses. *Z* or *z* is the letter least frequently used in books, newspapers, and other printed material in English. *Z* is often used to denote the last of anything, as in the phrase "from A to Z." *Z* is used to denote *atomic number* in chemistry and *zenith distance* in astronomy. *Zone* and *zero* are also represented by *z.*

Pronunciation. In English, a person pronounces the normal consonant *z* sound, as in *zone,* by placing the tongue blade near the edges of the upper front teeth, with a narrow chink left over the tip. The velum, or soft palate, is closed, and breath is expelled through the chink and against the front teeth. The vocal cords vibrate. The letter *z* may also have a *zh* sound in English as in *azure* or *glazier.* In German, *z* has a *ts* sound. In most of the other European languages, *z* sounds are like those in the English language. See **Pronunciation.**

Marianne Cooley

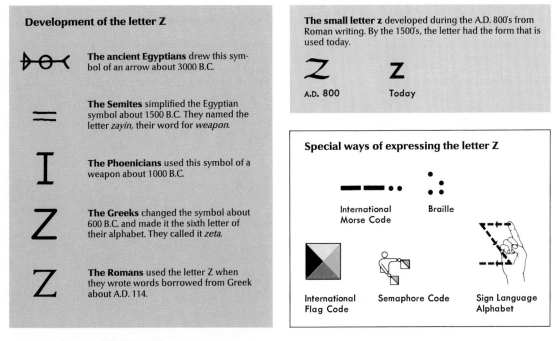

Development of the letter Z

The ancient Egyptians drew this symbol of an arrow about 3000 B.C.

The Semites simplified the Egyptian symbol about 1500 B.C. They named the letter *zayin,* their word for *weapon.*

The Phoenicians used this symbol of a weapon about 1000 B.C.

The Greeks changed the symbol about 600 B.C. and made it the sixth letter of their alphabet. They called it *zeta.*

The Romans used the letter Z when they wrote words borrowed from Greek about A.D. 114.

The **small letter z** developed during the A.D. 800's from Roman writing. By the 1500's, the letter had the form that is used today.

A.D. 800   Today

Special ways of expressing the letter Z

International Morse Code

Braille

International Flag Code

Semaphore Code

Sign Language Alphabet

Common forms of the letter Z

Handwritten letters vary from person to person. *Manuscript* (printed) letters, *left,* have simple curves and straight lines. Cursive letters, *right,* have flowing lines.

Roman letters have small finishing strokes called *serifs* that extend from the main strokes. The type face shown above is Baskerville. The italic form appears at the right.

Sans-serif letters are also called *gothic letters.* They have no serifs. The type face shown above is called Futura. The italic form of Futura appears at the right.

Computer letters have special shapes. Computers can "read" these letters either optically or by means of the magnetic ink with which the letters may be printed.

Zagreb, *ZAH grehb* (pop. 763,293), is the second largest city in Yugoslavia and a major trade and industrial center. Only Belgrade, the nation's capital, is larger. Zagreb is the capital of Croatia, one of Yugoslavia's six republics. It stands on the Sava River, about 230 miles (370 kilometers) northwest of Belgrade. For location, see **Yugoslavia** (political map). Industries in the city manufacture leather, machinery, paper, and textiles.

Zagreb is one of Yugoslavia's most important centers of culture. The city has art galleries, museums, and theaters. It is also the home of Zagreb University.

A Slavic tribe settled an area in present-day Zagreb in the A.D. 600's. A religious community was founded nearby in 1094. In 1557, the two towns merged into one city, called Zagreb.   Alvin Z. Rubinstein

Zagros Mountains. See Iran (The mountains).

Zaharias, *zuh HAIR ee uhs,* **Babe Didrikson,** *DIHD rihk suhn* (1911?-1956), is generally considered the greatest woman athlete in sports history. She gained her most enduring fame in golf and track and field, but she also competed in basketball, baseball, pocket billiards, tennis, diving, and swimming. In a 1932 track and field meet, she set four world records in three hours. At the 1932 Olympic Games, she set world records in the 80-meter hurdles, the javelin throw, and the high jump.

Didrikson began concentrating on golf in the early 1930's. Her style of play dramatically changed women's golf. Her powerful swing, low scores, and showmanship attracted many new fans to women's golf. Didrikson won the U.S. Women's Amateur tournament in 1946. In 1946 and 1947, she won 17 tournaments in a row, including the 1947 British Women's Amateur tournament. She became the first American to win this event. Didrikson turned professional in 1947. She was one of the founders of the Ladies Professional Golf Association (LPGA). She won the U.S. Women's Open in 1948, 1950, and 1954. The 1954 victory came a year after she had cancer surgery.

Wide World
Babe Didrikson

Mildred Ella Didrikson was born in Port Arthur, Tex. She was nicknamed Babe after baseball slugger Babe Ruth because of the many home runs she hit playing baseball as a child. She married George Zaharias, a wrestler, in 1938.   Marino A. Parascenzo

Additional resources

Johnson, William O., and Williamson, N. P. *Whatta-gal! The Babe Didrikson Story.* Little, Brown, 1977.
Knudson, R. Rozanne. *Babe Didrikson: Athlete of the Century.* Viking, 1985. For younger readers.
Zaharias, Mildred D. *This Life I've Led: My Autobiography.* Dell, 1975. First published in 1955.

Zaire, *zah IHR,* is a large country in the heart of Africa. A narrow strip of Zaire borders the Atlantic Ocean. But most of the country lies deep in the interior of Africa, slightly south of the center of the continent. The equator runs through northern Zaire.

One of the world's largest and thickest tropical rain forests covers about a third of Zaire. The mighty Congo River (called the Zaire River in Zaire) flows through the forest and is one of the country's chief means of transportation. Many kinds of wild animals live in Zaire.

The vast majority of Zaire's people are black Africans. Most of the people live in small rural villages and farm the land for a living. But each year, many villagers move to Zaire's cities, and so the cities are growing rapidly. Kinshasa is Zaire's capital and largest city.

Belgians ruled Zaire from 1885 until it became an independent nation in 1960. The nation was called Congo until 1971, when it took its present name. Europeans greatly influenced Zaire's economic and cultural life at the time of independence. In addition, deep divisions existed among Zaire's people, and the country faced severe economic problems. Since independence, Zaire's leaders have worked to reduce European influence, unite the people, and improve the economy.

Government

Zaire's Constitution provides for a presidential form of government. It gives the nation's president almost complete control over the government.

National government. The president makes all major policy decisions in Zaire and also appoints the officials who operate the government. The president is elected by the people to a five-year term. By law, the president may serve only two terms. But Mobutu Sese Seko, who has been president since 1965, is allowed by a special provision to serve an unlimited number.

The *Mouvement Populaire de la Révolution* (Popular Movement of the Revolution) is Zaire's only political party. Commonly called the MPR, it supports and promotes the president's policies. All citizens belong to the party. Citizens may not openly criticize the government. Instead, they must privately pass their criticisms on to MPR officials. Zaire's president heads the MPR.

Jacques Jangoux
Zaire is a country in the heart of Africa. Many of its rural areas lack good roads and bridges. The children above use boats to cross a swampy area in order to get to school.

About 20 executive departments direct the operations of Zaire's national government. A commissioner appointed by the president heads each department. Zaire's legislature, called the National Legislative Council, meets for a few weeks each year to debate details of the government's budget and to pass laws proposed by the president. The council has 310 members. MPR leaders choose all candidates for council seats. The people elect the council members to five-year terms.

Local government. Zaire is divided into eight regions, plus the separate district of Kinshasa, for purposes of local government. The regions are divided into about 30 subregions, and the subregions into about 150 zones. An administrator governs each of these local government units. All the administrators are appointed by the president. Zaire's zones are divided into hundreds of smaller units called collectivities, in which tribal chiefs are responsible for maintaining order.

Courts. The Supreme Court is Zaire's highest court. It hears appeals from lower courts. The president appoints its members. Zaire also has three other appeals courts and a variety of lower courts.

Armed forces. Zaire's military forces include about 50,000 members. Military service is voluntary.

People

Population and ancestry. Zaire has a population of about 35,330,000. About 60 per cent of its people live in rural areas, and about 40 per cent live in urban areas. Kinshasa, the country's largest city, has about $2\frac{1}{4}$ million people.

More than 99 per cent of Zaire's people are black Africans. Most of them are descendants of people who began moving to the area from other parts of Africa at least 2,000 years ago. At that time, other black Africans, including Pygmies, lived in what is now Zaire. The Pygmies, known for their small size, number about 50,000 in Zaire today (see **Pygmies**). About a million black African refugees—chiefly from Angola, Burundi, and Rwanda—live in Zaire. The population also includes about 50,000 Europeans, mostly Belgians.

Zaire's people belong to many different ethnic groups. At times, conflicts between groups have flared up. Since 1965, Zaire's government has made progress toward overcoming ethnic divisions and giving the people a sense of national unity.

Facts in brief

Capital: Kinshasa.
Official language: French.
Area: 905,365 sq. mi. (2,344,885 km²). *Greatest distances*— north-south, about 1,300 mi. (2,090 km); east-west, about 1,300 mi. (2,090 km). *Coastline*—25 mi. (40 km).
Elevation: *Highest*—Margherita Peak, 16,762 ft. (5,109 m) above sea level. *Lowest*—sea level along the coast.
Population: *Estimated 1990 population*—35,330,000; density, 39 persons per sq. mi. (15 per km²); distribution, 60 per cent rural, 40 per cent urban. *1984 census*—29,671,407. *Estimated 1995 population*—41,156,000.
Chief products: *Agriculture and forestry*—bananas, cassava, cocoa, coffee, cotton, corn, palm oil, peanuts, rice, rubber, tea, timber. *Manufacturing*—beer, cement, processed foods, soft drinks, steel, textiles, tires. *Mining*—cadmium, cobalt, copper, gold, industrial diamonds, manganese, oil, silver, tin, zinc.
Money: *Basic unit*—zaire. See **Money** (table: Exchange rates).

Editorial Photocolor Archives, Inc.

Kinshasa is the capital, largest city, and main business center of Zaire. It has many wide boulevards and tall, modern buildings.

Zaire's flag was adopted in 1971. The torch stands for progress and honors those who died in Zaire's conflicts.

The coat of arms, adopted in 1971, bears a leopard's head and the French words for justice, peace, and work.

WORLD BOOK map

Zaire is a large country that lies near the center of Africa. The equator runs through the northern part of the country.

Languages. Most of Zaire's ethnic groups have their own local language. About 200 local languages are spoken in the country. Most of them belong to the Bantu language group and are closely related (see **Bantu**).

Most Zairians also speak at least one of the country's four regional languages—Kikongo, Lingala, Swahili, and Tshiluba. French is Zaire's official language. Government officials often use French in their work, and many students learn it in school.

Way of life. Most rural Zairians live in small villages that range in size from a few dozen to a few hundred people. The vast majority of village families farm a small plot of land. They raise almost all their own food, including cassava, corn, and rice. Some rural people also

catch fish. Few families can afford farm machinery, and so most use hand tools. As a result, farm production is low, and most farm families are poor.

Since 1960, large numbers of Zairians—especially young people—have moved from rural areas to cities. They have been attracted to the cities by the opportunity for jobs in business, industry, and government. The rapid growth of cities has led to such problems as unemployment and crowded living conditions. Also, many people who have jobs earn low wages and find it difficult to support themselves and their families.

During Belgian rule, few Zairian women received more than a few years of education or held a job outside the home. Since independence, the government

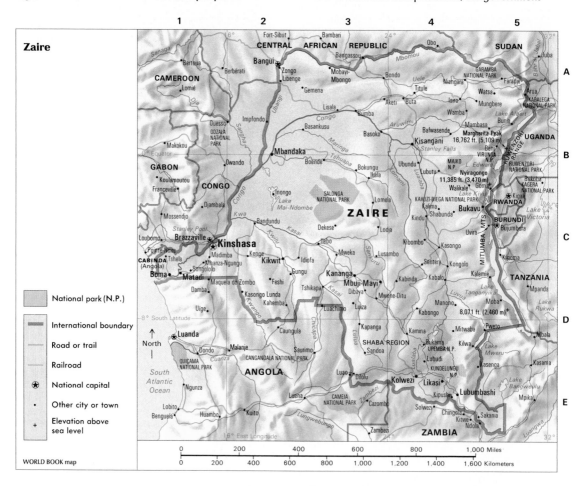

Cities and towns

Aketi	22,963	A 3
Bandundu	55,967	C 2
Basankusu	18,039	B 2
Basoko	20,947	B 3
Beni	36,978	B 5
Boende	12,791	B 3
Boma	210,784	D 1
Bondo	11,925	A 3
Bukama	16,493	D 4
Bukavu	158,920	C 5
Bumba	75,156	B 3
Bunia	57,876	B 5
Buta	38,378	A 4
Dibaya	24,916	D 3
Dilolo	8,974	E 3
Faradje	11,086	A 5
Gemena	73,234	A 2
Goma	87,550	B 5

Source: 1984 official estimates.

Gungu	12,170	C 2
Idiofa	26,180	C 2
Ikela	8,173	B 3
Ilebo	72,803	C 3
Inongo	18,641	C 2
Isiro	111,193	A 4
Kabalo	25,025	D 4
Kabinda	72,360	D 4
Kahemba	7,135	D 2
Kalemie	65,476	D 5
Kalima	45,156	C 4
Kamina	111,069	D 4
Kananga	460,091	D 3
Kasenga	17,977	E 5
Kasongo	30,339	C 4
Kenge	19,740	C 2
Kikwit	150,677	C 2
Kindu	72,708	C 4
Kinshasa	2,222,981	C 1

Kipushi	38,417	E 4
Kisangani	316,310	B 4
Kolwezi	223,524	E 4
Kongolo	28,550	C 4
Libenge	15,168	A 2
Likasi	208,299	E 4
Lisala	61,396	B 3
Lodja	26,215	C 3
Lomela	6,627	C 3
Lubumbashi	596,297	E 4
Lubutu	6,084	B 4
Luiza	10,156	D 3
Lusambo	16,628	C 3
Manono	51,755	D 4
Matadi	177,357	D 1
Mbandaka	180,298	B 2

Mbanza-Ngungu	54,505	C 1
Mbuji-Mayi	391,845	D 3
Moba	21,217	D 5
Mwene-Ditu	105,549	D 3
Niangara	15,453	A 4
Pweto	13,789	D 5
Sandoa	6,562	D 3
Shabunda	12,755	C 4
Songololo	7,963	C 1
Tshela	20,517	C 1
Tshikapa	107,394	D 3
Ubundu	7,642	B 4
Uvira	76,451	C 5
Wamba	17,461	B 4
Watsa	26,119	A 5
Zongo	21,046	A 2

Physical features

Aruwimi (River)		B 4
Congo (River)		C 2
Kasai (River)		D 3
Lake Albert		B 5
Lake Edward		B 5
Lake Kivu		C 5
Lake Mai-Ndombe		C 2
Lake Mweru		D 5
Lake Tanganyika		D 5
Lomami (River)		C 4
Lualaba (River)		E 4
Margherita Peak		B 5
Mitumba Mountains		C 5
Nyiragongo (volcano)		B 5
Shaba Region		D 4
Stanley Falls		B 4
Ubangi (River)		B 2

Harrison Forman

Small rural villages dot Zaire's countryside. Most of the village families farm a small plot of land for a living. They live in small houses with thatched roofs, like the one above.

Christian Vioujard, Gamma/Liaison

Zaire's cities are growing at a rapid rate. City people often shop in outdoor marketplaces. The busy marketplace shown above is in Goma, a city in eastern Zaire.

has increased educational and job opportunities for women.

Housing. Most rural Zairians live in houses made from mud bricks or dried mud and sticks. The majority of the houses have thatched roofs. The houses of some well-to-do rural families have metal roofs.

In Zaire's cities, important government officials, business managers, and merchants—as well as many Europeans—live in attractive bungalows. But large numbers of factory and office workers live in crowded areas of small, cheap houses and apartments made from cinder blocks or baked mud bricks.

Clothing. Zaire's government discourages people from wearing Western-style clothing as part of its program to reduce European influence. Since independence, most Zairian men who hold important jobs have adopted a kind of "national costume." They wear trousers with a matching collarless jacket that buttons at the neck. No shirt or tie is worn with this costume. Most male workers and farmers wear long or short trousers with a shirt. Zairian women usually wear a long, one-piece dress of cotton cloth or a blouse and long skirt.

Food and drink. Corn, rice, and *manioc meal*—which is made from cassava—are the basic foods of most of the people. Zairians serve these foods mostly as a thick porridge flavored with a spicy sauce. They add fish or meat to the porridge when they can afford to do so. Beer is a popular beverage among adults. The diet of many Zairians lacks important nutrients, especially protein. Thus, many people suffer from malnutrition.

Recreation. Rural Zairians enjoy social gatherings that feature drum music and dancing. Many city people spend much leisure time in barrooms. There, they dance and listen to Zairian jazz provided by a phonograph or small band. Soccer ranks as the country's most popular spectator sport. Large crowds attend Sunday afternoon soccer matches in Zaire's main cities.

Religion. More than three-fourths of all Zairians are Christians. Roman Catholics make up the largest Chris-

tian group, followed by Protestants and *Kimbanguists*. Kimbanguists are members of an independent Christian church called the Church of Jesus Christ on Earth. Other Zairians are Muslims or practice local African religions.

Education. Zairian law requires children from 6 to 12 years old to attend school. But many areas lack enough schools, and the law is not strictly enforced. Most parents value education as a key to a better life for their children. The percentage of children who attend elementary school has risen from about 65 per cent in 1960 to about 75 per cent today. In the same period, secondary school enrollment has risen from approximately 1 per cent to 50 per cent. A secondary school student must pass a nationwide examination to receive a diploma. Schools in Zaire's remote rural areas are poorly equipped compared with those in other parts of Zaire. Many students from those areas fail the exam.

Zaire has three major universities, at Kinshasa, Kisangani, and Lubumbashi, and has several other specialized institutes of higher education. Since independence, the number of Zairian university students has increased from a few hundred to about 13,000.

The arts. Carved wooden statues and masks are the best-known Zairian works of art. Art critics praise such works for their delicate form and balance and rich symbolism. Music is also a major art in Zaire. The rhythm of drums dominates Zairian music. Urban Zairians have developed their own form of jazz, which blends elements of modern jazz and traditional Zairian music.

Land and climate

Zaire covers 905,365 square miles (2,344,885 square kilometers). Among Africa's countries, only Sudan and Algeria are larger than Zaire. Zaire's land includes three distinct kinds of regions: (1) a tropical rain forest, (2) savannas, and (3) a highland.

The tropical rain forest covers most of the northern part of Zaire. It is one of the world's largest and thickest rain forests and has an extraordinary variety of trees and

Jacques Jangoux

Zaire's tropical rain forest is an area of thick vegetation. Its weather is hot and humid throughout the year. Because of the weather and lack of open space, few people live in the forest.

other plants. The forest is so thick that sunlight seldom reaches parts of its floor. The equator runs through the rain forest, and the area has hot, humid weather all year. Daytime temperatures average about 90° F. (32° C). Annual rainfall often totals 80 inches (203 centimeters) or more. Much of it falls in heavy thunderstorms.

Savannas. A savanna covers much of southern Zaire. Another savanna covers a strip of land north of the rain forest. The savannas are chiefly grasslands, and a variety of grasses grow there. Small groups of trees are scattered throughout the savannas, and forests grow in some valleys. Daytime temperatures in the savannas average about 75° F. (24° C). The savannas receive little or no rain for several months each year. Annual rainfall averages about 37 inches (94 centimeters).

The highland is an area of plateaus and mountains along Zaire's eastern and southeastern borders. Plant life varies with the elevation. Margherita Peak, the highest point in Zaire, rises 16,762 feet (5,109 meters) there. Daytime temperatures average about 70° F. (21° C). Annual rainfall totals about 48 inches (122 centimeters).

Rivers and lakes. The Congo River is Zaire's most important waterway. It rises near the southeast corner of the country. It flows northward to northern Zaire and is called the Lualaba River until it reaches Stanley Falls near the equator. It then flows westward across northern Zaire. Finally, it flows southwestward until it empties into the Atlantic Ocean in far western Zaire. The world's fifth longest river, the Congo flows for 2,900 miles (4,667 kilometers). It carries more water than any other river except the Amazon. Many other rivers branch out from the Congo. They include the Ubangi and Aruwimi to the north and the Lomami and Kasai to the south.

Several deep lakes lie along Zaire's eastern border. The largest is Lake Tanganyika.

Animal life. Zaire has a spectacular variety of wild animals. Baboons, chimpanzees, gorillas, and many

kinds of monkeys live in areas with trees. Antelopes, leopards, lions, rhinoceroses, and zebras roam open areas. Crocodiles and hippopotamuses live in or near water. The okapi, a forest-dwelling animal related to the giraffe, lives nowhere else in the world but Zaire. It has become a national symbol of the country. Through the years, hunters have killed many animals in Zaire and have endangered some species. The government has set aside large areas of land as part of a national park system where animals are protected from hunters. Many wild animals also still live outside the parks, especially in thinly populated areas in the east.

Economy

Zaire is a poor country with a developing economy. But it has many valuable resources that give it the potential of becoming a wealthy nation. Mining ranks as Zaire's most important economic activity.

Mining. Copper is Zaire's most important mineral. The country ranks among the world's leading copper-producing nations. Zaire leads the world in the production of industrial diamonds, its second most important mineral. Zaire produces oil from deposits off its coast. The country's other economically valuable minerals include cadmium, cobalt, gold, manganese, silver, tin, and zinc.

Agriculture and forestry. Agriculture in Zaire centers around small plots, where families struggle to produce enough food for their own needs. The chief food crops include bananas, cassava, corn, peanuts, and rice. Crops raised for sale include cocoa, coffee, cotton, and tea. The trees of Zaire's rain forest yield palm oil, rubber, and timber.

Agence Hoa-Qui from Tom Stack & Assoc.

The Congo River is Zaire's main waterway and the fifth longest river in the world. The people in the picture above are setting traps in the Congo in order to catch fish.

Agence Hoa-Qui from Tom Stack & Assoc.

A huge copper mine operates near Likasi, in southeastern Zaire. Copper is Zaire's chief product.

Manufacturing. Zaire produces relatively small amounts of manufactured goods. Its chief products include beer, cement, processed foods, soft drinks, steel, textiles, and tires. Since independence, manufacturing has grown in importance in Zaire.

Foreign trade. Copper is Zaire's chief export by far. Other exports include cobalt, coffee, industrial diamonds, and palm oil. Imports include food, oil, textiles, and manufactured goods. Zaire trades chiefly with nations of Western Europe, especially Belgium.

Transportation and communication. Most roads in Zaire are unpaved and many are badly rutted, especially in rainy seasons. Less than 1 per cent of all Zairians own an automobile. The Congo River plays an important role in Zaire's transportation system, especially in the rain forest where there are few good roads. The river and its many branches are navigable for about 7,200 miles (11,500 kilometers) in the country.

Zaire's railroads operate mostly in the southeastern part of the country. They link mining areas there with several river ports. Matadi is Zaire's chief seaport. Airlines serve Zaire's major cities and connect Kinshasa with several countries in Africa and Europe.

The development of inexpensive transistor radios has made radio the most important means of communication in Zaire. In some rural areas, however, people communicate from village to village by means of drum signals. Television broadcasts serve Zaire's largest cities, but few people can afford TV sets. Only about 7,000 Zairians own a television. Four daily newspapers are published in Zaire.

History

Early days. Pygmies were the first known inhabitants of what is now Zaire. They have lived there since prehistoric times. At least 2,000 years ago, people from other parts of Africa moved into the area. In the A.D. 700's, well-developed civilizations grew up in southeastern Zaire. In the 1400's—or perhaps earlier—several separate

states developed in the savanna south of the rain forest. The largest were the Kongo, Kuba, Luba, and Lunda kingdoms. In the 1600's or 1700's, other kingdoms grew up near the eastern border. They carried on long-distance trade with people on the east and west coasts.

The coming of the Europeans. In 1482, Portuguese seamen began stopping at the mouth of the Congo River. Portugal soon established diplomatic relations with the Kongo kingdom, which then ruled the coastal region. Representatives of the kingdom visited Portugal and the Vatican—the headquarters of the Roman Catholic Church—in the late 1400's. The kingdom soon adopted Roman Catholicism as its religion, and many Kongo men became Catholic priests.

In the early 1500's, the Portuguese began enslaving black Africans. They bought many of the slaves from the leaders of the Kongo kingdom. Other Europeans soon began taking part in the slave trade. From the early 1500's to the early 1800's, hundreds of thousands of people were enslaved in the Zaire area. Most of them were sent to North or South America.

In 1876, Henry M. Stanley, a British explorer, crossed Zaire from east to west. Other explorers crossed the area at about the same time. The explorations gave Europeans and Americans their first detailed information about the interior of what is now Zaire.

Belgian rule. In 1878, King Leopold II of Belgium hired Stanley to set up Belgian outposts along the Congo River. Through skillful diplomacy, Leopold persuaded other European leaders to recognize him as the ruler of what is now Zaire. The recognition stated that Leopold himself—not the Belgian government—was the ruler. The area became Leopold's personal colony on July 1, 1885, and was named the Congo Free State.

The people of the Congo Free State suffered under Leopold's rule. The king's agents treated the people cruelly and forced them to work long hours at such jobs as collecting rubber in forests and building a railroad. Many people died as a result of the harsh treatment.

Leopold's rule brought many protests, especially from Great Britain and the United States. In response, the Belgian government took over control of the Congo Free State from Leopold in 1908. Belgium renamed the colony the Belgian Congo. The Belgian government's rule was often harsh, but the government improved working and living conditions somewhat.

By the 1920's, Belgium was earning great wealth from the Belgian Congo's copper, diamonds, gold, palm oil,

Important dates in Zaire

A.D. 700's Well-developed civilizations grew up in what is now Zaire.

c. 1400 The Kongo and other kingdoms were established in the area.

Early 1500's The slave trade began in what is now Zaire.

1885 King Leopold II of Belgium took control of the area and named it the Congo Free State.

1908 The Belgian government took control of the Congo Free State and renamed it the Belgian Congo.

1960 The Belgian Congo gained independence from Belgium and was renamed Congo.

1965 President Joseph Mobutu came to power.

1971 The country's name was changed to Zaire.

1977 and 1978 Katanga rebels invaded Zaire from Angola, but were defeated.

and other resources. The worldwide Great Depression of the 1930's crippled the colony's economy as prices and demand for its resources fell sharply. In 1940, Belgium entered World War II on the side of the Allies. During the war, the Belgian Congo provided the Allies with valuable raw materials.

After World War II ended in 1945, the Belgian Congo's economy again developed rapidly as prices for its exports soared. The Belgians made efforts to improve education and medical care for the colony's people. But they refused to give them a voice in the government.

Independence. In the 1950's, many Africans in the Belgian Congo began calling for independence from Belgium. In 1957, Belgium allowed the colony's people to elect their own representatives to some city councils. But the demand for independence continued. In 1959, rioting broke out against Belgian rule. On June 30, 1960, Belgium granted the colony independence. The new country was called Congo.

In Congo's first general elections—held about a month before independence—nine political parties won seats in the national legislature. No party received a majority. This splitting of votes weakened the power and unity of Congo's government. In a compromise on the eve of independence, two opposing leaders agreed to share power. Joseph Kasavubu became president and Patrice Lumumba became prime minister.

Civil disorder broke out in Congo following independence. Belgian officers still held power in the army, and many Belgians retained important government posts. Five days after independence, Congolese army troops near Léopoldville (now Kinshasa) revolted against their Belgian officers. The revolt spread throughout Congo. Most Belgian government workers then fled.

In July 1960, Katanga Province (now the Shaba Region) *seceded* (withdrew) from the new nation and declared itself independent. This copper-producing province in the south ranked as Congo's wealthiest area. The diamond-producing province of Kasai seceded in August. In September, President Kasavubu dismissed Prime Minister Lumumba. Lumumba was imprisoned and, in 1961, he was assassinated. Lumumba's supporters established a rival government to that of Kasavubu and claimed to rule the country.

Fighting broke out between the rival groups in Congo. United Nations (UN) troops—at the invitation of the Congo government—were sent to the country to restore order in 1960. In August 1961, the rival groups reached a compromise that united all of the country except Katanga Province. Cyrille Adoula headed the new government as prime minister.

UN troops finally brought an end to the Katanga secession in January 1963. Many of the Katanga rebels fled to neighboring Angola. The UN forces were withdrawn in June 1964. In a surprising political settlement in July, Moise Tshombe, who had led the Katanga secession movement, became prime minister of the reunited country. At about the same time, a wave of new revolts broke out in Congo. White *mercenaries* (hired soldiers) helped the government end the revolts by 1965.

National elections were held in March 1965. A loose coalition headed by Tshombe won the elections. But the coalition soon fell apart, and disagreements among the leaders halted government operations. In November,

the Congolese army took control of the government. General Joseph Désiré Mobutu became president.

Rebuilding the nation. The civil disorder of the early 1960's severely damaged Congo's economy. Fighting among the country's people resulted in bitterness and deep divisions. President Mobutu took steps to try to solve the country's problems. He set up a strong national government that extended its authority throughout the nation. The government's authority helped end fighting among people and lessen the ethnic divisions of earlier years. The economy improved steadily in the late 1960's.

Mobutu also tried to strengthen the nation by encouraging pride in its African heritage and reducing European influence. Many cities, towns, and physical features in the country had European names. Mobutu's government gave all of these African names. In 1971, the government changed the country's name from Congo to Zaire. The government also required all Africans in the country who had European names to adopt African names. Mobutu changed his own name from Joseph Désiré Mobutu to Mobutu Sese Seko in 1972.

Recent developments. In the early 1970's, the worldwide problems of recession and inflation caused new economic hardships in Zaire. The price of copper fell sharply, greatly reducing the country's revenues. At the same time, the prices of food and oil—which Zaire imports—rose dramatically.

In 1977, Katanga rebels who had been living in Angola invaded Zaire in an attempt to take over the former Katanga Province. By then, the province had been renamed the Shaba Region. Zairian government troops, aided by Moroccan troops and French military equipment, defeated the rebels. Katanga rebels invaded Zaire again in 1978, but were defeated. French and Belgian troops played a leading role in helping the Zairian forces turn back the invasion.

In spite of its problems, however, Zaire still has great economic potential. Its valuable natural resources give it the possibility of becoming one of Africa's wealthiest nations.   M. Crawford Young

Related articles in *World Book* include:

Africa (pictures)	Lake Albert	Sculpture (African)
Clothing (picture: Traditional costumes)	Lake Tanganyika	Stanley and Living-
	Luba	stone
Congo River	Mobutu Sese Seko	United Nations
Kinshasa	Mythology (African (picture: Fetish figures))	(The Congo emergency)

Outline

I. Government
   A. National government
   B. Local government
   C. Courts
   D. Armed forces
II. People

A. Population and ancestry	C. Way of life	G. Recreation
	D. Housing	H. Religion
	E. Clothing	I. Education
B. Languages	F. Food and drink	J. The arts

III. Land and climate
   A. The tropical rain forest   D. Rivers and lakes
   B. Savannas   E. Animal life
   C. The highland
IV. Economy
   A. Mining   B. Agriculture and forestry

C. Manufacturing
D. Foreign trade
V. History

E. Transportation and
communication

Questions

What is Zaire's most important economic activity?
What problems has Zaire faced since it gained independence from Belgium?
Why is farm production low in Zaire?
Why has the government discouraged Western-style clothes?
What is the role of Zaire's only political party?
What were the roles of Henry M. Stanley and King Leopold II in the area's history?
What is the chief river in Zaire?
Why do few people live in Zaire's tropical rain forest?
What is the most important means of communication in Zaire?
How has the government sought to protect wild animals?

Zama, Battle of. See Army (table: Famous land battles); Scipio, Publius Cornelius.

Zambezi River, *zam BEE zee,* is the fourth longest river in Africa. Only the Nile, the Congo, and the Niger rivers are longer. The Zambezi rises in Zambia, near the border between Zaire and Angola. The river follows a winding 1,700-mile (2,736-kilometer) course, separating Zambia from Zimbabwe and crossing Mozambique to empty into the Mozambique Channel (see **Africa** [map]). The Zambezi has many branches, and drains more than 500,000 square miles (1,300,000 square kilometers).

The upper course of the river lies in level land, where the water supply depends on equatorial rains that fall from October to March. From this plateau, the Zambezi plunges to a lower level over Victoria Falls, a mighty cataract of water. A hydroelectric plant has been in operation there since 1938. Kariba Dam, completed in 1959, lies in Kariba Gorge, about 200 miles (320 kilometers) downstream. It forms a lake that covers 2,000 square miles (5,200 square kilometers).

Early geographers knew of the Zambezi region, prob-

ably through Arab traders. The first European to explore the Zambezi River was David Livingstone. He explored the river in the 1850's and 1860's.   Hartmut Walter

See also **Stanley and Livingstone; Victoria Falls.**

Zambia, *ZAM bee uh,* is a country in south-central Africa. It ranks as one of the largest producers of copper. Zambia exports copper to many parts of the world and gains much income from the exports. Without copper, it would be one of the poorest countries in Africa.

Zambia takes its name from the Zambezi River, which forms most of its southern border. Mighty Victoria Falls, one of the world's most beautiful waterfalls, lies on the river. The great Kariba Dam, one of the world's largest hydroelectric projects, and Kariba Lake also are located on the Zambezi, serving both Zambia and Zimbabwe.

Zambia was formerly a British protectorate called *Northern Rhodesia.* From 1953 to 1963, it formed part of the Federation of Rhodesia and Nyasaland with Nyasaland (now Malawi) and Southern Rhodesia (now Zimbabwe). Zambia became an independent nation in 1964. Lusaka is its capital and largest city.

Government. The people of Zambia elect the president as head of state and government. The people also elect 125 members of the National Assembly, the country's legislature. The president nominates 10 extra assembly members to represent particular interests. Assembly members serve five-year terms. The president appoints the Cabinet from among the Assembly. All citizens over the age of 18 may vote.

Zambia has only one political party, the United National Independence Party (UNIP). Usually, voters have at least two UNIP candidates from which to choose for each elected office. The party's leaders have a key role in establishing the government's policies.

The country is divided into eight provinces. Each province is administered by a provincial minister.

WORLD BOOK map

Zambia

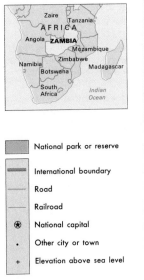

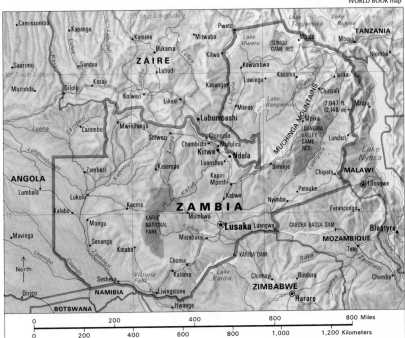

Facts in brief

Capital: Lusaka.
Official language: English.
Official name: Republic of Zambia.
Area: 290,586 sq. mi. (752,614 km²). *Greatest distances—* east-west, 900 mi. (1,448 km); north-south, 700 mi. (1,127 km).
Population: *Estimated 1990 population—*8,459,000; density, 29 persons per sq. mi. (11 per km²); distribution, 56 per cent rural, 44 per cent urban. *1980 census—*5,679,808. *Estimated 1995 population—*10,193,000.
Chief products: *Agriculture—*cassava, corn, millet, peanuts, sorghum grain. *Fishing—*perch, whitebait. *Manufacturing and processing—*cement, copper products, flour, wood products. *Mining—*copper, cobalt.
Flag: The flag has an orange eagle in the upper right corner over three vertical stripes of red (for freedom), black (for the people), and orange (for mineral wealth) on a field of green (for natural resources). See **Flag** (picture: Flags of Africa).
Money: *Basic unit—*kwacha. See **Money** (table).

People. Most Zambians are black Africans who speak Bantu languages (see **Bantu**). There are more than 70 ethnic groups represented and eight major local languages spoken in Zambia. Many people also speak English, the official language.

In remote parts of the country, village life goes on much as it has for hundreds of years. The people live in circular, grass-roofed huts, and raise food crops on the surrounding land. However, the development of mining has caused thousands of Zambians to move to mining towns.

Corn is the main food. A favorite dish is *nshima,* a thick porridge made from corn. In the *bush* (rural areas), where most Zambians live, the people plant their crops in November and December.

The majority of Zambians are Christians, but traditional local beliefs still have a strong hold on the village people. However, witchcraft and old customs such as *polygyny* (marrying several wives) and *bride price* (paying the parents for a bride) are slowly dying out in the towns.

Most Zambian children attend elementary school. But

Robert Harding Picture Library Ltd.

Copper is Zambia's major export. This picture shows copper being processed in one of the country's refineries.

only a fifth of them go to high school. Zambia's only university, the University of Zambia, was founded in 1965. Zambia also has several trade and technical schools.

Land. Most of Zambia is flat and covered with trees and bushes. It lies on a plateau about 4,000 feet (1,200 meters) above sea level. The plateau is broken by the 7,000-foot (2,100-meter) Muchinga Mountains in the northeast. In the south, the trees are smaller, and there are large open areas. The Zambezi River flows south through western Zambia, and forms much of the southern border. Every year it floods a broad, sandy plain in Western province in the southwest.

Because of its altitude, Zambia has a milder climate than might be expected. The hot season lasts only from September through November. Midday temperatures then range between 80° and 100° F. (27° and 38° C). From November through April, Zambia has a rainy season. Violent storms flood the rivers by March. From May through August, temperatures range from 60° to 80° F. (16° to 27° C). Northern Zambia gets about 50 inches (130 centimeters) of rainfall a year. The south gets 20 to 30 inches (51 to 76 centimeters).

Economy. Copper accounts for more than 80 per cent of Zambia's export earnings. Four large copper mines and several smaller mines lie in an area called the *copperbelt,* along Zambia's border with Zaire. Valuable amounts of cobalt are obtained as by-products of copper mining. Zambia has a lead and zinc mine at Kabwe, and large coal deposits near Kariba Lake. The production of copper products is the country's most important manufacturing activity. Farming in Zambia is made difficult by poor soil. Corn is the country's most important farm product. Other leading crops include cassava, millet, peanuts, and sorghum.

Zambia has no outlet to the sea. Railroads connect the country with seaports in Angola, Mozambique, and Tanzania. The railroad to Angola passes through Zaire, and the one to Mozambique passes through Zimbabwe. The railroad to Tanzania was built in the early 1970's with millions of dollars of aid from China.

Robert Harding Picture Library Ltd.

Lusaka, Zambia's capital and commercial center, is a modern city with tall buildings and busy streets.

History. In 1851, the Scottish missionary David Livingstone crossed the Zambezi from the south. He spent nearly 20 years exploring the region.

In the late 1800's, Cecil Rhodes's British South Africa Company made treaties with African chiefs in the area. The company named the area Northern Rhodesia to distinguish it from the region south of the Zambezi, which they called Southern Rhodesia.

In 1924, the British government took over the administration of Northern Rhodesia and appointed a governor. The discovery of large copper ore deposits during the late 1920's brought a rush of Europeans to the area. Ten years later, mining was an established industry.

After World War II ended in 1945, the Europeans asked Great Britain for greater control of the government. Many wanted the merger of Northern Rhodesia with Southern Rhodesia. The Africans of Northern Rhodesia opposed these demands. But in 1953, Britain formed a federation of Northern Rhodesia, Southern Rhodesia, and Nyasaland. The Africans opposed the federation, because the European minority controlled the government in Southern Rhodesia. Britain dissolved the federation in 1963. On Oct. 24, 1964, Northern Rhodesia became the independent nation of Zambia. Kenneth Kaunda was elected president in 1964. He was reelected in 1968, 1973, 1978, and 1983. In 1972, the UNIP became the only legal political party in Zambia.

Southern Rhodesia came to be called Rhodesia after the federation was dissolved. In 1965, Rhodesia declared its independence in defiance of Great Britain. Relations between Zambia and Rhodesia became severely strained, because Rhodesia's white minority government refused to give the African majority a greater voice in government.

Zambia experienced serious economic problems in the 1970's and 1980's. In 1973, Rhodesia prohibited Zambia from shipping goods across its territory, eliminating one of Zambia's main outlets to the sea. Rhodesia soon lifted the ban. But until 1978, Zambia refused to ship goods across Rhodesia. In 1980, blacks gained control of Rhodesia's government, and the country's name was changed to Zimbabwe. Relations then improved between Zambia and Zimbabwe. Zambia's economy also suffered from low market prices for copper and a reduction in copper ore reserves. *J. Dixon Esseks*

See also **Kaunda, Kenneth D.; Lake Bangweulu; Lusaka; Victoria Falls; Zambezi River.**

Zamboanga, *SAHM boh AHNG gah* (pop. 343,722), is a beautiful city in the Philippines. It lies on the western tip of Mindanao Island, 550 miles (885 kilometers) south of Manila (see **Philippines** [map]). The city is the chief port and trading center for a region that produces abacá, rubber, coconuts, lumber, and rice. The Spaniards built a fort at Zamboanga in 1635. The city served as a base for Japanese troops in World War II (1939-1945).

Russell H. Fifield and Carlos P. Romulo

Zane's Trace. See **Ohio** (Transportation).
Zanzibar. See **Tanzania.**
Zanzibar, *ZAN zuh BAHR* (pop. 133,000), is a historic seaport city on the west coast of Zanzibar Island, which is part of Tanzania (see **Tanzania** [map]). Zanzibar's main exports are cloves and clove oil. In the old section of the city, buildings with ornate, brass-studded carved wooden doors line narrow, winding streets. Huge con-

crete block apartment buildings stand inland.

In the 1500's, the Portuguese established a trading center at Zanzibar. In the early 1800's, the sultan of Oman, who controlled much of the East African coast, established his capital in Zanzibar. He built up an economy based on clove plantations, the slave trade, and the ivory trade. The sultan's palace still stands in the center of the city. *John A. Rowe*

Zapata, *sah PAH tah,* **Emiliano,** *EH mee LYAH noh* (1880?-1919), was a leader of the Mexican Revolution. He was an Indian, and his main goal was to gain land for his people. After forced service in the army, he joined the revolt in 1910 against President Porfirio Díaz. Zapata refused to lay down his arms until the revolutionary leader, Francisco Madero, distributed land. He also refused to recognize Victoriano Huerta, Madero's assassin. With Pancho Villa, he occupied Mexico City in 1914. Zapata was murdered by Colonel Jesús Guajardo in 1919. He was born in Anenecuilco, Morelos. See also **Mexico** (The constitution of 1917). *Donald E. Worcester*

Zapotec Indians, *ZAH puh tehk,* developed an empire in what is now the state of Oaxaca in southern Mexico from about 1500 B.C. to A.D. 750. There, they built their capital city, Monte Albán, on a mountaintop. The city had a ceremonial district that included temples and ball court. Numerous elaborate tombs and many urns with human features have been found at the site of Monte Albán. The Zapotec also produced the earliest written texts in Middle America. They carved on stone slabs records of conquests, sacrifices, and relations with other peoples. After the disintegration of their empire, the Zapotec abandoned Monte Albán. But a number of smaller Zapotec kingdoms developed. Mixtec Indians gained control of several of these kingdoms by conquering or marrying into Zapotec ruling families. Some of the Zapotec kingdoms were conquered by the Aztec Indians.

Thousands of Zapotec still live in the state of Oaxaca and speak Zapotec dialects. Most are farmers. Some Zapotec are also skilled potters and weavers. Their products are sold worldwide. *William O. Autry*

See also **Rivera, Diego** (picture).
Zaragoza. See **Saragossa.**
Zarathustra. See **Zoroastrianism.**
Zebra is a striped, horselike animal found wild in Africa. It stands 4 to 5 feet (1.2 to 1.5 meters) high at the withers. The zebra differs from all other members of the horse family because of its startling color pattern. It has alternating white and black or dark-brown stripes. These stripes run all over its body, meeting diagonally down the sides of the head. The lines may appear even on the zebra's long ears, short thick mane, and down its tail to the tuft of hair. The lines help to hide the zebra from its enemies. The zebra's chief foe is the lion. Some kinds of zebras live on open grassy plains, and some in rough mountains. Zebras are grazing animals. They live in small bands, each of which is led by a stallion. Zebras are savage fighters. They are difficult to tame and train to work. They are sometimes tamed in South Africa because they appear immune to *nagana,* a disease that attacks most domesticated animals in Africa. Nagana is carried by the tsetse fly (see **Tsetse fly**).

Great numbers of zebras once lived over most of eastern Africa, from southern Egypt to Cape Colony.

Giuseppe Mazza

Zebras resemble horses but have a wild nature and are difficult to tame. Most zebra mares have one colt every spring.

They were killed for their meat and hides. Their meat is said to have an excellent taste and their hides are used to make leather. The *quagga,* a type of zebra that once inhabited southern Africa, is extinct. Some kinds of zebras are nearly extinct, but others are numerous.

Scientific classification. The zebra belongs to the horse family, Equidae. It is classified as genus *Equus.*

Duane A. Schlitter

See also **Mammal** (pictures).

Zebu. See **Cattle** (Beef cattle).

Zebulun, *ZEHB yuh luhn,* was the name of one of the 12 tribes of Israel. It occupied an area in southwestern Galilee just north of the Plain of Esdraelon. In the 1100's B.C., Zebulun, with neighboring tribes, played a leading part in the defeat of the Canaanites by Deborah and Barak (Judges 4-5). Later, it was a part of the northern kingdom of Israel. In 733 B.C., Zebulun was taken by the Assyrians with the rest of Galilee. Jesus' home, Nazareth, lay in what had once been the tribe's territory. Zebulun was named for the tenth son of Jacob, the sixth and youngest born to him by Leah (Gen. 30:20). The tribe claimed that it descended from him. H. Darrell Lance

Zechariah, *zehk uh RY uh,* **Book of,** is a book of the Old Testament or Hebrew Bible. It is named for a prophet who lived in Jerusalem and prophesied from 520 to 518 B.C. Chapters 1-8 are usually attributed to Zechariah himself. Chapters 9-14 are considered a slightly later collection written anonymously by an individual or group.

Zechariah lived about the same time as the prophet Haggai. But Zechariah's message goes beyond the encouragement to rebuild the Temple that Haggai provided to Israelites returning from exile. Zechariah elaborated the plan upon which the community must be reestablished. In the first section (1:1-8:23), a series of visions and oracles help the Israelites understand and accept the new form of government by high priest and governor that the Persian authorities had permitted. Central to the plan was the recently refounded Temple of Yahweh that dominates all the visions and oracles of the first section.

The second section (9:1-14:21) focuses on the struggle in the Jewish community that emerged after the Persian Empire experienced rebellions in Babylon and Egypt by 450 B.C. Eric M. Meyers

Zeeman, *ZAY mahn,* **Pieter,** *PEE tuhr* (1865-1943), a Dutch physicist, became known for his discoveries in spectroscopy. In 1896, he discovered what is now called the *Zeeman effect,* the splitting of spectral lines by a magnetic field (see **Zeeman effect**). The theory for this phenomenon was developed by Hendrik A. Lorentz, and the two scientists shared the 1902 Nobel Prize in physics for their work (see **Lorentz, Hendrik A.**). It is by means of the Zeeman effect that astronomers can measure the strength of the magnetic field on the surface of the sun or other stars. Zeeman was born in Zonnemaire, in Zeeland, the Netherlands. R. T. Ellickson

Zeeman effect, *ZAY mahn,* is the splitting of a spectral line when a source of light is placed in a magnetic field. Spectral lines of light are produced when the electrons in atoms change from one energy level to another (see **Light** [Sources of light]). The pattern of spectral lines thus indicates the energy levels of the atoms. Because the lines split into parts when the atoms are in a magnetic field, the Zeeman effect indicates that the energy levels of the atoms have changed.

The Zeeman effect was first observed in 1896 by Pieter Zeeman, a Dutch physicist. Scientists did not completely understand its importance until the development of quantum mechanics in the 1920's. Physicists can learn about such things as the magnetic properties of atoms and the electrons in them by observing the split spectral lines. The Zeeman effect can also be used to study molecules and nuclei. Gerald Feinberg

Zen is an East Asian form of Buddhism. Zen Buddhism is practiced primarily in Japan and has greatly influenced Japanese culture. Since the mid-1900's, Zen has gained many followers in the United States.

The goal of Zen is the attainment of a state of spiritual enlightenment called *satori.* Zen Buddhists believe meditation is the key to achieving satori. There are two major schools of Zen, *Rinzai* and *Soto.* Followers of Rinzai meditate on the meaning of baffling riddles called *koans* while sitting cross-legged. People who practice Soto meditate in the same position. They also read from the sacred works of Mahayana Buddhism, another East Asian form of the religion. Zen Buddhists believe physical labor contributes to the attainment of enlightenment. They work closely with a teacher called the *master,* who guides their search for satori.

According to tradition, Zen began in India. During the A.D. 500's, an Indian monk named Bodhidharma established Zen in China, where it was called Chan. Two Japanese priests, Eisai and Dogen, introduced Chan into Japan. Eisai founded the Rinzai school in the 1100's, and Dogen established the Soto school in the 1200's. Zen quickly became a major religious and cultural force in Japan. Frank E. Reynolds

See also **Buddhism** (Zen).

Additional resources

Bancroft, Anne. *Zen: Direct Pointing to Reality.* Thames & Hudson, 1987. First published in 1979. A beginner's introduction.
Kasulis, Thomas P. *Zen Action: Zen Person.* Univ. Press of Hawaii, 1981.
Suzuki, Daisetz T. *Zen and Japanese Culture.* 2nd ed. Princeton, 1959. *Manual of Zen Buddhism.* Grove, 1960.

Zenger, *ZEHNG uhr,* **John Peter** (1697-1746), gained the first major victory for freedom of the press in the American Colonies. Political opponents of British governor William Cosby established Zenger as printer of the *New-York Weekly Journal* in 1733. These opponents, including Chief Justice Lewis Morris, belonged to the Popular Party, and used the *Journal* to oppose the Government Party. In 1734, when Cosby abruptly dismissed Morris from his office, the *Journal* criticized Cosby severely. Zenger shielded Cosby's enemies by refusing to reveal who had written the critical articles.

Because they could find no one else to prosecute, the British arrested Zenger and tried him in 1735 for criminal libel. Zenger's lawyers were disbarred, and he was left almost defenseless. Finally, Andrew Hamilton, a famous Philadelphia lawyer, came to New York to aid Zenger. Hamilton presented a brilliant and powerful speech that persuaded the jury to find Zenger "not guilty" by arguing that Zenger had printed the truth, and that truth is not libelous. After his acquittal, Zenger published *A Brief Narrative of the Case and Tryal of John Peter Zenger* (1736).

Zenger was born in Germany, and came to New York at the age of 13. He was apprenticed to a printer, and set up his own printing shop in 1726.   Jethro K. Lieberman

See also **Freedom of the press** (In the United States).

Zenith, *ZEE nihth,* in astronomy, is any point directly above a person on the earth. Zeniths lie on the *celestial sphere,* which can be pictured as an imaginary sphere that encloses the universe. A zenith is opposite to a *nadir,* which is a point directly below a person on the earth (see **Nadir**).

Astronomers speak of two kinds of zeniths, *astronomical zeniths* and *geocentric zeniths.* An astronomical zenith is any point where a *plumb line,* if it were extended, would intersect the celestial sphere (see **Plumb line**). A geocentric zenith is any point where a line drawn from the earth's center through a person on its surface would intersect the celestial sphere. The angular distance of a star or other celestial body from a zenith is called the *zenith distance.* This information can be used to determine the position of such an object.   Lee J. Rickard

Zeno of Citium, *ZEE noh, SIHSH ee uhm* (335?-265? B.C.), was the founder of Stoic philosophy in Athens. He was born in Citium on the island of Cyprus. It is reported that he was originally a merchant, but was shipwrecked and lost all his property traveling to Athens in 314 B.C. He stayed there, and took up the study of philosophy, meeting his students on a *stoa* (porch), from which the name *stoic* came (see **Stoic philosophy**).

Zeno taught that it is foolish to try to shape circumstances to our desires. The world process is not like a blindly running machine. Instead, a divine intelligence guides and governs it, and directs all things ultimately toward what is good. Wise people will "follow nature" and fit their desires to the pattern of events. They will find happiness in freedom from desire, from fear of evil, and in knowing that they are in tune with the divine purpose directing all things. The Stoic philosophy spread to Rome and flourished there for several centuries after the birth of Christ.   S. Marc Cohen

Zeno of Elea, *ZEE noh, EE lee uh* (490?-430 B.C.), was a Greek philosopher who lived in the Greek colony of Elea in southern Italy. He defended the doctrine of his teacher, the philosopher Parmenides, who believed that what exists is one, permanent, and unchanging (see **Parmenides**). Zeno tried to prove that motion, change, and *plurality* (reality consisting of many substances) are impossible. He used a method of arguing called *reductio ad absurdum.* By this method, he would derive impossible conclusions from the opinions of his opponents.

Zeno is believed to have devised at least 40 arguments, but only 8 have survived. His four *paradoxes* concerning motion make up his most famous surviving arguments. In one of these paradoxes, Zeno argued that a runner can never reach the end of a race course. He stated that the runner first completes half of the course, then half of the remaining distance, and so on infinitely without ever reaching the end. Zeno's apparently simple arguments raise profound issues about time, space, and infinity. These issues continue to interest philosophers and scientists.   S. Marc Cohen

Zephaniah, *zehf uh NY uh,* **Book of,** is a book of the Hebrew Bible, or Old Testament. It is named for the prophet Zephaniah, whose ministry in the Kingdom of Judah probably occurred between about 630 and 625 B.C.

During Zephaniah's ministry, Palestine was invaded by the Scythians, a barbarian people. Zephaniah equated their arrival with God's judgment on Judah and on all humanity. He stated, however, that God's wrath was principally directed against Judah so that people might repent. Zephaniah forecast a destructive "Day of the Lord," when the wicked would be punished. This theme is a central element in Biblical prophecy. The prophet predicted that a faithful few would be spared God's anger and be preserved in Jerusalem and in the rest of Judah. There God would gather them and they would accept His rule.   Eric M. Meyers

See also **Bible** (Books of the Old Testament).

Zeppelin. See **Airship** (The Zeppelins).

Zeppelin, *ZEHP uh lihn or, TSEHP uh LEEN,* **Ferdinand von** (1838-1917), was a famous German pioneer in lighter-than-air vehicles. He designed aircraft that were primarily gas bags, supported internally by a light framework. Engines powered and controlled his aircraft. These aircraft soon were named after him. Germany used zeppelins in air raids against Great Britain during World War I. These attacks were the first planned air raids against a civilian population (see **Airship**).

Zeppelin was born in Constance, Baden, and was trained to be an army officer. He visited the United States during the Civil War and went up in balloons with the Union forces. The balloons convinced him of the value of aircraft. Zeppelin served in the Franco-Prussian War in 1870. After his retirement in 1891, he devoted himself to aeronautics. He had spent most of his savings when Kaiser Wilhelm II became interested in his work and offered financial support.   Robert B. Hotz

Zero, in arithmetic, is the name of the digit 0, sometimes called *naught* or a *cypher.* It is used to indicate the absence of quantity. A zero is needed in a positional numeral system, such as the familiar system commonly used by most people today. In a *positional* system, the *position,* or place, of a digit determines the digit's value. Thus, in the numeral 246, the digit 2 stands for two hundred, the digit 4 stands for four tens (or forty), and the digit 6 stands for six units, or ones. The numeral represents the number 246. In order to write the number 206, a symbol is needed to show that there are no tens. The digit 0 serves this purpose. Zero added to or subtracted from a number gives the original number. A number multiplied by zero gives zero. Division by zero is undefinable. Zero is an even number.

On most scales, zero marks the starting point or the neutral position. Positive numbers are placed to the right or above zero, and negative numbers are placed to the left or below zero. But on some scales, zero is set arbitrarily. For example, on a Celsius thermometer, zero is set at the temperature at which water freezes.

The Maya Indians of Central America are believed to have invented the concept of the zero before the A.D. 300's. The Hindus developed the concept independently several hundred years later. The idea spread from India and was adopted in Europe during the late 1400's. The word *zero* probably came from *ziphirum,* a Latinized form of the Arabic word *sifr. Sifr* is a translation of the Hindu word *sunya* (void or empty).   John M. Smith

See also **Decimal system.**

Zero-base budgeting (ZBB) is a technique used to reduce spending in business and government. ZBB requires each department of an organization to justify annually every dollar it wishes to spend in the next year. It differs from *incremental budgeting,* which requires departments to justify only proposed changes from the previous year's *base* (budget). With ZBB, managers regard a program as though it never existed before—in other words, that it has a base of zero dollars.

Organizations that use ZBB prepare annual outlines called *decision packages.* The outlines set forth a program's current spending level and its proposed high and low spending levels. Using the outlines, executives decide how much money to spend on each program.

ZBB was introduced in the 1960's by Texas Instruments, Incorporated, an electronics company. Many federal agencies used ZBB during the administration of President Jimmy Carter, but President Ronald Reagan abandoned ZBB. Procedures called *sunset laws* have also been used to control spending.

Robert T. Golembiewski

See also **Sunset laws.**

Zero population growth. See **Birth and death rates; Ehrlich, Paul Ralph.**

Zeus was the king of the gods and the supreme ruler of people in Greek mythology. He originally was a god of the sky. In time, the Greeks regarded him as the only god who was concerned with the entire universe. They associated Zeus with justice and believed that he punished the wicked and rewarded the good. He had the same powers as the Roman god Jupiter.

Zeus was the son of Cronus and Rhea, members of a race called the Titans. Zeus and Cronus' other children overthrew their father during a war against the Titans. Zeus then took Cronus' place and ruled from Mount Olympus. He headed a family of 12 major gods and goddesses called the Olympians. Zeus's brothers were the gods Hades and Poseidon. Hades ruled the underworld, and Poseidon controlled the seas. The goddesses Demeter, Hera, and Hestia were Zeus's sisters. Zeus married Hera, who became queen of the gods. They had two children, the gods Ares and Hephaestus.

Zeus had many love affairs with goddesses and mor-

tal women. His children by them included the gods Apollo, Dionysus, and Hermes; the goddess Artemis; and the heroes Heracles (Hercules in Latin) and Perseus. In addition, Zeus gave birth to the goddess Athena, who sprang full-grown from his head. Zeus and the goddess Mnemosyne were the parents of the Muses, the nine goddesses of the arts and sciences. According to some myths, Zeus and the goddess Themis were the parents of the Fates (see **Fates**).

Artists have shown Zeus as a bearded and majestic man. His symbols were the eagle, the oak tree, the royal scepter, and the thunderbolt.   Robert J. Lenardon

See also **Mythology** (Greek); **Jupiter; Hera; Olympia; Olympus; Persephone; Titans.**

Zhao Ziyang, *jow zu yahng* (1919-   ), also spelled *Chao Tzu-yang,* served as general secretary of the Chinese Communist Party from November 1987 until June 1989. He had been acting general secretary since January 1987. As general secretary, Zhao held the highest post in the Communist Party, which controls China's government. But Deng Xiaoping is the country's most powerful leader (see **Deng Xiaoping**). Zhao was dismissed from his post in June 1989 after he showed support for a pro-democracy movement in China (see **China** [China after Mao]).

Zhao was born in Henan (Honan) Province. He joined the Communist Party in 1938. He rose through the ranks and, in 1965, was given the party post of first secretary of Guangdong (Kwangtung) Province. He was removed from office in 1967 during China's Cultural Revolution (see **China** [The Cultural Revolution]). Zhao regained his post in 1971. In 1975, he became the Communist Party's first secretary of

Michael Blackman, Camera Press
Zhao Ziyang

Sichuan (Szechwan) Province and helped improve the economy there. Zhao's work in Sichuan helped him advance rapidly in the Communist Party and the government. In 1980, Zhao became a member of China's most powerful policymaking body—the standing committee of the Communist Party's Politburo. Also in 1980, he became premier of China. The premier heads the operations of the government. Zhao held that post until he became general secretary in 1987.   Donald W. Klein

Zhou dynasty, *joh,* also spelled *Chou,* was a Chinese *dynasty* (family of rulers) that governed from about 1122 B.C. to 256 B.C. It was China's longest-ruling dynasty.

The dynasty began when the Zhou tribes of western China conquered the ruling Shang dynasty. Zhou rulers set up a society with three classes—aristocrats, commoners, and slaves. The commoners farmed their own land and that of the aristocrats. Zhou rulers divided the kingdom into many states. A local chief headed each state but enforced the central government's rules.

A weak Zhou ruler was overthrown by his enemies in 771 B.C. The dynasty then moved its capital east from Hao (near what is now Xi'an) to Luoyang. The move marked the beginning of the *Eastern Zhou period.* During this period, cities grew, a merchant class developed, and the use of money replaced *barter* (trade). The famous philosophers Confucius and Laozi developed their ideas during this time (see **Confucius; Laozi**).

The Zhou central government gradually lost power to its large states, and the dynasty finally ended in 256 B.C. Seven large states controlled China until 221 B.C., when the Qin dynasty took over.   Eugene Boardman

Zhou Enlai, *joh ehn ly* (1898-1976), also spelled *Chou En-lai,* became premier and foreign minister of China when the Communists won control of the country in 1949. He was replaced as foreign minister in 1959, but remained the most influential spokesman for China in international affairs.

Zhou was born in Jiangsu (Kiangsu) Province. He attended schools in China, Japan, and France, and became a spokesman for the international Communist movement. In 1931, Zhou joined Mao Zedong, leader of the Chinese Communists. Zhou took part in the *Long March* of 1934, when Mao led the Communists 6,000 miles (9,700 kilometers) across China. Zhou was a leader in the competition with the Nationalists for control of China in the 1940's. As premier, he became Mao's spokesman in foreign affairs. In 1972, Zhou held meetings with President Richard M. Nixon. It was the first time a U.S. President visited China while in office.   Marius B. Jansen

Audrey Topping, Rapho Guillumette
Zhou Enlai

Zhuangzi, *jwahng dzuh,* also spelled *Chuang Tzu,* was a Chinese philosopher of the 300's B.C. He ranks with Laozi (Lao Tzu) as the most important figure in the development of the philosophy called Taoism. Zhuangzi probably wrote parts of a book called the *Zhaungzi,* which was named after him. The book's wit and imaginative style make it one of the greatest works of Chinese literature. The *Zhuangzi* also helped shape the branch of Buddhism called Zen.

The *Zhuangzi* teaches the mystical doctrine that all things come together in an indefinable harmony called the *Tao* (Way). The book urges that people live spontaneously, calmly accepting inevitable changes—even death. One passage asks: "How do I know hating death is not like having strayed from home when a child and not knowing the way back?"   N. Sivin

See **Taoism; Laozi.**

Zhukov, *ZHOO kawf,* **Georgi Konstantinovich,** *gay AWR gih KAWN stahn TEE nah vihch* (1896-1974), became a Soviet military hero during World War II (1939-1945). He organized the defense of Moscow in 1941 and the Soviet victory at Stalingrad in 1942 and 1943. He led the Soviet forces that captured Berlin in 1945. Zhukov became a marshal—the highest rank in the Soviet army—in 1943.

Soviet dictator Joseph Stalin feared Zhukov's popularity after the war and assigned him to minor posts. Stalin died in 1953, and Zhukov rose to the post of defense minister in 1955. Zhukov helped Nikita S. Khrushchev in-

crease his power in the Communist Party in 1957. Khrushchev made Zhukov a member of the *Presidium* (now called *Politburo*), the highest Soviet governing body, but came to fear his influence. Khrushchev removed him from his high positions later that year. Zhukov was born in Strelkovka, near Moscow. He fought in World War I.   Albert Parry

Ziegfeld, *ZIHG fehld,* **Florenz** (1869-1932), was an American theater producer. He became famous for a series of musical revues, called the *Ziegfeld Follies,* which he presented annually from 1907 to 1927.

The *Ziegfeld Follies* featured a chorus line of beautiful women in lavish costumes performing in extravagant settings. Many Ziegfeld beauties became motion-picture stars, including Marion Davies, Irene Dunne, and Paulette Goddard. Ziegfeld also introduced many famous entertainers in the revues, notably Eddie Cantor, Fanny Brice, Will Rogers, W. C. Fields, and Bert Williams. Ziegfeld commissioned such composers as Irving Berlin and Jerome Kern to provide songs for the *Follies.* Ziegfeld also produced numerous musical comedies, such as *Rio Rita* (1927), *Show Boat* (1927), and *Rosalie* (1928). He was born in Chicago.   Daniel J. Watermeier

Ziggurat. See **Architecture** (Mesopotamian).

Zim, Herbert Spencer (1909-   ), is an author and educator. He wrote more than 60 children's science books, including *Elephants* (1946), *Dinosaurs* (1954), *The Universe* (1961), and *Sharks* (1966).

Zim was born in New York City. He earned B.S., M.A., and Ph.D. degrees from Columbia University. He taught science courses at a private school in New York City from 1932 to 1950 and at the University of Illinois from 1950 to 1957.   Eloise Rue

Zimbabwe, *zihm BAH bway,* formerly called Rhodesia, is a landlocked country in southern Africa. Most of the country is a high plateau. Zimbabwe lies in the tropics but has a pleasant climate because of the high altitude. Zimbabwe's beautiful scenery includes the famous Victoria Falls on the Zambezi River along the country's northern border. Zimbabwe is a leading mineral producer. Harare (formerly called Salisbury) is the capital and largest city.

Since the late 1800's, the area that is now the country of Zimbabwe has had a troubled, often violent, political history. The vast majority of Zimbabwe's people are

Facts in brief

Capital: Harare.
Official language: English.
Area: 150,804 sq. mi. (390,580 km²).
Population: *Estimated 1990 population*—9,700,000; density, 64 persons per sq. mi. (25 per km²); distribution, 72 per cent rural, 28 per cent urban. *1982 census*—7,550,000. *Estimated 1995 population*—10,630,000.
Chief products: *Agriculture*—cattle, coffee, corn, cotton, sugar, tea, tobacco, wheat. *Manufacturing and processing*—chemicals, clothing and footwear, iron and steel, metal products, processed foods, textiles. *Mining*—asbestos, chromite, coal, copper, gems, gold, nickel.
National anthem: "Ishe Komborera Africa" ("God Bless Africa").
Flag: The flag has seven horizontal stripes of green, yellow, red, black, red, yellow, and green. A white triangle on the left contains a yellow Great Zimbabwe bird on a red star. See **Flag** (picture: Flags of Africa).
Money: *Basic unit*—Zimbabwe dollar. See **Money** (table).

Zimbabwe

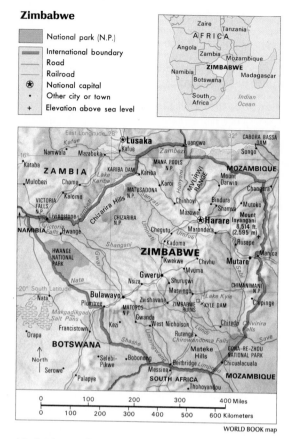

National park (N.P.)

International boundary
Road
Railroad
⊛ National capital
• Other city or town
+ Elevation above sea level

WORLD BOOK map

black Africans, but whites controlled the government from about 1890 to 1979. During the last years of white rule, black nationalists in Zimbabwe—then called Rhodesia—engaged in guerrilla warfare against the government. At the same time, the nation's economy was crippled by international trade *sanctions* (restrictions).

In the face of mounting opposition both at home and abroad, white Rhodesians finally agreed to hand over political power to the blacks. The first black-majority government was elected in 1979. However, many blacks rejected this government because they felt it was unrepresentative and that it allowed whites to retain many special privileges. Widespread guerrilla violence continued until late 1979, when the government and the rebels signed a peace treaty. In return for a cease-fire, the government agreed to hold new elections in February 1980. The political party of Robert Mugabe, one of the principal rebel leaders, won a large majority of votes in these elections. Mugabe then became prime minister of the independent republic of Zimbabwe.

Government. An executive president heads Zimbabwe's government. The first executive president, Robert Mugabe, was elected by Parliament in 1987. Succeeding executive presidents are to be elected by the people. The executive president appoints a vice president and Cabinet to carry out government operations.

Zimbabwe's laws are made by a Parliament that consists of a 100-member House of Assembly and a 40-member Senate. The members of the House are elected by the people to five-year terms. In the Senate, some

members are chosen by members of the House, some by local councils, and some by the executive president. The senators serve five-year terms.

Zimbabwe's constitution, adopted in 1979, included provisions that reserved a majority of the seats in Parliament for blacks and a minority of the seats for whites. These provisions for reserving seats on the basis of race were abolished in 1987.

People. About 98 per cent of Zimbabweans are blacks. About 1 per cent are whites. The rest are Asians and *Coloreds* (people of mixed ancestry). Over three-fourths of the blacks live in rural areas. Most of the whites, Asians, and Coloreds live in cities and towns. The largest black ethnic group is the Shona (often called the Mashona). The Ndebele (often called the Matabele) is the second largest. The Shona speak a language called Chishona, and the Ndebele speak Sindebele.

Most blacks in Zimbabwe are farmers who live in thatched huts. Most of them raise only enough food for their families. Their main crop, corn, is pounded into flour to make a dish called *mealies* or *sadza*.

Many blacks in Zimbabwe work on commercial farms owned by whites. Other blacks work in cities and towns. The whites include farmers, who own most of the high *veld* (grasslands), and business and professional people.

Land. Most of Zimbabwe is a high, rolling plateau from 3,000 to 5,000 feet (910 to 1,500 meters) above sea level. The High Veld, a central plateau, crosses the country from northeast to southwest. The Middle Veld lies on either side of the High Veld. The Low Veld consists of sandy plains in the Zambezi, Limpopo, and Sabi river basins. Mount Inyangani (8,514 feet, or 2,595 meters) is Zimbabwe's highest point.

Zimbabwe's summer lasts from October to April and is hot and wet. The winter, from May to September, is cool and dry. Temperatures range between 54° and 85° F. (12° and 29° C), and rainfall varies from 15 inches (38 centimeters) a year in the west to 50 inches (130 centimeters) in the east.

Economy. Zimbabwe is an important producer of gold, asbestos, and nickel. A smelter at Kwekwe (formerly Que Que) removes iron from ore mined in the area. Coal comes from the Hwange (formerly Wankie) region. The country also has deposits of chromite, copper, tin, and gems. Crops include coffee, corn, cotton, peanuts, sugar, sunflower seeds, tea, tobacco, and wheat. Cattle raising on large ranches is also important.

The Kariba Gorge hydroelectric complex on the Zambezi is one of the world's largest. Its dam forms Kariba Lake, which covers 2,000 square miles (5,200 square kilometers). Its power plant supplies electricity to most of Zimbabwe. It is operated by Zimbabwe and Zambia.

History. Bushmen paintings and tools found in the region indicate that Stone Age people lived in what is now Zimbabwe. By the A.D. 800's, people were mining minerals for trade. Shona people established their rule about A.D. 1000. They built a city called Zimbabwe, or Great Zimbabwe. The word *zimbabwe* means *house of stone* in the Shona language. The city's ruins lie near Masvingo (formerly Fort Victoria). They include a tower 30 feet (9 meters) high and part of a wall 800 feet (240 meters) around and up to 32 feet (10 meters) high. The city's structures were made of huge granite slabs, most of which were fitted together without mortar.

Harare, *left,* is the capital and largest city of Zimbabwe. This street in Harare's downtown area is lined with high-rise hotels and office buildings.

Cameramann International, Ltd. from Marilyn Gartman

During the 1400's, a branch of the Shona, called the Karanga, established the Mwanamutapa Empire. This empire included what is now Zimbabwe. At eastern African ports, the Karanga traded ivory, gold, and copper for porcelain from China and cloth and beads from India and Indonesia. The Rozwi, a southern Karanga group, rebelled in the late 1400's and founded the Changamire Empire. This empire became stronger than the Mwanamutapa Empire, and the Rozwi took over the city of Zimbabwe.The Rozwi built the city's largest structures. The Changamire Empire was prosperous and peaceful until Nguni people from the south conquered the empire in the 1830's. The city of Zimbabwe was abandoned after the fall of the Changamire Empire.

Portuguese explorers introduced Christianity to what is now Zimbabwe in the 1500's. But few people accepted Christianity until the 1850's when Robert Moffat, a Scottish missionary, set up a mission at Inyati. In 1888, the Ndebele granted mineral rights in the area to Cecil Rhodes, a British financier. By 1893, Rhodes's British South Africa Company occupied most of the region. In 1895, this company named its territory Rhodesia.

The British crushed black African uprisings in 1896 and 1897, and reports of gold brought more Europeans to the area. In 1898, Great Britain recognized Southern and Northern Rhodesia as separate territories. In 1922, the white settlers of Southern Rhodesia (now Zimbabwe) voted for self-government, and Southern Rhodesia became a self-governing British colony in 1923. In 1953, Britain set up the Federation of Rhodesia and Nyasaland, which included Southern Rhodesia, Northern Rhodesia (now Zambia), and Nyasaland (now Malawi).

In 1961, Britain and Southern Rhodesia approved a new constitution. But the leading black African party boycotted the first election, because it felt too few blacks could vote. Later, the government banned two black African parties, the Zimbabwe African People's Union and the Zimbabwe African National Union. Both demanded a greater part in government for blacks.

The Federation of Rhodesia and Nyasaland was dissolved in 1963. In 1964, Northern Rhodesia became the independent nation of Zambia, and Nyasaland became independent as Malawi. Southern Rhodesia became known as Rhodesia. Its government demanded independence in 1964. Britain declared that Rhodesia must first guarantee the black majority a greater voice in the government. Rhodesian talks with Britain finally broke down. On Nov. 11, 1965, Prime Minister Ian Smith declared Rhodesia independent. Rhodesia was the first colony to break with Britain without consent since the American Colonies did so in 1776. Britain called Rhodesia's action illegal and banned all trade with Rhodesia. Rhodesia rejected British proposals for a settlement. In 1966, the United Nations imposed economic sanctions against Rhodesia. Most countries then stopped or reduced their trade with Rhodesia.

In 1969, Rhodesian voters—mostly whites—approved a new constitution designed to prevent the black African majority from ever gaining control of the government. The constitution took effect in 1970. Rhodesia declared itself a republic on March 2, 1970. But no country recognized its independent status. Led by the United Nations, many countries continued to apply political and economic pressure to end white rule in Rhodesia.

In 1971, Britain and Rhodesia reached an agreement that included provisions to gradually increase black representation in the government. But most Rhodesian blacks opposed the pact, and it did not take effect. In the early 1970's, fighting erupted between government troops and black guerrillas in Rhodesia. In 1974, the two sides agreed to a cease-fire.

In 1976, fighting again broke out between Rhodesian government troops and black guerrillas. Mozambique and other black African nations joined in the demand for an end of white rule in Rhodesia. Clashes between Rhodesian government troops and troops of Mozambique broke out near the border between the countries.

In the mid-1970's, Rhodesia's white rulers, led by Prime Minister Smith, began making plans to establish a new government with a majority of black leaders. In 1978, the whites reached an agreement with moderate Rhodesian blacks to form a government. Voting procedures were changed to allow all people 18 years old or over to vote. Previously, strict economic and educational requirements had prevented most blacks from voting. Elections in April 1979 resulted in a government with a majority of black leaders. Abel T. Muzorewa, a Methodist bishop, became the first black prime minister. But many blacks rejected the new government as unrepresentative, and no other country officially recognized it.

Widespread fighting between black guerrillas and the government went on until September 1979, when Britain arranged a peace settlement between the government and the rebels. Both sides finally agreed to the formation of a new government. In elections held in February 1980, the Zimbabwe African National Union-Patriotic Front (ZANU-PF) party won a majority of the seats in the House of Assembly. Robert Mugabe, the party's leader, became prime minister. On April 18, 1980, Britain recognized the country's independence, and Rhodesia's name was officially changed to Zimbabwe. Most countries and the United Nations soon recognized the new government and lifted the remaining trade sanctions against the nation. Since the blacks gained control of the government, many whites have left.

In 1981, fighting broke out between the Shona and the Ndebele ethnic groups. In 1982, Prime Minister Mugabe—the leader of the Shona—dismissed Joshua Nkomo—the head of the Ndebele—from his Cabinet. Supporters of Nkomo deserted the national army and formed guerrilla groups that attacked government installations and security forces. During 1983, Shona military units put down most of the rebellion.

Mugabe's party won the 1985 national elections. In 1987, the office of prime minister was abolished. The office of executive president was created to replace it as the highest government post. Parliament elected Mugabe to the new office.

Negotiations begun in 1986 between Mugabe's ZANU-PF and Nkomo's Zimbabwe African People's Union led the parties to formally merge in 1988. The new party uses the name ZANU-PF.   J. Dixon Esseks

Related articles in *World Book* include:

Bulawayo	Rhodes, Cecil J.	Victoria Falls
Harare	Smith, Ian D.	Zambezi River
Mugabe, Robert G.		

Zinc, a chemical element, is a shiny, bluish-white metal. It is important in industry. Zinc can be worked into almost any shape using conventional metalworking methods. Such metals as iron and steel can be *galvanized*— that is, coated with zinc—to prevent rusting. Galvanized

Leading zinc-mining countries

Annual zinc production	
Canada	●●●●●●●●●●●●●●
	1,295,000 short tons (1,175,000 metric tons)
Soviet Union	●●●●●●●●●
	893,000 short tons (810,000 metric tons)
Australia	●●●●●●●●
	809,000 short tons (734,000 metric tons)
Peru	●●●●●●◖
	649,000 short tons (589,000 metric tons)
Mexico	●●●
	309,000 short tons (280,000 metric tons)

Figures are for 1985.
Source: *Minerals Yearbook, 1985,* U.S. Bureau of Mines.

metal is used in such products as roof gutters and tank linings. Zinc is also used in electric batteries. Plants and animals require zinc for normal growth and healing. Zinc is also a component of the hormone insulin.

Zinc can be combined with other metals to form many *alloys* (mixtures). For example, brass is an alloy of copper and zinc. Bronze is copper, tin, and zinc. Nickel silver is copper, nickel, and zinc. Zinc is also used in *solders* (easily melted alloys used for joining metals). Zinc and its alloys are used in *die-casting* (forming objects from liquid metal in molds), *electroplating* (coating an object by use of electricity), and *powder metallurgy* (forming objects from metal powder). Since 1982, United States pennies have been made from a predominantly zinc alloy coated with a thin layer of copper.

Moist air *tarnishes* (discolors) zinc with a protective coating of zinc oxide. Once a thin layer of this coating forms, air cannot tarnish the zinc below it. White, powdery zinc oxide is used in making cosmetics, plastics, rubber, skin ointments, and soaps. It is also used as a pigment in paints and inks. Zinc sulfide, a compound of zinc and sulfur, glows when ultraviolet light, X rays, or *cathode rays* (streams of electrons) shine on it. It is used on luminous dials for clocks and to coat the inside of television screens and fluorescent lamps. When mixed with water, zinc chloride, a compound of zinc and chlorine, protects wood from decay and insects.

Zinc is never found pure in nature. It occurs combined with sulfur in a mineral called *sphalerite* or *zinc blende.* Other zinc-containing minerals are *calamine, franklinite, smithsonite, willemite,* and *zincite.* Zinc is hard and brittle at room temperature. It is taken from its ores by heating them in air to convert them to zinc oxide. The oxide is heated with carbon to produce zinc.

Zinc's chemical symbol is Zn. Its atomic number is 30, and its atomic weight is 65.39. Zinc melts at 419.58° C and boils at 907° C. Alloys containing large amounts of zinc have been found in prehistoric ruins. By 200 B.C., the Romans were making brass from ores containing zinc and copper. The first complete study of zinc was published in 1746 by Andreas Sigismund Marggraf, a German chemist.   Raymond E. Davis

See also **Alloy; Galvanizing; Sphalerite.**

Zinjanthropus, *zihn jan THROH puhs* or *zihn JAN thruh puhs,* was a humanlike creature that most anthropologists believe lived about 1,750,000 years ago. A fossil skull of *Zinjanthropus* was discovered in 1959 by the British anthropologist Mary D. Leakey in the Olduvai Gorge in northern Tanzania. It was one of the first indications that primitive humanlike creatures once lived in eastern Africa. Scientists determined that such creatures existed about twice as long ago as had previously been estimated. The word *Zinjanthropus* comes from *zinj,* an ancient Persian word meaning *eastern Africa,* and *anthropos,* a Greek word meaning *human being.*

The *Zinjanthropus* skull came from a creature 16 to 18 years old that had a brain about a third the size of a modern human brain. *Zinjanthropus* was nicknamed "Nutcracker Man" because its teeth, though shaped like human teeth, were larger than those of modern apes or human beings. It ate mostly plants, and its teeth were worn down from grinding coarse vegetation. Many scientists believe it also may have butchered dead animals for meat, because stone tools and broken animal bones were discovered near the skull. *Zinjanthropus* probably became extinct about a million years ago.

Later findings in southern Africa indicated that *Zinjanthropus* was one type of humanlike creature called *Australopithecus.* In 1967, *Zinjanthropus* was renamed *Australopithecus boisei.* Most scientists believe it belonged to a species of *Australopithecus* that did not develop into modern human beings. Adrienne L. Zihlman

See also **Australopithecus; Leakey family.**

Zinnemann, *ZIHN uh muhn,* **Fred** (1907-   ), is a motion-picture director whose films are noted for their skillful character portrayal. He won Academy Awards for *From Here to Eternity* (1953) and *A Man for All Seasons* (1966). His other major films include *The Seventh Cross* (1944), *The Search* (1947), *The Men* (1950), *The Member of the Wedding* (1952), *High Noon* (1952), *Oklahoma!* (1955), *The Nun's Story* (1958), *The Sundowners* (1960), *The Day of the Jackal* (1973), and *Julia* (1977).

Zinnemann was born in Vienna, Austria. He learned film techniques while working in Paris. He moved to Hollywood in 1929. His short *That Mothers Might Live* (1938) won an Academy Award. Howard Thompson

Zinnia, *ZIHN ee uh,* is a genus of garden plants of the composite family. There are about 16 species. The zin-

Youth-and-old-age   Starlike   Hybrid
Zinnia   Zinnia   Zinnia

WORLD BOOK illustrations by Christabel King
Colorful zinnias are popular garden flowers.

nias are native to Mexico and the southwestern United States. The best-known zinnia is a garden plant that blooms in a wide variety of colors. Its stiff, hairy stem may grow 2 feet (61 centimeters) tall. The flowers are in tones of red, yellow, scarlet, crimson, pink, salmon, and bronze. This zinnia is one of the most successful summer annual flowers. It grows in three types. One is *youth-and-old-age,* which grows as high as 3 feet (91 centimeters). Another has golden, starlike flowers. The third is a miniature hybrid. Zinnias grow well in warm, sunny climates. They are grown from seed.

Scientific classification. Zinnias are in the composite family, Compositae. Youth-and-old-age is *Zinnia elegans.* The starlike flower is *Z. linearis;* the small hybrid, *Z. angustifolia.*

Margaret R. Bolick

See also **Flower** (picture: Garden annuals).

Zion, *ZY uhn,* is a word with many different meanings. It comes from the Hebrew word *Tsīyōn.* Originally, it was the name of a hill in the city of Jerusalem. After the Israelites captured the city from the Jebusites, Zion became the place where the royal palace of King David stood and where Solomon later built the Temple. It was the seat of Jewish worship and government. The name Zion also refers to the Israelites themselves. After their exile from the Holy Land, the word Zion meant to them their homeland, with Jerusalem, the Temple, and all Palestine's ancient glory. Among Christians, the name Zion means the church ruled by God, or a heavenly city or heavenly home. See also **Zionism.** Gary G. Porton

Zion National Park lies in southwestern Utah. It has many colorful canyons, some of which are extremely narrow and have steep, plunging walls. Rock formations range in color from dark red and orange to light purple and pink. These colors change continuously as the light changes. Wild plants and such animals as mule deer and bats flourish there.

Zion Canyon is the main feature of the park. It is about 10 miles (16 kilometers) long and from $\frac{1}{2}$ mile (0.8 kilometer) to less than 50 feet (15 meters) wide. Its walls tower as high as 3,000 feet (910 meters), in some places almost straight up and down. The canyon contains many unusual rock formations.

The park was set aside in 1909 as Mukuntuweap National Monument. In 1918, the park was enlarged and in 1919 it became Zion National Park. Zion National Monument, a vast area of rugged land adjoining the park, was added in 1956. For the area of the park, see **National Park System** (table: National parks). For location, see **Utah** (political map).

Critically reviewed by the National Park Service

Zionism is a movement aimed at establishing a national Jewish state in Palestine, the ancient Jewish homeland. Active Zionism began in the 1800's and led to the establishment of Israel in 1948. Zionism now supports various projects in Israel and acts as a cultural bridge between Israel and Jews in other countries. Zionists work to revive the national Jewish language and culture, and to establish the political and social institutions needed to recreate national Jewish life. *Zion* is the Hebrew poetic name for Palestine.

Movement to Palestine. A series of *pogroms* (organized persecutions of the Jews) in Russia in the 1800's spurred the first significant wave of Jewish emigration from Europe. In 1882, groups of Jewish youths calling themselves *Hoveve-Zion* (Lovers of Zion) formed a movement to promote immigration to Palestine. The Hoveve-Zion started what was called *practical Zionism,* which favored establishing Jewish settlements in Palestine. Theodor Herzl, an Austrian journalist, developed *political Zionism,* which worked for political recognition of the Jewish claim to a Palestine homeland.

Herzl was a reporter at the famous trial in 1894 of Alfred Dreyfus, the French army officer falsely convicted of treason. The Dreyfus affair convinced Herzl that, if anti-Semitism could be an active force in a country as enlightened as France, Jews could not assimilate in non-Jewish society. To him, the only remedy was to create an independent Jewish state.

Herzl organized the Zionist movement on a worldwide scale at the First Zionist Congress in Basel, Switzerland, in 1897. Since that time, Zionism has been opposed by those Jews who claim (1) that only God can restore the Jews to their homeland; and (2) that the Jews are a religious denomination, not a national group.

Practical Zionism dominated the movement until World War I. But the movement gained political recognition when Great Britain liberated the Middle East, including Palestine, from Turkish domination in World War I. Scientist Chaim Weizmann, who later became the first president of Israel, helped persuade the British government to issue the Balfour Declaration in 1917.

The Balfour Declaration pledged British support for a national homeland for the Jews in Palestine. It was included in the British *mandate* (order to rule) over Palestine that went into effect in 1920. Arabs fought against a Jewish state in Palestine, and severe fighting broke out several times in the 1920's and 1930's. The mandate recognized the Jewish Agency as the representative organization of the Jews in Palestine. The agency developed economic and cultural facilities, set up educational and scientific institutes, and encouraged Jews to settle there.

In 1939, the British set strict limits on Jewish immigration to Palestine to gain Arab support for the Allies during World War II. Palestine's Jews fought bitterly against the restrictions after World War II, and the British submitted the problem to the United Nations. In 1947, the UN approved the partition of Palestine into an Arab and a Jewish state. The Zionists proclaimed the State of Israel in 1948. Arab states attacked Israel almost immediately. Arab-Israeli fighting has broken out several times since then.   Joel L. Kraemer

See also **Palestine; Israel; Balfour Declaration; Hebrew language and literature** (Modern Hebrew literature); **Herzl, Theodor; Weizmann, Chaim.**

Additional resources

O'Brien, Conor C. *The Siege: The Saga of Israel and Zionism.* Simon & Schuster, 1986.
Schweid, Eliezer. *The Land of Israel: National Home or Land of Destiny.* Fairleigh Dickinson, 1985.

ZIP Code is a code system used to speed the sorting and delivery of mail in the United States. The name stands for *Z*oning *I*mprovement *P*lan.

The ZIP system uses five numerals that appear after an address. In the ZIP number 22207, for example, the first numeral—2—designates one of 10 geographical areas. Area 2 consists of the District of Columbia, Maryland, North Carolina, South Carolina, Virginia, and West Virginia. The second two numerals—22—indicate a metropolitan area or sectional center. In this case, the mail is going to the Arlington area of Virginia. The last two numerals—07—represent a small town or delivery unit from which the mail will be delivered. In 1981, the Postal Service introduced a voluntary nine-number ZIP code. High-volume business mailers that use this code receive a discount on their mailing rate.

The Post Office Department (now the United States Postal Service) introduced the ZIP Code in 1963. By that time, the volume of the mail in the United States had increased almost 900 per cent since 1900. The mail had also changed in nature from chiefly personal to about 80 per cent business correspondence.

Many companies use mechanized addressing systems. To help them, the Post Office Department in 1963 introduced two-letter abbreviations for states and some other areas. These abbreviations enable mechanized addressing systems to save space by putting a ZIP Code on the same line of an address as the city and state. For the two-letter state abbreviations, see the table with the **Post office** article.

The ZIP Code especially speeds up the handling and delivery of *bulk mail* (a huge number of identical pieces). Several other nations also use code systems for mail processing.   Critically reviewed by the United States Postal Service

See also **Post office** (Sorting).

Zipper is a term often used to mean any kind of slide fastener. These fasteners have two edges of teeth and hollows which fit into each other snugly. A slide draws the edges together and meshes the teeth into the hollows. The edges remain fastened until the slide is drawn back, unmeshing the teeth. Whitcomb L. Judson of Chicago patented the first slide fastener in 1893. It was a series of hooks and eyes that fastened together with a slider. Gideon Sundback obtained a patent on the meshed-tooth type of slide fastener in 1913. In 1922, the B. F. Goodrich Company gave the trade name *Zipper* to galoshes with slide fasteners. Zippers were first used in men's pants. They did not appear in women's clothing until the late 1920's.   Lois M. Gurel

Zircon, *ZUR kahn,* is a mineral composed chiefly of the elements silicon, oxygen, and zirconium. It is a *silicate* and has the chemical formula $ZrSiO_4$ (see **Silicate**). Zircon contains smaller amounts of other elements, including hafnium, iron, and the rare earths. Some zircons also contain the radioactive elements thorium and uranium. Zircon crystals may be reddish-brown, yellow, green, blue, or colorless. They resemble prisms with pyramid-shaped ends. The crystals occur in alkali basalts, granites, and other *igneous rocks* (see **Igneous rock**). Zircon is resistant to weathering, so it is also found in gravel and sand produced by the erosion of igneous rock.

Zircon is the world's main source of zirconium and hafnium. These metals are used in the ceramics industry and in making parts for nuclear reactors. Large zircon crystals are used for jewelry (see **Gem** (picture)). Zircon is a December birthstone.   Robert W. Charles

Zirconium, *zur KOH nee uhm,* is a grayish-white metal. It is found in nature as the silicate mineral *zircon* and the oxide mineral *baddeleyite.*

Zirconium is used to make the cores of nuclear reactors because it resists corrosion and does not readily absorb neutrons. *Zircaloy* is an important alloy developed for such nuclear applications as a coating for fuel parts. Baddeleyite can withstand extremely high temperatures. It is used for laboratory *crucibles* (melting pots for metals) and the linings for furnaces.

Zirconium has the chemical symbol Zr. Its atomic number is 40, and its atomic weight is 91.22. It melts at 1857° C and boils at 4200° C. At 25° C, its density is 6.51 grams per cubic centimeter (see **Density**). Martin Heinrich Klaproth, a German chemist, isolated the oxide of zirconium from zircon in 1789. Metallic zirconium was first prepared in 1824 by Jöns J. Berzelius, a Swedish chemist.   S. C. Cummings

Zither is a stringed musical instrument that consists chiefly of a flat, wooden box with 32 or more strings or wires stretched along its length. The zither is placed on a table when played. The five strings nearest the musician provide the melody. The other strings are used for accompaniment. The player strums the melody strings with a ring-shaped *plectrum* (pick) worn on the thumb of the right hand. The second, third, and fourth fingers on that hand pluck chords. The left hand presses the melody strings against a fingerboard with *frets* (ridges) to select the pitch.

Abram Loft

Cameramann International Ltd. from Marilyn Gartman

The zither

Zodiac, *ZOH dee ak,* is a band of stars that appears to encircle the earth. *Astrologers* (people who tell fortunes by studying the stars) believe that the zodiac influences people's lives. They use a representation of the zodiac to draw a chart called a *horoscope.* The chart supposedly reveals a person's character or future.

The signs of the zodiac. The zodiac consists of 12 divisions called *signs.* The signs are named for certain groups of stars called *constellations.* For example, the zodiac includes Aries (the Ram) and Taurus (the Bull). Astrologers believe that a person comes under the influence of a particular sign, depending on the person's date of birth. For example, people born during the period from June 22 to July 22 have Cancer as their sign. For the names of all the signs of the zodiac and their related dates, see the illustration with this article.

The influence of the signs. According to astrologers, the zodiac's influence on a person comes from several sources. Some influence comes from the plan-

ets. Each sign gets its main characteristics from one planet, called its *ruling* planet. For example, the planet Jupiter rules Sagittarius. Astrologers consider Jupiter "friendly" and "generous." Thus, people born under the sign of Sagittarius supposedly have these traits.

The zodiac also receives some of its influence from four "substances" called *elements:* air, earth, fire, and water. Ancient astrologers thought that all matter was made up of these four elements. Each element has certain qualities that it gives to three signs of the zodiac. For example, fire—considered forceful and restless—influences Aries, Leo, and Sagittarius.

History. Astrologers developed the idea of the zodiac more than 2,000 years ago. They observed the changing position of the stars that accompanied the change in seasons. They knew that if the stars could be seen in daytime the sun would appear to move through a series of constellations, entering a new one each month. These constellations made up the zodiac.

Ancient peoples believed there was a connection between seasonal changes and the constellations of the zodiac. At that time, for example, spring began when the sun was "in" Aries. Thus, Aries became associated with the energetic forces of spring. In time, astrologers developed ways to explain the supposed influence of the zodiac on people's lives.

The position of the earth in space has changed since ancient times. As a result, the dates for each sign no longer represent the time when the sun is in the related constellation. For example, on March 23, a date associated with Aries, the sun is actually in Pisces. However, most modern astrologers still use the traditional dates.

Christopher McIntosh

See also **Astrology; Constellation; Horoscope; House** (in astrology); and the articles on signs of the zodiac, such as **Aries.**

Zodiacal light, *zoh DY uh kuhl,* is a cone-shaped glow of faint light that is seen soon after twilight and

The signs of the zodiac
Astrologers believe that everyone is influenced by a particular sign, depending on his or her birthday. The chart below shows the dates and some characteristics associated with each sign.

WORLD BOOK diagram by Dick Keller

Apr. 20-May 20
Taurus ♉
Bull
Conservative, possessive, loyal

Mar. 21-Apr. 19
Aries ♈
Ram
Bold, courageous, energetic

Feb. 19-Mar. 20
Pisces ♓
Fishes
Artistic, emotional, sensitive

Jan. 20-Feb. 18
Aquarius ♒
Water bearer
Curious, outgoing, independent

Dec. 22-Jan. 19
Capricorn ♑
Goat
Ambitious, cautious, practical

Nov. 22-Dec. 21
Sagittarius ♐
Archer
Cheerful, generous, restless

May 21-June 20
Gemini ♊
Twins
Lively, talkative, intelligent

June 21-July 22
Cancer ♋
Crab
Emotional, patriotic, home loving

July 23-Aug. 22
Leo ♌
Lion
Cheerful, proud, powerful

Aug. 23-Sept. 22
Virgo ♍
Virgin
Modest, practical, tidy

Sept. 23-Oct. 22
Libra ♎
Scales
Companionable, diplomatic, pleasant

Oct. 23-Nov. 21
Scorpio ♏
Scorpion
Secretive, intense, passionate

just before dawn. The zodiacal light is brightest near the sun and shades off gradually. It can easily be traced half-way across the sky. It brightens again in an area just opposite the sun called the *Gegenschein,* which means *counterglow.*

The zodiacal light is so named because it is seen against the zodiacal constellations that lie along the *ecliptic,* the sun's apparent path around the earth. The accepted explanation of the light is that large numbers of small particles of material scattered about the inner solar system reflect sunlight and become visible when the sky is dark. These dust particles are believed to be debris from comets and asteroids.   Lee J. Rickard

Zola, *ZOH luh,* **Émile,** *ay MEEL* (1840-1902), made naturalism the leading form of literature in France in the late 1800's. He described life as he saw it, and his books and his life demonstrate his courage, intelligence, and sense of justice. Zola's open letter *J'accuse* (1898) helped win a new trial for Alfred Dreyfus, a French army officer unjustly convicted of spying. Zola was convicted of libel after publication of the letter. He fled to England for a year, but he later became a national hero for his part in the affair. Zola also tried to win acceptance for artist Edouard Manet and other impressionist painters who broke with artistic tradition.

Zola was born in Paris. He began his career as a journalist and novelist in the 1860's. His first novel of merit was *Thérèse Raquin* (1867). After the Franco-Prussian War of 1870, he started working on a long series of novels, *The Rougon-Macquart.* Zola subtitled the series the "natural and social history of a family in the Second Empire." Each of the 20 novels in the series describes the adventures of one or several members of the Rougon-Macquart family, and each treats a different profession, trade, or class of society.

The Belly of Paris (1873), the third volume in the series, gives a vivid picture of the central markets of Paris. *The Grog Shop* (1877) is a terrifying portrait of the effects of alcoholism on industrial workers in Paris. *Nana* (1880), a study of prostitution and other vice, caused a scandal when it was published. *Germinal* (1885) is probably Zola's best novel and perhaps the finest novel ever written on the life of miners. *The Crash* (1892) describes France's defeat by Germany in 1870.

Zola wrote a second series, *The Three Cities,* dealing with religious and social problems. A third series, *The Four Gospels,* was still unfinished at his death.

In his fiction, Zola tried to practice the scientific method. He argued that the novels of *The Rougon-Macquart* showed the effects of heredity and environment on society. However, the scientific basis of Zola's work is weak. But he used the documentary style skillfully and his novels are still valid portraits of various aspects of French life from 1860 to 1890.

Each of Zola's major novels is dominated by a symbol, such as the mine in *Germinal.* His style is somewhat heavy, but he excelled in writing descriptions, especially of crowds. Zola's characters often lack complexity, but they perform vividly in dramas of death and destruction.

Zola wrote several works of criticism defending the naturalist movement. These include *The Experimental Novel* (1880), *The Naturalistic Novelists* (1881), and *Naturalism in the Theater* (1881).   Thomas H. Goetz

See also **Naturalism; Dreyfus, Alfred.**

Zone melting is a method of removing impurities from solid materials that are used in industry and in research. Germanium metal was the first material to be refined commercially by zone melting. Germanium can be purified by zone melting until it contains only 1 atom of an impurity in every 10 billion atoms. If a boxcar of sugar were this pure, it would contain only one grain of impurity. Extremely pure germanium and other substances are used in making semiconductor electronic devices such as transistors and printed circuit boards.

The apparatus used for zone melting consists of a row of ring-shaped heaters that move slowly along a tube containing the solid to be purified. Each heater melts a narrow band of the material, forming a liquid "zone" that moves along with the heater. After each heater passes, the liquid cools and freezes. The impurities tend to stay in the liquid zone and are carried to one end of the tube. The material melts again when the next heater passes, and it becomes purer with each melting and freezing.

Scientists have found that many substances have unexpected properties in a highly pure state. Impurities in these substances had affected their properties in unsuspected ways.   David C. Armbruster

Zoning is a procedure that controls the use of land. Local legislative bodies pass laws that divide a town, city, or county into zones for commercial, industrial, residential, or other types of development. These laws generally limit building and lot dimensions in each zone. Many regulations require certain building features and limit the number and location of parking and loading areas and the use of signs. Other regulations provide space for schools, parks, or other public facilities.

Zoning helps city planners bring about orderly growth and change. It controls population density and helps create attractive, healthful residential areas. It also helps assure property owners and residents that the characteristics of nearby areas will remain stable.

People have regulated land use since ancient times. Zoning became increasingly important as population and industry grew in urban areas. In 1916, New York City enacted the first major zoning ordinance in the United States. Today, many cities around the world have zoning regulations.   Jack Meltzer

Zoning Improvement Plan (ZIP). See ZIP Code.

Zonta International is a worldwide service organization of executive women in business and the professions. It has more than 950 clubs in the United States and about 45 other countries. Zonta International works to improve the economic, legal, political, and professional status of women. The organization awards Zonta Amelia Earhart fellowships annually to women graduate students in aerospace-related sciences and engineering.

Zonta International was founded in 1919 in Buffalo, N.Y. International headquarters are at 557 W. Randolph, Chicago, IL 60606.

Critically reviewed by Zonta International

Zoo is a place where wild animals are kept and displayed. Most large zoos exhibit mammals, birds, reptiles, and amphibians from all parts of the world. Some also feature fish and insects. Many zoos have beautiful gardens and wide, tree-lined paths that lead from one animal display to another. The word *zoo* is a short form of *zoological garden.*

People have put wild animals on display since ancient times. Today, almost every large city has at least one zoo, and many smaller communities also have one. The Zoological Society of San Diego operates the two largest zoos in the world. The San Diego Zoo, which has about 3,200 animals of 800 species, owns one of the largest zoo collections. The San Diego Wild Animal Park, which covers 1,800 acres (728 hectares), ranks as the largest zoo in terms of area.

Size does not necessarily determine the quality or im-

Kenneth W. Fink, Bruce Coleman Inc.

Robert H. Glaze, Artstreet

Zoos vary greatly in size and kinds of animals. The enormous San Diego Wild Animal Park, *above,* features animals from many parts of the world, such as these African elephants. The much smaller Arizona-Sonora Desert Museum, *right,* exhibits only animals, including this coati, that live in the Sonora desert.

Robert H. Glaze, Artstreet

WORLD BOOK photo

Zoos acquaint city dwellers with nature. Visitors at Brookfield Zoo near Chicago, *left,* can see polar bears and other rare animals. Children's zoos, such as the one at the Milwaukee County Zoo, *right,* give youngsters an opportunity to see and touch various animals.

WORLD BOOK photo

Tigers and deer at the Milwaukee County Zoo live in areas that are side-by-side. A deep moat, which visitors cannot see, prevents the tigers from attacking the deer.

portance of a zoo. For example, the Arizona-Sonora Desert Museum in Tucson, Ariz., ranks as one of the finest zoos in the United States. Most of the animals in this small zoo come from the Sonora Desert. But the zoo's imaginative display techniques have been copied throughout the world.

The purposes of zoos

Entertainment and education. People of all ages enjoy visiting zoos. They delight in viewing creatures that they would never otherwise see. But zoos provide more than recreation. They help keep people aware of the beauties of nature and of the need to preserve wildlife. Many zoos offer educational tours and lectures for schoolchildren and other groups. Most large zoos include a special *children's zoo,* where youngsters can pet and perhaps even feed some animals.

Scientific research. Zoos have long served as living zoology laboratories. Zoologists have learned much about animal habits and diseases by studying them in zoos. Studies of live zoo animals, together with examinations of those that have died, have provided zoologists with information about the structure and function of animal bodies.

Zoos also function as collecting centers for facts about animals. The London Zoo, for example, has the largest zoological library in the world. Since 1864, this zoo has published *The Zoological Record,* a yearly index of zoological writings. Scientists in all parts of the world use this book.

Wildlife conservation has become one of the most important jobs of zoos. The breeding of animals in captivity may offer the only means of survival for many species that face extinction in nature. Zoos breed endangered species and subspecies in the hope that these creatures may someday be returned to the wild. Such

breeding has saved the European bison, the Hawaiian goose, Père David's deer, and Przhevalski's horse from extinction. At least two of these species, the European bison and the Hawaiian goose, have been returned to the wild. In the future, zoo breeding programs may help save such creatures as the orang-utan, the pygmy hippopotamus, and the tiger.

Caring for zoo animals

The life of most zoo animals differs greatly from that of their relatives in the wild. For example, zoo animals receive regular meals and medical care. Trained zookeepers take care of the animals' needs, and *curators* (zoologists employed by the zoo) carefully watch the animals. Also, zoo animals need not fear enemies called *predators,* which would eat them or their young. In zoos, predators and prey are kept apart.

On the other hand, the advantages of zoo life can become disadvantages. Regular care and safety make some animals less alert, and boredom causes many to become sluggish or nervous. A number of species will not breed in zoos.

Many institutions have acted to remedy the problems of zoo life. Zoologists, using their increased knowledge of animal behavior, have designed zoos that encourage animals to act as they would in the wild. This emphasis on naturalism has resulted in lively, more active animals. It also has increased the number of species that breed in zoos.

Display. Zoos exhibit animals in a variety of natural settings. One of the most widely used naturalistic display techniques is based on a moat. Heavy-bodied animals, such as bears, lions, and tigers, cannot jump far, and so zoos need not cage them. These creatures can be displayed in an outdoor area surrounded by a deep moat. Such displays not only encourage animals to behave more naturally, but also provide a better view of them. Leopards, mountain lions, and certain other animals that can jump long distances are usually kept in cages.

Many animal exhibits, both indoors and outdoors, include plants, play equipment, and pools and waterfalls. These features relieve the boredom of captivity and encourage the animals to act more as they would in nature.

Other display techniques include a cold barrier for reptiles. This method, developed by the Antwerp Zoo in Belgium, features a refrigerated area that separates the animals from the viewers. Reptiles are cold-blooded and cannot maintain their body temperature in cold surroundings. They will not normally enter the refrigerated zone, and for this reason they do not have to be caged.

Many animals, such as owls and raccoons, are usually active only at night, and they often appear sluggish to zoo visitors. But the Bronx Zoo in New York City developed a lighting system that enables these animals to be viewed under nighttime conditions. At night, a bright white light is shone in the animals' cages. The white light causes the animals to sleep, as they normally would do during the day. In the daytime, when people come to the zoo, the cages are lit only with red or blue light. The animals can barely detect these colors of light, and so they behave as they normally would at night.

During the late 1960's, drive-through zoos began to

be developed. These zoos do not display their animals in cages, but they do keep predators and prey apart. Visitors ride through the zoo in their automobile or aboard a bus or a monorail train. In a well-planned drive-through zoo, the animals live in spacious, naturalistic settings. But some drive-through zoos crowd the animals into smaller areas than traditional zoos do.

Wild-animal parks resemble drive-through zoos because the animals are not caged. But these parks are larger than most drive-through zoos, and they have less interest in exhibiting animals. They serve largely as breeding farms for zoo animals because they provide the natural surroundings required for mating. The San Diego Wild Animal Park, the first such establishment in the United States, opened in 1972. Animals in this huge park roam over large areas under the close watch of curators. Visitors ride a monorail train that travels through the park. The train's route is designed to skirt the areas where animals live, thus disturbing the herds as little as possible. Wild-animal parks have succeeded in breeding such animals as cheetahs and rhinoceroses, which do not breed well in traditional zoos.

Feeding. Zoo kitchens prepare meals designed to meet each animal's nutritional needs. The kinds and amounts of food given to different creatures vary greatly. Some reptiles are fed only once a week, but certain birds and small mammals eat several meals a day.

Zoo kitchens keep a variety of foods, including eggs, fish, fruit, meat, seeds, and vegetables. They also have such unusual items as insects and earthworms. Food supplements, such as vitamins and bone meal, are used to ensure a nutritious diet for every animal. Many animals receive cakes or pellets that consist of various foods and supplements mixed together. These mixtures assure a balanced meal for each animal.

An animal's diet may vary under certain conditions. For example, a male deer receives special food during the summer, when he grows antlers. Pregnant females and mothers nursing their young must also be given a special diet.

Some zoos have set aside areas where visitors may feed prepared foods to the animals. Except in these areas, people should not feed zoo animals. Candy, popcorn, and similar foods can make an animal sick. Thoughtless visitors often throw wrappers, tinfoil, and other objects to the animals. If an animal swallows these things, it could become ill, or it might even die.

Medical care. Nearly all large zoos employ a full-time staff veterinarian to care for their animals. The veterinarian examines the animals regularly and treats sick or injured creatures. Most large zoos have an animal hospital, complete with a nursery for zoo babies. Many smaller zoos employ a veterinarian on a part-time basis.

How zoos obtain animals

Zoos buy most of their animals from people called *animal dealers.* An animal dealer obtains specimens from other zoos and dealers, or from hunters who specialize in capturing wild animals. A dealer sends a list of animals to different zoos. If a zoo wants any of the animals, it buys them from the dealer. Zoos also deal directly with one another, buying and trading animals.

The United States government severely restricts the import of many animals, especially endangered species and those that may transmit diseases to livestock. Because of these restrictions, zoos must rely increasingly on breeding programs as a source of animals.

History

The earliest known zoo was established by Queen Hatshepsut of Egypt about 1500 B.C. About 500 years later, the Chinese emperor Wen Wang founded the Garden of Intelligence, an enormous zoo that covered about 1,500 acres (607 hectares). Between 1000 and 400 B.C., rulers from northern Africa, India, and China established many small zoos. These zoos were designed to display the wealth and power of the ruler.

The ancient Greeks established public zoos as places for the study of animal and plant life. Greek students visited the local zoo as part of their education. The Romans had many private zoos. They also kept a large public collection of wild animals for use in the bloody fights in the Colosseum (see **Colosseum**). During the Middle Ages, from about A.D. 400 to 1500, zoos became rare in Europe. The world's largest zoo at this time was in China.

By the end of the 1400's, global exploration and an increased interest in learning had renewed the desire of Europeans for zoos. Explorers brought back strange creatures from the New World. But these adventurers found more than just animals. In 1519, the Spaniards discovered a huge zoo built by the Aztec Indians in what is now Mexico.

During the next 250 years, a number of zoos were established in Europe. Some of them amounted to nothing more than small exhibits called *menageries.* These consisted of a few bears, lions, or tigers in small, gloomy cages or pits. Many people became disgusted with this treatment of animals and refused to visit menageries. Through the years, menageries were replaced by larger collections of animals that received better care. These institutions became centers of research as well as exhibitions of animals, and they developed into the first

Terence Spencer, Colorific

Zoo animals receive expert care. A zookeeper feeds milk to an infant monkey at Gerald Durrell's Zoo, *above,* on the British island of Jersey. Carefully balanced meals are prepared for the animals in zoo kitchens.

modern zoos. The oldest zoo still in existence is the Schönbrunn Zoo, which opened in Vienna, Austria, in 1752. The Madrid Zoo in Spain was established in 1775, and the Paris Zoo, the third oldest zoo in continuous operation, opened in France in 1793. The Berlin Zoo, which became a leader in research of animal behavior, opened in Germany in 1844.

The development of zoos in the United States began with the chartering of the Philadelphia Zoological Society in 1859. But the Civil War (1861-1865) delayed construction of the Philadelphia Zoo, which did not open until 1874. The Central Park Zoo in New York City opened in 1864, followed by the Buffalo Zoo in New York in 1870 and Chicago's Lincoln Park Zoo in 1874. In 1889, Congress established the National Zoological Park in Washington, D.C. This zoo is the only one operated by the federal government (see **National Zoological Park**). The first Canadian zoo opened in Toronto in 1887.

In 1907, a German animal dealer, Karl Hagenbeck, developed the moat technique of displaying animals (see **Hagenbeck, Karl**). The first children's zoo in the United States opened at the Philadelphia Zoo in 1938.

By the mid-1940's, zoologists knew that many species of animals faced extinction in the wild. Zoos realized that they could help preserve some of these species and began to develop breeding programs. Previously, most zoos had tried to display at least one member of as many different species as possible. Few zoos owned more than one or two animals of a rare species. Today, as a result of the policy of developing breeding herds, many zoos own several animals of the same species.

Clyde A. Hill

Zoogeography. See Geography (Physical geography).

Zoological garden. See Zoo (with pictures); **San Diego** (picture).

Zoology, *zoh AHL uh jee,* is the study of animals. Zoologists try to answer many questions about animals. For example, they conduct research to determine how animals carry out the activities of their lives. They also study how different species are related to one another and how species have *evolved* (changed over long periods). Zoologists observe the ways animals interact with one another and their environment. They also try to find out how people and animals affect one another.

The study of zoology has benefited people in many ways. Human beings and animals have many similar body parts and body functions. As a result, zoology forms a basis for understanding human medicine and other health-related fields. Some animals, such as certain insects and worms, can be harmful to people. Zoological research has led to better methods of dealing with such animals. Zoological studies also have helped in the management of wildlife and other natural resources and in the breeding of domestic animals.

What zoologists study

No one knows for certain how many kinds of animals there are in the world. More than 1 million species have been identified, and new ones are discovered every year. No zoologist can know more than a small part of all that is known about animals. As a result, most zoologists specialize in a certain area of study.

Many branches of zoology deal with a particular kind of animal. For example, *entomology* is the study of insects, the largest group of animals. *Mammalogy* deals with those animals that have hair and that feed their babies on the mother's milk. *Ichthyology* is the study of fish. A zoologist in any of these fields might spend an entire lifetime studying a single species of animal.

Other areas of zoology deal with certain characteristics that many animals have in common. *Taxonomy* is the study of naming and classifying animals. As part of their work, taxonomists establish relationships among different animal groups. For instance, they have shown that bats are more closely related to mice and other mammals than they are to birds. *Comparative anatomy* is the study of differences and similarities in the body structures of different animals. A comparative anatomist might compare the circulatory systems of sharks, frogs, and cats. *Paleontology* is the study of fossil organisms. Paleontologists and comparative anatomists have made important contributions to knowledge about the evolution of many animals.

Zoologists who study *embryology,* also called *developmental biology,* deal with the formation and development of organisms from fertilized eggs to birth. *Physiology* is the study of the functions of animals. Physiologists may observe how the heart pumps blood, how nerves transmit impulses, and how muscles contract.

Other areas of zoology include *genetics* and *ecology.* Genetics is the study of *heredity,* the passing on of characteristics from parents to their young. This field of zoology is important in breeding livestock and in understanding certain human diseases. In addition, through genetic engineering, scientists have been able to alter the *genes* (units of heredity) of various organisms (see **Genetic engineering**). *Ecology* is the study of the relationship of organisms to their environment. A knowledge of ecology helps in managing the limited resources of the earth without harming plant and animal populations.

How zoologists work

Many zoologists work in modern laboratories at universities, research centers, zoos, and museums. Other zoologists do *field studies* in the outdoors. These studies might be performed in a wildlife refuge, at the North Pole, in the jungle, at sea, or anywhere else animals live.

Like other scientists, zoologists conduct research by gathering information in an orderly way. Zoologists often begin their research with an observation that arouses different thoughts as to its meaning. For example, a zoologist working in a laboratory might notice that some rats are much smaller than others. Following this observation, the zoologist would attempt to explain why the rats are smaller by making a scientific guess called a *hypothesis.* The zoologist might hypothesize that the group of small rats lacked a substance that affects normal growth.

After making the hypothesis, the zoologist would test the hypothesis by a series of experiments. In this example, the zoologist might compare the blood of both groups of rats to see if any substance was missing in the blood of the smaller rats. Suppose, in this case, that a substance called growth hormone was absent in the small rats. Additionally, injections of growth hormone restored normal growth in the rats. At this point, the zoologist would develop a theory that would state a connection between this substance and growth. For example, the zoologist might state that growth hormone is necessary for normal growth in rats. Testing the theory in different situations for long periods of time might prove or disprove the theory.

When a zoologist adds to the knowledge of zoology, he or she writes a report of the findings. Such reports are published in scientific journals that are read by zoologists and other interested people.

History

People have always been interested in animals. Prehistoric people had an interest in those animals that were useful as food or clothing, as well as those that were dangerous. Early cave paintings show some of these animals.

During the 300's B.C., the Greek philosopher Aristotle described the structures and habits of animals found in Greece. He based his conclusions on his own observations and those of others. He is sometimes called the father of zoology. Galen, a Greek physician, studied anatomy and physiology in the A.D. 100's. He made observations of dissected animals and experimented with living animals. Galen's work greatly influenced the early medical profession.

After the fall of the Roman Empire in the A.D. 400's, zoology and the other sciences made little progress. During the 1500's and 1600's, however, there was a rebirth of learning. Andreas Vesalius, an anatomist born in present-day Belgium, argued against Galen in *On the Structure of the Human Body* (1543), a book that contained the first detailed portrayal of the human body. Many of Vesalius' careful observations are still accepted today. The development of the compound microscope led to many discoveries. Cells, bacteria, and protozoans were observed for the first time.

Many zoological discoveries occurred in the 1700's and 1800's. In 1758, the Swedish naturalist, Carolus Linnaeus, published a classification system for animals. The system enabled all scientists to use a universally accepted name for each animal that had been discovered. In the early 1800's, Baron Cuvier of France made important contributions to paleontology and comparative anatomy. Cuvier concluded that several animals had become extinct. See **Classification, Scientific.**

Until the end of the 1700's, most people believed that each species of life had remained unchanged and no new species had appeared since the world began. In 1809, the French naturalist Jean Baptiste de Lamarck proposed a theory of evolution of new species based on the influence of the environment. For example, Lamarck said that giraffes had developed long necks by stretching for leaves. Long necks, he said, would then be passed on to the next generation of giraffes. Discoveries in genetics later showed that Lamarck was wrong. But his ideas influenced many scientists, among them the British naturalist Charles Darwin. Darwin made tremendous contributions to zoology. In 1859, he published *The Origin of Species,* one of the most influential zoology books ever written. In it, Darwin presented the theory of *natural selection* to explain how evolution works. See **Evolution; Natural selection.**

Important findings have continued to occur in zoology during the 1900's. Many of these findings have been made in the areas of genetics, physiology, and developmental biology. An important area of zoology that developed in the mid-1900's is *ethology,* the study of the behavior of animals. The Austrian naturalist Konrad Lorenz helped found this field with his study of the behavior of geese.

Careers in zoology

Zoology offers a broad range of career opportunities. Most of these careers require a college education. In addition to zoology courses, students who wish to become zoologists must take courses in mathematics, chemistry, and physics. Many students also take courses in computer science. Certain careers in zoology require additional training in graduate or professional schools.

Many zoologists teach and conduct research in colleges and universities. Other zoologists work in zoos and museums. Many scientists with zoological training work to make more food available for people. These agricultural scientists work with cattle, hogs, sheep, and other farm animals. They use genetic engineering, selective breeding, and other methods to produce more and bigger animals for food. Zoologists with special training in fishery biology attempt to improve the production of fish for food.

Some zoologists work with animals in the field. These zoologists include game wardens, park managers, and ethologists. Manufacturers sometimes hire zoologists to test the effect that a product, such as a fertilizer or insecticide, will have on animals in their natural environment. Zoologists also may work as writers, illustrators, or photographers.   Lawrence C. Wit

Related articles. See **Animal** and its list of *Related articles.* See also the following:

Biographies

Broom, Robert	Haeckel, Ernst H.	Swammerdam, Jan
Cuvier, Baron	Huxley (Thomas)	Tinbergen,
Frisch, Karl von	Lorenz, Konrad	Nikolaas
Goodall, Jane	Schaller, George B.	Vesalius, Andreas

Branches of zoology

Anatomy	Ethology	Morphology
Biochemistry	Genetics	Ornithology
Biophysics	Helminthology	Paleontology
Cytology	Herpetology	Pathology
Ecology	Histology	Physiology
Embryology		

Other related articles

Classification, Scientific	Evolution	Taxidermy
	Fauna	Zoo

Additional resources

Macmillan Illustrated Animal Encyclopedia. Ed. by Philip Whitfield. Macmillan, 1984.
Ricciuti, Edward R. *They Work with Wildlife: Jobs for People Who Want to Work with Animals.* Harper, 1983.
Stewart, Darryl. *The North American Animal Almanac.* Workman, 1984.

Zoom lens. See Television (The cameras); **Photography** (Shooting a movie).

Zoroaster. See Zoroastrianism.

Zoroastrianism, *zawr oh AS tree uh nihz uhm,* is a religion founded between 1400 and 1000 B.C. by a Persian prophet named Zoroaster. *Zoroaster* is the Greek form of the Persian name *Zarathustra,* which means *He of the Golden Light.*

A winged god named Ahura Mazda is the symbol of Zoroastrianism. He was the chief god of the ancient Persians.

Beliefs. Zoroastrianism teaches a belief in one God, Ahura Mazda, who created all things. Devout people must seek and obey Ahura Mazda, who will judge everyone at the end of worldly time after their bodies have been resurrected.

The heart of Zoroastrianism is the belief in a battle between good and evil. Zoroaster taught that the earth is a battleground where a great struggle is taking place between Spenta Mainyu, the spirit of good, and Angra Mainyu, the spirit of evil. Ahura Mazda calls upon everyone to fight in this struggle, and each person will be judged at death on how well he or she fought. Each person should be dedicated to fighting for good thoughts, good words, and good deeds.

Zoroaster composed several hymns called *Gathas* that were collected into a sacred book known as the *Avesta.* These hymns are the only record of what Zoroaster believed, in his own words.

Some scholars believe that traces of Zoroaster's theology can be found in the concept of Satan as the personification of evil (Angra Mainyu). They also find similarities between the Zoroastrian belief in Fravashirs (guardian spirits) and the angels of Western religions.

History. Little is known of Zoroaster's life. Scholars believe he lived between 1400 and 1000 B.C. in what is now northeastern Iran. But Zoroastrian tradition teaches that he lived between the early 600's and the mid-500's B.C. He left his home in search of religious truth. After wandering and living alone for several years, he began to have revelations at the age of 30. In a vision, he spoke with Vohu Manah, a figure who represented the Good Mind. In the vision, Zoroaster's soul was led in a holy trance into the presence of Ahura Mazda.

In the years after his revelations, Zoroaster composed the *Gathas* and spread the teachings of Ahura Mazda. Zoroaster's conversion of Vishtaspa, a powerful ruler, strengthened the new religion. According to the Avesta, Zoroaster was assassinated at the age of 77.

Zoroastrianism thrived in Persia from about 550 to 330 B.C., when the religion seems to have lost some of its vitality. The Muslim conquest of Persia in the mid A.D. 600's led to a further decline in the practice of Zoroastrian rites and rituals. However, several groups continued to observe the religion's traditions. These groups have carried the faith into the 1900's in Iran, India, and other countries. In India, the followers are called Parsis. Modern Zoroastrians read from the *Avesta,* practice traditional purification habits, and attend rituals at fire temples. Fire is important in Zoroastrianism as a symbol of Ahura Mazda.   Robert William Smith

See also **Parsis; Persia, Ancient** (Religion, pictures); **Magi; Mithra.**

Zouaves, *zoo AHVZ,* were soldiers of certain light infantry regiments in the French Army. The name *Zouave* came from that of the *Zouaoua* tribe of Kabyles in Algeria, where the French first recruited Zouaves in 1830. At first, the Zouave regiments were battalions made up of tribesmen and Frenchmen. Later, the army separated the races, but the French Zouaves continued to wear their tribal dress. The Algerian regiments were called *Turcos.* The Zouaves fought with Free French forces in North Africa during World War II (1939-1945).

Napoleon III organized a group called the Papal Zouaves in 1860 for the protection of the Papal States. They were disbanded in 1871.   John W. Gordon

Zucchini, *zoo KEE nee,* is a type of squash that resembles a cucumber. Zucchini are cylindrical, and most have shiny green skin, though some varieties are golden colored. Their flesh is greenish-white. People eat zucchini raw in salads, including the skin. Zucchini also are eaten cooked and are used in making a kind of bread. They are low in calories, but a good source of calcium,

WORLD BOOK illustration by James Teason
A single plant produces several zucchini squash.

iron, vitamin C, thiamine, riboflavin, and niacin. The term *zucchini* means *little squashes* in Italian. It was first used in California for a type of Italian or Spanish squash.

Zucchini are popular garden vegetables and grow well in any climate that has at least two months of warm weather. Zucchini are planted from seeds after all danger of frost has passed. They grow on a bush that has a short stem and large leaves. Zucchini are picked when they are 6 to 8 inches (15 to 20 centimeters) long and their rind is still tender.

Scientific classification. Zucchini belong to the family Cucurbitaceae. They are *Cucurbita pepo.*   W. E. Splittstoesser

See also **Squash.**

Zuider Zee. See Netherlands (introduction).

Zukerman, *ZOO kur mahn,* **Pinchas,** *PIHNG kuhs* (1948-   ), is an Israeli-born violinist, violist, and conductor. He gained international recognition as a soloist and conductor with both symphony orchestras and chamber orchestras.

Zukerman was born in Tel Aviv, Israel. He began studying at the Israel Conservatory at the age of 8. In 1962, he went to New York City to study on an America-Israel Cultural Foundation scholarship. From 1965 to 1969, he studied music at New York's Juilliard School. Zukerman made his New York debut as a violinist in 1969. He first appeared as a conductor in 1974 with the English Chamber Orchestra. He served as director of the St. Paul Chamber Orchestra in Minnesota from 1980 to 1987. Zukerman became a United States citizen in 1976.   Reinhard G. Pauly

Zulu, *ZOO loo,* are one of the main Bantu-speaking peoples of Africa. About 7 million Zulu live in the province of Natal in the Republic of South Africa. They make up the largest language group in that country. Many Zulu live in urban areas. Others live in Kwazulu (Zululand), a homeland assigned to them by the South African government. The government subjects the Zulu and other black South Africans to a policy of severe racial segregation called *apartheid.*

During the early 1800's, a Zulu king named Shaka led his nation in a series of military conquests. In 1838, the Zulu clashed with invading Dutch settlers, called *Boers.* The Zulu remained independent until the British conquered them in 1879.

Before the British conquest, the Zulu were farmers and cattle herders. They lived in cone-shaped houses made of finely matted reeds and straw. They arranged these houses in circles to form villages. The Zulu had a powerful monarch and a well-disciplined army.

The Zulu have traditionally practiced *polygyny,* the custom of a man's having more than one wife at the same time. A traditional Zulu family consists of a man, his wives, his unmarried children, and his married sons and their wives and children. In urban areas, however, polygyny is becoming rare, and most families are much smaller.   Pierre L. van den Berghe

See also **Africa** (picture: Traditional African dancing); **Bantu; South Africa.**

Zuni Indians, *ZOON yee* or *ZOO nee,* are a tribe that lives in northern New Mexico near the Arizona border. They are one of several tribes of Pueblo Indians. Many tribal members live in the pueblo village of Zuni, which the tribe has inhabited since about A.D. 1000. Many Zuni are farmers. The Zuni are known for their silver, coral, and turquoise jewelry. Many live in traditional houses of stone. Others live in modern houses.

The Zuni religion is one of the most complex native religions in the Southwest. It centers around six cults, each with its own rituals. One colorful Zuni ceremony is the *Shalako.* It is held annually between Thanksgiving and mid-December to celebrate the arrival of winter.

The Zuni are descended from a prehistoric group called the Anasazi. In 1539, the first Spanish expedition to enter New Mexico met the Zuni. The explorers were searching for the fabled *Seven Cities of Cibola,* which were believed to be rich in gold (see **Cibola, Seven Cities of**). The Zuni resented the invasion by foreigners. They killed one of the explorers, a black guide named Estevanico (see **Estevanico**). The Spanish adventurer Francisco Coronado heard tales of riches reported by this earlier party. He came seeking the Seven Cities in 1540 and instead found six Zuni villages.

The Zuni came under U.S. authority after the Mexican War ended in 1848. That year, the United States acquired land from Mexico, including regions that later became parts of Arizona and New Mexico.

In 1969, the tribe established the Zuni Comprehensive Development Plan to create jobs and improve education and living conditions. In 1970, it became the first tribe to contract with the federal government to run tribal programs organized by the U. S. Bureau of Indian Affairs.
Alfonso Ortiz

Zunz, *tsunts,* **Leopold** (1794-1886), has been called the founder of the scientific study of Judaism. He was the first scholar to make a scientific study of the prayers and poetry used in the services of the synagogue. He also studied the intellectual life of European Jews. Zunz was born in Detmold, Germany, and spent most of his life in Berlin.   Clifton E. Olmstead

Zurbarán, *ZUR buh RAHN,* **Francisco** (1598-1664), was a Spanish painter of the 1600's. His calm, almost classical paintings seem simple, but they are intricately composed. Zurbarán was unsurpassed in his ability to create sculptural forms through the use of broad areas of light and shadow or color. His subjects for paintings included meditating monks, female saints, and still life objects such as earthenware jugs.

Zurbarán was born in Fuente de Cantos in the province of Estremadura. Many scholars believe the severity of the Estremadura landscape influenced his style. However, the paintings of Michelangelo Caravaggio, Jusepe de Ribera, and Diego Velázquez were probably more important in Zurbarán's development as an artist. Zurbarán's finest works were done between 1629 and 1645, principally for monasteries. His severely simple style made him the foremost interpreter of monastic life. In his own day, Zurbarán's paintings were exported to Latin America, where they had a decisive influence on colonial painting.   Marilyn Stokstad

See also **Moors** (picture).

Zurich, *ZUR ihk* (pop. 351,545; met. area pop. 834,299), is the largest city in Switzerland and the capital of the *canton* (state) of Zurich. It is a major manufacturing and commercial center. Zurich lies on the north end of Lake Zurich, along the Limmat River. For location, see **Switzerland** (map).

The old section of Zurich has many architectural treasures. These include two medieval churches, the

Shostal

The stately Grossmünster Church in Zurich, built between the 1000's and 1200's, towers over the Limmat River. Many architectural landmarks in Zurich date from the Middle Ages.

Grossmünster and the Fraumünster; beautifully restored houses used by associations of craftsmen called *guilds;* and the Baroque *Rathaus* (town hall). Bahnhofstrasse, a famous avenue, is flanked by stone palaces built in the 1800's that house Swiss banks, insurance companies, luxury stores, and fancy hotels. Zurich's schools include the Swiss Institute of Technology and the University of Zurich, the largest university in Switzerland.

Products made in Zurich include machine tools, paper, radios, and textiles. The city is one of the world's financial centers and a hub of the international gold trade. People from many countries deposit money in Zurich's banks (see **Switzerland** [Banking]).

According to archaeological evidence, a prehistoric settlement existed near Zurich, on the lake. The Romans built a fort at Zurich, possibly in the late A.D. 100's. In 1351, Zurich united with other Swiss areas in a political unit called the Swiss Confederation, which became modern Switzerland. New textile manufacturing and machine industries contributed to Zurich's growth in the 1800's. As the city has grown, it has expanded from the area around Lake Zurich and the Limmat River to neighboring valleys. Heinz K. Meier

Zwaanendael Museum. See Delaware (Places to visit).

Zweig, *zwyg* or *tsvyk,* **Stefan** (1881-1942), was a well-known Austrian writer of psychological novels, stories, biographies, and poems. His best-known stories include *Amok* (1922), *Conflicts* (1927), and *Beware of Pity* (1939). Some of his best biographies are *Romain Rolland* (1921), *Marie Antoinette* (1932), and *Erasmus of Rotterdam* (1934). Zweig was born in Vienna. The Nazis forced him to leave Austria because of his Jewish ancestry, and from 1934 to 1940 he lived in London. He and his wife committed suicide in Brazil because of their depression over world affairs. He described the tragic conflicts of his life in his autobiography, *The World of Yesterday* (published in 1943, after his death). Jeffrey L. Sammons

Zwingli, *ZWIHNG lee* or *TSVIHNG lee,* **Huldreich,** *HUL drykh* (1484-1531), was a leader of the Protestant Reformation. His career centered in Switzerland, but he influenced the Reformation in Germany, the Netherlands, and England.

His life. Zwingli was born in the Wildhaus Valley near St. Gall, Switzerland. In 1506, he was ordained a Catholic priest. By 1514, Zwingli had become a follower of the Dutch humanist Desiderius Erasmus. Zwingli studied Erasmus' edition of the Greek text of the New Testament and adopted the program of the Christian humanists for reforming the church. This program tried to follow what the humanists felt was the simple faith of the New Testament and of the early Christians.

In 1518, Zwingli was chosen to be a priest of the cathedral in Zurich. He became a forceful reform preacher, following the views of Erasmus. Soon he was reading works by the reformer Martin Luther. By 1520, Zwingli had worked out a Protestant theology unlike that of Luther. After the Catholic bishop of Zurich tried to silence Zwingli, the civil magistrates took charge of all the city's religious affairs. In 1523, the magistrates called a public meeting to decide between Catholicism and Zwingli's new Protestantism. Zwingli's side won.

During the next two years, the magistrates abolished religious images such as statues, adopted a Protestant liturgy, closed the monasteries, and substituted the Lord's Supper for the Mass. By 1528, the major German-Swiss cities had followed Zurich's lead. Rural areas remained Catholic. In 1531, Zwingli, serving as a chaplain with the Protestant troops, died during a war with Catholics.

His ideas. Zwingli agreed with other early reformers on many issues. These issues included salvation by faith rather than by good works, the supremacy of the Bible as the sole authority for Christianity, and the universal priesthood of all believers. The concept of universal priesthood declared that all believers were considered priests since they helped bring God's grace to others. Catholic priests were set apart from lay people by their power to perform the sacraments.

Luther and Zwingli disagreed on certain points, especially the Lord's Supper. Luther believed that Jesus Christ was really present in this sacrament, though not in the same way the Catholic Church taught. Zwingli considered the Lord's Supper a thanksgiving to God for grace already given in other ways, especially through God's gift of the Gospel. Luther was primarily concerned about individual salvation. Zwingli had greater concern about what he called the "renaissance of Christendom." By this he meant the total rebirth of humanity and society.

Zwingli became active in politics and in social reform. He supported radical changes in the church and worked successfully for the right of the people to control the church. Peter W. Williams

See also **Luther, Martin; Reformation** (Zwingli and the Anabaptists).

Zworykin, *ZWAWR uh kihn,* **Vladimir Kosma,** *VLAD uh MEER KAHZ muh,* (1889-1982), was a Russian-born American physicist and electronics engineer. He was responsible for many advances in radio, television, and the electron microscope.

He came to the United States in 1919. After learning to speak English, he went to work in 1920 for the radio tube department of the Westinghouse Electric Company in Pittsburgh, Pa. Zworykin studied at the University of Pittsburgh, where he received his Ph.D. degree in 1926.

At Westinghouse, Zworykin was put in charge of a group of young engineers to help develop the television camera and picture tube. His most important work there was the development of the *iconoscope,* an electronic tube that converts light rays into electric signals. The signals can then be changed into radio waves. He was also largely responsible for developing and perfecting the electron microscope (see **Electron microscope**). In 1929, he became director of electronics research for Radio Corporation of America (now RCA Corporation). He was made vice president of the company in 1947.

Zworykin was born in Murom, Russia, and graduated from the Petrograd Institute of Technology in 1912 with a degree in electrical engineering. He then went to Paris. There, he did X-ray research with the physicist Paul Langevin at the College of France, before returning to Russia in 1914. G. Gamow

See also **Electronics** (picture: A pioneer of television).

Zygote. See Fertilization.